# Springer Proceedings in Humanities and Social Sciences

Aims and Scope

Springer Proceedings in Humanities and Social Sciences collates the most current, selected research presented at international and regional conferences, seminars, and workshops to bring it to a global readership. The series features volumes (in electronic and print formats) of selected contributions from conferences in all areas of both the humanities and social sciences, including interdisciplinary work, covering philosophy, religious studies, history, language and literature, communications and cultural studies, anthropology, sociology, developmental studies and political science and policy. In addition to an overall evaluation by the publisher of the topical interest, research quality, and timeliness of each volume, each contribution is refereed to standards comparable to those of leading journals, resulting in authoritative contributions to the respective fields. Springer's production and distribution infrastructure ensures rapid publication and wide circulation of the latest developments in the most compelling and promising areas of research in HSS today. The series publishes both Open Access and non-Open Access works.

This series promotes the inclusion of 'Selected Proceedings', a middle ground between edited volumes and full conference proceedings. The series is specifically looking for submissions from conferences with a defined, focused theme, or a regional focus in a specific discipline.

The series offers the option for conferences to use Springer Nature's conference management platform, Equinocs, free of charge.

For more information, contact the listed publishing editor.

Nawawi · Athiqah Nur Alami · Julius Bautista ·
Maitrii Aung-Thwin · Deasy Simandjuntak ·
Yanu Endar Prasetyo
Editors

# Managing Disruption and Developing Resilience for a Better Southeast Asia

## The 4th SEASIA Biennial Conference 2022

CONSORIUM FOR
SOUTHEAST ASIAN STUDIES
IN ASIA

BRIN
BADAN RISET
DAN INOVASI NASIONAL

The 4th SEASIA Biennial Conference 2022

Springer

*Editors*
Nawawi
National Research and Innovation Agency (BRIN)
Research Center for Population
Jakarta, Indonesia

Athiqah Nur Alami
National Research and Innovation Agency (BRIN)
Research Center for Politics
Jakarta, Indonesia

Julius Bautista
National University of Singapore College
Singapore, Singapore

Maitrii Aung-Thwin
Department of History
National University of Singapore
Singapore, Singapore

Deasy Simandjuntak
National Chengchi University
Taipei, Taiwan

Yanu Endar Prasetyo
National Research and Innovation Agency (BRIN)
Research Center for Population
Jakarta, Indonesia

ISSN 2948-2526 ISSN 2948-2534 (electronic)
Springer Proceedings in Humanities and Social Sciences
ISBN 978-981-96-2115-6 ISBN 978-981-96-2116-3 (eBook)
https://doi.org/10.1007/978-981-96-2116-3



This Springer imprint is published by the registered company Springer Nature Singapore Pte Ltd.
The registered company address is: 152 Beach Road, #21-01/04 Gateway East, Singapore 189721, Singapore

# Introduction

Southeast Asian countries currently under challenges due to the ongoing political, regional, socio-economic and cultural dynamics. The political landscape of Southeast Asia has changed dramatically in the last two decades. Democracy remains "the only game in town" in a number of region's countries but its legitimacy and effectiveness have been under threat of predatory oligarchic network, military praetorian, and sectarian violence.

The region also witnessed the emergence of populist leaders that took repressive and unaccountable use of force as one of their political tools in silencing dissidents and opposition groups. Furthermore, security threats have also struck the region in fast pace and unpredictable forms. Strategic rivalries among extra-regional powers have dragged the region into dangerous—yet probably inevitable—great power politics that might hamper the realization of "one identity, one community" in Southeast Asia.

On the other hand, the current COVID-19 pandemic has made clear how difficult it is to manage a complex system of interconnected and dynamic components (economy, transportation, health care, and education) regarding risk perception, culture, attitudes, institutional and social trust, and socio-economic contexts. The pandemic of COVID-19 has also put social and physical distancing in place—as a new part of health protocols. It has brought a considerable new way of people in doing business, public services and consumption's behavior at the global practices. The crowd of people, social mobility, and close physical contact are now at high risk toward human life. In addition, it also affects people's income, jobs, health, life satisfaction, and education.

In the same vein, the impacts of digital transformation in Southeast Asian communities are amplified by ongoing global trends, like demographic change, rapid urbanization, increasing international migration, and strong reliance on digital technologies. The relationship of society and digital technology has been given greater and previously unimaginable significance within Southeast Asian countries.

We witness people's improved lives, more sophisticated public administration, good governance, inclusivity, and democratization. However, digital society also brings necessities on (cyber) security, discourse about personal and public boundaries, and the culture of consumption. New markets and jobs are being created, but many existing jobs are and will be eliminated, or will have to be significantly retooled in the production process as a result of automatization. The impact of digital transformation is also forcing governments to review their educational system, what skills that need upward the line, and how education can create flexible creativity and adaptive toward various risks.

In line to above changes and development in Southeast Asia, identities remain both an asset and a challenge for Southeast Asian countries in a nowadays globalized world. Most feuds, conflicts, and even wars are, quite often, linked to cultural, ethnic, or religious background. It is necessary to build global awareness of the diversity of humankind and responsibility for cultural, ethnic, and religious aspirations. In this context, recognition over minority rights represents the primary principles of a free and democratic society.

In addition to this is the issue of gender that still remains challenging within contemporary Southeast Asian societies. Thus, forging an inclusive form of citizenship would likely to be the important key to not only maintain social harmony but also ensure the fulfillment of the rights of all citizens. While its discourse has been discussed around the world, its realization and implementation remain challenging in many countries in Southeast Asia. Therefore, these shared various characteristics, changes, challenges, and development set Southeast Asian countries in politics, regional, economic, socio-culture importance at present and in the future.

## Southeast Asian as an Emerging Countries

There are many overlaps in the thematic focus of conferences, symposium, and workshops sponsored individually or jointly by area studies institutions. Some of the unintended consequences of this "noodle-bowl" phenomenon include intellectual fragmentation and segmentation even within one particular topic of "area studies" as can be experienced at some of the larger academic meetings that are frequently held. This fragmentation and segmentation can potentially impede the development of synergistic, inter- and multi-disciplinary research and ultimately hinder comparative approaches in terms of the goals and endeavors that are held and pursued in common by all of us scholars who are keen to promote area studies.

The study of Southeast Asia has been an integral part of Asian studies and is represented in various international academic meetings such as the Association for Asian Studies (AAS), International Convention of Asia Scholars (ICAS), and European Association for South East Asian Studies (EuroSEAS). Parallel to these meetings, which have until very recently been held outside of the region, there have also existed region-based institutions that have provided excellent platforms for promoting Southeast Asian studies.

The creation and rise of East Asian and Southeast Asian studies departments and research institutes within the region and in its vicinity are testimony to this. As

ASEAN comes of age through the creation of a regional community in 2015, there has never been a more compelling need to establish a region-based Consortium for Southeast Asian Studies institutions, one that can complement deepening economic, social and cultural integration and foster both regional and global efforts to network.

In North America and Europe, Southeast Asian studies constitute only one sub-regional branch of "area studies" among many other areas and is subject to the vicissitudes of funding and institutional imperatives specific to the countries in which they are based. But for scholars working on Southeast Asia who are based in East Asia, this "area" matters in geopolitical, economic, intellectual, institutional, social, cultural, and affective terms.

The study of Southeast Asia is not peripheral and external to what scholars, public intellectuals, policymakers, and activists are doing in the region. This consortium enables scholars who live and research within or close to the region to come together for regular meetings without the added expense of traveling outside of the region. In line with the principle of open regionalism, however, the consortium welcomes close linkages with institutions based outside the region and encourages scholars from different regions of the world to participate in the common endeavor of enriching knowledge of Southeast Asia and sharing this knowledge with the world.

To discuss these important issues, the Indonesia's Research Organization of Social Sciences and Humanities (OR-IPSH), National Research and Innovation Agency (BRIN), in Jakarta, to publish these conference proceedings on "Managing Disruption, Developing Resilience for a Better Southeast Asia." All chapters in this proceedings have been presented at the 4th SEASIA Biennial Conference on June 9-11, 2022 in Jakarta. This publication allowed the participants of the conference not only to discuss critical issues on economic, social, history, art, cultural, heritage, religion, politics, human rights, and international relations issues within Southeast Asian countries, but also to reflect on the experiences of Southeast Asian countries in developing resilience and building back better after the COVID-19 as well as to build networks among scholars on Southeast Asian studies.

## About the SEASIA Conference

The SEASIA Biennial Conference is an international conference organized by the Consortium for Southeast Asian Studies in Asia, consisting of thirteen leading educational and research institutions in the Asian region. This conference is an academic forum for scholars, researchers, and practitioners from Asia and other regions to enrich and share knowledge and contemporary strategic issues in Southeast Asia. The conference has been taking place since 2015 in Kyoto, Japan.

Continuing the success of previous conferences, the 4th SEASIA Biennial Conference brought a theme entitled "Managing Disruption, Developing Resilience for a Better Southeast Asia." The conference held in a hybrid event on June 9-11, 2022 in Jakarta, Indonesia, and organized by Research Organization of the Social Sciences and Humanities of the National Research and Innovation Agency (BRIN).

The host used a special application for virtual conference which allows all participants to watch live webinar and have many opportunities to ask questions, make comments, and download any materials presented in the conference. All the sessions have been recorded and available to watch at any time. The theme is important to be discussed at this conference as an effort to respond to the latest developments and challenges experienced by countries in Southeast Asia related to political, economic, and socio-culture dynamics in the region, including the impact of the COVID-19 pandemic that hit countries in the region.

The 4th SEASIA Biennial Conference specifically has three objectives. First, it aims to conduct critical analysis on economic, social, history, art, cultural, heritage, religion, politics, human rights, and international relations issues within Southeast Asian countries. The second objective is to investigate the challenge and prospect of Southeast Asian countries in managing turbulence and developing resilience in dealing with global health, climate change and environment, and socio-economic, cultural, and political development. Third, the conference aims to provide a platform for dialogue, share experiences and lessons learned, as well as build international network among scholars on Southeast Asian studies. The conference consists of a number of fascinating activities ranging from the presentation of Guest of Honor by the Coordinating Minister of Human and Culture Development of the Republic Indonesia, Prof Muhajir Effendi, Minister of Education and Culture Republic Indonesia, Nadim Makarim, and Keynote Speech by Prof. Bart Barenberg from Leiden University and representation from Ministry of Foreign Affairs of the Republic of Indonesia, Round Table Discussions from experts in their fields and panel discussions, to various supporting activities such as poster presentations, book fairs, and screenings of films about Southeast Asia.

## Structure of the Proceeding

All papers published in these proceedings have been presented and selected for publication. The author(s) has received various inputs during presentation at each panel discussion. All papers have also been reviewed during review process by editors. This proceeding covered nine sub-themes which are strategic issues in the Southeast Asia region. These nine sub-themes includes: (1) New Model of Economic Development in Southeast Asia; (2) Challenge to Education Quality, New Skills, Labor Market of Southeast Asia in Digital Era; (3) Demographic Changes and Critical Issues of Young and Elderly People in Southeast Asia; (4) Cascading Disaster as a Future Challenge for Risk Management in Southeast Asia; (5) Religions, Minority, Identity and Social Harmony in Southeast Asia; (6) Religions, Minority, Identity and Social Harmony in Southeast Asia; (7) Diaspora, Migration, Pandemic, Citizenship and Human Security in Southeast Asia; (8) Democracy, Security and Human Rights in

Southeast Asia: National and Sub-National Context; (9) Foreign Policy, Diplomacy and State Sovereignty in Contemporary Southeast Asia.

Research Organization of Social Sciences and Humanities
National Research and Innovation Agency (BRIN)

Nawawi
Athiqah Nur Alami

# Contents

**Challenge to Education Quality, New Skills, Labor Market of Southeast Asia in Digital Era**

# Message from the Chairman of National Research and Innovation Agency (BRIN)

Bismillahirrahmanirrahim.

Assalamu'alaikum warahmatullahi wabarakatuh.
Salam sejahtera bagi kita semuanya
Salom, Om swastiastu, Namo buddhaya, Salam kebajikan.

Excellencies,
Distinguished participants,
Ladies and gentlemen,
Good morning,
Welcome to the 4th SEASIA Biennial Conference 2022 and welcome to Jakarta, Indonesia.

I would like to thank everyone here today for being part of this prestigious event. As the Chairman of the National Research and Innovation Agency (BRIN), it is a tremendous honor to see so many members of the Consortium for Southeast Asian Studies in Asia, to have so many distinguished and high-level speakers on the agenda, and to welcome hundreds of delegates from all over the world.

I would like to thank our Chairman of the Institute of Social Sciences and Humanities (ISSH) BRIN Prof. Ahmad Najib Burhani, Head of the Research Center for Politics, Dr Athiqah Nur Alami, and Head of Research Center for Population, Dr Nawawi, for co-organizing this event, and the steering committee, and of course Dr Yanu Prasetyo, chair of organizing committee, for putting all this together.

I would also like to thank all those who have been involved in organizing this event, and what we see before us today is a testament to their hard work. Excellencies, Distinguished participants, Ladies and gentlemen, the coronavirus disease (COVID-19) pandemic has reversed many of Southeast Asia's hard-won gains in reducing poverty, creating jobs, and enhancing health and well-being, with the poor and vulnerable particularly hard-hit.

As countries begin to transition to a post-pandemic world, we hold our 4th SEASIA Biennial Conference 2022 to discuss experiences, innovations, and solutions that can restore our economies and social life, in order to lay the foundation for an equitable and enduring recovery. The 4th SEASIA Biennial Conference 2022 builds on the momentum to address unprecedented pandemic challenges. I believe this conference will provide a unique opportunity to discuss research and policy responses for a post-COVID-19 world.

The 4th SEASIA Biennial Conference 2022 Excellencies, Distinguished participants, Ladies and gentlemen. It was clear that no one could act alone in this era, and there is a need for wider cooperation to rebuild our national economy and community resilience to achieve a longer-term sustainability in our region. Without this cooperation and collaborative action, the world would have exhibited extreme uncertainty, with far-reaching negative consequences for our society. It is important to remember what happened over the past two years during the pandemic. While acknowledging some significant achievements we have made, we are also aware that our work is ongoing.

It is also clear that what we have witnessed underlines just how important collaboration is with all the main parties, including government, academic community, private sectors, and civil society especially in Southeast Asia to recover from the pandemic. In this regard, this 4th SEASIA Biennial Conference 2022 is part of our ongoing efforts to promote dialogue and cooperation with all SEASIA Consortium members, including scholars and students from higher education institutions, researchers, and activists who work with the issues related to economic, social, history, art, cultural, heritage, religion, politics, human rights, and international relations issues. We will investigate the challenge and prospects of Southeast Asia countries in managing disruption and developing resilience in dealing with global health, climate and environment, and socio-economic, cultural, and political development together.

Once again, this 4th SEASIA Biennial Conference 2022 is part of our attempt to provide platforms for dialogue, share experiences and lessons learned, as well as to build an international network among scholars and researchers on Southeast Asian studies in various research institutes in the region. As you might know that National Research and Innovation Agency (BRIN) is one of the prominent research institutes in Southeast Asia. Our establishment aims to build and develop a conducive science and innovation ecosystem in Indonesia as well as to make Indonesia as a global reference for science. BRIN is also expected to contribute to economic development in the country in order to achieve Indonesia's goals to be a developed country in 2045. Currently, BRIN consists of seven deputies, twelve research institutes, and eighty-five research centers that play role as facilitators and enablers for the development of research and innovation in Indonesia and collaboration with foreign research institutes, including with the member of SEASIA Consortium.

The 4th SEASIA Biennial Conference 2022 Excellencies, Distinguished participants, Ladies and gentlemen. Over the next three days in this conference, you will hear presentations and debates on how the state and society have managed disruption and developed resilience for a better Southeast Asia. Through the lively discussions that are sure to follow, we will undoubtedly learn from one another by exchanging valuable viewpoints and experiences.

I hope you all find the next two days and a half an enjoyable and rewarding experience. Don't forget also to explore Jakarta where you can find various tourist attractions, from cultural heritage, culinaries to fun world-class destinations. On that note, I would like to announce that the 4th SEASIA Biennial Conference 2022 is now officially open. May we all have a fruitful discussion.

Thank you very much! Wassalamu'alaikum Warahmatullahi wabarakatuh' Om santi-santi om

Dr. Laksana Tri Handoko, M.Sc.
The Chairman of the National Research and Innovation Agency

# Message from Chairman of the Institute of Social Sciences and Humanities BRIN

Welcome to the 4th SEASIA Biennial Conference 2022 on "Managing Disruption, Developing Resilience for a Better Southeast Asia."

On behalf of the National Research and Innovation Agency (BRIN), local organizers of SEASIA Biennial Conference, and the SEASIA Conference Committee, I would like to convey my gratitude and appreciation to all esteemed guests and participants to this year's conference in Jakarta, Indonesia.

Due to COVID-19, this 4th SEASIA Biennial Conference is moved from its earlier schedule in December 2021 to June 2022. One year ago, we were still not sure about the pandemic situation and, therefore, we decided to organize this conference in hybrid format: offline and online. The situation is much better now and hopefully we are in the final and recovery stage of the pandemic. We hope the theme of this conference can help us building our society better after the COVID-19.

We started distributing our Call for Paper (CfP) in August 2021 through our websites, academic mailing lists, social media, and also direct invitation to a number of scholars. We received almost 400 applicants from several countries and after selection we have 198 registered participants.

During the process of CfP, there was a huge change and transformation of research organization in Indonesia. The government dissolved the Ministry of Research, Technology and Higher Education (Kemenristek- Dikti) and bestowed the authority to oversee research in the country upon the National Research and Innovation Agency (Badan Riset dan Inovasi Nasional, or BRIN). Various research institutes, including LIPI, were merged or integrated into BRIN. We are grateful that the changing and transition of research management in Indonesia does not really affect the process of organizing the 4th SEASIA Biennial Conference.

The background of this conference is mostly related to the recent dynamics in Southeast Asia. Countries in this region currently under challenges due to the ongoing political, regional, socio-economic, and cultural dynamics. Democracy remains "the only game in town" in a number of region's countries but its legitimacy and effectiveness have been under threat of predatory oligarchic network, military praetorians, and sectarian violence.

On the other hand, the current COVID-19 pandemic has made clear how difficult it is to manage a complex system of interconnected and dynamic components (economy, transportation, healthcare, and education) regarding risk perception, culture, attitudes, institutional and social trust, and socio-economic contexts. In the same vein, the impacts of digital transformation in Southeast Asian communities are amplified by ongoing global trends, like demographic change, rapid urbanization, increasing international migration, and strong reliance on digital technologies.

The 4th SEASIA Biennial Conference 2022 specifically has three objectives. First, it aims to conduct critical analysis on economic, social, history, art, cultural, heritage, religion, politics, human rights, and international relations issues within Southeast Asian countries. The second objective is to investigate the challenge and prospect of Southeast Asian countries in managing turbulence and developing resilience in dealing with global health, climate change and environment, and socio-economic, cultural, and political development. Third, the conference aims to provide a platform for dialogue, share experiences and lessons learnt, as well as build international network among scholars on Southeast Asian studies.

I am sure this conference will certainly provide us with a valuable academic opportunity to share ideas with other researchers and scholars from many parts of the world. All presenters, chairs, and discussants will share their best research findings, experiences, and knowledge to this conference. Lastly, I would like to thank all presenters for participating in this conference and for presenting their papers. We are also grateful for the willingness of Professor Bart Barendregt of Leiden Institute of Cultural Anthropology and Sociology to give keynote speech in this conference. We hope that you will find the conference interesting and thought-provoking.

Ahmad Najib Burhani
Steering Committee of the 4th SEASIA Biennial Conference 2022
Chairman of the Institute of Social Sciences and Humanities, BRIN

# Message from Governing Board of the Consortium for Southeast Asian Studies in Asia (SEASIA)

It gives me great pleasure to represent the Governing Board of the Consortium for Southeast Asian Studies in Asia (SEASIA) in welcoming all participants to the 4th SEASIA Biennial Conference 2022.

The host for this conference, the Badan Riset dan Inovasi Nasional (BRIN, formerly known as Lembaga Ilmu Pengetahuan Indonesia, or LIPI), is one of the ten institutions which came together to establish SEASIA in Kyoto, Japan, in 2013. Since that time, the consortium has advanced its mandate of facilitating accessible platforms for Southeast Asianists to meet and interact in productive and meaningful ways.

This year's conference continues a tradition that has featured successful events held in Kyoto (2015), Bangkok (2017), and Taipei (2019). In 2022, we come together amid the difficulties and disruptions brought about by the global pandemic which has greatly affected our lives. In spite of these challenges, the conference call for proposals has attracted some 198 proposals from 15 academic institutions in Asia and beyond.

The conference program features a great diversity of topics, involving presentations from scholars from disciplines that range from natural science, anthropology, political science, sociology, economics, geography, law, and environmental studies to name just a few. The conference also features roundtable sessions which confront the most pressing issues in the region today.

I am confident that these presentations will exemplify the many ways in which Southeast Asian studies have been continuing to thrive, in spite of the disruptions brought about by our common predicament. A conference of this magnitude would not have been possible if not for the dedicated work of the SEASIA Conference Committee, which is made up of representatives from the University of the Philippines Asian Center, the Center for Southeast Asian Studies at Kyoto University, and Taiwan's Academia Sinica.

The Governing Board also wishes to acknowledge the tireless efforts of the members of the BRIN organizing team, who have worked synergistically with our own SEASIA Secretariat over the past four years in bringing this conference to fruition. We hope that you have a meaningful and enjoyable time at this year's conference.

Professor Hsin-Huang Michael Hsiao
Academia Sinica
SEASIA Chairman

# New Model of Economic Development in Southeast Asia

# Indonesia's Potential Trading Partners Under More Protective Global Markets During the Pandemic of COVID-19

**Zamroni Salim, Carunia Mulya Firdausy, Agus Syarip Hidayat, Panky Tri Febiansyah, Kanetasya Sabilla, Reninta Dewi Nugraheni, and Bintang Dwitya Cahyono**

**Abstract** Potential market exploration aims to increase competitiveness, expand Indonesia's products' exports globally, and obtain imported goods as supporting raw materials at more competitive prices. The expansion of potential trading partners is critical as a stepping stone to establishing further investment and production cooperation within a bilateral investment agreement, regional production network (RPN), and another economic diplomacy. This paper examines the possibility of investigating potential new markets for Indonesia and the existing main markets. We applied the Potential Market Composite Index (PMCI) to search for new potential markets based on several significant indicators. The PMCI is to provide an overview of the potential and performance of the destination country in issuing respective trade policies, following the direction, orientation, and competitiveness of export products. The PMCI is built using an aggregative framework and linear multivariate method. The potential country is determined by several economic conditions, trade policies, and infrastructure status of the destination country. The following indicators represent the PMCI framework of potential countries: (1) the size of the markets; (2) bilateral/regional cooperation agreements in the trade/investment sector; (3) performance of foreign direct investment (FDI); (4) the access to transportation/direct flights/direct calls; (5) status of trading partners (not as the main trading partner before the year of 2000); (6) the number of non-tariff measures (NTMs) applied by the potential trading partners to Indonesia. As a result, using the PMCI, Indonesia should expand its market to the existing main trading partner countries and potential markets such as some countries in West Asia, Eastern Europe, and Africa. Market expansion is significant for Indonesia, especially since global competition with other countries in attracting potential trading partners is getting more challenging amid the COVID-19 pandemic. In addition, the search for potential countries is a "hedging strategy" associated with the dynamics of the global economy.

Z. Salim (✉) · C. M. Firdausy · A. S. Hidayat · P. T. Febiansyah · K. Sabilla · R. D. Nugraheni · B. D. Cahyono
National Research and Innovation Agency—BRIN, Jakarta, Indonesia
e-mail: zamronisalim@gmail.com; zamr001@brin.go.id



Nawawi et al. (eds.), *Managing Disruption and Developing Resilience for a Better Southeast Asia*, Springer Proceedings in Humanities and Social Sciences,
https://doi.org/10.1007/978-981-96-2116-3_1

**Keywords** Trade · Potential markets · Trade partners · Potential market composite index · Competitiveness

## 1 Introduction: Why Do We Need Searching New Potential Markets?

The spread of COVID-19 was responded to through various health and economic policies by each country, causing the economy to contract. Maliszewska et al. [27] explained the impact of COVID-19 on GDP and trade, they concluded that the potential decline in GDP in the affected countries could be significant, global GDP decreased by 3.9%, and developing countries, on average, decreased around 4%; some have reached minus 6.5%. As the virus spreads worldwide, the global situation becomes increasingly uncertain; global foreign direct investment shrinks by 5–15% [44].

Amid the decreasing global economy due to the COVID-19 pandemic, open international trade is necessary for every country to achieve high growth and income, increase productivity and innovation, and expand opportunities for the population to develop their capabilities. However, with the trade war between America and China and the increasing number of countries that carry out trade protection [18, 22, 24, 33], as well as the COVID-19 pandemic, have led to a decreasing trend of international trade. Indonesia needs to change its international trade policy to respond to this trading trend. One form of policy that cannot be avoided is the policy of exploring potential trading partners.

Why does Indonesia, with so many trading partners, still need to look for other potential countries? Our thinking framework needs to be placed in the context of a strategic and holistic national interest in searching for new potential markets. We are placing the motivation to seek new markets as something strategic means that in addition to achieving goals in the trade sector, the expansion of potential partners must be able to make strategic contributions in various other aspects. A holistic national interest emphasizes the selection of potential trading partners. We need to include multidimensional factors such as economic aspects, non-economic aspects (culture, politics, citizen protection), and aspects of the political geo-economic constellation of trading blocks in Indonesia with various regions.

It is a critical note that the concept of searching for potential markets is generally placed in a traditional context, namely state-driven. The state-driven approach tries to choose countries that have not become major trading partners or whose trade and investment cooperation percentage is still low [5, 28, 42]. This is something logical. However, in the future, it will be better if efforts to find potential markets are built by combining the concepts of state-driven and sector-driven [11, 30]. In the sector-driven concept, the selection of potential partners is more emphasized to find potential markets based on specific sectors or products that have potential but have not been included in regional and multilateral liberalization schemes and excluded sensitive sectors or products. The scope of trade and potential partner countries will be broader.

This paper examines efforts to find potential new markets for Indonesia and the existing main markets. The search for new markets is based on the Potential Market Composite Index (PMCI) based on several indicators. The PMCI provides an overview of the potential and performance of the destination country in managing their respective trade policies. It can also provide alternatives and choices for the relative destination country under the direction, orientation, and competitiveness of export products. The PMCI approach uses a linear multivariate method.

## 2 Research Method: Country Ranking of Indonesia's Potential Trading Partners

Ranking of potential countries is an urgent matter to be done in Indonesia. The rating is expected to provide an overview of the potential and performance of the destination countries in managing their respective trade policies. Then, the ranking of potential countries can also provide alternatives and choices of relative destinations following the direction, orientation, and competitiveness of export products.

According to Harris [20], a potential trading country is a country that has the possibility of trade relations, which can be traced through an abstract index value and can be approximated by market access (by looking at the level of income and population) and distance (transportation costs). Geographical distances that reflect transportation costs must be considered when assessing trading partners. Jacks and Novy [23] explain that trading partner countries have several external and internal supporting factors, especially demand in importing countries, and also need to pay attention to transportation costs in the trade process. Specifically, Hanson [19] and Redding and Venables [35] pay attention to the importance of economic size (GDP per capita) as the main criteria in determining partner countries.

On the other hand, Beise and Cleff [7] pay attention to several relative advantages that can be obtained concerning the innovative idea of developing a particular product in the destination country. Liu and Meissner [25] underlined that the potential market is a function of trade barriers that need to pay attention to foreign purchasing power. There are many prerequisites that Indonesia needs to consider in sorting out and selecting these potential trading partner countries. The potential partner countries chosen should not be limited to countries with significant market size but also need easy trade access, adequate logistics services, and fast tax settlement procedures. On the other hand, Indonesia must also make structural improvements in various fields so that the potential trading partners are interested in joining [34, 46]. Moreover, Indonesia's competition with other countries in attracting potential trading partners is getting more challenging amid the pandemic of COVID-19.

In this study, for Indonesia, we define a potential country as a country with several main supporting factors to become a trade and investment partner out of the countries that have been the main trading countries since 2000. The main supporting factors are used as indicators in constructing the Potential Market Composite Index (PMCI). The composite index started to be recognized and used more often because it can become a tool for policy analysis and public communication [6]. This index will make identifying the general trend of the various forming indicators easier and is relatively accurate as a benchmark [37, 41]. The composite index is built using an aggregative framework. Meanwhile, the PMCI approach uses a linear multivariate method.

The PMCI method is designed as follows, where the potential country is described as the ability and potential of the destination country for Indonesia's trade performance. PMCI as an indicator of a potential country is determined by economic conditions, trade policies, and infrastructure status of the destination country relative to Indonesia. Therefore, based on literature review and input from stakeholders, potential country PMCI frameworks are represented from the following compiling indicators: (1) export performance to destination countries (X); (2) market size (MZ); (3) trade agreement (TA); (4) performance of foreign direct investment (FDI); (5) direct flights/calls (DFC); (6) trading partner status (TP); and (7) number of non-tariff measures (NTM). For the record, the coverage of the country sample is highly dependent on the data availability in each destination country.

Specifically, X represents the value of Indonesia's exports to destination countries. MZ is compiled based on the ratio of Indonesia's imports from destination countries to world imports. Then, TA is the number of cooperation between Indonesia and the destination country, government to government, business to business, and government to business. The foreign investment performance (FDI) is formed from the ratio of foreign investment from the destination country to the total foreign investment in Indonesia. Meanwhile, DFC shows direct flights and direct ship shipping to destination countries and vice versa. TP is the status as a significant trading partner based on ranking in 2000. Finally, NTM is the number of non-tariff measures in the destination country. It should be noted that MZ and FDI are ranked with upper, middle, and lower criteria, and DFC contains a dummy, number 1 has direct transportation and number 0 does not.

$\text{PMCI}_{\text{NP}}^{X}$ can be shown as below:

$$\text{PMCI}_{\text{NP}}^{X} = \beta_{\text{MZ}}\text{MZ}_i + \beta_A\text{TA}_i + \beta_{\text{PMA}}\text{FDI}_i + \beta_{\text{DFC}}\text{DFC}_i + \beta_{\text{TP}}\text{TP}_i + \beta_{\text{NTM}}\text{NTM}_i \quad (1)$$

Where $\beta_{\text{MZ}}, \beta_{\text{TA}}, \beta_{\text{FDI}}, \beta_{\text{DFC}}, \beta_{\text{TP}}, \beta_{\text{NTM}}$ are the weight of each indicator $\text{MZ}_i$, $\text{TA}_i$, $\text{FDI}_i$, $\text{DFC}_\text{i}$, $\text{TP}_i$, $\text{NTM}_i$. In addition, $i$ represents selected countries. So far, $\text{PMCI}_{\text{NP}}^{X}$ still requires the development of methodologies, data, and theoretical frameworks. The data used are 2019 data for partners' country export performance (X), market size (MZ), and FDI ratio (FD). Trade agreement (TA) and direct flight/calls data (DFC) are existing data in 2019/2020; NTM data accumulate the existing NTMs until 2020 [45]. Trade Partners (TP) is data on the trade partners' status in 2000 as main trading partners for Indonesia or not.

The process of indicators' development has systematical steps while methodologically facing some challenges. Reliability and accuracy are essential in propagating composite indicators in policy areas [32, 37, 41]. We deal with the broad scope of the theoretical framework and carry a different nature of data on a general group of indicators. Since the study has been preliminary in building a potential partner index, we stressed using multivariate analysis while constructing the aggregation of indicators. The primary purpose is that the composite indicators will point out as an initial start for introducing discussion in public concern about the importance of the country's potential partner measurement.

The controversy of composite indicators arises when weights are put into the context of having either relative or equal values. Freudenberg [15] suggested that relative weights are suitable to have aggregate indicators more precise and reliable in presenting the degree of indicators' importance. The enactment of relative measures is valid only inside a specified information area, reflecting the scientists' choices on how to examine reality [17]. This allows composite marker development to follow subjectivity depending on either policy interest, data availability, or theoretical framework. Furthermore, Box [9] and Sen [40] also described that the function of composite indicators is still valid even though the statistical fitness is low as long as the theoretical background sustains. Box and Sen's suggestions were represented in the earlier development of the UN Human Development Index.

Multivariate regression is a standard method to deal with the relative weights of indicators. A relative impact of variables is desirable to convey the weighting process [29, 39]. This technique approximates the degree of importance of variables and avoids equal weights. In this case, the motive of regression is to find weighting values resulting from interrelationship indicators with the policy target without considering the statistical significance of each variable [10]. Following the work of Rogge [36], the procedure method of our study adopts the benefit of the doubt (BOD) model to construct composite indicators by undertaking regression to achieve a practical policy setup with a lack of performance for the individual indicator.

## 3 Country Ranking of Indonesia's Potential Trading Partners

In the context of trade interests, potential market exploration aims to expand export markets and obtain imported goods at more competitive prices. High exports can drive growth in the industrial and related sectors, increase employment, and encourage economic growth. The external component (export–import of goods and services) will play an essential role in driving economic growth when domestic and international markets are integrated in the future.

In addition to trade interests, the expansion of potential trading partners needs to be used as a stepping stone to establishing investment and production cooperation within the framework of a bilateral investment agreement and regional production network

(RPN). Learning from China's experience, the Indonesian government needs to give more roles to the emergence of micro, small, and medium enterprises (MSMEs) in every market penetration, expansion, and investment process. This is urgent considering that SME exports' contribution to total national exports is still around 15%, while MSME business entities account for 98% of the total business units. MSMEs are a symbol and the main instrument in inclusive development. Currently, big business players still dominate the use of bilateral, regional, and multilateral FTA trade and investment schemes.

The search for potential countries in international trade needs to be placed to diversify the market and a "hedging strategy." This action becomes essential when it is associated with the dynamics of the global economy, which is vulnerable to financial and economic crises. Many of the countries affected by the crisis are Indonesia's main trading partners. Various crises such as the subprime mortgage, which triggered the US recession in 2007, the prolonged economic crisis in European countries, and the slowdown in Japan's economic growth have contributed to Indonesia's exports.

On the other hand, Indonesia's cooperation with several main trading partners, such as China (in the ASEAN-China FTA/ACFTA framework), and potential trade partners, such as India (in the AIFTA framework), is expected to stimulate growth in exports of primary and secondary products to these countries, which has not shown a positive trend. Hedging strategies are also needed amid the increasing trade protection regime [13, 24]. Potential market exploration aims to expand the export market and obtain imported goods as raw materials/supporting raw materials at more competitive prices. The expansion of potential trading partners needs to be a stepping stone to establishing further investment and production cooperation within a bilateral investment agreement, regional production network (RPN), and economic diplomacy.

In this study, the search for Indonesia's potential trading partner countries is carried out by listing several existing trading partner countries. The list of trading partners is based on several determining variables which are considered to have a role in determining the potential of a country or not. Potential countries are intended as potential destination countries with some supporting factors to become Indonesia's new (more intensive) trading partners. Several variables include: (1) the size of the markets; (2) bilateral/regional cooperation agreements in the trade/investment sector; (3) performance of foreign direct investment (FDI); (4) the access to transportation/direct flights/direct calls; (5) status of trading partners (not as the main trading partner before the year of 2000); (6) the number of non-tariff measures (NTMs) applied by the potential trading partners to Indonesia.

**The size of the markets**: A country's economic size determines its ability to cooperate with its trading partners. The bigger the size of the country, the more attractive it will be. More specifically, the size of this country's economy can also be seen through GDP per capita, which shows purchasing power (the more significant the demand in the country). Ekanayake [12] found that an importing country's GDP and per capita income affect the amount of trade with the partner country (exporting country) because the demand for products in the importing country will be more numerous and varied. Market size is seen based on the ratio of imports of trading partner countries to total world imports (grouped into three groups: upper = 3,middle = 2; and lower = 1).

**Bilateral/regional cooperation agreements in trade**: Bilateral and regional trade cooperation will facilitate the process of a more intensive trade increase and a wider range of trade products. Trade cooperation (such as an FTA) will directly eliminate trade barriers, especially tariffs. Also, a more comprehensive FTA (in the form of a closer economic partnership—CEPA) enables trading partner countries to actively remove or at least reduce these barriers [38]. Other obstacles include non-tariff measures and other cooperation such as trade facilitation to facilitate trade flow in goods and services between trading partner countries. Based on research on two trade agreements between two different countries/regions, trade agreements can increase the value of trade between countries and provide a better economic impact for both [14, 26]. FTA/bilateral agreement/business to business: free trade agreement (FTA = 5, preferential trade agreement (PTA = 4; MoU government to government (GtoG = 3; government to business (GtoB = 2; business to business (BtoB = 1.

**Performance of foreign direct investment (FDI)**: The existence of FDI can be an accelerator for increasing trade between two countries that have investment relations (FDI). Often trade relations are closely related to foreign companies entering a country (Indonesia). The higher the FDI from a partner country in Indonesia, the higher the existing trade volume. The existence of FDI can also support a country's participation in the global value chain (GVC) and regional production network (RPN), which in turn also increases the volume of trade between countries. Several previous studies [4, 31] found that FDI positively relates to trade value between countries, especially for manufactured products. In preparing this index, the value of FDI is calculated based on the ratio of FDI to Indonesia's total FDI (grouped into upper = 3, middle = 2; and lower = 1).

**Access to direct flights/direct calls**: In international trade, the existence of a direct sea shipping line (direct call) with a supporting marine fleet (cargo, shipping company) will simplify the process of logistic at the port and of course in terms of costs, direct calls tend to be cheaper in terms of cost compared to shipping lines via transit, likewise for the flight path. Direct flights also facilitate trade flow in goods and services (via air cargo). The operation of shipping liners and flights has a local economic impact because it can potentially increase the use of airports/ports for international trade. Shipping and air access also impact the supply chain in trade [3]. Better airline/shipping accessibility is measured by the supply of flight/vessel routes, increasing productivity in various sectors [1]. Furthermore, Ahn et al. [2] and Bernard et al. [8] show that ease of access to airports reduces costs by facilitating direct connections to export markets.

**Status of trading partners**: The status of the trading partner filters the countries to be potential or not (a country that has been Indonesia's main trading partner).

Suppose a country has specific characteristics with higher productivity in a particular sector. There is a higher possibility that the country may enter the export market due to the "learning by exporting" effect [21]. The status of not being a major trading partner does not necessarily mean that the country does not have the potential to be Indonesia's main trading partner. In compiling the index of potential countries, we used the limit of "not as a major trading partner country" until 2000. So countries that are the main trading partners get a score of "1", while those that have not become major trading partner countries until 2000 are assigned a value "0."

**Non-tariff measures (NTMs)**: NTMs implemented by trading partner countries will affect the level and intensity of trade between two trading partners in terms of bilateral and regional trade. These NTMs have become a means for trading countries to protect the domestic industry and economy from global competition. In the context of support for increasing trade, the existence of NTMs is thought to reduce the trade flows between two trading partners (Table 1).

NTMs can have quantitative implications such as anti-dumping measures, quantitative restrictions, and safeguards (directly change the amount traded goods and services or prices) or have a qualitative impact on international trade [43]. A qualitative NTM can indirectly impact the emergence of better regulations and higher standards in line with technological developments, standards, domestic innovations, health, and the environment [16].

The NTM value of the index is the cumulative value of the number of NTMs until 2021. In the composition of countries based on PMCI, the smaller the PMC value, the more potential the country will become Indonesia's trading partner country more intensively. The higher the PMCI value, the countries not included in the potential group of countries.

The emergence of several countries that Indonesia has not widely looked at as main trading partners should receive extra attention when Indonesia wants to expand the global export market and accelerate the national economy's recovery through the external trade sector. The top ten most potential countries are indicated by smaller index values. The first ten countries with relatively small PMCI are Iran, Mauritius, Niger, Taiwan, Tunisia, Qatar, Yemen, Netherlands, United Arab Emirates, and Egypt.

The countries with relatively low PMCI scores are South Africa and Russia. Some countries with relatively small PMC values can be grouped into two large groups: countries in the West Asia—Middle East region and the Africa Region. Meanwhile, some export destination countries we know today are considered less potential. The status does not mean that we do not have trade relations, nor that the trade value is low; it could be that these countries have been the main trading partner countries, such as the USA, Japan, China, South Korea, and several ASEAN countries.

**Table 1** Country ranking of Indonesia's potential trading partners

| Country | V1 | V2 | V3 | V4 | V5 | V6 | PMCI scores |
|---|---|---|---|---|---|---|---|
| Iran* | 0 | 3 | 1 | 0 | 0 | 0 | 5,358 |
| Mauritius | 1 | 3 | 1 | 0 | 0 | 3.4965 | 13,925 |
| Niger | 1 | 3 | 1 | 0 | 0 | 3.6109 | 14,161 |
| Taiwan*** | 0 | 3 | 2 | 1 | 0 | 6.9791 | 16,102 |
| Tunisia | 1 | 4 | 1 | 0 | 0 | 3.8918 | 16,927 |
| Qatar | 1 | 3 | 1 | 1 | 0 | 6.5236 | 17,736 |
| Yemen** | 1 | 3 | 1 | 0 | 0 | 5.3799 | 17,804 |
| Netherlands | 3 | 3 | 3 | 1 | 1 | 6.5250 | 18,306 |
| United Arab Emirates | 2 | 3 | 1 | 1 | 0 | 6.3784 | 18,804 |
| Egypt | 1 | 3 | 1 | 0 | 0 | 5.8749 | 18,823 |
| South Africa | 1 | 3 | 1 | 0 | 0 | 6.1654 | 19,421 |
| Russia | 2 | 3 | 1 | 0 | 0 | 5.6699 | 19,767 |
| Hong Kong** | 3 | 5 | 3 | 1 | 0 | 5.5722 | 20,473 |
| Singapore | 3 | 5 | 3 | 1 | 1 | 5.4848 | 20,541 |
| Saudi Arabia | 2 | 3 | 1 | 1 | 0 | 7.2619 | 20,623 |
| Pakistan | 1 | 5 | 1 | 0 | 0 | 4.8040 | 20,994 |
| Vietnam | 2 | 5 | 1 | 1 | 0 | 5.6095 | 21,597 |
| Malaysia | 2 | 5 | 1 | 1 | 1 | 5.7714 | 22,178 |
| New Zealand | 1 | 5 | 1 | 1 | 0 | 6.6503 | 22,374 |
| Australia | 2 | 5 | 2 | 1 | 0 | 6.8013 | 22,845 |
| Philippines | 2 | 5 | 1 | 1 | 0 | 6.5453 | 23,524 |
| Thailand | 2 | 5 | 1 | 1 | 0 | 6.9489 | 24,355 |
| India | 3 | 5 | 1 | 1 | 0 | 6.3081 | 24,402 |
| South Korea | 3 | 5 | 3 | 1 | 0 | 7.4866 | 24,415 |
| Japan | 3 | 5 | 3 | 1 | 1 | 7.5219 | 24,736 |
| China | 3 | 5 | 3 | 1 | 0 | 7.9146 | 25,297 |
| USA | 3 | 5 | 3 | 0 | 1 | 8.6154 | 29,410 |

*Notes* V1–V6 are Market Size, FTA, FDI, Direct Flight/Direct Call, Trading Partners, and NTMs. * Market size and NTM data were not available; ** export data were not available; *** export data and market size data were not available

## 4 Conclusion and Policy Recommendation

The construction of the Potential Market Composite Index (PMCI) is based on several significant indicators to search for new potential markets based on some indicators including economic conditions of the targeting countries, trade policies, and the level of infrastructure development in the export destination countries relative to Indonesia. The following constituent indicators represent the composite index of potential countries: (1) export performance to destination countries; (2) market size (size of the markets); (3) Bilateral/regional cooperation agreements in the trade/ investment sector; (4) Performance of foreign investment (FDI); (5) access to transportation/direct flights/direct call; (6) status of trading partners; and (7) number of non-tariff measures (NTM) between Indonesia and potential countries.

Using PMCI, we get the order from potential countries to expand Indonesia's export market. The top ten countries have the most potential (indicated by a smaller index value). The first ten countries with relatively small PMCI are Iran, Mauritius, Niger, Taiwan, Tunisia, Qatar, Yemen, Netherlands, United Arab Emirates, and Egypt. The countries with relatively low PMCI scores are South Africa and Russia. Several countries with relatively small PMC values can be grouped into two large groups: countries in the West Asia—Middle East region and the Africa Region.

Various improvements need to be made by Indonesia to expand the export market to potential trading partners based on PMCI (of course, not to exclude several countries that have been Indonesia's main trading partners). Some strategic actions in line with essential indicators that support market expansion include: first, the importance of Indonesia in improving inefficiencies or weaknesses in the transportation, logistics, and customs systems; second, improve the quality of telecommunications infrastructure, financial markets, and information technology; and third, improving regulations in encouraging the entry of new investments. Some examples of improvements in the trade facilitation policy above are more important for Indonesia than Indonesia's efforts to find potential trading partner countries. Using the composite index of potential trading partner countries, Indonesia should expand its market to the existing main trading partner countries and consider expanding the market to some countries in West Asia—the Middle East and Africa. Market expansion is significant; especially Indonesia's competition with other countries in attracting potential trading partners is getting more challenging amid the COVID-19 pandemic.

## References

1. Ahlberg K, Dyvnas M, Eliasson K (2007) Commercial real estate: different aspects of rent setting, no December. Jonkoping University
2. Ahn J, Khandelwal AK, Wei S (2011) The role of intermediaries in facilitating trade. J Int Econ 84(1):73–85. https://doi.org/10.1016/j.jinteco.2010.12.003
3. Airports Commission (2014) Local economy: literature review, no November
4. Aizenman J, Noy I (2006) FDI and trade-Two-way linkages? Q Rev Econ Finan 46(3):317–337. https://doi.org/10.1016/j.qref.2006.02.004
5. Baier SL, Bergstrand JH (2004) Economic determinants of free trade agreements. J Int Econ 64:29–63. https://doi.org/10.1016/S0022-1996(03)00079-5
6. Bandura R, Campo CM del (2006) A survey of composite indices measuring country performance : 2006 update
7. Beise M, Cleff T (2004) Assessing the lead market potential of countries for innovation projects. J Int Manag 10:453–477. https://doi.org/10.1016/j.intman.2004.08.003
8. Bernard AB, Grazzi M, Tomasi C (2012) Intermediaries in international trade: direct versus indirect modes of export. SSRN Electron J. https://doi.org/10.2139/ssrn.1692586
9. Box GEP (1954) Robustness in the strategy of scientific model building

10. Cherchye L, Moesen W, Puyenbroeck van T (2004) Legitimately diverse, yet comparable: on synthesizing social inclusion performance in the EU. J Common Mark Stud 42(5):919–955. https://doi.org/10.1111/j.0021-9886.2004.00535.x
11. Coe NM, Yeung HW (2019) Global production networks: mapping recent conceptual developments. J Econ Geogr 19:775–801. https://doi.org/10.1093/jeg/lbz018
12. Ekanayake EM (2001) Determinants of trade: the case of Mexico. Int Trade J 15(1):89–112. https://doi.org/10.1080/088539001300005468
13. Erbahar A, Zi Y (2017) Cascading trade protection: evidence from the US. J Int Econ. https://doi.org/10.1016/j.jinteco.2017.06.006
14. Francois J, Norberg H, Thelle M (2007) Economic impact of a potential free trade agreement (FTA) between the European Union and South Korea, no March
15. Freudenberg M (2003) Composite indicators of country performance: a critical assessment. No 16, STI Working Paper Series. https://doi.org/10.1787/405566708255
16. Ghodsi M, Stehrer R (2022) Non-tariff measures and the quality of imported products. World Trade Rev 21(1):71–92. https://doi.org/10.1017/S1474745621000392
17. Gough C, Castells N, Funtowicz S (1998) Integrated assessment: an emerging methodology for complex issues. Environ Model Assess 3:19–29
18. Gunnella V, Quaglietti L (2019) The economic implications of rising protectionism: a euro area and global perspective
19. Hanson GH (2005) Market potential, increasing returns and geographic concentration. J Int Econ 67:1–24. https://doi.org/10.1016/j.jinteco.2004.09.008
20. Harris CD (1954) The market as a factor in the localization of industry in the United States. Ann Assoc Am Geogr 44(4):315–348
21. Harris R, Li QC (2005) Review of the literature: the role of international trade and investment in business growth and development (Issue September)
22. IMF (2017) World economic outlook: gaining momentum? (Issue April)
23. Jacks DS, Novy D (2018) Market potential and global growth over the long twentieth century. J Int Econ. https://doi.org/10.1016/j.jinteco.2018.07.003
24. Kinzius L, Sandkamp A, Yalcin E (2018) Trade protection and the role of non-tariff barriers, vol 7419, no December
25. Liu D, Meissner CM (2015) Market potential and the rise of US productivity leadership. J Int Econ. https://doi.org/10.1016/j.jinteco.2014.11.012
26. Mai Y, Adams P, Fan M, Li R, Zheng Z (2005) Modelling the potential benefits of an Australia-China free trade agreement. In: Working Paper No. G-153 (G-153; Issue October 2005)
27. Maliszewska M, Mattoo A, Mensbrugghe van der D (2020) The potential impact of COVID-19 on GDP and trade a preliminary assessment, vol 9211, no April
28. Mansfield ED (2013) The expansion of preferential trading arrangements. Int Stud Quart 57:592–604. https://doi.org/10.1111/isqu.12064
29. Mazziotta M, Pareto A (2013) Methods for constructing composite indices: one for all or all for one ? Rivista Italiana Di Economia Demografia e Statistica, vol LXVII
30. Menon J (2008) Dealing with the proliferation of Bilateral trade agreements: consolidation, multilateralization, harmonization, or dilution? no 123
31. Min BS (2003) FDI and trade: links in the case of Malaysia. J Asia Pacific Econ 8(2):229–250. https://doi.org/10.1080/1354786032000074749
32. Nardo M, Saisana M, Saltelli A, Tarantola S (2005) Tools for composite indicators building prepared by
33. OECD (2019) Rethink policy for changing world: economic outlook
34. OECD (2021) Global value chains : efficiency and risks in the context of COVID-19, no February. https://www.oecd.org/coronavirus/policy-responses/global-value-chains-efficiency-and-risks-in-the-context-of-covid-19-67c75fdc/#boxsection-d1e140
35. Redding S, Venables AJ (2004) Economic geography and international inequality. J Int Econ 62:53–82. https://doi.org/10.1016/j.jinteco.2003.07.001
36. Rogge N (2017) On aggregating benefit of the doubt composite indicators. Eur J Oper Res. https://doi.org/10.1016/j.ejor.2017.06.035

37. Saltelli A (2007) Composite indicators between analysis and advocacy. Soc Indic Res 81:65–77. https://doi.org/10.1007/s11205-006-0024-9
38. Salim Z, Pranata N, Sabilla K (2020) Benchmarking Singapore and Hong Kong to develop Indonesia's trade facilitation. Int J Bus Global 26(1/2):119–147
39. Salzman J (2003) Methodological choices encountered in the construction of composite indices of economic and social well-being
40. Sen A (1988) Development as capability expansion. In: Readings in human development, vol 987, pp 3–16
41. Sharpe A (2004) Literature review of frameworks for macro-indicators, no February
42. Spilker G, Bernauer T, Umana V (2016) Selecting partner countries for preferential trade agreements: experimental evidence from Costa Rica, Nicaragua, and Vietnam. Int Stud Quart 60:706–718. https://doi.org/10.1093/isq/sqv024
43. UNCTAD (2019) International classification of non-tariff measures
44. UNCTAD (2020) Impact of the coronavirus outbreak on global FDI, no March 2020. https://unctad.org/en/PublicationsLibrary/diae_gitm34_coronavirus_8march2020.pdf
45. WITS (2021) Non-tariff measures (NTM) by country. https://wits.worldbank.org/tariff/non-tariff-measures/en/ntm-bycountry
46. World Bank (2021) World development indicators. Worldbank.Org. https://databank.worldbank.org/source/world-development-indicators

# Government and Communities Roles in the Collaborative Governance for Ecotourism Policy

**Sanusi, Elfira Rosa Juningsih, Tommy Hendrix, Angga Wijaya Holman Fasa, Mahardhika Berliandaldo, and Rika Harini**

**Abstract** Ecotourism is one of the important aspects of the economic development of countries in various parts of the world, including in the Southeast Asia Region (ASEAN). Current conditions show that various policies implemented in Indonesia and several ASEAN countries have a diversity of ecotourism development governance, especially aspects of the partnership pattern between policymakers. Each country has its level of success in managing this partnership. This study focuses on government-community partnerships as the essential part of Ecotourism Partnership Governance. This paper used literature study and based on analysis of seminar paper and academic discussion summaries, taskforce reports from research, and journals on the good governance of tourism. Existing partnerships have the potential to serve as the framework for developing a model of partnership patterns, according to the study's findings. The analysis demonstrates that effective collaborative management adheres to several parameters, including the sustainable use of natural resources, community-based and community-run initiatives, equity, and the maintenance of partnerships in coordinating all stakeholders as part of the policy, thereby fostering commitment, synergy, and beneficial collaboration.

Sanusi (✉) · E. R. Juningsih
Research Center for Population, National Research and Innovation Agency, Jakarta, Indonesia
e-mail: mung.sanusi@gmail.com; sanusi484201@mail.ugm.ac.id; sanu002@brin.go.id

Sanusi
Research Center for Population, National Research and Innovation Agency, Jakarta, Indonesia

T. Hendrix · A. W. H. Fasa · M. Berliandaldo
Regional Research and Innovation Division, Regional Planning Research and Development Agency, Bogor Regency, Bogor, Indonesia

A. W. H. Fasa
Ministry of Tourism and Creative Economy of the Republic of Indonesia, Jakarta, Indonesia

R. Harini
Faculty of Geography, Universitas Gadjah Mada, Yogyakarta, Indonesia



Nawawi et al. (eds.), *Managing Disruption and Developing Resilience for a Better Southeast Asia*, Springer Proceedings in Humanities and Social Sciences,
https://doi.org/10.1007/978-981-96-2116-3_2

**Keywords** Ecotourism · Community-based collaboration · Successful partnership management

## 1 Introduction

Tourism is the world's largest industry. It employs 10% of all workers and accounts for 11% of the global GDP [33]. Tourism is a significant tool not merely to foster economic growth but significantly also to enhance sustainable development and environmental protection. Statista [41] states that the ecotourism industry worldwide was estimated at 181.1 billion U.S. dollars in 2019. The sector was estimated to reach 333.8 billion U.S. dollars in 2027 [41]. The contribution of ecotourism to economic and business development cannot be deemed absent favorable consideration of the society and structure of the society in which ecotourism development occurs [3]. Remarkably, the dominance, power, and control of certain actors in economic activities within a community, as well as capacity issues surrounding entry into the ecotourism sector, must be considered. Typically, a distinction is made between all stakeholders involved, particularly the term local community [2]. The approach to stakeholder management that conceptualizes the group community as a single social entity is contested. In this study, the collaborative management strategy as an egalitarian relationship between all stakeholders serves as the primary reference point.

Due to growing global sustainability concerns, ecotourism is a form of sustainable travel expanding quickly. In addition to conserving the local environment and culture, ecotourism has the potential to generate economic benefits and employment for host nations [24]. Ecotourism's significant share of the global economy is determined by global trends calculated using data from various organizations, along with short- and long-term projections, which indicate an increasing demand for ecotourism and forecast its significant growth. According to projections, the global ecotourism market could reach 333.8 billion U.S. dollars in 2027, up from 181.1 billion U.S. dollars in 2019. As each country integrates into the global tourism community, it strives to establish itself and strengthen its position in the ecotourism industry, thereby increasing the need to implement competitive strategies [23]. The competitiveness of a destination is primarily determined by the effectiveness of the partnership involved in the production of ecotourism products. Collaboration strategies and resource integration are essential for maximizing benefits and adding value. Collaboration between stakeholders is necessary for achieving and sustaining ecotourism competitiveness [13].

Ecotourism was also carried out to maintain sustainable resources and guide travelers to attain natural and ecological experiences which are environmentally friendly [20]. Several characteristics cause ecotourism to support environmental conservation. The primary motivation of the tourist is to appreciate nature and its cultural environment; education contains; and reduce the negative impact on nature and local culture; and increase the awareness of nature conservation [47].

Ecotourism's potential as a natural management tool can promote a greater societal awareness of the importance of protecting nature within a feasible development system, which is consistent with sustainability [48]. Despite the fundamental and vital role that control, planning, and other government activities play in complementing and supporting ecotourism planning and delivery, ecotourism governance has focused on the quality of ecotourism in order to address these issues [14]. The sustainable ecotourism model is based on the long-term survival and quality improvement of a well-managed environment that has an impact on a more productive and widespread culture of protecting the environment. Commonly, ecotourism is seen as a strategy to promote environmental friendliness to encourage the necessary changes in consumer behavior and become a strong reason for the development of environmentally friendly infrastructure. This is due to the belief of all stakeholders that ecotourism is beneficial for the environment [12, 28, 49]. Collaboration between stakeholders and active community participation is crucial to the development of sustainable ecotourism within the context of governance [42]. Community-based ecotourism (CBET) is the foundation for the use of natural resources, and intuition between the community, the local economy, and the environment is essential to the development of viable instruments for protecting natural heritage [31].

The Association of Southeast Asian Nations (ASEAN) has developed a strategic plan titled, the ASEAN Community-Based Tourism (CBT), in order to increase recognition of local communities' engagements and empower their vital role through community-based ecotourism schemes in the Southeast Asian Region [46]. The ASEAN Community-Based Tourism (CBT) Standard provides performance indicators for the coordinated management of tourism products offered by communities, several criteria such as community ownership and management, including effective and transparent governance, recognition of legitimate establishment, effective and transparent management, and effective partnerships. Moreover, the ASEAN CBT provides standard indicators for contributions to social well-being (maintaining human dignity, equitable sharing of benefits and costs, and linkage with regional equilibria) and environmental well-being (maintaining human dignity, equitable sharing of benefits and costs, and linkage with regional equilibria) (maintaining human dignity, equitable sharing of benefits and costs, linking with regional ecotourism networks) [5]. However, the primary obstacles to implementing the standards are inadequate governance, limited resources, and inadequate community capacity [29].

This study will elaborate on the various ecotourism development governance policies implemented in Indonesia and several ASEAN nations, focusing on the partnership pattern between policymakers, emphasizing government-community partnerships as the core of Ecotourism Partnership Governance. In addition, this study may have implications for the implementation of future policy for regional stakeholders and refers to other destinations where sustainable tourism development is possible.

## 2 Method

The study relied on secondary sources and reviews of the relevant literature and analyses of seminar papers and discussion summaries, taskforce reports from research, and journals on the good governance of tourism.

## 3 Literature Review

### 3.1 Sustainable Ecotourism

Environmental and conservation values are the objective of cultural and ecological preservation, which seeks to mitigate the damage caused by tourism-related activities such as increased waste, pollution, sanitation problems, and unethical travel [44]. It is proposed that sustainable tourism be developed by focusing on nature and the socio-cultural environment and putting public welfare first [15]. Moreover, in order to achieve sustainable development, three fundamental requirements must be met: sustainable ecology, socio-cultural, and economical. Sustainable tourism's primary goal is to balance utilization and generate economic, social, and human development while adhering to shared integrity standards and environmental preservation. Traditionally, culture and economic environment objectives have been regarded as crucial to progress [26]. The economic multiplier of tourism is higher than that of other development strategies because it is an essential component of the industry. Due to the wide variety of goods and services they require from various economic sectors, tourists, who are an essential actor in the business, have a significant impact on the local economy [25, 34]. To develop ecotourism, the collaboration of all these actors must be strengthened, as they regulate natural destinations tasked with preserving ecosystems, economic activities, and community welfare [2]. Unquestionably, local communities have the right to contribute to ecological sustainability-based resource management and revenue generated [50].

Currently, this is the golden age of sustainable tourism. Numerous nations and regions have developed distinctively modern tourist attractions, including types of tourism, such as developing tourist villages and other forms of artificial and digital tourism, marine tourism, mountain and sea travel, as well as halal tourism and travel for the purpose of adventure and as a way of life, have been spawned by numerous nations and regions around the globe [1, 35]. Engagement in resource management and connecting directly to the resulting funds are gaining significance for achieving the fundamental goal of promoting ecological sustainability [45]. Occasionally, however, peripheral priorities, particularly at the national and international levels, can ignore public requirements [11, 37]. Despite greenwashing, ecotourism is positioned to shape alternative tourism, which is typically portrayed as a distinct departure from mass tourism. Ecotourism continues on. Due to its long-term connection with the development, it has become the most popular tourist destination [22].

Principle community-based ecotourism (CBE) protects the public interest by fostering local management, ownership, and education. Moreover, this highlights the significance of local public entrepreneurship, deliberative decision-making, access to benefit sharing, equitable distribution, and a diverse local economy [42]. The challenge with ecotourism is ensuring that all stakeholders involved in its development interpret values, culture, and management authority appropriately [39]. Ecotourism may indirectly contribute to giving solutions to public-sector problems such as unplanned expansion, work opportunities, revenue uncertainty, leakage, criminality, social erosion and lack of community participation, and the involution of biodiversity.

## *3.2 A Strategic Approach to Sustainable Tourism*

The tourism industry has chosen effective development because it provides and employs a variety of growth-enabling characteristics. Sustainable tourism contributes to poverty reduction, infrastructure development, and social development, enhancing the quality of life. The majority of tourism alternatives are environmentally friendly and sustainable, and they coexist well with the environment. For example, sustainable tourism is travel that fully considers the effects it will have on the economy, society, and environment in the present and future, as well as the needs of tourists, businesses, the environment, and host communities [21]. Therefore, sustainable tourism must ensure optimal utilization of environmental resources, respect the socio-cultural characteristics of local communities, and provide socio-economic value to stakeholders [21, 47].

An intersectoral network of individuals and organizations carries out a variety of activities for the public good. The emphasis on stakeholder engagement in management and public services continues to shift toward high-potential, low-risk sectors like tourism [32]. Collaborative governance refers to a group of institutions that cooperate to achieve shared objectives and provide public value. Activity visitors determine the governance of a destination. Ecotourism is one of them, and it investigates tourism governance concepts. At the administrative level, examples of such governance include interrelated and inventive governance, economic performance governance, and social and environmental governance [30] (Mulyani 2021).

Ecotourism involves visiting relatively underdeveloped natural areas in order to admire natural landscapes, learn about wildlife, and experience authentic local culture while preserving the environment. Authorities of protected areas have significantly facilitated ecotourism in several countries, fostering sustainable tourism growth. As a result, stakeholder support is a crucial component of sustainable ecotourism because, when properly planned, ecotourism can provide substantial economic benefits to local communities. Ecotourism may therefore encompass five distinct criteria: bioproducts, low-impact management, environmental awareness, conservation, and social contributions. Furthermore, minimal management impact could replace with the implementation of integrity and sustainability [8].

A comprehensive ecotourism model incorporates a social dimension, culture, ecology, and sustainable characteristics that promote environmental advancement. Due to its function of promoting sustainable tourism, ecotourism is projected to increase environmental protection awareness, promote sustainability, reduce environmentally destructive activities, and improve control conditions [9]. Ecotourism is generally recognized as a type of tourism that encourages the sustainable use of natural resources and the natural environment [30] (Mulyani 2021). Ecotourism is essential for local communities because it enables them to rely on their internal strengths and resources to become self-sufficient, thereby significantly contributing to the economy and social welfare [3]. The assistance of stakeholders (government, national–international organizations, and businesses) concerning community friendliness has aided in developing ecotourism as a potential for accelerated expansion. In Indonesian villages and Southeast Asian countries, an absence of human resources, processing space, raw products, and competitive product quality impedes ecotourism. Therefore, assistance is required for the ecotourism industry's sustainable development and benefit enhancement.

In order to expand ecotourism, collaboration among stakeholders' interests must be strengthened, as it regulates natural destinations in a manner that simultaneously protects natural life, economic activities, and public welfare [43]. Suppose ecotourism has flourished in the region as a result of the stakeholders' sense of responsibility and dedication to its growth. Consequently, this is done for the benefit of society and as a model for other regions (Wondirad 2020). We map collaborative process work with studies in order to foster trust, process commitment, and implementation. Strengthening collaboration among all stakeholders is required to develop ecotourism because it controls natural destinations in a manner that protects natural life, economic activities, and public welfare. If ecotourism developed in the region due to stakeholders' awareness of their responsibilities and commitment to its growth, it would benefit society and serve as an example for other regions. This study maps collaborative activities such as establishing trust, committing to the process, and implementing.

## 3.3 Collaborative Management of Ecotourism

From the governance paradigm emerged collaborative management. In the implementation of country government, there is a paradigm shift from "government" to "governance" in the concept of "governance." Government administration of the state is no longer a monopoly; roles must be shared with the private sector and civil society [17]. State actors (government), the private sector, and the community must collaborate to build consensus, and the state's role has shifted from regulator to facilitator. This eventually became known as "good governance" [16, 19]. As a facilitator, the operations of government and communities reflect societal norms. Southeast Asian societies utilize social conventions and compromises to manage their natural resources. Since the year 2000, collaborative management initiatives have emphasized this point. Collaborative management generates social partner networks that negotiate and share resources. Conflicts of national interest plague conservation management, particularly ecotourism. Collaborative management can rationalize initiatives affecting protected areas that overlap (or are absent) by negotiating territories and responsibilities [11].

Multiple actors inside and outside of formal institutions collaborate to overcome challenges and seize opportunities through mutually agreed-upon management. Ansell and Gash [2] define collaborative management as a set of arrangements in which one or more public institutions engage non-government stakeholders directly in a formal, consensus-oriented, and deliberative policy-making process to develop or implement public policies or programs. Organize programs in managing public problems. Several phenomena influence the initial conditions of collaboration, including the shared interests of stakeholders and the vision to be realized, previous collaboration experiences, the existence of mutual respect for the existing cooperation, the trust of each stakeholder, the imbalance of power, the strength of resources, and knowledge, and previous collaboration experiences. Leadership is concerned with facilitating stakeholder discussions, establishing clear ground rules, fostering trust, facilitating stakeholder engagement, and distributing mutual benefits. It is crucial to have procedural law, process transparency, participant inclusion, and forum exclusivity in the collaboration process. Institutional design refers to cooperation's fundamental procedures and rules, facilitating stakeholder engagement and sharing mutual benefits. It is crucial to have procedural law, process transparency, participant inclusion, and forum exclusivity in the collaboration process. The procedures and rules of cooperation that facilitate stakeholder participation and the distribution of mutual benefits are referred to as collaborative management. Collaboration processes require procedural law, process transparency, participant inclusion, and forum exclusivity. It relates to the fundamental procedures and rules of cooperation.

Armitage et al. [4] associate this collaboration with a mutual trust-building process that is adaptive to each other to drive ecosystem management. Joint management conducted by various stakeholders is a crucial element of the governance of natural resources as shared property because the relationship between stakeholders substantially impacts governance performance [51]. However, adaptive co-management is not necessarily applicable in all ecosystem governance cases in many global locations. Carlsson and Sandstrom [10] conclude that the government must facilitate and adapt as a partner in the collaborative process, seeking ways to influence new policies collaboratively and adaptively. Certain government agencies and local interests play a significantly more prominent role in most collaborative management. According to Berkes [6], to overcome this, collaborative management must be viewed as a problem-solving process and not a rigid rule. However, negotiations, discussions, knowledge updates, and joint studies exist. The impact of various institutional arrangements and management systems is a central topic of interest in contemporary research on human–environment interactions. Sustainable management systems must relate to and adapt to a complex and ever-changing environment because natural resources are affected by various changing social and ecological variables [36].

### 3.4 *Collaborative Management of Ecotourism*

Tourism is one industry that uses collaborative governance to advance tourism's long-term growth [7]. Tourism governance has an essential function of organizing and developing destinations based on the active participation of local stakeholders, encouraging commitment, synergy, and beneficial collaboration among stakeholders in the public and private sectors, and assisting policymakers in implementing sustainable development. Governance is concerned with the structures and procedures used to manage diverse determinants, including systemic structure, interpersonal relations, and collective connections [38]. Nonetheless, tourism governance frequently places commercial and government interests ahead of the interests of numerous stakeholders. According to previous research, participation, legitimacy, transparency, and effectiveness are all aspects of good governance. Pragmatism drives collaborative governance to resolve this issue that has not been resolved through the application of conventional theories that were believed to resolve the issue [2]. Tourism collaborative governance is not limited to coordinating the public, private, and civil society. Instead, it involves coordination between public agencies with authority to influence the tourism industry [40].

The nature of the tourism industry, which is currently highly fragmented and interdependent across geographical spaces, leads to a situation in which the state and numerous actors and groups are responsible for governance and regulation. Consequently, there is a new emphasis on the need for coordination and collaboration among various (public and private) actors in tourism governance and regulation. Due to the fragmented nature of the tourism industry, in which multiple stakeholders share similar interests in providing services, a collaboration between stakeholders is essential for good governance. In this context, it is crucial to managing stakeholder relationships to ensure legitimacy and acceptance. However, the numerous and diverse interests of stakeholders' interactions could impact inefficient. To analyze these drivers and barriers, we review the planning and implementation processes that underpin collaborative governance, specifically ecotourism. Ecotourism is utilized with an emphasis on sustainable development.

## 4 Discussion

The primary objective of the central government is to implement regulations for equal development. Each region is granted the authority to establish its own rules for maximizing its potential based on the conditions of its territory. The travel and lodging industry is the second private sector participant. The relationship between ecotourism and these two stakeholders is strong. Using a mountainous geographical terrain with a natural atmosphere, environment, and cold climate, these stakeholders promote ecotourism in a tourist area. Despite the local government's lack of institutional authority, it has functions to promote and provide tourist accommodations.

In addition, tourism service providers like souvenir shops, tour guides, tourist attractions, and restaurants have strong ties to the local community and small business groups. The local government has authorized the provision of tourist services by local communities. Due to their respective role as authoritative actors, local governments have functions to provide permits for agricultural, natural, river, and mountain tourism attractions that provide adventure tourism within the destination. The authorization permits the use of tourist attractions and services [5]. This credential is obtained through government-sponsored training, development, and primary education prior to establishing a tourist attraction. Ecotourism activities are inextricably linked to the interests of the three key stakeholders.

Ecotourism stakeholders, including local governments, commercial enterprises, and society, are involved in the implementation and provision of service travel. Tourism services, as well as guides and infrastructure, necessitate the direct participation of stakeholders. Due to the unique limitations of these stakeholders, it is also possible to form collaborative connections that result in synergy between the three pillars. This cooperative relationship can take on a variety of forms, from which collaboration-required tasks can be identified. Due to the limitations of the stakeholders, these collaborative interaction phenomena can be viewed as a complex engagement relationship. According to the constructed theory, the complexity of this connection is a crucial aspect of governance, as previously stated.

Strong collaboration and stakeholder support are required for sustainable ecotourism management, which can aid in focusing on planning, implementation, and utilization of instruments to achieve sustainable ecotourism. Future evaluations and emphasis must be placed on enhancing stakeholder engagement and government participation. Government assistance is only provided when progress has been made at established destinations. Therefore, more research is required to highlight the role of local governments in responding to, managing, and maximizing the region's potential to develop a well-being-based society due to the fact that the development of ecotourism destinations starts with raising public awareness of how to boost the regional economy. Through the exploitation of natural resources, residents and the private sector are essential to the planning and implementation process. Then there is the participation of business or private actors in financing and mutual agreements with outside parties to ensure the continuous empowerment and development of local communities, as well as frequent monitoring and the maintenance of ecotourism. Moreover, local communities possess human resources with comparable characteristics that can aid in developing ecotourism destinations. Qualities that can improve ecotourism destination development collaboration.

The increased use of ecotourism sites has provided local governments with additional revenue to supplement local tax revenue and reduce unemployment and poverty. The benefits gained by corporate or private actors are also substantial, investment opportunities are abundant, and actors in the tourism service industry are increasingly eager to improve ecotourism destinations. In addition, ecotourism has numerous advantages for local communities, such as enhancing local economic activity, reducing unemployment, and enhancing local communities' ability and capability to compete with other regions in ecotourism development.

## 5 Conclusion

- Collaborative management in ecotourism regulates the course of coordination and maintains partnerships in coordinating all stakeholders as part of the policy, fostering commitment, synergy, and beneficial collaboration.
- Collaborative management is expected to produce management policies that can overcome and resolve problems of adequate governance and damaging biodiversity. Inadequate community capacity ensures that CBT in ASEAN countries satisfies the agreed-upon standards.
- Sustainable ecotourism requires strong collaborative management involving all stakeholders, including communities, in the planning, implementation, and monitoring processes. Ecotourism development must start with community awareness of boosting local economies through natural resources management.
- Further studies are needed to emphasize the capacity of local governments in responding to, managing, and enhancing regional potential so that a prosperous society can be developed.

## References

1. Andespa R, Andespa N, Andespa R (2020) Halal tourism development in West Sumatera. In: Proceedings of tourism development centre international conference, pp 221–233
2. Ansell C, Gash A (2007) Collaborative governance in theory and practice. J Public Admin Res Theor 18(4):543–571
3. Anup KC (2016) Ecotourism and its role in sustainable development of Nepal. In: Butowski L (ed) Tourism—from empirical research towards practical application. IntechOpen, London
4. Armitage DR, Plummer R, Berkes F, Arthur RI, Charles AT, Davidson-Hunt IJ, Diduck AP, Doubleday NC, Johnson DS, Marschke M et al (2009) Adaptive co-management for social ecological complexity. Front Ecol Environ 7(2):95–102
5. ASEAN, ASEAN Community Based Tourism Standard. ASEAN Secretariat. https://asean.org/book/asean-community-based-tourism-standard-2. Last accessed 14 May 2022
6. Berkes F (2009) Review: evolution of co-management: role of knowledge generation, bridging organizations and social learning. J Environ Manage 90(5):1692–1702
7. Bichler B, Lösch M (2019) Collaborative governance in tourism: empirical insights into a community-oriented destination. Sustainability 11:1–13
8. Boley B, Green T (2016) Ecotourism and natural resource conservation: the 'potential' for a sustainable symbiotic relationship. J Ecotour 15(1):36–50
9. Butarbutar RR, Sumarno M (2013) Environmental effects of ecotourism in Indonesia. J Indonesian Tour Dev Stud 1:97–107
10. Carlsson L, Sandström A (2008) Network governance of the commons. Int J Commons 2(1):33–54
11. Cochrane J (2007) Chapter 15, critical issues in ecotourism. Ecotourism and biodiversity conservation in Asia. Institutional challenges and opportunities
12. Dimitriou C (2017) From theory to practice of ecotourism: major obstacles that stand in the way and best practices that lead to success. Euro J Tour Hospital Recreat 8(1):1–12
13. Fathimath A (2015) The role of stakeholder collaboration in sustainable tourism competitiveness: the case of Auckland, New Zealand. Thesis for PhD at School of Hospitality and Tourism, Auckland University of Technology

14. Fennell DA (2014) Ecotourism, 4th edn. Routledge, London
15. GhulamRabbany M, Afrin S, Rahman A, Islam F, Hoque F (2013) Environmental effects of tourism. Am J Environ Energy Power Res 1(7):117–130
16. Haris S (2019) Governance: Perubahan Paradigma Pada Penyelenggaraan Pemerintahan. Sosfilkom Jurnal Sosial, Filsafat Dan Komunikasi 13(01):33–47
17. Ikeanyibe OM, Ori OE, Okoye AE (2017) Governance paradigm in public administration and the dilemma of national question in Nigeria. Cogent Soc Sci 3(1):131691
19. Kharisma B (2014) Good governance Sebagai Suatu Konsep dan Mengapa Penting dalam Sektor Publik dan Swasta: Suatu Pendekatan Ekonomi Kelembagaan. Buletin Studi Ekonomi 19(1):9–30
20. Kiper T (2013) Role of ecotourism in sustainable development. In: Özyavuz M (ed) Advances in landscape architecture. InTech, London
21. Kisi N (2019) A strategic approach to sustainable tourism development using the A'WOT hybrid method: a case study of Zonguldak, Turkey. Sustainability 11(4):964
22. Klak T (2007) Sustainable ecotourism development in central america and the caribbean: review of debates and conceptual reformulation. Geogr Compass 1(5):1037–1057
23. Lesik I, Lesik M, Tishechkina K, Ushkarenko I, Soloviov A, Lahoiskyi A (2021) Analytical evaluation of the prospects for sustainable development of environmentally oriented tourism business. Bus Theory Pract 22(2):318–329
24. Ly TP, Bauer T (2016) Ecotourism in mainland Southeast Asia: theory and practice. Tour Leisure Glob Chan 1:61–80
25. Mayer M, Vogt L (2016) Economic effects of tourism and its influencing factors: an overview focusing on the spending determinants of visitors. Zeitschrift für Tourismuswissenschaft 8(2):169–198
26. Mazilu M (2013) Tourism and culture—a vital role in the development of Romanian's destinations. Int J Energy Environ 1(7):27–36
28. Mulyani S, Ahsani R, Wijaya D (2021) Collaborative governance on ecotourism: towards sustainable tourism development. Jurnal Borneo Administrator: Media Pengembangan Paradigma dan Gaya Baru Manajemen Pemerintahan Daerah 17(3):319–334
29. Novelli M, Klatte N, Dolezal C (2017) The ASEAN community-based tourism standards: looking beyond certification. Tour Plan Dev 14(2):260–281
30. Pambudi S, Suryono A, Setyowati E (2020) Collaborative governance towards development of eco-based tourism village in Kalipucang Village, Pasuruan Regency. Wacana J Soc Human Stud 23(2):129–141
31. Phelan A (Anya), Ruhanen L, Mair J (2020) Ecosystem services approach for community-based ecotourism: towards an equitable and sustainable blue economy. J Sustain Tour 28(10):1665–1685
32. Rahmawati R, Apriliani A, Sastrawan B (2020) Stakeholder involvement through a partnership model for sustainable tourism development. Int J Psychosoc Rehabil 24(8):8153–8168
33. Rosas-Baños M (2014) Networks in strengthening community-based ecotourism in the Sierra Norte of Oaxaca, Mexico. Pertanika J Soc Sci Human 2(3):24–32
34. Rasool H, Maqbool S, Tarique M (2021) The relationship between tourism and economic growth among BRICS countries: a panel cointegration analysis. Futur Bus J 7(1):1–11
35. Ruoss E, Alfare L, Vallone R, Moscatelli M, Zumaglini M, Grünner R, Klementschitz R (2013) Sustainable tourism as driving force for cultural heritage sites development. Planning, managing and monitoring cultural heritage sites in Southeast Europe
36. Sandstrom A, Rova C (2010) Adaptive co-management networks: a comparative analysis of two fishery conservation areas in Sweden. Ecol Soc 15(3):150314
37. Sarr B, González-Hernández MM, Boza-Chirino J, de León J (2020) Understanding communities' disaffection to participate in tourism in protected areas: a social representational approach. Sustainability 12(9):3677
38. Scott N, Marzano G (2015) Governance of tourism in OECD countries. Tour Recreat Res 40:1–13

39. Sentanu I, Prabowo A, Kumalasari K, Galih A, Wismanu R (2021) Stakeholder collaboration model for ecotourism development in indonesia: case study from Batu City East Java Province. J Govern Civ Soc 5(2):214–236
40. Septiana AD (2022) Collaborative governance in enhancing surabaya's tourism through sister city cooperation. Jurnal Pesona Pariwisata 1(1):39–44
41. STATISTA: ecotourism market size worldwide 2019–2027. https://www.statista.com/statistics/1221034/ecotourism-market-size-global. Last accessed 11 Apr 2022
42. Stone MT (2015) Community-based ecotourism: a collaborative partnerships perspective. J Ecotour 14(2–3):166–184
43. Sulistyadi Y, Eddyono F, Hasibuan B (2017) Model of sustainable tourism development strategy of the thousand islands tourism area—Jakarta. J Econ Manag Trade 19:1–17
44. Sunlu U (2003) Local resources and global trades: environments and agriculture in the Mediterranean region. Environ Impacts Tour 263–270
45. Sutresna IB, Suyana U, Saskara IA, Setyari NP (2019) Community based tourism as sustainable tourism support. Rus J Agric Soc-Econ Sci 94:70–78
46. Suyanto A, Haryono E, Baiquni M (2020) The community-based conservation management in Gunungsewu UNESCO global Geopark cased study of Nglanggeran Geoheritage. IOP Conf Series: Earth Environ Sci 451(1)
47. UNWTO: ecotourism and protected areas. https://www.unwto.org/sustainable-development/ecotourism-and-protected-areas. Last accessed 29 May 2022
48. Wearing S, Adjunct H, Schweinsberg S, Lecturer S (2019) Ecotourism: transitioning to the 22nd century, 3rd edn. Routledge, London
49. Weaver D (2005) Comprehensive and minimalist dimensions of ecotourism. Ann Tour Res 32
50. Wondirad A, Tolkach D, King B (2019) Stakeholder collaboration as a major factor for sustainable ecotourism development in developing countries. Tour Manag 78
51. Yamaki K (2014) Network governance of endangered species conservation: a case study of Rebun Lady'S-Slipper. J Nat Conserv 24(4):83–92

# The Main Drivers of Local Business Internationalization During the COVID-19 Pandemic

**Agus Syarip Hidayat, Zamroni Salim, Carunia Mulya Firdausy, Panky Tri Febiansyah, Kanetasya Sabilla, Reninta Dewi Nugraheni, and Bintang Dwitya Cahyono**

**Abstract** This study investigates the main drivers of the internationalization process of local business champions during the COVID-19 pandemic. PEST-BCL approach (political, economic, social, technology, business, climate, and law) is employed to examine the primary data gathered through in-depth interviews in three provinces of South Sulawesi, Bali, and North Sumatera. The pandemic, which most economic sectors see as a disaster, is not the case with some creative local businesses. In Bali, a group of youths called "Petani Muda Keren" (Cool Young Farmers) has become a driving force for the agricultural sector revival during the pandemic and succeeded in exporting several fruit commodities such as mangosteen to many countries. In South Sulawesi, porang farmers and seaweed cultivators have existed during the crisis and even exported or established cooperation with exporting companies during the pandemic. Meanwhile, in North Sumatra, many creative farmers intensify farming activities in specific vegetable crops (such as chili and ginger) and fruit crops (such as salak and durian), thereby contributing significantly to agricultural commodities export growth. This study found that three main drivers of local business champions' internationalization success are innovator entrepreneurs' emergence, appropriate technology application, and the adaptation and proliferation of social innovation policy to the broader community and sectors. This study fills the existing knowledge gap that has not fully addressed the interaction effect among the theory of social innovation, entrepreneurship, and ERBV theory in building back better sectors slumped by the pandemic.

**Keywords** Local business champions · Internationalization · COVID-19 pandemic · Innovator entrepreneurs · Appropriate technology · Social innovation policy

---

A. S. Hidayat (✉) · Z. Salim · C. M. Firdausy · P. T. Febiansyah · K. Sabilla · R. D. Nugraheni · B. D. Cahyono
National Research and Innovation Agency—BRIN (Formerly known as Indonesian Institute of Sciences—LIPI), Jakarta, Indonesia
e-mail: agus110@brin.go.id



Nawawi et al. (eds.), *Managing Disruption and Developing Resilience for a Better Southeast Asia*, Springer Proceedings in Humanities and Social Sciences,
https://doi.org/10.1007/978-981-96-2116-3_3

# 1 Introduction

The outbreak of the COVID-19 pandemic globally since early 2020 has caused a massive contraction on the demand and supply sides, leading to the disruption of domestic and international trade. The pandemic has also prompted many countries to take temporary protective measures on export and import activities. UNCTAD [57] reported that international merchandise and services trade declined about 7.4 and 20% in 2020. For the Indonesia case, the pandemic decreased export by about 2.7% in 2020 and dropped economic growth to −5.3% in 2020Q2. The trend of negative growth continued until 2021Q1, sending the economy into a recession. This painful condition has pushed millions of people to lose their businesses and jobs and eventually fall into poverty.

Amid the pandemic, it is fortunate that new business opportunities have emerged. Some local entrepreneurs turned this situation around creatively and reaped considerable economic benefits through internationalization. In Bali, for instance, a group of youths called "Petani Muda Keren" (Cool Young Farmers) has become a driving force for the agricultural sector revival during the pandemic and succeeded in exporting several fruit commodities such as mangosteen to many countries. In South Sulawesi, porang farmers and seaweed cultivators have been able to exist during the crisis and even export or established cooperation with exporting companies during the pandemic. Meanwhile, in North Sumatra, many creative farmers are taking advantage of the pandemic by intensifying farming activities in specific vegetable crops (such as chili and ginger) and fruit crops (such as salak and durian) and exporting the commodities to new markets.

The strategy of local entrepreneurs, especially those in small-medium enterprises (SMEs), to compete in the export market under challenging conditions is a kind of non-predictive strategy (NPS), a term popularized by Sarasvathy et al. [48]. The application of NPS entails improvisation efforts [2], creativity and purposeful creation [5], flexibility and openness to divergence from the original course of action, and spontaneous commitment [38]. Furthermore, Bai et al. [5] mention that NPS leads entrepreneurs to become more open-minded, explore unusual ways, think outside the box, and improvise solutions when chances and challenges arise. The increase in their export capabilities is also inseparable from the emergence of entrepreneurship leaders trying to start a new Business Model Innovation (BMI). Colovic [15] mentions that SMEs' model innovation led by innovative leadership yields a timelier foreign market entry.

Research discussing the phenomenon of the internationalization process of SMEs outside the normal business cycle processes during a pandemic is still rare. As is the general view, SMEs are generally identified as businesses with various limitations in the internationalization process. This limitation happens because they face multiple obstacles such as lack of access to finance [27, 29, 44], low capacity to innovate [9, 42, 56], and weak business networks among the supply chains [26, 31, 49]. The obstacles have been even getting harder during the pandemic time.

Considering the abovementioned background, this study aims to investigate the main drivers of the internationalization process of local business champions during the COVID-19 pandemic.

## 2 Literature Review

Business internationalization is a complex process that involves many competitive factors affecting company performance and supply chain cooperation, social environment, and business ecosystem. Thus, the perspective examining the business internationalization process needs various views. Therefore, this study is underpinned by theories supporting the internationalization process that represent various factors from internal firms, external linkages, and social innovation perspectives.

### *2.1 Theory of Social Innovation*

The severe economic impacts during the COVID-19 pandemic have been caused by the lockdown and physical distancing of large parts of social and economic life into a stay-at-home economy [41] or less contact economy [13]. These measures further affect the core of human behavior and lead to individual isolation [22], particularly the vulnerable groups. Fortunately, the crisis caused by the COVID-19 pandemic also offers businesses and/or entrepreneurial opportunities, especially for social innovation[1] that is oriented toward social needs and emerges because of pressing social-economic problems [11, 33, 36, 50, 54, 55, 59] (Anheir et al. 2019). Of the many ways of social innovation, digital social innovation is one way to address physical distancing. Another way of social innovation is establishing stronger links to local communities [17]. On the institutional or organizational level, this can be in the forms of the improvement of business infrastructure [39], adjusting their supply chains [34], and experimenting with their business models [11] to ensure the survival of their businesses to mitigating the consequences of crises in general and COVID-19 in particular.

Empirically, social innovation has also shown able to alleviate the social and economic consequences of the COVID-19 pandemic crisis [7, 8]. Social innovation even has given contributions beyond its (potential) contributions to economic recovery, as typically addressed in the literature [10, 60]. This may also suggest that social innovation can open up new business opportunities that existing market or state activities are unable to address [20, 24]. Therefore, the social innovation caused by

[1] *S*OCIAL innovation theoretically can be defined in three distinct ways: (1) as a form of social value creation, capture, and distribution; (2) as a polysemous concept that creates networks of meaning necessary in cross-sector collaborations; and (3) as striving for institutional change (see, [36], for details).

COVID-19 is not only lucrative opportunities but can be construed as opportunities from a variety of evaluative criteria [23], offering room for innovation that benefits society [4] (Nichols and Murdock 2012).

While the social innovation theoretically and empirically discussed above sounds promising, the nexus between the social-economic conditions provoked by the COVID-19 crisis and the business opportunities for social innovation, for instance, cannot be simply defined. This is partly because of the social problems that social innovation seeks to address frequently involve multiple and diverse actors, from different fields, across systems with multiple interdependencies. Furthermore, social innovations, be they new products, processes, or business models, require a change in or affect existing relational and social structures, including routines, resource and authority flows, governance, and values [36]. Thus, caveats apply when employing the theories of social innovation.

## *2.2 Theory of Entrepreneurship*

The uncertainty during the COVID-19 pandemic has promoted the idea of entrepreneurship. Entrepreneurship is perceived as one essential element in achieving a nation by fundamental means, especially economically: for its strong correlation with the economic growth [58], the acquirement of new sources for productivity enhancement, the employment of human resources, and the contribution in reducing poverty [6]. Ratten [46] strongly promotes entrepreneurship, claiming that it generates positive and dynamic energy. Entrepreneurship maintains the competitiveness of a nation's economy. Moreover, an entrepreneur is characterized by his/her perseverance and risk-taking ability, even in a pandemic situation.

Entrepreneurship drives the structural transformation of a nation with profiles of low-income society. It heavily relies on the primary sector for a nation with a better income society based on service and technology [40]. During the pandemic, many entrepreneurs also conduct innovation [46] and adopt new technologies and digitalized systems to improve product and service quality (Stephen et al. 2021).

There are plenty of variables in the concept of entrepreneurship, such as the motivation and support from family and economic conditions (capital), the dimension of the market, the change and shifting of technology, the structure of the market, and a nation's demographic [1]. Some influential factors include the functions of institutions, culture, and social values. The entrepreneurship environment also requires the cooperation and harmony of its stakeholders, namely the society, related institutions with legal status, and the environment (cluster and economy agglomeration if present) [16]. The approach to entrepreneurship is unquestionably complex [18], considering its starting point is strictly possible only by human initiation, not merely by the economic or technological situation, or even by normative and demographic changes.

## 2.3 *Extended Resources-Based View (ERBV) Theory*

A framework of resources-based view (RBV) documents ownership's role in controlling resources and using them to create economic value using strategic activities [43]. Other studies make a similar definition of RBV, as Amit and Schoemakers [3] defined RBV as controlled resources by a firm. In addition, the pioneering work of RBV belongs to Penros. They described RBV as bundles of heterogeneous resources that a firm uses to produce goods or services with a high value compared with other firms' products [37].

Several studies mention that RBV focuses its analysis only on an internal firm [14, 21, 30]. This internal view of the firm makes several limitations when current business processes become more complex. For example, one of the main limitations is assuming resources are heterogeneous and have imperfect mobility. It means that firms will have a comparative advantage when they own non-transferable and unrivaled resources [32]. Today, most literature has moved its framework from traditional RBV to extended RBV. According to Kiwala et al. [32], the first extended RBV framework was introduced by Lavie [35]. An extension made by Lavie [35] explains that firms can benefit from their value from internal sources and external sources. Collaboration within two or more firms relaxes the assumption of non-transferable resources. When an alliance of firms is formed, each firm shares its resources. Usually, an alliance of firms has the same goals to generate additional benefits from shared resources.

Managing own resources and collaborating among firms are the basic drivers of the industrial system. Mathews [37] argued that learning is a process that runs beyond resources and collaboration. In the context of firm-level, Mathews [37] defined the learning process as economic learning. Economic learning can be described as firms' capabilities to adapt to new circumstances and create new opportunities. In addition, learning is a dynamic process. Firms accumulate their capabilities by changing business processes or standard operating procedures from what they learn from external sources or past mistakes.

# 3 Methods

To explore the driving factors for the internationalization process in business, especially SMEs engaged in some primary sectors such as agriculture and fisheries (in South Sulawesi, Bali, and North Sumatera), we apply the PEST analysis. PEST is an acronym for four sources of change: political (P), economic (E), social (S), and technological (T). PEST is a powerful analytical tool widely used to assess strategic risk related to the external macro-environment for companies that can affect their business [47]. Due to the nature of the external environment beyond the company's control (larger ecosystem), the company has to respond well. The company's macro-environment (or organization) has to be addressed by minimizing risks and increasing opportunities through strategic policies [47]. Those three provinces were selected as the case study because many local entrepreneurs in these areas have survived and even expanded their businesses during the pandemic time.

PEST analysis has several variants adapted to the object of analysis and the study's purpose. Rastogi and Trivedi [45] explain the flexibility in using PEST as an analysis tool that can be adapted to the purpose and character of the study. Several modifications to the PEST analysis include other indicators in the fundamental PEST analysis, such as PESTEL or PESTLE, with additional environmental and legal attributes. The PEST analysis variant is also used to look at the macro-environment of an industry that allows companies to identify the risks around them with the PESTLE model [52].

In this study, we use the PEST variant by entering the essential variables PEST (political (P), economic (E), social (S), and technological (T)) and adding some variables, namely in behavior (B), climate/environment (C) and legal (L)—(BCL). We conducted in-depth interviews with several relevant stakeholders to collect PEST-BCL analysis data. The stakeholders include the farmers, group of farmers, business community members of ALFI, KADIN, and appropriate local government officials (Agriculture Service, Trade and Industry Office, Regional Investment Office, Tourism Office, Marine, and Fisheries Office, Regional Quarantine Institute), Fisheries Certification Agency, and Academicians.

## 4 Findings and Discussion

Internationalization in the business process can move the local economy beyond the usual business practices. Internationalization is very helpful in the economic recovery process, especially for the local economy. Internationalization cannot work without internalizing culture, ideas, and technology adoption within the company. Factors outside the company influence internalization and internationalization. However, external macro factors affect the business processes inside the companies. These external factors are uncontrollable factors that go beyond the ability of businesspeople to control them. Table 1 describes several external factors presented using the extension of the PEST method [45, 51] and developed into PEST-BCL, which is adapted to the character of the business entities in the area of the study.

**Political**: Political factors affect the competitiveness of SMEs expanding to new markets. There are negative campaigns for agricultural and fishery products with environmental damage and deforestation issues searching for new markets. Some fundamental issues in the political aspects include standardization, certification, and NTMs.

**Economic**: The pandemic affects the distribution chain of agriculture and fisheries products. A further impact of the pandemic is that there is often a shortage of containers during the COVID-19 pandemic [28], increasing cargo costs that can reach 1000%. During the pandemic, international shipping costs (including cargo)

**Table 1** PEST'—BCL analysis

| | |
|---|---|
| Political | – There is a negative campaign for agricultural and fishery products with environmental damage and deforestation issues<br>– Standardization is part of the protectionism of importing countries to protect domestic consumers<br>– The political approach is to establish a Mutual Recognition Arrangement (MRA) for several agricultural and fishery products |
| Economic | – International trade relations can be started by establishing B-to-B relations through business networks<br>– Border closures during the pandemic increase additional costs (changes in the distribution chain and container scarcity, operations cancellation of several liners)<br>– Direct calls/direct flights follow the law of supply and demand and the availability of transshipment routes |
| Social | – Leadership and entrepreneurship in the farmers' community significantly impact the business direction, including the ability to export<br>– Less commitment of many farmers to maintain their products (according to the specified grade)<br>– Need for training related to certification and quality control of farming and fishery products |
| Technology | – The use of technology (IT) accelerates technology adoption to assist the agricultural production process (control of humidity, water requirements, air temperature, and others), seed selection and fertilization, and marketing that utilizes technology applications. Appropriate technology also increases productivity<br>– Many farmers lack access to the appropriate technology<br>– Need cargo consolidation for MSMEs with fewer shipments and many shippers (MSMEs) |
| Behavioral | – The average export problem is about coordination<br>– Business networks often start from personal relationships, diaspora, and young businesspeople (school alumni)<br>– Export decisions are not in the hands of farmers but are still in the hands of collectors; farmers only produce |
| Climate/ environment | – Land carrying capacity helps maintain sustainable production (agriculture, fisheries) and indirectly helps protect the environment<br>– Limited land and the need for participation of business actors in the form of social business (cooperatives)<br>– Environmental issues (deforestation, wildlife protection) are often used as material for negative campaigns on Indonesian agricultural products |
| Legal | – Government guidelines are needed, especially from the Ministry of Trade, to support efforts to expand export markets to Eastern Europe, Latin America, and other potential markets<br>– Government support is needed in conducting MRA with trading partners (agricultural products: coffee) |

contributed significantly to the increase in transportation and logistics costs, the rise in freight was 400–1000% due to a shortage of cargo. Indonesia's exports are demand-driven: The reason for choosing a country to be the export target is the existing demand from the destination country. Trade relations (export destination countries) can be started by establishing business-to-business relations through business networks that trigger exports [53]. Often, the status of direct calls/direct flights follows the law of supply and demand. The business instincts of buyers and sellers and the presence of ship routes determine the characteristics of direct or indirect exports.

**Social**: The issue of NTMs and ignorance about NTMs is still a big problem for many exporters in the region (a common problem of exporters from North Sumatra and other regions). The exporter usually relents if there is a rejection of export goods due to the NTM factors. The solution is to sell the export goods to other buyers or lower prices to minimize losses. The exporters (from North Sumatra and Bali) experienced the rising issues of deforestation, forest protection, and environmental sustainability that hindered the CPO exports. One example is about "Cup Test" [25] for coffee products. This cup test has a very high level of subjectivity. The tester assigned by the importer tends to make decisions for the benefit of his boss (importer).

**Technology**: The use of appropriate technology (IT) increases productivity and accelerates the development and innovation in agriculture and fisheries businesses in marine fishing, as well as assists agricultural production (control of humidity, water requirements, air temperature, and others), seed selection, and fertilization and marketing that utilizes technology applications. One of the main issues is many SMEs lack the ability to afford appropriate technology. In addition, the support from the government, universities, and research institutes on technical aspects is also limited.

**Behavior**: One of the crucial problems of exports is hampered by a lack of coordination among government agencies. Here, the government's presence facilitates and lets businesses move according to their business instincts. Another issue is that many export decisions are not in the hands of farmers but the hands of collectors; farmers only produce the products. Leadership plays a fundamental role in changing many farmers' groups; for instance, having an excellent leader has pushed a group of young farmers in Bali (*Petani Muda Keren*) and Medan to go through the boundaries. Here, *Petani Muda Keren* has tried to overcome the problems of production and supply chain at their company level [34] and further go outside the typical behavior of other entrepreneurs by designing their business model [11] in line with the local culture of Bali and structural land ownership in Bali community.

Personal behavior within the entrepreneur also determines the company's success in carrying out internationalization. Business networks often start from personal relationships, diaspora, and young businesspeople. Here, in Bali, social innovation [10, 60] could be working well with the young business leaders of *Petani Muda Keren*.

**Climate/Environment**: The carrying capacity of the environment/land helps maintain sustainable production (agriculture, fisheries) and indirectly helps the protection of the environment. Agricultural business systems and patterns often experience limited land [12, 19]. These problems are standard features of agriculture-farming systems in Bali, Medan, and Makassar. Environmental variables become a central issue when national companies (of all sizes) expand their business overseas. Environmental issues (deforestation, wildlife protection) are often used as material for negative campaigns on Indonesian agricultural and fishery products. The government and the business need to cooperate in explaining environmental problems proportionally and responsibly and counter the black campaign globally.

**Legal**: Macro problems in Indonesia's business and investment world are still waiting to implement the Job Creation Law and its derivative products supporting the business and investment climate. Implementing the Job Creation Law could strengthen the fisheries and agriculture sectors. Government guidelines, especially from the Ministry of Trade, are needed to support overseas markets expansion to Eastern Europe, Latin America, and other potential markets. The concrete forms of trade cooperation such as FTA, CEPA, and others may facilitate this global expansion. The existing problems, such as protection through NTMs, can be resolved through trade negotiations in the form of trade cooperation. In particular, the effort to overcome NTMs is through the MRA scheme. In this case, the business world needs government support in conducting MRA with trading partners (such as agricultural products: coffee and other featured products).

Based on the above PEST-BCL findings and also the in-depth interview results, we select three factors as the main drivers of local business champions' internationalization:

## 5 The Emergence of Innovator Entrepreneurs

As the COVID-19 pandemic negatively impacted the economy, many entrepreneurs faced resource constraints, especially for those small-scale businesses. The significant decrease in product demand was the main problem during the pandemic. This situation led to a drop in income and caused a lack of capital to adjust to the economic shock. Their vulnerability forced them to apply an adaptive strategy.

In theory, the entrepreneurs were the innovators who were open to risks and applied adaptive strategy by trying new ideas. As the shock occurs, these entrepreneurs develop new ideas in business processes or products, or both of them to be their survival strategy. This strategy even could cause better performance during the shock period. The strategy may also be done by the community or most local farmers with or without government intervention. According to the field research in Bali, South Sulawesi, and North Sumatera, entrepreneurship innovation became the main driver of the export business during the pandemic.

In Bali, Petani Muda Keren (Cool Young Farmers) became successful entrepreneurs during the COVID-19 pandemic. The young farmers had successfully exported their farm products by adopting innovations in their farming technology, known as smart farms, based on the Internet of Things. This community also broke the recent trend that young people tend to avoid working in the agricultural sector. They proved that young people could crucially contribute to the farming process mainly due to a better understanding of technological adoption. Their innovation solved the problem of the young people's contribution to the agricultural sector and technology adoption in the farming process.

In South Sulawesi, the government intervention supported the innovation to export their new potential product. While maintaining to export profitable commodities like seaweed, the government supported farmers to diversify their export commodities. The rise of *porang* demand from other Asian countries due to its nutritional content made some farmers apply different strategies by growing *porang* instead of other commodities. The government had contributed to this shift by conducting socialization, education, and extensification of *porang* commodities. The export potential of *porang* is also bolstered by the existence of exporting companies of the same item.

In North Sumatera, product shifting also occurred during the pandemic. Besides the stability of plantation crops, mainly the palm oil commodity, the increase in agricultural products during the COVID-19 pandemic is also caused by horticulture products' intensification. At least two vegetable crops (chili and ginger) and two fruit crops (snake fruit/salak and durian) became the primary commodities for export. The farmers of those commodities' major innovation strategy were the application of processing more healthy crops or organic products and the utilization of the Internet to find a new market, mainly the Middle East countries.

Although their strategy was quite different, the similarity among those local champions was in their spirit of innovation. In entrepreneurship, their bravery to face the risks and adopt new ideas was crucial to surviving the economic shock. While *Petani Muda Keren* established the idea of a new business process in the form of farming technology by young farmers, the farmers in South Sulawesi followed the government's instruction to grow new commodities; hence they could export new products. Lastly, a new adaptation of new healthier products and new business processes by using the Internet led to excellent export performance in North Sumatera. These findings also proved that an adaptive innovation strategy could solve resource constraints.

## 6 The Application of Appropriate Technology

The use of technology by local entrepreneurs in the primary sector in the provinces of South Sulawesi, Bali, and North Sumatra during the COVID-19 pandemic has increased productivity and sales. Two types of technology that can help local entrepreneurs penetrate international markets during COVID-19 are appropriate technology and digital technology. Appropriate technology plays a role in increasing productivity on-farm and post-harvest, while digital technology is mainly used for market expansion and finding new markets.

In the case of Bali, the adoption of digital technology has been used by farmers in business processes from upstream to downstream. One of the main actors in applying digital technology is the younger generation of farmers who call themselves Cool Young Farmers (PMK). The agricultural concept that they are stretching is smart farming based on the Internet of Things (IoT). In the upstream, they apply the concept of smart farming through digitalization and IoT. This technology can be used in watering and fertilizing plants using an application on smartphones to set the volume and time as needed. This technology also serves as a weather sensor that can function as a soil moisture sensor, soil PH sensor, rain sensor, and air sensor.

Furthermore, the electricity used for this purpose comes from solar cell energy, so energy costs are also more efficient. This smart farming model has increased land productivity by 15%. While in the downstream, they utilize cooperative business units such as offline retail, online, exhibitions, and exports. Their export capacity has increased from 3 to 10 ton every shipment to countries in Asia and Europe.

Meanwhile, in the case of farmers in North Sumatra, technology is more widely used in handling post-harvest activities during the pandemic. The Provincial Agriculture Office initiated the use of such technology. The technology used includes providing warehouses with many large cold storages to help store crops and maintain the stock-flow of horticultural products. Another technology that is intensively used during the pandemic is post-harvest product preservation technology. In addition, to increase productivity and encourage exports, farmers also get technical support from the Local Agriculture Office to provide fertilizers, superior seeds, pesticides for pest eradication, and agricultural technical assistance and intensification of extension services.

During the pandemic, farmers also intensively utilize digital technology for marketing and finding new markets. They create websites to provide information regarding export products and prices and actively engage in social media to interact with potential customers in domestic and export markets. The farmers and collectors can expand the market to countries that have not been entered, including countries in the Middle East. The Middle East was chosen as the target for market expansion because of the country's high demand for healthy plant commodities. Exports of North Sumatra Province for agricultural products (in a broad sense) experienced a significant increase of 38% in 2020–2021. Plantation-based products and horticultural products experienced the most considerable portion of the agricultural export increase. Palm oil is one of the mainstays of exporting plantation products. Some of the mainstays of exporting horticultural products include vegetable crops (such as chili and ginger) and fruit crops (such as salak and durian). The largest export markets for agricultural products of North Sumatra Province are countries in the Middle East Region, Japan, and the Netherlands.

## 7 The Adaptation and Proliferation of Social Innovation Policy to the Wider Community and Sectors

Local businesses in North Sumatera, Bali, and South Sulawesi performed adaptive strategies in dealing with the pandemic COVID-19. Their effort broke out the impact of the crisis. They have realized that working in the agricultural sector was beneficial and significantly needed in the current global economy. An attempt of survival intuition led to achieving export performance and absorbing unemployment-related pandemics in their neighborhood.

Individual innovation and collective action developed by local entrepreneurs are critical components for surviving a business. According to the interview with business actors, the pandemic enables social learning to emerge in uncertain situations that rely on stakeholders' engagement. Active engagement between local businesses, community, and local government empowers the local economy to sustain livelihood and well-being and avoid the consequence of health crises.

The group of youths called *Petani Muda Keren* (PMK) in Bali adopts the social-business system that benefits local agriculture products in the international market. This group has shown that social innovation could deliver a resilient business and adaptive capacity during a crisis. The interplay between the government of Bali Province and PMK benefits local farmers by intensifying fruit commodities to increase product competitiveness in the global market. This collaborative attempt has successfully exported some fruits to many countries while other regions struggled to survive the pandemic effect.

A case study in South Sulawesi provides another story of collaborative action. Exporter companies take a step to build a transitional analysis of niche management. They encourage the interrelationship between the local government of South Sulawesi and farmers to accommodate an international demand for *porang* and seaweed commodities. Its social innovation process seems to thrive because firms undertake learning processes from the associated experience and culture. As a result, governmental-business collaboration in commodities conveys community practices in the pattern of farmers' responses to their values incorporated with external dynamics.

The evidence from North Sumatera is different from Bali and South Sulawesi case studies. Social innovation is flourished from farmers' actions, which creatively initiated adaptive management of their business process. They develop power structures with local governments to channel global needs of particular commodities into their carrying capacity of product diversification. An intensive nexus between actors has facilitated the building of international networks between farmers and foreign businesses, resulting in impressive export performance for vegetable and fruit commodities during the pandemic.

The distinct features of case studies showcase how social innovation works. Adaptive and collaborative frameworks are necessary to increase social learning in dealing with the crisis. Three conceiving agents in different cases lead the social innovation process. Each actor carries a discourse and a practice. Its varied experiences reflect local characteristics and values with a similarity: the inclusion of government interference. It means that the governmental role can enhance the process of social innovation if the socioeconomic ecosystem supports it.

## 8 Conclusion

During the COVID-19 pandemic, local creative entrepreneurs have turned adversity into opportunity by advancing the internationalization of small and medium enterprises (SMEs). Many SMEs that are still facing various political, economic, social, technological, business, climate/environmental, and legal challenges can survive in the domestic markets and even expand to new export markets. By implementing a no n-predictive strategy (NPS) and applying Business Model Innovation (BMI) supported by innovative entrepreneurship, many local business champions in the provinces of South Sulawesi, Ball, and North Sumatra are able to carry out the internationalization process during the pandemic.

Grounded in theories of social innovation, entrepreneurship, and the extended Resource-Based View (RBV), and analyzed through the PES T-BCL framework, the study identifies three key factors that enabled SMEs to internationalize during the pandemic: (a) the emergence of i nnovator entrepreneurs; (b) the application of appropriate technology; and (c) the adaptation and proliferation of social innovation policy to the broader community and sectors.

To sustain and expand this momentum, urgent policy support is needed to build a more enabling Innovation and business ecosystem. This includes designing fiscal, monetary, certification, and innovation linkage instruments that improve SMEs' access to affordable technologies and simplify export processes. Strengthening collaboration between SMEs, universities, and research institutions, particularly through the e stablishment of local SME Innovation Centers, is also essential. These centers should be equipped with both hard and soft infrastructure to nurture innovation where SME growth potential is high. In the global trade context, three policy priorities are recommended: (1) standardi zation (certification, NTMs, and Mutual Recognition Arrangement (MRA) for many agricultural and fishery products); (2) cost efficiency (shi pping cost and cargo consolidation); and (3) environmental concern.

While this study focuses on the internationalization of primary sector SMEs during the pandemic, further research is needed to examine th e social structures and governance mechanisms underlying social innovation, Exploring these deeper drivers will be key to understanding h ow to replicate and scale successful SME internationalization across both primary and secondary sectors and their supply chains.

## References


1. Acs Z, David Audretsch (2010) Discoverers of the role of small firms in innovation and creators of the small business economics. Springer, Boston, MA. https://doi.org/10.1007/0-387-23633-3_8
2. Alsos GA, Clausen TH, Mauer R, Read S, Sarasvathy SD (2020) Effectual exchange: from entrepreneurship to the disciplines and beyond. Small Bus Econ 54(3):605–619. https://doi.org/10.1007/s11187-019-00146-9
3. Amit R, Schoemaker PJ (1993) Strategic assets and organizational rent. Strateg Manag J 14:33–46. https://doi.org/10.1002/smj.4250140105
4. Anheier H, Krlev G, Mildenberger G (2019) Social innovation: comparative perspectives. Routledge, New York. https://www.taylorfrancis.com/books/oa-edit/10.4324/9781315158020/social-innovation-helmut-anheier-gorgi-krlev-georg-mildenberger
5. Bai W, Johanson M, Oliveira L, Ratajczak-Mrozek M, Francioni B (2022) Where business networks and institutions meet: internationalization decision-making under uncertainty. J Int Manag 28(1):100904. https://doi.org/10.1016/j.intman.2021.100904
6. Baptista R, Escaria V, Madruga P (2005) Entrepreneurship, regional development, and job creation: the Case of Portugal. SSRN Electron J. https://doi.org/10.2139/ssrn.666842
7. Bapuji H, Patel C, Ertug G, Allen DG (2020) Corona crisis and inequality: why management research needs a societal turn. J Manag. Online first 1–18
8. Barki E, Campos JG, Lenz A-K, Kimmitt J, Stephan U, Naigeborin V (2020) Support for social entrepreneurs from disadvantaged areas navigating crisis: insights from Brazil. J Bus Venturing. Insights 14
9. Baumann J, Kritikos AS (2016) The link between R&D, innovation, and productivity: are micro firms different? Res Policy 45(6):1263–1274. https://doi.org/10.1016/j.respol.2016.03.008
10. Bishop P (2019) Knowledge diversity and entrepreneurship following an economic crisis: an empirical study of regional resilience in Great Britain. Entrep Reg Dev 31:496–515
11. Bjo€rklund TA, Mikkonen M, Mattila P, van der Marel F (2020) Expanding entrepreneurial solution spaces in times of crisis: business model experimentation amongst packaged food-beverage ventures. J Bus Venturing. Insights 14
12. Boyd CE, D'Abramo LR, Glencross BD, Huyben DC, Juarez LM, Lockwood GS, McNevin AA, Tacon AGJ, Teletchea F, Tomasso Jr JR, Tucker CS (2020) Achieving sustainable aquaculture: historical and current perspectives and future needs and challenges. J World Aquaculture Soc 51(3):578–633. https://doi.org/10.1111/jwas.12714
13. Brodjonegoro B (2020) Ekonomi Minim Kontak. Kompas 23(6/2020):6
14. Cao M, Zhang Q (2011) Supply chain collaboration: impact on collaborative advantage and firm performance. J Oper Manag 29(3):163–180. https://doi.org/10.1016/j.jom.2010.12.008
15. Colovic A (2022) Leadership and business model innovation in late internationalizing SMEs. Long Range Plan 55(1):102083. https://doi.org/10.1016/j.lrp.2021.102083
16. Dau LA, Cuervo-Cazurra A (2014) To formalize or not to formalize: entrepreneurship and pro-market institutions. J Bus Ventur 29(5):668–686. https://doi.org/10.1016/j.jbusvent.2014.05.002
17. Doern R, Williams N, Vorley T (2019) Special issue on entrepreneurship and crisis: business as usual? An introduction and review of the literature. Entrep Reg Dev 31:400–412
18. Eckhardt JT, Shane SA (2003) Opportunities and entrepreneurship. J Manag 29(3):333–349. https://doi.org/10.1177/014920630302900304
19. FAO (2020) The state of world fisheries and aquaculture 2020. Sustainability in action, Rome. https://doi.org/10.4060/ca9229en
20. Farhoud M, Shah S, Stenholm P, Kibler E, Renko M, Terjesen S (2020) Social enterprise crowdfunding in an acute crisis. J Bus Venturing. Insights 15. https://www.mendeley.com/catalogue/4efc24f7-0726-3716-a777-441da54438fd/
21. Frenz M, Ietto-Gillies G (2009) The impact on innovation performance of different sources of knowledge: evidence from the UK community innovation survey. Res Policy 38(7):1125–1135. https://doi.org/10.1016/j.respol.2009.05.002

22. Gibson C (2020) From "social distancing" to "care in connecting": an emerging organizational research agenda for turbulent times. Acad Manag. Discoveries 6:165–169. https://journals.aom.org/doi/10.5465/amd.2020.0062
23. Gümüsay AA (2018) Unpacking entrepreneurial opportunities: an institutional logic perspective. Innovation 20:209–220
24. Gümüsay AA, Harrison P (2020) Never let a crisis go to waste: entrepreneurship in the age of coronavirus. Int Bus Rev
25. HQTS (2021) Evaluating coffee quality with the cupping test. 10 Dec 2021. https://www.hqts.com/coffee-quality-cupping-test/
26. Hanna V, Walsh K (2008) Interfirm cooperation among small manufacturing firms. Int Small Bus J 26(3):299–321. https://doi.org/10.1177/0266242608088740
27. Hidayat AS, Pok WC (2021) The effect of credit rationing on the probability of SMEs investing. Rev Dev Financ 11(2):18–38. https://doi.org/doi:10.10520/ejc-rdfin_v11_n2_a2
28. Jakarta Post (2021) The pandemic drives sea freight prices to record high. 4 Jul 2021. https://www.thejakartapost.com/news/2021/07/04/pandemic-drives-sea-freight-prices-to-record-high.html
29. Jinjarak Y, Wignaraja G (2016) An empirical assessment of the export-financial constraint relationship: how different are small and medium enterprises? World Dev 79:152–163. https://doi.org/10.1016/j.worlddev.2015.11.012
30. Khanna T, Palepu K (2000) The future of business groups in emerging markets: long-run evidence from Chile. Acad Manag J 43(3):268–285. https://doi.org/10.2307/1556395
31. Kim J-J, Hemmert M (2016) What drives the export performance of small and medium-sized subcontracting firms? A study of Korean manufacturers. Int Bus Rev 25(2):511–521. https://doi.org/10.1016/j.ibusrev.2015.09.002
32. Kiwala Y, Olivier J, Ismail K (2022) Antecedents and enablers of supply chain value creation: an analysis of trust and competences. Dev South Afr. https://doi.org/10.1080/0376835X.2022.2029356
33. Krlev G, Anheier H, Mildenberger G (2018) Social innovation—what is it and who makes it?. In: Social innovation. Routledge, pp 3–35
34. Kuckertz A, Bra€ndle L, Gaudig A, Hinderer S, Morales Reyes C, Prochotta A, Steinbrink KM, Berger ES (2020) Startups in times of crisis—a rapid response to the COVID-19 pandemic. J Bus Venturing. Insights 13
35. Lavie D (2006) The competitive advantage of interconnected firms: an extension of the resource-based view. Acad Manag Rev 31(3):638–658. https://doi.org/10.2307/20159233
36. Logue D (2019) Theories of social innovation. Edward Elgar Publishing, 192 p. https://ssir.org/books/excerpts/entry/theories_of_social_innovation
37. Mathews J (2003) Competitive dynamics and economic learning: an extend resource-based view. Ind Corp Chang 12:115–145. https://doi.org/10.1093/icc/12.1.115
38. Mauer R, Wuebker R, Schlüter J, Brettel M (2018) Prediction and control: an agent-based simulation of search processes in the entrepreneurial problem space. Strateg Entrep J 12(2):237–260. https://doi.org/10.1002/sej.1271
39. Munõz P, Naudé W, Williams N, Williams T, Frías R (2020) Reorienting entrepreneurial support infrastructure to tackle social crisis: a rapid response. J Bus Venturing. Insights 14
40. Naudé W (2008) Entrepreneurship in economic development Wim Naudé*. In Unu-Wider
41. Nummela N, Paavilainen-Ma€ntym€aki E, Harikkala-Laihinen R, Raitis J (2020) When all doors close: implications of COVID-19 for cosmopolitan entrepreneurs. Int Small Bus J. online first 1–7
42. Ofreneo RE (2016) Auto and car parts production: can the Philippines catch up with Asia? Asia Pac Bus Rev 22(1):48–64. https://doi.org/10.1080/13602381.2014.990212
43. Popli M, Ladkani RM, Gaur AS (2017) Business group affiliation and post-acquisition performance: an extended resource-based view. J Bus Res 81:21–30. https://doi.org/10.1016/j.jbusres.2017.08.003
44. Rahaman MM (2011) Access to financing and firm growth. J Bank Finance 35(3):709–723. https://doi.org/10.1016/j.jbankfin.2010.09.005

45. Rastogi N, Trivedi MK, DM M (2016) PESTLE technique—a tool to identify external risks in construction projects. Int Res J Eng Technol 3(1):384–387. https://www.irjet.net/archives/V3/i1/IRJET-V3I165.pdf
46. Ratten V (2021) COVID-19 and entrepreneurship: future research directions. Strateg Chang 30(2):91–98. https://doi.org/10.1002/jsc.2392
47. Sammut-Bonnici T, Galea D (2014) PEST analysis. Wiley encyclopedia of management, edited by Professor Sir Cary L Cooper. John Wiley & Sons, Ltd.https://doi.org/10.1002/9781118785317.weom120113
48. Sarasvathy S, Kumar K, York JG, Bhagavatula S (2014) An effectual approach to international entrepreneurship: overlaps, challenges, and provocative possibilities. Entrep Theory Pract 38(1):71–93. https://doi.org/10.1111/etap.12088
49. Shaw E (2006) Small firm networking—an insight into contents and motivating factors. Int Small Bus J 24(1):5–29. https://doi.org/10.1177/0266242606059777
50. Shepherd DA (2020) COVID-19 and entrepreneurship: time to pivot? J Manage Stud 57:1750–1753
51. Song J, Sun Y, Jin L (2017) PESTEL analysis of the development of the waste-to-energy incineration industry in China. Renew Sustain Energy Rev 80(March 2016):276–289. https://doi.org/10.1016/j.rser.2017.05.066
52. The University of Sydney (2022) Marketing: PESTLE analysis. https://libguides.library.usyd.edu.au/c.php?g=508107&p=5994242
53. The UK's Department for International Trade (DIT) (2021) Large business export barriers, support needs, and the role of DIT qualitative research findings November 2021. Department for International Trade. https://assets.publishing.service.gov.uk/government/uploads/system/uploads/attachment_data/file/1044976/large-business-export-barriers-support-needs-and-the-role-of-dit-qualitative-research-findings.pdf
54. Thorgren S, Williams TA (2020) Staying alive during an unfolding crisis: how SMEs ward off impending disaster. J Bus Venturing. Insights 14
55. Tracey P, Stott N (2017) Social innovation: a window on alternative ways of organizing and innovating. Innovation 19:51–60
56. Turner JR, Ledwith A, Kelly J (2010) Project management in the small to medium-sized enterprise: matching processes to the nature of the firm. Int J Project Manage 28:744–755
57. UNCTAD (2021) Global merchandise trade exceeds the pre-COVID-19 level, but services recovery falls short. Retrieved from https://unctad.org/news/global-merchandise-trade-exceeds-pre-covid-19-level-services-recovery-falls-short#:~:text=According%20to%20the%20report%2C%20world,when%20trade%20fell%20by%2022%25
58. Wennekers S, Van Stel A, Carree M, Thurik R (2010) The relationship between entrepreneurship and economic development: is it U-Shaped? Found Trends Entrep 6(3):167–237. https://doi.org/10.1561/0300000023
59. Van Wijk J, Zietsma C, Dorado S, de Bakker FG, Marti I (2019) Social innovation: integrating micro, meso, and macro-level insights from institutional theory. Bus Soc 58:887–918
60. Williams N, Vorley T (2015) The impact of institutional change on entrepreneurship in a crisis-hit economy: the case of Greece. Entrepreneurship Reg Dev 27:28–49. https://www.econbiz.de/Record/the-impact-of-institutional-change-on-entrepreneurship-in-a-crisis-hit-economy-the-case-of-greece-williams-nick/10011297386

# Revisiting Models of Economic Development in the Philippines in Light of the Pandemic

**Benjamin Velasco**

**Abstract** This chapter revisits critiques of the neoliberal model of economic development in light of the pandemic and proposes holistic social development as an alternative. The relevance of modernist and functionalist perspectives has been critically examined since the 2008 global crisis. Inequality amid sustained economic growth in the Philippines raises questions about development strategy. The massive expansion of State intervention and public provisioning during the pandemic furthers the necessity of interrogating new models of development. The paper argues that recovery from the pandemic and mitigation of inequality toward holistic social development rests on an extension of social protection, an enhanced unemployment insurance, provision of employment guarantees, promotion of social solidarity economy and a rights-based development strategy. The imposition of a wealth tax is proposed as a key mechanism to fund robust social development programs. Finally, the paper recommends how this alternative model of development can be concretized in an electoral agenda in view of the 2022 national polls in the Philippines.

**Keywords** Philippines · Economic development · COVID-19 pandemic · 2022 election

## 1 Modernist Perspective of Development

The idea that social development accrues primarily from economic growth is rooted in a modernist perspective or a functionalist strategy. Wealth is created through economic growth. When the economy is booming, people have jobs and earn wages or incomes, businesses generate profit and the government gets taxes. When the working population has income, then they can procure their daily necessities. When the government generates taxes, then it has the fiscal ability to fund social services and provide social goods. When enterprises and corporations are profitable, then they

B. Velasco (✉)
University of the Philippines Diliman, Quezon City, Philippines
e-mail: bbvelasco@up.edu.ph



Nawawi et al. (eds.), *Managing Disruption and Developing Resilience for a Better Southeast Asia*, Springer Proceedings in Humanities and Social Sciences,
https://doi.org/10.1007/978-981-96-2116-3_4

can expand and hire more workers who will buy more goods. In theory, these are the mechanisms by which economic growth benefits social welfare. In this manner, social development can be reduced to measuring increases in gross domestic product (GDP) [30].

However, GDP increase and per capita income are aggregate measures and cannot capture the distribution of the gains of economic growth [18, 30]. Thus, other indicators of social development such as poverty incidence and the Gini coefficient have been proposed. The Gini coefficient gauges the share of income between the rich and the poor [13]. Meanwhile, the poverty incidence has an element of subjectivity since the poverty threshold is a matter for authorities to fix, more or less arbitrarily [17]. However, the World Bank [35] has recently used USD 1.90 a day as a measure of absolute poverty.

Per capita income, poverty incidence and the Gini coefficient as indicators of social development imply a trickle-down theory of progress. The modernization paradigm posits that countries will progress through the same stages of economic development [27]. The neoliberal era starting in the 1980s continues this modernist perspective with development proceeding from the one-size-fits-all formula of privileging free markets and free trade [34].

In the decades since, the promises of the neoliberal model have been unfulfilled and modernization theory has been discredited. Less developed countries remained mired in poverty and debt, and even in developed countries, an underclass grew as inequality has worsened [32, 34].

The Philippines is not an exception as inequality persists despite sustained economic growth. Looking at income distribution in 2015, the richest 20% took 45% of the income and just 10% of Filipinos amassed 30% of the total. On the other hand, the poorest 20% had to make do with just 7.5% of total income. Comparing the two extremes, the richest 10% earned seven times the poorest 10% [16]. One key mechanism for reproducing inequality has been wage suppression. From 2001 to 2016, real wages stagnated while labor productivity increased by about 50% and GDP doubled [19]. Economic growth streamed up to capital owners and did not trickle down.

As a result, for last three decades, the Philippines had the slowest growth in its Human Development Index (HDI) among a set of middle to low-income Asian countries. Among the same group, the Philippines was the third most unequal society based on the Gini coefficient [16].

Thus, other functionalist strategies of development have been initiated which innovate the basic model but do not contradict the basic tenet of trickle-down progress. For example, conditional cash transfers—called Pantawid Pamilyang Pilipino Program or 4Ps in the Philippines—and rudimentary forms of social protection like senior citizen allowances have been implemented in Global South countries [28]. These have been pioneered by the neoliberal State as forms of mitigation amid the persistence of poverty and exclusion but still within the framework of economic growth as social development.

In the context of the pandemic, the modernist and functionalist perspective can be clearly shown in the prioritization of economic growth as the basis for recovery from the crisis. At the height of the pandemic lockdowns in the Philippines, export processing zones and business process outsourcing firms were the sectors earliest allowed to resume face-to-face work. This is clearly due to the fact that these are dollar-earning industries and thus crucial to economic growth.

All of these imply that recovery from the crisis is less a matter of State intervention and instead more the subject of individual effort. If the economy recovers, then people will have jobs and using their income they can adapt to the new normal. The State may assist the poorest of the poor and the most vulnerable sectors but only to a point. The majority of the population is expected to fend for themselves since they have jobs and incomes. And for people to be employed, businesses must be prioritized in recovering since it is the private sector that is the engine of economic growth and thus of social development.

## 2 Holistic Social Development

Several social development concepts proceed from a critique of the modernist theory and functionalist strategies. Among these are the human development and sustainable development perspectives which are based on the idea that development must be directly measured in terms of outcomes and not indirectly through GDP growth.

The HDI is a composite measure of per capita income, life expectancy and mean years of schooling. It aims to directly measure health, education and well-being [18, 34]. However, wages, income and wealth are not equitably distributed between men and women. In fact, even within households, there are stark differences in well-being between females and males. Thus, the Gender Development Index compares the HDI for males and females to highlight this quest for parity in social development [13, 34]. Social development as well-being of the people must be directly measured by improvements in nutrition, health and education as basic needs and other more substantive rights such as political freedoms and capability to participate in social life.

The recovery of the economy from the crisis wrought by the pandemic is necessary. But social interventions that target improvement of the well-being of the poor and marginalized must be undertaken. And in these social interventions, the State is the primary actor. The private sector is an actor in social development of course but the State directs it through purposive interventions.

How can the gains of economic growth and recovery from the pandemic redound to mitigation of inequality and holistic social development?

First, by an expansion of social protection. Elements of social protection already exist at present. There are forms of assistance for people who are at risk or vulnerable to shocks and challenges in terms of sickness, disability, unemployment or old age. These must be radically expanded. For example, universal health care (UHC) is already provided for by a law passed just before the onset of the pandemic [20]. But it has not been fully implemented due to budget constraints. Another is the unemployment insurance scheme provided through the Social Security System which has certain requirements and limited benefits.

These rudimentary forms of social protection must be further developed. First, by expanding the pandemic aid or *ayuda* and the 4Ps program into a universal basic income (UBI). Through a UBI, everyone is entitled to a State subsidy that will be enough to provide for the most basic needs. In this way, absolute poverty will be abolished. The wages and income of those gainfully employed can then provide for further improvements in their well-being, such as spending for better housing.

Second, an enhanced unemployment insurance and its flipside, an employment guarantee. Those who have lost their jobs must be assisted. But this can only be sustainable if gainful employment is indeed available to people. In the neoliberal model, it is expected that the private sector will provide these jobs. However, the recent decade and a half economic boom, characterized by around 5% annual GDP increases, have been jobless growth [14]. It is the State that must ensure there are enough jobs and full employment is attained.

Full employment is possible since there are millions of jobs needed to respond to social needs. Unfortunately, the private sector does not invest in the provision of these social needs because it is not profitable. For example, there is a glut in high-end housing since condominiums and subdivisions are lucrative for real estate developers. But there is a five million backlog in low-end and socialized housing [1]. A massive public housing program for the working class and the urban poor will not only provide affordable housing to the homeless but also employ millions in public construction work.

Another sector for public employment is climate adaptation and mitigation. Solarizing homes and buildings, and retrofitting buildings are labor-intensive industries. Likewise, reforestation in rural areas and cleanup of rivers, waterways and beaches will employ millions of otherwise unemployed or discouraged workers [11].

Third, a social solidarity economy must be promoted. In this, the State does not have to be the actual lead actor such as in the provision of enhanced social protection. The State only has to provide the legal scaffolding for these grassroots initiatives and encourage civil society to step up. Amid the pandemic, community pantries sprouted all over the Philippines. Starting from an individual initiative in one street in Quezon City, community pantries were set up in a few thousand places [9]. The community pantry exhibits the best elements of a social solidarity economy. In the solidarity economy, non-market transactions transpire between individuals and groups with the aim of providing for social needs. The International Labour Organization annual conference in 2022 had social solidarity economy and decent work as its main themes.

In the community pantry, the market has been totally displaced as basic needs like food are provided gratis instead of sold. But other types of solidarity economy involve market transactions as for example, direct buying between urban communities and farmers cooperatives [22]. Affordable agricultural products are made available to the poor in the towns and cities since the mark-up of merchants is absent. Likewise, production cooperatives based in the urban areas like garment homeworkers producing face masks or clothes can sell their inexpensive goods to both urban and rural areas. This can be enabled by new technologies like the Internet through online selling. The State can encourage this by providing training and capital to these community-based "start-ups" and cooperatives.

The State promoting forms of social solidarity economy initiatives can make up for the period when the more expansive social protection measures that still being setup are not yet fully implemented. But the solidarity economy is not just a stop gap measure. It should be a bedrock of the better normal too.

Finally, robust social protection schemes and a social solidarity economy must be framed in terms of a rights-based development strategy [1, 6]. These forms of social assistance to the population, especially the poor and marginalized, should be understood as entitlements that are due to everyone. They are human rights that must be enjoyed by all. The Philippine constitution and international conventions from the UDHR, ICCPR, ICESCR and CEDAW all provide the legal scaffolding for a rights-based social development strategy.

Funds for a comprehensive package of social assistance can be immediately generated by imposing a wealth tax on the richest Filipinos. Arguably the first to issue the call in the Philippines in late 2020, the labor coalition Nagkaisa advocated for imposing on Filipino billionaires a graduated tax. The wealth tax will generate enough funds for supporting MSMEs and initiating a UBI [31]. This is one crucial step toward rolling back regressive taxation in the form of VAT and the recent lowering of estate taxes and corporate income taxes. Other than a wealth tax, other forms of asset reform are needed. To cite just one example, agrarian reform must be completed and rural development must be assisted. This will resolve the historical demand of the rural population for wealth redistribution.

## 3 Alternative Electoral Platform

In light of the 2022 national polls in the Philippines, the alternative model of development can be concretized in an electoral agenda. The following proposal borrows from the key advocacies of various workers groups, social movements and human rights organizations that the author has engaged with as a labor educator and rights defender.

### *3.1 Drug War*

President Duterte made no secret of the fact that the drug war will be bloody. The killings of drug addicts, overwhelmingly residents of depressed urban communities, even started weeks before he assumed power. With the end of his term, it is clear as day that the drug war was a failure in terms of eradicating the scourge of drugs. Drug addiction should be approached as public health concern not as a peace-and-order problem needing a militarized or securitized solution.

Social development is best served by respecting human rights, including the right to life and the right to fair trial and due process. The authorities responsible for the bloody drug war must be made responsible for their crimes. The response to drug addiction must involve social intervention using the tools of social workers and medical practitioners like psychologists and psychiatrists.

## 3.2 *Human Rights*

No doubt the narrative of human rights has suffered under the Duterte administration as he personally made a crusade against it using the argument that it protects criminals. Yet, the Universal Declaration of Human Rights was drafted in the wake of the horrors of the Second World War. It sought to ensure that basic and fundamental rights and freedoms can be enjoyed by all. From a more limited framework of political freedoms and civil liberties, human rights have become expansive in terms of covering even economic, social and cultural rights. Many of the major social reforms at the national and international level have been implemented under the rubric of furthering human rights.

The goal of reviving human rights as a principle of good governance must be put front and center. And to contest the narrative that human rights defend criminals instead of the innocent, the new administration must ensure that human rights are expansive. That is, social programs and public services should be framed as elements of human rights. The Commission of Human Rights (CHR) must continue to be the lead agency in the observance of human rights. But its leadership in promoting political rights should extend and expand to the economic, social and cultural dimensions of human rights. The CHR already has an economic, social and cultural rights office but it is practically inactive. That office must be reanimated so as to be as prominent as the understanding of human rights as involving political freedoms and civil liberties.

## 3.3 *West Philippine Sea*

Under the Duterte administration, the Philippine claim to the West Philippine Sea was practically abandoned. Under a new administration, the legal victory of the country must be asserted in the face of transgressions by China. However, the pitfalls of a policy on the West Philippine Sea that favors the United States as against China must be avoided. The Philippines must not be a pawn in the geopolitical maneuverings of both China and the United States. Instead, the country must pursue an independent foreign policy that is reflected in a policy on the West Philippine Sea.

Assertion of Philippine claim to the WPS should be for the purpose of assisting small fishers to avail of the resources of the area. From the perspective of sustainable development, it would be a mistake for the assertion of sovereignty over the WPS to result in oil exploration and mining by multinational corporations. Extracting the oil and gas under the WPS will merely exacerbate climate change. A strategic resolution to the West Philippine Sea issue should be undertaken under a multilateral not bilateral framework.

### *3.4* Ayuda *and Universal Basic Income*

The pandemic has shown that social assistance is an utmost necessity so that masses of Filipinos do not fall under the cracks. But even in so-called normal times, social assistance in the form of a guaranteed income for Filipinos should be set up.

UBI has already been piloted in some countries and communities [33]. In the Philippines, mass poverty and mass unemployment—even without the threat of Industry 4.0—necessitate a solution like UBI. The organizational and bureaucratic systems for a UBI already exist in the 4Ps. But for 4Ps to blossom into a UBI, the coverage should be universal not targeted. Also, the benefits must expand to cover the costs of basic needs [2].

### *3.5 Jobs and Contractualization*

Duterte famously promised to end contractualization or precarious jobs the moment he became president [29]. The pledge notoriously ended with him vetoing the proposed Security of Tenure bill that Congress passed [8].

Regular employment must be the norm once more in both the private and public spheres. Ending contractualization will go a long way in improving decent work in the country. But it is not enough. A public employment program must be implemented so that all able-bodied Filipinos, men and women, of proper age will have gainful employment. This will be a historic leap toward attaining the Sustainable Development Goal on decent work and economic growth. This public employment program should be State-led and similar to the NREGA of India [5]. Workers can be employed for the construction of mass housing and also for climate adaptation and mitigation. These concrete programs are major steps toward solving unemployment, poverty, homelessness and environmental degradation.

### *3.6 National Living Wage*

Another populist promise of Duterte that remained unmet was his pledge to abolish regional wages. In conjunction with promoting regular jobs, abolishing regional wages and ensuring living wages will advance decent work and inclusive growth.

It will further human development as wages and income are key instruments in improving well-being.

Organized labor, farmers' organizations and social movements as well as employers' groups should have voice and participation in this program of fixing and instituting living wages. The system of tripartism can be the venue for the dialogue between the stakeholders in setting living wages.

## 3.7 Land Reform

Despite numerous attempts at land reform, landlessness and rural poverty remain daunting challenges to this day. The Comprehensive Agrarian Reform Law and then its extension, the so-called CARPER, came and went without land redistribution being completed [4]. Likewise, even agrarian reform beneficiaries face difficulties due to lack of capital and low prices in the face of global competition and cheap agricultural imports.

A new and radical land reform program must be earnestly pursued as an asset reform and wealth redistribution mechanism. In this way, it becomes a step toward social development that it is transformative and not just a token reform.

## 3.8 Environment and Climate Change

A welcome development in the early part of the Duterte administration was the appointment a pro-active Environment and Natural Resources secretary who used her position to assiduously protect the environment by closing mines that had been reckless polluters and violative of standing laws. But she was ousted after a short period and her initiatives died under a new secretary [12].

The Philippines is among the nations severely affected by climate change [7, 10, 15]. Sustainable development does not only ensure the well-being of the present generation but also the future generations of humans. A program that immediately closes down mines, extractive industries and business establishments that violate the environmental laws must be implemented unrelentingly by the new administration. This will set the tone for the advancement of sustainable development and other initiatives protective of the environment.

## 3.9 Mass Housing

A glut in high-end housing contrasts with the shortfall in socialized housing. That is the unfair and unequal state of the housing sector in the Philippines. The forcible occupation by poor informal settlers of an unutilized government housing project during the early part of the Duterte administration exposed the housing problem in the country [23]. Millions of Filipinos survive in informal settlements in vacant or unoccupied land in the cities where jobs are available.

The only solution to the problem is State-led public housing development since real estate developers do not engage in low-income and socialized housing. A public housing program does not only provide homes for the homeless but also employ the unemployed. Such a massive construction program necessarily needs hundreds of thousands if not millions of workers. Again, informal settler groups must be given voice and representation in the planning and implementation. Some urban poor organizations implement so-called people's plans in undertaking on-site housing development. These grassroots initiatives must be supported and scaled-up.

### *3.10 Women's Rights*

It is ironic that under the Duterte administration pro-women initiatives like the Safe Spaces Act [24] and Expanded Maternity Leave Law [21] were passed even as the president flagrantly disrespected women's rights through sexist and misogynist jokes and acts [26]. In this climate of misogyny, online sexual harassment and bullying of women who were critical of the administration festered.

A new administration can definitely do better by matching deeds with words. The government must consistently promote women's rights and gender equality. Much has been done in terms of advancing women's rights and development in the country in the post-1986 period. Much of this is due to the struggles of a strong women's movement. No doubt this has led to a good standing for the Philippines in terms of gender development indices. This of course fell under the term of Duterte [25]. Several key reforms remain. One is the legalization of divorce. Another is enactment of a bill on sexual orientation, gender identity and expression. Both of these are practical and realizable goals under a gender responsive administration.

## 4 Conclusion

The paper revisited the critiques of the neoliberal model of economic development in light of inequality amid economic growth and the pandemic-induced crisis. It proposed an alternative that is framed in holistic social development. Recovery from the pandemic and mitigation of inequality toward holistic social development rests on an extension of social protection, an enhanced unemployment insurance, provision of employment guarantees, promotion of social solidarity economy and a rights-based development strategy. The imposition of a wealth tax is a key mechanism to fund robust social development programs. This alternative model of development can be concretized in a progressive electoral agenda. Elements of this electoral agenda but not its entirety are reflected in the platform of the 2022 opposition candidate Leni Robredo.

The 2022 election in the Philippines was arguably the most important since the 1986 transition from one-man rule to elite democracy. The space for civil society and social movements became severely constricted with the turn toward authoritarianism under the Duterte administration. With the landslide victory of the son of the former dictator Marcos as president and the daughter of Duterte as vice-president, the current regime of killings and impunity is bound to be consolidated.

Thus, the prospects are gloomy in terms of actually changing the course of social development in the Philippines. Even worse, the scenarios are grim as far as the flourishing of civil liberties and democratic rights is concerned. In the next six years, the social movements in the Philippines will have to bundle their advocacy for an alternative social development with the defense of democratic spaces.

## References

1. Bastagli F, Lowe C (2021) Social protection response to Covid-19 and beyond: emerging evidence and learning for future crises, ODI. https://cdn.odi.org/media/documents/ODI_Synthesis_final.pdf. Last accessed 30 Jun 2021
2. Cabegin E (2020) Policy reforms in Philippine social protection and labor systems beyond COVID-19. Philippine J Labor Ind Relat 37:45–75
3. Congressional Policy and Budget Research Department of the House of Representatives: The Philippine Housing and Household Statistics, CPBRD (2021) https://cpbrd.congress.gov.ph/images/PDF%20Attachments/Facts%20in%20Figures/FF2021-40_Phil_Housing_and_Household_Stats.pdf . Last accessed 30 Jun 2021
4. Cruz JPD, Manahan MAB (2014) CARPER diem: a socio-legal analysis of the state of the comprehensive agrarian reform program in the Aquino administration. Ateneo Law J 59(3):930–1006
5. De Venanzi A (2022) Can Latin America learn from India's efforts at fighting poverty? The case of the Mahatma Gandhi National Rural Employment Guarantee Act. J Int Comparat Soc Policy 36(2):159–74. Last accessed 01 May 2022
6. Devereux S, Sabates-Wheeler R (2004) Transformative social protection. IDS working paper 232. https://www.ids.ac.uk/download.php?file=files/dmfile/Wp232.pdf. Last accessed 30 Jun 2021
7. Eckstein D, Künzel V, Schäfer L, Winges M (2019) Global climate risk index 2020, Germanwatch. https://www.germanwatch.org/sites/default/files/20-2-01e%20Global%20Climate%20Risk%20Index%202020_14.pdf. Last accessed 30 Jun 2021
8. Esguerra DJ (2019) It's official: Duterte vetoes Security of Tenure bill, Inquirer.net. https://newsinfo.inquirer.net/1146631/its-official-duterte-vetoes-security-of-tenure-bill. Last accessed 30 Jun 2021
9. Espartinez A (2021) Emerging community pantries in the Philippines during the pandemic: hunger, healing, and hope. Religions 12(11):926–935
10. Fortaleza W (2019) Is the Philippines getting green and just?: A baseline study on the application of just transition framework in the Philippines, Friedrich Ebert Stiftung—Philippine Office. http://thecentre.ph/pdf/Fin-Publication-%20Is%20the%20Philippines%20Getting%20Green%20and%20Just%20(Just%20Transition%20Framework%20in%20PH).pdf. Last accessed 30 Jun 2021

11. Fortaleza W (2021) Greening the pandemic response—A labor agenda on recovery through green employment in rebuilding (LARGER) programs, Friedrich Ebert Stiftung—Philippines Office. http://library.fes.de/pdf-files/bueros/philippinen/17278.pdf. Last accessed 30 Jun 2021
12. Gutierrez J (2019) Gina Lopez, who led crackdown on mines in the Philippines, Dies at 65, The New York Times. https://www.nytimes.com/2019/08/19/obituaries/gina-lopez-philippines-dies.html. Last accessed 30 Jun 2021
13. Hall A, Midgley J (2004) Social policy for development. SAGE, London
14. International Labour Organization Country Office for the Philippines (2017) Decent work country diagnostics: Philippines 2017. ILO, Philippines
15. Just Transition and Equitable Climate Action Resource Center: Philippines (n.d.) A Whole-of-government Approach to Creating Green Jobs, World Resources Institute. https://www.wri.org/just-transitions/philippines. Last accessed 30 Jun 2021
16. Lim JA (2020) Towards a better normal: a study on inequalities and the lack of development in the Philippines, Oxfam Philippines. https://oi-files-cng-prod.s3.amazonaws.com/philippines.oxfam.org/s3fs-public/file_attachments/SUMMARY%20(Online)%20Oxfam%20Pilipinas%20Inequality%20Report%20Oct%202020.pdf. Last accessed 28 Jul 2022
17. Mangahas M (2014) The will to measure poverty, Inquirer.net. https://opinion.inquirer.net/74139/the-will-to-measure-poverty. Last accessed 28 Jul 2022
18. Midgley J (2014) Social development: theory and practice. SAGE, Los Angeles
19. Monsod S (2018) Productivity rising—but not wages. Inquirer.net. https://opinion.inquirer.net/115767/productivity-rising-not-wages. Last accessed 28 Jul 2022
20. Official Gazette (2019a) Republic Act 11223, Official Gazette. https://www.officialgazette.gov.ph/downloads/2019/02feb/20190220-RA-11223-RRD.pdf. Last accessed 30 Jun 2021
21. Official Gazette (2019b) Republic Act 11210, Official Gazette. https://www.officialgazette.gov.ph/downloads/2019/02feb/20190220-RA-11210-RRD.pdf. Last accessed 30 Jun 2021
22. Ofreneo RP, Hega MD (2016) Women's solidarity economy initiatives to strengthen food security in response to disasters: insights from two Philippine case studies. Disaster Prev Manag 25(2):168–182
23. Pasion P (2017) Occupy Bulacan: how the urban homeless won shelter, Rappler. https://www.rappler.com/nation/166293-kadamay-housing-issue-briefer/. Last accessed 30 Jun 2021
24. Philippine Commission on Women (2019a) Republic Act 11313: safe spaces act, PCW. https://pcw.gov.ph/republic-act-11313/. Last accessed 30 Jun 2021
25. Philippine Commission on Women (2019b) Philippines drops 8 places in gender equality, remains top in Asia, PCW. https://pcw.gov.ph/philippines-drops-8-places-in-gender-equality-remains-top-in-asia/. Last accessed 30 Jun 2021
26. Ranada P (2021) Duterte, fond of sexist jokes, issues women's month message, Rappler. https://www.rappler.com/nation/duterte-womens-month-2021-message/. Last accessed 30 Jun 2021
27. Rostow WW (1960) The stages of economic growth: a comparative manifesto. Cambridge University Press, Cambridge
28. Saguin K, Howlett M (2019) Policy transfer and instrument constituency: explaining the adoption of conditional cash transfer in the Philippines. Asia Pacific Policy Stud 6(3):352–366
29. Santos EP (2018) Ending 'endo': How's Duterte's campaign promise?, CNN Philippines. https://www.cnnphilippines.com/news/2018/04/24/president-rodrigo-duterte-dole-endo-contractualization-kmu.html. Last accessed 30 Jun2021/06/30.
30. Seers D (1969) The meaning of development. IDS Commun 44:1–26
31. Serrano M, Fortaleza W, Esguerra J, Miraflor M, Castillo C (2021) State of labor and its agenda on recovery (SOLAR): stimulating the economy by protecting workers. Nagkaisa, Philippines
32. Standing G (2011) The precariat: The new dangerous class. Bloomsbury Academic, London
33. Stanford Basic Income Lab (2020) Updated: global map of UBI experiments: where have we been, where are we now, and where are we Going?, Stanford basic income lab. https://basicincome.stanford.edu/news/lab-updates/global-map-of-ubi-experiments-where-have-we-been-where-are-we-now-and-where-are-we-going/. Last accessed 30 Jun 2021

34. Trask BS (2014) Women, work and globalization: challenges and opportunities. Routledge, New York
35. World Bank (2018) Poverty and shared prosperity, WB. https://www.worldbank.org/en/publication/poverty-and-shared-prosperity-2018. Last accessed 30 Jun 2021

# Village Economic Mapping for Capturing Economic Sectors: Case Study in Tegal Regency

**Muhammad Iqbal Maulana and Muhammad Ilham Maulana**

**Abstract** Analyzing village economy in Tegal Regency, this paper demonstrates village economic mapping that is used as a new economic tool. It suggests the policymakers in the Indonesian government and Tegal Regency government formulate the right public policies for economic optimization. In order to realize local potential optimization, Tegal Regency needs initial mapping to find out the economic potential of its village with the support of community empowerment. This research aims to identify the specific economic potential of villages in Tegal Regency. The study is also using spatial analysis. The results of the study showed village economic mapping can be an initial step of economic optimization for many sectors and how it can be a new paradigm of public policy for local government in Indonesia.

**Keywords** Mapping · Village economy · Spatial analysis

## 1 Introduction

Todaro and Smith [31] put forward the paradigm of development planning. There are three aspects of development, such as people-centered development, resource-based development, and institutional development [29]. The key to economic development lies in the management of economic resources that can be managed by the public and the private sector [3]. The Indonesian government has engaged in development with the community through the Village Law. Ulumiyah [33] argues that village development can run well because there are four determining factors, including economic empowerment, human resources quality, village infrastructure, and village institutions. These are in line with the superior economic theory which states that regional growth, labor, and added value act as the main drivers.

M. I. Maulana
Urban and Regional Planning, Diponegoro University, Semarang, Indonesia

M. I. Maulana (✉)
Ministry of Finance, The Republic of Indonesia, Jakarta, Indonesia
e-mail: mm.ilhammaulana@gmail.com



Nawawi et al. (eds.), *Managing Disruption and Developing Resilience for a Better Southeast Asia*, Springer Proceedings in Humanities and Social Sciences,
https://doi.org/10.1007/978-981-96-2116-3_5

Gul and Chaudhry [14] once created inequality mapping that photographed the lack of resource distribution in a village in the Tribal Region of Pakistan. They call this a new paradigm in economics to determine the distribution of socio-economic inequality. Seeing this, economic mapping becomes an important thing to be used as a tool of public policy [7, 13]. In particular, the village economy is currently a priority for the Indonesian government.

## 2 Literature Review

Basically, mapping is the process of visualizing and becoming a representation collectively to increase transparency and visibility processes [17]. Maps play a role in assisting the work process, interrupting system elements for process improvement [9]. Typically, a map shows what will be done, who is doing it, when and where it is done, and who or what depends on it. The benefits of mapping are focused on improving some of the revision processes based on future circumstances [26]. Mapping is becoming a new paradigm in economics [21 ] because many researchers from various countries have implemented mapping to help their work processes. For example, mapping is used for the spatial distribution of poverty in Vietnam and codifies key areas for poverty reduction [5]. Then, mapping is used to reduce socio-economic and economic disparities by predicting distribution in the region [1]. Economists Li and Zhao have used mapping to investigate levels of inequality in some countries and determine their relationship to economic characteristics [19, 34]. In addition, mapping is also used as an economic planner and makes a policy to overcome poverty [30].

Then in special cases such as spatial econometrics and demographics, dynamic spatial panel models can be used to characterize population dynamics in Brazil [8]. In addition, economic development and population growth in 28 European countries between 1960 and 2010 also used spatial models that resulted in a relationship between the two variables [2]. According to Nieto and Cardenas Alonso [22], spatial analysis techniques can be used for decision-making in Extremadura, such as very low returns on leaders' funds, which are obtained from rural areas with underdeveloped socio-economic conditions. In addition, in the same case, [28] studied the model of population growth by identifying the phenomenon of rural depopulation and its relationship to agricultural welfare and subsidies, where he discovered the seriousness of the problems, causes, and dependency relationships of several variables involved, as well as determining territorial policies and specific actions in each region. Spatial or mapping techniques can also determine rural development policies that have uneven effects, accentuate center-periphery differences, and contribute to rural depopulation in remote areas due to the influence of profits in more dynamic areas, to the detriment of those who lack centrality and exacerbate differences between them [6].

Maps play a role in providing information and are useful in representing the information consequently. In economics, mapping can demonstrate a causal role in shaping social and economic outcomes. In addition, the role of mapping has the potential to have an influence on regional natural resource investment because it is able to facilitate the identification of the entire geography so that it can predict the existence of regional economic potential. Then the mapping can be used as a basis for decision-making in an area [11]. The importance of understanding the role of policy is considered important because it can explore information and its use so that its objectives can be achieved. Thus, innovation in policymaking is an important part in achieving accelerated development in a region. Jordan and Huitema [16] explain policy innovation as a process and product of efforts to develop new policies that are widely adopted, which can have a significant impact due to the poor performance of existing policies.

## 3 Data and Methods

### *3.1 Research Area*

Based on satellite imagery in Fig. 1, Tegal Regency is located in The Province of Central Java Indonesia with its location on the north coast of Java (Pantura). The area of Tegal Regency is 87.79 km$^2$ which is divided into 18 districts and 287 villages. Tegal Regency is flanked by clear natural boundaries, such as the northern part of the Java Sea and Tegal City, the southern part of Mount Slamet and Banyumas Regency, the eastern part of Pemalang Regency, and the western part of Brebes Regency. The capital of Tegal Regency is located in Slawi District. The district with the farthest distance to the district capital is Warureja District which reaches 42 km. In addition, the shape of the earth surface of Tegal Regency ranges from 0 to 1000 m above sea level (masl) which is formed into 3 groups, namely land morphology, hills, and highlands. Lowland areas have a height of < 50 masl to coastal areas with a height of 0–1 masl. The medium–low bumpy hill area has a minimum height of about 350 masl, where most of it occupies the central part such as the Jatinegara District. While the highland area has a height ranging from 500 to 1000 masl, covering Bojong District 686 masl and Bumijawa District 947 masl. Then the Tegal Regency area is adjacent to the equator which divides the hemisphere vertically so that it has two seasons, namely drought and rain. As a result, Tegal Regency has a fluctuating rainfall cycle every time. When calculating on an annual basis, the volume of rainfall during 2019 was recorded at 2,006.6 mm. Then the air humidity level of Tegal Regency is relatively high with the monthly average ranging from 69 to 82% with a change in temperature between 23.2 °C and 32.9 °C. The geographical location of Tegal Regency also feels the direct effects of the pseudo-movement of the sun, where the average length of sunlight in 2019 ranges from 4.2 h to 9.1 h per day. Sunlight is dimming in January with an average shine of 4.2 h per day and in March with an average shine of 4.3 h per day. Based on the geographical location and climate [4], Tegal Regency will determine the direction of economic development of the village in the future.

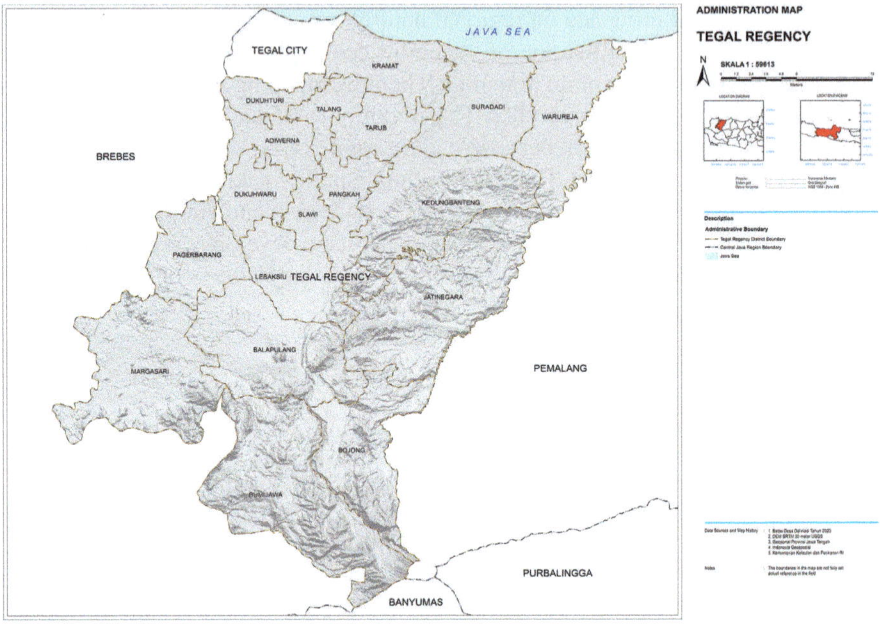


**Fig. 1** Tegal regency administration map

## 3.2 *Data*

To generate new economic growth in Tegal Regency, it must know the potential in each economic sector through mapping so that it is easy to analyze in detail. Data mapping analysis of economic sectors must first look for data sources in each sector of the economy, such as agriculture, fisheries, plantations, tourism, and industry. Data sources are divided into two, namely literature studies and agencies/institutions. Investment data [10] includes data on agriculture, fisheries, plantations, tourism, and industry that are analyzed through the GIS application to produce maps in each sector of the economy. In addition, other supporting data to help the analysis process is obtained from open sources, such as GIS web and satellite imagery [12]. Then the literature review data aims to validate the existing data so that it is accurate. The data that has been collected consists of villages, districts, and location and distribution areas. Thus, the source of economic sector data in Tegal Regency was obtained, as follows (Tables 1, 2, 3, 4 and 5).

**Table 1** Table of fishery economic sector

| Districts | Village | Fishery economic sector | |
|---|---|---|---|
| | | Large (Ha) | % |
| Kramat | Bongkok | 14.67 | 2.23 |
| Kramat | Dampyak | 198.09 | 30.07 |
| Kramat | Kramat | 77.86 | 11.82 |
| Kramat | Maribaya | 57.46 | 8.72 |
| Kramat | Munjungagung | 43.42 | 6.59 |
| Kramat | Padaharja | 48.03 | 7.29 |
| Suradadi | Bojongsana | 25.06 | 3.80 |
| Suradadi | Suradadi | 2.2 | 0.33 |
| Warureja | Demangharjo | 65.71 | 9.97 |
| Warureja | Kedungkelor | 126.25 | 19.17 |
| Total area | | 658.75 | 100.00 |

*Source* Geoportal, Central Java

## *3.3 Spatial Approach: Dividing Study Area into Economic Sector Zones*

Based on the literature and data obtained, we made a number of methodological choices, such as Handayani et al. [15], where several approaches to spatial analysis [20, 23, 27] coupled with judgment. Spatial analysis methods use a qualitative approach. The characteristic of spatial analysis is combining attributes and usually consists of vector data and raster data, but we use vector data with three types of geometry, namely point, line, and area. Analyzing the zone of the economic sector in each village involves several functions of spatial analysis used to create an economic sector zone. This spatial analysis function is in the form of reclassifying, which is the activity of reclassifying data that eventually becomes a new spatial data with certain criteria and attributes [24]. Then we also use the overlay method to display the economic sector of each village in Tegal Regency. The overlay process is carried out by two or more thematic maps with the same area that form a new map layer of the economic sector of each village in Tegal Regency [25]. All of the above explanations can be described by flowchart as follows (Fig. 2).

**Table 2** Table of agriculture economic sector

| Districts | Village | Agriculture economic sector | |
|---|---|---|---|
| | | Large (Ha) | % |
| Adiwerna | Bersole | 90.91 | 0.20 |
| Adiwerna | Adiwerna | 24.38 | 0.05 |
| Adiwerna | Gumelar | 99.93 | 0.22 |
| Adiwerna | Harjosari Kidul | 88.84 | 0.19 |
| Adiwerna | Harjosari Lor | 58.54 | 0.13 |
| Adiwerna | Pecangakan | 60.08 | 0.13 |
| Adiwerna | Kaliwadas | 96.23 | 0.21 |
| Adiwerna | Kedungsukun | 86.92 | 0.19 |
| Adiwerna | Lemah Duwur | 41.38 | 0.09 |
| Adiwerna | Lumingser | 80.2 | 0.17 |
| Adiwerna | Pagiyanten | 108.31 | 0.24 |
| Adiwerna | Pedagangan | 41.17 | 0.09 |
| Adiwerna | Penarukan | 95.79 | 0.21 |
| Adiwerna | Pedes Lohor | 275.73 | 0.60 |
| Adiwerna | Tembok Lor | 15.14 | 0.03 |
| Adiwerna | Pesarean | 56.85 | 0.12 |
| Adiwerna | Tembok Banjaran | 5.78 | 0.01 |
| Adiwerna | Tembok Kidul | 23.1 | 0.05 |
| Adiwerna | Tembok Luwung | 33.53 | 0.07 |
| Adiwerna | Ujungrusi | 33.4 | 0.07 |
| Balapulang | Bukateja | 157.52 | 0.34 |
| Balapulang | Balapulang Kulon | 484.75 | 1.05 |
| Balapulang | Balapulang Wetan | 92.3 | 0.20 |
| Balapulang | Cilongok | 128.63 | 0.28 |
| Balapulang | Banjaranyar | 504.45 | 1.10 |
| Balapulang | Batuagung | 295.73 | 0.64 |
| Balapulang | Cenggini | 381.39 | 0.83 |
| Balapulang | Cibunar | 90.98 | 0.20 |
| Balapulang | Danareja | 176.91 | 0.38 |
| Balapulang | Darawarih | 152.61 | 0.33 |
| Balapulang | Pamiritan | 157.04 | 0.34 |
| Balapulang | Harjowinangun | 204.66 | 0.44 |
| Balapulang | Kalibakung | 94.41 | 0.21 |
| Balapulang | Kaliwungu | 199.22 | 0.43 |
| Balapulang | Sangkanjaya | 105.35 | 0.23 |
| Balapulang | Karangjambu | 251.9 | 0.55 |

(continued)

**Table 2** (continued)

| Districts | Village | Agriculture economic sector | |
|---|---|---|---|
| | | Large (Ha) | % |
| Balapulang | Pagerwangi | 72.76 | 0.16 |
| Balapulang | Sesepan | 60.27 | 0.13 |
| Balapulang | Tembongwah | 97.14 | 0.21 |
| Balapulang | Wringinjengot | 157.06 | 0.34 |
| Bojong | Batunyana | 170.78 | 0.37 |
| Bojong | Gunungjati | 145.32 | 0.32 |
| Bojong | Bojong | 171.43 | 0.37 |
| Bojong | Buniwah | 138.12 | 0.30 |
| Bojong | Cikura | 76.64 | 0.17 |
| Bojong | Danasari | 60.66 | 0.13 |
| Bojong | Dukuhtengah | 27.3 | 0.06 |
| Bojong | Kajenengan | 92.12 | 0.20 |
| Bojong | Kalijambu | 112.16 | 0.24 |
| Bojong | Karangmulyo | 216.82 | 0.47 |
| Bojong | Lengkong | 219.38 | 0.48 |
| Bojong | Pucangluwuk | 140.99 | 0.31 |
| Bojong | Suniarsih | 58.51 | 0.13 |
| Bojong | Rembul | 283.42 | 0.62 |
| Bojong | Sangkanayu | 73.1 | 0.16 |
| Bojong | Tuwel | 386.69 | 0.84 |
| Bumijawa | Traju | 110.23 | 0.24 |
| Bumijawa | Begawat | 77.47 | 0.17 |
| Bumijawa | Carul | 134.92 | 0.29 |
| Bumijawa | Bumijawa | 119.18 | 0.26 |
| Bumijawa | Cawitali | 216.36 | 0.47 |
| Bumijawa | Cempaka | 216.43 | 0.47 |
| Bumijawa | Cintamanik | 15.92 | 0.03 |
| Bumijawa | Dukuhbenda | 225.63 | 0.49 |
| Bumijawa | Guci | 53.16 | 0.12 |
| Bumijawa | Gunungagung | 241.1 | 0.52 |
| Bumijawa | Jejeg | 145.61 | 0.32 |
| Bumijawa | Muncanglarang | 152.94 | 0.33 |
| Bumijawa | Pagerkasih | 235.57 | 0.51 |
| Bumijawa | Sumbaga | 242.89 | 0.53 |
| Bumijawa | Sokasari | 306.66 | 0.67 |

(continued)

**Table 2** (continued)

| Districts | Village | Agriculture economic sector | |
|---|---|---|---|
| | | Large (Ha) | % |
| Bumijawa | Sokatengah | 320.75 | 0.70 |
| Dukuhturi | Dukuhturi | 121.93 | 0.26 |
| Dukuhturi | Kademangaran | 49.55 | 0.11 |
| Dukuhturi | Pekauman Kulon | 6.21 | 0.01 |
| Dukuhturi | Kepandean | 57.05 | 0.12 |
| Dukuhturi | Ketanggungan | 56.43 | 0.12 |
| Dukuhturi | Kupu | 146.2 | 0.32 |
| Dukuhturi | Lawatan | 103.31 | 0.22 |
| Dukuhturi | Pagongan | 12.38 | 0.03 |
| Dukuhturi | Sidakaton | 227.1 | 0.49 |
| Dukuhturi | Sidapurna | 27.8 | 0.06 |
| Dukuhturi | Pengarasan | 72.81 | 0.16 |
| Dukuhwaru | Blubuk | 239.11 | 0.52 |
| Dukuhwaru | Bulakpacing | 190.39 | 0.41 |
| Dukuhwaru | Dukuhwaru | 368.37 | 0.80 |
| Dukuhwaru | Kabunan | 120.71 | 0.26 |
| Dukuhwaru | Gumayun | 309.89 | 0.67 |
| Dukuhwaru | Kalisoka | 115.29 | 0.25 |
| Dukuhwaru | Pedagangan | 94.69 | 0.21 |
| Dukuhwaru | Selapura | 126.37 | 0.27 |
| Dukuhwaru | Sindang | 82.28 | 0.18 |
| Dukuhwaru | Slaranglor | 305.33 | 0.66 |
| Jatinegara | Argatawang | 197.61 | 0.43 |
| Jatinegara | Capar | 135.77 | 0.29 |
| Jatinegara | Cerih | 130.87 | 0.28 |
| Jatinegara | Kedungwungu | 207.87 | 0.45 |
| Jatinegara | Lebakwangi | 233.4 | 0.51 |
| Jatinegara | Dukubangsa | 312.86 | 0.68 |
| Jatinegara | Penyalahan | 216.67 | 0.47 |
| Jatinegara | Gantungan | 88.65 | 0.19 |
| Jatinegara | Jatinegara | 120.5 | 0.26 |
| Jatinegara | Lembasari | 126.08 | 0.27 |
| Jatinegara | Luwijawa | 192.5 | 0.42 |
| Jatinegara | Mokaha | 150.22 | 0.33 |
| Jatinegara | Padasari | 242.05 | 0.53 |

(continued)

**Table 2** (continued)

| Districts | Village | Agriculture economic sector | |
|---|---|---|---|
| | | Large (Ha) | % |
| Jatinegara | Sitail | 110.99 | 0.24 |
| Jatinegara | Sumbarang | 128.87 | 0.28 |
| Jatinegara | Tamansari | 145.32 | 0.32 |
| Jatinegara | Wotgalih | 137.66 | 0.30 |
| Kedungbanteng | Kebandingan | 171.57 | 0.37 |
| Kedungbanteng | Dukuhjati Wetan | 146.23 | 0.32 |
| Kedungbanteng | Karanganyar | 103.48 | 0.22 |
| Kedungbanteng | Karangmalang | 291.03 | 0.63 |
| Kedungbanteng | Kedungbanteng | 203.84 | 0.44 |
| Kedungbanteng | Sumingkir | 126.89 | 0.28 |
| Kedungbanteng | Tonggara | 182.94 | 0.40 |
| Kedungbanteng | Margamulya | 229.48 | 0.50 |
| Kedungbanteng | Penujah | 83.86 | 0.18 |
| Kedungbanteng | Semedo | 152.15 | 0.33 |
| Kramat | Babakan | 74.04 | 0.16 |
| Kramat | Bangungalih | 91.71 | 0.20 |
| Kramat | Dinuk | 113.33 | 0.25 |
| Kramat | Kertaharja | 94.45 | 0.21 |
| Kramat | Bongkok | 140.06 | 0.30 |
| Kramat | Dampyak | 142.5 | 0.31 |
| Kramat | Kepunduhan | 100.27 | 0.22 |
| Kramat | Jatilawang | 140.3 | 0.30 |
| Kramat | Kemantran | 46.47 | 0.10 |
| Kramat | Kemuning | 117.52 | 0.26 |
| Kramat | Kertayasa | 287.43 | 0.62 |
| Kramat | Ketileng | 94.11 | 0.20 |
| Kramat | Kramat | 170.97 | 0.37 |
| Kramat | Maribaya | 177.43 | 0.39 |
| Kramat | Mejasem Timur | 216.72 | 0.47 |
| Kramat | Mejasembarat | 18.13 | 0.04 |
| Kramat | Munjungagung | 143.17 | 0.31 |
| Kramat | Padaharja | 164.39 | 0.36 |
| Kramat | Plumbungan | 131.49 | 0.29 |
| Kramat | Tanjungharja | 198.17 | 0.43 |
| Lebaksiu | Balaradin | 382.49 | 0.83 |

(continued)

**Table 2** (continued)

| Districts | Village | Agriculture economic sector | |
|---|---|---|---|
| | | Large (Ha) | % |
| Lebaksiu | Dukuhdamu | 195.56 | 0.42 |
| Lebaksiu | Dukuhlo | 170.89 | 0.37 |
| Lebaksiu | Jatimulya | 131.44 | 0.29 |
| Lebaksiu | Kajen | 173.81 | 0.38 |
| Lebaksiu | Kambangan | 96.91 | 0.21 |
| Lebaksiu | Kesuben | 0.68 | 0.00 |
| Lebaksiu | Lebakgowah | 161.44 | 0.35 |
| Lebaksiu | Lebaksiu Kidul | 159.39 | 0.35 |
| Lebaksiu | Slarangkidul | 339.12 | 0.74 |
| Lebaksiu | Lebaksiu Lor | 402.56 | 0.87 |
| Lebaksiu | Pendawa | 115.02 | 0.25 |
| Lebaksiu | Tegalandong | 331.83 | 0.72 |
| Lebaksiu | Timbangreja | 241.58 | 0.52 |
| Lebaksiu | Yamansari | 219.7 | 0.48 |
| Margasari | Jembayat | 460.66 | 1.00 |
| Margasari | Kaligayam | 303.05 | 0.66 |
| Margasari | Danaraja | 53.74 | 0.12 |
| Margasari | Dukuh Tengah | 218.19 | 0.47 |
| Margasari | Jatilaba | 211.42 | 0.46 |
| Margasari | Kalisalak | 500.46 | 1.09 |
| Margasari | Karangdawa | 329.88 | 0.72 |
| Margasari | Margaayu | 542.17 | 1.18 |
| Margasari | Margasari | 220.36 | 0.48 |
| Margasari | Pakulaut | 526.63 | 1.14 |
| Margasari | Prupuk Selatan | 284.1 | 0.62 |
| Margasari | Prupuk Utata | 177.25 | 0.38 |
| Margasari | Wanasari | 263.46 | 0.57 |
| Pangkah | Bogares Lor | 39.46 | 0.09 |
| Pangkah | Curug | 75.28 | 0.16 |
| Pangkah | Depok | 102.54 | 0.22 |
| Pangkah | Dermasandi | 39.72 | 0.09 |
| Pangkah | Dukuhsembung | 45.7 | 0.10 |
| Pangkah | Grobog Kulon | 60.76 | 0.13 |
| Pangkah | Bedug | 26.2 | 0.06 |
| Pangkah | Grobog Wetan | 161.28 | 0.35 |

(continued)

**Table 2** (continued)

| Districts | Village | Agriculture economic sector | |
|---|---|---|---|
| | | Large (Ha) | % |
| Pangkah | Jenggawur | 40.03 | 0.09 |
| Pangkah | Kalikangkung | 83.75 | 0.18 |
| Pangkah | Kendalserut | 89.09 | 0.19 |
| Pangkah | Pener | 170.21 | 0.37 |
| Pangkah | Balamoa | 106.08 | 0.23 |
| Pangkah | Dermasuci | 46.6 | 0.10 |
| Pangkah | Dukuhjati Kidul | 112.01 | 0.24 |
| Pangkah | Paketiban | 58.65 | 0.13 |
| Pangkah | Pangkah | 135.84 | 0.29 |
| Pangkah | Pecabean | 71.11 | 0.15 |
| Pangkah | Penusupan | 275.34 | 0.60 |
| Pangkah | Pubayasa | 28.65 | 0.06 |
| Pangkah | Rancawiru | 44.97 | 0.10 |
| Pangkah | Talok | 78.22 | 0.17 |
| Pangkah | Bogares Kidul | 143.42 | 0.31 |
| Pagerbarang | Karanganyar | 152.22 | 0.33 |
| Pagerbarang | Pagerbarang | 242.8 | 0.53 |
| Pagerbarang | Pesarean | 211.57 | 0.46 |
| Pagerbarang | Semboja | 209.68 | 0.46 |
| Pagerbarang | Rajegwesi | 141.64 | 0.31 |
| Pagerbarang | Randusari | 484.47 | 1.05 |
| Pagerbarang | Sidomulya | 138.74 | 0.30 |
| Pagerbarang | Surokidul | 126.62 | 0.27 |
| Pagerbarang | Kedungsugih | 237.22 | 0.52 |
| Pagerbarang | Srengseng | 437.74 | 0.95 |
| Pagerbarang | Kertaharja | 116.47 | 0.25 |
| Pagerbarang | Mulyoharjo | 84.95 | 0.18 |
| Pagerbarang | Jatiwangi | 434.37 | 0.94 |
| Slawi | Dukuhsalam | 31.42 | 0.07 |
| Slawi | Dukuhwringin | 164.51 | 0.36 |
| Slawi | Kagok | 37.48 | 0.08 |
| Slawi | Slawi Kulon | 30.73 | 0.07 |
| Slawi | Kalisapu | 197.04 | 0.43 |
| Slawi | Kudaile | 12.52 | 0.03 |
| Slawi | Pakembaran | 37.77 | 0.08 |

(continued)

**Table 2** (continued)

| Districts | Village | Agriculture economic sector | |
|---|---|---|---|
| | | Large (Ha) | % |
| Slawi | Rocot | 15.48 | 0.03 |
| Slawi | Slawi Wetan | 45.1 | 0.10 |
| Slawi | Trayeman | 28.1 | 0.06 |
| Suradadi | Purwahamba | 481.42 | 1.05 |
| Suradadi | Bojongsana | 371.37 | 0.81 |
| Suradadi | Gembongdadi | 312.59 | 0.68 |
| Suradadi | Harjasari | 702.89 | 1.53 |
| Suradadi | Suradadi | 551.12 | 1.20 |
| Suradadi | Jatibogor | 564.38 | 1.23 |
| Suradadi | Jatimulya | 309.64 | 0.67 |
| Suradadi | Karangmulya | 567.46 | 1.23 |
| Suradadi | Karangwuluh | 81.09 | 0.18 |
| Suradadi | Kertasari | 667.25 | 1.45 |
| Suradadi | Sidaharja | 195.17 | 0.42 |
| Talang | Bengle | 63.23 | 0.14 |
| Talang | Kaligayam | 48.85 | 0.11 |
| Talang | Kebasen | 42.57 | 0.09 |
| Talang | Langgen | 14.78 | 0.03 |
| Talang | Pacul | 126.85 | 0.28 |
| Talang | Pasangan | 19.68 | 0.04 |
| Talang | Pegirikan | 35.79 | 0.08 |
| Talang | Pekiringan | 24.72 | 0.05 |
| Talang | Pesayangan | 18.22 | 0.04 |
| Talang | Tegalwangi | 53.37 | 0.12 |
| Talang | Wangandawa | 153.42 | 0.33 |
| Talang | Dawuhan | 169.68 | 0.37 |
| Talang | Cangkring | 101.24 | 0.22 |
| Talang | Dukuhmalang | 15.37 | 0.03 |
| Talang | Kaladawa | 73.95 | 0.16 |
| Talang | Gembongkulon | 48.05 | 0.10 |
| Talang | Getaskerep | 75.73 | 0.16 |
| Tarub | Kabukan | 63.09 | 0.14 |
| Tarub | Kalijambe | 64.45 | 0.14 |
| Tarub | Kedungbungkus | 58.43 | 0.13 |
| Tarub | Kemanggungan | 69.38 | 0.15 |

(continued)

**Table 2** (continued)

| Districts | Village | Agriculture economic sector | |
|---|---|---|---|
| | | Large (Ha) | % |
| Tarub | Kesadikan | 89.36 | 0.19 |
| Tarub | Kesamiran | 83.47 | 0.18 |
| Tarub | Lebeteng | 73.77 | 0.16 |
| Tarub | Mangunsaren | 117.66 | 0.26 |
| Tarub | Margapadang | 88.28 | 0.19 |
| Tarub | Mindaka | 82.31 | 0.18 |
| Tarub | Purbasana | 42.79 | 0.09 |
| Tarub | Setu | 49.58 | 0.11 |
| Tarub | Tarub | 45.17 | 0.10 |
| Tarub | Brekat | 104.15 | 0.23 |
| Tarub | Bulakwaru | 226.85 | 0.49 |
| Tarub | Bumiharja | 87.2 | 0.19 |
| Tarub | Jatirawa | 131.77 | 0.29 |
| Tarub | Karangjati | 96.32 | 0.21 |
| Tarub | Karangmangu | 132.24 | 0.29 |
| Tarub | Kedokansayang | 160.08 | 0.35 |
| Warureja | Banjaragung | 323.14 | 0.70 |
| Warureja | Sidamulya | 164.07 | 0.36 |
| Warureja | Banjarturi | 612.35 | 1.33 |
| Warureja | Demangharjo | 231.7 | 0.50 |
| Warureja | Sigentong | 662.95 | 1.44 |
| Warureja | Kedungjati | 310.72 | 0.67 |
| Warureja | Kedungkelor | 573.12 | 1.24 |
| Warureja | Sukareja | 203.78 | 0.44 |
| Warureja | Kendayakan | 414.75 | 0.90 |
| Warureja | Kreman | 536.23 | 1.16 |
| Warureja | Rangimulyo | 412.06 | 0.89 |
| Warureja | Warureja | 449.9 | 0.98 |
| Total area | | 46,053.11 | 100.00 |

*Source* Geoportal, Central Java

**Table 3** Table of plantation economic sector

| Districts | Village | Plantation economic sector | |
|---|---|---|---|
| | | Large (Ha) | % |
| Adiwerna | Adiwerna | 1.54 | 0.02 |
| Adiwerna | Gumelar | 8.03 | 0.11 |
| Adiwerna | Harjosari Kidul | 1.86 | 0.03 |
| Adiwerna | Harjosari Lor | 2.97 | 0.04 |
| Adiwerna | Kalimati | 4.28 | 0.06 |
| Adiwerna | Kaliwadas | 3.62 | 0.05 |
| Adiwerna | Kedungsukun | 12.88 | 0.17 |
| Adiwerna | Lemah Duwur | 0.63 | 0.01 |
| Adiwerna | Lumingser | 10.88 | 0.15 |
| Adiwerna | Pagiyanten | 11.32 | 0.15 |
| Adiwerna | Pedagangan | 3.68 | 0.05 |
| Adiwerna | Penarukan | 3.71 | 0.05 |
| Adiwerna | Pedes Lohor | 3.98 | 0.05 |
| Adiwerna | Pesarean | 1.7 | 0.02 |
| Adiwerna | Ujungrusi | 2.2 | 0.03 |
| Balapulang | Bukateja | 7.68 | 0.10 |
| Balapulang | Balapulang Kulon | 36.16 | 0.49 |
| Balapulang | Balapulang Wetan | 0.81 | 0.01 |
| Balapulang | Cilongok | 128.67 | 1.73 |
| Balapulang | Banjaranyar | 1.74 | 0.02 |
| Balapulang | Batuagung | 34.88 | 0.47 |
| Balapulang | Cenggini | 36.39 | 0.49 |
| Balapulang | Cibunar | 14.55 | 0.20 |
| Balapulang | Danareja | 129.41 | 1.74 |
| Balapulang | Darawarih | 0.12 | 0.00 |
| Balapulang | Pamiritan | 5.02 | 0.07 |
| Balapulang | Harjowinangun | 32.39 | 0.44 |
| Balapulang | Kalibakung | 15.48 | 0.21 |
| Balapulang | Kaliwungu | 19.53 | 0.26 |
| Balapulang | Sangkanjaya | 28.5 | 0.38 |
| Balapulang | Karangjambu | 77.17 | 1.04 |
| Balapulang | Pagerwangi | 20.52 | 0.28 |
| Balapulang | Sesepan | 53.42 | 0.72 |
| Balapulang | Tembongwah | 164.07 | 2.21 |
| Balapulang | Wringinjengot | 5.15 | 0.07 |
| Bojong | Batunyana | 34.56 | 0.46 |

(continued)

**Table 3** (continued)

| Districts | Village | Plantation economic sector | |
|---|---|---|---|
| | | Large (Ha) | % |
| Bojong | Gunungjati | 72.66 | 0.98 |
| Bojong | Bojong | 47.8 | 0.64 |
| Bojong | Buniwah | 2.79 | 0.04 |
| Bojong | Cikura | 40.87 | 0.55 |
| Bojong | Danasari | 96.26 | 1.29 |
| Bojong | Dukuhtengah | 65.58 | 0.88 |
| Bojong | Kajenengan | 75.55 | 1.02 |
| Bojong | Kalijambu | 117.93 | 1.59 |
| Bojong | Karangmulyo | 71.61 | 0.96 |
| Bojong | Lengkong | 2.85 | 0.04 |
| Bojong | Kedawung | 186.93 | 2.51 |
| Bojong | Pucangluwuk | 70.36 | 0.95 |
| Bojong | Suniarsih | 39.39 | 0.53 |
| Bojong | Rembul | 84.56 | 1.14 |
| Bojong | Sangkanayu | 36.96 | 0.50 |
| Bojong | Tuwel | 98.24 | 1.32 |
| Bumijawa | Traju | 129.17 | 1.74 |
| Bumijawa | Batumirah | 9 | 0.12 |
| Bumijawa | Begawat | 233.62 | 3.14 |
| Bumijawa | Carul | 24.65 | 0.33 |
| Bumijawa | Bumijawa | 165.56 | 2.23 |
| Bumijawa | Cawitali | 86.4 | 1.16 |
| Bumijawa | Cempaka | 130.02 | 1.75 |
| Bumijawa | Cintamanik | 217.87 | 2.93 |
| Bumijawa | Dukuhbenda | 61.43 | 0.83 |
| Bumijawa | Guci | 38.95 | 0.52 |
| Bumijawa | Gunungagung | 59.65 | 0.80 |
| Bumijawa | Jejeg | 3.61 | 0.05 |
| Bumijawa | Muncanglarang | 86.25 | 1.16 |
| Bumijawa | Pagerkasih | 2.13 | 0.03 |
| Bumijawa | Sigedong | 1.29 | 0.02 |
| Bumijawa | Sumbaga | 134.71 | 1.81 |
| Bumijawa | Sokasari | 87.86 | 1.18 |
| Bumijawa | Sokatengah | 73.86 | 0.99 |
| Dukuhturi | Dukuhturi | 0 | 0.00 |

(continued)

**Table 3** (continued)

| Districts | Village | Plantation economic sector | |
|---|---|---|---|
| | | Large (Ha) | % |
| Dukuhturi | Pengarasan | 3.71 | 0.05 |
| Dukuhturi | Kepandean | 7.59 | 0.10 |
| Dukuhturi | Ketanggungan | 5.17 | 0.07 |
| Dukuhturi | Kupu | 5.11 | 0.07 |
| Dukuhturi | Pagongan | 2.82 | 0.04 |
| Dukuhturi | Sidapurna | 10.4 | 0.14 |
| Dukuhwaru | Bulakpacing | 0.01 | 0.00 |
| Dukuhwaru | Kabunan | 1.54 | 0.02 |
| Dukuhwaru | Kalisoka | 11.89 | 0.16 |
| Dukuhwaru | Pedagangan | 9.44 | 0.13 |
| Dukuhwaru | Sindang | 0.61 | 0.01 |
| Dukuhwaru | Slaranglor | 9.02 | 0.12 |
| Jatinegara | Argatawang | 79.07 | 1.06 |
| Jatinegara | Capar | 17.62 | 0.24 |
| Jatinegara | Cerih | 137.59 | 1.85 |
| Jatinegara | Kedungwungu | 94.46 | 1.27 |
| Jatinegara | Lebakwangi | 153.52 | 2.06 |
| Jatinegara | Dukubangsa | 56.58 | 0.76 |
| Jatinegara | Penyalahan | 139.48 | 1.87 |
| Jatinegara | Gantungan | 93.75 | 1.26 |
| Jatinegara | Jatinegara | 101.03 | 1.36 |
| Jatinegara | Lembasari | 72.06 | 0.97 |
| Jatinegara | Luwijawa | 67.19 | 0.90 |
| Jatinegara | Mokaha | 73.02 | 0.98 |
| Jatinegara | Padasari | 151.35 | 2.03 |
| Jatinegara | Sitail | 106.66 | 1.43 |
| Jatinegara | Sumbarang | 181.72 | 2.44 |
| Jatinegara | Tamansari | 101.78 | 1.37 |
| Jatinegara | Wotgalih | 135.04 | 1.82 |
| Kedungbanteng | Kebandingan | 0 | 0.00 |
| Kedungbanteng | Dukuhjati Wetan | 0.01 | 0.00 |
| Kedungbanteng | Karanganyar | 94.54 | 1.27 |
| Kedungbanteng | Karangmalang | 20.4 | 0.27 |
| Kedungbanteng | Kedungbanteng | 4.03 | 0.05 |
| Kedungbanteng | Sumingkir | 2.32 | 0.03 |

(continued)

**Table 3** (continued)

| Districts | Village | Plantation economic sector | |
|---|---|---|---|
| | | Large (Ha) | % |
| Kedungbanteng | Tonggara | 137.69 | 1.85 |
| Kedungbanteng | Margamulya | 1.72 | 0.02 |
| Kedungbanteng | Penujah | 93.39 | 1.26 |
| Kedungbanteng | Semedo | 26.46 | 0.36 |
| Kramat | Dampyak | 0.07 | 0.00 |
| Kramat | Padaharja | 11.08 | 0.15 |
| Kramat | Plumbungan | 9.45 | 0.13 |
| Kramat | Tanjungharja | 3.97 | 0.05 |
| Lebaksiu | Balaradin | 3.04 | 0.04 |
| Lebaksiu | Dukuhlo | 0.34 | 0.00 |
| Lebaksiu | Kajen | 27.93 | 0.38 |
| Lebaksiu | Kambangan | 14.49 | 0.19 |
| Lebaksiu | Lebaksiu Kidul | 246.74 | 3.32 |
| Lebaksiu | Slarangkidul | 6.68 | 0.09 |
| Lebaksiu | Lebaksiu Lor | 40.37 | 0.54 |
| Lebaksiu | Pendawa | 4.89 | 0.07 |
| Lebaksiu | Tegalandong | 11.18 | 0.15 |
| Margasari | Jembayat | 21.37 | 0.29 |
| Margasari | Kaligayam | 63.7 | 0.86 |
| Margasari | Danaraja | 25.9 | 0.35 |
| Margasari | Dukuh Tengah | 10.89 | 0.15 |
| Margasari | Jatilaba | 59.15 | 0.80 |
| Margasari | Kalisalak | 19.8 | 0.27 |
| Margasari | Karangdawa | 11.37 | 0.15 |
| Margasari | Margaayu | 5.44 | 0.07 |
| Margasari | Margasari | 22.01 | 0.30 |
| Margasari | Pakulaut | 7.08 | 0.10 |
| Margasari | Prupuk Selatan | 41.37 | 0.56 |
| Margasari | Prupuk Utata | 45.68 | 0.61 |
| Margasari | Wanasari | 22.86 | 0.31 |
| Pangkah | Bogares Lor | 1.89 | 0.03 |
| Pangkah | Depok | 0.02 | 0.00 |
| Pangkah | Grobog Kulon | 4.75 | 0.06 |
| Pangkah | Bedug | 1.15 | 0.02 |
| Pangkah | Grobog Wetan | 5.13 | 0.07 |

(continued)

**Table 3** (continued)

| Districts | Village | Plantation economic sector | |
|---|---|---|---|
| | | Large (Ha) | % |
| Pangkah | Kalikangkung | 31.97 | 0.43 |
| Pangkah | Kendalserut | 12.65 | 0.17 |
| Pangkah | Pener | 1.79 | 0.02 |
| Pangkah | Bogares Kidul | 3.27 | 0.04 |
| Pangkah | Balamoa | 3.46 | 0.05 |
| Pangkah | Dermasuci | 199.92 | 2.69 |
| Pangkah | Dukuhjati Kidul | 32 | 0.43 |
| Pangkah | Penusupan | 13.34 | 0.18 |
| Pagerbarang | Kertaharja | 3.59 | 0.05 |
| Pagerbarang | Mulyoharjo | 2.64 | 0.04 |
| Pagerbarang | Jatiwangi | 5.65 | 0.08 |
| Pagerbarang | Karanganyar | 6.2 | 0.08 |
| Pagerbarang | Pagerbarang | 6 | 0.08 |
| Pagerbarang | Pesarean | 11.7 | 0.16 |
| Pagerbarang | Semboja | 1.06 | 0.01 |
| Pagerbarang | Rajegwesi | 6.44 | 0.09 |
| Pagerbarang | Randusari | 8.16 | 0.11 |
| Pagerbarang | Sidomulya | 12.56 | 0.17 |
| Pagerbarang | Surokidul | 7.61 | 0.10 |
| Pagerbarang | Srengseng | 17.43 | 0.23 |
| Slawi | Dukuhwringin | 3.75 | 0.05 |
| Slawi | Kagok | 2.2 | 0.03 |
| Slawi | Kalisapu | 2.65 | 0.04 |
| Slawi | Pakembaran | 2.07 | 0.03 |
| Slawi | Rocot | 10.75 | 0.14 |
| Suradadi | Purwahamba | 20.11 | 0.27 |
| Suradadi | Bojongsana | 2.41 | 0.03 |
| Suradadi | Gembongdadi | 12.62 | 0.17 |
| Suradadi | Harjasari | 23.98 | 0.32 |
| Suradadi | Suradadi | 4.16 | 0.06 |
| Suradadi | Jatibogor | 1.43 | 0.02 |
| Suradadi | Jatimulya | 11.43 | 0.15 |
| Suradadi | Karangmulya | 0 | 0.00 |
| Suradadi | Karangwuluh | 21.47 | 0.29 |
| Suradadi | Kertasari | 19.13 | 0.26 |

(continued)

**Table 3** (continued)

| Districts | Village | Plantation economic sector | |
|---|---|---|---|
| | | Large (Ha) | % |
| Suradadi | Sidaharja | 4.21 | 0.06 |
| Talang | Gembongkulon | 1.9 | 0.03 |
| Talang | Kajen | 0.16 | 0.00 |
| Talang | Langgen | 3.1 | 0.04 |
| Talang | Pasangan | 1.56 | 0.02 |
| Talang | Pegirikan | 5.53 | 0.07 |
| Talang | Pesayangan | 6.63 | 0.09 |
| Tarub | Brekat | 5.93 | 0.08 |
| Tarub | Bulakwaru | 6.53 | 0.09 |
| Tarub | Jatirawa | 2.3 | 0.03 |
| Tarub | Karangjati | 28.23 | 0.38 |
| Tarub | Karangmangu | 0.23 | 0.00 |
| Tarub | Kabukan | 14.27 | 0.19 |
| Tarub | Kesadikan | 25.67 | 0.35 |
| Tarub | Kesamiran | 4.36 | 0.06 |
| Tarub | Lebeteng | 55.16 | 0.74 |
| Tarub | Margapadang | 0.31 | 0.00 |
| Tarub | Purbasana | 0.35 | 0.00 |
| Warureja | Banjaragung | 32.01 | 0.43 |
| Warureja | Sidamulya | 1.05 | 0.01 |
| Warureja | Banjarturi | 3.37 | 0.05 |
| Warureja | Demangharjo | 34.93 | 0.47 |
| Warureja | Sigentong | 3.79 | 0.05 |
| Warureja | Kedungjati | 31.53 | 0.42 |
| Warureja | Kedungkelor | 11 | 0.15 |
| Warureja | Sukareja | 14.01 | 0.19 |
| Warureja | Kendayakan | 56.15 | 0.75 |
| Warureja | Kreman | 3.64 | 0.05 |
| Warureja | Rangimulyo | 3.11 | 0.04 |
| Warureja | Warureja | 17.72 | 0.24 |
| Luas total | | 7439.79 | 100.00 |

*Source* Geoportal, Central Java

**Table 4** Table of tourism economic sector

| Districts | Village | Tourism economic sector |
|---|---|---|
| Adiwerna | Pesarean | Wisata Religi Sunan Amangkurat |
| Adiwerna | Harjosari Lor | Wisata Religi Makam Pangeran Hanggawan |
| Adiwerna | Pagiyanten | Wisata Religi Makam Suroponolawen |
| Bumijawa | Jejeg | DESA WISATA CURUG JEJEG |
| Bumijawa | Muncanglarang | DESA WISATA MUNCANGLARANG |
| Bumijawa | Dukuhbenda | DESA WISATA DUKUH BENDA |
| Bumijawa | Cempaka | Tuk Mudal Desa Cempaka |
| Bumijawa | Guci | Curug Jedor |
| Bumijawa | Guci | Curug Penganten |
| Bumijawa | Sigedong | Curug Cantel |
| Bumijawa | Cempaka | Pasar Tradisional Slumpring |
| Bumijawa | Gunungagung | GUNUNG CORONG |
| Bumijawa | Guci | Guci |
| Balapulang | Kalibakung | Wisata Kesehatan Jamu Kalibakung |
| Balapulang | Sesepan | WISATA BUKIT RANGKOK |
| Balapulang | Harjowinangun | Gua Lawa |
| Balapulang | Bukateja | Sawah Batu |
| Balapulang | Kalibakung | Wana Wisata Clirit View |
| Bojong | Cikura | DESA WISATA RELIGI CIKURA |
| Bojong | Rembul | Curug Si Geong |
| Bojong | Tuwel | Curug Luhur |
| Bojong | Rembul | WISATA LEMBAH REMBULAN |
| Bojong | Danasari | Wana Prabanlintang Danasari |
| Dukuhwaru | Pedagangan | Wisata Religi Makam Syech Atas Angin |
| Jatinegara | Gantungan | Water Park Gunung Gantungan |
| Jatinegara | Luwijawa | Pasar Sawah Luwijawa |
| Kedungbanteng | Tonggara | Waduk Cacaban |
| Kedungbanteng | Semedo | Museum Semedo |
| Kramat | Mujungagung | Pantai Larangan Indah |
| Lebaksiu | Lebaksiu Kidul | WISATA BUKIT SI TANJUNG |
| Pagerbarang | Pesarean | Wisata Religi Makam Abdulrachman Ibrahim Alzamzami |
| Pagerbarang | Srengseng | WISATA BENDUNG GONDANG |
| Pangkah | Balamoa | Wisata Religi Makam Pangeran Benowo |
| Talang | Kaligayam | DESA WISATA RELIGI GIREN |
| Slawi | Pakembaran | Gor Trisanja |
| Suradadi | Purwahamba | Pantai Purwahamba Indah |

*Source* Investment Profile of Tegal Regency, 2020

**Table 5** Table of industry economic sector

| Districts | Village | Industry economic sector | References |
|---|---|---|---|
| Balapulang | Balapulang Wetan | PT. Sakura Gifts Indonesia | Toys |
| Bumijawa | Bumijawa | PT. Tirta Sukses Perkasa | Commercial mineral water |
| Kramat | Maribaya | PT. SAS Kreasindo Utama | Wood furniture |
| Kramat | Dampyak | PT. Samone Abadi Indonesia | Textile |
| Kramat | Kramat | PT. Multiwell Embroidery | Embroidery garment |
| Kramat | Munjungagung | PT. Hamana Works Indonesia | Car manufacturing |
| Kramat | Maribaya | PT. Mutiara Busana Indah | Fashion |
| Margasari | Jembayat | PT. Sung Him International | Eyelashes Manufacturing |
| Margasari | Margasari | PT. Ken Lee Indonesia | Textile |
| Margasari | Margaayu | PT. New HopeFarm Indonesia | Commercial chickens breeding |
| Margasari | Margaayu | PT. Winners International | Textile and convection |
| Margasari | Pakulaut | PT. Charoen Pokphand Jaya Farm | Agrobusiness |
| Margasari | Kaligayam | PT. Java Energi Eoliana | Renewable energy |
| Slawi | Slawi Wetan | PT. Sketch Tegal Elektronik | Electronics |
| Suradadi | Sidaharja | PT. Nam Kyung Korea Indonesia | Frozen Surimi (Seafood) |
| Pangkah | Talok | Shuttlecock | Shuttlecock |
| Warureja | Kedungkelor | PT. Sai Garments Industries | Apparel, textile, and fashion |

*Source* Investment Profile of Tegal Regency, 2020

# 4 Results and Discussion

## *4.1 Results*

The fishery economic sector of Tegal Regency is located in the north which has a direct border with the Java Sea. Kramat District is the area that has the largest fishery development area, whereas Dampyak Village is the largest village with 198.09 Ha or 30.07% of the total distribution area of the fishery sector (Fig. 3).

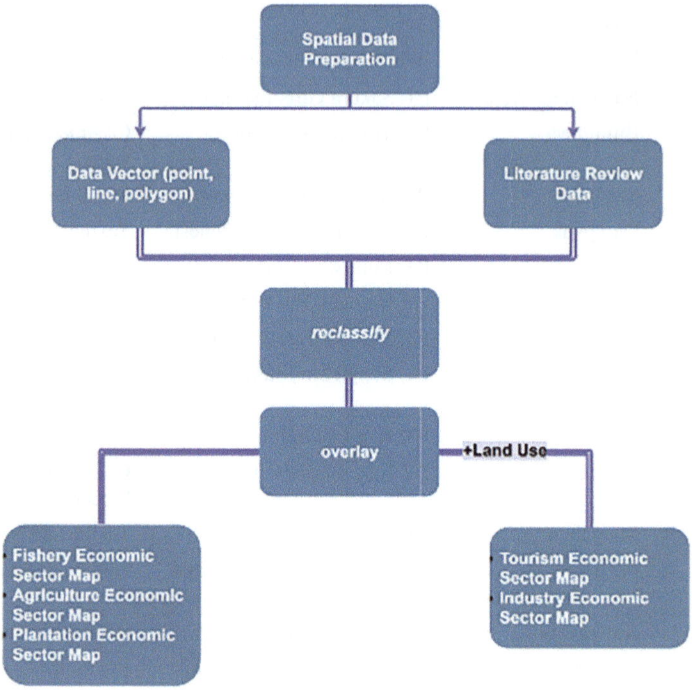


**Fig. 2** Working process with spatial analysis approach

The agricultural economy sector of Tegal Regency is the main sector with a total area of 46,053.11 Ha or 46.29% of the total area. This shows agriculture as a primary base sector that continues to be developed. In addition, most of the agricultural land is located in the lowlands, near the coast, and adjacent to the center of population activity. Harjasari Village, Suradadi District is the largest agricultural area among villages in Tegal Regency with an area of 702.89 Ha or 1.53% of the total area (Fig. 4).

The plantation economy sector in Tegal Regency as a whole has an area of 7439.79 Ha or 7.48% of the total area. The plantation sector is growing most rapidly in Bumijawa District, Bojong District, and Jatinegara District because it is located in the hills and highlands. In addition, the three districts are at the foot of Mount Slamet so it is very suitable to be developed into plantations. Then Begawat Village, Bumijawa District is the village with the largest plantation area among other villages, where the area is 233.62 Ha or 3.14% of the area of all plantations in Tegal Regency (Fig. 5).

Tegal Regency has many tours that support economic growth, where the tour is very complete ranging from beaches, waterfalls/waterfalls, reservoirs, hot springs, tourist villages, hill tourism, caves, traditional markets, religious tourism, museums, and sports venues (GOR). The existence of tourism potential can increase the country's foreign exchange and equitable development of Tegal Regency. Not only

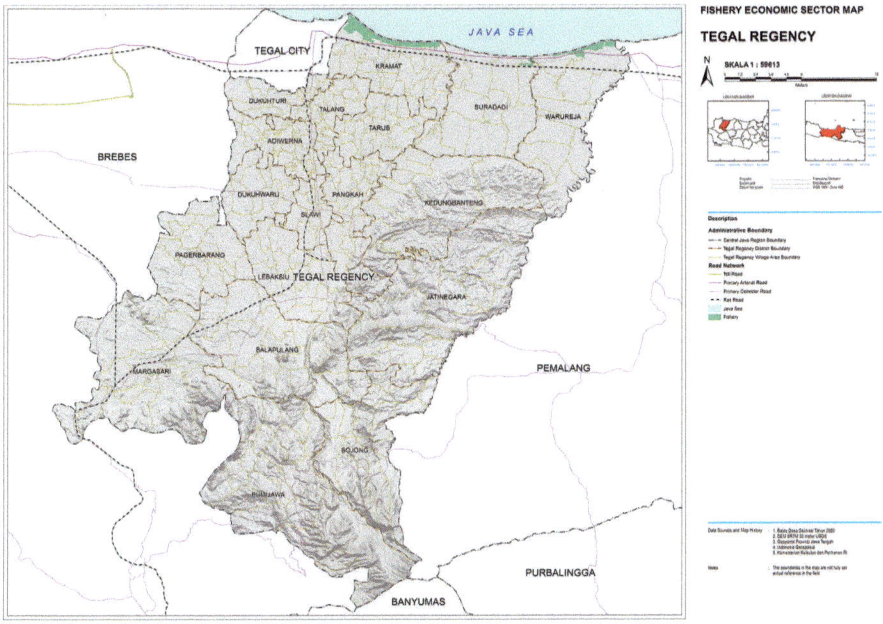


**Fig. 3** Fisheries economic mapping in Tegal regency

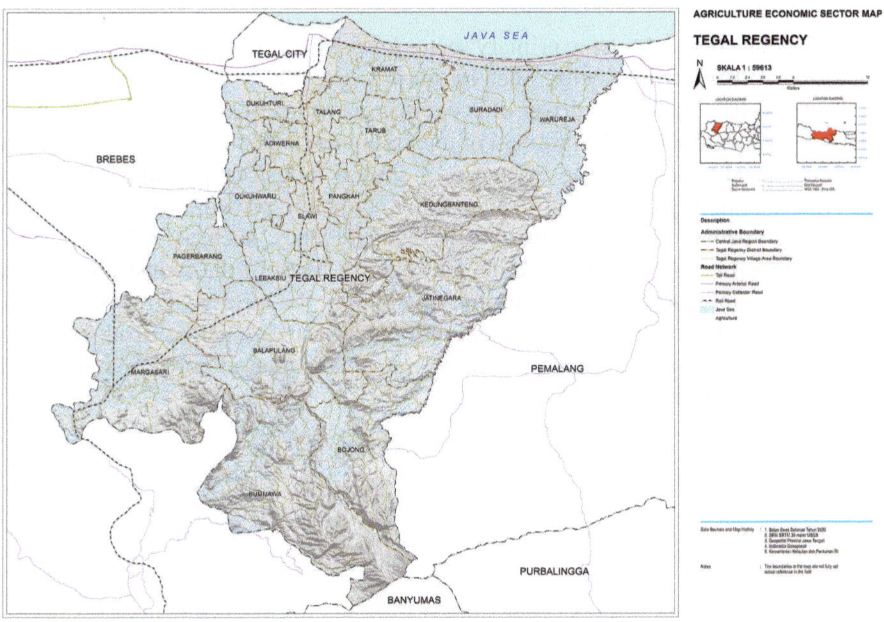


**Fig. 4** Agriculture economic mapping in Tegal regency

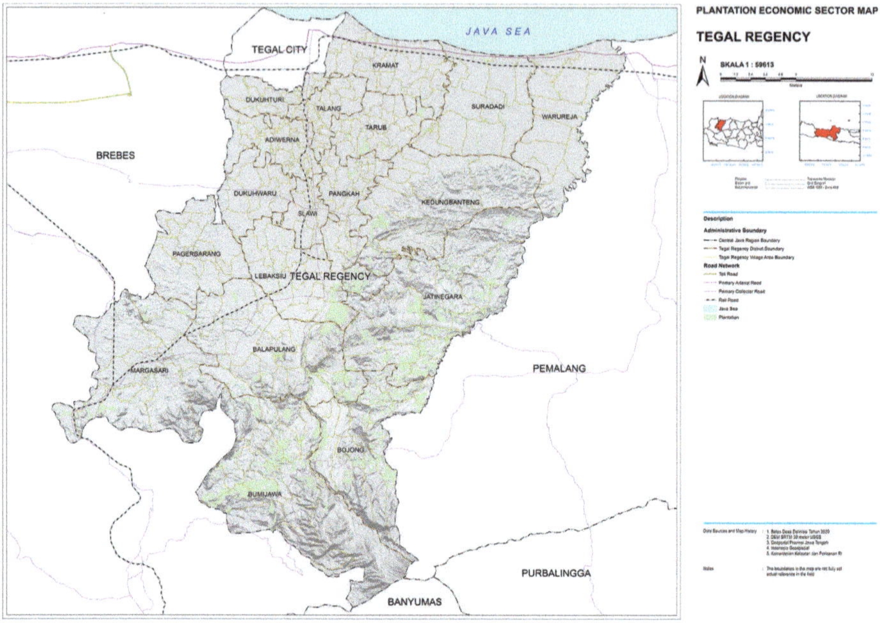


**Fig. 5** Plantations economic mapping in Tegal regency

Tegal Regency depends on the primary sector (agriculture, fisheries, and plantations) but also on other leading sectors such as tourism (Fig. 6).

The industrial sector is a driver of economic growth in Tegal Regency because it has a role in overcoming the problem of unemployment and the creation of a natural resource-based economy. The existence of several industries provides investment opportunities in Tegal Regency in increasing economic growth. There are several outside companies that have invested in Tegal Regency, such as Belgium, South Korea, Singapore, Japan, Hong Kong, and France. Most of the industries in Tegal Regency are textiles and manufacturing. In addition, the local government has also been concerned about the improvement of local industries, such as drinking water, shuttlecock, tea, and food, thus increasing the equalization of economic growth in Tegal Regency (Fig. 7).

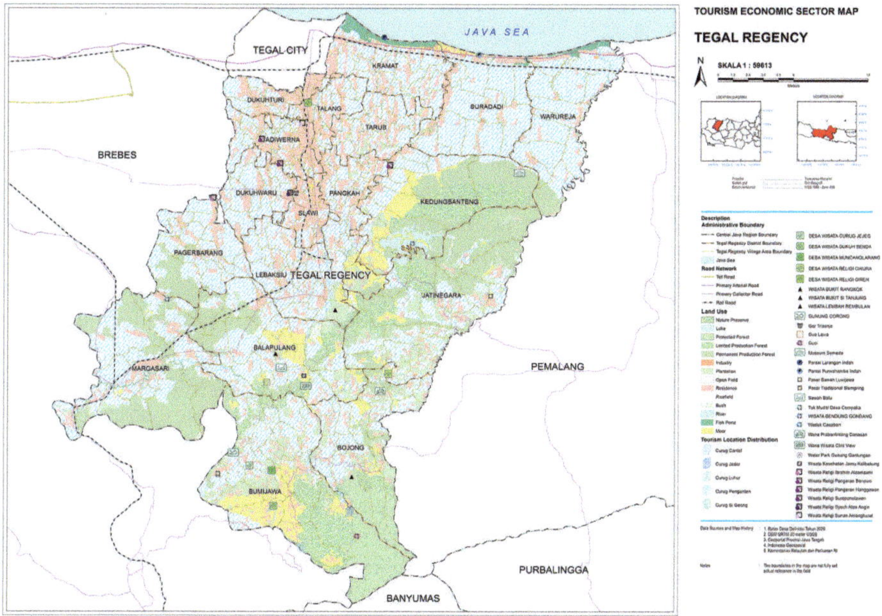


**Fig. 6** Tourism economic mapping in Tegal regency

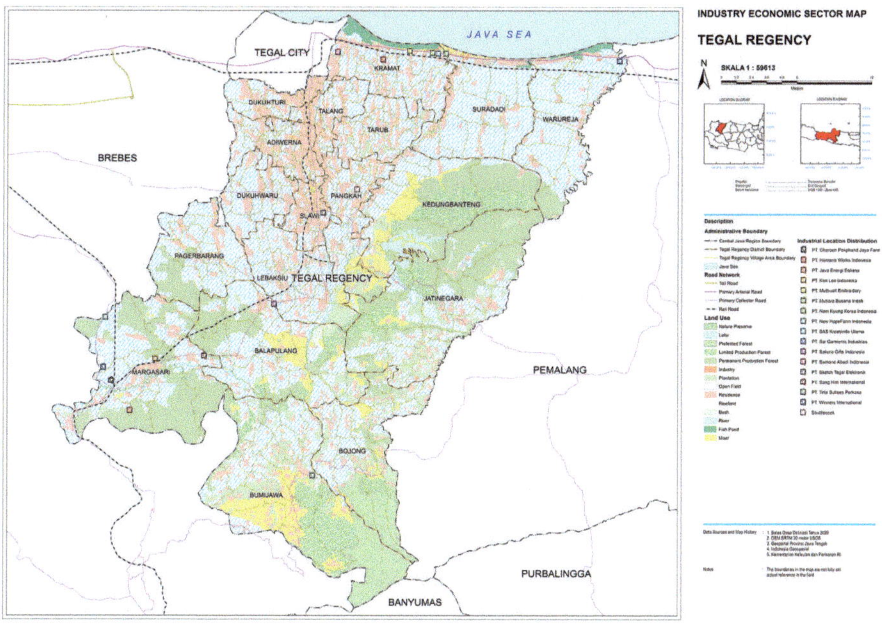


**Fig. 7** Industry economic mapping in Tegal regency

## 4.2 Discussion

Looking at the economic structure of villages in Tegal Regency, economic dominance still rests mostly on the primary sector (fishery, agriculture, and plantations) which shows weak structural transformation so that regional development growth becomes very slow [18]. Although there are industrial sectors (secondary sector) and tourism (tertiary sector), not many village economies depend on these things. In addition, villages that excel in the primary sector are located in each other's arms, namely Dampyak Village and Harjasari Village are in the north while Begawat Village is in the south. The tourism and industrial center of Tegal Regency is also located in the western part. This leads to a lack of economic integration. Todaro [32] states that growth increases whenever output also increases. Increased growth also depends on three aspects, namely infrastructural investment and human resources, advanced technology, and labor supply [32]. Referring to the results of village economic mapping, we argue that the progress of villages in Tegal Regency can occur when the local government is able to make the right public policies as follows:

1. fill the village land space that is still empty for economic expansion;
2. integrate all sectors of the village's economy through village infrastructure building;
3. provide increased competence and capacity of the community in the village based on its economic sector, financial and business knowledge, and technological knowledge;
4. apply the use of advanced technology to the primary sector (fishery, agriculture, and plantations);
5. increase the quantity of investment in the secondary sector, including manufacturing, water and electricity supply, and construction;
6. increase the quantity of investment in the tertiary sector, including goods trading, services industry (high-competency skills), transport, and communication.

Here are the public policy choices for each type of village referring to Todaro [32] that combined by our judgment.

| Policy Choices for Villages | land use | villages infrastructure | human development | technology | labor supply |
|---|---|---|---|---|---|
| Fishery Villages | fish port | reliable road conditions, dock/boat mooring, industrial growth for the fishery in the village, banking services, internet access, village enterprises | fishery training, financial and business knowledge, internet dan technological knowledge | Bycatch Excluder Device (BED), gillnet, lift net, stage trap, bamboo split, cast net, hybrid energy, internet of things, and other technologies | young generation, skilled labors |
| Agricultural Villages | productive land | reliable road conditions, industrial growth for agriculture in the village, banking services, internet access, village enterprises | agriculture training, financial and business knowledge, internet dan technological knowledge | transplanter, indo combine harvester, superior seed picking machine, soybean dryer, waste processing installation, internet of things, autonomous tractor, agricultural management system, hybrid crop, RFID technology, and other technologies | young generation, skilled labors |
| Plantations Villages | productive land | reliable road conditions, industrial growth for plantations in the village, banking services, internet access, village enterprises | plantations training, financial and business knowledge, internet dan technological knowledge | clones/superior varieties, integrated pest control technology, productivity improvement technology, cultivation technology, organic products, and biotechs, equipment engineering, downstream industrial technology, plantation plant rejuvenation model, waste control technology, plantation agribusiness information system, plantations biotechnology, and other technologies | young generation, skilled labors |
| Tourism Villages | tourist villages | reliable road conditions, tourist village, banking services, internet access, village enterprises | tourism and hospitality training, financial and business knowledge, internet dan technological knowledge | internet of things, QR Code, and other technologies | young generation, skilled labors |
| Industrial Villages | manufacturing land | reliable road conditions, industrial growth in the village, banking services, internet access | manufacturing training, financial and business knowledge, internet dan technological knowledge | mobile ERP, real-time operations, internet of things, and other technologies | young generation, skilled labors |

## 5 Conclusions

Village economic mapping provides a comprehensive and clear picture of the condition of a region. Tegal Regency has a fairly complete village economic structure, including fishery, agriculture, plantations, tourism, and industry. The greatest potential is in the primary sector economy, especially the fishery, agriculture, and plantations sectors. Unfortunately, secondary and tertiary economic structures have not been widely built in Tegal Regency. Referring to the economic mapping of the village, policymakers can formulate policy choices reliably and on target so that the economy of Tegal Regency can be optimized properly. Mapping the village's economy is also a public policy tool that can later be followed by many local governments.

## References

1. Alesina A (2005) Corruption, inequality and fairness. J Monet Econ 52:1227–1244
2. Alvarez-Diaz M, D'Hombres B, Ghisetti C, Pontarollo N, Dijkstra L (2018) The determinants of population growth: literature review and empirical analysis. In: JRC working papers in economics and finance, No 2018/10 European commission joint research centre. JRC, Ispra
3. Arsyad L (2010) Ekonomi Pembangunan, Edisi Kelima. UPP STIM YKPN, Yogyakarta
4. BPS Kabupaten Tegal (2020) Geografi dan Iklim Kabupaten Tegal
5. Baulch B (2002) The spatial distribution of poverty in Vietnam and the potential for targeting. World Bank Working Paper 2829
6. Cejudo Garcia D, Navarro Valverde F (2009) La inversion en los programas de desarrollo rural. SU reparto territorial en la provincia de granada. Anales de Geografia 29(2):37–64
7. Cienfuegos OLA, Sánchez AIO (2022) Spatial approach to contribution of public policies to the dynamization of the rural population. Appl Spat Anal Policy 15(1):215–240. https://doi.org/10.1007/s12061-021-09398-z
8. Costa da Silva D, Elhorst J, Silveira Neto R (2016) A spatial economic model and spatial econometric analysis of population dynamics in Brazilian MCAS. In: Anais do XLII Encontro Nacional de Economia (proceedings of the 42nd Brazilian economics meeting), ANPEC, p 158
9. Curtis B, Kellner MI, Over J (1992) Process modeling. Commun ACM 35:75–90. https://doi.org/10.1145/130994.130998
10. Dinas Penanaman Modal dan Pelayanan Terpadu Satu Pintu Kabupaten Tegal (2020). Buku Profil Peluang Investasi Kabupaten Tegal
11. Eden C, Ackermann F (2004) Cognitive mapping expert views for policy analysis in the public sector. Euro J Oper Res 152(3):615–630. ISSN 0377-2217, https://doi.org/10.1016/S0377-2217(03)00061-4
12. Geoportal Central Java Province, Indonesia @ geoportal.jatengprov.go.id (n.d.). https://geoportal.jatengprov.go.id/
13. Goyal N, Taeihagh A, Howlett M (2022) Whither policy innovation? Mapping conceptual engagement with public policy in energy transitions research. Energy Res Soc Sci 89:102632. ISSN 2214-6296, https://doi.org/10.1016/j.erss.2022.102632
14. Gul, Ejaz, Chaudhry, Imran Sharif (2022) Islamabad Spatial distribution of socio-economic inequality: evidence from inequality maps of a village in Tribal region of Pakistan. Pakistan Institute of Development Economics The Pakistan Deve 54(4)
15. Handayani D, Soelistiajadi R, Sunardi (2005) Pemanfaatan Analisis Spasial untuk Pengolahan Data Spasial Sistem Informasi Geografi

16. Jordan A, Huitema D (2014) Innovations in climate policy: conclusions and new directions. Environ Politics 23(5):906–925
17. Klotz LE, Horman MJ, Bi HH, Bechtel J (2008) The impact of process mapping on transparency. Int J Product Perform Manag 57:623–636
18. Kuznets S (1966) Modern economic growth. Yale University Press, New Haven, CT
19. Li H (2006) Income, income inequality and health: evidence from China. J Comp Econ 34:668–693
20. Lovrak A, Pukšec T, Duić N (2020) A geographical information system (GIS) based approach for assessing the spatial distribution and seasonal variation of biogas production potential from agricultural residues and municipal biowaste. Appl Energy 267(January):115010. https://doi.org/10.1016/j.apenergy.2020.115010
21. Nagaraj A, Stern S (2020) The economics of maps. J Econ Perspect 34(1):196–221. https://www.jstor.org/stable/26873535
22. Nieto Masot A, Cardenas Alonso G (2018) The rural development policy in extremadura (SW Spain): Spatial location analysis of leader projects. ISPRS Int J Geo-Inf 7(2)
23. O'Donoghue C, Buckley C, Chyzheuskaya A, Green S, Howley P, Hynes S, Upton V, Ryan M (2021) The spatial impact of rural economic change on river water quality. Land Use Policy 103(C)
24. Prahasta E (2009) Sistem informasi geografis: konsep-konsep dasar (perspektif geodesi & geomatika)/Eddy Prahasta. Informatika, Bandung
25. Rojas F, Rubio C, Rizzo M, Bernabeu M, Akil N, Martín F (2020) Land use and land cover in irrigated drylands: a long-term analysis of changes in the Mendoza and Tunuyán River Basins, Argentina (1986–2018). Appl Spat Anal Policy 13(4):875–899. https://doi.org/10.1007/s12061-020-09335-6
26. Rother M, Shook J (1999) Learning to see: value stream mapping to create value and eliminate muda, The Lean Enterprise Institute, Brookline, MA
27. Salmivaara A, Kummu M, Varis O, Keskinen M (2016) Socio-economic changes in cambodia's unique tonle sap lake area: a spatial approach. Appl Spat Anal Policy 9(3):413–432. https://doi.org/10.1007/s12061-015-9157-z
28. Sanchez Reyes B (2011) Evolucion de la poblacion de los municipios de extremadura: aplicaciones parametricas y semiparamtricas. PhD thesis, Facultad de Ciencias Economicas y Empresariales. Universidad autonoma de Madrid
29. Suswanto B, Handoko W, Sabiq A (2013) Model community development sebagai strategi pemberdayaan berbasis Kearifan Lokal. Jurnal Review Politik 03:298–312
30. Swinkels R (2007) Poverty mapping in Vietnam, Chapter 14. In more than a pretty picture: using poverty maps to design better policies, The World Bank
31. Todaro MP, Smith SC (2012) Economics development, 11th edn. Pearson Education Inc., Boston
32. Todaro M (2011) Ekonomi Pembangunan. Edisi kesebelas, Jilid 1. Jakarta: Penerbit Erlangga
33. Ulumiyah I (2013) Peran pemerintah desa dalam memberdayakan masyarakat desa (studi pada Desa Sumberpasir Kecamatan Pakis Kabupaten Malang). Jurnal Administrasi Publik 1(5):890–899
34. Zhao Z (2006) Income inequality, unequal health-care access, and mortality in China. Popul Dev Rev 32:461–483

# How Do Social Entrepreneurs Establish Sustainable Value Chains? A Model of Social Entrepreneurs-Induced Social Network to Develop Resilient Rural Economy

**Luh Putu Mahyuni and Gusti Ayu Ketut Surtiari**

**Abstract** The economy of Bali has been largely impacted by the COVID-19 pandemic. Researchers have emphasised that there is a need for Bali to diversify their income sources for a more sustainable and resilient economy. Even though the COVID-19 pandemic has inflicted severe economic crises, it has acted as a push for transformation. It is observed that a large number of young tourism workers, who are laid off, return to their hometowns. They are working on either farming, fisheries, or small creative industry sectors for a living, sectors that have long been abandoned by young people due to more lucrative tourism industry. The pandemic has shifted the centre of economic development, from cities to rural areas. While this shifting has provided great opportunities to boost rural economic development, the rural communities are still facing various challenges, such as limited innovation, management, and marketing capability, as well as limited market access. These factors contribute to the very low bargaining power of producers and unfair prices for farmers/fishers/craftsmen. This study aims to explore how social entrepreneurs build social networks to develop a resilient rural economy, particularly through establishing sustainable value chains. Guided by social entrepreneurship, social network, and transformative theory, this study uses qualitative case studies on farmer, fisher, and craftsman communities in Bali. This study finds that social entrepreneurs play a significant role as network builders to connect producers and consumers directly by introducing the latest technology and innovation, as well as connect producers and universities, village-owned enterprises, state-owned enterprises, and private companies. By establishing this sustainable value chain, the producers gain fair prices, thus increasing their income significantly. A more resilient rural economy could be established. A model offered by this study could also be relevant and implemented

L. P. Mahyuni (✉)
Universitas Pendidikan Nasional, Denpasar, Indonesia
e-mail: mahyuniluhputu@undiknas.ac.id

G. A. K. Surtiari
Badan Riset dan Inovasi Nasional, Jakarta, Indonesia
e-mail: gust003@brin.go.id



Nawawi et al. (eds.), *Managing Disruption and Developing Resilience for a Better Southeast Asia*, Springer Proceedings in Humanities and Social Sciences,
https://doi.org/10.1007/978-981-96-2116-3_6

in other South East Asia countries that have a similar context to the context of this study.

**Keywords** Sustainable business · Sustainable economy · Sustainable value chain · Rural economic resilience · Social entrepreneur · Social entrepreneurship theory · Innovation · Social network theory · Transformative theory

## 1 Introduction

Rural areas are home to about 47.74% of the South East Asia population (The Global Economy 2020). Despite having abundant natural resources, rich culture, and strong social capital, the poverty rate in rural areas remains high [10]. Lack of access to quality education, health, and basic services for rural populations has contributed to the low level of the human development index in rural areas [25]. This, in turn, limits rural populations' capability to take advantage of their resources and increase the value added to the products they produce for better income.

Rural development is essential to achieving sustainable development goals. The United Nations calls for a stronger commitment from the government bodies to push the rural development agenda to the centre stage [38]. Various rural development models have been suggested to reduce urban–rural economic disparity. One of the models is 'in situ urbanisation' [38] which involves extensive government intervention to minimise the gap in the urban–rural standard of living. By improving the quality of living in rural communities, the urbanisation rate is expected to be reduced [6, 26].

In an institutional void context—a typical emerging economy setting—grassroot initiatives led by local champions are effective in improving the quality of living of rural populations [8]. The advent of digital and frontier technologies enables grassroot initiatives to boost the rural economy even further [20, 21]. It is documented [23] that during the pandemic of COVID-19, there were significant changes in urban–rural social structure, particularly in the South East Asia context which is very much dependent on the tourism industry. [38], for instance, reported significant numbers of migration of young people from cities to rural areas. Some of these young people have no other choice but to return to their hometown due to the loss of their job in the city, and some others decide to work in rural areas as they are given an option to work from anywhere [14]. Besides the significant changes in social structure, it is reported that the pandemic has also shifted travel and tourism preferences [33]. Tourists prefer to visit and stay longer in rural areas which are supportive of improving their wellness by reconnecting with nature [18, 41]. These phenomena, in turn, open a lot more opportunities and support for grassroot initiatives to bring rural development to the next level.

Literature has documented various grassroot initiatives which are successful in developing rural economies (see, UNDP 2021), such as youth activities, leadership and women empowerment, intensive agriculture activities, small loans for livestock farming and trading, and connecting indigenous women and defending rights [27], including social entrepreneurship.

Social entrepreneurship has gained momentum recently as a lot of businesses have realised the importance of aligning the economic goals of a business with social and environmental goals. Businesses that incorporate social and environmental issues into their core strategies enjoy better support and legitimacy from stakeholders, a significant improvement in brand reputation, and better overall business performance [26–30].

Compared to entrepreneurship which has a sole focus on financial gain, social entrepreneurship is more interesting in the eyes of sustainable investors [40]. Thus, it is relatively easier for social entrepreneurship to attract funding from investors. Moreover, due to the nature of social entrepreneurship which builds businesses around social and environmental missions, it is also relatively easier for social entrepreneurship to develop an ecosystem of multi-stakeholders for business scale-up purposes, as well as for developing a resilient rural economy.

Resilient rural economic development could be driven by capital-intensive or labour-intensive local capacities [9, 37]. In developed countries, shifting completely to a capital-intensive rural economy might be viable. It is not the case for emerging economies, such as Indonesia where a labour-intensive rural economy is still preferable. Transformation into a more innovative approach, as well as empowerment of rural communities, is needed for the labour-intensive rural economy to thrive.

The terminology of resilience itself is an agenda of policy and in addition to discourse in the academic field [4]. The essence of resilience is being able to do self-management in dealing with change, learn from experiences, and utilise various resources to recover better when faced with pressures and crises [7, 11]. In this regard, researchers have paid much attention to understanding ways to improve rural communities' capability to manage themselves [3, 4, 12].

The ability to organise oneself or a community is closely related to social networks [34]. Building a network can be in a polycentric form that considers the interaction of various stakeholders at various levels. The polycentric approach is multi-stakeholder and multi-level with an emphasis on collaboration and integration [39]. Interaction between stakeholders at different levels needs to occur in synergy so that it can develop the capacity of one system to be able to deal with changes that occur outside the system and within the system [16]. Collaboration between stakeholders can also increase the optimisation of the resources used, namely by complementing each other [17].

This paper focuses on understanding how social networks are developed to create sustainable values and welfare for farmers, fishers, and craftsmen. Accordingly, the research questions are: (1) How do social entrepreneurs grow in the local communities? (2) How do social entrepreneurs establish a sustainable value chain? How do social entrepreneurs build a resilient rural economy? This study uses the concept of resilience as its origin defined as a term to describe the system's ability to absorb disturbances and recover from damages to continue on its current path, as well as the ability to shift and transform to a new state [11].

There are various interpretations of the resilience concept as it is a local-specific context and involves multi-stakeholder and multi-level systems (Ibid.). In general, the basic concept of rural economic resilience considers the capacity of a system to be static by removing or overcoming the perturbation, the capacity to "bounce back" to a steady-state condition such as the capacity of farming system and an agriculture community to return to its original state after affected by stressors and shocks [22]. Rural economic resilience is an ability possessed by residents in rural areas to face external pressures by responding, adapting, organising themselves, and recovering after experiencing pressure or when facing changes. Building resilience is a complex process and local context following the characteristics of the individual and the community and also the level of vulnerability and capacity possessed varies from one individual to another and one group to another [19].

Departed from the resilience concept developed by Holling [15], a healthy system can invent and explore, profiting from inventions that create opportunities while staying safe from those that destabilise due to their nature or excessive exuberance. It occurs in different levels and each level is free to operate at its own pace, with slower, larger levels protecting it from above while faster, smaller cycles of invention energise it from below [15]. They have creativities to interact between the cycles to maintain their capacity to adapt. The creativities are arranged based on their ability to organise themselves [24]. The capacity to organise themselves in the complexity of systems is based on experiences and knowledge [15]. In the process of self-organising, transformation is an opportunity to recover better after experiencing perturbation. Transformation leads to a sustainable pathway in the long term and facilitates the successful adaptation to the changes.

In the concept of community resilience, it is stated that three main things will determine resilience at the community level that can be built [2]. The first is learning, which consists of perception, knowledge, reflection, monitoring, and evaluation. Second, actions include the ability to reduce the level of vulnerability and increase capacity in the process of managing environmental change [1]. The third is resources and capacities consisting of financial, physical, socio-political, and also human. Resources, lessons learned as well as action are critical to success in building resilience considering a large population.

In the pathway to transform through self-organisation, it needs a provision of resource accumulation, subsequent growth, and storage for the unprecedented and uncertain conditions [13]. There is a strong relation between ecological resilience and regulation as a social process. Moreover, Holling [15] elaborates that innovation is prominent to respond the high uncertainty with weak control. Innovation is an opportunity which can fail and success depends on the inputs and the regulation within the system. The social and human systems try to stabilise the system by optimising the opportunities such as the business entrepreneur combined with the local culture or local traditions [5].

In the panarchy systems as a nature of rural economic resilience, there are features namely multiple connections in nested and across levels. The successful process of one system to another system in creating a larger structure to potentially widen sustainable assets. Self-organising encompasses agency, efficacy, proactive, responsibility, and collective capacity which are represented through empowerment, inability, engagement, responsibility, participation, partnership, independence, and local development [34]. In addition, building rural economic resilience can be constructed through social capital which consists of networks, connectedness, support structures, and cohesion to represent inclusion, exclusion, cohesion, connectedness, network, and social innovations (Ibid). The resilience is high when the accumulation of assets not limited to natural capital is sufficient [15].

## 2 Methods

We use multiple case studies for our research since it is likely to provide more comprehensive and varied perspectives. A case study is an ideal approach to studying a complex phenomenon in a comprehensive way [35].

Following Stake's [35] suggestion in selecting cases, we selected individual cases which could provide relevant and varied information to the multi-case phenomenon under study and could also offer opportunities to learn about complexity and contexts. Accordingly, we selected three cases of social enterprises that have developed certain networks within three different types of communities, namely farming, fisheries, and creative industry communities. All cases selected are located in Bali, Indonesia. The context of Bali is significant as during the pandemic of COVID-19 Bali has experienced the largest economic downturn compared to other provinces in Indonesia. Regional domestic product growth of Bali Province from 2019 to 2020, was recorded at $-10.22\%$, It was far below the national figure, which was $-3.15\%$ [36]. Grassroot initiatives, such as those initiated by social entrepreneurs which have contributed to maintaining rural economic resilience amidst a crisis could shed some light on the topic under study.

We collected our data through semi-structured in-depth interviews with social entrepreneurs, community leaders and members, officials of local governments, village enterprises, and state-owned enterprises. The duration of the interviews ranged from 45 to 120 min. All interviewees were given sufficient information related to the purpose of the study and were asked to sign an informed consent form prior to the interviews. Interviews were audio recorded and notes were taken during the interviews with interviewees' permission. To minimise the possibility of social desirability bias, we guarantee the anonymity of the interviewees and social enterprises participating in our research. We interviewed social entrepreneurs, community leaders, and officials of local governments, village enterprises, and state-owned enterprises in their offices, while the community members were interviewed informally in their workplaces or home. As there are three cases investigated in this study, interviewees of cases A, B, C are assigned codes starting with A, B, C, respectively, then followed by the number.

We also collected data through social enterprises' websites and social media platforms. Fieldwork observations were also conducted to capture physical setting descriptions, formal and informal activities and interactions. Interviews with various stakeholders enable us to obtain a variety of perspectives. Moreover, a combination of data collected through interviews, documents, and fieldwork observations facilitated data validation and cross-check findings [28].

We analysed our data using inductive analysis. Meaningful themes are allowed to emerge from the pattern found in the case studies, without predetermining in advance what those important themes will be. A system theory with a holistic perspective was applied as a framework to understand how a system is formed and works. We analysed the cases as a complex system and searched for the unifying nature of cases. A system perspective is particularly appropriate to study a community of practice, like the focus of this study. The community of practice is an interconnected and interacting network of people [28].

# 3 Results and Discussion

## 3.1 Within Case Analysis

**Case A**. Our first case is a social entrepreneur who works intensively with farmers. He has succeeded in developing a complex social network which integrates farming suppliers, farmers, consumers, and various related stakeholders. Powered by the latest digital technologies, such a social network has been contributing to the improvement of farming ecosystem quality and farmers' welfare.

Started as a movement to raise awareness of the benefits of natural farming, the social network has been slowly formed and grown through several stages and processes as explained by the social entrepreneur who initiated the network (A1). In the initial stage, A1 mapped current problems of the farming ecosystem in Indonesia and then identified possible solutions, "*I observed that current farming practices have caused significant depletion of organic contents in the top soil. This results in lower crop productivity and at the same time higher cost to maintain the same level of productivity. I also learned that natural farming is effective in turning back this situation*" (A1). He realised that raising awareness is very important before suggesting changes in current farming practices. Therefore, in the initial stage, his focus is on raising awareness of the importance and benefits of natural farming. Convincing the farmers is a major challenge in this stage, "*The farmers want to be shown the prove of successful natural farming practices*" (A1). He resolved this issue by involving some successful natural farmers as speakers in various seminars and workshops conducted to raise awareness. Besides raising awareness among the farmers, in this initial stage, A1 also campaigns healthy lifestyle by consuming organic/natural foods, "*We educate people how to live a healthy life through healthy foods consumption*" (A1).

In the second stage—the formation stage, A1 invited all successful natural farmers to establish a foundation called Bali Young Farmer Forum. The forum hosts two regular events every year, namely farmer camp and farmer convention. While farmer camp focuses on delivering various practical trainings for farmers, farmer convention provides a forum for farmers to exchange knowledge and experiences, as well as broaden their network. In this stage, various players in natural farming ecosystem find a forum to connect, as stated by A1, "*Through this forum, we meet many champions who are excel in various area, such as those who produce very good natural fertiliser, natural pesticide, successful organic fruits and vegetables growers*" (A1). Though direct connections and transactions have happened between players at this stage, it is still unorganised. A1 then identified an opportunity to create larger impacts by creating a social venture in the third stage of complex social network development.

In the third stage, a social enterprise (SE) was established. This SE takes a form of a cooperative. Major players in the natural farming ecosystem are members of this cooperative, including thousands of farmers spread across various districts in Bali. Powered by a digital marketplace, the cooperative plays a significant role as an orchestrator connecting all actors within the ecosystem. Such a digital marketplace allows direct transactions between farmers and consumers, hence creating a fair and transparent trade. Moreover, with only one intermediary (the cooperative) within the value chain, the farmers could get a better price, as explained by a farmer, "*[name of the cooperative] has helped us getting higher prices for our produces. We used to sell our produces to a middle man who come and take our produces. At that time, we did not have any other options, so most of the time we could not sell our produces at good prices*" (A2).

In the fourth stage, advanced technologies were introduced within the ecosystem, namely: (1) Smart farming powered by Internet of Things (IOT) and Artificial Intelligence (AI) application; (2) Blockchain technology and big data implementation within the digital marketplace. Smart farming practices increase cost efficiency significantly, "*Our farmers could save up to 70% for labour and water cost by introducing IOT and AI technology*" (A1). Whereas blockchain technology and big data implementation within digital marketplace allow better traceability of products sold in the marketplace and better business planning, "*Consumers could trace the produces they bought up to the source. They could get detail information about the farmer or group of farmers who produce the products*" (A1).

Under the umbrella of a foundation called Bali Young Farmer Forum, social venture in Case A grows significantly in a short amount of time. The foundation serves as social network builder, while the social venture captures the economic benefits created by the social network. The foundation and social venture in Case A have created a self-sustaining and sustainable farming ecosystem. The farmers could obtain latest technical know-how, technology support, natural fertiliser and pesticide, and good quality seeds within the ecosystem. They could also obtain support to open wider market with fair prices. This, in turn, improves farmers' welfare significantly, creates a more resilient rural economy, and ensures the sustainability of healthy food supply within the community.

**Case B**. Our second case is a social entrepreneur who works intensively with fishers. He (B1) established a social venture in 2017 which has been successful in aligning coral reef conservation initiatives with volunteer tourism development in the small fishing village of Tianyar on the North East coast of Bali. After many years working in city of Denpasar with foreigners, B1 decided to return and develop his hometown in 2015. With support from his previous connections, he established a foundation which focuses on delivering free informal education for children of Tianyar. Initially, B1 foreign friends came to visit him, stayed at his house, and offered free English course. Then, some of his friends who are marine scientists suggested him to raise local community awareness and participation towards marine environment, including coral reef conservation. B1 explained, "*When I returned in 2015, I saw people dump their waste anywhere, including the beach. [...] our coral was badly destroyed, leaving bare sands covering vast area of our sea*" (B1).

Through the foundation, B1 and his friends raised funds to build a community plastic recycling centre and centre for coral reef conservation. A lot of foreign volunteers come to Tianyar village regularly to support coral reef conservation initiatives since then. At that time, there were no decent accommodations and restaurants for volunteers available in the village. The volunteers had to stay at Tulamben—a well-established underwater tourist destination, 22 kms away from the village. Understanding the needs of foreign volunteers, B1 and fisher groups then established a social venture. All members of this social venture invested some money to build accommodation, restaurants, and other tourist facilities. One of B1's foreign friends, who is a marine scientist from the UK (B2), became a co-founder of this social venture. B2 connects this social venture with several prominent travel agents in the UK and Europe, then the travel agents promote volunteer tourism programme in Tianyar. B2 explained that volunteer tourism is currently on trend, particularly among young people in the UK and Europe, "*They [youngsters] want to travel on purpose. So, they are not interested to travel just for relaxing on the beach, do nothing. They want to do something meaningful for local people and the environment*" (B2). The volunteers pay some money to the social venture for accommodation, meals, and volunteering programmes. The fishers of Tianyar village obtain significant additional income from volunteer tourism, as explained by one fisher (B3), "*Since volunteers come to our village, I get some money from renting my boat and guiding them to the sea*" (B3).

Volunteer tourism developed by social venture in case B improves the economy of the village significantly. This, in turn, raises local support for marine environment conservation in general and coral reef conservation initiative in particular, as described by head of the village (B4), "*Our people now see the importance of keeping the village clean. They also understand the negative impact of destructive fishing practices. They stop practise that now*" (B4).

Social entrepreneur in case B uses a social venture to develop connections with travel agents, volunteer tourists, local leaders, local government, and organisations with the aims of conserving marine environment and developing village economy.

**Case C**. Our third case is a social entrepreneur who works intensively with bamboo craftsmen. Having laid off from the hotel due to COVID-19 pandemic, he (C1) decided to return to his hometown, a small village in the North of Bali. In his village, almost all households do bamboo craft traditionally, a craft art that has been passed on from generation to generation. They produce simple bamboo baskets, the same design as their ancestors did, without any innovation. Their products are mostly sold for Bali's ceremony purposes, to contain offerings. Due to lack of market access, the craftsmen are much dependent on middleman who come and take their products in the village. As a consequence, the craftsmen have no other choice but to accept whatever the price set by the middleman.

Understanding this problem, C1 with the help of his previous connections at the hotel where he used to work introduces some innovations in product design. C1 trains the villagers to make fancy interior decorations made of bamboo, including tumbler made of bamboo, and many other creations. Having some connections with foreigners and national businessmen, C1 could open up a market for these brand-new designs of bamboo crafts.

As the orders rose significantly, C1 decided to establish a social venture in which all craftsmen in his village would become members. This social venture received social responsibility grants from a state-owned enterprise in 2020 to build a workshop and showroom, buy some machinery, and run various trainings to improve craftsmen's capability. With better innovation and management, bamboo crafts could be sold at much better price. Craftsmen's welfare improves significantly and so does the village economy.

## 3.2 Cross-case Analysis

The three cases in this study exemplify social entrepreneurs' significant roles in developing resilient rural economy amidst the COVID-19 pandamic. Through a social venture, they are able to build a social network connecting various actors with the aims of improving the economy of all members, economy of the village, and at the same time improving the quality of the environment. Supporting Aldrich and Meyer [2] argument, this study finds that social entrepreneurs develop and enforce social network through learning process, collaborative actions, and resources orchestration, initiated and facilitated by social entrepreneurs. Social enterprises are used to capture the economic benefits created by the social network.

The social enterprises in the cases of this study could grow relatively fast, due to several factors, Firstly, social enterprises model offered fits in Balinese spirit of "*menyama braya*" (kinship), "*salunglung sabayantaka*" (cooperativeness), and "*gilik-saguluk*" (togetherness). In all cases, social enterprises are built and managed as cooperative model where all members have shares in the enterprises. Secondly, social enterprises are established not only for economic purposes, but also for social support and environmental protection purposes. Such broad purposes attract various organisations to offer assistance and funding, particularly through social responsibility programmes.

The growth of social enterprises is not without challenges. Several challenges for continuity are identified in this study. Firstly, young people might be tempted to leave the villages to work in the tourism industry once the industry recovers from the crisis. This, in turn, could disrupt the operation of current social enterprises. Secondly, unstable and unpredictable global as well as national economy create enormous challenges for social enterprises to maintain their marketing and financial performance.

While the three cases have similar purposes and processes, they are quite different in terms of the size and the growth speed of the social network. Case A has the largest network, followed by case B and case C. This study indicates that the size and the growth speed of social network to some extent are determined by the number of champions within the system. Case A has the largest number of champions, followed by case B (2 champions) and case C (1 champion).

## 4 Conclusion

This study aims at exploring how a social entrepreneur could develop a resilient rural economy through establishing a social network. Social entrepreneurs in this study have social sensitivity to figure out problems in their community and find solutions to the problems identified. Then they walk the talk, being the example, showing the proof to the community. By doing so, the community is convinced to work together and create a network. A social venture is established to capture the economic benefits of the social network and at the same time to create an impact on the local environment and the local economy. This social venture reinforces the social network further. As members of the network have a share in the social venture, all profits created by social venture from business activities in the network are returned to the members of the network. Rural economic development driven by grass root initiative, particularly by social entrepreneurship could be effective in creating a resilient rural economy. As the business is fully owned by the community, they would actively take part in the process.

## References

1. Abeling T, Huq N, Chang-Seng D, Birkmann J, Wolfertz J, Renaud F, Garschagen M (2019) Understanding disaster resilience. In: Framing community disaster resilience. John Wiley & Sons Hoboken NJ and Chichester, West Sussex, pp 9–25
2. Aldrich DP, Meyer MA (2015) Social capital and community resilience. Am Behav Sci 59(2):254–269
3. Anzola D, Barbrook-Johnson P, Cano JI (2016) Self-organization and social science. Computat Math Organ Theor 23(2):1–37. https://doi.org/10.1007/s10588-016-9224-2

4. Berkes F, Ross H (2013) Community resilience: toward an integrated approach. Soc Nat Res 26(1):5–20. https://doi.org/10.1080/08941920.2012.736605
5. Berkes F, Colding J, Folke C (2008) Navigating social-ecological systems: building resilience for complexity and change. Cambridge University Press
6. Boncinelli F, Riccioli F, Casini L (2015) The determinants of quality of life in rural areas from a geographic perspective : the case of tuscany the determinants of quality of life in rural areas from a geographic perspective : the case of tuscany (July). https://doi.org/10.1111/rurd.12035
7. Bousquet F, Botta A, Alinovi L, Barreteau O, Bossio D, Brown K, Staver C et al (2016) Resilience and development: mobilizing for transformation. Ecol Soc 21(3). https://doi.org/10.5751/es-08754-210340
8. Brauer R, Dymitrow M (2014) Quality of life in rural areas : a topic for the rural development policy ? 25(25):25–54
9. Chapin FS, Robards MD, Huntington HP, Johnstone JF, Trainor SF, Kofinas GP, Naylor RL et al (2006) Directional changes in ecological communities and social-ecological systems: a framework for prediction based on alaskan examples. Am Nat 168(s6):36–49. https://doi.org/10.1086/509047
10. Erlando A, Dwi F, Masakazu S (2020) Heliyon financial inclusion , economic growth, and poverty alleviation : evidence from eastern indonesia. Heliyon 6(May):e05235. https://doi.org/10.1016/j.heliyon.2020.e05235
11. Folke C (2016) Resilience (republished), vol 21
12. Fuchs C (2003) Some implications of pierre bourdieu's works for a theory of social selforganization. Euro J Soc Theor 6(4):387–408. https://doi.org/10.1177/13684310030064002
13. Gunderson LH, Holling CS (2002) Panarchy: understanding transformations in human and natural systems. Island Press, Washington, D.C
14. Hannah B, Emmanouil T (2022) Working from home and digital divides: resilience during the pandemic. Ann Am Assoc Geograph 112(4):893–913. https://doi.org/10.1080/24694452.2021.1939647
15. Holling CS (2001) Understanding the complexity of economic, ecological, and social systems. Ecosystems 4(5):390–405. https://doi.org/10.1007/s10021-001-0101-5
16. Homsy GC, Liu Z, Warner ME (2019) Multilevel governance: framing the integration of top-down and bottom-up policymaking. Int J Public Adm 42(7):572–582
17. Innes JE, Booher DE (2016) Collaborative rationality as a strategy for working with wicked problems. Landsc Urban Plan 154:8–10
18. Jiricka-pürrer A, Brandenburg C, Pröbstl-Haider U (2020) City tourism pre- and post-covid-19 pandemic—messages to take home for climate change adaptation and mitigation? J Outdoor Recreat Tour 31. https://doi.org/10.1016/j.jort.2020.100329
19. Kirmayer S, Whitley D, Isaac (2000) Departed from the resilience concept developed by Holling, a healthy system
20. Labianca M, Rubertis SDE, Belliggiano A, Salento A, Union E, Observatory LE, Leader T (2016) Innovation in rural development in Puglia, Italy : critical issues and potentialities starting from empirical evidence 118:38–46
21. Neumeier S (2017) Social innovation in rural development: identifying the key factors of success 183(1):34–46. https://doi.org/10.1111/geoj.12180
22. Nguyen MT, Renaud FG, Sebesvari Z, Nguyen DC (2019) Resilience of agricultural systems facing increased salinity intrusion in deltaic coastal areas of Vietnam. Ecol Soc 24(4):n–a
23. Oecd (2021) Oecd regional outlook 2021: addressing covid-19 and moving to net zero greenhouse gas emissions, oecd publishing, Paris. https://doi.org/10.1787/17017efe-en
24. Olsson P, Gunderson LH, Carpenter SR, Ryan P, Lebel L, Folke C, Holling CS (2006) Shooting the rapids: navigating transitions to adaptive governance of social-ecological systems. Ecol and Soc 11(1)
25. Ophi and Undp (2021) Global multidimensional poverty index 2021: unmasking disparities by ethnicity, caste and gender. In: report

26. Orsini F, Kahane R, Nono-Womdim R, Gianquinto G (2013) Urban agriculture in the developing world: a review. Agron Sustain Dev 33(4):695–720. https://doi.org/10.1007/s13593-013-0143-z
27. Patrick-Agulonye UV (2021) Common causes in grassroot development : a case for community-based and community-driven response in the postpandemic era. https://doi.org/10.1108/frep-09-2021-0056
28. Patton MQ (2015) Qualitative research and evaluation methods: integrating theory and practice, 4th ed. Sage Publications, Inc.
29. Porter ME, Kramer MR (2002) The competitive advantage of corporate philanthrophy. Harv Bus Rev 80(12):56–68
30. Porter ME, Van Der Linde C (1995) Green and competitive. Harv Bus Rev 73(5):120–134
31. Porter ME, Kramer MR (2006) The link between competitive advantage and corporate social responsibility. Harvard Bus Rev 1–13
32. Porter ME, Kramer MR (2011) Creating shared value. Harvard Bus Rev 89(1–2). https://doi.org/10.32591/coas.ojss.0201.04037b
33. Qiu H, Wu J, Hong L, Luo Y, Song Q, Chen D (2020) Clinical and epidemiological features of 36 children with coronavirus disease 2019 (COVID-19) in Zhejiang, China: an observational cohort study. Lancet Infect Dis 20(6):689–696
34. Roberts E, Anderson BA, Skerratt S, Farrington J (2017) A review of the rural-digital policy agenda from a community resilience perspective. J Rural Stud 54:372–385
35. Stake R (2006) Multiple case study analysis. Guilford Press
36. StatisticsIndonesia (2021) [Seri 2010] Laju Pertumbuhan Produk Domestik Regional Bruto Per Kapita Atas Dasar Harga Konstan 2010 (Persen). https://www.bps.go.id/indikator/indikator/view_data/0000/data/296/sdgs_8/1
37. Tanner T, Lewis D, Wrathall D, Bronen R, Cradock-Henry N, Huq S, Thomalla F (2015) Livelihood resilience in the face of climate change. Nat Clim Chan 5(1):23–26
38. United Nations, Department of Economic and Social Affairs (2021) Highlights 2020–2021: towards sustainable development for All. UN DESA, New York, USA
39. Vedeld T, Hofstad H, Solli H, Hanssen GS (2021) Polycentric urban climate governance: creating synergies between integrative and interactive governance in Oslo. Environ Policy Gov 31(4):347–360
40. Verkerk MJ (2013) Social entrepreneurship and impact investing. Philos Ref 78(2):209–221
41. Zenker S, Kock F (2020) The coronavirus pandemic—a critical discussion of a tourism research agenda. Tour Manag 81(June):104164. https://doi.org/10.1016/j.tourman.2020.104164

# Challenge to Education Quality, New Skills, Labor Market of Southeast Asia in Digital Era

# Challenges and Strategies for Development of Fishery Training and Counseling in Ambon, Maluku Province

**Anggi Afriansyah, Fikri Muslim, Ruth Meilianna, and Vera Bararah Barid**

**Abstract** Indonesia has a good potential for marine resources. Ambon, the capital city of Maluku province, is a part of the area targeted to become the National Fish Barn. This position requires both skilled human resources in mastering knowledge and skills in the fishery sector. This article aims to describe the existing condition of the fishery sector workforce in the city of Ambon. First, this article describes the demographic characteristics of the fishing workforce. Second, the existing condition of vocational training in the fishery sector. Third, analysis of needs and training schemes for workers in the fishery sector. This research uses a mix method approach. Field data collection was carried out using a survey method using a questionnaire to 200 respondents in the Ambon City area who work in the fishery sector. Qualitative data collection was also carried out using in-depth interviews to explore in-depth information related to interesting issues obtained from the survey results. The research findings illustrate that the majority of workers in the fishery sector are male, more than half are in the 35–44 and 45–54 years age groups, and most of them are fishermen. The majority of fishery workforce education is high school education. Most respondents have not had the opportunity to attend training due to lack of information and time constraints. Proposals for training needs for fishery sector workers include: use of modern fishing gear, ship engine repair, business management, and marketing, and catch processing.

**Keywords** Fishery training · Fishery counseling · Worker · Vocational training

A. Afriansyah (✉) · F. Muslim · R. Meilianna
Research Center for Population, National Research and Innovation Agency, Central Jakarta, Indonesia
e-mail: afriansyah.anggi@gmail.com

V. B. Barid
Research Center for Law, National Research and Innovation Agency, Central Jakarta, Indonesia



Nawawi et al. (eds.), *Managing Disruption and Developing Resilience for a Better Southeast Asia*, Springer Proceedings in Humanities and Social Sciences,
https://doi.org/10.1007/978-981-96-2116-3_7

# 1 Introduction

In the first period, the government of Joko Widodo expressed its hope to make Indonesia the world's maritime axis [4]. Then, in 2017, the Presidential Regulation of the Republic of the Republic of Indonesia Number 16 of 2017 was released on Indonesian Marine Policy [18, 19]. Article 1, paragraph 2 of the Presidential Regulation explains that the World Maritime Axis is a vision of Indonesia to become a maritime country that is sovereign, advanced, independent, strong, and able to make a positive contribution to regional and world security and peace by national interests. Then, on the Roadmap for Indonesia's Maritime Policy toward the World Maritime Axis, in the pillars of human resource development, it was stated that several main programs become priorities, among which are closely related to educational programs. One of them is developing competency standards for human resources in the marine sector.

Indonesia is an archipelagic state entity with vast territorial waters. Based on the national reference to territorial data of the Republic of Indonesia released on the press release page of the Coordinating Ministry for Maritime Affairs and Investment, it is stated that the area of Indonesian waters reaches 6.4 million km$^2$ (Bureau of Communication of the Coordinating Ministry of Maritime Affairs and Investment, 2018). In addition, Referring to the Performance Report of the Ministry of Maritime Affairs and Fisheries in 2020, it was explained that fish resources in Indonesia's seas cover 37% of fish species in the world, with several types having high economic value. It is estimated that there are 12.54 million tons per year of sustainable potential for marine fish resources scattered in the territory of Indonesia and the waters of the Indonesian Exclusive Economic Zone (ZEEI).

Meanwhile, the Permitted Catch (JTB) is 10.03 million tons per year, or about 80% of the sustainable potential. Currently, only 6.98 million tons are used in 2019, or only 69.59% of JTB, while the total production of capture fisheries (in sea and inland waters) is 7.53 million tons. According to Latuny [11], Maluku Province as the largest producer of fish with the best quality, encourages the central government to designate this area as a national fish barn, which of course has an impact on the volume and value of fishing, increasing the volume and value of trade and also has a positive value for food marketed in hotels [11].

Even though the potential is excellent, various kinds of problems still face the management of marine resources in Indonesia. There are at least five characteristics of the fishery sector workforce in Indonesia [1], including low levels of education, the dominance of male workers, old age workers, limited access, and low-income levels. According to Zaelany [23], there are six main problems in preparing the quality of the fishery workforce such as: (1) there is no planning for human resources needs in the fisheries sector, (2) the number of workers in the fisheries sector is decreasing, (3) the training programs carried out tend to be top-down, (4) the curriculum and training infrastructure are not sufficient and do not follow the required skills needs, (5) the lack of synergy between institutions causes overlapping types of training, (6) fishery instructors are limited in number and not proportional to the comprehensive coverage of the target area, and some are approaching retirement [23].

Residents of coastal areas with low education affect the use of coastal areas [6] and their awareness of health [20]. In addition, a study from Masri [14] states that the education of fishermen's children on the Donggala coast is not following the needs of the work and the situation at hand. Christiawan [3] mentions that socio-economically coastal communities have weaknesses in terms of demographics with population density and many family members and low-income levels, savings, and education levels. It is in line with Siburian's [19] research for the coastal community of Hajoran Induk Village, Central Tapanuli Regency, North Sumatra Province, which stated that the education level of fishermen in this location was low and low-income levels caused the low level of family welfare. Amin et al. [2] state that fishermen's skill and knowledge level in Karangantu Banten is still relatively low because almost 80% of fishermen do not understand what competencies they should have.

The implementation of training and counseling in the fishery sector by the government is a mandate of Law Number 31 of 2004 concerning Fisheries. Based on Article 57, paragraph 1, the implementation of fishery training and counseling aims to increase the capacity of human resources working in the fishery sector. Operational limitations regarding training and extension of the fishery sector in Indonesia are regulated in Government Regulation Number 62 of 2014 [5]. The regulation defines fishery training as an overall activity to improve and develop knowledge, skills, and work attitudes in fisheries in a structured and tiered manner.

The fundamental problem in the implementation of fishery training and counseling in Indonesia is that there is no grand design of training and counseling that should be a reference for implementing fisheries training and counseling programs and activities. The authority for the preparation of education, training, and counseling plans is divided between the central and regional governments. National education and training/counseling plans are under the authority of the Central Government through the Minister who carries out government affairs in the fishery sector. Then planning at the provincial level becomes the authority of the Governor, and planning at the district/city level becomes the authority of the Regent/Mayor. The absence of a standard reference for the implementation of fishery training has the potential to cause program overlap at the time of its implementation, especially training that targets fishery workers. Both training and training programs are organized by ministries/ agencies at the central level or those organized by the regions.

In addition to the routine targets and objectives of the program, the results of the training also do not support efforts to open up market opportunities. Regulation of the Head of the Marine and Fisheries Research and Human Resources Agency Number 12/PER-BRSDM/2020 states a Strategic Plan for the Research and Human Resources Agency for Marine and Fisheries (BRSDM) for 2020–2024. The document presented various strategies for developing marine human resources under the authority of the Marine and Fisheries Ministry. The training is supported by the presence of 5 Fisheries Training and Counseling Centers (BPPP) in Medan, Tegal, Banyuwangi, Bitung, and Ambon [9, 10]. In that year, 112 marine and fishery groups were targeted to be upgraded, while the achievement reached 118 groups. In addition, in the first quarter of 2021, 2232 marine and fisheries groups were formed, while the target was only 1120 groups. The effectiveness of this BRDSM can be assessed by the graduates who are absorbed in the business world. Moreover, the achievement of BRDSM Ambon won the best award for achieving the performance and work productivity of the 4th BRDSM KP scope of work based on the 2021 SAKIP Evaluation Test with a score of 81.07 (A). This high achievement can indicate that the effectiveness of training and counseling by BRDSM Ambon is considered very good (A) if judged by the government's evaluation assessment.

Based on this background, this study aims to answer some questions. First, what are the demographic and employment characteristics of the fishing workforce? Second, what are the existing vocational training conditions in the fishery sector? Furthermore, how is the analysis of needs and training schemes for workers in the fishery sector? This study will be divided into several parts. In the first part, this research will explain the demographic and employment profile through a survey that we have conducted. Second, Participation in fisheries training and counseling in Ambon and source of training information and motivation to attend the training and counseling of respondents. Then continued with training needs by fishery workers in Ambon City. Finally, this research will discuss conclusion suggestions for training development strategies.

## 2 Method

This research uses a mixed method approach. Field data collection was carried out using a survey method using a questionnaire to 200 respondents in the Ambon City area who work in the fishery sector. Qualitative data collection was also carried out using in-depth interviews to explore in-depth information related to interesting issues obtained from the survey results. The research results are described in this article in a quantitative descriptive manner, accompanied by qualitative arguments obtained from the interviews.

## 3 Demographic and Employment Profile: Based on Research Survey

Based on the results of the research survey "Design of Fisheries Sector Education to Support the Capacity Building and Productivity of Maritime Human Resources 2021" conducted in the Ambon City area, it is known that the respondents consisted of 187 males, which is equivalent to 93.5% of the total respondents. (N: 200 respondents). Very few female respondents, namely only 13 people (6.5%). The dominance of male workers who are respondents is very likely related to the potential characteristics of the Ambon area which tend to be capture fisheries. The work of fishing to catch fish

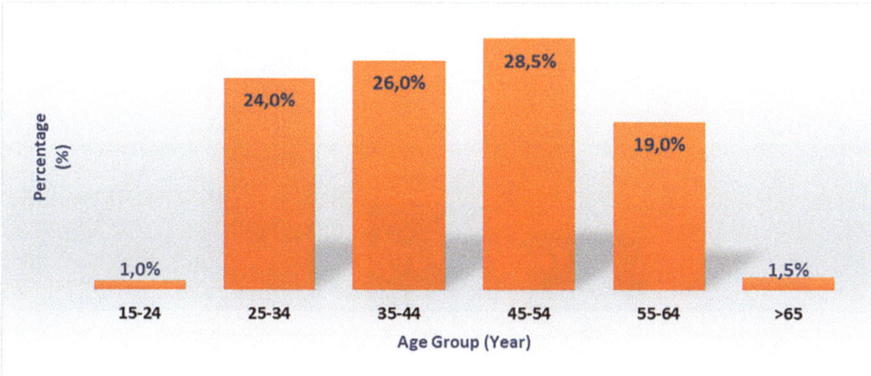


**Fig. 1** Respondents by age. *Source* Results of Survey Data Processing in Ambon City, 2021

is more likely to be done by men. Female workers very rarely go to sea to catch fish, these women are more involved in selling the caught fish in the market or processing it into smoked fish.

According to age group, survey results show that the majority of research respondents are workers in the 25–64 year age group. The proportion of respondents in that age group reached 97.5% of the total respondents. When viewed based on age per 10 years, respondents in the 45–54 year age group were the most dominant at 28.%, followed by the 35–44 year age group as much as 26%, the 25–34 year age group as much as 24% and age 55–64 years as much as 19%. Meanwhile, respondents in the age group 15–24 years and age group 65 years and over are only 1% and 1.5%, respectively (Fig. 1).

When viewed by education level, 55.5% of respondents to this research survey have graduated from senior high school and 22.5% have completed junior high school. Respondents with higher education (Diploma III and Bachelor) are very few in number, namely 3% of the total respondents (Fig. 2).

Respondents to this survey are distributed in six main types of occupations, namely: (i) entrepreneur/owner of fishing boats, (ii) capture fisherman, (iii) fish farming fisherman, (iv) business actor/fishing industry, (v) seafood trader, and (vi) port worker/fish auction/fish market. The survey results show that most of the respondents work to capture fishermen as many as 167 people or 83.5% of the total research respondents. For the status of their work, 90% of the fishing fishermen are fishermen with independent business status. This is closely related to the marine potential in the Ambon region which is still very dominant for capture fisheries (Table 1).

The survey results also show that the length of time worked on the type of work occupied. The majority of respondents have worked for a relatively long period of time, more than 75% of respondents have worked more than 5 years in the field of work they are engaged in. The most dominant respondents are those who have worked between 6 and 15 years, as many as 42% of the total respondents. Respondents who have worked between 16 and 25 years are 31%. (Fig. 3).

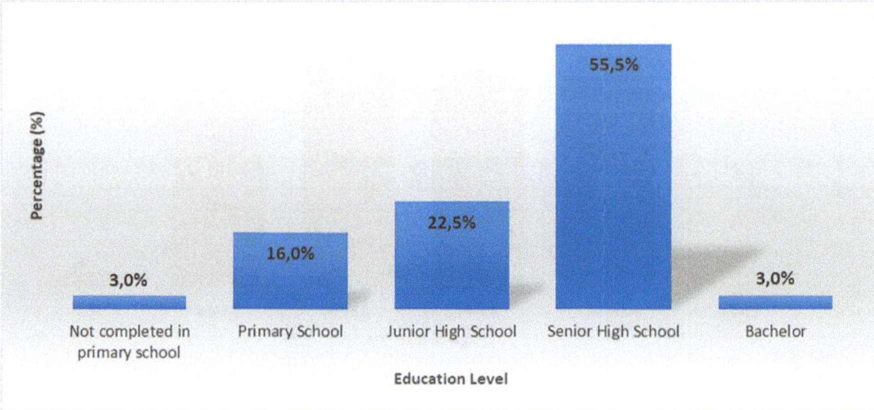


**Fig. 2** Respondent by education level. *Source* Results of Survey Data Processing in Ambon City, 2021

**Table 1** Respondents by occupation

| No. | Main job type | | Main employment status | | | | | Grand total |
|---|---|---|---|---|---|---|---|---|
| | | | Independent worker | Workers assisted by temporary workers | Workers assisted by permanent/paid workers | Labor/employee | Free worker on farm | |
| 1 | Entrepreneur/owner of fishing boats | Amount | 1 | – | 1 | – | – | 2 |
| | | percentage | 50.0% | 0.0% | 50.0% | 0.0% | 0.0% | 100.0% |
| 2 | Capture fisherman | Amount | 151 | 5 | 5 | 4 | 2 | 167 |
| | | Percentage | 90.4% | 3.0% | 3.0% | 2.4% | 1.2% | 100.0% |
| 3 | Fish farming fisherman | Amount | 2 | 6 | 8 | 1 | – | 17 |
| | | Percentage | 11.8% | 35.3% | 47.1% | 5.9% | 0.0% | 100.0% |
| 4 | Business actor/fishing industry | Amount | 3 | – | – | – | – | 3 |
| | | Percentage | 100.0% | 0.0% | 0.0% | 0.0% | 0.0% | 1000% |
| 5 | Seafood trader | Amount | 6 | – | – | – | – | 6 |
| | | Percentage | 100.0% | 0.0% | 0.0% | 0.0% | 0.0% | 100.0% |
| 6 | Port worker/fish auction worker/fish market worker | Amount | 2 | – | – | 3 | – | 5 |
| | | Percentage | 40.0% | 0.0% | 0.0% | 60.0% | 0.0% | 100.0% |

*Source* Results of Survey Data Processing in Ambon City, 2021

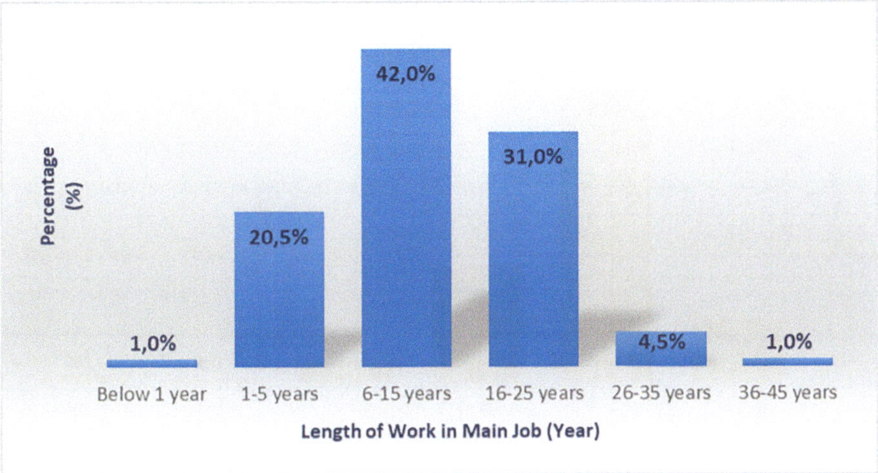


**Fig. 3** Respondent by length of work in main job. *Source* Results of Survey Data Processing in Ambon City, 2021

Maluku Province is ranked 32nd out of 33 provinces based on the amount of GRDP generated by each province in Indonesia. Three main sectors have dominated the economic structure of Maluku Province since 2000. The three sectors are the agricultural sector, the trade sector, hotels and restaurants, and the services sector. The superiority of the agricultural sector is mainly due to the very large contribution of the fisheries sub-sector, which reaches 65% of the entire sector [11]. Based on the survey results, some fishermen in Ambon city still receive wages below the average (12.5%). However, more than half of them (57.5%) range from 1.1 million to 3 million rupiahs (Fig. 4). Even though the Province Minimum Wage in Maluku province based on the Decree of the Governor of Maluku Number 672 of 2021 concerning the Determination of the Maluku Province Minimum Wage in 2022 is approximately 2,619,312 rupiahs.

The number of catches of traditional fishermen greatly affects the level of income of traditional fishermen. The income level of traditional fishermen certainly impacts spending for daily needs and the level of livelihood of traditional fishermen and their family members. The increase in fishery production will lead to the improvement and welfare of fishermen. Income, one of the economic factors, is highly dependent on fishermen's social factors (age, education, number of dependents, and work experience) and vice versa. The number of catches is also reflected in the amount of income received. Most of this income is for family consumption purposes; thus, the level of fulfillment of family consumption or minimum physical needs (KFM) is largely determined by the income received [15].

Based on the survey results that have been conducted, it can be concluded that the average working hours of fishermen in Ambon City, almost a quarter of respondents have a working duration of 41–55 h per week or 7–8 h per day. It is very possible if

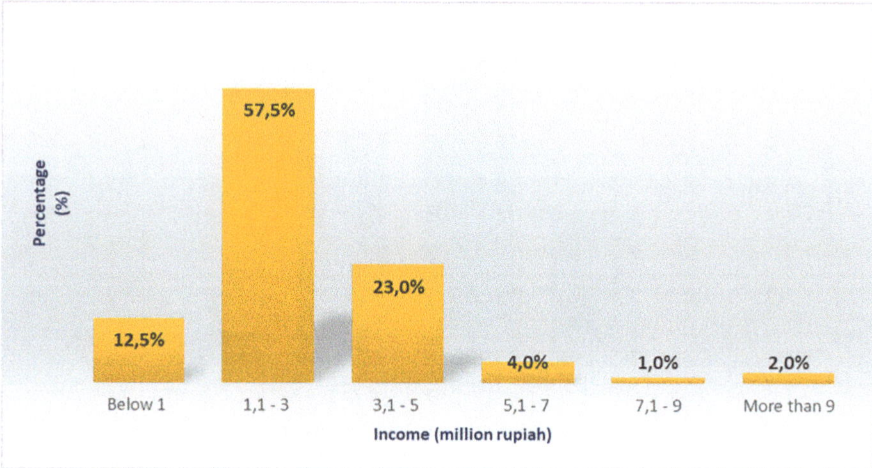


**Fig. 4** Average wages per month. *Source* Results of Survey Data Processing in Ambon City, 2021

the fishermen take the time to increase their knowledge by participating in training or the like organized by the government or other agencies. Working hours for workers in the private sector are regulated in Law No. 13 of 2003 concerning workforce, especially articles 77 to with article 85. Long time at sea in the life of fishermen in Indonesia is determined by the duration of fishing operations ranging from 2 to 17 h and this fishing is done at the same time varies. However, according to Metekohy, the variable working hours do not significantly affect the income received by fishermen on the coast of Ambon Island [15] (Table 2).

**Table 2** The average working hours during a week

| No. | Duration (h) | Amount | Percentage (%) |
|---|---|---|---|
| 1 | Less than 10 | 1 | 0.5 |
| 2 | 11–25 | 37 | 18.5 |
| 3 | 26–40 | 45 | 22.5 |
| 4 | 41–55 | 49 | 24.5 |
| 5 | 56–70 | 28 | 14.0 |
| 6 | 71–85 | 36 | 18.0 |
| 7 | 86–100 | 4 | 2.0 |
| Grand total | | 200 | 100.0 |

*Source* Results of Survey Data Processing in Ambon City, 2021

## 4 Participation in Fisheries Training and Counseling

There are only 5% who have attended training and counseling of all worker respondents we interviewed in Ambon City. Most of the fishery workers in Ambon City have not received any fishery training/counseling (Table 3) in the last five years. As many as 95% of fishery workers have not received fishery training or counseling in at least the last five years.

The results of this survey indicate that fishery training is still not evenly distributed to all fishery workers in Ambon City. This is directly proportional to the results of our interview with one of the extension workers at BPPP Ambon who stated that the extension workers in Ambon City were still limited and not evenly distributed in number or in terms of skills. This condition certainly makes it difficult and encourages inequality in training between locations. Furthermore, the 2021 First Quarter Performance Report shows data on the number of fishery instructors at BPP Ambon amounting to 252 people in 2020, which has decreased compared to the previous year, which amounted to 287 in 2019 and 299 in 2018. Besides that, there was a widyaswara of 5 people, 14 instructors, and 4 technical personnel. The number of teachers and extension workers oversees five regions, namely Maluku, Southeast Sulawesi, North Maluku, West Papua, and Papua. The number of instructors and extension workers of 276 is relatively small considering that the number has to oversee five provinces. Besides that, based on interviews with BPP Ambon, a limited number of teaching staff need to master teaching materials that are not their expertise, besides they need to do other tasks besides teaching assignments. This of course burdens the teaching staff at BPP Ambon.

Besides that, actually, fishery training in Ambon City actually covers a fairly broad training from fishing training, fishing vessel machinery, fish cultivation, processing and marketing of marine and fishery products and water conservation, but the problem of the limited number of trainers makes it difficult for all people to receive training on a regular basis equally. In addition, based on interviews, trainers, and extension workers not only work as trainers, but also they have to do various administrative work which also burdens them. The complexity of the work of trainers and extension workers should be one of the focuses that needs to be considered so that the productivity of trainers in the main job of training can be increased. Moreover, BPPP is also faced with the problem of recruiting extension workers and faced with the problem of budgeting for training for extension workers which can only be managed by the

**Table 3** Percentage of participation in training/counseling

| No. | Participation in training/counseling | Amount | Percentage (%) |
|---|---|---|---|
| 1 | Have attended training/counseling | 10 | 5.0 |
| 2 | Never attended training/counseling | 190 | 95.0 |
| Grand total | | 200 | 100 |

*Source* Results of Survey Data Processing in Ambon City, 2021

central government, so that they do not have the flexibility to improve the competence of extension workers. They are also faced with the difficulty of reaching fishing locations which are quite remote. Problems from the extensionist and BPPP side also contributed to the uneven distribution of training between locations (Table 3).

In addition to discussing trainer and institutional issues, it is necessary to analyze the reasons why the majority of workers still have not attended training. Based on the survey data, several main reasons were generated as to why the community did not attend the training. Not getting information, not being interested, having difficulty accessing training sites (geographical factors), not having training support facilities and limited time are factors that encourage people not to take fishery training (Table 4). Lack of information (33%) and time constraints (23%) are the main reasons why fishery workers do not participate in fishery training and counseling. In addition, it is logical for workers who still have low incomes to spend more of their time working than attending education considering that the time they have must be allocated to work compared to attending training, where participating in training takes time and costs. Panjaitan [17] stated that low income often makes fishermen reluctant to attend training (Table 4).

Furthermore, as many as 19% of all fishery workers who did not attend training, admitted that they did not do the training because they did not have training support facilities. Coupled with the current pandemic conditions, most of the training is conducted online, which requires workers to be more active in seeking information online and using extensive internet facilities and networks to participate in training. The next problem that becomes an obstacle for fishery workers to participate in training is the difficulty of accessing training sites (by 15%). The remaining 8% of workers who did not attend the training admitted that they were not interested in participating in the training and fishery counseling. Tan et al. [21] quite support our study. The results of their research indicate that fishermen workers in coastal areas are not trained and they do not want to go to school and complete their education, nor do they receive training to improve their knowledge and skills. Tan et al. [21] showed several research results that could be related to the limited condition of fishermen workers in coastal areas to have the desire and be able to attend education or training. First, on average, they get married at a young age and have two children at age 20.

**Table 4** Percentage of the reasons for not attending the training

| No. | The reasons for not attending the training | Amount | Percentage (%) |
|---|---|---|---|
| 1 | Not getting information | 167 | 33.7 |
| 2 | Not interested | 42 | 8.5 |
| 3 | Difficult to access training venues (geographical factor) | 76 | 15.3 |
| 4 | Do not have training support facilities | 94 | 19.0 |
| 5 | Limited time | 117 | 23.6 |
| Grand total | | 496 | 100 |

*Source* Results of Survey Data Processing in Ambon City, 2021

Apart from that they are burdened with loans or debts, due to their seasonal work. They are trapped and in debt.

There is more that fishermen have a lazy nature, are unproductive and not innovative, and are not creative because they are born naturally like that [22], someone who is poor will find it difficult to have plans and expectations. Moreover, Tan et al. [21] stated that they are not trained. Moreover, they are faced with living in isolated areas and faced with a shortage of infrastructure, and facilities such as roads, schools, training facilities. There are important things that cause them not to take part in the training because the training programs held by the government are not evenly distributed. Training is only given to fishermen who are already advanced, while fishermen who are not yet developed do not receive training from the local government. And the training model, and the technical assistance provided are not relevant to real needs [21]. Apart from the uneven training, some of the above conditions make it difficult for them to have more desire to be able to attend training and education, because they are much more focused on the conditions of poverty they face. The OECD [16] states that one of the important things in wanting to participate in training is the support of families and teachers, but this becomes a difficult thing when there is a lack of time and inadequate digital skills as well as a lack of curricular guidelines during the COVID-19 pandemic. This is also one of the participants who participated in the training.

Maslow in Panjaitan [17], states that there are several things that can increase the motivation of fishermen in participating in training from the beginning to the end, namely: (1) Free stationery supplies, (2) Free work clothes in the field; (3) Provision of transportation money from home to the training site; (3) Provision of free lunch and children in the morning and evening; (4) Giving pocket money as a substitute because they don't go to sea; (5) Provision of a certificate of completion of the training for free.

This statement is in line with the recommendations from the ILO on vocational training for fishermen, which states that in terms of financing, the government needs to provide financial assistance for training such as assistance for fishing boats, machines, navigational equipment, and fishing gear, as well as the provision of free instructors and reimbursement of costs when fishermen are concerned with training [7]. These two references indicate that incentives are important enough to increase the motivation of fishery workers to participate in training and reduce their barriers to accessing training (Table 5).

We questioned the willingness of workers who did not attend training if they were given the opportunity to be given training and most answered that they were willing to take part in the training, which was 72.6% (Table 7). Then 14.2% admitted that they are still unsure or still need consideration in deciding whether to take part in training if fishery training is provided. The remaining 13.2% are not willing to take part in the training. The compositions in Tables 7 and 8 indicate that they actually want training but they have limitations. This limitation needs to be facilitated so that the percentage of fishery workers participating in training increases.

This conclusion is actually in line with our in-depth interviews with several fishermen's wives in the Laha area who work as fish smokers. They claimed that they

**Table 5** Percentage of the willingness to take part in training/counseling when there is an offer

| No. | Willingness to take part in training/ counseling when there is an offer | Amount | Percentage (%) |
|---|---|---|---|
| 1 | Willing to take part in training/ counseling | 138 | 72.6 |
| 2 | Doubtful/needs consideration | 27 | 14.2 |
| 3 | Not willing | 25 | 13.2 |
| Grand total | | 190 | 100.0 |

*Source* Results of Survey Data Processing in Ambon City, 2021

**Table 6** Percentage of sources of information about training

| No. | Sources of information about training | Percentage (%) |
|---|---|---|
| 1 | From family/friends/coworkers | 12.0 |
| 2 | From the organization/community | 12.0 |
| 3 | From social media | 13.9 |
| 4 | From digital communication media | 13.9 |
| 5 | From electronic media | 13.9 |
| 6 | From school | 13.9 |
| 7 | From government officials | 7.5 |
| 8 | Other | 12.6 |
| Grand total | | 100.0 |

*Source* Results of Survey Data Processing in Ambon City, 2021

**Table 7** Percentage of motivation to participate in training

| No. | Motivation to participate in training percentage | Percentage (%) |
|---|---|---|
| 1 | Improve skills and knowledge at work | 10.0 |
| 2 | To get job access | 13.4 |
| 3 | Driven by Parents/family/community | 16.8 |
| 4 | Get training incentives/pocket money | 15.1 |
| 5 | Get a relationship | 11.7 |
| 6 | Get a certificate | 14.2 |
| 7 | Other | 18.4 |
| Grand total | | 100.0 |

*Source* Results of Survey Data Processing in Ambon City, 2021

wanted to receive training in processing fish catches but needed to be accompanied by the assistance of the goods being trained. They get training to smoke fish with modern tools. This tool makes them smoke fish faster but they don't have the modern fish smoking device so that the training becomes less effective and not on target. Besides, so far they have only received training in smoking fish and it has been

**Table 8** Types of training/counseling required according to survey respondent's proposal

| No. | Type of training (number of $N = 200$) | Needed | | Not needed | |
|---|---|---|---|---|---|
| | | Amount | Percentage (%) | Amount | Percentage (%) |
| 1 | Fishing techniques | 138 | 69.0 | 62 | 31.0 |
| 2 | Mechanical engineering | 82 | 41.0 | 118 | 59.0 |
| 3 | Cultivation and seeding | 20 | 10.0 | 180 | 90.0 |
| 4 | Processing and quality of fishery products | 14 | 7.0 | 186 | 93.0 |
| 5 | Marketing and fishery business management | 25 | 12.5 | 175 | 87.5 |
| 6 | Entrepreneurship | 18 | 9.0 | 182 | 91.0 |
| 7 | Product packaging | 3 | 1.5 | 197 | 98.5 |
| 8 | Basic safety | 14 | 7.0 | 186 | 93.0 |
| 9 | Fishery Conservation | 1 | 0.5 | 199 | 99.5 |
| 10 | Digital technology | 4 | 2.0 | 196 | 98.0 |
| 11 | Automatic machine | 5 | 2.5 | 195 | 97.5 |

*Source* Results of Survey Data Processing in Ambon City, 2021

for a very long period of time. They admitted that they really wanted to get training in other fish processing besides smoking fish, such as making fish balls, fish crackers, shredded meat, and many more, but keep in mind that training must also provide tools so that they are able to use and apply them individually. Besides that, considering that the market for processed food made from fish in Ambon is actually very small. The people of Ambon City prefer fresh fish to processed food. This reminds us that processing training must be accompanied by marketing and entrepreneurship training because product distribution outside the region must receive attention.

## 5 Source of Training Information and Motivation to Attend the Training and Counseling

Based on the survey results, it was found that the sources of information regarding training and counseling were obtained from several sources. Even so, the percentages from each source are calculated relatively almost the same number, nothing is too prominent. Sources from social media, digital communication media, electronic sources, and schools are the main sources for people surveyed to get information on fisheries training and counseling (Table 6). Meanwhile, sources of information from family/friends/coworkers and from organizations/communities are the second highest sources of information (Table 6). In addition, information from government officials is the source that provides the lowest contribution in providing information on fishery training and counseling. This is reinforced by the research of Tan et al.

[21] which states that the training programs held by the government have not been well distributed.

Besides the source of information, it is also important to know the motivation for participating in the training. Encouragement by parents/groups/communities is the main motivation for a person to take part in the training. After that, getting incentive money/pocket money is the second biggest motivation for someone to want to take part in fishery training and counseling. This is supported by research by Maslow and Panjaitan (2015) which states that there are several things that can increase the motivation of fishermen, namely the provision of transportation money from home to the training site and the provision of pocket money because they cannot go to the sea. The next motivation that drives someone to want to work is to get a certificate. This is also in line with Maslow and Panjaitan (2015) research which states that giving a certificate of graduation from training is one thing that can be given to increase a person's motivation to take part in training or counseling. Gaining access to work and increasing skills and knowledge at work are the smallest motivations for a person to participate in fishery training and counseling (Table 7).

## 6 Training Needs by Fishery Workers in Ambon City

Based on the data, there are various pieces of training needed by fishery workers, including fishing techniques, mechanical techniques, cultivation and hatcheries, processing and quality of fishery products, marketing and management of fishery businesses, entrepreneurship, product packaging, basic safety, fisheries conservation, digital technology, and automatic machines. From these data, fishing (69%) and mechanical engineering (41%) dominate the needs conveyed by respondents. This condition occurs because the majority of respondents are fishermen who need fishing skills and mechanical techniques. These two skills are needed to support the daily needs of fishermen while at sea. From discussions with some fishermen, they stated that so far the skills they have related to the fishing process are based on the skills they have learned from their parents.

From the survey results, it can also be seen that there is a need for cultivation and seeding (10%). This need was conveyed by fish farmers that they need new knowledge about fish farming and hatchery processes. However, when examined through interviews, one of the farmers complained about the lack of support from the Fisheries Service in Ambon City and the Fisheries Service in Maluku Province regarding the assistance of fish seeds and new skills regarding cultivation. One of the representatives of the cultivators stated that so far, they had carried out the cultivation process independently. They learn independently the skills needed to carry out the cultivation process, superior seeds, the size of the floating cage needed, the spawning process, egg hatching, maintenance and development, rearing, and harvesting processes. They also spend their capital to manage the fish farming process.

Table 1 The skills that received attention from the respondents' proposals were processing and quality of fishery products (7%), marketing and management of fishery businesses (12.5%), entrepreneurship (9%), and basic safety. Processing and quality of fishery products, marketing and management of fishery businesses, and entrepreneurship are needed by most fishery workers. The need for these skills is closely related to the increase in the added value of fishery products which seems to have not been optimized by fishery workers. For the processing and quality of fishery products, for example, there are still very few fishery products that are processed properly. Marketing skills are very supportive to sell fishery products and processed fishery products from fishery workers. Meanwhile, the need for basic safety-related skills was also suggested by the workers. From discussions with several fishermen, it was conveyed that attention to safety issues had not been a concern. Even though the work, especially for fishermen, is very risky. They should have basic safety skills (basic safety training). Other proposed skills are product packaging (1.5%), fisheries conservation (0.5%), digital technology (2.0%), and automatic machines (2.5%). All three received less attention from respondents even though these three skills are excessively needed by fishery workers today. From discussions with fishery workers, attention to conservation issues, digital technology, the use of automatic machines, and product packaging have not become major issues (Table 8).

Taking into account the survey results regarding the need for skills improvement, the government needs to pay attention to several aspects. First, the government needs to do a more thorough mapping of the types of fishing jobs in Ambon City. Mapping the types of work becomes an important part of designing the training needs that can be provided to fishery workers. An understanding of the types of work that fishery workers do in Ambon City will make it easier for the government to design training that is needed and relevant for fishery workers.

Second, the training and counseling provided must be sustainable by taking into several aspects such as regional conditions; type, pattern, working time; and basic skills possessed by fishery workers. Continuous training/counseling activities must be carried out to increase the capacity of each fishery worker. This is to make the training/counseling contextual to the needs of workers. It is no longer possible to hold training/counseling that is carried out uniformly. Regional conditions can determine the type of work undertaken by workers; the type, pattern, and time off work greatly determine the training, methods, teaching materials, curriculum, location, as well as the right time for the implementation of training/extension; and basic skills determine targeted training/counseling interventions.

Third, training/counseling needs to pay attention to women and youth. Workers in fisheries are dominated by men. Therefore, attention to women should be a priority. The women in Ambon City have participated enough in activities to help their husbands work, but they have not become an important part of fishing activities. Even though they have been supporting the activities carried out by the husbands. By providing adequate training/counseling for women, it is hoped that they can contribute to family welfare. In addition, capacity building and skills gained through training/counseling activities will empower women. In addition, in the context of regeneration, youth also need to be involved in training/counseling activities. Through this process, it is hoped that the sustainability of the fishery business in the family can be maintained and its capacity increased so that it can contribute to the fishery business.

Fourth, training/counseling activities need to target financial management or management issues, not only related to technical skills improvement. Management ability or financial management has a significant effect because as revealed in various kinds of literature, fishing communities have problems with money management. Financial literacy is an important thing that is conveyed in training/counseling. Regarding technical skills, for example, in some cases, fishermen can learn this independently based on long experience at sea. Research by Mahdavikya and Tjahjono [13] shows that fishermen have above-average knowledge and skills in using GPS.

Fifth, the need for evaluation and monitoring that is scheduled in a structured manner to monitor the progress of each training/counseling program carried out. Evaluation and monitoring activities are an important part so that every program implementation is following the plan. Through evaluation and monitoring activities, the government knows the pace of development of activities and the effectiveness of training/counseling activities.

## 7 Conclusion

Based on the survey results, the demographic characteristic of respondents is the majority of workers in the fishery sector are male, more than half are in the 35–44 and 45–54 years age groups, and most of them are fishermen. The majority of fishery workforce education is high school education. Of the average working hours of fishermen in Ambon City, almost a quarter of respondents have a working duration of 41–55 h per week or 7–8 h per day. In addition, more than half of the respondents (57.5%) have the wage range from 1.1 million to 3 million rupiahs; meanwhile, the Maluku Province Minimum Wage is approximate 2,619,312 rupiahs.

Participation in training and counseling is still low in Ambon. This is a complex matter because it is caused both in terms of the limited number of extension workers and the limitations of workers in the fishery sector. However, the survey results show that most respondents are willing to attend training if they are allowed to receive training. Looking away from the side of the respondents who attended the training, most of the respondents who participated in the training were motivated to get incentives. This is reinforced by previous research where incentives are important for workers in the fisheries sector to attend training as an opportunity cost of the time they can use to work. Considering that only a small proportion of the respondents attended the training, we tried to examine how they got the training information. Most get information from electronic media or social media. This can indicate that social media is very important in deepening information about training. This of course can be useful for policymakers to deepen information through social media and electronic media. Deepening information and increasing incentives for fishery workers can certainly increase the probability of these workers participating in training besides there are indeed many problems that prevent them from participating in training and counseling.

Increasing the capacity of fishery workers in Ambon City through training and counseling requires intensive attention from the government. The results showed that the training and extension programs obtained by fishery workers were not always relevant to the needs of fishery workers. Several things need to be considered by the central government and local governments. The government needs to map the types of fishing jobs in Ambon City more carefully. Mapping the types of work becomes an important part of designing the training needs that can be provided to fishery workers. Second, the training and counseling provided must be carried out sustainably by taking into account several aspects such as regional conditions; type, pattern, working time; and basic skills possessed by fishery workers. Third, training/extension needs to pay attention to women and youth. Fourth, training/counseling activities need to target financial management or management issues, not only those related to technical skill improvement. Fifth, the need for evaluation and monitoring that is scheduled in a structured manner to monitor the progress of each training/counseling program carried out.

**Acknowledgements** The authors conveyed their gratitude, especially for PRN and LPDP Research grants program through the activity of Excellence Research that has been supporting the funding for this study. The gratitude is also sent to the local enumerator team in Ambon who have been involved during the data collection

## References

1. Afriansyah A (2021) Reformasi pasar tenaga kerja sektor perikanan: desain dan tata kelola pelatihan vokasional pada lapangan ekonomi informal. Policy brief. Tim Riset, Pusat Penelitian Kependudukan—LIPI
2. Amin M, Purwangka F, Mawardi W (2018) Skillfulness and knowledge fishermen level in Karangantu, Banten. ALBACORE Jurnal Penelitian Perikanan Laut 2(1):107–121
3. Christiawan PI (2017) Entitas permukiman kumuh di wilayah pesisir. Jurnal Ilmu Sosial Dan Humaniora 6(2):178–187
4. Fahmi I (2014) Poros maritim: jokowi tetapkan 5 pilar andalan. https://ekonomi.bisnis.com/read/20141113/9/272659/poros-maritim-jokowi-tetapkan-5-pilar-andalan
5. Government Regulation Number 62 of 2014 Concerning implementation of fisheries training and education counseling
6. Hiariey LS, Romeon NR (2013) Peran serta masyarakat pemanfaat pesisir dalam pengelolaan wilayah Pesisir Teluk Ambon Dalam. Jurnal Matematika Sains dan Teknologi 14(1):48–61
7. ILO—Recommendation concerning the vocational training of fishermen R126 (formazione professionale pescatori), 21 giugno 1966
8. Kementerian Kelautan dan Perikanan KK (2017) Kebijakan kelautan Indonesia. Kementerian Kelautan dan Perikanan, Jakarta
9. Kementerian Kelautan dan Perikanan KK (2021) Laporan kinerja triwulan I tahun 2021 Kementerian Kelautan dan Perikanan Badan Riset dan SDM Kelautan dan Perikanan Pusat Pelatihan dan Penyuluhan Perikanan KP Balai Pelathan dan Penyuluh Perikanan Ambon. Kementerian Kelautan dan Perikanan, Jakarta

10. Kementerian Kelautan dan Perikanan KK (2021) Laporan kinerja triwulan II Tahun 2021 Kementerian Kelautan dan Perikanan Badan Riset dan SDM Kelautan dan Perikanan Pusat Pelatihan dan Penyuluhan Perikanan KP Balai Pelathan dan Penyuluh Perikanan Ambon. Kementerian Kelautan dan Perikanan, Jakarta
11. Latuny EM (2014) Analisis sektor unggulan di provinsi maluku. Cita Ekonomika. Jurnal Ekonomi VIII(2):148–157
12. Law Number 31 of 2004 concerning Fisheries
13. Mahdavikya M, Tjahjono H (2021) Pengetahuan dan keterampilan nelayan menggunakan alat navigasi global navigation system (GPS) untuk aktivitas melaut di Kecamatan Kragan Kabupaten Rembang. Edu Geogr 9(1):66–77
14. Masri A (2017) Pendidikan Anak Nelayan Pesisir Pantai Donggala (The education for coastal fishermen children in Donggala). Asian J Environ Hist Herit 1(1)
15. Metekohy S (2020) Determinan Pendapatan Nelayan di Pulau Ambon. Cita Ekonomika, Jurnal Ekonomi XIV(1):1–10
16. OECD (2020) Strengthening online learning when school are closed: The role of families and teachers in supporting students during the Covid-19 crisis. OECD Working Paper
17. Panjaitan H (2015) Motivasi peserta pelatihan di balai pelatihan penyuluhan di balai pelatihan dan penyuluhan perikanan Medan. https://kkp.go.id/an-component/media/upload-gambar-pendukung/BPPP%20Medan/MOTIVASI%20PESERTA%20PELATIHAN%2018_1.pdf
18. Presidential Regulation of the Republic of the Republic of Indonesia Number 16 of 2017 on Indonesian Marine Policy
19. Rahmadani S, Siburian JP (2020) Socio economic study of coastal communities in Hajoran Induk Village Central of Tapanuli Regency, North Sumatera Province. PELAGICUS 1(2):53–61
20. Susanti N, Siregar PA, dan Falefi R (2020) Hypertension's determinant in coastal communities based on socio demographic and food consumption. Jurnal Ilmiah Kesehatan 2(1):43–52
21. Tan WF, Nesti L, Yonnedi EY, Ridwan ER (2021) Strategy to improve economic condition of fisherman living in the coastal area in Kabupaten Pesisir Selatan. J Bus Soc Econ Dev Emer Publish Ltd, 2635–1374.
22. Tan F, Prima Putra F, Sartika D (2012) Kajian Sistem Manajemen Pengembangan UMKM/UIKM Berbasis local economic resources development. A research report. Published by West Sumatra Regional Planning Board (BAPPEDA) Padang, pp 1–223
23. Zaelany AA dkk (2014) Kualitas Tenaga Kerja Perikanan. IPB Press. Cetakan ke-1, Bogor

# Effectiveness of Online Learning Models for Engineering Courses at Civil and Environmental Engineering Department, Faculty of Engineering, Universitas Indonesia (CEE FTUI)

**Amilia Novitasari, Idqan Fahmi, and Cindy Rianti Priadi**

**Abstract** Engineering education is required to apply innovation in its teaching method while the trend of online learning becomes very dramatic during the COVID-19 pandemic. This study aims to analyze the level of effectiveness and the factors that influence the level of effectiveness of using online learning models and formulate strategies to increase effectiveness for engineering courses at CEE UI as a recommendation for the blended learning method towards the new normal era. This study used quantitative methods with questionnaires and saturation sampling techniques with 117 students for sampling (both offline and online). The data analysis technique used Mann–Whitney test, SEM PLS, and Cartesian diagrams. The results show that the effectiveness of online learning from the variables of learning implementation and time management is considered quite effective, although from the learning effectiveness variable itself the results are not significant, which means that there is no difference between offline and online learning. Based on the SEM PLS analysis, the indicator of effective learning time gives the largest contribution to the variable of time management, while the indicator of the use of learning media has the largest contribution to the variable of learning implementation. Hypothesis testing has been done to prove that the implementation of learning and time management has a significant effect on the effectiveness of online learning. Although time management has the largest loading factor, it has a low respondent's perception value, so it is in the high-priority quadrant or is a concern for improvement.

**Keywords** Learning effectiveness · Online learning · Structural equation model—partial least square (SEM PLS)

---

A. Novitasari (✉) · C. R. Priadi
Center for Engineering Education (CEE) FTUI, Universitas Indonesia, Jakarta, Indonesia
e-mail: amilia.novitasari31@ui.ac.id

I. Fahmi
IPB University, Jawa Barat, Indonesia



Nawawi et al. (eds.), *Managing Disruption and Developing Resilience for a Better Southeast Asia*, Springer Proceedings in Humanities and Social Sciences,
https://doi.org/10.1007/978-981-96-2116-3_8

## 1 Introduction

The significant impact in the teaching process has been felt as a result of the development of Information and Communication Technology (ICT) in the Industrial 4.0 era. Easy access to technology has been utilized by lecturer to facilitate the learning process. Access to technology can also improve the quality of education. Internet technology almost allows everything in the world of education. Currently, students can use the existing online learning model facilities, not only in any place but also at any time. Now, both in developed and developing countries, especially in Indonesia, the online learning model is considered as a way to overcome problems in the field of education and training.

Similarly, in universities and universities, in terms of providing lecture materials, grades, and presentations, online learning models have been used in the world of education. Due to the paradigm shift in the field of education in the era of globalization, online learning models have become trends and choices. The online learning model can be a bridge in terms of space and time between educators and learners. The use of online learning models can support the process of knowledge transformation [17]. Model online learning provides good results, namely the improvement of competency results and increased understanding of lecture materials by students [10]. As has been conveyed by Keengwe and Georgina [6], technological developments have brought changes to the implementation of teaching. Can receive information technology as a medium of educational process, including helping the teaching and learning process including finding sources of information and references [20].

The online learning model was also adopted by the University of Indonesia, one of which was with innovative and adaptive *engineering education* applied by the Department of Civil and Environmental Engineering, Faculty of Engineering, Universitas Indonesia (DTSL FTUI). Engineering education is currently required to apply innovation in teaching so that the competencies promised by an engineering study program can be achieved effectively. The condition of millennial students today which is increasingly critical with increasingly difficult focusing skills also demands various innovations in teaching so that students' motivation and interest are maintained. According to Ivanova et al. [3], online learning means learning carried out using *online* learning applications and social networks.

Online learning is becoming increasingly competitive with traditional face-to-face teaching, both in promoting learning and keeping costs down. That trend became an option in 2020, when the *COVID-19* pandemic caused universities to cancel face-to-face classes and forced lecturer to implement online learning models, with or without training or previous online learning model experience. One way to overcome face-to-face problems is to implement a distance education system considering the problems of *physical distancing* rules, time, location, distance, and cost that are major obstacles today [8].

Universitas Indonesia also implemented an education policy with online methods during this pandemic in accordance with the Circular Letter of the Rector of the Universitas Indonesia Number SE-723/UN2. R/OTL.09/2020 concerning Vigilance and Prevention of the Spread of *COVID-19* Infection in the Universitas Indonesia Environment. Where in the circular stipulates the change of face-to-face teaching and learning activities to distance or online learning. Even for the semester 2020/2021, it has been determined to continue to carry out distance or online learning in accordance with the Circular Letter of the Directorate General of Higher Education, Ministry of Education and Culture Number 6 of 2020 concerning the Implementation of Learning in the Even Semester of the Academic Year 2020/2021.

The implementation of online learning policies during the *COVID-19* pandemic began to bring up many things that were previously unpredictable, one of which was related to new problems that are rarely encountered when face-to-face learning takes place. The problem that is often encountered is the selection of learning methods by lecturers that are not suitable be done online so that the two-way interaction between lecturers and students produced becomes less effective. The selection of methods by these lecturers tends to make many students feel saturated because they only use lecture methods in the online learning process. Providing material for online learning models can be interactive so that students are able to interact with computers as a learning medium.

Engineering courses have their own challenges to be delivered with an online learning model, where engineering courses require practicum and field practice to support learning. Because all courses taken in the first and second semesters are prerequisite courses to continue the course in the next semester.

Referring to the importance of basic Engineering compulsory courses in the first semester and the second semester to be able to continue to the next semester because it is a prerequisite, then this is what researchers feel is important to analyze the effectiveness of online learning models for engineering courses at DTSL FTUI, especially during this pandemic. DTSL FTUI also needs to get an idea of the effectiveness of online learning models during this pandemic and in the *next new normal* period after the end of this pandemic, especially for mandatory technical basic courses carried out in the first and second semesters as one of the managerial implications to determine strategies for improving online learning models for engineering courses in the future to implement *blended learning* in the future. *New normal.*

This study aims to analyze the level of effectiveness and factors that affect the level of effectiveness of the use of online learning models and to announce effectiveness improvement strategies for engineering courses at DTSL FTUI as a recommendation for the implementation of *blended learning* in the *new normal* in the future.

# 2 Method

## 2.1 Research Design

This research refers to a quantitative descriptive research approach. While this type of research is a quantitative type of analytical survey through a *cross-sectional* approach, it emphasizes the time of collection and measurement, and observation of variable data only once at a time [13].

## 2.2 Sampling, Population, and Sample Techniques

The sampling technique in this study will use *non-probability sampling* with *saturation sampling* or census sampling techniques, namely by using all samples in the population. In this case, the entire class of 2018, 2019, and 2020 participated in compulsory technical basic courses, which have the same criteria, because they have a tightness value and an average of relatively the same learning outcomes. The research population consists of undergraduate program students' class of 2018, 2019, and 2020 DTSL FTUI who have taken compulsory basic engineering courses. Each of the 117 samples was online and offline.

## 2.3 Variables and Indicators

This research consists of two exogenous (independent) variables, namely the implementation of learning and time management, while endogenous (dependent) variables are the effectiveness of online learning and offline learning. The indicators of each variable will be measured with a 5-point Likert Scale, a 1 for disagreeing and 5 for strongly agreeing.

## 2.4 Data Processing and Analysis

The data analysis technique used in this study is SEM PLS (*Structural Equation Model—Partial Least Square*) to analyze factors that affect the effectiveness of the use of online learning models for engineering courses at DTSL FTUI. In order to analyze the effectiveness of the use of online learning models offline for engineering courses for students at DTSL FTUI, *the Mann–Whitney* test was used and formulate strategies to increase the effectiveness of the use of online learning models for engineering courses at DTSL FTUI, analysis was carried out using Kartesius Diagram.

**Table 1** Normal test table

| One-sample Kolmogorov–Smirnov test | | | | |
|---|---|---|---|---|
| | | X1. implementation of learning | X2. time management | Y. effectiveness of learning |
| N | | 908 | 908 | 908 |
| Normal parameters[a,b] | Mean | 66.0646 | 65.7369 | 65.2643 |
| | Std. deviation | 6.23040 | 6.89695 | 7.31574 |
| Most extreme differences | Absolute | 0.179 | 0.172 | 0.200 |
| | Positive | 0.179 | 0.172 | 0.200 |
| | Negative | −0.108 | −0.107 | −0.117 |
| Test statistic | | 0.179 | 0.172 | 0.200 |
| Asymp. Sig. (2-tailed) | | 0.000[c] | 0.000[c] | 0.000[c] |

a. Implementation of learning
b. Time management
c. Effectiveness of learning

# 3 Results and Discussions

## *3.1 Result*

To determine the level of effectiveness of the online learning model, a normality test is carried out on the distribution of questionnaire data as in Table 1.

Normal test results show the value of asymp sig. (2-tailed) $< 0.05$ on each variable means that each variable does not spread normally, so the different test is done by the non-parametric method, namely the *mann–whitney* different test. The *Mann–Whitney* test is an alternative to the t-test, which is a non-parametric test used to compare two mean populations coming from the same population. The *Mann–Whitney* test can also be used to test whether two population mean is the same or not [18].

## *3.2 The Effectiveness Level of Use of Online Learning Models is not Offline*

Comparison between non-practicum online learning and non-practicum offline shows that the results of the *Mann–Whitney* test have a p-value of $< 0.05$, namely in variables X1 Learning Implementation and X2 Time Management, but not significant for the effectiveness of learning itself as seen in Table 2.

The same results were obtained by comparing practicum online learning with practicum offline. The *Mann–Whitney* test showed a *p*-value of $< 0.05$, namely in variable X1 Learning Implementation and X2 Time Management, but not significant for the effectiveness of learning itself as seen in Table 3.

**Table 2** Mann-Whitney test statistics table of online and non-practicum offline learning

| | X1. Implementation of learning | X2. Time management | Y. Effectiveness of learning |
|---|---|---|---|
| Mann–Whitney U | 19,184.000 | 21,813.500 | 24,539.500 |
| Wilcoxon W | 46,679.000 | 49,308.500 | 52,034.500 |
| With | −4.699 | −2.829 | −0.872 |
| Asymp. Sig. (2-tailed) | 0.000 | 0.005 | 0.383 |

**Table 3** *Mann–Whitney* test statistics table of online learning and practicum offline

| | X1. Implementation of learning | X2. Time management | Y. Effectiveness of learning |
|---|---|---|---|
| Mann–Whitney U | 19,607.500 | 21,497.000 | 24,279.000 |
| Wilcoxon W | 47,102.500 | 48,992.000 | 51,774.000 |
| With | −4.396 | −3.058 | −1.062 |
| Asymp. Sig. (2-tailed) | 0.000 | 0.002 | 0.288 |

The results of the *Mann–Whitney* test for both *clusters* are significant ($p$-value $< 0.05$) and then it will be followed by descriptive analysis using mean values. The average of scores for both learning methods, where for the implementation of learning and time management, non-practicum online methods have a greater mean value compared to non-practicum offline methods, as well as the implementation of learning and time management with practicum online methods that have mean values greater than offline practicum as in Table 3.

The comparison of mean value between online and offline learning for the implementation of learning and time management can be seen in Table 4 that the value of online learning is greater than offline, which means that online learning is considered **effective** compared to offline learning.

**Table 4** Mean values of non-practicum and practicum online and offline learning

| | X1. Implementation of learning | X2. Time management | Y. Effectiveness of learning |
|---|---|---|---|
| | Mean | Mean | Mean |
| Online—non-practicum | 67.58 | 66.70 | 65.47 |
| Luring—non praktikum | 64.89 | 64.86 | 65.02 |
| Online—practicum | 67.31 | 66.80 | 65.70 |
| Luring—internship | 64.64 | 64.70 | 64.91 |
| Daring | 67.45 | 66.75 | 65.58 |
| Luring | 64.77 | 64.78 | 64.96 |

### 3.3 *Factors Affecting the Effectiveness of Using Online & Offline Learning Models*

As for the evaluation of the measurement model (*outer model)* if there is an indicator that has a *loading factor* value of < 0. 5, a recalculation of the model must be carried out to produce *a loading factor* of all reflective indicative indicators' worth > 0.5 as the criteria of the latent variable convergent validity test [1]. In addition, the model shared has good validity if each latent variable with a reflective indicator has an AVE > 0.5. Model measurements must also qualify for reliability and discriminant validity. After going through several iterations, the final measurement model was obtained in Fig. 1 for online learning and Fig. 2 for offline learning.

X1 Learning Implementation affects Y Learning Effectiveness of 0.140 means that the higher X1 Learning Implementation as measured through X1.02, X1.05, X1.08 and X1.15 then Y Learning Effectiveness increases. Likewise, the variable X2 Time Management affects Y Learning Effectiveness of 0.447 means that the higher the X2 Time Management measured through X2.1 and X2.2, the Y Learning Effectiveness will increase. Structural model Y Learning Effectiveness produces an R-square value of **29.6%** meaning the diversity of Y Learning Effectiveness can be

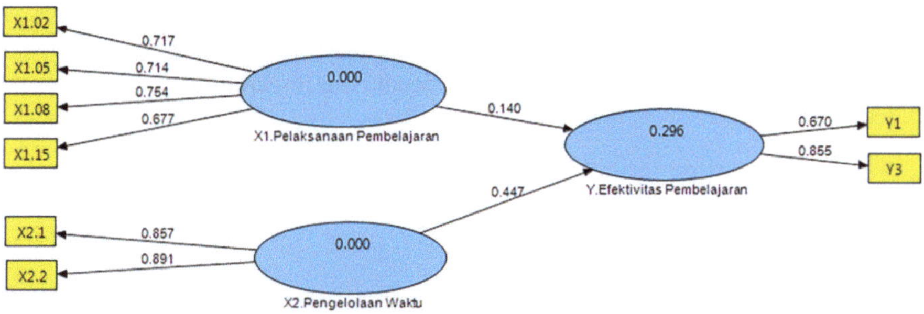


**Fig. 1** *Loading factor* on the online learning final measurement model

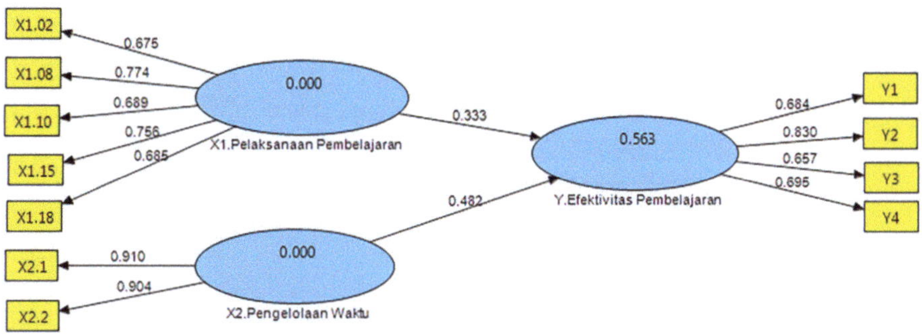


**Fig. 2** *Loading factor* on offline learning final measurement model

explained by the model by 29.6% while the remaining 70.4% is explained by other factors outside the model as presented in Fig. 1.

The GoF index value of the online learning PLS model > 0.36, which is 0.429 which means that the GoF value is large or has a research model feasibility level of 43%, or it can be concluded that the feasibility level of the model is 0.429. A large study can be seen in Table 24.

X1 Learning Implementation affects Y Learning Effectiveness of 0.333 means that the higher the X1 Learning Implementation as measured through X1.02, X1.08, X1.10, X1.15 and X1.18 then Y Learning Effectiveness increases. Likewise, the variable X2 Time Management affects Y Learning Effectiveness of 0.482 means that the higher X2 Time Management measured through X2.1 and X2.2, the Y Learning Effectiveness will increase. Structural model Y Learning Effectiveness produces an R-square value of 56.3% meaning the diversity of Y Learning Effectiveness can be explained by the model by 56.3% while the remaining 43.7% is explained by other factors outside the model as presented in Fig. 2.

Based on Fig. 3, there are several managerial strategy recommendations that can be given to DTSL FTUI management to improve the effectiveness of online learning. This recommendation only focuses on the *High-Priority* quadrant because the indicators located in the area have a great influence on the effectiveness of online learning but have low perceptual values (Tables 5 and 6).

Nilai GoF index of offline learning PLS model > 0.36, which is 0.590 which means a large GoF value or has a research model feasibility level of 59%, or it can be concluded that the feasibility level of the model big research (Fig. 4).

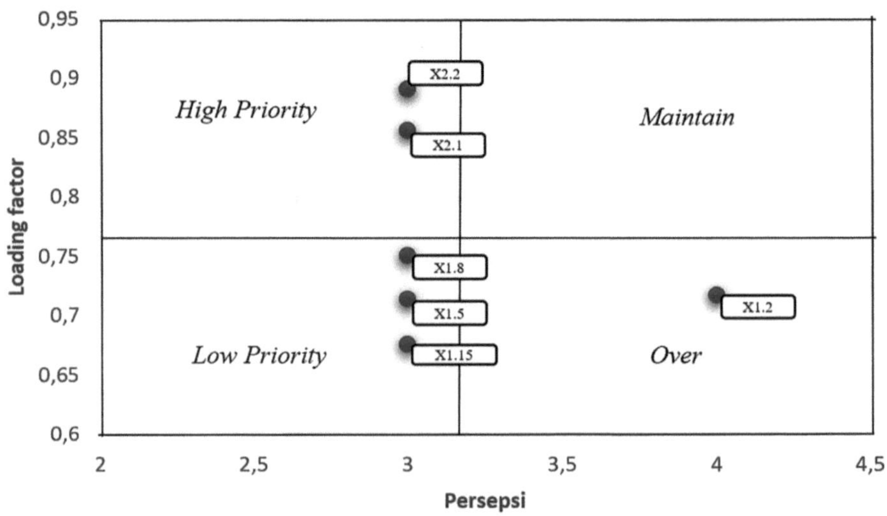


**Fig. 3** Perception matrix of online learning indicators

**Table 5** Calculation table GoF index online learning PLS model

| | R square | Communality | Value GoF |
|---|---|---|---|
| X1. Implementation of learning | | 0.513 | |
| X2. Time management | | 0.764 | |
| Y. Learning outcomes | 0.296 | 0.589 | |
| | | | **0.429** |

**Table 6** Calculation table GoF index model PLS offline learning model

| | R square | Communality | Value GoF |
|---|---|---|---|
| X1. Implementation of learning | | 0.514 | |
| X2. Time management | | 0.822 | |
| Y. Learning outcomes | 0.563 | 0.518 | |
| | | | **0.590** |

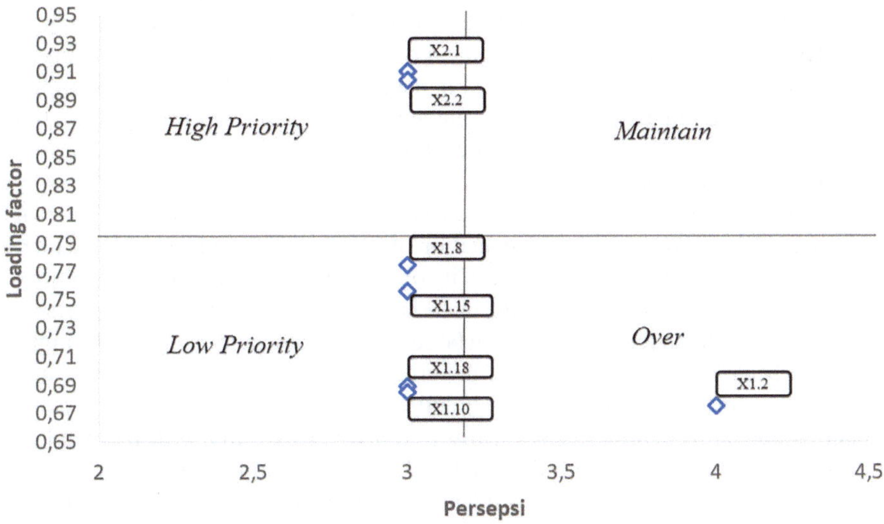


**Fig. 4** Perception matrix against offline learning indicators

## 4 Discussion

The average score for both learning methods, where for the implementation of learning and time management, non-practicum online methods have a greater mean value compared to non-practicum offline methods, as well as the implementation of learning and time management with practicum online methods that have a greater mean value compared to offline practicum. The mean value of online learning is greater than offline, which means that **online learning is considered effective compared to offline learning.**

Based on the results of the PLS SEM Analysis for **online learning**, the most influential indicator on the effectiveness of online learning is effective communication (X1.02). This indicator has a *loading factor* value of 0.717 which contains a statement about students' perception of lecturer who provide online teaching using a sound volume that can be heard clearly by all students in delivering learning materials and using clear language in delivering learning materials. In this indicator, it is described that in the online learning process, clear and directed communication is one of the factors that affect the effectiveness of online learning. Effective communication focuses on the core concepts and principles of a discipline, facilitating students to investigate, solve problems, and other meaningful, student-centered tasks, and produce real products. Effective communication has an influence to improve student learning outcomes which is one of the innovative learning models [19].

A positive attitude toward students (X1.05) has a *loading factor* value of 0.714 where this indicator contains student statements about lecturer who can receive active student responses both right and wrong as an effort to learn and provide support in accordance with student ability levels. This illustrates that online learning can run effectively if lecturer is able to show a positive attitude or provide feedback to students during online learning. This is in accordance with Haryoko's research [2] that learning implementation, learning outcome assessment, and feedback are three components that are inseparable from each other. Giving feedback is one form of reinforcement and strategy in learning.

The use of learning media (X1.08) has a *loading factor* value of 0.754 and is the highest *loading factor* in the implementation of learning. This indicator is considered the most influential by students because it contains statements about the selection of learning media in accordance with the material taught, the use of interesting learning media, and easy to understand. This can be seen as the indicator that gives the highest influence because in online learning, the crucial thing is the learning media itself, both synchronously and *asynchronously* and *user friendly.* Learning media is needed to help students in facilitating the learning process, especially with the pandemic as it is today [15]. In line with the results of Rosmiati and Lestari's research [16], learning provision can also attract students' attention during the learning process to make learning meaningful.

Conformity with the procedure (X1.15) is the last indicator to have the lowest *loading factor*, which is worth 0.677. This indicator contains a statement about the student's perception of the workmanship of the task given in accordance with the correct steps and practicum work by the order of steps that have been given by the teacher.

The next variable, namely time management, is a variable that has the highest *loading factor* in *bootstrapping,* which means that time management has a dominant role in influencing the effectiveness of online learning. This is in line with Kwon's [9] research that time management is a prominent factor for success in *e-learning* and finding a relationship between student action levels, time management, and learning outcomes, suggests that understanding time management is the key to *e-learning* success. The first is Perseverance (X2.01); this indicator has a *loading factor* value of 0.857, where this indicator contains a statement of student perception before starting learning to prepare the required learning equipment. In online, learning equipment can be interpreted as computer preparation and other tools, as well as students' perception of statements to focus on participating in learning activities. Then in this indicator also contains a statement of student perception regarding perseverance to relearn the material that has been taught, the use of discussion activities to exchange information, and find the source of reading materials and reference books needed.

Effective study time (X2.02) is an indicator that has the highest loading factor value of 0.891, where this indicator contains the effective use of time to affect the effectiveness of online learning. Student perception of attending lectures on time later follows learning activities until the end of the lecture and use the study time in accordance with the time given and the existence of Study independently outside of lecture hours. In addition, there is also a perception about meeting the needs of time. Learned and the availability of study time is quite high, in accordance with the theory of TSEM (*Time and Study Environment Management)* which is the ability to manage learning time effectively [5, 14] and the Environment [21]. Specifically, it is related to learners' ability to prioritize learning tasks, allocate time to sub-tasks, and revise their plans if needed [12]. Students with high TSEM are proactive in organizing not only their study time, but also their learning environment and resources [12]. For example, students who manage time and learning environments efficiently demonstrate high functionality and choose appropriate learning tools.

Furthermore, for **offline learning,** the most influential indicator on the effectiveness of offline learning is the implementation of learning: (a) Effective communication (X1.02) this indicator has a *loading factor* value of 0.675, (b) The use of learning media (X1.08) of this indicator has a *loading factor* value of 0.774 and is the highest *loading factor* in the implementation of learning, (c) High teaching motivation (X1.10) indicator with loading factor value *of 0.689,* (d) Conformity with the procedure (X1.15), this illustrator has a loading factor worth 0.756, (e) Mastery and enthusiasm for the subject matter (X1.18) this indicator has a loading factor value of 0.685.

The next variable, namely time management, is a variable that has the highest *loading factor* on *bootstrapping,* which means that time management has a dominant role in influencing the effectiveness of offline learning: a) Perseverance (X2.01)—this indicator has a *loading factor* value of 0.910 b) Effective learning time (X2.02) i—this indicator is an indicator that has the highest *loading factor* value of 0.904, where this indicator contains the effective use of time to affect the effectiveness of offline learning. Student perception of attending lectures on time later follows learning activities until the end of the lecture and use the study time in accordance with the time given and the existence of Study independently outside of lecture hours. In addition, there is also a perception about meeting the needs of time. Learned and the availability of study time are quite high.

As for the results of the cartesian diagram to formulate a strategy, there are 2 (two) indicators in the *high-priority* area, namely X2.1 and X2.2, where the indicator is included in the time management variable. X2.1 is perseverance and X2.2 is effective learning time. Perseverance indicators include the preparation of learning equipment before learning begins and the level of focus of students in participating in learning activities, so that in this case, the management of DTSL FTUI can help borrow or procure learning equipment needed by students in online learning, by previously recording and finding out what difficulties related to learning equipment experienced by students so that with the fulfillment of adequate learning equipment. It is expected to increase the level of focus of students in participating in learning activities.

Indicators of perseverance also include student awareness to relearn the material that has been taught by utilizing discussion activities to exchange information. Based on this, management can help socialize online discussion activities *asynchronously* through the University's online platform that has been available outside *of synchronous* learning. So that response activities that are usually done offline can be accelerated with *asynchronous* online activities. This is in accordance with the results of Lee et al. research [11], which states that when a university decides to use *e-learning,* then the decision involves knowledge management both synchronously and *asynchronously.*

The last indicator of perseverance is related to the source of reading materials and reference books needed. Management can collaborate with university libraries to socialize the use of *digital* libraries to students, making it easier for students to find references and other reading sources related to learning.

Effective learning time indicators include the perception of students to attend lectures on time and follow learning activities until the end of the lecture; in this case, management can monitor through the student attendance system, so that an evaluation can be carried out at the end of the semester what obstacles students face in following this online learning. This can also be done by monitoring the frequency of student logins into *asynchronous* systems [7].

In terms of the use of independent time in online learning, in order to remain well monitored, management can maximize the use of *asynchronous* media to provide large tasks, carry out assistance, respond, and evaluate the implementation of the learning every month if possible through *synchronous* media so that every deficiency can find a solution so as not to drag on and affect the effectiveness of learning. According to the research of Jo et al. [4] to complement students' self-learning in virtual classes, offline meetings are held once a month to give students the opportunity to ask directly to the instructor.

## 5 Conclusion

The attitude of respondents, namely students in assessing the learning they follow, both offline and online, practicum and non-practicum is considered quite effective. Although online learning has been considered more effective than offline learning, there is no value that is too significant. The dimension of the effectiveness of this online learning is the competence of *executing* with the highest *loading factor* value, then the provision of fair values, implementing competencies, and finally formative assessment. This indicates that students have gained and understood new knowledge from the lectures they participated in. In line with that, students have also been able to answer questions given by lecturers related to learning materials to successfully get grades that are in accordance with their abilities. And able to apply the new knowledge he has gained while learning to follow the next lecture.

Factors that affect the effectiveness of online learning are effective communication, positive attitude toward students, use of learning media, conformity to procedures, perseverance, and effective learning time. The combination of these factors is positive for the effectiveness of online learning, which means that if these factors increase, the effectiveness of online learning will increase.

Strategies to increase the effectiveness of online learning are to provide online learning media support to students and conduct more intensive socialization about online learning platforms to students and lecturer so as to maximize the use of *synchronous* and *asynchronous* learning media.

## References

1. Ghozali I, Latan H. (2015) *Partial least square* (Konsep, Tehnik, dan Aplikasi) Menggunakan program SmartPLS 3.0. Universitas Diponegoro, Semarang (ID)
2. Haryoko S (2011) Efektivitas Strategi Pemberian Umpan Balik Terhadap Kinerja Praktikum Mahasiswa D-3 Jurusan Teknik Elektronika. Jurnal Cakrawala Pendidikan. 11(1):103–115
3. Ivanova T, Gubanova N, Shakirova I, Masitoh F (2020) Educational technology as one of the terms for enhancing public speaking skills. Universidad y Sociedad 12(2):154–159
4. Jo IH, Park Y, Yoon M, Sung H (2016) Evaluation of online log variables that estimate learners' time management in a Korean online learning context. Int Rev Res Open Distrib Learn 17(1):195–213
5. Kearsley G (2000) Online education: learning and teaching in cyberspace. Wadsworth, Belmont, CA.
6. Keengwe J, Georgina D (2012) The digital course training workshop for online learning and teaching. Educ Inf Technol 17(4):365–379. https://doi.org/10.1007/s10639-011-9164-x
7. Kim Y, Lee CK, Lee HU, Lee SN (2013) The effects of learning strategies on academic achievement. J Korea Assoc Yeolin Educ 19(3):177–196
8. Kusuma JW, Hamidah H (2020) Perbandingan Hasil Belajar Matematika dengan Penggunaan Platform Whatsapp Group dan Webinar Zoom dalam Pembelajaran Jarak Jauh pada Masa Pandemik Covid-19. Jurnal Ilmiah Pendidikan Matematika. 5(1):65–74
9. Kwon S (2009) The Analysis of differences of learners' participation, procrastination, learning time and achievement by adult learners' adherence of learning time schedule in e-Learning environments. J Learn-Center Curr Instruct 9(3):61–86
10. Laipaka R, Kasma U (2017) Penerapan Teknologi Informasi Pembelajaran E-Learning Menggunakan Addie Model. JUPITER: Jurnal Penelitian Ilmu Dan Teknologi Komputer 9(1):1–12. https://doi.org/10.5281/zenodo.3411828
11. Lee CS, Tan DTH, Goh WS (2004) The next generation of E-learning: strategies for media rich online teaching and engaged learning. J Dist Educ Technol 2(4):1–17
12. Lynch R, Dembo M (2004) The relationship between self-regulation and online learning in a blended learning context. Int Rev Res Open Distrib Learn 5(2)
13. Nursalam (2008) Konsep dan Penerapan Metodologi Penelitian Ilmu Keperawatan Pedoman Skripsi, Tesis dan Instrumen Penelitian Keperawatan. Salemba Medika, Jakarta

14. Phipps R, Merisotis J (1999) What's the difference? A review of contemporary research on the effectiveness of distance learning in higher education. The Institute for Higher Education Policy, Washington, D.C.
15. Rahmatika YM, Agung L (2021) The effectiveness of Youtube as an online learning media. J Educ Technol 5(1):152–158
16. Rosmiati U, Lestari P (2021) Inovasi model Pembelajaran PBI (problem based instruction) Berbasis Whatsapp Sebagai Langkah Solutif Pembelajaran di Masa Pandemi Covid-19. Jurnal Nasional Pendidikan Matematika. 5(1):188–197. https://doi.org/10.33603/jnpm.v5i1.3708
17. Seliana N (2019) Evaluasi keberhasilan penggunaan e-learning di fakultas teknik Universitas Riau [tesis]. Institut Pertanian Bogor, Bogor
18. Spigel M (2004) Statistik. Terjemahan. Penerbit Erlangga, Jakarta
19. Suprapto N, Chang TS, Ku CH (2017) Conception of learning physics and Self-efficacy among Indonesian university students. J Balt Sci Educ 16(1):7–19. https://doi.org/10.33225/jbse
20. Wekke IS, Hamid S (2013) Technology on language teaching and learning: a research on Indonesia pesantren. Procedia – Soc Behav Sci 83. https://doi.org/10.1016/J.SBSPRO.2013.06.111
21. Zimmerman BJ, Martinez-Pons M (1986) Development of a structured interview for assessing student use of self-regulated learning strategies. Am Educ Res J 23:614–628

# Model of the Favorite Madrasah Ibtidaiyah with Islamic Boarding School Base in Sleman District Case Study MI Afkaruna

**Nugroho Eko Atmanto, Aji Sofanudin, A. M. Wibowo, and Umi Masfiah**

**Abstract** This research reviews the best practices of one of the basic education institutions, namely Madrasah Ibtidaiyah (MI) Afkaruna, located in Sleman. This study uses a qualitative approach that is described descriptively and aims to determine the practice of implementing management in improving student achievement and to identify various factors that can increase public trust in the madrasah institution. Data was collected by means of interviews, observations, and document studies. The results of this research show that MI Afkaruna is positioned as an international standard educational institution, which is of global quality while maintaining aspects of local culture and Islamic boarding school method religious content. Learning activity is conducted by adopting the Cambridge University Curriculum combined with the National Curriculum and the Ministry of Religious Affairs Curriculum. Meanwhile, the Indonesian aspect and religious material strengthen students' character in accordance with religious teachings and the true personality of the Indonesian nation. The implication is that as an international standard institution, the language of communication in the school environment uses English, while the aspect of local religious content adopts the traditional Islamic boarding school method, namely learning the *kitab kuning* (The *kitab kuning* is interpreted as a reference to classical Arabic religious books, the contents of which include knowledge of Islamic religious sciences. The *kitab kuning* is usually studied in Islamic boarding schools, madrasas, ta'lim assemblies. In general, the *kitab kuning* is printed on yellow paper, but the meaning of the *kitab kuning* also includes Arabic books printed on white paper [Thoha in Kitab Kuning dan Dinamika Studi Keislaman. Duta Media Publishing, 2018, 28)]

N. E. Atmanto (✉) · A. Sofanudin · A. M. Wibowo · U. Masfiah
National Research and Innovation Agency, Jakarta, Indonesia
e-mail: nugr012@brin.go.id

A. Sofanudin
e-mail: ajis004@brin.go.id

A. M. Wibowo
e-mail: amwi001@brin.go.id

U. Masfiah
e-mail: umim001@brin.go.id



Nawawi et al. (eds.), *Managing Disruption and Developing Resilience for a Better Southeast Asia*, Springer Proceedings in Humanities and Social Sciences,
https://doi.org/10.1007/978-981-96-2116-3_9

lettered *pegon* in a *sorogan* way [*Sorogan* is one of the methods of delivering subject matter which is generally found in Islamic boarding schools, where the kiai/ustadz teach students individually, taking turns and taking turns. Previously the kiai/ustadz read the yellow book then translated word for word and explained the meaning, then the students read and repeated it in front of the kiai/ustadz (Abror in Kurikulum Pesantren: Model Integrasi Pembelajaran Salaf dan Khalaf. Dee Publish, 2020 29)].

**Keywords** Madrasah ibtidaiyah · Islamic school · Excellent madrasa

## 1 Introduction

Madrasah/madrasa is a formal educational institution that has the same position as other schools that are regulatory integrated into the national education system (Law Number 2 of 1989), mandating that madrasas transform from religious educational institutions into religiously characterized schools. This law has brought rapid progress to madrasas with various programs, including excellent madrasas, model madrasas, and funding assistance programs from the government. However, madrasa face a number of challenges in catching up, including: (1) the stigma that considers madrasas as second-class educational institutions, (2) madrasas are left behind from other general educations [1].

This integration requires madrasas to create a conducive learning environment in order to achieve the national education goals as stated in Law Number 20 of 2003. It is stated in the regulation that education is a conscious and planned effort to create a learning environment and learning process, in which students actively develop their potential for religious spirituality, self-control, personality, intelligence, noble character, and skills they themselves, society, nation, and state need. In response to this regulation, Government Regulation Number 19 of 2005 concerning National Education Standards was issued. The regulation contains provisions on eight educational standards, which are as follows: (1) Graduate Competency Standards, (2) Content Standards, (3) Process Standards, (4) Education and Education Personnel Standards, (5) Facilities and Infrastructure Standards, (6) Management Standards, (7) Education Financing Standards, and (8) Educational Assessment Standards.

Finally, the success of educational institutions will be determined by the achievement of educational outputs as evidenced by the achievement of competency standards in accordance with those set by school leaders and targets set by the government in accordance with their authority in developing education. The targets are stated in the curriculum and learning syllabus document.

As madrasas integrated into the national education system develop and more people prefer education that includes more religious knowledge for their children. Private schools that provide religious material have proliferated. Some of these schools have a lot of religious material as local content as an attraction for the community to send their children to these places. These advantages strengthen the Islamic school's position and bargaining power in the madrasa's existence.

Along with the development of religious schools, the number of madrasas today is increasing, as proven by the increasing number of institutions and students [2]. Today, the prestige of madrasa education is rising, as proven by the achievements of madrasa students in various fields. Madrasas are starting to improve to catch up with other schools to compete in producing the output of students who excel. There are excellent madrasas in some areas that can compete with regular schools.

Excellent madrasas do not arise overnight, but rather over time. Therefore, it needs to be subjected, and it is important to understand the potential for the development of a better madrasa, so that it can be used as a model for other madrasas to follow. Best practice studies are also expected to provide input for competent officials to consider when making policy decisions. It is hoped that as madrasah developed, they will be able to participate more efficiently, on par with schools, and the demand by people will increase. Thus, the motto "Madrasah is Better, Better Choose Madrasah" [3] will be actualized.

Excellent Madrasas are those whose excellence is recognized by the government and the people. The government acknowledges both verbally and empirically the education quality, the accreditation value, and the various achievements of madrasas. In addition, they are recognized by people because they have the quality, so for education, people prefer madrasas to send their children to, even for basic education. It is because they believe that religious education at the basic level is essential. They are willing to spend more money to send their children to the madrasah.

MI Afkaruna is one of the excellent Islamic madrasas in the Special Region of Yogyakarta. This madrasah is in Sleman Regency and was established in 2017. MI Afkaruna won a prestigious championship [4] two years after its establishment, among other achievements. Unlike other madrasas, MI Afkaruna has branded itself as an international madrasa, because it has international curriculum standards while maintaining the contents of the madrasa and the spirit of Islamic boarding schools. The expected outcome is to create students with global perspectives and graduates of international standard while maintaining aspects of local culture. Because it is an international standard educational institution, English is the language of instruction and communication during learning activities and communication.

This study aims to explore the best practices and experiences of madrasah ibtidaiyah to learn about the practice of implementing management to improve student achievement as well as the various factors that can increase public trust in MI institutions. This study is a case study conducted by selecting excellent madrasah ibtidaiyah in the Special Region of Yogyakarta. The data was collected from various sources, including officials from the Special Region of Yogyakarta Regional Office of the Ministry of Religious Affairs, the Sleman Regency Office of the Ministry of Religion, and the madrasah.

## 2 Theoretical Framework

### 2.1 *Madrasah Ibtidaiyah*

Madrasah Ibtidaiyah is a formal institution for primary education. It is equivalent to elementary school. This institution is a formal educational institution with the same curriculum as elementary school, but with additional religious material. Madrasah Ibtidaiyah is the first step in the process of Islamic education [5]. This demonstrates the significance of Madrasah Ibtidaiyah in the process of religious education, as it marks the beginning of the next stage, namely at the Madrasah Tsanawiyah level.

It is necessary to improve the management of madrasas because there are changing demands from the community. At the moment, parents or the community expect madrasah graduates to be able to master general knowledge besides the religious knowledge [6]. This change in demands should be met quickly through innovation in changes in madrasa management. Changes in madrasa management affect the behavior, attitudes, and perspectives of madrasa human resources, starting from the madrasa principal, teachers, education staff, and all parties involved in managing a madrasa [7].

The effective madrasa management will increase the quality of madrasa education and public trust since there are many advantages that madrasas have. Therefore, excellent madrasas should be able to fulfill: (1) optimizing madrasa institutional management (2) developing entrepreneurs (3) optimizing madrasa principal leadership [8].

Facilities and infrastructure also play an important role in the success of educational activities at madrasas. Therefore, facilities and infrastructure managements are important. Management of infrastructure must be organized in an integrated manner from planning, procurement, maintenance, inventory, and removal. Procurement planning must be responsive to the needs and technological developments [9].

### 2.2 *Excellent Madrasa/School*

According to Syuhud [10], excellent schools are those that constantly improve their performance and use all their potential to maximize overall student achievement. Furthermore, Syarifah Rahmah [11] defined that excellent schools are those that are able to deliver their students to excel intellectually, emotionally, and spiritually.

Novita and Solihin [12] investigated the nature of superior schools. This study discovered that although student input is not good (bad) but if the superiority process is + (positive), the output attends to be + (excellent). The superiority process in the process includes: (1) the ability of good, professional teachers, competence in learning, mentoring, and student communication, (2) a differentiated curriculum that is relevant to today's modern inventions, (3) extracurricular programs that encourage the development of interests and talents, (4) and collaborative networks with other parties.

According to Wahed [13], there are four simple steps to make a school/ madrasah excellent, namely (1) improving management, (2) resource management (3) curriculum management, (4) and student management. Furthermore, it is also necessary to explore the potential that schools/madrasas have, namely by (1) generating motivation, because this motivation is the foundation of the goals to achieve (2) viewing opportunities, (3) time management skills, (4) and being diligent and tenacious.

On the other hand, excellent international standard schools/madrasas try to provide the best educational services for their students. In contrary, it is alleged to create an environment with an elite environment for certain people. Therefore, Prastowo [14] suggests the reconstruction of excellent school/madrasah education through as follows: first, its development takes into account the issues of conflict (and compromise) between groups caused by different views on race, class, and gender.

Second, the curriculum is redesigned to provide knowledge and materials to raise awareness of the dominant's class domination and exploitation. Third, it is necessary to democratize school access and administration. Fourth, it is aimed at the public's view. Fifth, students' understanding and awareness of the real world and their future must be developed. Sixth, schools/madrasah should be a productive force, rather than a reproductive force. Lastly, the government implements affirmative action to accommodate poor and less-smart children in these excellent schools/madrasahs.

## 2.3 *Madrasa Branding*

The continuity of stable students is critical to the madrasah's sustainability. A consistent number of students indicates that the madrasa has good educational management. One of the important aspects in this case is the madrasa branding to introduce the institution to the community, so that they will choose madrasah.

Branding is the process of communicating a name, term, sign, symbol, or design as a marker to distinguish an institution or product from other institutions or products [15]. The branding strategy of educational institutions evolves along with the demands over time; whereas, the previous era used manual methods (distribution of procedures, banners, mouth to mouth promotion), but now, it is necessary to transform through online promotion by social media. This change is required to reach a larger community and increase the visibility of educational institutions [15].

## 2.4 *Best Practice*

Best practice is an idea of a technique, method, process, activity, incentive, or award that is more effective to achieve extraordinary success compared to other techniques, methods, and processes [13]. Another understanding of best practice is that it is the experience of the best success in solving problems when carrying out tasks as educators. Alternatively, if interpreted as best practice at school/madrasah, it is the best experience in the successful implementation of tasks related to the principal's duties madrasah [13].

Meanwhile, according to the Ministry of Education and Culture, Best Practice is the best experience that is the result of a person or group's success in carrying out tasks and overcoming problems [16]. Thus, best practice is an exposure to the best experiences and successes in carrying out their duties as a teacher, as well as the best experiences in managing schools/madrasahs. This explanation is expected to be beneficial for both the institution and various parties providing ideas in the educational institutions management.

Best practice research has numerous benefits for education. For teachers, it is useful as a medium to improve the development of learning models in the classroom, especially with a contextual learning approach using audio-visual recording media. Teachers obtain a deeper understanding of creative, innovative, and fun-learning models. Best practice research is also useful for students to increase creativity and appreciation to achieve their full potential [17, 18].

## 3 Previous Research

Research on leading madrasas based on Islamic boarding school was examined by Siswanto [20], stating that the development of excellent madrasas, especially Islamic boarding house is aimed at combining excellence in the intellectual and skill fields with excellence in religious knowledge, personality, faith, and piety. Meanwhile, Jemani et al. [21] conveyed the findings of the research that there is an influence of madrasah head leadership on teacher performance at excellent madrasas in MA Unggulan Hikmatul Amanah Bendunganjati Pacet Mojokerto, which are (1) the madrasah principal's leadership style, (2) the madrasah principal's motivation. The research conducted at MI Sambas, Purbalingga Regency [21] emphasizes the innovation aspect of strict quality control management through several stages, as well as learning strong religious aspects. Quality control is a priority, so that even though the incoming students have average abilities, they can produce maximum output.

As an educational institution, Madrasah Ibtidaiyah requires a branding strategy to introduce its institution to the wider community. A branding strategy is even still needed for popular schools such as state schools with zoning system [18]. According to research at SMP N 3 Mrebet, Purbalingga school strategies for dealing with zoning are needed, specifically: (a) building a school's branding image; (b) the "pick up the ball" strategy; (c) improving school performance; (d) scholarships [22].

Another study conducted in Surabaya [18] found that although the branding of educational institutions is important, there are several educational institutions that have not made this branding strategy something that needs to be jointly aware of. This even occurs in schools considered favorites by the public [23]. Schools that have quite a huge number of students and sometimes even reject prospective students are still stuck on how to improve the output quality with satisfactory school test scores that increase public confidence.

## 4 Research Method

This study used a qualitative approach, with the type of field research. This study reveals the success of MI Afkaruna in managing its educational institution to provide academic and religious education in the implementation of Indonesian characters.

Data was collected through observation, interviews, and document studies. Observations were made by observing learning activities and student and teacher activities in madrasahs. Interviews with teachers and madrasah principals were conducted. Meanwhile, the study of documents was obtained by observing the documents, books, brochures, and others in the madrasah.

## 5 Research Findings

### *5.1 Afkaruna Islamic School*

The formal name of this educational unit that is recorded at the Ministry of Religion is Madrasah Ibtidaiyah Afkaruna (MI Afkaruna), indicating that the institutional format is a madrasah. Meanwhile, to introduce to the public, they use their branding name, Afkaruna Islamic School. MI Afkaruna is located at Kaliurang Street Km 12.5, Hargobinangun, Pakem, Sleman Regency. This institution tries to present as an international standard educational institution by highlighting various benefits to its students.

MI Afkaruna was founded in 2016, with the idea to establish an international school perspective, but focus on the religious aspects and character development in accordance with Indonesian culture. Therefore, it aims to align the three main pillars, namely Islam, Internationality, and Locality.

The founder of this madrasah, Syamsul Maarif Mujiharto, after attending doctoral education in Australia, felt that nothing matched the criteria expected when looking for an educational institution for his children. Mujiharto wanted his children to attend an international standard institution but with Indonesian cultural roots. Unfortunately, he had not found what he wanted. Many schools that provided strong religious education are lacking in preparing students to face the global society. On the other hand, there are schools with good academics and global insight, but are lacking in religious and cultural characters [24].

As a manifestation of the great ideals of its founder, MI Afkaruna develops a vision to prepare students to become *insan kamil* human and as part of the global community while still rooted in local culture. Through this vision, this madrasah wants to build the concept of integration among religious (Islamic) values, local values, and international mindsets.

To achieve maximum educational outcomes, MI Afkaruna's religious curriculum is compiled which is a combination of 3 curricula: (1) The Ministry of Religious Affairs curriculum which includes the Qur'an and Hadith, Akidah and Akhlak, Fikih (Jurisprudence), and Islamic Cultural History, (2) Hifdzul Quran, i.e., memorizing the holy book (Al-quran) and comprehending Arabic books (*al Kitabah al Arabiyah*), (3) adopting Islamic boarding schools, i.e., learning to read classical Islamic books (*qiraah al kutub*) and Arabic conversation (*al muhadatsah al yaumiyah*) [25].

Managers and parents synergize with teachers through innovative learning methods, emphasizing learning experiences to stimulate and inspire students. Students are also encouraged to explore and ask questions, which boosts creativity, independence, and learning. As a result, Afkaruna's student curiosity is very high, and the students are active in asking questions and discussing every learning process at the Madrasah.

## 5.2 Application of Curriculum

MI Afkaruna, as a formal educational institution in madrasah format, in principle implements the curriculum in accordance with the provisions where the Ministry of Education and Culture is currently applying the 2013 Curriculum. Meanwhile, as madrasah institution, it follows the Ministry of Religious Affairs Curriculum in its religious subjects. Then, for character and personality development, MI Afkaruna employs a local curriculum developed by the internal madrasah in collaboration with the foundation that houses it. Dealing with curriculum, as a form of international madrasah, Afkaruna adopts the International Primary Curriculum (IPC) combined with the National Curriculum (Curriculum 2013). In this case, Afkaruna uses the Cambridge curriculum which is combined with a learning package that includes English, *Dirasah Islamiyah*, and local values. The use of the Cambridge curriculum is adjusted to MC (Main Competence) and BC (Basic Competence) of the 2013 Curriculum.

MI Afkaruna graduates will have a double diploma, which are national diploma and a Cambridge diploma. The awarding of this Cambridge standard diploma is to provide evidence that MI Afkaruna graduates have international standards that can be used to continue studying abroad (Interview with the Head of Madrasah, April 6, 2022). Even though the students' parents had no idea that their children would continue their studies abroad, the madrasah principal advised them to be optimistic as a motivator, because no one knows what the future holds. Life skills are developed through skills, character building, physical education, and art. Learning skills include independent learning, innovative creative, critical, communicative, and collaborative thinking. Life skills include self-management, literacy, numeracy, finance, social field, and community involvement [25].

The concept of learning at the Afkaruna institution can generally be divided into 3: (1) *ta'allama* (2) *tafaqqaha* (3) *tashawwafa. Ta'allama* is creating a generation that is muhibbul ilmi, the one that has a strong desire to learn. This is achieved through fun-learning to be able to master various kinds of knowledge. Therefore, an integrated STEM (Science, Technology, Engineering, and Mathematics) approach, conversational skills training and expressing opinions, and mastery of Information Technology are used. The aspect of *tafaqqaha* is directing students to become *faqih* individuals, inviting students to understand various sources of knowledge, both from the *kauniyah* verse (proof of phenomena in life and natural phenomena) and the *qauliyah* verse (written in the holy Qur'an). In this case, students learn *Dirasah al-Islamiyyah* which includes *Qira'ah al-Qur'an, al-Kitabah al-'Arabiyyah, Hifdzul Qur'an, Qira'ah al-Kutub, as- Shirah an-Nabawi*, and Islamic History. in Indonesia) synchronized systematically with several subjects including Science, Social Sciences—including History, Geography, Society, *Pancasila* and Citizenship Education) as well as Arts and Performance, and Physical Education. Meanwhile, the *tashawwafa* aspect is forming a generation that has an Islamic personality and masters 7 competency skills and main characteristics involving: skills, independent learning, communication, critical thinking, creativity, and collaboration. In addition to forming life skills, students are trained with practical skills, literacy skills, numeracy skills, financial skills, and social awareness as society. [25].

## *5.3 International Madrasah*

As an international madrasah, the overall learning is in English except for Indonesian lessons and *pegon* translation). According to the Madrasah's head, it takes about a month of language adaptation in grade 1 before students can understand and communicate in English. Some students who still have difficulty in language are given special assistance by a team in charge. Likewise, all student handbooks are in English. Books for Cambridge curriculum lessons are purchased from abroad. Meanwhile, Afkaruna develops its own module with English text for other subjects (religious material and skills). The adapting period is anticipated to last one month in grade 1, during which time, continuous evaluation is also carried out. The learning and adaptation of English communication in Afkaruna happen through making communication effective and forbidding the use of languages other than English in all communications (except only for Indonesian lessons).

Therefore, Afkaruna applies learning by doing and saying and without translating in Indonesian in all conversations in class. English instructions are used throughout the class, from students entering the room to the teacher greeting them and asking them to sit. Sometimes the teacher also needs to demonstrate an example by doing (e.g., sitting down) and the teacher says: "sit down," then signaling the students to sit down (Interview with the head of the madrasa, May 6, 2022).

The madrasa principal has said that there is no selection to enter MI Afkaruna, neither based on intelligence nor based on English ability. There are observations to determine prospective students' English proficiency, but this step is only done for mapping and placing groups of students, making it easier for teachers to choose techniques that fit with the students' ability in English. The goal is to improve the effectiveness of the habit of using foreign languages.

Furthermore, students are trained to master Islamic materials, such as the ability to read books, through the *pegon* book. Mastering the *pegon* and *kitab kuning* includes skills for writing and reading. Furthermore, for reading skills, students are trained using the traditional method that is well-known by Islamic boarding schools, which is the *sorogan* method.

As an educational institution that devotes itself to a rural environment, Afkaruna students pay relatively affordable tuition fees. Although it is still considered pricey, the tuition fee at MI is still relatively normal compared to other favorite schools in Yogyakarta. The headmaster of madrasah stated that the tuition fees at MI Afkaruna are proportional to the educational outcome students obtain.

The madrasah has a big responsibility to maintain the educational quality, with the proper facilities and infrastructure as well as adequate teacher welfare. The madrasah also provides quota opportunities to local residents who wish to become MI Afkaruna students by providing fee waivers, even free of charge. However, they have not taken advantage of this opportunity.

## *5.4 Discussion*

Madrasah Ibtidaiyah Afkaruna brands itself as an international school. It is an effort to increase the bargaining value of the institution in the community while also maintaining the institution's quality. Through branding as an international, hopefully, it will be people's choice for high-quality education and a religious (Islamic) character.

The efforts toward international quality madrasah begin with effective English communication. It is beneficial because it combines the national curriculum (2013 Curriculum) with the Cambridge University curriculum, the Ministry of Religious Affairs Curriculum, as well as the Islamic boarding school curriculum. The curriculum integration aims to ensure that graduates have a strong understanding of modern science and are prepared to be members of a global society from an early age. Meanwhile, mastering religious material by adopting the Islamic boarding school teaching system is intended to provide students with basic religious knowledge to face the challenges of the global world. Indirectly, the spirit of the establishment of MI Afkaruna is aimed to contribute so that Muslims can take part in global without abandoning the religious aspects. According to Mujiharto, the *Kitab Kuning* teaching method using *sorogan* method is still relevant amid the presence of various kinds of learning methods. Mujiharto has said that there is no other country that has the method of reciting the Al-Qu'ran which is better than Indonesia, namely the *sorogan* method [24].

As a manifestation of an excellent madrasah, MI Afkaruna has equipped itself with facilities and infrastructure. Classroom buildings and administrative offices look simple, far from the impression of a favorite school/madrasah which usually has a magnificent building. However, it has a clean and tidy impression. Some parts of the building are still under construction, and it is targeted that the new semester year 2022/2023 can fully operate. Despite the simplicity caused by limited funding sources, the teachers and school administrators seem enthusiastic and optimistic to move forward together for the expected quality of education. In this case, the manager's support by paying attention to the welfare of the teachers is one of the factors that contribute to the institution's progress. One aspect to practice is English mastery where all activities in madrasas are required to use English as the language of communication. Since grade 1, students must be accustomed to speaking English during adaptation period. Learning through this habituation will also minimize various obstacles in teaching foreign languages often encountered in schools [26, 27]. MI Afkaruna also wishes to respond to the numerous complaints that English instruction at the elementary school or madrasah Ibtidaiyah level is unsatisfactory [11]. It is hoped that by learning English as an effective language of instruction, students will quickly master English as an international language.

## 6 Conclusion

MI Afkaruna as a modern educational institution always tries to improve and maintain the quality of educational services and is always responsive to developments, by providing innovations both in institutional management and in learning. MI Afkaruna is positioning itself as an international standard educational institution, which has global quality and strengthens the religious and local cultural aspects simultaneously. It emphasizes more aspects of Indonesian character and Islamic boarding to form a global quality person, but to remain rooted in the culture of the Indonesian nation.

MI Afkaruna's programs that follow an international curriculum provide students with academic skills as well as global perspectives. Furthermore, the Indonesian and Islamiyah materials help to strengthen students' character in accordance with religious teachings and the true personality of the Indonesian nation.

To summarize, things that can increase public trust in a madrasah include: (1) having proud achievements, (2) having attractive superior programs, (3) management professionalism in fostering innovations, innovation in both teaching and organizational management, (4) good teacher competence, and (5) community culture that tends to support madrasah.

## References

1. Pratama YA (2019) Integrasi Pendidikan Madrasah Dalam Sistem Pendidikan Nasional (Studi kebijakan Pendidikan Madrasah di Indonesia). Al-Tadzkiyyah J Pendidik Islam. https://doi.org/10.24042/atjpi.v10i1.3838

2. Tholkhah I (2013) Potensi Intoleransi Keagamaan Siswa Sekolah Di Jawa Dan Sulawesi (Potential for Religious Intolerance Among Students in Schools in Java and Sulawesi. EDUKASI J Penelit Pendidik Agama dan Keagamaan. https://doi.org/10.32729/edukasi.v11i1.422
3. Kemenag P (2014) Madrasah Lebih Baik, Lebih Baik Madrasah. In: 26 Agustus 2014. http://pendis.kemenag.go.id/index.php?a=detilberita&id=7072#.YSYGWddR1dh
4. Sleman K (2019) MI Afkaaruna Islamic School Borong Piala di "Al-Azhar 55 Expo 2019." Yogyakarta
5. Sirojudin A (2019) Manajemen Pendidikan Madrasah Ibtidaiyah (Madrasah Ibtidaiyah Education Management). Model J Prog Stud PGMI 6:204–219
6. Muhaimin D (2015) Manajemen Pendidikan (Aplikasinya dalam Penyusunan Rencana Pengembangan Sekolah/Madrasah), 5 ed. Prenada Media Group, Jakarta
7. Harmanto B (2015) Manajemen Pembelajaran Bahasa Inggris di Sekolah Dasar/Madrasah Ibtidaiyah Kategori Unggul (Analysis Best Practice Pengajaran Bahasa Inggris untuk Anak). J. Dimens. Pendidik. dan Pembelajaran Januari
8. Wahib A (2018) Penguatan Mutu Madrasah Swasta Menuju Madrasah Unggul (Strengthening the Quality of Private Madrasahs Towards Excellent Madrasahs). Nidhomul Haq J Manaj Pendidik Islam. https://doi.org/10.31538/ndh.v3i1.181
9. Nurhasanah S (2019) Manajemen Sarana Prasarana Madrasah (The Infrastructure Management of Islamic Elementary School). J Isema Islam Educ Manag. https://doi.org/10.15575/isema.v1i2.4991
10. Syuhud S (2019) Sekolah Unggulan Tuntutan Pendidikan Global (Excellent Schools Demand of Global Education.) Bidayatuna J Pendidik Guru Madrasah Ibtidaiyah. https://doi.org/10.36835/bidayatuna.v2i1.359
11. Rahmah S (2016) Mengenal Sekolah Unggulan. ITQAN J. Ilmu-Ilmu Kependidikan 7
12. Novita M, Solihin M (2020) The role of education management in improving the quality of excellent school education. Innov J Relig Innov Stud. https://doi.org/10.30631/innovatio.v20i1.104
13. Wahed A (2018) Strategi Mewujudkan Sekolah Dan Madrasah Unggulan Di Era Global (Strategies for Realizing Excellent Schools and Madrasa in The Global Era). AL—IBRAH 3(1):3
14. Prastowo A (2020) Fenomena pendidikan elitis dalam sekolah/madrasah unggulan berstandar internasional (The phenomenon of elitist education in international standard schools). J Pendidik Islam. https://doi.org/10.14421/jpi.2011.11.31-54
15. Suryawan A, Umam AK, Prasetyo AD, Pranata MRA, Setyawan BH, Ahmady F (2021) Optimalisasi Media Sosial untuk Eksistensi SD Muhammadiyah Sirojudin dalam Penerimaan Peserta Didik Baru (Social Media Optimization for Muhammadiyah Elementary School Existence in New Student Admission). Community Empower. https://doi.org/10.31603/ce.3884
16. Kemendikbud (2016) Pedoman Lomba Penulian Best Practice bagi Kepala ekolah/Madrasah. Jakarta
17. Azis A (2021) Peningkatan Apresiasi Konsep Karya Tari Berbantuan Media Rekaman Audio Visul pada Siswa Kelas IX Semester 2 SMPN 1 Pecalungan Tahun Pelajaran 2019/2020 (Enhancement of Appreciation for Dance Work Concepts Using Audio-Visual Rcording Media Among 9TH Grade Students Smester 2 SMPN 1 Pecalungan Academic Year 2019/2020. PAEDAGOGY J Ilmu Pendidik dan Psikology. https://doi.org/10.51878/paedagogy.v1i1.333
18. Munawaroh I (2019) Penggunaan Media Sosial sebagai Upaya Meningkatkan Hasil Belajar Matematika Peserta Didiki mKelas IX di SMP Negeri 1 Sindangkasih Kabupaten Ciamis Tahun Pelajaran 2017/2018 (The Use of Social Media as an Effort to Improve Methematics Learning Outcomes of Grade IX Students at SMPN 1 Sindagkasih, Ciamis Regency, 2017/2018 Academic Year). In: Pros. Nas. Call Pap. Progr. Stud. Magister Pendidik. Mat. Univ. Siliwangi Tasikmalaya. Tasikmalaya, hal 267
19. Siswanto S (2017) Madrasah Unggulan Berbasis Pesantren (Excellent Islamic Boarding School-Based Madrasa). Ulumuna. https://doi.org/10.20414/ujis.v18i1.157

20. Jemani A, Ismail AG, Darim A (2020) Pengaruh Gaya Kepemimpinan dan Motivasi Kepala Sekolah Terhadap Kinerja Guru di Madrasah Aliyah Unggulan Hikmatul Amanah (The Influence of Leadership Style and Motivation of School Principals on Teacher Performance at Madrasah Aliyah Unggulan Hikmatul Amanah). Tadbir J Manaj Pendidik Islam. https://doi.org/10.30603/tjmpi.v8i2.1401
21. Suprapto S (2015) MI Istiqomah Sambas: Profil Madrasah Unggul di Kabupaten Purbalingga (MI Istiqomah Sambas: Profile of Superior Madrasah in Purbalingga Regency). EDUKASI J Penelit Pendidik Agama dan Keagamaan.vol 13 No. 2. https://doi.org/10.32729/edukasi.v13i2.244
22. Habibullah AH (2019) Strategi Sekolah Dalam Menghadapi Sistem Zonasi Studi di SMP Negeri 3 Mrebet Purbalingga (School Strategies in Dealing with The School Zonong System at SMP Negeri 3 Mrebet Purbalingga). J. El- Hamra (Kependidikan dan Kemasyarakatan) 4
23. Zulaikha Z (2017) Perlukah Branding pada Sekolah? Studi Kasus pada SMP Swasta di Surabaya (Is School Branding Necessary? Case Study on Private Junior High School in Surabaya). J Komun Prof. https://doi.org/10.25139/jkp.v1i2.425
24. Republika (2016) Afkaaruna Islamic School Bangga Gunakan Sistem Sorogan. Republika.com
25. Afkaaruna Integrated Education System [AfIES]. In: afkaruna.ch.id. http://www.afkaaruna.sch.id/page/Afkaaruna-Integrated-Education-System/17. Accessed 17 Nov 2021
26. Maili SN, Hestiningsih W (2017) Masalah-Masalah Pembelajaran Bahasa Inggris pada Sekolah Dasar (The Problems of English Learning in Elementary School). Media Penelit Pendidik J Penelit dalam Bid Pendidik dan Pengajaran. https://doi.org/10.26877/mpp.v11i1.2607
27. Listia R, Kamal S (2013) Kendala Pengajaran Bahasa Inggris di Sekolah Dasar (Problems of English Teaching Inelementary School). Media Penelitian Pendidikan Vol.11 / No.2, 2017.
28. Thoha M (2018) Kitab Kuning dan Dinamika Studi Keislaman (Yellow Book and The Dynamics of Islamic Studies). Duta Media Publishing, Pamekasan
29. Abror D (2020) Kurikulum Pesantren: Model Integrasi Pembelajaran Salaf dan Khalaf. Dee Publish, Yogyakarta

# Field Schools (FS) Effectiveness on Productivity of Paddy Irrigated Systems in Aceh Besar Regency, Indonesia

**Mira Handayani, Azhar, and Irfan Zikri**

**Abstract** The purpose of this study was to analyze the factors that influence the effectiveness of the field school program implementation and the level of effectiveness of the field school program to increase rice productivity of irrigated rice farmers in Aceh Besar District. The implementation of the field school began to be implemented in 2020 until now in the Montasik District which consists of three villages and five farmer groups with a total of 125 SL participants. This study systematically analyzes the factors that affect the effectiveness of the implementation of field schools (FS) using multiple linear regression analysis approach. This study observed and interviewed farmer members of the field school (FS) using questionnaires and collecting secondary data obtained through literature studies as well as through notes and reports from the Agricultural Extension Center (BPP) involved in the implementation of FS activities. The results showed that there was no effect of age, land area, ownership status, motivation, participation, intensity of counseling, and financial assistance with the effectiveness of the field school implementation program. Education and innovation characteristics have a positive effect on the effectiveness of the field school implementation program. The effectiveness of the field school program has a positive effect on increasing the productivity of irrigated paddy in Aceh Besar District ($p \leq 0.05$). Based on the results of the study, it can be concluded that the factors that most influence the effectiveness of the implementation of field schools (FS) are education and innovation characteristics.

**Keywords** Effectiveness · Field schools · Paddy rice productivity

M. Handayani (✉) · Azhar · I. Zikri
Master of Agribusiness Departement, Syiah Kuala University, Banda Aceh, Indonesia
e-mail: mirahandayani303@gmail.com



Nawawi et al. (eds.), *Managing Disruption and Developing Resilience for a Better Southeast Asia*, Springer Proceedings in Humanities and Social Sciences,
https://doi.org/10.1007/978-981-96-2116-3_10

## 1 Introduction

The integrated participatory irrigation management and development program for a period of 6 years (2017–2022) aims to improve the capacity of irrigation managers, water user farmers, and other irrigation beneficiaries in implementing effective, efficient, and sustainable irrigation management by involving community participation in irrigation system implementation. This program is designed to support the Indonesian government's efforts to overcome various obstacles and increase agricultural productivity, as well as reduce rural poverty, promote gender equality, and improve nutrition. Its services include irrigation areas which are being rehabilitated through an irrigation management program, namely with the support of intensive counseling, including through Field Schools (FS) for farmers. The Government of Indonesia, the international Fund for Agricultural development (IFAD), and the Asian Development Bank (ADB) have collaborated to support an integrated participatory irrigation development and management project. The project is designed to achieve the agricultural development goals in Indonesia. The program adopts an inclusive targeting approach in irrigated areas so as to benefit all active farmers.

The Field School Program is a place for learning for farmers which is carried out directly on farmers' agricultural land, where 12 components of agricultural technology produced by research institutions are applied. In the application of this technology, it is adjusted to local conditions or specific locations [1]. Indicators of success of FS can be seen from the increase in knowledge, skills, and changes in farmers' attitudes, the application of good and correct cultivation, and increased rice productivity and sustainability. So through this FS program, it is expected that farmers' rice productivity will increase which has implications for increasing farmers' income and welfare. Rice self-sufficiency is still the main focus of the government in dealing with the threat of a food crisis. Increased productivity and food production are expected to be able to overcome the threat of a food crisis [2].

Aceh Besar District is one district in Aceh Province that has received Field School activities. The implementation of FS began to be implemented in 2020 until now in 18 villages spread across seven sub-districts with a total of 34. Farmer groups and the number of FS participants are 850 people. The field school activities are expected to be able to improve the understanding of farmers and farmer groups regarding the importance of correct technological innovation, resulting in an increase in productivity, but in fact, in the field, the integrated crop management innovations that have been studied in field schools have not been fully implemented by farmers.

This study aims to analyze the factors that affect the effectiveness of the FS program implementation and the level of effectiveness of the FS program on increasing rice productivity of irrigated rice farmers. Seeing the above conditions, Field School (FS) activities in irrigated rice fields are expected to realize food security and farmers' welfare through increasing rice productivity in Aceh Besar District. A feasibility study on the implementation of the Field School has been carried out by the Aceh Besar District Government, where BPP makes a printed report after the activity is completed. Meanwhile, based on data and reports from the Department of

Agriculture, the productivity of paddy in 2020 in the sub-districts that have carried out SL activities is an average of 5.7 tons/ha. [3].

Effectiveness is the relationship between output and goals, the greater the contribution of the output contribution to the achievement of goals, the more effective the organization, program, or activity [4]. Effectiveness is the main element to achieve the goals or targets that have been determined in each organization, activity, or program. It is said to be effective if the goals or objectives are achieved as determined. Efforts to evaluate the course of an organization can be done through the concept of effectiveness. This concept is one of the factors to determine whether it is necessary to make significant changes to the form and management of the organization or not. In this case, effectiveness is the achievement of organizational goals through the efficient use of available resources, in terms of inputs, processes, and outputs. In this case, what is meant by resources includes the availability of personnel, facilities, and infrastructure as well as the methods and models used. An activity is said to be efficient if it is carried out correctly and in accordance with procedures, while it is said to be effective if the activity is carried out correctly and provides useful results [5].

The field school is one of the components in the national rice production improvement program implemented by the Ministry of Agriculture in 2009–2014 with large budget support [6]. The implementation of SL is expected to have a real impact on increasing food production. The participation of farmers in the Rice Field School program has been shown to only be correlated with improving farmers' attitudes and mindsets, but has no correlation with its application. One of the causes is the limited number and quality of extension workers even though their role is very important to assist farmers in implementing the technology components of integrated crop management field schools.

## 2 Research Methods

This study uses quantitative methods. The research design is in the form of an explanatory research where the researcher tries to explain the influence of the research variables. This research was conducted in Aceh Besar District with the determination of Districts and Villages carried out purposively and gradually by considering the location where the Field School Development Program and Integrated Participation Irrigation Management Program were being implemented. The population of this study is farmers who are participants in the 2020 Rice Field School in Aceh Besar District, a case study in Montasik District, which consists of three villages and five farmer groups with 125 SL participants. Quantitative data analysis using multiple linear regression approach.

# 3 Result and Discussion

## 3.1 *Factors Affecting the Effectiveness of the Field School Implementation Program*

**Simultaneous Test Results (F Test)**

To test the hypothesis regarding the factors that affect the welfare of farmers, it can be seen in Table 1.

In this study, the number of independent variables (independent) is 9 with a sample of 60 data, so the Degree of Freedom (DF) 1 is 9 and DF2 is 60 − 9 − 1 = 50. By looking at table F, the $F_{table}$ value is 2.070. Furthermore, from the test, the $F_{count}$ value is 10.134, then $F_{count} > F_{table;}$ 10.134 > 2.070 and the probability level is 0.000. Thus the results of this calculation can be taken a decision that the proposed alternative hypothesis is acceptable and the null hypothesis is rejected, meaning that age ($X_1$), education ($X_2$), land area ($X_3$), ownership status ($X_4$), motivation ($X_5$), participation ($X_6$), intensity of counseling ($X_7$), characteristics of innovation ($X_8$), and financial assistance ($X_9$) together have a significant effect on the effectiveness of field schools.

**Partial Test Results (*t* Test)**

The results of the *t*-test in this study can be seen in Table 2 as follows:

Based on the statistical description above, it shows that the variables that affect the effectiveness of field schools are education and innovation characteristics.

Formal education of farmers has an important role in the level of understanding of information during the field school program. The level of education is an important element in assessing a person's sociographic aspect [7]. Education greatly determines the level of competence of farmers in carrying out agricultural activities. Reference [8] put forward the characteristics of innovations that can affect the fast or slow acceptance of innovations, namely (1) Relative advantage, namely the extent to which the innovation is considered profitable for its recipients., satisfaction, or because it has a very important component, (2) Compatibility is the degree of conformity of the innovation with the values, experiences, and needs of the recipient. Innovations that are not in accordance with the values or norms that are believed by the recipient will not be accepted as quickly as innovations that are in accordance with existing norms, (3) Complexity is the level of difficulty to understand and use the innovation for the recipient. An innovation that is easy to understand and easy to use by the

**Table 1** F. Test results

| Model | Sum of squares | df | Mean square | *F* | Sig |
|---|---|---|---|---|---|
| Regression | 736.981 | 9 | 81.887 | 10.134 | 0.000[a] |
| Residual | 404.003 | 50 | 8.080 | | |
| Total | 1.140.983 | 59 | | | |

**Table 2** T. Test result

| Model | Unstandardized coefficients | | Standardized coefficients | *t* | Sig. |
|---|---|---|---|---|---|
| | B | Std. error | Beta | | |
| (Constant) | 10.063 | 6.509 | | 1.546 | 0.128 |
| Age | 0.505 | 1.126 | 0.058 | 0.448 | 0.656 |
| Education | 1.666 | 0.686 | 0.328 | 2.430 | 0.019 |
| Land area | 1.388 | 1.578 | 0.079 | 0.879 | 0.383 |
| Ownership status | 0.276 | 0.830 | 0.030 | 0.332 | 0.741 |
| Motivation | 0.551 | 0.699 | 0.133 | 0.788 | 0.434 |
| Participation | −1.403 | 0.981 | −0.160 | −1.430 | 0.159 |
| Extension intensity | −0.684 | 0.521 | −0.438 | −1.313 | 0.195 |
| Innovation characteristic | 0.593 | 0.620 | 1.137 | 3.857 | 0.000 |
| Aid | −0.514 | 0.593 | −0.192 | −0.868 | 0.389 |

recipient will spread quickly, while an innovation that is difficult to understand or difficult to use by the recipient will spread slowly, (4) Trialability is whether or not an innovation can be tried by the recipient, which will be quickly accepted by the community than innovations that cannot be tried first, (5) Observability is whether or not an innovation is easily observed. An innovation whose results are easy to observe will be more quickly accepted by the community, and conversely an innovation whose results are difficult to observe will be accepted by the community for a long time.

### Correlation Coefficient and Determination

The results of the correlation coefficient and determination can be seen in Table 3.

The correlation coefficient (R2) = 0.646 which indicates that the degree of relationship (correlation) between the independent and the dependent variable is 64.6%. Thus, if all these variables increase, it will increase the effectiveness of the field school. Meanwhile, the coefficient of determination obtained with a value of 0.804 means that 80.4% of changes in the dependent variable can be explained by changes in the independent variable, while the remaining 19.6% is explained by other factors outside the variables studied.

**Table 3** Correlation and determination coefficient results

| Model | R | R square | Adjusted R square | Std. error of the estimate |
|---|---|---|---|---|
| 1 | 0.804[a] | 0.646 | 0.582 | 2.84254 |

**Table 4** T. Test analysis results

| Model | Unstandardized coefficients | | Standardized coefficients | *t* | Sig. |
|---|---|---|---|---|---|
| | B | Std. error | Beta | | |
| (Constant) | −1.947 | 0.865 | | −2.252 | 0.028 |
| Effectiveness | 0.311 | 0.033 | 0.778 | 9.419 | 0.000 |

### *3.2 Factors Affecting the Effectiveness of the Field School Implementation Program*

The results of testing the effect of the effectiveness of the field school program on increasing rice productivity of irrigated rice farmers in Aceh Besar District can be seen in Table 4.

Based on the statistical description above, it shows that there is an effect of the effectiveness of the field school program on increasing rice productivity of irrigated farmers in Aceh Besar District ($p \leq 0.05$). The results of this study are in line with research conducted by Mulyanti which in the learning process shows that the only real difference is the stages of farmer motivation between Balinese-Javanese ethnicities. Together, the probability of the effectiveness of the SL learning process for lowland rice in the three ethnic groups is influenced by the level of education, self-efficacy beliefs, the level of courage to take risks, the level of intelligence, the expectation of results, the competence of the model, and the role of the farmer group. The implication is that it is necessary to prepare learning materials that can increase the motivation of farmers, it is necessary to increase the empowerment of farmer groups and empower the role of role models, and farmer community leaders.

## 4 Conclusions

Based on the results of the research above, it can be concluded that the factors that affect the effectiveness of the field school program are education and innovation characteristics, namely ($p \leq 0.05$), because the level of education is quite risky to improve its condition, the efforts that can be made are to grow the level of intelligence of farmers by learning directly in the field through the field school program. The characteristics of the innovations applied during the field school program have not been able to be adopted by farmers. There is a significant effect between the effectiveness of the field school program on increasing the productivity of irrigated paddy in Montasik District, Aceh Besar District ($p \leq 0.05$).

## References

1. Kementan. Petunjuk Teknis Lapang Pengelolaan Tanaman Terpadu (PTT) (2013) Padi Sawah Irigasi. Badan Penelitian dan Pengembangan Pertanian. Kementerian Pertanian, Jakarta
2. Mulyani SI, Jumiati E (2015) Peningkatan Produktivitas Padi Melalui Pendekatan Sekolah Lapang Pengelolaan Tanaman Terpadu (SLPTT) di Kecamatan Sesayap Hilir Kabupaten Tana Tidung. J AGRIFOR 16(1):1–10
3. Distan. Daftar Produksi Padi TA (2020) dan Penggunaannya serta Kondisi Ketersediaan. Dinas Pertanian Aceh Besar, Aceh Besar
4. Mahmudi (2013) Manajemen Kinerja Sektor Publik. UPPSTIM YKPN, Yogyakarta
5. Rosalina I (2012) Efektivitas Program Nasional Pemberdayaan Masyarakat Mandiri Perkotaan Pada Kelompok Pinjaman Bergulir Di Desa Mantren Kecamatan Karangrejo Kabupaten Magetan 1(1)
6. Yofa R, Ariani M, Kaniaya IS (206) Rancangan dan Implementasi Sekolah Lapang Pengelolaan Tanaman Terpadu padi. J Anal Kebijak Pertan 14(1):35–55
7. Mayamsari IM (2014) Karakteristik Petani dan Hubungannya Dengan Kompetensi Petani Lahan Sempit. Agrisep 15(2):58–74
8. Rogers EM (1995) Diffusion of innovation. Edisi Ke-4. New York, London, Toronto, Sydney, Tokyo. The Free Press, Singapore

# “Birds of A Feather Flock Together”: Ethnic Communities and Social Capital of Migrants in Batam

**Inayah Hidayati, Meirina Ayumi Malamassam, Bayu Setiawan, Ade Latifa, Haning Romdiati, and Irin Oktafiani**

**Abstract** Social capitals are essential components in the migration process that can be formed among migrants through their ethnic communities in the destination areas. This research aims to examine the role of ethnic communities in the formation of migrants’ social capital in Batam, one of the main migration destination areas in Indonesia that provides various employment opportunities and relatively higher income. By utilizing data from the study of “Migration and Human Development” by Research Center for Population, Indonesian Institute of Sciences in 2017 and 2019 in Batam, this study applies both quantitative and qualitative approaches for the data analysis. The preliminary finding of this study shows that migrants with similar ethnic backgrounds tend to be engaged in a similar type of work field. The segregation of work fields by migrant workers’ ethnicity is influenced by social support within ethnic communities. It can be said that ethnic backgrounds have become a critical social capital for migrants, particularly the less educated ones, in helping their adjustment process post-migration. However, this situation can also lead to the social exclusion of migrants from the broader community in the destination area.

**Keywords** Social capital · Ethnicity · Migration process · Labor migrant

## 1 Introduction

Chain migration is formed by access to information from previous migrants who generally have the same hometown. The chain pattern is formed because prospective migrants obtain transportation, accommodation, capital, and job opportunities from previous migrants who are bound in primary social relationships [1]. Prospective migrants who migrate to big cities are usually triggered by the emergence of success

I. Hidayati (✉) · M. A. Malamassam · B. Setiawan · A. Latifa · H. Romdiati · I. Oktafiani
Research Center for Population BRIN, Jakarta Selatan, Indonesia
e-mail: inay001@brin.go.id

M. A. Malamassam
School of Demography, Australian National University, Canberra, Australia



Nawawi et al. (eds.), *Managing Disruption and Developing Resilience for a Better Southeast Asia*, Springer Proceedings in Humanities and Social Sciences,
https://doi.org/10.1007/978-981-96-2116-3_11

stories from previous migrants when they return home. Migrants from various regions are interested in migrating because of the vast job opportunities in the areas of destination. The network owned by prospective migrants can be seen as social capitals that facilitate the accessibility of prospective migrants to find work in urban areas [2].

For those moving within Indonesia with the intention of working or looking for a job, Batam is one of the primary destinations. Therefore, it is not surprising that the proportion of migrant workers in this area is quite large. In the 2000s, when there was a lot of investment, Batam's economy grew quickly due to the strong flow of labor in-migration. The industrial sector's presence in Batam generates industry-based jobs and necessitates a large labor force. The requirements for the quantity of workers required in this city are particular, and locals are unable to supply them. Due to this circumstance, many people migrate in order to work in the manufacturing sector [3].

Our 2017 survey results have shown that the majority of the respondents were migrants who were born outside Batam City. More than half of the migrants (65%) were born in other areas on Sumatra Island or areas around Batam City. About 30% of them are workers born in cities/districts on the island of Java. The birthplaces of the remaining 5% are spread across the islands of Kalimantan, Sulawesi, Nusa Tenggara, and Maluku. When viewed from the length of stay, nearly 50% of the sample (48.2%) is classified as having lived in this city for less than five years. Meanwhile, around 26.5% of respondents have lived in Batam for five to ten years, and the rest (25.3%) have lived in Batam for more than ten years or their whole life.

Furthermore, when viewed from the ethnicity of the working respondents in this survey, the workforce in Batam is dominated by those of Javanese ethnicity (29%), followed by Batak (22%) and Minang (17%). In general, ethnic groups from Sumatra Island still dominate the distribution of respondents based on ethnicity. Although the largest proportion of the workforce comes from Javanese ethnicity, this condition does not reflect that they have lived in Java before. This is because there are quite a lot of Javanese respondents who were born and spent their time in adulthood outside Java. This situation also indicates that their parents may have carried out the experience of interregional migration.

The diverse ethnicities of the population in Batam form various types of groups and social capital. Migration flows that increase from year to year create community groups based on areas of origin and ethnicity. This group can be used as social capital for migrants in Batam, especially those who come without information from current migrants. In the migration process, social capitals are crucial elements that might develop between migrants through their ethnic communities in the destination areas. In Batam, one of Indonesia's key migration destinations that offers a variety of career options and a relatively higher income, this study attempts to investigate the function of ethnic communities in developing migrants' social capital.

## 2 The Impact of the Social Networks on Batam City's Labor Migration Dynamics

One of the factors that encourages migration is the existence of social networks. The presence of migrants who return periodically brings stories, styles, and appearances that symbolize the identity of advanced and modern city residents. The symbols are considered indicators of progress in economic and social status in society. Whether we realize it or not, the picture of developments in urban areas also encourages other residents to migrate to cities. At this point, the existence of social networks tends to strengthen. The former migrants can be a point of formation of social networks that strengthen the psychology of other villagers to migrate. On the other hand, research on social relations is useful to find out the ways and reasons for each individual to gain access to sources of capital to use them for migration purposes [4].

A key step in the migration process is the use of social networks. Former migrants and new migrants, as well as migrants and the local population, develop social networks [5, 6]. Past migrants include family members, close friends, neighbors, and neighbors of new migrants. A migration doesn't happen before social networks are established. A person's drive to move is increasingly encouraged by and influenced by social networks. The presence of relatives and friends from the place of origin and the invitation from them serve as pull factors for new migrants.

Social media plays a part in assisting migrants in preparing for their migration, particularly in discovering more about the destination city before and after they arrive in Batam City. Career opportunities, cost of living, housing, public amenities, an introduction to the area, and potential residences, as well as financial and work-related information, are just a few examples of the various sorts of migration-related information that migrants find valuable [7]. The ideal source of information would include both mainstream (newspapers, TV, and magazines) and internet media, as well as the family, friends, and coworkers of migrants who have lived in or have moved to Batam City.

## 3 Methods

This research was conducted in Batam City, Riau Islands Province. This province is one of the main destinations for internal migration in Indonesia. Based on the Intercensal Survey 2015, around 65% of the population in this city had lived in another city/regency before, the majority of whom had lived outside the Riau Archipelago Province [8]. Likewise, the majority of immigrants (71%) in this city are between the ages of 20 and 34.

The main motivation for the entry of immigrants into Batam is related to work, 54% of the immigrant population enters Batam to look for work, and the other 15% aims to work. The high proportion of migrants who enter Batam to work and look for work is supported by quite good economic opportunities. Moreover, the good accessibility of information and communication enables this region to become one of the main nodes in Indonesia from an increasingly global situation. Migrants who work in this city mainly carry out economic activities in the manufacturing sector (69%). Only about a third of migrant workers in Batam are in the service sector, and less than two percent work in agriculture.

In 2017, there were 600 survey participants. Three-stage Probability Proportional Size (PPS) sampling is the technique used to pick the sample in this investigation. The process of choosing sub-districts at random is the initial step in this sample selection method (five sub-districts). Four villages were then randomly chosen from among the sub-districts that had been chosen in the first stage in the second step. Respondents were lastly chosen at random in each chosen village during the last stage. The questionnaire will be completed if the chosen respondent fits the requirements of being between the ages of 20 and 34 and having worked most of the previous week.

To gain a deeper understanding, a qualitative technique was also used in focus group discussions (FGD) and in-depth interviews. To learn more about the dynamics of population migration in this region, FGDs and in-depth interviews were conducted with stakeholders who are familiar with the challenges surrounding migration in this area, such as local governments, community leaders, and migration actors. The paper's qualitative data were collected in Batam City in 2017 and 2019.

## 4 Results and Discussions

One of the destinations for internal migration in Indonesia is the city of Batam [8, 9], where the majority of the migrant population is young and productive, ranging between the ages of 20 and 34. Young people in particular are motivated to migrate as a part of enhancing their competitiveness. They will be able to improve their human capital through migration and become more competitive. In addition to economic causes, each person's personal motivations, such as goals for education, job advancement, relocating back to their hometown, and seeking out new experiences, all have an impact on migration [10]. As a destination for migration, Batam has met the demands of labor migrants by satisfying their reason for moving.

According to the survey, most respondents are immigrants (92%). These people move to Batam for a variety of reasons, such as job searching, moving closer to family, and pursuing higher education. Figure 1 demonstrates that 69% of migrants who arrive in Batam are driven to hunt for employment. The remaining migrants, in contrast, move to this city for a variety of other reasons, including personal reasons like following their family and changing their place of employment (mutation).

Because of its crucial role as a significant industrial and commerce location in Indonesia, Batam City has a very high attractiveness for job seekers. This condition is consistent with the idea of economic push and pull forces, which show that the majority of migration is motivated by economic factors [11]. Batam has a tremendously potent pull factor that draws employees to relocate as a source of

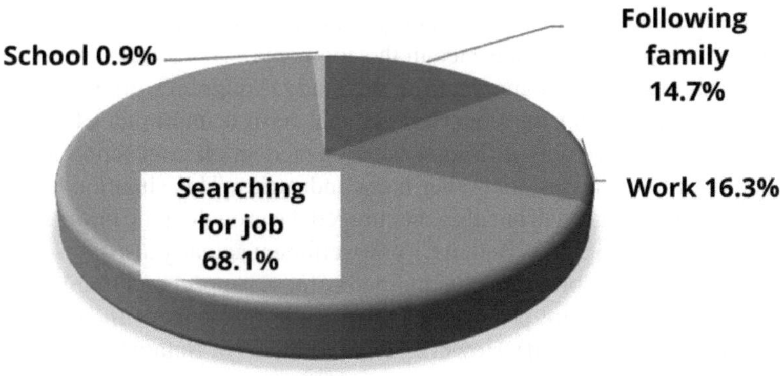


**Fig. 1** Distribution of migrants entering Batam City by migration motivation, $N = 552$, 2017 (%)

economic prospects. Given the employment prospects and relatively higher income level compared to the area of origin, Batam has become more appealing to labor migrants.

According to the survey, migrants play important roles and make significant contributions in helping to meet the demand for workers with specialized skills that are not owned by local workers. Some migrant respondents are skilled in shipyard or underwater welding, among other specialties. The majority of workers in all types of jobs, particularly in the shipbuilding industry, are from Central Java and East Java. The study’s findings in 2019 in Batam and Karimun City revealed that business owners had more faith in Indonesian workers since they were thought to have high enough skill levels, even if they had to compete with international workers. The sole barrier for Indonesian workers compared to foreign workers is the different language, yet Indonesian workers may be trusted in terms of their talents. Through a self-taught learning process or extensive job experience, it has been demonstrated that Indonesian workers occasionally possess skills that are above the certification norm. Ironically, only a few Indonesian workers have official work recognition or certification.

Some companies require formal legal evidence such as a skill certificate. This condition causes workers who do not have certification to be vulnerable to be terminated. However, obtaining certification is not an easy thing, because it takes a lot of money to get it. The local government, in this case the Batam City of Manpower Office, has made efforts to facilitate skill improvement by holding certification training for free and in collaboration with assessors at the national level. However, due to limited budget allocations, this effort is only accessible to a small number of workers. The company actually also provides training and certification related to work skills needed by the company. However, the recognition of expertise issued by the company can only be used within the company’s internal scope, not recognized in xfa wider work scale. Therefore, most of the migrant labor should spend a lot of money from their own saving to join the training in order to obtain the skill certificate.

The formal certificate is important not only to upgrade the worker skill level but also to maintain their position or presence in the company.

Another interesting phenomenon from this study is migrant workers are even able to play a role in creating job opportunities that have a multiplier effect on other jobs. For example, migrants in Batam have opened small convection shops, food stalls, batik craft businesses, and other home industries. This situation has not only accelerated industrial growth but also encouraged the growth of the informal sector to support the needs of migrants. Batam City Government actually also pays attention to local residents. Various programs, including business support and training for small and medium industries, are provided exclusively to residents of the city of Batam (having a Batam City ID card). However, local residents of Batam City tend to prefer formal types of work.

As mentioned above, the main motivation for migration to Batam is indeed economic interests, especially to work or to look for work. The findings of the focus group discussion (FGD) with union organizations and regional community organizations demonstrated that Batam became a migratory hotspot because of the presence of businesses that can take on a large number of workers. Numerous immigrants believe that coming here is necessary if they wish to work in industries.

> Compared to my hometown, there are more factories here. I was invited by a Garut's people acquaintance of mine. I first had trouble finding employment. I'm still going to gamble and look for it. Anyway, I'm coming here to work. So, certainly, I attempted to register at some factories. In addition, I received the job thanks to God. You could be unable to work at a factory if you are at home. There are many tales in the village, but if you want to work, head to Batam. That simple and only require your instinct. (FGD Community Association, Batam City)

Figure 2 demonstrates that more than half of Batam's labor migrants arrived in the city alone, without the help of their families or other close relations. The majority of migrants in Batam are people between the ages of 20 and 24 who are single and migrate in search of or for employment. Migrants still have close social ties with the families they leave behind even when they relocate alone. According to this poll, more than a quarter of migrants from the previous year were still able to make at least one yearly trip back to their place of origin. The primary motivation is to see family during holy days.

Job seekers are expected to be pushed to travel to Batam via the social network established by the migrants. Additionally, news from friends or family members, particularly those who have previously been successful in finding work, encourages migrants to move. In terms of employment, new migrants typically take jobs that aren't all that dissimilar from others in their network. The knowledge that recent immigrants obtain through their social networks is relevant to this situation. This context explains why migrants from the same region may occasionally hold the majority of positions in a city (see Fig. 3).

The findings of the FGD with community groups also demonstrated that selecting employees and coworkers from similar backgrounds was done in order to comprehend the behavior of the workers in question.

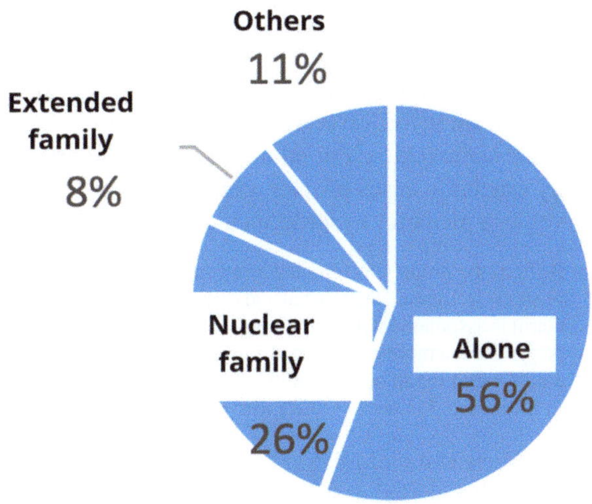


**Fig. 2** Distribution of migrants entering Batam City according to parties accompanying interregional migration, $N = 552$, 2017 (%)

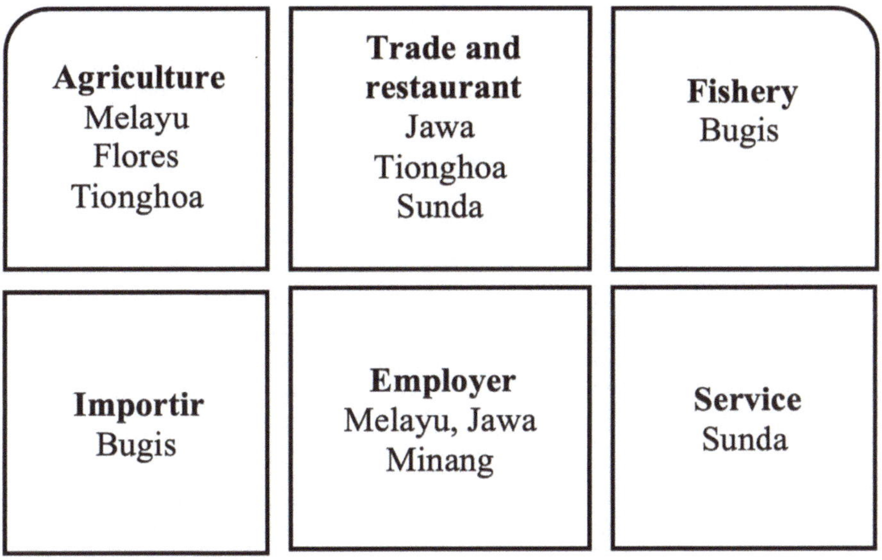


**Fig. 3** Illustration of types of work based on ethnicity/region of origin of migrants in Batam City

Migration to Batam comes from a variety of ethnic and geographic origins. Every ethnic group and geographic region has an organization or society whose goal is to foster connections. Every association has a set schedule for holding member meetings. This involves inviting coworkers from the community to work together. We could make suggestions to the boss. (FGD with migrant associations, Batam City)

Social networks are important for migrants' adaption strategies in their new communities. For new immigrants, past migrants can serve as guides in every situation. Existing immigrants can assist with housing, offer advice on where to live and work, and aid in the job search. A community or alliance forms among migrants who have the same regional or ethnic heritage. The existence of this community is especially crucial in cases of inter-ethnic conflict, as the association's leader frequently serves as a mediator to settle such disputes.

> At first, the group was founded as a location for social gathering. Over time, it evolved into business, religion, and cultural and creative pursuits (economics). This is Asgar, for instance. Garut is associated with it. Economic and business activity are welcomed by this association. Asgar Cafe, a mobile basic food enterprise founded in early 2017 that empowers its members and is preparing to open a health clinic, is now operating. Most Garuti migrants (80%) work in the clothing industry. (FGD with migrant associations, Batam City)

The interaction of migrants with their environment, especially the location where they live and work, has a significant impact on the social network of migrants in the destination area. The majority of the migrants at the study locations typically work. This demonstrates that the only people with whom they interact are their neighbors and coworkers. In the destination country, different forms of social contact can be seen as a result of the migrants' participation in social activities in their home community, such as religious activities, sports, skills, social gatherings, cooperation, funerals, and others. The more people who are actively involved in their surroundings, the more people will know, which will make it easier for migrants to adapt to their new environment.

Data from the survey reveals that 72% of migrants in the area engage in social gathering activities. The following interview extracts demonstrate how closely connected (strong ties) migrants are to their social network:

> In most cases, if we don't have any cash, we can borrow some to eat at the community event. For kids who reside on their coasts, in particular, this is incredibly beneficial. Only your neighbors and friends are there for you if something goes wrong. No relatives. (L, Housewife, Batam City)

Economic, social, and informational functions have been separated into three categories in previous research on social networks [12]. When migrants need it, especially during the first few weeks in a new home, the economic function includes having access to financial and material aid. Relatives or close friends who have already migrated typically perform economic functions. Socialization at work and a sort of social security are the following social functions. Social security involves having access to housing, food, and help from prior migrants, whereas job socialization is knowledge of the specifics of the jobs that migrants perform. The information function, which forwards any information about the job, is the final step.

Based on the information from migrant workers who work in the shipyards, in terms of work, there is a lot of assistance in terms of transferring knowledge or skills from workers who previously worked in that field. The shipbuilding sector mostly accommodates workers from high school graduates and generally, they do not have special skills. Meanwhile, the company does not have the budget to provide training for them. This condition causes workers to rely heavily on other workers who already have work experience to teach them skills related to work in the industry. From the experience of migrants who are brought from their hometowns by their relatives to work in Batam, it can be said that there is also an attitude of cooperation instead of competition among them within their working environment. There was even a case when a migrant who worked in a mining industry passed away and all the workers in the mine stopped their activities because they wanted to share their sorrow. Although their staff manager instructed that the machine should not stop at all and there must still be workers on duty, the sense of solidarity among the fellow workers has encouraged them to take a day off.

Migrants typically learn about social networks' functions from family, friends, and online media at the beginning of the migration process. Migrants will use a variety of information they gather to inform their decisions on where to go and how they will do it. Family and friends were consulted for information on career chances (63%), and internet media was consulted for data on the cost of living (74%). The majority of the early migrants in Batam received support from their family members and social networks. It was discovered that there was a very strong family tie based on ethnicity or background in the area of origin. Even migrants from their home countries have received employment assistance from one restaurant owner. This deep familial connection can provide support for needy migrants.

## 5 Conclusion

Batam is a major hub for internal migration between Indonesian provinces. Because of the numerous career prospects, migrants from diverse locations are interested in opting to relocate. Batam's industrial sector generates industry-based jobs and necessitates a labor-intensive workforce. The workforce in Batam is dominated by those of Javanese ethnicity (29%), followed by Batak (22%) and Minang (17%). In general, ethnic groups from Sumatra Island still dominate the distribution of respondents based on ethnicity. According to the preliminary findings of this study, migrants from similar ethnic backgrounds tend to work in related fields. The ethnicity of migrant workers influences the segregation of employment fields. Migrants also have an important role and contribution to fill in the shortage of workers with special skills that are not owned by local workers. Migrant workers are even able to play a role in creating job opportunities and creating a multiplier effect for other jobs.

## References

1. MacDonald JS, MacDonald LD (1964) Chain migration ethnic neighborhood formation and social networks. Milbank Mem Fund Q 42(1):82–97

2. Prayitno G, Matsushima K, Jeong H, Kobayashi K (2014) Social capital and migration in rural area development. Procedia Environ Sci 20:543–552
3. Nasution AP (2016) Peran dan kompetensi kemampuan pemerintah terhadap perkembangan ekonomi dan kesejahteraan masyarakat di Kota Batam. DIMENSI 3(1)
4. Thieme S (2006) Social networks and migration: far West Nepalese labour migrants in Delhi, vol 7. Lit Verlag Münster.
5. Massey DS, España FG (1987) The social process of international migration. Science 237(4816):733–738
6. Hidayati I (2019) The process of migration and communication technology roles among labor migrants in Batam-Indonesia. Society 7(2):173–184
7. Hidayati I, Latifa A, Setiawan B, Malamassam MA (2019) Keputusan Migrasi Pekerja Muda ke KOTA SORONG, Papua Barat. Masyarakat Indonesia 45(2):158–171
8. Badan Pusat Statistik [BPS] (2016) Statistik migrasi Kepulauan Riau: Hasil survei penduduk antar sensus 2015. BPS, Jakarta
9. Badan Pusat Statistik [BPS] (2016) Statistik migrasi Indonesia: Hasil survei penduduk antar sensus 2015. BPS, Jakarta
10. Malamassam MA, Romdiati H, Noveria M, Latifa A, Setiawan B, Fitranita RL, Hidayati I (2015) Pemetaan isu-isu mobilitas penduduk kontemporer dalam situasi dunia global dan perubahan lingkungan. *Laporan Penelitian* DIPA. P2 Kependudukan LIPI, Jakarta
11. Fratzscher M (2012) Capital flows, push versus pull factors and the global financial crisis. J Int Econ 88(2):341–356
12. Bell AR, Calvo-Hernandez C, Oppenheimer M (2019) Migration, intensification, and diversification as adaptive strategies. Socio-Environ Syst Modell 1:16102–16102

# Informal Sector Workers' Income and Access to Social Security in Indonesia

**Triyono, Lengga Pradipta, Vera Bararah Barid, Fuat Edi Kurniawan, and Fikri Muslim**

**Abstract** Income is one of the important factors affecting the economic empowerment of informal sector workers. Income is also closely related to the ability of informal sector workers to participate in social security. Therefore, this article aims to dig deeper into how the income of informal sector workers affects the expansion of access to employment and social security. The information in this article comes from the findings of a 2019 study conducted in North Sumatra, West Java, Yogyakarta, East Java, South Sulawesi, and East Nusa Tenggara by the Research Center for Population, LIPI. This study used a mixed-methods approach by using quantitative and qualitative data. This study indicates that income in the informal sector is mostly less than one million rupiahs and impacts access to participation in social security. This condition will jeopardize the expansion of access of social security participants to jobs in the informal sector. An accident at work and the lack of social protection are significant sources of vulnerability for informal workers. If they do not have access to basic income security, they will be trapped in poverty and social exclusion. In comparison, the social security scheme should target this vulnerable group as the target of the expansion program. Besides the low income, it is also related to the lack of awareness of informal sector workers about the importance of social security participation. This is a big challenge for individual welfare and

Triyono (✉) · F. E. Kurniawan · F. Muslim
Research Center for Population, National Research and Innovation Agency, Jakarta, Indonesia
e-mail: triy013@brin.go.id

L. Pradipta
Institute of Asian Studies, University of Brunei Darussalam, Gadong, Brunei

Deputyship for Development Policy, National Research and Innovation Agency, Jakarta, Indonesia

L. Pradipta
e-mail: lengga.pradipta@ubd.edu.bn

V. B. Barid
Research Center for Law, National Research and Innovation Agency, Jakarta, Indonesia

F. E. Kurniawan
Yogyakarta, Indonesia



Nawawi et al. (eds.), *Managing Disruption and Developing Resilience for a Better Southeast Asia*, Springer Proceedings in Humanities and Social Sciences,
https://doi.org/10.1007/978-981-96-2116-3_12

Indonesia's economic development and social welfare. Therefore, serious efforts are needed in the form of a policy of assisting; promoting a comprehensive and integrated strategy for the extension of coverage; raising awareness, sharing information and enhancing trust; guaranteeing an adequate level of benefits; embedding social protection in an integrated approach to facilitate the transition from the formal to the informal economy.

**Keywords** Informal workers · Income · Access · Social security

## 1 Introduction

Social protection or social security is a fundamental right given to everyone to prevent poverty. This protection covers all beneficiaries, family members, workers, children and maternity women, the aging generation, and people with disabilities. ILO [1] has declared that social protection is a major part of promoting social equality and justice and achieving the SDG's agenda. Thus, to increase inclusive development and economic productivity, this scheme is crucially needed by more than 70% of the global population. Yoshida [2] mentioned that social security systems have to be provided by the State to reflect its economic stability. Still, this reality seemed contrary to the situation in developing countries that are always associated with high human growth but have fewer protection systems. Behrendt and Nguyen [3] also stated the significant gaps in the social security system. Although people realize the necessity of the social security system, they still face the burdens of accessing and participating in this scheme. For instance, social security programs could only cover half of the population in developing countries. It happened due to many low-skilled workers and a lack of government abilities.

In developed countries such as Japan and Germany, there is a social insurance system for nursing care for the elderly. Unlike private insurance, where premiums are determined based on risk and actuarial evaluations, most social insurance premiums are determined based on the amount of income. In this case, we can see the principle of social solidarity at work in the form of social insurance. Recently, many cases worldwide have shifted from public pay-as-you-go pensions to privately funded pensions. However, compulsory enrollment in private insurance is still regarded as a type of social insurance. Social security systems have been regarded as systems that exist in developed countries but that developing countries do not yet have. However, social insurance systems and social assistance programs exist in developing countries. Among the Newly Industrializing Countries (NICs), some countries' institutional development has been accelerating recently due to economic growth and political democratization [4]. Since World War II, developed Latin American countries have been developing social security systems based on social insurance. On the other hand, assistance for poor people in low-income countries is a main social security concern.

Countries in Asia are now trying to expand their social assistance program. For example, in Bangladesh, social security has been regulated and guaranteed by the government, but its implementation and effectiveness remain an obstacle. Similar conditions also occurred in Vietnam, where social security programs raised many challenges. In Indonesia, the social security system has been stipulated under central government policy, and it consists of health coverage and employment security. But these two ambitious plans are facing different circumstances, when the health protection system in Indonesia is quite successful and accepted by more than185 million people, the employment protection system is having the opposite [5]. Data from Indonesian Bureau of Statistics (2019) revealed that only 43% of Indonesian work for formal sectors, while others or about 57% work for the informal sector.

The dual-economy perspective claims that government intervention is needed in informal groups [6: 117]. Marginal groups have different vulnerabilities. Thus, the government must find specific strategies for the informal sector or other marginalized groups because poverty and vulnerability create barriers that prevent them from accessing social security schemes. Implementing a social protection and security system that is right on target and can cover all residents can increase the productivity of the population to improve the country's economy [7].

## *1.1 Research Objectives*

This study attempted to examine the tumultuous situation of Indonesia's informal sector employees, beginning with a mapping of their sources of income as well as their understanding and access to social security. This study aims to look at three key areas: first, the informal workers' perceptions of the benefits of social protection programs; second, to assess informal workers' willingness to participate in social protection programs; and finally, to investigate the impact of income on informal or unskilled labor, as well as how the social assistance program affected their job.

## *1.2 Literature Review*

Social protection for informal workers still faces many challenges. Due to that reason, the regulation that could bear the gaps and participation is crucially needed because problems still occurred until today. A study by Ofreneo [8] in the Philippines has stated that the government's commitment always contravenes economic conditions following its financial abilities. In order to achieve maximum participation and contribution to the social protection program, the system has to be more specific and moderate [3: 210]. The social protection for workers in Indonesia should make a greater impact and positively contribute to workers with permanent income or nonpermanent income.

Another issue that can be retrieved from the social protection system is validating data. Based on a study conducted by Sian Alice Summerto [9], in India, the urgency of valid data is related to the real beneficiaries. A similar situation also happened in North Sulawesi, Indonesia, where the data owned by the social protection authority is no longer valid and could not be proved by data phone tracking [7]. This validity made a big impact on the distribution of aid so that the vulnerable groups could not access the aid from the government.

Unlike European countries with a settled social protection system, developing countries in Asia remained unstable. Bilecen et al. [10] mentioned that in Spain, every person is served with all social protection benefits without differentiating their contribution and type of jobs. Since it is very different from Indonesia, this gap resulted in formal and informal workers' participation [7].

Then another complicated problem is that for countries with high poverty rates, the informal sector is a foothold for work and social security reinforcement [11]. It is because the informal sector is easy to enter without administrative procedures. Furthermore, work in the informal sector is easy for workers to enter because it does not require skills and is voluntary [12]. In addition, the definition of the informal sector, according to Chen (2005) as quoted by Pouri and Hilty [12], is that informal sector workers do not have formal contracts, worker benefits, or social protection and wages that are not under the legislation. If we look at this definition, informal sector workers have a very high vulnerability due to the absence of social security. Meanwhile, some researchers say that reform of the social security system encourages economic growth [13]. Therefore, it is necessary to collaborate on policies between the social security system and economic policies. When the social security program functions as intended, it will provide more benefits to participants.

Meanwhile, various innovations are needed in the implementation, such as the duration of transfers to claimants and application features that make it easy for participants. It is hoped that it will encourage workers to have a strong desire to participate in labor social security [14]. In addition, this convenience reduces the negative effects of information related to the implementation of social security. Therefore, it is necessary to provide complete information to workers. On the other hand, social security program schemes run by the government may be much more stable and durable than those run by the private sector [14]. The employee social security scheme, organized by BP Jamsostek, should have various advantages over the one run by the private sector. The program that is run must carry out effective communication with the community. The role of social security programs has numerous benefits for workers in the future. For example, it may assist workers in developing better financial planning and asset management strategies [15]. The existence of training on planning programs will help informal sector workers have insight into work risks and when they are no longer productive. Moreover, the informal sector does not have social security and does not have a fixed income; thus, the existence of this planning program is at least able to encourage informal sector workers to have the desire to be included in the employee social security scheme and can reap benefits when they experience work accidents and when they are not productive.

Moreover, the role of local government is also influential in the intervention of the participation of informal sector workers in the employment social security program. The role of local governments is to control the function of employment social security in times of crisis [16]. It is done, for example, through the Ministry of Manpower to be able to function as a bridge when there are problems with informal sector workers, both in registering programs and claiming employment social security benefits. Therefore, the synergy between the labor social security administration body and the workforce office has a very vital role so that workers can accept this program.

## 1.3 Methodology

The methodology used in writing this article uses quantitative methods and qualitative approaches sourced from primary and secondary data. The secondary data used are the National Socio-Economic Survey (SUSENAS), the National Labor Force Survey (SAKERNAS), and BP Jamsostek participation. Primary data were collected through surveys, in-depth interviews, and focused discussions. The sampling technique used in this study was a multi-stage sampling method considering the selection of the proportion of the productive age population in the six selected provinces. Each selected province will be determined by one city and one district representing urban and rural areas based on the number of participation in social security (employment) and/or the number of workers who have social security (sourced from 2018 Sakernas Data).

The provinces selected as research locations are (1) North Sumatra (covering the City of Medan and Deli Serdang Regency), (2) West Java (covering Bandung City and Sumedang Regency), (3) Special Region of Yogyakarta (covering Yogyakarta City and Bantul Regency), (4) East Java (covering Surabaya City and Malang Regency), (5) South Sulawesi (covering Makassar City and Gowa Regency), and (6) East Nusa Tenggara (covering Kupang City and South Central Timor Regency). The total number of respondents from this research survey is 1800. The criteria for determining respondents are people of productive age (aged 15–64 years) who have working status and work in the formal and informal economic sectors. However, we only use survey data for informal sector workers in this article, so the number of data samples analyzed is 1192 respondents.

In-depth interviews were conducted with policymakers, the private sector, and communities and individuals. The policy-making level includes the central government/relevant ministries, provincial governments, and regional governments/relevant agencies, such as Bappeda, Manpower Office, and BP Jamsostek. Private parties include companies/employers and insurance service providers. Resident communities include traditional institutions, community economic institutions, farmer/fisherman groups, and labor unions. Individuals include community leaders and religious leaders. In addition to in-depth interviews, data was collected through FGDs to see the perspectives of stakeholders and population groups on increasing productivity through the use of social security.

# 2 Discussion

## *2.1 General Knowledgement of BP Jamsostek*

BP Jamsostek is an institution that administers employment social security programs in Indonesia. The establishment of BP Jamsostek is under the mandate of Law Number 24 of 2011 concerning the Social Security Administering Body. The law also regulates the duties and functions of BP Jamsostek as the organizer of four employment social security programs, namely (1) work accident insurance, (2) old-age insurance, (3) pension insurance, and (4) death security. Employment social security itself is a protection program for workers and their families from risks while carrying out work.

Despite the establishment of institutional frameworks and the implementation of programs, the survey results indicate that the majority of respondents in the informal sector are unaware of the existence of BP Jamsostek or its programs. In the institutional context, of the 1192 informal sector workers, 68.8% of them admitted that they did not know about BP Jamsostek. Then when viewed according to the location of the respondent's residence, workers who live in rural areas tend to be less aware of BP Jamsostek's existence than workers who live in urban areas. 80% of respondents who live in rural areas claim to be unaware of BP Jamsostek, while 54.9% of respondents in urban areas claim not to know BP Jamsostek. This condition is closely related to infrastructure modernization, and the development of information and communication technology in urban areas is relatively better than in rural areas Revisi This condition is Respondent's knowledge of the employment social security program by place of resident (Table 1).

BP Jamsostek's physical offices and regional infrastructure (e.g., transportation networks) are primarily located in urban areas, so access to service coverage for

**Table 1** Respondents' knowledge of the employment social security program by place of residence

| No. | Type of program | Know/don't know | Respondent's knowledge of employment social security program (%) | | Total cases (*n*: 1.192) (%) |
|---|---|---|---|---|---|
| | | | Urban | Rural | |
| 1 | Work accident insurance | Know | 18.8 | 9.7 | 31.2 |
| | | Don't know | 81.2 | 90.3 | 68.8 |
| 2 | Death security | Know | 14.1 | 7.7 | 10.6 |
| | | Don't know | 85.9 | 92.3 | 89.4 |
| 3 | Old-age insurance | Know | 15.8 | 7.9 | 11.4 |
| | | Don't know | 84.2 | 92.1 | 88.6 |
| 4 | Pension insurance | Know | 13.5 | 65 | 9.6 |
| | | Don't know | 86.5 | 93.5 | 90.4 |

*Source* Results of survey data processing in six provinces Indonesia, 2019

workers in urban areas will be higher than for workers in rural areas located farther away. The availability of relatively more adequate information and telecommunications networks in urban areas also contributes to the level of knowledge of workers, where information on BP Jamsostek services online will be more easily accessible to those living in urban areas.

A relatively similar condition also occurs when one looks at the knowledge of informal sector workers about the social security programs provided by BP Jamsostek, where the majority of workers who are respondents also state that they are not aware of employment social security programs. The work accident insurance program is the most popular of the other three employment social security programs. Respondents of informal sector workers who claimed to know about the work accident insurance program reached 31.2%, while the other three programs were only known to about 10% of survey respondents. The death insurance program is only known by 10.6% of the respondents, the old-age insurance program is only known by 11.4% of the respondents, and the pension insurance program is only known by 9.7%.

The gap in respondents' knowledge of the employment social security program is increasingly visible when viewed according to the respondent's place of residence. However, in general, it has the same pattern that most respondents do not know about employment social security programs, both respondents who reside in urban and rural areas. However, based on data obtained by residents in rural areas aware of each employment social security program, it does not even reach 10% of the total respondents working in the informal sector. Only 9.7% of informal workers living in rural areas know about the work accident insurance program; only 7.7% know about the death insurance program; only 7.7% know about the old-age insurance program; those who know about the pension insurance program are only 7.7%. In the meantime, informal laborers who reside in urban areas and are aware of the work accident insurance program comprise 18.8%; those who know about the death insurance program are 14.1%; those who know about the old-age insurance program are 15.8%; and those who know about the pension insurance program are 13.5%. The low level of knowledge of informal sector workers about the employment social security program from BP Jamsostek is due to the low access to information about employment social security programs received by informal sector workers. Informal sector workers are also entitled to employment social security services because they also have the same risks to working as formal workers. Therefore, socialization and education regarding the employment social security program and the benefits that informal sector workers can obtain are still problems for BP Jamsostek. Its implementation needs to be improved to encourage the level of participation of informal sector workers in employment social security participation.

**Table 2** The number of informal sector workers in sampling provinces

| Province | Total |
|---|---|
| East Java | 12,662,574 |
| West Java | 10,019,837 |
| North Sumatra | 3,816,533 |
| South Sulawesi | 2,378,566 |
| Yogyakarta | 1,833,828 |
| East Nusa Tenggara | 1,152,685 |

*Source* BPS–Statistics Indonesia, 2018

## 2.2 Limitation

This research chose six provinces as follows because the number of informal sector workers is quite high. This also affects the number of employment social security participation. The level of participation in the informal sector is a determinant of our sampling to represent the broad characteristics of Indonesia, consisting of islands because it is the informal sector that is our focus in this study. The variable number of population with productive age, according to the main employment status in the largest informal sector in Indonesia, was chosen to show the level of participation in the informal sector. The six provinces were chosen, namely East Java, West Java, North Sumatra, South Sulawesi, Yogyakarta, and East Nusa Tenggara (Table 2).

## 2.3 Survey Respondent Profile by Employment Sector

In this research survey, respondents' occupations are classified into 16 categories of employment sectors, namely: (1) Agriculture, Forestry, and Fisheries; (2) Mining and Quarrying; (3) Processing Industry; (4) Procurement of Electricity, Gas, Steam/Hot Water, and Cold Air; (5) Water Supply, Waste Management and Recycling, Waste and Garbage Disposal and Cleaning; (6) Construction; (7) Wholesale, Retail, Repair, and Maintenance of Cars and Motorcycles; (8) Transportation and Warehousing; (9) Provision of Accommodation and Drinks; (10) Information and Communication; (11) Real Estate; (12) Company Services; (13) Government Administration, Defense, and Mandatory Social Security; (14) Education Services; (15) Health Services and Social Activities; (16) Other Services.

Of the 16 employment sectors, the most dominant survey respondents are informal workers in the Agriculture, Forestry, and Fisheries Sectors, 33.4%. The Trade Sector is the category of employment sector with the second-highest number of 27.8%, followed by the Other Services Sector as the third employment sector at 14.1% (Table 3).

**Table 3** Respondent profile by employment sector

| No. | Type of working fields/industries | Residential | | | | Total | Percentage (%) |
|---|---|---|---|---|---|---|---|
| | | Urban | % | Rural | % | | |
| 1 | Agriculture, forestry, and fisheries | 32 | 6.0 | 366 | 55.5 | 398 | 33.4 |
| 2 | Mining | 1 | 0.2 | | – | 1 | 0.1 |
| 3 | Manufacturing | 11 | 2.07 | 24 | 3.64 | 35 | 2.94 |
| 4 | Electricity, gas, heater, and air con providers | 2 | 0.4 | 1 | 0.2 | 3 | 0.3 |
| 5 | Water, waste management, and dumping providers | 9 | 1.7 | 6 | 0.9 | 15 | 1.3 |
| 6 | Construction | 32 | 6.0 | 34 | 5.6 | 66 | 5.5 |
| 7 | Big traders, reparation, vehicle maintenance | 217 | 40.8 | 114 | 17.3 | 331 | 27.8 |
| 8 | Transportation and Storage industry | 40 | 7.5 | 26 | 3.9 | 66 | 5.5 |
| 9 | Accommodation, food, and beverages providers | 50 | 9.4 | 29 | 4.4 | 79 | 6.6 |
| 10 | Information and communication | 4 | 0.8 | – | – | 4 | 0.3 |
| 11 | Real estate | 2 | 0.4 | 3 | 0.5 | 5 | 0.4 |
| 12 | Corporations | 4 | 0.8 | 1 | 0.2 | 5 | 0.4 |
| 13 | Gov administration, defense, and social security | 1 | 0.2 | – | – | 1 | 0.1 |
| 14 | Education | 1 | 0.2 | 4 | 0.6 | 5 | 0.4 |
| 15 | Health and social service providers | 8 | 1.5 | 2 | 0.3 | 10 | 0.8 |
| 16 | Others | 118 | 22.2 | 50 | 7.6 | 168 | 14.1 |
| Grand total | | 532 | 100 | 660 | 100 | 1.192 | 100 |

*Source* Results of survey data processing in six provinces Indonesia, 2019

## 2.4 *Income and Social Security Access*

Income is one of the factors in determining how the position of the informal sector workers is economically empowered. In addition, the position of laborers within the social structure of society is also influenced by their income. So far, informal sector workers are synonymous with low wages and protection, including access to social security participation. The problem of access to social security is also seen from the income level factor of informal sector workers. BP Jamsostek has an income limit policy for informal sector workers, a participant requirement, with a minimum income limit of one million rupiahs per month. Then how do informal sector workers in Indonesia have the requirements set by BP Jamsostek in terms of income?.

From the Table 4, it can be concluded that the income in the informal sector is mostly less than one million rupiahs with a percentage reaching 46.31%, and the lowest number with a percentage of 3.86% having an income of four million rupiahs. Based on the distribution of the table data above, it can be seen that the income of workers in the informal sector is unequal. The high-income rate of informal sector workers is less than one million rupiahs per month, reaching 46.31%, impacting access to employment and social security participation. Even access and opportunities are closed. The minimum income threshold for a participant is one million rupiahs. This condition will threaten the expansion of access to employment for social security participants. A solution from the government is crucially needed in this phase.

Moreover, this group with low income is vulnerable. The results [17: 9] show that vulnerable population groups to employment turnover of IAW are the youngest and the oldest, the less educated, and those with the lowest income. Nevertheless, these are precisely the groups that social protection schemes should fully cover. The problem of this vulnerable group with low incomes is not included in the employee social security scheme because it is hindered by the administration of the minimum income limit, further increasing the living burden of informal sector workers. Because of low incomes without social security when an accident occurs, these informal sector workers do not have social security. In comparison, the social security scheme aims to target this vulnerable group as one of the program targets.

On the other hand, from the above data, it can be seen from a geographical perspective that informal sector workers in rural areas are more vulnerable because the income level, which is below one million rupiahs, is greater in proportion than in urban areas with the percentage reaching 56.97%. It further adds to the problem of expanding access, especially in rural areas which are still far from access to

**Table 4** Respondent's data by income average and place of residence

| No. | Income | Type of residential | | | | Total | Percentage (%) |
|---|---|---|---|---|---|---|---|
| | | Urban | % | Rural | % | | |
| 1 | < 1,000,000 | 176 | 33.08 | 376 | 56.97 | 552 | 46.31 |
| 2 | 1,000,001–2,000,000 | 126 | 23.68 | 150 | 22.73 | 276 | 23.15 |
| 3 | 2,000,001–3,000,000 | 109 | 20.49 | 83 | 12.58 | 192 | 16.11 |
| 4 | 3,000,001–4,000,000 | 32 | 6.02 | 18 | 2.73 | 50 | 4.19 |
| 5 | 4,000,001–5,000,000 | 34 | 6.39 | 12 | 1.82 | 46 | 3.86 |
| 6 | 5,000,001–6,000,000 | 55 | 10.34 | 21 | 3.18 | 76 | 6.38 |
| Grand total | | 532 | 100.00 % | 660 | 100.00 % | 1192 | 100.00 |

*Source* Results of survey data processing in six provinces Indonesia, 2019

employment and social security services. Besides that, there are not many types of work compared to urban areas, making the informal sector workers in rural areas not have a greater opportunity to have more than two types of work than in urban areas.

## 2.5 *Aspirations and Income*

The aspiration of the desire to be included in the employee social security scheme is also faced with income. The correlation between informal sector incomes with the aspiration to become a participant in the social security of employment can be seen in the Table 5.

From the survey results above, there are more informal sector workers who do not want to be participants, with a total of 827 respondents from a total of 1192 respondents, which means more than 69% of informal sector workers are not interested. This data is very interesting because it turns out that informal sector workers are more disinterested even though social security participation provides great benefits to workers. It is very surprising, especially since the premium claim paid is also quite cheap—16,800 rupiahs per month with the type of work accident and death guarantee. Then, if viewed based on the amount of income, it is also in line with income less than one million rupiahs per month, which occupies the first place who does not want to be a participant in employment social security by reaching 45.59% of the total 827 respondents who stated that they did not want to be a participant in social security. This is in line with the minimum income limit of one million rupiahs for the informal sector that can become a participant in the employment social security program. This indicates that the wage issue is correlated with the ability of informal sector workers to have access as participants in the employee social security program.

On the other hand, the employee social security program is not an attractive option for most informal sector workers. This condition in Indonesia is also experienced in India. The results of the study in India conducted by Oleb [18: 114] "The study's

**Table 5** Respondent's data by income average and willingness to become participants

| No. | Income | The willingness to be participant | | | | | | Total | Percentage (%) |
|---|---|---|---|---|---|---|---|---|---|
| | | Want | % | Don't want | % | Not answer | % | | |
| 1 | < 1,000,000 | 168 | 51.85 | 377 | 45.59 | 7 | 17.00 | 552 | 46.31 |
| 2 | 1,000,001–2,000,000 | 65 | 20.06 | 200 | 24.18 | 11 | 26.83 | 276 | 23.15 |
| 3 | 2,000,001–3,000,000 | 50 | 15.43 | 135 | 16.32 | 7 | 17.07 | 192 | 16.11 |
| 4 | 3,000,001–4,000,000 | 17 | 5.25 | 28 | 3.39 | 5 | 12.20 | 50 | 4.19 |
| 5 | 4,000,001–5,000,000 | 12 | 3.70 | 31 | 3.75% | 3 | 7.32% | 46 | 3.86% |
| 6 | 5,000,001–6,000,000 | 12 | 3.70 | 56 | 6.77 | 8 | 19.51 | 76 | 6.38 |
| Grand total | | 324 | 100.00 | 827 | 100.00 | 41 | 100.00 | 1192 | 100.00 |

*Source* Results of survey data processing in six provinces Indonesia, 2019

findings, in conjunction with the focus group discussion, demonstrate that workers in a developing country (India) do not have the option or preference to access insurance, in contrast to developed countries." This condition is understandable because of workers with incomes below one million rupiahs. They only think about how they can survive amid uncertain economic conditions. This problem usually occurs in countries where the proportion of the number of workers in the informal sector is more dominant than in the formal sector. It is because, formally, the company must register its workers in the social security program scheme. According to Jessen and Kluve's research [19: 3] reveal that for workers, formality for workers can include being registered as employees by a law firm or having the firm make the requisite social security contributions. Formal sector workers have more access than the informal sector to employment social security. Because besides, the company also should include workers in the employment social security program.

The issue of social protection for informal sector workers is essential to get significant attention. In 2016, there were around 70% of informal sector workers from the total labor market in Indonesia [20]. The dual-economy perspective claims that government intervention is needed in informal groups [6: 117]. So the government needs to create special schemes and strategies for the informal sector or other marginalized groups because poverty and vulnerability create barriers that prevent them from accessing social security schemes.

These problems are specifically in the field caused by several limitations faced by labor social security providers. First, the affordability of the primary branch office/pioneer branch office services to informal workers is still very limited, especially for rural communities that do not obtain information about BP Jamsostek. Second, the socialization approach for participation focuses more on formal workers (Corporate-Based Orientation) because it is more accessible to reach membership than the informal sector segmentation, which is more numerous and diverse. The approach taken is also still conventional or the same as the approach in the formal sector. Third, BP Jamsostek overcomes the problem of low participation by developing a program of conscious villages, conscious markets, and social security awareness malls for informal workers. However, these services are still limited and only serve as pilot projects. Fourth, BP Jamsostek also recruits Shield Agents (Indonesian Social Security Movers) to increase membership, but the number of shield agents is not significant and often unsustainable.

The results of this research state that the level of wage income for informal sector workers is less than one million rupiahs, with a percentage reaching 46.31%. Of course, this will affect the level of participation. From a regulatory perspective, it is clear that 46.31% cannot be included in the employee social security scheme. Informal workers do not have the same routine income. Some are daily, monthly, or seasonal, and some are just harvesting; this makes informal workers have a diverse segmentation. This problem also forms the basis for informal workers' willingness and ability to pay because many informal workers still complain about this and do not know what benefits they will get.

In general, BP Jamsostek membership in six provinces shows three major groups of respondents according to membership, namely (a) being participants, (b) not participating but wanting to become participants, and (c) not participating but not wanting to become participants. The first group has the smallest percentage among the other groups, namely 11.4%. The average participation in these six provinces is lower than the national membership of 18% or 55 million participants. However, one province has a higher participation rate than the national one, namely North Sumatra. At the district/city level, three regions have participation above the national average, namely Medan, Yogyakarta, and Makassar. There is a high disparity between participation in the formal sector (27.6%) and the informal sector (3.2%). BP Jamsostek participation disparities also occur between education levels, ages, and districts/ cities. Most of the BP Jamsostek participants are active participants (85%), and the rest (15%) are inactive participants.

The group of respondents who are not members of BP Jamsostek but wish to become members is 27.6%. This group is a group of respondents who have great potential to become participants in the BP Jamsostek. Despite wanting to become a participant, there are several conveniences desired by respondents, namely: ease of payment schemes (61.6%), income limits (49.3%), and third-party assistance (78%). The level of respondents' desire is negatively correlated with age and positively correlated with education level. Young and highly educated groups have more significant potential to become BP Jamsostek participants in six provinces.

The group of respondents who are not participants in BP Jamsostek and do not wish to become members is 61%. This group has a low potential to become BP Jamsostek participants, so more extraordinary efforts are needed to attract them to become participants. The largest percentage of this group is in Gowa Regency and Bandung City, at 88% and 82%, respectively. On the other hand, the lowest percentages were found in Medan City and Deli Serdang Regency, at 35% and 39%, respectively. According to the formal–informal sector, the challenges in the informal sector are greater because 69% of respondents fall into this group, while in the formal sector, 43%.

Based on the survey results in general, it is found that the majority of informal workers still depend on the agriculture, forestry, and fisheries sectors, where around 33.3% of survey respondents work in this sector. The dominance of the type of work in the agricultural sector is increasingly prominent for informal workers who live in rural areas. It is known that more than 50% of respondents in rural areas work in this sector. This is closely related to the characteristics of rural areas, which are identical depending on the agricultural sector with the support of the availability of land to be developed for farm businesses. Meanwhile, for urban areas, the pattern of domination of the type of work is independent of the agricultural sector. The character of the urban area itself is morphologically dominated by built-up land, so the availability of land for agricultural businesses is more limited. Therefore, it is natural that most informal worker respondents in urban areas work in the trade and service sector.

The expansion of BP Jamsostek participation is faced with the high reality of community groups who do not want to become BP Jamsostek participants. The three main reasons that cause them not to want to become participants in the BP Jamsostek are that they do not know/do not understand BPJS for labor, feel they do not need it, and cannot pay. Not understanding BPJS for labor is the highest answer from respondents, so membership expansion needs to provide a solution to the lack of knowledge. Various socialization activities and increasing public knowledge need to be carried out massively with various media readily accepted by the community. Creating user-friendly and attractive applications for the community must also be done.

Efforts to expand the membership of BPJS for workers are faced with various structural and socio-economic constraints of the community, especially policies, institutions, accessibility, and knowledge of the population. Therefore, government intervention is needed, for example, by offering subsidies or other policies that can encourage an increase in the income of informal sector workers. In addition, the government and social security providers must also play a role in planning and asset management programs [15]. With this role, informal sector workers have insight into developing finances. It is hoped that informal sector workers can increase their income and enter as a participant in labor social security.

## 3 Conclusion

The Employment Social Security research that has been carried out has represented the western, eastern, and central regions of Indonesia by diversifying the number of informal jobs and education. The average participation in these six provinces is lower than the national membership of 18% or 55 million participants. However, one province has a higher participation rate than the national one, namely North Sumatra. Meanwhile, districts/cities with participation above the national average are Medan, Yogyakarta, and Makassar. Spatial distribution describes the different conditions between regions so that it affects social security. The high membership rate of BP Jamsostek in North Sumatra is due to the ease of access, facilities, and active socialization by the BP Jamsostek workforce.

Many informal sector workers associated BP Jamsostek with BPJS Health, so knowledge about this program is minimal, and many workers do not even know its benefits. The need for an employee social security program, both for informal workers who have more vulnerable characteristics, is essential because, under certain conditions, this program safeguards and helps informal sector workers. More than half of the respondents in this study were interested in becoming participants in the BP Jamsostek program. In addition, informal sector workers in rural areas are more vulnerable because the income level, which is below one million rupiahs, is greater in proportion than in urban areas. However, their income did not meet the specified minimum requirements. Hence, it was necessary to open an alternative membership so that this program could still cover all workers, such as a government assistance program similar to BPJS Kesehatan.

**Acknowledgements** The authors have conveyed their gratitude, especially for National Priority (PN) 2019, through the activity of Excellence Research supporting the funding for this study. The gratitude is also sent to the local coordinator and enumerator team, FGD participants, key informants, and all the parties involved in data collection in six provinces in Indonesia.

## References

1. ILO (2019) Executive summary: world social protection report 2017–19. Retrieved from https://www.ilo.org/wcmsp5/groups/public/---dgreports/---dcomm/---publ/documents/publication/wcms_605078.pdf
2. Yoshida K (2018) The stability of social security in the United States: the need for durable institutional design. J Soc Policy 47(2):397–415. https://doi.org/10.1017/S0047279417000599
3. Behrendt C, Nguyen QA (2019) Ensuring universal social protection for the future of work. Transfer: Europ Rev Labour Res 25(2):205–219. https://doi.org/10.1177/1024258919857031
4. Koichi U (2017) Social security systems in developing countries that support daily life. IDE JETRO. https://www.ide.go.jp/English/Research/Topics/Soc/Social_security/overview.html
5. ASEAN Briefing (2020) Indonesia increases social security premium for 2020. https://www.aseanbriefing.com/news/indonesia-increases-social-security-premium-2020/
6. La Porta R, Shleifer A (2014) Informality and development. J Econ Perspect 28:109–126
7. Triyono, Zaelany, A. A., Alihar, F., Ngadi, Ocktaviana, S., Pradipta, L., Barid, V. B., Muslim, F., Aruan, N. L., Kurniawan, F. E., Aini, Y. N., Meilianna, R., & Purba, Y. A. (2019). Perluasan akses dan partisipasi jaminan social ketenagakerjaan untuk mendukung produktivitas penduduk. Yayasan Pustaka Obor Indonesia.
8. Ofreneo ER (2013) Precarious Philippines: expanding informal sector, "flexibilizing" labor market. American Behav Scient 57(4):420–443 © 2013 SAGE Publications Reprints and permission: http://www.sagepub.com/journalsPermissions.nav; https://doi.org/10.1177/0002764212466237; http://abs.sagepub.com
9. Summerto AS (2020) Implications of the COVID-19 pandemic for food security and social protection in India. Indian J Human Develop 14(2):333–339. © 2020 Institute for Human Development Reprints and permissions: in.sagepub.com/journals-permissions-india. https://doi.org/10.1177/0973703020944585; journals.sagepub.com/home/jhd
10. Bilecen et al (2019) Gendered dynamics of transnational social protection. Comparative Migrat Stud 7:47. https://doi.org/10.1186/s40878-019-0161-3
11. Mughal SK, Schneider FG (2020) How informal sector affects the formal economy in Pakistan? A lesson for developing countries. South Asian J Macroecon Public Fin 9(1):7–21. © 2020 SAGE Publications India. https://doi.org/10.1177/2277978719898975; journals.sagepub.com/home/smp
12. Pouri MJ, Hilty LM (2021) The digital sharing economy: a confluence of technical and social sharing. Environ Innov Societal Trans 38:127–139. https://doi.org/10.1016/j.eist.2020.12.003
13. Li Q, Zhao Y, Li S, Zhang L (2021) Spatial-temporal characteristics of the coupling coordination of social security and economic development in China during 2002–2018. Reg Sustain 2(2):116–129. https://doi.org/10.1016/j.regsus.2021.04.001
14. Prencipe L, Houweling TAJ, van Lenthe FJ, Palermo T (2021) Do conditional cash transfers improve mental health? evidence from Tanzania's governmental social protection program. J Adolesc Health 69(5):797–805. https://doi.org/10.1016/j.jadohealth.2021.04.033
15. Haurin D, Moulton S, Loibl C (2022) The relationship of financial stress with the timing of the initial claim of U.S. Social Security retirement income. J Econ Ageing 21:100362. https://doi.org/10.1016/j.jeoa.2021.100362
16. Dutta A, Fischer HW (2021) The local governance of COVID-19: disease prevention and social security in rural India. World Dev 138:105234. https://doi.org/10.1016/j.worlddev.2020.105234

17. Guerra et al. (2018) Loss of job-related right to healthcare associated with employment turnover: challenges for the Mexican health system. BMC Heal Serv Res 18:457. https://doi.org/10.1186/s12913-018-3283-7
18. Banerjee S, Goswami K (2019) Whether the industrial workers of slums have access to job insurance? Int J Workplace Heal Manag 12(3):102–119. © Emerald Publishing Limited 1753–8351. https://doi.org/10.1108/IJWHM-08-2018-0110
19. Jessen J, Kluve J (2021) The effectiveness of interventions to reduce informationality in low-and middle-income countries. World Dev 138:105256. https://doi.org/10.1016/j.worlddev.2020.105256
20. Rothenberg AD, Gaduh A, Burger NE, Chazali E, Chandraningsih I, Radikun R, Weilant S (2016) Rethinking Indonesia's informal sector. World Dev 80:96–113

# Featuring Multi-generational Digital Workers in Indonesia

**Ngadi, Devi Asiati, and Zantermans Rajagukguk**

**Abstract** Internet-based digital technology has developed rapidly in Indonesia, including in the labor market. New employment relationships such as partnerships "Mitra" on online transportation and freelancers are increasing along with the use of the internet in the labor market. Research on employment in digital-internet-based is important so that policies can be taken following field conditions. This paper will discuss the feature of digital-internet-based workers across generations. The data used for the analysis is the 2021 National Labor Force Survey (Sakernas). Analysis was done through descriptive analysis. The results of the analysis show that Generation X workers are the biggest workers in Indonesia in 2021. Generation Z is a generation that is highly educated, mostly uses the internet for work, and is increasingly leaving the agricultural sector. On the other hand, the education level of female workers is increasing and even higher than that of male workers.

**Keywords** Digital · Labor market · Across generation · Indonesia

## 1 Introduction

Cross-generational differences in the world of work are factors that need to be considered in employment development because each generation has different characteristics and attitudes toward the world of work. Glass [1] shows that Generations X and Y have different views of the world of work than the baby boomers. Each generation has different characteristics based on basic life events and forms the values of work that are believed [2, 3]. Kratz [4] shows that the proportion of Generation Y in the workforce is increasing and dominant in 2020.

A generation is a group of people of approximately the same age, socialized at a similar time, and its members thus are inferred to share a similar way of thinking

Ngadi (✉) · D. Asiati · Z. Rajagukguk
Research Center for Population, National Research and Innovation Agency of Indonesia, Jakarta, Indonesia
e-mail: Ngad009@brin.go.id



Nawawi et al. (eds.), *Managing Disruption and Developing Resilience for a Better Southeast Asia*, Springer Proceedings in Humanities and Social Sciences,
https://doi.org/10.1007/978-981-96-2116-3_13

and lifestyle [5]. Broadly speaking, four generations characterize the creative workforce in Indonesia. These generations are (a) Baby boomers, namely those born in 1946–1964, (b) Generation X born in 1965–1980; Generation Y (millennials) born in 1981–1996; and Generation Z who were born in 1997–2012. Especially for Indonesia, in 2020, Indonesia's population will be dominated by Generation Z and the millennial generation (Y). In 2020, the number of Generation Z in Indonesia will reach 75.49 million people (27.94 percent of the total population of 270.2 million people). Meanwhile, the millennial generation reached 69.90 million people (25.87 percent).

Intergenerational labor cooperation is an integral part of the labor market in Indonesia. This collaboration provides various advantages at the level of companies, individuals, the job market, and competitiveness [6]. Technological advances that are very fast and have an impact on the quality standards of the workforce make intergenerational collaboration even more important. The internet-based digital job market that is currently developing in the world requires a better-qualified workforce. This digital job market is friendly to Generation Y who generally have a strong ambition to master all fields. They are known as a reliable generation in the use of technology. Generation Z grew up in an all-digital environment, making this generation grow into individuals with diverse characteristics, both in terms of interpersonal and academic relationships [7, 8].

The discussion of cross-generational employment in Indonesia is very important so that it can become the basis for the development of employment and the business world. The understanding will be able to illuminate strategic actions for Human Resources departments when facing generational diversity challenges [9], and knowledge transfer [10]. Therefore, this paper is intended to discuss the state of the workforce across generations, especially education, wages, and plans for COVID-19.

## 2 Method

The data used for analysis is the National Labor Force Survey data, August 2021. In this survey, workers are grouped into jobs that use the internet and do not use the internet (question R17B). Generations are grouped based on year of birth, namely: baby boomers generation: born in 1946–1964, generation X: born in 1965–1980, generation Y/millennials: born in 1981–1996, and generation Z: born in 1997–2012. The level of education in this paper is divided into low education (junior high school and below), medium (high school or equivalent), and high education (diploma and above). The wages/income of workers in this study is a combination of wages in the form of money and wages in the form of goods.

## 3 A Cross-Generational Worker in Indonesia

The state of the workforce in Indonesia across generations shows the dominance of workers from Generation X, namely those born between 1965 and 1980 or currently aged between 41 and 56 years. Currently, most of the baby boomers have retired or died, so the proportion is already low (16.7% for men and 15.4% for women). The dominance of Generations X and Y in the world of employment in Indonesia will be even greater in the next few years. For this reason, the government and companies need to prepare suitable working conditions to optimize labor productivity in the future. On the other hand, the number of generation Z workers is still small (less than 10%) because some of this generation are still in school and have not yet become the workforce. Okros [11] stated that the approach to work for baby boomers is a driven service-oriented team player who does not want to be micro-managed. They live to work. On another side, the work values of the X Generation are independent, self-reliant, unimpressed by authority, focused on self-development, and work to live. The work values of Y Generations are self-confident, optimistic, outspoken, and collaborative. They blend work and personal life.

The education level of the baby boomers generation (age 57–75) and X is dominated by workers with low education. This is understandable considering that the baby boomers who were born in the post-independence period (1946–1964) lived in a period of transformation with unstable security conditions so access and opportunities to get an education in school were very rare. As development progresses, access to education is increasingly open, as can be seen from the secondary and higher education owned by Generation X, which are 27.1% and 12.7%, respectively.

The educational condition of the Y and Z generations of workers is getting better, Generation Y or the millennial generation with secondary and higher education levels, respectively 35.2% and 21.4% high. Meanwhile, in Generation Z, which is currently a school-age population (10–24 years), the majority (60.6%) have completed secondary education. As many as 31.7% have elementary school education and, likely, most of them are currently undergoing secondary school education (SMP and SMA). The better level of education of the younger generation is supported by the construction of educational infrastructure, even the government has budgeted 20% of the state budget for education. This indirectly reflects the quality of the Indonesian workforce is getting better. In the next 5–7 years when all baby boomers retire and are replaced by Generation Z, the education level of workers in Indonesia will increase (Table 1).

Figure 1 shows the education level of the population between generations by sex. It can be seen that in the baby boomers generation, women with lower education are higher (84.8%) than men (80.2%). Likewise, for the secondary education level, the education of men is better than that of women, it can be seen from secondary education that men have 13.2% higher than women's 7.4%. The educational conditions of the boomer generation reflected the social and cultural situation and conditions that occurred in society at that time, which prioritized education for boys over girls. Several empirical studies show that at the beginning of independence, the opportunity

**Table 1** Education attainment of Indonesian workers across generations (%), 2021

| Generation | Education level (%) | | | *N* | % |
|---|---|---|---|---|---|
| | Low | Medium | High | | |
| Baby boomers | 81.70 | 11.30 | 7.00 | 67,718 | 16.24 |
| Generasi X | 60.20 | 27.10 | 12.70 | 166,306 | 39.88 |
| Generasi Y | 43.50 | 35.20 | 21.40 | 143,078 | 34.31 |
| Generasi Z | 31.70 | 60.60 | 7.60 | 36,004 | 8.63 |
| Others | 93.80 | 4.60 | 1.60 | 3916 | 0.94 |
| | 55.80 | 30.00 | 14.20 | 417,022 | 100.00 |

*Source* Sakernas, 2021

to continue education to a higher level was given to boys and girls were more likely to help with household chores.

In Generations Y and Z, women's access to higher education is very open, as can be seen from the percentage of women with secondary and higher education. In Generation Y, women with higher education (33.8%) are much larger than men (14.6%). Then in Generation Z, the level of secondary and higher education is higher for women, 67.3% and 13.8%, respectively, while men are 56.7% and 4%. Another

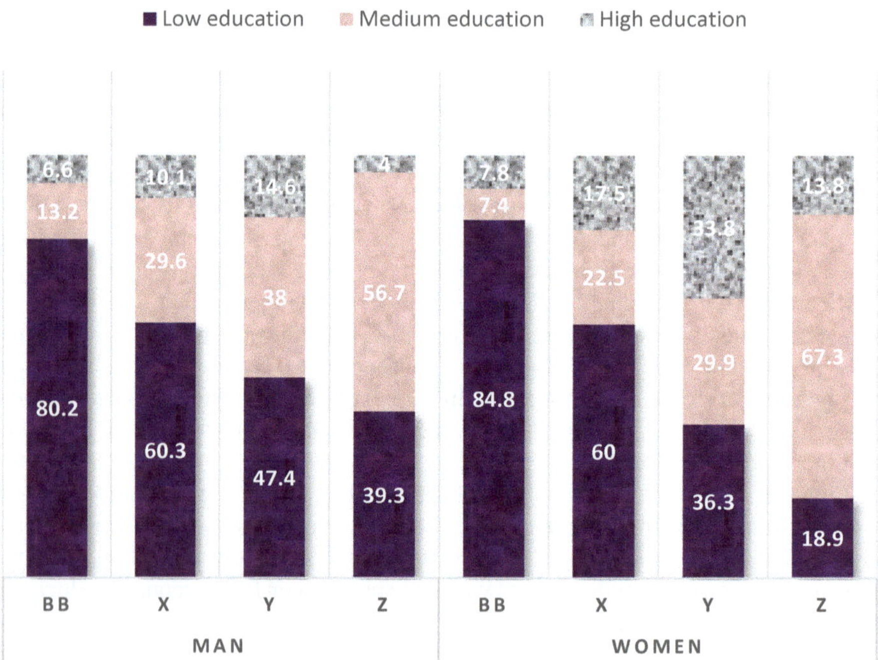


**Fig. 1** Workers in Indonesia by level of education and sex. *Source* Sakernas, 2021; BB is Baby Boomers

factor that affects the difference in education levels between men and women is the entry of men into the labor market is greater than that of women. Based on Susenas 2017 data, 18.7% of men did not continue their education on the grounds of working, while 13.6% of women did.

Based on the use of the internet for work, around 33.4% of workers use the internet for work. The proportion of Generation Z using the internet for work is 44.3%, while the baby boomers are only 12.5%. The younger the generation, the greater the level of internet use for work. Generations Y and Z are generations that were born simultaneously with technological advances, so they are accustomed to using technology in their work [12]. Even though they weren't born in a time of technological advancement, some Generation X workers still use the internet for work because they can learn to use the technology. The ability to use the internet for work decreases in the baby boomer generation as they age, so they find it difficult to keep up with mastery and use the internet for work (Table 2).

Education level is a major factor in using the internet for work. The majority of highly educated workers across all generations use the internet for work (83.4%). The proportion of highly educated Generation X, Y, and Z workers who use the internet at work looks almost the same. This situation shows that the use of the internet in the higher education group has occurred since Generation X. A lower proportion occurs in the generation of highly educated baby boomers. A different situation occurs for low-educated workers, where only a small proportion uses the internet for work.

# 4 The Feature of Multi-generational Workers

## *4.1 Workers by Main Industry*

Based on employment, the agricultural sector is the mainstay of work for all generations with low education, especially the baby boomers generation (56%) the percentage is lower for Generation X (44.3%), Generation Y (39.1%), and Generation Z (32.8%). However, there is a tendency to decrease the proportion of the workforce in the agricultural sector from baby boomers to Generation Z. The younger the generation, the less work in the agricultural sector. To be attractive to the younger generation, the agricultural sector must develop from a technology-poor one to one that uses technology [13]. The level of income of workers in the agricultural sector must also be competitive and ensure welfare.

The industrial sector absorbs more workers from generation Z, both those with low, middle, and high education compared to generations X and Y. Generation Z with low education absorbs 15.1% in the industrial sector and 18.1% with secondary education, while those with higher education are 6.1%. Younger age with a stronger workforce is one of the factors that many Generation Z absorb in the industrial sector. In recruiting workers, companies and industries limit young people, especially those with low and middle education (Table 3).

**Table 2** Workers in Indonesia by level of education and use of the internet at work

| Education | | Internet_users (%) | | *N* |
|---|---|---|---|---|
| | | Yes | No | |
| Low | Baby boomers | 4.9 | 95.1 | 55,335 |
| | Generasi X | 12.6 | 87.4 | 100,092 |
| | Generasi Y | 20.5 | 79.5 | 62,195 |
| | Generasi Z | 23.6 | 76.4 | 11,421 |
| | Others | 1.1 | 98.9 | 3675 |
| | Total | 13.2 | 86.8 | 232,718 |
| Medium | Baby boomers | 31.0 | 69.0 | 7651 |
| | Generasi X | 43.3 | 56.7 | 45,148 |
| | Generasi Y | 50.6 | 49.4 | 50,292 |
| | Generasi Z | 53.3 | 46.7 | 21,839 |
| | Others | 16.8 | 83.2 | 179 |
| | Total | 47.2 | 52.8 | 125,109 |
| High | Baby boomers | 70.8 | 29.2 | 4734 |
| | Generasi X | 85.2 | 14.8 | 21,077 |
| | Generasi Y | 84.0 | 16.0 | 30,597 |
| | Generasi Z | 85.1 | 14.9 | 2748 |
| | Others | 29.0 | 71.0 | 62 |
| | Total | 83.4 | 16.6 | 59,218 |
| Total | baby boomers | 12.5 | 87.5 | 67,720 |
| | Generasi X | 30.1 | 69.9 | 166,317 |
| | Generasi Y | 44.7 | 55.3 | 143,084 |
| | Generasi Z | 46.3 | 53.7 | 36,008 |
| | Others | 2.2 | 97.8 | 3916 |
| | Total | 33.4 | 66.6 | 417,045 |

*Source* Sakernas, 2021

In the trade sector, the percentage of Generation Z with low education is absorbed by the trade sector as much as 16.2%, more than Generation X, Y, and Boomers. Likewise, Generation Z, which is educated, is prominently absorbed in the trade sector (28.5%) which is higher than Generation X, Y, and boomers. This is influenced by advances in digital technology in business and transportation businesses. Digital-based (online) transportation such as Gojek, and Grab has been rife since 2011. In 2011, most of Generation Z was around 23 or 24 years old, many of whom were involved in the world of business and commerce with the support of digital technology. Advances in digital technology in the world of business and business encourage Generation Z to enter the business world.

**Table 3** Workers in Indonesia by generation and main industry

| Education | Generation | Main industry (%) | | | *N* |
|---|---|---|---|---|---|
| | | Agriculture | Manufacture | Services | |
| Low | Baby boomers | 56.1 | 15.5 | 28.4 | 55,335 |
| | X | 44.3 | 23.0 | 32.7 | 100,092 |
| | Y | 39.1 | 27.8 | 33.1 | 62,194 |
| | Z | 32.8 | 31.7 | 35.4 | 11,421 |
| | Others | 68.0 | 11.1 | 21.0 | 3675 |
| | Total | 45.5 | 22.7 | 31.7 | 232,717 |
| Medium | Baby boomers | 30.1 | 15.8 | 54.1 | 7651 |
| | X | 20.0 | 22.7 | 57.3 | 45,148 |
| | Y | 16.4 | 24.3 | 59.3 | 50,292 |
| | Z | 10.5 | 26.2 | 63.3 | 21,839 |
| | Others | 39.7 | 9.5 | 50.8 | 179 |
| | Total | 17.6 | 23.5 | 59.0 | 125,109 |
| High | Baby boomers | 15.8 | 5.7 | 78.6 | 4734 |
| | X | 3.6 | 7.1 | 89.2 | 21,077 |
| | Y | 3.5 | 7.7 | 88.8 | 30,596 |
| | Z | 2.8 | 9.9 | 87.3 | 2748 |
| | Others | 30.6 | 4.8 | 64.5 | 62 |
| | Total | 4.5 | 7.4 | 88.0 | 59,217 |
| Total | Baby boomers | 50.3 | 14.9 | 34.8 | 67,720 |
| | X | 32.6 | 20.9 | 46.5 | 166,317 |
| | Y | 23.5 | 22.3 | 54.2 | 143,082 |
| | Z | 17.0 | 26.7 | 56.3 | 36,008 |
| | Others | 66.1 | 10.9 | 23.0 | 3916 |
| | Total | 31.3 | 20.8 | 47.9 | 417,043 |

*Source* Sakernas, 2021

Trading businesses, such as food, clothing, and so on, cooperate with online transportation in distributing to consumers. The most widespread digital movement today is the startup business. Startup businesses that are developing in Indonesia are leading to businesses based on the internet, websites, and technology. Until 2016, there were 2000 local startups in Indonesia, which grew because they were inspired by the success of previous startup businesses [14]. Digital technology is also used in promoting businesses and businesses through digital, such as gadgets, and websites. The results of the Puskakom UI study by Asiati et al. [14] noted that from the demographic aspect, 49% of internet users were in the 18–25 year age range with an average education at the high school (SMA) level.

## 4.2 Wages

Theoretically, the wage level is influenced by the level of education and labor productivity. The amount of wage rate reflects the level of worker productivity. In the current era of globalization, the use of internet technology at work can increase work efficiency and productivity. On the other hand, the ability to use internet technology is usually owned by those who have a higher level of education. Generation Y or the millennial generation is the first generation to grow up in the era of technological progress. By far they are seen as the most educated generation in the workforce and represent the fastest growing segment of the workforce. (https://www.indeed.com/career-advice/career-development/generations-in-the-workplace). BPS data shows that 78% of Generation Y and 79% of Generation Z use the internet. Then as many as 93% of the highly educated Generations X, Y, and Z use the internet, while in the boomer generation, it is slightly lower at 88%. The same trend is found in those with secondary education, but the percentage is smaller (Fig. 2).

In one workplace, it is possible for a workforce consisting of various generations to work side by side. Each generation has different characteristics, both educational background and experience. Mastery and use of the internet at work can affect the level of wages. In Fig. 3, it can be seen that workers who master the internet have a higher wage rate than those who do not master the internet. Across all generations, highly educated workers have higher wages than those with lower and middle education. This condition occurs both for internet users and not.

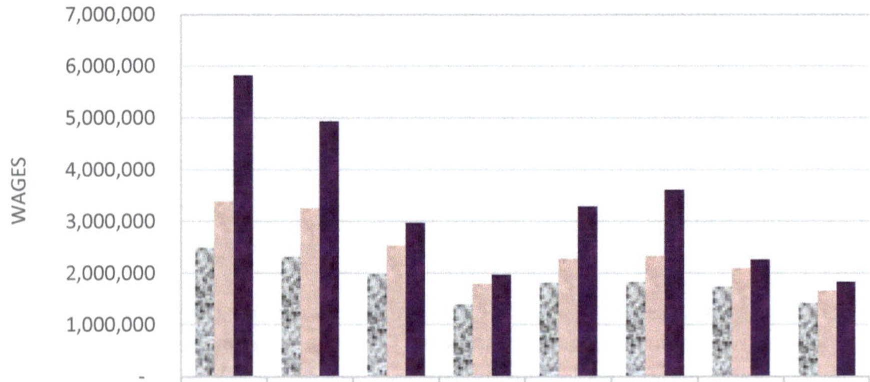


| | Internet user | | | | Not internet user | | | |
|---|---|---|---|---|---|---|---|---|
| | BB | X | Y | Z | BB | X | Y | Z |
| Low education | 2,492,1 | 2,317,1 | 1,984,4 | 1,391,4 | 1,817,1 | 1,830,7 | 1,738,5 | 1,414,4 |
| Medium education | 3,383,8 | 3,251,4 | 2,534,3 | 1,797,2 | 2,282,3 | 2,330,3 | 2,092,0 | 1,659,6 |
| High education | 5,816,2 | 4,932,4 | 2,970,9 | 1,970,3 | 3,284,5 | 3,600,6 | 2,258,0 | 1,827,9 |

**Fig. 2** Workers in Indonesia by wages, internet usage for work, generation, and education. *Source* Sakernas, 2021; BB is Baby boomers

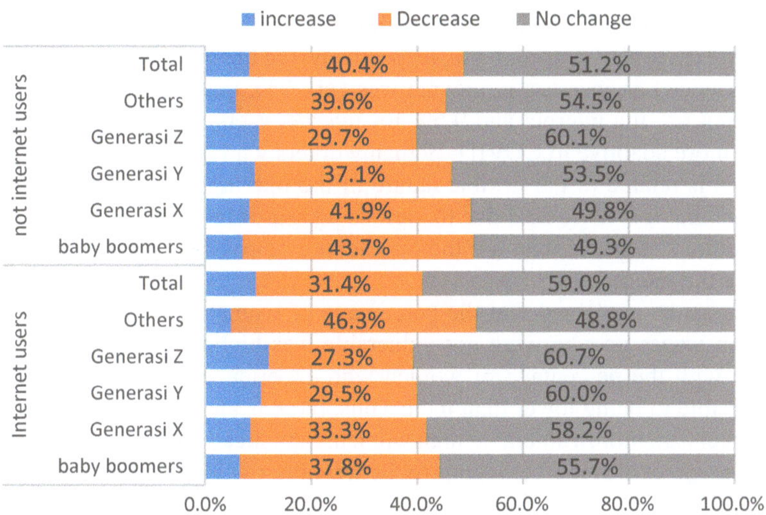


**Fig. 3** Condition of income of workers in Indonesia compare with August 2020. *Source* National Labor Force Survey, 2021

Figure 3 also shows that at the same level of education, the average wage for baby boomers is higher than for generations X, Y, and even generation Z. This shows that age and work experience have a significant effect on wage levels. Generations Y and Z even though they have good internet technology adaptability, have less work experience than workers from the baby boomers generation who have longer work experience. Rood [15] in his research on generational diversity in the tourism industry shows that baby boomers have a very good work ethic, are passionate at work, are responsible, and are financially supported.

## 5 Vulnerability to the Pressure (COVID-19)

COVID-19 has impacted the condition of the labor market in the world. ILO [16] found that in the first half of 2020, as a result of the COVID-19 crisis, downward pressure on the level or growth rate of average wages was observed in two-thirds of the countries for which recent data are available, in other countries, average wages increased, largely artificially as a reflection of the substantial job losses among lower-paid workers. In Indonesia, Ngadi et al. [17] found that COVID-19 caused job loss and decreased income of workers. This impact varies according to province, and main industry.

The various impacts of COVID-19 on workers in Indonesia also depend on digital technology. Figure 3 shows that the income of all workers, internet users and not internet users, is declining when compared to 2020. However, the percentage of workers who experience this decline is higher among workers who do not use the internet, which is 40.4% and 31.4%, respectively. On the other hand, the percentage that experienced an increase in income was very low, that is about 8% of workers who did not use the internet and 9.6% for internet users. That shows that internet users are more adaptive to COVID-19 than workers who do not use the internet for work. This is related to the flexible nature of the internet, not limited by time and location so that it is more adaptive to various pressures including COVID-19. In all the generations, workers who use the internet are more adaptive than workers who do not use the internet.

It can also be explained that the percentage of women who did not experience changes in wages or who were not vulnerable was higher than that of men. This is in line with the percentage of women who experience a decrease in wages or are vulnerable to being lower than men. Thus, there is an indication that in general male workers are more vulnerable than women. Statistically, this is possible because the percentage of women belonging to Generation z is higher than men, which is 9.24% compared to 8.31%. Qualitatively, another possibility that could be the cause is that women's wages were lower than men's before the COVID-19 pandemic, so companies are more likely to reduce men's wages. Another possibility is that women are more concentrated in companies that have not been hit too hard, such as garment, cigarette, tobacco, food-beverage, footwear, and other community service businesses on a small and medium scale.

## 6 Conclusion

In 2021, the workforce in Indonesia consists of four generations, namely baby boomers, X, Y, and Z. Among these four generations, Generation X, or workers born 1965–1980 are dominant in the labor market. Most of the baby boomers have retired. In the next 15 years, Generation Y will become dominant in the job market followed by Generation Z because most of Generation X have retired. Mapping the composition of the workforce between generations is an important part of workforce development because each generation has different attitudes and behaviors toward work.

The younger the generation, the more familiar they are with using the internet for work. However, in terms of wages, the workforce of the baby boomer generation is still higher than other generations. This means that the period of service remains the main consideration in providing workers' wages. In addition, the agricultural sector is becoming a sector that is increasingly being abandoned by Generations Z and Y. Various programs need to be carried out so that the agricultural sector is attractive to the younger generation. Technology-based agriculture and using the internet need to be developed. Cross-generational collaboration in various government institutions and private companies is very important.

## References


1. Glass A (2007) Understanding generational differences for competitive success. Ind Commer Train 39(2):98–103. https://doi.org/10.1108/00197850710732424
2. Smola KW, Sutton CD (2002) Generational differences: revisiting generational work values for the new millennium. J Organ Behav 23:363–382
3. Howe N, Strauss W (2000) Millennials rising: the next great generation. In: Matson RJ (ed) Cartoons. Vintage Books, New York
4. Kratz H (2013) Maximizing millennials: the who, how, and why of managing gen Y [Thesis]. University of North Carolina, United States
5. Levickalitė R (2010) Generations X, Y, Z: how social networks form the concept of the world without borders (The case of Lithuania). LIMES 3(2):170–183
6. Farkačová L (2020) Cross-generational cooperation in the workplace development of networks of cross-generational teams of individual EU states, as a tool to achieve the EU's competitive advantage in the global market
7. Kaifi BA, Nafei WA, Khanfar NM, Kaifi MM (2012) A multi-generational workforce: managing and understanding millennials. Int J Bus Manage 7(24):2012
8. Binus (2022) https://onlinelearning.binus.ac.id/2021/12/06/begini-perbedaan-generasi-baby-boomers-x-y-z-dan-alpha/(diakses 12 Mei 2022)
9. Sobrino-De Toro I, Labrador-Fernández J, De Nicolás VL (2019) Generational diversity in the workplace: psychological empowerment and flexibility in Spanish companies. Front Psychol. www.frontiersin.org
10. Joy A, Haynes BP (2011) Office design for the multi-generational knowledge workforce. J Corporate Real Estate 13(4):216–232
11. Okros A (2019) Harnessing the potential of digital post-millennials in the future workplace. Canadian Forces College Canada, Toronto
12. Latkovikja MT, Popovska MB (2010) How millennials, Gen Z, and technology are changing the workplace design? In: Proceedings of the 6th International Workshop on Socio-Technical Perspective in IS Development (STPIS 2020), June 8–9, 2020
13. Gandasari D, Dwidienawati D, Suwardi S, Pertamasari RB (2020) Generation Z working interest in agriculture sector: the case for vocational school students in Bogor. Int J Adv Sci Tech 29(3):7697–7703. Retrieved from http://sersc.org/journals/index.php/IJAST/article/view/8233
14. Asiati D, Aji GB, Ningrum V, Ngadi N, Triyono T, Kurniawan FE, Aruan NL, Purba YA (2018) Employment opportunities and human resources development in digital era: a case study in industrial sector. J Indones Soc Sci Humanit 8(2):159–167
15. Rood AS (2011) Understanding generational diversity in the workplace: what resorts can and are doing. J Tourism Insight 1(1)
16. ILO (2020) Global wage report 2020–21: wages and minimum wages in the time of COVID-19. ILO, Geneva
17. Ngadi MR, Purba YA (2020) The impact of COVID-19 on worker layoffs and income in Indonesia. Jurnal kependud Indonesia

# Effectiveness of Vocational Training on Minimizing School—Job Mismatch

**Beni Teguh Gunawan, Ivan Lilin Suryono, Hennigusnia, and Ardhian Kurniawati**

**Abstract** Job mismatch is one of the big issues regarding the labor market in Indonesia. The Mismatch is defined as the unsuitable job level and type for formal education output. According to research, the mismatch in Indonesia has been getting bigger in some sectors for the last 5 years. This problem can be caused by the rapid transformation of the demand side and/or unadaptive in supply-side skill facing to the transformation. Government policies try to minimize the mismatch in various ways, and one of the policies is vocational training. This research aims to determine whether vocational training can minimize the school-job mismatch. Individual data of the labor force from the National Labor Force Survey (Sakernas) is used to inspect this objective. As Sakernas held twice a year, in February and August, we use the August publication data because of the size of sample survey data. This research analyzes a quantitative logit regression model with the probability of mismatch as the dependent variable. The mismatch between school and job measures using vertical mismatch with vocational training as the dummy variable.

**Keywords** Vocational training · School · Jobs · Mismatch

## 1 Introduction

There is voluminous research about education and job mismatch. Job mismatch is defined as the failure of the formal education regarding the needs of industry sector. This failure is related to the inability of education to be adaptive to the time

B. T. Gunawan (✉) · I. L. Suryono · Hennigusnia · A. Kurniawati
National Research and Innovation Agency, Jakarta, Indonesia
e-mail: beni.teguh.gunawan@brin.go.id

I. L. Suryono
e-mail: ivan.lilin.suryono@brin.go.id

A. Kurniawati
e-mail: ardhian.kurniawati@brin.go.id



Nawawi et al. (eds.), *Managing Disruption and Developing Resilience for a Better Southeast Asia*, Springer Proceedings in Humanities and Social Sciences,
https://doi.org/10.1007/978-981-96-2116-3_14

changes [1]. Researchers found that mismatch does not only occur in developing countries with relatively lagging education systems compared to developed countries. However, in some developed countries, the mismatch is still a serious problem [2]. For example, the mismatch in the Netherlands has tended to increase due to the rise in supply of higher education graduates in the last decade [3]. Different from Cabus & Somers [3], Morgado et al. [4] investigated the mismatch conditions in several developed countries in Europe actually found that most of the mismatches were caused by the lower workers' skills compared to the demands of the labor market, known as undereducation.

The mismatch has a wide impact on the economy. At the individual level, optimal productivity by each worker is not obtained due to inappropriate skills [5]. The worst negative impact related to productivity is generally caused by a mismatch in the category of undereducation or education that is lower than the job requirements [4]. The negative impact of mismatch are not only takes by the company side, but also by the workers. Mismatch workers case don't have the proper level of wages [6], job satisfaction [7], and workers' career sustainability [8].

Mismatch case in Indonesia is caused by the shift in the composition of the workforce. The trend of the highly educated workforce in Indonesia has been increasing in recent decades [9]. In comparison, 20 years ago the labor structure in Indonesia was dominated by junior high school education or less. Based on BPS data in the period between 2008 and 2018, the number of graduates from higher education increased to 131.33%, vocational school graduates 67.47%, and high school graduates 28.31%. Meanwhile, the proportion of junior high school workers and below continues to decline [6]. In 2015, for example, as many as 18.17% of the unemployed at that time were junior high school graduates. When compared to current conditions, the workforce is dominated by the high school graduates, with 5% of the unemployed being high school graduates [10].

Another factor regarding the high level of mismatch in Indonesia is the heterogeneity of demand for skills in the labor market. Each sector in the labor market has its characteristics that require specific skills. Prayudhani [10] found that the level of mismatch in Indonesia is different by sector. According to the study, in general, the mismatch rate in Indonesia is 44.8%, with 18.83% working above their competence and the rest 35.48% working below their competence. If viewed by sector, government services have the highest level of non-compliance, which is 74.24%. Meanwhile, the education services sector has the lowest level of non-compliance at 27.5%.

Cases of mismatch can be grouped into 3 types, namely excess education, lack of education, and occupation mismatch. According to Safuan and Nazara [11], excess education indicates a condition in which supply of labor has a higher qualification than market demand. On the other hand, lack of education is a condition when market demand is higher than the skills possessed by the workforce. While the occupation mismatch is related to irrelevant education major and the job sector.

The government continues to strive to minimize the negative impact of the mismatch. The Indonesian government develops the policies to both prevent and repress the mismatch in Indonesian labor market. Preventive policy is reforming the formal education curriculum to be more adaptive to times changing. Repressive policy is related to the quality improvement of graduates and linking skill suitability during the school-job transition. At the repressive side, vocational training conducted by both government and private agencies is expected to be the right solution. This study aims to identify the effectiveness of vocational training, both organized by government and private agencies. The scope of this study is only for pre-employment training. The skill improvement during employment is not included in this study.

## 2 Literature Review

There are at least two theories that discuss mismatch in the labor market. One of them is the theory used by Hartog [12] which states that the mismatch of qualifications and work of the workforce is a temporary condition caused by imperfect information. The workforce does not have sufficient information about available job vacancies and will try to find jobs that are more suitable to their qualifications or skills (searching and matching). Therefore, the incidence of overeducation is often found in new workers who are going through school-to-work transition phase. This theory is used in several studies, including [4, 7, 13].

The second theory is about the labor surplus that occurs in the labor market. Labor surplus occurs because of the high supply of labor. Cabus and Somers [3] is one of the studies that use this theory. The research assumes that mismatch occurs due to skill shifts in the job market. The shift in question is the dominance of certain education graduates who replace the role of lower education in the labor market. As a result of this shift, the labor market responded too late, so that workers with higher skill levels were forced to accept jobs that required substandard skills.

The second theory is more in line with conditions in Indonesia considering that currently, Indonesia is also experiencing a labor surplus. Historically, the structure of the workforce in Indonesia has undergone various shifts. In the early decades of the country's formation, the dominance of a low-educated workforce was still high. The 1990s were as a period of transformation from the the primary sector to the secondary sector [14]. This condition is in line with the economic transformation from the agricultural sector to the industrial sector. There has been a decline in demand for labor from the agricultural sector and shifting to the industrial sector [15]. This shift in the composition of the labor market impacted abundant supply of labor at a high level. The imperfect labor market condition to accommodate specific skills makes job seekers downgrade their standard of job.

Competition in the job market that has an impact on mismatch conditions can be caused by several things. Labor market indicators used to identify competition include the number of labor force, percentage of formal workers, and industrial sector workers. The number of labor force describes the competition to enter the labor market, while the percentage of formal workers and industrial sector workers is assumed to be an indicator of the chances of success in entering the ideal labor market. In addition to macro variables, micro variables attached to each individual worker also determine the mismatch process. These micro variables include education level [16], age [17], gender [7, 13], and marital status [18].

## 3 Data and Method

This study uses data from the National Labor Force Survey (Sakernas) in August 2019. Sakernas is conducted by National Statistical Agency of Indonesia. Sakernas data is individual survey data for the best employment indicators currently available in Indonesia. Sakernas is conducted twice per year, in February and August. The August data provides a more detailed estimate down to the district/city level. In addition, the August Sakernas publication took a much larger sample than February. Another consideration for the use of data for 2019 is because that year has not been affected by the COVID-19 pandemic.

The classification of positions at Sakernas is often known as the Indonesian Standard Classification of Occupation (KBJI). KBJI also has several versions, of which the latest version is KBJI 2014. KBJI 2014 was adapted from the International Standard Classification of Occupation (ISCO) 2008. The code in the one-digit KBJI is divided into 10 groups, starting with code 0 for members of military and police, up to code 9 for blue collar workers and related. This research does not include the position groups of military and police members because the recruitment mechanism is different from that of workers in general.

To inspect the matching based on education and occupation, the research used a vertical mismatch method. The vertical mismatch is calculated by adjusting the education level of the workforce with the position occupied. The level of education is seen from the highest education attainment. While the positions occupied are seen from the ISCO adopted in the KBJI 2014. All employees are selected based on job tenure and work experience. Mismatch criteria are taken for workers with less than one year of job tenure and no previous work experience.

Workers with qualifications that do not pass elementary school will be declared matched if they have positions in the lowest group, codes 8 and 9, while other positions are included in the overeducation category. Likewise, elementary school graduates will be categorized as a match if they occupy positions with codes 7, 8, or 9, and are declared overeducated if they occupy other positions. Junior high school education equivalent is declared match if occupy positions with codes 6 and 7, declared overeducation if occupy positions with codes 1 to 5, and declared undereducation if occupy positions with codes 8 and 9, and so on as shown in Table 1.

The empirical statistical method used to calculate the effect of independent variables on the probability of occurrence of the value of the dependent variable is logistic regression. Logistic regression has a binary response. The response is usually coded with 1 for a successful event and 0 for a failure event. As explained earlier, in the context of this paper, a successful event is a condition where job seekers get a job and 0 vice versa. According to Agresti [19], the equation model for logistic regression is:

**Table 1** Measurement of *Matching* between position and education

| Education | Position | | | | | | | | |
|---|---|---|---|---|---|---|---|---|---|
| | 1 | 2 | 3 | 4 | 5 | 6 | 7 | 8 | 9 |
| Maximal elementary school equivalent | *Undereducation* | | | | | | | | *Matching* |
| Junior high school equivalent | *Undereducation* | | | *Matching* | | | | | *Over education* |
| Senior high school (General) equivalent | *Undereducation* | | | *Matching* | | | | | *Over education* |
| Senior high school (Vocational) equivalent | *Undereducation* | | | *Matching* | | | | | *Over education* |
| Diplomas 1, 2, and 3 | *Matching* | *Under education* | *Matching* | *Overeducation* | | | | | |
| Undergraduate and postgraduate | *Matching* | | *Overeducation* | | | | | | |

*Source* [23]
*Notes* 1: Legislative Officers, Senior Officials and Managers, 2: Professionals, 3: Technicians and Assistant Professionals, 4: Administrative Personnel, 5: Service Businesses and Sales Personel in Shops and Markets, 6: Agricultural Business Personnel and Animal Husbandry, 7: Processing and Craft Workers and related, 8: Machine Operators and Assemblies, and 9: Blue Collar and Related Workers

$$log\left(\frac{p_i}{1-p_i}\right) = \alpha + \beta_1 dTraining_i + \beta_2 dVocational_i + \beta_3 dVocational_i * dTraining_i + \gamma_i X_i \quad (1)$$

where dTrainingi is a dummy indicating that a worker has received previous training. This dummy variable is coded 1 if worker *i* has received training and 0 otherwise. dVocationali is a dummy variable for the highest level of education attainment in the category of vocational education. In Indonesia, there is vocational education that is prepared for those who will directly enter the labor market, including vocational education and diploma level. The model also includes an interaction variable between vocational education and training. This variable is coded 1 if a worker has vocational education and has attended training. Other variables included in the model are variables that indicate the demographics of the respondents such as age, age squared, marital status, gender, and the highest level of education completed. In addition to demographic variables, the model also includes provincial-level macro variables which aim to determine the labor market conditions of the province where the respondent works. The variables are the number of the provincial workforce, the percentage of industrial sector workers, and the percentage of formal workers.

The operational definitions of control variables in logistic regression that will be used in this study are.

| | | |
|---|---|---|
| Labor force | : | The absolute number of the workforce in the province where the respondent lives |
| Industry | : | Percentage of respondent working in the industrial sector in the province where the respondent lives |
| Formal | : | Percentage of formal workers who work in the province where the respondent lives |
| Age | : | Age variable, which indicates the age of the respondent at the time the survey was conducted, the age unit measurement is in years with the rounding down option |
| Agesq | : | Age variable squared, to determine the quadratic effect of the variable age |
| Marstat | : | *Dummy* variable of marital status, code 1 indicates that respondents are married and 0 otherwise. Married status includes married, divorced, or separated |
| Sex | : | *Dummy* variable, indicate gender, 1 for male and, 0 otherwise |

Logistic regression interpretation is to compare the probability of success and failure or we used to call it as the odds ratio (OR). The odd ratio is used to interpret the number of times the probability of success with certain treatments in the independent variable [20]. In the case of mismatch, 0 is the condition where the employee is mismatched and 1 is the matched worker. Therefore, the logistic regression interpretation is the probability of a worker being matched with a certain treatment in the independent variable has the higher odds ratio than the one without treatment. Measurement of significance in logistic regression using the Z statistic. The probability Z value which is smaller than 5%.

## 4 Results and Discussion

The number of individual units of analysis used in this study is 4932,931 people. This number represents workers who have worked less than one year and have no previous work experience. This study assumes that the group of workers is a fresh graduate which reflects the output of formal education. The descriptive analysis shows that participation in training has no impact on the level of job matching. The sample of respondents who were training participants was only 7.41% of the total respondents. Only 5.45% of fresh graduate workers who have attended training match, the level of education and the position occupied. Meanwhile, 8.59% who never attended the training experienced conformity (Fig. 1).

Meanwhile, based on the highest level of education completed, the largest number of respondents had general high school education and the equivalent. Of the majority, 43.56% of them matched. Based on all levels of education, the highest matching rate is the equivalent of elementary school graduates reaching 51.87%. Meanwhile, the

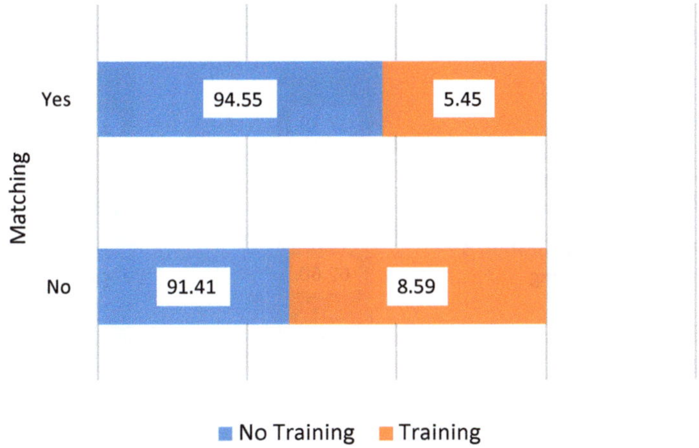


**Fig. 1** Matching level with training participation

lowest matching level is the undergraduate/postgraduate level where all of them are not matched with the position occupied (Table 2).

Figure 2 describes the matching level of the combination of workers who graduated from vocational education and had attended training with workers who were not graduates of vocational education and had received training. From the results of data processing, it can be seen that workers who are not vocational graduates and have received training have a higher matching rate (58.79%) compared to the matching rate of workers who graduated from vocational education and have received training (41.21%). Similar to the matching level, the discrepancy level also describes similar conditions. Workers who are not vocational education graduates and have attended the training have a higher dissonance rate (62.60%) compared to the group of workers with vocational education graduates who have received training (37.39%).

**Table 2** Education level and matching level of workers

| Education level | Matching | |
|---|---|---|
| | No | Yes |
| Less than elementary school | 63.13 | 36.87 |
| Elementary school and equivalent | 48.13 | 51.87 |
| Secondary school and equivalent | 68.78 | 31.22 |
| General senior high school and equivalent | 56.44 | 43.56 |
| Vocational senior high school | 55.33 | 44.67 |
| Diploma 1 and 2 | 57.90 | 42.10 |
| 3-year diploma | 55.26 | 44.74 |
| Undergraduate and postgraduate | 100.00 | 0.00 |

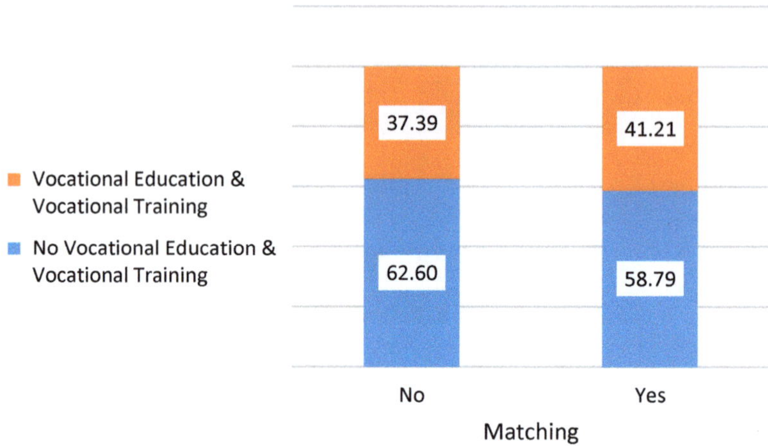


**Fig. 2** Vocational training and education combination with worker matching level

The results of the logistic regression showed that all variables showing individual characteristics were significant. This means that all these variables affect the matching. Meanwhile, the province's macro variables are not entirely significant. The main issue regarding the effectiveness of training shows that vocational training has a significant effect on matching. However, when viewed from the value of OR value is relatively smaller than the other variables. The OR interpretation of this variable is that workers with training have a matching rate of 0.5 times or 50% higher than those without training. Meanwhile, the combination of vocational training and vocational education provides the best results for matching in the job market. Both combinations have a matching rate of 1.88 times or a 188% higher probability of being matched (Table 3).

**Table 3** Odds ratio of effectiveness of training on matching

| Variable | Odds ratio | *Z* value | *P* value |
|---|---|---|---|
| Vocational training | 0.50421 | −8.83 | 0.000 |
| Vocational education | 1.17047 | 3.60 | 0.000 |
| Vocational training*Vocational education | 1.88937 | 4.96 | 0.000 |
| Age | 0.96626 | −4.76 | 0.000 |
| Age_square | 1.00033 | 3.70 | 0.000 |
| Sex | 1.08035 | 2.47 | 0.014 |
| Marstat | 1.11378 | 2.43 | 0.015 |
| Laborforce | 1.00000 | 0.80 | 0.422 |
| Industry | 0.99444 | −1.24 | 0.214 |
| Formal | 1.00068 | 0.35 | 0.728 |
| _cons | 1.14011 | 1.00 | 0.318 |

If we look at the results of the empirical analysis, it is found that training does not have a significant impact on increasing the chances of matching workers. Training has a lower level of effectiveness compared to vocational schools. The combination of vocational schools and training provides a better impact to minimize mismatches.

This problem has comprehensive implications for the improvement of education in Indonesia. On the vocational education side, vocational teachers in Indonesia found it difficult to implement the curriculum in a number of areas [21]. This difficulty is related to several indicators of success assessment required by the government. The Indonesian government changed the ratio of senior high schools and vocational education from 70: 30 to 30: 70. The establishment of a new school was not balanced with a feasibility study, and this impacted graduates in finding a job. They learned approaches that tended to be theoretical and less relevant in the labor market. In addition, 74% of students were bored during learning due to numerous social lessons. Some of the challenges faced were inadequate facilities, teachers, and industry support [22].

Meanwhile, from the point of view of providing training, after-work training is considered more effective in enhancing a worker's career [8]. This effectiveness relates to specific things that are urgent to learn in specific types of work. The on-the-job training model during work is claimed to increase worker productivity [2].

## 5 Conclusion

Empirical analysis results found that vocational training impacts significantly in parameters but not in number. It impacts 0.5 times higher than the labor without training on job matching. In another view, vocational education gives a better impact to mismatch with 1.17 times higher regarding the general equivalent school. The combination between vocational school and training produces the highest impact on job matching, which is 1.88 times more likely to match. This condition illustrates that vocational education graduates have the competencies required by the labor market. However, vocational education alone is not enough, job training is still needed to improve work competence.

Recommendations to minimize school-job mismatch are: improve the effectiveness of vocational education and training, both organized by government and private agencies. Vocational education should prioritize practical training which is very dependent on educational tools/facilities. Therefore, it is important to carry out improvements and reforms in the field of vocational education and training in an integrated and integrated manner, namely by collaborating between industry/companies and vocational education institutions. One of the forms of collaboration is to create a joint curriculum. So that graduates have the competencies required by industry, not only hard skills but also soft skills.

## References


1. Dimian GC, Begu LS, Jablonsky J (2017) Unemployment and labour market mismatch in the European Union Countries. Zbornik Radova Ekonomskog Fakultet au Rijeci 35(1):13–44. https://doi.org/10.18045/zbefri.2017.1.13
2. Georgellis Y, Lange T (2007) Participation in continuous, on-the-job training and the impact on job satisfaction: longitudinal evidence from the German labour market. Int J Hum Resour Manag 18(6):969–985. https://doi.org/10.1080/09585190701321112
3. Cabus SJ, Somers MA (2018) Mismatch between education and the labour market in the Netherlands: is it a reality or a myth? The employers' perspective. Stud High Educ 43(11):1854–1867. https://doi.org/10.1080/03075079.2017.1284195
4. Morgado A, Sequeira TN, Santos M, Ferreira-Lopes A, Reis AB (2016) Measuring labour mismatch in Europe. Soc Indic Res 129(1):161–179. https://doi.org/10.1007/s11205-015-1097-0
5. Turrell A, Speigner B, Djumalieva J, Copple D, Thurgood J (2018) Using job vacancies to understand the effects of labour market mismatch on UK output and productivity [Online]. Available: www.bankofengland.co.uk/working-paper/staff-working-papers
6. Hasibuan E, Handayani D (2021) Pengaruh qualification mismatch terhadap Upah Tenaga Kerja Di Indonesia. Jurnal Ekonomi dan Pembangunan 29(1):1–16. https://doi.org/10.14203/jep.29.1.2021.1-16
7. Mcguinness S, Sloane PJ (2009) Labour market mismatch among UK graduates: an analysis using REFLEX data. Swansea [Online]. Available: http://hdl.handle.net/10419/50044www.econstor.eu
8. Prasetyo I, Aliyyah N, Rusdiyanto, Tjaraka H, Kalbuana N, ur Rochman AS (2021) Vocational training has an influence on employee career development: a case study Indonesia. Acad Strat Manag J 20(2):1–14. https://doi.org/10.20944/preprints202104.0153.v1
9. di Gropelo E, Kruse A, Tandon P (2011) Skills for the labor market in Indonesia: trends in demand, gaps, and supply. The World Bank, Washington
10. Prayudhani O (2020) Peta Ketidaksesuain Kualifikasi Sektoral Di Indonesia. Ketenagakerjaan 15(2)
11. Safuan S, Nazara S (2005) Identifikasi Fenomena 'Overeducation' di Pasar Kerja di Indonesia? Jurnal Ekonomi dan Pembangunan Indonesia. https://doi.org/10.21002/jepi.v6i1.152
12. Hartog J (2000) Over-education and earnings: where are we, where should we go? [Online]. Available: www.elsevier.com/locate/econedurev
13. Mavromaras K, Mcguinness S, O'leary N, Sloane P, Wei Z (2013) Job mismatches and labour market outcomes: panel evidence on university graduates. Adelaide
14. Tentua MN, Winarko E (2020) Applying Data Mining to Analysis of Mismatch between Education and Labor Market in Indonesia. In: IOP Conference Series: Materials Science and Engineering, March 2020. vol 771, no. 1. https://doi.org/10.1088/1757-899X/771/1/012020
15. Hill EJ (2005) Work-family facilitation and conflict, working fathers and mothers, work-family stressors and support. J Fam Issues. https://doi.org/10.1177/0192513X05277542
16. di Pietro G, Urwin P (2006) Education and skills mismatch in the Italian graduate labour market. Appl Econ 38(1):79–93. https://doi.org/10.1080/00036840500215303
17. Dimian GC (2015) Economic Insights-trends and challenges labour market mismatches and age group unemployment in Romania and other six CEE countries. Economic Insights—Trends and Challenges
18. Pholphirul P (2017) Educational mismatches and labor market outcomes: evidence from both vertical and horizontal mismatches in Thailand. Education + Training 59(5):534–546
19. Agresti A (2007) An introduction to categorical data analysis. https://doi.org/10.1002/0471249688
20. Hailpern SM, Visintainer PF (2003) Odds ratios and logistic regression: further examples of their use and interpretation

21. Retnawati H, Hadi S, Chandra Nugraha A (2016) Vocational high school teachers' difficulties in implementing the assessment in curriculum 2013 in Yogyakarta Province of Indonesia [Online]. Available: www.e-iji.net
22. Suharno S, Pambudi NA, Widiastuti I, Harjanto B (2019) Apprenticeship implementation of productive teacher at vocational school in Indonesia. https://doi.org/10.2991/ictvet-18.2019.20
23. Stoevska, V (2018, October) Measurement of qualifications and skills mismatches of persons in employment. 01 24, 2021, from International Labour Retrieved Organization: https://www.ilo.org/wcmsp5/groups/public/ --- dgreports/ --- stat/documents/meetingdocument/wcms_636052.pdf

# Employment Mismatch Trends in the Digitalization Age: Indonesia Case Studies

**Ivan Lilin Suryono, Beni Teguh Gunawan, Hennigusnia, and Ardhian Kurniawati**

**Abstract** Digitalization has become a phenomenon that has attracted attention in the last few decades. The impact of digitalization is seen in almost all sectors including employment. Disruption and changes on the demand side are forcing the world of employment to transform. The transformation includes the upstream side or the output of the world of education which is an input in the job market. This study aims to look at the mismatch trend in the world of employment in the last decade where digitalization is increasing along with the creation of industry 4.0. This study uses secondary data from the 2011–2020 National Labor Force Survey to see mismatch trends in the world of education and the world of work. Vertical mismatch analysis is used to see the suitability between the level of education and the level of the position occupied. The results show that the mismatch rate of Indonesian workers is still quite high in line with the increasingly rapid development of digitalization in the last decade. Overall, the level of overeducation in Indonesia is higher than the level of undereducation, especially at the level of Academy/Diploma and University education which occupies a portion of more than 50%.

**Keywords** Employment · Mismatch · Digitalization · The world of work

I. L. Suryono (✉) · B. T. Gunawan · Hennigusnia · A. Kurniawati
National Research and Innovation Agency, Jakarta, Indonesia
e-mail: ivan.lilin.suryono@brin.go.id

B. T. Gunawan
e-mail: beni.teguh.gunawan@brin.go.id

Hennigusnia
e-mail: hennigusnia@brin.go.id

A. Kurniawati
e-mail: ardhian.kurniawati@brin.go.id



Nawawi et al. (eds.), *Managing Disruption and Developing Resilience for a Better Southeast Asia*, Springer Proceedings in Humanities and Social Sciences,
https://doi.org/10.1007/978-981-96-2116-3_15

## 1 Introduction

Employment mismatch is still an issue of concern in both developing and developed countries. Globalization, rapid changes in the job market, labor migration, digitalization, and demographic changes have prompted policymakers to pay more attention to these issues. The seriousness of policymakers in responding to the issue of mismatch can be seen among others in the 2030 Agenda for Sustainable Development, particularly in Sustainable Development Goals (SDGs) target 4.4 "*By 2030, substantially increase the number of youth and adults who have relevant skills, including technical and vocational skills, for employment, decent jobs, and entrepreneurship*;" and target 8.5 "*By 2030, achieve full and productive employment and decent work for all women and men, including for young people and persons with disabilities, and equal pay for work of equal value*" [1].

The mismatch is a complex phenomenon that deserves attention because it affects individuals, companies, and output from the labor market and ultimately impacts the economy. A mismatch indicates poor resource utilization. If this condition continues, it can harm workers' and employers' economic and social costs [2]. Skill mismatch is a mismatch between education and work. Mismatches can have serious consequences for individuals, employers, countries, and regions. At the individual level, mismatch causes a wage penalty, especially for overqualification, which eventually affects job and life satisfaction. In addition, skill deficiencies decrease the chances of landing a job altogether. For entrepreneurs, mismatch has an impact on the decline in productivity and competitiveness of the company, lack of innovation, and high labor turnover. At the country and region level, mismatches can have an impact on unemployment, competitiveness, and investment, which in turn will have an impact on productivity and job creation. Underskilling and under qualification can ultimately slow down economic growth due to a lack of knowledge and skills to adapt to technological changes [2–9].

A mismatch can occur because of the adoption of new technology. The adoption of new technologies requires skills that are not readily available in the job market. This causes a difference in skills between workers and the skills needed in the work they fill [8, 10, 11]. On the other hand, the match between skills and work is very important in adapting to change [5]. Adaptation to new technologies is growing rapidly along with the digitalization that has occurred in the last few decades. Digitization is defined as a change from an analog system to a digital system. This simple change had a huge impact not only on the technology itself, but also on all aspects including the job market. It is undeniable that the digitalization that has occurred in the last few decades has sparked fear, speculation, and how it will impact the future. Possible impacts include growing inequality in the labor market which can be seen in the difference in wages, dualization of the labor market through typical or "precarious" employment, the substitutability of human labor by robots and machines, and emerging new forms of work in the platform of the gig economy [12]. The emergence of new forms of work as one of the impacts of digitalization requires new knowledge that must be continuously updated. Digitization can't be denied and will create gaps in the workers' knowledge and skills. In line with the development of digitalization, the labor market will experience changing requirements. The skills of workers that were previously used to do a job may no longer be suitable due to digitization [13, 14]. Changes in labor market requirements by technological developments with digitization can of course have an impact on mismatch conditions.

As far as we know, there are still not many studies that analyze how the mismatch trend is in line with the development of digitalization. Existing research to date has focused more on overeducation and undereducation, how to measure mismatch, description of mismatch in developing and developed countries, and the impact of mismatch [2, 4, 5, 9, 15–28]. Likewise, research on a mismatch in Indonesia is still very limited. Research that has been carried out includes analyzing mismatch profiles at the national level without distinguishing sectors [3, 29], the national level in all sectors in Indonesia [30], and focusing on the island of Java only [31]. Another study that was conducted in Indonesia analyzed the impact of mismatch on wages and found a wage penalty for mismatch [32–34]. Apart from having an impact on wages, the mismatch would extend the length of time someone was looking for work [35]. The majority of these studies conducted their study at one point in time using one year of data except for research conducted by Safuan and Nazara [34] which uses 3 data series. The majority of studies measure mismatch by comparing years of schooling with the average length of schooling plus the standard deviation of one type of work except those performed by Hasibuan and Dwini [33]. This study will try to fill the research gap on a mismatch in Indonesia by using a longer data series to provide an overview of the mismatch trend in the digitalization era. This study identifies the vertical mismatch by comparing the type of work and the level of education required for that type of work.

## 2 Literature Review

To date, there has been no attempt to develop a unified theory of education or skills mismatch [8]. Several theories can be used to understand the mismatch. These theories include human capital, technological change, career mobility, job search, signal, job competition, labor market segmentation, and assignment theories. The theory that allows and is following conditions in Indonesia is the theory of job competition. The Job Competition Model says that with the limited number of available job vacancies, job seekers will compete to get jobs based on their level of education. This competition will create a job queue based on the training cost of the job seeker. For companies, job seekers with higher education are considered to have lower training costs than job seekers with low education. Therefore, job seekers with higher education can be hired with suitable job specifications (matched) or below their level of education (overeducation) [19].

A mismatch is a condition that describes a mismatch between the skills offered and the skills needed in the world of work [21]. Every individual in the world of work can experience two types of mismatches. The two types of mismatches are qualification mismatch and skill mismatch. Qualification mismatch is a condition where there is a mismatch between job qualifications and the qualifications of the worker occupying the job. Qualification mismatch is divided into two, namely mismatch by the level of education (vertical mismatch) and mismatch by fields of study (horizontal mismatch). Mismatch by the level of education occurs when a worker's level of education is higher than the level of education required to carry out the job (overeducation) and vice versa (undereducation). The horizontal mismatch is a condition where the fields of study of workers do not match the fields of study required to carry out their work. Skill mismatch is a mismatch between the skills possessed by workers and the skills required for their work. Skill mismatch covers all skills or only certain types of skills. The mismatch of certain types of skills in question is a mismatch of job-specific/technical skills, a mismatch of basic skills, and a mismatch of portable skills. Workers are likely to experience conditions where the level and/or type of skill is higher than the level and/or type of skill required to carry out their work (over skilled), and vice versa (underskilled) [2].

Measuring education and skills mismatch between workers and jobs is not an easy task. The literature on skill mismatch is still limited when compared to the literature on qualification mismatch. This is because measuring skill mismatch is more difficult and no skill data is available [8, 36]. Most of the available skills data only cover literacy and numeracy. Even self-assessments of reported skill mismatches are rare [8].

The literature on the measurement of educational mismatch has been found. To measure educational discrepancy, the key component is to compare the education of workers. Verhaest and Omey [9] stated that there are at least four ways to measure educational mismatch. The 4 (four) methods are Direct Self-Assessment (DSA), Indirect Self-Assessment (ISA), Job Analysis, and Realized Matches. In general, the four methods can be grouped into self-declared, normative, or statistical approaches [8, 16, 19]. The normative approach (Job Analysis) uses the assumption of compatibility between education and position by the agreed description, for example, the International Standard Classification of Occupation (ISCO). The Statistical Approach (Realized Matched) is an analysis that objectively determines the level of education required based on the estimated distribution of educational attainment in each occupational group by calculating the average, median, or mode of education of the job in which the worker is employed and then comparing the education level of the worker with the average mean, median or mode. The self-declared approach uses individuals' opinions about whether their job matches their educational level, either through direct questions (Direct Self-Assessment/DSA) or by asking individuals about their current job requirements and then comparing the respondent's education level (Indirect Self-Assessment/ISA) [8, 19].

## 3 Research Method

This study uses secondary data sourced from the National Labor Force Survey (Sakernas) issued by the Central Statistics Agency (BPS). The data to be used is data from 2011 to 2020. This period was chosen because in the last decade, digitalization has entered almost all human activities. Sakernas data is an individual survey containing information on employment indicators, including demographic information, education, occupation, and work experience. This study uses current education and employment information as the main data for measuring mismatch in several business fields.

This research will focus on discrepancies in 3 business fields (sectors). The three business fields are a simplification of the 17 (seventeen) business fields in Indonesia. The simplification was made to make it easier to see the mismatch trend that occurred during the 2011–2020 period. The three business sectors are the primary sector (hereinafter referred to as agriculture in this study) which is a combination of agriculture, forestry, fisheries, mining, and quarrying. The secondary sector (hereinafter referred to as industry) is a combination of the manufacturing sector, electricity and gas supply, water supply, waste management, waste and recycling, and construction. The third sector is the tertiary sector (hereinafter referred to as services) which is a combination of trade, transportation and warehousing, accommodation, information and communication, financial and insurance services, real estate, corporate services, government administration, defense, and mandatory social services, security service, education, health services, social activities, and other services.

In addition to simplifying 17 (seventeen) business fields, this research is also limited to workers with certain criteria. The criteria are workers who work in the formal sector and have a working period of less than one year and have no previous work experience. These considerations are carried out to eliminate the possibility of changes in skills acquired along with work experience and to determine whether the output of education is by the needs of the labor market. This study does not include workers with TNI/POLRI positions in its analysis because TNI/POLRI has a special recruitment mechanism.

The method used to determine the mismatch in this study is a vertical mismatch. The mismatch is measured based on education and position occupied. The level of education is seen from the highest education attainment. Meanwhile, the position occupied is seen from the 2008 Standard Classification of Occupation (ISCO) adopted in the 2014 KBJI. The mismatch criteria refer to the criteria used by Stoevska [2]. Workers with a maximum qualification of elementary school will be declared match if they have positions in the lowest group, namely code 9, while other positions are included in the undereducation category. Likewise for the workforce. Junior high school education equivalent is declared match if they occupy positions with codes 4 to 8, declared overeducation if they occupy positions with code 9, and declared undereducation if they occupy positions with codes 1–3, and so on as shown in Table 1.

**Table 1** Measurement of matching between position and education

| Education | Position | | | | | | | | |
|---|---|---|---|---|---|---|---|---|---|
| | 1 | 2 | 3 | 4 | 5 | 6 | 7 | 8 | 9 |
| Maximal elementary school equivalent | *Undereducation* | | | | | | | | *Matching* |
| Junior high school equivalent | *Undereducation* | | | *Matching* | | | | | *Over education* |
| Senior high school (general) equivalent | *Undereducation* | | | *Matching* | | | | | *Over education* |
| Senior high school (vocational) equivalent | *Undereducation* | | | *Matching* | | | | | *Over education* |
| Diplomas 1, 2, and 3 | *Matching* | *Under education* | *Matching* | *Overeducation* | | | | | |
| Undergraduate and postgraduate | *Matching* | | *Overeducation* | | | | | | |

*Source* Stoevska [2]
*Notes* 1 Legislative Officers, Senior Officials, and Managers, 2: Professionals, 3: Technicians and Assistant Professionals, 4: Administrative Personnel, 5: Service Businesses and Sales Personal in Shops and Markets, 6: Agricultural Business Personnel and Animal Husbandry, 7: Processing and Craft Workers, 8: Machine Operators and Assemblies, and 9: Rough Workers, Cleaning and Workers

## 4 Result and Discussion

The mismatch between education and work is one of the causes of the increasing number of unemployed in Indonesia. Education and work are inseparable parts. Education prints people so they can compete for decent jobs. Based on processed data from Sakernas August 2011–2020 (Fig. 1), the Open Unemployment Rate (TPT) according to the latest education shows a downward trend over the last nine years. However, in 2020, the Open Unemployment Rate (TPT) according to the latest education in all lines has increased from the previous year. This condition may be due to the first time Indonesia faced the threat of the COVID-19 virus. The decline in the unemployment rate indicates that the number of jobs can accommodate the increase in the labor force and vice versa.

The above conditions are supported by data on the working population according to the education attainment. Sakernas August 2011–2020 data illustrates the trend

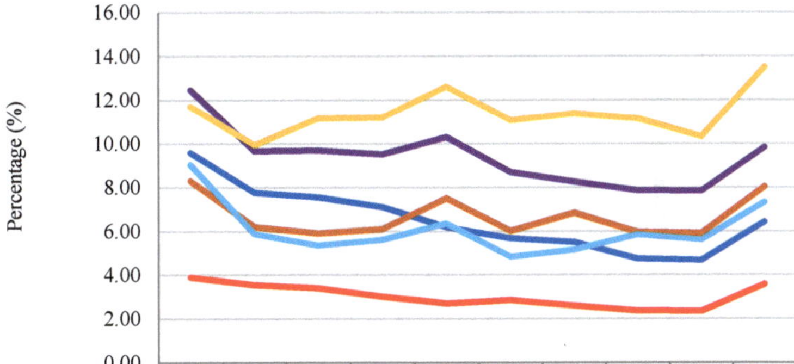


| | 2011 | 2012 | 2013 | 2014 | 2015 | 2016 | 2017 | 2018 | 2019 | 2020 |
|---|---|---|---|---|---|---|---|---|---|---|
| <= Elementary School | 3.93 | 3.59 | 3.44 | 3.04 | 2.74 | 2.88 | 2.62 | 2.40 | 2.39 | 3.61 |
| Junior High School | 9.62 | 7.80 | 7.59 | 7.15 | 6.22 | 5.71 | 5.54 | 4.77 | 4.72 | 6.46 |
| Senior High School (General) | 12.49 | 9.69 | 9.72 | 9.55 | 10.32 | 8.72 | 8.29 | 7.90 | 7.87 | 9.86 |
| Senior High School (Vocational) | 11.74 | 9.97 | 11.21 | 11.24 | 12.65 | 11.11 | 11.41 | 11.18 | 10.36 | 13.55 |
| Diploma/Academy | 8.35 | 6.23 | 5.95 | 6.14 | 7.54 | 6.04 | 6.88 | 6.00 | 5.95 | 8.08 |
| University | 9.06 | 5.92 | 5.39 | 5.65 | 6.40 | 4.87 | 5.18 | 5.88 | 5.64 | 7.35 |

**Fig. 1** Open unemployment rate by education attainment. *Source* Sakernas, BPS (The author's calculation)

of the working population in Indonesia according to the education attainment, experiencing a significant change for the better (Fig. 2). This can be seen from the indications that the working population with elementary education levels and below has decreased from 49.76% in 2011 to 38.89% in 2020. Meanwhile, the working population with junior high school education and above tends to increase. This indicates that the condition of the last education owned by the working population tends to improve. However, this condition is also sufficient to show that higher education in Indonesia has not fully guaranteed it to be easy to find work. This can also be possible because there is no link and match between the world of education and the world of industry/work.

The Indonesian labor market has not been able to provide a reliable and competent workforce. This proves that the world of education is still difficult to implement harmony between the world of education and the world of work in the labor market, which causes a mismatch between the needs of the labor market and education graduates. Figure 3 shows that the mismatch level of Indonesian workers is still quite high. The academic/diploma education level and above dominates the trend of vertical or education mismatch in the last 10 (ten) years (2011–2020), with a mismatch rate above 50%. Meanwhile, the trend (in 2011–2020) is that the vertical or education mismatch at the high school level and below is less than 50%. The conditions described in Fig. 3, should be a challenge for the world of education so that graduates from education, especially at the Academy/Diploma and University levels, have the competence and capability so that they can work according to their level of education and provide open access to a more comprehensive job market.

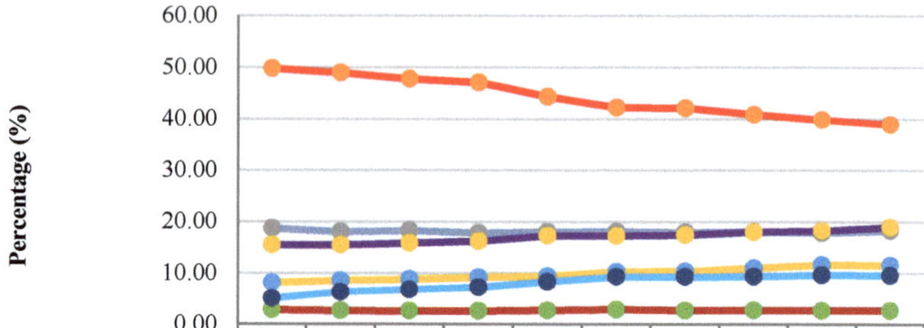


| | 2011 | 2012 | 2013 | 2014 | 2015 | 2016 | 2017 | 2018 | 2019 | 2020 |
|---|---|---|---|---|---|---|---|---|---|---|
| <= Elementary School | 49.76 | 48.96 | 47.72 | 47.07 | 44.27 | 42.20 | 42.12 | 40.82 | 39.83 | 38.89 |
| Junior High School | 18.71 | 18.03 | 18.24 | 17.75 | 18.03 | 18.04 | 17.94 | 18.04 | 17.85 | 18.27 |
| Senior High School (General) | 15.50 | 15.48 | 15.85 | 16.21 | 17.26 | 17.24 | 17.46 | 17.96 | 18.26 | 18.95 |
| Senior High School (Vocational) | 8.13 | 8.56 | 8.84 | 9.18 | 9.44 | 10.28 | 10.40 | 11.02 | 11.69 | 11.56 |
| Diploma/Academy | 2.83 | 2.67 | 2.60 | 2.58 | 2.69 | 2.88 | 2.72 | 2.77 | 2.69 | 2.70 |
| University | 5.07 | 6.30 | 6.75 | 7.21 | 8.32 | 9.36 | 9.36 | 9.38 | 9.69 | 9.63 |

**Fig. 2** Workers in Indonesia based on education attainment. *Source* Sakernas, BPS (The author's calculation)

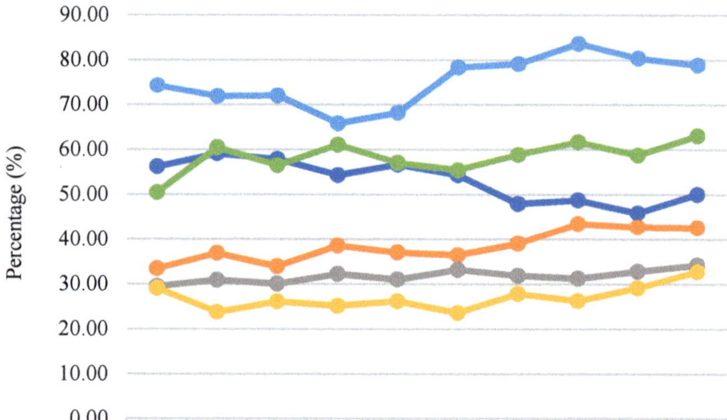


| | 2011 | 2012 | 2013 | 2014 | 2015 | 2016 | 2017 | 2018 | 2019 | 2020 |
|---|---|---|---|---|---|---|---|---|---|---|
| <= Elementary School | 56.24 | 59.14 | 57.87 | 54.27 | 56.63 | 54.28 | 47.94 | 48.72 | 45.84 | 49.98 |
| Junior High School | 33.45 | 36.90 | 33.96 | 38.58 | 37.07 | 36.41 | 39.01 | 43.40 | 42.72 | 42.54 |
| Senior High School (General) | 29.47 | 30.86 | 30.03 | 32.23 | 31.01 | 33.14 | 31.84 | 31.24 | 32.82 | 34.22 |
| Senior High School (Vocational) | 29.07 | 23.77 | 26.09 | 25.14 | 26.15 | 23.57 | 27.79 | 26.20 | 29.07 | 32.73 |
| Diploma/Academy | 74.30 | 71.89 | 71.99 | 65.81 | 68.17 | 78.41 | 79.18 | 83.60 | 80.38 | 78.87 |
| University | 50.46 | 60.48 | 56.46 | 61.02 | 57.08 | 55.41 | 58.85 | 61.67 | 58.71 | 63.05 |

**Fig. 3** Mismatch trend in Indonesia based on the education attainment. *Source* Sakernas, BPS (The author's calculation)

The availability of quality human resources is a hope that continues to be echoed in facing the current digital era. Given that digital technology in Indonesia has experienced significant development after going through the 2010s era, there has been a debate between work and technology, where there are concerns about how automation and digitalization make finding work even more difficult [29]. Based on Fig. 3, we can see that the educational qualifications of workers are not in line with the number of jobs requiring higher education. In the absence of skills competency measures, the results of this analysis cannot be considered conclusive, but only indicative. The skills gap is very worrying because it will affect Indonesia's competitiveness in an increasingly knowledge-based and technology-intensive world economy [29].

The phenomenon of Overeducation and Undereducation is a gap that may occur in the workforce. This gap can be one of the considerations in entering the job market. Figure 4 shows that from 2011 to 2020, Indonesia was included in the overeducation category. Overall, at the last education level attainment, the percentage of overeducation is higher than undereducation, especially at the Academy/Diploma and University education levels which occupy a portion of more than 50%. This shows that these overeducated workers believe that even though a job is not matching their education level, this condition is better than being unemployed, because by working they can fulfill, maintain, and maintain their lives [37]. On a macro level, this has implications for the existence of untapped human resources in the economy.

The phenomenon of overeducation and undereducation also illustrates the consequences or consequences of a shift in the distribution of workers' education in the labor market in certain occupations or business sectors. Figure 5 shows that over 10 (ten) years, the number of workers who have matched the level of education they have and the required job in the business sector is around 56–61%. Meanwhile, the trend of workers experiencing a vertical qualification mismatch for ten years is around 39–44%, of which around 20–28% are overeducated and 15–20% are undereducated. If the education of workers who work in a certain type of work/business sector is matching with the level of education required by the type or sector of business, it is called required education or adequate education [34].

Figure 6 shows the trend of the percentage of qualification matches in each business sector for the last 10 (ten) years (2011–2020). The three business sectors, namely agriculture, industry, and services, have a trend in the percentage of vertical employment suitability that is not much different. The service sector has the highest match education compared to other sectors, although it has decreased during the observation period. This also occurs in the industrial sector, but the trend of Matcheducation in the agricultural sector generally has increased, although the number is the least compared to the other two sectors. The trend of overeducation shows an increase during the observation period, with the largest trend in the agricultural sector. Overeduction in 2011 amounted to 13.92% to 30.58 in 2020, approaching the amount of overeducation in the industrial sector. Meanwhile, overeducation in the service sector has the least trend of increasing overeducation.

In the agricultural sector, there was a sharp decline in the trend of undereducation in the 2011–2016 period, then stagnant until 2020 at 18.59. The magnitude of the

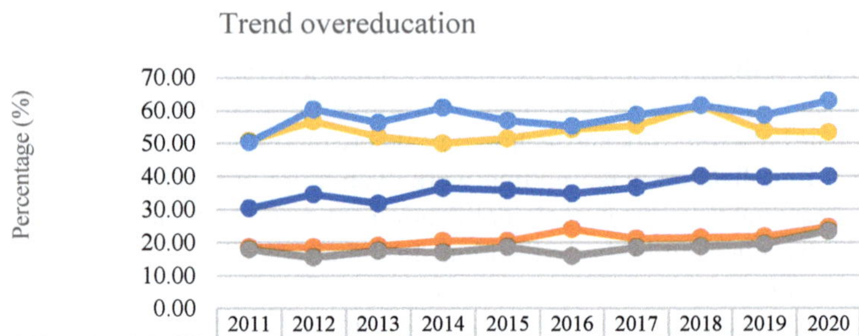


| | 2011 | 2012 | 2013 | 2014 | 2015 | 2016 | 2017 | 2018 | 2019 | 2020 |
|---|---|---|---|---|---|---|---|---|---|---|
| Junior High School | 30.52 | 34.73 | 31.97 | 36.59 | 35.87 | 34.91 | 36.73 | 40.22 | 39.94 | 40.08 |
| Senior High School (General) | 18.85 | 18.81 | 19.25 | 20.63 | 20.58 | 24.20 | 21.31 | 21.58 | 21.91 | 24.74 |
| Senior High School (Vocational) | 17.98 | 15.51 | 17.52 | 16.98 | 18.58 | 15.89 | 18.42 | 18.70 | 19.48 | 23.37 |
| Diploma/Academy | 50.98 | 56.98 | 52.21 | 50.15 | 51.61 | 54.40 | 55.53 | 61.60 | 53.90 | 53.55 |
| University | 50.46 | 60.48 | 56.46 | 61.02 | 57.08 | 55.41 | 58.85 | 61.67 | 58.71 | 63.05 |

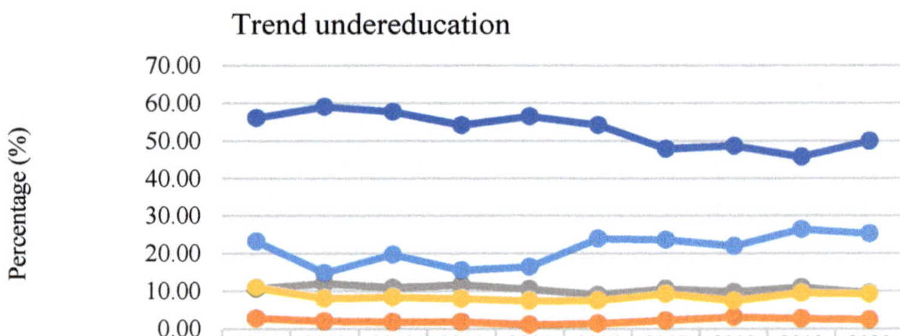


| | 2011 | 2012 | 2013 | 2014 | 2015 | 2016 | 2017 | 2018 | 2019 | 2020 |
|---|---|---|---|---|---|---|---|---|---|---|
| <= Elementary School | 56.24 | 59.14 | 57.87 | 54.27 | 56.63 | 54.28 | 47.94 | 48.72 | 45.84 | 49.98 |
| Junior High School | 2.93 | 2.18 | 1.99 | 1.99 | 1.20 | 1.50 | 2.27 | 3.19 | 2.78 | 2.45 |
| Senior High School (General) | 10.62 | 12.04 | 10.78 | 11.60 | 10.43 | 8.94 | 10.52 | 9.66 | 10.90 | 9.48 |
| Senior High School (Vocational) | 11.10 | 8.26 | 8.57 | 8.16 | 7.57 | 7.68 | 9.36 | 7.50 | 9.59 | 9.36 |
| Diploma/Academy | 23.32 | 14.92 | 19.78 | 15.66 | 16.56 | 24.01 | 23.66 | 22.01 | 26.48 | 25.31 |

**Fig. 4** Overeducation and undereducation trend in Indonesia based on the education attainment. *Source* Sakernas, BPS (The author's calculation)

decline was the largest compared to the other two sectors. The service and industrial sectors show almost the same trend, although the number of undereducation is greater than in the service sector. The dynamics of matching education between the three sectors show that the agricultural sector has a lower percentage trend of match education but experiences a higher trend of overeducation and lower undereducation compared to the other 2 (two) sectors in the last 10 (ten) years.

An interesting finding regarding the pattern of overeducated or undereducated in the labor market is that in the last ten years (2011–2020) the percentage of overeducated in Indonesia tends to increase, while the percentage of undereducated tends to decrease. This is understandable considering that access to education continues to be improved. However, there are several things to note regarding the phenomenon

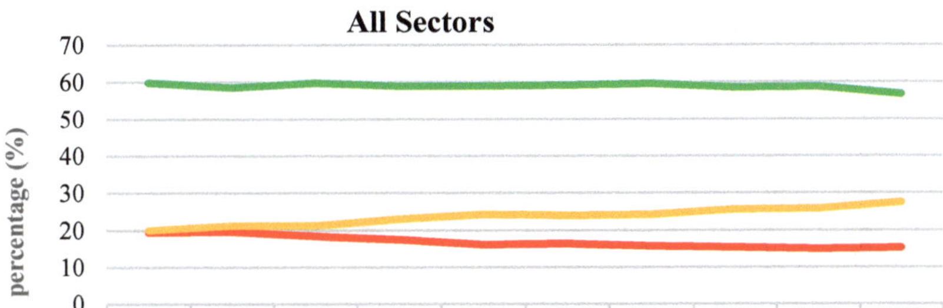


| | 2011 | 2012 | 2013 | 2014 | 2015 | 2016 | 2017 | 2018 | 2019 | 2020 |
|---|---|---|---|---|---|---|---|---|---|---|
| undereduc | 19.68 | 19.85 | 18.57 | 17.63 | 16.36 | 16.55 | 15.88 | 15.51 | 15.09 | 15.47 |
| overeduca | 20.21 | 21.42 | 21.42 | 23.24 | 24.51 | 24.16 | 24.4 | 25.75 | 25.94 | 27.69 |
| match-edu | 60.12 | 58.73 | 60.01 | 59.13 | 59.14 | 59.29 | 59.72 | 58.74 | 58.97 | 56.84 |

**Fig. 5** Match education, overeducation, and undereducation trend in Indonesia

of overeducation, namely: overeducation is interpreted as a sign or evidence of a decrease in the level of economic return in education; overeducation is associated with the occurrence of credential education, namely the public's assessment of a type of education that is not related to the increase in skills required by a particular field or type of work (education is only used as a social status symbol); and overeducation is an indicator of an occupational mismatch or the presence of workers who do not get jobs that can maximize their level of education and abilities [38].

Based on this analysis, we can see that the educational qualifications of workers are still not in line with those required by the business sector. The trend of the proportion of overeducated workers has increased over the last 10 (ten) years, but the trend of the proportion of workers who are undereducated shows a decline. This shows that the quality of education for Indonesian workers is low, especially at the Academy/Diploma and University levels of education. Whereas in the twenty-first century, in the era of the fourth industrial revolution (IR 4.0), where there is a fusion of various technological advances (nanotechnology, digital technology, and biotechnology) [39], Indonesian human resources must be able to adapt quickly. To face the 4.0 era, human resource reform is a must to minimize the impact of the mismatch between education output and industrial needs.

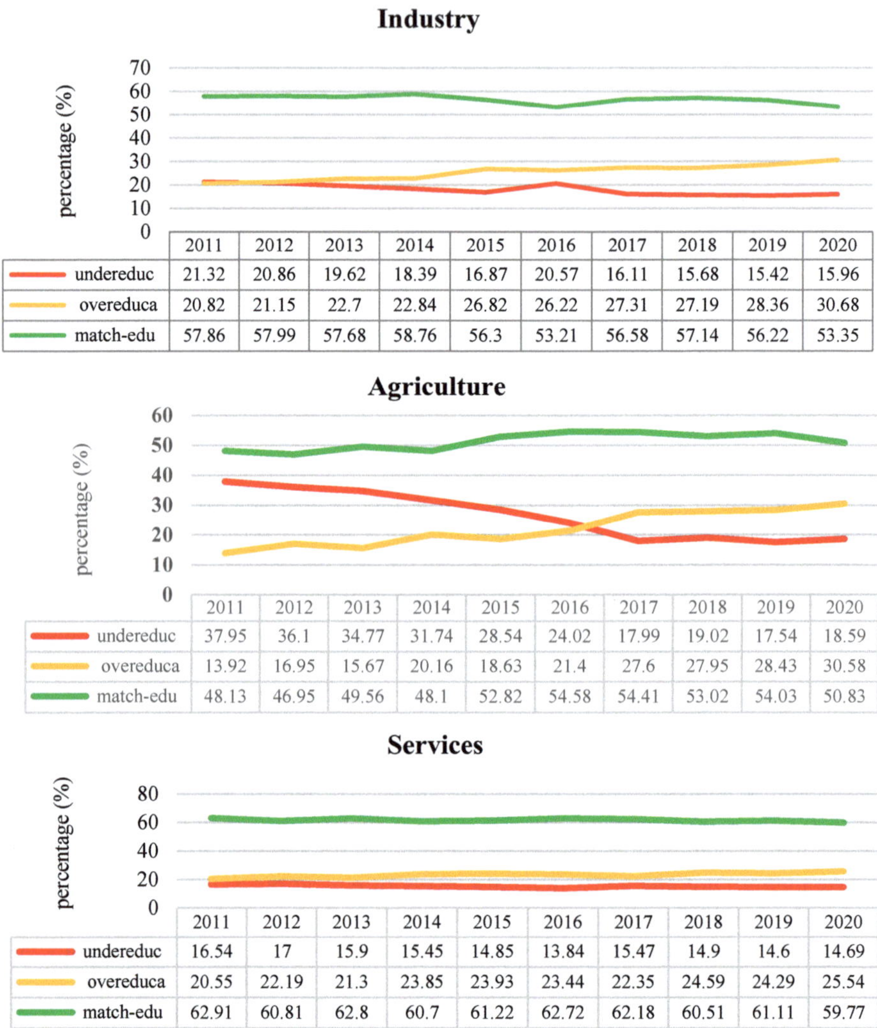


Industry

| | 2011 | 2012 | 2013 | 2014 | 2015 | 2016 | 2017 | 2018 | 2019 | 2020 |
|---|---|---|---|---|---|---|---|---|---|---|
| undereduc | 21.32 | 20.86 | 19.62 | 18.39 | 16.87 | 20.57 | 16.11 | 15.68 | 15.42 | 15.96 |
| overeduca | 20.82 | 21.15 | 22.7 | 22.84 | 26.82 | 26.22 | 27.31 | 27.19 | 28.36 | 30.68 |
| match-edu | 57.86 | 57.99 | 57.68 | 58.76 | 56.3 | 53.21 | 56.58 | 57.14 | 56.22 | 53.35 |

Agriculture

| | 2011 | 2012 | 2013 | 2014 | 2015 | 2016 | 2017 | 2018 | 2019 | 2020 |
|---|---|---|---|---|---|---|---|---|---|---|
| undereduc | 37.95 | 36.1 | 34.77 | 31.74 | 28.54 | 24.02 | 17.99 | 19.02 | 17.54 | 18.59 |
| overeduca | 13.92 | 16.95 | 15.67 | 20.16 | 18.63 | 21.4 | 27.6 | 27.95 | 28.43 | 30.58 |
| match-edu | 48.13 | 46.95 | 49.56 | 48.1 | 52.82 | 54.58 | 54.41 | 53.02 | 54.03 | 50.83 |

Services

| | 2011 | 2012 | 2013 | 2014 | 2015 | 2016 | 2017 | 2018 | 2019 | 2020 |
|---|---|---|---|---|---|---|---|---|---|---|
| undereduc | 16.54 | 17 | 15.9 | 15.45 | 14.85 | 13.84 | 15.47 | 14.9 | 14.6 | 14.69 |
| overeduca | 20.55 | 22.19 | 21.3 | 23.85 | 23.93 | 23.44 | 22.35 | 24.59 | 24.29 | 25.54 |
| match-edu | 62.91 | 60.81 | 62.8 | 60.7 | 61.22 | 62.72 | 62.18 | 60.51 | 61.11 | 59.77 |

**Fig. 6** Match education, overeducation, and undereducation trend in Indonesia based on sector

## 5 Conclusion

The mismatch rate of Indonesian workers is still quite high in line with the rapid development of digitalization in the last decade. Overall, the level of overeducation in Indonesia is higher than the level of undereducation, especially at the level of Academy/Diploma and University education which occupies a portion of more than 50%. The trend of the proportion of overeducated workers has increased over the last 10 (ten) years, but the trend of the proportion of workers who are undereducated shows a decline. If we look further by sector, the agricultural business sector experiences a trend of higher overeducation and lower undereducation compared to the industry and service sectors in the last 10 (ten) years. The mismatch condition that still occurs in Indonesia amid increasingly rapid technological developments needs to get attention from various parties considering the mismatch describes the existence of human resources that have not been utilized effectively and efficiently in the economy. In this article, we have not seen individual considerations in choosing a job that is matched with the education and skills possessed based on the business field. In addition, how does the agricultural sector have an attractive job or become a place of compulsion to work so that it can be developed in further research.

From the results of this study, the authors propose several policy recommendations that can be carried out, especially in the field of reform in the development of human resources and labor market institutions to address the mismatch that still occurs in the era of digitalization which is growing rapidly.

- The need to strengthen links and match the vocational education system and vocational training appropriate to the needs of the labor market. Manpower graduates from vocational education, vocational training, and universities must have qualifications and competencies that can follow the trend of the labor market era 4.0 which is based on data and information processing.
- Transformation of the labor market during the 4.0 era to a more dynamic direction which resulted in the transformation of industry by sector. This has resulted in a change in the character of the business, where there are several types of conventional jobs that disappear, but also new types of jobs, skills, and skills appear.

## References

1. United Nation (2015) Transforming our world: the 2030 Agenda for sustainable development. United Nation
2. Stoevska V (2018) Measurement of qualification and skill mismatches of persons in employment. In: 20th international conference of labour statisticians, ICLS/20/2018/Room Document15. Geneva
3. Allen ER (2016) Analysis of trends and challenges in the Indonesian labor market. ADB Working Paper No.16
4. Bol T, Ciocca Eller C, Van De Werfhorst HG, DiPrete TA (2019) School-to-work linkages educational mismatches, and labor market outcomes. Am Sociol Rev 84(2):275–307. https://doi.org/10.1177/0003122419836081
5. Choi A, Guio J, Escardibul JO (2019) The challenges of mapping overeducation and overskilling across countries: a critical approach using PIAAC. Comp: J Comp Int Educ. https://doi.org/10.1080/03057925.2019.1600400
6. —. What is skills mismatch and why should we care? April 01, 2020. https://www.ilo.org/skills/Whatsnew/WCMS_740388/lang--en/index.htm
7. McGuinness S (2006) Overeducation in the labor market. J Econ Surv 20(3)
8. Quintini G (2011) Over-qualified or under_skilled: a review of existing literature. OECD Social, Employment and Migration Working Paper No. 121. https://doi.org/10.1787/5kg58j9d7b6d-en

9. Verhaest D, Omey E (2006) The impact of evereducation and its measurement. Soc Indic Res 77:419–448. https://doi.org/10.1007/s11205-005-4276-6
10. Brana F-J (2019) A fourth industrial revolution? Digital transformation, labor and work organization: a view from Spain. J Ind Bus Econ 46:415–430. https://doi.org/10.1007/s40812-019-00122-0
11. de Oliveira MM, Santos MC, Kiker BF (2000) The role of human capital and technological change in overeducation. Econ Educ Rev 19:199–206. https://doi.org/10.1016/S0272-7757(99)00020-5
12. Eichhorst W, Hinte H, Rinne U, Tobsch V (2017) How Big is the Gig? Assessing the preliminary evidence on the effects of digitalization on the labor market. Manag Rev 28(3):298–318
13. Glotova IA, Lushnikova TY, Kokanov NA (2020) Development of the qualification institute as the strategy element of the national employment policy: impact factors in the conditions of coronavirus infection (Covid-19) and innovative economy. In: Proceedings of the research technologies of pandemic coronavirus impact (RTCOV 2020). Atlantis Press
14. Walwei U (2016) Digitalization and structural labour market problems: the case of Germany. ILO Research Paper No.17
15. Abraham KG (2015) Is skill mismatch impeding U.S. economic recovery? ILR Rev 68(2):291–313. https://doi.org/10.1177/0019793914564962
16. Battu H, Bender KA (2020) Educational mismatch in developing countries: a review of existing evidence. Econ Educ 269–289. https://doi.org/10.1016/b978-0-12-815391-8.00020-3
17. Cappelli P (2015) Skill Gaps, skill shortages, and skill mismatches: evidence and arguments for the United States. ILR Rev 68(2):251–290. https://doi.org/10.1177/0019793914564961
18. Choi SK, Hur H (2020) Does job mismatch affect wage and job turnover differently by gender? Educ Econ. https://doi.org/10.1080/09645292.2019.1710464
19. Desjardins R, Rubenson K (2011) An Analysis of skill mismatch using direct measures of skills. OECD Education Working Papers, No. 63, OECD Publishing. https://doi.org/10.1787/5kg3nh9h52g5-en
20. Handel MJ, Valerio A, Puerta MLS (2016) Accounting for mismatch in low-middle-income countries: measurement, magnitudes, and explanations. Directions in Development. World Bank, Washington, DC
21. —. Skill Mismatch in Europe (2014) ILO, Geneva
22. Kleibrink J (2016) Inept or badly matched? Effect of educational mismatch in the labor market. Labour 30(1):88–108. https://doi.org/10.1111/labr.12065
23. Kracke N, Rodrigues M (2020) A task-based indicator for labour market mismatch. Soc Indic Res 149:399–421. https://doi.org/10.1007/s11205-019-02261-2
24. McGowan MA, Andrews D (2017) Labor market mismatch and labor productivity: evidence from PIAAC data. Res Labor Econ 45:199–241. https://doi.org/10.1108/S0147-912120170000045006
25. McGuinness S, Pouliakas K, Redmond P (2017) Skill mismatch: concepts, measurement, and policy approaches. J Econ Surv 00:1–31. https://doi.org/10.1111/joes.12254
26. Pholphirul P (2017) Educational mismatches and labor market outcomes: evidence from both vertical and horizontal mismatches in Thailand. Education + Training 59(5). https://doi.org/10.1108/ET-11-2016-0173
27. Sam V (2020) Impacts of Educational mismatches on job satisfaction: the case of university graduates in Cambodia. Int J Manpow 41(1). https://doi.org/10.1108/IJM-07-2018-0229
28. Verhaest D, Sellami S, van der Velden R (2017) Differences in Horizontal and vertical mismatches across countries and fields of study. Int Labour Rev 156(1)
29. ILO (2017) Indonesia jobs outlook: harnessing technology for growth and job creation. ILO, Jakarta
30. Prayudhani O (2020) Peta Ketidaksesuaian Kualifikasi Sektoral di Indonesia. Jurnal Ketenagakerjaan 15(2):Edisi Juli-Desember
31. Suryono P, Pitoyo AJ (2013) Kesesuaian Tingkat Pendidikan dan Jenis Pekerjaan Pekerja di Pulau Jawa. Analisis Data Sakernas Tahun 2010. Jurnal Bumi Indonesia

32. Hartato (2020) The analysis of vertical mismatch and manufacturing labor wage by using Cramer's V method. Jurnal Public Policy 6(1). https://doi.org/10.35308/jpp.v6i1.1564
33. Hasibuan E, Handayani D (2021) Pengaruh Qualification Mismatch terhadap Upah Tenaga Kerja di Indonesia. Jurnal Ekonomi dan Pembangunan 29(1). https://doi.org/10.14203/JEP.29.1.2021.1-16
34. Safuan S, Nazara S (2005) Identifikasi Fenomena 'Overeducation' di Pasar Kerja di Indonesia? Jurnal Ekonomi dan Pembangunan Indonesia 6(1):79–92
35. Friska M, Damayanti A (2021) The effecct of overeducation on unemployment duration in Indonesia. Berdikari: Jurnal Ekonomi dan Statistik Indonesia 1(1):1–13. https://doi.org/10.11594/jesi.01.01.01
36. Shahidan A, Ismail R (2021) A critical review of the literature on the concept of job mismatch and overeducation. J Econ Sustain (JES) 3(1):33–41
37. Kurniawati DI (2014) Masa Kerja dengan Job Engagement pada Karyawan. Jurnal Ilmu Terapan Psikologi 2(2):311–324
38. Saputra W, Junaidi J (2011) Fenomena over education dan under education dalam pasar kerja wanita. Jurnal Ekonomi Pembangunan Universitas Muhammadiyah Surakarta 12(2):212–220
39. Schwab K (2016) The fourth industrial revolution. World Econ Forum

# The Challenges and Obstacles of the Indonesian Gen-Z in Meeting Future Work Needs in the Southeast Asia Labor Market

**Mirza Ayunda Pratiwi, Maya Mustika, and Nurul Hilda Syani Putri**

**Abstract** A pandemic causes massive changes in any behaviors regarding education and work. Numerous studies revealed a set of skills needed in the post-COVID-19 pandemic. In May 2021, the Organisation for Economic Co-operation and Development (OECD) Southeast Asia regional forum revealed three changing skill needs in Southeast Asia that should be adapted. These are cognitive and metacognitive skills, social-emotional skills, and technical skills. This study aims to create a roadmap that explores the challenges and obstacles of Generation Z in Indonesia in preparing themselves to meet these three needs. The method used is qualitative with NVIVO 12 software analysis tools. Triangulation analysis data were collected from documents, observation, and open-ended questionnaire of the 126 informants from various regions in Indonesia. This study indicates that their challenges and obstacles in meeting these skill needs are economic levels, infrastructure (such as signal stability, public learning facilities, school, or institutional support), informal education, non-formal education, and mastery of foreign languages. This research also provides several policy implications and efforts to address these challenges.

**Keywords** Future work needs · Future skills · Gen-Z skills · Learning obstacles

M. A. Pratiwi (✉)
Faculty of Economy, Universitas Maritim Raja Ali Haji (UMRAH), Riau Islands Tanjungpinang, Indonesia
e-mail: mirzaayunda@umrah.ac.id

M. Mustika
Faculty of Education, Universitas Palangka Raya, Kalimantan Tengah Palangka Raya, Indonesia

N. H. S. Putri
Faculty of Education, Universitas Maritim Raja Ali Haji (UMRAH), Riau Islands Tanjungpinang, Indonesia



Nawawi et al. (eds.), *Managing Disruption and Developing Resilience for a Better Southeast Asia*, Springer Proceedings in Humanities and Social Sciences,
https://doi.org/10.1007/978-981-96-2116-3_16

## 1 Introduction

The world megatrend includes technological progress, demographic change, migration, climate change, and 17 items of sustainable development goals—the latest megatrend includes unforeseen shocks, such as the COVID-19 pandemic [1]. These megatrends drive the necessity of skill to overcome complex problems. People who can adapt and have a set of skills appropriate to work needs and life will be able to survive and turn the challenge into an opportunity.

The Fourth Industrial Revolution (4IR) in Indonesia affects the loss of 23 million jobs replaced by automation in 2030. The new job is emerging for around 27–46 million [2]. Indonesian must prepare themselves to deal with these challenges, especially for the youth who will occupy the future labor market. The population census of Indonesia in 2020 shows that Generation Z (Gen-Z), born from 1997 to 2012, dominates the population, reaching 74.93 million people or 27.94% of the total population. A demographic bonus can be an opportunity as well as a challenge. If Gen-Z Indonesia is not well prepared, is it possible that Indonesia's dream of becoming a developed country can be achieved?

Gen-Z must know what future skills need to be prepared. Many studies revealed and predicted a set of future skills. Kotsiou et al. [3] conducted a systematic literature review that shows nine future skill needs: higher-order thinking skills, dialogue skills, digital and STEM literacy, values, self-management, life-long learning, enterprise skills, flexibility, and leadership. Davies et al. [4] revealed ten skills or abilities are proposed for the future workforce: sensemaking; social intelligence; innovative and adaptable thinking; intercultural skills; computational thinking; digital literacy; multidisciplinary; design mentality; knowledge management; and virtual collaboration. Alsenaidi [5] revealed six future skills appropriate for undergraduate students: problem-solving; safety and security; communication; time management; economic; decision-making. Seattle Office of Economic Development [6] revealed the workforce's new skill sets appropriate to the post-pandemic COVID-19 condition: digital skills; adaptability; socio-emotional skill; and creativity.

To avoid confusion about the future skills to be used, this study focuses on using the future skills in Learning Compass 2030 designed by the Organization for Economic Co-operation and Development (OECD). *Cognitive and metacognitive skills, social and emotional skills,* and *physical and practical skills* are the three types of skills identified by the OECD Learning Compass 2030 [7]. Cognitive and metacognitive skills are an individual's critical thinking, creative problem-solving, thinking creatively, self-regulation, and how they learn to learn. Cognitive skills are a set of thinking strategies to use in verbal and nonverbal communication, language ability, and numeric processing, and how they process the knowledge they have acquired as well [7]. Metacognitive skills include learning-to-learn skills and recognizing one's knowledge, skills, attitudes, and values [7]. Metacognition is also called "cognition about cognition," "thinking about thinking," "knowing about knowing," "becoming aware of one's awareness," and higher-order thinking skills (HOTS) [8].

Emotional skills are an individual's ability to manage their emotions properly, including empathy. It also refers to a person's ability to recognize and regulate themselves, including leadership skills, self-efficacy, self-confidence, and self-awareness. Social skills refer to an individual's ability to build relationships with others, including collaboration, cooperation, and responsibility. Social and emotional skills are a set of individual capacities that are embodiment through consistent patterns of thoughts, feelings, and behaviors that allow people to develop themselves, cultivate relationships, and fulfill civic responsibilities [7]. This skill differs from cognitive abilities such as literacy or numeracy. They focus on how people manage their emotions, see themselves, and interact with others rather than their raw capacity to process information. However, like reading and numeracy, they are situationally sensitive and responsive to change and development through formal and informal learning experiences. Importantly, social-emotional skills have a long-term impact on various personal and societal outcomes.

Practical skills are also known as technical skills [1]. Practical skills are required to utilize and manipulate materials, tools, equipment, and artifacts to achieve specific results [7, 9]. Physical skills refer to employing physical tools, procedures, and functions. They include manual skills such as using information and communication technology devices and new machines, playing musical instruments, crafting artworks, and participating in sports and moreover also include life skills such as dressing oneself, preparing food and drink, keeping oneself clean, and mobilizing one's capacities such as strength, muscular flexibility, and stamina [7]. Physical skills also include a person's ability to maintain physical and well-being. In the future, technology will be more dominant in helping human physical work, thus enable humans rarely move and use technology more intensely. The complexity of the problems and the many life demands make young people vulnerable to depression and stress. Therefore, the skill to maintain physical health and well-being is a global priority. Young people are required to have good habits in maintaining their health.

To achieve the ASEAN 2025 Vision in line with the United Nations 2030 global agenda for sustainable development in Southeast Asia region, there are 5 development priorities have been formulated, namely poverty eradication, infrastructure and connectivity, sustainable management of natural resources, sustainable production and consumption and resilience [21]. The development advocates an integrated and inclusive approach, sustainability-oriented, and collaborative partnerships for Southeast Asian countries. The development is expected not only to focus on advanced technology and innovation, but also human resource development to serve high-value industries such as digitalization and automation. For this reason, ASEAN should place a lot of emphasis on social investment to enable digital literacy and capacity building or education training for the younger generation in particular.

In the recent past, a larger supply of young employees has resulted in rapid economic transformation in many Southeast Asian countries through well-suited education systems to create job-related skills [10]. However, because of the fast-changing demand for skills, the existing paradigm of education and production will no longer be able to sustain rapid expansion in the following decades. Thus, countries in Southeast Asia have begun to adapt by transforming their education systems to provide human resources that can occupy future work needs. The best education system in Southeast Asia is Singapore. Singapore's education system makes its young generation better prepared to meet future challenges. Singapore has implemented a digital learning system since 2015 and has been developing the *Singapore Student Learning Space*—an online learning platform—for two to three years [11].

Meanwhile, in Indonesia, digital-based learning transformation has been implemented massively recently due to the lockdown during the COVID-19 pandemic. Therefore, the COVID-19 pandemic is an "unexpected lesson" for schools and universities still stuck with the conventional learning system. Indonesian students learned many things during the COVID-19 pandemic, especially regarding the use of digital-based technology. They have become more familiar with digital-based learning over the last two years. It was recorded that at least one-third (39%) of Indonesian respondents considered the success of educational institutions in presenting a better digital experience than before the disruption due to the pandemic that hit. Then, 36% of consumers in Indonesia see the success of educational institutions in improving the overall user experience. As many as 37% say they are happy and are ready to implement the digital interaction model with educational institutions [12].

To face the future, the skills needed are not limited to being able to operate digital devices. There are many skills that Indonesia's younger generation must prepare for when facing rapidly sustainable change. The Indonesian Ministry of Education, Nadiem Makarim, in early 2020, formulated a curriculum named "Free Learning-Independent Campus." It is designed to enable Indonesian students to gain knowledge directly from competent partners and explore the industry's knowledge and skills. Nevertheless, does *Free Learning-Independent Campus* program is enough to meet the challenges of future work in Indonesia and internationally? As already mentioned, the younger generation must be ready for the demands of the future skills needed, namely cognitive and metacognitive skills, social and emotional skills, and physical and practical skills. It is necessary to know what students experience when required to prepare themselves to deal with future work needs. So, this study will explore the Indonesian Gen-Z challenges in dealing with changing future skill needs. In addition, this study also explores the obstacles experienced by Indonesian Gen-Z when preparing themselves to meet the needs of the future labor market.

## 2 Research Methodology

This study used a qualitative-phenomenological method. The approach of the research is to understand or explain the experiences of Indonesian Gen-Z (born 1997–2012) in the learning process (formally, informally, and non-formally) to face future work needs. An open-ended survey, interviews, internet (news, videos, and audio), and observation were all used to gather the data. An open-ended survey was distributed through electronic mail, WhatsApp, and Telegram. The minimum target of informants was 100, and in the end, we were able to collect 126 informants from various regions in Indonesia. Informants came from university students and several high school students. There are twelve open-ended questions related to their challenges and obstacles in mastering cognitive and metacognitive skills, social and emotional skills, and practical-physical skills (technical skills). Questions were also asked about their experience of obstacles in undergoing the online learning process during the COVID-19 pandemic.

The data analysis method used thematic analysis, adapted by Virginia Braun and Victoria Clarke [13]. Thematic analysis is the process of identifying patterns or themes within qualitative data [14]. A thematic analysis aims at finding themes or patterns in the data that are significant or relevant and applying these themes to address the study or make a statement about a problem. An effective thematic analysis interprets and makes sense of the data rather than simply summarizing it. Analysis method uses six-phase: (1) data familiarization and writing familiarization notes; (2) systematic data coding; (3) generating initial themes from coded and collated data (4) developing and reviewing themes; (5) refining, defining, and naming themes; and (6) writing the report [13]. This research used qualitative software, NVIVO 12, to organize the data, make codes, and create concept maps.

## 3 Result and Discussion

### *3.1 The Challenges Faced by Indonesian Gen-Z Today*

The challenges meaning in this study arise when Gen-Z finds the difficulties out of their control. Challenges, on the other hand, might be seen as opportunities to go forward. People who can overcome the challenges will be able to become outstanding compared to others who cannot. Based on the data collected, the obstacles to meeting Indonesian Generation Z's future work needs are as follows: Megatrend, politics, boundary-less, regional disparities, and qualification and skill mismatched.

**Megatrend.** The twenty-first century is changing rapidly. Changes and developments globally are currently called "megatrends." The forms of megatrends are technological progress, demographic change, migration, climate change, and the COVID-19 pandemic. *Technological progress.* Southeast Asian countries have a vulnerability to automation, especially in the manufacturing, construction, wholesale, retail, hotel, and restaurant industries (OECD, 2021). Examples of vulnerable jobs include sewing machine operators in Cambodia and Vietnam, food waiters in Thailand, shop assistants in the Philippines, and office workers in Indonesia [1]. *Demographic change.* The demographic bonus is expected to create an economic boom. The instance, Japan experienced a demographic bonus in 1950 and made Japan become the third highest economic power in the world in the 1970s, after the United States and the Soviet Union. Indonesia also currently had the same human capital as Japan in 1950 [15]. The demographic bonus in Indonesia predicted will be the economic leverage for Indonesia in 2050. "The World in 2050" by Price Water Cooper (PWC) predicts that Indonesia will become an economic powerhouse, the fourth largest in the world, in

2050 [16]. Demographic bonuses may have two sides. On the one hand, this will provide Indonesia with a large amount of human capital, allowing it to expand its national economy. On the other side, if the national labor market cannot handle the extra productive workers, this offers a risk of excessive unemployment. *Migration.* National or international migration both influence the mobility of people with particular skills. The home region or country will lose and move its human capital to another place. A location that attracts many people to migrate will accommodate individuals with a variety of skills. *Climate change.* The increase in the Earth's temperature impacts various aspects of nature and human life. The melting of ice at the Earth's poles causes the global water level to rise and flood many countries. Recently, extreme weather often caused a prolonged dry season. Several areas in Indonesia are directly affected by global climate change. Drought and crop failure occurred emerge in several farming lands. Unpredictable weather makes going out to sea difficult for fishers. Some jobs become challenging to do. As a result, Gen-Z loses interest in working in sectors vulnerable to the impacts of climate change. Climate change challenges also require Gen-Z to take care of their health concerns and physical well-being. They also must be able to innovate and work using environmentally friendly and sustainable systems. Therefore, green living must also be practiced in their daily life. *COVID-19.* The pandemic adds new challenges besides megatrends. Disruption of technology has become faster than ever. Ways of working, economic transactions, and learning have changed during the COVID-19 pandemic. The pandemic makes skills to use technology tools develop quickly. As these changes become rapid and unpredictable, individuals must be able to adapt in the long term, even though the COVID-19 pandemic is over.

**Politics.** The unstable global politics is also troubling the younger generation. Starting from US President Donald Trump's collaborative policies, Trump's feud with North Korean leader Kim Jong Un, China's global ambitions, the volatile situation in the Middle East, and the issues of Ukraine and Russia. Political turmoil between major countries will also affect civilian life in many countries, including Indonesia. Political problems are not something that individuals can control. So international conflicts are also a concern and a mental burden for the Millennial and Gen-Z. This political condition makes the younger generation worry about their safe and comfortable life in the future.

**Boundary-less.** Gen-Z is also labeled as a boundary-less generation. They explore and connect with many people in various places virtually through an internet connection. They easily communicate with audio or video via technological devices. The ease of communicating without boundaries has a positive impact, such as a more open-minded attitude, global insight, mastering foreign languages, and more tolerance. They comfortably roam to different parts of the world without moving from their place. As a result, this causes their experience of limited experience to travel geographically. Gen-Z needs to do more exploring and move around to explore different places.

**Regional Disparities.** For an archipelagic and with a large population like Indonesia, facing megatrends and achieving equity is very challenging. There is a gap between regions regarding economic development and education quality distribution. Development of economy and education are more developed on Java Island, while the Sumatra and the eastern part of Indonesia are still being managed to make it even better. Today's technology requires internet stability and an adequate electrical power supply, but not all parts of Indonesia distributed and well-established infrastructure in all regions. The challenges were more impactful for Gen-Z, who live in areas with inadequate infrastructure and low quality of education. Educational and economic disparities also occur between ASEAN countries. Indonesia is behind Singapore, Malaysia, Brunei, and Thailand regarding global education rank. If Gen-Z wants to compete in the ASEAN labor market, they must be able to compete with Gen-Z from other ASEAN countries. Improving the way to learn is the key to overcoming this matter.

**Qualification and Skill Mismatched.** A *qualification mismatch* arises when a worker's level of education is higher or lower than that required for their job. If they are more educated than their job requires, workers are classified as "overqualified." Otherwise, if they are less educated than the job requires, they are classified as "underqualified." Meanwhile, *skills mismatch* arises when workers have a higher or lower skill level than their job requires. If they have more excellent skills than their job requires, workers are classified as "overskilled." If their skills are below the minimum, they are classified as "underskilled" [17]. Indonesia Central Bureau of Statistics reported that primary school graduates dominate the Indonesian workforce. Between 2014 and 2018, at least a quarter, or 28.75% of the workforce with primary school graduates. Nevertheless, then it declined to 25.21% in 2018. They were next, followed by the secondary school graduates ranging from 17 to 18% annually. It means that the total composition of primary and secondary school graduates reaches 43% as a workforce. Indonesia Central Bureau of Statistics reported also noted that the manufacturing industry is the third-largest sector in absorbing Indonesian workers, amounting to 22% or 18.25 million people. Interestingly, 23.06% of them are primary school graduates with low skills. The dominance of workers with low education, especially in the manufacturing industry sector, is a big challenge for the Indonesian workforce in facing fourth revolution industry related to the digital economy and robotic technology.

## *3.2 The Obstacles for Gen-Z in Meeting Future Work Needs*

The results of data collection were processed and organized using NVIVO 12 software. The results were gathered through an open-ended survey and interviewed several informants. We get various information from the data collection process. Then, we conducted a coding process according to the themes of the informant's answers. After being classified based on the theme, we interpret the data and conclude into several categories that will be discussed: obstacles in dealing with online learning during COVID-19 and the informants' obstacles in facing future needs, namely cognitive and metacognitive skills; social and emotional skills; and technical skills. A summary of all the constraints can be seen in Table 1.

**Online Learning.** Before pandemic COVID-19, most Indonesian students were unfamiliar with online learning and tended to learn conventionally. The socioeconomic problem is one of the reasons to consider implementing online learning in the educational system. However, COVID-19 positively impacted the acceleration of technology-based learning (TBL) at schools and universities. Many students and teachers were reluctant and complained about doing this at first. Nevertheless, they were eventually able to adapt. However, the adaptation faces various obstacles that cause the teaching and learning process to be ineffective. The learning and teaching process becomes ineffective, and the mastery of knowledge and skills is not optimal during online learning. Pandemic COVID-19 triggered many online learning platforms to arise. Remote work is also becoming more widely available. The companies consider using the hybrid method to conduct learning and development programs due to the reduced operational cost. Hence, autonomous online learning is a must-have skill for the present and future.

**Table 1** The Indonesian Gen-Z constraints in preparing future skills based on the results of the open-ended survey

| Future skill needed | Obstacles |
|---|---|
| Cognitive and metacognitive skill | |
| • Language (English) | Grammar, lack of interest, less practicing, low of learning ability in English, no English-speaking partner, less confidence, poor vocabulary, unavailability affordable-accessible-quality English course, unsupportive environment |
| • Reading | Boredom, gadget distraction, hard to understanding, laziness, less motivation, library access, not used to it since childhood, prefer to use google, prefer online or digital media, too busy, unaffordable quality book |
| • Math | Hard to memorize the formula, laziness, less interest, low ability of learning about number, teacher quality |
| • Self-directed learning | confusing, incomplete material, laziness, less learning facilities, less motivation |
| Social and emotional skill | Less non-formal learning such as seminar, workshop or training. Less informal learning such as home education, reading, and self-taught |
| Technical skill | External: Infrastructure support, lack learning facilities, rapid changing, technological knowledge burden, unreliable free course |
| | Internal: Budget constraint, not mastering English language, unsupportive facilities, low of self-directed learning |

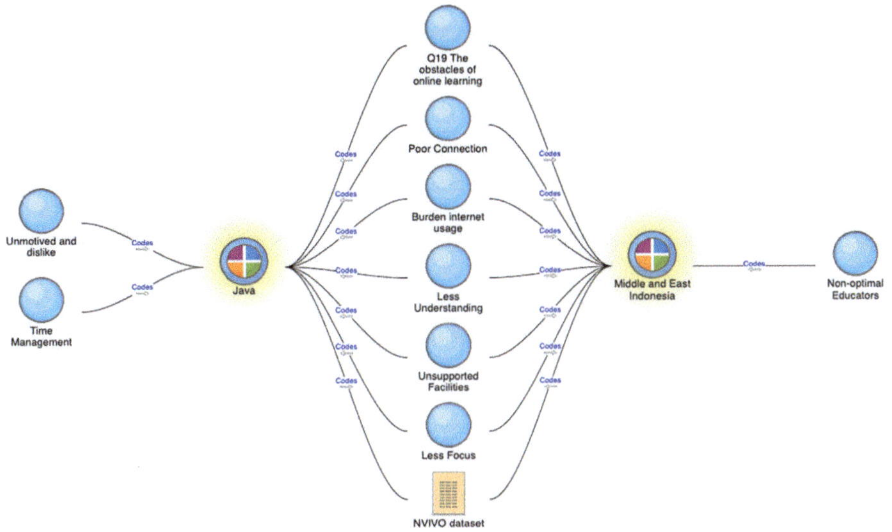


**Fig. 1** A diagram proceeded by NVIVO 12 about the differences of the obstacles in experiencing online learning between Java Island and Middle and East Indonesia

In code form, we classified the informants' answers about their learning difficulties during the COVID-19 pandemic. The coding transformed into eleven themes: Assignment overload, the boredom of studying, the burden of internet usage, lack of interaction and communication, less focus, less understanding, non-optimal educator, poor internet connection, time management, unmotivated and dislike, and unsupported facilities (Fig. 1).

We also compare the coding between the island of Java and the island of Sumatra, and it can be seen in Fig. 2. Informants from Central and Eastern Indonesia, when compared to Java, they experienced problems with the attributes of non-optimal educators. While comparing Java and Sumatra, informants from Sumatra experienced attributes of non-optimal educators, the boredom of studying, lack of interaction and communication, and assignment overload. We can also conclude that Java has the advantage of having better teaching resources than other islands.

**Cognitive and Metacognitive Skills.** We asked the informants about the obstacles in developing their cognitive abilities such as literacy or reading, numeracy skills, and the ability to master foreign languages. We asked about their ability to regulate self-study and understand independent learning or self-taught regarding metacognitive abilities. *Language.* We have nine coding themes about the obstacles in terms of mastery of foreign or English language: Grammar, lack of interest, less practicing, low of learning ability in English, no English-speaking partner, less confidence, poor vocabulary, unavailability affordable-accessible-quality English course, unsupportive environment. *Reading.* Indonesia has a low interest in reading. Based on a survey conducted by the Program for International Student Assessment (PISA)

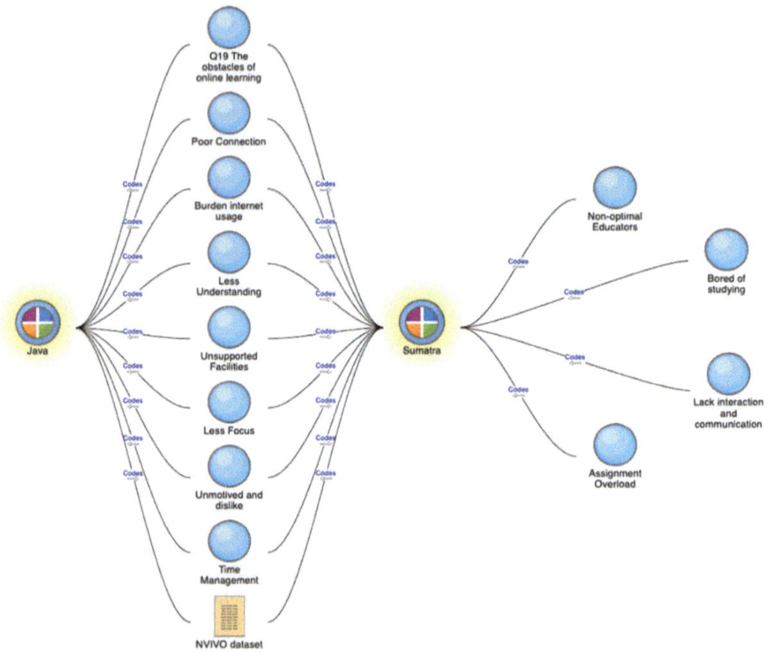


**Fig. 2** A diagram proceeded by NVIVO 12 about the differences of the obstacles in experiencing online learning between Java Island and Sumatra Island

released by the Organization for Economic Co-operation and Development (OECD) in 2019, Indonesia is ranked 62 out of 70 countries or in the bottom ten countries with low literacy levels. Of the 79 countries surveyed involving 600,000 children aged 15 years, Indonesia is ranked 74th in reading ability with an average score of 371. So, we gather information on what reasons the informants are not interested in reading. We found eleven coding themes: Boredom, gadget distraction, hard to understand, laziness, less motivation, library access, not being used to it since childhood, preferring to use google, preferring online or digital media, too busy, and unaffordable quality book. *Math.* Indonesia has a low literacy rate in the global rankings. PISA notes that on mathematical ability, Indonesia is ranked 73 with an average score of 379. Furthermore, on science ability, Indonesia is ranked 71 with an average score of 396. We have five coding themes regarding why they are not engaging in a study related to numbers: Hard to memorize the formula, laziness, less interest, low ability to learn about numbers, and teacher quality. *Self-directed learning.* Self-directed learning is a process in which people plan, continue, and evaluate their learning independently. Self-directed learning is a must-have skill to survive in future work needs. We have five coding themes: Cannot asking, confusing, incomplete material, laziness, less learning facilities, and less motivation.

**Social and Emotional Skills.** Social and emotional skills are not easy to measure. It needs a particular measurement tool to determine a person's social and emotional level. Social and emotional skill is the ability of individuals to build a relationship with others, as well as the ability to understand others. These skills will be needed in the future because humans will face complex problems in the Fourth Industrial Revolution era. So to have the ability to overcome complex problems, it is necessary to have good social and emotional skills. OECD [1] reported that Indonesia has a low social and emotional level compared to the cognitive and technical skills. These skills can be formed and developed through formal, non-formal, or informal education. So, we asked the informants whether they had ever tried to improve their skills in developing social and emotional skills. Forty-four informants acknowledge they have attended any seminar, workshop, or training to develop their social and emotional skills. Thirty-seven informants stated that they developed these skills through learning at home or self-taught from books or social media. However, other informants admitted that they never and rarely attended seminars, workshops, or social and emotional skills training. Some informants more often attend seminars, workshops, or training to improve their technical skills rather than social and emotional skills. In addition, the informants also said that they did not receive knowledge about social and emotional skills in their homes. They were never taught or taught by their parents related to social and emotional skills. The informant's self-awareness regarding the need of social and emotional skills is quite low. They admitted that they rarely read books about self-development. They also stated that they thought that improving cognitive and technical skills were much more critical than social and emotional skill.

**Technical Skills.** Regarding the ability to improve technical skills, we divide coding themes into two forms, namely external and internal. External are obstacles out of control by the informant, and it is difficult for them to control individually. There are five external obstacles to developing technical skills by informants. First, the lack of adequate infrastructures, such as poor internet connection and limited electric power supply. Second, lack of learning facilities, such as no lab or practice facilities in their university study programs, or they have a computer lab but are not maximally empowered for students use. Third, rapid change, several informants said they were very confused because the changes were too fast. They were just about to learn new one thing, but there have to reach something other new they had to learn. They find it difficult to run after the change in this digital age. Fourth, the technological knowledge burden, the development of technology is very rapid. Nowadays almost all aspects are related and use technology based. They feel that there is too much knowledge to learn about technology, which makes it difficult for them to master it. Fifth, unreliable free course, the informant told me that he had participated in the free training several times, but the results were not optimal. In contrast, learning outcomes tend to be satisfied. When it held commercially or paid. However, technology-related training costs are costly for some of them.

From the internal attribute, we have four coding themes. First, budget constraints, those who come from low-income families find it challenging to master technical skills because they do not have more budget to pay for courses and buy supporting facilities. Second, not mastering the English language, informants said that to master technology, one must master English because the language used in various tools and manuals primarily uses English. The inability to speak English is one of the obstacles that cause them to have difficulty mastering technical skills. Third, unsupportive facilities are an obstacle because the facilities have low specifications, such as laptops with low specs or smartphones with low Random-Access Memory (RAM). Fourth, low self-directed learning, and lack of independence in learning will make them fall behind. Some informants stated they are not able to learn independently to develop their technical skills.

## 3.3 Conclusion

From the results of data collection, results, and discussion, we conclude that first, Indonesian Generation Z to compete in the ASEAN labor market, they need to be good at three primary skills: cognitive and metacognitive skills, social and emotional skills, and technical skills. Second, the obstacles to online learning are identical in every region in Indonesia, but compared between regions, the Sumatra, and the Middle and Eastern regions of Indonesia experience quality educator problems. Third, social and emotional skills in Indonesia still need to be improved. Many informants still think that this skill is not more important than cognitive and technical skills. Fourth, the Infrastructure issues significantly discriminate between regions in the learning process. Students from areas with an adequate electrical power supply and a good internet connection have fewer learning obstacles.

We provide several recommendations that related stakeholders can implement to improve the quality of Gen-Z in preparing for future work needs: *Learning strategies*, Gen-Z needs to be taught well. Teachers need to know how Gen-Z thinks and acts. By knowing what makes them unique, teachers will be able to change the way they teach. If teachers use the wrong learning style, Generation Z will get bored with school and lose interest in learning. If Generation Z does not like the learning environment, it will be harder to learn and remember what they have learned. Some suggestions for learning styles that can be used with Generation Z are project-based learning, real case studies, collaboration, technology-based learning, and hybrid learning methods. *Free Space*, Gen-Z needs to be stimulated and supported by their creativity. Campuses and city governments need to create "free space" to channel various Gen-Z creativity. *Learning and development center (LnD Centre),* universities need to develop learning and development centers on their campuses. We asked the informants if their university had a place to provide particular training and development for students. However, few informants acknowledge that their university has an LnD center. *Career guidance,* we also asked whether the university had a career consulting center. Most of them acknowledge that their university does not provide any place to consult about their future career. So, universities and schools should consider providing a career guidance center for their students.

## References


1. OECD (2021) Adapting to changing skill needs in Southeast Asia [2021 OECD Southeast Asia Regional Forum Discussion Note] [Online]. Available: https://www.oecd.org/southeast-asia/events/regional-forum/OECD_SEA_RegionalForum_2021_Discussion_Note.pdf
2. Dedy (2021) Hadapi Tantangan Pendidikan dalam Megatrend 2045. Universitas Negeri Yogyakarta. https://www.uny.ac.id/id/berita/hadapi-tantangan-pendidikan-dalam-megatrend-2045. Accessed 21 Apr 2022
3. Kotsiou A, Fajardo-Tovar DD, Cowhitt T, Major L, Wegerif R (2022) A scoping review of future skills frameworks. Irish Educ Stud 41(1):171–186. https://doi.org/10.1080/03323315.2021.2022522
4. Davies A, Fidler D, Gorbis M (2011) Future work skills 2020. Univ Phoenix Res Inst p 19 [Online]. Available: http://cdn.theatlantic.com/static/front/docs/sponsored/phoenix/future_work_skills_2020.pdf
5. Alsenaidi SF (2020) Teaching future skills for undergraduate university students and its effectiveness in developing future job skills to meet labor market requirements. Univers J Educ Res 8(11B):5790–5800. https://doi.org/10.13189/ujer.2020.082213
6. Seattle Office of Economic Development (2020) COVID-19 and the future of work
7. OECD (2019) OECD future of education and skills 2030 concept note
8. Sujak A (2020) Mengajar Generasi Z. Pustaka Insan Madani, Yogyakarta
9. OECD (2019) Learning compass 2030
10. Sudan FK (2021) Fourth industrial revolution and future of work in Asia. Glob Econ Sci 98–111. https://doi.org/10.37256/ges.222021783
11. Mada PSSATUG (2020) Covid-19: Wajah Pendidikan Singapura dan Indonesia. Pusat Studi Sosial Asia Tenggara Universitas Gadjah Mada. https://pssat.ugm.ac.id/id/covid-19-wajah-pendidikan-singapura-dan-indonesia/. Accessed 23 Apr 2022
12. Mamduh M (2021) Masa Depan Pendidikan di Asia Tenggara. https://www.medcom.id/teknologi/news-teknologi/JKRW26QN-masa-depan-pendidikan-di-asia-tenggara. Accessed 23 Apr 2022
13. Braun V, Clarke V (2021) One size fits all? What counts as quality practice in (reflexive) thematic analysis? Qual Res Psychol 18(3):328–352. https://doi.org/10.1080/14780887.2020.1769238
14. Braun V, Clarke V (2006) Using thematic analysis in psychology. Qual Res Psychol 3(2):77–101. https://doi.org/10.1191/1478088706QP063OA
15. Lubis B, Sos S, Si M, Mulianingsih S, Pd S, Pd M (2019) Keterkaitan Bonus Demografi Dengan Teori Generasi. J Regist 1(1):21–36 [Online]. Available: http://ejournal.ipdn.ac.id/jurnalregistratie/article/view/830
16. Tulung JM, Syahid A, Janis Y, Kalampung YO (2019) Generasi Milenial: Diskursus Teologi, Pendidikan, Dinamika Psikologis dan Kelekatan pada Agama di Era Banjir Informasi
17. OECD (2019) Skills matter additional results from the survey of adult skills. Paris

# Modified Teaching Factory (Motefa): the Best Practice of Life Skill Program in MAN 2 Kulonprogo

**Siti Muawanah and Aji Sofanudin**

**Abstract** MAN 2 Kulonprogo, which is also known as MANDAKU, is an Islamic senior high school (MA) in Yogyakarta which provides life skill programs for the students. It becomes the most favorite because most surrounding students are coming from lower middle class who mostly do not pursue their study into university. With other 82 MA throughout Indonesia, the madrasah has conducted the program since 1998 with the full support of MoRA and UNDP. When some MAs quitted the program because the ministry stopped the final support to the program, MANDAKU could survive the program without financial support of the MoRA. Even, due to the school's good achievement, MANDAKU is given a chance to become the only MAKN (State Vocational Madrasah Aliyah) in Yogyakarta Province, or one of the only three MAKN in Indonesia. Based on qualitative research conducted in 2021, it is found that MANDAKU has special program which becomes the best strategy. The program is the MAN de Motefa. It is created by the vocational teachers of MANDAKU. It consists of four components: block schedule system, job sheet, product oriented, and working attitudes. The essence of this strategy is combining *akhlaqul karimah* (Islamic values which become a characteristic of madrasah) with teaching factory in the school. Even by this program, MANDAKU became the representative of the MoRA in National Innovative Public Services Competition held by Ministry of in 2020. In this article, what *motefa* is and how it works in MANDAKU will be described.

**Keywords** Modified teaching factory · MAN 2 Kulonprogo · Life skill program

S. Muawanah (✉) · A. Sofanudin
National Research and Innovation Agency, Jakarta, Indonesia
e-mail: siti087@brin.go.id

A. Sofanudin
e-mail: ajis004@brin.go.id



Nawawi et al. (eds.), *Managing Disruption and Developing Resilience for a Better Southeast Asia*, Springer Proceedings in Humanities and Social Sciences,
https://doi.org/10.1007/978-981-96-2116-3_17

## 1 Introduction

Madrasah is an Islamic educational institution which continously improves education quality in order to meet the demand of the time. Therefore, it is not surprising if there are always changes in madrasah, especially in the curriculum [1–6]. In addition, the Ministry of Religious Affairs (MoRA) as a govermnet department which is responsible for the quality of madrasah is always making diversifications in education, such as giving life skills in madrasah aliyah (Islamic senior high school) which is a kind of educational diversification in vocational MA [7, p. 204]. According to Murray, et.al, only about 30% of MA graduates pursue their study into higher education, while the rest is working in informal sector or even unemployed [8, p. iii]. It means that MA students need skill to face their life after finishing their study.

Actually, life skill program has become a part of MA curriculum since a half and three decades ago, when the MoRA made an agreement with UNDP/UNESCO on 14 December 1987 with the project number INS 85/036. The agreement was in the form of making pilot project on life skill program in *madrasah aliyah* consisting of three kinds of life skill: electronics, automotive, and fashion [9, p. 203, 10, p. 1]. The agreement run up to three periods. In the first period, three MAs were addressed as the pilots: MAN (State Madrasah Aliyah) Garut, MAN Kendal, and MAN Jember [10, p. 1]. At the second period, five MAs were added to become new pilot madrasahs. In the first and second period, the project was funded by UNDP. In the third period, however, the project was funded by Islamic Development Bank (IDP) with the document number INDO 053 dan 054 signed on 30 November 1995 [9, p. 188, 10, p. 1] and 82 MA were addressed to participate in the program (interview, informant 3 and 4, 9 September 2021). During the agreement periods, the program was fully supported by the MoRA and those cooperating institutions. The teachers, materials, and workshops were provided by the project. MA which provides life skill program for their students are called as "MA Keterampilan".[1]

As the agreement ended, the MA which had joined the program, had to struggle for the continuity of life skill program in the schools, because there were no more financial supports from the ministry. Due to some reasons, some MA continued the life skill program while some others did not. As an illustration, in Lampung, there were 11 MA registered as "MA Keterampilan" in 2016 but in 2020 the number decreased into 5 MAs. So were in Banten and Bali. In 2016, there were 19 and 9 MA which provided life skill program for the students, but in 2020 the number changed into 7 and 3 respectively [11, 12].

Moreover, even some certain MAs which joined the program at early phase, especially at the third phase, when the program was still fully funded by the

[1] We prefer using the term "MA Keterampilan" to "vocational MA" because MA Keterampilan is not the same as MA Kejuruan (Vocational MA). If it is compared to educational institution under the Ministry of Education, Culture, Research and Technology, "Vocational High Schools (SMK) is equivalent to "Vocational Islamic Senior High Schools" (MAK). Although the term "vocational MA" may be more familiar and more appropriate but the Decree of Minister of Religious Affairs identifies them into different categorization. Therefore, I used "MA Keterampilan" to avoid confusion and interchangeable.

ministry, seemed to be less encouraged to continue the program. Some of them that were addressed as the piloting madrasas were not considered as *MA Keterampilan* anymore. They prefer other types of MA (such as Research MA, Digital MA, Academic MA, etc.) to *MA Keterampilan.* MAN 3 Yogyakarta, for example, which was also addressed as *MA Keterampilan* together with MAN 2 Kulonprogo, is not recognized as *MA Keterampilan.* The school is more famous as research MA and digital MA. The MA was neither listed in the Decree of General Director of Islamic Education Number 4924/2016 nor 2831/2020).

By contrast, MAN 2 Kulonprogo (which is usually called as MANDAKU, so is in this writing) is still encouraged to pursue the program. The school is continuously creating innovation to develop the program. Even, in the future, the school will be projected as vocational Islamic senior high school (*MA Kejuruan*) and becomes the only *MA Kejuruan* in Yogyakarta Province and one of three state vocational Islamic senior high schools (*MA Kejuruan Neg*eri) in Indonesia.

One of MANDAKU's innovation is *Motefa* (modified teaching factory), a modified-characterized teaching learning model in vocational school. By this innovation, MANDAKU became the representative of the MoRA of Republic of Indonesia in the Public Service Competition held by the Ministry of Administrative and Bureaucratic Reform of Republic of Indonesia (Kementerian PAN-RB) in 2020. The innovation also become the Top 45 public service innovations [13]. These are appreciable factors to lead MANDAKU an important madrasah among other MA Keterampilan. In addition, the school is also reported as having some good points, such as good at making network, life skill education and training [8, p. 38] and marketing [14, p. 40]. Therefore, it is considerable to dig more information about education practice in the school.

This article is discussing about *motefa*, one of MANDAKU's strategies to develop life skill program in the madrasah. The study is important to inspire especially other 333 MA Keterampilan in Indonesia to make innovation in the field. It also will present a more comprehensive picture of life skill teaching learning process in the school.

As far as we are concerned, based on literature search, there is no study about this modified teaching factory yet. Most writing about vocational and life skill programs talk about policies [15], program design [16–18], implementation [9], [19–22] evaluation [7, 23], mapping [8], and public perception on the program [24]. So rare are articles discussing about features of certain vocational teaching learning method in certain school. The most common (and somehow similar to this article) is writings talking about the implementation [25–29], development [30–32], and evaluation [23–33] of the teaching factory in vocational schools. Although they are also discussing about teaching factory, this study, however, is different because of the term "modified" itself in the "motefa". Therefore, there is something really unique from the teaching factory applied in MANDAKU from teaching factory conducted by other vocational schools.

Teaching factory is a concept which got much attention in the last three decades. In America, the concept has resulted in many piloting projects in education and business spheres [34, p. 31], while in Indonesia, the teaching factory concept took its simplest form with the development of production unit in vocational senior high schools in 2000 [35, p. 4]. The term "teaching factory" then become a "standard" concept in teaching learning process in vocational schools in 2011, when Indonesian government eagerly developed a conceptual framework of "factory as a learning center" in vocational schools [35, p. 3].

At the same time, Indonesian government also made agreement with Germany to develop teaching factory. The agreement project was called as Technical and Vocational Education and Training (TVET). The program basically adapted the dual teaching system which was previously applied in Germany and Swiss. By the system students are provided with two environments at the same time, namely school environment and manufacture environment. With this system students can sharpen their basic competence (in school environment) and practice their skills (company environment) at the same time [35, p. 4]. In other words, teaching factory is a teaching learning model which bridge theoretical field and practical one; a model which trains students as if they are working in real industrial world.

The concept "teaching factory" itself stems from medical world, especially in terms of medical school which operates in parallel with hospitals [34, p. 32–36, p. 190] so that students can practice their knowledge in practical world. Therefore, the students can integrate academic field with working field where they can attain more relevant experiences (more realistic).

There are two models in applying teaching factory, namely "factory-to-classroom" and "academia-to-factory/lab-to-factory" [34, p. 32–36, p. 191], [37, pp. 2–3]. The "factory-to-classroom" model, as it is named, is transferring industrial environment into learning environment (classes). By the first model, students will know more about industrial atmosphere, daily production process, and any other industrial matters in detail [34, p. 32–36, p. 191]. Through this first model, students are provided with a set of tasks in product/production lifecycle, such as line balancing new production line. This is then broken down and distributed into some students who are grouped into teams. The students have to work to find solution to the problem. They can communicate to each other, using technologies to communicate with engineers, or using modern tools for developing and validating their ideas and solution.

In order to run the "factory-to-classroom" model, there are two approaches: "one to one" or "one to many". By one-to-one approach means one factory for one classroom, while by the other means one factory for more than one classrooms. In other words, one factory interacts with some classes at the same time [34, p. 32–36, p. 191] (Rentzos, dkk. 2014:191; Rentzos, dkk. 2015:32).

The other model of teaching factory is "academic-to-factory" which is also called as "lab-to-factory". This is different from the first model. By the second model, knowledge is transferred from academic realm into industrial environment. Equipment and facilities used in learning process is to be validated by students and researchers. The new knowledge is then transferred back to industrial world to support making decision process or introduce management team with new concept or technology in industrial world. By "academic-to-factory" any equipment or technologies installed in classes can be used as demonstrators for new technologies or concepts. According to Rentzos, et. al, [34, p. 32], the second model is suitable for training because there are many new concepts/technologies in industrial world which is too costly and time consuming to be industrially tested on their actual production. By teaching factory, the new concept can be validated by students and researchers. Therefore, teaching factory becomes a bridge to the gap between industrial and academic innovation [38, p. 6.943.1].

The main purpose of teaching factory is providing students with complete knowledge and skills in manufacture world, not only learning what is written on books (theoretical matters) but also direct experiences in working fields with all its management and problems, such as making proposals, making prototypes, making solution and decision, dealing with deadlines, making interpersonal communications, team working, etc. [39, p. 3]. In short, as it is stated by Nurtanto, et.al. [32, p. 451], teaching factory has double benefits: a place for learning as well as a place for working (entrepreneurship).

## 2 Method

This is a qualitative study. In order to gain sufficient data, the researcher conducted some techniques, such as document study, observation, and interviews. Study document was performed to any relevant written sources relating to the needed data, especially related to the MANDAKU, such as school profile, schedule, and curriculum documents. Observation was conducted in the madrasah environment. Unfortunately, due to the pandemic situation and some medical procedures, the researcher could not observe the program neither directly nor naturally. Therefore, the data which ideally gained from observation technique was completed by another technique, namely interviews, which was conducted to the principal, the program coordinator, the teachers of the subjects for life skill program, teachers of Islamic education, students, and local peoples.

Interview applied in this research was unstructured interview in which the questions listed in interview guideline were not raised in sequence. In addition, by using unstructured interview, the researcher and informants were in equal position so that two-way interaction was highly possible [40, p. 61]. Moreover, the researcher also conducted focused-group discussion to explore more information about the program. The focused-group discussion was conducted once in the meeting room of MANDAKU with the program supervisor, four program instructores, one external researchers, and two other teachers of life skill program.

In terms of data analysis, this study used Miles' and Huberman's model which is divided into three main steps: data reduction, data display, and drawing conclusion/verification. Although this analysis model consists of three steps, it does not mean that the step one has to be completely done before the second and the third steps. It also does not mean that the researcher had to finish collecting field data before analyzing them. By using this interactive model, the researcher conducted data analysis before, during, and after field-data collection. In certain condition, the researcher could move from data reduction to data display and came back to data reduction, but in other condition, the researcher moved from data reduction to verification [41, p. 83].

The research was conducted in September 7, 2022,–October 21, 2022.

# 3 Result and Discussion

## *3.1 MANDAKU and Its Life Skill Program*

MANDAKU is one of 11 MA Keterampilan in Yogyakarta Province or 333 in Indonesia. The madrasah was addressed as MA Keterampilan in about 1998/1999, in the third period of agreement between Indonesian government and UNDP (interview, informant 3 and 4, 9 September 2020) which was funded by IDB [9, 10, p. 1].

At the beginning, MANDAKU served 3 programs for the students: electronics, fashion, and agricultural technology. However, when this study was conducted, MANDAKU had provided five life skill programs: fashion, audio visual technology, visual communication design, agribusiness and agriculture technology, and cooking. Audio visual technology and visual communication programs were actually the development of electronics, while agribusiness and agricultural technology was previously agricultural technology. In other words, from the beginning, MANDAKU has provided no totally new programs but cooking which was begun in 2017/2018.

Each group (class) of the program contains of 24–26 students. Since MA Keterampilan is different from regular school, student organization into classes is also different. The students of life skill programs are distributed into some different classes. A regular class may contain students from two life skill programs. However, on the schedule of certain program, the students will group into same classes of the same program to learn materials (Table 1).

Although distributed into some classes, the number of the students are relatively the same as presented by Table 1.

**Table 1** The number of students of each life skill programs

| No | Programs | Grade | | |
|---|---|---|---|---|
| | | **X** | **XI** | **XII** |
| 1 | Audio visual technology | 25 | 24 | 25 |
| 2 | Agribusiness and agriculture technology | 26 | 25 | 25 |
| 3 | Fashion | 25 | 25 | 24 |
| 4 | Visual communication design | 26 | 25 | 25 |
| 5 | Cooking | 26 | 24 | 24 |
| **Total** | | **128** | **123** | **123** |

## 3.2 *Motefa: Modified Teaching Factory in MANDAKU*

Motefa had been implemented in MANDAKU since 2018. According to Imam Muttaqien, there are four main pillars in motefa. They are block system schedule, job sheet, product oriented, and working attitude. These four pillars are inspired by a meeting held by the ministry of education and culture in 2017, when some vocational teachers were trained to upgrade their skills in teaching. At that meeting one of the presented materials was about teaching factory which outlined procedures and principals in conducting teaching factory model in vocational schools.

### 3.2.1 Block System Schedule

This system is a characterized learning schedule and popular enough in vocational schools but not in other school types. The main principal of this system is giving students same materials continuously in a longer period of time, one or two weeks depending on the material difficulties or other considerable factors. It means that the teacher will not give new materials before the earlier materials are completely studied. This schedule system is different from the schedule of other subjects where in the later the materials could be divided into some parts and delivered separately. By separately here means the materials are not given continuously and consequentially.

In order to run this system, a class is divided into some smaller groups consisting of 5–6 students. Each group is taught or trained different materials and skills so that in certain period of times competence or skills needed to make a certain product are fulfilled. In other words, in a same time, the students of a certain major are not taught same materials. That is the striking difference between the block system schedule in vocational schools in general or in MANDAKU in particular and schedule system from other majors.

To make it more understanding the block system in MANDAKU, here is the sample of the schedule of audio-visual technology grade X, XI, and XII. From the schedule we can see that a student is taught same material for one or two weeks. He/she will not get new materials before the earlier materials completely taught. Moreover, we also know that students in the same class are taught different materials (Table 2).

### 3.2.2 Job Sheet

The second component of motefa is job sheet. It is a list of activities as a guidance for students to make a certain product. This job sheet consists of some working sheets which guide students to make a certain product. It lists some procedures and the technical guidance. Therefore, the students have to obey the listed procedures. The teacher supervises and controls the procedures done by the students and will

**Table 2** The schedule of audio-visual technology program using block system

| Group | No | Meeting | | | | | | | | | | | | | | | | | |
|---|---|---|---|---|---|---|---|---|---|---|---|---|---|---|---|---|---|---|---|
| | | Week I | | | | | | Week II | | | | | | Week III | | | | | |
| | | Mon | Tue | Wed | Thu | Fri | Sat | Mon | Tue | Wed | Thu | Fri | Sat | Mon | Tue | Wed | Thu | Fri | Sat |
| 1 | 1–5 | CD | CD | CD | CD | CD | CD | elk | elk | elk | elk | elk | elk | elk | elk | elk | elk | elk | Elk |
| 2 | 6–10 | LA | LA | LA | LA | LA | LA | elk | elk | elk | elk | elk | elk | elk | elk | elk | elk | elk | elk |
| 3 | 11–15 | elk | elk | elk | elk | elk | elk | CD | CD | CD | CD | CD | CD | elk | elk | elk | elk | elk | elk |
| 4 | 16–20 | elk | elk | elk | elk | elk | elk | LA | LA | LA | LA | LA | LA | elk | elk | elk | elk | elk | elk |
| 5 | 21–25 | elk | elk | elk | elk | elk | elk | elk | elk | elk | elk | elk | elk | CD | CD | CD | CD | CD | CD |
| 6 | 26–30 | elk | elk | elk | elk | elk | elk | elk | elk | elk | elk | elk | elk | LA | LA | LA | LA | LA | LA |

put the sign on each procedure if he/she finds the students performed the activity well according to the guidelines. By this job sheet and putting teachers' sign on each procedures the product created by students is suitable for competence required for students and the quality of the product is guaranteed.

### 3.2.3 Product Oriented

The third component of motefa is product oriented. The product has to fulfill quality and consumers' standards. At the beginning, the targeted consumers are the MANDAKU community (the students, staffs, teachers) and the other is wider community. By wider community here is community outside the MANDAKU. In order to reach wider community, the MANDAKU products are sold in local markets or entrusted to some shops to be sold. The products for internal consumers are usually the products made by the tenth-grade students, while the products to be sold to external consumers (wider community) are the products of the eleventh and twelfth grade students. This policy is based on the consideration the students from higher grades are considered to be more capable and competent than that of the lower grade.

Some products made by the MANDAKU students are mask, mask connector, madrasah uniform, pisgrow (pizza growol), stikgrow (stik growol), various keripik (chips), some bread, instant drink from ginger extract, pin, mug, and robot. The related fashion products were made by the students of fashion class, meal products were made by the students of Agribusiness and Agriculture Technology, pin and mug were done by the students of Visual Communication Design.

Discussing about the products of MANDAKU, this madrasah has more positive image than other madrasah because it has characterized products, namely some products made from "growol", such as "stik growol", "pizza growol", and "pizza growol". The "growol" is local comestibles which is made from cassava. It needs long process to make growol. Although growol is so popular for the local people, the growol by MANDAKU is different in terms of the texture and ingredients. The story behind "growol" production by MANDAKU was an accidental story when a teacher of life skill program in MANDAKU soaked the cassava for too long. As a result, the texture of the soaked cassava was over soft. Confused with the unexpected texture, the teacher then thought to make "growol" stick, a sort of growol products of MANDAKU which is licensed halal by the BPJPH (Badan Penyelenggara Jaminan Prodduk Halal, a governmental institution dealing with issues halal of products in Indonesia. The license was handed to the MANDAKU principal on 27 May 2020. The halal license will be valid for five years [42, 43].

The second factor making "growol" products of MANDAKU different from other "growol" products lies on the mixed ingredients. If the mixed ingredients of growol of other people is tapioca flour, the "growol" products of MANDAKU were mixed with wheat fluor.

### 3.2.4 Working Attitude

The last component of the motefa in MANDAKU is working attitude. By working attitude here is that students are taught and treated as if they were in real industrial environment, as if they were working in the real factory in which they have to work in high discipline, serious, and full of responsibility. They have to work according to standard operating procedures including using personal protective equipment.

These are the common attitudes in industrial environment which are considered not enough for the students of life skill program in MANDAKU. MANDAKU gives other good attitudes to be performed by the students during the process of teaching learning life skills, good Islamic attitudes which are named as akhlaaqul kariimah (good behaviors). This is additional positive attitudes implemented in the teaching factory model in MANDAKU.

In order to implement akhlaqul kariimah, the MANDAKU has some programs, such as 5 S (Senyum, Salam, Sapa, Sopan, dan Santun; Smile, Salutation, Greeting, Polite, and ethical), morning greeting (making shaking hands) between teachers and staffs in the madrasah, morning literacy activities in the form of reading the Qur'an or other selected books, reciting asmaul husna, performing morning prayer (shalat dhuha), morning dhikr, performing dhuhur prayer in congregation, kultum (short religious sermon after dhuhur prayer), and clean Friday.

These good behaviors are integrated in teaching factory and become the positive values for the MANDAKU as well as identity which make the madrasah different from other vocational schools.

According to the teachers of life skill program in MANDAKU, these good Islamic characters are so important in industrial environment. In addition, the integration of the good characters into teaching factory will give benefits to the students of MANDAKU and will elevate their acceptance level, especially after they finish the study and step into working place. When two applicants come to an employer, the first is a skillful person with lack of good characters and the second is a skillful with good characters, the employer must choose the second one. Even if the two applicants are a skillful person and less-skillful with good characters, the employer should choose the later over the first, because a less-skillful people could be trained in two or three months to reach better technical competence, while good character could not be implemented quickly. It needs a long habituation and cultivation from the early life (informant 2 and 3, interview, 9 September 2022).

In order to emphasize the importance of akhlakul karimah (good characters) in the life skill program, more specifically in teaching factory model, they become a considerable factor in evaluation. In other word, the final score of the students do not merely come from theoretical and practical aspects, but also from akhlakul kariimah aspect. Therefore, the life skill program teachers ask other teachers (especially the teachers of Islamic education and Pancasila and civic education) and staffs to take a part in evaluating the students.

## 4 Conclusion

Modified Teaching Factory (motefa) is a new breakthrough created by the teachers of life skill program in MANDAKU. It has helped the madrasah existed in maintaining the program which was not financially supported by the Ministry of Religious any longer. It contains of four components, namely block system schedule, job sheet, product oriented, and working attitudes emphasizing on akhlakul karimah (Islamic good characters) in addition to professional characters in industrial environment. The fourth component becomes the identity which differentiate the madrasah from others.

In addition, due to the product oriented, this madrasah has produced some processed food made from "growol", a characterized comestibles from Kulonprogo. Although the "growol" is so popular in the area, the product made by the MANDAKU is different from other growol in terms of texture. Moreover, the processed-food products from MANDAKU are halal licensed by the BPJPH (Badan Penyelenggara Jaminan Produk Halal), a governmental institution which deals with the issue of halal for food in Indonesia, starting from the registration, verification, and supervision of halal for various products in Indonesia.

## References


1. Rhoyachin M, Wahyuni S (2019) Dinamika Perubahan Kurikulum Madrasah Diniyah Pondok Pesantren Putri Lirboyo Al-Mahrusiyah Kediri. J Pemikir Keislam. https://doi.org/10.33367/tribakti.v30i1.665
2. Hikmawati SA (2018) Pendekatan dan Model-Model Pengembangan Kurikulum Bahasa Arab pada Madrasah/Sekolah di Indonesia. J Ihtimam. https://doi.org/10.36668/jih.v1i2.170
3. Kusmawati H, Surachman AI (2019) Glokalisasi Kurikulum Pendidikan Agama Islam Madrasah Aliyah Keagamaan di Era Revolusi Industri 4.0. J. Ilm. Pendidik. Dasar, https://doi.org/10.30659/pendas.6.2.98-115
4. Mukaffa Z (2017) Pengembangan Model Madrasah Inklusif (Studi atas Kesiapan dan Model Pengembangan Kurikulum Madrasah Inklusif MI AL-Hidayah Margorejo Surabaya). *Edukasia J. Penelit. Pendidik. Islam*, https://doi.org/10.21043/edukasia.v12i1.2051
5. Almu'tasim A (2018) Menakar model Pengembangan Kurikulum di Madrasah. *At-Tuhfah*, https://doi.org/10.36840/jurnalstudikeislaman.v7i2.140
6. Nasir M (2009) Pengembagan Kurikulum Berbasis Madrasah. HUNAFA J Stud Islam. https://doi.org/10.24239/jsi.v6i3.138.273-300
7. Muzayanah U (2021) Evalusai Program Keterampilan di Madrasah Aliyah Menggunakan Model CIPPO. J. Penamas Balai Litbang Agama Jakarta, 34(02):203–220, https://doi.org/10.31330/penamas.v34i2.496
8. Murray R et al. (2017) Pengembangan Keterampilan Vokasional di Madrasah Aliyah. Jakarta: Education Sector Analytical and Capacity Development Partnership (ACDP)
9. Suprihatiningsih S (2015) Implementasi Kurikulum Pendidikan Keterampilan Vokasi di Madrasah Aliyah (Studi pada Madrasah Aliyah di Provinsi DKI Jakarta). J INDO-ISLAMIKA. https://doi.org/10.15408/idi.v5i2.11746
10. Bahroji MMS (2018) Eksplorasi Kesiapan Siswa Memasuki Dunia kerja pada Program Keterampilan Madrasah Aliyah (MAN) 1 Garut. Universitas Pendidikan Indonesia

11. Direktorat Jenderal Pendidikan Islam (2020), Keputusan Direktur Pendidikan Islam Nomor 2851 Tahun 2020 tentang Penetapan Madrasah Aliyah Plus Keterampilan. Jakarta
12. Direktorat Jenderal Pendidikan Islam (2016) Keputusan Direktur Pendidikan Islam Nomor 4924 Tahun 2016 tentang Penetapan Madarasah Aliyah Penyelenggara Program Keterampilan. Jakarta
13. Kanwil Kemenag DIY (2020). MAN de MOTEFA Terima Penghargaan Top 45 Inovasi Pelayanan Publik 2020. https://diy.kemenag.go.id/10406-man-de-motefa-terima-penghargaan-top-45-inovasi-pelayanan-publik-2020.html Accessed 13 Oct 2021
14. Puslitbang Pendidikan Agama dan Keagamaan (2021) Penelitian best practice life skill di Madrasah Aliyah. Jakarta
15. Safitri NA, Marlina R (2019) Kebijakan Penyelenggaraan Madrasah Aliyah Kejuruan. Madrasa J Islam Educ Manag. https://doi.org/10.32940/mjiem.v2i1.44
16. Verawadina U, Jalinus N, Asnur L (2019) Kurikulum Pendidikan Vokasi Pada Era. J. Pendidik
17. Suarta IM (2013) Pengembangan konstruk sistem pembelajaran pada pendidikan tinggi vokasi. J Pendidik Vokasi. https://doi.org/10.21831/jpv.v2i1.1012
18. Penulis T (2018) Sistem Pendidikan Vokasi di Inggris, 1st edn. Kantor Atase Pendidikan dan Kebudayaan Kedutaan Besar Republik Indonesia, London
19. Masruroh Z (2017) Manajemen Pendidikan Keterampilan (Vocational Skill) di MAN Kembangsawit. Muslim Herit. 1(2):417–438
20. Sarbiran H (ed) (1998) Pelaksanaan Program Keterampilan di Madrasah Aliyah Negeri di Jawa Tengah. J. Kependidikan,. Khusus, pp. 99–108,.
21. Junardi N (2007) Program Pendidikan Keterampilan di Madrasah Aliyah Ummatan Wasathon Imogiri (Studi tentang Proses dan Efektifitas Program. Pascasarjana UIN Sunan Kalijaga Yogyakarta
22. Wahyudi I (2019) Pembelajaran Berintegrasi life skill dalam Pelajaran Prakarya dan Kewirausahaan untuk Mengembangkan Potensi Diri Siswa Kelas XI IPS di MAN Kota Batu. Universitas Islam Negeri Maulana Malik Ibrahim Malang
23. Fajaryati N (2012) Evaluasi Pelaksanaan Teaching Factory SMK di Surakarta. J. Pendidik. Vokasi 2(3):325–337
24. Sriwardani N (2011) Persepsi mahasiswa terhadap perkembangan pendidikan vokasi di program pendidikan teknik mesin. J Pendidik Vokasi. https://doi.org/10.21831/jpv.v1i1.5813
25. Rohmah W, Efita Sari D, Wulansari A (2019) Pembelajaran Berbasis teaching factory di SMK Negeri 2 Surakarta. J. Pendidik. Ilmu Sos, https://doi.org/10.23917/jpis.v29i2.9171
26. Fitrihana N (2019) Rancangan Pembelajaran Teaching factory Di Smk Tata Busana. Home Econ J. https://doi.org/10.21831/hej.v2i2.23293
27. Sudiyanto S, Sampurno YG, Siswanto I (2017) Teaching factory di SMK St. Mikael Surakarta. Taman Vokasi, https://doi.org/10.30738/jtvok.v1i1.134
28. Siswanto I (2015) Teaching factory SMK program Keahlian Teknik Otomotif
29. Siswanto I (2011) Pelaksanaan teaching factory di SMK RSBI Daerah Istimewa Yogyakarta. Universitas Negeri Yogyakarta
30. Diwangkoro E, Soenarto S (2020) Development of teaching factory learning models in vocational schools. https://doi.org/10.1088/1742-6596/1456/1/012046
31. Azizah DN et al (2019) Development of teaching factory model at vocational high school (VHS) In Indonesia. Indones J Learn Educ Couns. https://doi.org/10.31960/ijolec.v2i1.115
32. Nurtanto M, Ramdani SD, Nurhaji S (2017) Pengembangan model teaching factory di Sekolah Kejuruan. In: Prosiding Nasional seminar Pendidikan, pp 447–454
33. Supriyantoko I, Jaya A, Kurnia V, Habiba PGS (2020) Evaluasi Implementasi Kebijakan teaching factory dengan model Evaluasi CIPP di SMK Negeri DKI Jakarta. J. Vocat. Tech. Educ.
34. Loukas R, Dimitris M, George C (2015) A two-way knowledge interaction in manufacturing education: The teaching factory. In: The 5th Conference on Learning Factories, pp 31–35, https://doi.org/10.1016/j.procir.2015.02.082
35. Direktorat Pembinaan Sekolah Menengah Kejuruan (2017). Tata Kelola Pelaksanaan Teaching Factory. Jakarta: Direktorat Pembinaan Sekolah Menengah Kejuruan Direktorat Jenderal Pendidikan Dasar dan Menengah Kementerian Pendidikan dan Kebudayaan RI

36. Loukas R, Doukas M, Dimitris M, Mavrikios D, George C (2014) Integrating manufacturing education with industrial practice using teaching factory paradigm: a construction equipment application. In: Proceedings of the 47th CIRP Conference on manufacturing systems, pp 189–194, https://doi.org/10.1016/j.procir.2014.01.126
37. Dimitris M, Georgoulias K, Chryssolouris G (2018) The teaching factory paradigm: Development and outlook. In: 8th Conference on learning factories 2018-addvanced engineering education and training for manufacturing innovation. pp. 1–6, 8th Conference on learning factories 2018-Addvanced engineering education and training for manufacturing innovation
38. Alptekin SE, Pouraghabagher R, McQuaid P, Waldorf D (2001) Teaching factory. In: Proceeding of the 2001 American society for engineering education annual conference and exposition, pp 6.943.1–6.943.6. https://doi.org/10.18260/1-2--9863
39. Diwangkoro and Soenarto E (2020) Development of teaching factory learning models in vocational schools. J. Phys. Conf. Ser., pp 1–5
40. Sidiq U, Choiri MM (2019) Metode Penelitian Kualitatif di Bidang Pendidikan. Ponorogo: Natakarya
41. Rijali A (2018) Analisis data Kualitatif. J. Alhadharah, 17(33):81–95. [Online]. Available: http://jurnal.uin-antasari.ac.id/index.php/alhadharah/article/viewFile/2374/1691
42. Krjogja.com, "UP MAN 2 Kulonprogo Terima Sertifikat Halal," 2021. [Online]. Available: https://www.krjogja.com/berita-lokal/diy/kulonprogo/up-man-2-kulonprogo-terima-sertifikat-halal/.
43. Kanwil Kemenag DIY, "UP MAN 2 Kulonprogo Terima Sertifikat Halal," 2021. https://diy.kemenag.go.id/14787-up-man-2-kulon-progo-terima-sertifikat-halal.html Accessed 11 May 2022

# Demographic Changes and Critical Issues of Young and Elderly People in Southeast Asia

# ‘Always on the Move’: Commuting Behavior of Migrants in Indonesia

**Dian Wahyu Utami and Meirina Ayumi Malamassam**

**Abstract** Commuting is an important aspect of urban life. It plays a vital role in how people can enhance their quality of life and subjective well-being. However, from a regional development perspective, commuting is considered a reflection of the high occurrence of spatial mismatch due to occupation and residential segregation. Moreover, migrants are suggested to have a higher likelihood of experiencing spatial mismatch due to their limited access to affordable housing in areas of origin. While internal migration and commuting are often examined separately, previous studies have shown that these two spatial mobility patterns are interrelated. By utilizing data from Intercensal Survey 2015, this study aims to understand the characteristics of commuting migrants, particularly the recent ones, and to what extent their socio-demographic background can explain their commuting behavior. About a third of Indonesian commuters are long-term migrants, while around 14.6% are recent migrants. These commuting migrants are mainly well-educated and work as employees in tertiary and quaternary sectors. This study finds that commuters’ socio-demographic characteristics can strongly predict their commuting behaviors. Highly educated recent migrants, in particular, have the highest likelihood of commuting in the shortest time compared to their highly educated counterparts. They also have the highest propensity to commute by using private transportation. Understanding the relationship between commuting and migration not only can help explain spatial mismatch in employment and housing among migrant workers in Indonesia, but also signal challenges in population mobility dynamics and transportation system development.

**Keywords** Commuting · Recent migrants · Spatial mismatch · Indonesia

D. W. Utami (✉)
Department of Political Science, Yonsei University, Seoul, South Korea
e-mail: dian064@brin.go.id; utami.dw@yonsei.ac.kr

D. W. Utami · M. A. Malamassam
Research Center for Population, National Research and Innovation Agency, Jakarta, Indonesia
e-mail: meir001@brin.go.id



Nawawi et al. (eds.), *Managing Disruption and Developing Resilience for a Better Southeast Asia*, Springer Proceedings in Humanities and Social Sciences,
https://doi.org/10.1007/978-981-96-2116-3_18

## 1 Introduction

Rapid economic growth and urbanization in many developing countries, including Indonesia, has been a critical attractor to in-migration to metropolitan cities and urban areas. While this situation may positively affect human capital accumulation in areas of destination, the presence of the migrants can also cause residential segregation [1]. Commuting has become an important feature of population dynamics within the framework of urban life systems due to its annual growing number. Workers' choice to rent or buy residentials in peripheral areas due to restricted access to housing space at the center of economic activities has been argued as the critical reason for the increasing number of commuters toward metropolitan areas and big cities. Further, the high intensity of commuting flows would impact a variety of factors, including the demand for transportation investment to facilitate their journey [2] and regional spatial inequities.

Commuting is argued as an outcome of spatial mismatch between the distribution of economic activities and the residential of corresponding workers [1]. The spatial mismatch happened due to the gaps of location of living and viable occupation [3]. Additionally, spatial mismatch is argued to have mainly occurred among migrants who lived in urban areas. While the decision to migrate is strongly driven by the motivation to improve individuals' welfare, residential segregation in areas of destination might hinder the migrant group from gaining optimal return to their spatial movement.

With the rapid urbanization and advancement of transportation means in Indonesia, it is expected that the number of commuters is continued to increase over time. In Indonesia, the number of working commuters increased from 6,310,835 (5.7%) to 7,080,845 (6.0%), according to data from the 2015 National Labor Force Survey. West Java has the highest proportion of commuters (25.5%), and Jakarta is accounted for 15% of that total (1,062,127). Figure 1 shows the distribution of commuter in Indonesia, with Java having the largest percentage of commuters.

Migrants are suggested to experience greater spatial mismatch and higher intensity of commuting than local workers [4]. However, there is a gap in knowledge of the migration-commuting nexus within the Indonesian context. Thus, this study aims to examine the characteristics of commuting migrants and understand to what extent the socio-demographic backgrounds of the migrants influence their commuting behavior. The findings of this study are significant for a better understanding of how populations with distinctive spatial mobility patterns also differ in their job-housing relationships, resulting in their distinct commuting behavior. Moreover, this study can work as a basis for planning and formulating regional policies that consider the variations of spatial distributions of populations' socio-economic activities.

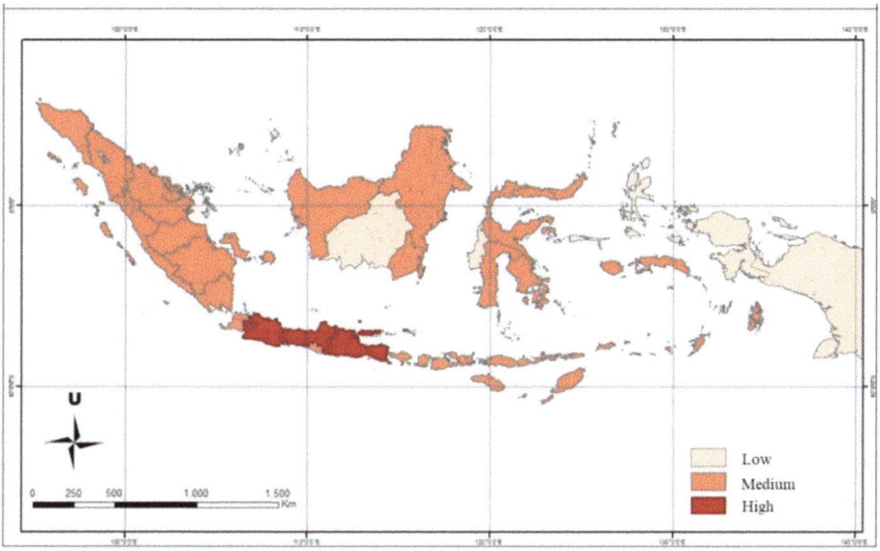


**Fig. 1** The distribution of commuters in Indonesia. *Source* Indonesian labour force survey, 2015

## 2 Literature Review

Internal migration and commuting are the two primary forms of population mobility across regions within a country. Migration can be defined as a permanent or temporary change of residence within a particular duration and geographical distance [2–5], while commuting is a type of population mobility that involves a daily trip across regions between residence and workplace [6]. In other words, commuting is continuous mobility between home and work or traveling from one place and back to another place in a day [2]. Migration and commuting are rarely discussed jointly since they are assumed to be independent forms of population mobility [7]. Some migration theories explain that migration is population mobility beyond the individuals' daily limits; thus, commuting is not part of the migration. However, migration and commuting have a close relationship due to their substituting roles. Commuting is regarded as an alternative to migration and vice versa [8]. Moreover, previous studies also show that commuting is a complimentary follow-up action to rural–urban migration [1, 4, 9].

Commuting mainly occurs in metropolitan areas due to its high in-migration rate and low capability to accommodate living in urban centers. Transformation of employment from the agricultural to non-agricultural sector motivates people to move from rural to urban areas, encouraging people to live in suburban areas and decide to commute due to the unavailability of land for workers to reside in the city center. Commuting habits and patterns are strongly linked to employment and residential location selections [2]. Moreover, commuting patterns result from spatial mismatch between individuals' job and housing choices that are greatly influenced by their socio-demographic attributes, such as sex, age, occupation, education level, and household size [1]. For example, low educated individuals are estimated to have the highest likelihood of experiencing spatial mismatch [4]. Hence, the workers from this group are mainly found among the commuting groups. Alternatively, the occurrence of spatial mismatch is suggested due to uneven spatial distribution of certain industries and workers [10]. It is also suggested that the spatial mismatch between home and work in developing countries is mainly due to economic reasons [11].

Migrants, in particular, are suggested to have distinctive commuting behavior [9, 12]. They are more likely to have a more balanced jobs-housing relationship and shorter commuting duration and distance than local population. However, migrants with a higher level of education are predicted to commute over the longer distance and duration compared to the lower educated ones [9–11]. This situation can be attributed to the institutional obstacles that may restrict the labor market mobility of the higher educated migrants. Migration history also significantly affects commuting duration. It is suggested that the longer of duration living in a migration destination, the longer the commuting duration that a migrant would have [11]. It is also apparent that married migrants are more willing to have long commutes in comparison to their single counterparts [11]. Further, the relationship between the housing market, labor market, and the decision to commute based on travel time and location of residence [13]. Moreover, the location of housing selections is strongly linked to transportation costs. However, commuting costs would be minimized if labor and housing markets were ideal. Longer and more expensive commutes would be offset by marginal rewards such as higher income or cheaper housing unit prices [2, 13]. Additionally, migrants who perform manual labor and service-oriented work are more likely to commute over a shorter distance in comparison to their local counterparts. Meanwhile, less-skilled local workers tend to have the longest commute distance among all the worker groups [1].

Variations in commuting behavior, including commuting duration, distance, and means, may result in commuting burdens and affect commuters' quality of life. Several studies on commuters have found that heavy commuting burdens due to transport inequity negatively influence life satisfaction, sleep quality, and subjective health conditions [13–15]. Migrants with limited specific-context knowledge and restricted financial capacity are more prone to face these disadvantages. Thus, it can be said that spatial disaggregation experienced by the migrants can hinder this group's efforts to fulfil their migration aim, i.e., welfare improvement.

## 3 Method

This study utilizes migration and spatial mobility information from Intercensal Survey 2015. Different from population census and other national surveys conducted by Statistics Indonesia, the intercensal survey provides more extensive information mobility trajectories of its respondents. Besides collecting data on birthplace and place lived five years ago, the intercensal survey also records place lived before current residential if respondents ever migrate. Information on commuting activities is also available in this dataset through the questions on whether respondents commute daily to conduct their main activities, their commuting destination, and the duration of their daily commuting.

This study focuses on those aged 15 years old and above who commute daily for work. In total, there are 40,220 observations included in the analysis that represent about 5,771,892 commuting workers in Indonesia. This study applies both descriptive and inferential statistics for the data analysis. The first analysis discusses the summary statistics of socio-demographic and commuting characteristics of the observations in three spatial mobility sub-groups, namely stayers (never migrate or moved to current residential during childhood age – below 15 years old); long term migrants (moved to current residential after the age of 15 years more than five years ago); and recent migrants (moved to current residential after the age of 15 years within the last five years). The second part of the analysis estimates the determinants of commuting behavior by applying multinomial logistic regression. Two regression models are run with the dependent variables of commuting duration and commuting means. In contrast, the independent variables are spatial mobility type, sex, age group, marital status, working sector, working status, education level, and residential region.

## 4 Findings and Discussion

Table 1 summarizes commuters' socio-demographic characteristics and mobility patterns in Indonesia in 2015. More than half of commuters are those who never migrated or had their last migration experience before they turned 15 years old. Further, about a third of commuters are migrants who have lived in their current residence for more than five years. About 14.6% of commuters have just moved into their current city within the last five years. It can be said the major proportion of commuters is those who have lived in their current residence for a long time. This situation may also depict the tendency of stayers to access the labor market beyond their residential areas. Commuting is considered a strategy to substitute migration since they prefer to remain living in their native communities. Moreover, migrants, particularly the recent ones, are more likely to buy or rent a house within the workplace region. In other words, migrants tend to have a more balanced job-housing relationship than the native population [9].

Commuters are dominated by males within all three types of spatial mobility. However, there is a higher proportion of female commuters in the stayer group than in the other two migrant groups. This situation illustrates the less tendency of female migrants to experience spatial mismatch. Moreover, younger recent migrants have a higher chance of experiencing a spatial mismatch between their job and housing choices, resulting in their commuting behavior. Meanwhile, most of the commuters are married. Married migrants have a higher propensity to commute, and this situation is highly influenced by their life-course stages [11]. Life-cycle events

**Table 1** Summary statistics of commuters by their spatial mobility type

| | Stayers | Long-term migrants | Recent migrants |
|---|---|---|---|
| % | 54.4 | 31.0 | 14.6 |
| **Sex** | | | |
| Male | 68.5 | 75.8 | 73.8 |
| Female | 31.5 | 24.2 | 26.2 |
| **Age group** | | | |
| < 25 years old | 25.3 | 1.4 | 14.9 |
| 25 – 34 years old | 38.0 | 17.6 | 49.8 |
| 35 – 44 years old | 21.7 | 39.0 | 24.6 |
| ≥ 45 years old | 15.0 | 42.0 | 10.7 |
| **Marital status** | | | |
| Never married | 39.9 | 6.3 | 17.2 |
| Married | 56.2 | 90.0 | 80.9 |
| Widow/divorced | 3.9 | 3.7 | 1.9 |
| **Working sector** | | | |
| Primary sector | 3.2 | 3.3 | 3.5 |
| Secondary sector | 31.0 | 24.4 | 24.5 |
| Tertiary sector | 47.3 | 43.1 | 50.2 |
| Quaternary sector | 18.5 | 29.2 | 21.8 |
| **Working status** | | | |
| Self-employed | 7.6 | 9.1 | 8.1 |
| Employer | 4.0 | 5.7 | 4.9 |
| Employee | 84.0 | 83.2 | 83.9 |
| Freelancer | 4.4 | 2.0 | 3.1 |
| **Education level** | | | |
| Low secondary or below | 29.1 | 19.2 | 19.1 |
| High secondary | 46.2 | 43.5 | 47.0 |
| Tertiary | 24.7 | 37.3 | 33.9 |
| **Current residential region** | | | |
| Java & Bali | 83.9 | 85.5 | 80.0 |
| Sumatera | 9.5 | 9.1 | 13.3 |
| Kalimantan | 2.0 | 2.0 | 2.7 |
| Sulawesi | 3.1 | 2.3 | 2.9 |
| Eastern Indonesia | 1.5 | 1.1 | 1.1 |
| **Commuting duration** | | | |
| ≤ 30 min | 38.4 | 32.7 | 39.5 |
| 30 – 60 min | 41.3 | 40.0 | 40.3 |
| > 60 min | 20.3 | 27.3 | 20.2 |

(continued)

**Table 1** (continued)

| | Stayers | Long-term migrants | Recent migrants |
|---|---|---|---|
| **Commuting means** | | | |
| Private transportation | 78.6 | 80.7 | 82.4 |
| Shared transportation | 6.4 | 6.1 | 5.6 |
| Public transportation | 15.0 | 13.2 | 12.0 |

like marriage and family growth would drive residential migration decisions due to changing housing requirements [16]. Married workers might have a higher tendency tend to have permanent residences beyond their workplace regions due to their need to have larger housing spaces attributed to the increase in their family sizes and more balanced relationships between work, housing, and other domains of family life, such as children's education.

This study classifies the working sector of the respondents into primary, secondary, tertiary, and quaternary sectors. The primary sector includes the working field engaged in the extraction and harvesting of natural resources, such as agriculture and mining. The secondary sector comprises manufacturing and construction activities, while the tertiary sector consists of economic activities that mainly provide retail and financial services. Lastly, the quaternary sector is the type of work engaged in knowledge-based services, such as education, health, and government services. Commuters mainly work in the tertiary sector in all three migration groups. However, there are higher proportions of migrants, both long-term and recent, who work in the quaternary sector than the stayer commuter. In contrast, the percentage of commuters who work in the secondary industry is the highest for the stayer group among the three spatial mobility groups. In addition, most of the commuters in all three groups work as employees. The small proportion of commuters among self-employed, employers, or freelancers shows that those types of working statuses give than a better chance to match the spatial distribution between their housing and workplace.

Commuting is a consequence of urban growth in almost every major city in Indonesia [17, 18]. Java-Bali is the region with the most significant number of commuters. This is in line with urban growth and population growth in Indonesia centered in this region. The Java-Bali region has also been the main destination of in-migration flows in Indonesia. The availability of more diverse jobs in urban centers in Java triggers high in-migration followed by high commuting. The high demand for housing will also increase along with in-migration, which will increase house and land prices, causing residents to look for housing outside the city at relatively low affordable prices [19]. The cost of housing in the inner city rises due to the increased demand for housing brought on by living close to a job and better wages after deduction of travel expenses [3].

About a fifth of commuters travelled more than an hour each way daily. For these commuters, mainly the recent migrants, commuting behaviour is regarded as the result of interrelated decisions when looking for an appropriate mix of a place of residence and employment. A non-optimal commuting trip distribution has ramifications for the spatial distribution of homes and economic activity and the structure of a city and its environment [2]. The option to live outside the workplace region and commute for an extended period daily are mainly driven by the motive to get cheaper housing [19]. The extremely high share of commuting by using private transportation that simultaneously occurred with the least preference to use public transportation, particularly by the recent migrants, signals challenges in transportation management in metropolitan areas and urban cities in Indonesia. This situation can illustrate the growth of population through migration that results in the growth of private transportation means, which is likely not accompanied by the growth of transportation networks.

This study subsequently ran multinomial logistic models to estimate the duration and means of commuting activities based on the socio-demographic attributes of the commuters (Table 2). The time spent commuting and the choice of the transportation means act as reliable indicators to reflect the degree of spatial mismatch experienced by the commuters [20]. Among all the determinants, sex is the only variable that consistently affects commuting duration and means. Females are estimated to have the highest likelihood of commuting for a shorter duration and using public transportation. It indicates the tendency for women commute over shorter distances than men [21]. Meanwhile, recent migrants are less likely to commute longer than their local counterparts. The former group also has a lower propensity to commute by using public transportation than the stayer and long-term migrant groups. There is no significant influence of commuters' working sector in differentiating their short- and mid-time commuting duration. However, workers in the quaternary sector have a slightly lower propensity to have a long commute than their counterparts in the agricultural sector. In terms of education background, it is apparent that the most educated group is less likely to commute under 30 min each way and more likely to travel more than an hour to go to their workplaces. This finding aligns with a previous study that suggested higher education increases commuting time [21]. Although longer commuting duration might illustrate the greater degree of spatial mismatch experienced by the tertiary educated group, their housing and job choices are argued to have a strong association with their access to housing and labor markets [13]. Longer commuting are argued to be compensated with higher income or lower housing unit prices [2]. Moreover, the lowest propensity of highly educated commuters to travel by shared and public transportation not only illustrates their high capacity to cover the high costs of private transportation but can also depict the flaw in transportation management across the region that may hinder the utilization of public transportation for commuting.

In order to have a better understanding of commuting behaviour by both spatial mobility type and education background, the multinomial regression models also incorporated interaction terms between these two independent variables. The illustrations of the effect of these interaction terms on commuting duration and commuting means are presented in Figs 2, 3 respectively.

Figure 2 shows that recent migrants tend to have a more balanced jobs-housing relationship than stayers and long-time migrants. For the travel time of more than

**Table 2** Results of multinomial logistic estimates for the commuting duration and commuting means

| Variables | Commuting duration | | | | Commuting means | | | |
|---|---|---|---|---|---|---|---|---|
| | Less than 30 min | | More than 60 min | | Shared transportation | | Public transportation | |
| | RRR | SE | RRR | SE | RRR | SE | RRR | SE |
| **Spatial mobility type** (ref.: stayers) | | | | | | | | |
| Long-time migrants | 0.907* | 0.500 | 0.895 | 0.062 | 0.654*** | 0.065 | 0.832*** | 0.057 |
| Recent migrants | 1.099 | 0.080 | 0.763*** | 0.077 | 0.772** | 0.101 | 0.753*** | 0.075 |
| **Female** | 1.347*** | 0.035 | 0.733*** | 0.023 | 2.071*** | 0.095 | 3.633*** | 0.115 |
| **Age group** (ref.: < 25 years old) | | | | | | | | |
| 25 – 34 years old | 0.892*** | 0.034 | 0.994 | 0.048 | 0.949 | 0.070 | 1.130** | 0.564 |
| 35 – 44 years old | 0.862*** | 0.039 | 1.168*** | 0.064 | 1.142 | 0.097 | 1.426*** | 0.085 |
| ≥ 45 years old | 0.867*** | 0.043 | 1.263*** | 0.074 | 1.445*** | 0.130 | 2.093*** | 0.132 |
| **Marital status** (ref.: unmarried) | | | | | | | | |
| Married | 1.098*** | 0.039 | 1.005 | 0.042 | 1.000 | 0.067 | 0.556*** | 0.025 |
| Widow/divorced | 1.167** | 0.082 | 1.140 | 0.094 | 1.274** | 0.151 | 0.915 | 0.071 |
| **Education background** (ref.: low secondary and lower) | | | | | | | | |
| High secondary | 0.656*** | 0.025 | 0.778*** | 0.037 | 0.599*** | 0.039 | 0.557*** | 0.027 |
| Tertiary | 0.439*** | 0.021 | 1.086 | 0.058 | 0.449*** | 0.039 | 0.565*** | 0.032 |
| **Work sector** (ref.: primary) | | | | | | | | |
| Secondary | 1.050 | 0.072 | 0.759*** | 0.059 | 0.477*** | 0.044 | 0.764*** | 0.694 |
| Tertiary | 0.922 | 0.062 | 0.942 | 0.071 | 0.329*** | 0.303 | 0.995 | 0.088 |
| Quaternary | 1.058 | 0.075 | 0.819** | 0.649 | 0.373*** | 0.374 | 0.852* | 0.079 |
| **Work status** (ref.: self-employed) | | | | | | | | |
| Employer | 1.014 | 0.068 | 1.205** | 0.096 | 1.523*** | 0.236 | 0.702*** | 0.664 |

(continued)

**Table 2** (continued)

| Variables | Commuting duration | | | | Commuting means | | | |
|---|---|---|---|---|---|---|---|---|
| | Less than 30 min | | More than 60 min | | Shared transportation | | Public transportation | |
| | RRR | SE | RRR | SE | RRR | SE | RRR | SE |
| Employee | 0.731*** | 0.033 | 1.076 | 0.058 | 2.788*** | 0.315 | 1.131** | 0.654 |
| Freelancer | 0.810*** | 0.059 | 0.834* | 0.080 | 2.366*** | 0.357 | 1.304*** | 0.125 |
| **Spatial mobility # Education** | | | | | | | | |
| Long-time migrants # high secondary | 1.055 | 0.071 | 1.552*** | 0.126 | 1.723*** | 0.208 | 1.409*** | 0.122 |
| Long-time migrants # tertiary | 1.124 | 0.083 | 1.334*** | 0.112 | 1.513*** | 0.205 | 1.087 | 0.099 |
| Recent migrants # high secondary | 0.987 | 0.086 | 1.365*** | 0.161 | 1.402** | 0.224 | 1.549*** | 0.188 |
| Recent migrants # tertiary | 1.176 | 0.112* | 1.362** | 0.165 | 1.330 | 0.240 | 1.272* | 0.163 |
| **Constant** | 1.708*** | 0.143 | 0.589*** | 0.052 | 0.086*** | 0.013 | 0.183*** | 0.020 |
| Base category is commuting duration between 30 – 60 min | | | | | Base category is private transportation | | | |

N = 40,220; *, **, *** indicates significance at the 90%, 95%, and 99% level, respectively

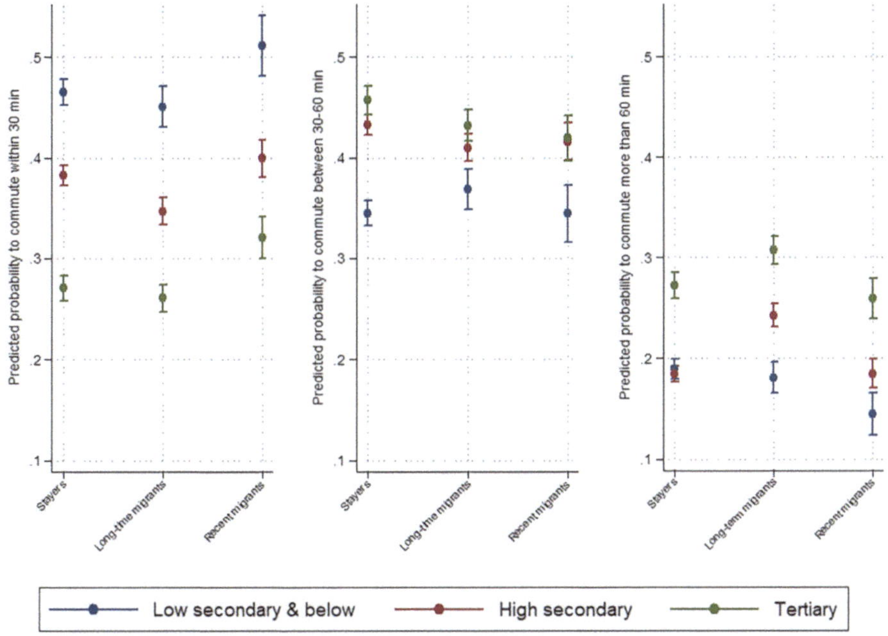


**Fig. 2** Predicted probabilities of commuting duration by spatial mobility type and education background

30 min, recent migrants are shown to have the least likelihood regardless of their education background. The new residents who commute are more likely to travel under 30 min. Migrants, particularly those who just moved in, are mostly renters, and they might have greater freedom and flexibility in their choices of housing and travel to work [1]. Therefore, they tend to experience less spatial mismatch than the local population, leading to shorter commuting times [9]. It is also shown that the least educated recent migrants have the highest likelihood to commute in a shorter time. Less commuting time can critically impact the urbanization process and might lessen the negative impact of spatial disaggregation on regional development [22]. The low-educated workers who usually perform unskilled manual labor and service-oriented work tend to commute in a shorter time than their highly skilled counterparts [1]. The low-skilled labors would have an easier job-labor match than the highly educated workers whose jobs are usually more specialized and concentrated in certain areas.

Among all the spatial mobility groups, long-term migrants, particularly the more educated ones, have a higher propensity to commuter over a longer duration. Unlike the recent migrants, those who have moved into areas of destination for a longer time might already live in a more permanent residence, either by house purchasing or long-term lease. Their higher likelihood of having a long daily commute might reflect their preference to live in peripheral regions that offer much cheaper housing and their limited access to affordable housing within their workplace regions. However, the

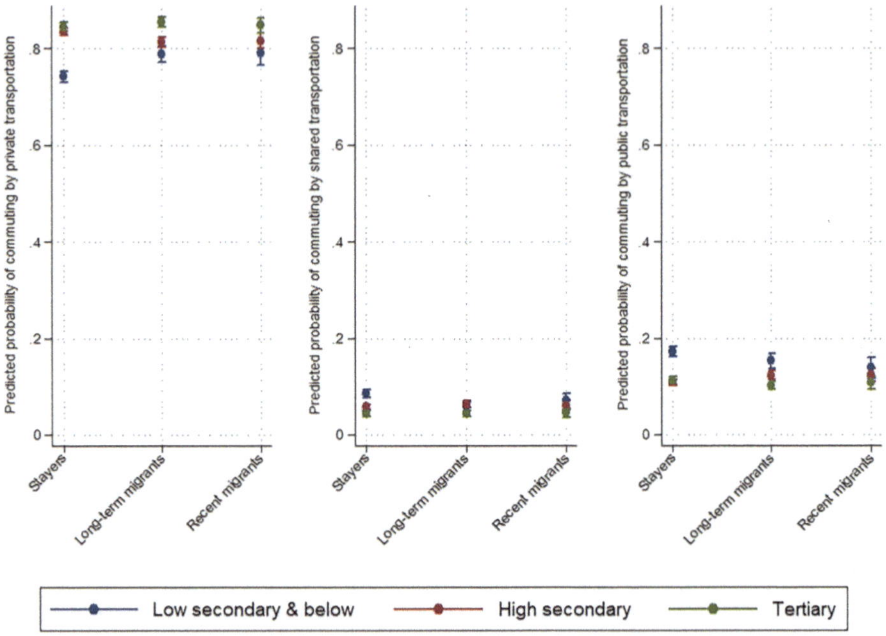


**Fig. 3** Predicted probabilities of commuting means by spatial mobility type and education background

long duration of commuting by the long-term migrants can depict heavy commuting burdens faced by this migrant group and might decrease their quality of life [23].

In terms of transportation means, Fig. 3 shows the much higher tendency to commute by private transportation across all spatial mobility groups. The low propensity to use shared and public transportation for commuting might indicate the imbalanced development between housing and public transportation infrastructures. On the other hand, the use of private vehicles for commuting that might affect the increasing travel costs can be seen as a trade-off for cheaper housing and shorter commuting time. Additionally, tertiary-educated individuals have a slightly higher propensity to commute by private transportation. Also, it is estimated that the most educated groups are those with the lowest probability of using shared and public transportation.

## 5 Conclusion

This study examines the socio-demographic characteristics of commuters by their migration history and analyses whether those characteristics affect commuting behavior. While most commuters are local population, there are also considerable proportions of long-term and recent migrants who commute on a daily basis to work. Those who commute are mainly males, married, well-educated, and work as employees in tertiary and quaternary sectors. This study subsequently explores whether demographic background and migration characteristics affect commuting behavior, i.e., duration and means.

The illustrations of the interaction terms between spatial mobility type and education emphasized the tendency of recent migrants to commute in a shorter duration and use private transportation. A shorter commuting time is more pronounced among the least educated and, among them, recent migrants have the highest likelihood of commuting in a shorter time. This situation may reflect the lesser degree of spatial mismatch between their jobs and housing options. The differences in housing situations between long-term and recent migrants seem to influence their job-housing relationship, which is reflected in their commuting behavior. Further, commuters, particularly the most educated ones, have an extremely high tendency to travel by private transportation. This situation might indicate practical issues regarding public transportation infrastructures in Indonesia. The higher travel costs embedded in private vehicles' travelling are compensated with cheaper housing and shorter commuting time.

Commuting and migration are important keys in examining population distribution and spatial disparities. It can be said that the number of commuters is increased along with population growth through migration and spatial mismatch between working and living spheres. Commuting behavior shown by the migrant groups has also shown how their presence can have a critical role in shaping regional planning on housing and transportation infrastructures. The increasing pressure on transport infrastructure across the city center and housing development in its peripheral regions are reflected in the tendency to commute for a longer duration with private transportation by the migrant populations. Also, the high use of private vehicles by commuters on a daily basis would pose challenges related to urban carbon emissions and road and public transport investments.

Due to the data limitation, several key issues related to the migration-commuting nexus in the Indonesian contexts remain to be explored. Future studies are encouraged to have a more comprehensive understanding of the relationship between migration and commuting, particularly research that sheds light on the distribution of benefits and costs of commuting among the local and migrant populations.

## References

1. Li Y, Geertman S, Hooimeijer P, Lin Y, Yang H (2021) Do migrants and locals differ in commuting behavior? A case study of Xiamen, China. Transport policy, 108:1–10. https://doi.org/10.1016/j.tranpol.2021.04.020
2. Haas A, Osland L (2014) Commuting, migration, housing and labour markets: Complex interactions. Urban Studies 51(3):463–476. https://doi.org/10.1177/0042098013498285
3. Houston D (2005) Employability, skills mismatch and spatial mismatch in metropolitan labour markets. Urban Studies 42(2):221–243

4. Fan Y, Allen R, Sun T (2014) Spatial mismatch in Beijing, China: Implications of job accessibility for Chinese low-wage workers. Habitat Int 44:202–210. https://doi.org/10.1016/j.habitatint.2014.06.002
5. Long L (1988) Migration and residential mobility in the United States. Russel Sage
6. Green A (2004) Is relocation redundant? Observations on the changing nature and impacts of employment-related geographical mobility in the UK. Reg Stud 38(6):629–641. https://doi.org/10.1080/0034340042000240941
7. Brown DL, Champion T, Coombes M, Wymer C (2015) The migration-commuting nexus in rural England. A longitudinal analysis. J. Rural Stud. 41:118–128. https://doi.org/10.1016/j.jrurstud.2015.06.005
8. Sandow E, Westin K (2010) The persevering commuter—Duration of long-distance commuting. Transportation Research Part A: Policy and Practice 44(6):433–445. https://doi.org/10.1016/j.tra.2010.03.017
9. Zhang M, He S, Zhao P (2018) Revisiting inequalities in the commuting burden: Institutional constraints and job-housing relationships in Beijing. J Transp Geogr 71:58–71. https://doi.org/10.1016/j.jtrangeo.2018.06.024
10. Zhou X, Yeh AG, Li W, Yue Y (2018) A commuting spectrum analysis of the jobs–housing balance and self-containment of employment with mobile phone location big data. Environment and Planning B: Urban Analytics and City Science 45(3):434–451. https://doi.org/10.1177/2399808317707967
11. Zhu P, Zhao S, Wang L, and Al Yammahi S (2017) Residential segregation and commuting patterns of migrant workers in China. Transp. Res. Part D: Transp. Environ. 52:586–599. https://doi.org/10.1016/j.trd.2016.11.010
12. Li S, Liu Y (2016) The jobs-housing relationship and commuting in Guangzhou, China: Hukou and dual structure. J Transp Geogr 54:286–294. https://doi.org/10.1016/j.jtrangeo.2016.06.014
13. Choi J, Coughlin JF, D'Ambrosio L (2013) Travel time and subjective well-being. Transp. Res. Rec. 2357(1):100–108. https://doi.org/10.3141/2357-12
14. Friman M, Olsson LE, Ståhl M, Ettema D, Gärling T (2017) Travel and residual emotional well-being. Transport Res F: Traffic Psychol Behav 49:159–176. https://doi.org/10.1016/j.trf.2017.06.015
15. Hansson E, Mattisson K, Björk J, Östergren P-O, Jakobsson K (2011) Relationship between commuting and health outcomes in a cross-sectional population survey in southern Sweden. BMC Public Health 11:834. https://doi.org/10.1186/1471-2458-11-834
16. Rossi P (1955) Why Families Move. MacMilian, New York
17. Giuliano G, Small KA (1993) Is the journey to work explained by urban structure? Urban Studies 30(9):1485–1500. https://doi.org/10.1080/00420989320081461
18. Baum-Snow N (2010) Changes in transportation infrastructure and commuting patterns in US metropolitan areas, 1960–2000. Am Econ Rev 100(2):378–382. https://doi.org/10.1257/aer.100.2.378
19. Brueckner JK, Šťastná L (2020) Commuting and migration. J. Reg. Sci 60(5):853–877. http://ideas.repec.org/a/bla/jregsc/v60y2020i5p853-877.html
20. Bi L, Fan Y, Gao M, Lee CL, Yin G (2019) Spatial mismatch, enclave effects and employment outcomes for rural migrant workers: Empirical evidence from Yunnan Province, China. Habitat international, 86:48–60. https://doi.org/10.1016/j.habitatint.2019.02.008
21. Cassel SH, Macuchova Z, Rudholm N,and Rydell (2013) A willingness to commute long distance among job seekers in Dalarna, Sweden. J. Transp. Geogr. 28:49–55. https://doi.org/10.1016/j.jtrangeo.2012.10.011
22. Sorek G (2009) Migration costs, commuting costs and intercity population sorting. Reg Sci Urban Econ 39(4):377–385. https://doi.org/10.1016/j.regsciurbeco.2009.03.003
23. Zhao P, Cao Y (2020) Commuting inequity and its determinants in Shanghai: New findings from big-data analytics. Transp Policy 92:20–37. https://doi.org/10.1016/j.tranpol.2020.03.006
24. Rouwendal J, Meijer E (2001) Preferences for housing, jobs, and commuting: A mixed logit analysis. J Reg Sci 41(3):475–505. https://doi.org/10.1111/0022-4146.00227

# Elderly People Issues in Indonesia: Determinant of Working Elderly in Demographic Transition

**Darojad Nurjono Agung Nugroho, Arga Nugraha, Syahmida S. Arsyad, Rahmadewi, Robani Catursaptani, Ikhsan Fahmi, and Putu Wira Wirbuana**

**Abstract** Demographic transition in Indonesia resulted in increasing the proportion of elderly population. Population aging is becoming a demographic challenge in many parts of the world. The issue becomes a challenge is the existence of an increasingly elderly workforce. This study aims to determine some key factors of the elderly population still working. The elderly population who are still working is the unit of analysis and uses The National Labor Force Survey (Sakernas) 2020 data. The analysis uses binomial logistic regression. More than half of the elderly are still working. The education, marital status, sex, place of residence, disability, number of household members, head of household, ID number, recent migrant status have a significant relationship with the working elderly population. The elderly population with normal physicality tends to work 14.7 times compared to those with disabilities. This supports the conceptual framework of productive and active aging approaches for the workforce of the elderly population as an asset that is physically and mentally capable of meeting its needs. Government policies both central and regional related to the productive elderly population who are still working are needed in terms of ability development, skills, health insurance so that the productivity of the elderly population is maintained.

**Keywords** Elderly · Population aging · The national labor force survey (Sakernas) 2020

D. N. A. Nugroho (✉) · A. Nugraha · S. S. Arsyad · Rahmadewi · R. Catursaptani
National Research and Innovation Agency, Jakarta, Indonesia
e-mail: darojad104@gmail.com

I. Fahmi · P. W. Wirbuana
Statistics Indonesia, Jakarta, Indonesia



Nawawi et al. (eds.), *Managing Disruption and Developing Resilience for a Better Southeast Asia*, Springer Proceedings in Humanities and Social Sciences,
https://doi.org/10.1007/978-981-96-2116-3_19

# 1 Introduction

The declining fertility and mortality rates will increase the life expectancy. Then it will guide to changes in the structure of the population. The population is living longer were based on the WHO 2019 data. Elderly population who aged 60 years old become 2.1 billion in 2050 which previously1.4 billion in 2030 and 1 billion in 2019. This proportion of the elderly population is projected to continue to increase, especially in developing countries [1]. These significantly changes in the global population need adjustment in all aspects, such as: housing, transportation health and social care, public facility to create a friendly environment for any age including elderly people where this is an important part of situation of demographic changing. Therefore, now in this world it is recognized that the condition of population aging a new challenge to face, including Indonesia.

The demographic transition in Indonesia is identified by increasing life expectancy as a result of declining fertility and mortality rates. This condition causes changes in the structure of the population. This condition causes changes in the structure of the population, namely the younger population decreases, while the productive age population increases and on the other hand the elderly population increases steadily. It shows that Indonesia is not only getting a demographic bonus but also entering the phase of population which is getting older. According to Law No. 13 1998 [2] and WHO, 2018 [3], the elderly people is who are reach 60 years old and over. In Indonesia, the elderly population continues to increase then it will attain almost one-fifth of the total population of Indonesia by 2045 [4].

The elderly population in Indonesia is still dominated by those with low education, namely 32.48% did not finish elementary school and even 13.96% never went to school. Meanwhile, there are only about 13.77% of the elderly population who have a high school education and above. The issue that becomes a challenge is the presence of an elderly workforce which is increasing and reaches 51.04%. Among the working elderly population, 42.29% finished elementary school and 38.34% did not finish elementary school; 85.83% work in the informal sector; 62.28% became the head of the family and 91.29% were male and 35.81 female [5]. Many of the elderly population are still working and working in the informal sector are issues that need to be observed and require necessary policies to protect them. It is necessary to analyze them. The research questions that arise are: Who are they and what are their conditions and what keeps them working? This analysis aims to find out: (1). Social, economic, demographic conditions of the working elderly population; (2). the relationship between social democracy and the working elderly; (3). The significant and most powerful factor influencing them is still working. The results of this analysis are expected to be useful for policy makers to formulate policies for the elderly who are still working because of how they contribute to the situation of economy in the country.

As we know, there are two demographic changes which contributes significantly to the aging population, namely: (1). Decreasing of the total fertility rate; (2). Increasing of life expectancy [1, 6, 12]. Both of these demographic changes occur for a long time period and will happen naturally in countries that achieve economic, social and health development [13]. The total fertility in the global recognized at 1950 is 4.9 births per woman, and in 2010 decline to 2.6, then it is estimated by 2.0 births in 2050. This decreasing condition of fertility rates has occurred mainly in Europe and Asia at the regional level. The situation specially in Europe, the fertility rate came down from 2.7 births per woman in 1950 to 1.5 births in 2010, and approximate will slightly decline to 1.5 births by 2050. In the other side, the figure in the Asia, the fertility rate by 1950 was 5.8 births per woman, then in 2010 it decreased to 2.3. It is estimated in 2050 to become 1.9. The condition in Africa is a little bit different where the fertility rate remain high, namely 4.8 births per woman and projected will be decreasing to 3.1 births per woman [14].

As we know, the second demographic cause of aging population is increasing life expectancy. In the word now, the average of life expectancy is increasing from 46.8 years to 68,8 years in six decades that is from 1950 to 2010. In fact, the life expectancies in Asia reached greater than the average of world, scilicet in1950 is 42.1 years rose up to 71.6 years in 2010. Northern America and Latin America was the countries with longest life expectancy where 51.2 years and 68.6 years in 1950 then in 2010 rose up to 74.5 years and 79.2 years, respectively. Europe and Oceania experienced an increase to 77.5 in 2010 also. Africa also experienced increases although still below world average in 2010, from 37,3 years in 1950 to 56,5 years in 2010 [15]. Total fertility rate and life expectancy are main contributor to population aging. The demographers define population aging is the average age of the population increases or there is a change in the age structure of the population, so that the elderly population can represent the overall age structure of a country. However, the aging population is a condition where people can live longer than previous generations. This is because life expectancy continues to increase and life is better than in the past [16].

Approach issued by the World Health Organization that to help the elderly population still active and in good health is the most important need. Countries are required to put in place policies and programs regarding with active aging which promote the participation and health in safety of elderly people. [11, 17, 18].

Active ageing hinges on determinants or various aspects that included to individuals, even families and nations also. Regarding these determinants, it can assist us to develop successful policies and to design programs. The determinant can be implemented in terms of health on all age groups, even though focus to quality of life and health of the elderly population. The determinants can explain the relationships or interactions within those variables of health and show the dominant variables on aging individuals and populations. In order to explain the role of each determinant variables and the relationship then interaction between the variables, the specific research is needed. Furthermore, knowing these determinants can affect to health and well-being is needed. Then, analyse the effect of determinants variables in order to get te benefit of transitions and "windows of opportunity" to enhance participation, health and security at various levels. Example, some key factors, such as work which is determine to a person's financial readiness in old age. Long-term care is essential for the next future life. The gender and culture are important determinants of knowing active aging. Long-term care is essential for the next future life. The gender and culture are important determinants of knowing active aging. Culture influences the way people become old and relate to the other determinants of active aging. Gender is another variables to specified the proper policy and will affect men and women well-being. The as usually in lower social status and less access to several aspects such as education, food, health services and employment opportunity. Traditional and modern women can play the role in contributing the health and family income [11, 17–20].

The global phenomenon is population aging that need action of international, national, regional and local both government and private sectors. The United Nations Principles for Older People (the outer circle) has the policy framework for active ageing, namely independence, participation, care, self-fulfillment and dignity.

An understanding of how the determinants of active ageing influence the way that individuals and populations age as a key to make the decision [11, 17, 18]. The policy framework needs implementing in three basic domains, namely: (1). Access to the entire range of health and social services that address the needs and rights of women and men as they age; (2). People and community participation will continue to make a productive contribution to society in both paid and unpaid activities as they age; (3). Financial and physical security needs and rights of people as they age in which older people are guarantee of dignity, protection and care in the event that they are no longer able to protect and support themselves[11, 17–19].

## 2 Research Methods

Source of the data is the results of National Labor Force Survey (Sakernas) in the August 2020 which is specially designed to collect employment data conducted by the Central Statistics Agency. The scope of Sakernas August 2020 is 514 districts/cities in Indonesia with a sample size of 300,000 households. The August 2020 Sakernas estimate can be bring out to the district/city level (BPS, 2020). The unit of analysis of this research is the population aged 60 years and over as dependent variable, which are grouped into the working elderly population and the elderly population not working. Independent variables are gender, education, marital status, place of residence, disability, number of household members, ID ownership, household head relationship status, and recent migrant status, are used to provide information on the background characteristics of the elderly.

Univariate descriptive analysis was conducted to describe the condition of the elderly in general by presenting a percentage table according to characteristics. Furthermore, bivariate analysis was carried out by presenting a tabulation of the percentage of the elderly population working and not working on their characteristics. Multivariate analysis with binary logistic regression is implemented to predict the ratio of the tendency of the elderly to work and not work using the elderly population who worked or did not work with several characteristics (independent) together. The binary logistic regression model is a regression model consisting of a response variable that produces two categories which are denoted as $y = 1$ representing the occurrence of "success" or $y = 0$ representing the occurrence of "failure" and the response variable following the Bernoulli distribution [21]. According to Hosmer, Lemeshow, and Sturdivant (2013), the stages in binary logistic regression analysis are coexistent test, partial test, and odd ratio [22]. Simultaneous test or as a likelihood ratio examine is implemented to consider the overall relation of independent variables in order to response the simultaneous model. Odds ratio is a measure to determine the level of risk in the comparison between events that fall into the category of success or failure. In this study, the dependent variable is the working status of the elderly population, namely working (1) and not working (0). From the variables used in this study, the logistic regression model that will be formed is

$$\begin{aligned} g(D) = & 0 + 1D1 + 2D21 + 3D22 + 4D31 + 5D32 \\ & + 6D4 + 7D5 + 8D6 + 9D7 + 10D8 + 11D9 \end{aligned}$$

## 3 Results and Discussion

The elderly population in this study in terms of working status, 51% of the elderly population work. The characteristics of the elderly population are: 52% of the elderly population are male; Almost 79% have low education. Sixty-two percent of the elderly population are married; 54.31% live in urban areas; Nearly 95% of the old people is not disabled; 78% of the elderly population has less and equal to 4 household members; 95% of the elderly population has the ID; Nearly 65% of the elderly population is the head of the household; and 99% of the elderly population are migrants, meaning that they have lived in the area for more than 5 years.

Analysis of the relationship between characteristics and working status showed that all characteristic variables had a statistically significant relationship ($p < 0.05$) with the working status of the elderly population. Five variables show positive coefficient signs, namely gender, marital status, disability, ID ownership, and the relationship of the head of the family. The findings of this relationship analysis are strengthened by the framework developed by WHO. [11, 17–19, 21, 23]. Variables such as education, place of residence, number of household members, and recent migration status have negative coefficients, which means that elderly people with secondary and higher education are less likely to work than those with low education. Elderly in urban is likely less to work than those in rural areas. Elderly people who have many household members have less opportunity to work than those who have few household members. Meanwhile, elderly people who migrate are less likely to work than non-migrant elderly people.

Multiple logistic regression analysis showed that the most dominant independent variable making the elderly population have the opportunity to work was the disability variable ($p < 0.05$). Population with disability is a description of the inability or deficiency that exists both physically and mentally, causing limitations in an activity. Elderly people who do not have disabilities are 14.7 times more likely to be able to work compared to elderly people who have disabilities. This is supported by the results of Triana's research conducted in NTB which showed that the variable that had the greatest influence on the elderly workforce was the health status of the elderly [24]. Montero (2021) explains that elderly people who have physical activity and are healthy have a tendency to have better daily performance, especially at work [25]. Lee (2017) added that it is important to support the elderly population who work in an age-friendly working environment because heavy work pressure, long working hours, physical risks at work and the absence of social security at work make the elderly vulnerable to health problems that result in they are not productive [26]. The health aspect contributes positively to the elderly population to remain productive. This is explained in detail by the concept of WHO [11, 17–19, 21]. On the other hand, elderly people with disabilities tend not to work due to declining health conditions as a result of the lack of physical activity to support their health [27]. Elderly residents who do not work because of disabilities are also found to generally have health complications due to inactivity [28].

The elderly population as the head of the household has a tendency of 2.6 times to work compared to the elderly population who are members of the household. The elderly population who is the head of the household has the responsibility and role of the main breadwinner of the family will have a tendency to work when compared to other family members [29, 30]. Pribe and Howell (2014) also explain that the elderly population who is the head of the household will try to work to meet their basic needs and the basic needs of their family members [20]. On the other side, elderly people who do not have the status of head of household tend not to work because they have poor health conditions and do not feel they are considered important in their families [31]. The elderly population who are still married have 1.4 times the opportunity to work compared to the elderly population who are not married. Married elderly people have the responsibility to meet the needs of their families. Several other studies have found that elderly people who have unmarried status are more susceptible to health problems and disabilities [32].

The male elderly population has a tendency of 1.4 times greater to work than the female elderly. This result is in accordance with Tomioka et al., which states that there are still gaps and differences in opportunities of employment among the elderly population based on gender [33]. The male elderly people is significantly higher than the female in the paid work category. It was further explained that work as one of the social participations needed by parents needs to pay attention to instrumental activities of daily living (IADL) where female parents receive a stronger impact than men. work as IADL decreases [34]. In addition, Minami sees that the male elderly population works as a recommendation from family members as well as the need to pay debts, on the other hand, the female elderly population looks for work as an effort to improve their welfare or mere social participation [35]. Other results show that on average women elderly feel they have less workplace chance rather than men[36]. Furthermore Nolan Anna and Allan Barret mentioned after 65 years old, women are significantly likely less to work instead of men [37] [38]. This effect is stronger among the married elderly than the single households. This is consistent with the explanation where older women without immediate access to family-provided financial need to work to support themselves. It might also be the case that older married women have caring responsibilities that reduce their employment in older age [22].

The similar situation in Thailand, old people work in the lower quality jobs and they have more riskier job. Elderly population are tending to be a self-employment where the rates is higher on them. In fact, older were self-employed and around two-thirds of workers 65 in 2019. Self-employment in past time has lacks of stability and job-linked with wage. The prevalence of less stable condition of employment, older people have much higher rates of informality also, that is indicate they lack access to social protection. In addition, 91 percent of those 65 and over and three-quarters of workers between 55 and 64 work in informal jobs [23].

In the Sri Lanka, there was a duality in the elderly people labor market which carries over into old age: low casual workers and the self-employed are working until very old age or until they are death because they are very poor people and have to get their living, and they will stop working when they have a health problem. In other side, civil employee and workers of formal private sector will stop work early which generally before they reach 60 years of age. It because they are pressure to mandatory pension provisions [39]. Other study between 2004 and 2011 in Sweden shows there is an increase in proportion of individuals aged 55–64 in the workforce. Majority the elderly people employment is a professions with lower education requirement and lower salary[40]. Other study explain that the elderly who live in rural areas work more because there is still open jobs, especially in the agricultural sector [41]. Also in Thailand, elderly population in rural tend to work in lower quality jobs [42].

Based on the analysis of the relationship between all characteristic variables and the working elderly, it shows that the health of the elderly is very important. Elderly residents who have good health status or do not have disabilities have a great chance of being able to continue working. Therefore, an understanding of healthy living and health insurance is the main thing in improving the quality of potential human resources and will eventually reach a potential and resilient elderly population (Table 1)

## *3.1 Conclusion and Recommendation*

The elderly population is increasing and in fact many of them are working. This shows that the elderly population aged 60 years and over still has potential and has a great opportunity to work. Elderly people who do not have disabilities tend to have high opportunities to work. This condition certainly shows that they still have the physical ability to produce something. This need to be facilitated by both the central government, local and private parties to ensure that the health status of the elderly population is optimal. Routine and affordable health insurance facilities really help improve the health quality of the elderly population which in turn contributes to

**Table 1** Variables that have opportunities for the elderly population to work

| Characteristic | P Value | 95% CI from exp value(B) | | exp(B) |
|---|---|---|---|---|
| | | Lower Limit | Upper Limit | |
| **Gender** | | | | |
| Men | 0.00 | 1.359 | 1.435 | 1.397 |
| Women | | | | |
| **Education** | | | | |
| Low | | | | |
| Middle | 0.00 | 0.577 | 0.647 | 0.612 |
| High | 0.00 | 0.254 | 0.377 | 0.316 |
| **Marital Status** | | | | |
| Not Married | | | | |
| Married | 0.00 | 1.306 | 1.525 | 1.416 |
| Divorce On/Dead | 0.00 | 0.358 | 0.580 | 0.469 |
| **Place of Residence** | | | | |
| Urban | 0.00 | 0.552 | 0.607 | 0.579 |
| Rural | | | | |
| **Disability** | | | | |
| Disability | | | | |
| Non Disability | 0.00 | 14.597 | 14.781 | 14.689 |
| **Number of Household Member** | | | | |
| $< = 4$ | | | | |
| $> 4$ | 0.00 | 0.859 | 0.924 | 0.892 |
| **ID Owner** | | | | |
| Have ID | 0.00 | 1.341 | 1.467 | 1.404 |
| Don't Have ID | | | | |
| **Head of Household Status** | | | | |
| Yes | 0.00 | 2.598 | 2.675 | 2.636 |
| No | | | | |
| **Recent Migrant Status** | | | | |
| Migrant | 0.047 | 0.718 | 1.008 | 0.863 |
| Non Migrant | | | | |

increasing the productivity of the elderly population in the labor market. Another interesting finding is that elderly people with low education are more likely to work. Those with low education generally work in the informal sector. The implication is central, local government and private sectors are needed to open up employment opportunities in the informal sector workface and guarantee the presence of the elderly population in the sector. Policies regarding health insurance, welfare and safety of the elderly population are urgently needed.

There are many things that need to be explored more deeply about the elderly population because of course this research has a limited scope, especially related to limited variables. For example, elderly people with low education have a great opportunity to work. The question arises, who are these lowly educated people? What factors cause them to work? What kind of sector do they work in? Is it formal or informal? Then the elderly population who migrate are less to work rather than elderly population who are non-migrants. For this reason, further and deeper research is needed to analysis the cause or the greatest opportunity to contribute to the non-migrant elderly population having a higher chance of working. In addition, there is a need for further research on the second phase of the demographic transition, that assumes the life expectancy will be higher so that the population will live longer. So the proportion of the Indonesian population is increasing. This condition requires the intervention of the government and the private sector to ensure the quality of the population's health and facilitate appropriate employment opportunities for the elderly population which in the end in a broader scope will contribute to the country's economy.

## References


1. World Population Ageing 2020 Highlights: Living arrangements of older persons [Internet]. New York: United Nations; 2020. Available From: Https://Www.Un.Org/Development/Desa/Pd/Sites/Www.Un.Org.Development.Desa.Pd/Files/Undesa_Pd-2020_World_Population_Ageing_Highlights.Pdf
2. Badan Pembinaan Hukum (1998). Undang-Undang Republik Indonesia Nomor 13 Tahun 1998tentangkesejahteraan Lanjut Usia
3. United Nations, World Population Ageing 2019 (2019) World population ageing 2019 [Internet]. Economic and social affairs, population division. P 1–111. Available from: Http://Link.Springer.Com/Chapter/https://doi.org/10.1007/978-94-007-5204-7_6
4. Badan Pusat Statistik (2018). Proyeksi Penduduk Indonesia 2015–2045: Hasil Supas 2015. Badan Pusat Statistik. P 464
5. Badan Pusat Statistik (2021) Statistik Penduduk Lanjut Usia 2021. Stat Pendud Lanjut Usia Di Indones 2021. Xxvi + 288 Halama
6. Kudo S, Mutisya E, Nagao M (2015) Population aging: An emerging research agenda for sustainable development. Soc Sci 4(4):940–966
7. Centre E (2008) Features and challenges of population ageing. : The European perspective. (1):1–16
8. Lee S, Mason A, Park D (2011) Why does population aging matter so much for Asia? Population aging, economic growth, and economic security in Asia (284)
9. Oec (2008) Trends shaping education
10. United Nations Population Fund (2012) Ageing in the twenty-first century : A celebration and a challenge. In Unfpa
11. World Report and Ageing On Health (2015)
12. Bloom De, Luca Dl (2016) The global demography of aging. P 3–56
13. Marko Mrsnik, David T Beer And Im (2010) Global aging 2010 : An irreversible truth global aging 2010 : An irreversible truth. P 1–49
14. Dobriansky Pj, Suzman Rm, Hodes Rj (2007) Why population aging matters—A global perspective. Us Dep State [Internet]. 1–32. Available From: Papers2://Publication/Uuid/4b8865db-5866–4285-A74d-168f45ed1109

15. Shrestha Lb (2000) Population Aging In Developing Countries
16. Harper S (2014) Ageing societies: Myths, challenges and opportunities
17. Organization Wh (2002) Non communicable diseases and mental health cluster noncommunicable disease prevention and health promotion department ageing and life course: Active ageing a policy framework. Madrid, Spain
18. Rudnicka E, Napierała P, Podfigurna A, Męczekalski B, Smolarczyk R, Grymowicz M (2020) The World Health Organization (Who) approach to healthy ageing. Maturitas 139(May):6–11
19. Jhala N, Christian Ma (2013) Active ageing. Int J Humanit Soc Sci Invent. 2(1):1–4
20. Priebe J, Howell F (2014) Old-age poverty in Indonesia: Empirical evidence and policy options: a role for social pensions. Tnp2k Working Paper 07
21. Pa S (2019) Grosch J, Scholl Jc, Tamers Sl. Fram. Considering Prod. Aging Work. 60(5):440–448
22. Argesti A. Categorical Data Analysis Second Edition. Vol. 9. New Jersey: John Wiley & Sons; 2002. 9–12 P.
23. Rantanen T, Saajanaho M, Karavirta L, Siltanen S, Rantakokko M, Viljanen A, et al. (2018) Active aging—resilience and external support as modifiers of the disablement outcome : Agnes Cohort Study Protoc. 35:1–21
24. Hosmer DW, Lemeshow S, Sturdivant Rx (2013) Applied logistic regression third edition. New Jersey: John. Wiley and Sons, Inc
25. All KNE (2016) Has the participation of older employees in the workforce increased? Study of the total Swedish population regarding exit from working life. Scand J Public Health. 44:506–516
26. Lee B (2017) Effects of working environment and socioeconomic status on health status in elderly workers: A comparison with non-elderly workers. J Korean Acad Community Heal Nurs. 28(4):472–481
27. Minami U, Nishi M, Fukaya T, Hasebe M, Nonaka K, Koike T et al. (2017) Effects of the change in working status on the health of older people In Japan. Plos One 10(12):E0144069
28. Tyagi R, Paltasingh T (2017) Determinants of health among senior citizens: Some empirical evidences. J Health Manag. 19(1):132–43
29. Rizqi M, Nur F, Oktora Si (2020) Analisis Kurva Roc Pada Model Logit Dalam Pemodelan Determinan Lansia Bekerja Di Kawasan Timur Indonesia. Indones J Stat Its Appl. 4(1):116–35
30. Fs S (2015) Analisis Partisipasi Kerja Penduduk Lanjut Usia. J Ilm Mhs Fak Ekon Dan Bisnis Univ Brawijaya. 4(1):1–21
31. Srivastava S, Singh SK, Kumar M, Muhammad T (2021) Relationship between physical activity and cognitive functioning among older Indian adults. Bmc Geriatrics. 21:304
32. Hirve S, Juvekar S, Lele P, Agarwal D (2010) Social gradients in self-reported health and well-being among adults aged 50 and over in Pune District, India. Indepth Who-Sage Supplement. Glob. Health. Action 3
33. Tomioka K, Kurumatani N, Hosoi H (2017) Age and gender differences in the association between social participation and instrumental activities of daily living among community-dwelling elderly. 1–10
34. Fujiwara Y, Nishi M, Fukaya T, Hasebe M, Nonaka K, Koike T, Suzuki H, Murayama Y, Saito M, Kobayashi E (2017) Synergistic or independent impacts of low frequency of going outside the home and social isolation on functional decline: A 4-year prospective study Of Urban Japanese older adults. Geriatr Gerontol Int 17:500–508
35. Minami U, Suzuki H, Kuraoka M, Koike T, Kobayashi E et al (2016) Older adults looking for a job through employment support system in Tokyo. Plos One 11(7):E0159713
36. Damman M, Henkens K (2020) Gender differences in perceived workplace flexibility among older workers in the Netherlands: A brief report. J Appl Gerontol 39(8):915–921
37. Anne Nolan Ab (2019) Work at older age in Ireland. Esri research Bulletin
38. Wright R (2011) Baby boomers paying for retirement : Sex differences In. 52(2):231–244
39. Arunatilake Mv, N (2008) The impact of population aging on the labor market: The case of Sri Lanka. Iza Discuss Pap. 3456

40. Nilsson K et all (2016) Has The participation of older employees in the workforce increased? Study of the total Swedish population regarding exit from working life. Scandinavian J. Public Health. 44:506–516
41. Utomo A, Mcdonald P, Utomo I, Cahyadi N, Sparrow R (2019) Social engagement and the elderly in Rural Indonesia. Soc. Sci. Med [Internet] 229:22–31. Available From: https://doi. Org/https://doi.org/10.1016/J.Socscimed.2018.05.009
42. Hosmer Jr, David W, Lemeshow S, Sturdivant RX (2013) Applied logistic regression. John Wiley and Sons

# What Causes Young Mothers of Twenties with Two or More Children Still Think of Having More in Indonesia

**Rindang Ekawati, Omas Bulan Samosir, and Mugia Bayu Rahardja**

**Abstract** The desire for more children is very important for population and family planning program. It helps us to know the fertility pattern and understand the population dynamic. This study aimed to identify the impact of family planning program, socioeconomic factors, and modernity on the desire to have more children. The data used were derived from the results of the Indonesia Demographic and Health Survey 2017 focusing on specific target which were women at safe motherhood age of 20–29 years who had two or more children. The dependent variable was the fertility preference, while the independent variables were socioeconomic, program, and modernity variables. The data were analyzed using the binary logistic regression. The results of the study indicate that women aged 20–29 years with two or more children who lived in urban areas and who had some secondary or higher education were less likely to want more children than other women. Higher odds of wanting more children among women aged 20–29 years with two or more children was associated with obtaining family planning information from the internet and the socio-economic variables and modernity cause young mothers still think of having more.

**Keywords** Family planning · Young mothers · Wanting more children · Internet · Indonesia

R. Ekawati (✉)
National Research and Innovation Agency, Republic of Indonesia (BRIN RI), Jakarta, Indonesia
e-mail: rindang.eka1@gmail.com; rind004@brin.go.id

O. B. Samosir
Faculty of Economics & Business, Department of Economics, University of Indonesia, Depok, Indonesia
e-mail: omas.bulan@ui.ac.id

M. B. Rahardja
National Research and Innovation Agency (BRIN), Jakarta, Indonesia
e-mail: mugi004@brin.go.id; raharja82@gmail.com





Nawawi et al. (eds.), *Managing Disruption and Developing Resilience for a Better Southeast Asia*, Springer Proceedings in Humanities and Social Sciences,
https://doi.org/10.1007/978-981-96-2116-3_20

## 1 Introduction

The study of desire for more children helps us to know the fertility patterns and understand the trend of population dynamics. The results of the Indonesia Demographic and Health Survey (IDHS) show that the ideal family size in Indonesia declined from 2.8 children in 2007 to 2.6 in the 2012 and 2017 [1]. In addition, there was a gap between the total wanted fertility rate (2.1 children) and the actual fertility rate (2.4 children).

Some factors that may associate with the overachieved fertility preference are husbands' higher fertility preference, child mortality, and frequency of marriage [2]. The level of women's formal education, area of residence, and religion were also found to be associated with the desire for more children [3]. Women characteristics such as socioeconomic characteristics and their environment which are program variables and modernity may also contribute to the desire to have more children. Women with higher ideal number of children and lived in rural areas tend to have higher children ever born than others [4]. Source of information about family planning program may affect the desire to have more children, as revealed by the same study that women who were exposed to radio and TV had lower children ever born.

Having children is a logical consequence for couples in Indonesia. Children are the successor of the lineage and strengthen the love in the family. Wives will be loved more by their husbands if they have more children [5]. The decision to have children involve both husbands and wife. Accordingly, communication within couples had a strong correlation with the achievement of desired number of children [6]. In a high fertility region, it was found that the desire to have more children was higher among husbands than that's of their wife [7]. Men had considerable reasons to have more children, such were financially safe, couple wanted to have children, couple was of worth to have children, and personal reason [8].

Among socio-economic variables, area of residence and positive point of view of having more children had an important effect on the demand for the third child. Women's education and age at first marriage also contributed to desire for the third child [9]. Fertility desire was associated with whether they had reached their ideal family size and also the level of education [7]. Wife's intention to have second or third child was higher than their husband's intention. This condition was associated with cost and benefit of having more children among couples [10].

The study on the fertility preference in Indonesia revealed that desire for an additional child was strongly related with the number of living children [11]. In addition, modernity, that is the availability of broadband, allowed women to get information on contraceptive behaviors and the consequences of whether becoming a parent or not [12]. Increased broadband access explained at least 7% of the decline in the teen birth rate between 1999 and 2007 [13]. Highly educated women who had access to broadband were more likely manage time equally between work and motherhood [14].

Studies on the determinants of fertility preference among younger mothers aged 20–29 years with two or more children in Indonesia were limited. Therefore, the objective of this study was to investigate the association between socioeconomic and programmatic factors as well as modernity on the fertility preference among younger mothers aged 20–29 years with two or more children in Indonesia.

## 2 Methods

This study used the data from the results of the Indonesia DHS 2017 cross-sectional data, a national representative survey conducted during July–September 2017. The unit of analysis of the study was currently married women at safe motherhood age 20–29 years who had already two and more children. The total weighted sample was 2785 women.

The dependent variable in this study was fertility preference that is whether women age 20–29 years who already had two and more children wanted more children. Therefore, it was a categorical variable. The independent variables were grouped into three: program variables, socioeconomic variables, and modernity variable. The program variables consisted of source of family planning (FP) from art events, discuss FP with husband, and husband wanted more children than wife. Socioeconomic variables were area of residence, wife's education, wealth index, and wife's work status. The modernity variable was source of FP information from internet.

The research analytical framework of the determinants of fertility preference among women age 20–29 years who had two or more children is presented in Fig. 1. It was hypothesized that socioeconomic, program, and modernity factors affect fertility preference among women age 20–29 years who had two or more children in Indonesia.

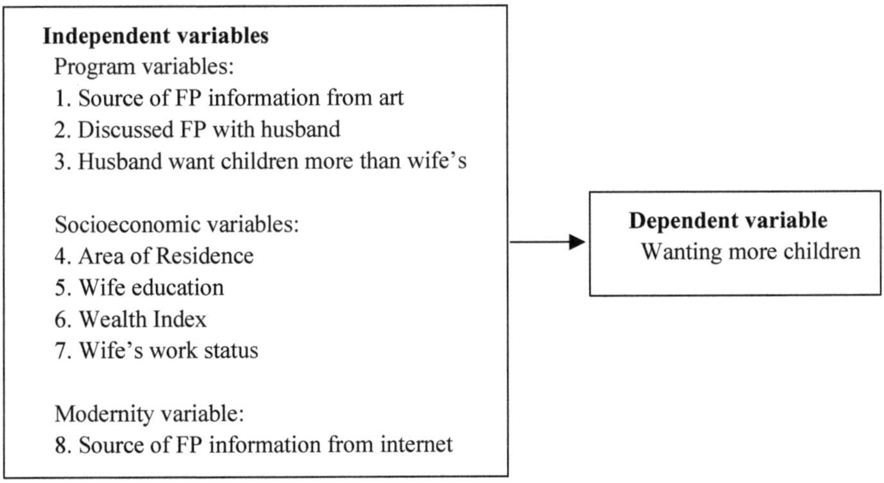


**Fig. 1** Research analytical framework of the determinants of fertility preference among women age 20–29 years who had two or more children

The data in this study were analyzed employing descriptive and inferential analyses. Percentage distribution of respondents of the study was presented. A bivariate and multivariate analyses between independent and dependent variables were also given. A binary logistic regression was carried out to examine the association between program, socioeconomic, and modernity factor with fertility preference. Multicollinearity test was also done.

## 3 Results

Percentage distribution of respondents of the study was presented in Table 1. It can be seen that one in two married women age 20–29 years who have at least 2 children still wanted more children. In addition, only about 10 percent of them stated that they had received information about family planning through art events. One of 3 women discussed family planning with their husband. One of 5 women stated that the husband wanted more children than the wife wanted. Almost half of women lived in urban areas. The majority of women had some secondary education. Based on the percent distribution of the wealth index, 33 percent were at the lowest level of wealth index. Nearly half of all women were working. Six out of 100 women got family planning information from the internet.

The results of bivariate analyses were displayed in Table 2. It can be seen that the percentage of women age 20–29 years with two or more children who wanted more children was higher among those who did not receive family planning information through art events, who discussed family planning with husband, whose husbands did not want more children than wives, who lived in rural areas, who had secondary or higher education, who came from households with lowest wealth index, who were working, and who obtained family planning information from the internet.

The results of multicollinearity test showed that there was no multicollinearity among independent variables. The correlation between independent variables were all less than 0.8. In addition, only three of eight factors examined had significant association with fertility preference statistically, that is place of residence, education, and obtaining family planning information from the internet.

Other things being the same, urban women age 20–29 years with two or more children had lower odds of wanting more children than their urban counterpart. Meanwhile, after controlling for other factors, women age 20–29 years with two or more children who had secondary or higher education had higher odds of wanting more children than lower educated women age 20–29 years with two or more children. Further, ceteris paribus, women age 20–29 years with two or more children who obtained family planning information from the internet had higher odds of wanting more children than women age 20–29 years with two or more children who did obtain family planning information from the internet.

**Table 1** Percentage of married women age 20–29 by research variables, IDHS 2017

| Variables | | Frequency | Percentage (%) |
|---|---|---|---|
| Wanting more children | Yes | 1452 | 52.1 |
| | No | 1333 | 47.9 |
| Source of FP information from art | Yes | 272 | 9.8 |
| | No | 2513 | 90.2 |
| Discussed FP with husbands | Yes | 1013 | 36.4 |
| | No | 1772 | 63.6 |
| Have a mobile phone | Yes | 2191 | 78.7 |
| | No | 594 | 21.3 |
| Use of internet | Yes | 1230 | 44.2 |
| | No | 1555 | 55.8 |
| Husband needs children more than wife | Yes | 632 | 22.7 |
| | No | 2153 | 77.3 |
| Area of residence | Urban | 1220 | 43.8 |
| | Rural | 1565 | 56.2 |
| Wife education | Less than primary | 259 | 9.3 |
| | Completed primary | 513 | 18.4 |
| | Some secondary | 924 | 33.2 |
| | Completed secondary | 803 | 28.8 |
| | Secondary+ | 286 | 10.3 |
| Wealth index | Lowest | 914 | 32.8 |
| | Second | 584 | 21.0 |
| | Middle | 504 | 18.1 |
| | Fourth | 456 | 16.4 |
| | Highest | 327 | 11.7 |
| Wife's work status | Yes | 1326 | 47.6 |
| | No | 1459 | 52.4 |
| Source of FP information from internet | Yes | 169 | 6.1 |
| | No | 2616 | 93.9 |

## 4 Discussion

### Education and Fertility

The level of education influence women's mindset on regulating their fertility. Moreover, for young generation they are more likely to expose to more access of information which is provided by media including the internet.

Fertility behavior is associated with several factors such as women education, economic, social environment, and the spread of information through various social

**Table 2** Unadjusted and adjusted Odds Ratio (OR), 95% Confidence Interval (CI) and *p* value of the binary logistic regression model of the determinants of fertility preference among women age 20–29 years who had two or more children, Indonesia DHS 2007

| Covariates | | Unadjusted | | | | Adjusted | | | |
|---|---|---|---|---|---|---|---|---|---|
| | | OR | 95% CI. for OR | | *p*-value | OR | 95% CI. for OR | | *p*-value |
| | | | Lower | Upper | | | Lower | Upper | |
| Source of FP information from art | Yes | 0.96 | 0.74 | 1.23 | 0.72 | | | | |
| | No | 1.00 | | | | | | | |
| Discussed FP with husbands | Yes | 1.08 | 0.93 | 1.26 | 0.31 | | | | |
| | No | 1.00 | | | | | | | |
| Have a mobile phone | Yes | 0.99 | 0.83 | 1.19 | 0.98 | | | | |
| | No | 1.00 | | | | | | | |
| Use of internet | Yes | 1.01 | 0.87 | 1.17 | 0.89 | | | | |
| | No | 1.00 | | | | | | | |
| Husband need children more than wife | Yes | 0.93 | 0.78 | 1.11 | 0.39 | | | | |
| | No | 1.00 | | | | | | | |
| Area of residence | Urban | 0.75 | 0.64 | 0.87 | 0.00 | 0.76 | 0.65 | 0.88 | 0.00 |
| | Rural | 1.00 | | | | 1.00 | | | |
| Wife education | Less than primary | 0.84 | 0.60 | 1.18 | 0.33 | 0.75 | 0.53 | 1.06 | 0.10 |
| | Completed primary | 0.80 | 0.59 | 1.08 | 0.14 | 0.76 | 0.56 | 1.02 | 0.06 |
| | Some secondary | 0.68 | 0.52 | 0.89 | 0.00 | 0.66 | 0.51 | 0.87 | 0.00 |
| | Completed secondary | 0.61 | 046 | 0.80 | 0.00 | 0.62 | 0.47 | 0.82 | 0.00 |
| | Secondary+ | 1.00 | | | | 1.00 | | | |
| Wealth index | Lowest | 1.14 | 0.88 | 1.47 | 0.32 | | | | |
| | Second | 0.92 | 0.70 | 1.21 | 0.55 | | | | |
| | Middle | 0.93 | 0.70 | 1.23 | 0.61 | | | | |
| | Fourth | 0.83 | 0.63 | 1.11 | 0.21 | | | | |
| | Highest | 1.00 | | | | | | | |
| Wife's work status | Yes | 1.11 | 0.96 | 1.29 | 0.16 | | | | |
| | No | 1.00 | | | | | | | |
| Source of FP information from the internet | Yes | 1.82 | 1.31 | 2.52 | 0.00 | 1.78 | 1.28 | 2.47 | 0.00 |
| | No | 1.00 | | | | 1.00 | | | |

media. Women with higher educational level have a higher chance to enter the labor market. They start considering the cost and benefit of having children as working women. The desire to have the third child and more declines on certain level of education [15]. Previous research found that most of women of secondary or higher education have fewer children than their ideal [16]. Research in Europe found that there was a correlation between women education and lifetime fertility intention [17]. Women with lower education were more likely to want more children than those of higher level of education [18]. However, our findings show that women with higher level of education had higher probability to have additional child. After controlling educational level and desire for additional child it was revealed that women who already have two children wanted more additional child than those who already have three children (Table 3). This study confirmed that fertility preference among those who already have two children is higher than those who already have three. It may mean that their ideal number of children is three. Government should rethink three children for highly educated women to prepare better educated future generation.

**Area of Residence and Fertility**

The dynamic of urban–rural fertility differences is associated with government's policy to control population growth by campaigning small family size and the use of modern contraceptive. Meanwhile, the speed of spreading information have led to a bigger difference in rural–urban fertility where fertility is higher in rural areas than in urban areas [19]. Age at first marriage, contraceptive use, and level of education differentiated urban and rural fertility [20]. The relationship between urbanization and fertility have been widely observed. There is a correlation between women's participation at work and fertility both in the urban and rural area [21]. The results of this study confirm these findings where fertility preference was higher in rural areas

**Table 3** The desire of another child by controlling education and number of existing children

| Education level | Number of living children | Wanted more children? | | | |
|---|---|---|---|---|---|
| | | No | | Yes | |
| | | *n* | % | *n* | % |
| Less than primary | 2 children | 66 | 39.3 | 102 | 60.7 |
| | More than 2 children | 48 | 52.7 | 43 | 47.3 |
| Completed primary | 2 children | 160 | 42.1 | 220 | 57.9 |
| | More than 2 children | 72 | 54.1 | 61 | 45.9 |
| Some secondary | 2 children | 355 | 46.7 | 405 | 53.3 |
| | More than 2 children | 100 | 61.0 | 64 | 39.0 |
| Completed secondary | 2 children | 318 | 48.0 | 344 | 52.0 |
| | More than 2 children | 100 | 70.9 | 41 | 29.1 |
| Secondary+ | 2 children | 93 | 36.5 | 162 | 63.5 |
| | More than 2 children | 21 | 67.7 | 10 | 32.3 |

than in urban areas indicating rural dwellers still adhere to larger ideal family size for various reasons, including supporting agricultural works.

**Internet and Fertility**

The information about family planning has an important role in equipping women about their reproductive health, fertility, and family formation planning. Source of information about family planning includes health provider, family planning field worker, mass media, television, and the internet. Previous research found that the higher the frequency of internet usage, the lower the fertility intention [22]. Our research finding was the opposite. Women who got family planning information from the internet had higher probability to want another additional child. Meanwhile, mobile phone ownership is related with smaller ideal family size. It was proposed that this relationship works through role modeling, preference change, and access to information [23]. Other research on the role of media on fertility, which is MTV 16 Pregnant, shows that there was a correlation between this program and fertility. The MTV 16 Pregnant was a program that broadcast the difficulties of being a teenage mother. The exposure to this program reduced 4.3 percent of teenage pregnancy [24]. To prevent unintended pregnancies, the intervention delivered by mobile phone is conducted to improve various health behavior. It was found that it is feasible to develop an intervention by mobile phone for young people in a resource limited setting.

**Interrelation Between Education, Area of Residence, and Internet with Fertility**

The level of education and area of residence influence fertility behavior. The fertility behavior such as desire for more child was obtained from various source of information. In the digital era, the source of information is more easily available, especially in urban community [25]. The study about fertility-related knowledge and information-seeking behavior found that most of the respondents used internet as source of information [26]. The internet was used as preliminary information, then they asked friends, family, or health professional to confirm their concerned. To seek information from the internet people should have digital literacy. Other research revealed that the digital literacy level of millennial mothers at some big cities in Indonesia was in the moderate level [27].

## 5 Conclusion

The desire for another child of young mothers who have two or more children was influenced by level of education, place of residence, and source of family planning information from the internet. Based on these findings it is recommended that, in order to manage fertility level in Indonesia, the government should strengthen family planning information, education, and communication particularly through digital technology so that eligible couples can obtain comprehensive family planning information for their quality family development.

## References


1. National Family Planning and Population Board, Indonesia; Statistics Indonesia; Ministry of Health Republic Indonesia; ICF International, Indonesian Demographic and Health Survey, 2017. Jakarta, 2018
2. Id IY, Kwankye SO, Frempong-ainguah F (2021) Predictors of underachieved and overachieved fertility among women with completed fertility in Ghana. PLoS ONE 16(6):1–16
3. Ahinkorah BO, Seidu AA, Kwesi E, Ansah A, Ameyaw EK, Budu E et al (2021) Socio economic and demographic factors associated with fertility preferences among women of reproductive age in Ghana: evidence from the 2014 demographic and health survey. Reprod Health 18(2):1–10
4. Adhikari R (2010) Demographic, socio-economic, and cultural factors affecting fertility differentials in Nepal [Internet]. Adhikari BMC Preg Childbirth 10. Available from: http://www.biomedcentral.com/1471-2393/10/19
5. Msoka AC, Pallangyo ES, Brownie S, Holroyd E (2019) My husband will love me more if I give birth to more children: rural women's perceptions and beliefs on family planning services utilization in a low resource setting. Int J Africa Nursing Sci 10:152–158
6. Babalola S, Oyenubi O, Speizer IS, Cobb L, Akiode A, Odeku M (2017) Factors affecting the achievement of fertility intentions in urban Nigeria: analysis of longitudinal data. BMC Public Heal 17(1)
7. Matovu JKB, Makumbi F, Wanyenze RK, Serwadda D (2017) Determinants of fertility desire among married or cohabiting individuals in Rakai, Uganda: a cross-sectional study. Reprod Heal 14(1)
8. Roberts E, Metcalfe A, Jack M, Tough SC (2011) Factors that influence the childbearing intentions of Canadian men. Hum Reprod 26(5):1202–1208
9. Bagheri A, Saadati M (2019) Factors affecting the demand for a third child among Iranian women. J Midwifery Reprod Heal 7(1):1536–1543
10. Duvander AZ, Fahlén S, Brandén M, Ohlsson-Wijk S (2020) Who makes the decision to have children? couples' childbearing intentions and actual childbearing. Adv Life Course Res 1:43
11. Samosir OB, McDonald P, Utomo A, Hull T, Herartri R, Fadila W, Rachmad SH et al (2018) Fertility preferences in Indonesia. In: Family demography in Asia. Edward Elgar Publishing, pp 138–152
12. Guldi M, Herbst CM (2017) Offline effects of online connecting: the impact of broadband diffusion on teen fertility decisions. J Popul Econ 30(1):69–91
13. Billari FC, Rotondi V, Trinitapoli J (2020) Mobile phones, digital inequality, and fertility: longitudinal evidence from Malawi. Demogr Res 42:1057–1096
14. Billari FC, Giuntella O, Stella L, Billari FC, Giuntella O, Stella L (2019) Does broadband Internet affect fertility? does broadband Internet affect fertility? 4728
15. Lazzari E, Mogi R, Canudas-Romo V (2021) Educational composition and parity contribution to completed cohort fertility change in low-fertility settings. Popul Stud 75(2):153–167
16. Channon MD, Harper S (2019) Educational differentials in the realisation of fertility intentions: is sub-Saharan Africa different? PLoS ONE 14(7):e0219736
17. Testa MR (2014) On the positive correlation between education and fertility intentions in Europe: Individual- and country-level evidence. Adv Life Course Res 1(21):28–42
18. Beaujouan E, Berghammer C (2019) The gap between lifetime fertility intentions and completed fertility in Europe and the United States: a cohort approach. Popul Res Policy Rev 38(4):507–535
19. Lerch M (2019) Fertility decline in urban and rural areas of developing countries. Popul Dev Rev 45(2):301–320
20. Ogaboh A, Ushie EM, Olumodeji, Attah FM (2011) Socio-cultural and economic determinants of fertility differentials in rural and urban Cross Rivers State, Nigeria. J Geography Regional Plann [Internet] 4(7):383–391. Available from: http://www.academicjournals.org/JGRP
21. Desta CG (2019) Rural-urban differential in fertility and maternal work participation: a study in Northwestern Ethiopia. African Popul Stud 33(2)

22. Liu P, Cao J, Nie W, Wang X, Tian Y, Ma C (2021) The influence of internet usage frequency on women's fertility intentions—the mediating effects of gender role attitudes. Int J Environ Research Public Heal 18(9)
23. Billari F, Rotondi V, Trinitapoli J (2020) Mobile phones, digital inequality, and fertility: longitudinal evidence from Malawi. Demogr Res 11(42):1057–1096
24. Kearney MS, Levine PB (2015) Media influences on social outcomes: the impact of MTV's 16 and pregnant on teen childbearing. Am Econ Rev 105(12):3597–3632
25. Prasanti, P. (2017). Portrait of health information media for urban communities in the digital era 19. Health Information Media for the Community. Sumedang, 2017
26. Hammarberg K, Zosel R, Comoy C, Robertson S, Holden C, Deeks M et al (2017) Fertility-related knowledge and information-seeking behaviour among people of reproductive age: a qualitative study. Hum Fertil 20(2):88–95
27. Jati, WDP (2021). Digital Literacy of Millennial Generation Mothers on Child and Family Health Issues. Journal of Global Communication 10(1):1–23

# Medical Students' Flourishing, Resilience, and Well-Being: Phenomenological Perspective from Indonesia

**Andre S. G. Samosir**

**Abstract** Despite being a burgeoning research topic, well-being is still a neglected issue to a large degree in Indonesia. In educational context, well-being may play an important part in students' resilience, achievements, and future flourishing in life. Moreover, while there have been rapid changes in the landscape of Indonesian medical education, there is an assumption that those who succeeded in entering medical school were amongst the most talented, competent, and capable component of the society, and as such more impervious to well-being issues. A paucity in the literature concerning the well-being of the medical student population in Indonesia was identified. The purpose of the study was to gain an understanding of the well-being of medical students with a focus on the students themselves. Specifically, the well-being of Indonesian medical students is explored using semi-structured interviews of 46 third and fourth-year undergraduate students in 10 Indonesian medical schools, acquired by means of purposive and snowball sampling methods. After Giorgian descriptive phenomenological analysis of the data, an essence of what being well is for the students emerged: it is being fulfilled, empowered, and grateful. The students acquired a sense of flourishing as a person throughout medical school, and their resilience developed along the way. There are many contributors that influence both the students' well-being and resilience. Resilience-related issues were interestingly pronounced when participants discussed negative aspects of their lives and were closely related to sense of deficiency. Echoing scholars' concern, mention of systematic intervention from the schools in developing and maintaining students' well-being and resilience was scarce. Overall, the findings helped rectifying the Euro-American bias in the literature regarding the topic, while to some extent agreeing with previous studies. Further recommendations are presented.

**Keywords** Well-being · Quality of life · Resilience · Medical students · Higher education · Lived experience · Phenomenology

A. S. G. Samosir (✉)
Faculty of Medicine and the Centre for Medical Science and Technology and Health Equity, Parahyangan Catholic University, Bandung, Indonesia
e-mail: dr.andresamosir@unpar.ac.id



Nawawi et al. (eds.), *Managing Disruption and Developing Resilience for a Better Southeast Asia*, Springer Proceedings in Humanities and Social Sciences,
https://doi.org/10.1007/978-981-96-2116-3_21

# 1 Background

## *1.1 Medical Education in Indonesia*

Education is a vital tool in improving people's well-being. Education improves people's quality of life (QOL) and assists people in learning how to improve their well-being [1]. Being the largest provider of international medical practitioners in the region, and with the backdrop of Indonesian disaster-prone geography, unequal development, huge and unequally distributed population, very low doctor/population ratio, and double burden of communicable and non-communicable diseases, Indonesian medical education needs to be especially tailored to build medical professionals' resilience and provide adequate support for Indonesian people [2–5]. There were also rapid changes in Indonesian medical education system, e.g. the fast growth of private medical schools; adoption of problem-based learning systems and continuing medical education; changes in laws governing medical practice and education; and changes in professional competence regulation [6–10].

Medical undergraduates in Indonesia are usually aged 18–25 years. Obtaining the bachelor's degree takes at least 3.5–4 years. Via a spiral curriculum [11], students are taught pre-clinical—mostly involving basic sciences—aspects of medicine in the first two years, and the clinical sciences in the next two years. Daily teaching and learning involves problem-based discussions amongst ten to fifteen students facilitated by a tutor, clinical skills practice with either mannequins or simulated patients, and traditional lectures. Subsequently, clinical clerkship rotations in multiple hospitals and healthcare centres follow for 1.5–2 years under consultants' supervision. After that they must pass a national competence examination authorised by the government, to be registered as qualified general practitioners.

While much attention has been given to the regulation of institutional and curricular affairs [12–14], less has been given to medical students' well-being. Data regarding medical students' mental health in Indonesia are lacking [15]. Shamionov [16] contended that transitioning to higher education may decrease students' life satisfaction. Students' QOL may have an impact on their motivation and achievement, and academic burnout and faculty's attitude towards students were correlated with the students' QOL [17–22]. It is also suggested that students in Asia may suffer from extreme pressure to achieve [23].

## *1.2 Well-Being and Resilience*

Studying well-being is a way to improve the condition of a population, and it is critical for a nation to have an interest in well-being [24–26]. Scholars noted that most well-being studies were both mostly conducted in a western (i.e. Euro-American) culture and grounded in western theories, and the practice of applying them as a universal yardstick is questionable [27–30]. Past approaches presumed authorities were more

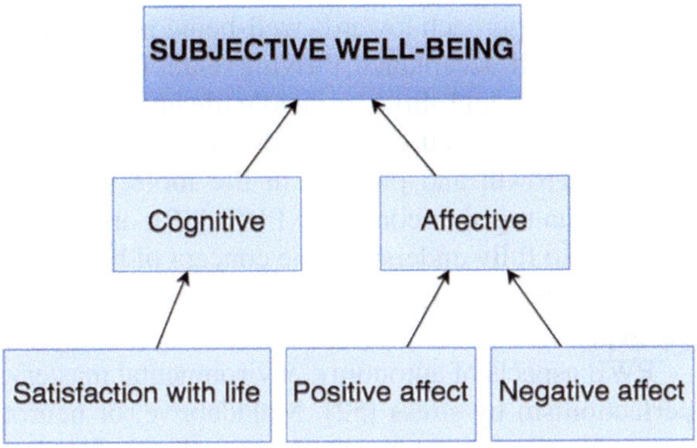


**Fig. 1** Subjective well-being: basic building blocks

qualified to judge a person's well-being (i.e. "top-down") and the experience of the people was of little relevance [29].

Both well-being and QOL are technical terms for what people usually recognise in popular parlance as happiness, or how one judges their life favourably. QOL concept came from studies in economics; it is more technical, global, top-down, and calls for measurable numbers, usually involving expedient regional or national data. The relationship between these objective data and happiness is not straightforward. The tendency now is to re-examine the researchers' attitude of treating QOL as a function of only material resources [31, 32]. Various disciplines are interested in the subject, emphasising the multidimensionality of QOL and the preferred holistic approach towards the issue [27, 32, 33].

Well-being, particularly subjective well-being (SWB), is more personal and closer to individuals' lived experience. SWB has been found to comprise momentary feelings—affective reactions to life events—and cognitive evaluation of one's whole life-termed satisfaction with life [34–40]. As such, well-being is more than what happiness usually means in popular parlance, i.e. hedonia—the gain in pleasant/positive affect and evasion from unwanted/negative affect (Fig. 1).

A counterpart to hedonia, in well-being discourse there is also the concept of eudaimonia: the fulfilling of purpose in life and the aspiration for excellence. Regarding this, scholars argued that more extrinsic aspirations—e.g. recognition or financial success—interfere with SWB and are positively correlated with anxiety and depression, while more intrinsic purposes—e.g. personal growth—are related to increase in SWB [40–42]. It will be useful to know what values the Indonesian medical students consider important. Available evidence regarding well-being suggests that personal factors are more important than external ones, and researchers suggested that QOL research should explore personal strengths that may play a role in increasing well-being [43, 44]. As such, it seems the development of character strength needs to be integrated into well-being appraisal and interventions. Understanding it further will help identify potentially vulnerable students and support them in their academic endeavour.

Another approach towards well-being is psychological well-being (PWB). PWB comprises self-acceptance, thriving relationship, personal growth, having purpose in life, autonomy, and ability to handle life intricacies (environmental mastery) [45–49]. PWB is sometimes used interchangeably with SWB, but PWB seems to emphasise personal growth and purpose in life more [47]. Other views stated hedonia and eudaimonia together constitute PWB [50], or suggested integrating PWB and SWB literature to fully understand the concept of happiness [51]. In line with the existing literature, the terms QOL, well-being, and SWB will be used interchangeably within this report.

PWB aspects of autonomy, environmental mastery, and life purpose are related to perfectionism by stress [52]. Maladaptive, or neurotic, perfectionism—i.e. excessive self-criticism and persistent feeling of failure—makes students inflexible with circumstances, and is linked with hopelessness and depression [53]. This, understandably, may also decrease resilience.

Gratitude, i.e. tendency to appreciate the good in life, has been found as a reliable link to SWB [18, 37, 54, 55]. In a sample of undergraduate students, gratitude partly moderates the positive relationship between SWB and emotional intelligence, the ability to effectively process and regulate emotion [56]; it is possible that people with emotional intelligence will be able to evaluate their lives and satisfaction in a more rational and positive way, in contrast to people with emotional inflexibility and maladaptive perfectionism. I found it notable that these attributes of continual appreciation and regulation of emotion, existing within an emotionally intelligent individual, are also relevant to the concept of mindfulness known in eastern culture for a long time but only recently flourishing in western literature. Mindfulness can be summarised as a continual awareness of phenomena, i.e. internal and external experiences, as they take place without being judgmental. Mindfulness is found to associate with higher SWB and lower anxiety [57, 58]. Furthermore, it is argued that mindfulness builds acceptance and resilience [57], which is important for students' well-being in medical school.

Resilience can be summarised as the ability to adapt, restitute, and even flourish, in the presence of stressors [15, 59–61]. Resilience is a crucial part of well-being and affects QOL and life satisfaction [60], and it may limit stress effects on students' mental health [15]. Despite this, similar to well-being research, apparently resilience literature on medical and other health professions students in Indonesia is limited. Most resilience studies, including in Indonesia, seemed to focus on disasters or environmental systems [62], and lately the COVID-19 pandemic [63–66]. The existing body of research regarding Indonesian medical students' resilience was cross-sectional, thus did not show causal relationship between resilience and other measured constructs; needs replicating with more sampling and areas; and was quantitative and "top-down" using instruments from Euro-American contexts, thus not sensitive to subtle personal facets and might lose the fuller picture, something educators urged to ameliorate [15, 59].

While resilience is important to medical and other health professions students and that it can be learned and improved—therefore should have been of concern to educators—our understanding of resilience and what contributes to it within Asian health professions students' context is largely unknown [15, 59, 67]. A case study found Indonesian factory workers maintain resilience through religious activity, supportive people and job environment, and chances to do self-care and pursue goals [61]. Another study suggested that people who enjoys art have both better resilience and propensity to help others [66]. Resilience is associated with lower depression and anxiety despite work-related stress [15, 67]. Resilience or the lack of it may even affect future work, e.g. quality of care, or job retention especially in rural areas [60, 68], something important considering Indonesian demogeographics. Grit—i.e. consistency in effort and interest; arguably a facet of resilience—is consistently positively linked with SWB, happiness, self-esteem, optimism, resilience, health, higher grades, and graduation rates amongst college students and negatively correlates with negative affect [40, 43, 69, 70].

Personal, social, and environmental factors play their parts in one's resilience makeup, for example in Rahiem's study on university students' motivation to learn [64]. Nevertheless, differences in resilience capability seem more endogenous, i.e. determined by an individual's personality, rather than exogenous, i.e. determined by the environment [60, 66]; similar to that of well-being [34, 71, 72]. It is found that adaptive coping ability contributes most to cultivating resilience within Indonesian medical students' context, followed by personality traits [59]. To complicate the issue, it is contended that social and environmental factors affect one's personality [15].

### *1.3 Well-Being and Resilience in Medical School*

There are plenty observations that getting into higher education, and medical school in particular, can be harmful. New environment, vulnerable age range, high workload, demanding schedule, financial pressure, and uncertainty about the future play a part in causing students' mental health deterioration [15, 16, 37, 67, 73–75]. Bullying and harassments, living away from family, maladaptive coping, and low resilience can also worsen well-being [15]. A similar finding in dental school environment was reported, where they found that dental students have poorer health compared to the general population and they are prone to burnout [71]. Anxiety, depression, and frustration, which in medical students are more prevalent than in general population or other student groups [59, 73], have been associated with lower academic performance in medical students [76]. Indonesian's hierarchical and collectivist culture may provide additional challenge against students' QOL [59]. Stress is a predictor of suicidal behaviour in research involving 2074 university students [77]. On a more positive note, academic and social engagements in university environment correlate positively with students' well-being [78]. Scholars uniformly urged medical schools in Indonesia to introduce screenings and programmes which assist students to deal with academic stress and improve resilience [15, 59, 60, 67], and even invited students to voice their ideas concerning this [15]. Nevertheless, medical schools in Indonesia seem to not have specific courses or interventions as part of their curricula to improve medical students' resilience. Only one study focused on a support programme to reduce stress, depression, and anxiety—in 30 medical students—through eight sessions of problem-focused and emotion-focused coping skills training [68]. Bustamam et al. mentioned that for medical students, the greatest source of stress is the heavy burden of curriculum and examinations [68].

There were studies in other contexts, including RCTs and a meta-analysis, which showed that higher education students' well-being may be modulated through various interventions, especially some strands of meditation and mindfulness practice [79–83]. It is argued that with mindfulness, resilience can be developed and be the target treatment in maladaptive and depressed students [40]. Other potential well-being interventions are intra-curricular wellness and positive psychology courses [84, 85], reflective writing [86], and positive emotion intervention—i.e. boosting positive emotions whether in frequency, intensity, or duration [83]. Lastly, regular light-hearted student get-together was suggested to improve, respectively, well-being and resilience [59, 87]. In general, the strategies involve identifying high-risk students, improving resilience and coping ability, and community support.

## 2 Methodology

The study employed a qualitative, exploratory approach to uncover views concerning a multidimensional topic existing within the literature but within a novel context [88–90]. Adhering to single theoretical basis of well-being was deliberately avoided to prevent introducing presuppositions.

The study aimed to explore Indonesian undergraduate medical students' understanding of the concept of well-being and QOL and their perceptions of the state of their well-being. The aim was articulated through these research questions:

1. What are the ways in which the students define QOL?
2. What is the meaning that the students ascribe to the concepts they consider as significant in contributing to their QOL?
3. What changes happen to the ascribed meaning throughout the students' study years?

Data collection took place from August 2016 until May 2017. 46 medical students (29 females, 17 males; age 18–23 years) in their third or fourth year, from five public and five private medical schools within five provinces and accreditation levels A to C, were interviewed. Interview times were 20–110 min (averaging 40 min). Audio recordings of the interviews were transcribed, member-checked, anonymised, and then analysed using Giorgian descriptive phenomenology [91], to obtain the essence of how they made sense of their lived experiences as medical students. The methodology was chosen to obtain as plural situations and as general an understanding as possible regarding the lives, experiences, and inner mental states of individuals relative to the topic [91–98]. An overview of distilling style in Giorgian analysis is as follows (Fig. 2).

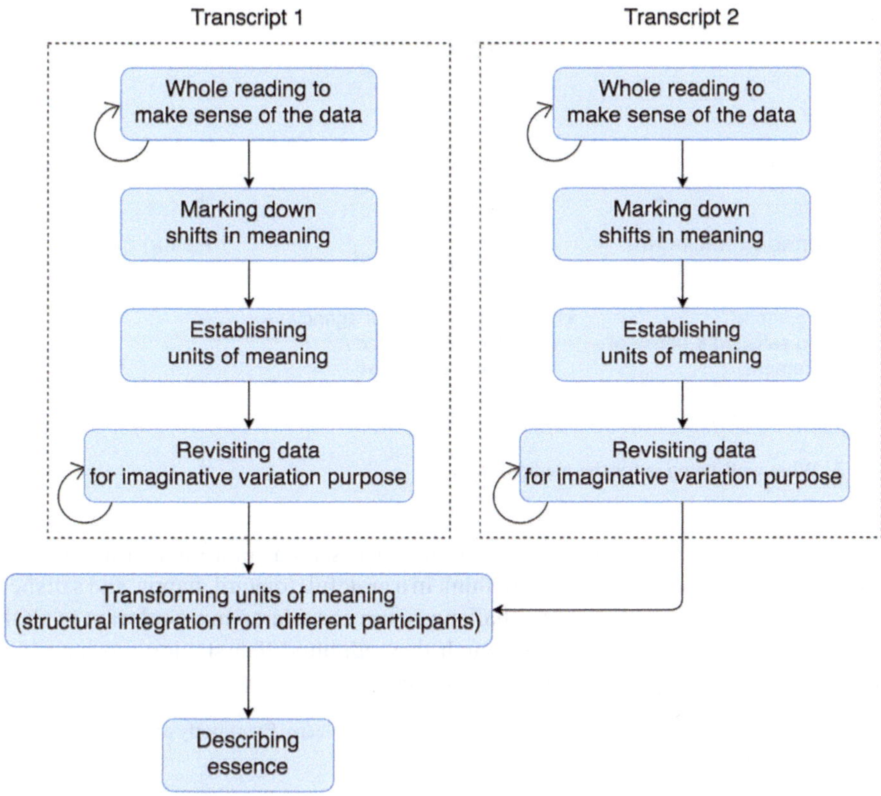


**Fig. 2** Iterative data analysis in Giorgian descriptive phenomenology

# 3 Findings

Indeed, the participants viewed well-being as a subjective concept. A part in the produced essence of well-being reflects resilience.

> [...] being comfortable or enjoying doing daily activities, even after taking into account both happy and sad events in life; [and] balance between stressors/responsibilities and the capacity to handle stressors/responsibilities. [99]

The main structures of well-being for the participants are depicted below (Fig. 3).

A major structure of students' well-being with regards to maintaining resilience is having a sense of agency and being empowered/adequately resourced, which included understanding their own weaknesses and strengths and the ability to improve on them.

> Because education can change someone's standards of living [...] It all can be achieved through adequate education. [Also] if we have money, and know how to use it well, we can improve our QOL, for example by buying things that support [our work]. (M14)

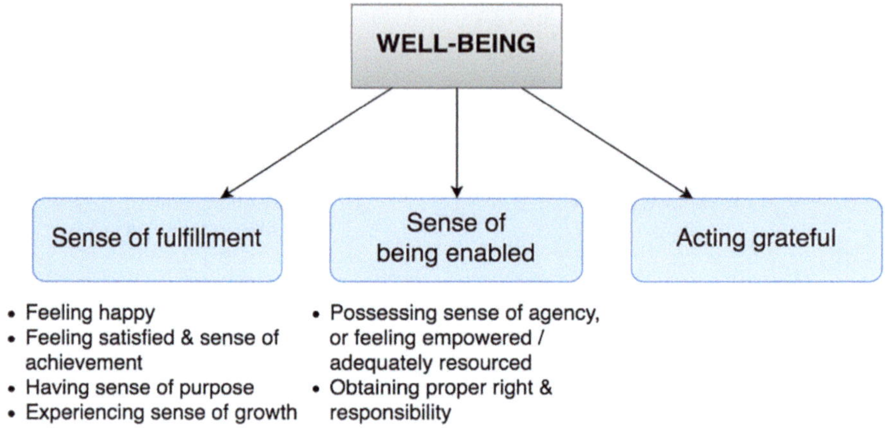


**Fig. 3** What well-being is for the medical students

Also of note, for the participants gratitude was seen as more than a feeling, but also action; it involves the decision to think in a grateful, tranquil, happy, and satisfied way. How the students respond to challenges was considered more relevant to QOL than the challenges themselves, although they admitted that staying too long in a negative situation may change a person for the worse.

> The important thing is doing the positive things [...] We can learn. Everybody makes mistakes; we learn from the mistakes. (F14)

Of note, all participants mentioned that supportive relationship or connectedness in its various forms strengthened them, thus improving their QOL and helped them stay resilient.

> For example, when I am sick [...] it's impractical contacting parents or friends [far away, but] there are neighbours that may be able to take care of me. (M8)

The next table lists other life aspects beneficial towards the participants' well-being (Table 1).

**Table 1** Influences ameliorating well-being

| Structure | Aspects |
|---|---|
| Constructive activities | Regular exercise and lifestyle; enough rest and vacation; doing hobbies and work/career; learning; treating others well; contemplation; fulfilling religious obligations |
| Conducive environment | Physical security; decent accommodation and healthy meals; access to places, transportation, and other services; stable job/finance |
| Personal domains | Self-acceptance; emotional stability; open-mindedness; feeling safe; being motivated and healthy; freedom and chance to explore; achieving; planned life; longevity; faith |

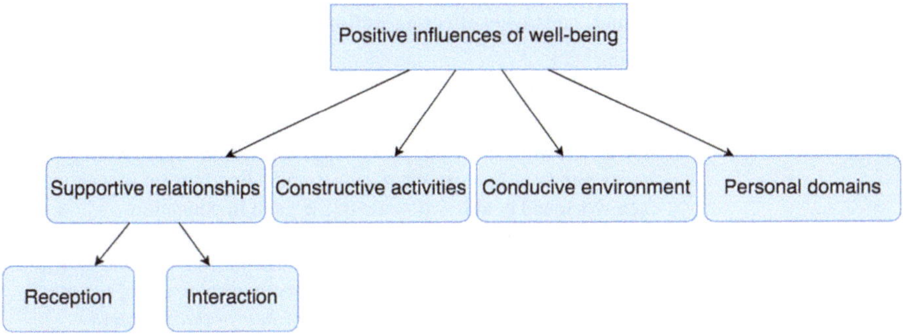


**Fig. 4** Positive influences towards well-being

What follows is the summary of positive influences towards students' well-being (Fig. 4).

Interestingly, aspects pronouncedly closer to the concept of resilience emerged when participants discussed negative issues in their lives, and noticeably were closely related to sense of deficiency, as shown below (Table 2).

Other negative influences towards participants' well-being are as follows (Table 3).

A summary of negative influences towards students' well-being is shown in the following figure.

Remarkably, part of the essence of well-being from this study demonstrates that the students have indeed been developing resilience as they study medicine (Fig. 5).

> During students' time in medical school, students grow as a person and become more capable to manage their life domains, despite facing challenges. [99]

A quote below exemplifies their thriving.

> So I feel that the changes were very significant, especially in the first year as I still tried to adapt, still tried to understand how to be a proper medical student; if we compare to other students, or other faculties, being a medical student is very different. And then the next years; in second year, we understand more how to regulate ourselves as a medical student, it formed—it is very important to be involved in organisations, or to know more people, because in the medical world, later I will be involved in a social environment. Finally, I'm thinking—in the third and fourth years, I'm thinking of where I want to go [emphasis]. After I graduate, after internship, what am I going to do? It is starting to come in mind. So there are these different... levels of thinking. (M6)

What is most fascinating is how the students throughout the changes in their lives, for the most part, were able to build their own personal strength and purpose in life, and thus were on the right track to improve their well-being. Some of the clearest development areas are shown within the next table (Table 4).

More areas of the participants' flourishing throughout the participants' time studying medicine are within the following table (Table 5).

**Table 2** Resilience-related issues, negatively affecting well-being

| Topic | Meaning<br>*(Illustrative Quote)* |
|---|---|
| Disorganised | Being irresponsible or failure in balancing life or managing time (e.g. religious worship, studying, socialising, and within organisations) prevents one from focusing, achieving, and being present in a situation; it even worsened health and made oneself fail in education<br>*I did find imbalances, where my academic [achievement] deteriorated, while I was at the busiest in organisations. At those moments, in my opinion my QOL is in disarray [...] Too much organisation, too much socialising, but diminishing academically, in my opinion doesn't improve QOL (M9)* |
| In non-conducive environment | Bad or non-suitable infrastructure for growth or reaching goals (e.g. uncomfortable accommodation and transportation system); which steals time and energy that should have been used for something productive; being "technologically stuttered."<br>*Can you imagine a crowded city where we have to go to school at 4 in the morning, and staying in the traffic jam? (F9)* |
| Insolvent | Financial, income, or job instability; which means inability to fulfil daily goals and brings stress, preoccupation, and disappointment<br>*If we're [financially] hampered we won't be able to conduct daily activities, and later fulfil our targets for that day, which in turn makes us stressed, burdened(M7)* |
| Physically and mentally deprived | Lack of food, rest, recreation, or exercise; physical illness (self or family; one student mentioned that being on period also annoyed her); low mood, and mental stress or instability; these make one weaker, prone to mistakes, jaded, uncomfortable, and also reduce the students' ability to think and work to reach life goals<br>*Not meeting needs, like not eating when hungry, not sleeping when sleepy. [It] simply makes us ill. Being ill means our QOL—like we can do nothing, non-functioning (F20)*<br>*My mum's sick, then died. Then there're so many tasks I couldn't finish. They're pressures. It made me* [voice trembling] *suffer from depression. I had to repeat semesters and all. It really deteriorated QOL (M12)* |
| Lacking control | Not having enough command of emotion, infrastructure, and time; which makes them feel controlled by the situation<br>*I feel low or less well when I can't manage time well. Bad health, inadequate sleep, it's all because our self-management not being good enough [...] When we can manage time well, our mind will focus on one thing [at a time]; thus we'll be wholly present in an event, or we'll do a job well, and the impact is our QOL increases (M14)* |
| Lacking faith/ religiosity | With lack of faith in/devotion to God, students feared there will be many trials and obstacles that cannot be overcome, make them feel failed, and worsen self-confidence and happiness<br>*When my devotion is lacking quantitatively or qualitatively, I consider my QOL as decreasing too. [T]here's power beyond us humans. That means God is involved. Unlucky, for example [...] not passing [...] practice exam, because of trivial stuff that I [already] know everyday but I failed [to do] in practice [...] I'll go back [thinking], maybe my devotion is lacking (M9)* |

(continued)

**Table 2** (continued)

| Topic | Meaning<br>*(Illustrative Quote)* |
|---|---|
| Lacking wisdom or learner attitude | Lack of knowledge or inability to make informed decisions and solve problems; which lowers confidence and makes life and interaction more difficult<br>*When we're unwilling to learn, we automatically won't know new things. We won't be able to discern between good and bad […] we can get lost [while] as humans we have to take responsibility for all our choices […] We'll be in difficulties, we'll also be confused (M10)* |
| Pessimistic | Pessimism and listening to negative words made oneself unhappy and ungrateful, unproductive, lazy, and waste time; similarly, sense of failure without enough fortitude, self-confidence, acceptance, and patience brought discomfort, unrest, frustration, even suicidal thoughts<br>*Like, hearing others or ourselves speaking negatively [or] being pessimistic with life; [it can be] depressing, and really, made our outlook of the world ugly. When our outlook of the world is bad, we might be—unhappy and unable to enjoy life, unable to be grateful of the smallest things. [It's already] hard to find something to be grateful of, even harder if we're used to listening to bad stuff [and] we became really unproductive (F20)* |
| Undriven | Non-existence of motivation or purpose, lack of discipline, laziness, procrastination, unwillingness to sacrifice, and despair as they prevent one from achieving goals; being coerced or sudden/unplanned changes in schedule, which may make one work unpurposefully, half-heartedly, irresponsibly, or suboptimally; not solving problems, which may pile up and worsen<br>*The most important strength is [from within] ourselves […] If we don't want to sacrifice [some aspects of our life], our qualities will just be run-of-the-mill (F17)* |
| Unfocused | Distraction, preoccupying thoughts, ruminating about past or future, or not doing meditative activities (e.g. praying) waste time for the participants, and they made oneself complain, feel lethargic, unable to focus and do the best, and less able to control emotions<br>*I […] I should've focused on just one activity. [I] sometimes went home late at night, or my mind became distracted; distracted mind made us […] stressed (M11)* |

**Table 3** Influences deteriorating well-being

| Structure | Aspects |
|---|---|
| Dysfunctional relationship | Peer pressure, contradiction with parents/tradition, conflict, feeling lonely or not enough |
| Bereavement | Someone's passing away |
| Appraisal issues | Complaining; complacency; incompetence/not achieving; feeling unconfident; self-blaming |

**Fig. 5** Negative influences towards well-being

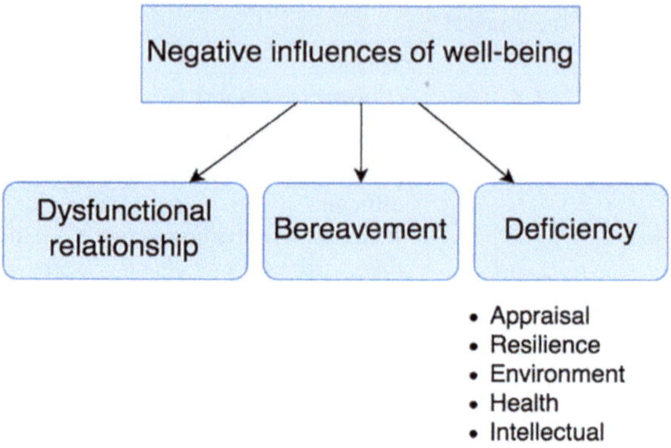


**Table 4** Some life skills learned

| Topic | Meaning<br>*(Illustrative Quote)* |
|---|---|
| Financial | Students felt more capable in managing money<br>*Ever since [I] became a boarding student, well—it's good that I can manage [my] own finance; it's still difficult at times, [I even] lost track sometimes. But now it's good! It was horrible at first (M8)* |
| Independent | Students have been learning to live by themselves<br>*Now it's all by myself. Scheduling life, doing things. [I] adapt. [I] at first was often homesick. [Now I] become used to the long distance, feel more comfortable, and not too worried (F12)* |
| Reflective | Students were more critical, open-minded, and learned better from past actions to inform their present decisions, developed problem-solving ability, and valued not just results but the progress<br>*If I didn't change my way of thinking, I wouldn't survive […] until becoming a doctor. So the ability [to think] is honed with problems [I experienced]. Rather than blaming others, […] I must find my mistakes and find solutions by myself. Sort of understanding differences [between me and other people] (F17)* |
| Social | Students built leadership and managerial abilities, in order to help people and to realise dreams<br>*[Medical] school is a plural environment and we're faced with different conflicts […] I learned a lot from that. So for example when I want to criticise a policy. It can't just be seen from one side (F25)*<br>*[Being in medical school] opened my mind regarding dealing with people whose backgrounds we don't know. [I'm] more understanding of others' situation. This relates to future profession as a doctor, where we can't choose who our patients are (M7)* |

**Table 5** Areas of growth

| Topic | Meaning |
|---|---|
| Personality | Becoming responsible and purposeful, and confident and proud; made fewer negative assumptions; more forgiving towards the past and self |
| Relationship | Consideration towards others and empathy; genuineness; giving and forgiving; more relationship (including romantic); acceptance towards impermanence; learning socialising skills, even after discomposure in new situation |
| Time | Appreciation both towards time and the usefulness of time management; not dwelling/ruminating; yet students mentioned losing time for rest (and thus also losing health), leisure, and people |
| Studying | Gaining knowledge and prestige; there are also physical, mental, and financial costs, tensions with family/friends |
| Religiosity | More devotion by those who are religious |

## 4 Discussion

Studies suggest that good awareness of personal strengths and weaknesses, while altogether not being restrained by doubts, ruminations, and over-criticism with self, can only be useful for a person's well-being as they become able both to improve on those strengths and to prepare for future contingencies [39, 53, 100]; these respectively equate to personal growth and environmental mastery in PWB. Taken as a whole, this is another cue to other scholars' sentiment that we should explore personal strengths in relation to how well-being may be improved.

Students' attitude showed the impact of collectivity culture in Indonesia [23, 46, 100, 101]. Relationships and other people were repeatedly thought to impact participants' well-being, which can also affect their resilience. Students want their relationships to be supportive, and conflicts, be it with teachers, partners, friends, and especially parents, were detrimental. Being away from family to start studying medicine was a problem at first. Students' conveying of feeling lonely and lacking after comparing self with others specifically indicated that at times relating with others might injure someone even without the existence of an external agent actively doing the insult. This asserts the need for treatments directed to self, i.e. improving personal strengths, as this involves a person's internal locus of control which plays a good deal of importance for someone's well-being [46, 48, 72, 102].

Further findings concerning studying medicine and relationships might add to generally Euro-American perspective within the literature. For many students, studying medicine/becoming a doctor was a way to please their parents. Students also observed that there were teaching situations where they felt held back from being themselves or discussing with their teachers and seniors out of cultural expectations. These conformation and authority issues can lower well-being [23, 59, 101], and participants stated that for them it created anxiety, which inversely correlates to resilience [15, 67]. Indeed, some students remarked they experienced suicidal thoughts regarding this push to conform. It is encouraging that later the students, for the most part, found ways to accept the past and live in the present, a mindful attitude that has been found to alleviate anxiety and improve well-being [57, 58, 79–83]. Lastly, students repeatedly said they want to be more useful towards other people, including by being a doctor. Further studies looking at how exactly resilience is affected by relationships will be useful.

Students described developments in their problem-solving and coping abilities, learning strategies, and openness to learn new things and to new situations. Students also showed development of their autonomy, life purpose, empathy and intent of being beneficial to others, and religiosity for religious participants. These are beneficial towards their resilience and well-being, mirroring existing studies [60, 65]. Yet, there were mentions as well that not fulfilling religious obligations and lacking faith would mean future obstacles and failures for the students and filled them with fear. It can mean that religiosity is actually an external pressure and not internal purpose for the participants, which can understandably harm them [40–42]. It may be of note that while religiosity/spirituality helped to cope with stress or gave them a sense of order or purpose, students did not discriminate between religiosity and spirituality (cf. Abdel-Khalek [28]). More studies into these issues are needed.

More findings that add to the literature also emerged. A key aspect improving the students' well-being is gratitude as an action instead of mere feeling. Together with purposefulness, this seems to tip the balance of well-being concept to more "eudaimonic" instead of "hedonic" for the medical students interviewed. Students' grateful attitude, a main structure of the findings, also enhances PWB aspects of mastery, autonomy, and relationship quality, which in turn will boost well-being [103]. This is fortuitous as it has been noted being grateful can be a self-reinforcing habit that maintains and even heightens one's well-being [56]. Students also showed flourishing in knowledge and mastery, which involves the improvement of positive affect and SWB as a whole, and emotional stability/psychological flexibility, which is related to a decrease in negative affect [59]. These are heartening and have been shown to build resilience.

The students considered studying medicine a rather gruelling endeavour. There were mentions of high expectations to achieve, personally or from others, especially parents, reflecting hints in the literature [23]. Studying took away their energy, social life, rest and leisure time, and money, something also mentioned in the literature [15, 16, 37, 67, 68, 73–75]. Students experienced anxiety with their achievements, being seen as incompetent, being inflexible with situations they faced, and being unable to experience fulfilment in the past and even present. This may harm their QOL and contribute to depression, hopelessness, and even suicide [53, 77, 104]. Signs of serious mental health decline, including depression and suicidal ideations, indeed were mentioned. There is a paucity in the student reports regarding medical schools' interventions towards increasing the students' physical and/or mental health, which is alarming. It will be helpful if medical schools are able to identify whether students practice maladaptive or adaptive types of perfectionism, which students respond worse against stress, and place interventions.

All in all, the findings of this study generally reflect existing literature; e.g. that well-being involves multiple contributing factors, or that studying medicine presents challenges. It is encouraging that while each participant was aware of the ups and downs of their daily life as a student and person, they also appeared to be building long-term understanding of themselves and the world around them, competencies in how to manage their lives, a more stable self, and satisfaction with self and their surroundings. The participants became more resilient in their academic endeavour and life, but these must also be balanced with medical schools actively providing ways to support students' growth, and society gently accommodating their flourishing.

## 5 Limitations and Suggestions

This study was done before COVID-19 pandemic; the development in medical students' well-being might be affected by the outbreak. As an exploratory study, this research wanted to achieve understanding of a phenomenon in a particular context. Generalisability and establishing cause-and-effect are not its aims. To obtain a fuller picture, studies with medical students in the first and second undergraduate years and in clerkship will be useful. As well, studies involving students in other health professions or allied health schools will only do good. A more ambitious project would be following cohort(s) of medical students throughout their years studying in medical school. Furthermore, in conjunction with studies with similar focus, it is hoped that systematic measures can be established to maintain and improve the well-being and resilience of medical students in Indonesia.

**Acknowledgements** The author would like to express thanks to Susan Jamieson and Jill Morrison, University of Glasgow, and Bill Spence, University of Dundee, for their insights on being a sharp researcher.

## References

1. Power C (2015) The power of education: Education for all, development, globalisation and UNESCO. Springer, Singapore
2. Badan Pusat Statistik (Statistics Indonesia) (2016) Population by region and religion. Available at https://sp2010.bps.go.id/index.php/site/tabel?tid=321&wid=0. Accessed 6 Nov 2016
3. Badan Pusat Statistik (2020) Dynamic table for subject health. Available at https://www.bps.go.id/subject/30/kesehatan.html#subjekViewTab5. Accessed 20 Aug 2020
4. Hsu S, Perry N (2014) Lessons in sustainable development from Malaysia and Indonesia. Palgrave Macmillan, New York
5. Kanchanachitra C, Lindelow M, Johnston T, Hanvoravongchai P, Lorenzo FM, Huong NL, Wilopo SA, de la Rosa JF (2011) Human resources for health in southeast Asia: shortages, distributional challenges, and international trade in health services. Lancet 377(9767):769–781. Available at: https://doi.org/10.1016/S0140-6736(10)62035-1. Accessed 26 Jan 2016
6. Adityo P (2016) Kartu Jakarta Pintar bisa untuk kuliah gratis. Available at: http://metro.tempo.co/read/news/2016/01/18/231737178/kartu-jakarta-pintar-bisa-untuk-kuliah-gratis. Accessed 26 Jan 2016

7. Denura F (2012) Fakultas kedokteran: mutu pendidikan dan ancaman ditutup. Available at: http://www.scholae.co/web/read/248/fakultas.kedokteran.mutu.pendidikan.dan.ancaman.di. Accessed 26 Jan 2016
8. Hendika R (2015) Kuliah gratis di fakultas kedokteran Unpad. Available at: http://www.tempo.co/read/news/2015/07/14/273683872/kuliah-gratis-di-fakultas-kedokteran-unpad. Accessed 26 Jan 2016
9. Lestari TRP (2012) Kebijakan pendidikan kedokteran di Indonesia. Info singkat kesejahteraan social. P3DI (Jakarta), 4(8):9–12. Available at: http://berkas.dpr.go.id/pengkajian/files/info_singkat/Info%20Singkat-IV-8-II-P3DI-April-2012-27.pdf. Accessed 26 Jan 2016
10. Rasmin M (2010) Dokter Indonesia: kualitas dan kuantitas. Available at: http://edukasi.kompas.com/read/2010/09/16/03565925/Dokter.Indonesia.Kualitas.dan.Kuantitas. Accessed 26 Jan 2016
11. Harden RM (1999) What is a spiral curriculum? Med Teach 21(2):141–143. Available at: https://doi.org/10.1080/01421599979752. Accessed 27 Nov 2021
12. Findyartini A, Werdhani RA, Iryani D, Rini EA, Kusumawati R, Poncorini E, Primaningtyas W (2015) Collaborative progress test (cPT) in three medical schools in Indonesia: the validity, reliability and its use as a curriculum evaluation tool. Med Teach 37(4):366–373. Available at: http://www.tandfonline.com/doi/abs/10.3109/0142159X.2014.948831. Accessed 26 Jan 2016
13. Miller LA, Chen X, Srivastava V, Sullivan L, Yang W, Yii C (2015) CME credit systems in three developing countries: China, India and Indonesia. J Eur CME 4:27411–27417. Available at: http://www.jecme.eu/index.php/jecme/article/view/27411/xml_8. Accessed 26 Jan 2016
14. Widyandana D, Majoor GD, Scherpbier AJJA (2011) Comparison of three clinical environments for pre-clinical clinical skills training. Med Teach 33:928–932. Available at: http://www.tandfonline.com/doi/full/10.3109/0142159X.2011.558141. Accessed 3 Feb 2016
15. Ramadianto AS, Kusumadewi I, Agiananda F, Raharjanti NW (2022) Symptoms of depression and anxiety in Indonesian medical students: association with coping strategy and resilience. BMC Psychiatry 22(92). Available at: https://bmcpsychiatry.biomedcentral.com/articles/10.1186/s12888-022-03745-1/. Accessed 1 Apr 2022
16. Shamionov RM (2014) Adaptational potential and subjective well-being of comprehensive school graduates and first year students of higher educational institutions. Procedia Soc Behav Sci 131: 51–56. Available at: http://linkinghub.elsevier.com/retrieve/pii/S1877042814029887. Accessed 30 Aug 2016
17. Henning MA, Hawken SJ, Krägeloh C, Zhao Y, Doherty I (2011) Asian medical students: quality of life and motivation to learn. Asia Pac Educ Rev 12(3):437–445. Available at: https://doi.org/10.1007/s12564-011-9148-y. Accessed 27 Jan 2016
18. Eklund Karlsson L, Crondahl K, Sunnemark F, Andersson Å (2013) The meaning of health, well-being, and quality of life perceived by Roma people in West Sweden. Societies 3(2):243–260. Available at: https://doi.org/10.3390/soc3020243. Accessed 28 Jan 2016
19. Monk-Turner E (2013) Quality of life among Thai sex workers: how important are work, educational and personal characteristics in shaping subjective well-being? J Int Women's Stud 14(3):1–13. http://go.galegroup.com.ezproxy.lib.gla.ac.uk/ps/i.do?p=EAIM&u=glasuni&id=GALE|A347968424&v=2.1&it=r. Accessed 3 Feb 2016
20. Pagnin D, de Queiroz V (2015) Influence of burnout and sleep difficulties on the quality of life among medical students. SpringerPlus 4(1):676–682. Available at: https://doi.org/10.1186/s40064-015-1477-6. Accessed 12 Nov 2015
21. Tempski P, Santos IS, Mayer FB, Enns SC, Perotta B, Paro HBMS, Gannam S, Peleias M, Garcia VL, Baldassin S, Guimaraes KB, Silva NR, da Cruz EMTN, Tofoli LF, Silveira PSP, Martins MA (2015) Relationship among medical student resilience, educational environment and quality of life. PloS one 10(6):e0131535–e0131547. Available at: https://doi.org/10.1371/journal.pone.0131535. Accessed 27 Jan 2016
22. Yalçın İ (2011) Social support and optimism as predictors of life satisfaction of college students. Int J Adv Couns 33(2):79–87. Available at: https://doi.org/10.1007/s10447-011-9113-9. Accessed 28 Jan 2016

23. Diener E, Suh EM, Smith H, Shao L (1995) National differences in reported subjective well-being: why do they occur? Soc Indic Res 34(1):7–32. Available at: https://doi.org/10.1007/BF01078966. Accessed 29 Aug 2016
24. Glatzer W (2015) Monitoring and analyzing quality of life—an introduction. In: Glatzer W, Camfield L, Møller V, Rojas M (eds) Global handbook of quality of life: exploration of well-being of nations and continents. Springer, Dordrecht. Ch. 1
25. Land KC (2015) The human development index: objective approaches (2). In: Glatzer W, Camfield L, Møller V, Rojas M (eds) Global handbook of quality of life: exploration of well-being of nations and continents. Springer, Dordrecht. Ch. 7
26. Maggino F (2015) Assessing the subjective wellbeing of nations. In: Glatzer W, Camfield L, Møller V, Rojas M (eds) Global handbook of quality of life: exploration of well-being of nations and continents. Springer, Dordrecht. Ch. 37
27. Abdel-Khalek AM (2010) Quality of life, subjective well-being, and religiosity in Muslim college students. Qual Life Res Int J Qual Life Asp Treat Care Rehabil 19(8):1133–1143. Available at: http://link.springer.com/10.1007/s11136-010-9676-7. Accessed 29 Aug 2016
28. Abdel-Khalek AM (2013) The relationships between subjective well-being, health, and religiosity among young adults from Qatar. Ment Health, Relig Cult 16(3):306–318. Available at: http://www.tandfonline.com/doi/abs/10.1080/13674676.2012.660624. Accessed 30 Aug 2016
29. Rojas M (2015) Poverty and people's wellbeing. In: Glatzer W, Camfield L, Møller V, Rojas M (eds) Global handbook of quality of life: exploration of well-being of nations and continents. Springer, Dordrecht. Ch. 14
30. Wong YJ, Ho RM, Li P, Shin M, Tsai PC (2011) Chinese Singaporeans' lay beliefs, adherence to Asian values, and subjective well-being. Pers Individ Differ 50(6):822–827. Available at: https://doi.org/10.1016/j.paid.2011.01.003. Accessed 29 Aug 2016
31. Assi J, Lucchini M, Spagnolo A (2012) Mapping patterns of well-being and quality of life in extended Europe. Int Rev Econ 59(4):409–430. Available at: https://doi.org/10.1007/s12232-012-0147-z. Accessed 28 Jan 2016
32. Salvador-Carulla L, Lucas R, Ayuso-Mateos JL, Miret M (2014) Use of the terms "Wellbeing" and "Quality of Life" in health sciences: a conceptual framework. Eur J Psychiatry 28(1):50–65. Available at: https://doi.org/10.4321/S0213-61632014000100005. Accessed 28 Jan 2016
33. Charlemagne-Badal SJ, Lee JW, Butler TL, Fraser GE (2015) Conceptual domains included in wellbeing and life satisfaction instruments: a review. Appl Res Qual Life 10(2):305–328. Available at: https://doi.org/10.1007/s11482-014-9306-6. Accessed 28 Jan 2016
34. Abdel-Khalek AM, Lester D (2010) Personal and psychological correlates of happiness among a sample of Kuwaiti muslim students. J Muslim Ment Health 5(2):194–209. Available at: http://www.tandfonline.com/doi/abs/10.1080/15564908.2010.487725. Accessed 30 Aug 2016
35. Correia I, Batista M, Lima ML (2009) Does the belief in a just world bring happiness? Causal relationships among belief in a just world, life satisfaction and mood. Aust J Psychol 61(4):220–227. Available at: http://doi.wiley.com/10.1080/00049530802579515. Accessed 29 Aug 2016
36. Emmons RA (1986) Personal strivings: an approach to personality and subjective well-being. J Pers Soc Psychol 51(5):1058–1068. Available at: http://doi.apa.org/getdoi.cfm?doi=10.1037/0022-3514.51.5.1058. Accessed 30 Aug 2016
37. Macaskill A, Denovan A (2014) Assessing psychological health: the contribution of psychological strengths. Br J Guid Couns 42(3):320–337. Available at: http://www.tandfonline.com/doi/abs/10.1080/03069885.2014.898739. Accessed 29 Aug 2016
38. Molnar DS, Busseri MA, Perrier CPK, Sadava SW (2009) A longitudinal examination of alcohol use and subjective well-being in an undergraduate sample. J Stud Alcohol Drugs 70(5):704–713. Available at: http://www.jsad.com/doi/10.15288/jsad.2009.70.704. Accessed 29 Aug 2016
39. Robak RW, Chiffriller SH, Zappone MC (2007) College students' motivations for money and subjective well-being. Psychol Rep 100(1):147–156. Available at: http://prx.sagepub.com/lookup/doi/10.2466/pr0.100.1.147-156. Accessed 26 Aug 2016

40. Satici SA (2016) Psychological vulnerability, resilience, and subjective well-being: the mediating role of hope. Pers Individ Differ 102:68–73. Available at: https://www-sciencedirect-com.ezproxy.lib.gla.ac.uk/science/article/pii/S0191886916308078. Accessed 30 Aug 2016
41. Nishimura T, Suzuki T (2016) Aspirations and life satisfaction in Japan: the big five personality makes clear. Pers Individ Differ 97:300–305. Available at: https://www-sciencedirect-com.ezproxy.lib.gla.ac.uk/science/article/pii/S019188691630126X. Accessed 29 Aug 2016
42. Oishi S, Diener E, Suh E, Lucas RE (1999) Value as a moderator in subjective well-being. J Pers 67(1):157–184. Available at: http://doi.wiley.com/10.1111/1467-6494.00051. Accessed 30 Aug 2016
43. Eklund K, Dowdy E, Jones C, Furlong M (2011) Applicability of the dual-factor model of mental health for college students. J Colle Stud Psychother 25(1):79–92. Available at: http://www.tandfonline.com/doi/abs/10.1080/87568225.2011.532677. Accessed 30 Aug 2016
44. Proctor C, Maltby J, Linley PA (2011) Strengths use as a predictor of well-being and health-related quality of life. J Happiness Stud 12(1):153–169. Available at: http://link.springer.com/10.1007/s10902-009-9181-2. Accessed 29 Aug 2016
45. Bechtel RB, Corral-Verdugo V (2010) Happiness and sustainable behavior. In: Corral-Verdugo V, Garcia-Cadena CH, Frias-Armenta M (eds) Psychological approaches to sustainability: current trends in theory, research and applications. Nova Science Publishers, New York. Ch. 21
46. Cooper H, Okamura L, McNeil P (1995) Situation and personality correlates of psychological well-being: social activity and personal control. J Res Pers 29(4):395–417. Available at: http://linkinghub.elsevier.com/retrieve/pii/S0092656685710239. Accessed 30 Aug 2016
47. Durkin J, Joseph S (2009) Growth following adversity and its relation with subjective well-being and psychological well-being. J Loss Trauma 14(3):228–234. Available at: http://www.tandfonline.com/doi/abs/10.1080/15325020802540561. Accessed 29 Aug 2016
48. Owusu-Ansah FE (2008) Control perceptions and control appraisal: relation to measures of subjective well-being. Ghana Med J 42(2):61–67. Available at: http://www.pubmedcentral.nih.gov/articlerender.fcgi?artid=PMC2631269. Accessed 29 Aug 2016
49. Páez D, Mendiburo Seguel A, Martínez-Sánchez F (2013) Incremental validity of alexithymia, emotional coping and humor style on happiness and psychological well-being. J Happiness Stud 14(5):1621–1637. Available at: http://link.springer.com/10.1007/s10902-012-9400-0. Accessed 29 Aug 2016
50. Rugira J, Nienaber AW, Wissing MP (2013) Psychological well-being among Tanzanian university students. J Psychol Afr 23(3):425–442. Available at: https://www-tandfonline-com.ezproxy.lib.gla.ac.uk/doi/abs/10.1080/14330237.2013.10820647. Accessed 29 Aug 2016
51. Compton WC (2001) Toward a tripartite factor structure of mental health: subjective well-being, personal growth, and religiosity. J Psychol 135(5):486–500. Available at: http://www.tandfonline.com/doi/abs/10.1080/00223980109603714. Accessed 29 Aug 2016
52. Ashby JS, Noble CL, Gnilka PB (2014) Multidimensional perfectionism, depression, and satisfaction with life: differences among perfectionists and tests of a stress-mediation model. J Colle Couns 15(2). Available at: http://link.galegroup.com.ezproxy.lib.gla.ac.uk/apps/doc/A299343270/EAIM?u=glasuni&sid=EAIM&xid=9fb1314c. Accessed 26 Aug 2016
53. Gnilka PB, Ashby JS, Noble CL (2012) Adaptive and maladaptive perfectionism as mediators of adult attachment styles and depression, hopelessness, and life satisfaction. J Couns Dev 91(1):78–86. Available at: http://link.galegroup.com/apps/doc/A320069053/EAIM?u=glasuni&sid=EAIM&xid=828b6e1e. Accessed 26 Aug 2016
54. Allan BA, Steger MF, Shin JY (2013) Thanks? Gratitude and well-being over the Thanksgiving holiday among college students. J Posit Psychol 8(2):91–102. Available at: http://www.tandfonline.com/doi/abs/10.1080/17439760.2013.776623. Accessed 29 Aug 2016
55. Chen LH, Chen MY, Tsai YM (2012) Does gratitude always work? Ambivalence over emotional expression inhibits the beneficial effect of gratitude on well-being. Int J Psychol 47(5):381–392. Available at: http://doi.wiley.com/10.1080/00207594.2011.632009. Accessed 29 Aug 2016

56. Geng Y (2018) Gratitude mediates the effect of emotional intelligence on subjective well-being: a structural equation modeling analysis. J Health Psychol 23(10):1378–1386. Available at: https://doi-org.ezproxy.lib.gla.ac.uk/10.1177/1359105316677295. Accessed 20 May 2020
57. Bajaj B, Pande N (2016) Mediating role of resilience in the impact of mindfulness on life satisfaction and affect as indices of subjective well-being. Pers Individ Differ 93:63–67. Available at: https://www-sciencedirect-com.ezproxy.lib.gla.ac.uk/science/article/pii/S0191886916301416. Accessed 29 Aug 2016
58. Crowley C, Kapitula LR, Munk D (2020) Mindfulness, happiness, and anxiety in a sample of college students before and after taking a meditation course. J Am Colle Health (ahead of print). Available at: https://doi.org/10.1080/07448481.2020.1754839. Accessed 5 May 2020
59. Findyartini A, Greviana N, Putera AM, Sutanto RL, Saki VY, Felaza E (2021) The relationships between resilience and student personal factors in an undergraduate medical program. BMC Med Educ 21(113). Available at: https://www.ncbi.nlm.nih.gov/pmc/articles/PMC7890950/. Accessed 1 Apr 2022
60. Handoyo NE, Rahayu GR, Claramita M, Ash J, Schuwirth LW (2020) Personal resilience and rural doctors retention: a study in Indonesia. Rural Remote Health 20(6097). Available at: https://www.rrh.org.au/journal/article/6097/. Accessed 1 Apr 2022
61. Purba EJ, Abdullah SMS (2017) Overcoming workplace challenges: a qualitative study of resilience factors of Indonesian women factory workers in Malaysia. J Bus Soc Rev Emerg Econ 3(2):169–178. Available at: https://publishing.globalcsrc.org/ojs/index.php/jbsee/article/view/188/330. Accessed 1 Apr 2022
62. Pauwelussen A (2016) Community as network: exploring a relational approach to social resilience in coastal Indonesia. Marite Stud 15:e2. Available at: https://link.springer.com/article/10.1186/s40152-016-0041-5. Accessed 1 Apr 2022
63. Pristiarawati M, Prameswari A, Hartanti H (2021) Pelatihan resiliensi untuk menurunkan perceived stress selama masa pandemi Covid-19. Psychocentrum Rev 3(2):218–226. Available at: https://journal.unindra.ac.id/index.php/pcr/article/view/632/pdf. Accessed 1 Apr 2022
64. Rahiem MDH (2021) Remaining motivated despite the limitations: University students' learning propensity during the COVID-19 pandemic. Child Youth Serv Rev 120:e105802. Available at: https://www-sciencedirect-com.ezproxy.lib.gla.ac.uk/science/article/pii/S0190740920322246?via%3Dihub. Accessed 1 Apr 2022
65. Rahiem MDH, Krauss SE, Ersing R (2021) Perceived consequences of extended social isolation on mental well-being: narratives from Indonesian university students during the COVID-19 pandemic. Int J Environ Res Public Health 18(19):e10489. Available at: https://www.mdpi.com/1660-4601/18/19/10489/htm. Accessed 1 Apr 2022
66. Tubadji A (2021) Culture and mental health resilience in times of COVID-19. J Popul Econ 34:1219–1259. Available at: https://link-springer-com.ezproxy.lib.gla.ac.uk/article/10.1007/s00148-021-00840-7. Accessed 1 Apr 2022
67. Devi HM, Purborini N, Chang HJ (2021) Mediating effect of resilience on association among stress, depression, and anxiety in Indonesian nursing students. J Prof Nurs 37(4):706–713. Available at: https://www-sciencedirect-com.ezproxy.lib.gla.ac.uk/science/article/pii/S8755722321000545?via%3Dihub. Accessed 1 Apr 2022
68. Bustamam N, Theresa RM, Wahyuningsih S (2020) Student support program to reduce stress, anxiety, and depression on medical students. Jurnal pendidikan kedokteran Indonesia 9(2):170–181. Available at: https://jurnal.ugm.ac.id/jpki/article/view/51245/28265/. Accessed 1 Apr 2022
69. Akbağ M, Ümmet D (2017) Predictive role of grit and basic psychological needs satisfaction on subjective well-being for young adults. J Educ Pract 8(26):127–135. Available at: https://iiste.org/Journals/index.php/JEP/article/view/38908/40009. Accessed 5 May 2020
70. Datu JA, Mateo NJ (2017) How to combat the negative impact of discrimination in a collectivist context? The safeguarding function of peer-oriented hope. Psychol Health Med 22(3):345–351. Available at: https://doi.org/10.1080/13548506.2016.1164875. Accessed 5 May 2020

71. Montasem A, Brown SL, Harris R (2013) Do core self-evaluations and trait emotional intelligence predict subjective well-being in dental students? J Appl Soc Psychol 43(5):1097–1103. Available at: http://doi.wiley.com/10.1111/jasp.12074. Accessed 29 Aug 2016
72. Tuzgöl Dost M (2006) Subjective well-being among university students. Hacet Univ J Educ 31:188–197. Available at: http://uvt.ulakbim.gov.tr/uvt/index.php?cwid=9&vtadi=TSOS&c=ebsco&c=summon&c=ebsco&ano=71909_ad0d08f2872e4b3887878c8cca16c9ac. Accessed 30 Aug 2016
73. Ahmed I, Banu H, Al-Fageer R, Al-Suwaidi R (2009) Cognitive emotions: depression and anxiety in medical students and staff. J Crital Care 24(3):e1–e7. Available at: https://www-sciencedirect-com.ezproxy.lib.gla.ac.uk/science/article/pii/S0883944109001348. Accessed 29 Aug 2016
74. Mazzucchelli TG, Purcell E (2015) Psychological and environmental correlates of well-being among undergraduate university students. Psychol Well-Being 5(1):6. Available at: http://www.psywb.com/content/5/1/6. Accessed 29 Aug 2016
75. Oguz-Duran N, Yuksel A (2010) The effects of coping humour and gender on college adjustment in Turkish freshmen. Education 130(3):470–478. Available at: http://web.b.ebscohost.com.ezproxy.lib.gla.ac.uk/ehost/detail/detail?sid=8628989c-5509-4cc9-b8d2-bb812a1a005e%40sessionmgr103&vid=0&hid=107&bdata=JnNpdGU9ZWhvc3QtbGl2ZQ%3D%3D#AN=EJ917131&db=eric. Accessed 30 Aug 2016
76. Tucker P, Jeon-Slaughter H, Sener U, Arvidson M, Khalafian A (2015) Do medical student stress, health, or quality of life foretell Step 1 scores? A comparison of students in traditional and revised preclinical curricula. Teach Learn Med 27(1):63–70. Available at: http://www.tandfonline.com/doi/abs/10.1080/10401334.2014.979178. Accessed 29 Aug 2016
77. Lew B, Huen J, Yu P, Yuan L, Wang DF, Ping F, Abu Talib M, Lester D, Jia CX (2019) Associations between depression, anxiety, stress, hopelessness, subjective well-being, coping styles and suicide in Chinese university students. PLoS one 14(7):e0217372. Available at: https://doi.org/10.1371/journal.pone.0217372. Accessed 5 May 2020
78. Boulton CA, Hughes E, Kent C, Smith JR, Williams HTP (2019) Student engagement and wellbeing over time at a higher education institution. PLoS one 14(11):e0225770. Available at: https://doi.org/10.1371/journal.pone.0225770. Accessed 5 May 2020
79. de Vibe M, Bjørndal A, Fattah S, Dyrdal GM, Halland E, Tanner-Smith EE (2017) Mindfulness-based stress reduction (MBSR) for improving health, quality of life and social functioning in adults: a systematic review and meta-analysis. Campbell Syst Rev Available at: https://doi-org.ezproxy.lib.gla.ac.uk/10.4073/csr.2017.11. Accessed 20 May 2020
80. de Vibe M, Solhaug I, Tyssen R, Friborg O, Rosenvinge JH, Sørlie T, Bjørndal A (2013) Mindfulness training for stress management: a randomised controlled study of medical and psychology students. BMC Med Educ 13:107–117. Available at: http://www.biomedcentral.com/1472-6920/13/107. Accessed 29 Aug 2016
81. Rajagopal M, Pugazhanthi SS, George LS (2012) A study on effectiveness of meditation on subjective well-being, anxiety and study habits of undergraduate nursing students. Int J Nurs Educ 4(2):137–140. Available at: http://content.ebscohost.com.ezproxy.endeavour.edu.au/ContentServer.asp?T=P&P=AN&K=104394679&S=R&D=rzh&EbscoContent=dGJyMNHr7ESeqK84y9f3OLCmr0%2Bepq5Ss6y4S7eWxWXS&ContentCustomer=dGJyMPGqs1Czr7ZLuePfgeyx43zx%5Cn. Accessed 30 Aug 2016
82. Shapiro SL, Brown KW, Thoresen C, Plante TG (2011) The moderation of mindfulness-based stress reduction effects by trait mindfulness: results from a randomized controlled trial. J Clin Psychol 67(3):267–277. Available at: http://doi.wiley.com/10.1002/jclp.20761. Accessed 29 Aug 2016
83. Weytens F, Luminet O, Verhofstadt LL, Mikolajczak M (2014) An integrative theory-driven positive emotion regulation intervention. PloS one 9(4):e95677. Available at: http://www.pubmedcentral.nih.gov/articlerender.fcgi?artid=PMC3997402. Accessed 29 Aug 2016
84. Higgins JW, Lauzon LL, Yew A, Bratseth C (2009) University students' wellness—What difference can a course make? Colle Stud J 43(3):766–778. Available at: http://www.freepatentsonline.com/article/College-Student-Journal/206687069.html. Accessed 26 Aug 2016

85. Maybury KK (2013) The influence of a positive psychology course on student well-being. Teach Psychol 40(1):62–65. Available at: http://top.sagepub.com/lookup/doi/10.1177/0098628312465868. Accessed 30 Aug 2016
86. Marlo H, Wagner M (1999) Expression of negative and positive events through writing: implications for psychotherapy and health. Psychol Health 14(2):193–215. Available at: http://www.tandfonline.com/doi/abs/10.1080/08870449908407323. Accessed 30 Aug 2016
87. Diener E, Colvin CR, Pavot WG, Allman A (1991) The psychic costs of intense positive affect. J Pers Soc Psychol 61(3):492–503. Available at: http://doi.apa.org/getdoi.cfm?doi=10.1037/0022-3514.61.3.492. Accessed 30 Aug 2016
88. Marshall C, Rossman GB (2016) Designing qualitative research, 6th edn. SAGE Publications Inc., Thousand Oaks
89. Ritchie J, Ormston R (2014) The applications of qualitative methods to social research. In: Ritchie J, Lewis J, Nicholls CM, Ormston R (eds) Qualitative research practice: a guide for social science students & researchers. SAGE Publications Ltd, London. Ch. 2
90. Schutt RK (2015) Investigating the social world: the process and practice of research, 8th edn. SAGE Publications Inc., Thousand Oaks
91. Giorgi A (2009) The descriptive phenomenological method in psychology: a modified Husserlian approach. 5th reprint. Duquesne University Press, Pittsburgh
92. Ashworth P (2015) Conceptual foundations of qualitative psychology. In: Smith JA (ed) Qualitative psychology: a practical guide to research methods, 3rd edn. SAGE Publications Ltd, London. Ch. 2
93. Brinkmann S, Kvale S (2015) InterViews: learning the craft of qualitative research interviewing, 3rd edn. SAGE Publications Inc., Thousand Oaks
94. Cohen L, Manion L, Morrison K (2018) Research methods in education, 8th edn. Routledge, Abingdon
95. Gray DE (2014) Doing research in the real world, 3rd edn. SAGE Publications Ltd., London
96. King N, Horrocks C, Brooks J (2019) Interviews in qualitative research, 2nd edn. SAGE Publications Ltd., London
97. Langdridge D (2007) Phenomenological psychology. Pearson Education Limited, Essex
98. May T (2011) Social research: issues, methods, and process, 4th edn. Open University Press, Berkshire
99. Samosir ASG (2021) The meaning of well-being for undergraduate medical students: perspective from Indonesia (Doctoral thesis, University of Glasgow)
100. Yamaguchi A, Kim MS (2015) Effects of self-construal and its relationship with subjective well-being across cultures. J Health Psychol 20(1):13–26. Available at: http://ezproxy.lib.gla.ac.uk/login?url=http://search.proquest.com.ezproxy.lib.gla.ac.uk/docview/1683509091?accountid=14540. Accessed 29 Aug 2016
101. Tam KP, Lau HPB, Jiang D (2012) Culture and subjective well-being: a dynamic constructivist view. J Cross-Cult Psychol 43(1):23–31. Available at: http://jcc.sagepub.com/cgi/doi/10.1177/0022022110388568. Accessed 30 Aug 2016
102. Van de Vliert E, Janssen O (2002) "Better than" performance motives as roots of satisfaction across more and less developed countries. J Cross-Cult Psychol 33(4):380–397. Available at: http://journals.sagepub.com/doi/pdf/10.1177/00222102033004002. Accessed 30 Aug 2016
103. Wang Y (2020) College students' trait gratitude and subjective well-being mediated by basic psychological needs. Soc Behav Pers: Int J 48(4):e8904. Available at: https://doi.org/10.2224/sbp.8904. Accessed 5 May 2020
104. Abdel-Khalek AM (2010) Religiosity, subjective well-being, and neuroticism. Ment Health, Relig Cult 13(1):67–79. Available at: http://www.tandfonline.com/doi/abs/10.1080/13674670903154167. Accessed 30 Aug 2016

# Another Meaning Behind the Differences Between Median Age at First Marriage and Median Age at First Sexual Intercourse

**Teguh Widodo, Mario Ekoriano, and Edy Purwoko**

**Abstract** Sexual intercourse before marriage may affect to the child whom was born. It will make on the absence of recognition biological father legally. It means that woman herself will bear her child from getting pregnant, giving birth, educating, and until raising them. This study aims to examine the median age at first marriage and the experience of having sex for the first time against trends that have occurred in decades of Demographic and Health Survey (DHS) data collection results. This study used DHS secondary data from 72 countries that posted their survey on its website. Data series got from website were vary in each country. It might be caused by the related country had not conducted survey at that time. The analysis was conducted by regarding trend of time between median age at first marriage (MAFM) and median age at first sexual intercourse (MAFSI). Normally, the country which still uphold religious and traditional values, there is relatively no different time between MAFM and MAFSI or MAFSI is little bit longer than MAFM. This study shows the trend that MAFM had increased simultaneously from 1991 till 2017, on the other hand MAFSI had decreased, and even interval between them have been getting further. There is a positive time gap that the state or its people still uphold the dignity of women. It means that women are treated legally even though some of them married before 18. The society still uphold religious norms. On the other hand, if MAFSI less than MAFM indicates that the society are permissive and ease of religious norms. This study recommends that preventing sexual intercourse before marriage is the duty of the state and it needs collective action to participate in care, besides having a positive impact on lineage. It will also protect women and their children from the loss of legal inheritance rights in the family.

**Keywords** Women's dignity · Median age at first marriage and median age at first sexual intercourse

T. Widodo · M. Ekoriano (✉) · E. Purwoko
National Research and Innovation Agency (BRIN), Jakarta, Indonesia
e-mail: mari036@brin.go.id



Nawawi et al. (eds.), *Managing Disruption and Developing Resilience for a Better Southeast Asia*, Springer Proceedings in Humanities and Social Sciences,
https://doi.org/10.1007/978-981-96-2116-3_22

# 1 Background

Marriage naturally is the sexual relation between man and woman legally both in the context of religion, custom, and state. There are rights and obligations of the couple that must be fulfilled between the two parties in accordance with the law of marriage. If sexual relations man and woman are not legalized, then there are no rights and obligations between the two. In the event of pregnancy, there is no obligation for a man to provide living cost for the woman during her pregnancy and even grows into a human being, even though the sexual relationship is consensual.

Previous researches related sexual intercourse before marriage find the trend of increasing sexual transmission diseases, disorders of pregnancy, and HIV/AIDS [5, 7]. The other research conducted by Dunne et al. [2], and Odeyemi et al [6] found that the first sexual intercourse before marriage contributes to the genetics. Then, it little bit forces to the woman. Unfortunately, the researches related to the same topics are not to analyze the decreasing woman's dignity. In other words, these researches are rarely conducted, because by allowing promiscuity such as the permissively of sexual relations without marriage ties, women potentially lose their rights in child care and nurture.

Investigating MAFM in the country is to indicate potential human hazard in terms of violence to the woman because married under 18 years old. On the other hand, maturing at first marriage is to invest girls' education, growing awareness of the legal age of marriage (18 years) and community efforts to highlight the health and economic risks of child marriage and early childbearing [4].

This study aims to analyze furtherly the median age at first marriage and the median age at first sexual intercourse in developing countries so that it can describe the form of the decline in women's dignity in terms of women's rights (Table 1).

# 2 Theoretical Review

Girgis et al. [3] view marriage in two perspectives. The first is a *conjugal view:* That marriage is the union of a man and a woman who make a permanent and exclusive commitment to each other of the type that is naturally (inherently) fulfilled by bearing and rearing children together. Second, *revisionist view:* Marriage is the union of two people (whether of the same sex or of opposite sexes) who commit to romantically loving and caring for each other and to sharing the burdens and benefits of domestic life.

The first view is legalization to a man and a woman as in terms of sexual intercourse. It means that sexual intercourse cannot be conducted before marrying. It needs legalization because impact of it is children that have identity of heredity to prevent incest. Many biological scholars admit such as Cohen and Mannarino [1]. Incest is a particular type of child sexual abuse that often has severe consequences

**Table 1** Median Age at First Marriage and Median Age at First Sexual Intercourse (Women 25–49)

| Country | Survey | Median age at first marriage (Women): 25–49 | Median age at first sexual intercourse (Women): 25–49 | Time interval |
|---|---|---|---|---|
| | | Total | Total | |
| Afghanistan | 2015 DHS | 18.5 | 18.7 | 0.2 |
| Albania | 2017–18 DHS | 22 | 20.9 | −1.1 |
| Albania | 2008–09 DHS | 21.8 | 20.9 | −0.9 |
| Angola | 2015–16 DHS | 20.5 | 16.6 | −3.9 |
| Armenia | 2015–16 DHS | 21.4 | 21.2 | −0.2 |
| Armenia | 2010 DHS | 21.1 | 21.1 | 0 |
| Armenia | 2005 DHS | 20.7 | 20.7 | 0 |
| Armenia | 2000 DHS | 20.5 | 20.5 | 0 |
| Azerbaijan | 2006 DHS | 21.9 | 22 | 0.1 |
| Bangladesh | 2017–18 DHS | 16 | 16.2 | 0.2 |
| Bangladesh | 2014 DHS | 15.8 | 15.9 | 0.1 |
| Bangladesh | 2011 DHS | 15.5 | 15.6 | 0.1 |
| Benin | 2017–18 DHS | 19.4 | 17.3 | −2.1 |
| Benin | 2011–12 DHS | 19.8 | 18.4 | −1.4 |
| Benin | 2006 DHS | 18.6 | 17.8 | −0.8 |
| Benin | 2001 DHS | 18.8 | 17.3 | −1.5 |
| Benin | 1996 DHS | 18.4 | 17.3 | −1.1 |
| Bolivia | 2008 DHS | 20.9 | 18.6 | −2.3 |
| Bolivia | 2003 DHS | 20.6 | 18.6 | −2 |
| Bolivia | 1998 DHS | 20.9 | 18.9 | −2 |
| Bolivia | 1994 DHS | 20.6 | 18.9 | −1.7 |
| Brazil | 1996 DHS | 21.1 | 19.5 | −1.6 |
| Burkina Faso | 2010 DHS | 17.8 | 17.7 | −0.1 |
| Burkina Faso | 2003 DHS | 17.7 | 17.5 | −0.2 |
| Burkina Faso | 1998–99 DHS | 17.6 | 17.5 | −0.1 |
| Burkina Faso | 1993 DHS | 17.5 | 17.4 | −0.1 |
| Burundi | 2016–17 DHS | 20.3 | 19.6 | −0.7 |
| Burundi | 2010 DHS | 20.3 | 20 | −0.3 |
| Cambodia | 2014 DHS | 20.5 | 20.7 | 0.2 |
| Cambodia | 2010 DHS | 20.3 | 20.8 | 0.5 |
| Cambodia | 2005 DHS | 20.1 | 20.4 | 0.3 |
| Cambodia | 2000 DHS | 20 | 19.9 | −0.1 |
| Cameroon | 2018 DHS | 20 | 17 | −3 |
| Cameroon | 2011 DHS | 18.5 | 17 | −1.5 |

(continued)

**Table 1** (continued)

| Country | Survey | Median age at first marriage (Women): 25–49 | Median age at first sexual intercourse (Women): 25–49 | Time interval |
|---|---|---|---|---|
| | | Total | Total | |
| Cameroon | 2004 DHS | 17.6 | 16.4 | −1.2 |
| Cameroon | 1998 DHS | 17.4 | 15.8 | −1.6 |
| Cameroon | 1991 DHS | 16.5 | 16 | −0.5 |
| Central African Republic | 1994–95 DHS | 17.3 | 15.9 | −1.4 |
| Chad | 2014–15 DHS | 16.1 | 16.2 | 0.1 |
| Chad | 2004 DHS | 15.9 | 15.7 | −0.2 |
| Chad | 1996–97 DHS | 15.8 | 15.5 | −0.3 |
| Colombia | 2015 DHS | 21.4 | 17.7 | −3.7 |
| Colombia | 2010 DHS | 21.5 | 18.1 | −3.4 |
| Colombia | 2005 DHS | 21.7 | 18.4 | −3.3 |
| Colombia | 2000 DHS | 21.5 | 19.2 | −2.3 |
| Colombia | 1995 DHS | 21.4 | 19.6 | −1.8 |
| Colombia | 1990 DHS | 21 | 20 | −1 |
| Comoros | 2012 DHS | 20.7 | 21 | 0.3 |
| Comoros | 1996 DHS | 18.5 | 18.3 | −0.2 |
| Congo | 2011–12 DHS | 19.7 | 16.2 | −3.5 |
| Congo | 2009 AIS | 20.2 | 16.1 | −4.1 |
| Congo | 2005 DHS | 20.4 | 15.8 | −4.6 |
| Congo DR | 2013–14 DHS | 18.7 | 16.8 | −1.9 |
| Congo DR | 2007 DHS | 18.6 | 16.8 | −1.8 |
| Cote d'Ivoire | 2011–12 DHS | 19.7 | 17 | −2.7 |
| Cote d'Ivoire | 2005 AIS | 19.2 | 16.4 | −2.8 |
| Cote d'Ivoire | 1998–99 DHS | 18.7 | 16.1 | −2.6 |
| Cote d'Ivoire | 1994 DHS | 18.1 | 15.8 | −2.3 |
| Dominican Republic | 2013 DHS | 19.2 | 18.2 | −1 |
| Dominican Republic | 2007 DHS | 18.8 | 18.1 | −0.7 |
| Dominican Republic | 2002 DHS | 19 | 18.4 | −0.6 |
| Dominican Republic | 1999 DHS | 19.3 | 18.6 | −0.7 |
| Dominican Republic | 1996 DHS | 19.3 | 18.7 | −0.6 |

(continued)

**Table 1** (continued)

| Country | Survey | Median age at first marriage (Women): 25–49 | Median age at first sexual intercourse (Women): 25–49 | Time interval |
|---|---|---|---|---|
| | | Total | Total | |
| Dominican Republic | 1991 DHS | 19 | 19 | 0 |
| Eritrea | 2002 DHS | 18.2 | 17.9 | −0.3 |
| Eritrea | 1995 DHS | 16.7 | 16.8 | 0.1 |
| Eswatini | 2006–07 DHS | 23.7 | 18 | −5.7 |
| Ethiopia | 2016 DHS | 17.1 | 16.6 | −0.5 |
| Ethiopia | 2011 DHS | 16.5 | 16.6 | 0.1 |
| Ethiopia | 2005 DHS | 16.1 | 16.1 | 0 |
| Ethiopia | 2000 DHS | 16 | 16 | 0 |
| Gabon | 2012 DHS | 22 | 16.9 | −5.1 |
| Gabon | 2000 DHS | 19.7 | 16.1 | −3.6 |
| Gambia | 2019–20 DHS | 19.4 | 18.5 | −0.9 |
| Gambia | 2013 DHS | 18.6 | 18.6 | 0 |
| Ghana | 2014 DHS | 20.7 | 18.4 | −2.3 |
| Ghana | 2008 DHS | 19.8 | 18.4 | −1.4 |
| Ghana | 2003 DHS | 19.4 | 18.2 | −1.2 |
| Ghana | 1998 DHS | 19.1 | 17.7 | −1.4 |
| Ghana | 1993 DHS | 18.8 | 17.1 | −1.7 |
| Guatemala | 2014–15 DHS | 19.5 | 18.6 | −0.9 |
| Guatemala | 1998–99 DHS | 19.3 | 18.3 | −1 |
| Guatemala | 1995 DHS | 19 | 18.2 | −0.8 |
| Guinea | 2018 DHS | 18.5 | 16.6 | −1.9 |
| Guinea | 2012 DHS | 17 | 16.4 | −0.6 |
| Guinea | 2005 DHS | 16.2 | 16 | −0.2 |
| Guinea | 1999 DHS | 16.4 | 16 | −0.4 |
| Guyana | 2009 DHS | 20.7 | 18.5 | −2.2 |
| Guyana | 2005 AIS | 20.5 | 18.4 | −2.1 |
| Haiti | 2016–17 DHS | 22.8 | 17.7 | −5.1 |
| Haiti | 2012 DHS | 21.8 | 18 | −3.8 |
| Haiti | 2005–06 DHS | 20.4 | 18.1 | −2.3 |
| Haiti | 2000 DHS | 20.5 | 18.2 | −2.3 |
| Haiti | 1994–95 DHS | 20.8 | 19 | −1.8 |
| Honduras | 2011–12 DHS | 19.3 | 18.4 | −0.9 |
| Honduras | 2005–06 DHS | 18.9 | 18.2 | −0.7 |

(continued)

**Table 1** (continued)

| Country | Survey | Median age at first marriage (Women): 25–49 | Median age at first sexual intercourse (Women): 25–49 | Time interval |
|---|---|---|---|---|
| | | Total | Total | |
| India | 2015–16 DHS | 19 | 19 | 0 |
| India | 2005–06 DHS | 17.4 | 17.6 | 0.2 |
| Indonesia | 2017 DHS | 20.8 | 20.9 | 0.1 |
| Indonesia | 2012 DHS | 20.4 | 20.6 | 0.2 |
| Indonesia | 2007 DHS | 19.8 | 20.1 | 0.3 |
| Indonesia | 2002–03 DHS | 19.2 | 19.5 | 0.3 |
| Indonesia | 1997 DHS | 18.6 | 18.6 | 0 |
| Indonesia | 1994 DHS | 18.1 | 18.1 | 0 |
| Indonesia | 1991 DHS | 17.7 | 17.8 | 0.1 |
| Kazakhstan | 1999 DHS | 21.2 | 20.8 | −0.4 |
| Kazakhstan | 1995 DHS | 21 | 20.8 | −0.2 |
| Kenya | 2014 DHS | 20.2 | 18 | −2.2 |
| Kenya | 2008–09 DHS | 20 | 18.2 | −1.8 |
| Kenya | 2003 DHS | 19.7 | 17.6 | −2.1 |
| Kenya | 1998 DHS | 19.2 | 16.5 | −2.7 |
| Kenya | 1993 DHS | 18.8 | 16.8 | −2 |
| Kyrgyz Republic | 2012 DHS | 20.6 | 20.5 | −0.1 |
| Kyrgyz Republic | 1997 DHS | 20.4 | 20.4 | 0 |
| Lesotho | 2014 DHS | 20.3 | 18.5 | −1.8 |
| Lesotho | 2009 DHS | 19.9 | 18.5 | −1.4 |
| Lesotho | 2004 DHS | 19.1 | 18.6 | −0.5 |
| Liberia | 2019–20 DHS | 21.2 | 16.1 | −5.1 |
| Liberia | 2013 DHS | 18.8 | 16.2 | −2.6 |
| Liberia | 2007 DHS | 18.4 | 16.2 | −2.2 |
| Madagascar | 2008–09 DHS | 18.9 | 17.3 | −1.6 |
| Madagascar | 2003–04 DHS | 19.1 | 17.5 | −1.6 |
| Madagascar | 1997 DHS | 18.5 | 16.9 | −1.6 |
| Madagascar | 1992 DHS | 18.2 | 16.7 | −1.5 |
| Malawi | 2015–16 DHS | 18.2 | 16.8 | −1.4 |
| Malawi | 2010 DHS | 17.8 | 17.2 | −0.6 |
| Malawi | 2004 DHS | 17.9 | 17.3 | −0.6 |
| Malawi | 2000 DHS | 17.8 | 16.8 | −1 |
| Maldives | 2016–17 DHS | 20.9 | 20.7 | −0.2 |

(continued)

**Table 1** (continued)

| Country | Survey | Median age at first marriage (Women): 25–49 | Median age at first sexual intercourse (Women): 25–49 | Time interval |
|---|---|---|---|---|
| | | Total | Total | |
| Maldives | 2009 DHS | 19 | 19.6 | 0.6 |
| Mali | 2018 DHS | 17.8 | 16.5 | −1.3 |
| Mali | 2012–13 DHS | 18 | 17 | −1 |
| Mali | 2006 DHS | 16.6 | 16.1 | −0.5 |
| Mali | 2001 DHS | 16.5 | 15.8 | −0.7 |
| Mali | 1995–96 DHS | 16 | 15.8 | −0.2 |
| Mauritania | 2000–01 DHS | 17.1 | 17 | −0.1 |
| Moldova | 2005 DHS | 20.4 | 20 | −0.4 |
| Mozambique | 2015 AIS | 18.2 | 16.8 | −1.4 |
| Mozambique | 2011 DHS | 18.8 | 16.1 | −2.7 |
| Mozambique | 2009 AIS | 17.7 | 16.6 | −1.1 |
| Mozambique | 2003 DHS | 17.5 | 16.1 | −1.4 |
| Mozambique | 1997 DHS | 17.1 | 15.9 | −1.2 |
| Myanmar | 2015–16 DHS | 22.1 | 22.5 | 0.4 |
| Namibia | 1992 DHS | 24.8 | 19.2 | −5.6 |
| Nepal | 2016 DHS | 17.9 | 17.9 | 0 |
| Nepal | 2011 DHS | 17.5 | 17.7 | 0.2 |
| Nepal | 2006 DHS | 17 | 17 | 0 |
| Nepal | 2001 DHS | 16.7 | 16.7 | 0 |
| Nepal | 1996 DHS | 16.2 | 16.3 | 0.1 |
| Nicaragua | 2001 DHS | 18.2 | 17.8 | −0.4 |
| Nicaragua | 1998 DHS | 18.3 | 18.2 | −0.1 |
| Niger | 2012 DHS | 15.7 | 15.9 | 0.2 |
| Niger | 2006 DHS | 15.5 | 15.6 | 0.1 |
| Niger | 1992 DHS | 14.9 | 15.1 | 0.2 |
| Nigeria | 2018 DHS | 19.1 | 17.2 | −1.9 |
| Nigeria | 2013 DHS | 18.1 | 17.6 | −0.5 |
| Nigeria | 2008 DHS | 18.3 | 17.7 | −0.6 |
| Nigeria | 2003 DHS | 16.6 | 16.2 | −0.4 |
| Nigeria | 1990 DHS | 16.9 | 16.9 | 0 |
| Pakistan | 2017–18 DHS | 20.4 | 20.7 | 0.3 |
| Papua New Guinea | 2016–18 DHS | 20.4 | 19.7 | −0.7 |
| Paraguay | 1990 DHS | 20.9 | 19.4 | −1.5 |

(continued)

**Table 1** (continued)

| Country | Survey | Median age at first marriage (Women): 25–49 | Median age at first sexual intercourse (Women): 25–49 | Time interval |
|---|---|---|---|---|
| | | Total | Total | |
| Peru | 2012 DHS | 21.6 | 18.7 | −2.9 |
| Peru | 2011 DHS | 21.6 | 18.7 | −2.9 |
| Peru | 2010 DHS | 21.5 | 18.8 | −2.7 |
| Peru | 2009 DHS | 21.8 | 18.8 | −3 |
| Peru | 2007–08 DHS | 21.7 | 18.8 | −2.9 |
| Peru | 2004–06 DHS | 21.6 | 19 | −2.6 |
| Peru | 2000 DHS | 21.4 | 19 | −2.4 |
| Peru | 1996 DHS | 20.9 | 18.9 | −2 |
| Peru | 1991–92 DHS | 21.1 | 19.4 | −1.7 |
| Philippines | 2017 DHS | 22.5 | 21.2 | −1.3 |
| Philippines | 2013 DHS | 22.3 | 21.5 | −0.8 |
| Philippines | 2008 DHS | 22.2 | 21.5 | −0.7 |
| Philippines | 2003 DHS | 22 | 21.9 | −0.1 |
| Philippines | 1998 DHS | 22.1 | 22.1 | 0 |
| Philippines | 1993 DHS | 21.6 | 21.8 | 0.2 |
| Rwanda | 2014–15 DHS | 21.9 | 21 | −0.9 |
| Rwanda | 2010 DHS | 21.4 | 20.7 | −0.7 |
| Rwanda | 2005 DHS | 20.7 | 20.3 | −0.4 |
| Rwanda | 2000 DHS | 20.7 | 20.1 | −0.6 |
| Rwanda | 1992 DHS | 20 | 19.7 | −0.3 |
| Sao Tome and Principe | 2008–09 DHS | 18.8 | 17.8 | −1 |
| Senegal | 2019 DHS | 20 | 19.7 | −0.3 |
| Senegal | 2018 DHS | 20.4 | 19.8 | −0.6 |
| Senegal | 2017 DHS | 20.2 | 19.7 | −0.5 |
| Senegal | 2016 DHS | 19.9 | 19.5 | −0.4 |
| Senegal | 2015 DHS | 19.5 | 19 | −0.5 |
| Senegal | 2014 DHS | 19.8 | 19.3 | −0.5 |
| Senegal | 2012–13 DHS | 19.3 | 18.9 | −0.4 |
| Senegal | 2010–11 DHS | 19.3 | 18.8 | −0.5 |
| Senegal | 2005 DHS | 18.3 | 18.4 | 0.1 |
| Senegal | 1997 DHS | 17.4 | 17.3 | −0.1 |
| Senegal | 1992–93 DHS | 16.2 | 16.2 | 0 |
| Sierra Leone | 2019 DHS | 19.5 | 16 | −3.5 |

(continued)

**Table 1** (continued)

| Country | Survey | Median age at first marriage (Women): 25–49 | Median age at first sexual intercourse (Women): 25–49 | Time interval |
|---|---|---|---|---|
| | | Total | Total | |
| Sierra Leone | 2013 DHS | 18 | 16.4 | −1.6 |
| Sierra Leone | 2008 DHS | 17 | 16.1 | −0.9 |
| South Africa | 1998 DHS | 24.2 | 18.4 | −5.8 |
| Tajikistan | 2017 DHS | 20.2 | 20.2 | 0 |
| Tajikistan | 2012 DHS | 20.2 | 20.3 | 0.1 |
| Tanzania | 2015–16 DHS | 19.2 | 17.2 | −2 |
| Tanzania | 2011–12 AIS | 19.1 | 17.9 | −1.2 |
| Tanzania | 2010 DHS | 18.8 | 17.4 | −1.4 |
| Tanzania | 2007–08 AIS | 18.8 | 17.3 | −1.5 |
| Tanzania | 2004–05 DHS | 18.6 | 17 | −1.6 |
| Tanzania | 2003–04 AIS | 18.7 | 17.5 | −1.2 |
| Tanzania | 1999 DHS | 18.1 | 16.6 | −1.5 |
| Tanzania | 1996 DHS | 18.2 | 16.7 | −1.5 |
| Tanzania | 1991–92 DHS | 17.9 | 16.7 | −1.2 |
| Timor-Leste | 2016 DHS | 21.7 | 20.5 | −1.2 |
| Timor-Leste | 2009–10 DHS | 20.9 | 20.9 | 0 |
| Togo | 2013–14 DHS | 20 | 18.2 | −1.8 |
| Togo | 1998 DHS | 18.8 | 17.3 | −1.5 |
| Turkmenistan | 2000 DHS | 21.5 | 21.6 | 0.1 |
| Uganda | 2016 DHS | 18.7 | 16.9 | −1.8 |
| Uganda | 2011 AIS | 18.2 | 17 | −1.2 |
| Uganda | 2011 DHS | 17.9 | 16.8 | −1.1 |
| Uganda | 2006 DHS | 17.6 | 16.4 | −1.2 |
| Uganda | 2000–01 DHS | 17.8 | 16.6 | −1.2 |
| Uganda | 1995 DHS | 17.4 | 16 | −1.4 |
| Ukraine | 2007 DHS | 20.7 | 19.6 | −1.1 |
| Uzbekistan | 1996 DHS | 20.1 | 20.1 | 0 |
| Vietnam | 2005 AIS | 21.2 | 21.2 | 0 |
| Zambia | 2018 DHS | 19.1 | 16.6 | −2.5 |
| Zambia | 2013–14 DHS | 18.4 | 17.3 | −1.1 |
| Zambia | 2007 DHS | 18.2 | 17.2 | −1 |
| Zambia | 2001–02 DHS | 17.8 | 16.8 | −1 |
| Zambia | 1996 DHS | 17.7 | 16.4 | −1.3 |

(continued)

**Table 1** (continued)

| Country | Survey | Median age at first marriage (Women): 25–49 | Median age at first sexual intercourse (Women): 25–49 | Time interval |
|---|---|---|---|---|
| | | Total | Total | |
| Zambia | 1992 DHS | 17.4 | 16.3 | −1.1 |
| Zimbabwe | 2015 DHS | 19.8 | 18.7 | −1.1 |
| Zimbabwe | 2010–11 DHS | 19.7 | 18.9 | −0.8 |
| Zimbabwe | 2005–06 DHS | 19.3 | 18.6 | −0.7 |
| Zimbabwe | 1999 DHS | 19.3 | 18.7 | −0.6 |

*Source* dhs

for the child, the perpetrator, and the family as a whole. Then, Webster's Dictionary defines incest as "sexual intercourse between persons who are closely related to marry." Both in religion perspective and tradition, they ban it.

Unfortunately, the second view is very contradictory with either religious perspective or natural norms because basically one of marriage purposes is reproductive for human sustainability. The second perspective, as long as the same sex, the marriage is not normative, so that it is potentially out of natural family. The consequence of their children doesn't come their genetic as well.

In practice, sexual intercourse is often carried out before marriage. If it is happened, it is possible that a child will be born about 42 weeks after conception. Once born alive, the child has rights as human beings such as a decent life, education, and so on. Of course, the parents will responsible for the fulfillment of these rights first. If the sexual intercourse is not legalized first, then woman will be harmed in several ways, including the cost of living during pregnancy and childbirth. In some countries that still uphold religious and customary values, woman's virginity is sacred before marriage. It will be dedicated to the man only who marries her.

## 3 Methods

This study used secondary data from 72 countries that uploaded the data to the Demographic and Health Survey (DHS) website. The analysis was conducted by looking at the time difference between the median age at first marriage and the median age at first sexual intercourse. In general, countries are considered to uphold women's dignity if the median age at first sexual intercourse is higher (positive value) or at least equal to the median age at first marriage, as it is normatively expected that marriage should precede sexual intercourse. It means that the age of marriage is younger or relatively the same as the first sexual intercourse. Furthermore, the results of the analysis per country are communicated with some of the research literature that been conducted in that country.

## 4 Results

The research findings indicate that countries with a negative difference between the MAFSI and MAFM indicate that the country has experienced loosening of norms and is permissive to acts that deviate from religion or customs. With the meaning of the word, many women have sexual intercourse before marriage. Communities with this condition have an individualistic tendency, not communal.

Research shows that there is a decrease in the distance between the median age at first marriage and the median age at first sexual intercourse. Armenia, Kyrgyzstan, and Indonesia have tended to decrease. It means that it is possible that there will be an increase in sexual transmission infection and the prevalence of HIV/AIDS. Countries that experienced a decrease in the median distance also indicated that both customary and religious norms in that country experienced permissiveness and relaxation. And the next possibility is the decline in the dignity of women and children. A small part of them will lose custody. There will be an increase in single parents. Cases such as in Indonesia, especially people who are Muslim, children who are born without marriage ties both in religion and the state will make children lose their rights as heirs or guardianship rights.

For countries whose people have experienced the median age at first sexual intercourse under 18 years of age, it is possible that the infant mortality rate and maternal mortality rate will increase. This is because physically women at that age are not ready to get pregnant. And it is possible that when giving birth there will be bleeding—and this can result in the death of both the mother and the child.

Meanwhile, countries where the difference in positive values is too far, such as Afghanistan and Bangladesh, indicate that marriages are often hampered by opportunities to have sexual relations because of the possibility of war or women are menstruating or sick at the time of the marriage. In addition, because there are several customs that should exist, it is recommended that sexual relations be carried out a few days after the marriage occurs.

Colombia, the Philippines and Rwanda show a trend of increasing pre-marital sexual relations since 1993. This is also the possibility of an easing of religious or customary values. On the other hand. Cambodia, Chad, Comoro, and Congo showed a decline in sexual relations outside of marriage. India (2005 and 2015) and Indonesia from 1991 to 2017 show that sexual relations were carried out after the marriage took place.

From the data series, it can also be analyzed in terms of age of marriage and age of sexual intercourse. Countries that have entered the maturity age of marriage include Armenia, Bolivia, Brazil, Kyrgyz Republic, Indonesia, Pakistan, Papua New Guinea, and Peru. The age of marriage is over 20 years, where marriage in the context of human rights is carried out after someone has exceeded the age limit of 18 years. While countries that still allow child marriage include Afghanistan, Angola. Bangladesh, Benin, Chad, Republic of Africa, Nepal, and Nigeria.

Although their sexual relationship in this context is consensual, the consequences that must be borne are more detrimental to women, including (1) the child who is born has no legal status with the man who impregnated her. This means that there is no inheritance law to inherit. (2) A man who gets pregnant does not have any legal obligations toward the woman he impregnates. (3) Women must raise and educate the children they give birth to.

Variables entered/removed[a]

| Model | Variables entered | Variables removed | Method |
|---|---|---|---|
| 1 | MAFSI[b] | | Enter |

[a]Dependent Variable: MAFM
[b]All requested variables entered

Model summary[b]

| Model | R | R square | Adjusted R square | Std. error of the estimate |
|---|---|---|---|---|
| 1 | 0.743[a] | 0.552 | 0.550 | 1.19936 |

[a]Predictors: (Constant), MAFSI
[b]Dependent Variable: MAFM

ANOVA[a]

| Model | | Sum of squares | df | Mean square | F | Sig |
|---|---|---|---|---|---|---|
| 1 | Regression | 410.073 | 1 | 410.073 | 285.077 | 0.000[b] |
| | Residual | 332.285 | 231 | 1.438 | | |
| | Total | 742.358 | 232 | | | |

[a]Dependent Variable: MAFM
[b]Predictors: (Constant), MAFSI

Coefficients[a]

| Model | | Unstandardized coefficients | | Standardized coefficients | t | Sig |
|---|---|---|---|---|---|---|
| | | B | Std. Error | Beta | | |
| 1 | (Constant) | 4.857 | 0.857 | | 5.666 | 0.000 |
| | MAFSI | 0.795 | 0.047 | 0.743 | 16.884 | 0.000 |

[a]Dependent Variable: MAFM

| Residuals statistics[a] | | | | | |
|---|---|---|---|---|---|
| | Minimum | Maximum | Mean | Std. deviation | N |
| Predicted value | 16.8641 | 22.7484 | 19.2691 | 1.32949 | 233 |
| Residual | −1.96414 | 4.71180 | 0.00000 | 1.19677 | 233 |
| Std. predicted value | −1.809 | 2.617 | 0.000 | 1.000 | 233 |
| Std. residual | −1.638 | 3.929 | 0.000 | 0.998 | 233 |

[a]Dependent Variable: MAFM

## Charts

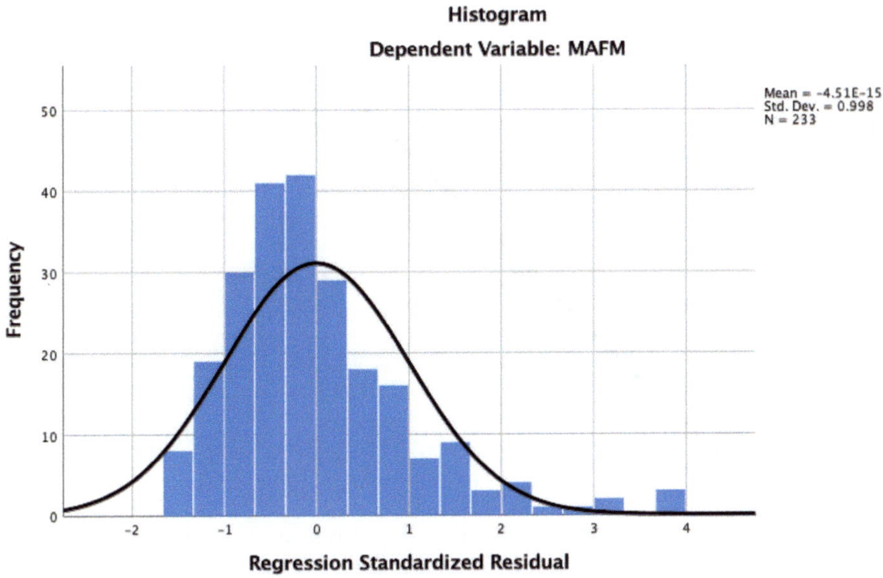

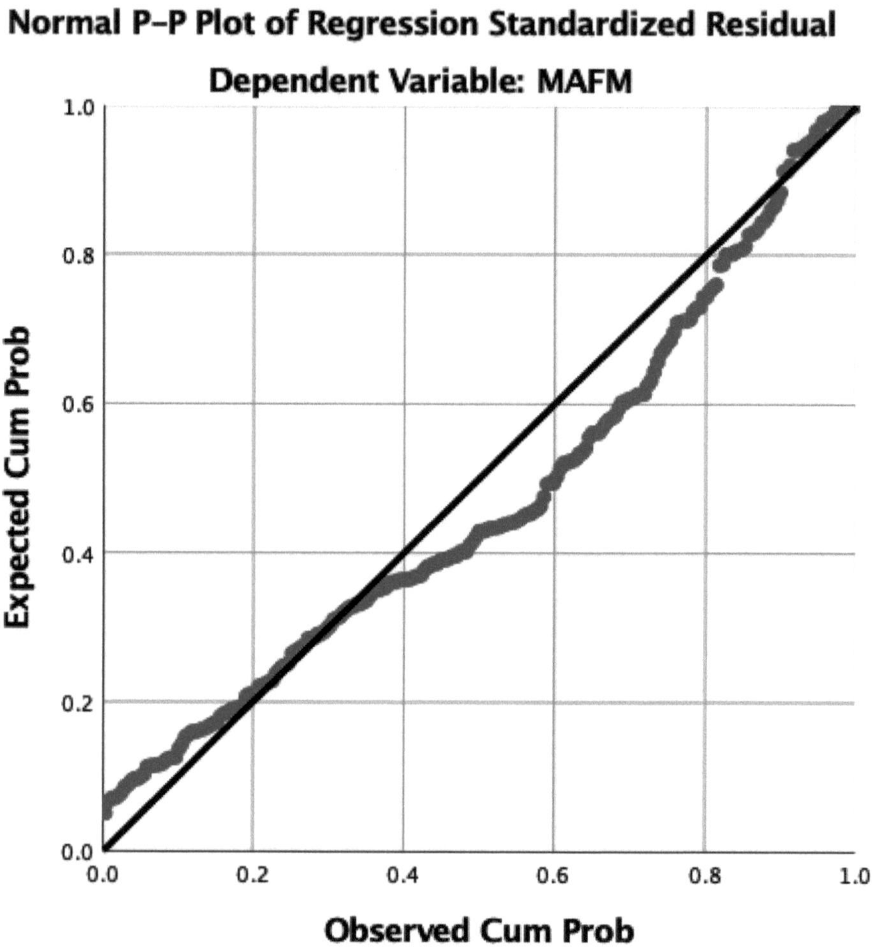


## 5 Discussion

Normatively, the main purpose of marriage is to form a family. Then, through this family, the regeneration will be done by sexual intercourse legally. Currently, many sexual intercourses are conducted illegally so that marriage is not important anymore in a sexual intercourse, while in some countries which have been keeping the norm, religion and tradition, sexual intercourse must be conducted after marriage to keep their lineage. In other words, the first marriage age will increase if the country is permissive in terms of violating toward norm, belief and tradition. Then, MAFSI will be conducted earlier than the country which still keep the norm, tradition, and belief.

## 6 Concluding Remarks

Traditionally and religiously, maintaining the dignity of women and lineage is by conducting legal marriages. There is a trend of an increase in the median age at first marriage but on the contrary, there is a decrease in having sexual intercourse for the first time, whereas the first sexual intercourse in religion is done after marriage. In developing countries that still hold religious values, it is very good to keep genetics in the family. In developing countries, there is a good trend that MAFM is increasing, but on the other hand. MAFSI is declining. This implies that the increase in MAFM if it is not accompanied by an awareness of maintaining the dignity of women will destroy human genesis and existence. MAFM should no longer as a measure of reducing the risk of infant mortality if it is not followed by a similarity between MAFM and MAFSI or a slightly higher MAFSI. Increasing MAFM will not have any impact if it is not accompanied by keeping MAFSI also increasing. Increasing MAFM and decreasing MAFSI will actually worsen public morale. This can be proven by decreasing moral values, increasing sexual violence against both children and women.

## References

1. Cohen JA, Mannarino AP (2000) Incest. In: Ammerman RT, Hersen M (eds) Case studies in family violence. Springer, Boston. MA. https://doi.org/10.1007/978-1-4615-4171-4_11
2. Dunne MP, Martin NG, Statham DJ, Slutske WS, Dinwiddie SH, Bucholz KK, Madden PAF, Heath AC (1997) Genetic and environmental contributions to variance in age at first sexual intercourse. Psychol Sci 8(3):211–216. https://doi.org/10.1111/J.1467-9280.1997.TB00414.X
3. Girgis S, George RP, Anderson RT (2010) What is marriage? Harv J Law Public Policy 34(1):245–287. https://doi.org/10.1177/009164717400200108
4. Jones N, Presler-Marshall E, Kebede Hateu M (2020) Constrained choices: exploring the complexities of adolescent girls' voice and agency in child marriage decisions in Ethiopia. Prog Dev Stud20:298–311. https://doi.org/10.1177/1464993420958215
5. Laguna-Torres A, Aguayo N, Aguilar G, Ampuero JS, Galeano A, Barboza A, Villafane M, Jimé Nez L, Perez J, Kochel TJ, Halsey ES (2014) HIV infection and high-risk behaviours in a Paraguayan military population 25(12):866–877. https://doi.org/10.1177/0956462414523741
6. Odeyemi K, Olufunlayo T, Ogunnowo B, Onajole A (2016) Sexual violence among out-of-school female adolescents in Lagos. Nigeria. SAGE Open. 6(4). https://doi.org/10.1177/2158244016669972
7. Yaya S, Bishwajit G (2018) Age at first sexual intercourse and multiple sexual partnerships among women in Nigeria: a cross-sectional analysis. Front Med 5:171. https://doi.org/10.3389/fmed.2018.00171

# Generations: Demographic Trends in Workforce Indonesia

**Sonyaruri Satiti, Umi Listyaningsih, and Agus Joko Pitoyo**

**Abstract** Indonesia's younger population, the so-called Gen Z and the millennials, now make up more than half of its citizens, according to the latest Statistics Indonesia (BPS) census, demonstrating the peak of the country's demographic bonus period, which experts warned could make or break the economy. Their transition into the labor market has long-term impacts on their lives as well as or the socio-economic development of their countries. It is thus essential to understand their pathways into the world of work and how they are engaging—or not, as the case may be in employment. This study aims to provide an overview of the employment profile of the productive age population by generation in Indonesia. To support the analysis, the main data used came from the Central Statistics Agency (BPS), namely the 2020 Population Census and the 2020 and 2021 National Labour Force Surveys. The results of the analysis show that in 2020, most of the productive age population who are actively involved in the Indonesian economy are Generation Y, which is 39.89% of the total working age population. In terms of education, there is a tendency that the younger the generation, the higher the level of education taken by the working population of productive age. To be able to gather the demographic bonus, a general strategy is needed, namely that young people who are not included in the category of being educated, working, or participating in training commonly known as NEET (Not in Education, Employment, or Training) must be reduced.

**Keywords** Generations · Demographic bonus · Workforce

S. Satiti (✉) · U. Listyaningsih · A. J. Pitoyo
Center for Population and Policy Studies, Universitas Gadjah Mada, Yogyakarta, Indonesia
e-mail: sonyaruri_satiti@ugm.ac.id

U. Listyaningsih
e-mail: umilis@ugm.ac.id

A. J. Pitoyo
e-mail: aguspit@ugm.ac.id

U. Listyaningsih · A. J. Pitoyo
Department of Environmental Geography Faculty of Geography, Universitas Gadjah Mada, Yogyakarta, Indonesia



Nawawi et al. (eds.), *Managing Disruption and Developing Resilience for a Better Southeast Asia*, Springer Proceedings in Humanities and Social Sciences,
https://doi.org/10.1007/978-981-96-2116-3_23

## 1 Introduction

Indonesia has experienced rapid demographic changes in which the number of productive age population continues to increase and reaches a peak in around 2030. During this period, Indonesia became one of the countries with the largest labor force in Asia (Bappenas, 2018). Population of Indonesia in 2020 will reach 270.20 million with a total workforce of 128.06 million (BPS, 2020). A large population is a development asset to be managed optimally in order to produce quality Human Resources (HR). The blast of the productive age population (15–64 years) during the Demographic Bonus period will generate profits or bonuses which can be used to boost the national economy. The productive age population has a major contribution to the nation's economy by becoming workers, business actors, or owners of capital. The number of productive age population tends to increase over time. Based on the results of the 1961 Population Census, the population of productive age is 53.4 million people and in 2020, it will reach 187.2 million, an increase of more than 3 times (BPS, 2020). With such a large productive age population, Indonesia has the potential to become a country with an important economic power not only in Southeast Asia, but also in the world. Currently, Indonesia is ranked fourth as one of the largest population-of-productive age after China, India, and the United States.

Advancing toward the 100th anniversary of Indonesia's independence, which will be in 2045, the number of productive age in Indonesia based on the 2015 SUPAS population projection is predicted to reach 207.9 million people. This number is equivalent to about 38% of the total productive age population in ASEAN [19]. With a sizeable population of productive age at the ASEAN level, Indonesia has the potential to fill in the workforce needs for countries with a declining proportion of the working age population, such as Singapore, Korea, Japan, and Australia.

At the global level, Indonesia is predicted to have the opportunity of becoming one of the five countries with the largest economy in the world by 2045. The UN report predicts that in 2045, the population of Indonesia will be 318 million people with a GDP per capita of 29 thousand US dollars per year [19]. The accumulation of the demographic bonus over the previous few years is expected to lift up the Indonesian economy through increased production, consumption, savings, and investment, as well as human and technological capacity, so that the GDP of Indonesia is predicted to be ranked 4th in the world by 2045.

In terms of employment, the momentum of the Demographic Bonus will be prospective with the presence of the Millennial Generation population which continues to grow. Seeing from the total population of Indonesia, around 25.87% or 69.38 million people are Millennial Generation (BPS, 2020). This refers to the fact that almost a third of the total population of Indonesia is a millennial generation. The demographic bonus is basically inseparable from the millennial generation. Based on the results of the 2020 Population Census (SP2020), Indonesia's dependency ratio in 2020 is 41.00, which is the lowest so far, and it also implies that the percentage of the productive age population is around 1% of the total population. Furthermore, if the percentage of the population of productive age is associated with the percentage of the millennial generation in 2020 which is 25.87% of the total population, it means that their contribution in shaping the structure of the population of productive age is quite high. It is due to the fact that more than 50.00% of the population of productive age is basically the millennial generation.

Millennials are population who were born between 1980 and 2000 and in 2020, they are by the age of 20–40 years old. This condition turns the millennialsto be at their most productive age to make the best contribution to the Indonesian economy. The second largest population after Millennial Generation is Generation Z or those who were born after 2000. However, in regard of a productivity perspective, only a small part of Generation Z is at their productive age so that the Millennial Generation will remain the economic foundation for the next ten years. Before the Millennial Generation, there were Generation X and Generation Baby Boom + Pre Boomers who had contributed to the national economy first. As the largest population, of course, the millennial generation will play a major role in the demographic bonus era. This generation will be in control of the development, especially in the economic sector, which is expected to be able to bring Indonesia toward a more advanced and dynamic development. In essence, the millennial generation is a big capital to realize the independence of the nation in all aspects.

This is in accordance with the research by [16] which shows that in the world of employment nowadays, organizations are faced with two different generations: Generation X and Generation Y. Kratz [12] stated that the potential proportion of Generation Y will also increase in the future. In 2014, the portion of Generation Y was around 36.00% in the world of employment. Furthermore, there is a possibility that by 2020, 46.00% of Generation Y will dominate the world of employment.

The employment concept used in this article refers to the 13th International Conference of Labour Statistics (ICLS) issued by the International Labour Organization (ILO). In terms of employment, the Indonesian population is divided into two, namely the working age population and the non-working age population. The working age population is the population aged 15 years and more. Based on the main activities carried out by the population, the working age population is divided into two, namely the labor force and the non-labor force. The population included in the labor force is the population of working age who are economically active, either working or employed, but temporarily not working and unemployed. Meanwhile, population who are not included in the labor force are those of the working age who are still in school, taking care of the household, or carrying out other activities other than personal activities [18].

In this discussion, population refers to the population of working age or man power, while the labor force is part of man power, which is called the labor force [22]. The term of working age is determined as the age when one is to be able to work if there is a job offer to get benefits or wages which are useful for the community. In Indonesia, since 1961, the age limit was 10 years and it lasted until the early 1990s. After 1990, the lower limit was increased to 15 years [26].

The objective of this article is to provide an overview of the employment profile of the productive age population in Indonesia by generation while considering that the productive age population is the largest human resource in the era of the demographic bonus. From this profile, it can be seen the weaknesses and strengths of the productive age population by generation from the employment dimension. The data and information Population Census (SP) and National Labour Force Survey (Sakernas) from Central Statistics Agency (BPS) presented in this article refer to 2020 and 2021. To see the development of the employment profile of the Post Gen Z Generation, Generation Z, Millennial Generation, Generation X, Baby Boomer Generation, and Pre-Boomer Generation, the information is presented during the last two years (2020–2021). The data and information presented in this article describe conditions at the national and provincial levels.

To support the analysis of the employment profile of the productive age population by generation (Post Gen Z Generation, Generation Z, Millennial Generation, Generation X, Baby Boomer Generation, and Pre-Boomer Generation), various data sources are used. The main data came from the Central Statistics Agency (BPS), namely the Population Census (SP) and the National Labour Force Survey (Sakernas). Other sources outside of BPS are obtained from survey results of research institutions and other references related to and supporting the need for data on the employment profile of the productive age population by generation.

## 2 Coverage of Productive Age Population Based on Generation in Indonesia

Demographic balance affects the success of development in a region. The productive age population as development agents is expected to be distributed evenly and proportionally, so that economic activity can also be distributed throughout the region. Thus, development will not be concentrated in certain areas, but will be evenly distributed throughout the region. With an even distribution, the benefits of development are expected to be experienced fairly by all Indonesian people.

With a fairly large range of age, the productive age population has different characteristics. These characteristics are influenced by experience and development of the era. In order to make it easier to understand the characteristics of the population, experts put the categorization of the the population based on several generations according to the period of year of birth. People who were born in a certain range of years are considered to have the same characteristics. On the other hand, generations who were born in different time periods have different characteristics. This is due to the fact that the historical experiences experienced by the population in certain generations affect their growth phase [13]. Generational groupings in the world of employment will emerge following the development of human resource management. Research on this generational difference was first conducted by [17]. According to Manheim, generation is a social construction in which there is a group of people who have the same age and historical experience. Individuals who are part of one generation are those who have the same year of birth in a span of twenty years and are in the same social and historical dimensions. This definition was specifically developed by Ryder [23] who mentioned that a generation is an aggregate of a group of individuals who experience the same events in the same period of time.

Theoretically, a generation is formed as a group which has a common year of birth, age, location, and significant life events at a critical stage of development. So, a generation becomes different from other generations since there are factors of change which come along with it.

One of the generational grouping theories put forward by William H. Frey divides the population into six generations, as shown in Table 1. From these six generations, the productive age population is spread over four generations, namely the Baby Boomer generation, Generation X, Generation Y, and Generation Z. If it is ordered from the smallest age, the youngest productive age population is in Generation Z. This generation was born in the range of 1997 to 2012 or by the age of 8 to 23 years in 2020. However, the productive age population is in the age of 15–23 years.

The following is Generation Y or Millennials. This generation was born between 1981 and 1996. In 2020 as the year the demographic bonus begins, the millennials are in the age range of 24–39 years old. That age is the productive age which will become the backbone of the Indonesian economy. Three years before that era occurred (2017), the number of millennials was already dominant when compared to other generations. According to the 2017 Susenas, the number of millennials reached around 88 million people or 33.75% of the total population of Indonesia. This proportion is greater than the proportion of the previous generation, such as the X generation (25.74%) and the baby boom + veteran generation (11.27%). Likewise, the number of new Generation Z reached around 29.23% (BPS, 2017). Next is Generation X, who were born between 1965 and 1980 or 40–55 years old in 2020. The last one is the Baby Boomer generation who were born between 1946 and 1964 or in 2020, they were by the age of 56–74. Similar to Generation Z, not all of this generation is included in the productive age population, namely only those aged 56–64 years.

The majority of Indonesia's productive age population in 2020 belongs to Generation Y, which is 37.23%. Furthermore, the second highest number of productive age population belongs to Generation X in 30.21%, followed by Generation Z in 21.62% and the least belongs to the Baby Boomer generation, which is 10.94%. Each province will have its order of the population of productive age by generation

**Table 1** Generation categorization of population according to William H. Frey

| No | Generation | Year of birth | Age by the year 2020 |
|---|---|---|---|
| 1 | Post generation Z | 2013–now | 0–7 y.o |
| 2 | Generation Z | 1997–2012 | 8–23 y.o |
| 3 | Generation Y (Millenial) | 1981–1996 | 24–39 y.o |
| 4 | Generation X | 1965–1980 | 40–55 y.o |
| 5 | Baby boomer generation | 1946–1964 | 56–74 y.o |
| 6 | Pre-boomer generation | Before 1945 | 75 + y.o |

*Source* William H. Frey, *Analysis of Census Bureau Population Estimates* (June 25, 2020) as quoted by BPS (2021a)

from the largest to the smallest. By knowing the composition and distribution of the productive age population by generation, the government can map the potential of the productive age population by generation in all regions, so that each region can utilize the demographic bonus more optimally.

The distribution of the productive age population by province in each generation does not differ much. Most of the productive age population in each generation is West Java, East Java, Central Java, and North Sumatra, while the lowest are in North Kalimantan, Gorontalo, West Papua, and North Maluku. However, this is not the case when the percentage of the productive age population of a generation is relative to the total productive age population in each province. When compared to the total population of productive age in each province, it is found that Generation Z is mostly located in Maluku, West Sulawesi, and East Nusa Tenggara Provinces. Furthermore, Generation Y is mostly found in Papua, West Papua, and the Riau Islands. Meanwhile, Generation X and Baby Boomers are mostly located in Yogyakarta Special Region, East Java, and Bali. Figure 1 shows the variation in the percentage of the population of productive age relative by generation in each province. The figure is ordered from the largest percentage of Generation Y, so it shows that Yogyakarta Special Region has the lowest percentage of productive age population in Generation Y compared to other provinces. In addition, the percentage of Generation Z in this province is also the least. Meanwhile, the proportion of Generation X and Baby Boomers is the largest compared to other provinces. It proves that the productive age population in Yogyakarta in proportion is considered older when compared to other provinces.

When compared by gender, the older the generation, the higher the percentage of the female productive age population, and vice versa for the male productive age population. The male productive age population in Generations X, Y, and Z in 2020 is more than the female productive age population. Meanwhile, in the Baby Boomer generation, there are more women of productive age than men.

Based on research by the Association of Indonesian Internet Service Providers (APIII), 65% of Indonesia's total internet users are dominated by users in Java Island.

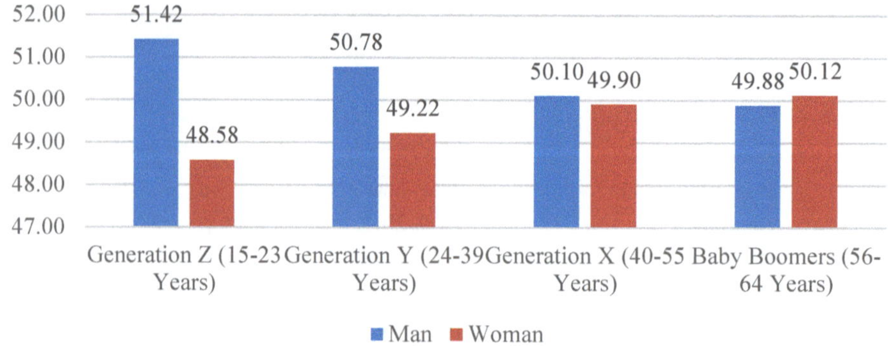


**Fig. 1** Percentage of productive age population in each generation toward total number of productive age population in each province in Indonesia 2020. *Source* Population Census 2020 (SP2020) Results, BPS

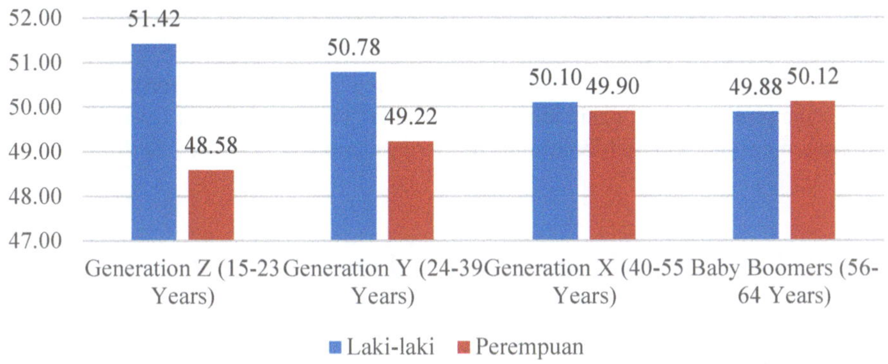


**Fig. 2** Proportion of productive age population based on gender in each province (percentage), 2020. *Source* The National Labour Force Survey (Sakernas), BPS

The data on the distribution of internet users from APIII provides an illustration that the population of internet users is concentrated in Java. This digital inequality may be caused by the unequal availability of supporting infrastructure. As explained earlier, the millennial generation were born and grew up in the strong current of technological development. Tapscott (1998) calls the millennial generation as the Digital Generation. Many of their attitudes and behaviors are influenced by gadgets and the internet. They tend to be more concerned with the use of technology, music taste, and lifestyle. The choices they make are based on information from the internet, especially social media. Therefore, it is unsurprisingly that the number of millennial residents is also concentrated on Java Island (Fig. 2).

The dominance of the male productive age population in Generations X, Y, and Z also occurs in several provinces. In Generation Z, the dominance of the male productive age population occurs in all provinces. As for Generation Y, the dominance of the male productive age population occurs in 32 provinces, while the other 2 provinces (West Nusa Tenggara and East Nusa Tenggara) have a slightly higher number of female productive age population, namely 50.47% in West Nusa Tenggara and 50.28% in West Nusa Tenggara. Furthermore, talking about Generation X, only 23 out of 34 provinces were dominated by male productive age population. Meanwhile, the other 11 provinces (Aceh, North Sumatra, West Sumatra, Central Java, Yogyakarta Special Region, East Java, Bali, West Nusa Tenggara, East Nusa Tenggara, South Sulawesi, and Maluku) have slightly higher female productive age population. In the Baby Boomer generation, only 20 out of 34 provinces are dominated by male productive age population. Meanwhile, the other 14 provinces (Aceh, North Sumatra, West Sumatra, DKI Jakarta, Central Java, Yogyakarta Special Region, East Java, Bali, West Nusa Tenggara, East Nusa Tenggara, South Sulawesi, Gorontalo, West Sulawesi, and Maluku) has a slightly more female productive age population.

The dominance of the female productive age population in Generation X and Baby Boomers in several provinces shows that women have a longer life expectancy than men. In 2020, Life Expectancy of the female population of Indonesia is 74.46 years, higher than the Life Expectancy of the male population of 69.59 years (BPS, 2020c). Therefore, gender inequality in all sectors, especially the economy sector, such as opportunities to be employed, needs to be minimized. At present, efforts to eliminate gender inequality in Indonesia are commendable. This can be seen from the gender empowerment index which continues to increase and reaches 75.57 in 2020.

## 3 Age Productive Population Based on Generation in the World of Employment

The contribution of the productive age population in development can be comprehended through their involvement in the labor market. Most of the productive age population who are actively involved in the Indonesian economy are Generation Y, which is 39.89% of the total working age population (see Fig. 3). The entry of the millennial generation into the Indonesian labor market will certainly bring transformation from an economic, political, social and cultural perspective. Furthermore, 36.53% of Generation X, then 11.98% of Generation Z, and finally 11.60% of the Baby Boomer generation. This order of composition of the productive age population by generation also applies in many provinces. Only four provinces have different compositions, namely Yogyakarta Special Region, East Java, Bengkulu, and Central Java. As for Yogyakarta Special Region and East Java, these two provinces have more Generation X workers than Generation Y and more Baby Boomer generation workers than Generation Z.

In terms of education, there is a tendency that the younger the generation, the higher the level of education taken by population of productive age who are employed. The productive age population who are employed in Generations Z and Y have a better education than Generation X and Baby Boomers. The majority of the productive age population of Generations Z and Y who work have a high school education/equivalent

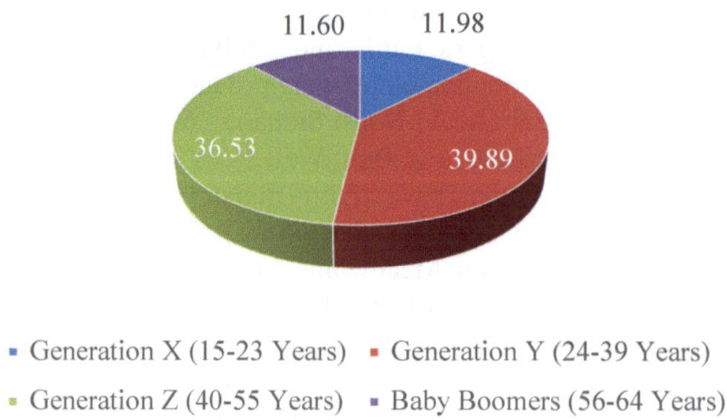


**Fig. 3** Percentage of productive age population who are employed in Indonesia in 2020. *Source* The National Labour Force Survey (Sakernas) 2020, BPS

with a percentage of 56.05% and 36.58%, respectively, while the workforce who are not in school or have not finished elementary school in these two generations each less than five percent, namely 3.15% in Generation Z and 4.66% in Generation Y. Meanwhile, the productive age population who work in Generation X and Baby Boomers are dominated by elementary school graduates/equivalent with a percentage of each of 33.96% and 41.56%.

According to Sukamdi [24], there has been a quite encouraging change in the quality of the workforce during the period 1980–1990, for example, there has been an improvement in the quality of the workforce which is quite encouraging (based on formal education). This can be seen in the decrease in the percentage of the workforce with low education (elementary level and below) and an increase in the workforce with junior high school education and above.

Tjiptoherianto et al. [25] stated that the quality of the Indonesian workforce based on the level of education was still low from 2009 to 2014 that around 50% of the Indonesian workforce only had elementary school education or did not attend school. On the other hand, the proportion of those with diploma and undergraduate education is less than 10%. Although the proportion is still low, the trend of the workforce with university diploma from 2009 to 2014 has increased. Likewise, vocational education which has been used as a second-class choice by junior high school graduates, the trend of the workforce of vocational school graduates is also increasing.

The research conducted by Adioetomo (2018) using data from the 2003, 2009–2012 National Labor Force Survey (Sakernas) showed that the Indonesian labor force in 2012 was still characterized by low education. 47.4% and 18.6% of the workforce were elementary school graduates or even less and junior high school graduates. However, there is a tendency to have an increase in education from year to year, which is shown by a decrease in the percentage of the workforce which has completed elementary and junior high schools, which is accompanied by an increase in the percentage of the workforce who graduate from high school and associate degree (D1, D2, D3) and universities. This brings hope that the quality of human resources will be better in the future although this improvement is too slow because the accomplishments for 9 years from 2003 to 2012 seem to be too low.

The development of technology and the internet requires massive implementation and adaptation in employment. Among the four generations of the productive age population, the use of the internet in the employment is mostly done by Generation Y, which is 41.60% of the total workforce in Generation Y. This is followed by Generation Z (36.30%), Generation X (27.73%), and those who use the internet the least at work are the Baby Boomer generation (13.70%) (see Fig. 4).

The usage of the internet at work is inevitable. Various online services began to be improved, especially after the COVID-19 pandemic spread out. Gradually, various needs can be accessed and fulfilled through online services. Workers who are unable to adapt to using the internet will be left behind and will find it difficult to enter the labor market.

In connection with the development of this technology, the types of work performed also experienced a shift. The younger the generation, the percentage of workers in the primary sector tends to decrease. The opposite condition occurs in the

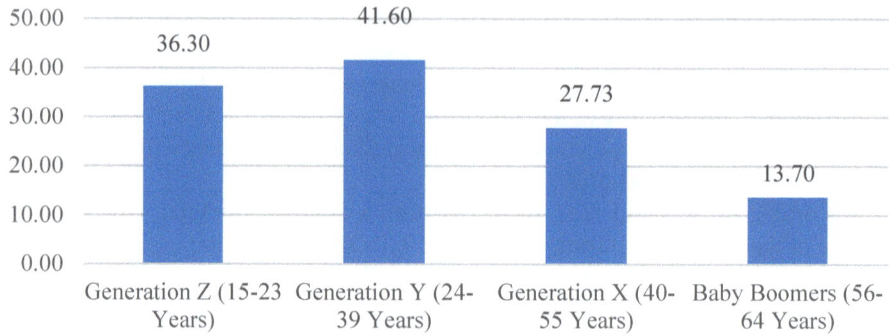


**Fig. 4** Percentage of internet usage by productive age population workforce in each generation 2020. *Source* The National Labour Force Survey (Sakernas) 2020, BPS

tertiary sector. Workers from Baby Boomer generation still predominantly work in the primary sector, which is 46.35% of the total workforce. Meanwhile, Generation X and younger are more involved in service-related jobs.

Based on the characteristics of the productive age population by generation, Generations Y and Z have the potential to become the driving force of the economy today and in the future. The research by Lindh and Malmberg (1999) found that these generations' productive age group had the most significant impact on economic growth. Apart from the quality and competence sides, their number currently also dominates the population in Indonesia. More than half of Indonesia's population are Generations Y and Z, as well as among the entire productive age population. The role of Generations Y and Z in Indonesia's workforce is still constrained by problems with the quality of labor for the productive age population. This quality problem which includes education and expertise then has an impact on the problem of unemployment. Increasing education and skills alone is not sufficient if it is not in accordance with the needs of the labor market.

Unstoppable urbanization causes problems in the employment sector, such as the increasing unemployment rate due to incomplete absorption of labor. Employment in urban areas generally requires skill and higher education which cannot be fully absorbed from the available workforce and eventually causing a large number of unemployed workers. Sakernas in August 2021 data shows that the Millennial Generation's Open Unemployment Rate is still quite high (6.70%). Millennials tend to choose not to work rather than work in the informal sector. This is influenced by the level of education of the millennial generation which is higher than the previous generation so that they have the hope of getting a better job. In addition, the millennial generation, both male and female, tend to be more selective in choosing a job (Fig. 5).

As a human resource which is expected to be empowered in the future, the condition of unemployment in the young population requires a close attention. The NEET (Not in Education, Employment, or Training) indicator shows that in 2020, there are 24.28% of the young population who are not in school, not working, and not

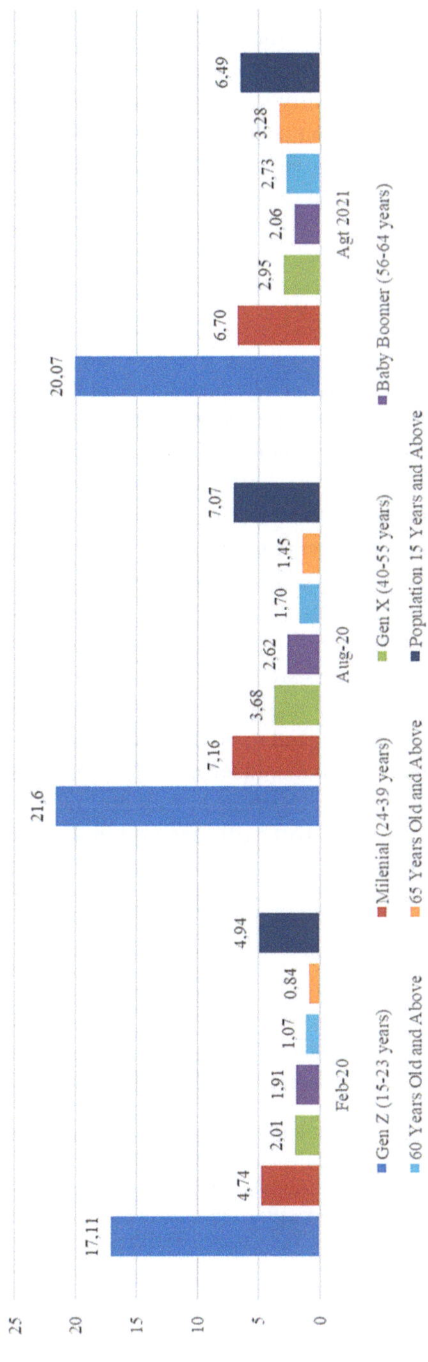


**Fig. 5** Open unemployment rate based on generation, 2020–2021. *Source* The National Labor Force Survey (Sakernas), 2020–2021, BPS

attending training (BPS, 2021c). If the issue of young people with this condition is not being addressed, it can lead to various development problems.

The potential of youth, in this case including Generations Z and Y, needs to be optimized to meet the challenges of the demographic bonus. One of the optimization efforts is through improving the quality of youth. Along with these efforts, various problems of today's young generation need to be addressed immediately. The problems of the young generation today are relatively low levels of education, young marriage, cigarette consumption, and drug abuse.

## 4 Conclusion

The active contribution of the productive age population in the economy will increasingly have a positive impact on development if it has good quality. The quality of the workforce has an essential role in increasing productivity. However, to realize a quality workforce requires joint efforts, both from the government, the community, and each individual. The government's efforts in preparing employment opportunities will not have an optimal effect on employment if the productive age population does not have the appropriate quality. The productive age population who take up the world of work are expected to meet the standard of ability or competence, thus enabling them to compete in an increasingly competitive labor market.

Increasing skills and competencies are related to increasing self-potential through increasing knowledge. Ideally, this corresponds to the demands of the dynamic labor market. Abilities and competencies need to be improved on both sides in a balanced way, namely between hard and soft skills. In terms of hard skills, people of productive age can improve their skills by participating in training, taking quality education, and taking certification. Meanwhile, soft skills can be acquired or improved through activities that increase creativity, innovation, optimism, and positive thinking.

## References

1. Adioetomo SM, Indrayanti R (2018) Entering the world of work and employment conditions in Indonesia. Picking demographic bonuses building humans from an early age. Rajawali Pers, Depok
2. Central Bureau of Statistics (2021) Portrait of the 2020 Population census towards one Indonesian population data. Central Bureau of Statistics, Jakarta
3. Central Bureau of Statistics (BPS). (2020). Indonesian Population Results of the 2020 Population Census Long Form. Jakarta: BPS.
4. Central Bureau of Statistics (BPS). (2021a). Condition of the Indonesian Labor Force February 2021. Jakarta : BPS
5. Central Bureau of Statistics (BPS). (2021c). Condition of the Indonesian Labor Force August 2021. Jakarta : BPS
6. Central Bureau of Statistics (2017) Publication of the results of the 2017 national socio-economic survey. Central Bureau of Statistics, Jakarta

7. Central Bureau of Statistics. Retrieved from social and population: https://bps.go.id/indicator/40/455/1/angka-harapan-hidup-ahh-menurut-kabupaten-kota-dan-tipe-kelamin.html
8. Central Bureau of Statistics (2020) The state of the workforce in Indonesia 2020. Central Bureau of Statistics, Jakarta
9. Central Bureau of Statistics (2021) The state of the workforce in Indonesia 2021. Central Bureau of Statistics, Jakarta
10. Egnatoff WJ, Tapscott D (1998) Growing up digital. The rise of the net generation. McGraw Hill, New York
11. Egnatoff WJ, Tapscott D (1998) Growing up digital. The rise of the net generation. New York: McGraw Hill. xii +338. ISSN 0-07-063361-4. Educ Inf Techno 4, 203–205 (1999). Web site: https://www.growingupdigital.com. https://doi.org/10.1023/A:1009656102475
12. Kratz H (2013) Maximizing millennials: the who, how, and why of managing generation Y. University of North Carolina, United States
13. Kupperschmidt B (2000) Multigeneration employees: strategies for effective management. Health News 19:65–76
14. Lindh T (1999) Age structure effects and growth in the OECD 1950–1990. J Popul Econ 12(3):431–449
15. Lindh T, Malmberg B (1999) Age structure effects and growth in the OECD, 1950–1990. J Popul Econ 12, 431–449. https://doi.org/10.1007/s001480050107
16. Madiistriyatno H, Hadiwijaya D (2019) Millennial generation: the challenge of building work/business commitment and adversity quotient (AQ). Indigo Media, Tangerang
17. Manheim K (1952) The problem of generations. Essay Sociol Knowl 24(19):276–322
18. Mantra IB (2000) General demographics. Pustaka Pelajar, Yogyakarta
19. Ministry of Education and Culture (2017) Indonesia golden generation roadmap 2045. Ministry of Education and Culture
20. Ministry of National Development Planning/National Development Planning Agency (2018) Development demographic. Ministry of National Development Planning/National Development Planning Agency, Jakarta
21. Ministry of National Development Planning/Bappenas. (2018). Demografi Pembangunan. Jakarta : Ministry of National Development Planning/Bappenas
22. Ross JA (1982) International Encyclopedia of population. The Free Press, New York
23. Ryder NB (1985) The cohort as a concept in the study of social change. Am Sociol Rev 30(6):843–861. https://doi.org/10.2307/2090964
24. Sukamdi (1996) Structural transformation and employment issues in Indonesia. In: Agus Dwiyanto et al (eds) Population and development. Aditya Media, Yogyakarta
25. Tjiptoherianto P, Yasin M, Wiyono NH (2016) Employment challenges after 2015. Demographic mosaic: thoughts on population and development. Salemba Empat, Jakarta
26. Tukiran (2010) Population. Universitas Terbuka, Yogyakarta

# Cascading Disaster as a Future Challenge for Risk Management in Southeast Asia

# The Strategy of Enhancing Plantation Production in the Food Estate Area of Central Kalimantan

**Sri Wahyuni, Nyak Ilham, Sahyuti, Miftahul Azis, and Sri Suharyono**

**Abstract** One of the government's efforts to achieve food security in Indonesia in 2020–2024 is through the Food Estate (FE) Program in Central Kalimantan. Therefore in 2020, a baseline survey focused on rice farming areas. In 2021, a survey also covered plantation areas considering that plantation is a strategist commodity to reach the farmers' welfare. Research on the existing condition of plantation areas in FE has been carried out in Kahayan Kuala Sub-District of Pulang Pisau District and Kapuas Barat Sub-District of Kapuas District. Data were collected through focus group discussion with the related institutions, individuals interviewed with 40 farmers' households, and field observation then analyzed qualitatively. Results showed: (1) The characteristics of the Household (Family members are four people, age 50 years old, education seven years); (2) The land asset is own land (rice field 1.21 Ha and plantation 0.41 Ha) and rented rice field 0.63 Ha; (3) The Income contribution from rice field asset is 24.5% while plantation land is 22%; (4) The plantation crop in the locations are coconut and rubber, with income contribution from rice/Ha is 20.08% while plantation/Ha is 50.00%. They concluded that plantations had a significant contribution. Therefore, production should be enhanced. The strategy for developing plantation commodities is to improve the quality of plantation seeds and introduce modern planting system technology. To get appropriate technology and efficient achievement of the plantation program, the technology should be based on the results of gender analysis.

**Keywords** Food estate · Central Kalimantan · Farmers' income · Plantation contribution

S. Wahyuni (✉) · N. Ilham · Sahyuti
National Research and Innovation Agency, Bogor, Indonesia
e-mail: maloleyayuk@yahoo.com

M. Azis · S. Suharyono
Indonesian Center for Agricultural Socioeconomic and Policy Studies, Bogor, West Java, Indonesia


Nawawi et al. (eds.), *Managing Disruption and Developing Resilience for a Better Southeast Asia*, Springer Proceedings in Humanities and Social Sciences,
https://doi.org/10.1007/978-981-96-2116-3_24

# 1 Introduction

## *1.1 Background*

One of the government's efforts to achieve food security in Indonesia is through the National Strategic Projects in 2020–2024, such as the Food Estate (FE), which is located in ex-peatland development or *Pembangunan Lahan Gambut* (PLG) in Central Kalimantan Province that covering about 165,000 hectares in Kapuas and Pulang Pisau District [1]. The target of FE is to develop and manage the area sustainably to achieve the national food reserves and reach the farmers' welfare. The expected outputs of FE [2] are: (1) Increasing farming efficiency, production, productivity, added value, and competitiveness, (2) Establish Farmers' enterprises or *Badan Usaha Milik Petani* (BUMP) and farmer' corporations as food estate managers, (3) The application or implementation of modern technology and digitalization systems, (4) Availability of facilities and infrastructure in supporting FE, and (5) Establish a modern management system in FE.

To achieve these targets, some studies have been done, such as implementing a demonstration of modern agriculture on an area of 2000 hectares known as the Center of Excellence (CoE) in 2020. The modern agriculture demonstrated was based on the results of the action research that had been carried out in the CoE area [3]. Other research about technical aspects was also reported. Among them is Christian [4], who reported on the importance of land use aspects, sustainability of the program, and one map policy project across all agencies. While Fahmid et al. [5] reported on water management, infrastructure rehabilitation, land management, adaptive and potential commodity selection, and farmer institution strengthening and facilitation. Additional information such as the maps of the farmers' location, the distribution of pyrite depth, and the recommendations for land management have been reported by Husnain and Mulyani [6]. The social aspect was described spatially and holistically and focused on the base strategy for the related Ministries/Institutions in the implementation of the future program that pays attention to the rights of the people in Central Kalimantan proposed by Yestati and Noor [7]. An appreciation of the FE Program was delivered by Lasminingrat and Efriza [8], who concluded that the FE program in Central Kalimantan could be used as an example for FE development in other regions.

## *1.2 Problem*

In addition to various positive responses toward the FE, Program has been described in the introduction. There were reports of opinions that were against the implementation of the program. There were reports on worries, doubts, and failures in the success of the FE program were found. Adil and Lestari [9] conveyed the demands of the people of Central Kalimantan, such as "the government should not repeat mistakes of the past program (peatland development or *Pembangunan Lahan Gambut),* the FE program will increase the national losses, damaged the nature and people propose that the government should let farmers to handle food matters as well as give them rights on land." Responding to these community's commands or concerns, the governor of Central Kalimantan assures that FE provides a multiplier effect in improving the people's economy and will prosper the people of Central Kalimantan [10] as long as the implementation of the program accommodates the interests of the community, providing protection and guarantee on their rights to access the agricultural corporation mechanism from the Constitution in Central Kalimantan.

As an effort to support the achievement of the expected outputs of FE No 1, such as Increasing farming efficiency, production, productivity, and added value/competitiveness and refers to the design of FE as an integrated farm that also includes plantation, therefore in 2021, a research was conducted in some locations outside of CoE area which has plantation commodities [11]. Another reason to explore plantation is that this sub-sector was one of the main drivers of the positive GDB growth in agriculture, which amounts to IDR163.49 trillion (28.59%) of GDP and the largest contributor to total exports with a contribution of 90.92% or IDR359.5 trillion that 11.6% higher compared to 2019 (IDR 322.1 trillion). In which the biggest increase was contributed by rubber and coconut as well as palm oil, cocoa, and coffee commodities. Therefore, the government targeted to enhance these commodities to have tripled production [12].

### *1.3 Research Objectives*

This paper provides information on the existing condition of plantation areas in FE. The information includes (1) The characteristics of the farmers' Household; (2) Farmers' assets on land (3) Income contribution from plantation assets; and (4) The existing plantation crops and the income contribution/Ha land. Based on the information on the existing plantation conditions, a base strategy to enhance production would be derived to enhance the plantation production.

## 2 Methodology

### *2.1 Theoretical Framework*

To derive appropriate interventions, this research implemented qualitative research methods refer to Busetto et al. [13], who explain how to use and assess information. The qualitative information was collected from the related institutions through group discussion, completed with secondary data. The information consists of the agroecosystem and the socioeconomic potential as well as the prospect of agriculture

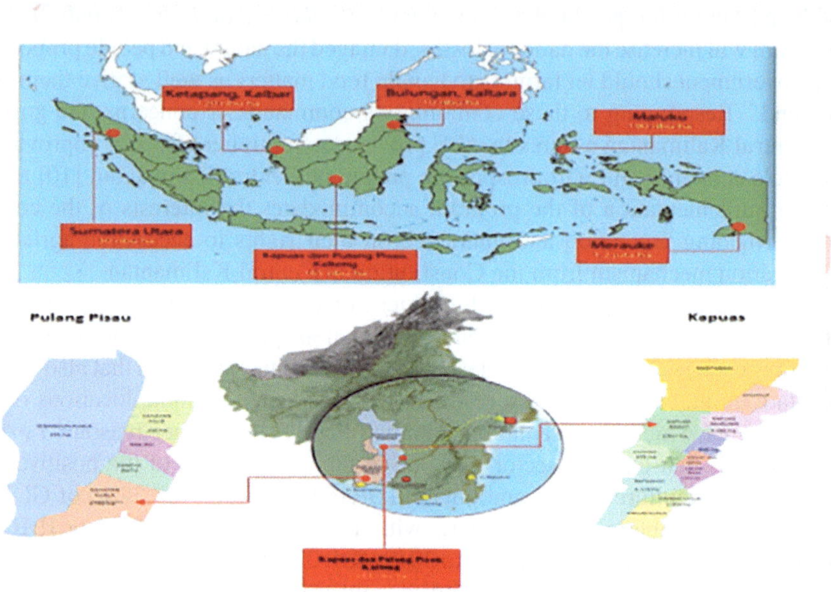


**Fig. 1** The location of the research

development. During the survey, field observation (non-participant) and individual interviews with farmers were also done based on a structured questionnaire.

## 2.2 *Locations*

The research location was selected for purposes such as in FE of Central Kalimantan, which is located in two districts, namely Pulang Pisau and Kapuas. Each district consists of 2 clusters and 4 clusters, respectively. From each district, 1 cluster was selected, namely Kahayan Kuala Sub-district of Pulang Pisau District and West Kapuas Sub-district of Kapuas District (Fig. 1). Those two sub-districts were selected because plantation areas were found as part of the farmers' source of income.

## 2.3 *Data Collection and Analysis*

Data consisted of secondary and primary information. The secondary data such as agroecosystem and socioeconomic potential as well as the prospect of the plantation development were collected from the related institutions. Meanwhile, the primary data were collected through field observation and individual interviews with 40 farmers' households in each Sub-district. The questions were referred to a structured questionnaire that consist of (1) Characteristics of the farmers' Household; (2) farmers' assets on land (3) Plantation crops as the Sources of farmers' household income; and (4) The Contribution of rice compared to plantation farming/Ha. Furthermore, the data were analyzed qualitatively to get a good understanding of the existing conditions as the base of appropriate intervention that should be implemented Douglas [14].

## 3 Results

### *3.1 The Characteristics of the Farmers' Household*

Kahayan Kuala is a sub-district in Pulang Pisau District of Central Kalimantan Province-Indonesia, with a population of about 20,940 people and an average population density of 12 people per $km^2$. The number of households is 5221 with an average household member of 4 people (population report in the Kahayan Kuala sub-district). About 25% of the population is more than 50 years old, of which 2.5% are over 75 years old with a life expectancy of 68 years with the majority of school enrollment rate at high school being 61.63% (BPS Kabupaten Pulang Pisau, 2021) [15]. The characteristics of farmers' families in the research location might reflect the figure of the sub-district level namely consisting of more than 4 family members (Table 1).

The head of Household is classified as productive age with an average age of 50 years, had completed education from elementary school (7.8 years) and some farmers have graduated from high school meaning they could read to help them get access to information about agriculture extension services. The farmers' family member who participates in farming activities is at least one person and a maximum of three people, which reflects that the agricultural sector is their main occupation. Meanwhile, Kapuas Barat Sub-district has a similar demographic figure to Kahayan Kuala in the average household member of 4 people, but the percentage of the population who are more than 50 years old is 50%. The characteristics of the farmers' family are relatively only slightly different compared to Kahayan Kuala Sub-district. The farmers' family's main occupation is also in agriculture, with the member who participates in farming activities being at least one person and a maximum of three people.

### *3.2 Farmers' Assets on Plantation Land*

All farmers have their tidal rice fields, an average of 1.21 Ha, and plantations land of 0.41 Ha which is owned by 11% of farmers (Table 2). Farmers also rented tidal rice

**Table 1** Characteristics of farmer in Pulang Pisau and Kapuas district, 2021

| Characteristics of the head of household | Pulang Pisau district<br>Kahayan Kuala Sub-district | Kapuas district<br>Kapuas Barat Sub-district | Average |
|---|---|---|---|
| 1. Number of family members (head) | | | |
| • Average | 4.09 | 3.52 | 3.8 |
| • Min | 2 | 1 | 1,5 |
| • Max | 6 | 6 | 6 |
| 2. Age (years) | | | |
| • Average | 49.12 | 51.55 | 50.33 |
| • Min | 24 | 29 | 26.5 |
| • Max | 78 | 72 | 75 |
| 3. Education (years) | | | |
| • Average | 7.30 | 8.31 | 7.8 |
| • Min | 2 | 3 | 2.5 |
| • Max | 12 | 12 | 12 |
| 4. Participation of family members in agriculture (Person) | | | |
| • Average | 1.12 | 0.97 | 1.05 |
| • Min | 1 | 1 | 1 |
| • Max | 3 | 3 | 3 |

*Source* Primary data

fields with an average area of 0.63 Ha, but there were no farmers who rent plantation land; the reason was that farmers concerned about the availability of rice to meet the food needs of the family.

The existence of these plantation crops (Table 3), according to ILO [16], is that coconuts as a tropical plant have long been known by the people of Indonesia that spread out in almost all regions of the archipelago. Coconut is a strategic commodity that has a social, cultural, and economic role in the life of the Indonesian people. The benefits of coconut plants are not only located in the flesh of the fruit, but also all parts of the coconut plant have great benefits. All parts of the coconut can be used for various purposes. Moreover, the government of Central Kalimantan also urges the community not to replace coconut with other crops and the government will help to increase coconut plantations which have prospects for very good Norjani [17].

Rubber has the same case as coconut crops. According to Josiano and Jelfi [18], rubber is a commodity that is cultivated from generation to generation in Indonesia. Central Kalimantan has approximately 83% of the total population who are involved in developing natural rubber as their main occupation. Based on the potential analysis and previous studies, it is clear that the economic potential of rubber can be further developed [19], which is supported by the statistical data that the rubber plantation

**Table 2** The farmers' assets on land in Kahayan Kuala and West Kapuas Sub-districts in 2021

| Descriptions | District | | Average |
|---|---|---|---|
| | Kahayan Kuala | Kapuas Barat | |
| Own land | | | |
| 1. Tidal rice field (ha) | | | |
| • Average | 1.47 | 0.95 | 1.21 |
| • Min | 0.20 | 0.20 | 0.20 |
| • Max | 5.70 | 2.00 | 3.85 |
| • Owners of a tidal rice field (%) | 100 | 100 | 100 |
| 2. Plantation land (ha) | | | |
| • Average | 0.37 | 0.45 | 0.41 |
| • Min | 0.10 | 0.09 | 0.09 |
| • Max | 0.50 | 0.60 | 0.55 |
| • Owners of Plantation land (%) | 12.1 | 10.0 | 11.05 |
| Rented land | | | |
| 1. Tidal rice field (ha) | | | |
| • Average | 0.97 | 0.29 | 0.63 |
| • Minimal | – | 0.20 | 0.10 |
| • Max | 0.97 | 0.43 | 0.70 |
| Tenant of Tidal rice field (%) | 100 | 100 | 100 |
| Total cultivated land (ha) | | | 2.25 |

*Source* Primary Data

area in central Kalimantan has positive growth from 2018 to 2022 (288,866; 291,142; 295,858; 301,038; and 303,799) or growth 1.62% from 2020 over 2019 [20].

### 3.3 *Plantation Crops as Farmers' Household Source of Income*

Farmers' source of income was influenced by their agroecosystem. Kahayan Kuala sub-district is divided into two parts by the Kahayan River. One part is a rice field to grow local varieties of rice, namely "*Siam*" with a monoculture cropping pattern once a year. The other parts are areas that are close to the river, planted with plantation crops. These crops also function to prevent the entry of excessive water into the rice field (Fig. 2).

Historically, the coconut plantation business played a major role in the farmers' household income which was used to pay for the pilgrimage. Unfortunately, the changing coconut plantation into oil palm has caused disturbance to the monkeys' habitat such as a loss of food resources, therefore, the monkeys look for food in

**Table 3** Plantation area commodities and production in Kahayan Kuala and Kapuas Barat Sub-district in 2021

| No | Estate Crop | Pulang Pisau district | | Kahayan Kuala Sub-District | | Kapuas district | | Kapuas Barat Sub- District | |
|---|---|---|---|---|---|---|---|---|---|
| | | Planted area (Ha) | Production (Ton) | Planted area (Ha) | Production (Ton) | Planted area (Ha) | Production (Ton) | Planted area (Ha) | Production (Ton) |
| 1 | Oil palm | 4163 | 416.00 | – | – | 656.00 | 923.00 | – | – |
| 2 | Coconut | 5449 | 5,924.68 | 4119 | 4991.63 | 153.00 | 57.50 | 258.00 | 58.00 |
| 3 | Rubber | 41,422 | 20,950.40 | 92 | 9.35 | 3865.00 | 60.50 | – | – |
| 4 | Coffee | – | | – | | 13.00 | 2164.00 | – | – |

*Source* BPS Kalimantan Tengah

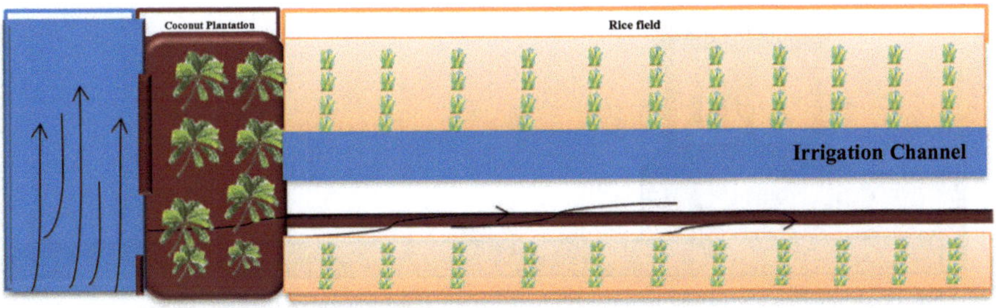


**Fig. 2** Position of rice fields and coconut plantations in Kahayan Kuala sub-district, Pulang Pisau district, 2021. *Source* Field observation

the coconut crop areas and become pests. According to Herminayati et al. [21], this fact is considered proof of the improper implementation of the Regulation Of The Minister Of Environment And Forestry of the Republic Of Indonesia (*Permen* LHK No. 24/2020) which caused marginalizes the people. The reason is that the regulation was not adjusted to the socio-ecological needs of Central Kalimantan as a whole, therefore, it was emphasized that environmental and socioeconomic aspects are the biggest threats to implementing policies. However, farmers continue to plant coconut trees, considering the various benefits obtained from coconut. The coconut trees were planted along the rice field as the border between the river and the rice fields to prevent water overflow and at the same time make it easier for farmers to monitor the condition of coconut plants in addition to rice (Photo 1).

In Kapuas Barat sub-district, similar to Kahayan Kuala, farmers generally cultivate the local variety *"Siam"* with a monoculture pattern of rice—fallow cropping once a year; therefore, the rice production is only sufficient to meet the family consumption needs. The difference between Kapuas Barat with Kahayan Kuala Sub-district is that in West Kapuas, rubber plantations are more dominant with the land used, as Fig. 3.

In Village *Sei Pitung,* rubber was a reliable commodity as a source of income. This village has about 20 hectares of rubber plantations, planted with local varieties found from plants that are found around the existing rubber plantations, then planted

**Photo 1** The existing condition of the integration of rice and coconut plants in the Harapan Tani farmer group, Bandar Raya Village. *Source* Private documentation, 19 June 2021

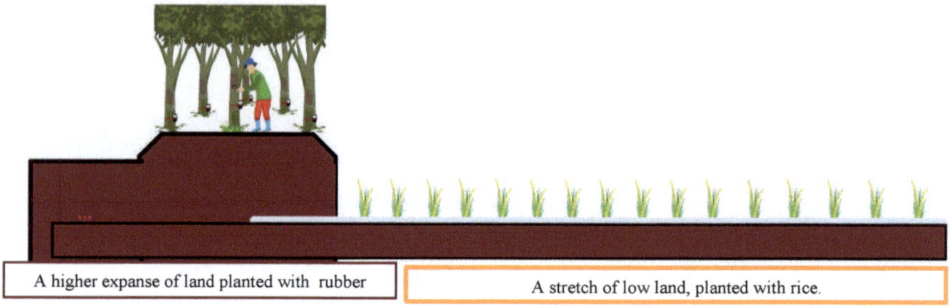


**Fig. 3** Land used pattern of rice field and rubber plantation in Pulang Pisau district in 2021. *Source* Field observation

at a 3 × 3 m distance. The maintenance of rubber plants is done only by cleaning the shrubs around the rubber plants, therefore, many plant pest organisms or *Organisme Pengganggu Tanaman (OPT)* namely termites grow wildly and cause a minimum of rubber production. The product of the sliding of the rubber is collected using used aqua bottles and then sold to the local market in Mandumai village (Photo 2).

Under these existing agroecosystems and traditional farming, the research showed that income from rice farming is IDR 19,526.000 per 1.21 Ha owned land (24.76% contribution to household income) while plantations crops IDR 8310.000 per 0.41 Ha own land (21.84% contribution to household income) respectively (Table 4). Table 4 also illustrates that the highest source of family income comes from their rice farming, the second was salary from rice farming labor, the third was rented tidal rice land and the plantation has the lowest contribution to farmers' household income.

These facts need further analysis, such as income per Ha of land which results from IDR 16,137,190 for rice and IDR 20,268,292 for plantation crops, meaning that the income from the plantation is higher than rice. To prove that this income is the rationale or makes sense, the publication review reported by Herminayati et al. [21] as already cited, supports this finding. Stating that even though coconut is planted

**Photo 2** The existing condition of the integration of rice and rubber in the Harapan Tani farmer group, Bandar Raya Village. *Source* Private documentation: 19 June 2021

**Table 4** Plantation crops as the sources of farmers' household income in Kahayan Kuala and Kapuas Barat Sub-district in 2021

| Source of household income | Income contributions | | | | Average | |
|---|---|---|---|---|---|---|
| | Sub-district Kahayan Kuala | | Sub-district Kapuas Barat | | | |
| | (%) | IDR. (000) | (%) | IDR. (000) | (%) | IDR. (000) |
| 1. Tidal rice field/ 1,21Ha land | 30.93 | 13,213 | 18.16 | 6313 | 24.76 | 9763 |
| 2.Plantation/0,41 Ha own land (coconuts and rubber) | 18.52 | 7915 | 25.17 | 8750 | 21.84 | 8310 |
| 3. Tidal rice land (Rented) | 24.13 | 10,310 | 27.53 | 9570 | 25.83 | 9904 |
| 4. Rice field labor | 26.42 | 11,287 | 29.13 | 10,125 | 27.77 | 10,706 |
| Total | 100.00 | 42,725 | 100.00 | 34,758 | 100.00 | 28,685 |

*Source* primary data

without fertilizer, it will bear fruit throughout the year and reach an exchange rate of 1 kg of copra that equivalent to 3 kg of rice. Meanwhile, Mu'alim and Astuti [22] found that through intensive farming of coconuts (*Cocus lucifer L*) until the year of production of 25th-year farmers get profit with an average of IDR 82,986,534/Ha/year. The highest income was obtained in the 12th year (IDR 140,086,396) while the lowest was in the 25th year (IDR 75,018,182) with a B/C ratio of 6.31. Based on these findings, it is very logical if the profits obtained from farming without investment and operational costs generate 25% of the intensive one. This fact implies that the production of coconut farming could be enhanced to reach maximum production. Therefore, it is very understandable if farmers feel very disadvantaged by the replacement of oil palm in their coconut plantations. Besides the economic aspect, Syahni [23] also warns that the changing of coconut land to oil palm disturbs the productivity of coconuts and other plantation crops such as soil quality degradation, reduced biodiversity, and the attack of plant pests.

It has been stated previously that in addition to coconut, farmers also grew rubber which is planted on the same land as coconut crops (categorized as *lahan Kebun* or plantation land or non-rice fields). It is difficult for farmers to mention the area of land planted with coconut and rubber separately but they can mention the amount of money received from each crop from their plantation land. The reason is although planting coconuts and rubber is a part-time activity, the production provides significant contributions to them. That is why farmers always remember the amount of money they get from selling the products. Farmers reported that in 2021, they got money from selling coconuts IDR 3408.000 and rubber IDR 4902.000; therefore, the total money from plantation land (0.41 Ha) was IDR 8310.000. During the interview, farmers mention the amount of money they earned proudly and emphasized that they did not spend any special costs as well as labor for planting the crops. But, fortunately, income from coconut and rubber production contributed to financing the capital of rice farming, stated by 16% of farmers in Kahayan Kuala Sub-district and 20% in West Kapuas (Table 5). While income from rice farming was prioritized for rice farming capital in the next season stated by 54% and 37% of farmers in Kahayan Kuala and Kapuas Barat respectively. From these two sources of income, the capital for rice farming was not sufficient yet therefore farmers work as farm laborers in the rice fields. Utilization of the results of farm labor as capital for rice farming was reported by 30% of farmers in Kahayan Kuala and 31% of farmers in West Kapuas. This fact makes it clear that plantation crops have the potential to be developed in the two research locations.

Regarding the contribution of rubber crops to household income, to analyze the extent that the information from the farmers is reasonable or logical, the report of Hendrawati and Syamsudin [24] informs that in intensive rubber farming, the profits from the management of rubber plantation land amounting to IDR 20,731,558/ha/year. This report was very close to reports of farmers who earn income profit from rubber crops through the existing management per hectare land is IDR 20,268,292/ha under the existing conditions. This fact indicates that rubber plantations have the potential to increase their production through intensive cultivation. The potential of rubber development in Central Kalimantan has been reported by Sudarta et al. [25] that the leading commodities in Central Kalimantan based on the superior plantation crops in production and planted area, rubber is the first, followed by coffee, areca nut, cocoa, and candlenut. To see the real contribution of plantation crops to family income, the analysis of income per hectare of land from rice crops compared to plantation commodities is presented in Fig. 4. The result showed that the contribution of income from plantation farmers in Pulang Pisau Sub-district is 2.3 times compared to rice farming, while in West Kapuas even reached 2.9 or 3 times.

Besides the economic benefit, coconuts are also playing an important role in social life such as in family consumption. Coconuts were processed into various types of snacks and cooking oil. Coconut flesh could also be consumed as chips and sold to increase the farmers' income [26]. Meanwhile, coconut water is trusted by the community as a nutritious food that can improve health and even cure various diseases. These reports also confirmed with results of experimental studies by Zulaihah [27] that Coconut has 11 functions as consuming coconut water showed

**Table 5** Contribution of plantation crops as a source of rice farming capital

| No | Source of capital | Sub-district Kahayan Kuala (%) | Sub-district Kapuas Barat (%) |
|---|---|---|---|
| 1 | Benefits from the previous rice farming | 54 | 37 |
| 2 | From selling plantation production | 16 | 20 |
| 3 | From moneylender | | 12 |
| 4 | Farm labor | 30 | 31 |
| | Total | 100 | 100 |

*Source* Primary Data

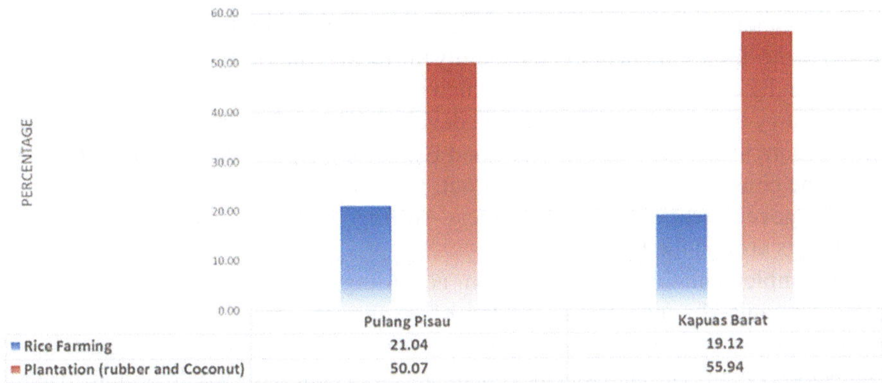


**Fig. 4** Contribution of rice farming versus plantation farming/Ha at Pulang Pisau and Kapuas Barat Sub-District (%), in 2020–2021

that it can be used to prevent oxidative stress, Antioxidant activity, Lipid peroxidation Activity, Improve Lipid Profile, Blood Pressure, Cardioprotective activity, Anti-inflammatory effects, Diarrhea Therapy, Increase hemoglobin levels, Antidiabetic activities, and Antithrombotic Activities, etc. The additional function of coconut water was also reported by Ariestini et al. [28] that regularly in the third trimester of pregnancy can prevent Meconium Staining of amniotic.

## 4 Conclusions

Plantation crops in the research location are coconuts and rubber which are managed in traditional farming but provide a significant contribution to farmers' income. Plantation crops have multi functions such as economic as well as social functions, especially for farmers in Central Kalimantan. Plantation production was also sold to outside provinces such as Banjarmasin and Palangkaraya. Both coconuts and rubber have good prospects to be developed to increase the farmers' welfare as well as for the agricultural sector.

## 5 Policy Implications

To achieve the maximum development of plantation in FE in Central Kalimantan, it is necessary to implement The Ministry of Agriculture planning on the use of technology in managing a food estate in Central Kalimantan. The technology was presented in a conceptual framework for swampland development in Indonesia according to the characteristics of the swamps area [29].

The implementation of the technology should refer to [30], involving the main actors in the development of FE and mainly the local farmers. The government should help them by creating a condition in which these development actors are willing and able to carry out successful Food estate developments as expected. Every farmer has the freedom to choose what type of Food Estate development they will do, how and when the construction will be carried out, what the results will be used for, and so on. The government only directs farmers' suffrage rights by regulating the existing conditions around the farmers.

The implementation of the program, according to Wulandari et al. [31] should be accompanied by mentoring activities of the farmers' group to improve the group bookkeeping administration which includes such as activity bookkeeping and financial bookkeeping. Through this mentoring, farmer institutions would be able to apply the benefits of the administrative book records to control the progress of the farmer institutions that farmers follow so that these institutions can be strong, resilient, and independent.

Referring to the three policies mentioned above, the strategy of involving farmers (male and female) in development, starting from planning, implementing, monitoring, and evaluating as well as enjoying the benefit of the development, first must implement the gender mainstreaming [32]. To implement Gender mainstreaming, first, gender analysis should be conducted in the study areas to get appropriate technology for the development. Through an analysis of gender, an outstanding achievement was obtained.

## References


1. Pemerintah Republik Indonesia (2020a) Peraturan Presiden Republik Indonesia Nomor: 122 tahun 2020, tentang Pemutakhiran Rencana Kerja Pemerintah Tahun 2021. Jakarta (ID)
2. Pemerintah Republik Indonesia (2020b) Peraturan Presiden Republik Indonesia Nomor: 86 tahun 2020, tentang Rencana Kerja Pemerintah Tahun 2021. Jakarta (ID)
3. Syahyuti, Handewi Purwati Saliem, Tri Pranadi, Kurnia Suci Indraningsih, Herlina Tarigan, Roosganda Elizabeth, Sri Suharyono, Annisa Rika Racmita, Rangga Ditya Yofa, Miftahul Azis, Eddy Supriyadi Yusuf, Ahmad Makky Arrozi (2020) Strategi Penumbuhan dan Pengembangan kelembagaan Ekonomi Petani Berbasis Kawasan Pertanian, Bogor
4. Christiawan R. Tata Guna Lahan Proyek Lumbung Pangan, https://katadata.co.id/redaksi/indepth/5f34fb6522108/tata-guna-lahan-proyek-lumbung-pangan, last accessed 2022/04/28
5. Fahmid IM, Wahyudi, Agustian A (2022) The Potential Swamp Land Development to Support Food Estates Programmes in Central Kalimantan, Indonesia. Environ Urban ASIA J April (4):1–12
6. Husnain, Mulyani A (2021) Dukungan Data Sumberdaya Lahan dalam Pengembangan Kawasan Sentra Produksi Pangan (*Food Estate*) di Provinsi Kalimantan Tengah. Jurnal Sumberdaya Lahan 15:23–35
7. Yestati A, Noor RS (2021) Food Estate dan Perlindungan Terhadap Hak-Hak Masyarakat di Kalimantan Tengah. Morality 7(1):52–73
8. Lasminingrat L, Efriza E (2020) Pembangunan Lumbung Pangan Nasional: Strategi Antisipasi Krisis Pangan Indonesia. Jurnal Pertahanan dan Bela Negara 10(3):243–260
9. Adil dan Lestari. Pernyataan Sikap Masyarakat Sipil: Hentikan Proyek Cetak Sawah/ Food Estate di Lahan Gambut Di Kalimantan Tengah, Jangan Menciptakan Malapetaka

Baru!. http://walhikalteng.org/2020/06/14/pernyataan-sikap-masyarakat-sipil-hentikan-proyek-cetak-sawah-food-estate-di-lahan-gambut-di-kalimantan-tengah-jangan-menciptakan-malapetaka-baru-!!/, last accessed 2022/04/29
10. Ichsan Emrald Alamsyah. Kalteng H Sugianto Sabran: PSN Food Estate di Kalteng akan Wujudkan Kedaulatan Pangan Nasional. https://mediaindonesia.com/nusantara/477885/gubernur-kalteng-h-sugianto-sabran-psn-food-estate-di-kalteng-akan-wujudkan-kedaulatan-pangan-nasional. Senin 14 Maret 2022, 07:25 WIB
11. Nyak Ilham, Syahyuti, Tahlim Sudaryanto, Sahat M Pasaribu, Bambang Irawan, Endro Gunawan, Miftahul Aziz,Sri Suharyono. Strategi Pengembangan Korporasi Petani Mendukung Food Estate di Kalimantan tengah. Laporan Akhir, Bogor (2021).
12. Directorate General of Plantation (2020) Plantation export opportunities still survive, Directorate General of Plantation, Jakarta
13. Busetto L, Wick W, Gumbinger C (2020) How to use and assess qualitative research methods. Neurol Res Pract 2(14):1–10
14. Ezzy D (2013) Qualitative Analysis. 1st edn. Imprint Rotledge, London
15. Badan Pusat Statistik (2021) Provinsi Kalimantan Tengah Dalam Angka 2020 Penyediaan Data untuk Perencanaan Pembangunan. CV APP Digital Printing. Kalilmantan Tengah
16. ILO—PCdP2 UNDP (2021) Kajian Rantai Nilai Kelapa dan Iklim Investasi Sarmi Proyek Pelembagaan Pembangunan Matapencaharian yang Berkelanjutan
17. Nurjani (2019) Potensi perkebunan kelapa Kotim masih besar. Senin, 4 November 2019 14:55 WIB. https://kalteng.antaranews.com/berita/352014/potensi-perkebunan-kelapa-kotim-masih-besar
18. Josiano, MM, Jelfi. Mengembalikan Kejayaan Karet Rakyat Di Kalimantan Tengah. Usaid Lestari: Cerita Dari Lapangan. https://www.lestari-indonesia.org, https://www.lestari-indonesia.org/wp-content/uploads/2018/05/USAID_LESTARI-CDL-Mengembalikan_Kejayaan_Karet_Rakyat_di_Kalimantan_Tengah.pdf
19. Masliani, Ludang Y (2020) Potential development of sheet rubber as an economic commodity in central Kalimantan. Int J Manag 11(4):62–67. http://www.iaeme.com/IJM/issues.asp?JType=IJM&VType=11&IType=
20. Direktorat Jenderal Perkebunan (2022) Luas Areal Karet Menurut Provinsi di Indonesia, 2018–2022, Kementerian Pertanian, Jakarta
21. Herminayati M, Erlina Y, Ludang Y, Adji FF, Darung U (2020) Socio-economic perspective to increase coconut productivity in central Kalimantan. Int J Manag 11(6):963–971
22. Mu'alim M, Astuti A (2018) Perbandingan Pendapatan Usahatani Kelapa Sayur (Cocos Nucifer L) Dengan Kelapa Kopyor Di Kecamatan Dukuhseti Kabupaten Pati. Jurnal Ilmiah Agritas 2(2):53–63
23. Syahni D. Questioning the Tugging of Domestic Coal Ration Policy. http://www.mongabay.co.id/2018/08/15/menyoal-tarik-ulur-kebijakan-jatah-batubaradomestik/. Last accessed 2020/06/20
24. Tri Yuni Hendrawati, Syamsudin AB (2016) Analisis Kelayakan Industri Kelapa Terpadu. Jurnal Teknologi Universitas Muhamadiyah Jakarta 8(2):61–70 (2016). ISSN: 2085–1669. E-ISSN: 2460–0288. HTTPS//doi.org/10.24853/jurtek.8.2,61-70
25. Ary Sudarta, Andi Tenri Sompa, Muhammad Riduansyah Syafari (2021) Analysis of Leading Commodities in the North Barito District, Central Kalimantan Province. Saudi J Econ Financ 5(2):72–75
26. Junaidi J, Ramdhan TW, Putera KB (2020) Membangun Ekonomi Pasca Covid 19 Di Desa Sadah Tanah Merah Bangkalan Melalui Pelatihan Pembuatan Keripik Kelapa. Lp3m Stai Darul Hikmah. Bangkalan. Http://Ejournal.Kopertais4.Or.Id/Madura/Index.Php/Dharma/Article/View/4136http://Ejournal.Kopertais4.Or.Id/Madura/Index.Php/Dharma/Article/View/4136
27. Zulaikhah ST (2018) The effect of tender coconut water on free radical due to Mercury exposure. June 2018. Int J Public Health Sci (IJPHS) 7(2). https://doi.org/10.11591/ijphs.v7i2.11849
28. Ariestini TR, Adriani M, Purnomo W, Devy S (2020) Prevention Of meconium staining of amniotic fluid using coconut water based on culture: a qualitative study. Pak J Med Health Sci 14(3):1559–1561

29. Sulaiman AA, Sulaeman Y, Minasny B (2019) A framework for the development of Wetland for agricultural use in Indonesia. Resources 8(1):34; pp 1–16. https://doi.org/10.3390/resources8010034. https://www.mdpi.com/2079-9276/8/1/34#cite
30. Mukti A (2020) Pemberdayaan Pertanian Lokal Dalam Menopang Keberhasilan Program Food Estate Di Kalimantan Tengah. J Socio Econ Agric (Agustus) 15(2):97–107
31. Wulandari A, Abdussamad A, Septiana N (2020) Partisipasi Petani dalam Kegiatan Kelompok Tani pada Usahatani Jeruk Siam di Kecamatan Astambul Kabupaten Banjar 21–26. Frontier Agribisnis 2(4), Juni 2020. 21–26. https://ppjp.ulm.ac.id/journals/index.php/fag/article/view/2650
32. Kementerian Pemberdayaan Perempuan dan Perlindungan Anak (2022) https://www.kemenpppa.go.id/lib/uploads/list/eb8d4-0ffb0-1.-gender-mainstreaming.pdf

# Roles of Local Government in Community Forest Management and Resilience: A Case Study of Ban Pee Community, Phayao Province, Thailand

**Kunanon Pannil and Wanwalee Inpin**

**Abstract** Community forests are forests that provide direct benefits to communities, such as the consumption of herbs and other forest products. In Thailand, the role of community forests is becoming more critical, and the number of community forests is increasing year by year. The study explores the community context and forest management of community and local organizations' role in forest management for community resilience in Ban Pee community forest, Chiang Kam district, Phayao province, as well as in addition, studying the role of local organizations in participating in community forest management through Ban Pee community forest management. The research uses the qualitative methodology to study and analyze based on the literature reviews for policy implementation on community forest resilience under the Sendai Framework (2015). Also, the research studies the resilience of community and community forest management. According to the study's findings, the community forest in Ban Pee has supported people and livelihoods, and the local government has been active in forest conservation. People in the community have formed a strong volunteer that unifies villagers in forest conservation and fire prevention to avoid future forest fire disasters and ensure their livelihood by reducing wildfire damage, including the haze pollution in the area. Therefore, the benefit of this study is to promote community forest management of local organizations by building the resilience of well-managed community forests to increase the local disaster risk reduction strategies in Thailand.

**Keywords** Sustainable community forest · Community forest management · Role of local government · Thailand

K. Pannil (✉) · W. Inpin
School of Social Innovation, Mae Fah Luang University, Chiang Rai, Thailand
e-mail: 6352301001@lamduan.mfu.ac.th

W. Inpin
e-mail: Wanwalee@mfu.ac.th



Nawawi et al. (eds.), *Managing Disruption and Developing Resilience for a Better Southeast Asia*, Springer Proceedings in Humanities and Social Sciences,
https://doi.org/10.1007/978-981-96-2116-3_25

# 1 Introduction

## *1.1 Background*

In Thailand, Forest is the fundamental resource for people and the basis of economic, social, security, and environment [11]. The management of forests is a vital issue that the government is concerned with to sustain the country's benefit. In 1895, the Royal Forest Department (RFD) establishment was the first government agency to officially undertake forest management in Thailand. At that time, the forest policy by RFD mainly focused on timber production for use in domestic and export for foreign traders [16].

During the 1970s, the country's forest area has been decreased continuously due to the problem of deforestation and unfair allocation of forest land [11]. Throughout the 1970s, the country's forest area decreased steadily due to deforestation and unfair forest land allocation, with the percentage of total forest area at 43.21% in 1970 and remaining at 25% in 1998 [11]. In 2000, Thailand's forest area was 33.15% and in the 2018 survey, it was forested at 33.15%. 31.68% [11]. Moreover, the increasing degradation of forest areas in natural resource reserves is another problem. The leading cause is the increase in domestic population, economic expansion, housing construction, illegal deforestation, and forest burning for agriculture [14]. According to Thaphracharoen [18], the degradation of the forest area is affecting the ecosystem and biodiversity, including the effect on the soil and water source. Moreover, its consequences impact natural disasters such as floods and drought [18].

The country's rapid increase in deforestation encourages the government to find a solution to decrease the deforestation impact and increase the forest area. One of the measurements was the recognition of community forestry to encourage participation in environmental protection and sustainable forest management. By 1989, there were an estimated 8000 sites, and there were more than 10,000 in 2011 [20]. In 2021, 12,217 community forest sites existed [12]. However, the authority to operate any forest management is still in compliance with the central government. In other words, the community needs government permission to use or maintain that community forest first. This incident caused conflict between people and the government regarding authority and rights.

So, the idea of community forest management could be enhanced by studying resilient communities to promote community capability for the change and uncertainty of the environment. The resilience perspective is fundamentally different from traditional approaches to sustainability because it seeks to build the adaptive capacity of social-ecological systems to respond to future surprises. In contrast, traditional approaches have sought control over systems assumed to be stable. The resilience framework assumes that change will always occur, but the drivers of change are not necessarily predictable ([1], as cited by Nelson et al., 2007). It is necessary to understand better how local communities rely on forests and how sustainable forest management strategies can support the resilience of local communities [20]. According to Akamani [1], the forest communities are social-ecological in the concern for one type of resilience system, which means it is necessary to build adaptive capacity in its system because it seeks to build the adaptive capacity of forest communities' systems to respond to future surprises [1].

## 2 Literature Review

### *2.1 Public Policy*

Policies are written statements of ideas, goals, and plans of action proposed or adopted by several agencies. The term policy represents the method of action from the governmental and non-governmental organizations to achieve in pursuit of their concern. The agenda of organizations that propose their policy in each sector is caused by fulfilling needs and public policy [2]. According to Lasswell (1956), the policy cycle is still considered one of the essentials in the conceptual toolbox of public policy to study policy analysis.

According to Pressman and Wildavsky (1973), implementation of the policy is the fulfillment of tasks and total productivity, which is a process of interaction between goal setting and action to achieve it. Also, Van Horn and Van Meter's (1976) policy implementation encompasses all activities carried out by governments and private individuals, both individuals and groups, that contribute to achieving the objectives predetermined by policy decisions (as cited by [15]).

According to Kenaphoom & Jandaeng [6], the theoretical models of policy implementation can be classified into two major groups: (1) Top-down approach,the idea emphasizes the policy implementation process beginning with the government as an actor in decision-making under the political system. The Top-Down approach relies on centralization and central government holding the policy formulation power, including separating the order for any practitioner to apply. (2) The Bottom-Up itself concentrates more on the involvement and participation of stakeholders in the purpose and the needs of the policies. The service delivery asks about the goals, planning, action, and associates, then tries to develop a technical link to categorize local, regional, and national actors included in the policy implementation [6].

According to Kotchapong et al. [8], Public policy is regarded as a guideline of the government sector in providing public services in solving problems or developing or meeting people's needs in various matters [8]. In the local government context, Local government delegation, which is decentralization, is a method by which a state is partially delegated to provide public services within the territory of each locality with specific budgets and officials [19]. In Thailand, the local government can be divided into various categories such as Provincial Administrative Organization (PAO), Subdistrict Administrative Organization (SAO), and municipality [19]. These entities have autonomy and legal rights to self-govern and do public affairs in important areas.

Under the "Act Prescribing Plans and Procedures for Decentralization to Local Administrative Organizations, 1999," the local government has a role in delivering public service in areas such as economic, social, and cultural development, education, public health, and environment. According to Wisitsath [22], Decentralization to Local Administrative Organizations Act Section 16 of this Act, stated about the powers and duties in organizing the public service system, especially the environment of local government, are stated as: "...local government organizations have the authority to make local development plans and must protect, manage, maintain and utilize forests, including land, natural resources, and the environment, as well as manage pollution and promote other activities that for the benefit of the local people..." Therefore, sub-local administrative organizations have the powers and duties to promote and maintain the quality of the environment according to the law [22].

## *2.2 Sendai Framework for Disaster Risk Reduction 2015–2030*

The Sendai Framework for Disaster Risk Reduction 2015–2030 is the successor of the Hyogo Framework for Action (HFA) 2005–2015: Building the Resilience of Nations and Communities to Disasters. The Hyogo Framework for Action (HFA) 2005–2015 was conceived to give further force to the global work under the International Framework for Action for the risk reduction of natural disasters and strengthening of resilience (UNDRR, 2015).

According to Sendai Framework (2015), one statement emphasizes incentive factors for promoting resilience, "...To support the implementation of the present Framework, the following is necessary...Local Government organization and other relevant bodies of local governments to continue supporting cooperation and mutual learning among local governments for disaster risk reduction and the implementation of the present Framework..." (UNDRR, 2015). Moreover, the local government is vital to achieving the strengthening disaster risk governance to manage disaster risk in priorities two, "... To establish and strengthen government coordination forums composed of relevant stakeholders at the national and local levels for disaster risk reduction to designated national focal points for implementing the Sendai Framework for Disaster Risk Reduction 2015–2030. Such mechanisms must have a strong foundation in institutional frameworks with clearly assigned responsibilities..." (UNDRR, 2015). Also, the local government plays a crucial role in building awareness and knowledge of disaster risk through sharing and dissemination of non-sensitive disaster risk information and data, including contributing to and coordinating reports on disaster risk, facilitating and supporting local multi sectoral-cooperation, and contributing to the determination of and reporting on national and local disaster risk management plans and all policies relevant for disaster risk management. These responsibilities should be established through laws, regulations, standards, and procedures (UNDRR, 2015).

### 2.3 *New Public Governance (NPG): Concept and Application for Local Governance*

According to Mala [9], New Public Governance (NPG) is a public sector management concept mentioned in the late twentieth century. The challenges such as disaster, climate change, and terrorism are that problems need more collaboration [9]. The increase in non-traditional security is a threat to the traditional bureaucracy system to cope with these challenges consistently.

New Public Governance (NPG) is rooted in institutional and network theory, which considers states diverse within their own or plural states. The concept sees the state as an actor of organizations and jobs that depend on each other. Many levels and forms play a role in providing public services [9]. According to Cheema (2005), the application of the NPG concept in local governance encourages the locality to change the structure and operational processes to the changing situation as a basis for the regional and national level ([9], as stated by Cheema 2005). The state must decentralize its power over local governments in terms of freedom of decision-making and also provide opportunities for other sectors to participate in policy-making and local public service delivery on specific issues ([9], as stated by Cheema 2005).

The government must believe that participation is a key process in the development of democracy by examining transparent government operations and empowering civil society and local communities ([9], as stated by Cheema 2005). In addition, the concept of NPG could influence the dissemination of power as well as enhance the effectiveness of local governance in the management of the challenges [9]. Also, it has changed the role of the government according to the NPG concept, making the state smaller with power and obligations but increasing social networks in public affairs [9]. It can be applied to local governance that can transform management from the traditional concept of bureaucracy and chain of command to network management that allows for collaboration of all local sectors in the process of issuing policies and public services or other public activities to empower and strengthen communities and local governments [9].

## 3 Methodology

This research uses the qualitative method to study and analyze based on the concept of community forest management and resilience. The data collection gathers information based on sources acquired from documentary research and in-depth and group interviews.

The purpose of using documentary research and interview for understand community forests in the development of community forest management, including the role of different stakeholders. This research uses documentary research and interview as the data collection. There are interviewees 12 people: 5 in-depth interviews and 7 group interviews, consisting of 10 males and 2 females. 3 of the interviewees are from the government authorities, 5 of the interviewees are from community forest administration and 4 are community members. There is demographic information of the interviewees as shown in Table 1.

The target interview was aimed at local government officers and local community leaders who contribute to community forest management. The gathered information focused on (1) how local governments work on community forest management, (2) the development of community forest management, and (3) the problems of community forest management in the past. There were 2 groups of interviewees; the first group was an in-depth interview on the issue of forest management participation in a management community forest from a community leader, stakeholders, and other community organizations. The second group was community members and community forest committees, which gained and shared the benefit of how to manage sustainable community forests and their perspective on community forest management.

This research was conducted in the "Ban Pee community forest" Wiang subdistrict, Chiang Kam district, Phayao, Thailand, located in the country's northern part. Ban Pee community is located in the Chiang Kham district. The community has a total population of 516 in 184 households (personal informant 27 January 2022).

**Table 1** Interviewees demographic information

| No | Gender | Occupation | Position |
|---|---|---|---|
| 1. | Male | Retired | Community forest committee chairman |
| 2. | Male | Bureaucrat | Head of the department of public health and environment, Wiang Chiang Kham municipality, |
| 3. | Male | Bureaucrat | Head of provincial community forest department, Phayao forest center, Royal forest department |
| 4. | Male | Village headman | Community forest committee |
| 5. | Male | Village headman | Community forest committee |
| 6. | Male | Assistant village headman | Community forest committee |
| 7. | Female | Assistant village headman | Community forest committee |
| 8. | Female | Assistant village headman | Community forest committee |
| 9. | Male | Farmer | Community member |
| 10. | Male | Farmer | Community member |
| 11. | Male | Retired | Community member |
| 12. | Male | Farmer | Community member |

The "Ban Pee community forest" is located on the east side of the community with an approximate area of 375.6 acres, covered by two villages [3, 5].

# 4 Results

In the study result, the collected data can be categorized regarding the research objectives for the understanding of the role of local government in the management of community forests. There are 2 objectives of the research; (1) To study the Ban Pee community's community and forest management, and (2) To study the role of local organizations in participation in the forest management of the Ban Pee community.

## *4.1 The Community and Forest Management of the Ban Pee Community*

In 1999, the community established a community forest called "Ban Pee Community Forest," initially located in Ban Pee villages No.1 and No. 10, with 257 acres of community forest. Later, in 2018, the forest area expanded the community forest area to 375 acres (In-depth interview, 27 January 2022).

According to the personal informants (2022), in 2002, the community had a consensus on the establishment of the first official executive body known as "Ban Pee Community Forests Committees" to manage tasks and keep the interest of the community forest. The committees consist of 15 representatives of Ban Pee village number 1 and number 10 (In-depth interview, 27 January 2022). The committees' tasks produced a substantial impact on the benefit of the community. It was initiated by launching "Rules of Ban Pee Community Forest," the mandatory regulation to control the community activity in the community forest. Also, they were providing punishment for anyone who violated the rules (In-depth interview, 27 January 2022), as below in Table 2:

In Ban Pee Community, seven activities are the method of managing their community forest. All of the work has proceeded in different ways and consists of the following activities.

(1) Community Forest route and Fire protection line maintenance. This activity benefits the community as it becomes the village's fire line that helps prevent forest fires in the community forest. So, it required maintenance for the sustainability of forest fire mitigation. (2) Community Youth Guide Project encourages the youth generation to love and preserve community forests. (3) Forest Fire patrol is the task force to investigate and extinguish forest fires around the community forest. (4) Forest ordination is the forest preservation stratagem and prevents people in the community from destroying forests by representing the importance of trees as much as a Buddhist monk. (5) Reforestation of the forests in the damaged area of

**Table 2** List of rules and penalty of Ban Pee community forest

| Rules of Ban Pee community forest | The penalty for Ban Pee community forest |
|---|---|
| 1. Prohibited cutting and collecting firewood without permission from the Community Forest Committee<br>2. Hunting of any kind of wildlife in the community forest is prohibited<br>3. Forest collection is permitted but in a limited number and must be kept sustainably | 1. The amount of the fine would adjust according to the damage (Minimum 500 baht)<br>2. The items seized from offenders will be left in the forest, but they will be taken to the community's temple (Wat Ban Pee)<br>3. The fine will be charged to the Community Forest Development Fund<br>4. If the charges are serious, they will be passed to the government authority for legal prosecution |

deforestation and degradation. (6) Worship ceremony; pray and offer respect for the holy spirit who lived in the forest. In return, the holy spirit would bless villagers and help conserve the abundance of forest and water. (7) Weir construction is the construction of a weir to reduce the water flow level, including storage water for the dry season.

In addition, according to personal informants (2022), the management of the community forest of Ban Pee proceeds more efficiently after the promulgation of the Community Forest Act. 5 of 5 respondents said the "Community Forest Act" empowers the committee authority in forest management and greatly benefits the community (In-depth interview, 7 February 2022). "In the past, villagers had to make many requests through provincial authorities, and it took a long time to get approval for an activity in forest management" (In-depth interview, 9 February 2022). So, the community forest act provides a lot of positive effects on forest management to be more autonomous and an opportunity to promote the development of community forests.

## *4.2 The Role of Local Organizations in Participation in Community Forest Management of the Ban Pee Community*

According to the Wiang municipality (2018), the municipality must set up a five-year development plan for the development direction of the subdistrict. The plan itself consists of development aspects to improve economic, socio-cultural, and environment (Wiang Municipality, 2018). The current development plan (2018–2022) stated that the development strategy in the region is one of the strategies for environmental conversation and management of natural resources to substantiality. So, Budget support is provided by the municipality in many activities such as worshiping ceremonies and forest fire patrolling. As well as support the training of human capacity of community and local organizations to ensure the practical outcome of environmental protection [21].

In the past, the municipality managed and coordinated community development budget projects. However, the attention to community forests declined since 2007; 4 of 5 respondents about the budget once subsidized for forest fire was transferred to another environmental protection sector (In-depth interview, 21 April 2022). The municipality mainly focuses on waste management and reducing the household waste burning method rather than the forest fire extinguisher and community forest. Due to the change in the law of local government to support forest management became irrelevant to the local government's duty (In-depth interview, 21 April 2022). Also, the municipality considers the community forestry in Ban Pee in villages 1 and 10 as a positive effect on the community and sub-district as a whole by being an example of a community that is strong and united in forest protection. So, the budget of the municipality for the environment and natural resource management must cover the area of all 10 villages under their responsibility (In-depth interview, 18 April 2022).

Moreover, the community forest area also initiated the overlapping dispute between the two subdistricts. In 2007, the new draft of the subdistrict map and the new map made the boundary of the community overlap with another subdistrict. So, the dispute has led to the debate between two local governments that two local governments should sponsor local maintenance taxes. This problem results in discontinuous development and causes difficulty for the financial support from local government to the community forest.

On the other hand, according to the personal informants, 3 out of 10 respondents believe that the role of the local government has changed and has less important in community forest management, even though the rest of 7 respondents still believe that the local government is necessary for managing the community forest alongside the community. Even though the local government's role has changed, 9 of 12 respondents still think that the local government is a necessary actor in managing the community forest alongside the community (focus group interview, 2022). This is because the local government is also one of the keys to achieving a sustainable community forest. However, the respondents are concerned about a solution with the local government as a mediator to resolve the dispute. Despite the present, there is more budget support from other sectors, such as the private sector. However, the overlapping area affects the claimant from another subdistrict to take advantage without helping to maintain the community forest. Moreover, most respondents stated the necessity of the municipality for support for building sustainable income for continued development, whether budget, human resources, and training program.

## 5 Conclusion and Discussion

In conclusion, the community forest management in Ban Pee enhances the unity of people through forest management activities that rely on the help and unity of everyone in the community to conserve the community forest. As a result, the community forest management of the Ban Pee community provides benefits to the community and people. For instance, the fertility of forests reduces the chance of forest fire, including having volunteers to patrol and quench fires which helps to reduce the damage of haze pollution to the whole region. So, the Ban Pee community forest management's activities create impacts on the community and environmental conservation in many ways such as socio-cultural, economic, and food security.

According to Thapa [17], the role of local government represents the decentralization of government and encourages participation [17]. Therefore, the local government is necessary for its executive function to support and maintain the locality's interests. So far, the local government is a crucial notion for contemporary society for sustainable development. Thus, it is worth supporting and ensuring disaster risk reduction and with the local government's support, the development could continue and benefit greater than its area.

According to informants, the local government contributes to community forestry management. Even though the role in the past was different from the present, the existence of local government could benefit the community through budget support, human resources, and training program. Moreover, the local government also includes the effective community forest as one of the grand strategies to reduce the problems of haze pollution in the province. The provincial office plans to decrease the amount of haze pollution impacted by household garbage incineration in every district (In-depth interview, 2022).

Meanwhile, the municipality also encourages the campaign to stop forest fires and haze pollution. However, they could not provide a budget or workforce to extinguish forest fires as much as they should. According to informants, 11 of 12 respondents said forest fire prevention needs more financial support and men. However, the municipality cannot support it either due to a lack of staff and budget. Also, the conflict from overlapping areas undermines the capacity of local government the work for community forest management (In-depth and group interview, 2022).

However, the problems of the overlapping area of community forest since 2007 questioned the effectiveness of the work of local organizations as government bodies are supposed to be trusted by local people. According to informants, 8 of 12 respondents requested a solution to the dispute to eliminate conflicts and lead to sustainable development in community forestry. Moreover, one of the respondents said, "...the problems are somehow beyond the municipality's authority to solve; it must be the provincial authority to fix it...however, the community forest committee requested a solution from the provincial officer but never received any news from them..." (In-depth interview, 2022). Hence, the local government could use this circumstance as an opportunity rather than a problem to bridge the conflict between the two subdistricts.

Moreover, NPG adaptation promotes participation and empowerment of local organizations [9]. As a result, the connection between the local people and the central or provincial executive body defines the character of local government. Establishing an excellent relationship to gain the locals' trust is critical, and it improves the effectiveness of local officials' work [17]. Because the longer this situation persists, the more difficult it will be to resolve, and it will not achieve the desired effects in community forest management.

Another way, the character of local government is the connection between the local people and the central or provincial executive body. It is crucial to build up an excellent relationship to obtain trust of locals, and it enhances the work of local officials to be more effective. Because the longer this situation is allowed to go on, the more complex the chances of resolving it will be, and it will not achieve the desired effects in community forest management. So, the local government seems to catch this attention and consider the solution to this circumstance.

In addition, according to Sendai Framework (2015), the emphasis is on risk reduction goals, disaster risk management, and preparedness for natural disaster mitigation. It is urgent and critical to anticipate, plan for, and reduce disaster risk to more effectively protect persons, communities, and countries and their livelihoods (UNDRR, 2015). The intense awareness of the concern of forest fire around the Ban Pee community is still intact. Somehow, it might affect the community forest and the nearby forest that frequently burns during the dry season in Thailand (February to April). Therefore, the issue of forest fire prevention needs to be on account of the local government as one concern alongside reducing the problems of haze pollution from the household's garbage incineration solely. The idea of resilience thinking is necessary because the studying of adaptive capacity will help the community forest management work more about how to adapt to further challenges So, preparedness and cooperation are required in the province area yet confront the problems of haze pollution and forest fire yearly. The support for the training program, budget allocation, and volunteers for forest fire extinguishing needs to be done.

## References


1. Akamani K (2012) A community resilience model for understanding and assessing the sustainability of forest-dependent communities. Hum Ecol Rev 19(2):99–109. Retrieved from https://opensiuc.lib.siu.edu
2. Capano G, Pritoni A (2020) Policy cycle. The Palgrave Encyclopedia of Interest Groups, Lobbying and Public Affairs (pp.1–7). Retrieved from https://doi.org/10.1007/978-3-030-13895-0_69-1
3. Department of Forestry (2021) Ban Pee Community Forest Information. Information technology center and communications department of forestry. Retrieved from http://forestinfo.forest.go.th/fCom_detail.aspx?id=2033
4. Forest Protection Network (2022) Thailand Forest Protection Volunteers Information. Retrieved from https://www.forest.go.th/forest-protection
5. Department of Forestry (2021) Summary of the establishment of the provincial community forest project. Retrieved from http://forestinfo.forest.go.th/fCom_area.aspx
6. Kenaphoom S, Jandaeng B (2019) Theory model of public policy implementation. J Local GovAnce Innov 3(1):January–April. Retrieved from https://so03.tci-thaijo.org/index.php/JLGISRRU/article/view/215982
7. Klongdumnoenkit S (2019) Public policy evaluation if unsuccessful, it fails? Humities Soc Sci 36(3):September–December. Retrieved from https://so01.tci-thaijo.org
8. Kotchapong S, Pongpaeo D, Bunklanson K, Rojanatrakul T (2021) Public Policy Implementation of Local Government Organizations. J Mod Learn Dev 6(5):September–October. Retrieved from https://so06.tci-thaijo.org/index.php/jomld/article/download/249269/170204/

9. Mala T (2018) New Public Governance (NPG): concept and application for local governance. Valaya Alongkorn Rev (Humities Soc Sci) 8(1):January–April. Retrieved from https://so06.tci-thaijo.org/index.php/var/article/view/146949
10. Ministry of Interior (2017) Regulations of the Ministry of Interior on the preparation of development plans of local government organizations 2005, third revised 2017. Retrieved from http://www.lp-pao.go.th›book›Plan_Law_3
11. Ministry of Natural Resources and Environment (2019) National Forest Policy. Subcommittee on the drafting of the National Forest Policy and the drafting of the National Forest Development Master Plan. Retrieved from http://forestinfo.forest.go.th
12. Ministry of Natural Resources and Environment (2022) Summary of the establishment of the community forest project by province. Retrieved from http://forestinfo.forest.go.th/fCom_area.aspx
13. Samukkethum S (2015) The Crisis of Deforestation and Public Governance of Community Forest in Thailand. Thammasat Rev 18(1):27–45. Retrieved from https://sc01.tci-thaijo.org
14. Singharak P (2018) Overlapping problems in forest areas in natural resource conservation areas. Office of the Council of State. Retrieved from https://lawforasean.krisdika.go.th/Content/View?Id=441&Type=1
15. Somboon S (2012) Implementing the tablet PC policy for Thai education: a case study of university demonstration schools Srinakharinwirot (primary division). Master of Public Administration Program for executives Graduate School of Management Studies Sripatum University. http://dspace.spu.ac.th/handle/123456789/4893
16. Sritanatorn P (2009) Sustainable Community Forest management in Local development: community practice, people participation, and the success of forest conservation. National Institute of Development Administration. Retrieved from http://libdcms.nida.ac.th/thesis6/2009/b166940.pdf
17. Thapal (2020) Local government: concept, roles, and importance for contemporary society. Public Administration Campus, Tribhuvan University, Nepal. https://doi.org/10.13140/RG.2.2.23009.33123
18. Thaphracharoen N (2015) Key success factors in the forest management of Baan chongkheap, Thasao Sub-District, Saiyork District, Kanchanaburi Province. Retrieved from http:/202.28.75.7/xmlui/handle/123456789/9970
19. Tongsukmak C (2020) The roles and authorities of local administrative organizations in promoting and protecting geographical indications according to the principles and relevant laws. NITIPAT NIDA Law J 9(1). Retrieved from so04.tci-thaijo.org
20. RECOFTC (2011) Community forestry in Thailand. Retrieved from https://archive.recoftc.org/basic-page/community-forestry-thailand
21. Wiang Sub-District Municipality (2018) Wiang Sub-District Municipality Development Plan, Chiang Kham district 2018–2022. Retrieved from http://www.wianglocal.go.th
22. Wisitsath K (2011) Sustainable Forest Fire and Smog Pollution Management, Puea sub-district, Chiang Klang district, Nan Province. Retrieved from lib.more.go.th

# Mainstreaming Disaster Risk Reduction and Resilience Education in Thailand: A Case Study of Comprehensive School Safety (CSS) Framework in Chiang Rai Province

**Reni Juwitasari**

**Abstract** In Chiang Rai province, the intensity of heavy rain causes flash floods to increase, and children are particularly vulnerable to natural disasters. Because school is one of the locations where children spend substantial time during their formative years, school safety in disaster and emergency preparedness should be prioritized and managed effectively. This study examines the Comprehensive School Safety (CSS) Framework in Thailand with a case study from schools in Chiang Rai, with three pillars, (1) Safe Learning Facilities, (2) School Disaster Management, and (3) Risk Reduction and Resilience Education. By applying the qualitative method, this study reviews the literature from peer-reviewed journal articles on Disaster Risk Reduction (DRR) and School Safety in Thailand for two decades (2000–2020) to identify good practices and challenges in DRR and School Safety fields. The study applies in-depth interviews and develops survey questionnaires to the respondents' administrators and teachers in one primary school in Chiang Rai regarding its CSS framework implementation. Results show that the school has created and implemented a student curriculum on DRR as endorsed in the CSS Framework. The basic core curriculum of DRR learning in Thailand starts from pre-school grade 6 to grade 12. However, there is still a lack of teacher training programs and school children's participation in drills and training. Several challenges include financial and human resources limits. Moreover, with the increasing frequency and intensity of disasters in Thailand, the DRR in education should cover multi-hazards preparedness to help school children gain preparedness knowledge and readiness attitude and mitigate emergencies effectively.

**Keywords** Disaster risk reduction · School safety · Resilience

---

R. Juwitasari (✉)
Disaster Resilience and Environmental Sustainability (DRES) Program, Asian Research Center for International Development (ARCID), Mae Fah Luang University, Chiang Rai 57100, Thailand
e-mail: reni.juw@mfu.ac.th



Nawawi et al. (eds.), *Managing Disruption and Developing Resilience for a Better Southeast Asia*, Springer Proceedings in Humanities and Social Sciences,
https://doi.org/10.1007/978-981-96-2116-3_26

# 1 Introduction

## *1.1 Background*

In connection with vulnerable populations, floods and other natural catastrophes greatly influence children, youth, and education systems. Studies of catastrophe patterns and the expected implications of climate change imply that 175 million children are projected to be impacted by natural hazard-related disasters alone (Bastidas 2011). In fact, 3.8 million children from 13.6 million people were impacted by floods in Thailand in 2011 (USAID 2011). For example, severe and adverse flooding happened in 2011 with the longest duration of 158 days, and 7.5 flood magnitude affected the entire country, including Chiang Rai, from the Nam Mae Kok river [1]. Chiang Rai is one of the prone areas to flooding located in the northern part of Thailand. As reported by MRC in 2016, from 2000 to 2015, Chiang Rai faced flooding events.

Security, safety, and prevention in educational institutions have long piqued the educational community's concern and attention (Vicario 2017). UNISDR developed a framework for disaster risk reduction that emphasizes the capacity building of vulnerable societies and promoting sustainable development. The Hyogo Framework for Action (HFA) intends to minimize catastrophe losses significantly and is endorsed by 168 UN member states. The HFA is divided into five Priorities for Action, with this thesis focusing on DRR instruction in primary schools, which falls under Priority 3 (knowledge, innovation, and collaboration to foster a culture of safety and resilience at all levels) [2]. The literature discusses school safety regarding how secure pupils feel at school [3]. Moreover, the successor of HFA, the Sendai Framework for Disaster Risk Reduction (SFDRR), has continued school safety as one of the priorities, especially in Priority 1, Understanding Disaster Risk [4].

In realizing children as one vulnerable group and the international disaster global framework of HFA and SFDRR, UNDRR (United Nations for Disaster Risk Reduction), along with the Worldwide Initiative and the Global Alliance for Disaster Risk Reduction and Resilience in the Education Sector, established a framework of Comprehensive School Safety (CSS) in 2017 with three pillars of (1) Safe Learning Facilities, (2) School Disaster Management, and (3) Risk Reduction and Resilience which aims to foster safe school implementation globally (Green et al. 2020). By applying these three pillars of CSS, this research becomes substantial for the case of Chiang Rai schools to build school safety through the enhancement of disaster risk understanding and resilience. Chiang Rai is located in the northern part of Thailand, particularly hill areas and prone to flooding. One disaster, for instance, flooding, did not merely happen, but another disaster occurred with a cascading effect of landslide. Due to that, school children have to deal with the "double impacts of disasters," where education plays a crucial role in enhancing preparedness. Consequently, this research emphasizes compulsory education to reflect the Thai existing disaster education for disaster preparedness with a holistic view, ensuring disaster knowledge, readiness attitude, and emergency mitigation.

## 1.2 Conceptual Framework

To develop a successful learning and working environment, educational institutions must offer a safe and secure environment for students, teachers, and non-teaching workers. School safety is defined as the safety within the school setting, which entails examining the individual and collective safety for emotional, physical, and social elements to achieve safety for all members of the educational community, particularly the most vulnerable pupils [5]. To incrementally improve school safety, it is necessary to develop physical, social, and emotional security [6].

To comprehend safer school creation, the Comprehensive School Safety (CSS) framework was established to protect students and teachers from injury, death, and damage in schools, to ensure that students have consistent access to education and education continuity regardless of anticipated natural or human-made hazards, to safeguard education sector investments for quality basic education, and to strengthen students' capability for disaster risk reduction through education [7].

Comprehensive school safety is addressed via education policies and practices integrated with disaster management at the national, subnational, and local school site levels. Three pillars support it, as follows (UNISDR 2017):

1. Safe School Facilities include education authorities, architects, engineers, contractors, and school members in the safe site, design, selection, building, and facility maintenance (including uninterrupted and safe accessibility to the facility).
2. School Disaster Management is formed through cooperation between national and regional education parties and local school societies (including students) to preserve safe learning facilities and prepare for continuous education according to international standards.
3. Risk Reduction Education should be structured in such a way that it fosters a culture of safety and resilient communities.

In the nexus of CSS pillars as the cornerstone of Comprehensive School Safety planning, there are three elements, as follows; (1) multi-hazard risk assessment, (2) education sector analysis, and (3) child-centered assessment and planning. Those three pillars are part of a larger examination of educational policy and administration to provide a foundation for planning and action (UNISDR 2017). Ideally, this is encouraged to be integrated into national, subnational, and local educational management information systems.

The integrity influences the school actions, which can significantly contribute to the attainment of the Sendai Framework for Disaster Risk Reduction (SFDRR) and Sustainable Development Goals (SDGs), especially referring to education for safety in the context of sustainable development (ESD) [7]. In fact, ESD, in link with safety education, assists acquire students' knowledge, skills, and attitudes to learn the sense of safety for an emergency, such as rapid-onset disasters, even daily life in terms of building preparedness toward resilience [8]. Therefore, in this study, the Comprehensive School Safety Framework (CSS) is used to investigate the implementation and practical actions at the school levels, especially in the northern part

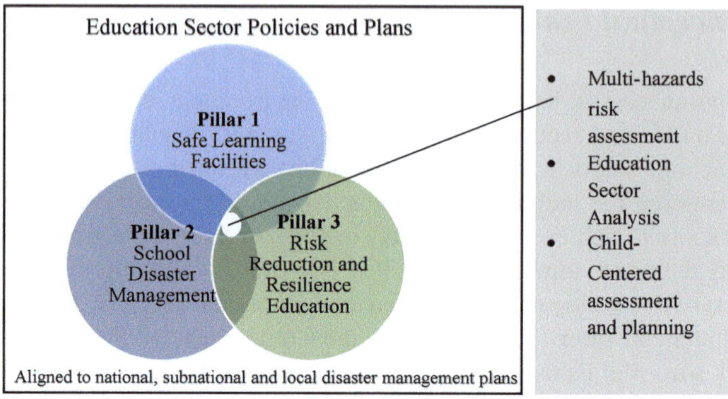


**Fig. 1** The nexus of the three pillars of the Comprehensive School Safety (CSS) Framework from UNISDR in 2014

of Thailand, in each pillar of safe learning facilities, school disaster management, risk reduction, and resilience education. The CSS reflects the importance of integrating disaster education policymaking from national, subnational, and local disaster management levels. Moreover, this study examines these pillars' reflection incorporated into everyday action developed by the educational institution as part of its culture, especially disaster resilience among school members, students, teachers, and administrators (Fig. 1).

## 2 Methodology

This study applied qualitative methods with two steps of approaches, such as a systematic literature review and a survey questionnaire, including in-depth interviews in Chiang Rai school. The systematic literature review aimed to elaborate on the empirical studies of good practice and challenges for Comprehensive School Safety (CSS) in Disaster Risk Reduction (DRR). To identify literature reviews, the data derived from Web of Science limited between 2000 and 2020 uses three pillars of CSS as keywords:

> safe learning facilities "OR" school disaster management "OR" risk reduction and resilience education.

The first stage was to gather 371 articles that included these three keywords. The data were chosen after reading the abstracts, with an emphasis on Thailand's background. As a result, 29 articles were selected to be related. The entire articles chosen for consideration were continually scrutinized for information pertaining to formal education. The remaining articles included just six empirical investigations on school safety in Thailand. In summary, those six articles were included in the in-depth examination.

The second phase included conducting an in-depth examination using a survey questionnaire and interviews in conjunction with a qualitative case study. A qualitative case study is a method of research that enables the examination of phenomena [9]. Purposive sampling is used to pick the target, consisting of 10 key respondents from two administrative schools, three teachers from the science learning group, three teachers from the social studies learning group, and two teachers from the health education learning group. Sueksa Songkhro Mae Chan School is situated in the Mae Chan district of Chiang Rai Province, one of the active fault zones and by the Mekong River's tributary, the Khong River Basin [10]. As a result, the Mae Chan district has been identified as a high-risk location for flash floods and landslides, including a Chiang Rai earthquake.

Numerous questions on Comprehensive School Safety (CSS) were posed to important respondents, focusing on three pillars: safe learning environments, school disaster management, and risk reduction and resilience education. Demographic data, such as position, gender, age, duration of employment, and educational background, are collected using this survey questionnaire. Table 1 summarizes this information.

The questionnaire was delivered to key respondents and was constructed as a closed-ended question. Additionally, an in-depth interview was done in person and online to elicit significant information that cannot be dwelt upon in light of the likely response to the pertinent material. The interview lasted between forty and sixty

**Table 1** Demographic information

| Category | N = 10 (100%) |
|---|---|
| **Position** | |
| School executive | 2 (2%) |
| Teacher | 8 (8%) |
| **Gender** | |
| Men | 4 (4%) |
| Female | 6 (6% |
| **Age** | |
| Below 30 years | 1 (1%) |
| Between 31 and 40 years | 1 (1%) |
| Between 41 and 50 years | 5 (5%) |
| Above 51 years | 3 (3%) |
| **Length of working period** | |
| Between 2 and 5 years | 2 (2%) |
| Between 6 and 10 years | 3 (3%) |
| Between 11 and 15 years | 2 (2%) |
| More than 16 years | 3 (3%) |
| **Educational background** | |
| Bachelor degree | 6 (6%) |
| Master degree | 4 (4%) |

minutes. An inductive interpretation was used to assess the interview data to ascertain the respondents' subjective perspectives (Akinyode and Khan 2018). The data was categorized using comparable types of information and coding methodologies for identifying and designating the underlying concepts [11] associated with the CSS notion. This research made use of the codebook.

## 3 Results

Due to the two-stage methodology used in this study, the study resulted in a summary of the literature review presented in Table 2, which was sorted by relevant keywords and interpreted as school safety in Thailand using three indicators of safe learning facilities, school disaster management, and risk reduction and resilience education.

The findings from this six-selection of the literature suggested that Thai educational practitioners attempt to establish appropriate practices and models for school safety building consistent with the CSS's three pillars. The first pillar, school disaster management, refers to establishing a model for school safety management. Four of the six publications expounded fully on this three-pillar structure. Safe learning environments underscored the critical nature of school-level disaster management policies, evaluations, and activities. Finally, the third pillar is efforts to maintain ongoing resilience programs, including mitigation, waste management, and child-centered DRR active participation.

These publications focused on natural catastrophes in general, emphasizing tsunamis, fire prevention, and other concerns like bullying and school violence. The Japanese value becomes a lesson for complete school safety beyond crisis management. However, waste management of mura, muda, and muri inspired the development of seven school safety management systems (refer to literature numbers 2 and 5), and another (refer to paper number 6) emphasized the global framework's implications for regional DRR agendas, including school safety in Asia. The investigation was conducted in Bangkok, Chiang Mai, Nakhon Ratchasima, and South Thailand.

Additionally, Table 3 summarizes significant responses to Comprehensive School Safety (CSS) implementation and practices, including maintaining safe learning facilities, developing school disaster management, and enhancing risk reduction and resilience education. Every pillar assigned a set of questions that the key respondents must answer.

The first pillar of safe learning environments highlights the importance of physical structure in simulating students' desire for learning and teaching. Positive emotion, social and academic achievement, particularly healthy psychology and well-being have blossomed in a safer school or learning environment [12]. According to key responders, the school is well-located in a safe neighborhood, as shown by its placement in Muang Mae Chan or Mae Chan city, which occupies 400 m of the Nam Mae Chan River's surface [13]. Indeed, several important responders expressed confusion about the resilient school design. However, seven significant responders indicated

**Table 2** Summary of literature review of school safety in Thailand

| Author year | Title | Comprehensive school safety | | |
|---|---|---|---|---|
| | | Safe learning facilities | School disaster management | Risk reduction and resilience education |
| 1. Siripong, A. (2010) | Education for disaster risk reduction in Thailand | Protective and preventive measures such as disaster risk analysis (vulnerability assessment); disaster prediction; warning system, mapping of the hazards; assistance from teachers; assistance from parents | Dissemination of education programs on natural disaster awareness and preparedness; assistance from scientists; Assistance from teachers, parents, and psychologists | Mitigating social, emotional, and psychological impacts of disasters in the community |
| 2. Srichai, P., Yodmongkol, P., Sureephong, P., & Meksamoot, K. (2013) | Managing school safety in Thailand: assessing the implications and potential of a lean thinking framework | School should be an inviting place across a set of five key areas (people, place, processes, policies, and programs) | The seven management: Financial Implications; Time; Leadership; Communication; Stakeholder Understanding; Culture; Commitment | Lean and safety derive from the Japanese values mura, muda, and muri, which mean "safety" and "leverage," respectively |
| 3. Musigapong, P., & Phanprasit, W. (2013) | Knowledge, attitudes, and practices relating to fire prevention among students in the elementary schools of Muang Nakhon Ratchasima, Thailand | – | – | Design guidelines for incident reduction and the potential human improvement, especially in the case of fire prevention |
| 4. Kruger, L. (2014) | The Significant Influence of School Safety Management on School Safety in Selected International Schools in Bangkok, Thailand | Safe classrooms, safe facilities, safe playgrounds, and prevention against violence and to ensure that disaster and emergency preparedness is well managed | The four traditional functions of management are: Planning, Organizing, Leading, and Controlling | Encourage waste reduction activities |

(continued)

**Table 2** (continued)

| Author year | Title | Comprehensive school safety | | |
|---|---|---|---|---|
| | | Safe learning facilities | School disaster management | Risk reduction and resilience education |
| 5. Srichai, P., Yodmongkol, P., Chakpitak, N., Meksamoot, K., & Sureephong, P. (2015) | A framework for improving school safety management: Applying lean thinking to a case study in Thailand | Appropriate and dynamic legislation to facilitate the appropriate management of safety | The seven management: Financial Implications; Time; Leadership; Communication; Stakeholder Understanding; Culture; Commitment | Effective communication management among disaster stakeholders (e.g., students, parents, staff community); a safe environment achieved through the role of school leaders to implement effective school policy; and curriculum safety management for lifelong learning |
| 6. Chatterjee, R., Shiwaku, K., Das Gupta, R., Nakano, G., & Shaw, R. (2015) | Bangkok to Sendai and beyond: Implications for disaster risk reduction in Asia | – | – | Children and Youth as Agents of Change; Science and Technology as a Key Actor for Information Sharing and Warning Systems |

**Table 3** Comprehensive school safety questions indicators

| Category | Question Indicators | Response (n = 10) |
|---|---|---|
| Safe learning facilities | 1. The school is located in a safe area<br>2. The school is designated resiliently<br>3. The school has a regular building monitoring<br>4. The school implements environmentally friendly practices to increase energy, food security, and water, e.g., school gardens<br>5. The school has continuous budgeting as well as monitoring for the safety and maintenance of facilities | Yes 10<br>Yes 7; No 3<br>Yes 10<br>Yes 10<br>Yes 10 |
| School disaster management | 1. The school establishes policies, guidance, and planning to reduce disaster risk and preparedness<br>2. The school has a program of response preparedness, for instance, stimulation drills<br>3. The school has an early warning system<br>4. The school engages with other stakeholders in the disaster management sector<br>5. The school is functional during disaster occurrence, e.g., temporary shelters | Yes 10<br>Yes 10<br>Yes 2; No 7<br>Yes 10<br>Yes 10 |
| Risk reduction and resilience education | 1. The school integrates risk reduction and resilience into the curriculum<br>2. The school encourages teachers to develop quality learning and teaching materials, for instance, mitigation and a culture of safety and resilience<br>3. The school curriculum is designated to stimulate critical thinking for all types of disasters<br>4. The school engages students and school members actively in real-life disaster management activities | Yes 10<br>Yes 4; No 6<br>Yes 10<br>Yes 4; No 6 |

that the school is resiliently designed by elevating the classroom and student dormitories above the soil level, roughly 1, 5 to 2 m to the first floor. It has proved beneficial in saving lives during floods.

Additionally, they said the space class is enough for the 20: $5 \times 4.5$ m student–teacher ratio. While three important respondents said that in the event of an earthquake, higher levels might pose a hazard to children and school personnel; for example, the 2014 earthquake may have caused some damage to the school building. The school has continuously examined the complete facility yearly to maintain a safe physical environment for ongoing instruction, and all major responders responded similarly, including the allocation budget for school building maintenance. Additionally, a significant push is to establish ecologically friendly practices, particularly with regard to trash management and school gardens. Students who live in dormitories may cultivate vegetables to ensure their food security. There are many varieties of morning glory, including chili, spinach, and tomato. Another option is to build the three draw wells. Consequently, a massive physical structure, appropriate learning space, universal access to the school, regular building maintenance, food security, and adequate water access are all critical components of a secure school building, and the school site is built to be resistant to flooding.

In the second pillar of school disaster management, key respondents elaborated that school administrators, primarily the School Division of General Administration, establish concrete disaster policies at the school level by integrating intra- and extra-curricular disaster studies, for example, by organizing activities on safe school projects and connecting disaster studies to social studies, religion, and culture subjects, as well as Boys and Girls Scouts. The school collaborates with external networks such as the Bureau of Disaster Prevention and Mitigation, the Organization for Sub-district Administration, the Department of Land Development, and non-governmental organizations (NGOs). Typically, the disaster program is conducted at least once a year. The school serves as a temporary shelter during disasters, most notably earthquakes. However, the early warning system remained in need of improvement.

Risk reduction and resilience education are two of the school's primary objectives. The school has included disaster education in its curriculum by offering students a variety of crisis scenarios. The school encourages instructors to take part in disaster-related education and training. The school's dedication to catastrophe resilience and knowledge capacity has sparked students' critical thinking in decision-making and emergency capabilities. Additionally, the pupils do not experience panic and are not capable of surviving an emergency. The institution holistically instills a spiritual world and strengthens pupils' immunity to mitigate the disaster's effects. Additionally, the school creates the material, infographics, video clips, and visualizations to aid students' learning. In practice, real-world disaster management measures are rarely implemented due to challenges in quantification, and training for teachers is seldom provided.

## 4 Discussion and Conclusion

According to the literature review, disaster education research has been conducted in several locations throughout Thailand, most notably in major cities such as Bangkok, Chiang Mai, Nakhon Ratchasima, and South Thailand, with an emphasis on the impact of typical natural disasters such as flood and tsunami, as well as other school safety concerns, on students' psychological well-being. As a result, the growth of research in Chiang Rai as a case study remains speculative. Chiang Rai has developed into a crucial research development site due to its topography in a mountainous and deep catastrophe zone, prone to earthquakes, floods, landslides, and drought, despite the fact that earthquakes do not occur regularly in the region [14]. When it comes to numerous catastrophe occurrences, a cascading disaster occurrence significantly impacts disaster preparation and response. According to Djalante and Lassa in 2019, catastrophe is not a solution to a single issue but a complex system including interactions between humans and all physical objects in the environment. It might occur as a consequence of hazard multiplicity interlinking.

According to the three pillars of CSS, the primary priority for school safety is protecting children from risks and threats and developing children's resilience. Consequently, the inclusion of disaster management at all organizational levels is encouraged to strengthen adaptive capability. The previous study focuses on school administration, leaving child-centered and child-participatory concerns like CSS objectives unaddressed. Additionally, the apparent rationale for CSS literacy at the school level is unidentified in reflection of school activities. Furthermore, insufficient teacher training for disasters can impact the knowledge of teacher capacity, which simultaneously affects students' knowledge. The budget allocation is utilized more for physical school building rather than training. Therefore, the training conduction has been held irregularly.

Each phase of a catastrophe has diverse goals and a different complexity level, including time constraints, organizational engagement, and functional coordination requirements [15]. As seen in the outcome, the majority of actors involved in permitted disaster management are governmental organizations. As a result, the top-down strategy dominates the disaster management operation. However, the intricacy shown above underscores the critical nature of mainstreaming Community-Based Disaster Risk Management (CBDRM) as a benchmark for community participation. CBDRM exemplifies a bottom-up approach to disaster management since it actively includes communities in identifying, analyzing, solving, monitoring, and evaluating catastrophe risks to minimize their vulnerabilities and strengthen their capabilities [16]. Indeed, participative decision-making, policy formulation, and planning remain the purview of the executive level. Teachers and the institution's community cannot be acknowledged in this regard. Consequently, school-based disaster management has been ineffectively structured compared to real-world catastrophe situations, which affects the results of disaster education.

In this case study, the CBDRM concept revealed the lack of a higher education network. Higher education is critical for establishing credibility in application-oriented teaching, environmental research, and catastrophe risk reduction [17]. Additionally, higher education participation is crucial in DRR education as a knowledge provider for environmental friendliness [18]. Since an educational and research institution, the university is compelled to participate in all stages, as it is tasked with the goal of making a significant contribution to society [19]. Consequently, enhancing partnership with higher education becomes critical for disaster risk reduction and resilience efforts.

In conclusion, the research stated that comprehensive school safety has to be mainstreamed in Thailand, particularly in the event of a tragedy. The school now has a larger physical structure from the three CSS pillars of safe learning facilities, school disaster management, and risk reduction and resilience education. However, school disaster management, risk reduction, and resilience education need improvement and development in the Thai context to ensure the school's lifelong learning education continuity. As a consequence, resilience capability is not yet quantifiable. As a result, the study suggests persistent disaster risk reduction planning and measures at the school level, including a prolonged commitment to providing disaster stimulation drills, enhancing disaster networks, and conducting inclusive research development activities across Thailand. Encouraging the development of networks from the bottom up, for example, through higher education and non-governmental organizations, is critical for achieving contextual and efficient disaster management, particularly disaster education. Its connection to higher education plays a critical role in knowledge generation by boosting teachers' disaster knowledge transmission to elementary school children.

## References


1. Gale EL, Saunders MA (2013) The 2011 Thailand flood: climate causes and return period. Weather 68(9):233–237
2. Willmott E (2014) DRR education in Indonesia: how does the organisation of DRR and DRR education in Indonesia affect the implementation of DRR education programmes? And does it contribute to a reduction of children's vulnerability?. MS thesis. University of Stavanger, Norway
3. Srichai P, Yodmongkol P, Sureephong P, Meksamoot K (2013) Managing school safety in Thailand: assessing the implications and potential of a lean thinking framework. SAGE Open 3(2):2158244013489985
4. Selmi A et al (2015) The Sendai framework for disaster risk reduction: renewing the global commitment to people's resilience, health, and well-being. Int J Disaster Risk Sci 6:164–176
5. Mubita K (2021) Understanding school safety and security: conceptualization and definitions. J Lexicogr Term 5(1):76–86
6. Devine J, Cohen JD (2007) Making your school safe: strategies to protect children and promote learning
7. Mamon MAC (2019) Implementation and practices of the comprehensive school safety framework: views of senior high school students. Intern J Educ Res 10(3):49–60
8. Kitamura Y (2014) The possibility of holistic safety education in Japan: from the perspective of education for sustainable development (ESD). IATSS Res 38:40–47
9. Baxter P, Jack S (2008) Qualitative case study methodology: study design and implementation for novice researchers. Qual Rep 13(4):544–559
10. Kanthiya S et al (2019) Structural interpretation of Mae Suai Basin, Chiang Rai Province, based on gravity data analysis and modelling. Elsevier 5:e01232
11. O'Connor H, Gibson N (2003) A step-by-step guide to qualitative data analysis. Pimatiziwin J Abor Ind Comm Health 1:64–90
12. Kutsyuruba B et al (2015) Relationships among school climate, school safety, and student achievement and well-being: a review of the literature. Rev Educ 3(1):103–135
13. Scholten JJ, Boonyawat W (1971) Detailed reconnaissance soil survey of the northern part of Chiang Rai Province. Dept of Land Development, Bangkok
14. Nasaku T (2017) Natural disaster, and disaster management in Thailand: status, risks, and trends. In the 13th International Conference on Thai Studies, Chiang Mai, Thailand
15. O'Sullivan TL et al (2013) Unraveling the complexities of disaster management: a framework for critical social infrastructure to promote population health and resilience. Soc Sci Med 93:238–246
16. Tanwattana P (2018) Systematizing community-based disaster risk management (CBDRM): case of urban flood-prone community in Thailand upstream area. Intern J Dis Risk Reduct
17. Shaw R et al (2011) Essentials of higher education in disaster risk reduction: prospects and challenges. Environment and Disaster Risk Management. Emerald Group Publishing, United Kingdom, In Community
18. Thayaparan M et al (2014) Disaster management education through higher education—industry collaboration in the built environment. Proc Econ Fin 18:651–658

19. Ahmad R (2007) Roles of the university in disaster management. Malays J Med Sci 14(2):1–3
20. Chatterjee R et al (2015) Bangkok to Sendai and beyond: implications for disaster risk reduction in Asia. Intern J Dis Risk Sci 6(2):177–188
21. Green RP et al. (2019) Comprehensive school safety policy: a global baseline survey. Intern J Dis Risk Red 44
22. Kruger L (2014) The significant influence of school safety management on school safety in selected international schools in Bangkok, Thailand. In the International Conferences held by the Australian Society for Commerce Industry and Engineering (SCIE), Phuket 10
23. Musigapong P, Phanprasit W (2013) Knowledge, attitudes and practices relating to fire prevention among students in the elementary schools of Muang Nakhon Ratchasima, Thailand. J Educ Soc Res 3(7):288–288
24. Siripong A (2010) Education for disaster risk reduction in Thailand. J Earthq Tsunami 4(02):61–72
25. Srichai P et al (2015) Framework for improving school safety management: applying lean thinking to a case study in Thailand. Intern J Manag Educ 9(1):47–69
26. UNISDR (2017) Comprehensive School Safety. https://schools.aidr.org.au/media/4853/unisdr_css-framework_0117.pdf, last accessed 2022/05/02
27. USAID (2011) Success story: child-centered preparedness in Thailand. https://www.usaid.gov/sites/default/files/documents/1866/Sucess-Story-Thailand.pdf, last accessed 2022/4/27

# Root Causes, Dynamic Pressure, and Unsafe Living Conditions of Thai Rural Farmers to Climate-Based Drought in Chiang Rai Province: A Social Vulnerability Perspective

**Wanwalee Inpin and Maya Dania**

**Abstract** The rainfed lowland areas in Northern Thailand develop drought during the rice-growing season. This study analyzes the Thai farmers' vulnerability to socio-economic drought in Chiang Rai province in Northern Thailand. Socio-economic drought refers to a condition in which a decrease in precipitation affects the population's well-being and is linked to underlying vulnerability. This research was conducted in Phan District, Chiang Rai province, where the worst drought occurred in the area for more than a decade. An exploratory case study in the qualitative analysis was utilized to analyze the socio-economic vulnerability model by Blaikie et al. [6]. Data were collected from interviews with affected farmers (n = 50) and stakeholder engagement. The findings feature root causes, dynamic pressure, and unsafe living conditions explaining Thai farmers' social vulnerability to drought. The root causes implicated in the rice system in Thailand are characterized by rainfed lowland where the water supply is unpredictable by too much and too little water in the same season. Dynamic pressure involved the government's policy-related drought management response, which was not adequately responsive to safety nets and social protection assessment in strategic plans and actions. Furthermore, rural Thai are less likely to migrate, particularly poor farmers and families with limited income, exposing them to unsafe conditions from consecutive droughts. As climate change impacts result in more extreme drought events, it is also crucial to understand the institutional context of governance responding to climate change mitigation and adaptation measures in broader livelihoods diversification strategies.

**Keywords** Drought · Social vulnerability · Northern Thai farmers

W. Inpin · M. Dania (✉)
Mae Fah Luang University, Chiang Rai 57100, Thailand
e-mail: Maya.Dan@mfu.ac.th



Nawawi et al. (eds.), *Managing Disruption and Developing Resilience for a Better Southeast Asia*, Springer Proceedings in Humanities and Social Sciences,
https://doi.org/10.1007/978-981-96-2116-3_27

# 1 Introduction

## *1.1 Background*

Drought is a slow-onset natural disaster that affects the population in nearly all region on earth and may result in immense and long-lasting impacts on the livelihoods of individuals, communities, and the environment. In Thailand, a drought might be meteorological, caused by low rainfall and seasonal climate variability, but it could also be hydrological with the lack of water resources accessible to the people. Human activities (i.e., urbanization and industrialization) have threatened the important natural water resource and groundwater and contributed to the shortage of water supply in urban and rural areas [1]. The frequency and intensity of disasters have escalated since the turn of the twenty-first century in Thailand, and the local community will be immensely vulnerable to the hazard threats.

In Thailand, costs and losses from a drought event are significant to the agricultural environment. The most tangible examples are decreasing food production because of affected crop fields and reducing rural farmers' income from harvest failure. This study was conducted in Phan District, Chiang Rai province, where the worst drought occurred in the region for more than a decade. In 2020, the Department of Disaster Prevention and Mitigation (DDPM) declared disaster areas prone in 25 provinces to severe drought, which Chiang Rai province included in the emergency measures. In Chiang Rai province, the Governor declared disaster zones after the provincial DDPM office confirmed that the province experienced a full-scale drought, affecting thousands of households with water shortages.

The study is significant because drought is persistent in Chiang Rai province, yet very little research has been done to assess drought risk management and local farmers' socio-economic vulnerability to drought. Each year in the province, the agricultural sector is often the first to be affected by drought as rice crop production declines. This study of drought focused on local farmers because they are most directly affected by lost agricultural productivity. In Chiang Rai province, more and more places are experiencing water shortages at an increasing rate. As climate change impacts result in more extreme drought events, it is crucial also to understand the local context of drought and policies that respond to effective climate change adaptation toward resilience at the local level in rural areas.

## *1.2 Conceptual Framework*

Social vulnerability is a multidimensional concept that represents the susceptibility of a community to experience losses because of hazards. The impact of social vulnerability drivers differed greatly depending on the stage of the disaster, emphasizing the relevance of policy and practice context in understanding social vulnerability determinants, mechanisms, and consequences. The conceptual circumstances were derived from the social vulnerability model by [2], which assumes that vulnerability is a social condition that highlights Root Causes (RC), Dynamic Pressure (DP), and Unsafe Living Conditions (UL). In this conceptual framework, the social vulnerability is intertwined with drought hazards as the primary risks of climate change for the local farmers, as shown in Eq. (1) below.

$$Hazard\ x\ Vulnerability\ (RC + DP + UL) = Social\ Risk \tag{1}$$

A drought event represents a hazard in this study. A drought event is considered a hazard because its intensity, duration, and spatial extent affect the environment and well-being that affect community resilience. Natural disasters also have a dynamic effect on social vulnerability reflected in socio-economic and demographic aspects. It is a multidimensional entity that's difficult to pin down with a particular element [3]. The social vulnerability was first used in disaster management in the 1970s when researchers realized that vulnerability includes socio-economic factors that impact community resilience [4]. It measures a population's sensitivity to natural hazards and its ability to adapt to and recover from the effects of hazards. Many factors increase vulnerability to a hazard, including age (elderly and children), home tenure (renter or owner), educational attainment, and gender. When communities, families, and individuals' lives are threatened by drought, they feel vulnerable and helpless. Social risk refers to the social impacts of a drought event. Disasters disproportionately afflict economically disadvantaged people. The most vulnerable persons are generally those whose needs are not considered enough in local reaction and relief preparations. The impoverished are less likely to have the income or assets necessary to prepare for a disaster or recover after one has occurred [5]. Therefore, social vulnerability is crucial for disaster preparedness, immediate reaction, mitigation planning, and long-term recovery.

### *1.3 Social, Economic, and Environmental Impacts of Drought*

Drought is one of the most devastating natural disasters, affecting communities' economic, environmental, and social aspects characterized by spatial and temporal constraints [6]. Drought is a "creeping phenomenon" [7], making it difficult to anticipate when it will begin or finish. Unlike other climate-related phenomena, drought develops slowly and quietly, with no obvious consequences. The exact timing of the beginning or end is difficult to determine. As in the case of small-scale farming or subsistence agriculture, a lack of visibility, understanding, and definition of the hazards can result in a great deal of human suffering and significant economic losses at the local level [8]. Drought's relevance should not be separated from its social context. The severity of a drought is primarily determined by society's sensitivity to drought at the time. Even if the intensity, length, and spatial aspects of subsequent droughts in the same place are comparable, they will almost certainly have distinct impacts [9].

Natural disasters, such as drought, can have direct and indirect consequences. Drought causes several indirect costs in addition to direct losses. These costs and losses vary greatly from one drought year to the next in the same location, depending on the drought's timing, intensity, and geographic scope. The precise measurement of the financial costs of drought is a tremendous challenge due to many impacted organizations and sectors, the large geographic region affected, and the challenges in measuring environmental damages and personal losses. Direct costs of drought were confined to the loss of crops, harvests, land, buildings, and other agricultural-related machinery, while indirect costs included business disruption and economically regressive effects [3]. The agriculture sector is the most affected by drought, marked by dried crops, abandoned farmland, and withered and yellow pastureland. Drought-induced soil moisture shortages also cause harm to crops and pastures. Local farmers were the focus of this drought study since they are the ones who are most affected by the loss of agricultural productivity.

### *1.4 Drought and Vulnerability in Thailand Context*

Drought is a slow-onset natural disaster caused by economic, environmental, political, and social elements by weather events (Zarafshani et al. 2007). Drought can be characterized in various ways, including the effects of drought on people and their activities [1]. Several Thailand-based pieces of research related to drought management have been done and given important remarks to be developed in the future. [10] conducted research about climate trends and drought index in the Mun River Basin in Thailand by describing the importance of drought management research in the Northeastern part of the country because people in Isaan relied on their lives on 90% rice cultivation activities. Therefore, according to Prabnakorn, the analysis of the rice yield is important for establishing proper adaptation and mitigation measures to enhance productivity. In his research, Prabnakorn focused on the relationship between rice yield and a drought indicator. His research resulted in the importance of spatial and temporal resolutions in detecting climate trends and impacts on yields.

Seeboonruang [1] has also undertaken a study on the influence of climate change on groundwater and drought vulnerability in Eastern Thailand and the previously described studies. Seeboonruang focused his research on the relevance of natural water resources in the Eastern portion of Thailand, specifically groundwater, which may be used as a backup water source during natural droughts. According to the study, many groundwater supplies have been threatened by urbanization, industrialization, seasonal climate variability, and climate change. The study proposed a variety of risks, impacts, and vulnerability maps for Eastern Thailand, concluding that better groundwater management and planning will improve decision-making.

On a larger scale, Jongdee's [11] research found that many of Thailand's poor farmers face an erratic water supply and a dry season. According to the study, Thailand's rainfed lowland rice accounted for 6.2 million acres or 67% of the country's total rice-growing area. In the same season, farmers in Thailand were characterized by their reliance on too much and too little water, resulting in yearly drought losses of up to 45%, particularly in the country's northern half. The study found that in the lowland rice environment of Northern Thailand, there had been a shift in the seed production in the rice-growing method and that this was attributable to people who had combined their expertise and adaptation to water deficit. The study identified three terrace paddy levels: upper (susceptible to drought), middle (vulnerable to drought-prone to favorable), and lower (vulnerable to drought-prone to favorable) (vulnerable to flood). Finally, Phan District in Chiang Rai Province is susceptible to climate change with extreme climatic drought events. Based on several studies elaborated above, there are limited works of literature concerning drought management, local resilience, and disaster risk governance in Northern Thailand.

## 2 Methodology

Qualitative research is a process of analysis that aims to provide an in-depth interpretation of a social phenomenon [12]. This study uses a qualitative method in an exploratory case study design to evaluate the impact of a drought occurrence in the Phan District of Chiang Rai, Thailand, and to obtain new insights. The explanatory approach was appropriate for a more in-depth investigation of a catastrophic event. As a result, the case study methodology is excellent for investigating phenomena in a real-world situation that relies on various sources of evidence and benefits from creating theoretical propositions to guide data gathering and analysis [13]. This work received ethical approval from the university's human research ethics committee, and it was carried out in compliance with research ethics standards.

The population for this research was selected from 5 villages in the Phan District, consisting of 10 households from each village (n = 50). The villages and participants were selected with a purposive sampling technique from the information obtained from the farmer group leaders. The selected participants were farmers with more than ten years of farming experience to gain insight into their experience in a drought event in at least one decade. The interview was also conducted with the policymakers and officers at the local governments in Phan District, Chiang Rai Province.

A survey is useful to access many participants in standardized questions such as demographic questions to describe socio-economic dimensions into specific indicators of Age, Gender, Monthly Income, Educational Attainment, Household Dependents, and Experience of Drought in Farming, as shown in Table 1.

From the demographic data, most farmers in the Phan District who participated in this study were women aged more than 50 years with an educational background in elementary school. All participants were initially contacted and gathered in the appointed places. The questions were formulated to suit an interview and a survey

**Table 1** Demographic information

| Category | Indicators | N = 50 (100%) |
|---|---|---|
| Age | 25–40 years old | 10 (20%) |
| | 41–50 years old | 4 (8%) |
| | Over 50 years old | 36 (72%) |
| Gender | Female | 27 (54%) |
| | Male | 23 (46%) |
| Monthly Income | Less than 10,000 THB | 21 (42%) |
| | Between 10,000 and 20,000 THB | 28 (56%) |
| | More than 20,000 | 1 (2%) |
| Educational | Elementary School | 36 (72%) |
| Attainment | Secondary School | 8 (16%) |
| | Bachelor's degree | 6 (12%) |
| Household | None | 5 (10%) |
| Dependents | 2–5 persons | 2 (4%) |
| | 5–10 persons | 39 (78%) |
| | More than ten persons (including farm employees) | 4 (8%) |

as a data collection tool for this study [14]. The questions used in the survey to reflect the demographic conditions were closed-ended. In the closed-ended questions, possible answers were listed for the participants to select all the pertinent choices. The interview was conducted more interactively and formulated with open-ended questions. Each interview highlighted answers from the concise questions reflecting multidimensional aspects of drought impacts on social vulnerability divided into three main questions theme: environment and well-being, institutional supports, and social conditions, as shown in Table 2.

The object of qualitative analysis can be any recorded communication, such as transcripts of interviews. The topic guide helped ensure that the research covered themes identified as relevant. The interview data were analyzed in an inductive and holistic approach. The interviews were taped, transcribed, and coded inductively to detect emerging themes to capture specific meaning, key, and contextual information [15]. All text components related to the research themes were compiled in the first step of the analysis. Data analysis in the phenomenological method consists of several steps: drawing attention to key remarks from the interview transcripts to understand how the participants felt about the phenomena, forming themes from meaning clusters derived from significant statements; writing a textural and structural description of what the participants experienced; and developing a compound explanation that provides the kernel of the phenomena foci [16].

**Table 2** Matrix of interview questions

| Questions theme | Socio-economic circumstances |
|---|---|
| Environment and well-beings Economic conditions | How is your access to clean water?<br>Were you affected by food consumption during the drought?<br>Did any member of your family fall sick during the drought period?<br>Have you experienced increased harvesting losses since the drought started?<br>Do you spend extra costs because of the drought? What type of extra cost was incurred?<br>Do you take a loan because of impacts from drought? From where do you get the source of the loan?<br>Do you employ temporary or permanent staff for your farming activities? Furthermore, were there cases of letting-off staff/unemployment caused by decreased production? |
| Social conditions | Did you/your family members have to move from your household village because of drought? |

# 3 Results

## *3.1 Root Causes of Social Vulnerability in Thai Rural Context*

Phan District in Chiang Rai province is a lowland area with the Mae San River flowing through the municipality. Most areas are covered with agricultural land where rice and vegetables are grown. The climate in Phan District is tropical, with an average temperature of 24–43 degrees Celsius and an average rainfall of 58.50 mm/year. Due to the lack of rain during the last three months, the main rivers have dried up, and thousands of farmland have gone dry. The district is in the grip of a severe drought because rainfall has decreased, resulting in a water shortage for home usage and crops. Rainfed lowland rice with shallow favorable, and drought-prone soils characterize farms in the Phan area. Drought occurs seasonally from March to May. However, in the previous decade, residents have reported that droughts have lasted longer and caused more acute water scarcity from January to June when the rainy season is meant to be. The drought-threatening effect of rising temperatures has been amplified, with 10 to 12% of days exceeding 35 °C.

According to the interview, the drought in 2010 in Thailand was the impetus for the worst drought in the province. From the Interior Ministry's Disaster Prevention and Mitigation Department report in 2010, 53 provinces in Thailand were hit by severe drought, and the extreme dry season has affected 1,755,100 households or 6,482,602 people. The changing climate patterns in Thailand have resulted in insecurity and challenges for the people and infrastructure. As shown in Table 3, drought is a severe constraint to rice production in the Chiang Rai region, and it is one of the biggest sources of risk and uncertainty in Thai rural agriculture. Drought is now a serious issue in agricultural crop production, reducing land productivity and, as a result, threatening food security [11]. Drought has substantially impacted the livelihood of rainfed lowland rice farmers in northern Thailand due to changes and fluctuations in the normal climate [17].

Water shortages resulting from global warming are predicted to significantly impact populations, particularly farmers who rely on their harvest and water supply for subsistence. The locals bought water after freshwater reservoirs dried up during the hazard event. Lowland rice culture is one of the crops expected to suffer from climate change. Thailand exports the most rice globally, and the agricultural industry consumes 70% of the country's total water supply. This has become an emerging problem because farmers have extended cultivation outside irrigated zones. Many farmers also do not preserve water and do not effectively plan agricultural output. On the other side, Thailand is experiencing a flood problem during the rainy season, with several areas seeing prolonged periods of severe rain, harmed agriculture and cattle, and impacted people's health.

Furthermore, heat stress negatively influences livestock reproductive and immunity and downstream effects from a lack of feed. The spread of disease and herd loss will be hastened when flood events become more frequent. Small-scale commercial poultry and pig businesses and smallholder cattle/buffalo systems are among the methods that are expected to be impacted. Thailand's forests and watersheds have suffered a hit as rains continue to be delayed and farmers struggle to make ends meet. Grasslands that were once lush and green have turned grey and parched. The rivers that supply them with water have dwindled in size—the likelihood of fires increases. Chiang Rai also set records for the worst air quality in the world earlier this year. Community members are working hard to create firebreaks while the drought continues. Wildfires could become more likely due to a lack of rainfall and water reserves, which would be an intertwined disaster affecting the health of the local people and farmers in the Phan District.

**Table 3** Interview key results (Environmental Root Causes)

| Impacts from drought | Keywords from the interview | N = 50 (100%) |
|---|---|---|
| Impacts on river | The water resources are dry for rice farming | 37 (74%) |
| | Decrease number of fish | 7 (14%) |
| | Loss of biodiversity in the water area | 6 (12%) |
| Impacts on soil | The soil is dry, and cannot plant anything | 18 (36%) |
| | Reduce in quality and quantity of rice | 21 (42%) |
| | Crops failure and low yield production | 11 (22%) |
| Impacts on food | No water for human consumption | 29 (58%) |
| Consumption | No water for animals consumption | 12 (24%) |
| | Limited variations of foods for the family | 9 (18%) |
| Impacts on health and | Reduce in quality of water and sanitation | 42 (84%) |
| Well-Beings | Reduce in quality of air (smog pollution) from wildfire | 8 (16%) |

## 3.2 Dynamic Pressure of Disaster Governance in Thailand

Water scarcity is one of the worldwide concerns that Thailand will face in 2025. Consequently, the country requires a long-term strategy to address this impending threat, beginning with a comprehensive water management system [18]. The government has established a water crisis center in response to the severe drought that many Thai provinces are experiencing this year, which is worse than the previous year's. The Office of National Water Resources (ONWR) revealed that 6,255 villages in 24 provinces had been drought-affected, although dams and reserves are only 49% complete. Only 26% of the available water may be utilized. The ONWR is trying to implement a 20-year national strategy to supply people and enterprises with clean, sustainable water resources, avoid flood damage, and balance water resource usage and public cooperation [19].

As shown in Table 4, a drop in agricultural productivity due to water scarcity in drought events will set off second-round impacts in rural areas where agriculture is a key source of income and employment due to backward agricultural connections with other sectors. According to the National Statistical Office (NOS), Thai rice farmer debt increased from 2.4 trillion baht in 2016 to 2.8 trillion baht in 2017. The government has offered assistance, but rice farmers could not escape from debts due to crop uncertainty, unforgiving weather, droughts and floods, shifting prices, and growing costs. From the interview, the local farmers explained that the rural farmers in Thailand are normally authorized to borrow agricultural credits from the Bank for Agriculture and Agricultural Cooperatives (BAAC) for a year in 10,000–50,000 baht (about $300–1,500 USD), based on their investment capacity and demands [4]. Farmers account for 1.1 million of the 3.8 million creditors with state-backed loans.

Due to debt, many rural farmers in the Phan District rent land to plant rice. During drought, farmers in Phan had to spend more money on extra production expenditures, such as tractor oil, chemical herbicides, chemical fertilizers, and seeds. Farmers use

**Table 4** Interview Key Results (Economic Conditions)

| Impacts from drought | Keywords from the interview | N = 50 (100%) |
|---|---|---|
| Impacts on agricultural | Loss in Plants Harvest (Crop Failures) | 37 (74%) |
| Loss | Loss in Poultry Products | 13 (26%) |
| Impacts on extra cost | Household Expenses (Water Pumping, Fuel, and Electricity) | 31 (62%) |
| | Fertilizer Costs | 19 (38%) |
| Impacts on loans | Government Bank | 18 (36%) |
| | Private Bank Debt | 2 (4%) |
| | Village Fund (Farmer Union) Debt | 29 (58%) |
| | Family/Colleagues Debt | 1 (2%) |
| Impacts on employment | Letting-off Staff | 12 (24%) |
| | Stop Farming | 38 (76%) |

the extra costs to borrow money for various reasons, including building or purchasing a home or residential plot, schooling, strengthening the farming business, doing business, general consumption, and other uses. If agricultural revenue declines, the demand for items from agro-processing firms that cater to local markets will be reduced. As a result, income and employment in this sector will decrease.

Similarly, rural households that provide agricultural inputs would see a fall in their income. The impoverished, whose consumption levels are already low, may see a reduction in consumption due to a loss in household income. Farmers may try to cope with the loss by selling off productive assets, pulling their children out of school, traveling to distant locations searching for work, or going into debt. All of these repercussions can have extremely high economic and social implications. The overall economic loss from drought may be many times greater than what is suggested by the loss in the agricultural output alone by the time these consequences are fully realized.

## *3.3 Unsafe Living Conditions from Consecutive Drought*

Thailand's rice business is crucial, accounting for almost a quarter of the worldwide rice trade. Nonetheless, due to climate change susceptibility, the country faces food security challenges. According to local farmers, droughts are significant drivers of land degradation in the Phan District, negatively affecting resource-dependent rural populations and potentially leading to livelihood losses and subsequent migration out of affected areas due to debt trap and the loss of crops, harvests, land, buildings, and other agricultural-related machinery.

Many communities in Phan District's rural areas rely on natural resources for their livelihoods, including soil, water, and plant and animal husbandry. Rural households cannot adequately protect against shocks such as drought due to these limits and deep-seated poverty and consequently suffer large decreases in well-being [20]. Droughts are becoming increasingly common and severe due to ongoing worldwide climate changes, resulting in the loss of farmland, decreased agricultural yields, and livestock losses, expanding Thailand's fragile physical environment. Droughts are expected to become more frequent and severe due to climate change. Droughts are common in Chiang Rai, and their consequences are exacerbated by deep rural poverty, low local government capability, and other political, economic, and health shocks [21].

During this drought, the Thai Government will pay some compensation to affected farmers, but it is unlikely to match their expenditures. Rice growers in areas designated as disaster assistance zones could get up to US$36 per rai of land (0.16 hectares). According to farmers, the expense of growing one rai is around triple that amount. The local farmer mentioned that "(the aid). It will just be enough to keep us going for a while and buy food because rice is not grown here, so we will have to buy it." Another farmer said that "(The government). They will compensate you, but it will be insufficient." Some farmers have given up their lands and planned to move to other provinces to get other work on construction sites for income. However, due to unfinished loans and debts and the number of family dependents that rely on farming as their main household income, the local farmers could not migrate and waited for the rain. A local farmer also said, "If I cannot handle it, I will have to look for work in town. I will trust my father to manage independently in terms of the fields. Unfortunately, he is a senior citizen, and I need someone to take care of him." Finally, in the Phan District, farmers have taken various steps to improve access to water and reduce their reliance on irrigation water, and attempt other risk-reduction methods, such as non-agricultural enterprises, although they only offered little money.

## 4 Discussion and Conclusion

In Thailand, drought management occurs on a macro, meso, and micro-scale. In governing the drought hazards' impacts, the Royal Thai Government has given the Ministry of Interior the responsibility through the Department of Disaster Prevention and Mitigation (DDPM) of developing measures to deal with the drought. In the case study of drought in the Phan District, the National governments also implemented drought-relief programs, laws, and regulations at the macro level, frequently enlisting international assistance. They are in charge of alleviating suffering by coordinating relief efforts, giving loans, and creating employment opportunities for sufferers. Local governments at the meso level aim to reduce drought by considering national opportunities and local challenges. Farmers are at the vanguard of drought management, and they are the ones who bear the brunt of the effects. As a result, micro-level management is critical, such as farmers' reactions to drought. Social, institutional, cultural, religious, economic, environmental, hydrologic, geographic, educational, and political elements all have a role in designing efficient drought management policies and tactics [22].

**Acknowledgements** This article received funding support from Mae Fah Luang University Research Fund (2021–2022), Mae Fah Luang University, Chiang Rai, Thailand.

## References

1. Seeboonruang U (2016) Impact assessment of climate change on groundwater and vulnerability to drought of areas in Eastern Thailand. Environ Earth Sci 75(1):1–13
2. Blaikie P, Cannon T, Davis I, Wisner B (1994) Disaster pressure and release model. At risk: Natural hazards, people's vulnerability, and disasters, 21–45
3. Ding Y, Hayes MJ, Widhalm M (2011) Measuring economic impacts of drought: a review and discussion. Dis Prev Manag Intern J
4. Juntunen L (2005) Addressing social vulnerability to hazards. Disaster Safety Review 4(2):3–10
5. Cutter SL, Barnes L, Berry M, Burton C, Evans E, Tate E, Webb J (2008) A place-based model for understanding community resilience to natural disasters. Glob Environ Chang 18(4):598–606

6. Motamed MK, Devisti H (2012) Environmental and socio-economic impacts of drought from the viewpoint of Guilan Paddy farmers, North of Iran. Caspian J Environ Sci 10(2):227–235
7. Gillette HP (1950) A creeping drought underway. Water Sewage Works 104(5)
8. Guha-Sapir D (2011) Natural disasters in countries with very high human development. CRED Crunch 24:1–2
9. Wilhite DA, Glantz MH (1985) Understanding: the drought phenomenon: the role of definitions. Water Intern 10(3):111–120
10. Prabnakorn S, Maskey S, Suryadi FX, de Fraiture C (2019) Assessment of drought hazard, exposure, vulnerability, and risk for rice cultivation in the Mun River Basin in Thailand. Nat Hazards 97(2):891–911
11. Osti S (2016) Effect of drought condition on the technical efficiency of rice farms in Thailand. EC Agricult 3(3):674–680
12. Klenke K (2016) Qualitative research as method. In Qualitative research in the study of leadership. Emerald Group Publishing Limited
13. Yin RK (1994) Discovering the future of the case study. Method Eval Res Eval Pract 15(3):283–290
14. Babbie E (2013) The practice of social research (13th ed). Belmont, California: Wadsworth Cengage Learning
15. Strauss A, Corbin J (2008) Basics of qualitative research: Grounded theory procedures and techniques, 3rd edn. Sage, Newbury Park, CA
16. Creswell JW, Hanson WE, Clark Plano VL, Morales A (2007) Qualitative research designs: selection and implementation. Couns Psychol 35(2):236–264
17. Jain VK, Pandey RP, Jain MK (2015) Spatio-temporal assessment of vulnerability to drought. Nat Hazards 76(1):443–469
18. Suwal N (2019) Research on optimal operation of cascade hydropower stations considering ecological flows (Doctoral dissertation, Hohai University)
19. Prabnakorn S, Ruangpan L, Tangdamrongsub N, Suryadi FX, de Fraiture C (2021) Improving flood and drought management in agricultural river basins: an application to the Mun River Basin in Thailand. Water Policy 23(5):1153–1169
20. Dercon S (2002) Income risk, coping strategies, and safety nets. World Bank Res Obs 17(2):141–166
21. Kazianga H, Udry C (2006) Consumption smoothing? Livestock, insurance, and drought in rural Burkina Faso. J Dev Econ 79(2):413–446
22. Viljoen MF, DuPlessis LA, Booysen HJ, Weepener HJ, Braune M, Van Bladeren D, Butler M (2001) Flood damage management aids for integrated sustainable development planning in South Africa. WRC Report No. 889/1/01, Pretoria
23. Alston M, Kent J (2004) Coping with a crisis: human services in times of drought. Rural Soc 14(3):214–227
24. Amekawa Y (2010) Rethinking sustainable agriculture in Thailand: a governance perspective. J Sust Agricult 34(4):389–416
25. Buckley BM, Palakit K, Duangsathaporn K, Sanguantham P, Prasomsin P (2007) Decadal scale droughts over northwestern Thailand over the past 448 years: links to the tropical Pacific and Indian Ocean sectors. Clim Dyn 29(1):63–71
26. Cutter SL, Johnson LA, Finch C, Berry M (2007) The US hurricane coasts: increasingly vulnerable?. Env Sci Policy Sust Devel 49(7):8–21
27. Jongdee B, Pantuwan G, Fukai S, Fischer K (2006) Improving drought tolerance in rainfed lowland rice: an example from Thailand. Agric Water Manag 80(1–3):225–240
28. Mohanty S, Wassmann R, Nelson A, Moya P, Jagadish SVK (2013) Rice and climate change: significance for food security and vulnerability. Intern Rice Res Inst 14:1–14
29. Wilhite DA (2011) National drought policies: addressing impacts and societal vulnerability
30. Zarafshani K, Sharafi L, Azadi H, Hosseininia G, De Maeyer P, Witlox F (2012) Drought vulnerability assessment: the case of wheat farmers in Western Iran. Global Planet Change 98:122–130

# New Challenges of Flood Management and Resilience Building at Border Communities: A Case Study of Floods Over the Transboundary Sai River Between Mae Sai, Thailand and Tachileik, Myanmar

**Yuki Miyake**

**Abstract** Thailand of tropical monsoon and savanna climates faces floods every year somewhere in the country and thus had their own traditional ways of coping strategies, especially in terms of architectural style and community building. However, floods, which had been traditionally a part of daily life in Thailand, began to be recognized as disasters in recent years, and the case of recent annual floods from the Sai river of Mae Sai District, Chiang Rai Province is not an exception. The northernmost city of Mae Sai District, Thailand, and its neighboring town Tachileik Township in Myanmar had rapidly developed and urbanized since around 1990 as border cities thanks to trade and tourism. The border markets on both sides around the border checkpoint have been the most popular tourist spots and have always been very crowded with small shops, vendors, and tourists. However, there is a transboundary river, called the Sai-Ruak river, between Mae Sai and Tachileik and it sometimes causes heavy floods to the border market areas almost every year during the rainy season in these 10 years although the scales of the floods and damages differ every year. With a socio-anthropological approach, this paper firstly argues the rapid urbanization of the riparian communities of the Sai-Ruak river as the cause of the recent floods in comparison with the rural border area in the past as well as the traditional resilient community building in northern Thailand. The rapid economic development without a good disaster management plan made the community vulnerable to the disaster. It secondly shows the difficulties and challenges of the flood management of the transboundary river, which requires the cross-border corporation and thus is different from the domestic river management. By doing so, it thinks about the way to build community resilience in the border city of Mae Sai District, Thailand in the future.

**Keywords** Disaster management · Flood · Community resilience · Transboundary river · Northern Thailand

Y. Miyake (✉)
School of Social Innovation, Mae Fah Luang University, Chiang Rai, Thailand
e-mail: yuki.miy@mfu.ac.th



Nawawi et al. (eds.), *Managing Disruption and Developing Resilience for a Better Southeast Asia*, Springer Proceedings in Humanities and Social Sciences,
https://doi.org/10.1007/978-981-96-2116-3_28

## 1 Introduction

A large-scale flood disaster in Bangkok and Ayutthaya in 2011 is still remembered by Thai people as one of the worst floods in decades in Thailand with 823 people dead and about 13.6 million people displacement ([1], p. 2260). Although it may not be such a large scale as this, as a tropical monsoon and savanna climate region, floods are recognized every year in whole areas of Thailand including the northern region. In this sense, good flood-disaster management is important for Thailand both for economic development and for environmental sustainability.

Mae Sai City, Chiang Rai Province is the northernmost city of Thailand and it shares a border with Tachileik Township, Shan State of the Republic of the Union of Myanmar. The Sai-Ruak river flows between Mae Sai and Tachileik as a transboundary river. Its width is 10 to 20 m around the border bridge in the city while 20 to 40 m outside of the city, and it flows about 60 km in total as a borderline from the west to the east between two border cities, rural communities, and paddy fields, changing its name from the Sai to the Ruak river in mid-course. The Ruak river runs until it meets the well-known international Mekong river at Sop Ruak or Golden Triangle of Chiang Saen District, Chiang Rai Province.

The occurrence of floods from the Sai river was a natural phenomenon in the history of the river, and yet the recent flood disasters from the Sai river at the border towns of Mae Sai and Tachileik, such as in August 2017 [2] and in August 2018 [3], were big ones for the areas. Many local people, as well as government officers on both sides of the river, needed the outsiders' help as humanitarian aid.

As the objectives of the paper, it firstly argues the rapid, unplanned urbanization of the riparian communities of the Sai-Ruak river as the cause of the recent floods in comparison with the traditional resilient community building in northern Thailand and Tachileik, Myanmar. The rapid economic development of the border region without a good disaster management plan made the community vulnerable to the flood disaster. It secondly shows the difficulties and challenges of the flood management of the transboundary river, which requires the cross-border corporation and thus is different from the domestic river management. By doing so, it thinks about the way to build community resilience in the border city of Mae Sai District, Thailand in the future.

In terms of research method, this article is based on socio-anthropological field research at the border of north Thailand between mid-2019 and the beginning of 2021. Two border cities are Mae Sai District, Chiang Rai Province, Thailand, and Tachileik Township, Shan State, Myanmar. The field information comes largely from in-depth interviews with approximately 10 people in Mae Sai, Thailand, and 10 local people of the riverside communities in Tachileik, Myanmar in addition to field observations in two riparian communities. In terms of the research ethics, all participants' names (interviewees) are kept anonymous except for the then Mae Sai District Chief and other government officers for whom I used their titles in their organization.

# 2 Theoretical Background

## *2.1 Concept of Resilience and Urban Resilience*

It has been already three decades since the concept of "resilience" has become increasingly popular ([4], p. 152) to develop policies and practices both in the human psychological fields such as human health, well-being, and quality of life at the micro-level and in the social and environmental fields at the macro level. And yet, there seems no single definition of it even today [4–6]. With a focus on social and environmental resilience, based on ([4, 7] , p. 155) defines "social resilience" as "the ability of groups or communities to cope with external stresses and disturbances as a result of social, political, and environmental change," and she pays attention to the relationships "between social processes (e.g. informal networks within civil society and the private sector) and ecological dynamics, and to the extent of their disturbance (or non-disturbance)" ([4], p. 155; [8]). Furthermore, Windle pursues the concept more and suggests the importance to look at resilience as "a dynamic process of positive adaptation" ([4, 9], p. 156). For this, the literature mainly talks about psychology, but the author thinks that it is applicable to environmental resilience as well.

Since this article deals with the case of flood disaster, the concept of "disaster resilience" is important. While its basic definition in this article follows the one in the above paragraph, Patel et al. provide nine core elements for disaster resilience. Those are: "local knowledge, community networks and relationships, communication, health, governance and leadership, resources, economic investment, preparedness, and mental outlook" ([6], p. 1). Furthermore, as a difference between "disaster resilience" and "disaster vulnerability," ([6], p. 2; [10]) explain that the concept of "disaster resilience" shows more proactive and positive attitudes toward community engagement for disaster risk reduction than the concept of "disaster vulnerability."

The definition of the concept of "urban resilience" also comes under or takes the same line as socio-environmental resilience mentioned above. According to ([5], p. 164), "Urban resilience generally refers to the ability of a city or urban system to withstand a wide array of shocks and stresses." Likewise, according to ([11], p. 9), "The concept of urban resilience is based on the inherent capacity of cities to bounce back, or recover, after disasters." In this sense, the concept of urban resilience and disaster resilience is similar (Sharma et al. [11], p. 9) say that they are "closely related to the concept of the risk reduction," which is important to "build resilience in cities."

## *2.2 Unplanned Urbanization, Urban Vulnerability, and an Increase in Disaster Risk*

Urbanization is a phenomenon either "(c)ities are growing naturally, through migration," or "through redesignation of rural areas as urban" ([11], p. 2). It grows and develops very fast in both "population concentration" and economic "development densities," and in such a process, ill-managed land use and development can bring high risk to people there, especially to the poor. Due to lack of land, the poor have more possibility to move their livings to the more risky place ([11], p. 3).

As the emergence of risk in the urbanization process, ([11], p. 2) explain that when people migrated to a new place and settled there as strangers due to economic reasons, "their physical as well as social risk levels rise" by losing "traditional social safety nets." Migrants become "urban poor" or the "vulnerable people" in the city "who live in marginal settlements, in substandard housing, with limited infrastructure and services, and with very little assets." One of the possible high hazardous locations of this is a "riverbank," which is applicable to this case of floods. Thus, they argue that "urban disaster risks are key concerns," especially in high population-dense areas ([11], p. 2).

Beringer and Kaewsuk [12] are other scholars who talk about the relations among "unplanned urbanization," an increase of risk or "flood risks and livelihood vulnerability," and the creation of "new poverty patterns in peri-urban areas." By studying Khon Kaen City which is a secondary city in northeastern Thailand, they say that Khon Kaen "has rapidly urbanized over the past 20 years without an effective and ecologically sound development plan" ([12], p. 1). For them, "unplanned urbanization" especially due to "lack of land use regulations, inefficient monitoring of land, and house elevations" increased "flood risks," "ineffective water governance, and insufficient wastewater treatment," etc.

As a measure to build urban resilience, ([11], p. 2) suggest the importance of "integrated disaster risk reduction approaches and disaster risk management at the local level." Urban communities must be the main stakeholders to plan and implement action. In a different part, they also propose "community participation" or "participatory approaches" both in planning and implementing actions for urban development ([11], p. 12).

Lastly, concerning the urban resilience to the flood disaster, ([1], p. 2261) argue that "floods would be less of a problem if cities respect the water," not controlling the water. They propose the incorporation of "rivers and water into the everyday urban experience," "(s)mall-scaled 'green' engineering" along with the modification of "the material landscape" ([1], p. 2261). This view can be linked to the idea or attitude of "traditional resilience community building in northern Thailand" below.

## 3 Traditional Resilient Community Building in Northern Thailand

With a case study of the historical capital of northern Thailand, named Wiang Kum Kam, during the thirteenth and sixteenth centuries in the Lanna period, [1] show the importance of the rivers in terms of sustenance and defense as well as for religion and cultures, and also the existence of the unavoidable floods from the river in northern Thailand. They say that "(h)istorically, water was one of the primary concerns of city planners in northern Thailand. The establishment of a town in northern Thailand was highly dependent on the proximity of rivers" ([1], p. 2248).

Not only Wiang Kum Kam, the major three cities of northern Thailand, Chiang Mai, Chiang Rai, and Chiang Saen, have been all built next to rivers. According to [1], the river has been important for northern Thailand, first, for the traditional irrigation system, second, as a water resource and for transportation, and third, as a high cultural value not only for the north but for the whole Thai people. Thai people often build spirit houses near the rivers and the canals and also pay respect to the rivers through the famous annual Thai nationwide festival named *Loy Krathong* in November.

Due to the tropical monsoon and savanna climates, floods are a seasonal phenomenon in Thailand during the rainy season between May and October (e.g. [1], p. 2250). Under such a climate condition, floods are also a traditionally common natural disaster and a part of daily life in Thailand ([13], p. 328). Thus, it is a common understanding that northern Thai people, for example, have traditionally developed ways to cope with floods architecturally since the Lanna period, one of which is single-story, wooden stilted houses (e.g. [13], p. 328, [1], p. 2250). Those elevated houses make it possible for people to avoid floodwaters from inundating their living spaces above floor level.

Although [13] use the case of central Thailand for this, its view is applicable to northern Thailand including Mae Sai in Chiang Rai as well. It can be said that the traditional stilted house in Thailand comes from local knowledge to avoid the negative consequences of flood disasters and is a traditional way of resilience community building.

## 4 The Sai River and its Floods in the Border Areas

The Sai-Ruak river has been always flooded since the people's settlement in the riverside areas about 60 years ago and sometimes changed its river course [14], but flood disasters have occurred recently near the border checkpoint area both in Mae Sai City and Tachileik Township every year since 2012 till now. In most years, there were floods not only one time but several times per year in the rainy season of the region (from May to early October).

The scales of the floods depend on the case, sometimes small but sometimes big enough for the water level to reach one meter high or up until the waist level of adults. The causes of heavy rains sometimes come from a long stay of low atmospheric pressure in the region or are sometimes related to the pass of cyclones over the Andaman Sea or the South China Sea. When it rained heavily in the upstream area of the river in Myanmar, water from the mountain reaches Mae Sai City in one day [15]. The river becomes very narrow at the Border Bridge and causes floods for both riparian communities. Once a big flood occurred, the products of markets got wet. Since the water brought mud as well, it was also very hard to clean up the floors, roads, etc.

The big floods reached not only the border market area but also the communities in a little bit distant areas. According to a [15], the flood water used to reach the Mae Sai downtown area along Route 1 from the Border Bridge. There is a median strip to divide the highway, but it dammed water west side or the upstream side of the road, making the west side have more water than the opposite side. All the shops in the border market areas got wet.

After the Sai river flooded around the First Border Bridge, the flood water reached the areas about one kilometer downstream from the Bridge of both Mae Sai and Tachileik sides (Koh Chang Subdistrict Chief; [16]). Based on my field interview, Tachileik people reported the flood disaster in the areas about 3 km downstream from the bridge around in 2018. They stated that the flood problems were serious at that time.

According to my interviews, the Myanmar authority began to problematize three weirs in the Sai-Ruak river constructed by Mae Sai farmers for irrigation around 2012 [17]. It means that there have been floods even a few decades ago, but Myanmar authorities did not pay much attention or problematize it until then somehow. It might be related to Myanmar's democratization process that largely started in November 2010 [18]. That is to say, after democratization, both the central government of Myanmar as well as the local institutions and people of Tachileik had more time to pay attention to local development such as flood management of Tachileik.

## 5 Rapid Economic Development and Urbanization of Riparian Communities

Although Chiang Saen, a part of the riparian areas of the Sai-Ruak river, has a history that once flourished as the Lanna Kingdom between 1325 and 1328, besides it, many Mae Sai farmers say that their parents and grandparents moved to Mae Sai from the Lamphun and Lampang Province (the mid-province in northern Thailand) before or after 1950 in the modern history. Since then, both Mae Sai city and Tachileik town alongside the Sai-Ruak river grew up together till now (Koh Chang Subdistrict [19, 20]).

The commercial area of Mae Sai District began to develop well after 1991 when Thailand and Myanmar signed a Memorandum of Understanding (MOU) on the fixed border line between them. In 2007, as a next turning point, the Thai government announced the Five "Chiang" Strategy to develop these "Chiang" cities together along the border, whose policy promoted the Mae Sai development further.

The Sai river around the First Friendship Bridge (the Mae Sai Border Checkpoint) is one of the narrowest at 10 to 20 m wide today while the Ruak river, outside of the city area, is much wider than it. Before 1990, the Sai river even at the First Bridge was much wider than today, wide enough for boats to go by (Koh Chang Subdistrict [19, 20]). The width of the river can also be recognized from the old photos of the First Bridge area and other parts of the river in the 1950 and 1960s.

The area near the First Bridge was still a residential quarter in the 1990s [19], but both sides of the border developed together as a border market in the last 25 years, called the Sai Lom Joy market on the Mae Sai side and the Tha Lor market on the Tachileik side. Many interviewees of this research told me that the Tha Lor Market area in Tachileik was so flourished and crowded between 2000 and 2010. It was notorious for counterfeit goods such as brand-name bags, CDs, and so on, and attracted both domestic and foreign tourists a lot although those counterfeit goods have gradually decreased due to strict restrictions and measures in Thailand [19].

The economic growth of the city areas gradually brought new problems, namely, encroachments of the market and housing plots to the Sai river. The border markets' invasion of the riverbeds has been done from both Mae Sai and Tachileik sides, which made the river narrower and narrower [19, 21], although the encroachment at the half downstream is only from the Tachileik side because the Mae Sai side is a large agricultural field there. The encroachment can be said as a result of economic development and urbanization of the border areas. When the water had no way to go in the narrow river due to the encroachment, the river naturally flooded the lower areas, which was the Tachileik side in the case of the Mae Sai border bridge area. The Sai Lom Joy Market area also flooded because it was an area under the bridge.

Concerning this, the head of the Irrigation Branch of Chaing Rai Royal Irrigation Project said:

> The river was normally very wide. Water flew easily. It could have had little floods but there was no problem. However, because of the invasion of the river area, the Sai river became very narrow, so the drainage is difficult in comparison with the past.
>
> (Head of Irrigation Branch of Chiang Rai [22])

He also continued that the amount of water was the same as in the past, but that the river course became narrower, made the water level much higher, and caused floods eventually. A leader of the 3rd Mae Sai Farmers Group also said:

> Actually, an important cause of the floods is an encroachment of the river banks with the buildings from both sides, which made riverbanks much narrower. When there is heavy rain, the water in the Sai river cannot drain easily.
>
> (Leader of the 3rd Mae Sai Farmers Group [23])

Another area that often had floods is between the First and the Second Border Bridge. People there, especially on the Tachileik side, had built high walls by now so that the river would not overrun their accommodation. Pang Ha Village [24], Koh Chang Subdistrict said:

> Now people of both Thailand and Myanmar made high walls along the river. If there were any low areas, they put more soil. In the past, the river was much wider, more than 30 meters. But now, both sides continue to reclaim land over the river. Thus, the river became narrower. We can see a tall building on the Thai side of the First Mae Sai Border Bridge that encroached the transboundary river. Actually, it can be demolished. But it is still there for a long time.
>
> (Pang Ha Village [24])

Furthermore, the Deputy Chief of Koh Chang SAO [19], who used to often go to the border shopping area since a young boy, mentions the different ways of urban building (infrastructure) between Tachileik, Myanmar, and Thailand. From his words, the vulnerability to the floods of the Tachileik infrastructures and buildings is expected. He said:

> (For the Tachileik side,) people built buildings without filling in the river, which was different from the Thai process. For the Thai side, they first filled in the river, constructed the road, and then built some houses or buildings for shops. (For the Tachileik side,) they constructed a lot of houses in the areas that could be flooded. They should have surveyed the area before. I could foresee the issue of poor drainage in those communities.
>
> (Deputy Chief of Koh Chang SAO [19])

The traditional, flood resilient structure mentioned before is not recognized in recent border market areas anymore both in terms of infrastructures and house buildings. From my observation, most buildings are simple, modern-style buildings with blocks and concretes. There might be pillar houses, but not the stilted ones, with the first floor also occupied either for the living or shopping space.

After all, related to the rapid expansion of the market as well as a whole town, four causes of flood disasters are found mainly: (1) the narrowing river course due to people or buildings' encroachment on the river; (2) construction of higher concrete walls which after all blocked up the river in the narrow path at any time without taking into account the necessity of spare space in case of the increase of water amount in the rainy season; (3) the drainage system in Tachileik Township is not good including the market area near the First Border Bridge; and lastly (4) the deforestation of the upper stream of the Sai river related to the economic development. These problems without good urban planning made the areas vulnerable to flood disasters.

## 6 Difficulties and Challenges of Flood Management of the Transboundary River

For Mae Sai people, the concept of the "international" river became familiar in 1991 when the MOU on fixed border demarcation in Chiang Rai Province was concluded between Thailand and Myanmar. Till then, neither local people nor many local government officers did not have a consciousness that the Sai-Ruak river was international.

Even though the border demarcation with a clear fixed borderline was implemented in 1992, the relationship or the local practice had not changed soon, and the business went on as usual for long years. Such a situation changed when more floods were recognized by the Myanmar authority around 2012 onward, and people of the riparian communities faced transboundary problems and some conflicts due to floods.

Regarding the Sai-Ruak river, it is said that there is no international treaty for the Sai-Ruak transboundary river management [22]. Normally, the Thai border security is under the control of the Royal Thai Armed Forces, and likewise, in Tachileik, there is a Township Border Committee (TBC), which is under Myanmar military sections. TBC oversees the border security and plays a role to coordinate with Thailand for including the Sai transboundary river management. As a meeting space between Thailand and Myanmar, the Thailand-Myanmar Joint Border Committee (JBC) was formed with representatives at the state and the local levels of each state and held twice a year. And yet, there seems no international institution for river management except for occasional discussions in the meeting.

Related to it, the Mae Sai farmers complained that they were required to inform the Myanmar authority through the TBC of whatever they do in the Sai-Ruak river since around 2012 [25]. However, according to them, they felt that the reporting system works only one way, from Thai to Myanmar, and did not work the other way around.

Communication, discussion, negotiation, agreement, etc. for the river management might be easier among riparian people if the river is domestic. But since the Sai-Ruak river is the transboundary river, the other riparian community is foreign. To make the situation further complex, Myanmar is not politically stabilized well yet, and its governance capacity is not well either in the peripheral border region. Thus, transboundary flood management is challenging in the case of the Sai-Ruak river.

## 7 Transboundary Cooperation for Humanitarian Aid

Although the former section showed the difficulties of effective transboundary river management, the flood disasters are at the same time an opportunity for cross-border cooperation. Mae Sai District Chief said:

> As another issue of cooperation, when Myanmar had floods, they requested Thailand for assistance. So, we prepared materials and manpower to assist immediately. We put importance on the neighboring country whose local communities are connected. It must have positive dimensions because we still have international trades.
>
> (Mae Sai District [19, 20])

According to his words, although the Mae Sai farmers' three weirs were demolished by Myanmar as a cause of floods from the Sai-Ruak river, the discussion and the negotiation process related to the weirs and the floods were also a signal of good cooperation between Thailand and Myanmar. That was why when heavy floods occurred, the Mae Sai district government sent some humanitarian aid such as water and food to the Tachileik people.

Besides aids, a cross-border cultural exchange festival is also held every year between two riparian communities organized by the Mae Sai government and the TBC. Two state government officers also went to study transboundary river management together.

In addition, as another aspect of cooperation related to the floods, in the case of downstream Pang Ha Village and Sanna Village in Koh Chang Subdistrict, whose areas face the Ruak river, both the Deputy Chief of Koh Chang SAO [19] and Pang Ha Village [24] think that the rice fields can become the areas to receive flooded water by opening the canal gate. They told me that if they want to share the burden of floods with other areas including the Tachileik side, the farmers had better open the canal gate to receive the water. All farmers of the area need to cooperate with this so that they receive water on a full scale for two to three days. If only a few days, the rice would not be damaged by floods. Therefore, it would not be a big problem for the farmers in comparison with floods in the market areas [19, 24].

These local farmers' ideas are closer to the traditional idea of a "resilient community" which comes from "local knowledge," but it would be possible to realize when a better cross-border corporation has been promoted, and when local participation was supported in the process for resilient buildings.

## 8 Discussion and Conclusion

With a socio-anthropological case study of the flood disaster of the Sai-Rauk transboundary river between Mae Sai, Thailand, and Tachileik, Myanmar, this article thought about the problems and challenges in flood management and resilient building in border communities while comparing the traditional and contemporary buildings.

As is shown in traditional resilient community building in northern Thailand, both the traditional Thai architecture of the stilted house and the way arranged infrastructure of the community were flood-friendly, not controlling and managing the floods, but rather co-existing with them. In the time when people had close relations and developed together with the Mae Sai people a couple of decades ago, the Tachileik people's living styles, buildings, and community were also similar to the Thai ones.

Along with the rapid economic development, however, such traditional ways of flood-resilient building houses and communities were left behind, especially on the Tachileik side. In the case of the riparian communities of the Sai river, the Mae Sai, Thailand side has relatively slowly developed since around the 1950s with certain government management and controls. Thus, Mae Sai City seems relatively resilient to flood disasters besides the border market areas which developed rapidly including new migrant traders. Furthermore, the area 10 to 15 km downstream and more from the Border Bridge in Mae Sai District still keeps the traditional, rural lifestyles and is much more resilient to floods ([1], p. 2261) say that "floods would be less of a problem if cities respect the water." ([6], p. 1) also pay attention to the "local knowledge, community networks." Though not cities, the rural Mae Sai circumstance seems to fit this claim and can provide one way to build a resilient community in Thailand and others.

Compared to Mae Sai, the Tachileik, Myanmar has developed rapidly in these 20 to 30 years without much organized political institution mainly due to long-time domestic political conflicts. The theory of [11] on the emergence of disaster risk in the urbanization process is precisely applicable to the Tachileike case in that various ethnic groups, both the rich and the poor, have immigrated from other regions to Tachileik, being attracted to its rapid economic development as a border town. Due to the unique political circumstances of Myanmar, the transboundary riverside areas have economically developed without better urban planning and became vulnerable to flood disasters.

Mae Sai City, Thailand may have coped well with the floods to some extent at all four stages of disaster management, mitigation, preparedness, response, and recovery if the Sai-Ruak river was the domestic river. But since it is the international river whose other riparian community is Tachileik, Myanmar, its management and controls are not so simple, still less building disaster-resilient communities [11]. Suggest integrated disaster risk reduction approaches at the local level as a measure to promote urban resilience with an emphasis on "community participation." But either Mae Sai or Tachileik could not well achieve integrated disaster risk reduction management at the transboundary level.

However, it is also true that there is a discussion opportunity between Thailand and Myanmar including through the semiannual meeting of the Thailand-Myanmar Joint Border Committee (JBC). As is shown in the former section, there is also cross-border cooperation such as transboundary cooperation for humanitarian aid on the occasion of heavy floods as well as annual cultural exchange activity. Thus, if people discussed and cooperated well, it would also be possible to find some other measurements for floods. Some of the words from Mae Sai farmers show such intentions although it has not been realized yet.

**Acknowledgements** This article is based on two research projects: First one is funded by the Area-based Social Innovation Research Center (Ab-SIRC), School of Social Innovation, Mae Fah Luang University which received a fund from Thailand Research Institute; and the second one is funded by Mae Fah Luang University; to all of which I am grateful.

## References

1. Ng S, Wood SH, Ziegler AD (2015) Ancient floods, modern hazards: the Ping River, pale of loods and the 'lost city' of Wiang Kum Kam. Nat Hazards 75:2247–2263
2. Vipaporn Pooritanasarn, Itiporn Lakarnchua (2017) Heavy Rains Cause Mai Sai River to Burst its Banks Flooding Border Market. *Chiang Rai Times*. Accessed on 20th December 2018 at https://www.chiangraitimes.com/heavy-rains-cause-mai-sai-river-to-burst-its-banks-flooding-border-market.html
3. Chiang Rai Times Editor (2018) Mae Sai Market aread floods once again after heavy rains. Chiang Rai Times (18 August 2018)
4. Windle G (2010) What is resilience? A review and concept analysis. Rev Clin Gerontol 21(02):152–169
5. Leichenko R (2011) Climate change and urban resilience. Curr Opin Environ Sust 3:164–168
6. Patel SS, Rogers MB, Amlôt R, Rubin GJ (2017) What do we mean by 'Community Resilience'? A systematic literature review of how it is defined in the literature. *PLOS Currents Disasters*, 1–34
7. Adger WN (2000) Social and ecological resilience: are they related? Prog Hum Geogr 24:347–364

8. Goldstein BE (2008) Skunkworks in the embers of the cedar fire: Enhancing resilience in the aftermath of disaster. Hum Ecol 36:15–28
9. Luthar SS, Cicchetti D, Becker BB (2000) The construct of resilience: a critical evaluation and guidelines for future work. Child Dev 71(3):543–562
10. Cutter SL, Barnes L, Berry M, Burton C, Evans E, Tate E, Webb J (2008) A place-based model for understanding community resilience to natural disasters. Glob Environ Chang 18(4):598–606
11. Sharma A, Surjan A, Shaw R (2011) Overview of urban development and associated risks. In Shaw R, Sharma A (eds.) *Climate and Disaster Resilience in Cities: Community, Environment and Disaster Risk Management*. (Chapter 1). Bingley, UK: Emerald Group Publishing Limited
12. Beringer A, Kaewsuk J (2018) Emerging livelihood vulnerabilities in an urbanizing and climate uncertain environment for the case of a secondary city in Thailand. Sustainability 10(1452):1–22
13. Mongkonkerd S, Hirunsalee S, Kanegae H, Denpaiboon C (2013) Comparison of direct monetary flood damages in 2011 to pillar house and non-pillar house in Ayutthaya, Thailand. Procedia Environ Sci 17:327–336
14. Suebsakun Kidnukorn (2017) Dynamics on conflict, contradiction and cooperation in transboundary water resource management in a context of sustainable development?: A case study of Sai and Ruak River, Mae Sai, Thailand and Tachileik, Myanmar (in Thai). In *Sustainable Development: The Third Anniversary of the Establishment of School of Social Innovation.* Chiang Rai: School of Social Innovation, Mae Fah Luang University
15. BBC. (2015). Timeline: Reforms in Myanmar. 8 July 2015. Accessed on 21st July 2020 at https://www.bbc.com/news/world-asia-16546688

## *Interview list cited in this article*

16. Chairperson of the Mae Sai Chamber of Commerce, 2019: *Ditto*, interviewed on 26th October 2019
17. Chiang Rai Irrigation Project. (2019). A written reply from Chiang Rai Irrigation Project to the questions by the researcher (in Thai)
18. Deputy Chief of Koh Chang SAO, 2019: A Deputy Chief Executive of Koh Chang Sub-district Administrative Organization (SAO), interviewed on 6 October 2019
19. Head of Irrigation Branch of Chiang Rai, 2019: A Head of Water Management and Irrigation System Improvement Branch, Chiang Rai Royal Irrigation Project, interviewed on 6 August 2019
20. Head of Mae Sai Irrigation Branch, 2019: A Head of Operation and Maintenance Branch 5, Chiang Rai Royal Irrigation Project, interviewed on 6 August 2019
21. Koh Chang Sub-district Chief, 2019: Subdistrict Headman or *Kamnan* in Thai, Koh Chang Sub-district, Chiang Rai Province, interviewed on 26th Oct 2019
22. Leader of the 3rd Mae Sai Farmers Group, 2019a: A leader of Water Using Management Group (farmers group) of Mae Sai Agricultural Development Project Area, interviewed on 15 August 2019
23. Leaders of Mae Sai Farmers Group, 2019: Three leaders of the 1st, 2nd, and 3rd Water Using Management Group (farmers group) of Mae Sai Agricultural Development Project Area, a group interviewed on 15 August 2019
24. Mae Sai District Chief, 2019: Mr. Somsak Kanakham, Mae Sai District Chief, interviewed on 10 July 2019
25. Pang Ha Village Headman, 2019: A Village Headman of Pang Ha Village, Koh Chang Sub-district, Chiang Rai Province, interviewed on 6th Oct 2019
26. Tachileik people, 2020: Various people in Tachileik, interviewed on 12, 18, 23, and 24 January 2020

# Child Rights Protection Regarding Safe Learning Facilities in Accordance with the Comprehensive School Safety Framework: A Case Study of Schools in Phan District Areas, Chiang Rai Province

**Areerat Kosit and Wanwalee Inpin**

**Abstract** This research aims to study the protection of children's rights concerning safe learning facilities under the framework of surrounding safety in schools under the Comprehensive School Safety Framework (CSS Framework) in Phan District, Chiang Rai Province. This district is located on the Phayao earthquake fault, previously destroyed by a 6.3 magnitude earthquake on May 5, 2014. The perspective applied in this study is the policies and laws of Thailand. Using qualitative research, in-depth interviews were used with administrators and group representatives involved with school design, school construction, and school maintenance in Phan District. The study found that the request for land use in the affected area must be under the Town Planning Act B.E. 2522 (1979). The schools still have buildings constructed decades before the promulgation of the latest 2021 Ministerial Regulations. In addition, the design and calculation of building structures for earthquake resistance in the seismic area at present are under the Ministerial Regulations, which specify load-bearing, resistance, the durability of buildings, and the ground support for buildings in the earthquake resistance (B.E. 2564 (2021) issued under the Building Control Act B.E. 2522 (1979)). Effective school disaster management and education to reduce disaster risk will be the key to Disaster Risk Reduction (DRR) within the school's comprehensive safety framework. Therefore, the Initial Risk Assessment Guide requires a preliminary risk assessment for buildings subject to severe earthquake damage issued by the Department of Public Works and Town and Country Planning.

**Keywords** Comprehensive school safety framework · Child rights protection · 2014 Chiang Rai earthquake · Disaster management · Thailand

A. Kosit (✉)
School of Law, Mae Fah Luang University, Chiang Rai 57100, Thailand
e-mail: areerat.kos@mfu.ac.th

W. Inpin
School of Social Innovation, Mae Fah Luang University, Chiang Rai 57100, Thailand
e-mail: wanwalee@mfu.ac.th





Nawawi et al. (eds.), *Managing Disruption and Developing Resilience for a Better Southeast Asia*, Springer Proceedings in Humanities and Social Sciences,
https://doi.org/10.1007/978-981-96-2116-3_29

# 1 Introduction

## *1.1 Background*

The Comprehensive School Safety Framework (CSS Framework) is part of Thailand's Education Sector Policies and Plans. It is congruent with disaster management at the national, provincial, and local levels, including schools that use a child-centered approach to hazard risk assessment. The CSS Framework sets the scene for the analysis, divided into three pillars: Pillar One: Safe Learning Facilities, Pillar Two: School Disaster Management, and Pillar Three: Risk Reduction and Resilience Education [1]. According to the framework, its implementation is under the aims of the Worldwide Initiative for Safe Schools and the Global Alliance for Disaster Risk Reduction and Resilience in the Education Sector (GADRRRES). Moreover, it is also consistent with the Sustainable Development Goals (SDGs), the Sendai Framework for Disaster Risk Reduction 2015–2030 (SFDRR), and the Convention on the Rights of the Child 1989: CRC, which aims to protect children and enhance safety from disasters in schools, thereby reducing social, economic, and environmental losses caused by disasters and preventing future risks, including an understanding of disaster safety in schools.

In 2014, a 6.3 magnitude earthquake struck seven provinces in northern Thailand, including Chiang Rai Province. The quake, which had a depth of 7 km, impacted the Phan District in Chiang Rai Province, which was close to the epicenter and was the most severe hit. According to the assessment report by the Chiang Rai Office of Public Works and Towns & Country, in 2015, one hundred twenty-six educational institutions were damaged, according to the assessment. Furthermore, Phanpittayakhom School, Mae Lao Wittayakhom School, Pong Prae Wittaya School, and Mae Suai Wittayakom School had their school buildings severely damaged and needed to be demolished in order to construct new replacements. Standard school building designs for schools affiliated with the Office of Basic Education (Referred to by abbreviation as OBEC) were planned and constructed following the OBEC's specifications. In the past, school buildings planned and built prior to the proclamation of Ministerial Regulation No. 49 B.E. 2540 issued under the Building Control Act B.E. 2522 were not equipped to withstand earthquake shocks.

Thailand is currently planning for disaster response by requiring the usage of school buildings in seismic zones. Specific multipurpose constructions were also designed to facilitate development in an earthquake zone. Of course, it must comply with the Ministerial Regulations Indicating the Weight, Resistance, and Durability of the Structure and the Ground that Supports the Building in Earthquake Resistance 2564 B.E (From now on, it will refer to as Ministerial Regulation B.E. 2564). This was issued under Building Control Act B.E. 2522. Furthermore, on November 9, 2021, the Ministry of Interior announced the Design and Calculation of Building Structures to Resist Earthquake Vibrations, which specifies the criteria for designing and calculating earthquake resistance buildings that mention technical details and academic principles of earthquakes to ensure the safety of building construction and alteration in earthquake-prone areas. This announcement was mandated for schools that were given permission or informed of building development prior to Ministerial Regulation B.E. 2564.

Ministry of Education (2021), property owners may apply for a building renovation permit to improve their structure's stability and ability. There is already a ministerial law outlining the conditions for approval to alter the structure to increase its stability so it can withstand earthquakes (B.E. 2555). According to the Child Protection School standards by the Office of the Basic Education Commission for school safety and child protection in the usage of buildings or surrounding areas of the school, they must follow the Child Protection Act B.E. 2546 and the Child Protection School Standards established by OBEC. This means that the physical environment and people who may harm pupils in the school will be subject to regulations, methods, or guidelines for guaranteeing safety that prevents harm from within and outside the school and reduces the risk of environmental catastrophes (Safety Rules).

However, the researchers found that if Thailand's regulations and legislation are reviewed and practical efforts are taken, school buildings and premises in earthquake-prone regions will be safe from seismic shocks. The information acquired will be beneficial in formulating policies and rules, laws, and recommendations to decrease the loss caused by catastrophes in schools in terms of building structures or school grounds, therefore protecting children's rights following Pillar One: Safe Learning Facilities. This is because it can improve disaster management, which is one of the methods of improving disaster management and reducing the risk of future catastrophes.

## *1.2 Comprehensive School Safety Framework: CSSF*

The Minimum Standard Guide for a safety school in Chiangrai (under the CSSF) (pp. 8–15) aims to reduce the social, economic, and environmental losses caused by disasters and minimize future risks, including an awareness of school disaster safety, which emphasizes children's involvement and education for long-term development and disaster preparedness. The Comprehensive School Safety Framework is organized into three categories known as "pillars" according to the safety framework around the school. They are connected by a direction of disaster risk reduction activities that follow local and national disaster management plans:

- Pillar 1: Safe Learning Facilities
- Pillar 2: School Disaster Management
- Pillar 3: Risk Reduction and Resilience Education

This study is directed to Pillar 1 Safe Learning Facilities, which refer to school buildings, assembly buildings, area management, building design, construction, and maintenance. This includes school administrators, architects, engineers, contractors, builders, and educational institution employees, as shown in Fig. 1.

The following management guidelines are included in Pillar 1:

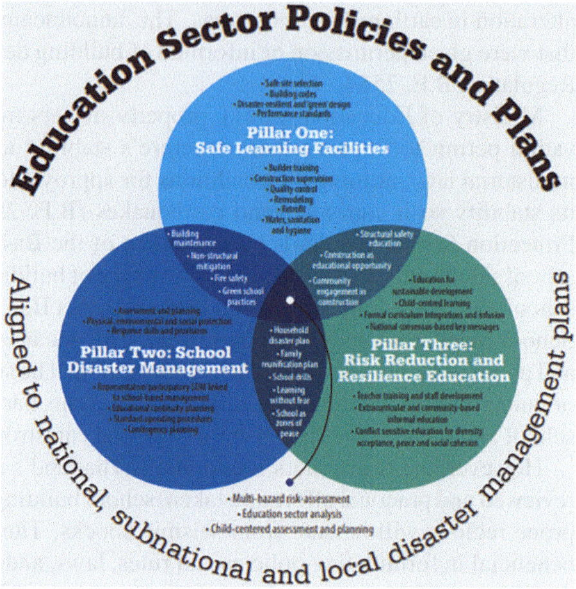


**Fig. 1** Education Sector Policies and Plans, Aligned to national, subnational, and local disaster management plans. *Source* Comprehensive School Safety: The Global Alliance for Disaster Risk Reduction and Resilience in the Education Sector and The Worldwide Initiative for Safe Schools, in preparation for the 3rd UN World Conference on Disaster Risk Reduction (UNISDR), 2015

1. Select a safe location for an educational institution and plan and construct disaster-resistant structures to ensure that every new building or site is safe from disaster.
2. The implementation of building control regulations (building codes) and the reinforcement of school buildings through different techniques, construction control, and construction worker training, including relocating the school to a more secure location.
3. Implementation of structural and non-structural risk reduction strategies. This includes maintaining the school's infrastructure to be utilized as a safe evacuation place in an emergency.
4. The design, installation, and supply of disability facilities at educational institutions to establish a friendly environment for the disabled and the elderly.
5. The building's architecture should allow for the usage of the educational institution area as a temporary shelter for the victims . This also involves establishing a designated area for teaching and learning management to minimize disruptions in teaching and learning due to educational facilities being used as temporary shelters.
6. Ensuring that students arrive at school safely and without incident.
7. Improving drinking water and sanitation in educational institutions.

**Global Framework for Comprehensive School Safety**

The United Nations' Sustainable Development Goals connected with overall school safety in the Disaster Risk Reduction context include SDGs 1, 3, 4, 6, 9, 10, 11, 12, 13, 16, and 17 (corresponding to some points). Moreover, the Sendai Framework, which evolved from the Hyogo Framework, is based on the continuity of government operations and stakeholder groups. The Third United Nations World Conference on Disaster Risk Reduction, held in Sendai, Japan, between March 14 and 18, 2015, voluntarily accepted the Sendai Framework for Disaster Risk Reduction, which was adopted as an extension of the Hyogo Framework for Action. There are seven objectives and four priorities for action. Simultaneously, it presented innovations that developed through the debates and negotiations of the Global Disaster Risk Reduction Framework, which specifies the timescale for achieving the targets based on internally determined indicators. Fifteen years, from 2015 to 2030, with seven goals, the Sendai Framework Priorities for the Education Sector aims to reduce the number of injuries and deaths caused by school hazards and the number of schoolchildren affected by disasters of all sizes. In addition, it aims to reduce the amount of educational investment lost due to disasters and the number of school closure days caused by disasters. (UNISDR, 2017).

### *1.3 Literature Review*

According to the literature review and related research, Thailand primarily focuses on building earthquake disaster courses at the local level and teacher development. Through learning activities, this curriculum was created for target schools [2]. A national policy and legal overview study on disaster management have also been conducted [3]. However, no studies have been conducted to protect children's rights in accordance with the Comprehensive School Safety Framework regarding Safe Learning Facilities.

## 2 Method

The descriptive qualitative method is applied in this type of study. In qualitative research, data processing is inductive, and qualitative research findings prioritize implication overviews. This research employs a phenomenological approach since they are closely related to the indicators resulting from the in-depth examination. The data was collected directly from the field research sites, like school buildings in Thailand's Chiang Rai area in Phan District. Purposive sampling and snowball sampling were used in this study. Data collection methods such as observation, interviews, and documentation are used. A qualitative sentence was then applied to interpret the study's findings. The study concluded that the data analysis approaches have some observed and collected processes. The categories of data have significance, seek and require a pattern and correlations, and create additional conclusions. This study looked at how far the Comprehensive School Safety Framework policy has been implemented in Chiang Rai Province with a case study from a rapid-onset disaster such as an earthquake.

# 3 Research Findings and Analysis

## *3.1 Part One: Policies and Laws*

1. Policy on protecting children's rights regarding safe learning facilities in Thai schools, in accordance with a comprehensive safety framework.

Thailand has signed the Sendai Framework for Disaster Risk Reduction—SFDRR 2015–2030, an international framework for implementing the Sustainable Development Goals (SDGs). The country used this framework as a guideline for its National Disaster Mitigation B.E. 2558, which is the country's master plan for disaster management, under the National Social and Economic Development Plan No. 12, and to supervise the operation drive under the Disaster Prevention and Mitigation Act framework 2007. Implementing the Disaster Prevention and Mitigation Plan 2015 emphasizes disaster risk reduction (DDR), emergency management integration, and sustainable recovery optimization (Build Back Better and Safer). Furthermore, strengthening international cooperation in disaster risk management is the critical guideline for attaining the plan's goals to contribute to the successful management of disaster risk, which is the foundation of sustainable development.

Through the Office of Basic Education (OBEC), the Ministry of Education has tasked each primary education area office with requesting cooperation from the directors of all schools under their jurisdiction to complete the educational institution's natural disaster preparedness questionnaire. The Ministry of Education's mission in disaster management has been outlined in five categories in the National Disaster Prevention and Mitigation Plan B.E. 2558:

1. Development of disaster prevention and mitigation teaching and learning curriculum at all levels, from elementary to higher education.
2. Support education organizations that aid with disaster prevention and mitigation.
3. Increase knowledge and raise awareness among students and the general public about disaster prevention and mitigation.
4. Encourage educational staff, such as Boy Scouts and Girl Scouts, to support the The National Disaster Prevention and Mitigation Headquarters and the Department of Disaster Prevention and Mitigation in the region.
5. Conduct a survey and create a database of educational institutions that can serve as temporary shelters.

Thailand has already undertaken various efforts to support disaster management at the school level and disaster risk reduction and recovery education, including:

1. Translating school-level disaster management guidelines from English to other languages into Thai;
2. Conducting surveys and data collection on Thai schools;
3. Developing an animated cartoon "Radar" to educate students about safe schools;
4. Organize a Champion School Model activity on DRR activities;
5. Conduct disaster preparedness and management youth camps;

6. Create disaster safety instructions for educational institutions and instructors in schools;
7. Develop minimal pilot standards for school safety;
8. Create safety guides for vulnerable students; and
9. Chiang Rai Province's model safe schools and others.

# 4 Laws Relating to Building Safety in the Vicinity of Schools

## *4.1 Laws Relating to the Control of the Usage of Space*

A. *The Town Planning Act B.E. 2562*

The Town Planning Act B.E. 2562 is a statute that establishes rules and regulations for the administration and development of places. It is concerned with deciding or controlling the use of land through planning both present and future land use projects while taking into consideration the economic conditions, resources, population, and public services, roads, bridges, parks, water, electricity, industrial sites, commercial sites, housing, and agriculture, as well as the country's natural beauty [4]. In summary, the law of town planning is one of the strategies used to manage and solve problems caused by a lack of control in public spaces in society [5].

B. *The Forestry Act B.E. 2484*

The Forestry Act B.E 2484 shall be implemented if there is a request for the use of a government agency or any government agencies operating inside the national forest reserve.

## *4.2 Laws Relating to Building Control (Building Code)*

Building control laws provide norms or standards for building safety to avoid incidents such as building collapse, fire, or disaster. The building control legislation aims to ensure that buildings are stable and sturdy and provide a safety system for building inhabitants. An ordered, elegant, and environmentally sound management system is in place. Acts, ministerial rules, and local ordinances are all examples of building control legislation. Laws relating to building control (Building Code) are:

- Building Control Act, B.E. 2522
- Building Control Act (No. 2) B.E. 2535
- Building Control Act (No. 3) B.E. 2543
- Building Control Act (No. 4) B.E. 2550 and
- Building Control Act (No. 5) B.E. 2558

The Building Control Act cannot be implemented alone but must be coupled with a Royal Decree to employ the Building Control Act, also known as the "Building Control Area." As a result, when the Royal Decree is issued in any area or locality that has been proclaimed to enforce town planning under the town planning legislation, the use or modification in the use of the building to restrict the use in that locality, one must first get permission from the local authority [6].

### *4.3 Laws Relating to Prescribing Regulations or Requirements for Building Structure Safety in Resisting Earthquake Vibrations*

The Ministerial Regulation has defined principles or requirements for the seismic resistance of school building structures. It also set out to determine the earthquake risk area, type of building design, and earthquake resistance calculation of building structures. Furthermore, the Ministerial Regulation (From now on, referred to by abbreviation as "Ministry Regulations") increases the criteria for calculating the load capacity, resistance, and durability of buildings to endure earthquake shock for the building to be more modern and safer for people to access (as Issued by the Building Control Act B.E. 2522, published in the Government Gazette on March 4, 2021, and effective on August 31, 2021).

a. Ministerial Regulations Outlining the Load-Bearing Capacity, Resistance, and the Durability of Structures and the Ground that Supports Them in the Earthquake Resistance of 2021.

The ministerial regulation identifies places or areas at risk of needing to monitor for earthquakes by considering the probability and risk that buildings in such regions will be damaged during an earthquake tremor. The ministerial regulation divides the surveillance area into three sections:

- Area 1: is a zone or location that must be watched because buildings may be affected by the strength and stability of earthquakes.
- Area 2: Zones or locations where the building may be moderately affected by seismic strength and stability.
- Area 3: Zones or locations where the building may be influenced by a high degree of strength and stability in the case of seismic disturbances.

b. Notification from the Ministry of Interior dated November 9, 2021

As Notification from the Ministry of Interior dated November 9, 2021: Design and Calculation of Building Structures to Resist Earthquake Vibrations (as referred to as Article 1), this notification shall come into force from the day following the date of its publication in the Government Gazette (Published in the Government Gazette on November 9, 2021, Volume 138, Special chapter 275).

Determine the specifics of earthquake-resistant building structure design and calculation. By classifying buildings according to their relevance, such as type 1 low importance, type 2 normal importance, type 3 high importance, and type 4 high importance, rapid transformation improves the safety of building construction and modification in earthquake-prone areas (as issued by Sect. 8 paragraph two of the Building Control Act, B.E. 2522 as amended by Building Control Act (No.3) B.E. 2543 in conjunction with Article 6 of Ministerial regulations specifying load-bearing, resistance, the durability of buildings, and the ground supporting the building in the earthquake resistance B.E. 2564 issued by the Building Control Act B.E. 2522 as amended by Building Control Act (No.5) B.E. 2558).

## 4.4 Part 2: General Spatial and Practical Data

1. General Geographic Information

All primary schools in Phan District, Chiang Rai Province, are divided into three categories: (1) schools operated by the Office of the Basic Education Commission: OBEC, which is also known as the Chiangrai Primary Educational Service Area Office 2, (2) schools run by the local government organization (Local Administration Organization), and (3) schools run by the Office of the Private School. (OPEC Education Commission). Chiang Rai Primary Educational Service Area Office 2 has 37 schools divided into 22 Kindergarten-Elementary Schools, 11 Kindergarten-Lower Secondary Schools, 1 Primary-Lower Secondary school, and 3 Primary Schools.

In terms of educational establishment size, there were 21 small schools, 15 medium-sized schools, and one large school discovered. The study found that the school is associated with the Chiangrai Primary Educational Service Area Office 2, which was founded before the year 1957. Twenty-five schools and 12 schools were founded after 1957, most of them were established no later than 1967, and only one school was established after 1967, in 1997. The earthquake damaged many schools in Phan and surrounding areas on May 5, 2014, which had 6.3 on the Richter scale. Furthermore, several school structures have been seriously damaged and must be removed to construct new replacements. However, the research team discovered that many schools were either minimally or completely unaffected by the earthquake. School buildings are still built before Ministerial Regulation No. 49, B.E. 2540. They were not constructed to endure seismic vibrations, according to the Building Control Act B.E. 2522. As a result, these school buildings are particularly vulnerable to natural disasters.

2. Information on Practice

The initiative to request permission and the budget to build or expand a school's building usually starts from requesting a budget, investing the money, cost of equipment, land, and buildings. The request will then be considered by the local Educational Service Area Office and the school, including the request for a budget for the construction of school buildings, other buildings (obligated budget), a budget for renovation costs, and a budget for the case of emergency. In order to submit the request for permission to construct a school building to the local administration where the school is located, the school must submit two copies of an accurate area plan, building plan, and a list of technical specifications (this is not the request for permission).

For the plan of disaster-resistant structures, the schools in the Chiangrai Primary Educational Service Area Office 2 are considered in the earthquake risk area, as mentioned. The construction must comply with earthquake-resistant building structure design and calculation defined by the Office of Basic Education Commission or follow the ministerial regulation B.E. 2564 on building design and earthquake resistance calculation for Safe Learning Facilities building structures. In case of renovation of buildings in earthquake risk areas, the buildings of an earthquake risk area include the existing buildings and the buildings that received the permission for construction before November 30, 2007, which are exempted from the Building Construction Control Act and do not have to comply with ministerial regulation.

## 5 Discussion and Conclusion

The study of protecting children's rights concerning safe learning facilities under the framework of surrounding safety in schools has shown that Thailand has prioritized the Comprehensive School Safety Framework (CSS Framework) under Pillar 1: Safe Learning Facilities. Thailand also enforced the Building Control laws to strengthen the learning facilities by controlling the construction and reducing the risk in school structures. The construction of school buildings in the earthquake risk area since August 31, 2021 must comply with the building design regulated by OBEC only or use the building design and earthquake resistance calculation of building structures for Safe Learning Facilities. In case of renovation of buildings in earthquake risk areas, the schools must follow the ministerial regulation B.E. 2564.

For the schools that get permission to build or the Notification of construction before the ministerial regulation, B.E. 2564, comes into force, there is a regulation (B.E. 2555) that determines the criteria for permission to modify the building and strengthen it to endure seismic vibrations. This regulation allows the owners of any building and any size to submit a request to renovate a building that can endure seismic vibrations. However, in practice, the OBEC has released the handbook of budgeting in the fiscal year B.E. 2568 on investment budget, cost of equipment, land, and building to set the guidelines on construction budgeting for the affiliated schools. For example, using the number of students as a criterion, the school must have at least 400 students and lack classrooms. In addition, if it is a small school, a primary school where students come to study together, or a stand-alone school or school that suffers flood every year, these schools can request one school building to replace the existing building allowed for dismantling only. In order to set the budget to replace the existing building that needs dismantling, the school must seek an opinion from a licensed engineer from the government agency that says "should be demolished" for consideration before the school can request the budget for a replacement building. The school must get permission to demolish the existing building and construct a new building simultaneously. In the case of assignment of duties and responsibilities for the school, the school director and teachers must conduct a survey, budgeting, control and inspect the construction, expanding, dismantling of the school building, and other construction which causes a burden to the teachers who get involved in the pricing committee, construction control committee, and inspection committer, etc. If there was a mistake in one step, those involved must be held legally liable. So, these criteria and conditions are practical obstacles to removing the old buildings built before the Building Control Act came into force. That leads to the ineffective attempt to have safe learning facilities under the surrounding safety in schools and cannot strengthen the disaster management as planned.

There are several feedbacks and recommendations, as follows. Firstly, OBEC should reconsider and revise its practical guidelines of criteria for construction budgeting of affiliated schools in the earthquake risk area by focusing on the safety of school buildings and facilities more than the number of students and the achievement or quality of the students. Next, the schools in earthquake risk areas should receive a proper budget for construction (including the cost of construction, renovation, and demolition) to be consistent with the risk of school buildings and should allocate the budget to demolish the school buildings older than 25 years or the buildings built before the Building Control Ace has become effective. OBEC should set up a department mainly responsible for constructing affiliated schools without causing the burden of construction on the school. Furthermore, OBEC should have personnel with specific expertise working in its affiliation, such as licensed engineers in each district and other related officers responsible for a survey, budgeting, control, and inspection of construction and demolition. Finally, there should be research on establishing an organization or department responsible mainly for the construction, renovation, and demolition of school buildings and other buildings in OBEC and a study on establishing an agency that has to supervise the construction. This regulatory agency may be under the Office of the Permanent Secretary, Ministry of Education, or another involved organization for management efficiency. At the same time, it will balance or audit the work of an established agency.

## References

1. UNISDR, GADRRRES, Comprehensive School Safety A global framework in support of The Global Alliance for Disaster Risk Reduction and Resilience in the Education Sector and The Worldwide Initiatives for Safe Schools, [Online] Retrieved from https://www.undrr.org/publication/comprehensive-school-safety (accessed December 15 2021)
2. Jantakoon Jakkrit (2019) The development of local earthquake disaster curriculum for school in the earthquake risk zone based on knowledge management. The Thailand Research Fund (TRF)
3. Chaikan, Chanwit et al. (2015) Public liability for natural disaster: comparative study of Japan and Thailand. The Thailand Research Fund (TRF)

4. Wongsawatgul E (2020) Description of the town planning law, Bangkok: textbook and teaching materials project. Thammasat University, Faculty of Law
5. Krutdilakanan Theeraphong (2020) Document for draft constitution on town planning. Bangkok. Tuesday, October 20
6. Sanseera Worachai (2009) Building Control Act, Paper Tiger Law? Legal reflection, Chulniti Journal, March-April
7. ASEAN COMMON FRAMEWORK FOR COMPREHENSIVE SCHOOL SAFETY [Online]. Retrieved from https://www.rcrc-resilience-southeastasia.org/wp content/uploads/2016/11/ publication_ASEANCommonFramework.pdf (accessed 15 November 2021)
8. Department of Disaster Prevention and Mitigation, Ministry of Interior (2015) Chiangrai earthquake, will it happen again? How to cope with it next time? Disaster Profile magazine, year 2, volume 2 July
9. Kosit Areerat (2020) Japan as it is. The 8th, protection of children's rights in disaster situations under international law: case study Japan. Bangkok: Faculty of Political science, Thammasat University
10. Office of the Basic Education Commission (OBEC) and Department of Disaster Prevention and Mitigation. School and Teach Handbook COMPREHENSIVE SCHOOL SAFETY. No printed date. No publisher listed
11. Suwith Kosuwan, Weerachat Wiwegwin. Mae Lao earthquake, Chiangrai and the Northern Phayao fault. (Mae Lao part) (presentation slide) No printed date. No publisher listed.
12. TCIJ, school buildings in risk area were not designed to withstand earthquakes. News team: February 5, 2017, Online access at https://www.tcijthai.com/news/2017/05/watch/6725 (February 10, 2017)
13. UNICEF, Save the Children, Office of the Basic Education Commission, Basic Education Sector Snapshot for Comprehensive School Safety and Education in Emergencies in Thailand (May 2016)
14. United Nations Office for Disaster Risk Reduction (UNDRR), Comprehensive School Safety, [Online] Retrieved from https://www.undrr.org/publication/ comprehensive-school-safety (accessed 11 November 2021)
15. United Nations, Disaster Risk Reduction-Related SDGS, [Online] Retrieved from https://sdgs.un.org/topics/disaster-risk-reduction (accessed November 10 2021)
16. Working group on the framework of surrounding safety in schools in Chiangrai, Minimum standard guide for safety school. Comprehensive School Safety Framework (CSS Framework). No printed date
17. World Bank and the Global Facility for Disaster Reduction and Recovery, Ana Miscolta, Risk RED, GADRRRES Comprehensive School Safety Policy Case Studies Series: Guiding Local Governments to Strengthen Unsafe Schools in Japan. [Online] Retrieved from https://www.preventionweb.net/files/61551_csspolicycasestudyjapanguidinglocal.pdf (accessed November 15 2021)

## *Other information*

18. Bureau of Research and International Cooperation. Department of Prevention and Mitigation. Ministry of Interior
19. Chiangrai Primary Educational Service Area Office 2
20. Disaster Prevention and Mitigation Act, B.E. 2550
21. Building Control Act, B.E. 2522
22. Building Control Act (No. 2) B.E. 2535
23. Building Control Act (No. 3) B.E. 2543
24. Building Control Act (No. 4) B.E. 2550 and
25. Building Control Act (No. 5) B.E. 2558

26. Ministerial regulations specifying load-bearing, resistance, the durability of buildings, and the ground supporting the building in the earthquake resistance B.E. 2564

# Understanding Society and Culture in Contemporary Southeast Asia: Natural Resource and People, Digital Humanities, and COVID-19 Social Development

# Digital Marketing Strategy in Strengthening Destination Branding in the Thematic Village of Mulyaharja

**Diyan Putranto and Marhanani Tri Astuti**

**Abstract** Technological developments have led to changes in marketing trends in Indonesia. Throughout the COVID-19 pandemic, also changes in consumer behavior patterns caused by restrictions on human movement have caused the development of the use of digital technology as a marketing tool to take on a very important role in strengthening branding and marketing of products and services so that the company can live and develop. Likewise with the Mulyaharja Thematic Village which is a village located in the city of Bogor with the concept of Community-Based Tourism (CBT) which can be applied in the form of local community participation, by forming tourism village institutions, environmental formation, and community business activities. Mulyaharja's "Unique Tourist Destination" is the topic of this study, which examines how digital marketing tactics might be used to strengthen the village's "Destination Branding" through the use of the media website, Instagram, and social media (Facebook). A SWOT (Strength, Weakness, Opportunity, Threat) study of both internal and external elements is used in the destination branding analysis technique to determine the most effective digital marketing strategy. Research findings, literature studies, and digital marketing media are examples of primary and secondary sources. The branding of a tourist destination is a very important aspect of tourist decision making. Digital marketing must be able to communicate the uniqueness, and uniqueness of the attraction, facilities, and attractiveness of a destination so that it can produce a positive and significant influence on customer behavior and ultimately attract tourists to visit.

**Keywords** Tourism · Digital marketing · Destination branding · Thematic village

D. Putranto (✉)
Sahid Polytechnic, Jakarta, Indonesia
e-mail: diyanputranto@polteksahid.ac.id1

M. T. Astuti
Indonesia's Minister of Tourism and the Creative Economy/Tourism and Creative Economy Agency Deputy for Strategic Studies, Jakarta, Indonesia
e-mail: marhananitria@kemenparekraf.go.id2



Nawawi et al. (eds.), *Managing Disruption and Developing Resilience for a Better Southeast Asia*, Springer Proceedings in Humanities and Social Sciences,
https://doi.org/10.1007/978-981-96-2116-3_30

# 1 Introduction

The COVID-19 outbreak affects tourism. Tourism-based regions face many economic problems. Indonesia's Tourism and Creative Economy Ministry predicts 74.84 percent fewer international tourists in 2020 than in 2019 (16,108,600) [1]. To recover tourism, a program must demand creativity, teamwork, and adaptation, which will boost the economy. The Ministry of Tourism and Creative Economy's tourism village development initiative is one of the national development agendas. In line with the emergence of a new trend during the pandemic is the increasing interest of tourists to travel in the open. Tourist villages can be an option for tourists to be able to enjoy the outdoors, by experiencing the experience of traveling in the midst of rural community life.

Likewise, in Bogor Municipality, the Bogor City Government has built and developed a tourism village called the Mulyaharja Thematic Village. The Thematic Village Mulyaharja is located in the southern part of Bogor, just 10.3 km from the city of Bogor. Mulyaharja Thematic Village originally has thematic attractions based on education and organic rice cultivation, and since then the village has been typical of nature, culture, creation, organic farming education, fashion events, performing arts, and nature panoramas. The theme-based village has evolved into a base-based souvenir and unique local cuisine. And outdoor tightrope walking.

The COVID-19 pandemic forced the government to impose restrictions on community activities; it caused changes in consumer behavior. Online culture has become a necessity, and digitalization has become a technology that is needed by people's activities in all aspects of life, including searching for information, shopping, communication, and work to education [2]. Indonesia's Internet users reached 196.7 million, or 73.7% of the population, by the second quarter of 2020, according to APJII (Indonesian Internet Service Providers Association) [3]. According to the survey results Booking.com, 44% of tourists search for accommodation and tourist destination information via Internet technology, and 57% plan their trips using online applications [4]. This is consistent with Ajina. Digital marketing and social media have a significant impact on consumer behavior when making purchase decisions [5]. In digital marketing, the process of strengthening destination branding, both identity (uniqueness) and image, must be formed with interesting and communicated content and create a clear message with most interactions (website, social media, etc.) to the intended target segment [6].

This project uses media websites, Instagram, and social media (Facebook) to boost Mulyaharja's destination branding and establish a "unique tourism destination" that integrates eco-tourism, educational tourism, and sports tourism. Digital marketing for Bogor's rural style.

## 2 Material and Methods

### 2.1 *Branding/Destination Branding*

Brand is one of a company's most significant intangible assets for selling products and services. Marketing obligations to properly manage its value. Kotler's definition of "brand" quotes the American Marketing Association (AMA) as saying that it can be any of these things. This is a combination of these to identify a vendor or a group of merchants' "goods or services." And make it stand out from the crowd [7]. Differences in product performance may be functional, reasonable, or significant. With regard to what the brand performs, it can also be more symbolic, emotive, or intangible. To express or mean in a more abstract sense. How the ability of a company to be able to form the uniqueness of a product that is of value to the market for the desire to buy the product. In addition, building a brand must be in line with the image and associations want to appear in the minds of consumers [7]. A brand is a unique name and/or symbol (such as a logo, trademark, or packaging design) used to differentiate one vendor's goods or services from those of competitors. A brand tells the customer where the product comes from and protects both the customer and the manufacturer from imitators [8]. Branding in this case is the process of designing, planning, and communicating names and identities to establish or maintain a reputation [9]. It becomes important for a company to be able to communicate branding, images, and also its attributes to the targeted market segment. Therefore, digital marketing takes a very important role to carry out this communication.

Place branding is branding in a specific region, such as a region, city, and country [10], which refers to marketing in that area or region by analyzing competitors for tourists, visitors, investors, residents, and other resources [11]. Destination branding is a process of identifying, describing, distinguishing from other tourist destinations and communicating the image that is the attraction of the destination to tourists, and providing an experience of the characteristics of the area [12]. Activities that assist the development of names, icons, logos, slogans, or other images that easily identify and distinguish places are part of the destination brand. Two, we'll keep expressing our desire for a trip of a lifetime that is entirely dependent on chance. Emotional connection is built between tourist and destination by using this method. Make it less likely that consumers will think of this fee as a search expense. As a result of these operations, a destination brand that influences consumer travel decisions is formed [13].

### 2.2 *Tourism Village/Thematic Village*

As a priority government effort to recover from a pandemic, the development of a tourist village is underway. A tourist village is a rural place with unique characteristics that make it a popular tourist attraction. Supportive aspects such as traditional food, agriculture, and social systems characterize the area of the tourist village, with residents still maintaining largely original traditions and cultures [14]. A tourist village is a type of community living structure that incorporates established customs and traditions while also incorporating attractions, lodging, and support services [15]. Tourism village is a type of tourism that combines rural experiences, natural features, traditions, and one-of-a-kind aspects to appeal to a broad range of tourists. Meanwhile, thematic villages are proactive in the community by exploring economic potential, addressing basic needs, and forming unique and distinctive ideas to support the local economy. It is the development of the village based on the involvement [16, 17]. There are three stages to working in a thematic village. The first step is to map out the problem. This means you may collaborate with the community to come up with new ideas for village development, create jobs, and improve local engagement. When the topic for Seeta Community was established in the second phase, a group of people was created who were interested in working together to put ideas and themes into action in the village. The third step involves establishing and adjusting boundaries based on ideas and themes. The many actors involved will modify them until they are finally implemented in that location. It also describes how theme villages can emerge from the viability of ideas and subjects via three stages of development. This can also be influenced by factors such as economic and social characteristics, the existence of potential in the region being nurtured, external financial support, community leader initiatives, increased income, and community initiatives [18].

## 2.3 Digital Marketing

In order to communicate with the market, branding necessitates the use of a procedure known as marketing. Marketing is the process of improving information, influencing a product, and developing an appealing product in order to get market acceptance [19]. To put it another way, the technology used to attract and retain customers. Branding seeks to attract more important and valuable customers, but most importantly, to keep them. Modern marketing is a type of economic activity that integrates production and consumption in order to meet the needs of market participants in a lucrative manner. Brand messaging is innovative and reaches consumers through a variety of media, including television, newspapers, and, in certain cases, email [20].

Consumer behavior has shifted as a result of COVID-19 pandemic. The pandemic crisis is hastening the digitization era, requiring consumers to conduct all of their transactions online or digitally through the Internet, mobile phones, and other digital gadgets [21]. Working and manufacturing practices must also alter as a result of digitization. A business model that responds to market demands, adapts to market conditions, improves competitiveness, and, eventually, gives a competitive advantage [22]. Digital essence is a continuous interaction with the target population, and the benefit is that the outcome of digital campaigns is easy to measure in real time, which has a significant impact on the creative process. create. If the measure outcomes are unacceptable, you can generate better inventive right away till you achieve what you desire. The core of digital marketing is a continuous communication with the target audience. Furthermore, the outcome of digital advertisements is easier to track in real time, which has a significant impact on the creative process. create. If the outcomes are favorable, if the outcomes are unsatisfying, you can make better creative right away till you have what you desire [20].

It's all about leveraging digital tools like social media, mobile devices, blogs, feeds, and podcasts to get your message out to your target audience. According to Chaffey, digital marketing includes all of these things. To help in marketing efforts. Customer retention and acquisition are critical to the long-term financial success of any business (in the multi-channel purchasing process and customer life cycle) [22]. Enhancing social media for a business includes sustaining and strengthening client relationships, focusing on Facebook clients, and producing cash and profits [23]. With social media improving the relationship between customers and enterprises by providing recommendations, enterprises must respond by engaging in fun, open, and empathetic two-way communication as well as sportsmanship if relationships with consumers are to be maintained from the company's brand awareness [24].

## *2.4 Method*

A qualitative description approach with SWOT analysis (Strength, Weakness, Opportunity, Threat) was used to evaluate the strengthening of destination branding through digital marketing. The SWOT analysis will inform future strategy. SWOT analysis, according to Rangkuti, is a methodical examination of a variety of aspects in order to develop a strategy. This SWOT can help you optimize your strengths, opportunities, and even opportunities that come from your weaknesses and threats. In the Word matrix, the strategy formulation yields four different options:

1. Strengths and Opportunities Strategy (SO Strategy)

The Strengths and Opportunities Strategy exploits internal strengths and external opportunities. All leaders want their organizations to use internal characteristics to benefit from external trends and events.

2. Strategies on Weaknesses and Opportunities (WO Strategy)

The goal of the Shortcomings and Chances Strategy is to take advantage of external opportunities to strengthen internal weaknesses. If a corporation has enormous external potential, its internal limitations prohibit it from taking use of them.

3. Strategies on Strength and Threat (ST strategy)

External risks can be avoided or minimized by utilizing the company's strengths as a defense. As a result, this does not imply that strong businesses must always encounter external dangers in order to grow.

4. Strategies on Weakness and Threat (WT strategy)

Internal flaws and external threats are the focus of the Weakness Threat approach. There are several hazards to a company, both external and internal [25].

Brand usage information in the form of (1) articles, visuals, instructions, and attachments is reinforced by digital marketing metrics (PDF, PPT). Articles, images, tutorials. (2) A communication video that introduces the company's goods and services and a customer's "experience." (3) Goods and services are easily available. Ads (5) A website where users may connect using hashtags, likes, comments, and testimonials. (6) Phone and email customer service options. (7) Node for placing orders and making payments. (8) Capability to develop a favorable brand image. (9) Capability to find and attract new consumers. (10) Boost your brand's power, grow your base and node availability, and make new friends. Suggestion-making skill [23, 26, 27]. And external variables and external environments are composed of three types of environments: general environment and operational environment (economy, society, interest and technology, environment, industrial/tourism environment) [28].

## 3 Results and Discussion

Kampung Thematic Mulyaharja has a special community to build and maintain seized marketing on Instagram and Facebook. Agrotourism Eduwisata Organik (@visit-mulyaharja) on Instagram, and Ciharashas Mulyaharja on Facebook. Berikut adalah SWOT analisis untuk Kampung Mulyaharja. Mulyaharja village's SWOT analysis is provided below.

### *3.1 SO Strategy*

1. Manage visitor data bases to increase the number of tourists.
2. Increase customer engagement in each campaign to generate online word of mouth (WOM) and thus broaden the reach.
3. Improve interpersonal relationships with customers, resulting in the formation of a network or community and the strengthening of the Mulyaharja village's branding.
4. Participate actively in being a follower of a huge Instagram community or account by commenting on their posts, as well as posting updates on your own account.
5. Conduct market research to identify new target markets by adjusting the segment's attractions, amenities, and accessibility requirements.

### 3.2 WO Strategy

1. Continuing to increase the uniqueness and differentiation of the Mulyaharja village's brand image and identity.
2. Create and distribute comprehensive information about package deals, especially for individual travelers.
3. Provide payment options transactions or payment media variations with facilities or links.

### 3.3 WO Strategy

1. Strengthen the image and identity of the experience of the products and services created, and interact actively with the market and society through social media.
2. Map social media use by market segment for a competitive market.
3. By enhancing originality and difference, create an event calendar based on numerous targeted segment goals.

### 3.4 WT Strategy

1. Implement regular training to increase service abilities and skills in anticipating intense competition.
2. Keep a close eye on market and competition activity to determine the best course of action.

## 4 Conclusion

Tourist decision making is heavily influenced by a tourist destination's branding. To have a good and meaningful impact on customer behavior and ultimately entice tourists to visit, digital marketing must be able to express the uniqueness of the attraction, facilities, and attractiveness of a destination.

Several strategies, both for boosting branding and for using social media to communicate, have a strong link to increasing tourist traffic. The pattern of creating and managing visitor data bases, improving consumer engagement in order to generate online word of mouth (WOM), generating networks and communities, and diversifying products based on new segments.

Strengthening destination branding by mapping the use of digital marketing and social media according to the target market segment, as well as strengthening human resources and frequently analyzing market behavior and rivals to determine the best plan.

**Table 1** Digital marketing matrix SWOT Kampung thematic Mulyaharja

| IFAS | Strength | Weakness |
|---|---|---|
| **EFAS** | 1. Product information or articles that support and provide product guidance for consumers are available on social media and websites Kampung Mulyaharja<br>2. Supporting pictures, such as photos or product illustrations, are available on social media and the website of Kampung Mulyaharja<br>3. Social media and website Kampung Mulyaharja available service assistance to consumers<br>4. Online opinion support is offered through Mulyaharja's social media and website community<br>5. Testimonials are available on social media and on the village website Mulyaharja<br>6. Visitor records are available on Kampung Mulyaharja's social media and website<br>7. Special deals are available on Kampung Mulyaharja's social media and website<br>8. Kampung Mulyaharja's social media and online sites have the power to increase visibility and brand awareness<br>9. Kampung Mulyaharja's social media and websites have the capacity to identify and attract new clients<br>10. Kampung Mulyaharja's social media and websites have the power to boost the brand image obtained by consumers by availability of facilities/ buttons to refer friends | 1. Lack of diversity of packages, uniqueness, and details of package information, particularly for individual travelers<br>2. Transaction payment options or variations of payment media are not available on social media or websites in Kampung Mulyaharja<br>3.Skills shortage for services |

(continued)

**Table 1** (continued)

| IFAS | Strength | Weakness |
|---|---|---|
| 1. Through digital marketing, economic and socio-cultural<br>2. Factors could support an increase in the number of tourists<br>3. Technology advancements and digital marketing promote brand awareness, which leads to a growth in the number of tourists<br>4. Government policies, as well as Kampung Mulyaharja's digital marketing, support an increase in the number of tourists<br>5. There are still numerous segments and luminosities that can be targeted | **SO Strategy**<br>1. Manage visitor data bases to increase the number of tourists<br>2. Increase customer engagement in each campaign to generate online word of mouth (WOM) and thus broaden the reach<br>3. Improve interpersonal relationships with customers, resulting in the formation of a network or community and the strengthening of the Mulyaharja village's branding<br>4. Participate actively in being a follower of a huge Instagram community or account by commenting on their posts, as well as posting updates on your own account<br>5. Conduct market research to identify new target markets by adjusting the segment's attractions, amenities, and accessibility requirements | **WO Strategy**<br>1. Continuing to increase the uniqueness and differentiation of the Mulyaharja village's brand image and identity<br>2. Creating and delivering extensive information regarding packages, particularly for individual tourists<br>3. Provide payment options transactions or payment media variations with facilities or links |
| **Threats**<br>1. Bogor's tourism destinations are growing in popularity, as is the city's competition | **ST Strategy**<br>1. Strengthen the image and identity of the experience of the products and services created, and interact actively with the market and society through social media<br>2. Social media mapping for market segmentation<br>3. By enhancing originality and difference, create an event calendar based on numerous targeted segment goals | **WT Strategy**<br>1. Implement regular training to increase service abilities and skills in anticipating intense competition<br>2. Keep a close eye on market and competition activity to determine the best course of action |

## References


1. Pariwisata Kementerian (2020) https://www.kemenparekraf.go.id/statistik-wisatawan-mancanegara/Statistik-Kunjungan-Wisatawan-Mancanegara-2020 [Online] // https://www.kemenparekraf.go.id/statistik-wisatawan-mancanegara/Statistik-Kunjungan-Wisatawan-Mancanegara-2020. https://www.kemenparekraf.go.id, 08 february 2021. - 17 02 2022. https://www.kemenparekraf.go.id/statistik-wisatawan-mancanegara/Statistik-Kunjungan-Wisatawan-Mancanegara-2020
2. Refachlis M. Ilham [et al.] (2020) Perubahan Perilaku Konsumen Di Indonesia Selama COVID-19 [Jurnal]. - Surabaya : Universitas Airlangga Surabaya
3. Jatmiko Leo Dwi , Pradana Rio Sandy (2022) teknologi.bisnis.com/read/20201110/101/1315765/apjii-1967-juta-warga-indonesia-sudah-melek-internet. [Online] // Bisnis.com. - Bisnis.com, 10 November 2020. - 24 february 2022. - https://teknologi.bisnis.com/read/20201110/101/1315765/apjii-1967-juta-warga-indonesia-sudah-melek-internet
4. Setiawan Bram, Kustiani Rini Kustiani, https://travel.tempo.co [Online] // https://travel.tempo.co/. https://travel.tempo.co/, 25 may 2019. - 24 february 2022. https://travel.tempo.co/read/1209221/riset-tren-wisata-booking-com-semua-diatur-lewat-internet/full&view=ok
5. Ajina Ahmed S (2019) The perceived value of social media marketing: an empirical study of online word of mouth in Saudi Arabian context [Jurnal]. Saudi Aarabia, 3: Vol. 6. http://jssidoi.org
6. Parlov Natalija, Perkov Davor (2016) Sičaja Željko new trends in tourism destination branding by means of digital marketing [Jurnal]. Croatia : Acta Economica Et Turistica, 101–236: Vol 2
7. Kotler P, Keller KL (2012) Marketing management . New Jersey : Prentice Hal
8. Aaker David A (1991) Managing brand equity [Jurnal]. Division of Simon & Schuster Inc., hal. 21
9. UNWTO (2015) Alholt Simon Handbook On Tourism Destination Branding [Jurnal]. Madrid : unwto.org
10. Avraham Eli, Ketter Eran (2008) Media strategies for marketing places in crisis: Improving the image of cities, countries and tourist destinations [Journal]. - London : Routledge, 248: Vol. I
11. Hospers Gert-Jan Hospers (2004) Place marketing in Europe - The branding of the Oresund region [Jurnal]. Oresund : Springer, pp 271–279 : Vol 39
12. Ritchie JR Brent, Ritchie Robin JB (1998) The branding of tourism destinations [Jurnal] // A Basic Report Prepared for Presentation to the 1998 Annual Congress of the International Association of Scientific Experts in Tourism Marrakech, Morocco, September 1998
13. Pike Steven Pike (2009) Destination brand positions of a competitive set of near-home destinations [Jurnal]. Brisbane : Elsevier, 857–866: Vol 30
14. Zakaria Faris; Suprihardjo Rima Dewi Konsep Pengembangan Kawasan Desa Wisata di Desa Bandungan Kecamatan Pakong Kabupaten Pamekasan [Jurnal] (2014) Surabaya : JURNAL TEKNIK POMITS, Vol 3, No 2: 2337–3520 (2301–9271 Print)
15. Nuryanti Wiendu Concept (1993) Perspective and Challenges [Jurnal] // makalah bagian dari Laporan Konferensi. - Yogyakarta : Gadjah Mada University, hal. 2–3
16. KłoczKo-GAjewsKA Anna (2013) General characteristics of thematic villages in Poland [Jurnal]. - Warsaw : Visegrad J Bioec Sust Devel. https://doi.org/10.2478/vjbsd-2013-0012
17. Tamara Anindya Putri Kajian Pelaksanaan Konsep Kampung Tematik diKampung Hidroponik Kelurahan Tanjung Mas Kota Semarang [Jurnal]. (2018) Semarang : JURNAL WILAYAH DAN LINGKUNGAN UNDIP, 6 Nomor 1, April 2018, 40–57
18. Atkočiū nienė V, Kaminaitė G (2017) The drivers of thematic village's development in strengthening their vitality. Manag Theory Stud Rural Bus Infrast Devel [Jurnal]. - [s.l.] : mts.asu.it, 39(2):139–147. https://doi.org/10.15544/mts.2017.10
19. Tjiptono Fandy Pemasaran Jasa (2011) Malang [Buku]. - [s.l.] : Bayu Media Publishing
20. Borić Slađana [et al.] (2016) Analysis of digital marketing and branding for the purpose of understanding the consumers in digital age [Jurnal]. - Zrenjanin, Serbia : International Conference on Applied Internet and Information Technologies, https://doi.org/10.20544/AIIT2016.45

21. Slywotzky JA (1996) Value migration: how to think several moves ahead of competition [Jurnal]. - Boston : Harvard Business School Press
22. Chaffey D, Smith PR (2008) E marketing Excellence [Buku]. - Burlington : Elsevier, Vol. III
23. Kumar Ashish [et al.] (2015) The effects of firm generated content in social media on customer behavior [Jurnal], [s.l.]. Am Market Assoc
24. Moriansyah La (2015) Pemasaran Melalui media sosial: antecedents dan consequences [Jurnal]. – Jakarta. doi.org/https://doi.org/10.33299/jpkop.19.3.346, https://jurnal.kominfo.go.id/
25. Rangkuti Freddy (2017) Teknik Membedah Kasus Bisnis Analisa SWOT [Buku]. Jakarta : PT Gramedia Pustaka Utama, Vol 23
26. Taneja S, dan Toombs L (2014) Putting a face on small business: visibility, viability, and sustainability the impact of social media on small business marketing. [Jurnal]. [s.l.] : Academy of Marketing Studies Journal, 217–227:18(1)
27. Wardhana Aditya (2015) STRATEGI DIGITAL MARKETING DAN IMPLIKASINYA PADA KEUNGGULAN BERSAING UKM DI INDONESIA [Buku]. Bandung, Vol IV, fkb.akuntansi.upi.edu/prosiding
28. Pearce John A, Robinson Richard B (2014) Manajemen Strategis: Formulasi, Implementasi, dan Pengendalian. [Jurnal]. - Jakarta : Nia Pramita Sari, Vol 4

# The Destruction of Priangan Cinchona Production as a Cultural Problem

**Lia Nuralia and Iim Imadudin**

**Abstract** The cinchona industry had connected Priangan to the world when colonialism was at its peak. Bandung became the epicenter of the world's cinchona, known as the cinchona capital. Priangan supplies more than 90 percent of the world's cinchona needs. This study aimed to reveal the destruction of Priangan cinchona production in global dynamics and find a way out through a cultural perspective. The method used is descriptive qualitative, with historical, archeological, and anthropological approaches, and used Social Engineering Concept from James C. Scott. The destruction of cinchona production is not only an economic problem but also a cultural problem. Traces of cinchona culture are now largely lost, so important historical evidence of cinchona's past glory is also lost. From a cultural perspective, the development of cinchona can still be developed considering that the downstream industry is still producing regularly. The cinchona waste produced can be used to develop the creative economy. The garden workers who have lived for generations in the plantation environment still survive. Loyalty is valued for maintaining the previous generation's legacy, which is practiced in everyday life. Plantation societies that are increasingly besieged by global penetration are able to survive.

**Keywords** Cinchona · Priangan · Cultural problem

L. Nuralia (✉) · I. Imadudin
Research Organization for Archeology, Language, and Literature, Research Center for Prehistoric and History Archeology, National Research and Innovation Agency, Jakarta, Indonesia
e-mail: lian004@brin.go.id

I. Imadudin
e-mail: iimi001@brin.go.id



Nawawi et al. (eds.), *Managing Disruption and Developing Resilience for a Better Southeast Asia*, Springer Proceedings in Humanities and Social Sciences,
https://doi.org/10.1007/978-981-96-2116-3_31

# 1 Introduction

## *1.1 Background*

Indonesia has rich natural resources, but there is a gap between reality and expectations in practice. These natural resources cannot be used optimally for the welfare of society. For example, the scarcity and high price of cooking oil is a unique phenomenon nowadays because Indonesia is one of the world's largest palm oil-producing countries. This situation is also a problem for other export commodities, namely quinine (quinine is the main alkaloid from the cinchona bark). The word quinine became a popular term for products from the quinine plant, one of the substances contained in the quinine tree. In Indonesia, it is known as kina, while the word cinchona is the quinine plant or quinine tree (Cinchona spp.). Quinine began to reappear and became known to the general public after WHO on March 12, 2002, officially announced that chloroquine (synthetic from quinine) was one of the drugs for the treatment of COVID-19. However, the quinine substance contained in chloroquine results in more dangerous side effects than the benefits. This situation has turned attention to the substance quinine from the cinchona bark, a natural substance with fewer side effects. However, cinchona in Priangan, West Java, in the past, became an important commodity crop. The quinine industry connected Priangan to the world when Dutch colonialism was at its peak in the late nineteenth and early twentieth centuries.

Cinchona bark, for the manufacture of quinine pills under government regulation, began operations in the late 1850s [1]. Furthermore, other cinchona plantations were established: Cinyiruan, Kertamanah, Cikembang, Riunggunung, Pasirmalang, Rancabali, and others [2]. The cinchona plantation entrepreneurs formed a coalition to support the upstream industry and succeeded in establishing a downstream quinine factory, namely Bandoengsche Kininefabriek (BKF) in 1896. Subsequently, Nederlandsch Kininefabriek (NKF) and Amsterdamsche Chininefabriek (ACF) were established [3]; the Bandung Quinine Factory produces quinine salts and derivatives. Its products are massively exported abroad, so Bandung has become the epicenter of quinine in the world and is known as the capital of quinine. Priangan became a supplier of more than 90 percent of the world's quinine needs in the twentieth century [4].

Today, the role of the Bandung Kina Factory has been replaced by PT Sinkona Indonesia Lestari (PT SIL). The cinchona plantation in Priangan is still the supplier of the raw material for quinine to be processed at the quinine factory in Bandung. The Quinine Bandung Factory is now a joint venture of Kimia Farma, PTPN VIII, and PT SIL since February 25, 1986. The current shareholders are PT. Kimia Farma, Tbk (51%) and PTPN VIII (49%). In 2021, only 20% of upstream (local) industrial factories will meet the demand for raw materials, while 80% will be supplied from outside (imports). The Quinine Bandung Factory produces 5% of its products for the chemical industry, 30% for the pharmaceutical industry, and 65% for the beverage industry [5]. PTPN VIII has now been integrated into PTPN I as a Sub-Holding

SupportingCo, responsible for managing plantation assets, including Bukit Unggul Plantation

The sustainability of the quinine and cinchona industry activities in the country and the global market demand in the international world are two things that synergize with each other. The global market is still in dire need of high-quality quinine from Indonesia. High world demand for quinine should trigger domestic flour of cinchona bark production to increase. However, in reality, cinchona bark production has declined drastically and is on the verge of collapse. The plantation area continues to shrink and the cinchona bark factory is only available at the Bukit Unggul Factory in Bandung, the Bintang Factory in Cianjur, and the community. The Bintang Plantation is a cinchona plantation established in the Dutch era. Now the old Dutch buildings are gone. At the Bintang Factory, cinchona bark is still produced where it is processed in a new factory (Yanuar, Bintang Plantation Employees 2022). Community-owned cinchona plantations are private property from East Java (Munajat, PT SIL 2022).

Based on this background, the issues in this research are how the destruction of cinchona production from a cultural perspective is related to the sustainability of the activities of the cinchona industry in the country and the global market in the international world. Thus, this study aims to reveal the destruction of Priangan cinchona production in global dynamics through a cultural perspective.

## 1.2 Method

The research method used is descriptive qualitative, with historical, archaeological, and anthropological approaches, and applies the concept of Social Engineering developed by James C. Scott. Data sources come from Research Results Reports 2018, 2019, and 2020; colonial archives; interviews; and literature. The historical approach is carried out by utilizing colonial archive sources in the form of old documents, old photos, and old maps. The archaeological approach is indicated by the presence of industrial plantation buildings in the form of factories, offices, warehouses, residences, and other archaeological objects. Meanwhile, the anthropological approach is related to the socio-cultural life of plantation communities, where cultural values and production traditions still persist today.

Sources of archaeological data discovered in the field during the survey (direct observation) in the form of former cinchona plantations, former cinchona bark factories, cinchona bark factories still in operation, and old buildings supporting cinchona production. Research on colonial plantation sites includes industrial archaeological research, so the data collection technique during the research refers to the industrial archaeological framework, namely surface surveys, excavations, archival research, and oral history interviews [6]. This research no excavation was conducted, as the above-ground sources were deemed sufficient.

## 2 Result and Discussion

### 2.1 *Cinchona Production in the Cinchona Bark Factory and the Quinine Bandung Factory in Priangan*

The old factory building (cinchona bark factory) in the plantation that is still operating is the Bukit Unggul Factory (East Bandung), while the Bintang Factory (Cianjur) is a new building. The Bukit Unggul Factory includes an old Dutch building as a trace of material culture, which is hundreds of years old and can be called the industrial heritage of plantation. Then the old building of the Kimia Farma Factory (Bandung City center) which became a symbol of the glory of pharmaceuticals in the past, is no longer operating and has been designated as a cultural heritage building. The city government plans to revitalize the former quinine factory building into a creative economic zone (https://Bandung.Merdeka.Com/Halo-Bandung/Pemkot-Akan-Revitalisasi-Eks-Pabrik-Kina-Jadi-Zona-Ekonomi-Kreatif-170222n.html, *accessed 15 April 2022*, n.d.) (Fig. 1).

The Bukit Unggul Factory produces starting from the supply of wet cinchona bark (Kulit Kina Basah/K2B) in the garden and the processing of dried cinchona bark at the factory (Kulit Kina Kering Tepung/K3T). The flour of cinchona bark is the raw material for the Bandung Quinine Factory (PT SIL Kimia Farma), which produces quinine salts and derivatives. These manufacturing industry products are exported to more than 35 countries to meet the needs of pharmaceuticals at 30%, chemicals at 5%, and beverages at 65% [5] (Fig. 2).

Cultural traces of cinchona industrial consist of former garden lands and settlement emplacement with their artifacts. Cinchona gardens are still found in Bukit Unggul Plantation in Bandung with the old building factory, and Bintang Plantation in Cianjur with a new factory building [8]. The Bukit Unggul Plantation, which was established in 1912 (Wardini et al. 2010), in the past is a combination of six of cinchona gardens with six factories, which were established in the 1870-1880s (see Table 1).

There are hundreds of cinchona plantations and cinchona bark factories that were established during the Nederlandsch-Indies era, located in the Priangan area

**Fig. 1** Bukit Unggul factory [7]

**Fig. 2** Old Building of the Quinine Bandung Factory (Bandoengsche Kininefabriek Hoofdgebouw Oostzijde. BKF-636–36-KIT) in Bandung, Priangan-West Java, masa lalu dan masa kini

**Table 1** Cinchona plantation/factory joined in Bukit Unggul plantation

| No | Name of factory/garden | Time of establishment factory/garden |
|---|---|---|
| 1 | Sukamanah (Sukamanah I, Sukamanah II, Sukamanah III) | 1876; 13 August 1881; 29 April 1887 |
| 2 | Cisarua | 21 March 1881 |
| 3 | Gegersunten (Cikapundung I, Cikapundung II) | 22 August 1881 dan 4 June 1884 |
| 4 | Panglipur Galih | 3 February 1833 |
| 5 | Gunung Kasur | 1 August 1884 |
| 6 | Pangparang | 27 May 1884 |

*Source Regeerings Almanak* [2, 4]; dan Archaeological Research Report in 2019 [7]

of West Java [2, 4]. The cinchona bark, or Peruvian bark produced in plantation under Nederlandsch-Indies government regulation, began to move in the late 1880s. However, thanks in large part to the efforts of private planters, who have worked hard to increase total export volumes. Cinchona plantation area by the 1930s contained about 16,000 hectares of land and produced about 12,000 tons a year. During the malaise era, these numbers dwindled and production remained very low [9, 10].

The Quinine Bandung Factory also contributes to the destruction of cinchona production. Synthetic materials replace quinine and quinidine substances. Natural substances are being pushed aside because many buyers turn to synthetic materials. In addition, domestic-derived products have not yet developed, so they cannot sustain these changes. However, it wasn't long before the potential for natural substances came back because research results showed that synthetic materials had more adverse effects on health. Natural substances are getting fresh winds to be developed again, and cinchona bark factories should be ready to resume production, with patience waiting for the cinchona to grow and ready to harvest (Fig. 3).

**Fig. 3** Cinchona gardens and former cinchona production buildings were successfully traced in 2019. [11] *Source* Research Documentation and Google Terrain

## 2.2 *Cultural Remains and the Destruction of Cinchona Production as a Cultural Problem*

The local cinchona plantation area is shrinking along with the reduced processing of the cinchona bark factory. Most of the land has been converted to other commodity crops, such as oil palm, tea, coffee, and various fruits and vegetables. Land shrinkage is very significant because of the central government's policy of no longer making cinchona a leading commodity. Since 2021, Bukit Unggul Plantation has become part of the Ciater Plantation, cinchona bark production has been officially removed, and cinchona commodity has been zeroed out (Ervi Permana, HR Admin 1 and General Plantation Ciater PTPN VIII 2022).

The disappearance of traces of the cinchona industry provides evidence of the destruction of cinchona. This situation is a cultural problem in which the cause and effect of an event involving material and immaterial cultural remains. The production of cinchona stopped, and the cultural remains slowly decayed and eventually disappeared. The loss of cultural traces is also related to cultural politics, namely how the state frames, interprets, and organizes culture according to its interests. According to Ignas Kleden, cultural politics views culture as a political culture of resistance and opposition. Culture becomes very political, a place for the struggle for social change, trying to penetrate the establishment with hidden unfair practices. In the present and the future, culture is expected to be a framework or reference for thinking [12].

The cultural traces of the cinchona industry are in the form of gardens, factories, offices, residences, and others. The factory becomes the most important cultural object as the main production building. There are about 20 traces of quinine factories, including the Bukit Unggul Factory which is still operating, and the land and foundations of former factories, such as the Cinyiruan. Then the traces of the Kertamanah Factory are in the form of an iron frame structure and the Cikembang Factory is in the form of a stone structure. In 2019, the iron frame is still standing in its place. In 2020, the iron frame was no longer there; the land had been planted with vegetables and the coffee field. Furthermore, traces of other cinchona factories are in the form of vacant land or changing functions into tea, coffee, and vegetable gardens [7].

Immaterial cultural remains can be found in the technology and social lives of the actors in the production or plantation industries. The technology used is current, with specific machinery and production tools. Drying, roasting, milling, and packing were the four processing phases in the past and now. The technique of preparing cinchona bark in the factory has become a hereditary legacy, with knowledge passed down from generation to generation.

Recruitment past and present are similar in some respects and have become a continuing tradition. Most of the workers come from their own environment, which has genealogical or kinship relationships. If the parents become workers in factories or plantations, their children will continue working or take their place in the future. Not only children but nephews, brothers, sisters, and other relatives have this opportunity. This situation occurs, especially among lower-level employees (unskilled workers). The social structure in plantation communities is created based on the type of work and their social status. It is divided into three social classes, namely upper social class, middle social class, and lower social class [13]. Currently, to meet the needs of employees at the management level and leadership elements, most have shifted to professional workforce recruitment based on expertise at certain educational levels and company needs [10].

The destruction of cinchona production in Priangan, particularly in Indonesia in general, was not a natural occurrence. He did not come by itself but as a result of all the actions or treatment of the highest institution that issued regulations, namely state policy. The government's policy of eliminating cinchona as a leading commodity (Ervi Permana) ensures that production is no longer profitable. Cinchona can be harvested every 5–10 years, which is considered a long time to achieve production output targets. The rest of the cinchona is now preserved because it is considered a heritage plant of historical value. This situation does not guarantee that cinchona will continue to exist as a heritage in the future if the state does not manage it properly.

This situation has not only occurred in the present but since the birth of the policy of nationalizing foreign companies in 1958, during the Japanese era, and during the Dutch East Indies government. After the nationalization was carried out in stages, the company merged slowly in the 1970s. The world's demand for quinine as a natural malaria drug has increased rapidly [14, 15]. This situation did not last long because the world market's central policy and the state changed. The supply of local raw materials becomes very expensive because the production costs are not commensurate with the results obtained. Most of them are replaced by cheaper imported raw materials. There are 10 countries that import quinine raw materials, namely Nigeria, the United States, the United Kingdom of Great Britain, India, Ireland, Germany, France, Romania, Myanmar, and others [16].

During the Japanese reign, the Japanese war economic system, which converted plantation commodities into quinine, became a food provider (rice and secondary crops) for Japanese war soldiers during World War II. A war economy is a policy of mobilizing all economic power to support Japan's wartime war needs. The garden land is mostly used for rice farming and secondary crops. Many production buildings and their supporting facilities were abandoned or damaged. During this time, the majority of cinchona plantations switched functions, and the Indonesian cinchona industry lost its international market [5].

During the Dutch colonial period, the growth and development of large plantations in the eighteenth and nineteenth centuries was the peak of the triumph of Dutch colonial influence in the Dutch East Indies (*Nederlandsch-Indie).* Sartono Kartodirdjo [17] said that plantations were the real Dutch colonialism. The hands and feet of the colonized children were tied with ropes [18], controlled with full force to fulfill the interests of the Dutch mother country.

The presence of the colonists, who initially aimed to find trade commodities, has changed local residents' economic, social, and cultural systems (children of Dutch colonies). In the economic field, there has been a change from a barter system to a money economy system [10]. After the colonists were politically in power, the socio-cultural sector was also under their control. The Dutch colonial government was a state figure who tried to create a new identity for its colony, namely as a colony of the *Nederlandsch-Indie.*

The concept of James C. Scott, in his book entitled *Seeing Like a State, How Certain Schemes to Improve the Human Condition have Failed* [19], that everything is seen as a state sees it, namely with a powerful approach in the form of control. Like a "State" refers to the simplified, standardized way in which modern states seek to render society legible and administratively manageable, often at the expense of local knowledge and lived realities. This epistemic simplification, while useful for governance, frequently leads to the failure of large-scale state-led development projects. How the state makes certain schemes aimed at improving human living conditions by creating laws and various regulations. However, all of them could not be implemented properly and eventually failed. James Scott [19] reveals the state's perspective on various aspects of life, such as the way of life of the population, the way forests and agriculture grow, the shape of the rural and urban landscape, the layout of roads, the distribution of labor, and others [20].

There are three concepts in James Scott, namely: (1) Central Planning-Social Aspect, (2) Social Engineering, and (3) Authoritarianism. In this paper, the concept of Social Engineering is used with the following 4 elements: (1) orderly administration of social and natural resources, (2) application of the ideology of advanced modernity, (3) state control of power, and (4) the powerlessness of civil society to face all plans designed by the state. He discusses the identity of a city within a country. A city is a residential area that is a unitary place to live for various levels of society [21]. The city referred to in this paper is a city in a colonial country, referred to as a colonial city.

The plantation colonial cities were located in the hinterland, on the plains of mountain slopes, but functionally the city has fulfilled the requirements because of the diversity of jobs. The plantation settlement area was like an independent city during the colonial era because all kinds of buildings were erected in it for the sustainability of the company and the fulfillment of the living needs of its employees. The position of plantation companies is like a state within a country, a separate enclave, which emphasizes the amount of power owned by plantation entrepreneurs. The *Nederlandsch-Indie*, as a vast Dutch colony, had abundant natural wealth. Almost all areas are used as locations for exporting commodity-producing plantations. The plantation became a system the Dutch colonial government deliberately created to achieve goals that stemmed from the doctrine of glory, gold, and gospel [22].

Plantations were created as an extension of the development of Western agrarian capitalism, which was introduced through a commercial agriculture economic system of colonial style. This new agricultural system had an important impact on the processes of colonialism and modernization. The main mission was to increase the production of export crops [23]. Thus, there is a very close relationship between the history of plantations and the history of colonialism. The plantation is a modern (industrial) capitalist business with a market orientation, while the garden system is an agricultural business for subsistence (pre-industrial) [22].

The regulations issued by the colonial government regarding plantations in general were the cultivation systems, namely *prijanganstelsel* during the VOC (1600–1800), *landelijkstelsel* during the Conservative Government (1800–1830), and *cultuurstelsel* during the Cultivation System (1830–1870). *Suiker Wet* and *Agrarische Wet* followed (Boomgaard, 20) (July 21, *Staatsblad* 136; April 9, 1870, *Staatsblad* 55; *Koninklijk Besluit* July 20, 1870, *Staatsblad* 118). In the period of Liberal Political Economy (1870–1901), the Dutch East Indies underwent significant transformations in the economic, social, and political spheres. This period was marked by the transition from the Cultivation System (Cultuurstelsel) to an era of liberal colonial economic Policies, the rise of capitalism and plantation-based industries, the emergence of social awareness and early critiques of colonialism, as well as the development of infrastructure. The colonial government system underwent a change again with the birth of the Ethical Policy (1901), which had a major impact on the socio-economic and cultural life of the inhabitants of the plantation community.

The components in the plantation concept are land, labor, capital, technology, scale, organization, and purpose [10]. There are basic needs in implementing the plantation system. The unoccupied land was then turned into *erfpacht* land to be rented out to foreign private entrepreneurs (Europe and China) for a long period of up to 75 years. The lands that already have tenants are divided into parcels (*perceelen*) to be used by the population as forced labor. In addition, there are plantation lands called private lands (*Partikuliere Landerijen*) and land rental systems in Praja Kejawen (*Vorstenlanden*) [22]. In the following years, the land for coffee plantations will become cinchona and tea plantations.

Implementing the ideology of advanced modernity (high modernism) that occurs in plantations is the economic system of commercial agriculture. The use of modern machines and tools, as well as advanced production methods or processes, is also related to the availability of these machines. The ideology of the colonial government that developed in the colonies of the *Nederlandsch-Indie* refers to the ideology of the mother country of the Netherlands. The establishment of large private plantations originated from the conflict between conservative and liberal groups in the Netherlands. The conflict concerns the practice of conservative colonialism, which is considered very inhumane and violates human rights. The problem of injustice is widespread, propelling the liberals to victory. The liberals became powerful and significantly impacted colonial policies in the *Nederlandsch-Indie* [17].

One of the most influential was the issuance of the Agrarian Law of 1870, which allowed foreign investors to participate in opening up business opportunities by establishing plantations in the *Nederlandsch-Indie*. The law contains regulations on land use and labor, as well as other factors of production. The *Nederlandsch-Indie* government tried to simplify the complexities of culture related to the local conditions of each region in the Indies. This situation shows that the *Nederlandsch-Indie* government was dealing with the state's high modernism ideology [20].

Control of power by the state is characterized by the number of laws and regulations issued. In practice, various government (state) regulations or policies for a better life cannot be implemented. Plantation entrepreneurs had replaced the position of the government. Forced labor is replaced with paid work; compulsory land surrender is replaced with land rent. However, its realization did not benefit the natives because the farming community's traditional bond and semifeudal condition hindered the liberalization process in labor wages and land rent [22].

The existence of state and private plantations on erfpacht land is a manifestation of the political economy of the *Nederlandsch-Indie* government. The exploitation of colonized lands through the large-scale production of export commodities by plantation companies is true colonialism, not only economically but also culturally. Residents of the *Nederlandsch-Indie,* as children of the Dutch colony, were forced to follow a modern agricultural economic system that was colonial in nature, leaving old habits and merging into a commercial economic order that was very profitable for the state. The garden workers feel the little benefit, just to survive and carry out the orders of the authorities. This was a state of powerlessness for civil society at the time in plantation communities.

The powerlessness of civil society during the *Nederlandsch-Indie* period was not much different from today, facing all the plans designed by the state. The current powerlessness of the plantation community in facing the policy of eliminating cinchona commodities is also a reality. The land for cinchona plantations is getting narrower, production is decreasing, and finally it has an impact on the existence of cinchona industrial buildings. The longer it gets unkempt and no longer functions as it was originally. Especially now that the production of cinchona bark at Bukit Unggul Factory is only 2,500 kg, processed every 4 months after reaching 10,000 kg, it is only 7,500 kg per year. The total area of cinchona is about 700 ha, but the cinchona population has decreased a lot, leaving only 20% (Nana, *Afdeeling Assistant* of Bukit Unggul, 2022).

The present government policy is the production policy and strategy for quinine production at PTPN. The quinine salt processing plant carried out by PT SIL has a market share of 27% and a reasonably large added value. However, the raw materials in the form of dried cinchona bark rely on imports of around 85% planned until 2023 [16]. Should cinchona bark be fulfilled by a local factory, it will revive cinchona plantations in Priangan. The revival of the cinchona plantation in Priangan will positively affect the cultural footprint of the cinchona industry in the plantation area. The old factory buildings and other supporting buildings of historical value will be preserved and maintained. Likewise, the Dutch heritage cinchona garden area has become a heritage industrial landscape that is a source of knowledge.

The cinchona plantations in Priangan were mostly established after the Cultivation System ended. At the end of the nineteenth century, the Netherlands entered modern capitalism, and in the *Nederlandsch-Indie*, it is considered the beginning of liberal colonial politics [17]. Most of the cinchona plantations which were later established were privately owned in the form of *erfpacht land*. Some were also private land (*particulaire landerijn*). The government-owned cinchona plantations that were established during the Cultivation System are continuing and adapting to changing circumstances, such as the Cinyiruan Plantation. Traces of the former government-owned gardens can still be found. The Cinyiruan Plantation has been part of the Kertamanah Plantation since the 1970s. In 2022, it was merged into the Malabar Plantation (Manager of the Kertamanah Plantations 2022).

The merger is carried out based on the Rightsizing Policy of the PTPN directors. The regulations issued may differ from the objectives of the colonial period regulations to create the *rust en orde*. Currently, regulations are issued mainly to regulate production better and more efficiently. There are a lot of vacant lands that are neglected, gardens that are no longer producing, and commodity plants that are no longer superior products. In addition, the company's organizational restructuring was carried out to regulate the position and number of employees to save and achieve maximum production (Ramdhan, Dadang, employees of Kertamanah 2022).

The impact of the birth of the new regulation also occurs on other cultural objects, such as factory buildings and residential houses. The coffee factory in Cikembang is no longer operating and is being left alone. This coffee factory is part of the former *Administrateur* House of Cikembang Plantation of building in the past. Then the stone structure of the former Cikembang Factory is feared to be neglected in the future. Next is the official residence of the Manager of Kertamanah Plantation. After the Rightsizing Policy the function of the Administrator's House at the Kertamanah Plantation was purposed into a guest house located within the plantation area. It is also feared that the change in function will affect the physical form, thereby eliminating the original form. The original form of the old building has a typical plantation architectural style as a source of knowledge that has historical value. If a new policy is born, it is likely to impact the removal of the old buildings of historical and cultural value.

## 3 Conclusion

The production of cinchona bark in industrial plants is still ongoing, and the global market still requires quinine production. From an economic perspective, everything runs smoothly and produces a ready-to-use product. From a cultural perspective, cinchona production is a problem in terms of the cultural traces of the cinchona industry, which are now damaged, neglected, and lost. The destruction of cinchona production in the gardens area greatly impacted the destruction and loss of material and immaterial heritage culture. Immaterial culture concerns production traditions and the daily lives of garden managers and employees. The number of cinchona plantations in the past in Priangan reached 100. Currently, only one plantation and one factory remain in Bukit Unggul. Production is still ongoing, which produces the flour of cinchona bark as a raw material to be processed at PT SIL.

The existence of only one old cinchona factory building shows the real destruction of cinchona bark production. The destruction of cinchona production is an economic problem that affects cultural problems. And those two problems happen naturally and occur because there is a great controlling force. One force is in the form of Social Engineering, which aims to simplify the complexities of the situation to improve human life. However, this control was not appropriately implemented and eventually failed. This control is aimed at the orderly administration of social and natural resources, which is correlated with the application of advanced modernity ideology, and has a major influence on the control of power by the state, and has an impact on the powerlessness of civil society to face all plans designed by the state.

## References

1. Schrijver., van den (1928) *De Kina van Boschprodukt tot Kultuutgewas (Openbare Les Gehouden Op 27 September 1928 Bij Den Aanvang van Zijn College over De Kultures van den Ned. Indischen Archipel Door DR. Z. Kamerling, Privaat-Docent Aan DE Rijks-Universiteit Te Leiden). N.V. Boek-E*
2. Regerings Almanak voor Nederlandsch-Indie (1893) Eeerste Gedeelte, Grondgebied en Bevolking, Inrrichting Van Het Bestuur Van Nederlandsch-Indie En Bijlagen. Landsdrukker Batavia. (n.d.). ANRI.
3. Algemene Secretarie Serie Grote Bundel Missive Gouvernements Secretarie 1890–1942, No.4583). Inventaris Arsip. (2022). Arsip Nasional Republik Indonesia
4. Regerings Almanak voor Nederlandsch-Indie (1892, 1893,1900, 1901, 1902, 1906) Eeer-ste Gedeelte, Grondgebied en Bevolking, Inrrichting Van Het Bestuur Van Nederland-sch-Indie En Bijlagen. Landsdrukker Batavia. (n.d.). Jakarta: ANRI
5. Rahmi KI (2021) Prospek Bisnis Kina, Perspektif Budidaya, Hilirisasi, dan Peluang Kolaborasi. Webinar Tea and Cinchona Knowledge by PPTK Gambung, 13 Januari 2021

6. Casella EC (2005) Industrial Archaeology: Future Directions (E.C.C. and J.Symonds. (Ed.)
7. Nuralia L (2021) Kehancuran Produksi dan Hilangnya Pabrik Kina Masa Kolonial di Ban-dung: Bukti Bencana Budaya Dan Sosial. Prosiding Balai Arkeologi Jawa Barat 4(1):235–246. https://doi.org/10.24164/prosiding.v4i1.22
8. Syahrian H (2020) Sejarah Bahan Tanaman Kina (Cinchona ledgeriana) Klon Seri QRC. Webinar Riset Perkebunan Nusantara. Serah Terima Plasma Nutfah Kina Klon QRC 230, PPTK-KRC LIPI. Kebun Raya Cibodas, Cianjur, 2 Desember 2020
9. Nuralia L dkk (2019) *Bangunan Industri dan Produksi Perkebunan Kina Kabupaten Bandung Barat dan Sekitarnya, Provinsi Jawa Barat, Abad XIX – XX Masehi*
10. O'Malley WJ (1988) Perkebunan 1830–1940: Ikhtisar. In A. W. Anne Booth, William J. O'Malley (Ed.), *Sejarah Ekonomi Indonesia* (p. 136). LP3ES
11. Nuralia Lia et al. (2019) *Bangunan Industri dan Produksi Perkebunan Kina Kabupaten Bandung Barat dan Sekitarnya, Provinsi Jawa Barat, Abad XIX – XX Masehi*
12. Suratman M (2016) Politik Kebudayaan. *Majalah Nusantara, Edisi Januari-Februari 2016.* https://www.kompasiana.com/mamansuratman/575d65b5b37e61cd0abb2167/politik-kebudayaan?page=3&page_images=1. Dikases 16 April 2022
13. Nuralia L (2017) Struktur Sosial dan Nilai-Nilai Kolonial Pada Rumah Pejabat Tinggi Perkebunan Zaman Hindia Belanda di Jawa Bagian Barat. ,. *Jurnal Kapata Arkeologi, Vol. 13,*(No. 1, Juli 2017.), Halaman 1–20
14. Danoesastro H (1975) *Perkebunan Kina. Laporan Terjemahan dari Bahasa Belanda ke Bahasa Indonesia untuk Kebutuhan Intern Pusat Penelitian Teh dan Kina Gambung*
15. Kerbosch (1948) De Kinacultuur. In *De Landbouw in de Indische Archipal, IIA,* (pp. 747–865.). van Hoeve, 's-Gravenhage
16. Sita K dan DR (2021) Analisis Kinerja dan Prospek Komoditas Kina. *Radar Vol.2, No.2, Januari 2021*
17. Kartodirdjo S (1990) Pengantar Sejarah Indonesia Baru: Sejarah Pergerakan Nasional Dari Kolonialisme Sampai Nasionalisme. Jilid 2. Gramedia
18. Ingleson J (2004) *Tangan dan Kaki Terikat, Dinamika Buruh, SArekat Kerja dan Perkotaan Masa Kolonial. Terjemahan Iskandar P. Nugraha.* Komunitas Bambu
19. Scott J (1998) Seeing like a state: how certain schemes to improve the human condition have failed. Yale University Press
20. Santoso H (2017) Negara dan Sindrom Otak Kiri. *Wacana Jurnal Transformasi Sosial, No.35, in 2017*
21. Handoko ST (2002) Kriminalitas di Semarang 1906- 1942. Suatu Masalah Sosial Perkotaan Pada Masa Kolonial. Tesis Magister Ilmu Sejarah, Program Pas-casarjana Universitas Gadjah Mada
22. Kartodirdjo Sartono & DS (1991) Sejarah Perkebunan di Indonesia, Kajian Sosial Ekonomi. Aditya Media
23. Leirissa RZ (1990) *Nusantara di Abad ke-18 dan ke-19. Sejarah Nasional Indonesia IV.* Balai Pustaka
24. Boomgaard P (2004) *Anak Jajahan Belanda, Sejarah Sosial dan Ekonomi Jawa 1795–1880. Terjemahan Monique Soesman, Keosalah Soebagyo Toer.* KITLV-Jakarta dan Djambatan
25. Nuralia L (2018) Bangunan dan Produksi Perkebunan Panglejar dan Bukit Unggul-Sukawana Kabupaten Bandung Barat, Provinsi Jawa Barat
26. Nuralia L dan II (2021) Nilai Budaya pada Lanskap Industri Perkebunan Kina Cinyiruan Bandung Pada Masa Kolonial. Jurnal Patanjala, Vol 13
27. Nuralia et al. (2020) Laporan Penelitian Desk Study Arkeologi. Kajian Arsip dan Pustaka Penelitian Perkebunan Gutta Percha Cipetir, Sukabumi
28. Widjaya AS (2009) Ujung Berung Serambi Timur Bandung. Panitia Pameran Sejarah Ujungberung. https://www.infobdg.com/v2/sejarah-pabrik-kina-bandung/, accessed 15 April 2022. (n.d.)
29. https://bandung.merdeka.com/halo-bandung/pemkot-akan-revitalisasi-eks-pabrik-kina-jadi-zona-ekonomi-kreatif-170222n.html. *di akses 15 April 2022.* (n.d.)

# The Economics of Perception in the Internet: Why Herbal Supplements Are Highly Demanded During Indonesia Covid-19 Pandemic?

**Dimas Caraka Ramadhani, Sudarsono Hardjosoekarto, Radhiatmoko, and One Herwantoko**

**Abstract** Perception over herbal supplement, locally known as "Jamu," to help prevent or cure Covid-19 gets inclusively discoursed in Indonesia's internet-based news and social media. The paper demonstrates the debate over the functionality of Jamu to boost immune and protect one's against Covid-19 in social media, as results of cognitive anchoring produced by government, policy makers, medical experts, industry, academia, and community leaders on the internet-based news. The paper reveals that inclusive social media works as means on advocating the benefit of Jamu and its efficacy, and importantly shaping the market perception and price formation of Jamu during Indonesia Covid-19 pandemic.

**Keywords** Economic sociology · Herbal · Jamu · Social media · Internet · Covid-19

## 1 Introduction

Herbal supplements, locally known as "Jamu," are massively consumed by the population with deep tradition and heritage. Ministry of Health claimed that 49.53% of the population consume it and 95.6% of them experienced its efficacy ([1], p. 134). It's a culturally accepted worldview that Jamu could improve one's health, while to some it cures diseases. It comes in many forms such as concoction, drinks, pills, and tablets. Because the scientific evidence of herbal supplement efficacy is limited, the Indonesian government created pathways for herbal ingredients to pursuing clinical trials and get certified. Those passing the animal-trials called Standardized Herbal Medicine ("OHT"), while the ones passing human-trials called Fitofarmaka. Registered Jamu are available as Over-the-Counter ("OTC") drugs at pharmacies.

D. C. Ramadhani (✉) · S. Hardjosoekarto · Radhiatmoko · O. Herwantoko
Department of Sociology, Faculty of Social and Political Sciences, University of Indonesia, Jakarta, Indonesia
e-mail: dimas.caraka01@ui.ac.id



Nawawi et al. (eds.), *Managing Disruption and Developing Resilience for a Better Southeast Asia*, Springer Proceedings in Humanities and Social Sciences,
https://doi.org/10.1007/978-981-96-2116-3_32

The Covid-19 pandemic has brought a perception test over the worldview of Jamu efficacy against infectious virus. Many believe by consuming Jamu would help improving health immunity to prevent Covid-19 infection, not a few have believed that it could actually help to cure the disease, while others would disbelieve entirely. Social media and the internet-based news has captured the perception debate between the Indonesia internet population. From communications perspective, such debate could help people to be informed and educated, while to others can misled. Through a sociological lenses, an inclusive discourse helps society to form new perception equilibrium. Meanwhile for economic sociology, it could explain the factors that shaped Jamu markets.

This article intends to describe the reconfirmation of cognitive frames [2] that shaped market perceptions and price formation over Jamu's efficacy during Covid-19 in Indonesia's internet. It started with: (1) lining down the discourse framing set by quoted figures (i.e., government, policy makers, industry, academia) on the internet-based Bahasa Indonesia written news portal throughout 2020 and 2021; (2) picturing the structure and network connections that foster believes (or disbelieve); and (3) correlating the framing with the discourses in social media (i.e., YouTube) as cognitive anchoring. The YouTube text corpus that this article observed is LifestyleOne channel, titled "Do not panic! Ginger and Turmeric Are Effective Against Corona Virus" from March 2020 through March 2021 with $\pm$ 3,000 corpus text.

## 2 Framing

Highlighted framing over herbal supplements, or traditionally known as "Jamu," use and efficacy are broadly grouped into 3 topics: product development, promotion and campaign, and efficacy.

On product development, attention to the use of herbal supplements gets escalated after Minister of Research and Technology in early 2020, Bambang Brodjonegoro: Suggesting clinical trial timeframe for herbal supplements to be shorten, encouraging doctors to prescribe herbal-based drugs; on government to instruct the acknowledgment of OMAI (Indonesia Origin Modern Medicine: i.e., tested Jamu such as OHT and Fitofarmaka) being available for doctor's prescription in the national healthcare services [3, 4]. Chains of reactions then came from Chairperson of Drug and Food Supervisory Body ("BPOM"), Penny K. Lukito, stating her organization has increased numbers of Jamu for clinical trial, and introducing Fitofarmaka in the national healthcare drug list [5].

Researchers and academia also contributed scientific reports about Jamu. For instance, Dean of Medical Faculty of University Indonesia ("UI"), Ari Fahrial Syam, and Professor Irmanida Batubara of Bogor Agriculture University ("IPB") reported that guava, orange peel, and moringa contains hesperidin, rhamnetin, kaempferol, quercetin, and myricetin that could prevent Covid-19 infection [6]. Confirming private sector support and synergy on Jamu product development, PT Kalbe Farma,

Hermin Agustina Silalahi, claimed that her company is pursuing clinical trial on cordyceps militaris fungus for Covid-19 light pneumonia treatment [7].

Taking further step by promoting Jamu consumption, President of Indonesia, Joko Widodo, said he regularly consume Jamu, and during Covid-19 pandemic gets intensified to three times a day [8]. Inspired by the president, Minister of Health in early 2020, Terawan Agus Putranto, endorsed the use of OHT and Fitofarmaka for Covid-19 treatments, saying that xanthorriza in curcuma and phyllanthus niruri in chamber bitter can be effective to treat patients [9]. Similarly, Minister of Agriculture, Syahrul Yasin Limpo, endorsing the antivirus eucalyptus necklace, claimed that it kills 42% Covid-19 within 15 min of contact, and 80% within 30 min [10].

Academia, Professor Chairul Anwar Nidom—Chief of CoV and Vaccine at Airlangga University—argued that scientifically Covid-19 can be prevented by consuming ginger and curcuma, as they possess curcumin that could be effective to minimizing Covid-19 fatality risks after learning from SARS [11].[1] Conclusively, researcher from the Traditional Herbal Medicine Agency, Fanie Indrian Mustofa, presented a survey, reporting that from 1,524 respondents: 79% consumed Jamu to boost health immunity during Covid-19 pandemic; 55.7% intensified their Jamu consumption; while 78.5% recommended family and friends to consume Jamu to prevent Covid-19 infection [12]. Encouraging decisiveness, parliament member, Anggia Ermarini, called for the government to take strong actions for encouraging people to consume Jamu to prevent Covid-19 infection [13].

Some has gone further by confirming Jamu efficacy over Covid-19. Parliament member, Andre Rosiade, claimed that Herbavit-19 has proved to cure patients from Covid-19 virus [14]. Popular anti-graft investigator, Novel Baswedan, claimed for recovering from Covid-19 after consuming turmeric, galangal, honey, and eucalyptus concoction and probiotic [15]. Navy Chief Special Staff, Vice Admiral Suradi, claimed that have found herbal concoction and proven effective to cure Covid-19 patients [16]. Chairperson of Doctor Association for Traditional and Herbal Medicine, Inggrid Tania, claimed that Jamu can help to relieve cytokines on heavy lung inflammation according to patients' testimonies [17].

The private sector has also claimed the results. Sari Buah Merah distributor, David Hadiningrat, said that his product has been consumed by more than 300 Covid-19 patients in four hospitals, with 299 of them gets recovered [18]. Director of PT Bio Teknologi Indonesia, Setya Dwi Haryanto, claimed that his product, Fit-O, has helped many patients to recover from Covid-19 (Sarah 2020). Chairperson of Nahdlatul Ulama Affiliated Researcher Group, Asep Rukmana, said have invented Anti-Virus Corona (AVC) Jamu and proven to cure all treated Covid-19 patients [19].

Meanwhile, many have confronted Jamu's efficacy on treating Covid-19. For instance, Director of Standardization at BPOM, Togi Junice Hutadjulu, and Deputy for Traditional Medicine Supervision at the same agency, Maya Gustina Andarini, confirm that no Jamu has been accredited as Covid-19 medicine yet [20, 21].

[1] Severe Acute Respiratory Syndrome, or popularly known as Bird Flu.

## 3 Structure and Network Enablers

The comments and claims made by people identified on the internet-based news happen under a given structure context. That said, the network that connects such structure is dynamic, which enables opportunities to change each individual's perceptions and positions, and depends on their efforts and influence. Each individual has relations pattern that can be plotted into social network mapping with 4 sets of rules: (F(x): 3) high level of interdependency, i.e., working in same organization; (F(x): 2) medium level of interdependency, i.e., demand for endorsement or permit and approval; (F(x): 1) low level of interdependency, i.e., referred opinion; (F(x): 0) unknown level of interdependency (Fig. 1).

The social network mapping pictures the centralities of 2 groups: (1) Penny K. Lukito as Chairperson of BPOM, and (2) Bambang Brodjonegoro, which in 2020 was the Minister of Research and Technology,[2] while other centralities are relatively less concentrated. The first group with Penny K. Lukito in central represents the pro-status quo structure of Indonesian drug authority whom enforces clinical methods on Jamu before market consumption, with distribution permit and product registration as its coercive instrument to implement regulations. The second group with Bambang Brodjonegoro in central represents the contra-status quo structure whom suggest reforms on medical stakeholders to take affirmative actions of incorporating more (and locally originated) Jamu for patient treatments.

Both group are not solidly separated. Many individuals helped by taking role as middle person to facilitating both interests. For instance, the Ministry of Health's ("MoH") organization (i.e., Akhmad Saikhu, Chief of B2P2TOOT MoH), and Dwi Ranny Pertiwi, Chairperson of Jamu Industry Association ("GP Jamu"), or others that jointly worked on the OMAI Covid-19 guidelines Taskforce. Due to the fluidity of networks and middle person, it took relatively short period of 10 months (December 2020 through October 2021) for BPOM Chairperson to take open public statement confirming the increased numbers of Jamu for clinical trial and introducing human-tested Jamu, "Fitofarmaka," in the national healthcare drug list [5], and after the earlier criticism coming from the Minister of Research and Technology on both points [3, 4].

## 4 Cognitive Anchoring

The discourse among medical and government elites over Jamu on the internet-based news gets reflected as an cognitive anchoring [2] into the debate among internet population. With taking YouTube as sample, from the ± 3,000 corpus text, titled "Do not panic! Ginger and Turmeric Are Effective Against Corona Virus" from March 2020 through March 2021: 393 key or conceptual words were identified, where top

[2] Prior to the creation of National Research and Innovation Agency ("BRIN").

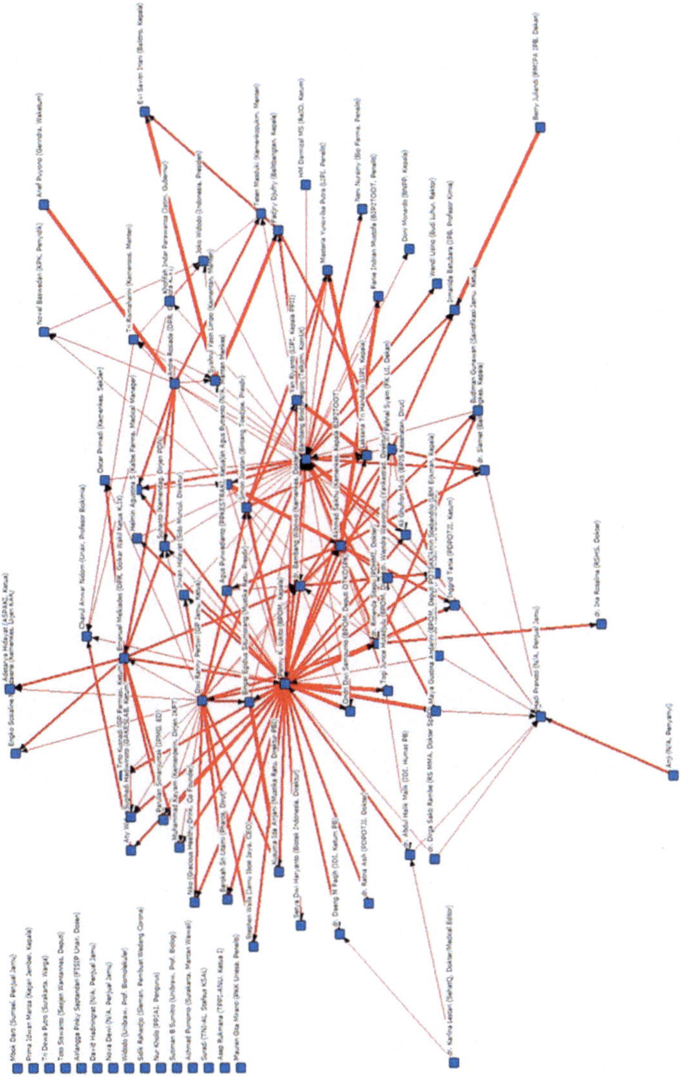

**Fig. 1** Social network mapping[3]

[3] UCI Net open software.

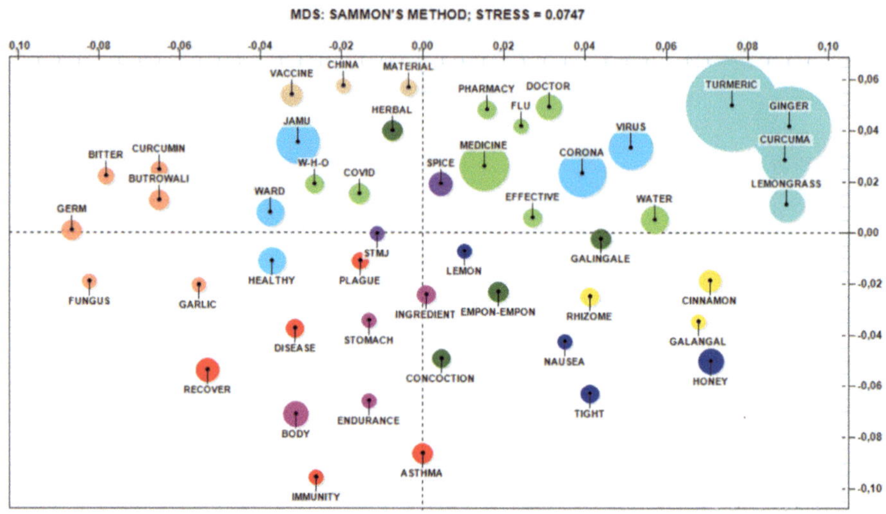


**Fig. 2** Multi-dimensional scaling[4]

five are turmeric (50 modus), ginger (43), medicine (23), corona (22), and curcuma (22) (FIg. 2).

Where the same corpus text gets plotted into multi-dimensional scaling ("MDS"), it has turmeric, ginger, curcuma, and lemongrass as herbal ingredients at the same quadrant with corona, virus, medicine, doctor, and effective. The similar quadrant tells distance of words in the text, while the color represents associations of words.

The cognitive anchoring of Jamu ingredients and concoction being associated to prevent and/or cure Covid-19 becomes the YouTube debate perimeter. For instance, many thank Professor Chairul Anwar Nidom—Chief of CoV and Vaccine at Airlangga University, for educating that ginger and curcuma (with curcumin) could be effective to minimizing Covid-19 fatality risks [11]. Many are confident that Jamu is effective for treating Covid-19, while Indonesia has vast spice resources; they had argued that Jamu needs to be globally promoted. Some would suggest to consume more local cuisine as many gets cooked with spices (i.e., Soto Ayam with turmeric). Some has shared their testimony of recovering from Covid-19 symptoms, such as nausea, short breath, and headache, after drinking turmeric and honey (examples of herbal substance). Some would go further by criticizing the medical stakeholder, as after 20 years being unable to take affirmative actions for more clinical testing and promote Jamu broadly, although Indonesian has hundred years of recorded history of consuming herbal concoction for curing disease.

[4] T-Lab open software.

## 5 Price Formation

The cognitive anchoring that frames the market perception has affected the price formation of Jamu and herbal commodity. Recorded on YouTube's corpus text, people in East Java have growing concerns over the inflation price of ginger, curcuma, and turmeric that gets doubled than normal price, due to high demand. That said, some of the internet population in YouTube's corpus text also criticized Indonesia's Covid-19 fatality rate although many have consumed herbal commodities and causing price inflation. Regardless of the efficacy results, the price inflation has benefiting small and medium herbal commodity sellers, as mentioned by Teten Masduki, Minister of Small and Medium Businesses and Cooperatives [22]. It pictures the inelastic demand of herbal commodities: when price of herbal commodities surges, the demand remains high.

Separately on the herbal supplement products, CEO of PT Jamu Iboe Jaya, Stephen Walla, said that Jamu sales surge up to 3 times than normal during Covid-19 pandemic, especially through internet marketplace and home delivery [23]: assuming that herbal supplement product prices remain the same or slightly increasing. Some sellers would share their profits to others by giving free products to help the population boost health immunity during Covid-19 pandemic, as pictured by the Herbal Jamu Association ("PPJAI") in Banyumas, Central Java [24]. As the demand for Jamu increases, government stakeholders started to encourage the promotion of Jamu as national brand, including marketing Fitofarmaka for Covid-19 treatment, as proposed by Budiman Gunawan, Chairman of the National Commission for Jamu Scientification [25].

## 6 Conclusion

This article has described the correlation between cognitive anchoring that influences herbal commodity inelastic demand, by setting perceived value of the transacted herbal commodity and Jamu, regardless efficacy for treating Covid-19 still debatable. The paper has explained the role of multiple middle-men advocating for the use of Jamu, which created the network dynamics and influencing the status quo structure that insisted on more use of Jamu for Covid-19 patient treatment.

## References

1. Andriati & Wahjudi (2016) Tingkat penerimaan penggunaan jamu sebagai alternatif penggunaan obat modern pada masyarakat ekonomi rendah-menengah dan atas. Masyarakat, Kebudayaan dan Politik 29(3):133–145
2. Beckert J (2010) How do field change? The Interrelations of Institutions, Network, and Cognition in the Dynamics of Markets. Sage Journals

3. Dinisari MC (2020) Kalangan Dokter Dukung Obat OMAI Masuk Program JKN. Posted: 21 December 2020 at 6.43pm. Downloaded: 2 May 2022 at 5.50pm. https://lifestyle.bisnis.com/read/20201221/106/1333879/kalangan-dokter-dukung-obat-omai-masuk-program-jkn
4. Yanwardhana E (2020) Gusur Obat China, Obat Made in RI Diusulkan Masuk Program JKN. Posted: 21 December 2020 at 8.21pm. Downloaded: 2 May 2022 at 5.48pm. https://www.cnbcindonesia.com/news/20201221142419-4-210615/gusur-obat-china-obat-made-in-ri-diusulkan-masuk-program-jkn
5. Simanjuntak MH (2021) BPOM Dorong Pengembangan Obat Herbal Terstandar dan Fitofarmaka. Posted: 13 October 2021 at 5.05pm. Downloaded: 2 May 2022 at 9.04pm. https://www.antaranews.com/berita/2456765/bpom-dorong-pengembangan-obat-herbal-terstandar-dan-fitofarmaka
6. Bempah RT (2020) Peneliti Gabungan IPB dan UI Temukan Senyawa Antivirus Corona. Posted: 1 April 2020 at 10.19pm. Downloaded: 2 May 2022 at 9.13pm. https://megapolitan.kompas.com/read/2020/04/01/22191801/peneliti-gabungan-ipb-dan-ui-temukan-senyawa-antivirus-corona
7. Nuraini D (2020) Jamur Cordyceps Antivirus Corona Minim Efek Samping. Posted: 1 July 2020 at 2.22pm. Downloaded: 2 May 2022 at 9.25pm. https://lifestyle.bisnis.com/read/20200701/106/1260110/jamur-cordyceps-antivirus-corona-minim-efek-samping
8. Asmara CG (2020) Jokowi: Sejak Ada Virus Corona Saya Minum Jamu 3 Kali Sehari. Posted: 12 Maret 2020 at 11.02am. Downloaded: 2 May 2022 at 9.30pm. https://www.cnbcindonesia.com/news/20200312105647-4-144295/jokowi-sejak-ada-virus-corona-saya-minum-jamu-3-kali-sehari
9. Putri BU (2020) Terawan Contohkan Ekstrak Temulawak Ikan Gabus Suplemen Covid-19. Posted: 14 July 2020 at 9.14pm. Download: 2 May 2022 at 9.38pm. https://nasional.tempo.co/read/1365252/terawan-contohkan-ekstrak-temulawak-ikan-gabus-suplemen-covid-19
10. Rosana FC (2020) Menteri Pertanian: Bulan Depan Kalung Antivirus Diproduksi Massal. Posted: 4 Juli 2020 at 7.33pm. Downloaded: 2 May 2022 at 9.46pm. https://bisnis.tempo.co/read/1361297/menteri-pertanian-bulan-depan-kalung-antivirus-diproduksi-massal
11. Dewi RK (2020) Professor Unair Klaim Ramuan Jahe Dapat Cegah Penularan Corona, Ini Penjelasannya. Posted: 20 February 2020 at 4.04pm. Downloaded: 2 May 2022 at 9.58pm. https://www.kompas.com/tren/read/2020/02/20/160437365/profesor-unair-klaim-ramuan-jahe-dapat-cegah-penularan-corona-ini?page=all
12. Winahyu AI (2020) Peneliti: Semakin Banyak Orang Minum Jamu Karena Covid-19. Posted: 20 Juli 2020 at 6.25pm. Download: 2 May 2022 at 10.25pm. https://mediaindonesia.com/humaniora/329999/peneliti-semakin-banyak-orang-minum-jamu-karena-covid-19
13. Rochim A (2020) DPR Minta Pemerintah Kampanyekan Bahan Tradisional Untuk Penangkal Covid-19. Posted: 30 September 2020 at 1.09am. Download: 2 May 2022 at 10.09pm. https://nasional.sindonews.com/read/180696/15/dpr-minta-pemerintah-kampanyekan-bahan-tradisional-untuk-penangkal-covid-19-1601395755
14. Maliana I (2020) Andre Rosiade Jelaskan Efek Jamu Herbavid-19 Pada Pasien Corona: Hari Ke-2 Membaik, Hari Ke-7 Sehat. Posted 3 May 2020 at 9.03pm. Download: 2 May 2022 at 10.35pm. https://www.tribunnews.com/nasional/2020/05/03/andre-rosiade-jelaskan-efek-jamu-herbavid-19-pada-pasien-corona-hari-ke-2-membaik-hari-ke-7-sehat
15. Nurfajriani R (2020) Novel Baswedan Bagi Tips Sembuh Covid-19, Salah Satunya Minum Campuran Minyak Kayu Putih. Posted: 11 September 2020 at 7.34am. Download: 2 May 2022 at 10.40pm. https://www.pikiran-rakyat.com/nasional/pr-01733704/novel-baswedan-bagi-tips-sembuh-covid-19-salah-satunya-minum-campuran-minyak-kayu-putih
16. Detikcom (2020) Laksma Suradi Klaim Punya Raman Anti Corona, Siap Diproduksi Massal. Posted: 27 April 2020 at 6.46pm. Download: 2 May 2022 at 10.45pm. https://news.detik.com/berita/d-4993418/laksma-suradi-klaim-punya-ramuan-anti-corona-siap-diproduksi-massal
17. Wuragil Z (2020) Jamu Cina Masuk RS COVID-19, Jamu Indonesia Minta izin Uji Klinis. Posted: 28 April 2020 at 1.25pm. Downloaded: 2 May 2022 at 10.52pm. https://tekno.tempo.co/read/1336460/jamu-cina-masuk-rs-covid-19-jamu-indonesia-minta-izin-uji-klinis/full&view=ok

18. Aryanto A (2020) 300 Pasien Covid-19 Sembuh dalam 3 Hari Berkat Obat Herbal Ini! Posted: 11 July 2020 at 9.30pm. Download: 2 May 2022 at 10.56pm. https://wartaekonomi.co.id/amp/read294247/300-pasien-covid-19-sembuh-dalam-3-hari-berkat-obat-herbal-ini
19. Buana G (2020) Peneliti NU Klaim Temukan Jamu Antivirus Korona. Posted: 14 May 2020 at 9.29pm. Download: 2 May 2022 at 11.06pm. https://mediaindonesia.com/humaniora/313084/peneliti-nu-klaim-temukan-jamu-antivirus-korona
20. Firdausya I (2020) Tangani Covid-19, Obat Tradisional Tak Dapat Gantikan Peran Vaksin. Posted: 5 August 2020 at 9.59pm. Download: 2 May 2022 at 11.12pm. https://mediaindonesia.com/humaniora/334280/tangani-covid-19obat-tradisional-tak-dapat-gantikan-peran-vaksin
21. Pebrianto F (2020) BPOM: Tidak Bisa Begitu Saja Klaim Obat Herbal Penangkal Covid-19. Posted: 10 August 2020 at 12.11pm. Download: 2 May 2022 at 11.16pm. https://bisnis.tempo.co/read/1374256/bpom-tidak-bisa-begitu-saja-klaim-obat-herbal-penangkal-covid-19/full&view=ok
22. Ramli RR (2020) Akibat Virus Corona, UKM Produsen Jamu Diuntungkan. Posted: 9 March 2020 at 5.46pm. Download: 3 May 2022 at 12.50pm. https://money.kompas.com/read/2020/03/09/174640726/akibat-virus-corona-ukm-produsen-jamu-diutungkan
23. Hakim L (2020) Dampak Corona, Perusahaan Jamu Ini Alami Lonjakan Permintaan. Posted: 24 May 2020 at 2.33pm. Download: 3 May 2022 at 12.17pm https://daerah.sindonews.com/read/44398/704/dampak-corona-perusahaan-jamu-ini-alami-lonjakan-permintaan-1590303952
24. Zain FM (2020) Cegah Virus Corona, Pengguna Jalan di Banyumas Dapat Jamu Gratis. Posted: 5 May 2020 at 4.23pm. Download: 3 May 2022 at 12.56pm. https://regional.kompas.com/read/2020/03/05/16234451/cegah-virus-corona-pengguna-jalan-di-banyumas-dapat-jamu-gratis?page=all
25. Kagama (2021) Kagama Open Kitchen 1: Kearifan Lokal dalam Olah Rempah dan Jamu. Posted: 20 March 2021 at 11.38pm. Download: 3 May 2022 at 1.07pm. https://kagama.id/kagama-open-kitchen-1-kearifan-lokal-dalam-olah-rempah-dan-jamu/
26. Saroh DN (2020) Tangani Covid-19, Pemerintah Dukung Produk Jamu dan OHT Jadi Fitofarmaka. Posted 11 July 2020 at 2.11pm. Download: 2 May 2022 at 11pm. https://www.jpnn.com/news/tangani-covid-19-pemerintah-dukung-produk-jamu-dan-oht-jadi-fiofarmaka?page=2

# Indigenous People in the Global Pandemic: Responses of Various *Adat* Communities in Indonesia During COVID-19 Pandemic

**Irin Oktafiani and Herry Jogaswara**

**Abstract** The transmission of COVID-19 has become a global pandemic in 2020. Communities and nations tried their best to cope with this virus, including indigenous people in Indonesia, who are considered more vulnerable than others. However, some indigenous people have only recorded a minimum of zero cases and have successfully protected their members from the virus. This article describes and analyses the responses of some indigenous people in Indonesia during the COVID-19 pandemic. We found that indigenous people can apply the local lockdown effectively and have some local knowledge when responding to the global pandemic. One of which is *besesandingon* to keep a distance from the seriously ill patients in the community of Orang Rimba in the Province of Jambi. However, in order to transfer the sense of crisis, the activists and people who care need a specific strategy to translate the situation to the indigenous people in Indonesia. Therefore, we are concerned that the government needs to learn from the indigenous people's local wisdom and create a specific regulation on how to transmit such an urgent situation but still be understood by the indigenous people.

**Keywords** Indigenous people · Indonesia · COVID-19 · Pandemic

## 1 Introduction

As this paper explains, there are more than one million people in Indonesia who have tested positive for COVID-19. The number of COVID-19 patients in Indonesia has been increasing since early February 2020 [1]. The first case of COVID-19 in Indonesia started at a dance club in South Jakarta. The virus was transmitted,

I. Oktafiani (✉)
Research center for Population, National Research and Innovation Agency, Jakarta, Indonesia
e-mail: irin.oktafiani@gmail.com

H. Jogaswara
Archaeology, Language, and Letters Research Organization, National Research and Innovation Agency, Jakarta, Indonesia





Nawawi et al. (eds.), *Managing Disruption and Developing Resilience for a Better Southeast Asia*, Springer Proceedings in Humanities and Social Sciences,
https://doi.org/10.1007/978-981-96-2116-3_33

suspiciously, from Japanese tourists who came to the event to a dancer who worked there. Another person who got infected too was her mother, and they got medical treatment and isolation in the Sulianti Saroso Infection Center Hospital (Rumah Sakit Pusat Infeksi Sulianti Saroso). Since the first case, the number of positive cases has been rising, and Indonesia has become the highest country in Southeast Asia with COVID-19 positive cases.

Day by day, the number of people with COVID-19 is increasing, and the government announced a large-scale social restriction. The regulation was adopted since the central government did not want to apply a national lockdown like in other countries. Each regional government was accountable for putting their people in order, and consequently, the tension was quite different depending on the regional order. The cities in Jabodetabek became stricter in applying the social restrictions than the others because their COVID-19 cases were higher than the others. However, the decision is somewhat wrong because the sense of crisis and the need to obey the social restrictions were not well socialised all over the country. The COVID-19 seemed to be just a threat to the townspeople, outweighing the villagers.

Furthermore, the effect of the COVID-19 pandemic in Indonesia was like a domino effect. The pandemic has successfully forced the government to make some mobility restrictions and also some business sectors were stuck because they could work normally. The manufacturing and tourism sectors lost their charm since the pandemic, and consequently, many people lost their jobs. There was a lot of unemployment in the cities, so they tried to return back to their village and to bet their luck. This kind of situation made the COVID-19 virus spread widely among the villagers, while they were not aware enough of the health protocol and the health facilities were very insufficient. The COVID-19 virus then became a national problem in Indonesia. Citizens in villages and cities are at risk of this novel virus. In addition to that, the resilience of the people varies depending on the situation of the communities, their ages, and the geographical landscape. The fact that Indonesia has a wide variation of conditions led this paper to find how the indigenous people responded to the COVID-19 transmission. In particular, we argue that indigenous people need a special treat in order to preserve their uniqueness, culture, and value.

Relating to the indigenous people, there is a report from Cultural Survival, a global civil society organisation (CSO) that has been advocating for indigenous people since 1972. The Cultural Society has an overall picture of the communities. First and foremost, there are many members of the indigenous people who make some smoke as part of their ritual and for food preparation. However, the smoke has a negative impact on their respiratory systems. The second is the limitation on access to medical facilities because of the geographic situation or because they live in a remote area. The third issue is the difficulty in obtaining safe drinking water and sanitation facilities. The fourth is the indigenous people living in the communal space so that it is difficult to apply social or physical distance. Lastly, it is very challenging to spread medical information to indigenous people because the information does not come in their language. So, they are struggling to know its meaning [2]. Furthermore, the indigenous people who live near mines are intensively contacting the outsiders.

Also, for some, their region becomes a tourist destination, making the indigenous people at risk of COVID-19.

Indigenous people around the world are facing a risk amid COVID-19, as some communities in Indonesia are. The lack of medical facilities in remote areas has become one of the problems. For example, there is no pulmonologist in the Mentawai Islands district, even more so in Enggano, where only a part of the sub-district is in North Bengkulu. The condition might be worse in the remote areas of Papua. However, the risk comes from the social and physical contact with the migrants, mining workers, or other manufacturers' workers and tourists. Furthermore, the tradition of the communities and the sanitation issues have put them in double jeopardy, but there is no single regulation focused on the condition of indigenous people itself.

As mentioned above, the Indonesian government does not take any official measures to keep the indigenous people safe, but there are some social movements helping them to face this situation. On the national level, some CSOs are raising the issue actively. The General Secretary of the Indigenous Peoples' Alliance of the Archipelago or Aliansi Masyarakat Adat Nusantara (AMAN) has released a statement about whatever should be done by the indigenous people facing the pandemic. On the other hand, the AMAN special task force for COVID-19 had already worked in the various regions of indigenous people nationally. On the community level, we found that there are some communities which are locking down their areas before the Pembatasan Sosial Berskala Besar (PSBB) or Large Social Restriction is officially applied in Indonesia. One of which is kasepuhan Cipta Gelar. The community has been officially closing its area to outsiders since March 16th, 2020. Furthermore, the AMAN task force in Enggano asked the government of North Bengkulu to close passenger access to the island in order to avoid the COVID-19 transmission there. Apart from that, it is reported by AMAN that some communities held some rituals to avoid the illness entering their areas. The indigenous people already sense the COVID-19 threat.

This paper describes the actual condition of some indigenous people and analyses the way they understand the COVID-19 pandemic and how they cope with the situation by applying their local values. However, the COVID-19 pandemic is a special condition that everyone is new to, so this paper will analyse what the government should do to give the right information and to raise awareness in the communities.

## 2 Methodology

This article is based on our research from May until June 2020 about the COVID-19 pandemic's effects on indigenous people in Indonesia. Due to the limitations amid the pandemic, our research is conducted by virtual meeting with the Zoom meeting application. We arranged two virtual focus group discussions (FGD) to gain an understanding of the existing condition of indigenous people in the COVID-19 pandemic. We wanted to know if indigenous people activists had any additional information to share about current regulations and what the government should do during this pandemic. The first virtual FGD was held on May 14th, 2020, and we focused on finding the perspective of some human rights and indigenous activists about the COVID-19 pandemic's impact on the indigenous people. For the first step, we invited four informants. There were two representatives of the Indigenous Peoples' Alliance of the Archipelago or Aliansi Masyarakat Adat Nusantara (AMAN), a male activist from the centre of Adat Land studies, and a female commissioner from the National Committee of Human Rights/Komisi Nasional Hak Asasi Manusia (Komnas HAM). From this discussion, we got some information about various activities from AMAN representatives in some regions in Indonesia, and we learned about the indigenous peoples' vulnerability and strength amid the COVID-19 pandemic.

Then, we held the second forum to learn more about the strength and resilience of indigenous people during the pandemic on May 29th, 2020. In the second discussion, we invited five people as the representatives of some indigenous peoples' communities in Indonesia. The discussants were a male university student as the representative of Orang Rimba in Jambi, a female activist from Sumba, a female AMAN's activist representing the Dayak ethnic group in West Kutai, East Kalimantan, a male local leader representative of Banua Lemo indigenous people, South Sulawesi, and a male local leader representative of Kei Island, Maluku. From this meeting, we knew that some indigenous people have already done some anticipatory acts to prevent COVID-19 spread into their areas. One of which is the local knowledge, called besesandingon, and the evaporation health treatment called ditongkok. They already have the local knowledge to interpret the pandemic and how to act towards it. Meanwhile, from those discussions, we found that there are some people who do not know about the COVID-19 risk, and some of them do not believe the government's regulation to prevent the COVID-19 spread optimally.

## 3 Indigenous People During the COVID-19 Pandemic

Since the first COVID-19 case occurred in Depok, West Java, the number of people with COVID-19 has been increasing in Indonesia, and the government created a national special task force for COVID-19 or Gugus Tugas COVID-19, four days after COVID-19 was announced by WHO as a pandemic situation. This ad-hoc committee is derived from the National Board of Disaster Management and is responsible for spreading the official news from the government to suppress the transmission of corona. The first information from the national special task force was about the pandemic situation and 3M medical protocol.

Given the WHO's declaration of a pandemic, the situation gradually evolved. People were more cognisant of the requirement to adhere to the 3M medical protocol. Some offices permit their employees to conduct virtual meetings and work from home. At this time, people spent the majority of their time at home, wore masks whenever they went outside, and avoided gatherings. In addition, hand sanitiser or temporary hand washing facilities are available in some stores or at the market's entrance. Some homes even provided a simple hand washing station consisting of a small plastic bucket and liquid soap in front of their homes. People are simple to locate or to become the soap police for. The good situation, however, will not last forever due to this medical protocol. A period of mask and hand sanitiser scarcity existed. According to the news, an evil person was hoarding stocks and selling them at exorbitant prices. Also, the second evil person attempted to sell recycled medical masks of questionable cleanliness.

Moreover, the financial situation was deteriorating daily, and virtually every industry was affected. First, the tourism industry was severely affected, with Bali Island suffering the most. This location, which was once the first choice for international tourists, became extremely quiet and temporarily lost its tourist soul. The second is from the manufacturing sector, as they were unable to export their goods to countries such as China, which effectively shut down the nation at the time. As people's purchasing power decreased, other industries, such as entertainment and food and beverages, struggled to survive, resulting in some job losses. Consequently, people attempted to live more economically during this period of hardship. Even though the situation was deteriorating, not everyone had the luxury of staying at home and working remotely. Some people are still required to work outside, and some of them must also use public transportation, making it nearly impossible to travel the necessary distance. They were unable to work from home because they feared losing their jobs like the others.

As announced by the COVID-19 special task force, the initial policy of the Indonesian government was not to secure the national border but rather to implement PSBB (pembatasan sosial berskala besar or large-scale social restriction). Foreigners were welcome to visit Indonesia for any reason. The purpose of this regulation was to ensure normal investment and business operations in Indonesia. On the social level, there was no clear sanction or fine for every medical protocol violation. People without masks in public received only a verbal warning, and not every office or 50% of attendees were granted work from home on the same day. It was easy to find people without masks in the traditional market, where only a few officers were present. Obviously, this circumstance increases the incidence of COVID-19 each day. Some academics and activists believed that the government failed to make the public aware of the COVID-19 crisis.

There is a segment of the population in Jakarta that believes that COVID-19 is an actual pandemic. At the onset of the pandemic, it was believed that wealthy individuals were the source of COVID-19. This is due to the fact that the initial contact was an individual who works with foreigners. In addition, some people believe that the virus originated in other countries; therefore, only wealthy Indonesians who can travel abroad could have brought the virus into Indonesia. However, when the PSBB was implemented, working-class people did not appear to have the option to work from home, and some of them believed that the virus would only affect those who travelled abroad. The traditional market functioned normally, as crowded as usual, until official security arrived to disperse it. They stated that if they did not go to market, they would be unable to sell or purchase the necessary items. On the other hand, some individuals had the luxury of working from home and purchasing their goods via an online shopping platform. As a result, people's perceptions of the

COVID-19 pandemic varied, as their backgrounds and opportunities varied. Then, how about the situation of the indigenous people?

First of all, we have to make a clear definition of the indigenous people—what it is and who they are. Regardless of all the conceptual meanings to define indigenous people in Indonesia, the author used the definition of indigenous people that was defined by Kingsburry [3] as the people or community that already inhabited a region before it was invaded by the migrants (mostly colonialists in history). Although the term "indigenous" brings the painful memory of colonialism and alienism, in fact, many Asian countries do recognise this term to separate the local (native) with the migrants. As a result, even if the term "indigenous" is coined to protect native rights, discrimination against them persists, even in the face of a pandemic.

Due to the limited access during the pandemic, we tried to map the risk of COVID-19 to indigenous people nationally by comparing official data from BNPB, or Indonesian National Board for Disaster Management, and BRWA, or registration board for indigenous land. The BNPB publishes updated data on districts that are threatened by COVID-19 on a regular basis. However, the data only provided the level of risk that the regions had to face, and there was no specific detail that the place was inhabited by indigenous people. Meanwhile, BRWA provides registered land for indigenous people. As a result, we used those data to map the regions of indigenous people that are at medium and high risk of COVID-19. The result is from 716 registered indigenous people in Indonesia. There are 255 regions matched with BNPB's data where the district name is registered nationally. Then, from the 255 regions, half of them were categorised as COVID-19 low-level risk, and 40% of them were medium risk (see Fig. 1).

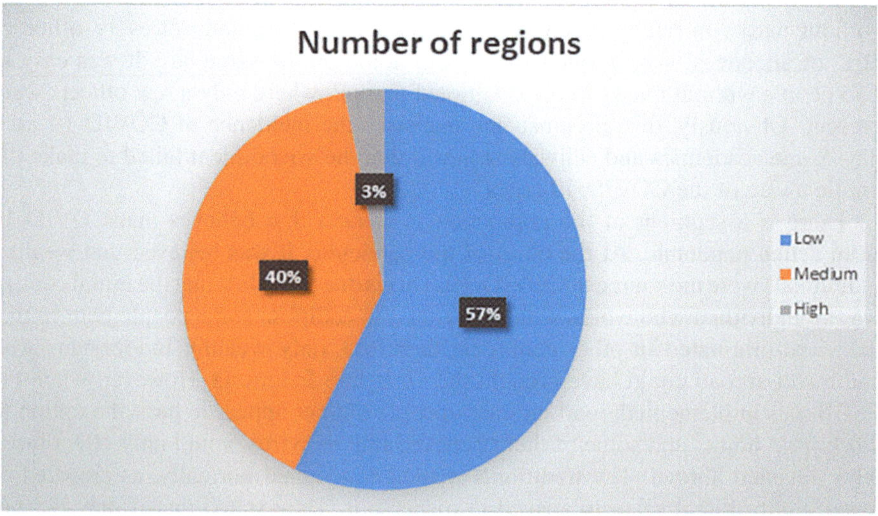


**Fig. 1** Regions in Indonesia with different risk possibilities (*Source* Researcher, 2020)

It can be seen from the data that almost half of indigenous people face the risk of a pandemic. All indigenous people share the same risk as all other people in Indonesia.

At the beginning of the pandemic, many non-profit organisations and government institutions tried to share and raise awareness about health protocols, one of which is AMAN. AMAN tried their best to teach and remind the people in remote areas about 3M. They helped the indigenous people produce and distribute masks and soaps. Furthermore, they remind people to avoid gatherings, some of which were suggested to stop holding rituals or ceremonies. The hefty indigenous people accepted the 3M protocol very well and they obeyed it day by day.

However, there was a stumbling block along the way. Some communities faced the problem of translating the health protocol to the elderly. The youngsters absorbed the information fast, but the older generation somehow found it difficult to know the purpose of health protocol, especially the regulation to stay away from gathering. The elderly still have a communal mindset and like to share and discuss everything in groups. Even more, they love to hold ceremonies that invite a wave of people. Some people in AMAN admitted that it was a little difficult at the moment, but as the day went on, the elderly slowly accepted why they had to stay away from the crowds.

## 4 Discussion

### *4.1 Indigenous People and Vulnerabilities*

Indigenous people in Indonesia face a variety of challenges, making many of them vulnerable to pandemics. Annie Wilkinson and contributors [4] stated that there are various kinds of vulnerabilities for people in urban settlements during COVID-19 pandemics, particularly in the lower- and middle-income countries (LMIC), such as (1) epidemiological vulnerability, (2) transmission vulnerability, (3) health system vulnerability, and (4) vulnerability to control measures. Those problems are related to the limited number of people and the geographical conditions in which they live. Indigenous people usually live in the forest and remote places. This condition makes many of them difficult to access any kind of facilities like education and healthcare services. Also, small numbers in the community make strong bonds within each other, and they have close contact to communicate and gather in several situations. Actually, the situation is ideal and good for them as long as they have sufficient food stock and live in a supportive environment, which they get mainly from the forest. Unfortunately, indigenous people have to face another problem. Minne Degawan [5] added that there is an issue of deforestation. For example, the indigenous people in Northern Thailand face fire ravaging and deforestation even in the period of the COVID-19 pandemic. Those problems endangered their living space, food supply, and clean water. According to BNPB, in 2019, it was found that around 1.6 million hectares of land were on fire and the number decreased to 300,000 hectares in 2020 and 527,000 hectares in 2021. Although the number has decreased yearly, the indigenous people are still in jeopardy. It comes from the pandemic situation. Hence, in the time of the COVID-19 pandemic, indigenous people are living in more dangerous situations than before.

From the problems mentioned, it can be said that indigenous people are vulnerable, especially in a pandemic situation. In general, there are, at least, three aspects to be concerned about: (1) access to healthcare facilities; (2) sufficient food and safe drinking water; and (3) a good understanding of COVID-19 health protocol. As mentioned earlier, indigenous people live in remote areas with limited access to proper health facilities. Some villages in Indonesia only have extended community health centres, which have limited health resources and facilities. The main health centre nearby or hospital can be found at the sub-district level or higher. In addition to that, some villages in Indonesia are separated by the sea or river. For example, Oktafiani, Suyadnya, and Triyono (2019) mentioned that people in Liki Island in the province of Papua have to travel around one hour to get to the main health centre or hospital in SARMI regency by boat. The people only have sub-health centre facilities on the island and they are served by one midwife and one nurse. They can only treat simple illnesses with limited facilities, and for acute illnesses requiring special treatment, they will make an appointment with the main health centre in SARMI. The distance becomes a problem in itself, not to mention the geographical condition. They have to sail for one hour in the Pacific Ocean, and it is too dangerous if there is an emergency situation.

Furthermore, there should be enough food and drinkable water for all indigenous people. Some indigenous people rely on the forest for their livelihoods. They believe that forests will supply enough food for them. Also, some people in the communities are farming and raising some chickens or cattle. Meanwhile, the others still hunt and depend on what they can catch in the forest or sea. Some communities, like Baduy and Kasepuhan in Southern Banten, have a settled farming and food supply mechanism, while others do not.

## *4.2 Indigenous People Capabilities and the Government Response*

Some indigenous people have their own coping strategy from the very beginning of the COVID-19 spreading in Indonesia. Through the discussion, we found that in general, the first priority from them is to limit mobility, particularly outside the village. Many of them can do lockdown that mostly to prevent the outsider to enter their own territory. They did it by using a modest system like guarding the border in shift or taking a big barrier on the village border. The second thing that became their coping strategy was to keep the food stock. The indigenous people knew that the food became the priority to overcome the situation. In Banualemo, South Sulawesi, the community had maintained the sago and corn to fulfil the people's needs. Furthermore, for some communities, like Dayak in West Kutai, Melak, they were even raising the chicken and catfish for village food stocks. Therefore, it seemed at the very first start that they secured the basic needs to overcome the crisis.

Without dismissing the high risk of COVID-19 to the indigenous people, the authors of this study conclude that each indigenous people has its own understanding of each disease, such as the Orang Rimba's *besesandingon*, in order to limit the distance between a sick person and the rest of the community. The message is straightforward: if a person contracts an infectious disease, he or she must withdraw from the community. For them, every disease is contagious, and they must maintain a safe distance of 100–200 m [6]. Surprisingly, the entire world employs a similar method to prevent the spread of COVID-19: maintaining a safe distance of 1–2 m. In fact, based on their knowledge, it is evident that the indigenous people already have a fixed cosmology to explain the illness. Consequently, the government could utilise the indigenous people's knowledge and interpretation to create more effective regulations in response to the pandemic.

There are various strategies to prevent COVID-19. Several stories came from West Kutai and South Sulawesi which had implemented "lockdown" and successfully prevented COVID-19 in those areas, emerge lockdown was not their main priority. They tried to adapt with the difficult situation by producing their own food during lockdown. The effort was keeping food stock through raising chicken, catfish in ponds, harvesting sago, planting corn, and basic staple foods. Additionally, they also planted herbs and medicinal plants as the first aid for the people within the community. Eventually, COVID-19 pandemic was also give lesson to be learned importance of traditional medicine through using medicinal plants for local garden.

Furthermore, the COVID-19 pandemics have changed and exposed the various pandemic awareness and preparedness levels in many countries. The Global Health Security Index noted in 2020 that the United States and the UK marked the highest rank for pandemic preparedness level, while countries in Latin America and Asia were in the middle level and African countries in the bottom [7]. However, this statement is somewhat correct in Indonesia from the national perspective. Before the official statement of COVID-19 as a world pandemic, Indonesia's government believed that its people were strong enough to face COVID. On February 17th, 2020, Indonesian president Joko Widodo tweeted about the coronavirus as the moment to give tourism incentive to develop the tourism industry. Furthermore, he stated that jamu (Indonesian's traditional herbal drink) is effective to prevent the virus after the first COVID patient had recovered from it by consuming jamu. In May 2020 [8], the Indonesian security minister, Mochamad Mahfud M.D., said that "Corona is like your wife; if you try to control it, then you realise that you can, then you learn to live with it." His statement went viral and caused serious tensions among people, because it showed how the government's side saw the pandemic as a non-serious thing and had a misogynist tendency. In that sense, governments that seem too slow to impose public health movement restrictions or are too quick to relax them have been accused of callousness, it is like "playing roulette with the public's lives" [9].

Thus, it can be seen that the government of Indonesia was not aware enough of the COVID-19 pandemic.

From the FGD, the authors found that each community of indigenous people had their own interpretation of the COVID-19 pandemic. Firstly, they understood that COVID-19 is a serious disease that can be problematic for them. Although they already interpreted COVID-19 as a serious disease, they already had certain knowledge to overcome the situation. For the Orang Rimba, the COVID-19 pandemic was treated like an infectious disease, and they did their best to deal with it. On the other hand, the indigenous Dayak Melak tried to make sure they had enough food, and they locked down their area to stop COVID-19 from getting in. Each of them had an exact strategy because they knew what their people needed at that time. Therefore, the indigenous people can protect their people from COVID-19 using their own knowledge.

In fact, unfortunately, the government seemed slow to spread the sense of crisis at the beginning of the COVID-19 pandemic. The evidence has shown that at the beginning of a pandemic, the government tried to create a calm environment that was even dangerous for all citizens. It was a different story of what the indigenous people did since the beginning of the pandemic. As Pipi [10] witnessed from Dayak Melak, they tried to translate the meaning of the COVID-19 pandemic into their local term and they ensured the elderly on how to obey all the regulations regarding limiting the COVID-19 spread. Contrary to this, at the beginning of the pandemic, the government was busy giving statements that had no relation to handling the situation.

## 5 Conclusion

The COVID-19 pandemic provided valuable insights into the capacity of indigenous people to confront the problem. In the early stages of the pandemic, the government did not provide sufficient treatment for the indigenous population. On the other hand, some local knowledge is utilised by communities to prevent pandemics. On the other hand, it is evident that the Indonesian government requires a more effective coping strategy in order to anticipate future pandemics, and they can learn from the indigenous people. Even though there were numerous risks associated with their daily lives, it has been demonstrated that some indigenous people had already developed effective coping mechanisms.

## References


1. *kompas.com* Homepage. https://nasional.kompas.com/read/2021/02/16/16352281/update-tambah-10029-kasus-covid-19-indonesia-kini-1233959-orang?page=all, last accessed 2021/02/17
2. https://www.culturalsurvival.org/news/indigenous-communities-adjust-new-normal-during-covid-19-pandemic, last accessed 2020/5/5
3. Kingsburry B (1998) Indigenous peoples, in International law: a constructivist approach to the Asian controversy. Am J Intern Law 92(3):414–457
4. Wilkinson, Annie, contributors (2020) Local response in health emergencies: key considerations for addressing the COVID-19 pandemic in informal urban settlements. Environ Urban 32(2):503–522
5. Degawan Minnie (2020) Vulnerable yet resilient. In: Agnès Bardon, Katerina Markelova, Chen Xiaorong (eds.) The UNESCO Courier, pp 29–31. UNESCO
6. Tampung M (n.d) Online interview, Unpublished, 30 May 2020
7. Khoo Su-ming (2021) COVID- 19 Pandemic Ignorance and the 'Worlds' of Development. In: Pádraig Carmody, Gerard McCann, Clodagh Colleran and Ciara O'Halloran (eds.) COVID- 19 in the Global South: Impacts and Responses, pp. 7–16. Bristol University Press, Great Britain
8. Thejakartapost.com Homepage. https://www.thejakartapost.com/news/2020/05/28/corona-is-like-your-wife-minister-mahfud-slammed-for-sexist-comment.html, last accessed 2020/06/30
9. Horton R (2020) 'The UK government—Matt Hancock and Boris Johnson—claim they are following the science'. Twitter, https://twitter.com/richardhorton1/ status/1237282270685380613, last accessed 2020/03/10
10. Supeni Pipi (n.d) Online interview, Unpublished, 30 May 2020

# The Characteristics of Pregnant Women and Contributing Factors to Pregnancy During COVID-19 Pandemic in Deli Serdang, North Sumatera

**Evalina Franciska Hutasoit and Muhammad Ancha Sitorus**

**Abstract** The COVID-19 pandemic, which is spreading rapidly throughout the world, is labeled as a public health emergency of international concern. Pregnant women are one of the groups that are vulnerable to COVID-19 infection due to the physiological changes they experience during pregnancy. During the COVID-19 pandemic, prevention efforts included a limitation to routine health services such as maternal health, and, therefore, a campaign regarding pregnancy prevention was also implemented. This study aims to determine the characteristics of mothers who experience pregnancy during the pandemic and examine contributing factors related to pregnancy. This study implemented a cross-sectional design. Data collection was performed in November 2020 using a questionnaire in Sub-District Sunggal and Sub-District Hamparan Perak. The number of respondents was 156 pregnant women who were taken using a simple random sampling method. Data were analyzed using multiple logistic regression with $\alpha = 0.05$. The result showed that 60.9% of women had intended pregnancies. The logistic regression analysis showed that women who have two or fewer children ($p < 0.05$), women who were married for the first time at 21 years or older ($p < 0.05$), women with a partner educated primary or lower ($p < 0.05$), and women who did not use any contraception ($p < 0.05$) are significantly related to intending pregnancies during COVID-19 pandemic. The study concluded that factors associated with getting pregnant during COVID-19 are having two children, age at first marriage $\geq$21 years old, married partner with primary education, and not using contraceptives.

**Keywords** Age at marriage · COVID-19 · Contraception · Intended pregnancy · Pregnancy

---

E. F. Hutasoit (✉)
National Research and Innovation Agency, North Sumatera, Indonesia
e-mail: eval001@brin.go.id

M. A. Sitorus
National Population and Family Planning Board, North Sumatera, Indonesia


Nawawi et al. (eds.), *Managing Disruption and Developing Resilience for a Better Southeast Asia*, Springer Proceedings in Humanities and Social Sciences,
https://doi.org/10.1007/978-981-96-2116-3_34

# 1 Introduction

The novel Coronavirus infection, first found in Wuhan in December 2019, known as COVID-19, has spread rapidly, and by The World Health Organization, was announced as a public health emergency of international concern [1]. As generally happens during times of crisis, women are included in a population group that is vulnerable to adverse impacts of disease outbreaks as women play the vital role of unpaid workers as the majority of caretakers looking after other household members [2]. Among the vulnerable group, pregnant women and their fetuses are also the most at risk during a disease outbreak [2–4] because women who experience pregnancy are generally more susceptible to disease and the adverse effects of infection. This may occur due to the physiological changes in women during pregnancy [3].

Studies over the decades have repeatedly shown that pregnant women experienced disproportionate morbidity and mortality caused by the adverse effect of infection, particularly infectious diseases that develop various symptoms in the respiratory tract, such as during the 1989 influenza [3, 5]. A similar pattern was shown during the H1N1 influenza pandemic, which resulted in increased hospitalization and death in pregnant women compared to women who were not pregnant [6, 7]. Furthermore, comparable patterns emerge in the COVID-19 outbreaks where the infectious disease attacks the respiratory system, increasing the susceptibility of pregnant women [8].

Indonesia reports two positive COVID-19 cases for the first time in March 2020 [9]. Based on the data obtained by an official report from the COVID task force team in Indonesia, on 31 March 2020, there were 1.528 positive confirmed cases of COVID-19 and 136 deaths due to COVID-19 [10]. To prevent the spread of a wider pandemic, the Indonesian government has designated COVID-19 as a national disaster [11]. Furthermore, Government Regulation No. 21 of 2020 [12] was implemented, where prevention and control measures were performed through social restrictions, primarily aimed at vulnerable population groups, including pregnant women. The community is facing limited information about COVID-19, including data on COVID-19-positive cases among pregnant women in Indonesia [9]. Moreover, the implementation of the government policy limiting almost all routine community services and the lack of information also causes anxiety among pregnant women, so they delay pregnancy checks [13, 14].

Research by Davis-Floyd [15] found that COVID-19 has changed pregnant women's and health practitioners' behavior in carrying out care practices, including using protective equipment (masks and gloves), reducing in-person visits, and increasing virtual prenatal and postpartum visits. Meanwhile, several studies indicated that the COVID-19 pandemic has resulted in a change in the fertility plans, including but not limited to contraceptive use, the desire to have children, the desire for parenthood, and preference for healthcare provision [16–20]. The studies further indicate that the shift in the fertility plan caused by the COVID-19 pandemic occurred on various scales, with about 18% in Australia, 37% in Italy, and 40% of women in the United States changing their plan to become pregnant [17–19]. While several women wanted more children sooner than planned before the pandemic, most studies found that the COVID-19 outbreak was associated with a decline in intention to get pregnant.

During the COVID-19 pandemic, several studies regarding pregnancy have been conducted in North Sumatera and Indonesia, consisting of study of the social distancing policy [9], knowledge and behavior in the COVID-19 prevention [21–23], provision of healthcare and contraception during the pandemic [13, 24], as well as the mental health of pregnant women [25]. Before the pandemic, unwanted pregnancies in Indonesia ranged between 14 and 19% [26, 27]. The limitation of essential health services and maternal and child health services including contraceptive services during the COVID-19 pandemic [14, 24] will likely increase unintended pregnancies. Knowing the risk of the adverse effects of infection for pregnancy during the pandemic, it is necessary to research the incidence of pregnancy and the pregnancy intention during the COVID-19 pandemic. Although a study of the prevalence of pregnancy during pandemic has been conducted in Pekanbaru [28], there is still room for additional information regarding the contributing factors associated with pregnancy intention with a larger sample size and broader analysis. This study aims to determine the characteristics of mothers who experience pregnancy during the COVID-19 pandemic and examine contributing factors related to that in Deli Serdang, North Sumatera Province.

## 2 Methods

This study implemented a cross-sectional design using primary source data. Data collection was performed in November 2020 using a questionnaire in Sub-District Sunggal and Sub-District Hamparan Perak, Deli Serdang Regency. The number of respondents was 156 pregnant women, taken using a simple random sampling method. All the pregnant women who participated in the study gave their consent before the interviews, and the health protocol (using a face mask, 2-m distance, and no physical contact) was applied during the interview.

The dependent variable of this study was intended pregnancy. Intended pregnancy was defined as the pregnancy intended and wanted to happen at that time. In contrast, unintended pregnancy was defined as a pregnancy that was wanted later or unwanted because the participants did not want to have more children. The independent variables of this study were age, age at first marriage, education, employment, household income, health insurance, number of children desired, current number of children, modern contraceptive use, knowledge of delaying pregnancy during the pandemic, spouse age, and spouse education.

Age was classified into age ideal for pregnancy (21–35 years old) and unideal (20 years or less and 36 years or older). Age at first marriage was divided into ideal (21 years or more) and unideal (20 years or less). Education was classified into primary education (no education or educated until primary school) and secondary education (high school and vocational college/university). Modern contraceptive use was divided into not using modern contraception methods before pregnancy and using other methods before pregnancy. The number of children and the number of children desired were categorized as more than two and two or less. Household income was divided based on the regional minimum wage regulated by the government.

## 3 Data Analysis

Participants' characteristics were displayed descriptively using frequency and percentage. Bivariate associations between dependent and independent variables were assessed using simple logistic regression analysis. The association between a sociodemographic variable and pregnancy intention was shown by the proportion of intended pregnancy, odds ratio, and p-value. A significant association was determined if a p-value was < 0.05. Each independent variable associated with the dependent variable from the bivariate analysis was put into multivariate analysis. Multiple regression analysis was performed to test the effect of independent variables on pregnancy intention, and a significant association was determined if the p-value was <0.05.

## 4 Results

Table 1 shows the characteristics of participants based on the sociodemographic. The total number of participants in this study was 156. Only 60.9% were reported to have intended pregnancy during the COVID-19 pandemic, while 30.1% reported unintended pregnancy. Around 80% of the pregnant women fell within the ideal age for pregnancy (21–35 years) and were having two children or less. The number of children desired is almost equal, with 50.6% of women who reported wanting to have two or fewer children. One in two pregnant women fell in the third trimester, while 4 of 5 pregnant women received antenatal care (ANC) from midwives. While all 100% of spouses were working, only 20% of the pregnant women were working. Most participants have a household income under the regional minimum wage with a 3 million monthly income. Half of the participants and their spouses have had secondary education, with 3% of the pregnant women and spouses having no education. All 100% of the participants commuted using a personal vehicle.

Table 2 describes the pregnant woman's characteristics based on pregnancy intention (intended or unintended). The proportion of intended pregnancy was slightly higher among women whose age is ideal for pregnancy (61.1%) than those who are too young or too old to get pregnant (60%). Women who married at 21 years or older also had a higher proportion of intended pregnancy (68.5) than those who married at a younger age (50.7%). The proportion of intended pregnancy was higher among participants who attained secondary education or above (65.6%) compared to women of lower school attainment (55%). Still, the proportion was lower in women

**Table 1** Characteristics of the participants

| Variable | Frequency (f) | Percentage (%) |
|---|---|---|
| **Pregnancy intention** | | |
| Intended pregnancy | 95 | 60.9 |
| Unintended pregnancy | 61 | 39.1 |
| **Age** | | |
| ≤20 | 6 | 3.8 |
| 21–35 | 126 | 80.8 |
| ≥36 | 24 | 15.4 |
| **Age at first marriage** | | |
| ≤20 | 67 | 42.9 |
| ≥21 | 89 | 57.1 |
| **Education** | | |
| No education | 6 | 3.8 |
| Primary education | 53 | 34.0 |
| High school/higher education | 97 | 62.1 |
| **Employment** | | |
| Working | 32 | 20.5 |
| Housewife | 124 | 79.5 |
| **Health insurance** | | |
| Yes | 106 | 67.9 |
| No | 50 | 32.1 |
| **Number of children** | | |
| ≤2 | 132 | 84.6 |
| > 2 | 24 | 15.4 |
| **Term of pregnancy** | | |
| trimester 1 | 17 | 10.9 |
| trimester 2 | 61 | 39.1 |
| trimester 3 | 78 | 50.0 |
| **Knowledge of delaying pregnancy** | | |
| Yes | 50 | 32.1 |
| No | 106 | 67.9 |
| **Place of ANC** | | |
| Obstetrician | 6 | 3.8 |
| Midwives | 130 | 83.3 |
| Primary healthcare | 13 | 8.3 |
| Hospital | 7 | 4.5 |
| **Desired children** | | |
| ≤2 | 79 | 50.6 |
| > 2 | 77 | 49.4 |

(continued)

**Table 1** (continued)

| Variable | Frequency (f) | Percentage (%) |
|---|---|---|
| **Modern contraceptive use** | | |
| Yes | 59 | 37.8 |
| No | 97 | 62.2 |
| **Household income** | | |
| ≤3.000.000 | 124 | 79.5 |
| > 3.000.000 | 32 | 20.5 |
| **Spouse age** | | |
| ≤35 | 98 | 62.8 |
| ≥36 | 58 | 37.2 |
| **Spouse employment** | | |
| Working | 156 | 100 |
| Not working | 0 | 0 |
| **Spouse education** | | |
| No education | 5 | 3.2 |
| Primary education | 51 | 32.7 |
| High school/higher education | 100 | 64.1 |
| **Mode of transportation** | | |
| Public transport | 0 | 0 |
| Personal vehicle | 156 | 100 |

who had spouses educated with secondary education (54.5%) compared to 71.9% among women who had a spouse of lower education.

The proportion of intended pregnancy during the pandemic was lower among working women (46.9%) compared to housewives (64.5%). Participants who use modern contraception before pregnancy also had a lower proportion of intended pregnancy (47.5%) than participants who did not use any modern contraception methods (69.1%). Furthermore, women with a spouse aged equal to 36 years or older had a lower proportion of intended pregnancy (53.45) than women with a younger spouse (65.3%).

Meanwhile, participants with health insurance had a higher proportion of intending pregnancy (66%) than those without health insurance (50%). While the proportion of intended pregnancy is doubled in women who have two or fewer children (65.2%) compared to 36.5% for women who had more than three children, the proportion of intended pregnancy was higher among women who stated that their desired number of children was more than two children (64.9%) compared to women who wanted less or equal to two children (57%). The proportion of intended pregnancy was higher in women who reported not knowing the program for delaying pregnancy during a pandemic (63.2%) than in women who reported knowing the program (56.3%). Also, women with a lower household income had a higher proportion of intending pregnancy (62.1%) than women with a higher household income

**Table 2** Association between sociodemographic and pregnancy intention

| Variable | Unintended pregnancy | | Intended pregnancy | | OR | *p-value* |
|---|---|---|---|---|---|---|
| | n | (%) | n | (%) | | |
| **Age ideal for pregnancy** | | | | | | |
| **No** | 12 | 40.0 | 18 | 60.0 | 1.048 | **0.911** |
| **Yes** | 49 | 38.9 | 77 | 61.1 | | |
| **Age at first marriage** | | | | | | |
| ≤ 20 | 33 | 49.3 | 34 | 50.7 | 2.114 | **0.025*** |
| ≥ 21 | 28 | 31.5 | 61 | 68.5 | | |
| **Education** | | | | | | |
| **Primary education** | 26 | 44.1 | 33 | 55.9 | 1.396 | **0.322** |
| **Secondary or higher** | 35 | 36.1 | 62 | 63.9 | | |
| **Employment** | | | | | | |
| **Housewife** | 44 | 35.5 | 80 | 64.5 | 0.485 | **0.071** |
| **Working** | 17 | 53.1 | 15 | 46.9 | | |
| **Health insurance** | | | | | | |
| **No** | 25 | 50.0 | 25 | 50.0 | 1.944 | **0.057** |
| **Yes** | 36 | 34.0 | 70 | 66.0 | | |
| **Number of children** | | | | | | |
| **> 2** | 15 | 62.5 | 9 | 37.5 | 3.116 | **0.013*** |
| ≤ 2 | 46 | 34.8 | 86 | 65.2 | | |
| **Number of children desired** | | | | | | |
| **> 2** | 27 | 35.1 | 50 | 64.9 | 0.715 | **0.308** |
| **≤ 2** | 34 | 43.0 | 45 | 57.0 | | |
| **Modern contraceptive use** | | | | | | |
| **Yes** | 31 | 52.5 | 28 | 47.5 | 2.473 | **0.008*** |
| **No** | 30 | 30.9 | 67 | 69.1 | | |
| **Knowledge of delaying pregnancy during pandemic** | | | | | | |
| **No** | 39 | 36.8 | 67 | 63.2 | 0.741 | **0.329** |
| **Yes** | 22 | 44.0 | 28 | 56.0 | | |
| **Household income** | | | | | | |
| ≤ 3.000.000 | 47 | 37.9 | 77 | 62.1 | 0.785 | **0.546** |
| **> 3.000.000** | 14 | 43.8 | 18 | 56.3 | | |
| **Spouse age** | | | | | | |
| ≥ 36 | 27 | 46.6 | 31 | 53.4 | 1.639 | **0.144** |
| ≤ 35 | 34 | 34.7 | 64 | 65.3 | | |
| **Spouse education** | | | | | | |
| **Secondary or higher** | 46 | 46.0 | 54 | 54.0 | 2.328 | **0.020*** |
| **Primary Education** | 15 | 26.8 | 41 | 73.2 | | |

**Table 3** Multivariate analysis of demographic variables affecting pregnancy intention

| Variable | OR | p-value | 95% CI |
|---|---|---|---|
| Age at the first marriage ≥ 21 | 2.994 | 0.004 | 1.411–6.351 |
| Number of children ≤ 2 | 2.999 | 0.029 | 1.122–8.015 |
| Not Using Modern contraceptive | 2.979 | 0.004 | 1.424–6.232 |
| Spouse education primary | 3.655 | 0.002 | 1.614–8.282 |

(56.3%). The bivariate analysis in Table 2 shows that age at the first marriage, number of children, modern contraceptive use, and spouse education were associated with pregnancy intention ($p < 0.05$) (Table 3).

Multivariate analysis indicates a statistically significant effect between all four variables and pregnancy intention, with a slight difference in the magnitude of risk of intending pregnancy. Women who first married at 21 years or older intending pregnancy by 2.994 times compared to those who married at 20 years or younger. Meanwhile, not using modern contraceptives increases the risk of intending pregnancy by 2.999 times than women who used any modern contraceptive before pregnancy. Women with two or fewer children intend to get pregnant almost three times more than those with three or more children. Spouse education shows the highest odds of contributing to pregnancy intention. Women with a spouse with primary education are 3.655 times wanting pregnancy compared to women with a partner educated secondary or higher.

## 5 Discussions

The study found that 60.9% of pregnant women reported having intended pregnancy, while 30.1% of women reported their pregnancy as unintended. The result shows a higher proportion of intended pregnancy based on the timing of pregnancy compared to currently pregnant women in Australia, who reported 50% of the pregnancy during the COVID-19 pandemic as intended to happen at the time of pregnancy [19]. The result shows a noticeably high proportion of unintended pregnancies, as much as 30.1% compared to the number of unintended pregnancies in Indonesia before the pandemic which was less than 20% [26, 29]. The number of unintended pregnancies is also higher than in a study in Southwest Ethiopia which found that around 19,5% of women experienced unintended pregnancy during the COVID-19 outbreak [30].

According to Bongaarts [31], several factors affecting the wanted fertility include but are not limited to the number of children desired, child composition within the household, and the time of pregnancy. Therefore, women will likely restrict their fertility when they reach the ideal number of wanted children. A study conducted in Italy found that the incidence of a pandemic reduced the intention to increase the number of children by 37% in Italy [18]. This means that every 1 in 3 couples who wanted additional children before the pandemic has canceled their intention to have a pregnancy after COVID-19. A similar finding was also found in the United States, which showed that 49.2% of women who were actively trying to get pregnant chose to stop trying the pregnancy program after the pandemic. That is, 1 in 2 women on a program for pregnancy stop intending to get pregnant, and 1 in 3 women planning a pregnancy also stopped trying to conceive [16]. A study in Australia also found that 18% of women who were trying to get pregnant before the COVID-19 pandemic had stopped their attempt to conceive [19]. The findings of those recent studies indicate that COVID-19 has affected pregnancy and fertility decisions for several reasons, including but not limited to the adverse outcomes of pregnancy during a disease outbreak, financial insecurities, and well-being concerns among women and their partners [16, 18, 19].

The shift in pregnancy intention during the COVID-19 pandemic might also be related to the adverse events women might face if they contract an infection during pregnancy. A previous study indicated the susceptibility of pregnant women to disease of respiratory virus [32]. Similarly, a study on Lebanese women also found that during the COVID-19 pandemic, there were 22% of women reported adverse events [33]. In addition, the COVID-19 pandemic potentially lessens access to healthcare, including but not limited to the reduced provision of mother and child health services and family planning/contraception services during the containment period [13, 14]. Moreover, the decreased number of contraceptive services during the implementation of large-scale social restrictions policy [24] might be related to the high numbers of unintended pregnancies during the COVID-19 outbreak such as shown by a study in Ethiopia which found that a lack of healthcare provision and family planning service during COVID-19 pandemic increases the risk of unintended pregnancy by two times and that not having adequate ANC from previous pregnancy was significantly associated with unintended pregnancy during the outbreak [30, 34].

This study shows that women's age at first marriage affects the intention to get pregnant during the COVID-19 pandemic, with women who first married at the age of 21 years or older wanting to get pregnant by 2.994 times compared to those who married at 20 years or younger. This might be because women who first married at 21 years or older would have felt in the older age group at the current time, and, therefore, they would want to get pregnant during their ideal age for pregnancy. This result corresponds with a study conducted in Australia which found that older women were less likely to delay pregnancy because of their limited time reflected on age. In comparison, younger women are more likely to postpone pregnancy and wait for the pandemic to have additional children [19]. However, this study found no significant association between women's age and intended pregnancy, opposite to previous research found that age is related to pregnancy intention [29, 35].

This study found that the number of children was significantly associated with pregnancy intention during the pandemic, with women who have two or fewer children having the odds of intending to get pregnant as much as three times greater than women who have three children or more. Studies have found that the number of children constantly contributes to both wanted and unintended pregnancy intention. Having more children was associated with a higher risk of unintended pregnancy because pregnancy intention is significantly affected by the amount of parity.

Hence, having fewer children is associated with women reporting their pregnancy as intended or wanted; reversely, women with more children will be more likely to report their pregnancy as unintended [36, 37]. In contrast, a study of Lebanese women reported that women who have had children are significantly associated with a decreased chance of getting pregnant during the COVID-19 pandemic [33]. During the pandemic, women with only one child might intend to have an additional child, therefore planning to conceive. A study among currently pregnant women in the United States indicated that women with fewer children are more likely to think about attempting to get pregnant [16]. The study in Australia also found that older women who had children were more likely to continue their attempt to conceive even during the pandemic, as they were concerned about the limited time of their reproduction age. In comparison, younger women are more likely to delay pregnancy [19].

The result shows that not using modern contraceptives is significantly associated with getting pregnant during COVID-19. Women not using any modern contraceptive are three times higher to have an intended pregnancy. This is because women who use contraception have a significant relationship with a decreased chance of getting pregnant during the COVID-19 pandemic [33]. Non-compliance with contraceptives is associated with a lack of intention to prevent pregnancy; hence, women who use contraceptives are more likely to report their pregnancy as unintended [26, 36]. Therefore, women were likely to use no contraception because they were intended to get pregnant.

It is found that lower education is significantly correlated with women's intention to get pregnant. Women with a partner-educated primary (junior high school or lower) were almost four times to have intended pregnancy compared to women with higher partner education. Women who attained primary education also had a higher risk of intending to get pregnant; however, the results show no significant association between women's education and intended pregnancy. The previous study has shown that low-educated women were more likely to experience unintended pregnancy [37]. On the contrary, it is found that during the COVID-19 pandemic, women who least ended the attempt to conceive were most on the higher education level, which is related to financial security among women of higher education attainment [16].

## 6 Conclusions

Among pregnant women studied, only approximately 61% of pregnant women in Sub-District Hamparan Perak and Sub-District Sunggal intended to get pregnant at the time of the pandemic. It is found that contributing factors to intended pregnancy during the COVID-19 outbreak are having $\leq$ two children, age of first marriage $\geq$ 21 years old, married to a partner with primary education, and not using modern contraceptives before pregnancy. The most dominant factor contributing to intended pregnancy is married to a partner with primary education.

## References


1. WHO (2020) COVID-19 Public Health Emergency of International Concern (PHEIC) Global research and innovation forum [Internet]. COVID-19 Public Health Emergency of International Concern (PHEIC) Global research and innovation forum. 2020 [cited 2021 Sep 4]. Available from: https://www.who.int/publications/m/item/covid-19-public-health-emergency-of-international-concern-(pheic)-global-research-and-innovation-forum
2. WHO (2007) Addressing sex and gender in epidemic-prone infectious diseases [Internet]. Geneva, Switzerland; 2007. Available from: https://www.who.int/csr/resources/publications/SexGenderInfectDis.pdf
3. Rasmussen SA, Jamieson DJ, Bresee JS (2008) Pandemic influenza and pregnant women. Emerg Infect Dis 14(1):95–100
4. Ramadhani HS, Islamy N, Yonata A (2020) COVID-19 in Pregnancy: Is it dangerous? Med Prof J lampung [Internet] 10(2):318–23. Available from: https://doi.org/10.53089/medula.v10i2.74
5. Reid A (2005) The effects of the 1918–1919 influenza pandemic on infant and child health in Derbyshire. Med Hist 49(1):29–54
6. Creanga AA, Johnson TF, Graitcer SB, Hartman LK, Al-Samarrai T, schwarz AG et al (2010) Severity of 2009 pandemic influenza a (h1n1) virus infection in pregnant women. Obstet Gynecol 115(4):717–726
7. Mosby LG, Rasmussen SA, Jamieson DJ (2011) 2009 pandemic influenza A (H1N1) in pregnancy: a systematic review of the literature. Am J Obstet Gynecol 205(1):10–18
8. Dashraath P, Wong JLJ, Lim MXK, Lim LM, Li S, Biswas A et al (2020) Coronavirus disease 2019 (COVID-19) pandemic and pregnancy. Am J Obstet Gynecol 222(6):521–531
9. Pradana AA, Casman C, Nur'aini N (2020) Pengaruh Kebijakan Social Distancing pada Wabah COVID-19 terhadap Kelompok Rentan di Indonesia. J Kebijak Kesehat Indones 9:2020
10. Satuan Tugas Penganganan COVID-19 (2021) Infogravis COVID-19 (31 Maret 2020) [Internet]. Available from: https://covid19.go.id/p/berita/infografis-covid-19-31-maret-2020
11. KEPUTUSAN PRESIDEN REPUBLIK INDONESIA NOMOR 12 TAHUN 2020 TENTANG PENETAPAN BENCANA NONALAM PENYEBARAN CORONA VIRUS DISEASE 2019 (COVID-19) SEBAGAI BENCANA NASIONAL (2020)
12. PERATURAN PEMERINTAH NOMOR 21 TAHUN 2020 TENTANG PEMBATASAN SOSIAL BERSKALA BESAR DALAM RANGKA PERCEPATAN PENANGANAN CORONA VIRUS DISEASE 2019/COVID-19 (2020)
13. Tristanti I, Kulsum U. Potret Perilaku Pemeriksaan Kehamilan di Masa Pandemi COVID-19. Mot J Ilmu Kesehat. 2021;16(1, Maret):17–23. Available from: ejournal.stikesmukla.ac.id
14. Saputri N selli, Anbarani MD, Tomayah N, Yumna A. Dampak (2020) Pandemi COVID-19 pada Layan Gizi dan keehatan Ibu dan Anak (KIA) Studi Kasus di Lima Wilayah di Indonesia [Internet]. Available from: www.smeru.or.id
15. Davis-Floyd R, Gutschow K, Schwartz DA (2020) Pregnancy, birth and the COVID-19 pandemic in the United States. Med Anthropol 39(5):413–427
16. Kahn LG, Trasande L, Liu M, Mehta-Lee SS, Brubaker SG, Jacobson MH (2021) Factors associated with changes in pregnancy intention among women who were mothers of young children in New York city following the COVID-19 Outbreak. JAMA Netw Open 4(9):e2124273–e2124273
17. Lindberg LD, VandeVusse A, Mueller J, Kirstein M (2020) Early impacts of the COVID-19 pandemic: findings from the 2020 Guttmacher survey of reproductive health experiences. New York
18. Micelli E, Cito G, Cocci A, Polloni G, Russo GI, Minervini A et al (2020) Desire for parenthood at the time of COVID-19 pandemic: an insight into the Italian situation. J Psychosom Obstet Gynecol 41(3):183–190
19. Qu L (2021) Impacts of COVID-19 on pregnancy and fertility intentions. Available from: https://aifs.gov.au/sites/default/files/publication-documents/2106_4_fias_pregnancy_and_fertility_intentions.pdf

20. Dasgupta A, Kantorova V, Ueffing P (2020) The impact of the COVID-19 crisis on meeting needs for family planning: a global scenario by contraceptive methods used. Gates Open Res 40(102):102
21. Mujiburrahman M, Riyadi ME, Ningsih MU (2020) Hubungan Pengetahuan dengan Perilaku Pencegahan COVID-19 pada Masyarakat di Dusun Potorono Banguntapan Bantul D.I.Yogyakarta. J Keperawatan Terpadu (Integrated Nurs Journal) 2(2):130–40
22. Aritonang J, Nugraeny L, Sumiatik, Siregar RN (2020) Peningkatan Pemahaman Kesehatan pada Ibu hamil dalam Upaya Pencegahan COVID-19. J SOLMA 9(2):261–269
23. Siregar RN, Aritonang J, Anita S (2020) Pemahaman Ibu hamil tentang Upaya Pencegahan Infeksi COVID-19 Selama kehamilan. J Healthc Technol Med 6(2):798
24. Wijayanti UT, Nindiyastuti NAI, Najib (2021) Dampak Pandemi COVID-19 terhadap Pelayanan KB. HIGEIA J Public Heal Res Dev 5(3):470–478
25. Arinda YD, Herdayati M (2021) Masalah Kesehatan Mental pada Wanita Hamil Selama Pandemi COVID-19. J Kesehat Vokasional 6(1):32. Available from: https://jurnal.ugm.ac.id/jkesvo/article/view/62784
26. Supriyadi, Yanti L (2020) Factors analysis of unwanted pregnancies among women childbearing age in Indonesia: analysis of demographic and health survey data in 2017. MEDISAINS J Ilm Ilmu-Ilmu Kesehat 18(3):93–98.
27. Zulmahira S (2017) Faktor-faktor yang berhubungan dengan kehamilan tidak diinginkan (KTD) di Indonesia tahun 2012 (Analisis Data SDKI 2012). Universitas Andalas
28. Fitri L (2021) Gambaran Prevalensi Kehamilan Selama Masa COVID-19 dan Faktor Penyebabnya di Klinik Pratama Afiyah Pekanbaru. J Endur Jakian Ilm Probl Kesehat [Internet] 6(2):419–426. Available from: http://publikasi.lldikti10.id/index.php/endurance/issue/view/12
29. Hutasoit EF, Indraswari N (2021) Determinan Kehamilan Tidak Diinginkan pada Wanita Menikah di Provinsi Jawa Barat. In: Rahayuwati L, Nurhidayah I, Hendrawati S, (eds) Bunga Rampai Bangga Kencana: Perspektif dan Penelitian [Internet]. 1st ed. Bandung: UNPAD PRESS, pp 233–55. Available from: https://bit.ly/BungaRampaiBanggaKencana
30. Tenaw SG, Chemir F, Zewudie BT, Chekole B, Argaw M, Mesfin Y et al (2022) Unintended pregnancy and associated factors among women attending antenatal care in public hospital during COVID-19 pandemic, Southwest Ethiopia: a cross-sectional study. Open Access J Contracept 13:9–16
31. Bongaarts J (1990) The measurement of wanted fertility. Popul Dev Rev 16(3):487–506
32. Yang H, Wang C, Poon LC (2020) Novel coronavirus infection and pregnancy. Ultrasound Obstet Gynecol 55(4):435–437
33. Haddad C, Malhab SB, Sacre H, Malaeb D, Azzi J, Khachman D et al (2022) Factors related to pregnancy status and unwanted pregnancy among lebanese women during the COVID-19 lockdown: a cross-sectional study. Arch Public Heal 80(1):68
34. Asratie MH (2021) Unintended pregnancy during COVID-19 pandemic among women attending antenatal care in Northwest Ethiopia: magnitude and associated factors. Int J Womens Health. 13:461–466
35. Andini MA, Mutahar R, Yeni (2020) Trends and determinants of unintended pregnancy occurrence among married women aged 15–49 years in Indonesia. Adv Heal Sci Res 22:361–367
36. Curtis S, Evens E, Sambisa W (2011) Contraceptive discontinuation and unintended pregnancy: an imperfect relationship. Int Perspect Sex Reprod Health 37(2):58–66
37. Anggraini K, Wratsangka R, Bantas K, Fikawati S (2018) Faktor-faktor yang berhubungan dengan kehamilan tidak diinginkan di Indonesia. Promot J Kesehat Masy. 8(1):27–37

# Religions, Minority, Identity and Social Harmony in Southeast Asia

# Construction of the Piety of Women Adhering to the Tarekat Annaqshabandiyah Al-Khalidiyah Al-Mujaddadiyah in Banyumas

Umi Masfiah and Nugroho Eko Atmanto

**Abstract** This article argues that the construction of women's piety is a form of expression of their existence in the midst of men's piety domination. In tarekat organizations, women can only become students, without ever increasing to become badals or even tarekat's murshid. Even among the conditions for the implementation of tawajjuhan activities in a village mosque, at least six man followers of the tarekat are required. When this number is not fulfilled, the tawajjuhan activity cannot be carried out even though there are 40 women who are followers of the tarekat. Nevertheless, the composition of the number of the Annaqsyabandiyah al-Mujaddadiyah al-Khalidiyah adherents branch of Sokaraja, Banyumas Regency is still more than the number of men recently. This study uses a qualitative research approach with data collection using interviews, observation, and documentation. The results of interviews with 10 tarekat women stated that when they entered the world of tarekat, they were based on a strong desire and heart readiness to carry out the tarekat teachings well. They practice 5000 times remembrance sirr all day for tarekat students who have never participated in Suluk activities. The obligation of remembrance will be added 1000 times if they have participated in one time Suluk until twelve activities, or 11,000 times remembrance. Besides dhikr, the women who follow the tarekat fulfill the call of their heart by increasing the practice of obligatory and sunnah worship.

**Keywords** Construction · The piety of the *tarekat* women · The Annaqsyabandiyah al-Mujaddadiyah al-Khalidiyah · Banyumas

U. Masfiah (✉) · N. E. Atmanto
Research Center for Religion and Belief, Jakarta, Indonesia
e-mail: umim001@brin.go.id



Nawawi et al. (eds.), *Managing Disruption and Developing Resilience for a Better Southeast Asia*, Springer Proceedings in Humanities and Social Sciences,
https://doi.org/10.1007/978-981-96-2116-3_35

# 1 Introduction

The piety of the *tarekat* women is to fulfill their obligations as *tarekat* members. In addition, their piety is expressed and manifested in the public. The domestic role of women in household activities encourages themselves to express their religion more broadly in the public sphere through *tarekat*. In it, most of the tarekat women only become students, a few of whom have been able to reach the position of *badal* and even *murshid*. This is reflected in women who are adherents of the Annaqshabandiyah al-Mujaddadiyah al-Khalidiyah Sokaraja Lor congregation *tarekat*, Banyumas Regency. Those women are different from those who are adherents of the Naqsyabandiyyah Muzhariyah *tarekat* in Madura. In this tarekat community, several women who have met the requirements can become *tarekat* murshids independently so that they are given the trust to lead *zikir* (remembrance) and *Suluk* [1, 2].

The tarekat murshid position of the women shows that their piety is clearly expressed in the public sphere, and it is equal to that of men. They can achieve the highest pious position in the congregation because of the opportunity and socio-religious support from the community. As for other tarekat, such as the Annaqshabandiyah al-Mujaddadiyah al-Khalidiyah Sokaraja Lor congregation, Banyumas Regency, the position of the murshid of the Naqshbandiyah congregation can only be inherited by direct line male descendants and not sons-in-law [1]. In addition, the position of women who are followers of the tarekat in the implementation of tawajjuhan in a village mosque is also not taken into account because among the conditions for the implementation of the tawajjuhan activity is the presence of a minimum of six men who are followers of the tarekat. If this is not fulfilled, then the tawajjuhan activity cannot be carried out even though there are 40 women who are followers of the tarekat (interview, Ibu Is, 9th July 2020).

Despite that, the women who follow the Annaqshbandiyah al-Mujaddadiyah al-Khalidiyah tarekat remain committed to the tarekat. It can be seen based on the current composition of the number of followers of the Annaqsyabandiyah al-Mujaddadiyah al-Khalidiyah tarekat in Karang Tengah Village, Kembaran District, Banyumas Regency, showing that the number of female followers of the tarekat is more than the number of men, which is 115 women and 35 men. These tarekat women consistently carry out the provisions of the congregation's worship practices. They are committed to practice the obligation of zikir 5000 times a day and night for tarekat students who have never participated in Suluk activities. For followers of the tarekat who have participated in Suluk activities once, it is added 1000 times. This addition will continue if the tarekat adherents follow the 2nd, 3rd, and so on Suluk activities until the number 11,000 zikir. In addition, the women of the tarekat also fulfill the call of the heart by increasing the practice of obligatory and sunnah worship and avoiding immorality of body part.

The construction of piety among women who join the tarekat in Karang Tengah Village, Kembaran District, Banyumas Regency is so interesting to study that it shows how they express their piety. Many studies on tarekat adherents have been conducted based on the results of several articles. There are three trends in the study of tarekat: first, studies of tarekat women by looking at female figures [1, 3, 4]; second, several studies that concentrate on discussing social values developed in the teachings of the Naqsyabandiyah tarekat [5, 6]; and third, other studies about the value of education in the teachings of the Naqsyabandiyah tarekat [7–9]. Thus, the study of the construction of piety among women adherents of the Annaqshabandiyah al-Mujaddadiyah al-Khalidiyah congregation in Banyumas Regency can complement the study of the previous researchers.

## 2 Framework of Thinking

### *2.1 Piety Construction*

Studying construction will always be related to social reality and knowledge. Social reality is a phenomenon that cannot stand alone, but is closely related to a person's knowledge. This knowledge guides the behavior of a person and society in everyday behavior [10]. Berger states that there are three forms of activity to see a construction, namely: externalization, objectification, and internalization. The starting point for understanding a reality is internalization as an understanding or direct interpretation of an objective event as the expression of a meaning [10]. Internalization can only take place with identification. Identification made by one person will internalize it in others and make it have the same attitude as the other person. At this stage, he/she can identify himself/herself as the other person. Objectivation is interpreted as manifesting oneself in the products of human activity that are available, both to producers and to others as elements of the common world. In this objectivation process, there is an important part, i.e. significance. Significance is the making of signs by humans, although initially this sign is not made to indicate something desired [10]. Then there is also the process of externalization, which is when a person adapts and interacts with people.

Furthermore, dealing with the concept of piety, piety means a good deed [11, p. 246]. In the Qur'an, the definition of good deeds is tied to faith as mentioned in Surah al-Baqarah verses 76–82, and verses 277. A summary of the concept of piety in these verses, that faith is considered right if it is followed by righteous deeds, and vice versa because faith and righteous deeds are two things that cannot be separated. Good deeds have been described in detail in the Qur'an as: (1) not worshiping other than Allah, (2) doing good (ihsan) toward parents, close relatives, orphans, and people in need, (3) speaking nicely to everyone, (4) performing prayers, (5) paying zakat. Surah al-Kahf verse 110 states that: "Say: I am only a mortal like you. My Lord inspireth in me that your Allah is only One Allah. And whoever hopeth for the meeting with his Lord, let him do righteous work, and make none sharer of the worship due unto his Lord." (Surah. Al-Kahf: 110).

## 2.2 *Women's* Tarekat

According to Ma'luf and Louis [12], tarekat (Arabic: Tariqah) means the way; circumstances; sect; scratches/lines on something; shelter posts; umbrella stick; or the famous one from an umbrella [12]. Meanwhile, according to Woodward, tarekat is a mystical Sufi order that plays a socio-political and religious role in Muslim society since the twelfth century. Tarekat regulates male authority and transmission of mystical knowledge through spiritual connections to the Prophet Muhammad [13]. Historically, this tarekat has had a significant influence on the Islamic world. After the collapse of the Abbasid caliphate by the Mongols in 1258, it previously had the task of maintaining the unity and spread of Islam to various regions that fell into the hands of the Sufis (tarekat), including in Indonesia [14, p. A]. However, the birth of the tarekat cannot be separated from the existence of Sufism in general, especially the transition of Sufism which is individual to the tarekat as an organization, which is the development, practice, and expansion of Sufism teachings. The study of the tarekat itself is not possible without the existence of Sufism studies [14].

According to the history of tarekat in many Muslim countries, the role of women in tarekat is marginal, often women's work is limited to seeking blessings in the graves of saints or participating in public celebrations. Although Sufi teachers may give lectures to female audiences, it is rare to find men and women participating together in the teachings and prayers that characterize the doctrinal aspects of Sufism [2]. A number of tarekat Sufi also allow women to become regular members, but do not in their environment [15]. Tarekat that provides the greatest opportunities for women is the Bektas in Ottoman Turkey. They are here all considered equal to men; they have to undergo the same oath ceremony and participate in banquets and gatherings together [15]. Whereas in Indonesia, equality in tarekat is found in the Naqsabandiyah congregation in Madura as evidenced by the presence of female murshid (tarekat experts) [16].

# 3 Method

This research is a type of field research, conducted for 10 days from 6 to 16th July 2020. Data on the construction of piety among women who adhere to the tarekat were collected through interviews with 10 women adherents of the Annaqsyabandiyah al-Mujaddadiyah al-Khalidiyah tarekat, the caretaker of the tomb, the tarekat murshid around the location of the pesantren, rowang badal tarekat in Karang Tengah Village, and 1 woman who was a tarekat believer in charge of bathing and giving instructions to female tarekat students when they are about to take allegiance. The research instrument used as an interview guide contained questions about the knowledge of the tarekat women regarding their interest in participating in tarekat activities, the process of becoming a tarekat member, how long they have been a tarekat member, whether they have participated in Suluk activities, and what practices are performed after becoming tarekat students, as well as the benefits after participating in tarekat activities.

Observations were conducted by visiting Pondok Suluk, observing its location, and the environment around it including the mosque, the boarding house, the residence of the tarekat murshid, and the grave complex of the tarekat murshids. Data collection techniques were carried out through interviews, observations, and document studies. The data analysis technique was done in a qualitative descriptive manner, namely qualitative data analysis using the four steps of Miles and Hubberman's analysis in the form of data collection, data reduction, data presentation, and conclusion drawing/verification [17].

## 4 Findings and Discussion

### *4.1 Genealogy of Tarekat Al-Mujaddadiyah Al-Khalidiyah Sokaraja Lor*

Tarekat Annaqsyabandiyah Al-Mujaddadiyah Al-Khalidiyah Sokaraja Lor, Banyumas Regency, was founded by K.H. Raden Muhammad Ilyas. He is the son of Raden Mas Haji Ali Dipowongso, the grandson of H.P.A. Diponegoro II, and the great-grandson of H.P.A. Diponegoro I (Abdul Hamid). H.P.A Diponegoro is the son of Sultan Hamengku Buwono III. R.M.H Ali Dipowongso, the father of Kiai Ilyas, traveled to several cities in Java such as Pekalongan City, Madura, and West Java. Once upon a time, R.M.H Ali Dipowongso arrived in the Indramayu area and met a religious figure who advised him to go to the Purwokerto area, Banyumas. Then he headed to the Banyumas Regency area and married and settled in the village of Kedung Paruk. R.M.H Ali Dipowongso gave birth to two sons, namely K.H. Muhammad Ilyas and Sulaiman (interview with Kiai Musa Asy'ari, 08 July 2020, interview with Gus As'ad, supervisor of Bani Malik Islamic Boarding School).

Muhammad Ilyas first became acquainted with the knowledge of tarekat Naqsyabandiyah when he studied with Kiai Ubaidah and Kiai Abdurrahman in Surabaya. Both of these teachers received diplomas from Sulaiman al-Qirimi. These two teachers also brought the teenage Muhammad Ilyas to Mecca and studied with Sulaiman Zuhdi and lived there for approximately 45 years. Muhammad Ilyas obtained his tarekat diploma from his teacher and became the caliph of the main tirakat Naqshbandiyah in Java with Muhammad Hadi of Girikusumo. Muhammad Ilyas also established the rule that the position of the Naqshbandiyah murshid could only be inherited by a direct line male descendant and not a son-in-law [1].

On his return to Java, Muhammad Ilyas visited his colleague Abdullah and married his sister. Muhammad Ilyas then settled in Sokaraja and had many followers, but at that time, the Dutch government suspected him and put him in prison. Not long after, he was rescued by a Dutch landrat named Abu Bakar, who managed to convince the Dutch authorities that Muhammad Ilyas had no political ambitions and was not a threat to the government. After his release, Abu Bakar married Abu Bakar's daughter [1].

Kiai Muhammad Ilyas died around 29 Shafar 1334 H (around 1914 AD). His position as a murshid was continued by his descendants, starting from Kiai Muhammad Affandi then Kiai Ahmad Rifa'i (d. 1970s), Kiai Abdussalam, and Kiai Thoriq. Kiai Abdussalam was sworn in by his own father in 1946. Some of the rules applied by Kiai Abdussalam include stipulating that tawajjuhan activities are carried out two times a week on Tuesday and Friday ba'da Isha. For those who do Suluk in Pondok, tawajjuhan can be done as much as three times within 24 h. Kiai Abdussalam also stipulates that if there are no obstacles or due to illness, travel or otherwise, every student must recite zikir of ism-al dzat five thousand times [1].

### 4.2 Construction of the Piety of Women Adhering to Tarekat

The main source of the teachings of the Annaqsyabandiyah Al-Mujaddadiyah Al-Khalidiyah Sokaraja Lor is a book with title: Guidance Treatise of Thariqah Naqsyabandiyah Lughah Jawi Ngalap Saking Kitab Majmu' al-Rasail 'ala Ushul al-Khalidiyah Saking Sulaiman Zuhdi Kangge Para Ihwan Thariqah Naqsyabandiyyah Sentral Sokaraja. This book is a guide for women who are followers of the tarekat. Then, the construction of the tarekat for women who are adherents of the Tarekat Annaqshabandiyah Al-Mujaddadiyah al-Khalidiyah in Karang Tengah Kembaran Village Banyumas is based on their practice of tarekat.

The practice of the women begins with their willingness to take bai'at (allegiance). For women in Karang Tengah Village, they usually take bai'at at Pondok Jam'iyyah Thoriqah Annaqsyabandiyah Al-Mujaddadiyah Al-Khalidiyah Sokaraja Lor. Besides Pondok Suluk, there are also tarekat followers who make allegiance in the mosque and prayer room of Karang Tengah Village. These are the tarekat followers who join the tarekat during the leadership of Kiai Abdussalam, the father of the current tarekat mursyid. Kiai Abdussalam has a policy that allegiance does not have to be carried out in Pondok Suluk but can be at the village mosque provided that many villagers want to take allegiance. Data about this can be seen in Table 1.

Any woman who will take allegiance at Pondok Suluk usually comes in the afternoon or evening. They are accompanied by badals from their villages without being limited in number. Arriving at Pondok Suluk, the introductory badal conveys the intent and purpose of his arrival to the administrator, badal, or kiai there. After that, the women are instructed on the procedure for taking allegiance and handed over to the female administrator in Pondok Suluk. This female Suluk Pondok administrator also provides knowledge about the procedures for taking bai'at and what activities will be carried out before taking bai'at (interview with Ibu. Sul, 14th July 2020).

During their stay at Pondok Suluk, the women who will be the followers of the tarekat perform the obligatory prayers as usual. After completing the Isha prayer, they will bathe in repentance, perform optional prayer, and sleep. They wake up early in the morning, then perform the Fajr prayer, and continue following the oath

**Table 1** Place of allegiance

| No | Name | Place of allegiance |
|---|---|---|
| 1 | Ibu Is | Ponpes Pesulukan Sokaraja Lor |
| 2 | Ibu T | Masjid Desa Karang Tengah |
| 3 | Ibu Pon | Ponpes Pesulukan Sokaraja Lor |
| 4 | Ibu Sal | Ponpes Pesulukan Sokaraja Lor |
| 5 | Ibu Min | Masjid Desa Karang Tengah |
| 6 | Ibu Kham | Musala Grumbul Bendasari |
| 7 | Ibu Dar | Ponpes Pesulukan Sokaraja Lor |
| 8 | Ibu Y | Ponpes Pesulukan Sokaraja Lor |
| 9 | Ibu Mur | Ponpes Pesulukan Sokaraja Lor |
| 10 | Ibu E | Ponpes Pesulukan Sokaraja Lor |

after the Fajr prayer. After taking the pledge, every woman who is a member of the tarekat will receive the obligation of worshiping to do dhikr in a sirr manner as much as 5000 times. The number of zikir will continue to be added every time they finish participating in Suluk activities. The number of zikir for female members can be seen in Table 2.

Table 2 indicates that the number of zikir that must be carried out by each tarekat adherent is in accordance with her position whether she has followed Suluk or not. However, the length of time of tarekat has no effect on the willingness of tarekat adherents to follow Suluk. As an example, Ibu Is, although only 10 years old, has participated in Suluk three times. This is different from Ibu Kham, who has been in tarekat for 15 years but has never participated in Suluk activities. They said that they wanted to join the tarekat but it was hard to share 10 days to stay at Pondok Suluk Sokaraja Lorr. Likewise, Ibu T and Ibu Pon, although they have been in tarekat for 20 years, have only participated in Suluk once.

**Table 2** The number of Suluk

| No | Name | Term of doing tarekat | Suluk/not yet |
|---|---|---|---|
| 1 | Ibu Is | 10 year | 3 × Suluk |
| 2 | Ibu T | 20 year | 1 × Suluk |
| 3 | Ibu Pon | 20 year | 1 × Suluk |
| 4 | Ibu Sal | 5 year | 1 × Suluk |
| 5 | Ibu Min | 10 year | 1 × Suluk |
| 6 | Ibu Kham | 15 year | Not yet Suluk |
| 7 | Ibu Dar | 5 year | Not yet Suluk |
| 8 | Ibu Y | 4 year | Not yet Suluk |
| 9 | Ibu Mur | 1 year | Not yet Suluk |
| 10 | Ibu E | 1 year | Not yet Suluk |

The large number of zikir that must be completed by the women of the tarekat within a day and night makes them set aside a special time to complete it. They choose the time according to their habits and their physical health condition. Most of the tarekat women complete their dhikr activities in the last third of the night, and others finish their dhikr after the Isha prayer, after the Fajr prayer, and after the Duha prayer. Data about this can be seen in Table 3.

Table 3 shows that most of the tarekat women choose the time of zikir in the last third of the night, while a small number of others perform it at the time after the Fajr prayer, the Duha prayer, the Maghrib prayer, and the Isha prayer. Even though Ibu T and Ibu Pon often do dhikr during the third of the night, both of them sometimes do it after the Fajr prayer time when they are not healthy. Similarly, Ibu Kham and Ibu Dar feel unable to wake up in the last third of the night so they chose the time after the Maghrib prayer and after the Isha prayer. Ibu Mur prefers to do zikir at the time after the Duha prayer, when all her household chores have been completed.

**Factors that Encourage Women to Tarekat.** Several reasons for joining the tarekat are identified based on Table 4.

Table 4 shows that women who follow the tarekat in Karang Tengah Village follow the tarekat because there are internal and external driving factors. Internal driving factors come from within the women themselves. They stated that they were ready to join it after they felt they were physically and mentally ready and especially mental readiness coming from a strong impulse to join. Mental readiness does not just happen, but through a fairly long stage. The information above illustrates that some have actually been invited to join the tarekat for a long time, both by friends and the badal tarekat, but they said they were not ready until finally after their desire became very strong and felt that they were ready, they did not hesitate to tell the badal tarekat to be sent for allegiance.

**Table 3** Time of Zikir

| No | Name | Time of Zikir | Information |
|---|---|---|---|
| 1 | Ibu Is | the final third of the night | Always |
| 2 | Ibu T | the final third of the night | When unwell, it is done after the Fajr prayer |
| 3 | Ibu Pon | the final third of the night | When unwell, it is done after the Fajr prayer |
| 4 | Ibu Sal | the final third of the night | Always |
| 5 | Ibu Min | the final third of the night | Often |
| 6 | Ibu Kham | after Maghrib/Isha prayer | Unable to wake up doing dhikr in the last third of the night |
| 7 | Ibu Dar | after Maghrib/Isha prayer | Unable to wake up doing dhikr in the last third of the night |
| 8 | Ibu Y | the final third of the night | Always in spare time |
| 9 | Ibu Mur | after the sunnah Duha prayer | After doing housework |
| 10 | Ibu E | the final third of the night | Often |

**Table 4** Factors encouraging women to Tarekat

| No | Result of interview and translation | Information |
|---|---|---|
| 1 | Because my parents joined it, I feel very happy to do what they have done (interview with Ibu Is, 9 July 2020) | Follow the tradition of tarekat |
| 2 | I've been taking part for 5 years, I was invited for a long time but I was still busy. Intention remained, finally really eager (interview with Ibu. Dar, 10th July 2020) | Self-will step by step |
| 3 | Initially invited by a friend saying; while still young, let's go along, then other friends come along, so I finally join (interview with Ibu. Y, 11 July 2020) | Factor from a friend's invitation and self-will |
| 4 | Self-initiative to strongly join (interview with Ibu Min, 11th July 2020) | Already feeling to possess |
| 5 | It's the time, the term "*wes perek pacule*" is ready (it's near the hoe) (interview with Ibu. E, 13 July 2020) | Feeling ready |
| 6 | I wanted to come along, I was ready, my husband allowed so I said to badal tarekat of village; Sir, I want to "ngidul" (south, Pondok Suluk from the village is in the south) …(interview with Ibu. Pon, 14 July 2020) | Self-will, husband's permisson, feeling ready |
| 7 | Invited by badal Eyang Duri (interview Ibu Kham, 8th July 2020) | Invited by *badal* tarekat |
| 8 | It's time, what else do I want and I wonder if this will continue, and just spending time on kitchen matters. And when ask permission from my husband, he said yes please (interview with Ibu. Mur, 16 July 2020) | Self-will and husband's permission |
| 9 | Self-will (interview with Ibu Sal, 12th July 2020) | Self-will |
| 10 | Self-will and it's time to join (interview with Ibu. T, 12th August 2020) | Self-will and feeling ready to tarekat |

The external motivating factor for women to tarekat comes from outside, such as the husband's permission, and following the tradition of the congregation for generations from previous generations. Women who are going to take bai'at/allegiance must have permission from their husbands, while unmarried women cannot take allegiance (interview with Ibu Sul, 13 July 2020). The stipulation that unmarried women cannot be pledged allegiance does not apply to unmarried men. An adult male and unmarried male are allowed to follow the tarekat.

**The Impact of Women's Choices to Tarekat. For women who are followers of the tarekat, participating in tarekat activities has an impact on themselves and they have high hopes of getting help from a mursyid in the hereafter. Some of these impacts can be seen in Table 5.**

Table 5 shows that they feel serenity, because there is hope that tomorrow in the hereafter, they will get help from their murshid teacher, or because their mind and heart feel calm. There is also the impact of increasing religious knowledge because by

**Table 5** Benefits of attending tarekat

| No | Results of interview and translation | Coding |
|---|---|---|
| 1 | I feel happy, comfortable, so I have activities (zikir) because I am not working, (interview with Ibu. Is, 09 July 2020) | Serenity and comfort, kill the time |
| 2 | For peace of mind, (interview with Ibu Dar interview, 10 July 2020) | Peace of mind |
| 3 | Worship (interview with Ibu Dar, 10th July 2020) | Spirituality |
| 4 | To have a teacher to follow (as a role model). Anyway, tomorrow, if one of the students is not seen in heaven, the teacher will look for him/her until he finds him/her (interview with Ibu. Dar, 10th July 2020) | Murshid as a role model and savior in the hereafter |
| 5 | Avoiding bad deeds, introspecting his/her sins (interview with Ibu Is, 9th July 2020) | Introspection |
| 6 | Already to have a teacher to follow (a role model), seek the Prophet's intercession (interview with Ibu Min, 11th July 2020) | Murshid as a role model, and seeking for the Prophet's intercession |
| 7 | There is a difference, because we always ask forgiveness of all parts of the body every day (interview with Ibu. Y, 11th July 2020) | Medium of self-healing |
| 8 | The benefit is to worship Allah SWT. Sincere heart with the aim of Allah SWT. So that (always) call on Allah swt. (Interview with Ibu. T, 12 August 2020) | Medium of worship |
| 9 | Already to have a teacher priest, some are followed, there is a place to ask questions about worship, have a teacher. *Angger ora melu maring ngendi-ngendi arep melu sapa* (interview with Ibu. E, 13th July 2020) | Teacher as a role model and a place to ask questions about worship |
| 10 | After attending the tarekat, I became more diligent to the mosque for congregational prayers (interview with Ibu. Mur, 16 July 2020) | More diligent to workship |
| 11 | There are activities that can reduce *ngendong* activities (visiting) (interview with Ibu Kham, 08th July 2020) | Having activities |
| 12 | Getting help from teachers in the afterlife (interview with Ibu. Sal, 12 July 2020) | Getting help from teacher |

participating in Tuesday Morning Recitation activities, they get advice on religious knowledge from tarekat badals. When they decide to join the tarekat activities, they already have physical and spiritual readiness to carry out all their obligations as members of the tarekat. Some of these women took a long time to feel ready to become members of the tarekat. At first, they doubted whether they would be able to carry out their obligations as members of the tarekat, especially when they had to complete zikir at least 5000 times a day and night. This was conveyed by Ibu. E, but she was finally able to say that after becoming a member of the tarekat, she felt light and did not feel burdened by completing that activity (interview with Mrs. E, 13 July 2020).

Activities of tarekat allow women to improve their worship practices, both sunnah worship practices and obligatory worship practices. Ibu Mur, Ibu Kham, Ibu Y, and

Ibu Tin are more likely to pray on time. When the clock shows 11 o'clock in the afternoon, they are usually ready to go to the prayer room to perform congregational prayers. Usually, before going to the prayer room, Ibu. Kham would stop by Ibu. Y's house to ask her to pray at the nearest prayer room. Likewise, Ibu Tin is used to waiting for the call to prayer for Fajr prayer after completing the practice of zikir in the last third of the night. Ibu. Mur also feels that after joining tarekat, she motivates herself to be able to perform the Fajr Prayer in tarekat in the prayer room. Ibu. Mur also becomes diligent to perform the Duha Prayer because after the Duha Sunna Time, she would complete her zikir obligations. Ibu Is always prioritizes getting up at night to perform the sunnah prayers in the last third of the night before she fulfills her obligations of zikir. Ibu Is does it even though she is at her son's residence. She will wake up sneaking into the prayer place to do zikir and practice the sunnah prayers. She says her grandson once asked; "why do you have your head covered last night" (interview, 9th July 2020).

This religious activity cannot be separated from the influence of parents and ancestors of the people of Karang Tengah Village. They feel that they have this tradition because it has been implemented and passed down from generation to generation. From little, they know that their parents and grandmother every Tuesday morning went to the Suluk Islamic Boarding School to take part in recitation and tawajjuhan activities. Among these women, there is also communication that influences each other by inviting friends who have not joined the tarekat to want to join the tarekat. Badals and kiai often give advice that they will get teacher help in the afterlife (interview with Ibu Dar, 10th July 2020).

The role of the badals in the tarekat tradition in Karang Tengah Village is quite prominent so that these activities can take place continuously until now. The badals are taken from local village leaders. The data on the Annaqsyabandiyah Al-Khalidiyah badal in Karang Tengah Village that can be known are: (1) Mr. Mad Kerun (late), (2) Mr. Nuruddin (late), (3) Mr. H. Hajidin (late), (4) Mr. H. Rohidi (late), (5) Mr. H. Mahduri (late), (6) Kiai Nurwakhid (late), (7) Kiai Samsuhari (current badal), (8) Kiai Warsum (current badal representative) (interview with Warsum, 15 July 2020). These badals have an important role to transmit and invite women, especially to become followers of the tarekat.

The women who are followers of the tarekat in Karang Tengah Village not only have worship practices as part of creating a relationship with the Creator, but also have good social awareness. When their neighbors get sick and couldn't cook, they would gladly send the food every morning, even though the food is just rice and vegetables or other dishes (observation of the activities of Ibu Mur, Ibu Kham, Ibu Sal). In addition, the tradition of sharing is also practiced by Ibu Tin. When she visited Mrs. Sal's family who had just had their second grandchild, Mrs. Tin came to visit and gave a parcel containing food and other items. Not only Mrs. Sal's family were given gifts, but the neighbors whose houses were close to Mrs. Sal were also given food parcels (observation of Ibu. Tin's activities).

All of the women's kindness does not necessarily just grow but is also driven by the tradition of mutual assistance of the village community that has been going on so far. Even though they have done a lot of good, as humans, they also admit that they are still unable to maximally avoid bad things from their body parts, such as *ngrasani* (backbiting others) (interview, Ibu Mur, 16 July 2020). However, they still always try to keep their mouths from talking bad things and talking less about other people (interview with Ibu Kham, 08 July 2020).

## 5 Conclusion

The construction of the women of the Annaqsyabandiyah al-Mujaddadiyah al-Khalidiyah tarekat in Karang Tengah Village has become part of a community tradition that has been passed down from generation to generation for hundreds of years and is reflected in worship activities to the Creator and social relations in the community.

## References

1. van Bruinessen M (1992) *Tarekat Naqsyabandiyah di Indonesia*. Bandung: Mizan
2. Mulyadi A (2015) BUDAYA EGALITARIANISME PEREMPUAN MADURA DALAM TAREKAT NAQSYABANDIYAH. KARSA J Sos dan Budaya Keislam. https://doi.org/10.19105/karsa.v23i1.614
3. Sururin S (2017) Perempuan dalam Lintasan Sejarah Tasawuf. Ulumuna. https://doi.org/10.20414/ujis.v14i2.219
4. Habibi I (2019) Perempuan Dalam Thariqah (Studi Terhadap Peran Perempuan Dalam Thariqah Tijaniyah Bangka). Sci J Has Penelit 4(2):268–291. https://doi.org/10.32923/sci.v4i2.1020
5. Nurika BW (2018) NILAI-NILAI SOSIAL PADA PENGAMAL TAREKAT NAQSYABANDIYAH DESA TAWANG REJO WONODADI BLITAR," *Spiritualita*, vol. 1, no. 1. https://doi.org/10.30762/spr.v1i1.638
6. Firdaus F (2018) Tarekat Qadariyah Wa Naqsabandiyah: Implikasinya Terhadap Kesalehan Sosial. Al-Adyan J Stud Lintas Agama 12(2):55–72. https://doi.org/10.24042/ajsla.v12i2.2109
7. Salahudin M, Arkumi B (2017) APLIKASI AMALAN TAREKAT QADIRIYAH WA NAQSABANDIYAH DAN HASILNYA SEBAGAI NILAI PENDIDIKAN JIWA," *ESOTERIK*, vol. 2, no. 1. https://doi.org/10.21043/esoterik.v2i1.1619
8. Sayyi A (2017) Wasiat Pendidikan Sufistik Dalam Naskah Tanbih Mursyid Tarekat Qodiriyyah Naqsyabandiyah Suryalaya (Telaah Pemikiran Guru Mursyid Tqn Suryalay), *FIKROTUNA*, vol. 5, no. 1. https://doi.org/10.32806/jf.v5i1.2947
9. Fuad J (2013) PENDIDIKAN KARAKTER DALAM PESANTREN TASAWUF. J Pemikir Keislam 23(1). https://doi.org/10.33367/tribakti.v23i1.13
10. Berger T, Luckmann PL (1990) *Tafsir Sosial atas Kenyataan, Risalah tentang Sosiologi Pengetahuan*. Jakarta: LP3ES
11. Izutsu T (1993) *Konsep-Konsep Etika Religius dalam al-Quran*. Yogyakarta: Tiara Wacana
12. Fata AK (2011) "TAREKAT," *Al-Ulum*
13. Mark Woodward BJS (2014) De-colonizing Islam and Muslim feminism, in *Gender and Power In Indonesian Islam: Leaders, Feminists, Sufis and Pesantren Selves*
14. Saude, Rusdin, Nurhayati, Darlis (2018) Contributions of Tarekat towards Islam Nusantara Preservation (Study of Qadiriyah Tarekat in Palu City). https://doi.org/10.1088/1755-1315/175/1/012182
15. Sururin S (2017) Perempuan dalam Lintasan Sejarah Tasawuf. Ulumuna 14(2):299–322. https://doi.org/10.20414/ujis.v14i2.219

16. Khamim M (2019) Mursyid Perempuan Dalam Tarekat: Studi Kepemimpinan Perempuan dalam Tarekat Naqsyabandiyah Mazhariyah di Madura, UIN Sunan Ampel Saudaranya
17. Hartono J (2018) *Metoda Pengumpulan Data dan Teknik Analisis Data*. Yogyakarta: Andi
18. BPS B (2021) *Kecamatan Kembaran dalam Angka 2021*. Banyumas: Badan Pusat Statistik Kabupaten Banyumas

# The Politics of Exclusion Based on Religious Identity (Shiah Case in Indonesia)

**Anik Farida, Adison Adrianus Sihombing, Dede Syarif, Retno Kartini Savitaningrum Imansah, Juju Saepudin, Sabara, Muhammad Ali Saputra, and Suprapto Prapto**

**Abstract** The marginalization phenomenon of Shia groups happening after the reform is appealing to examine deeper. In the past, the relations between the state, society, and Shiite followers used to be harmonious and coexisting. They were not prohibited from performing religious rituals. Unfortunately, post-reform inclusion has shifted to exclusion. The current study aims to describe, explore, and analyze in depth the phenomenon of an exclusion act against Shia minority community by individuals or groups through black campaigns in the election. Field research has been carried out in 2020 within the areas with a frequent level of exclusion cases, Bandung and Jakarta. In these regions, there live sizeable Shia followers with frequent cases of political exclusion against them. It is a qualitative study grounded in primary and secondary data. They are obtained through in-depth interviews of Shiite followers

A. Farida · A. A. Sihombing (✉) · R. K. S. Imansah · J. Saepudin · Sabara · M. A. Saputra · S. Prapto
The National Research and Innovation Agency Jakarta, Jakarta, Indonesia
e-mail: sonadi2017@gmail.com; adis009@brin.go.id

A. Farida
e-mail: anik005@brin.go.id

R. K. S. Imansah
e-mail: retn024@brin.go.id

J. Saepudin
e-mail: juju001@brin.go.id

Sabara
e-mail: saba005@brin.go.id

M. A. Saputra
e-mail: muha260@brin.go.id

S. Prapto
e-mail: supr040@brin.go.id

D. Syarif
Islamic State University, Sunan Gunung Djati Bandung, Bandung, Indonesia
e-mail: dede.syarif@uinsgd.ac.id



Nawawi et al. (eds.), *Managing Disruption and Developing Resilience for a Better Southeast Asia*, Springer Proceedings in Humanities and Social Sciences,
https://doi.org/10.1007/978-981-96-2116-3_36

who directly encounter political exclusion as candidates for legislators, politicians, or members of political parties. It finds that certain strategies disqualify political opponents through religious identity issues. The strategies are intended that the candidates from the Shia groups are marginalized from political contestation. The political strategy of religious identity issues is an exclusion act against the Shia or suspected Shia politicians due to their close relationship with Shiite figures. Political exclusion occurs in the run-up to elections. This study contributes to provide a broad and deep horizon toward political and religious education, so it brings about a mature, civilized, religious, and cultural democratic life which accepts and appreciates differences.

**Keywords** Politics of exclusion · Religious identity · Shia · Election

## 1 Introduction

The politics of exclusion is one of the crucial and phenomenal issues in the reform regime. Minority groups, Shiites who used to live side by side with the community [1], have changed significantly. They are excluded from the political scene in the public sphere on the basis of religious identity. It becomes a problem in the relationship of the state with society and among groups in the political process [2]. There are estimated 5 million Shia followers in Indonesia, and around 2.5 million people who practice their teachings [3]. They do not appear to be Shiites because they hide their identity to avoid conflict, and they do not build certain houses of worship [4]. The exclusion of Shia groups is increasing in Indonesia as indicated in the report of several research institutions, such as Setara Institute [5], CRCS UGM [1], Research and Development of the Ministry of Religious Affairs [6]. Setara Institute (2014) reported that between the range of 2008 and 2012, there had been hundreds of violence cases against the Shia community [1]. They became the target of discrimination that began with physical violence, such as what happened in Batang (2002), Tegal (2003), Pasuruhan (2004), Bondowoso (2005), Bangil (2007), Sampang (2012 and 2013), Jember (2013), and Karimun (2014) [7]. There found even anti-Shia propaganda expanding to all sectors, including cyberspace [6].

The existing literature on Shia has so far focused on four perspectives. *First,* theological perspective-doctrine, which is conducted by Sofjan [8], that despite the pros and cons, this community has contributed significantly to the spread of Islam in Southeast Asia. They have instilled the light of Islam, consistent as straight followers who are obedient to Allah. *Second,* studies under the perspective of sociology [9, 10], which demonstrate the position of Shiites as a minority group struggling to gain recognition from the societies and the state. They adopt a strategy that fits the social system. It is performed as a way to counter the anti-Shiite sentiment organized systematically in the reform regime. *Third,* a study under the perspective of regulation [11], which shows inconsistency between the constitution and regulations as a reference and political implementation of state recognition of religion. The studies have not paid particular attention to the political issue of Shia exclusion, and they have not been properly mapped. *Fourth,* perspective politics. In perspective this found existence state policies that are exclude Shia. Farida's study (2022) found Circular Letter_Governor of South Sulawesi (Circular (SE) number 450/0224/B. Welfare issued on January 12, 2017) [12] which was followed up by Circular_Mayor of Makassar No. 400/402/Welfare/IX/2019 [13] about Appeal Watching and Anticipating Deployment Shia Regional Secretariat by the Makassar City Government. SE in Makassar City addressed the sub-districts of Makassar City about Appeal for Beware and Anticipate Shia. The issuance of the Circular Letter on Shia vigilance and anticipation has made this group inaccessible to public facilities, such as the use of mosques, and other public spaces.

Campaigns in political events such as regional head elections often use hate speech against candidates suspected of being Shiite members. Consequently, Shiites receive discriminatory treatment, are marginalized, and lose their political rights as citizens. Therefore, three questions are formulated: (a) how does the politics of exclusion happen against the Shia groups? (b) what kinds of politics of exclusion are encountered by the Shiites? and (c) what are the motives and how is the impact of political exclusion on Shia groups in the democratic life of Indonesia?

This study perceives that the exclusion occurs in the form of political praxis that leads to the loss of citizenship rights of Shia community. The stigmatization against Shia as a deviant and dangerous sect is reproduced on social media into a more political framing that "Shiites are as dangerous as communists" and "Shiites are anti-NKRI" [14]. It is a political issue that arises during the political events right before regional head elections and general elections. Shia became the new political capital, effectively used to gather political support and defeat opponents. In addition, some regional heads provide support activities rejecting their presence. For example, Garut government accommodates the declaration of Anti-Shiite National Alliance movement in the hall of Garut Regency as a political campaign [15]; the head of Bogor issues a circular prohibiting Shiites from celebrating Ashura around Bogor area [16]; and so does the head of South Sulawesi with the discriminatory regional regulations [17].

## 2 Literature Review

### *2.1 Politics of Exclusion*

Exclusion is a concept that possesses a lot of meanings [18, 19]. In this study, exclusion is intended to describe situations in which a certain social group is deliberately marginalized that they do not fain their rights. Exclusion is adopted to describe a political act by a group against particular individuals or group, so they lose their national rights. Correspondingly, Giddens [20] suggests that exclusion is a broad concept. It focuses attention on various factors preventing an individual or group from having opportunities as experienced by the Shiites.

The marginalization process during the reform occurred politically before the contestation of political activities. In politics, people with certain stigma, such as Shiites, may go into social exclusion [21]. Shiites, as a minority religious group, are excluded from the political contestation. Political exclusion is, therefore, defined as the process of political marginalization and neglect against the group with different religious understanding from that of the majority [22].

**Religious Identity**

Identity is part of a complex social process which brings up our characteristics, attitudes, or modes of action while distinguishing us from others [23]. Religious identity refers to the self-identity attached to certain individuals or group that creates a religious attitude from which they differ from others. Identity is dynamic and liquid. Castells [24] noted that identity is influenced and shaped by several factors, such as economy, society, politics, and culture. In this regard, the religious identity of Shiites is problematized for political interests. Therefore, they hide their identity for safety from the political act of exclusion. They are excluded in various ways, such as the prohibition for the Shiites to access public spaces like open fields, grand mosques, etc.

Shia community has been refused to use the grand mosques to carry out religious activities, such as the great day of Ashura to commemorate the death of Hasan and Husein [25, 26]. The exclusion is given for a religious identity. According to Bhargava [27], religious identity-based exclusion is categorized into two, exclusion from religion and exclusion based on religion. The first is marginalizing people from freedom and equality of rights in religion while the second is excluding society from the wider context beyond religious domain, such as what happens to the Shiites. The exclusion happens when religious identity is used as an excuse to exclude Shiites from legal and political rights.

*Shia, the Minority Group*

The concept of Shia is derived from Arabic, which means follower. It is derivated from the phrase *Shiatu Ali* or "the followers of Ali". It refers to Ali ibn Abi Thalib, the son-in-law of the Prophet Muhammad. Within the leadership series after the death of the Prophet Muhammad, Ali was the fourth and the last of the four Khilafah (656–661). While the Shiites view Ali as the first imam and position him and his descendants as the legitimate heirs of leadership after the Prophet Muhammad passed away. The Shiite followers organizationally shelter under several organizations, such as *The Association of Jama'ah Ahlul Bait Indonesia* (IJABI), the national Shiite organization established in 2000. Jalaluddin Rakhmat, the founder of IJABI, stated that the number of Shia members is around 2.5 million throughout Indonesia [28]. The other Shiite organization is *Ahlul Bait Indonesia* (ABI), which was established in 2010.

Shiite followers are called minority groups as their number is less than 50% of the population within the area of their domicile [29]. In general, a minority finds it hard to be accepted by the majority. However, they have the right to be represented in the government because minority rights are protected by international law [30].

Similarly, they have the right to vote and to be voted, the right to associate, to raise opinions, and the right to be represented in state organizations. A discussion on minority rights is not limited to the issue of political rights. In short, their human rights are protected and guaranteed in the constitution. Pasal 28 Bab XA Undang-Undang Dasar Republik Indonesia Tahun 1945 sebagaimana dirubah dalam amandemen ke-2 Undang-Undang Dasar 1945, menjamin hak-hak asasi manusia.

# 3 Method

## *3.1 Topic Selection*

The politics of exclusion against Shiites has caused difficulties, discriminations, and even loss of rights to a decent life equal to others. The issue is deliberately selected as the research object because it has received a broad response of public. A little attention is given that exclusion has led to oppression, injustice, and betrayal of the noble values of humanity, which are contrary to the spirit of democracy. Moreover, it is performed on the basis of religious identity to win political contestation. In addition, an analysis of the relevance of the political act of exclusion to the political interests of power is significant to respond to the insistence of public who feel such action is reasonable. In this condition, the potential for horizontal conflicts will continue to exist that may disrupt the life of Indonesian democracy. This reason shows that the politics of exclusion against Shiites is a crucial issue to understand as the foundation of democratic policies and the structuring of common life in diversity.

**Case Selection**

This study selected Shiite cases in Bandung and Jakarta because these areas contain a great number of Shia followers, and cases of political exclusion often systematically occur in the reform regime. They lost political rights and, even, citizenship rights. They are selected as the subjects of discussion, on the one hand, considering that Indonesia has adopted a democratic system of governance, and the leader is directly elected by the society. However, it is, on the other hand, common for them to receive the practice of political exclusion before the political events. The author intends to acknowledge the concrete experience of the adherents as parts of Indonesian citizens. Their experience of being the subject of research is expected to provide a comprehensive understanding and insight for solving the problem of Shiites in Indonesia.

*Research and Data Types*

It is a qualitative study grounded in primary and secondary data. The primary data are collected through interviews with informants of Shiite politicians who experience exclusion while participating in legislative elections, IJABI and ABI national boards, and the party boards. They are involved to see the dynamics of the politics of exclusion that happens to them. The research was conducted in 2020. It begins from desk-review and collection of secondary materials by mapping down the issue of political exclusion that occurs at the level of the text. Interviews are performed several times at Grand Galaxy Park Bekasi, at Hotel Sakti Bandung, and also by phone to confirm and ensure the information. The research is initially performed by asking permission and willingness of the informants to be interviewed. In the interview, the questions focus on the process, form, and motives of the politics of exclusion and its impact. Data are analyzed in two forms. First, data processing which starts from data reduction, data display through summary and synopsis based on the topic of the findings, and data verification for the conclusion drawing. Second, the analysis follows the interpretation technique that starts from data restatement, followed by description to find patterns or tendency, and ends with interpretation to reveal the meaning.

# 4 Results

## *4.1 Exclusion Process*

This study opens up an idea that the politics of exclusion happens to the informants in two modes. The first, exclusion from religion, which refers to the process of marginalizing Shiites from religious freedom and equality of rights. The second, exclusion from a broader context beyond the religious domain. Shiites are excluded for their religious identity. The process begins with stigma, for example, the Shiites are heretical to whom we need to be cautious. The stigma lets Shiites isolated. As a result, they are shunned so as not to be affected by their misguided understanding. Stigmatization causes Shiites to be discriminated against in aspect of social life, such as religion and politics, as encountered by the first informant when he was a member of a political party. His religious identity was not a problem, yet in the run-up to his candidacy as a legislative member, religious identity turned out to be crucial and traced by his political party. It is known that he had been witnessed as a Shia follower. Since then, his opportunities and access to continue his political career were stopped because there had been a political exclusion. Similarly, it also happened to the second informant who managed to pass the nomination of a legislative member. However, the black campaign, which brought up the Shia label, had a direct impact on the low vote gain for him in the 2014 election. It was different from the result of his candidacy in 2004, which did not highlight the politics of identity or Shiite issues as black campaign propaganda. As a result, he won the vote and managed to be a legislative member.

The third informant encountered a different experience, as a politician who had a political opportunity to finally be elected because he gained over 56% votes. Although at that time he was sued, he managed to gain high votes for the election area of West Java II, Bandung regency-West Bandung regency, so he was successfully sworn in as a member of the Central House of Representatives. It happened because the informant was persecuted with various negative campaigns against him. The persecution led to an advantage for him. He received sympathy from the wider community and eventually gained victory, as depicted in the following interview excerpts:

> *"....... the more intense the negative campaign that called me "the center of heresy", the more militant my followers are, and intuitively, people sided with the persecuted. It means that onced somebody is persecuted, people are then sympathetic to him/her" (interview, the third informant, July 18, 2020).*

## Forms of Exclusion

The form of exclusion against the Shiites is through the politics of identity as a black campaign. Identity as a Shia follower is politicized through extreme interpretation, as admitted by the first informant, a politician from Partai Keadilan Sejahtera (PKS). He failed to be a member of the provincial legislative because Shia became a legitimate reason for the politics of exclusion. Most PKS members disagreed with the existence of Shiites, even the party leaders strongly refused it. It is presented in the following interview excerpts:

> *My candidacy was obstructed, especially in the internal environment of the party because the leader of PKS in West Java province was antipathy against Shia. Let alone running as a member of the Legislative, my membership was also revoked, so I could not be nominated, let alone being witnessed into a Legislative representing PKS* (Informant 1, July 15, 2020).

The informant's failure was because he was suspected of being a member of Shia, even though according to Law no 1/1965 on Blasphemy Shia is a sect categorised as a blasphemous phrase.

> *Circular letter containing _ appeal to the public to be vigilant and anticipate understand Shia already should published by the government as state administrators. For it to happen order in society, because could prevent society not to infiltrated understand Shia. Backrest the law enough clear namely the PnPs Law No. 1/1965* [31], *namely: phrase religious blasphemy. The Blasphemy Law also contains: provision for warn people, adherents , members and/ or administrator organizations that do deviant things_from the trees religious teachings . Decision for warn the could taken based on consideration from the Minister of Religion, the Minister of Home Affairs, and the Attorney General. If rated still Keep going violate, then individual the could convicted a maximum of five years and the organization could disbanded at a time declared as organization or Genre forbidden* (Informant, 05 June 2021).

Another form of exclusion experienced by Shiites began from anti-Shiite propaganda by social media, Facebook. It was massively shared that Shiites are heretical, deviated from Islam. Once came up a candidate from Shia, he or she was accused as an intrusion that would destroy PKS from within. The propaganda was full of political interests, restraining the pace of the informant's political movement who kept going for the Legislative. Finally, the party managed to expel the informant from the nomination. The second informant is a member of PDIP who experiences a politics of exclusion through "Syiasisasi", which is a label attached as if he were a Shiite. Anti-Shia group views that people who are close to Shiites are automatically considered to support the presence of Shia in Indonesia. A political act of exclusion also happened to the third informant, a Shia cleric as well as one of the founders of Partai Demokrat (Democratic Party) in 2001. The informant did not get any political office. It is presented in the following interview excerpts:

> *Some party officials fear that if I have a political office or become a member of the Legislative, representing Partai Demokrat, the party's vote will get down, even abandoned by the constituents because I am a Shia. The informant refers such political calculation to the political practice of identity (interview with informants, July 4, 2020).*

Thus, the politics of exclusion closes the access of Shiites to engage in practical politics. There is no opportunity to run as a legislative member, even the nomination is hampered by the stigma that Shia is a heretical and dangerous religious group.

*Exclusion Motives and Effects*

According to the informants, in general, people make exclusion acts with political motives. It is about strengthening the hegemony of a community organization against others. The choice is political contestation. The ban on Shiite politicians is made, one of which is through the politics of exclusion designed to be a massive movement to prevent the spread of Shiites in Indonesia. The assumption developed among the community is that if we let the Shiites in, they will grow into a political elite and control the country. It is feared that if they become a political elite, a number of regulations with Shia tendency are formulated so that they can be detrimental to the Islamic majority group. In this context, the politics of identity becomes prominent for those who are anti-Shia.

The political practice of exclusion has a widespread impact on the lives of Shiites, with their political careers stopped. It is revealed by the second informant that he is harmed and interrupted after the nomination due to the propaganda of Shia issues on social media, since 2017. He is also treated unpleasantly, even he lost the attention and service of the government of Bandung. Whereas, they used to facilitate the activities of IJABI before. Everything has changed since the massive political exclusion against Shiites. Local governments and political figures accidentally become afraid and shun them. They even close a space and opportunity for Shiite followers, as presented in the following interview with the second informant:

> *A few months ago, I participated in the selection of members of the Regional Broadcasting Commission (KPID) of West Java. I was not accommodated due to a religious identity even though I am quite competent, within some reasons. Firstly, I'm an expert in communications. Secondly, I once worked in commission one. Thirdly, I wrote a field of study related to broadcasting communication in the media (interview with the second informant, July 25, 2020).*

## 5 Discussion

This study explains in more depth why Shia groups are marginalised, and what factors cause it, as well as the impact experienced by Shia groups. In the past, the relations between the State, Society, and Shiite followers are harmonious and coexisting.

They are not prohibited from performing religious rituals [1]. Unfortunately, post-reform inclusion has shifted to exclusion. The politics of exclusion always happens in the run-up to legislative elections. It is intended to stop the candidates considered Shiites because they are close to Shia figures. This act of exclusion has always been repeated because it proves effective in defeating the political opponents. The term ambiguous means that the state's attitude on the one hand guarantees freedom of religion in accordance with the constitution, but the rules under it are contrary to the constitution because they contain the marginalisation of religious-based minority groups, including Shia. It is indicated by the issuance of circulars that harm the Shia community [12, 15, 32]. Although the democratic country holds laws that guarantee the rights of all its citizens, it sometimes goes the other way around in practice.

The party's decision not to involve the informants in various political posts is in line with the rise of black campaigns about Shiites. Even, social media provides negative information about the Shia candidates [33, 34]. Some conversations that lead to the attitude of anti-Shiite sentiment also rise on social media, with the hashtag # *antiSyiah* on Twitter, the anti-Shia groups on *Facebook*, and also on the websites of anti-Shia organizations in the country. According to a report by BBC Indonesia, in 2015, the use of the word # *antiSyiah* reached up to 39,000 times. This number was more than the use of the same word during the years 2006–2011 in which anti-Shia was relatively rare. Even, in 2012, the anti-Shia expression did not reach 100 in the digital public space [35].

In cyberspace, Shiites are discriminated against in relation to not only religious but also local and global political issues. There found even a narrative that Shiites are as dangerous as PKI (Indonesian Communist Party). They are threats to religion, nation, and state [36]. Cyberspace, thus, becomes a vehicle for the shifting of conflictual relations between religious groups in the country, that previously happened in real life and now goes in the virtual space. The political opponents of the informants use cyberspace to attack, so they are excluded from the practical political events.

From the perspective of a democratic state, the politics of exclusion is not compatible with the spirit of democracy, which always holds freedom for the majority and minority groups. Freedom is a characteristic of a democratic country. Freedom is *the distinctive nature* of democracy from authoritarianism and totalitarianism [37]. So, an act of exclusion against a minority group means negating freedom. In this case, Indonesia's democracy can be said to have not been successful that Shiites need to work hard to obtain equal citizenship rights to others.

On the one hand, Indonesia is not a country of a certain religion. Consequently, it has to protect all religions without exception. In a theistic state, a domination of one religion over another is impossible. It is also impossible to be a monopoly of a religious interpretation of one particular religious group against another religious group [38, 39]. However, on the other hand, the state recognizes that religion is an integral part of the life of the nation and state. Indonesia is built on the plurality of religions professed by all the population. Therefore, the act of exclusion against Shiites is complicated to imagine. The state has legal instruments and policies to protect the rights of citizens to believe in a religion, including minority groups. The second precept of Pancasila firmly declares a just and civilized humanity. Furthermore, Law

No. 10 of 2016 on regional election has set a ban on the practice of the politics of identity. Article 69 letter (B) states that the campaign is prohibited from insulting an individual, religion, ethnicity, race, class of candidates, and/or also political party.

However, politics of identity is still rife with stigmatization and anti-Shiite propaganda that Shia is a cult which does not conform to the mainstream Islamic teachings, and it is a big threat [40]. If we look at the population data of Shia groups, the suspicion against Shiites as threats to Indonesian unity is less reasonable. The number of Shiites in Indonesia is very small, only around 2.5 million of the overall population of Indonesia [41]. They are divided into three groups: Ikatan Jamaah Ahlul Bait Indonesia (IJABI); Ahlul Bait Indonesia (ABI); and Organisasi Ahlul Bait Dukungan Sosial dan Pendidikan (OASE) [7]. Thus, the accusations addressed to the Shiites are closely related to political interests.

The widespread act of politics of exclusion is a precondition for the inhibition of the problem-solving on the protection of Shiites in Indonesia. Various efforts made to prevent the politics of exclusion against religious identity are not effective due to the unconducive response of society. Polarization and grouping are made by politicization of identity. The nature of diversity is betrayed and obliterated because the politics of identity seeks to magnify differences in order to generate new problems, hatred, and hostility. Politicization is conditioned to ostensibly intended to maintain the purity of Islam and the United State of the Republic of Indonesia [42, 43]. Whereas, the political goal is to marginalize the Shia groups from the practical political scene. Therefore, the phenomenon of the politics of exclusion always comes up before heading to the implementation of the democratic party. The immediate impact on Shiites is that they lose their political rights of citizenship, and the candidates who participate in the legislative nomination receive unfair treatment in the country with Pancasila democracy ideology.

This study confirms that the politics of exclusion always happens right before the general elections or regional elections to gain power and defeat the political opponents from Shia group. The negative narratives and stigma as misguided, heretical, dangerous groups are always reproduced by society who underestimate Shiites. They are also subjectively viewed by those who participate in political contestation. This study confirms the findings of previous studies that the issue of Shia is always interesting, sensitive, and effectively used in campaigns to attack political opponents [44–46]. It reveals the reproduction of the politics of exclusion by elite figures to create a wide range of public acts that result in the exclusion of Shiites at another level. The anti-Shia political motives are barriers for Shiites to sit and represent the public in the legislative. There has been anxiety from anti-Shia groups that the presence of Shiites in the political institutions, such as House of Representatives (DPR) and Regional People's Representative Assembly (DPRD), can result in various policies perceived as tools to fight for the presence of Shia in Indonesia.

The reproduced act of exclusion requires a plan on two levels. In addition to the anticipation, the exclusion act also helps them to live the same life as other citizens. As long as the Shia community is not protected by the state with various regulations and institutions, they will always be victims of political acts of exclusion and lose their citizenship rights. To address the religious identity-based political act of exclusion, a massive campaign is required through extension workers and speakers who are organically under the Ministry of Religious Affairs. They need to encourage the public not to involve religious issues in practical politics to prevent the possibility of social religious conflicts. In addition, it is necessary to develop a policy model for diversity management, such as religious moderation to prevent religious issues from causing religious conflict as a result of residual religious identity-based exclusion acts.

## 6 Conclusion

This study reveals that exclusion is a deliberate political act against Shiites who are actively involved in practical politics. It is employed against figures or candidates considered close to Shia. The action is made by political opponents with anti-Shia ideology to expel the Shiites in the political contestation, for example, a candidate for legislative members. It always happens repeatedly right before the implementation of the democratic party. The politics of exclusion is getting stronger because it gets the legitimacy of local government regulation which explicitly limits the religious freedom of Shia groups.

The current research opens up a perspective in viewing the political act of exclusion, not the static causal factors, but the dynamic process of how the politics of exclusion against Shiites is produced and reproduced right before the political contestation in the democratic party. They exploit various forms of misguided discourse, such as the issues regarding the danger of Shia candidate once they win the election and become a leader or member of the legislative. The social behavior of the people toward Shiites, which is always suspicious and antipathy, is continuously reproduced. It is depicted from the uncertain and unsupportive action of the government, who cannot protect their citizenship rights equally although the country adheres to a democratic system. As a result, social anxiety arises.

This research is limited in the data sources that rely only on Shiite informants who encounter exclusion, so it cannot be adopted as a strong and comprehensive foundation for policy formulation. Policy formulation requires extensive surveys and in-depth informant interviews. Surveys toward political figures, observations on the Shiite political rights services ahead of the democratic party, and interviews with informants on the experience of political exclusion of Shiites and their struggle in everyday life can be a strong basis for the purpose of improving services and protecting their rights to life. Further studies that accommodate a wider range of samples and diverse sources of information are highly recommended for a deeper understanding and better structuring of diverse social religious identities.

## References


1. Syarif D, Zulkarnain I, Sofjan D (2017) Anti Shi'Ism in Indonesia: genealogy, development, and methods. Harmoni 16(1):24–37. https://doi.org/10.32488/harmoni.v16i1.54
2. Hasan N (2018) Reformasi, religious diversity, and islamic radicalism after Suharto. J Indones Soc Sci Humanit 1(1):23–51. https://doi.org/10.14203/jissh.v1i1.2
3. Jalal (2022) Kang Jalal on Shia in Indonesia (Part 2). TEMPO.CO, 2012. https://en.tempo.co/read/427522/kang-jalal-on-shia-in-indonesia-part-2. Accessed 26 Mar 2022
4. Riadi S (2022) Pengikut Syiah di Indonesia diklaim capai 5 juta. Sindonews.com, 2012. https://nasional.sindonews.com/berita/668456/15/pengikut-syiah-di-indonesia-diklaim-capai-5-juta. Accessed 24 Mar 2022.
5. Firdaus A (2011) NEGARA MENYANGKAL Kondisi Kebebasan Beragama/berkeyakinan di Indonesia 2010. Jakarta, 2011. https://setara-institute.org/
6. Sugiyarto W (2018) Pertumbuhan Syi'Ah Dan Relasinya Dengan Non Syi'Ah Di Kota Medan Sumatra Utara. Harmoni 17(2):272–289. https://doi.org/10.32488/harmoni.v17i2.294
7. Rosidi A et al (2017) Dinamika Syiah Di Indonesia, 1st ed. Jakarta: Puslitbang Bimas Agama dan Layanan Keagamaan Badan Litbang dan Diklat Kementerian Agama RI, 2017
8. Sofjan D (2013) Sejarah dan budaya syiah di Asia Tenggara, 1st ed, vol 5, no. 2. Yogyakarta: Sekolah Pascasarjana Universitas Gadjah Mada.
9. Syarif D (2018) Contrasting trajectories of Shi'a emergence in post-new order Indonesia. J Shi'a Islam Stud 11(2):99–116. https://doi.org/10.1353/isl.2018.0007
10. Zulkifli Z (2009) The struggle of the Shi'is in Indonesia. Universiteit Leiden The Netherlands
11. Kholiludin T (2009) Kuasa Negara Atas Agama (Politik Pengakuan, Diskursus Agama Resmi dan Diskriminasi Hak Sipil. Semarang: Rasail Media Group
12. Akbar C (2017) Inilah Isi Surat Edaran Mewaspadai Syiah 'Berkop Propinsi Sulsel. Hidayatullah.com. https://hidayatullah.com/berita/nasional/read/2017/01/26/110492/inilah-isi-surat-edaran-mewaspadai-syiah-berkop-propinsi-sulsel.html. Accessed 06 Apr 2022
13. Ramadhan G (2019) Pemkot Makassar Rilis Edaran Antisipasi Penyebaran Syiah. tirto.id
14. Rachmah I (2016) Cyberculture and sectarianism in Indonesia: the rise of Shia Media and Anti-Shia Online Movements. J Komun Islam 6(2). http://jki.uinsby.ac.id/index.php/jki/article/view/118
15. Akbar C (2016) MUI Garut Mengaku Siapkan Fatwa Sesat Syiah. *Hidayatullah.com*. https://www.hidayatullah.com/berita/berita-dari-anda/read/2016/03/07/90678/mui-garut-mengaku-siapkan-fatwa-sesat-syiah.html. Accessed 25 Mar 2022
16. Nizar and Syaf (2015) Syiah Gugat Bima Arya dan ANNAS DKI Jakarta. *voa-islam.com*, Jakarta
17. Irfan (2018) DPRD Sulawesi Selatan Segera Rancang Perda Larangan Syiah. *Inews MCB*, Makassar
18. Sen A (2000) Social exclusion: concept, application, and scrutiny. Social Dev. Manila, Philippines: Asian Development Bank
19. Silver H (1995) Reconceptualizing social disadvantage: three paradigms of social exclusion. Social Exc. Geneva: Institute of International Labour Studies
20. Giddens A (2006) Sociology, 5th Editio. Polity Press
21. Lawang RMZ (2014) Beberapa Hipotesis Tentang Eksklusi Sosial di Indonesia. J Ilmu Sos Mamangan 2(1).
22. Voelkel J, Ren D, Brandt M (2019) Political inclusion reduces political prejudice
23. Torrissen W (2017) Staging cultural identities as political performance: Hålogaland Teater, North Norwegian stage language and the emancipation of North Norwegian identities staging cultural identities as political performance: Hålogaland Teater, North Norwegian stage l. Nord Theatr Stud 28(2):6–35
24. Castells M (2010) The power of identity: the information age; economy, society, and culture. Blackwell Company, United Kingdom

25. AdminKotabogor.id (2015) Pemkot Keluarkan Edaran Larangan Perayaan Asyura di Kota Bogor, *KotaBogor.go.id*. https://kotabogor.go.id/index.php/show_post/detail/2346/pemkot-keluarkan-edaran-larangan-perayaan-asyura-di-kota-bogor. Accessed 08 Apr 2022
26. Permana S (2015) Wali Kota Bogor Larang Warganya Rayakan Asyura. *TEMPO.CO*
27. Bhargava R (2004) Inclusion and exclusion in South Asia: the role of religion. Human Development Report Office
28. Formichi C (2014) 'From fluid identities to sectarian labels', a historical investigation of Indonesia's Shi'a communities. Al-Jāmi'ah J Islam Stud 52(1):101–126. https://doi.org/10.14421/ajis.2014.521.101-126
29. Nasution MI (2013) Demokrasi dan Politik Minoritas Di Indonesia. Politica 4(2)
30. Sofjan D (2016) Religious diversity and politico-religious intolerance in Indonesia and Malaysia. Rev Faith Int Aff 14(4):53–64. https://doi.org/10.1080/15570274.2016.1248532
31. Sukarno (1965) Penetapan Presiden Republik Indonesia NOMOR 1 Tahun 1965 Tentang Pencegahan Penyalahgunaan Dan/Atau Penodaan Agama Presiden. Indonesia, p. 2
32. Hidayat B (2015) Bima Arya Larang Pelantikan Pengurus Anti-Syiah Bogor. *Tempo.co*. https://nasional.tempo.co/read/720558/bima-arya-larang-pelantikan-pengurus-anti-syiah-bogor/full&view=ok. Accessed 06 Apr 2022
33. Facebook (2014) Dakwah islam - Ngeri !! PDIP & Jokowi Menang, Tokoh Syiah Jalaludin Rahmat Menjadi Menteri Agama, *facebook*. https://m.facebook.com/464819463662429/photos/ngeri-pdip-jokowi-menang-tokoh-syiah-jalaludin-rahmat-menjadi-menteri-agama-waja/486955708115471/?locale=ar_AR. Accessed 28 Mar 2022
34. Mianarulita (2014) Waspada Caleg Syiah, *Scribd*. Accessed 1 April 2022
35. Franciska C (2016) #TrenSosial: Menelusuri jejak percakapan anti-Syiah di dunia maya, *BBC News Indonesia*. https://www.bbc.com/indonesia/majalah/2016/01/151127_trensosial_antisyiah. Accessed 09 Apr 2022
36. Hikmah (2017) Syiah dan PKI Ancaman Bagi Agama, Bangsa dan Negara, *Ciledugonline*. https://www.ciledugonline.com/2018/02/syiah-dan-pki-ancaman-bagi-agama-bangsa.html. Accessed 01 Apr 2022
37. Lipson L (1964) The democratic civilization. Oxford University Press, New York
38. Kementerian Agama TP (2019) Moderasi Beragama, 1st ed. Kementerian Agama, Jakarta
39. Ropi I (2017) Religion and regulation in Indonesia
40. Makhsum A (2019) Stigmatisasi Dan Propaganda Anti-Syiah: Sorotan Deskriptif Gerakan Annas. J C 12(2):182. https://doi.org/10.20961/cmes.12.2.37894
41. Chadijah R (2018) Mengintip Warga Syiah di Jakarta Sambut Asyura. *BeritaBenar*. https://www.benarnews.org/indonesian/berita/syiah-asyura-09202018120625.html. Accessed 07 Apr 2022
42. Wahyudi J, Wahid M (2015) Peminggiran Minoritas Dan Absennya Multikulturalisme Di Ranah Lokal (Studi Kasus Komunitas Muslim Syiah Di Sampang). JPP (Jurnal Polit. Profetik) 3(1):65–81. http://journal.uin-alauddin.ac.id/index.php/jpp/article/view/823.
43. Farida A (2014) Di Bandung Jawa Barat Islamic Mass Organiza Tions ' Responses To Shi ' a Muslims in Bandung , West Java Anik Farida. Penamas 159–175
44. Besman A (2017) Perubahan Pola Pencitraan Ridwan Kamil dalam Pilwakot Bandung 2013 Dan Pemilihan Gubernur Jawa Barat 2018. J Ilmu Pemerintah Widya Praja 43(2):111–124. https://doi.org/10.33701/jipwp.v43i2.53
45. Haris A (2016) Perkawinan Lintas Aliran ( Sunni- Syi ' I ). Mebara Tebu Ireng 12(01):83–102
46. Hikmawan MD (2017) Politik Perbedaan: Minoritas Dalam Implementasi Kebijakan. JIPAGS J Indones Public Adm s Stud 1(1). https://doi.org/10.31506/jipags.v1i1.1268

# Where is Our Old Respect for Each Other? Reflection on Indonesia Society Towards Homosexuality at the Beginning of the 20th and 21st Centuries

**Amelia Rahmawati**

**Abstract** Gender and sexuality discourse has changed in Indonesian or the Dutch East Indies societies' perspective, specifically for homosexuals, during the beginning of the twentieth and twenty-first centuries. Nowadays, it is common to find cases that discriminate against gender and sexual minorities, including homosexuals. Either directly or the role of the media in strengthening stigma in society. It is a problem for Indonesia, which is considered an intolerant country, but on the other hand, it is also a country that upholds democracy. Therefore, this article aims to look at the process of changing perspective on gender and sexuality discourse with a focus on homosexuality. It starts by comparing and analyzing phenomena related to the existence of homosexuals in two different periods. During the research, historical methods have been used in data collection obtained from manuscripts, archives, official reports, newspapers, academic works, journal, and articles. This article found that a change in perspective on gender and sexuality discourse, especially homosexuality, occurred during the colonial government's hunt for homosexuals in the Dutch East Indies from 1938 to 39. Through this journey, acceptance and respect for homosexuals as part of social and cultural diversity in the Dutch East Indies were lost until now.

**Keywords** Homosexuality · Gender and sexuality discourse · History of homosexual · Dutch east indies · Indonesia · Homophobia · Sexual diversity · LGBT · Sexual politics

---

A. Rahmawati (✉)
Alumni History Department, Universitas Gadjah Mada, Yogyakarta, Indonesia
e-mail: amelia.rahmawati20@mail.ugm.ac.id





Nawawi et al. (eds.), *Managing Disruption and Developing Resilience for a Better Southeast Asia*, Springer Proceedings in Humanities and Social Sciences,
https://doi.org/10.1007/978-981-96-2116-3_37

## 1 Introduction

Recently, issues regarding gender and sexuality minority groups, known as the LGBT community, have been heating up in Indonesia. The spotlight on this group, one of which is homosexuality, occurred after the emergence of the phenomenon of legalization of same-sex marriage in several countries has triggered them [49] until their existence was increasingly easily found in public spaces [32]. There are two types of public space, namely the physical public space and the new one, virtual public space [28]. In the form of physical public space, the space for the homosexual community to express and show their identity openly is very risky. Rejection, discrimination, and violence will be things that they encounter frequently. This insecurity has prompted some homosexual communities to establish their own virtual space. According to [17], virtual public space has become an ideal choice for the homosexual community to be expressive and show their identity after the emergence of Lambda Indonesia in 1982—the first openly homosexual organization in Indonesia [36]. This phenomenon runs linearly with the development of homosexual communities or LGBT groups in the cyberspace who actively use this space as a safe space to interact and to speak out, demands regarding equality and equal rights.

The decision to be more open virtually isn't always a smoother one. The ease with which people can access information in cyberspace has benefited homosexual communities in various social classes to communicate, make friends, and gain virtual acceptance. On the other hand, it will also be easier for them to be known by the wider community, causing backlash [51]. As a patriarchal country that is also very heteronormative, it is not surprising that backlash can occur at any time. Everything the homosexual community does, virtual or not, their existence is still considered a moral threat [30].

Moral degradation, eastern norms, and religious doctrines always seem to justify the strengthening of sexual politics that discriminates against homosexuals. Even today, many Indonesian media narrate the homosexual or LGBT community in a discriminatory manner. As a country that promotes democracy, which should respect gender and sexual diversity, but at the same time intolerant, disrespectful, and discriminatory attitudes towards minority groups have also strengthened [37]. Oley [37] said that democracy and tolerance are two different things that cannot be used as a narrative that supports each other.

One online media editorial said that Indonesia as a nation is respectful and tolerant of diversity, including diversity in gender and sexuality [46]. If the assumption is true, it is necessary to look at Indonesia as a nation in the past. Was it true that the Indonesians in the past had great respect for diversity, including respect for the homosexual community? Then where did the respect go? What happened to the Indonesians in the past until they changed their perspective on homosexuality?

## 2 Method

This article is a history of sexuality in Indonesia using primary and secondary data. Manuscripts and archives of government reports are the primary data used, while newspapers, academic books, journals, and articles are secondary data that assist research in processing and analyzing data. Using this data is able to answer research questions about how the Indonesian people view the discourse of sexuality in general and homosexuality in particular? And how is the process of changing the Indonesian perspective on homosexuality, from respect and tolerance to the opposite?

By asking 'how,' we can see how the history of homosexual discourse itself in Indonesia or at the beginning of the twentieth century was known as the Dutch East Indies. By tracking historical data, it is found that the change in perspective on homosexuality was related to the global situation at the beginning of the twentieth century and became one of the factors in the formation of attitudes that have no respect for homosexuals or homophobic that continue to this day.

## 3 Results and Discussion

### *3.1 Sexual Practices: Homosexuality*

Homosexuality can conceptually be defined by the emergence of an emotional and sexual attraction to people of the same sex [36], regardless of the occurrence of sexual relations between the two. On the other hand, homosexual practice itself refers to sexual activity between two people of the same sex.

There is a binary dichotomy, namely homosexuality and heterosexuality, referred to as sexual orientation or sexual preference—in which gender is the sexual object's impulse in the current context. However, we should know that having such sexual behaviour does not necessarily generalize if the person has a sexual orientation or preference as homosexual as given or a 'natural' phenomenon from humans [34]. Homosexuals can also perform behaviours or activities like heterosexuals, so they are also known as bisexuals. Because for some people, being homosexual or bisexual refers to sexual practices rather than sexual identity, it is not surprising that many homosexuals have to live with fractured identities, in two worlds—as heterosexuals and homosexuals [31].

Homosexuals are often referred to homo. The concept was born and formed in a sexist and patriarchal society [25] and used by both men and women who are emotionally and sexually attracted to figures of the same sex. Although homosexuals are often attached to a man with a man or called gay, a woman with a woman is usually called a lesbian. Furthermore, this terminology continues to develop until it becomes a sexual identity or orientation. However, this article will be used as a homosexual rather than gay. It refers to the homosexual terminology that has been used since the early twentieth century—also as a time limitation in this article. Therefore, it will discuss homosexual behaviour carried out by men, both Europeans and natives themselves, who will ultimately inherit heteronormative discourses about sexuality.

### *3.2 Homosexual Practices in the Archipelago*

There are elements that support the formation of certain gender behaviour to certain sexual behaviour. These are elements linked to a particular culture. Likewise, local culture and traditions in Indonesia shape and enrich the diversity of gender and sexuality, such as homosexuality is a form of habit, including the tendency to practice homosexuality. This condition can be found in the anthropological writings of colonial government and missionaries in the nineteenth and twentieth centuries, who were interested to have sexual relations with boys and the practice of sodomy [2].

As in the report of Western research, [22, 23] mentioned the prevalence of sexual intercourse between men in Aceh. It started with homosexual practices carried out by uleebalangs with young Nias boys as slaves. Another form is found in the Sadati dance in Aceh—with poems that are notoriously erotic, most of them referred to same-sex sexual relations, in which the male slaves from Nias take on the role of the dancer to serve the desires of Acehnese men. More than that, the practice of institutionalized homosexuality by dance is inseparable from the conditions of poverty experienced by these children [36]. In addition, not a few Acehnese traders carry out homosexual practices around the local East Coast. Through Hurgronje's notes, it was explained that same-sex sexual relations, such as pederasty, have become a sociocultural phenomenon in this era [22, 23, 35], and this phenomenon is not something problematic to do.

Homosexual practice by indigenous has also been written by Julius Jacobs, a health official in Bali. He interviewed Balinese people from the late 19th to early twentieth centuries. He found that homosexual practices in Bali, both by men and women, both among white people as expatriates or even the indigenous themselves. It is not a problematic thing, but it is considered a harmless hobby [24].

It is different in Minangkabau, which frames homosexual relationships as patron-client. This relationship is manifested by the existence of a relationship between an adult male, called the *Induk-Jaw*i, and a teenage boy as his partner, called *Anak-Jawi,* within all-male life in the Surau. In the world of silat, it's known as a form of 'teacher-student relationship' [33]. Not only in Minangkabau, which frames this sexual practice as a power relation, but also in Java, *Mairilan* can be seen as an emotional-erotic relationship between students in Islamic boarding schools in Java that can also take the form of a relationship. By guidance in learning to help in their daily lives. This practice is still ongoing [35, 47]. *Mairilan* relationship is narrated in *Serat Centhini.* It talks about the diversity of Javanese people's sexual behaviour at that time [4]. Besides the *Mairilan, Serat Centhini* also explains the relationship between warok and gemblak in the Ponorogo by Reog tradition that also uses a form patron-client. This practice is in the context of performances carried out by waroks to gain supernatural powers. There is an assumption that waroks are prohibited from having sexual relations with the opposite sex. Cebolang and Nurwitri narrated that they had sexual relations with waroks in Ponorogo. The sexual adventure continued along with the dance journey, which also explains the practiced sodomy with Ki Adipati in Daha [4].

In the autobiography of a Javanese aristocratic child in Balongbendo, Surabaya Regency is also there is the idea of homosexuality. Through *Djalan Sampoerna* by Soetjipto—his writing found in a collection of works by Hans Overbeck, a German who was homosexual and both of them suspected of having a special relationship as a couple [15]. This manuscript describes the life of homosexuals in the Dutch East Indies in the 1920s. Soetjipto describes his adventures in gaining awareness as a homosexual when he was in fourth grade. This moment began when he met and had a relationship with a boy who was still in the seventh grade from Kediri. The closeness between the two started when they slept together, marking Soetjipto's first experience of having sex with a man. Although, Soetjipto became confused about his sexual orientation after that moment. Until that time, the man from Kediri told that there was an indigenous doctor in Kediri who confessed his love for him and justified his behaviour by saying,

*"...napsu itoe kena di poewasken dengan laki sama laki..."* (Perpustakaan Nasional 2014).

*"...that lust can be satisfied with men and men..."* (Perpustakaan Nasional 2014).

The statement from the doctor then makes Soetjipto's friend believe it. What they had done was common, especially since many of his friends were doing the same thing. This pattern, which later described the practice of paedophilia and homosexuality in the early twentieth century, then became a large phenomenon. His sexual adventures continued when he went to Surabaya. He met a Dutchman who mistook him for a lackey and ended up molested that night. What the Dutchman did made him think about how the Dutch—as a civilized nation—could do something like that. How could he know his habit? And did the Dutch have the culture to do something like that, invite the boy to his house and do it? [10]. This incident prompted Soetjipto to self-reflect on his same-sex attraction until he had time to become the *jongos* of the Dutchman when he met behind Societeit.

Through these historical facts and historiographical products that explain same-sex sexual activity as homosexuals, it seems the tendency to like the same sex or currently included in the category of sexual orientation or preference is not only carried out by white people who have been closely related to the labels of liberals and modernists, but also by the indigenous people themselves. Homosexual behaviour in the Dutch East Indies itself has become something common and not something new or foreign, when the practice of homosexuals is institutionalized as part of cultural heritage to get supernatural powers, sacred positions, become part of the performing arts heritage, or even just as a habit.

Along with changes in global sexual politics, the acceptance of the existence of homosexuals as part of the phenomenon and socio-cultural diversity at the beginning of the twentieth century in the Dutch East Indies did not last long. The hegemony of masculinity in colonial countries in this period with a patriarchal world frame, in the end, made heterosexuality a reference for a 'normal' or 'common' concept in sexual behaviour [44]. This understanding then injures the opposite dichotomy, in this case, homosexuality, as considered contrary to public morality and violates the provisions of heteronormative as a mainstream.

## *3.3 The Beginning of Loss of Respect for Sexual Diversity*

Using a transnational perspective to know a process of moral changes in European and colonial society and to know the impact on repressive actions against homosexuals. It can be drawn when changes in sexuality discourse occurred during the reign of Queen Alexandria Victoria. In the mid-nineteenth century, the leaders of the British Empire issued regulations that fundamentally repressed Western sexuality. It is not without reason, considering the private lives of a British official. They were often involved in sexual scandals in the past and it was considered discriminatory, insulting, and damaging to the image of the British Empire government with a new label as an unscrupulous official. Moreover, sexual scandals or homosexual scandals, in particular, are often associated with political considerations and power. As a practice of sodomy is believed to weaken or cleanse male virility in a country, in this case, it is considered a 'dangerous' behaviour [3]. This encouraged nationalists and conservative Christians a concept of puritan ethics or sexual morality; the necessity to refrain from sexual desire, to the prohibition of deviant sexual behaviour [38]. In fact, in its application, it also closes the circular spaces of discourse on sexuality as a science, such as the prohibition speak about the realm of sexuality openly, both in literacy products and in discussions of daily life, until the practice of homosexuality itself is then considered illegal.

The implementation of curbing or repression of sexuality among British people, in particular, does not necessarily make European society a moralist and 'civilized' figure in behaving or behaving like what Victoria wants. Otherwise, what happened was the disorganization of values and norms on sexuality. The form of hypocrisy of European aristocracy was increasingly exposed, especially several homosexual scandals within the British Empire during the Victorian era, one of which was the scandal of his crown prince, who would later become King Edward VII [38].

Victoria's puritan sexual morality doesn't ultimately apply only to England or their colonies but also very massively spread to other European countries. It can happen considering that the peak of Britain's glory as the largest empire in the nineteenth century played a role [44]. It was marked by the occurrence of the massive industrialization in the colonies, which took part in bringing and spreading repressive ideas against sexuality. There are assumptions that the European colony countries at the end of the 19th and early twentieth centuries were known to be places of refuge, hiding places for Europeans who have a preference for lovers of the same sex [3]. It was also supported by the condition that some of them left for the colony and ended up getting married late and even chose to reject a monogamous marriage that was identical to heterosexual—which is why they had avoided having sex with women in the beginning.

It should acknowledge if there is an imbalance in the sex ratio between European women and men in colonial countries that can trigger homosexual behaviour. This condition causes European men to be far away from the sexual attraction of European women, then the sexual desire can also be changed into other behaviours. In this case, triggering situational homosexual behaviour—both deliberately looking for male roommates, looking for his soulmate among his fellow countrymen or indigenous men [3]. However, there is also a group of European men who deliberately escape the European 'situation' by travelling abroad—which is where the region that is considered to have looser boundaries on morality and tolerance for the practice of homosexuality—and then engage in sexual relation by making 'friendships' or looking for men as partners.

Another trigger is the factor of geographical conditions. The tropical climate is also a destination favoured by many homosexuals besides being considered to offer an escape from the cruelty of European tyranny, freedom of thought, and creativity. In addition to the harsh colonial conditions, feelings of loneliness and boredom are prone to sexual excess. Some writers categorize homosexuality as a symptom of psychosis caused by a hot climate [3]. It's not surprising if many writers say that at the beginning of the twentieth century, the practice of homosexuality often occurred in remote areas or tropical areas—including in the Dutch East Indies—as young indigenous men became figures most sought after by Europeans.

A sexual practice carried out by a person of the same sex at that time was still in a humanist perspective and did not receive much attention from the colonial government, but in the end, it had to be regulated by the state. Since 1918, there has been a law prohibiting sexual relations between adults and men under the age of 21, by article 292 *Wetboek van Strafrecht (Dutch Indies Criminal Code (KUHP))* [8]. A criminal sanction imposed is five years in prison, a year more severe when enforced in the Netherlands. The application of the law in the Dutch East Indies, which made the existence of those who practice pederasty or generally considered a homosexual practice, also indirectly began to stigmatize homosexuals in Dutch East Indies society [8]. Along with exposure of homosexual behaviour by colonial officials in 1936, then triggered the arrest of homosexuals in the Dutch East Indies until 1939.

### 3.4 *Discriminating! 'Zedenschaandal' in the Dutch East Indies*

The issue of the colony was a hiding place like heaven for Europeans as homosexuals that were slowly becoming evident. It started with controlling of sexuality discourse in the British colonies, which was also carried out by the Dutch colony, Dutch East Indies. The waves of proving this issue in the Dutch East Indies began to appear when L.A. Ries, a high-ranking colonial official, had sex with an underage boy in May 1936 [9, 21]. L.A. case, which uncovered Ries, also known as Riesaffaire (the Ries Case), have triggered more investigation into the existence of homosexuals.

In October 1936, the local newspapers reported on the practice of homosexuality in several cities in Java and began to search for meeting places and even gatherings of homosexuals in Batavia. This condition prompted the Dutch to ask Governor-General A.W.L. Tjarda Van Strakenborgh Stachouwer to order the police to investigate the existence of homosexuals. In 1937, a Batavia Police Commissioner, P. Dekker, was asked to make a list of people considered homosexual. It turned out that he had made a list beforehand. However, Dekker denies that homosexual practices can spread and are harmful to the image of the colonial government [3]. However, political and cultural fears forced him to do so. Moreover, in the Sukabumi police academy, homosexuality has become a separate subject of discussion, then has been considered a disease, and a warning until the phenomenon became a real fear in the 1930s.

Starting with fears over something considered 'dirty' and uncivilized from the Ries Case. Along the way, there is petition by Christelijke Staatspartij or a Christian Party that cooperated with the Anti-Revolutionaire Partij to the Governor-General in December 1936 regarding the homosexual practice committed by people who had positions in the Dutch East Indies government as a form of sin [7]. The colonial morality politics in the early twentieth century became the beginning of stigmatization of the homosexual community, as were the labels 'dirty,' 'uncivilized,' 'disease' [44]. Uncontrollable reports from newspapers in 1937–1938, such as *De Ochtendpost* and *Java Bode*, exposed there had been summons to three senior civil servants in Surabaya who indicated had related to homosexual groups in the Netherlands, Schorer.

The gate to the investigation of the existence of homosexuals further is the case of W.G. Van Eyndthoven discovered. The man who often stayed at a hotel in Batavia with his boy as his partner in November 1938. At the same time, the police found a collection of Van Eyndthoven's correspondence letters connected to other homosexuals in the Dutch East Indies, even the Netherlands. This case was the key to police investigations into homosexual networks and to knowing the vocabulary or codes that show a behaviour they usually did—which later became a sub-culture of homosexuals. Even the letters revealed that a student from the Police School in Sukabumi was involved as the sender of the letter [6].

The Van Eyndthoven case marked the seriousness of the colonial government in addressing the homosexual scandal in the Dutch East Indies. Moreover, homosexual scandals are increasingly reported with various terms in newspapers. *Zedenschandaal* is one of them, which comes from the word *zeden,* namely matters related to morals [50]. Based on this understanding, *zedenschandaa*l has a meaning related to morality scandals that refer to sexual scandals. This incident involved underage victims, such as the indigenous children, even Chinese and Dutch children [20]. Those victims were put into a *werk camp* to gain learning and moral improvement (Sights 1938). Most of them are street children who have poor economic conditions, so they practice homosexuality for a fee—as Soetjipto tells in his autobiography. In addition, some of them have indeed become the lackeys of Dutchmen, with one of their duties being to satisfy their sexual desires (Irawati 2010).

The hunt of homosexuals carried out under the *van Onderwijs Department* has targeted various groups, even the parliament proposed to examine the Dutch civil servants or administrative officials themselves—for which there was a circular warning for civil servants involved in homosexual practices [26]. Apart from civil servants, it turned out that European doctors and artists, Arabian journalists, and Chinese merchants [40–42]. A well-known person that was caught and written in the mass media also came from several cities in the Dutch East Indies. One of them in Medan, as the roots of the van Eyndthoven case that related to homosexuals in Medan were finally exposed. The Resident of Batavia himself, Fievez de Mallnes van Ginkel [40–42]. In Bali, they also have an artist, Walter Spies, who had worked at the Yogyakarta Palace as a Javanese orchestra leader and lived with R.M. Jayadipura [18], then lived in Ubud, Bali [1]. In Malang, there was also a search of Dr L.S.A.M. von R, a sex specialist who has a wealth of literature related to sexual behaviour [20]. This control over sexual behaviour was also carried out in other cities in the Dutch East Indies, such as Surabaya, Yogyakarta, Jombang, and Semarang, until the middle of 1939.

The homosexual hunting incident has changed the perspective of homosexuality in the Dutch East Indies even until now. If the practice of homosexuals was previously considered a habit, a socio-cultural phenomenon, and that's common to find their existence without having to cover it up, it has finally changed. This incident instilled a new understanding in the colonial society of the Dutch East Indies that homosexuality was something 'dirty,' so it deserved to be 'cleaned' at that time [8] and violated heteronormative sexual morality as the mainstream. This legacy of understanding ultimately continues into the twenty-first century.

### 3.5 *The Continuity of Discrimination Against Homosexuals in the 21st Century: An Analysis*

When trying to look at the twenty-first century that has upheld the human rights of each individual, there is no room for homosexuals to feel it. As explained in the introduction, it is difficult for Indonesian society to use a humanist perspective on homosexuals and to show respect for their sexual behaviour or orientation. Moreover, the hunt of homosexuals in the 1930s changed the colonial society's perspective of homosexual discourse and practice [44]. One of the impacts is the mainstream mass media and government policies often narrated from the patriarchal and heteronormative perspective in the Reformation era.

During the Soeharto era, non-heteronormative sexuality had become the target of political Islam populist action as an effort to win political contestation [45]. Then Soeharto era became the antithesis. The Reformation era was born with upheavals stemming from the crisis of morality—including sexual morality—and Islam has been considered to be an important foundation in improving the nation's morale. In this case, homosexuality also understood according to the colonial legacy. It's the kind of sexual practice against puritan morals of community and needs to be corrected. It is not surprising that religious politics and Islamic politics began to rise. When Islamic politics in Indonesia extends to sexuality discourse, then sexual politics in Indonesia has become increasingly conservative.

On the other hand, the Reformation period was actually on two blades: progressive and conservatism. The liberalization of mass media makes it easier to show sexual identity, distribute knowledge about the diversity of gender and sexuality, and advocate for sexual rights. But on the other hand, democratization and the strengthening of religious politics have also strengthened the homophobic narrative. The separation of state, religion, and sexuality has become an empty hope, as in 2016, the LGBT crisis escalated [14]. Rejection, discrimination, and other repressive actions against LGBT or homosexuals occur in various sectors of life. The mass media and television programs often reinforce homophobic narratives [30]. Not surprised to know that there has been an increase in demonstrations and violence by militant Islamic groups who participate in repressing non-heteronormative sexuality. FPI is a group that has power and uses its power to disband participants of the International Lesbian and Gay Association (ILGA) conference [12].

Apart from religious reasons or specifically religious politics, the restrictions during the Reformation period in terms of government policies were the passage of the UU Anti-Pornography in 2006 [12], which also attacked the sexual rights of minority sexual orientations in the end. The situation has been exacerbated by decentralization, which allowed some regions to set their morals or laws. Through this, it seems there are efforts at the political level to discriminate against homosexuality. It is not only discriminatory in multidimensional but also systemically by a country. Regulations by the government can be supervised and monitored to control sexuality, which is robbing some groups of sexual rights, in this case, homosexuals.

Multidimensional and systemic forms of discrimination have made the diversity of gender and sexuality be reconsidered as a disease that must be cured [11, 27]. The assumption is that if homosexuality can threaten national resilience [12], then it is not surprisingly that [13] argues that the future for LGBT is bleaker than the hunt for homosexuals in the 1930s. Nowadays, it is not only stigmatizing homosexuals who violate puritanical morality, which places great importance on the image of a nation, but it is also coupled with a strong political religion to control the right to life, even in the private sphere called sexuality.

Power has shaped the discourse of sexuality by force. Both in the form of a state that exists to limit and regulate the sexuality of citizens in a discriminatory manner, the mass media that produces discourses on sexuality that are heteronormative and eliminate diversity, to the conservative groups who want conservative sexual politics and morality by revealing what is considered good or bad or shameful [14]. From an early age, romantic relationships or marriages of the opposite sex have been internalized. It indirectly regulates and controls same-sex relationships. Feelings of worry, shame, and confusion will also experience when there is turmoil that they consider ‘different’ from what has been internalized.

The heteronormative perspective has been influenced by the state and religion nowadays. So, it is natural for societies to have conservative moral panic when facing and understanding the reality of the presence of homosexuality which previously turned a blind eye to non-heteronormative life [31]. The presence of homosexuals is once again considered immoral and disrupts the stability and defence of the state. This condition also causes an increase in police violence against LGBT groups. Even Saskia [48] said that at this time, if two women are sleeping together, it could raise suspicion and could even become a target for raids. It seems that there has been a tremendous increase in homophobia in Indonesia.

Unnecessary fears of diversity in sexuality eventually continue to be produced during a way of thinking that only revolves around binary, clean–dirty, right–wrong oppositions [29]. This way of thinking should be abandoned when looking at the diversity of sexuality, politics, and sexual morality. Apart from having revoked the sexual rights and the right to live of homosexuals, this paradigm of thinking also makes people not think humanely in responding to diversity. Trying to understand each other and respect the decisions taken by each individual should be done again so that no more minority groups have difficulty in obtaining their rights as human beings due to discrimination.

## 4 Conclusion

To answer where the 'respect' for the existence of the homosexual community in Indonesia has gone, it is necessary to conduct historical research: first, by looking at local historiography and travel records from the end of the nineteenth century to the beginning of the twentieth century, which narrate the existence of homosexuals as part of a habit and socio-cultural phenomenon without any discriminatory and repressive narratives; second, by looking at the existence of homosexuals in the Dutch East Indies at the beginning of the twentieth century and the way of thinking of colonial society at that time, who still have respect and do not make a problem as something contrary to patriarchal and heteronormative values. Conditions changed during the colonial political situation, which affected European sexual politics that became puritan morality and made homosexuals the opposite of the moralist values they had believed. It had an impact on their colonized countries, which got a new perspective on the discourse of homosexuality and regarded it as something 'dirty,' 'wrong,' 'disease,' and made their respect for the homosexual community which the Dutch East Indies community go away, even previously considered as a form of habit, and socio-cultural phenomena. This perspective on homosexuals has become a form of colonial heritage that has survived to this day, especially with the political factor of religion being strengthened and there is no longer any separation between state religion and sexuality.

# References


1. Adnyana WK (2018) Pita Maha: Gerakan Sosial Seni Lukis Bali 1930-an. KPG (Kepustakaan Populer Gramedia), Jakarta.
2. Anderson BROG (1990) *Kuasa Kata: Jelajah Budaya-budaya Politik di Indonesia.* Mata Bangsa, Yogyakarta
3. Aldrich R (2007) Colonialism and homosexuality. Routledge Taylor and Francis e-Library, London dan New York (2007).
4. Amangkunagara III, Kanjeng Gusti Pangeran Adipati Anom (Sunan Paku Buwana V) (2010) Centhini: Tambangraras-Amongraga Jilid IV. Gadjah Mada University Press, Yogyakarta
5. Ariyanto, Triawan, Rido (2008) Jadi, Kau Tak Merasa Bermasalah!? Arus Pelangi dan Yayasan Tifa, Jakarta
6. Arsip Nasional Republik Indonesia (ANRI). *Binnenlands Bestuur.* No.3409.
7. Bloembergen M (2011) Polisi Zaman Hindia Belanda: Dari Kepedulian dan Ketakutan. Kompas, Jakarta
8. Bloembergen M (2011) Being clean is being strong: policing cleanliness and gay vices in the Netherlands Indies in the 1930s" Kees van Dijk dan, Taylor JG (ed) Cleanliness and Culture Indonesiam Histories. KITLV Press, Leiden
9. Bouman HJ (1936) Nota van Mr. H.J. Bouman betreffende der vervolgingvan den thesaurier-generaal Mr. L.A. Ries. SN. Royal Library
10. Budiman A (1989) Gay Pilihan Jalan Hidupku: Pengakuan Seorang Priayi Masa Penjajahan Belanda. CV. Mimbar Media Utama, Semarang
11. Damarjati D (2022) Ramai Isu LGBT, WHO dan Kemenkas Beda Penlitian soal Homoseksualitas. Detik News. 13 Mei 2022. Accessed https://news.detik.com/berita/d-6076454/ramai-isu-lgbt-who-dan-kemenkes-ri-beda-penilaian-soal-homoseksualitas
12. Davies SG (2018) Pengaturan Seksualitas di Indonesia. In: Bennet LR, Davies SG, Hidayana IM (eds) Seksualitas di Indonesia: Politik Seksual, Kesehatan, Keberagaman, dan Representasi. Yayasan Pustaka Obor, Jakarta
13. Davies SG et al (2018) Memetakan Seks dan Seksualitas di Indonesia Masa Kini. In: Bennet LR, Davies SG, Hidayana IM (eds) Seksualitas di Indonesia: Politik Seksual, Kesehatan, Keberagaman, dan Representasi, Yayasan Pustaka Obor, Jakarta
14. Davies S (2020) What's driving Indonesia's moral turn. New Mandala 25 May 2020. Accessed https://www.newmandala.org/whats-driving-indonesias-moral-turn/
15. *Djalan Sampoerna* (2014) Perpustakaan Nasional Republik Indonesia, Jakarta
16. de Lyon JMB (1941) Over de waroks and gemblaks van Ponorogo. Koloniaal Tijdschrift, vol 30
17. Febriani E (2020) Fenomena Kemunculan Kelompok Homoseksual dalam Ruang Publik Virtual. *Komunikologi* Volume 17 Nomor 01, Maret
18. Fibiona I dan S (2018) *R.M. Jayadipura Maestro Budaya Jawa 1878–1939: Sebuah Biografi.* Balai Pelestarian Nilai Budaya, Yogyakarta
19. Gunawan FXR (1997) *Pelacur dan Politikus.* Pustaka Utama Grafiti, Jakarta
20. Handayani A (2010) Perkara Mesoem: Penangkapan Para Pelaku Homoseksual di Beberapa Kota di Indonesia Tahun 1938–1939. Universitas Gadjah Mada, Yogyakarta
21. Heide A Van Der. *De Zaak Tegen Mr. L.A. Ries: Theausier-Generaal bij het Departement van Financien.* Den Haag (1916)
22. Hurgornje S (1906) The Acehnese, vol 1. E.J. Brill, Leyden
23. Hurgornje S (1906) The Acehnese, vol 2. E.J. Brill, Leyden
24. Jacobs J (1883) *Eenigen tijd onder de Baliers: eene reisbeschrijving met aantekeningen betreffde hygiene, land—en volkenkunde van de eilanden Bali en Lombok.* G. Kolff, Batavia
25. Kramarae C, dan Treicher PA (1985) A feminist dictionary. Pandora Press, London
26. KHP (2010) Widya Budaya Karaton Ngayogyakarta Hadiningrat. *Senarai Arsip Kraton Yogyakarta.* No. 1788, 1956

27. Kwok Y (2016) LGBT rights in Indonesia are coming unprecedented attack. TIME. Accessed 11 Aug 2016 https://time.com/4447819/indonesia-lgbt-rights-islam-muslim-gay-bi-transgender/
28. Lattanzio M (2011/2012) The future of public space: toward an integrated design of public space and information technology. Leeds Metropolitan University, Leeds
29. Levi-Strauss C (1968) Structural anthropology. Allen Lane, London
30. Listiorini D et al Moral panics on lgbt issues: evidence from Indonesia tv program. Jurnal Studi Komunikasi 3(3). https://doi.org/10.25139/jsk.3i3.1882
31. McNally S, Grierson J, Hidayana IM (2018) *Belonging,* Komunitas, dan Identitas: Laki-laki Gay di Indonesia. In: Bennet LR, Davies SG, Hidayana IM (eds.). Seksualitas di Indonesia: Politik Seksual, Kesehatan, Keberagaman, dan Representasi. Yayasan Pustaka Obor Indonesia, Jakarta
32. Mustangin (2018) Social media amongs homosexuals: a new era of gay life in the age of technology. *Masyarakat, Kebudayaan dan Politik,* vol 31, Issue 4, pp 410–417
33. Navis AA (1987) Anak Jawi di Kampung Kami. *Tempo* 10 Oktober
34. Oetomo D (1984) Gays in Indonesia. Sybylls Press, Australia
35. Oetomo D (1991) Homoseksualitas di Indonesia. *Prisma* No.7 Tahun XX, Juli
36. Oetomo D (2001) Memberi Suara pada yang Bisu. Galang Press, Yogyakarta
37. Oley JDB, Wahyu YFM (2019) How intolerance can persist in democratic countries: the case of Indonesia. The Conversation. Accessed 7 Mei 2019 https://theconversation.com/how-intolerance-can-persist-in-democratic-countries-the-case-of-indonesia-110607
38. Onghokham (1991) Kekuasaan dan Seksualitas: Lintasan Sejarah Pra dan Masa Kolonial. *Prisma* No.7 Tahun XX, Juli 1991
39. *Pemandangan.* Rabu. 28 Desember 1938.
40. *Pemandangan.* Kamis. 4 Mei 1939. Th. 7 No.99.
41. *Pemandangan.* Sabtu. 27 Mei 1939. Th.7 No.118.
42. *Pemandangan.* Selasa. 13 Juni1939. Th.7 No.131.
43. Soerijo SH (1961) Gemblakan Ponorogo. Universitas Gadjah Mada, Yogyakarta
44. Rahmawati A (2019) Wacana dan Praktik Homoseksualitas di Jawa: Studi terhadap Kemunculan Homofobia Pada Masa Kolonia. Universitas Gadjah Mada, Yogyakarta
45. Robinson K (2018) Maskulinitas, Seksualitas, dan Islam: Politik Gender Perubahan Rezim di Indonesia. In: Bennet LR, Davies SG, Hidayana IM (eds), *Seksualitas di Indonesia: Politik Seksual, Kesehatan, Keberagaman, dan Representasi,* Yayasan Pustaka Obor, Jakarta
46. The Jakarta Post, "Are Indonesians homophobic?" *The Jakarta Post.* Accessed 20 Apr 20 https://www.thejakartapost.com/academia/2021/04/19/are-indonesians-homophobic.html
47. Usman (2012) *Mairil: Phenomena Homoseksualitas di Pesantren.* Magister Psikologi UGM, Yogyakarta
48. Wieringa S (2018) Perdebatan Diskursif Mengenai Interseks di Stigma, Hak Asasi, dan Identitas. In: Bennet LR, Davies SG, Hidayana IM (eds), *Seksualitas di Indonesia: Politik Seksual, Kesehatan, Keberagaman, dan Representasi,* Yayasan Pustaka Obor, Jakarta
49. Wijoyo H Hegemoni dalam Emansipatory: Studi Kasus Advokasi Legalisasi Lesbian, Gay, Biseksual, dan Transgender di Indonesia. Indonesian Perspective 1(2):31–47
50. Wojowasito S (1995) *Kamus Umum Bahasa Belanda-Indonesia.* PT. Ichtiar Baru-van Houve, Jakarta
51. Yi BL (2016) Indonesia says 'no room' for LGBT rights movement. *Thomson Routers Foundation.* Accessed 11 Aug 2016 https://www.reuters.com/article/us-indonesia-rights-lgbt-idUSKCN10M19T

# State Archiving System Against Indigenous Religions Post Issuance of Constitutional Court Decree Number 97/PU-XIV/2016

**Harry Bawono**

**Abstract** The state has confirmed that indigenous religions and major religions are equal in Indonesia through Constitutional Court Decree Number 97/PU-XIV/2016. Furthermore, indigenous religious followers can record their religious identity in various state archives. The documentation of indigenous religious identities in state archives reflected the archiving system. It is a system that determines what information should be included, preserved, or excluded. However, a concept or a label used by archivers in archiving the archived is rarely discussed. This archiving process affected how the state serves citizens and how citizens receive state services. This research was conducted from December 2021 to April 2022 and employed qualitative techniques such as archive studies and textual network analysis (TNA). This paper argues that the Constitutional Court Decree affected the reform of the state archiving system for indigenous religions. This reform heralds a new era in which the country is becoming more accepting of indigenous religions. Furthermore, the state's efforts to ensure the civil rights of all indigenous religious followers become clear. Nonetheless, the activism of indigenous religious followers needs to be maintained.

**Keywords** Constitutional Court Decree Number 97/PU-XIV/2016 · Indigenous religions · Archiving system · Civil rights

## 1 Introduction

The state has recognized equality between major and indigenous religions through Constitutional Court Decree Number 97/PU-XIV/2016. Previously, the state "recognized" only major religions such as Islam, Christianity, Catholicism, Hinduism, Buddhism, and (Confucianism). Meanwhile, indigenous religions, defined as The

H. Bawono (✉)
National Research and Innovation Agency, Jakarta Selatan, Indonesia
e-mail: harry.bawono@brin.go.id



Nawawi et al. (eds.), *Managing Disruption and Developing Resilience for a Better Southeast Asia*, Springer Proceedings in Humanities and Social Sciences,
https://doi.org/10.1007/978-981-96-2116-3_38

Belief in God Almighty, are viewed as unequal and classified by the state as non-religious. This recognition can boost the restoration process of indigenous religious followers' civil rights that had been neglected.

At least two civil rights have the potential to be restored: the right to religious freedom and not to be discriminated against people. The indigenous religious followers have many obstacles in many ways to religious freedom. Usually, they are being "forced" to admit to being recorded as an "official" religion or leaving the religion column blank on the ID Card. With their choice to be the "unofficial" religious adherents, they face difficulty accessing some jobs and even burying their dead.

The restoration of civil rights began with the legalization of the registration of believers' identities in various state archives, beginning with identity cards, birth certificates, marriage certificates, and other archives. The state's recognition of indigenous religions set out in this manner. This mechanism then affected the state's current archiving system for indigenous religion.

The archiving system is a state technology for managing their citizens through recorded information. As part of administrative power, the archiving system is the most visible form of disciplinary efforts and state monitoring of citizens across time and space [1]. As part of the state's administrative power, the archiving system can play a role in the administration of justice or even injustice.

The Constitutional Court Decree Number 97/PU-XIV/2016 impacts the archiving system. The archiving system is crucial for tracking the dynamics of the Constitutional Court's decision in the field because it describes the administrative power of the state. Furthermore, researchers in this field have not extensively dissected the archiving system variable in the constellation of indigenous religious issues in the context of the 2016 Constitutional Court decree. This study concerns how the state archiving system for indigenous religions functions following the Constitutional Court's Decree Number 97/PU-XIV/2016.

## 2 Conceptual Framework

### *2.1 Indigenous Religion*

Indigenous religion refers to local religious practices frequently claimed to be animist, magical, customary, cultural, or other [2]. The paradigm of indigenous religion views oneself and the surrounding environment as intersubjective relations. In intersubjective relations, the knowledge of the human self as a being does not exist in and of itself but is dependent on and related to other beings [3].

In the language of regulations, indigenous religion is defined as the Belief in God Almighty (*Kepercayaan terhadap Tuhan yang Maha Esa*). Belief in God Almighty is stated in Article 1 Number 18, Government Regulation Number 37 of 2007 concerning the Implementation of Law Number 23 of 2006 concerning Population Administration. Belief in God Almighty is a statement and implementation of a personal relationship with God Almighty based on belief, manifested by the behavior of piety and worship of God Almighty and the practice of nobility whose teachings are sourced from the local wisdom of the Indonesian nation.

## 2.2 Archiving System

The archiving is preceded by the process of Archivalization. Archivalization is a conscious or unconscious action that determines whether something should be archived or not [4]. The system developer's use of socio-cultural factors or values determines archivalization as a preliminary of archiving. The socio-cultural conditions directly influence archiving. Archiving entails creating and linking recorded information (archives) from one transaction process to another in various physical and digital forms [5].

The sophistication of the archiving mechanism corresponds to technological advancements. The use of technology allows for more precise archiving so that the recorded information can be used later for the benefit of the state in managing its people [6]. In other words, a filing system is a socio-technological tool used by an organization, or in this case, the state, to exercise administrative power through the use of information to achieve state goals.

In the archiving context model, archiving is a relationship between mandate (why), business (what), people (who), and work processes (how). The entire process is influenced by societal challenges or the socio-cultural perspective used. This socio-cultural perspective will later influence how the archiving process operates.

## 2.3 Civil Rights

Civil rights are fundamental liberties for human existence [8]. Civil rights might be defined differently in different countries, but their meaning remains consistent due to their universal nature. In Indonesia, civil rights are written in the 1945 Constitution and, more specifically, in Law No. 12 of 2005 on Ratification of the International Covenant on Civil and Political Rights. As shown in Table 1. Civil Rights on Religion/Belief in Indonesia, three civil rights have been identified [9].

This study focuses on the three civil rights listed in Table 1. These three points are summed up in two civil rights formulations: the right to religious freedom and the right not to be discriminated against.

**Table 1** Civil rights on religion/belief in Indonesia

| No | Civil rights | Basis |
|---|---|---|
| 1 | Everyone has the right to embrace a religion and worship according to his religion, choose education and teaching, choose a job, choose a nationality, choose a place to live in the territory of the country and leave it, and has the right to return | Article 28 E paragraph 1, the 1945 constitution |
| 2 | Everyone has the right to believe in any beliefs they choose and to express their thoughts and attitudes following their conscience | Article 28 E paragraph 2, the 1945 constitution |
| 3 | Everyone is free from discriminatory treatment on any basis and is entitled to protection against such discriminatory treatment | Article 28 I paragraph 2, the 1945 constitution |

## 3 Method

This study was conducted from December 2021 to April 2022. This study employed qualitative methods such as archival research and Textual Network Analysis (TNA) using the Socioviz web-based application. Archival data were obtained by searching the archives of four institutions: PP Muhammadiyah Yogyakarta (1922–2001), the Ministry of Religion of the Republic of Indonesia (1950–1998), the Ministry of Education and Culture of the Republic of Indonesia (1959–2010), and Konstituante (1956–1960). Those four inventories contain indigenous religious issues, yet, they are open access archives. The archive is a collection of the National Archives of the Republic of Indonesia (ANRI). Meanwhile, TNA data was obtained in March 2022 by crawling Twitter using the hashtags #agama leluhur and #KTP penghayat kepercayaan.

## 4 Indigenous Religions in Indonesia

Indigenous or local religion and belief in God Almighty are frequently used interchangeably. The indigenous religion, in this context, is used to represent the belief in God Almighty as a separate entity from the major religions. This indigenous religion existed before Indonesia's independence.

According to data compiled by the Ministry of Education and Culture in 2017, there are currently 118 indigenous religious organizations with 11,288,957 adherents spread across 14 provinces and 72 regencies/cities [10]. A person from the Indonesia Supreme Council of Belief in Almighty God explained that our religion is an ethnic religion or is often called an indigenous or local religion. However, the policy documents formally used belief in Almighty God. So, we prefer to be called the followers of Belief in God Almighty (*Penghayat Kepercayaan terhadap*

*Tuhan yang Maha Esa)* [11]. Parmalim (North Sumatra), Sunda Wiwitan and Buhun (West Java), Sapta Darma (Central and East Java), Wetu Telu (West Nusa Tenggara), Marapu (Sumbawa), Kaharingan (Kalimantan), Tolotang (South Sulawesi), Tonaas Walian (North Sulawesi), and Naurus (Seram Island) are some examples of Indonesia's indigenous religions or Belief in God Almighty [12].

Based on historical data, indigenous religion has recognized the importance of uniting in an organization. From 1955 to the present, there are seven organizations [13]:

1. *Badan Kongres Kebatinan Indonesia (BKKI)* (1955–1965);
2. *Badan Koordinasi Karyawan Kerohanian Kebatinan Kejiwaan Indonesia (BK5I)* (1966–1970);
3. *Sekretariat Kerja sama Kepercayaan terhadap Tuhan Yang Maha Esa (SKK)* (1970–1979);
4. *Himpunan Penghayat Kepercayaan terhadap Tuhan Yang Maha Esa (HPK)* (1979–2014);
5. *Forum Komunikasi Penghayat Kepercayaan terhadap Tuhan Yang Maha Esa* (1999–2014);
6. *Badan Koordinasi Organisasi Kepercayaan terhadap Tuhan Yang Maha Esa* (1999–2014);
7. *Majelis Luhur Kepercayaan Indonesia (MLKI)* (2014–present).

The dynamics of the labels used to represent indigenous religions or belief communities are reflected in the names used by these organizations. Although it was called *kepercayaan* (belief) in the Constitution by Wongsonegoro, this community labeled itself as adherents of *kebatinan* (mysticism) from the start, then expanded to equate *kebatinan* (mysticism) with *kerohanian* (spirituality) and *kejiwaan* (psychology). At a national meeting in 1970, the concept of Belief in God Almighty was introduced, which later replaced all those labels.

Even today, the state is more familiar with the stream of belief (*aliran kepercayaan*). According to the person from MLKI, the stream of belief is similar to a label that we are a part of religious sects with main religions, so many groups, including the state, pressure us to return to the main religion. Meanwhile, because we are independent, adherents of the belief of God Almighty do not belong to any major religions [11].

It is not surprising that the concept of belief in God Almighty has always been at odds with the concept of religion. There are at least three interpretations of religion and belief that have emerged: (1) Religion and belief are distinct concepts, (2) Religion and belief are synonymous, and (3) Belief refers to religious belief or internal variations of religion [14]. Followers of indigenous religions (belief in Almighty God) understand this point (2). Meanwhile, the state and other groups are dynamic, but the dominants are in points (1) and (3). Points (1) and (3) require that belief of God Almighty be neither independent nor equal to religion.

Law No.1/PNPS/1965, which contains six major religions as religions embraced by the Indonesian people, is the earliest regulation that nullifies the existence of belief [15]. Particularly after the G30S/(Indonesian Communist Party-PKI) incident, society at the time stigmatized the followers of beliefs as communists because they were all non-religious. Belief adherents were not only labeled but also physically excluded because they were suspected of involvement in the G30S/(PKI) rebellion. As a result, many followers converted to one of the major religions, such as Christianity, Islam, or Hinduism.

When an individual basis chooses the conversion, Aluk Todolota (Alukta) in Toraja has implemented an integration mechanism. They formally united as a Hindu sect in 1969 [16]. This union is legally written on the Director-General of Hindu and Buddhist Guidance Decree Number: Dd/M/200-VII/1969, dated November 15, 1969 [16]. The archives also emphasize that Alukta is now a part of Hinduism, the official religion [16]. Attempts to integrate adherents of beliefs into "official" religions are common, including those made by Muhammadiyah, which systematically targeted the followers of beliefs or indigenous religions for their preaching [17].

Indeed, society is more tolerant of "official" religion adherents than of "non-official" religion adherents, such as Belief in God Almighty [18]. This condition is aided by the state's attitude toward the diversity of religions in Indonesia, which is more concerned with the formal reality than the sociological reality. The administrative boundaries established by the state in categorizing religion as official or unofficial constructed the formal reality. In the meantime, the sociological reality as an empirical reality concerning the true diversity of religions that exist in society is neglected [19].

The data in Table 2 was extracted from sociovizz in March 2022. To end all discrimination and be treated equally with other citizens, followers of indigenous religion engage in activism to change the situation. Activism takes place both online and offline. Offline activism, for example, is carried out when the indigenous religious community proposes a judicial review to the Constitutional Court. They argue that the 2006 Population Administration Law is considered contrary to the 1945 Constitution because these regulations impede the fulfillment of adherents' civil rights. The 2006 Population Administration Law regulates the emptying of the religious column in state archives for the followers of indigenous religion. Meanwhile, online activism is being carried out, one of which is through the Twitter account @agama_nusantara. As shown in Table 2, sentiment toward *agama leluhur* invokes at least three keywords: religion, ancestor, and culture. What's more, the emergence of the term *bangs*t* (b*st*rd) is intriguing. The word b*st*rd appeared 22 times, referring to the term resistance to the West Sumatra Ulema Council, which was considered at the time to be discrediting local or ancestral culture. In the case of KTP, for the followers of belief, three words appear frequently: religion, belief, and column. One of the issues that adherents of belief continue to face is the emergence of the identity of indigenous religious followers in ID cards, as well as the identity of major religions.

Until now, adherents of indigenous religions have remained dynamic in their pursuit of equality alongside other citizens. The first step is to be able to register the identity of indigenous religions/beliefs followers in various state archives.

**Table 2** Texts network analysis

| No | Hastag | | | |
|---|---|---|---|---|
| | Agama Leluhur | | KTP penghayat kepercayaan | |
| | Words | Sum | Words | Sum |
| 1 | Agama | 144 | agama | 45 |
| 2 | Leluhur | 104 | kepercayaan | 42 |
| 3 | Budaya | 47 | kolom | 36 |
| 4 | Ritual | 36 | wiwitan | 26 |
| 5 | Tradisi | 34 | sunda | 26 |
| 6 | Menghormati | 32 | penghayat | 25 |
| 7 | Local | 26 | aliran | 25 |
| 8 | Warisan | 24 | warga | 23 |
| 9 | Nusantara | 23 | menunjukkan | 19 |
| 10 | B*ngsat | 22 | penganut | 19 |

## 5 The Function of the State in Administering Religions

There are two pretexts that the state could legally intervene the religious affairs, ideological and formal. Ideologically, it is reflected in Pancasila, particularly the first principle, the Belief in One Godness. Formally, Article 29 paragraph (1) The State based on the One Godhead in the 1945 Constitution of the Republic of Indonesia. This principle is then operated by the Ministry of Religious Affairs.

The Ministry of Religious Affairs, formerly known as the Department of Religious Affairs, was established on January 3, 1946 [20]. The first Minister of Religious Affairs, H.M Rasjidi, stated that the Ministry of Religious Affairs was established to protect and preserve religion and its adherents [21]. The government used the Ministry of Religious Affairs to integrate the religious tasks previously managed by various ministries [21].

Indonesians have been debating the issue of religion since the State's Constitution was constructed. From May to August 1945, the idea of "religion" was augmented with the concept of "belief" following a lengthy discussion at the *Badan Penyelidik Usaha Persiapan Kemerdekaan Indonesia* (BPUPKI) and the *Panitia Persiapan Kemerdekaan Indonesia* (PPKI). Wongsonegoro, an indigenous religious actor, suggested the term "belief" to represent Indonesia's diverse religions [22]. Since then, the state has guaranteed each resident's independence to embrace their religion according to their religion and beliefs, as stated in Article 29 paragraph (2) of the Republic of Indonesia's 1945 Constitution. It is significant to convey, even though there have been various interpretations and debates around the relationship between religion and belief. However, the acceptance to include the concept of belief in the constitution has become an umbrella for various spiritual beliefs or indigenous religions that have existed in Indonesia.

The division of recognized and unrecognized religions has been formed culturally and formally among Indonesian people. On a cultural level, the development of the Agama Djawa Asli Republik Indonesia (ADARI) was a clear example. This group was known as Barisan Samadi Republik Indonesia. Once, they received a piece of information from somebody who explained that the state only recognized the fighter group when it was Muslim or Christian. To counter the issue, this organization declared to become a religion called ADARI on November 13, 1950 [23]. At a formal level, the Ministry of Religious Affairs issued a regulation on the definition of religion in 1952. In this definition, a group that wants to be recognized as a religion must have three elements: the existence of a prophet, scriptures, and worldwide acceptance [24]. This regulation was then used to select which was a religion and not. Between 1950 and 1965, many beliefs or mysticism groups were propagated in society, with over 360 beliefs/mysticism groups in the Java region alone, according to Ministry of Religion 1953 data [25]. This interplay between cultural and formal difficulties in assessing the constellation of indigenous religions to Indonesia's main religions has become a significant component of understanding the current situation.

Before the policy on religion definition, the Ministry of Religious Affairs established the *Lembaga Penelitian Gerakan/Aliran Keagamaan* in 1951 to investigate beliefs/mystics outside of the major religions [26]. In 1953, the *Pengawas Aliran Kepercayaan Masyarakat* (PAKEM) was created from this institution. Subsequently, in 1961, PAKEM unit was transferred to be under the Prosecutor's Office, and in 1964, it was reorganized into interdepartmental units consisting of the Ministry of Religious Affairs, the Attorney General's Office, and the Ministry of Home Affairs, and the Ministry of Justice [27]. Until now, PAKEM, also known as the *Badan Koordinasi Pengawas Aliran Kepercayaan Masyarakat* (BAKOR PAKEM), has become inherent in the function of the Attorney's Office.

State services for indigenous religions are also provided in addition to oversight. The state assigned the Department of Religious Affairs in 1975 to provide services for indigenous religious followers. However, in 1978, the unit service for indigenous religious followers then transferred to the Department of Education and Culture (now the Ministry of Education and Culture) and remained until today. The state's stance on religion and belief influences the transfer of service functions from the Department of Religious Affairs to the Department of Education. The state utilizes the perspective of major religions and indigenous religions as equals when placing indigenous religions in the service of the Department of Religious Affairs.

The use of perspective can be seen in the rule of *Garis-garis Besar Haluan Negara* (GBHN) from 1973 and 1978. The GBHN is significant because it was a governmental document that served as a reference for five-year progress during the Sukarno era (1945–1966) and the Suharto era (1966–1998) [28]. It contained equality between religion and belief in the 1973 GBHN or TAP MPR IV/1973. This measure has sparked outrage, particularly among Muslims. Muslims who are opposed to this do not agree that the Ministry of Religion is serving the followers of belief [29]. Mohammad Natsir is one of the Islamic figures who has spoken out against this approach. Muhammad Natsir's objections were clearly stated in his letter to the Chairman of the MPR. His objections to the inclusion of "stream of belief" content in the GBHN in a letter dated February 10, 1978 [30]. Because of these complaints, the GBHN of 1978 underlined that belief is not a religion, and the coaching process was implemented to ensure that belief did not become a new religion [31].

The 1978 GBHN's perspective became mainstream, and it was used and emphasized in the 1998 GBHN that believers must choose one of the major religions [32]. Following the implementation of this policy, discrimination against followers of the belief became increasingly severe. The most obvious form of discrimination is the requirement to include the major religion in various state archives concerning their identity. This situation improved slightly after the passage of Law Number 23 of 2006 on Population Administration [33]. This regulation that regulated the adherents of indigenous religions can choose to leave the religion/belief column blank on their Identity Cards or other state archives. The population database, however, still contains information about the beliefs held. The emptying of religious identity makes the indigenous religious followers regarded as non-religious and it could be difficult for them. Due to persistent discrimination issues, religious believers finally sought to improve regulations through the Constitutional Court. The Constitutional Court Decision Number 97/PU-XIV/2016 resulted from this. The decision emphasizes that because belief and religion are equal, they must be treated equally [34]. One form of equal treatment is allowing followers of indigenous religion to include their religious identity in various state archives. This constitutional recognition paved the way for the abolition of religious discrimination in Indonesia. However, the community of indigenous religions needs extra efforts to ensure the implementation of this regulation.

## 6 The Dynamics of Indigenous Religion Archiving by the State

The analysis is limited to two periods, 1978 to 2016 and 2017 to the present. First, 1978 to 2016, it was chosen because it represents a condition when belief and religion are considered unequal. Meanwhile, the selection of period from 2017 until the present to describe the situation after the Constitutional Court Decree Number 97/PU-XIV/2016 was issued.

The archiving context model (Fig. 1) will be used to identify the traces of the state's archiving system against indigenous religions. In the archiving context, four elements exist; societal challenge (socio-cultural perspective), mandate (why), affairs (what), people (who), and work processes (how). Because this element is a representation of knowledge that determines an archiving process, researchers equate societal challenges with socio-cultural perspectives [35]. Table 3. Analysis of the Archiving System summarizes the differences between archiving from 1978 to 2016 (pre-Constitutional Court Decree Number 97/PU-XIV/2016) and 2017 to the present (post-Constitutional Court Decree Number 97/PU-XIV/2016).

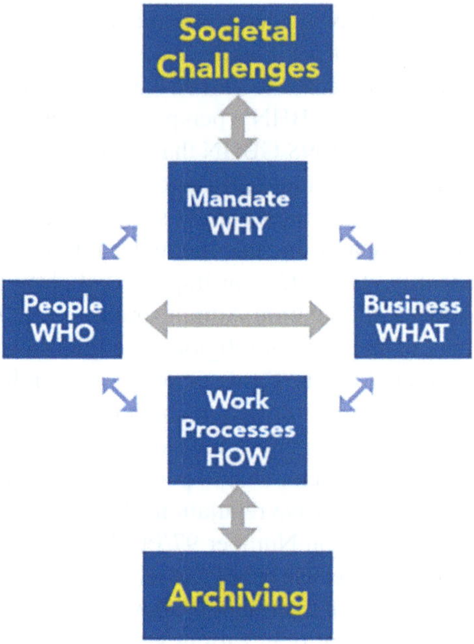


**Fig. 1** Archiving context [7]

The fundamental difference between the Pre-Constitutional Court's Decree archiving system and the post-MK decision archiving system is in the socio-cultural perspective and the work process, particularly the Ministry of Home Affairs' archiving actor. Previously, the recording in the database was done (implicit), but it was not displayed in the state archive (explicit); now, both the recording in the database and the appearance in the state archive are completed, indicating a shift from implicit to explicit.

Figure 2 of the Pre and Post Constitutional Court's Decree shows some examples of the inclusion of followers of belief/indigenous religious identities in state archives before and after the Constitutional Court's Decree.

Figure 2a depicts three models for inserting religious identity in ID cards for followers of belief/indigenous religion before the Constitutional Court's decision. The followers of indigenous religion could be: 1. choose one of the major religions; 2. labeled as a stream of beliefs; 3.—(strip symbol). Meanwhile, in Fig. 2b, it is clear that the model for inserting the identity of the religious column for indigenous religious believers is written Belief in God Almighty (*Kepercayaan terhadap Tuhan yang Maha Esa*). To make this transformation happen, it needs to change in both socio-cultural perspective elements and the work process or tools used in the work process. The example of how the Ministry of Home Affairs reformed its population administration system (SIAK) to follow the constitutional court's decree mandate is a clear example. As mentioned by the Director-General of Population and Civil Registry, Ministry of Home Affairs, our ministry will reform the SIAK application to implement the Constitutional Court's decree requirement [37].

**Table 3** Analysis of archiving system

| No | Element | Archiving on 1978–2016 | Archiving on 2017–present |
|---|---|---|---|
| 1 | Societal context (socio-cultural perspective) | Belief and religion are not equal | Belief and religion are equal |
| 2 | Mandate (why) | State administers religions (~~belief~~) and religious affairs | State administers religions/beliefs and religious affairs |
| 3 | Business (what) | (Religions) (~~Beliefs~~) | Religions and beliefs |
| 4 | People (who) | Archiver:<br>• Ministry of Religious Affairs<br>• Ministry of Education and Culture<br>• Ministry of Internal Affairs (Population and civil registry unit)<br>• Attorney Office (BAKORPAKEM) | Archiver:<br>• Ministry of Religious Affairs<br>• Ministry of Education and Culture<br>• Ministry of Internal Affairs (Population and civil registry unit)<br>• Attorney Office (BAKORPAKEM) |
| | | Archived:<br>• Followers of beliefs/indigenous religions;<br>• Organizations of beliefs/indigenous religions | Archived:<br>• Followers of beliefs/indigenous religions;<br>• Organizations of beliefs/indigenous religions |
| 5 | Work processes (why) | • Ministry of Religious Affairs: research and mapping<br>• Ministry of Education and Culture: Services and inventory<br>• Ministry of Internal Affairs (Population and civil registry unit): organizations registry and population and civil registry with **SEPARATING** the record on database and the state's archives such as Identity Card and so on<br>• Attorney Office (BAKORPAKEM): Intelligent research | • Ministry of Religious Affairs: research and mapping<br>• Ministry of Education and Culture: Services and inventory<br>• Ministry of Internal Affairs (Population and civil registry unit): organizational and population records and civil records by **APPOINTING** records in state databases and archives exactly the same as ID Cards and so on. Provide belief instead of religion column to record indigenous religious followers;<br>• Attorney Office (BAKORPAKEM): Intelligent research |

Inclusion of the identity of the indigenous religions in various state archives is the first step toward restoring adherents' difficult-to-obtain civil rights, particularly the right to freedom of belief and the right not to be discriminated against. The reform of the state archiving system for indigenous religions (Belief in God Almighty) was the first step in this improvement.

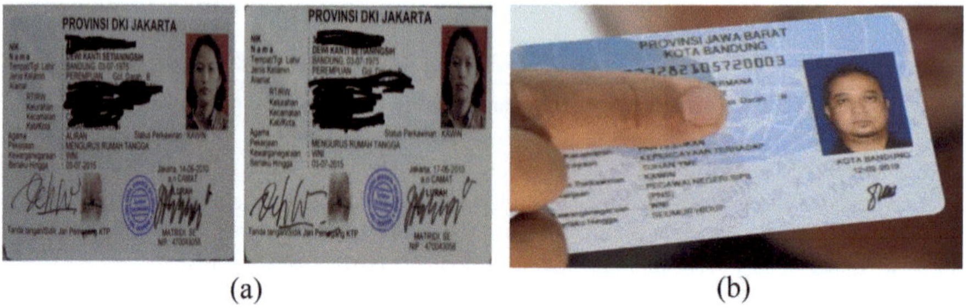


**Fig. 2** ID card before and after Constitutional Court's Decree [36]

## 7 Conclusion

Indonesia's archiving system for indigenous religions has been reformed following the 2016 Constitutional Court's Decree. The most noticeable shifts have occurred at the perspective and work process levels. This reform is significant because the archiving system is one of the state's administrative power tools for managing religions and religious affairs. However, the community of indigenous religions in Indonesia needs to continue their activism to ensure the implementation of the constitutional court's decree.

## References

1. Boyes-Watson C (1994) Recordkeeping as a technology of power. Berkeley J Sociol 39:1–32. Accessed 25 Apr 2022, http://www.jstor.org/stable/41035475; McKemmish S, Piggott M, Reed B, Upward F (2005) Archives: recordkeeping in society. Top Aust Libr Inf Stud 24:277–298; Giddens A (1985) The nation-state and violence. Polity Press, Cambridge
2. Maarif S (2017) *Pasang Surut Rekognisi Agama Leluhur dalam Politik Agama di Indonesia.* Yogyakarta: Center for Religious and Cross-cultural Studies, p 3
3. Maarif S (2015) *Kajian Kritis Agama Lokal, dalam Samsul Maarif, Studi Agama di Indonesia: Refleksi Pengalaman.* Pusat Studi Agama dan Demokrasi, Yayasan Paramadina, Jakarta, p 47
4. Ketelaar E (1999) Archivalisation and archiving. Arch Manuscr 26(1):54–61. Accessed https://publications.archivists.org.au/index.php/asa/article/view/8759
5. Ketelaar E (2020) Archiving people a social history of dutch archives. Stichting Archiefpublicaties, Gravenhage, p 16b
6. Ketelaar E (1999) Archivalisation and archiving. Arch Manuscr 26(1):54–61. Accessed https://publications.archivists.org.au/index.php/asa/article/view/8759; Ketelaar E (2020) Archiving people a social history of dutch archives. Gravenhage: Stichting Archiefpublicaties; Lupton D (2015) Digital sociology. Routledge, New York, p 33; Giddens A (1985). The nation-state and violence. Polity Press, Cambridge, pp 41–49
7. Ketelaar E (2020) Archiving people a social history of dutch archives. Stichting Archiefpublicaties, Gravenhage, p 19a
8. Institute for Criminal Justice Reform (2012, May 14). *publikasi.* Accessed 8 Apr 2022, from Institute for Criminal Justice Reform website: https://icjr.or.id/mengenal-kovenan-internasional-hak-sipil-dan-politik/

9. Afifah W (2017) Hukum dan Konstitusi: Perlindungan Hukum atas Diskriminasi pada Hak Asasi Perempuan di Dalam Konstitusi. Dih Jurnal Ilmu Hukum 13(26):210–216. https://doi.org/10.30996/dih.v0i0.1583; Presiden Republik Indonesia (2005) Undang-Undang Republik Indonesia Nomor 12 Tahun 2005 tentang Pengesahan Kovenan Internasional Tentang Hak-Hak Sipil dan Politik. *UU No. 12 Tahun 2005*. Jakarta, Indonesia: Dewan Perwakilan Rakyat Republik Indonesia.
10. Kementerian Pendidikan dan Kebudayaan Republik Indonesia (2017, no month no day). Rekapitulasi Jumlah Kabupaten/Kota, Jumlah Organisasi dan Jumlah Warga Penghayat Kepercayaan terhadap Tuhan yang Maha Esa Tingkat Pusat Seluruh Indonesia Tahun 2017. *Rekap Tingkat Pusat*. Jakarta, Indonesia: Kementerian Pendidikan dan Kebudayaan Republik Indonesia. Accessed 8 Apr 2022, from 10. https://kebudayaan.kemdikbud.go.id/ditkt/wp-content/uploads/sites/6/2018/09/REKAP-TINGKAT-PUSATok-.pdf
11. Pusat Riset Masyarakat dan Budaya BRIN (2022) Webinar Forum Diskusi Budaya tentang Agama Kepercayaan dan Paham Keagamaan. *Webinar Forum Diskusi Budaya*. Jakarta, Jakarta, Indonesia: Pusat Riset Masyarakat dan Budaya BRIN
12. Gatra (2016) Gatra. *Taman Sari Agama Marjinal*, p. no pages.
13. Damami M (2018) *Kepercayaan Terhadap Tuhan Yang Maha Esa Dewasa Ini*. Yogyakarta: Pusatak Pelajar.
14. Butt S (2020) Constitutional recognition “Beliefs” in Indonesia. J Law Relig 450–473:454. https://doi.org/10.1017/jlr.2020.39
15. Maarif S (2017). *Pasang Surut Rekognisi Agama Leluhur dalam Politik Agama di Indonesia*. Yogyakarta: Center for Religious and Cross-cultural Studies, p 36
16. ANRI, Inventaris Arsip Departemen Agama 1950 – 1998, No. 7607.
17. ANRI, Inventaris Arsip PP Muhammadiyah Yogyakarta 1922–2001, No.1961, 1970, 2101
18. Burhani AN (2005) Delimited Pluralisme: Kajian Sikap Pemerintah dan Masyarakat terhadap Agama Lokal di Indonesia. J Character Build 2(1):41–50
19. Bawono H (2019) Arsip Keagamaan, Narasi-Tandingan dan Memori Kolektif Keragaman Agama di Indonesia. J Kearsipan 12(1):37–50. Accessed http://jurnalkearsipan.anri.go.id/index.php/ojs/article/view/7
20. Maarif S (2017) *Pasang Surut Rekognisi Agama Leluhur dalam Politik Agama di Indonesia*. Yogyakarta: Center for Religious and Cross-cultural Studies, p 22
21. Rakhmat Nur Hakim (2021) *kompas news*. Accessed 8 Apr 2022, from kompas.com: https://nasional.kompas.com/read/2021/10/25/13480111/sejarah-lahirnya-kementerian-agama-di-indonesia?page=all.
22. Saafroedin B (1992) *Himpunan Risalah Sidang-Sidang Badan Penyelidik Usaha Persiapan Kemerdekaan Indonesia (BPUPKI), Panitia Persiapan Kemerdekaan Indonesia (PPKI), 29 Mei – 19 Agustus 1945 yang Berhubungan dengan Penyusunan Undang-Undang Dasar 1945*. Jakarta: Sekretariat Negara, p 196
23. ANRI, Inventaris Arsip Konstituante 1956–1960, No. 300.
24. Maarif S (2017) *Pasang Surut Rekognisi Agama Leluhur dalam Politik Agama di Indonesia*. Yogyakarta: Center for Religious and Cross-cultural Studies, p 25
25. Mulder N (1983) *Kebatinan dan Hidup Sehari-hari Orang Jawa: Kelangsungan dan Perubahan Kulturil*. Jakarta: Gramedia.
26. Sofwan R (2002) *Menguak Seluk Beluk Aliran Kebatinan: Kepercayaan Terhadap Tuhan Yang Maha Esa*. Semarang: Aneka Ilmu, p 2
27. Maarif S (2017) *Pasang Surut Rekognisi Agama Leluhur dalam Politik Agama di Indonesia*. Yogyakarta: Center for Religious and Cross-cultural Studies, p 112; Sofwan R (2002) *Menguak Seluk Beluk Aliran Kebatinan: Kepercayaan Terhadap Tuhan Yang Maha Esa*. Semarang: Aneka Ilmu, p 2
28. Subkhan I (2014) GBHN dan Perubahan Perencanaan Pembangunan di Indonesia GBHN. Aspirasi: Jurnal Masalah-Masalah Sosial 131–143. https://doi.org/10.46807/Aspirasi.V5i2.455.
29. Maarif S (2017) *Pasang Surut Rekognisi Agama Leluhur dalam Politik Agama di Indonesia*. Yogyakarta: Center for Religious and Cross-cultural Studies, p 50

30. ANRI, Inventaris Arsip PP Muhammadiyah Yogyakarta 1922–2001, No.1192.
31. Maarif S (2017) *Pasang Surut Rekognisi Agama Leluhur dalam Politik Agama di Indonesia.* Yogyakarta: Center for Religious and Cross-cultural Studies, p 53
32. Maarif S (2017) *Pasang Surut Rekognisi Agama Leluhur dalam Politik Agama di Indonesia.* Yogyakarta: Center for Religious and Cross-cultural Studies, p 62
33. Maarif S (2017) *Pasang Surut Rekognisi Agama Leluhur dalam Politik Agama di Indonesia.* Yogyakarta: Center for Religious and Cross-cultural Studies, p 81
34. Butt S (2020) Constitutional recognition "Beliefs" in Indonesia. J Law Relig 450–473. https://doi.org/10.1017/jlr.2020.39
35. Yeoh G (2021). Record-making and record-keeping in early societies. Oxon: Routledge, p xii. https://twitter.com/agama_nusantara/status/1447422791628693509/photo/1. Accessed 12 Dec 2021
36. Simbolon H (2019) *regional: liputan6*. Accessed 8 May 2022, from liputan6.com: https://www.liputan6.com/regional/read/3900180/senyum-lebar-warga-bandung-terima-e-ktp-pertama-dengan-kolom-kepercayaan
37. Antara (2017) *Beranda Nasional: Tempo.* Retrieved May 9, 2022, from nasional.tempo.co: https://nasional.tempo.co/read/1031991/kepercayaan-masuk-kolom-agama-kemendagri-benahi-aplikasi-siak.

# Prayer Poems for Reaching Happiness During Covid-19 Pandemic in Indonesia

**Indah Fadhilla and Syahirul Alim**

**Abstract** Restrictions on social space during the Covid-19 pandemic may disturb social harmony. If each person's religious consciousness is not strengthened, society may struggle to control the fear and anxiety they experience while a disease outbreak is underway. Literary works help to portray the shattered social reality as one of the efforts to preserve social peace. Prayer poems are included in this study as a literary text source since it is considered to be an artistic response to what people expected during the Covid-19 pandemic. A book collection of poems entitled *Peradaban Baru Corona* has various prayer poems that serve as the analytical source for this study. These poems inherently present prayers as a hope to achieve happiness. Prayer poems show another side of spiritual happiness in addition to portraying the realities of distress. This study was intended to illustrate that the Indonesian people have the hope of achieving happiness during the Covid-19 pandemic by increasing their sense of sincerity and gratitude to God through dialogues carried out in prayer. The language used in the collection of poems was analyzed using semi-miotic theory. By employing a prophetic literary approach, this research focuses on one of the intrinsic elements of literary works, namely the setting of the atmosphere depicted in the poems. This study discovered that improving sincerity and gratitude for God was one of the strategies to restore social harmony that had been disturbed by the Covid-19 outbreak. The author of the *Peradaban Baru Corona* book collection of poems used prayer poems to illustrate the closeness between humans and God to alleviate anxiety related to the Covid-19 pandemic in Indonesia.

**Keywords** Prophetic literature · Semiotics · Islam · And happiness

I. Fadhilla · S. Alim (✉)
Faculty of Da'wah and Communication Sciences, Universitas Islam Negeri Syarif Hidayatullah, Jakarta, Indonesia
e-mail: syahirulalm@uinjkt.ac.id

I. Fadhilla
e-mail: indahfadhilla@uinjkt.ac.id



Nawawi et al. (eds.), *Managing Disruption and Developing Resilience for a Better Southeast Asia*, Springer Proceedings in Humanities and Social Sciences,
https://doi.org/10.1007/978-981-96-2116-3_39

# 1 Introduction

One of Mark Woodward's articles on his personal social media website describes how religion responds to the conditions of human reality everywhere, including when the Covid-19 pandemic struck the world. This response is inherently connected to texts found in sacred literature, such as the Qur'an, the Bible, and other religious scriptures. When confronted with a grave threat, people instinctively seek spiritual guidance from religion and religious leaders. In these circumstances, the sacred text has the driving force of psychological reinforcement to support the "justification" in acting to carry out humanitarian jihad, even while society is threatened. Rereading religious texts sparked responses from various societal groups, including those in Indonesia. Prayers that fill literary spaces in a poem are symbolically an aesthetic answer to the fear and anxiety that disturbs social harmony in the Covid-19 pandemic situation in Indonesia.

Pandemics and infectious diseases constantly bring out new realities that provide constructive encouragement to society, reconstructing aspects of humanity that were nearly eroded in the face of terrifying pandemic threats. This new reality is the transcendental literary trend that emerged during the pandemic era by journalists who were compelled to respond to the Covid-19 situation through the poem with a strong spiritual nuance. The poet journalists that composed the poem in the poem collection book *Peradaban Baru Corona* have a similar background as a journalist who also writes the poem.

Journalists' sensitivity in reporting current conditions and situations can assist poets in presenting the conditions of the Covid-19 pandemic in Indonesia through the poems they write. There are at least a few poems that can represent traditional tendencies or to use Kuntowijoyo's definition, a type of transcendental literature that establishes tradition as a holistic knowledge system tied to the Transcendent in life (Hadi 1999).

Some of these works are described by researchers as poetic prayer, a new type of Sufistic literary tendency. Figurative language of a poem that utilizes all components of linguistic aesthetics to accomplish the power of pronunciation more readily transfers the flames of love (Hadi 1999). Thus, a series of poem prayer lines can elicit such intense feelings about the reality that the Transcendent is the only most beautiful entity to rely on for all hope and help.

Prayer poems created during the Covid-19 pandemic era, when analyzed semiotically, reveal not only an aesthetic nuance in each of the phrases but also a symbolic phenomenon in the context of spiritual experience, revealing the dimensions of God that exist in oneself and the surroundings. The following is an example of Uten Sutendy's poem:

*Hatiku merasa lebih damai, tentram dan hening bercengkrama dengan-Mu.*
*Justru pada saat aku sedang bertelanjang*
*tanpa jubah kebesaran dan kerudung keyakinan*

The prayers expressed in the *Peradaban Baru Corona* book collection of poems describe the atmosphere of fear and anxiety during the Covid-19 pandemic. It is obvious that the Covid-19 pandemic has not only had an impact on physical health but also on the mental health of the Indonesian people. The threat of depression comes as a result of social distancing or isolation, fear of being infected, infecting others, not receiving health care when needed, and even death threats [11]. To sustain mental health, each individual must be able to deal with pressure. During the Covid-19 pandemic, prevalent feelings include sadness, stress, bewilderment, anger, and fear. With good management, these emotions can be regulated so that they do not have a negative impact on humans.

Through a book collection of poems entitled "*Peradaban Baru Corona*", readers, in this case, the Indonesian people have the opportunity to manage their emotions well. The poems depict various feelings experienced during the Covid-19 pandemic. This book collection of poems was written by a poet journalist, curated by Remy Sylado, and financed by the Republic of Indonesia's Ministry of Education and Culture. The author attempts to demonstrate how to regulate emotions well in some of the poems that emerge. Anxiety and dread that developed during the Covid-19 pandemic were met with prayers that were meant to convey a message to the reader, allowing the reader to feel peaceful despite living amid a disease outbreak.

Responding to the pandemic situation with poems is done not only by poets in Indonesia but also by poets all around the world. In 2020, the Cape Comorin India publisher published a collection book of poems titled *Covid-19 Pandemic Poems: Volume I*. Poets from India, Australia, the United States, the Philippines, Sri Lanka, Pakistan, Indonesia, and other countries contributed to this book collection of poems [29]. The poems in the book illustrate the atmosphere that existed in various countries during the Covid-19 pandemic to elicit international humanitarian solidarity.

Ben Okri, a Nigerian poet, has also responded to the Covid-19 pandemic with a book collection of poems titled *A Fire in My Head: Poems for The Dawn*. Ratau [27] used this poem collection as a source of inspiration for his study *Art and Spirituality in the Covid-19 Epoch: An Exploratory Reading of Ben Okri's Poem*. Ratau [27] employs Hermeneutic theory to examine society's spirituality during the Covid-19 pandemic, focusing on issues of race, identity, healing, spirituality, and public awareness.

In Southeast Asia, Derak [8] conducted a study entitled *Impak Pandemik Covid-19 dalam Penulisan Puisi di Malaysia or* "The Impact of the Covid-19 Pandemic in Poem Writing in Malaysia". The analytical materials used are four books collection of poems entitled *Merentas Gempita Pandemik* 2020 by Lim Swee Tin; *Petaka Virus* by Munsy Mohammad Musip and friends; *Betapa berat* work by Munsy Mohammad Musip and his friends; and *Covid-19: Ibrah Buat the Ummah* by Dhiyah Alias and friends. Derak [8] states that poets have succeeded in conveying the psychological, social, religious, cultural, educational, health, and economic impacts of the Covid-19 pandemic.

According to some of the explanations above, the reflection of Covid-19 in the development of poems is carried out by poets all over the world. This has also piqued the interest of experts, who are looking into the topics that poets desire to address in their work amid the Covid-19 pandemic. In Indonesia, the poem is typically studied using a semiotic approach. A study of poem using the semiotic theory of Charles Sanders Peirce has been carried out by Santoso [28] with the *title "Religiusitas dalam Kumpulan Puisi Jawa Modern Sangarepe Ka'bah* by Nyitno Munajat". The religious behavior depicted in the collection of poems is belief in Judgment Day and belief in God's judgment. Both of these mindsets encourage Muslims to believe in the pillars of religion and Doomsday.

Putri [26] wrote a study of *"Konsep Kebahagiaan dalam Perspektif Al-Farabi"* or "The Concept of Happiness from Al-Perspective." According to al-Farabi, happiness is the sought good for the sake of the good itself. According to al-Farabi, there are four paths to happiness: intention and will, understanding of acceptable activities, possessing four virtues, and having intermediate (moderate) virtues. Furthermore, al-Farabi addresses the relationship between morality and enjoyment as a sign of a peaceful soul.

From the various messages that emerged as a result of the analysis of the poem using Peirce's semiotic theory, the emergence of the concept of Islam and Happiness in the poem of prayer has never been done. Thus, this research will look at how the concepts of Islam and Happiness might be used to alleviate the dread and anxiety of people who live in areas where disease epidemics occur. The poems were written by a poet journalist and published in a book collection of poems called *Peradaban Baru Corona.*

## *1.1 Concepts and Theories*

### 1.1.1 Islam and Happiness

Seyyed Hossein Nasr (2014), takes illustrates happiness through the concept introduced by Abu Nasr al-Farabi. According to him, al-Farabi had adopted Greek philosophical thought—especially Plato and Aristotle—reconstructed and integrated it with Islamic ethical values. He succeeded in building a theory of happiness which was later outlined in his work, *"Tahsil al-Sa'adah" (The Attainment of Happiness)* or to put it in another way, "Reaching Happiness". Not only has a political nuance, but the theory of happiness developed by al-Farabi also has a very strong emphasis on spiritual values, where the highest happiness is *"ukhrawi"* (paradisal) which is more important than the temporal happiness obtained by humans while living in this world.

Happiness in its paradisal connotation is always preceded by a positive emotional impulse in the form of continuous gratitude. Poetic literature with a prophetic undertone provides a happy stimulus to people who read it, as well as mental power to remind us of our appreciation to God for good and bad conditions. The expression of gratitude is frequently overlooked by us and undervalued in our larger social reality. In truth, gratitude not only receives high regard from all religions but in many great traditions, people have the highest quality ethical attitude as the most important to living a happy life [21]. Prayer poems will be placed as a form of gratitude for the authors. Gratitude in this case is in the form of positive emotions that grow through feeling happy and reaping the benefits of whatever is obtained.

A work of poem with a background of a prolonged disaster or a tense and frightening condition is born as a cognitive response when the author understands, feels, and how the words should be chosen and written. The choice of transcendental literary genres demonstrates a response in the form of submission as well as hope addressed straight to God. Anxiety and fear about the prolonged pandemic crisis appear to be beyond the reach of materialistic human approaches such as technology and current science. In such a case, the prophetic tendency, with its wide opening of spiritual channels, becomes the primary tool in resolving various anxieties, pressures, and fears. The arena of prophetic-transcendental literature becomes a spiritual space to awaken the spirit of life and push reality as hard as possible happiness that has so far been drowned in a gripping pandemic atmosphere. Prayer poems to bring the nuances of happiness in the midst of a sluggish spirit to continue living in a completely limited space can be an alternative to prophetic literature during a pandemic.

## *1.2 Poem Study*

According to the Great Indonesian Dictionary (KBBI), a poem is a literary genre whose language is defined by rhythm, dimension, rhyme, and the arrangement of lines and stanzas. A poem is a bound composition [25]. The limitations of the poem are based on the attachment to (1) the number of lines in each stanza, (2) the number of words in each line, (3) the number of syllables in each line, (4) rhyme, and (5) rhythm. Readers can enjoy different types of a poem with different meanings that the author wishes to impart to the reader.

Messages delivered through poems typically include values that highlight the wisdom of an event or stories that exist in poem statements. Because the poem is so intimately tied to philosophy and religion, its value can also aid the reader in shaping his perspective on life [6]. The author considers prayer poems to be a means of bringing the reader closer to the Creator. Poem poems with prayers will reflect on each reader's interpretation of the author's message.

To interpret a poem, the reader needs to grasp the structure of literary works, particularly poems, including intrinsic and extrinsic structures.

a. Intrinsic Structure

Intrinsic elements are those that directly contribute to the creation of a literary work (Eddy, 1991). Matters pertaining to this structure include plot, setting, center of storytelling, and characterizations, as well as matters about theme disclosure and mandate. It also contains issues of imagination and emotion. A poem's inherent characteristics include diction, rhyme, rhythm, stanzas, lines, and typography.

b. Extrinsic Structure

Extrinsic elements are all external factors behind the creation of literary works. It is the subjective property of the author which can be in the form of social conditions, motivations, and tendencies that encourage and influence one's authorship. In line with the two opinions above, Wellek and Warren (in [33]: 64) state that in this extrinsic element there are also factors such as (1) author biography, (2) psychology (creative process), (3) sociological (society) socio-cultural community, and (4) philosophical (the author's philosophical school).

After understanding the elements that make up a poem, the reader will find it easier to understand the message the author wants to convey about the poem. Each reader's interpretation of the same poem will differ depending on their talents and background information. In a poem study, various theories can be employed as analytical tools. The semiotic theory is one of the most commonly used theories.

### *1.3 The Semiotic Theory of Charles Sanders Peirce*

This study uses the theory of Charles Sanders Peirce which is called the triangle meaning theory. The following is a manifestation of the triangle meaning proposed by Peirce (Iskandar and Lestari, 2016).

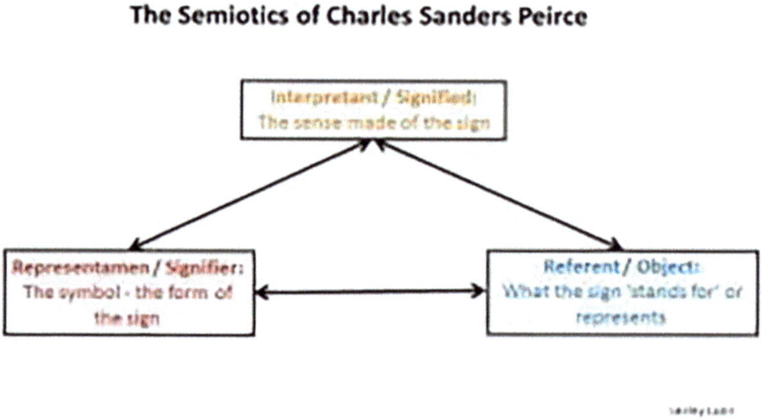


In his theory, Peirce divides it into three forms, namely:

1. Sign is a symbol that indicates to someone and makes an impact.
2. The object is a social context that becomes a reference or reference for a sign (representamen).
3. The interpretant is a person's concept of thinking by using a sign and using it as a meaning of something about the object referred to by the sign. In other words, the interpretant is the result of thinking from a sign that has been digested in the form of meaning.

In semiotics, Peirce's theory is also often called Grand Theory [34]. This is because the idea is global (comprehensive). Peirce identifies the basic particles of a sign and then combines them back into a single structure.

## 2 The Concept of Islam and Happiness in Poem with the Theme of the Co-Vid-19 Pandemic

Of the 99 poems written by poet journalists in the *Peradaban Baru Corona* poem collection book, several poems were selected that were used as objects of study in this study. To reduce this anxiety, the authors present poems containing prayers to God. Even though they are in the midst of a disease outbreak, these prayers are sent to God to achieve tranquility and peace of mind. The poem of prayer by these authors is one of the goals to be achieved from the concept of Islam and Happiness.

The first step in comprehending the concept of Islam and Happiness is to describe the inherent and extrinsic features of the chosen poems. The poems chosen were those that described the anxiety and terror felt by the Indonesian people during the outbreak. In addition to portraying anxiousness, the poems include pleas to God for readers to find peace and happiness.

The consideration of intrinsic aspects is limited to the atmosphere's surroundings. According to Fadhilla [12], the setting is made up of six elements: the event environment, visible background, time of day or year, climate or weather, historical period, and background people. In a literary work, the setting is used to define the themes, characters, and atmosphere both outside and inside the characters.

Of the 99 poems in the *Peradaban Baru Corona* book collection of poems, four poems were selected that were classified as prayer-poems, namely "*Bersujud di Rumah*" by Utten Sutendy; "*Laboratorium Doa (2)*" by Sihar Ramses Sakti Simatupang; "*Bersama Allah Aku Menghadapimu*" by Shafwan Hadi Umry; "*Jerit Corona dan Doa*" by Dimas Agoes Pelaz. The following describes the poet's depiction of fear and anxiety as a setting for the atmosphere of the Covid-19 pandemic. The poet then responds to the fear and anxiety with prayers to achieve serenity and happiness in the middle of a disease outbreak.

Utten Sutendy's first poem is titled "*Bersujud di Rumah.*" The poet describes the conditions of worshiping at home during the Covid-19 pandemic.

> Ya Rabbi
> Hari-hari ini aku merasa lebih dekat denganMu. Seolah bisa menyentuh
> danmemelukMu lebih erat. Justru saat aku sedang duduk bersila
> seorang diri di pojok sudut rumahku yang sepi.
>
> Aku merasa lebih bebas berbicara seolah sedang bercumbu
> denganMu. Justru saat aku duduk sendiri menatap langit berbintang di
> teras rumahku.
>
> Hatiku merasa lebih damai, tenteram, dan hening bercengkrama

denganMu. Justru saat aku sedang betelanjang tanpa jubah kebesaran
dan kerudung keyakinan.

Ya Rabbi
Kemesraanku bercinta denganMu terasa kian hangat.Justru saat aku
sedang bersujud panjang sendiri tanpa panggilan adzan, tanpa suara
nyaring dari balik mimbar khotbah.

Aku bersimbah di haribaanMu, menyerahkan sepenuh jiwa ragaku
bukan atas nama apapun, melainkan semata karena aku
membutuhkanMu.

Ya Rabbi
Kini aku mengerti mengapa Engkau memintaku harus pulang dan
bersujud di rumah saja, bukan di tempat-tempat mewah penuh
dengan simbol tentangMu yang kini sebagian sudah terkunci.

Ya Rabbi
Aku mengerti
Engkau ingin ajarkan kepadaku
Bahwa kasih sayangMu begitu dekat hingga raga yang membungkus
jiwa ini adalah rumah dan tempat ibadahku yang sebenar-benarnya
meski tanpa baju dan panggung keramaian ritual untukMu.

(BSD City 2020)

**The setting of fear or anxiety in the conditions of the Covid-19 pandemic:**

The setting of the atmosphere described in the poem above is in the first stanza / *seorang diri di pojok sudut rumahku yang sepi*/ or /alone in the corner of a quiet corner of my house/. The author wants to describe the quiet and tense situation of the Covid-19 pandemic. The character of "*Aku*" is confined at home together to fear and anxiety. The condition of the community described in the poem above is that there are pros and cons in society against the government's call to worship from home. Some people agree and some do not agree.

When the number of positive Covid-19 cases increased, MUI issued Fatwa Number 14 of 2020 on the application of worship during the Covid-19 pandemic. The fatwa received both positive and negative feedback from the general population and religious experts (Junaedi, 2020). During the Covid-19 pandemic, MUI advocates for the continuation of the five daily prayers in a congregation as well as Friday prayers. People are encouraged to pray at home and to substitute Zuhur prayers for Friday prayers. Amid these disagreements, this poem challenges the reader to realize the benefits of the policy of home worship. When performing worship at home, *Aku*'s character is defined as having a higher level of solemnity.

**Delivering the Message of Happiness:**

The author starts the line with /*Ya Rabbi*/. The author wishes to express to the reader through prayer poems that worshiping at home will provide you with a sense of comfort, calm, and solemnity. The author also encourages readers to be grateful for God's love and all the blessings they continue to get even though society is in the grip of a disease outbreak.

The second poem is entitled "*Laboratorium Doa* (2)" by Sihar Ramses. The poet intended to show the hope that will be achieved when the pandemic is over.

pada malam keberapakah kita mendapatkan cahaya dari tirai
kelam yang dilebarkan ini. ketika seluruh kota begitu sunyi.
dan gigil dari gigi bergemeletak hanya melahirkan lorong;
tempat sembunyi kita- kaum degil tanpa kepercayaan seolah
bukan makhluk ciptaan Tuhan.

padakelam.keberapakah kita mendapatkan terang dari
kelambu pekat yang terburai itu. ketika berada dalam
pintupintu itu- seolah kehidupan telah punah dan tak ada lagi
harap dari penciptaan ini.

ya Tuhan rawatlah kami. tubuh kami yang mencair jadi buih
pecah. dan tengkorak kami serupa tiang garam yang patah;
dan kelak terburai- ribuan jumlahnya.
orangorang berusaha mendengar bisikmu. tapi yang
berlahiran dari lubang telinga kami cuma cericit tikus. dan.
janji orang ingkar karena berharap tentang nasi yang terserak
dari langit.

ya Tuhan percayailah kami. sebagaimana Kau pernah karuniai
pokok kehidupan. tanpa embel cawat atau kelelahan si
pembawa batu ke puncak bukit- semua karena kedegilan.lalu
menjagaibuahbuah yang lenyap di ranting itu. siasia saja:
olehularularyangberlahiran di dada kami.

:ya Tuhan ratapi kami. ya Tuhan tangisilah kami. ya Tuhan
rahmati kami. ya Tuhan peluklah kami. ya Tuhan ciumi kami.
ya Tuhan..

(Medan 2020)

**The setting of fear or anxiety in the conditions of the Covid-19 pandemic:**

The setting of the atmosphere described in the poem above is in the first stanza/ *ketika seluruh kota begitu sunyi/* or /when the whole city is so quiet/. The chosen dictions, such as */gelap/, /sunyi/, /gigil* or/ dark/lonely/shiver, describe the fear felt by the narrator. The author wishes to describe the Covid-19 pandemic's quiet and tense atmosphere. The narrator and God are having a conversation about the meaning of life. During the Covid-19 pandemic, society is described as being in a state of chaos because of many polemics.

**Delivering the Message of Happiness:**

The author starts the line with */Ya Tuhan/* or /oh my god/. Through prayer poems, the author wants to convey a message to the reader that humans have hope that is dependent on God to protect humans even though they are in chaos. In this case, it represents the chaos that occurred during the COVID-19 pandemic. The author invites the reader not to put too much hope in human strength, but to pray to God for protection is the most appropriate step.

The third poem is entitled "*Bersama Allah Aku Menghadapimu*" by Shafwan Hadi. The poet encourages readers to be sincere and grateful for the life that is being lived despite being in the Covid-19 pandemic.

pada daun-daun roh yang hidup maupun mati
pada segala rasa cinta maupun benci
pada pintu yang terbuka maupun terkunci
engkau, merasuk tanpa kata-kata
menempel memagut memungut maut
bukankah tanda-tanda itu terbaca
virus kesepian
virus kematian
marilah kita tertawa, seperti komedi
yang membuat orang tidak terluka
marilah kita tafakur
yang membuat kita selalu bersyukur
karena ia adalah percobaan hati
jika hati bertafakur tentang kebaikan
"dan buahnya berupa pahala", kata seorang syekh
kita berburu mendapatkannya
jika hati berpikir tentang keburukan
"dan buahnya berupa azab", kata seorang syekh
kita menjauh meninggalkannya
karena itu, kawan!
tinggalkan dan jangan mendekat!,
inilahtafakurnya orang-orang abid
inilah tasyakur orang-orang yang sakit
pada Sang Kekasihnya
jika hati bertafakur tentang kefanaan
dan ketidakmampuan dunia
memenuhi keinginan nafsu carut-marut
mari tinggalkan dia untuk menjadi zuhud
-menjadi manusia
membaca tanda
virus yang membunuh dan mengeksekusi
Yallahi Rabbi
Kutatap, dan kuratap jua pesan-Mu ini

bagai anak nakal dilantai sesal
sementara Engkau tegak menatap ramah
sementara daku tertunduk resah
Menunggu cambuk cemeti-Mu
Menanti palu godam-Mu
Yainsanul kerdil!
Mari bertafakur tentang anugerah Allah
Cinta kasih dan sayang melebihi
Amarah dan Siksa-Nya,
mari bertafakur dan bersyukur
Mari kita tolong diri kita

(Medan, 25 April 2020)

**The setting of fear or anxiety in the conditions of the Covid-19 pandemic:**

The setting of the atmosphere described in the poem above is in the seventh line */virus kesepian/* or virus of loneliness/. The author wishes to depict the terrifying scenario caused by the Covid-19 pandemic. The author encourages the reader to be grateful and reflect on all of the challenges encountered during the Covid-19 pandemic. Humans are encouraged to use caution when coping with disasters. If humans perceive calamity as a test, they will be rewarded. If humans perceive calamity as a burden, they will be punished.

**Delivering the Message of Happiness:**

The author begins the prayer poems from the 32nd to the 44th line. The author wishes to express to the reader through prayer poems that, even amid anxiety, humans must stay grateful and contemplative to learn from every challenge that God has given. The author invites the reader to be grateful since our trust in God can aid us when we are in distress. Humans are invited to view the pandemic as a gift from God because God loves mankind, not because God is displeased. Even if we are in the midst of a disease outbreak, we are asked to be grateful for all the blessings that are still accessible from God.

The fourth poem is entitled "*Jerit Corona dan Doa*" or "The Screams of Corona and Prayer" by Dimas Agoes. The poet invites the reader to pray by praising God through Asmaul Husna.

Aku mendengar jerit menggerus
derita umat
Aku mendengar tangis mengharu
biru
Aku mendengar jerit tangis
membahana di bumi

Aku merasakan derita pilu di dada
Dunia menangis, Amerika nggegiris
Cina berborok luka menganga

Jutaan manusia terenggut paksa
Ribuan dokter, perawat
Para pekerja medis gugur menjadi
Syuhada

Do'ado'abersijingkat
Semua lebur menyatu dalam
permohonan, Ya Baari'.. engkaulah segala
perencana
Engkaulah segala pelaksana
Ya 'Aalim … Engkaulah yang maha mengetahui
segala kejadian dan peristiwa

Ya Samii' … Engkaulah Dzat yang
maha melihat mendengar
baik besar kecil jauh dekat halus
kasar, semua sama
Kami banyak bersalah
Kami dholim
Kami banyak berdosa

Ya Ghafuur … Engkau maha
Pengampun
Bagi hambanya yang mau bertobat
Ampunilah kami

Ya Tawwaab …. Engkaulah dzat
penerimataubat
Terimalah taubat kami
Ya..malikulMulk … Engkaulah dzat
pemilik kekuasaan
Ya DzulJalaaliWal
lkraam …. Engkaulah Dzat pemilik
segala kemuliaan
Dan kesempurnaan
Kabulkanlah do'a kami

(Jambi, 15 Maret 2020)

**The Setting of Fear or anxiety in Covid-19 Pandemic Conditions:**

The setting of the atmosphere described in the poem above is in the first and second stanzas. The author wants to describe the Pandemi Covid-19 situation which is very frightening because many health workers have died in facing COVID-19.

**Delivering the messages of happiness:**

The author starts the prayer poem in the third stanza. Through prayer-poems, the author mentions Asmaul Husna to praise God. The author invites the reader to pray for forgiveness for all the mistakes that have been made during life in the world. The reader is invited to repent to get peace of mind.

In addition to the intrinsic factor of depicting the atmosphere of the Covid-19 pandemic, this study also explored extrinsic elements such as the author's biography; Author Psychology; and social conditions in the process of creating works. The author who contributed to the *Peradaban Baru Corona* book collection of poems has the same biography or background, especially the poet who has or is still a journalist; the number was decided to be limited to 100 journalists, but from throughout Indonesia (Kemendikbud, 2020). Utten Sutendy is a journalist who started writing while studying at UIN Jakarta. Utten is now actively involved in writing poems, essays, and other forms of online media. Sihar Ramses is a lecturer at Multimedia Nusantara University. Some of his books' collections of poems have been published, including a collection of merely single poems, a collection of short tales, and novels. The Novel of *Bulan Lebam di Tepian Toba* received a nomination for a 2009 Literary Award as well as honors from Metropolid'asia, an Italian publisher. Ever worked as a journalist in the *Jawa Pos* Group opposition and rose to the rank of culture editor at *Harian Umum Sore Sinar Harapan*. Shafwan Hadi is a poet from Deli Serdang in Indonesia. Shafwan Hadi is an Indonesian poet from Deli Serdang. Shafwan had also been duty as a Bintang Sort Medan Daily reporter. At present Shafwan is a lecturer at UMN AI-Washliyah, Medan. Dimas Agoes is a poet who lives in Jambi. He writes a poem, short stories, and literary articles also with theater, but also became a journalist in various media. The media that first published his work was the education tabloid in the Media Guru, then the TIPS Poltabes Palembang Tabloid. He has also been a correspondent in the Hikmah tabloid.

There is also a similarity in the author's psychology in that both exhibit religiosity through prayer titles. The poem's four titles both exhort the reader to pray to God to find peace and happiness. Through the language of the prayer made, the author asks the reader to find happiness by enhancing the reader's spirituality. The social conditions of the community in the creative process in terms of the time and place of production of works both characterize the Covid-19 Pandemic condition in each Indonesian territory in 2020. The poem "*Bersujud di Rumah*" was created in BSD, one of the regions in the city of South Tangerang. The poem "*Laboratorium Doa* (2)" and "*Bersama Allah Aku Menghadapimu*" was created in the city of Medan. The poem "*Jeritan Corona dan Doa*" was created in the city of Jambi. Although different cities, the depiction of the atmosphere expressed by the poet is not much different from one city and another.

From the description above, it can be seen that the sign in this study was four chosen poems in the book collection of poems titled *Peradaban Baru Corona*. The *interpretant* of this study is hence an analysis of the research-related poem. Researchers observe the following depictions: the first, the community feels fear and anxiety during the Covid-19 pandemic; the second, the prayer poem Contains Prayers to Deliver a Message of Happiness, and the third one is that the readers of the prayer poem will find peace and happiness since the poem contains prayer. The object of this study is on four poems that show how, as a member of the community, the author experiences fear and anxiety during the Covid-19 pandemic; the author also uses these poems to describe fear and anxiety in the *Peradaban Baru Corona* book collection of poems, and the reader can access and read the collection of poems in the book collection of poems of *Peradaban Baru Corona* as a source of relief from fear and anxiety to feel peaceful despite the Covid-19 pandemic.

From the explanation above, the results have been obtained that first, the author of the prayer poem conveys to the reader a message of joy as an antidote for the fear and anxiety that are experienced during the Covid-19 pandemic. Second, the author uses poems to spread a message of happiness and serve as an antidote for the fear and anxiety that people experience during the Covid-19 Pandemic. To lessen the fear and anxiety experienced during the Covid-19 pandemic, the message of pleasure can thus be expressed through the prayer poem in the *Peradaban Baru Corona* book collection of poems.

## 3 Conclusion

To increase happiness in the community, the prophetic writing that emerged during the Covid-19 epidemic gave rise to a "new civilization" in the realm of the poem. The prayer poems have created an intrapersonal and interpersonal interaction that not only enhances awareness of how fragile the personal relationship between himself and his God is but also creates a "crack" in his relationship with other people and his surroundings. Through a series of phrases that flow and open a spiritual path to happiness, the Covid-19 outbreak's personal and social gap is bridged. People need to be happy since it is the most essential condition for building social capital and leading better lives. In terms of gaining either material pleasure (life satisfaction) or spiritual happiness (well-being and long-lasting happiness), Islam offers some theories of happiness that are strongly tied to all aspects of human existence. When the material needs of life are not met, prophetic literature is one of the social capitals that might produce spiritual satisfaction.

## References

1. Alquran Surat Hud Ayat 108
2. Alquran Surat Hud Ayat 105
3. Alquran Surat Al-Baqarah Ayat 69
4. Alquran Surat Yunus Ayat 58
5. Alquran Surat Al-Fajr Ayat 27—28
6. Aminuddin. 1987. *Pengantar Apresiasi Karya Sastra.* Bandung: Sinar Baru, 1987
7. Ansari MA (1963) "Miskawayh's Conception of Sa'dah", dalam. *Journal of Islamic Studies*: Islamabad: Islamic Research Institute, International Islamic University
8. Derak, Rosmah., dkk. (2021) "Impak Pandemik Covid-19 dalam Penulisan Puisi di Malaysia", in PENDETA Journal of Malay Language, Education and Literature, Vol (12), no (khas)
9. Eddy NT (1991) *Kamus Istilah Sastra Indonesia.* Yogyakarta: Nusa Indah.

10. Effendy, OnongUdjana (1994) *Ilmu Komunikasi Teori dan Praktek*, Cet-8. Bandung: Remaja Rosdakarya
11. Erlangga ND (2022) "Menjaga Kesehatan Mental Selama Pandemi Covid-19 dengan Self Empower" dalam buku *Jejak Pemikiran Pemuda Indonesia tentang Kesehatan Mental dan Covid-19*. Syiah Kuala University Press, Aceh
12. Fadhilla I (2014) Novel Persiden Karya Wisran Hadi: Analisis Latar Robert Stanton. Skripsi Sarjana Universitas Gadjah Mada, Yogyakarta
13. Fanani Z (2000) Telaah Sastra. Muhammadiyah University Press, Yogyakarta
14. Ibrahim RM (2009) Sa'adah al-Insan fi Alquran al-Karim. Tesis Master tidakdipublikasikan Universitas Islam Gaza, Palestina
15. Iskandar, Dudi Sabil dan Rini Lestari (2016) *Mitos dalam Jurnalisme*. Yogyakarta: Andi
16. Junaedi, Jujun., dkk (2020) Konflik Interpretasi Fatwa MUI dalam Pelaksanaan Ibadah selama Pandemi Covid-19. *Al-Taddabur: Jurnal Kajian Sosial, Peradaban, dan Agama, 6(2), hal.175—189*
17. Kamus Besar Bahasa Indonesia diakses pada 3 Mei 2022 pada link https://kbbi.kemdikbud.go.id/entri/puisi
18. Kementerian Pendidikan dan Kebudayaan Republik Indonesia. 2020. *Peradaban Baru Corona*. Diakses pada link http://repositori.kemdikbud.go.id/19367/
19. Leaman O (1980) IbnRushd on happiness and philosophy. *Journal StudiaIslamika*, No. 52. Tangerang Selatan: PPIM UIN Jakarta
20. Mayasari R (2014) "Religiusitas Islam dan Kebahagiaan" dalam *Jurnal Al-Munzir*, Vol. 7 no. 2, h. 81–100 (Kendari: IAIN Kendari Press)
21. McCullough ME, Emmons RA (eds) (2004) The psychology of gratitude. Oxford University Press, New York
22. Muriah S (2000) *Metodologi Dakwah Kontemporer*. Yogyakarta: Mitra Pustaka
23. Muthari AH (1999) *Kembali ke Akar Kembali ke Sumber: Esai-esai Sastra Profetik dan Sufistik*. Jakarta: Pustaka Firdaus
24. Nasr S (2014) Happiness and the attainment of happiness: an Islamic perspective. *Journal Law and Religion,* vol 29, no. 1. Cambridge: Cambridge University Press.
25. Pradopo RD (2020) *Pengkajian Puisi*. Yogykarta: UGM Press
26. Putri EW (2018) "Konsep Kebahagiaan dalam Perspektif Al-Farabi" dalam *Jurnal Thaqaffiyat*, Vol 18, no 1., (Yogyakarta: UIN Sunan Kalijaga Press)
27. Ratau N (2021) *Art and spirituality in the covid-19 epoch: an exploratory reading of Ben Okri's Poetry*. Pharos J Theology 102(2)
28. Santoso., dkk (2021) Religiusitas dalam Kumpulan Puisi Jawa Modern SangarepeKa'bah Karya Witno Munajat dalam. J Educ Dev 9(2):265–272. (Padang Sidempuan: Institut Pendidikan Tapanuli Selatan)
29. Silvest, Regin dan John Charles (2020) Covid-19 Pandemic Poems: Volume I. Cpe Comorin Publisher, Tamilnadu
30. Sobur A (2001) *Analisis Teks Media*. Bandung: Remaja Rosdakarya
31. Taufiqi, MuhammadAlfian (2021) *Pesan Dakwah AhmadunYosiHerfanda dalam Puisi tentang Sembahyang Rumputan di Media Sosial*. Skripsi Universitas Sunan Ampel Surabaya
32. Teeuw A (1984) *Sastra dan Ilmu Sastra: Pengantar Teori Sastra*. Jakarta: PT Dunia Pustaka Jaya
33. Waluyo HJ (1994) Pengkajian Cerita Fiksi. University Sebelas Maret Press, Solo
34. Wibowo I (2013) *Semiotika Komunikasi*. Jakarta: Mitra Wacana Media

# Dakwah Model in Millenial Generation Community (Study on Rumah Ta'arufqu, Bogor City)

**Nursalamah Siagian, Nur Alia, and Daniel Rabitha**

**Abstract** In recent years, ta'aruf has become a trend among the millennial Muslim generation along with the increasingly massive hijrah movement. This paper examines the da'wah model carried out by the millennial generation community, especially the ta'aruf community. The study focused on how the Rumah Ta'arufQu (RTQu) in Bogor City attracted the interest and attention of the millennial generation to become its congregation, what materials were studied and what was the profile of the teachers at RTQu. This paper is the result of research conducted with qualitative methods in the form of case studies. The results of the study show that the millennial Muslim generation is interested in Rumah Ta'arufQu apart from their desire to perform ta'aruf, also driven by a desire to explore studies on marriage that are packaged with interesting themes. Studies conducted by RTQu are carried out routinely by meeting face to face, not online. Social media is only used to publish the schedule and theme of the study. RTQu also facilitates congregants who want to perform ta'aruf by setting a number of requirements, as well as opening a consultation service for marriage issues. The speaker is not only an ustaz, but also a motivator, a national trainer in the field of digital marketing, and a psychologist.

**Keywords** Migrate · Ta'aruf · Millennial generation · Wedding

## 1 Introduction

In recent years, the hijrah movement has become a new trend among the millennial generation. Dozens of hijrah communities began to emerge and were enthusiastically welcomed by millennial youth, starting from local to national level communities [1]. Beginning with the existence of Pemuda Hijrah, a da'wah organization from

N. Siagian, N. Alia, and D. Rabitha: All authors have contributed equally to this paper.

N. Siagian · N. Alia (✉) · D. Rabitha
National Research and Innovation Agency, Jakarta, Republic of Indonesia
e-mail: nurs013@brin.go.id



Nawawi et al. (eds.), *Managing Disruption and Developing Resilience for a Better Southeast Asia*, Springer Proceedings in Humanities and Social Sciences,
https://doi.org/10.1007/978-981-96-2116-3_40

Bandung, in 2015, other young communities emerged whose scope extended to the national level. Among them are Indonesia Tanpa Pacaran (ITP) led by La Ode Munafar, The Strangers Al-Ghuroba initiated by former musicians, and the Hijab Squad pioneered by Muslim celebrities such as Shireen Sungkar, Alyssa Soebandono, Dewi Sandra, and others [2].

The word "hijrah" is generally interpreted in several ways, such as: changes in thinking, changes in appearance, converting to Islam, admiring scholars, attending recitations (online and offline), joining communities, attending gatherings, and participating in Islamic solidarity [3]. Meanwhile, hijrah for millennials is synonymous with changing the way they dress. Women, for example, who used to wear tight pants are now wearing wide headscarves covering their chests. Meanwhile, men wear pants above the ankles which make the impression more Islamic. In addition to the way they dress, the content they share on social media has changed. The content tends to be Islamic, for example, short lectures by famous clerics [4].

In line with this, Fajriani (2019) [5] found that Islamic studies from clerics who have an appeal to the congregation are supporting factors for the hijrah phenomenon. For example, Ustaz Abdul Somad, Hanan Ataqqi, Adi Hidayat, Khalid Basalamah, Mamah Dedeh, and so on. In addition, the massive hijrah movement among the younger generation has become a new phenomenon in the Islamic movement in Indonesia. The vision carried by this movement is to invite the younger generation to be closer to God. For this reason, the hijrah movement is actively carrying out da'wah using modern approaches, namely by utilizing social media, such as Facebook, as a symbol of media [6, 7].

The trend of the hijrah movement which has become increasingly widespread since 2015 has mainly emerged in big cities, including the city of Bogor. Many millennial generation religious movement communities have developed in the city of Bogor, including Rumah Ta'arufQu (RTQ), Sahabat Masjid, Komunitas Khadijah, Sahabat Karimah, Teman Hijrah, Yuk Ngaji, Laskar Sedekah, Yuk Nikah Syari, and many others (interview with the owner of Kalam TV, 20 August 2020).

Of these communities, there are several communities that discuss specific topics such as marital issues. One of them is the Rumah Ta'arufQu community, which specifically discusses from pre-wedding, the process, to post-wedding. This community is interesting to study in more depth, because the phenomenon of ta'aruf is increasingly emerging along with the emergence of the hijrah movement. This can be seen in the movement called #IndonesiaTanpaPacaran [8].

Ta'aruf in question is an introduction process in order to get to the level of marriage in accordance with the provisions of Islamic law. The understanding of ta'aruf itself in the Qur'an is knowing each other's personality, social background, culture, education, family, and religion [9]. Ta'aruf, which is now widely practiced by the millennial generation, can be done through friends, parents, relatives, or social media. Ta'aruf online is what makes the meaning of ta'aruf slightly shift because it no longer follows the stages of classical ta'aruf [10]. In fact, online ta'aruf is commodified by the perpetrators due to the demand of enthusiasts and the market [11]. It is different with the Rumah Ta'arufQu community which is still doing the ta'aruf stages directly or not online.

A number of studies on the hijrah and ta'aruf movements have been carried out. Among them were carried out by Saputra et al. [12] who found that the hijrah movement in the Sahabat Hijrahkuu community in Medan City could be positioned in the articulation typology of religiosity-based social movements. Aisyah et al. [7] conducted a study on da'wah messages on a Facebook account for Motivasi Hijrah. The da'wah activities carried out through Facebook use unique images to influence the attention of millennials in making hijrah. Likewise, the Terang Jakarta community is aggressively inviting young people to emigrate through the website, Instagram, and WhatsApp. They use attractive designs and everyday language so that the messages conveyed are easy to understand [13].

Of all these studies, not many have been able to show specifically how the profile of a hijrah community, especially the ta'aruf community, is followed by the millennial generation. What materials are studied by the community, teacher profiles, and how the community attracts the interest and attention of the millennial generation to follow it. For this reason, it is necessary to conduct a study that can reveal this. In detail, this research will answer the following research questions: (1) what are the motives of the congregation to join the millennial generation community of Rumah Ta'arufQu; (2) how is the da'wah model carried out by the Rumah Ta'arufQu community; (3) who are the clerics who usually fill studies in the Rumah Ta'arufQu community; and (4) what are the religious themes or materials commonly studied by the Rumah Ta'arufQu community.

## 2 Research Method

This research uses a qualitative approach in the form of a case study at the Rumah Ta'arufQu in Bogor City. The Rumah Ta'arufQu community was chosen based on the consideration that of all youth hijrah communities in Bogor City, only Rumah Ta'arufQu accommodates its congregation from the ta'aruf process to marriage. While other communities only provide study material on ta'aruf, but do not carry out the ta'aruf process. The data collection process was carried out from mid-August to early September 2020.

Research data were collected through interviews, observation, and documentation. Interviews were conducted with community leaders, coaches, government officials, and a number of members of the Rumah Ta'arufQu congregation. The aspects interviewed included the background of the establishment of the Rumah Ta'arufQu, the process of recitation and ta'aruf, existence, as well as the motivations and benefits of being a congregation. Observations are made when the community conducts routine studies. Meanwhile, documentation is carried out through website searches and social media accounts. The social media account of Rumah Ta'arufQu found by the researchers was a Facebook account with the name Rumah Ta'arufQu Bogor and an Instagram account, namely @rumahtaarufqu.official. Data analysis is done by reducing the data that has been obtained based on the research problem, so that it can be presented in the form of a description.

# 3 Results and Discussion

## 3.1 A Brief History of the Rumah Ta'arufQu (RTQ) Assembly

The community called the Majelis Rumah Ta'arufQu was founded in 2018, founded by Muhammad Haritsah as the Chair and Ustazd Suhendi Al-Khathab as the coach. This assembly is intended to provide education to millennials about how they have knowledge about ta'aruf, marriage, and post-marriage (household). Ustaz Suhendi, who acts as a coach, has a lot of experience in household consultations ranging from divorce, infidelity, domestic violence, and so on. This has motivated him to provide education to millennials so that they understand as early as possible that the household is not as beautiful as the virtual world. In addition, there are many tests that will be taken in the household so that it requires a lot of knowledge (interview with the chairman and builder of the Rumah Ta'arufQu, August 29, 2020).

In addition to conducting Islamic studies related to the theme of marriage, RTQ also becomes a facilitator for each member who will carry out ta'aruf to the wedding and post-wedding processions. These communities exist in the city of Yogyakarta and the city of Bogor. RTQ Bogor City conducts regular studies every Sunday morning with the segmentation of the younger generation. Social media is one of the media used by the RTQ community to inform all matters relating to the activities of the assembly. The social media that many netizens follow is the Instagram account @rumahtaarufqu.official which has around 3,899 followers. It is from this Instagram account that many young people know that they eventually became RTQ congregations.

Based on an interview with the RTQ Congregation (29 August 2020), there are several motivations for the congregation to take part in the study at RTQ. Among them is to prepare for marriage. For that, they need a study of all matters related to the household, from waiting for a mate, seeking a mate, to how to make a harmonious household, and in the pleasure of Allah. In addition, the congregation also wanted to learn about the correct rules and in accordance with Islamic law regarding pre, marriage, and after marriage. Another motivation is to study religion, improve oneself, and be in the circle of God's devout and pious servants. The congregation also wanted to know more about ta'aruf.

In its journey, RTQ has become a study assembly that is open to the public for the people of Bogor City and its surroundings. RTQ has appealed to the public for several reasons, as explained by the chairman of RTQ, Muhammad Haritsah (2 September 2020). First, because at every third meeting, a mass Ruqyah Syar'iyyah is held. Ruqyah Syar'iyyah is intended to detect the presence of jinn that hinders mate and interferes with household happiness. According to Ustadz Suhendi, one of the family splits is inseparable from the role or contribution of the devil or jinn. In addition, some brothers and sisters who find it difficult to find a mate are also due to interference from demons or jinn. Therefore, ruqyah is required for the congregation.

Second, the study material specifically discusses pre-marital, process, and post-wedding. The material discussed at RTQ is material that is needed by everyone as a provision for a family. The congregation is given special guidance and detailed discussion of ta'aruf to domestic life.

Third, the presentation of material at RTQ is delivered in a relaxed and interesting way, explains the theory of marriage with examples, and is full of kinship. Although the method used is similar to the lecture method, there is always a fluid interaction between the presenter and the study congregation. Ustaz Suhendi, for example, conveyed his study material by telling about his experience as a marriage consultant. In addition, it also uses the language of teenagers, so that the congregation finds it easier to understand the material presented. Fourth, the use of social media such as Instagram and Facebook to publish the theme of the study material and the presenters.

This RTQ community is open to all Muslims from various backgrounds of community organizations, both Nahdlatul Ulama (NU), Muhammadiyah, PERSIS, or others. At the time this research was conducted, there were around 150 members of the congregation from the RTQ assembly. Most of the congregation have graduated from college and are working.

In principle, this RTQ facilitates men and women from various circles to be able to find a mate in accordance with the guidance of Islamic law. Thus, the studies discussed are focused on marital problems, household problems, solving problems around domestic life, and facilitating singles who want to learn and want to be wise.

## *3.2 Study Pattern*

The study at the Bogor City RTQ was carried out not only to equip the congregation with an understanding of the material, but also as their main requirement to be able to submit biodata used for ta'aruf. Therefore, studies in RTQ have the following patterns.

First, the study at RTQ is carried out for one semester for each generation. In one semester, there are 15 meetings. Studies or meetings with a duration of three to four months. The implementation time is done once a week, every Sunday morning.

Second, at the end of each semester in each batch, there is a graduation ceremony. In this event, every congregation who has attended the study for 15 meetings is declared to have passed and is entitled to a graduation certificate, namely a premarital college certificate. In addition, they are also entitled to submit a biodata on ta'aruf.

Third, the congregation who has participated in the study, at least eight meetings for women and five meetings for men, has the right to submit biodata on ta'aruf. Ta'aruf biodata contains basic personal information for each congregation who performs ta'aruf. The biodata was then handed over to Muhammad Haritsah, the head of RTQ. This biodata is intended so that each candidate knows in advance what he needs to know from his potential partner.

Fourth, those who have registered as study congregations are advised to join a social media group that has been created by Rumah TaarufQu. The social media group has a stipulation that male congregations join fellow male groups (ikhwan), and female congregations join female groups (akhwat).

Fifth, RTQ conducted interviews with congregants who were already members and had filled out their biodata. This is done to get to know the congregation in detail and detail. Sixth, congregants who wish to become members register by paying an administration fee of Rp. 400,000—and thereafter, no additional fees are charged during the study.

Congregants who are already members get a number of privileges. Every Sunday morning, before the general study, members get Tahsin and Tahfizd Al-Qur'an. In addition, they can also study Arabic and Fiqh studies in depth, and can more freely ask questions to their ustaz and ustazah.

Activities carried out by the congregation on a regular basis are studies conducted every Sunday morning, starting from 09.30 to 11.30 WIB, and followed by the congregational noon prayer. The place of study is usually carried out at the Jami' Miftahul Jannah Mosque, Central Bogor District, Bogor City, and other mosques in Bogor City. Apart from being directly offline, the RTQ community also conducts online studies on Instagram. Another activity is carrying out Ta'arufQu Camp, such as taking place in the Tenjolaya stable village. There was also a food sharing activity for 300 members of the Majelis Taklim Insan Toda.

In addition to the RTQ community, the congregation also participated in studies in other communities such as the Teman Hijrah, Yuk Ngaji, Sahabat Masjid, Darul Quran, and Khadijah Community. But according to them, RTQ is different from other communities. Among these differences are that RTQ facilitates brothers and sisters who want to get married, upgrade themselves, and discuss marriage problems, household problems, and solve problems related to domestic life. While other communities are not like that. Other communities do not focus on discussions about marriage, nor do they facilitate singles who want to perform ta'aruf. In addition, at RTQ, the congregation is not only seeking knowledge, but also trying to prepare themselves to become better individuals, so that they can pick up a mate in a way that Allah is pleased with and build household life in an Islamic way (interview, September 4, 2020).

### *3.3 Themes and Materials*

The material taught at the RTQ assembly is about pre-marital, process, and post-wedding. For pre-marriage includes faith, rukiah, young marriage motivation, and pre-marital finances. Meanwhile, the material for the marriage process discussed started from ta'aruf, sermons, and marriage. Post-wedding material includes etiquette on the first night, psychology of husband and wife, health, husband's rights and obligations, parenting, financial management, divorce, and reconciliation. The themes are made as attractive as possible in accordance with current developments, such as: Be Happy, O Women Longing for Heaven (serial of Rights and Duties of Wives to

Husbands); *Babul Firosy* (Beautiful First Night); and issues related to the economy that are packaged with the learning material "Establishment First? Or Married First?".

The materials studied at RTQ, according to the results of interviews with several congregations, are very helpful for people who want to gain knowledge about marriage through regular meetings held every week. It also helps them to mediate those who want to be ta'aruf, because marriage with ta'aruf is very blessed by Allah (interview, 2 September 2020).

The congregation's views on ta'aruf are also often poured into study material. One of them is like the practice of attracting a mate which contains about fulfilling a vow (promise or oath). The relationship between humans and God, humans and humans, and humans and other creatures, is also used as study material.

Some of the books used as references by Ustaz Suhandi as the builder of the RTQ community are Sofwatut Tafasir by Ibnu Katsir, Tafsir Al Munir by Sheikh Mustafa Wahbah Az-Zuhaili, and Mu'tabarah books such as general books related to marriage. The schools used in conveying material related to ta'aruf, marriage, and domestic life refer to the Syafii School and the Hambali School. The Syafii School represents the congregation of the Syafii School, while the Hambali School represents the Hambali School congregation.

Adjusting the material based on the sect followed by the congregation will make the material more easily accepted by the congregation. Thus, the da'wah delivered to millennials is very effective. If viewed from the structural functional theory of Tallcott Parsons, this is an effort to adapt and adopt RTQ for the benefit of achieving da'wah [14].

### 3.4 Speaker Profile

As RTQ supervisor, Ustaz Suhendi Al-Khathab recruited several ustaz and other professionals to fill in the study material at RTQ. Of course, he is also the main speaker and consultant for married congregations. All presenters presented different study themes, which were adapted to the professions of each presenter. The following is the profile of the speakers who filled out the study in RTQ along with the theme of the study.

Ustaz Suhendi Al-Khathab is a preacher, marriage counselor, family consultant, and marriage counselor. His da'wah experience is not only at the national level but also at the international level. He once went on a da'wah safari in Hong Kong during the month of Ramadan in 2017.

In addition to RTQ, he also has a fixed study schedule in many places. Among them are the study of interpretation, aqidah, and Family Fiqh in a number of offices and mosques.

He currently serves as an administrator for the Indonesian Dai Daiyah Association Center, consultant for Keluarga Indonesia, muwajih for online study community, namely the Rumah Dakwah Indonesia, Kutub Hamba Allah, and Teman Hijrah.

Ustaz Obay Sobari is the founder of Cahaya Quran, a motivator, and a master of Public Speaking. Provide material about The Language of Love for Husband and Wife and Make Love with Charity.

Muhammad Farouq, DM. SLC, is the founder of the Powerful Digital Marketing Academy and the national trainer of the InspiRaadzi Digital Network Marketing Academy. The material that was given was related to Established or Married First?

Ustaz Hepi Andi Bastoni, is a teacher and author of "Betapa Romantis Rasulullah," entrepreneur, online business manager, and filler for WhatsApp online group studies. Filling out a study in the online RTQ community, the material taught is How the Prophet Faced Crisis. Dra. Tynsusi Nurhidayati, Psychologist, is the Head Psychologist of OPTIMA Bogor, the material given is the theme of Knowing the Character of a Partner.

## 3.5 *Ta'aruf Process*

As previously explained, apart from conducting studies, the Bogor City RTQ also facilitates congregants who wish to perform ta'aruf. Ta'aruf is an introduction process before deciding to get married, assisted by a mediator. The purpose of this taaruf is to get to know each other, both physically and non-physically [15].

To be able to apply for ta'aruf, the congregation is required to become a member first. Ta'aruf according to the RTQ community's view is that which is in accordance with the Shari'a, namely no *khalwat* (together, no appointments, no SMS or WA), not long-winded while doing ta'aruf, and only asking what is needed. One example is asking important things, for example about religion, the Koran, the vision and mission of marriage, and financial management. Then it is also forbidden to look for people's disgrace, but it is allowed to ask their parents about the candidate or seek information about the candidate through social media. All of them are required to be accompanied by a facilitator.

The stages of ta'aruf to walimah carried out at RTQ include five stages, namely: Taaruf → Nadzor → Khitbah → Marriage → Walimah. Meanwhile, the process of implementing ta'aruf includes several stages. First, congregants who wish to perform ta'aruf are required to submit their biodata to the head of the RTQ. Second, congregants who may fill out biodata for ta'aruf are those who have attended the study, at least eight times for brothers and five times for sisters. Third, the congregation is required to fill in the taaruf registration biodata honestly, according to the information contained in the biodata entry list. In addition, they also attach photos with polite poses and wearing neat and Islamic clothes.

Fourth, in determining the candidate to be invited for ta'aruf, the congregation cannot choose for themselves. The coach will decide based on information from the biodata filled in by the congregation as well as the results of interviews by the coach. In addition, there are rules that must be obeyed by couples who perform ta'aruf when communicating. Based on interviews with married congregational couples in a ta'aruf way at RTQ (6 September 2020), the regulations are: no direct communication with potential partners, either via chat or telephone; may not meet only the two of them (no seclusion); communication is only allowed through WhatsApp groups in which there is a mediator; and may not accept other taaruf.

Fifth, after the coach determines who is considered suitable between the two congregants who have filled out their biodata and were interviewed, then the facilitator (mediator) creates a WhatsApp group. The group consists of male candidates, female candidates, mediators, and RTQ leaders. They were then met (nazor) for the first time in a place, accompanied by a mediator. Then the mediator asked the two candidates if they still wanted to continue the ta'aruf process. If there is a match and want to continue, then the two congregants are still not allowed to meet together or chat directly, let alone secretly. To control this prohibition from being carried out, the RTQ management always reminds the congregation through the WhatsApp group. Then if there is a match, then the process is continued with the brotherhood's friendship to the brother's family home and the brother's friendship to the brother's family home. After that, do the application (*khithbah*) until finally the marriage contract. The whole process is always accompanied by a mediator.

Sixth, to convince the congregation of the importance of ta'aruf and its positive impact, the study committee from time to time presents married congregations through the Rumah Ta'arufQu. They were then asked to tell all their experiences from participating in the study at RTQ until then filling out their biodata and getting married. The various stories that were presented became the main attraction for the study congregation at RTQ so that indirectly this method made the congregation more interested in participating in the study at RTQ.

Couples who are doing the ta'aruf process don't always run smoothly. Disagreement over the choice of mediator is natural for every candidate. In RTQ itself, after a nazor occurs, the mediator always asks the ta'aruf pair whether to continue or not. This is because the candidate is allowed to end the ta'aruf process if there is a discrepancy. The mediator will then provide an explanation of the cancelation by one of the parties.

Until now, Rumah Ta'arufQu has succeeded in facilitating a number of men and women to find their soul mates to the level of marriage. There are about 15 married couples. The duration of ta'aruf in RTQ is approximately 2–5 months. The congregation has felt quite effective for the duration of time.

The total time to meet or meet face to face between brothers and sisters is about five times, namely when nadzor, gathering with the brothers' family wan, family gatherings, proposals, and marriage. The mediator plays an important role during the ta'aruf process as a guide, guide, and reminder if there are things that are not appropriate during the process. Also controls the process and provides motivation and useful knowledge (interview with married RTQ congregation, 2 September 2020).

The taaruf process at RTQ, as described above, provides an opportunity for potential partners to get to know each other. This can be seen by being given five opportunities to meet or meet face to face. Thus, potential partners who already know each other will have a positive impact on their married life. As also found by Sakinah and Kinanthi [13] that self-disclosure of married couples through the taaruf process has a contribution of 8.7% to marital satisfaction.

If you look at it, the establishment of the Rumah Ta'arufQu which conducts pre-marital studies or lectures and facilitates congregations for ta'aruf, is not much different from a matchmaking agency. Ilhami (2019) found that ta'aruf, which initially started from the contextualization of verses, has now become a community like a matchmaking agency for teenagers [16]. However, there are several things that distinguish RTQ from matchmaking agencies in general. Among them are matchmaking bureaus generally only facilitate the wishes of men or women who want to get a partner. This is done by providing a form that must be filled with identity, photo, and the desired partner criteria.

While the means used are usually social media [17]. However, this is not the case at RTQ, which also conducts pre-wedding, process, and post-wedding lecture studies. The material presented was mainly about how marriage according to Islamic teachings. Congregants who take part in the study are not automatically able to submit biodata to find and get the desired potential partner, before registering to become a member. One of the requirements to become a member is to attend the study at least eight times.

In addition, congregants who fill out their biodata at RTQ, even though they are in ta'aruf, are not allowed to make appointments alone, without any accompanying person. Unlike the case with matchmaking bureaus, they are allowed to make appointments to meet in person or through telecommunications networks. RTQ not only facilitates a meeting between two congregants who have both submitted biodata on taaruf, but also facilitates the process of khitbah (application) until the wedding. Congregants who have submitted biodata of ta'aruf and there is a match between them will continue to be guided by the mediator, up to the marriage and post-wedding process. While the matchmaking agency only provides information about someone who needs a partner.

In general, matchmaking agencies use online media to show the profile and identity of each matchmaker on their site [17]. While not so on RTQ. RTQ does not use online media and social media to inform the profile and identity of the ta'aruf congregation. Online media is only used to inform the study schedule, conditions for participating in the study, and other news about the study.

The emergence of the RTQ assemblies motivates and facilitates the congregation to carry out taaruf marriages in order to avoid and leave the dating culture. Marriage through ta'aruf is to find a partner in a syar'i way accompanied by a ustaz and ustazah. In the ta'aruf process, religious knowledge is also provided, to be used as provisions in building a household. In addition, it also contains the mission of Islamic da'wah in general.

The task of this da'wah is not easy because the target is young people who are definitely not all willing and willing to accept the programs and studies offered by RTQ. From here, RTQ got around this challenge by packaging studies with attractive packaging, such as packing the study themes in popular, interesting languages, and very close to the language of today's youth. Besides that, RTQ also presents young figures who are widely known by teenagers, as presenters.

RTQ not only provides an opportunity for its congregation to find a potential partner, but also becomes a place to gather and learn more about religion. The main thing is to learn family knowledge which they really need when they are married in the future. In addition, it can help congregants who have no acquaintances, are still having trouble finding a mate, or want to upgrade their knowledge. This community also helps congregants who are already members to consult about household problems (interview with congregation, 4 September 2020).

The da'wah carried out by RTQ by placing ta'aruf as the keyword, actually becomes a special attraction for the people millennial. By taking advantage of the millennial interest in taaruf that is becoming a trend, RTQ can attract many congregations. It is in the congregation who come from millennials that RTQ can then carry out its da'wah function. This is what Sunan Kalijaga did when he preached by using the Kidung Rumeksa Ing Wengi Fiber. The song contains one meaning which states that women who are difficult to match will find their soul mate by reading, listening, or listening to the song [18]. The mate issue raised in the kidung is the same as taaruf in RTQ. Both are attractive segments for society, especially for millennials.

In addition, RTQ also accommodates its congregations who have the desire to find, know, and find potential partners without having to deviate from Islamic teachings. The congregation can also protect themselves from things that are not prescribed by Islam and know the knowledge needed in marriage, pre, process, and post-wedding. Thus the marriage that is done does not invite the wrath of God.

When viewed from the form of da'wah which is now in great demand by urban Muslims, RTQ is a model for community recitation. This is in accordance with what was found by Dewi and Fata [1] that the community recitation model is a form of da'wah that has been prevailing in the middle class of Indonesian Muslims. Community studies occur when a number of Muslims want a more in-depth study so that they form a separate study group on a limited basis. Other models are the seminar and short course model, as well as the general recitation model.

RTQ is a recitation that specifically examines material about marriage. It even facilitates the congregation to get married through the ta'aruf process. This recitation community was formed based on the thought of its founder that millennial Muslims need to be educated about marriage. The focus of the study on marriage and ta'aruf is one of the characteristics of the community recitation model. Unlike other recitation models which generally discuss religious issues in general.

The RTQ congregation is a millennial Muslim generation who longs for a marriage that is blessed by Allah through the taaruf process. They generally find the RTQ community through social media which is indeed used as a means to publish study material by RTQ. The theme of the study material that is packaged using millennial languages can attract the attention and interest of the millennial generation to later become a congregation. This is in line with the findings of Rusdi (2019) that the attitude of student acceptance toward Taaruf arises due to several factors. Among them are social media, massive and interesting publications, and dreams of reaching an Islamic household.

# 4 Conclusion

Based on the research findings and analysis that have been described previously, several conclusions can be drawn. First, the millennial Muslim generation who are members of the RTQ study community is driven by several things. Among them is their desire to know more about ta'aruf which is a trend among the millennial generation. Another thing is their curiosity about everything about Islamic household life, which is comprehensively studied at RTQ. In addition, they certainly want to do ta'aruf facilitated by RTQ.

Second, the da'wah model carried out by the RTQ community is to conduct face-to-face studies by focusing on discussions about marriage, both before and after marriage. It is different from other communities which generally study religion extensively. RTQ also facilitates congregations who wish to perform ta'aruf with several provisions, including by applying a minimum limit of study that must be followed by congregants, before being allowed to apply for ta'aruf. It is intended that the congregation who will perform ta'aruf already understands well on how to build a household life in accordance with Islamic law. In addition, RTQ also opens a consultation room for congregants who have problems in the household, especially for congregants who are married through the taaruf process at RTQ. Social media is also RTQ's choice as a means of da'wah. However, not to submit the study online, but only to publish the schedule and theme of the study to be conducted.

Third, the materials studied at RTQ were delivered by a number of presenters from various elements. Not only an ustaz or dai, but also involving professionals such as motivators, national trainers in the field of digital marketing, and also psychologists. From the ustaz element, one of them is the founder of RTQ himself who has often filled religious studies in other millennial Muslim communities, as well as being a marriage consultant.

Fourth, the religious themes or materials studied at RTQ are packaged in interesting language, which can arouse the attention of the millennial generation. Among them are: Be Happy O Women Longing for Heaven (serial of Rights and Duties of Wives to Husbands); Babul Firosy (Beautiful First Night); Established First? Or Married First?

Based on the conclusions of this study, several things can be recommended. Communities or other institutions engaged in the field of da'wah need to increase studies on domestic life to strengthen the insight of the younger generation. This can ultimately support the family resilience program so as to create a prosperous family. In addition, the Office of Religious Affairs can collaborate with study communities such as RTQ to work together in providing pre-marital and post-wedding guidance services.

This research has several shortcomings. Among them is only to reveal the model of da'wah and the ta'aruf process carried out in the RTQ community. Not yet revealed how the marriage satisfaction of married couples through the taaruf process in RTQ, both qualitatively and quantitatively. In addition, it is not yet known in depth why not all who become members of the congregation then register for taaruf. These two things can be the focus of studies in further research, by targeting other millennial communities.

**Acknowledgements** The author expresses his deepest gratitude to all parties who have contributed to this research. Head of the Jakarta Religious Research and Development Center who has given the author the opportunity to conduct this research. The Ta'arufQu House Community in Bogor City has been the target of research.

## References

1. Dewi OS, Fata AK (2021) Beragam Jalan Menjadi Salih: model Dakwah Kelas Menengah Muslim Indonesia. *Jurnal Bimas Islam, 14*(1), 1–32. (2021). https://doi.org/10.37302/JBI.V14I1.325
2. Irfansyah A (2020) *Ketika Hijrah Bukan Sekadar Perbaikan Diri, tapi Juga Aksi Kolektif*. Tirto.Id. https://tirto.id/ketika-hijrah-bukan-sekadar-perbaikan-diri-tapi-juga-aksi-kolektif-fZPP
3. Syukur Y (2004) Tren Hijrah dan Halal Muslim Milenial. Academia, Edu
4. Meiranti M (2019) Fenomena Hijrah di Era Milenial dalam Media Sosial. *Ath-Thariq Jurnal Dakwah Dan Komunikasi*
5. Fajriani SW (2019) Hijrah Islami Milenial Berdasarkan Paradigma Berorientasi Identitas. *Sosioglobal : Jurnal Pemikiran Dan Penelitian Sosiologi.* https://doi.org/10.24198/jsg.v3i2.21643
6. Addini A (2019) fenomena gerakan hijrah di kalangan pemuda muslim sebagai mode sosial. J Islam CivIzation. https://doi.org/10.33086/jic.v1i2.1313
7. Aisyah AA, Fachruddin T, Aripudin A (2019) Dakwah Terhadap Kaum Milenial. Tabligh: J Komun Dan Penyiaran Islam 4(3):323–343. https://doi.org/10.15575/TABLIGH.V4I3.1053
8. Sari TY, Husein F, Noviani R (2020) Hijrah and Islamic movement in social media: a social movement study of anti-dating movement #IndonesiaTanpaPacaran. DINIKA : Acad J Islam Stud 5(1):1–26. https://doi.org/10.22515/DINIKA.V5I1.1673
9. Hamdi I (2017) Ta'Aruf Dan Khitbah Sebelum Perkawinan. JURIS (J Ilm Syariah) 16(1):43. https://doi.org/10.31958/juris.v16i1.959
10. Elysia E, Chatra E, Arif E (2021) Transformasi Makna Ta'aruf di Era Digital. J Komun Glob 10(1):24–53. https://doi.org/10.24815/JKG.V10I1.19717
11. Rahman F, Zulhaqqi GL (2020) Fenomena Ta'Aruf Online Dan Praktik Komodifikasi Perkawinan Di Dunia Digital. Kafaah: J Gend Stud 10(1):63. https://doi.org/10.15548/jk.v10i1.327
12. Saputra S, Pujiati P, Simanihuruk M, Ismail R, Sitorus H (2020) Gerakan Hijrah Kaum Muda Muslim di Medan (Studi Kasus Gerakan Komunitas Sahabat Hijrahkuu). Jupiis: J Pendidik Ilmu-Ilmu Sos 12(1):23. https://doi.org/10.24114/JUPIIS.V12I1.15009
13. Sakhinah S (2018) Strategi komunikasi persuasif pengurus komunitas terang jakarta dalam mengajak anak muda berhijrah melalui new media. https://repository.uinjkt.ac.id/dspace/handle/123456789/42745
14. Ihsani AFA, Febriyanti N (2021) Strategi Perencanaan Komunikasi Dakwah Masjid Peneleh Surabaya. J Kopis: Kaji Penelit Dan Pemikir Komun Penyiaran Islam 3(2):63–76. https://doi.org/10.33367/kpi.v3i2.1559
15. Islami P (n.d.) Ta ' ar uf dan Upaya Membangun Perjodohan Islami pada Kalangan Pasangan Muda Muslim di Yogyakarta Ta ' aruf and the Effort to develop an Islamic Matchmaking Amongst Young Muslim Couples in Yogyakarta
16. Ilhami N (2019) Budaya Ta'aruf dalam Pernikahan; Sebuah Tinjauan Sosiologi. KURIOSITAS: Media Komun Sos Dan Keagamaan 12(2):163–176. https://doi.org/10.35905/KUR.V12I2.1260

17. Rusdi. Kencan Islami: Studi Antusiasme Mahasiswa Mengikuti Kajian dan Praktik *Ta'aruf* di Rumah Ta'aruf Majelis Calon Ayah Amanah Yogyakarta. Pascasarjana UIN Sunan Kalijaga (2019)
18. Saroni, Faiz. Pesan Dakwah dalam *Serat Kidung Rumekso Ing Wengi* Karya Sunan Kalijaga (Kajian Semiotika Ferdinand De Saussure). Institut Agama Islam Negeri Ponorogo (2020)

# Online Da'wa During Pandemic COVID-19: An Alternative Approach to Deliver Islamic Teaching

**Zakiyah, Joko Tri Haryanto, Setyo Boedi Oetomo, Agus Iswanto, and Umi Muzayanah**

**Abstract** Pandemic COVID-19 has hit many countries in the world including Indonesia since the beginning of 2020. Since then, many activities have changed because there are several restrictions imposed by the government in order to minimize the spread of such virus. The Indonesian government has issued some regulations on how people should behave during this pandemic time; this includes regulations on the religious life. In addition, the Indonesian Ulama Council has produced several *fatwa* on how Moslem community should practice their prayer in the mosque and conduct Islamic teaching. Due to these matters, many face-to-face (offline) Islamic teachings have been postponed, and then some of them used online media to deliver Islamic teaching. Data were collected using interviews, observation, and analysis of online media content. This research was conducted in Yogyakarta Province at the end of 2020. Subjects of this research consist of two Islamic organizations namely Nahdlatul Ulama and Muhammadiyah, *majelis taklim* (Islamic teaching assemblies), and individual preachers affiliated with the office of religious affairs. Findings of this study show that some of those institutions and individual preachers have used digital media for da'wah before the pandemic COVID-19 and continued it during the pandemic COVID-19. Meanwhile, several of them have not used digital media before, and the pandemic drives them to use it. Those people and institutions use social media platforms such as YouTube, Facebook, Instagram, WhatsApp group,

---

Zakiyah (✉) · J. T. Haryanto · S. B. Oetomo · A. Iswanto · U. Muzayanah
University and Graduate School: Badan Riset Dan Inovasi Nasional (National Research and Innovation Agency), Jakarta, Indonesia
e-mail: zaki_smart@yahoo.com; zaki001@brin.go.id

J. T. Haryanto
e-mail: joko034@brin.go.id

S. B. Oetomo
e-mail: sety014@brin.go.id

A. Iswanto
e-mail: agus155@brin.go.id

U. Muzayanah
e-mail: umim002@brin.go.id



Nawawi et al. (eds.), *Managing Disruption and Developing Resilience for a Better Southeast Asia*, Springer Proceedings in Humanities and Social Sciences,
https://doi.org/10.1007/978-981-96-2116-3_41

Google meet, and Zoom meeting. The use of these media platforms becomes a bridge to transmit Islamic message and to communicate between preachers and audiences. However, the use of this digital media has faced several challenges, such as the lack of skill in digital technology including the ability to produce and upload content on the social media platform, and the readiness of *jamaah* (audiences) to access Islamic teaching through digital platform.

**Keywords** Online media · Da'wa · Pandemic COVID-19

## 1 Introduction

The fourth industrial revolution is part of human civilization continuum marked by the wave of significant digital technology development. Adliansah (2019) states that such technology development has altered the inter-human communication pattern to the digital media or the internet of things/the internet of people [1]. Information access and interpersonal communication at the global level have become easier and more intensive through the use of smartphone integrated with the internet. The global number of Internet users in 2020 reached 4.5 billion people or more than 60% of the total global population according to the data retrieved from We Are Social and Hootsuite.

The reports retrieved from both We Are Social and Hootsuite regarding Global Digital 2018 show that, in general, Indonesian people spend 3 h and 23 min a day accessing social media. With a total population of 265.40 million people, the active users among the Indonesian people have reached 130 million people with penetration rate 49%. YouTube has earned the first place with the penetration rate 43%, followed by Facebook on the second place with 41%, and WhatsApp on the third place with 41% while the remaining places are occupied by other social media platforms [2]. Then, in 2020, the number of Internet users in Indonesia reached 175.40 million people with the penetration rate 64%; in this figure, 171 million people or 98% of the total Internet users in Indonesia have benefitted the mobile devices. Furthermore, 96% of the same figure uses smartphones while the remaining 5.30% of the figure still uses the feature cell phone [3]. In sum, the total number of social media active users has reached 160 million people with the penetration rate 59% and the average Internet access activity is 4 h and 46 min, most of which have been spent accessing social media [4].

Looking at the above figure, a crucial question comes up to the surface: Does the change of communication pattern trigger the change in the religious activities? Specifically, does the change of communication pattern trigger the change for the Islamic da'wa? Budiantoro (2017), Usman (2018), Wibowo (2018), Yahya M and Farhan (2019), Adliansah (2019), Rohman (2019), Wahab, Muhammad, and Ismail (2019), Romadi (2020), Syah (2020), Prasanti and Karimah (2020), Munawara, Rahmanto and Satyawan (2020), and Ummah (2020) altogether argue that digital era has resulted in the change of da'wa pattern through the use of digital media. Nowadays, many da'wa or religious development activities have benefitted digital media by using numerous social media platforms such as Facebook, YouTube, Instagram, Zoom Meeting, Google Meet, WhatsApp Group, and alike; they use live streaming or recorded content as well. Religious institutions, religious mass organizations, da'wa institutions, and even religious figures perform their religious teachings or lectures through live streaming or recorded content that can be aired through many social media platforms [1, 5–15].

The use of digital media has increased significantly along with the pandemic COVID-19 in Indonesia at the beginning of 2020. As there is a social interaction restriction ruled out by the government, it has encouraged people to use digital media for their various activities including studying, working, and delivering religious teaching. At the same time, the Indonesian Ulama Council issued fatwa regarding prayer and religious activities in the mosque during the early period of pandemic, in which Moslem were encouraged to pray at home and in person religious teaching involving large number of people should be postponed. Due to many in person activities involving a large number of people have been prohibited from being performed, they have changed to online media, using various social media platforms such as YouTube, WhatsApp, Zoom Meeting, Google Meet, Facebook, and other platforms. During this pandemic time, many da'wa activities have been conducted using digital media.

The results of a study by Budiantoro (2017) on the da'wa development in the digital era depicted that in the era of digital media, the da'wa can be performed by means of citizen journalism media. Citizen journalism refers to the journalistic activity that has been developed based on the activity of the people who collect, report, and analyze news and information. As a da'wa medium, citizen journalism is able to facilitate the broadcast (*syi'ar*) to the public with regard to the dynamics of Islam and economic, social, and cultural changes [5]. In relation to the statement, the results of a study by Usman (2016) on the effectiveness of online media use show that online media have been an effective tool for the da'wa performance. The effectiveness of the online media use for the da'wa activity is shown by the correlation value between the use of smartphone and the activity of browsing information, which is very high at 0.8035 [6]. Furthermore, the results of a study done by Romadi (2020) and Syah (2020) on a number of *madrasah ibtidaiyah* students and university students found that the intensity of watching da'wa video through the online media platform is correlated to the level of religiosity [11, 12]. Meanwhile, the study done by Ditha Prasanti and Kismiyati El Karimah (2020) mentioned that during the COVID-19 pandemic time, the search for information on the da'wa of Islam has been mostly done by the young Moslems. They actively and selectively search the information on the da'wa of Islam through the online media and establish online discussion group using the online discussion platforms such as Google Meet, Zoom Meeting, and WhatsApp Video Call [13].

The results of a study conducted by Wahab, Muhammad and Ismail (2019) found that the development of communication technology and the Internet facility has provided the space for the Moslem preachers to establish interaction with the audience without limitation of space and time. Similarly, the results of a study by Wibowo (2018) found that the da'wa activities using social media platform YouTube consist of four typologies namely: (1) the affiliation between the Moslem preacher and the religious mass organization; (2) the management of official account by the Moslem preachers themselves; (3) the management by community of da'wa; and (4) the management of da'wa content by vlogger or any other YouTubers [10]. Other findings were also shown that the negative excess of da'wa freedom over the social media has become the arena to spread provocative content, hoax, and radical content. Furthermore, the results of a research done by Yahya and Farhan (2019) found that the virtual da'wa can decrease the physical interaction which can lead to anti-social, whereas the Moslem preachers are demanded to synergize the virtual and the cultural da'wa [8]. These results were supported by the findings of the study carried out by Adliansah (2019), which depicted those adolescents with relatively high social media use suffered from weak interaction with the social environment in the real world. On the contrary, the social environment within the virtual world has a huge influence on the self-concept formation of these adolescents, including the process of discovering their true identity [1].

Meanwhile, the study by Rohman (2019) found that da'wa activities using social media are considered effective and interesting in terms of social interaction pattern, persuasive pattern, and ethos or attraction of the da'wa activities through social media [9]. In addition, the results of a study by Ummah (2020) mentioned that the community of Arus Informasi Santri Nusantara has benefitted from digital media to disseminate the moderate Islam in the Islamic boarding schools for younger generations which can provide a more variative, modern, and interesting format of da'wa. Numerous da'wa messages are designed and delivered through multiple forms such as meme, video, picture, voice recording, and infographic so that the da'wa can deliver the messages to the audience (*mad'u*) more effectively [15]. With regard to the statement, the results of a study by Munawara, Rahmanto, and Satyawan (2020) stated that the use of digital media for da'wa to the surrounding community of the Islamic boarding schools can educate the Islamic boarding school students and the community on the importance of social media, deliver the trustworthy information, and realize the importance of delivering da'wa through a wise and well manner [14].

According to Barmawi (in Mutiawati, 2014), the development of religious activities refers to the communication activity between the Moslem preachers (*da'i*) and the audience (*mad'u*) in order to prepare the audience to practice the religious teachings so that they can attain better, more sincere, and more enjoyable life [16]. In his opinion, Falimu (2017) argued that communication refers to the process of meaning/message exchange from one person to another, to influence and persuade other people, to change, and to improve their attitudes and behaviors [17]. In this regard, the elements of communication consist of communicator (source and sender), message, media (channel), communicant (audience and receiver), and effect. The message itself can be information, ideas, emotions, skills, and alike through the use of symbols, words, pictures, graphics, numbers, and alike. On the contrary, Mubasyaroh (2016) explained that media refers to the objective tools that become the channel for linking ideas (materials) and audience/people or *mad'u*. Therefore, media can be a vital element of the da'wa [18].

Another term of da'wa is *tabligh* (delivering something or delivering religious teachings, opinions, and guidelines), *an-nasihat* (guidelines on good life and efforts to improve the behaviors of an individual or a group of individuals), *ad-diayah* (efforts to draw attention, sympathy, and happiness of an individual or a group of individuals toward certain attitudes, actions, and thoughts by using persuasions, compliments, and alike) [19]. According to Nafis (1989), the domain of da'wa includes the activities to embrace Islam, *ta'lim*, *tahsyir*, *tandzir*, *amar ma'ruf nahy munkar* and Islamic show of force. In another word, da'wa means the process of Islamic dissemination, understanding, and practice [20].

The exposure to the development of digital media users in Indonesia, the change in the da'wa media, and the theoretical review on the da'wa altogether mentioned that the phenomena of changing da'wa pattern in the digital era are very interesting to be studied. It is because the change in the pattern of certain religious dissemination has been followed by numerous problems from both the technical aspects and the social aspects. Therefore, this study focuses on the trend of Islamic religious development transformation and the model of da'wa through the digital media. Such religious development is assumed to be conducted mostly in the urban area since the use of Internet in the city has been supported by the Internet network infrastructure. In addition, the number of Internet users is relatively higher in the urban areas rather than in the village areas. Therefore, the study was conducted at the urban communities in Yogyakarta.

## 2 Method

The article was written based on the data from the field research that was done from August to September 2020 in Yogyakarta. This region was selected since it was representative for the typology of urban community that most of the residents are familiar with technology and digital media. This was qualitative research. According to Moeleong (2002), a qualitative study generates descriptive data in the form of oral or written information or in the form of policy action [21].

The primary data in the study were collected through interviews, observation, and documentation. The interviews are conducted with the informants who were selected purposively due to the pre-determined criteria. In this sense, the researchers select the representative parties who have the authority to explain the practice of da'wa through digital media. The interview itself is conducted using semi-structured interview guide. The informants in the study consist of religious figures, community figures, board members of Islamic organizations, board members of mosques, Islamic counselors, the director and board members of digital media organizers, as well as other community members who have been involved in the religious development activities through digital media.

In addition, the data are also gathered through digital ethnography, namely the observation toward several digital media, websites, and social media sites. The collected are analyzed by using descriptive analysis technique. Furthermore, searching the document related to the research themes was applied to know the history and the development of the use of digital media for da'wa activities. This includes browsing the data and the information from textbooks, research reports, journals' articles, and magazines. Meanwhile, the media analysis is conducted in order to identify the da'wa by the *da'i* including content productiveness, number of subscribers, number of viewers for each content, like / dislike responses by the audience (netizens), number of positive and negative comments, number of contents reposts and alike.

## 3 Findings and Discussions

### *3.1 Religious Context in Yogyakarta*

The Province of Yogyakarta Special Region is one of the provinces that has attained the "Special" status from the Republic of Indonesia for the merit and the service of the Yogyakarta Sultanate during the fight for the Indonesian independence. One of the specialties that the province has is that the Head of Regional Government is held by Sri Sultan Hamengku Buwono X, the reigning Sultan of Yogyakarta Sultanate. The historicity has made the people in Yogyakarta strongly hold the Javanese culture. In addition, Yogyakarta is also the witness for the religious movement, especially Islam since the Muhammadiyah organization was established by K.H. Ahmad Dahlan in Yogyakarta in 1924. The Muhammadiyah organization puts forward the concept of religious purification among the people of Yogyakarta who generally display the life orientation toward the Javanese tradition and culture. Muhammadiyah alone has gained success in being one of the biggest Moslem organizations in Indonesia along with Nahdlatul Ulama (NU), which was established in 1926 and accommodates the local cultures and traditions. Both Muhammadiyah and NU developed their influence in the religious life in Yogyakarta.

The Province of Yogyakarta Special Region consists of: (1) the Regency of Kulon Progo; (2) the Regency of Bantul; (3) the Regency of Sleman; (4) the Regency of Gunung Kidul; and (5) the City of Yogyakarta. Based on the Results of Interim Population Projection 2020–2023, the number of populations in the province is 3,713,000 people. Then, the religions that have been embraced by the people in Yogyakarta can be outlined as follows: (1) Islam 3,423,493 people; (2) Catholic 165,679 people; (3) Christian / Protestant 89,538 people; (4) Hindu 3,420 people; (5) Buddha, 3,093 people; and (6) Confucian 76 people (BPS DI Yogyakarta, 2022).

Despite the small number of population, the City of Yogyakarta itself has been the most densely populated area with the figure of 11,579 people / km$^2$, followed by the Regency of Sleman and the Regency of Bantul. The three regions serve as the center of government, trade, education, and crowd. Not to mention, the presence of many educational institutions has made Yogyakarta earn the title of "The City of Students." At least, there are 110 universities and 368,066 university students [22]. The oldest and yet most prominent state university in Indonesia is also located in Yogyakarta, namely Gadjah Mada University, along with Sunan Kalijaga State Islamic University, which is also a quite prominent university.

### 3.2 *Online Da'wa at the Beginning of the COVID-19 Pandemic Period*

The COVID-19 pandemic has driven the change of social communication model in a "revolutionary manner." The presence of COVID-19 pandemic has accelerated the Industrial Revolution 4.0 that has also been marked by the presence of digital technology. The combination of both aspects compels the da'wa activities that have previously been conducted through face-to-face meeting, be it in the general Koran recital, the religious oracy, the mosque, and the lectures in the *taklim* assembly, then it should shift into the cyberspace in which people do not meet each other physically. The da'wa through digital media does not only become an alternative in the pandemic time but also the certainty of the age in which digital technology should be benefitted to the fullest for the sake of the community.

The *mubaligh* and the *da'i* (Islamic preachers) before and after the COVID-19 pandemic have used digital media and social media for the da'wa activities. The *da'i* are encouraged to be more active in using the digital technology for greeting their *jamaah* (audiences) at the beginning of the pandemic era. In Yogyakarta, the religious development of Islam or the da'wa through online media has been done by the religious mass organizations, the *taklim* assembly, and mosque caretakers, and the Islamic preacher has been initiated long before the pandemic occurred, and it increased significantly during the COVID-19 pandemic time.

In performing the religious development activities, Nahdlatul Ulama relies mostly on the Bangkit Media team, one of the media under the caretaking of Ta'lif wan Nasyr Foundation of Nahdlatul Ulama Yogyakarta. The establishment of Bangkit Media began from the management of Bangkit Magazine, NU's internal media that was created in 1979. Along with the increasing use of social media, in 2016, Bangkit Magazine turned into Bangkit Media; consequently, all of the activities in Bangkit Magazine should be transferred to digital platforms such as websites, Facebook, Twitter, YouTube, and Instagram. Since the emergence of COVID-19 pandemic in 2020, da'wa activity and religious information in Bangkit Media has grown more actively. Outside the Bangkit Media, NU activists also start using digital media especially social media in performing the da'wa whether it was individually or communally.

The da'wa activities in the Muhammadiyah have been managed by the Tabligh Assembly of Muhammadiyah. The internal communication media in Muhammadiyah is Suara Muhammadiyah. In addition, the da'wa activities by Muhammadiyah through digital platform are performed through the official channel Mediamu.com. Thus, the da'wa activities by Muhammadiyah such as regular Koran recital should be transferred from the face-to-face meeting to the Zoom meeting. In addition, the routine Koran studies through the Zoom meeting are also uploaded on YouTube channel. The board members of Muhammadiyah Yogyakarta admit that in terms of digital media use the Muhammadiyah is a little bit late since they started using the online media after the implementation of social distancing during the pandemic period.

There are other Islamic organizations that also perform online media-based and digital-based da'wa activities in Yogyakarta. Furthermore, there are also groups that have been specifically established for religious learning or *taklim* assembly using online media. The Assembly of *Sahabat Cinta* is one of the *taklim* assemblies that have actively used digital media in their activities. The group was initiated by the young mothers and socialites in 2013 that is for studying the Koran; in 2015, the group officially used the name Assembly of *Sahabat Cinta.* This Assembly used social media long before the pandemic COVID-19. The activities and the studies of the Assembly have been broadcast through a live streaming service on Facebook. During the COVID-19 pandemic, the face-to-face studies that are usually held in hotels should be replaced with online studies through Zoom meetings and these online studies are uploaded to the social media of the Assembly.

The mosque has not only been a prayer place but has also been an organization with numerous programs and activities. Several mosques in Yogyakarta have actively performed several religious activities, including the da'wa through digital media. Some mosques have utilized digital media long before the COVID-19 pandemic happened, but there are also other mosques that have just recently used digital media. For example, the Jogokaryan Mosque has used the modern communication medium in performing da'wa for many years. The mosque has already had radio station and community television. Moreover, since 2012, Jogokaryan Mosque has used social media platforms such as YouTube, Facebook, and Instagram. The mosque has already had its own YouTube channel. Similarly, Gadjah Mada University Mosque and Suciati Saliman Mosque Sleman have also actively performed the da'wa activities through the online media due to the COVID-19 pandemic. Both Gadjah Mada University Mosque and Suciati Saliman Mosque have used the online media since 2018. They have used YouTube, Facebook, and Instagram. Both of these mosques have even had their own YouTube Channel (Table 1).

In Yogyakarta, there are also many preachers who individually conducted da'wa activities. In general, these preachers are activists from religious organizations such as NU, Muhammadiyah, campuses, as well as from the Islamic boarding schools. In addition, religious instructors from the Ministry of Religion are also active in religious teaching by using digital media and social media platforms. However, at that time, they did not really see the importance of da'wa activities using digital platform. When social restrictions were imposed due to the COVID-19 pandemic,

**Table 1** The da'wa or the religious development activities through digital media in Yogyakarta

| No | Name of institution | Digital activity |
|---|---|---|
| 1 | Board members of NU Yogyakarta / Bangkit Media | • From Bangkit Magazine, NU internal media (1979), and it changed to bangkitmedia.com in 2016<br>• Digital and social media platforms: website, Instagram, Facebook, Twitter (2012), and YouTube (joined in 2019)<br>• Bangkit TV Channel plays as the official channel of Nahdlatul Ulama and it was used for delivering information of the institutional and managerial activities of Nahdlatul Ulama<br>• Bangkit Live Channel is part of Bangkit TV that aims to accommodate the contents and the materials of not only the local but also the national level of NU figures<br>• Number of followers on Instagram 4,416 people, Twitter 1,533 people, and Facebook 6,381 people<br>• Number of YouTube Channel Bangkit TV view 19,128,960 times |
| 2 | Muhammadiyah, Yogyakarta province | • In general, the da'wa activities are under the coordination with the Tabligh Assembly of Muhammadiyah<br>• The communication activity through digital media, including the digital da'wa, is managed by the Literature and Information Assembly (*Majelis Pustaka dan Informasi*). They established media.mu as the official portal of Muhammadiyah since 2018<br>• The digital platforms used by Muhammadiyah are websites, Facebook, Instagram, Twitter, YouTube, and radio streaming service<br>• Number of followers on Instagram 912 people, Twitter 373 people, and Facebook 4,775 people<br>• Number of YouTube Channel Mediamu view 21,314 times |
| 3 | Assembly of Sahabat Cinta | • Began with the Koran studies in 2013, in 2015, the official name Majlis Sahabat Cinta started to be used<br>• The live streaming of Facebook service has been used long before the pandemic time and has been continued throughout the pandemic period<br>• Number of followers on Instagram 5,217 people and Facebook 4,775 people<br>• Number of YouTube Channel Majelis Sahabat Cinta Yogyakarta view 214,000 times with 60,193 audiences |
| 4 | Jogokaryan Mosque (*Masjid Jogokaryan*) | • Komunitas Masjid Jogokaryan TV (MJTV) with the 2.50 km-coverage VHF mode<br>• Facebook page of Masjid Jogokaryan has 173,052 likes, and is followed by 216,817 people<br>• Number of YouTube Channel subscribers 25,600 people and number of views 1,307,305 times<br>• Number of Instagram followers 177,000 people<br>• Number of Twitter followers 33,600 people<br>• Thematic da'wa and often invited national-level Moslem clerics who are viral on the digital media platforms |

(continued)

**Table 1** (continued)

| No | Name of institution | Digital activity |
|---|---|---|
| 5 | Gadjah Mada University Mosque | • YouTube Channel Masjid Kampus UGM joined on March 6, 2018<br>• Number of subscribers 20,900 people and number of views 1,464,876 people<br>• Number of Facebook Page Maskamugm followers 742 people<br>• Several religious studies, thematic studies<br>• Information on online activities (through Zoom meeting) is delivered through social media |
| 6 | Suciati Saliman Mosque, Sleman | • YouTube Channel Suciati Saliman Mosque joined YouTube on May 5, 2018<br>• Number of subscribers 29,100 people and number of views 1,862, 158<br>• Routine studies, thematic studies, Fiqh studies, Sirah Nabawiyah, and *tarawih* teaching |

*Source* Processed from interview sessions with the administrator of the institutions from August until September 2020 and digital browsing on March 21, 2022

they were initiated to use digital devices to do their da'wa tasks. However, they are not automatically able to do this, they must adapt first. For instance, Mahlani, one of the religious instructors in Yogyakarta, mentioned that at the beginning of the pandemic, he did coaching activities by writing materials and distributing them to his congregation. This written material is also shared through the WhatsApp group of the Islamic teaching assemblies; as it is hoped that this will be read by the members of the group. Then Mahlani was self-taught trying to make a short video containing religious guidance and then it was uploaded on his YouTube channel. Currently, Mahlani is actively making YouTube video content, whether it contains short Islamic teaching or *salawat* songs (Interview with Mahlani, Religious Counselor of the Ministry of Religion of Yogyakarta, 26 August 2020) (Table 2).

## *3.3 Opportunities for Digital Da'wa During the COVID-19 Pandemic Time*

The trend of Islamic religious development using digital media by mainstream Islamic groups is increasing during the COVID-19 pandemic time. One of the driving aspects is the social distancing policy which encourages people using digital media for Islamic religious development activities. The limitation of direct social interaction has become a stimulant for da'wa activists to find alternative solutions so that people (congregations) can still get religious teaching and at the same time, it can maintain the continuity of the study forum. This momentum is used by da'wa organizers to educate the congregation (Moslem people) to use digital media in Islamic da'wa.

**Table 2** Individual preachers using social media platform for their da'wa activities

| No | Name and profession | Digital/social media used | Description |
|---|---|---|---|
| 1 | Mahlani, S.Ag, M.Pd<br>Religious Counselor of the Ministry of Religious Affairs of Yogyakarta | • YouTube<br>• Recorded Video<br>• A booklet / short writing containing Islamic teaching<br>• Radio<br>• WhatsApp | • Video was created and uploaded to the YouTube channel independently<br>• As one of the preachers broadcasted in the Pro RRI radio Yogyakarta<br>• Used YouTube since 2011, and intensively used it for da'wa during the pandemic time<br>• YouTube mahlani jogja: 805 subscribers, 16.909 views<br>• Content of his YouTube channel; Islamic teaching, *salawat* songs, and religious activities |
| 2 | Rita Maesaroh<br>Religious Counselor of the Ministry of Religious Affairs of Yogyakarta<br>And the board member of Asyiyah, an Islamic organization, Yogyakarta | • WhatsApp Video Call<br>• Google Meet | • Class tahfidz and recitations of the Qur'an<br>• It was conducted regularly; once a week via Google Meet<br>• Before the pandemic, it was in person regular class, and it was continued online<br>• The class is for children/youth and parents<br>• There are 30 participants<br>• Participants who want to recite the Koran; asked to send a recording via WhatsApp video call. The time for the Koran recitation was determined by the agreement between them |
| 3 | Dr. Khoirudin Bashori<br>A lecturer at Ahmad Dahlan University, Yogyakarta, a psychologist, and a board member of Muhammadiyah Yogyakarta | • YouTube | • YouTube Channel: Khoirudin Bashori iru Tv, Joint in 2012<br>• It contains Islamic studies with a psychological perspective, Ramadan studies, syawal studies, etc<br>• Videos are made and uploaded independently, on Khoiruddin Bashori's YouTube channel iru TV<br>• Some of his da'wa videos have been uploaded to the Ahmad Dahlan University YouTube, and other YouTube channels such as Mediamu, youth TV, and Muhammadiyah channel<br>• Facebook Khoiruddin Bashori irutv: 1,027 followers, and 994 likes<br>• Instagram khoiruddin_bashori followed by 604. It contains religious and psychological messages |

(continued)

**Table 2** (continued)

| No | Name and profession | Digital/social media used | Description |
|---|---|---|---|
| 4 | KH. Sholehudin Manshur, S.Ag.,<br>Religious Counselor of the Ministry of Religious Affairs of Yogyakarta<br>And a board member of Nahdlatul Ulama, Yogyakarta | • YouTube | • Doing Islamic teaching managed by Bangkit TV (at YouTube channel)<br>• Islamic teaching broadcasted at; Kalam Ulama Bangkit TV<br>• Channel: Bangkit TV<br>• Video duration: 10–41 min |
| 5 | Ustad Ir.Nanung Danar Dono, M.P, Ph.D<br>A lecturer at the Department of Animal Husbandry, Gadjah Mada University,<br>And the director of halal center at the Faculty of Animal Husbandry Gadjah Mada University | • Zoom<br>• YouTube | • Halal class is conducted every Tuesday from 13.00 to 15.00 via Zoom meeting<br>• Halal class is also broadcast on YouTube channel managed by the Mosque of Gadjah Mada University |
| 6 | H Abdul Halim, S.Ag.,<br>Religious Counselor of the Ministry of Religion of Yogyakarta<br>And a board member of Nahdlatul Ulama, Yogyakarta | • YouTube<br>• RRI<br>• WhatsApp (booklet) | • Recorded Islamic teaching that was broadcasted for radio RRI Pro 1 and Pro 2<br>• YouTube channel: Abdul Halim Pusaka Sakinah<br>• Join YouTube 19 November 2013<br>• Subscribers: 3, Views: 84<br>• He also teaches Islam every Thursday night that was uploaded to YouTube Al Barokah mosque |

*Source* Processed from the results of interviews with research subjects in August–September 2020, and digital searches on March 21, 2022

In addition, social restrictions also created a problem for the audiences (object of da'wa) to access religious activities together. Congregations of the Islamic teaching assemblies could not gather together, even though both NU and Muhammadiyah congregants had regular in person meeting activities before the outbreak happened, such as Islamic teaching and performing religious traditions like *yasinan* and *tahlilan*.

Routine activities at Muhammadiyah office in Yogyakarta such as Saturday Morning Study (*Kajian Sabtu Pagi/KSP*), Saturday Night Study (*Kajian Malam Sabtu/Kamastu*), and Thursday Night Reading Books (*Malam Kamis Ngaji Kitab/ Mantap*) in the Muhammadiyah office were conducted with limited attendees and recorded. The recording is then uploaded to YouTube channel. The Islamic teaching activities during the month of Ramadan are carried out through a Zoom meeting and it was broadcast live streaming on Facebook, YouTube, and RadioMU Yogyakarta. Likewise, the Hajj rituals guidance activities for the Aisiyah Hajj Guidance Group (KBIH) congregation managed by the board member of Muhammadiyah Yogyakarta were organized using a Zoom Meeting, and broadcasted on YouTube channel

(Interview with the board members of Muhammadiyah Yogyakarta, August 29, 2020).

In general, in person da'wa activities tend to be interactive so that the *da'i* (the preacher) can measure whether their da'wa is effective in influencing the audience or not. However, da'wa through digital media platform, it is difficult to know the audience's response. What can be observed from the response of this digital media audience is the number of views, likes, subscribes, shares, and comments. However, various parties viewed the da'wa through digital media positively. This digital da'wa has many advantages and opportunities, in addition to the obstacles faced by the preachers and the audiences.

The advantages of the use of digital media for da'wa include organizational networks, such as NU and Muhammadiyah which have an organizational structure from the center to the village level. The strength of this network of organizational structures can make da'wa more effective and efficient in reaching very wide audiences. Likewise, NU and Muhammadiyah as the largest Islamic organizations in Indonesia certainly have adequate human resources, both media actors and figures who are able to become sources of da'wa.

The COVID-19 pandemic and the rules of social restrictions made local kyai of Nahdlatul Ulama, such as Gus Hilmy and KH. Hasan Mlangi in Yogyakarta, more proactive with da'wa strategies through online media and social media. The kyai are increasingly realizing that their roles have changed, it is not enough to rely on in person meetings. In support of this new phenomenon, the Bangkit Media team provides a lot of support, especially technical matters such as taking pictures, recording, and uploading their Islamic teaching content on the social media either through their own channel or Bangkit Media channel (Interview with the director and the board members of Bangkit Media, 28, 30 August 2020). Meanwhile in Muhammadiyah, generally the figures who appear in public are the board members of Muhammadiyah who have the authority to convey Muhammadiyah's religious views. In addition, institutionally Muhammadiyah supports the online da'wa by providing software and related amenities such as subscriptions for Zoom meetings, the development of a digital media team, and recruiting professional information technology supports, and developing digital media like MediaMU (Interview with the board members of Muhammadiyah Yogyakarta, August 29, 2020).

Digital da'wa has good opportunities in the future. People who are increasingly literate in digital media now tend to seek religious information through the internet. Even, there is a high demand of the Islamic content during the COVID-19 pandemic, for instance, practical Islamic religious content (such as sermons at home, being an imam for tarawih prayers during a pandemic, Eid prayers, and tahlil). Nahdlatul Ulama members really need the *tahlil* script, the number of people who accessed this type of script is relatively high. This is because during the COVID-19 pandemic who have to worship from home, it turns out that many NU members are unable to lead *tahlil* with their families.

### 3.4 The Challenges of Digital Da'wa

The COVID-19 pandemic has become an acceleration factor in the use of digital media for da'wa activities. It seems that the digital da'wa will get a bigger place in society along with the social change in the future, especially with the industrial revolution 4.0. However, this digital da'wa also has challenges, both internally in the form of weakness of da'wa managers and externally in the form of threats to the existence of moderate da'wa.

The challenges faced by the digital da'wa are mainly the problem of mastering technical and digital technology by kyai and religious leaders, as well as young generation. For this reason, Nahdlatul Ulama in Yogyakarta conducted several trainings on conventional and multimedia journalism. This training was managed by Bangkit Media team. However, the transfer of knowledge and technical skills is slow because participants of the trainings are mainly from the Islamic boarding schools affiliated with Nahdlatul Ulama and they have difficulty applying digital da'wa. It was because after returning to their respective Islamic boarding schools, there were no work partners and limited equipment including Wi-Fi and editing equipment to do digital da'wa (Interview with the director of Bangkit Media, August 30, 2020). Similarly, Muhammadiyah faced challenges related to digital technology. For example, the figures of Muhammadiyah who did da'wa had problems with the internet network and they were not familiar with social media. Another challenge was the gadgets owned by the congregation that were not compatible for accessing digital da'wa, and at the same, time they had a burden to purchase internet quota in order to participate in the online da'wa either by Zoom meeting, or livestreaming on YouTube, Facebook, or other social media platforms.

Digital da'wa also faced threats in which there is a battle for discourse and information capitalization. For instance, the competition between Islamic groups in producing and campaigning their religious ideas. As it is the fact that apart from the NU and Muhammadiyah organizations which are known as moderate Islamic organizations, there are also radical groups, such as the Hizbut Tahrir Indonesia (HTI) group, whose legal status was revoked on July 19, 2017, by the government through the Ministry of Law and Human Rights. The revocation of this legal status is because HTI has political views that are against the ideology of the state, thus it violated the law on community organizations. Although HTI has been declared an illegal institution, its followers are still active in new organizational forms and continue to spread their ideas. HTI and other radical groups actively attract public interest through various content on their social media, even rivaling the da'wa of moderate groups such as NU and Muhammadiyah (Interview the director and board member of Bangkit Media, August 30, 2020).

The threat of digital da'wa was not only the battle of discourse, but also attacks against moderate media by hacking and damaging websites. For instance, Bangkit Media once received a hacker attack when posting a case of burning the flag of a political party. The website of Bangkit media was suspended for a week. Besides, there was also an attack in the form of the cloning website Bangunpost.com which imitated the appearance of Bangkit Media. This fake website contained teaching on the caliphate. These radical groups also aim to network with various other Islamic groups that share an ideology that tends to be radical, including the Yogyakarta mosques. There are several mosques in Yogyakarta that are actively conducting studies by inviting figures from HTI. They also make a network in cyberspace by linking their links with other groups' websites or social media, even linking with the moderate groups (Interview the director and board member of Bangkit Media, August 30, 2020).

The next challenge faced by digital da'wa is related to media capitalization competition, as the large profit media company also uploads religious content. With digital algorithm analytic capabilities, those large companies are able to grab the first page in search engines for the religious themes compared to websites or social media owned by the religious organizations. As a result, the religious discourse accessed by the public does not come from the competent religious institutions, but from the news media. The Indonesian people tend to like bombastic titles which are used by the online profit media who pursue SEO (Search Engine Optimization), but pay less attention to the quality of information. This phenomenon often traps readers into non-authoritative religious teaching (Interview with the board member of Bangkit Media, August 28, 2020).

## 3.5 Discussion

The various factors that drive the changing trend of da'wa media will meet with all the internal weaknesses as well as challenges from the external factors. Therefore, there is a need for strategy to deal with these encounters by optimizing their potential to do digital da'wa. One of the strategies is to strengthen human resources for implementing digital media, through the transfer of knowledge and enhancing skills use information technology and social media, especially the younger generation. This can be done in both Muhammadiyah and Islamic boarding schools affiliated with Nahdlatul Ulama. Furthermore, the da'wa content should be proposed for the young generations too, as they are more intensive in accessing social media and are easier to follow information technology developments. The next strategy is the selection of social media platforms, it would be better to choose the more accessible media platform. For example, YouTube is easy to be accessed and more people use this platform for searching for religious information.

The next important aspect of digital da'wa is the message or content. It is necessary to choose simple and functional themes that are needed by the people in their daily life. For instance, practical content on sermons at home, being the imam of tarawih prayers during a pandemic, Eid al-Fitr prayers, and *tahlil*. It is because during a pandemic time, more internet users directly access practical religious content.

Regarding the challenges of competing against radicalism, these digital da'wa actors need coordination across moderate Islamic organizations such as NU and

Muhammadiyah to counter radicalism discourse in digital media, including collaborating with campuses and mosques. Moreover, kyai and moderate religious figures are encouraged to actively disseminate moderate Islam through digital media. This is an attempt to counter radicalism, as there are continuous attacks done by buzzer against moderate kyai and Islamic preachers.

## 4 Concluding Remarks

The COVID-19 pandemic cases since 2020 have indirectly encouraged the use of digital media in da'wa activities. Although da'wa through digital media was not started during the pandemic time, in recent years, many preachers, both individuals and da'wa institutions as well as religious organizations have used digital media in their activities to disseminate Islamic teaching.

The digital da'wa has various challenges during its implementation, both coming from the internal and external factors, for example; the ability of human resources to manage digital media is still limited, and the competition of religious discourse with radical groups, as well as media capitalization by big media companies. However, in the future, there will be opportunities in applying digital media for doing da'wa. This is because organizations such as NU and Muhammadiyah as well as other institutions have human resources both for media operations and resource persons. At the same time, the audiences are starting to be familiar with the digital media and they are eager to seek religious information and knowledge through digital media and social media. Therefore, it is necessary to improve the quality of human resources for handling digital da'wa.

## References

1. Adliansah W (2019) Person in environment remaja pada era revolusi industri 4.0. J Pekerj Sos 02(01):47–80
2. Gultom G, Atnan N (2019) Pemanfaatan media Sosial dan Komunikasi Interpersonal Guru dengan Murid Berkebutuhan Khusus. Commun: J Commun Stud 6(1):37–56
3. Ramadhan B (2020) Ini Data Pengguna Internet di Seluruh Dunia Tahun 2020. *Kompas*, Jakarta, 2020. Accessed 04 Aug 2020. https://teknoia.com/data-pengguna-internet-dunia-ac03abc7476
4. Kusuma W, Pertiwi (2020) Penetrasi internet di Indonesia Capai 64 Persen, *Kompas*, Jakarta, 2020. Accessed 04 Aug 2020 https://tekno.kompas.com/read/2020/02/20/14090017/penetrasi-internet-di-indonesia-capai-64-persen
5. Budiantoro W (2017) Dakwah di era digital. Komunika 11(02):263–281
6. Usman F (2016) Efektivitas Penggunaan media online sebagai sarana dakwah. Al-Tsiqoh: Jurnal Ekonomi dan Dakwah Islam 1(1):1–8
7. Wibowo A (2018) Kebebasan berdakwah di Youtube: Suatu analisis pola partisipasi media. mawa'izh J Dakwah Dan Pengemb Sos Kemanus 09(02):224–238
8. Yahya M, Farhan (2019) Dakwah 'Virtual' Masyarakat Bermedia Online. Briliant: J Ris dan Konseptual 4(2):249–259.

9. Rohman DA (2019) Komunikasi Dakwah melalui media sosial. Tatar Pasundan: J Diklat Keagamaan 13(02):121–132
10. Wahab N, Muhammad N, Ismail M (2019) Media sosial sebagai medium dakwah masa kini. Int Soc Sci Humlties J 02(01):14–24
11. Romadi P (2020) Intensitas Menonton Video Dakwah melalui Media Platform Online dengan Tingkat Religiusitas. Idarotuna: Jurnal Kajian Manajemen Dakwah 2(2):19–33. https://doi.org/10.24014/idarotuna.v2i2.9994
12. Syah AM (2020) Pengaruh Dakwah Media Sosial Youtube terhadap Religiusitas Remaja di MA. Al-Muhtadi Sendangagung. Busyro: Jurnal Komunikasi dan Penyiaran Islam 1(2):20–36
13. Prasanti D, el Karimah K (2020) Pencarian Informasi Dakwah Islam melalui Media Online Pada Masa Pandemi COVID-19 bagi Komunitas Muslim. J Ilmu Komun 18(03):292–302. https://doi.org/10.31315/jik.v18i3.4000
14. Munawara RA, Satyawan I (2020) Pemanfaatan Media Digital untuk Dakwah Pesantren Tebuireng (Studi pada Akun Media Sosial tebuireng.online). Komunika: J Dakwah Dan Komun 14(1):29–45
15. Ummah A (2020) Dakwah Digital dan generasi Milenial (Menelisik Strategi Dakwah Komunitas Arus Informasi Santri Nusantara). J Tasamuh 18(01):54–78
16. Mutiawati (2014) Strategi Komunikasi dan Pembinaan Keagamaan bagi Gelandangan dan Pengemis pada Unit Pelayanan Teknis Pelayanan Sosial Binjai. J Penelit Komun dan Pembang 15(1):33–44
17. Falimu (2017) Etika Komunikasi Pegawai terhadap Pelayanan Penerbitan Pajak Bumi dan Bangunan. J Komunikator 9(1):9–16
18. Mubasyaroh (2016) Dakwah dan Komunikasi (Studi Penggunaan Media Massa dalam Dakwah). At-Tabsyir: J Komun Penyiaran Islam 4(1):95–114
19. Syukir A (1983) Dasar-dasar Strategi Dakwah Islam. Surabaya: Al Ikhlas
20. Nafis (1998) Peranan Tarekat dalam Dinamika Dakwah pada Abad Pertengahan Islam. Semarang
21. Moeleong L (2002) Metode Penelitian Kualitatif. Bandung: Remaja Rosda-karya
22. BPS DI Yogyakarta (2022) Provinsi Daerah Istimewa Yogyakarta dalam angka 2022. Yogyakarta: BPS DI Yogyakarta

# Changing Gender Regime in Karen Community: A Case Study of Karen Women in Mae Ramat District, Tak Province, Thailand

**Chonnipa Amornwat and Yuki Miyake**

**Abstract** Karen is one of the ethnic groups that live mainly in Southeast Asia. They are diverse in ethnicity and linguistics within the Karen communities as there are many sub-groups with different customs, languages, and religions with about 500,000 Karen people in Thailand. Gender roles are practiced in every community, in Karen communities as well. Karen men have masculine character performance and male roles as leader of the family and breadwinner while Karen women's roles are kinship, childcare, recreation, sex, housekeeper, and provider. Karen women tend to express themselves at community and household levels rather than outside the community spaces. However, the changes in the world context over time have resulted in the shifting of gender roles and gender orders where the line between women's roles and men's roles become blurred, and yet, this can be considered as "changing in gender regime." This research aims to study the changes in gender regime of Karen women in Mae Ramat District, Tak Province. Karen women who settle in Thailand's border area can possibly distribute the new knowledge of gender study and ethnicity in the border area that perhaps present the different practices and thoughts of Karen women who settle in other areas. Gender regime is the fundamental concept to analyze the overall changes of Karen women in the area. The research employs a qualitative research approach, in which the key informants are 15 Karen women in their 20–60 s.

**Keywords** Karen women · Gender regime · Women empowerment · Community inclusion · Border · Thailand

C. Amornwat (✉) · Y. Miyake
School of Social Innovation, Mae Fah Luang University, Chiang Rai, Thailand
e-mail: 6352301002@lamduan.mfu.ac.th

Y. Miyake
e-mail: Yuki.miy@mfu.ac.th



Nawawi et al. (eds.), *Managing Disruption and Developing Resilience for a Better Southeast Asia*, Springer Proceedings in Humanities and Social Sciences,
https://doi.org/10.1007/978-981-96-2116-3_42

# 1 Introduction

## *1.1 Background*

Karen is one of the ethnic groups that live mainly in Southeast Asia. Karen people are diverse in ethnicity and linguistics within the Karen communities as there are many sub-groups with different customs, languages, and religions [1]. According to the (2002) data collection of the Cultural Office of Tak Province, Karens are the largest ethnicity that resides scattery among 15 provinces in Thailand (Cultural office Tak Province, 2014). The estimation of Karen population is between six and seven million Karen people in Myanmar [1] and there are about 500,000 Karens living in Thailand (Karen linguistics project, 2008) and probably more than this but in terms of irregular migrants, then it is impossible to know the exact overall number.

In Thailand, hill tribes are among the most vulnerable and disadvantaged groups in society (Fujioka 2002). Most hill-tribe people traditionally engage in agriculture as their main economic activity and in household-based handicraft production and also wage employment as their secondary sources of income. Their production inputs are limited, they lack access to basic social services, including health and education; and they also lack opportunities for systematic skill development, income, and employment (Fujioka 2002). However, besides the vulnerability status of Karens in Thailand, the status of Karen women themselves in the Karen community is interesting to be studied, that even though there are researches conducted on Karen women, this research is trying to deliver the updated phenomenon of Karen women. The traditional gender roles are obviously embedded in every society, in the form of family-scale to community-scale. Women are still expected to be a carer of the household while men are expected to be breadwinners of the family. The status of women according to traditional gender roles of Karen community may cause two-way discrimination toward Karen women in the case that they are struggling to act out of traditional beliefs on genders. Other than that, Karen women may continue to experience double burdens or when they take on dual responsibilities.

Karen women in Mae Ramat District, Tak Province in Thailand are selected to be a case study in this research. As the area of Mae Ramat is located near the Thai-Myanmar border, on the border area of Tak Province, it is an area where the mass flow of people from Myanmar comes to Thailand for various reasons, including political, economic, and human rights violations. Moreover, it is an area of interest for many Thai and foreign academicians who are interested in the study of the frontier and border. This Thai-Myanmar border area appears to provide many stories of the lives of people from various ethnic groups and statuses that have become an issue and research in various fields of study whether it is public health, political science, anthropology, and so on, or even useful for the topic of reports of various agencies. However, it is noticeable that feminist research as another form of social science studies is not so prevalent in studies on the Thai-Myanmar border [2]. Therefore, this area has the potential to be a case study and be able to contribute new knowledge in the field of gender studies and ethnicity. The information on the changing gender regimes and the model of Karen women in Mae Ramat District may not be able to represent and reflect the model of Karen women in other areas of Thailand but it can contribute in terms of academic knowledge of Karen women who live in the border area and it can possibly provide the model and points of view for Karen women in other areas of Thailand.

## *1.2 Theoretical Framework*

Gender regime is a significant concept that is used to analyze the changing of Karen women. It is playing as the main and fundamental concept to analyze the overall shifting and changing of gender roles and gender relations of Karen women. Gender regimes are operated at the state, economy, and society level, therefore, it influences the structure of gender relations within the family, the labor market, and state institutions [3]. Goff Boni-Le Isabel et al. [4] present that the focus on gender regimes can be at the macro-societal or national level which the concept captures the normative expectations and social structure that shape gender roles and gender relations in a given society and at a given moment in time. Gender regime is a big concept but can be used to explain the gender phenomenon in various levels of actors, from a single person to one family, community, and state. The changing gender regime here that will discuss is based on the changing of Karen women's roles to be the active actors in their families and even their community as well as it is associated with traditional gender assumptions (Sümer 2009), as a result of that, it can cause the inclusion and exclusion of each individual based on the belief and structure of gender that have been practiced in such way. The changing gender regime that this research mainly focuses on is not at the state level or national level but at the family and community level of the Karens. Changing gender regimes includes the small changes until the big changes that make the "different" pattern of living that has been continuing for generations to generations. The changes can be perhaps perceived as good changes or unpleasant changes that are due to the consideration of Karen family and community onwards.

Gender roles based on the feminist perspective point out not only simple ideas about appropriate behaviors for men and women but are also linked to different levels of power between men and women in society. Men experience greater economic control than women because men are expected to be the main breadwinners for their families while women often struggle with poverty if their marriage fails [5]. The issue of "breadwinning" is one of the clear examples of how gender relations, gender roles, and gender regimes are related. This mainstream concept is exercising and implementing "gender order" which provides particular action to individuals in society, nevertheless, the shifting in gender regimes can also influence the shifting in gender roles and gender relations as well. Breadwinning is one of the factors that can present the changing Karen women's roles, that is to say, the roles of women are beyond traditional gender roles where women are only the household carers. The breadwinning is also changing the gender relations among Karen women and their families, community, and Karen women themselves. The other factors that contribute to the changing of gender regimes are observed from the field observation and interview.

One of the reasons that held women's capability back is a gender stereotype. [6] stated that in Mavin (2009), gender stereotypes are actually hidden for women to be successful in their careers because the perceptions based on gender or sex roles are leading to what is considered appropriate or inappropriate behavior for women and men leaders. Moreover, the stereotypes based on gender are associated with conceptual beliefs and social predictions about the suitable traits and characteristics for women and men. In order to deal with such barriers to women's success in careers, "networking" is being seen as one beneficial way for advancing women's career paths. As well as Singh et al. (2006) also said that a network is important in terms of managerial career improvement and increases the success of an individual. Bourdieu (1986) and Lin (2001) cited in [6] think that relationships based on networks help performers to gain more value as it helps access the top resources from such beneficial relationships. Although, networking can benefit especially women as Coleman (2008) said that networking is an important element of women's career success and growth. Nevertheless, such networking that supposes to help women to deal with inequality structure is somehow identified as an "old boys network" (Coleman 2010), cited in [6]. Karen women's inclusion, in this case, can be considered as the result of women's networking. The integration of Karen women, raising their voice, and participating in community activities are ways to increase their position to be equal to men and be able to perform anything else outside of the household roles. It is also a sign for women to be accepted and included in the community. Community inclusion is significant to everyone because it means the rights that you are supposed to have will be reached and you will be protected by those rights.

## 2 Methodology

This research employs a qualitative research approach to collect information about the transition of Karen women's roles in their own families and community. The focus is particularly on Karen women's roles that are changing, such as Karen women who participate in the labor market, the participation in their community, women's agency, and the way they perceive their family, or the rights of women in the present day. In addition, it can also provide information about the impacts of gender roles on the Karen community and also attempts to find how Karen women are empowered.

This research primarily uses in-depth interviews. The interviewees selected for the interview are Karen women who live in Mae Ramat District, Tak Province. The social status of interviewees is not strictly limited while the age of interviewees expectation is between the 20 s and 60 s. With the contract, all data collected in this research will be kept confidential and used only for the purpose of this academic research. Since this research is an in-depth interview, the number of interviewees is 15 women as in Table 1. The process of the research also includes collecting online documents, and participatory observation. Online documents include news, websites, journals, and academic articles.

This research was conducted in Mae Ramat District, Tak Province Thailand. Tak Province is connected to the other nine provinces of the northern part of Thailand and has a border connected to Myanmar. It is the area with a diversity of races, religions, and cultures especially those who call themselves Karens or k'nyaw, they scattery reside in various districts of Tak Province including Mae Sot district, Phop Phra district, Mae Ramat district, Tha Song Yang district, Umphang district, Ban Tak district, and Sam Ngao district [7]. The History of Mae Ramat District is assumed that it was originally a village inhabited by the Karen people for more than 100 years. But from the rich in natural resources, people from the Northern part have immigrated down here, therefore, this area has developed to be a large village. (Tak.go, n.d.)

**Table 1** Data of interviewees

| Age | Education | Marital status | Jobs/careers | Women's group membership | Have children/do not have children |
|---|---|---|---|---|---|
| 30 | Non-formal education | Married | Village headman's assistant | Participate | Have children |
| 37 | Associate's degree | Widow | Entrepreneur | Participate | Have children |
| 39 | High school | Married | Unemployed | Not participate | Have children |
| 40 | Primary school | Married | Farmer | Participate | Have children |
| 36 | Vocational certificate | Married | Farmer/run a grocery shop | Not participate | Have children |
| 25 | Non-formal education | Married | Teaching assistant | Participate | Do not have children |
| 29 | Junior high school | Married | Farmer | Not participate | Have children |
| 38 | Unschooled | Married | Farmer | Participate | Have children |
| 32 | Non-formal education | Married | Farmer | Participate | Have children |
| 32 | Unschooled | Married | Farmer | Participate | Have children |
| 58 | Associate's degree | Married | Teacher | Used to participate | Have children |
| 43 | Bachelor degree | Single | Teacher | Used to participate | Not have children |
| 46 | Primary school | Married | Farmer/ run a grocery shop | Participate | Have children |
| 60 | Unschooled | Married | Unemployed | Used to participate | Have children |
| 55 | Unschooled | Married | Farmer | Used to participate | Have children |

It is rich in nature, forests, wildlife, and minerals, as well as beautiful scenery. It is a district that connects to Myanmar through the border on the west side. It is 120 km away from Tak Province and 33 km from Mae Sot district, covering an area of 1,475.54 square kilometers or about 999,014 rai (maeramadpolice, n.d.).

## 3 Results

### *3.1 Changing Gender Regime in Karen Community, Mae Ramat District, Tak Province*

Karens' way of building the family is in a monogamous relationship where husband and wife respect each other or the relationship is based on equal roles [8]. However, the changes in the world's context have influenced the new meaning of what is considered a respectful relationship between husband and wife. The interviewees have explained the gender phenomenon in their families from when they were young until now and that has shown the similarities between Karen families. In the past, in terms of a married couple, husbands were respected very much by their wives. The patriarchal social structure in Karen community influences the practices according to traditional gender roles where Karen women are tied to women's jobs which keep decreasing their power to participate in family decision-making and community inclusion afterward. This research has found the changing gender regime in Karen community, Mae Ramat District, and the changes are divided into four categories.

The first change that the interviewees mentioned is women's emancipation from domestic work. All of the interviewees mentioned in the same way that nowadays housework is shared between husband and wife. They go to work outside together and when they get home, they help each other with the housework. For example, one interviewee said, "Women work just like men … not like in the past when women did all the housework, Karen women have changed a lot" (Interview by the author in January 2022). There is no such clear line between women and men in housework anymore that in some households, men do the laundry by themselves. Even though women's roles in housework still exist but very little. Karen women today work outside just like Karen men, and they can do farming, for example. It is not like in the past when women only stay at home but both husband and wife are the breadwinners of the family, and they share most of the responsibilities together. However, the tasks which are considered men's work or have to use strength are still practiced such as cutting the trees and killing animals for the ceremony. Meanwhile, textile is considered a women's task, it is not for men one interviewee said "Weaving work was created for women to do. Men don't have to do it and this is according to the traditional belief. But this culture has changed because more talented women go to work such as farming, unlike in the past when women stayed at home and raised children" (Interview by the author in January 2022).

The second is the parenting and family planning of Karen's parents. The interviewees told that Karen parents in the past raised their children regardless of gender in the same way. The care and love are equally shared among their children and all of the children help with housework and farming all the same. However, if compared to the interviewees when they became parents, the changes in the world context seem to increase more sharing of responsibility for children between husband and wife. Moreover, Karen parents come to focus on education for their children more, for example, one interviewee said.

"Education also means going to higher society, meeting friends, and having broader experiences, so they can have many ideas and be active. To return home and live in a society like this they will blend in with the villagers, not doing anything" (Interview by the author in January 2022). According to the interview, the interviewees and their husbands are taking care of their children together. In terms of family planning, the interviewees who have children all agreed that there is no such favored demand for many children as in the past. In the past, Karens wanted to have many children to help with the work and income of the family, however, in the present time, the big concern of the number of children is the cost to raise them. The example statement from the interviewee, "Karen parents in the past did not want their children to study because there would be no one to help them with the work" (Interview by the author in April 2022).

Third, the personal belief in the traditional Karen way of practice is changing. Supawadee [9] explained the animism among Karen that Karen people have a strong belief in spirits. They believe that every good and bad event is produced by spirits. The events such as sickness, agriculture damage, or drought and the practices which are against the traditional beliefs will be punished not just the one who did it but the whole village. Similar to the interviewees in this research, this ritual is still practiced but not widely practiced anymore as they have turned to Buddhism more among the community, as well as the ritual needs delicacy preparation and together with adaptation to the changing mainstream culture. Therefore, the reason that can be found behind the changing of Karen personal beliefs is Karen women's flow on gender phenomenon is related to the world gender phenomenon. The belief and practice even though it was strongly embedded in the community, however, it is possible to change. Especially, when there is evidence that can prove the pros and cons as well as the causes and outcomes of the incident. Karen women have the choice to choose whether to believe and follow what has been done for generations or not, in this issue, their voice and opinion on personal beliefs do not turn out silent.

Fourth is the gathering of the Karen women's group. The Karen women's group that was informed by the interviewees is a group of Karen women around 10–20 people which spreads in many communities and are various in terms of group activities. The activities are mainly pig farming, textile, making rugs, and joining the community activities depending on each group. Those who have joined considered that the women's groups are quite beneficial, as they have the opportunity to meet other Karen women, share information, and specifically learn new skills from the experts that are invited to instruct the group. Karen women group is a sign of gender equality within the community, Karen women have space to increase skills and gain new knowledge together in the supportive environment provided by Karen women for Karen women.

The similarity that is noticeable after the interview is all of the interviewees' economic status when they were young was not so good. When they were telling their childhood stories, they were in the same line. Such as all of them have to help their parents with searching the food in the forest, helping with farming, and doing housework, and that sounds very normal when they were telling the story as it was what every household was doing at that time.

### *3.2 Karen Women's Overcoming the Patriarchal Gender Regime*

Despite the fact that originally the relationships of Karen women and men are respective, supportive, and based on equal roles [8], it is undeniable that Karen women are tied up to particular women's tasks which somehow causes their lives to not experience full freedom and ultimate opportunity. According to the interview, the 15 interviewees have reflected on the practice that they have used to overcome the strict gender roles and patriarchal gender regimes in which the practices are associated and surrounded by the change in the world context. In the present time, Karens in many areas started to work outside their community and come back with the outsider's cultures, as a result, the way of life that has been practiced among Karens for a long time started to change according to the current mainstream of the word [7]. For example, one interviewee said, "These days, Karen women do not stand it anymore because of the development of technology, advancement, and modernity. It has made women learn more. There are many examples to see from the past. As well as education also made women become better as they are able to use the knowledge to manage their life, make a living, and be able to weigh the term equality. In terms of ability, they become more assertive as well as be more courageous to express their own feelings" (Interview by the author in January 2022).

In the practices of Karen women, the commitment to the new changes is one of the most important foundations for other practices; otherwise, there will be no changes and improvement in women's roles at all if Karen women are not encouraged to do something. Together the changing of gender roles and gender relations in Karen community is considered one of the factors that build a supportive environment for Karen women to change, for example, to be able to access education and work in various fields of work.

"Karen women become more modern" one interviewee gave the opinion, the terms of "modern" she referred to does not only mean the clothing style that Karen's women do not often wear traditional Karen dress anymore but it also means that the roles of Karen become more modern, their way of life and thinking is changing from the traditional way of practices. Besides the gender roles of Karen women and men that have been discussed, the roles of Karen women when they have an opportunity to work their ambition is very inspiring and very active. As in the past, most of the Karen families only do the farming with various kinds of agriculture, but over and beyond that Karen women work more than just farming such as the interviewees who do farming also opened their own business; meanwhile, a few of them started the online business platform as an alternative platform to reach the customers. For example, one interviewee said: "Most Karen people focus on farming because to do farming they can earn a big amount of money at one time. People do not think that the profit from weaving is actually enough as they do not know about social media that can help with income generation" (Interview by the author in January 2022).

To break the stereotype image of Karen women, some groups of people might perceive this action as inappropriate and follow with concern about the fading of the traditional way of practices that few interviewees have noted. On the other hand, other groups of people are seeking for changes to overcome the things that are already provided to them and more opportunities to fulfill their own lives. For example, one interviewee said: "The combination of old and new cultures" is necessary, as the old culture cannot be completely abandoned but should be applied together (Interview by the author in January 2022). The interviewee uses this statement with the example of raising children that is related to other interviewees' concerns. One interviewee said: "The Karen children nowadays are not like in the past, they do not have to help their parents with plenty of housework and farming because they focus more on school as well as right now the water supply or the electricity is already reached, so their lives become easier, however, with the technology and internet they become lazier and cannot focus well" (Interview by the author in April 2022). The combination of the traditional and modern culture is brought to the table by the interviewees, their concern is to keep improvement of women's roles like nowadays, but at the same time try to protect the traditional culture and practices to not disappear which seems like an important challenge that they will have to resolve.

## 4 Discussion and Conclusion

The transition of traditional gender roles and gender orders is pervasively discussed in the public areas as well as in the field of research, the breakthrough of traditional gender roles where women are no longer biding with domestic work and household care. At the same time, the transition of gender roles also happened among ethnicities that this research focuses on Karens in Mae Ramat District, Tak Province.

The "shifting" in this research is used to reflect the situation where Karen women perform various roles besides the household carer, have more opportunities and choices for their lives, and share responsibility between husband and wife in their family. A situation like this can be considered as the change in gender regime. Based on the 15 interviewees, first, this research described the changing of gender regimes among Karens as women's emancipation from domestic work. The second showed the parenting and family planning of Karen's parents. The third was the changes in personal belief in the traditional Karen way of practice, and lastly, the gathering of Karen women's groups was shown.

In an attempt to find out the changing gender regime, following to the pattern of the definition of gender regime, this research has presented the current situation of the new pattern of gender regime in Karen community. In contrast to the original gender regime where the gender order is run under the traditional gender assumptions that keep dividing women and men in the current time, the traditional gender order is starting to be ambiguous. The pattern of gender roles and gender relations is changing due to the changing world trend where gender equality is becoming one of the significant goals to be achieved. Even in the midst of today's technology and materialist society, Karens have to face the rapid changes that come and challenge them with the confusion in choosing to accept or reject it, especially in terms of cultural traditions and beliefs being changed based on the influence of mainstream development in various forms [7]. However, as expected under the flow of Karen people that started working outside the community as well as the outcomes of globalization, people started to notice the new cultures and absorb them day by day and become a way of practice as a result.

The stories of 15 Karen women have demonstrated the clear statement that even traditionally, western societies believed that women are more nurturing than men. Therefore, the feminine gender role traditionally prescribes that women should behave in that way. One way for women to engage in the traditional feminine gender role could be by nurturing their family by working full-time rather than working outside the home. While men are traditionally presumed by the gender roles to be leaders [5], it is not really happening in the Karen community today. Karen women in this research are all the breadwinners of their own lives and share the breadwinner role with their husbands. It is not like in the past when the husband was the main breadwinner and controlled all the money situation of the family or used the same purse as one interviewee said, but right now, it is more like a different purse between husband and wife. Or in the case of a failed marriage, men experience greater terms of maintaining economic control than women because men are expected to be the main breadwinners for their families while women often struggle with poverty if their marriage fails [5], nevertheless, one interviewee has shown that it is not always true that she can take care of her child and can continue her business to be bigger, to jump on an online business platform and live her life in joy by being independent on herself.

## References

1. The Karen Buddhist Dhamma Dhutta Foundation (2010) The Karen people: culture, faith and history
2. Kanjanatiwat Pornpan (2016) Feminist research and gender perspective in Thai-Burma borderlands: the role of Karen displaced women in textile handicraft making. M.A. (Culture and Development), Research Institute for Languages and Cultures of Asia. Mahidol University

3. Chappell L, Guerrina R (2020) Understanding the gender regime in the European external action service. Coop Confl 55(2):261–280
4. Goff Boni-Le I et al. (2019) Do gender regimes matter? Gender, age and inequality in the professions, London. Routledge
5. Blackstone Amy. Gender roles and society. University of Maine
6. Wanigasekara WMSK (2016) Women's networking and career development: a systematic analysis of the literature. Department of human resource management, University of Kelaniya, Sri Lanka. Int J Bus Manag 11(11)
7. The Cultural Office Tak Province ( ประวัติอำเภอแม่ระมาด) (2014) Derived from; http://www.takculture.com
8. Wanlika S (2002) The study of changes in the mode of production and social relation system in gender aspect of the Karen community: a case study of Tipuyae Village Tongpabhum District. Thammasat University, Kanchanaburi Province
9. Supawadee K (2001) The family roles of Karen women in Samoeng District, Chiang Mai Province. Department of socio and anthropology, faculty of political science. Chulalongkorn University
10. Bamberry L (2015) Restructuring women's work; labor market and household gender regimes in the Greater Latrobe Valley, Australia. A J Fem Geogr
11. Booranaprasertsook Wichat (2012) Stories from the Thai-Burmese border: intellectual sparks for sustainable development. Karen linguistics project. The Thailand research fund. National Library of Thailand
12. Hayami Y (2006) Negotiating ethnic representation between self and other: the case of Karen and Eco-tourism in Thailand. Southeast Asian Studies, vol 44. No3
13. Karen ( กะเหรียง). Department of social development and welfare ( กรมพัฒนาสังคมและสวัสดิการ). Ministry of Social Development and Human Security ( กระทรวงการพัฒนาสงคมและความมันคงของมนุษย์). (2015)
14. The history of Mae Ramat District ( สำนักงานวัฒนธรรมจังหวัดตาก กระทรวงวัฒนธรรม). (n.d.). Derived from; http://www.tak.go.th/history_maeramad.htm, https://www.govesite.com/policmd/content.php?cid=20170713163551CbZ4nBM, https://www.maeramat.com/page/location.html

[illegible]

# Diaspora, Migration, Pandemic, Citizenship and Human Security in Southeast Asia

# African Trade Network in Southeast Asia: Identities, Transformation, and Complexities of African Trade Network in Tanah Abang

**Ahmad Helmy Fuady, Saiful Hakam, Erwiza Erman, Bondan Widyatmoko, Muzzar Kresna, and Angela Iban**

**Abstract** Africa is an essential non-traditional market for Indonesia. Unfortunately, long historical and cultural relation are not manifested enough into economic relation between the two. There are culprit factors for this, such as deficiency of diplomatic infrastructure, emotional and inter-generational gaps on development and historical relations as well as lack of academic studies focusing on African market penetration strategy. These factors explain the ongoing disinclination for general Indonesian investor to start new business in Africa as well as stigmatization toward African and the development of the region. In order to bridge it, rereading trade relation especially focusing on knowledge production and trade networks between Indonesia and Africa and vice-versa is important. A case study of Tanah Abang trade networks is used to show the important actors, the relationship among actors, and institutional contexts and problems for Indonesia's trade with African countries. It highlights the roles of the African, namely the Igbo's ethnic network and Malians (Mali's people) in Jakarta to facilitate trade between Indonesia and West Africa.

**Keywords** Indonesia · Economic diplomacy · Africa · Global production networks · Trade networks

## 1 Introduction

In the second term of President JokoWidodo's administration, it has been determined that Indonesia's Ministry of Foreign Affairs' main priority is economic diplomacy, particularly in potential or non-traditional markets. Weakening economic growth in Indonesia's main export markets (United States, Europe, and Japan) has forced the country to find new opportunities in potential export markets, such as Africa.

A. H. Fuady (✉) · S. Hakam · E. Erman · B. Widyatmoko · M. Kresna · A. Iban
Research Center for Area Studies, National Research and Innovation Agency (BRIN), Jakarta, Indonesia
e-mail: ahmad.helmy.fuady@brin.go.id; ahmad.helmy.fuady@yahoo.com



Nawawi et al. (eds.), *Managing Disruption and Developing Resilience for a Better Southeast Asia*, Springer Proceedings in Humanities and Social Sciences,
https://doi.org/10.1007/978-981-96-2116-3_43

Aiming Africa as non-traditional market comes with legitimate reasons. Historically, trade between Indonesia and countries in the continent has existed for a long time. There are even historical records that note that this relationship has been established since the third century. At that time, the merchants of the archipelago carried out activities in several ancient East African port cities, such as Kilwa and Zanzibar. In the seventeenth century, the Cape of Good Hope (now the Republic of South Africa), which was controlled by the *VereenigdeOostindischeCompagnie* (VOC), became a place of exile for political convicts from the archipelago, namely kings, nobles, and even scholars, such as Sheikh Yusuf from Makassar, who is the first cleric to spread Islam in South Africa. The presence and culture that they bring can be the main assets to open trade networks and further cooperation between Indonesia and Africa.

From an economic point of view, Africa is transforming from a region that was not considered much economically in the 1980s to become a continent of hope in the 2000s. Africa that was once associated with backwardness, poverty, and civil war, has now changed and has been seen as the future of the world economy. In addition to having 16.72 percent of the world's population (1.27 billion persons) of the 50 countries with the highest global economic growth in 2018, 40 percent came from Sub-Saharan Africa. However, the current figures and statistics for the Indonesia-Africa trade balance show that the long-term relationship did not result in an optimal economic relation. The total export–import of the 54 African countries in 2018 was USD 10.53 billion or only 2.85 percent of Indonesia's total international trade.

What went missing from Indonesia and African continent trade relation? There are several factors identified such as lacking in diplomatic infrastructure, emotional and inter-generational gaps in development and historical relations for both regions. These factors explain the ongoing disinclination for general Indonesian investor to start new business in Africa as well as stigmatization toward African and the development of the region. In order to bridge it, rereading trade relation especially focusing on knowledge production and trade networks between Indonesia and Africa and vice-versa is important. It will give current information and perspective regarding identities, transformation, and complexities of trade network and actors in global production network. This information is an initial strategy for penetrating the African market.

Academically, there is a very limited in-depth study on Indonesia's strategy to enter potential export markets, especially Africa. Previous studies on Indonesia-Africa relations are mostly from the perspective of history and international relations, especially concerning the Asia-Africa Conference (For example, [1–3, 10, 12, 18, 24, 26]). Studies on Indonesia-Africa economic relations are shown by Amalina et al. [4], Sabaruddin [22], and Rahmawati [21]. Sabaruddin [23] stated the need for Indonesia's economic diplomacy through clustering Indonesian export markets in traditional and non-traditional markets. Meanwhile, Rahmawati [21] specifically sees the importance of the Indonesia-Africa Forum for the expansion of Indonesian exports in non-traditional African markets. Road to Africa: Study of Economic Potential and Risk of African Countries compiled by the Indonesia Exim Bank Institute and the Directorate General of Asia Pacific and Africa, Ministry of Foreign

Affairs of the Republic of Indonesia [17] which was prepared for the Indonesia-Africa Forum 2018 is the only preliminary study about market potential, risks, and strategies for entering the African market. However, this study only provided analysis and overview of business opportunities and risks in Africa. There is no detailed study that analyzes production and trade networks in Africa that can show strategic hubs that can be used for the benefit of the Indonesian economy. In addition, the strategy of penetrating potential or non-traditional export markets has mostly been carried out with international relations and economics approaches in the macro realm.

This shortcoming creates a knowledge gap on the development of a long-built cultural, economic, and political relationship between Africa and Indonesia that has been shifting beyond the state realm. This shift requires observation on trade networks, commodities and actors' movement between two regions. Tanah Abang-which, located in Greater Region of Jakarta is a global site for textile and garment commodities trade. Many Africans successfully build their community and livelihood around the area. It takes production and logistic activities and infrastructure as well as cultural connectivity. Nevertheless, less we know about the community.

This article aims to fill the gap by commencing an analysis of African trade networks in Indonesia. By focusing on African in Tanah Abang, it purposely identifies influential African actors or groups in the society, exploring their peers and ties as well as historical and institutional context and facing problems in building and strengthening trade routes to Africa. In order to carry out the analysis, this article utilizes the Global Production Networks (GPNs) approach. This approach not only provides tools to investigate the structure of global production commodity and service but also observe various inter and intra relationships and engagements around the structure.

## 2 Identity, Transformation, and Complexity of Trade Network in GPNs Framework

The GPN approach combines analysis of global value chains (GVC), actor-networks theory (ANT), and varieties of capitalism (VoC). GVC supports an analysis to understand the relationships between companies in production and trade networks. ANT helps to identify and understand the various relationships between actors in the network. Meanwhile, VoC helps to comprehend the context of production and institutional governance.

This concept was mainly developed by the Manchester group in the 2000s (see for example [6–9, 16]. The production network is a nexus of interrelated functions, operations, and transactions in the production, distribution, and consumption of a product or service. GPNs are a production network that is 'interconnected nodes and links extend spatially across national boundaries and, in so doing, integrates parts of disparate national and sub-national territories' [7].

The concept of GPNs is similar to global commodity chains (GCC)[1] and global value chain (GVC),[2] however, there are two main differences [7]. First, GCC/GVC is essentially a linear structure, whereas GPNs seek to go beyond such linearity to incorporate all types of existing network configurations. Second, GCC/GVC focuses narrowly on the governance of intercompany transactions while GPNs seek to cover all relevant and related sets of actors.

The adoption of actor-networks theory (ANT) in the GPNs analysis allows us to identify various non-firm actors involved in the overall production system. These non-company actors can be political actors, NGOs, international donors, technology, infrastructure, or other relevant. In this perspective, network analysis does not start from categorization so that these actors do not have to come from the same category. The ANT network perspective also helps get out of the linear analysis, so that it can reveal the circulation of capital, knowledge, and people that underlie the production of all goods and services, more comprehensively. This can help to understand the process of adding value and commodity networks that are multidimensional, both vertical and horizontal with varying levels and scales.

In GPNs, the relationships between actors, both corporate and non-company, are located in different geographic areas, social contexts, and institutions, or can be said to represent various forms of capitalism. None of the elements in the GPNs exist in a vacuum. Therefore, the adoption of Variety of Capitalism analysis (VoC)[3] is an important part of the GPN. Traditionally, the VoC analysis shows the relationships and patterns of coordination between state and non-state actors (business, society). Institutions that are complex and related to production systems that are of concern in the VoC include the financial system, industrial and labor relations, the education system, relations between companies, and the role of the state in the economy.

There are three important elements in GPNs approach that link to the aspect of identity, transformation, and complexity. First, GPNs network analysis concentrates to see the flow and mobility of people, commodities, or values in a production and trade network, making it possible to answer questions related to production, relationship as well as cultural transformation. GPNs structure that is changing through upgrading process (production, supply chain, product type development, and value added) could open access for social upgrading [27]. This organizational production transformation leads to practices of worker capability advancement, worker rights, and working condition improvement. In this case, social upgrading places workers as social actors. By the same tokens, communities as social actors are interacting with upgrading process through inter-organizational reliability development which

[1] More about GCC see G. Gereffi and M. Korzeniewicz (Eds.), [13], Commodity Chains and Global Development. Westport: Praeger, pp. 95–122.

[2] Many of the writings on GVC have been developed from the book Michael [20], *Competitive Advantage: Creating and sustaining superior performance*

[3] More about VoC see Hall, P. A., & Soskice, D. (Eds.), [15]. *Varieties of Capitalism: The Institutional Foundations of Comparative Advantage. Academy of Management Review* (Vol. 28). Oxford: Oxford University Press.

further could be manifested into extended social responsibility program and standardization [25]. This is the transmission provided by the GPNs in identifying the transformation site, processes as well as related social actors.

Second, network analysis in the GPNs can show the position and power of actors in the social structure that surrounds them. This can help to explain the perceptions, attitudes, and behavior of each actor in the network. Actors in certain positions have certain roles. This role is particularly formed through placement of GPNs as an important structure of globalization processes. The structure induces reaction to social actors, cosmopolitan and reactant [14] social actors who are involved in global production structure, cosmopolitan, have tendency to make cooperation with others [5]. This type of reaction describes social actors' experiences shifting their motive and value of self-interest to group interest. It made them concerned more about the group welfare rather than individual [14]. Meanwhile, the reactant inclined more toward individual interest and traditional values [5]. The emphasis on the position, role, and power of these actors allows the GPN to explain the existing bargaining power and decision-making process, conflicts over resource allocation, or the dynamics of cooperation among social actors. Third, an understanding of the territorial and network *embeddedness* in the GPN makes it possible to observe various policy alternatives and solutions in economic diplomacy.

In the case of Africa, the concept of GPN can portray the global commodity circulation as well as people movement between Africa and Indonesia. Zanzibar, for example, which is known as a spice island in Africa, got the clove seed from Mollucan through a French trader. It then became a clove supplier for Indonesia to meet the demand from the cigarette industry in the 1970s [11]. This circulation shows trade relations between two regions which include people movement as well. The movement of Africans, especially to Asia, has gone through at least five periods, namely ancient period, the imperial era, the interaction of the spread of Islam, European colonization, and the contemporary period since decolonization [28]. This proves that the movement of Africans to Asia was a long historical process, rejecting the idea that Africa is very isolated from the rest of the world. Compared to America, the movement of Africa to Asia has a longer history because the pattern of movement is more varied and the process of movement is much more complex.

The new wave of African migration is now voluntary, not forced into slavery. In [28], it is explained that Africa is more African today than ever before. Africa today has been constructed and consumed by the continent itself, from sports to television to politics. The Africans in Jakarta are an example of a strong transnational power, they build business networks in Indonesia to open up markets in their own countries in Africa. Today, these connections are facilitated by developments in transportation, communication, and information technology. It is undeniable that these scattered Africans support the development of Africa's growing economic relations with Asia. It is these lines of relationship that are described in the ANT concept as the identification of actors who are interconnected in circulating capital, goods, services, culture, and values.

## 3 The Importance of Non-State Actors in Indonesia's Economic Diplomacy Trajectories to Africa

The Indonesia-Africa Forum (*Indonesia-Africa Forum*, IAF) in Bali, 10–11 April 2018, and the *Indonesia-Africa Infrastructure Dialogue* (IAID) in Bali, 20–21 August 2019 have been mentioned as important events that indicate the revival of Indonesia's economic diplomacy to Africa. The two forums are the continuation of cooperation between Asian and African countries through initiatives such as the Non-Alignment Movement and the 2005 New Asia-African Strategic Partnership (NAASP). Indonesia also seeks to strengthen relations between Asian-African countries through the commemoration of the 60th Anniversary of the Asia-Africa Conference in 2015, which delegates pledged commitments to build stronger, more inclusive, and sustainable.

IAF aims to explore various economic opportunities, strengthen technical cooperation, and enhance existing partnerships between Indonesia and Africa. From its official website, approximately 500 participants joined the forum, including business communities, high-level government officials, and other stakeholders from 53 countries. In the forum, business agreements worth USD 586.56 million occurred in the strategic industrial sector, infrastructure, finance, mining, textiles, aircraft maintenance, and commodity trading. The IAF also signed the Memorandum of Understanding (MoU) on Cooperation to Improve Economic Diplomacy between the Ministry of Foreign Affairs and Indonesia's Exim Bank as the Indonesian Export Guarantee Agency (*LembagaPenjaminEkspor Indonesia*, LPEI). Through cooperation with LPEI, it is hoped that relations with the business world can be improved, especially to convince them to willingly take measured risks, including entering African potential markets.

IAID is a continuation of the IAF with an emphasis on the infrastructure sector which is of particular concern in the previous forum. Significant developments in Africa's infrastructure sector are considered the right momentum to increase collaboration in infrastructure development between Indonesia and Africa. This forum is designed to be a platform for the business community, government officials, and other stakeholders from Indonesia and Africa to exchange ideas, explore possibilities of collaboration, and further engage in cooperation in the infrastructure sector and related sectors. The official IAID website states that during the first two days of the forum, several business agreements worth USD 822 million or around Rp.12.3 trillion were produced.

Previously, serious efforts to improve Indonesia's trade relations with Sub-Saharan Africa can be seen from the establishment of the Indonesian Trade and Promotion Center (ITPC) in Lagos, Nigeria in 2009 and in Johannesburg, South Africa under the Ministry of Trade. The ITPC was established to promote or introduce Indonesian products, attract new buyers or importers, maintain networking or cooperation with buyers or importers, and encourage as well as assist Indonesian business actors to export to Africa.

The ITPCs in Africa also provide technical information to Indonesian business actors, both individuals, and groups of small and medium businesses who are interested in entering the African markets. There are many cases of fraud or scams from Nigeria that must be watched out for by Indonesian business people, especially if they are beginners in entering the Nigerian market. Therefore, when it comes to exporting products from Indonesia, it is better for the Indonesian entrepreneurs to carefully study the buyer, and to comprehend Nigerian import regulations, Nigerian import taxes, and to communicate with buyers not only by email but also by telephone to ensure the seriousness of the business, and document legalization in Indonesia, including Nigerian Embassy in Jakarta. ITPC in Lagos, Nigeria, is very open and willing to help Indonesian entrepreneurs who are going to expand their business to Nigeria and West Africa (Focused Group Discussion with Head of ITPC Lagos, 15 September 2020).

In other African countries where ITPC is absent, the function of economic diplomacy is handled by the Trade Attaché and staff of the Indonesian Embassy. Currently, the role of the Indonesian Embassy is central in economic diplomacy because President JokoWidodo put economic diplomacy as a priority in the work of the Ministry of Foreign Affairs. The Indonesian Embassy in Mozambique, for instance, conducted a market access study for Indonesian Micro Small, and Medium Enterprises (MSMEs) products to Mozambique. They also meet potential buyers, distributors, or agents in Mozambique to explore possible cooperation with Indonesian entrepreneurs. They also facilitate Indonesian businessmen who visit Mozambique, as well as potential buyers, distributors, and agents from Mozambique to Indonesia to do business. The embassy also facilitated the participation of Indonesian MSMEs or displaying Indonesian MSMEs' products at the Trade Expo in Mozambique (HerrySudrajat, 3rd Webinar Routes to Africa, 22 October 2020).

In terms of economic cooperation agreements, until now there has only been one Preferential Trade Agreement (PTA) signed between the Indonesian government and African countries. The Indonesia-Mozambique PTA (IM-PTA) is the first trade cooperation that Indonesia has on the African continent and the first trade cooperation that Mozambique has with countries on the Asian continent. The PTA, which started on April 11, 2018, and was signed on August 27, 2019, in Maputo, Mozambique, covers trade in goods, including non-tariff measures, provisions on the origin of goods, and customs procedures [19]. According to Marthini, 217 Indonesian products received tariff preferences from Mozambique, which include palm oil, rubber, paper, furniture, fishery products, and processed food and beverage products. Meanwhile, Indonesia will give preference to 242 Mozambique products, including cotton, nuts, sunflower seeds, aluminum ore, coffee, fishery products, vegetables, and fruits. For Indonesia, IM-PTA is expected to be the entry point for Indonesian product markets not only in Mozambique but also in the African region. Even though it has been signed, the IM-PTA is still waiting for ratification. In addition to Mozambique which has been signed, Indonesia is still negotiating the PTA with Tunisia, Morocco, and Mauritius, as well as exploring the possibility of a PTA with Algeria, Djibouti, the South African Customs Union (SACU), the Economic Community of West African States (ECOWAS), and the East African Community (EAC).

Any attempts undertaken by the Indonesian government to cooperate with African countries should benefit not only Indonesian entrepreneurs, but should also give benefit to African governments and communities (Interview LI, 5 May 2020). The successful negotiation of the IM-PTA cannot be separated from the lobbying of the Indonesian Ministry of Trade providing confidence that this PTA will serve strategic benefits for the government and people of Mozambique (Interview LI, 5 May 2020). A principle of reciprocity or mutual benefits should be comprehended, and a model of cooperation in economic diplomacy should be clarified so that later will not be accused of carrying out colonialism (Interview PW, 29 July 2020).

Interestingly, Indonesia's economic diplomacy is not always linked to the efforts of the state or government. Business efforts carried out by Indonesian companies in Africa often do not start with what the government does. This can be seen, for example, in the business expansion of Indomie (instant noodle), B29 (detergent and cleaning liquids), TirtaAyu Spa (beauty care), or Wilmar (palm oil). They began to move to find markets in Africa regardless of the presence of economic diplomacy carried out by the Indonesian government. In addition to the government, there are private and individual roles that are important and need to be considered in Indonesia's economic diplomacy. So far, there is not much attention and research has been devoted to exploring the role of these non-state actors in Indonesia's economic diplomacy in Africa.

Indonesia's Economic Diplomacy to Africa must not forget the small actors that have often been ignored, namely the role of small private entrepreneurs who are quietly penetrating the African market. The stage of Indonesia-Africa diplomacy is not only controlled and filled by big actors and big collaborative projects but also small actors who are very strong in penetrating and seeking opportunities in the African market (Interview PS, 16 July 2020).

LH, a tenacious and hardworking entrepreneur, has successfully introduced beauty products to Nigeria, Cameroon, Ghana, and Eswatini which is a good example. LH introduced an Indonesian-style spa, in this case, Javanese women's beauty and health care as well as women's health among the middle and upper classes in the African countries. She has direct connections with several officials in African countries. In Africa, a new middle class has been born and a new lifestyle has emerged, especially body care and beauty (Interview LH, 28 August 2020).

## 4 Indonesia-Africa Trade Networks: The Case of Tanah Abang

There are two models of trade networks between Indonesia and Africa. The first is a conventional trade network or trade between exporters and importers. In this conventional trade, the exporter directly sends the goods to the importer. This conventional pattern of international trade is usually carried out on a large scale so it is quite easy to fill cargo containers. They are used to or able to take care of legality issues or the

**Table 1** Models of trade diplomacy, Indonesia to Africa

| Model | Leading actor | Supporting actor | Target |
|---|---|---|---|
| FTA/PTA | Ministry of trade | Ministry of foreign affairs, embassies, private sectors | Reducing trade barriers |
| Bilateral forums (IAF, IAID) | Ministry of foreign affairs, embassies | Ministry of trade, ministry of investment, private sectors, state owned enterprise (SOEs) | Investment and trade contract |
| Trade promotion and facilitation | Ministry of trade through ITPC | Embassies | Increasing exports, particularly from SMEs |
| Business to business | Private sectors, SMEs | Ministry of Trade, Ministry of Foreign Affairs | Investment and trade contract |

Source: Authors

**Fig. 1** Conventional trade

completeness of export–import documents. Therefore, this trading pattern is usually carried out by large-scale entrepreneurs or those who already have regular customers. Not many small and medium scale enterprises (SMEs) used this model. The export of palm oil or paper from Indonesian entrepreneurs to African entrepreneurs is an example of this conventional trading model (Fig. 1).

The second is the unconventional trade model or can be referred to as the 'Tanah Abang' model. Tanah Abang is an area in Jakarta where wholesale and retail markets, especially for textile and garment products. The Tanah Abang network is interesting to be explored further because this network can involve small-scale entrepreneurs or SMEs. The analysis in this paper will focus on this trade network to see how aspects of the global production networks approach can be used (Fig. 2).

Tanah Abang is an area where many Africans, mainly from Nigeria, Mali, and Senegal live or look for merchandise in Indonesia. A large number of Africans in the Tanah Abang area can also be seen by the presence of typical African food restaurants, such as the African Food Center, at K. S. Tubun Street, Petamburan, Jakarta. The African Food Center mainly caters to Africans who miss the food from their home country. Not only does it provide food with African tastes, such as Fufu with okra vegetables and beef or chicken, but the food portions at the restaurant are also quite large, adjusting to the portions of African food. Nigerian foods are plentiful in this restaurant because many Nigerians are active in this area, especially Nigerians from the Igbo tribe. The Igbos, who come from the East region of Nigeria, are known as an ethnic with entrepreneur skills. They controlled the trade networks from Tanah

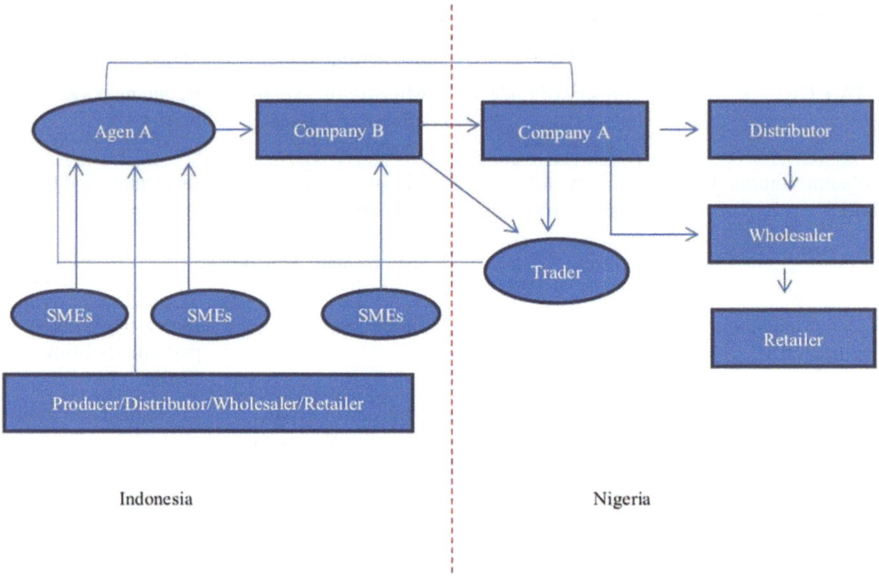


**Fig. 2** Tanah Abang network

Abang to the West African countries, not only throughout Nigeria, but also to Ghana and Cameroon (Online interview RD, July 2021).

For more than two decades, there have been many African traders from various countries going back and forth in the Tanah Abang market. They buy Indonesian products such as clothes, shoes, bags, and spices. They have established personal contacts with Tanah Abang traders and have even become regular customers. For Tanah Abang traders, the African traders, from various countries such as Nigeria, Mali, and Senegal, are no longer strangers. They seem to have become part of the Tanah Abang market. Apart from trading, they also participate in socio-religious activities in Tanah Abang. For example, traders from Mali, who actively pray in mosques around Tanah Abang and even actively donate and contribute to the restoration of the mosque. People also salute the merchants from Mali to always pray on time at the mosque. RD in an interview said that the name of Tanah Abang market is very fragrant, very well known, and very familiar among traders in Lagos, Nigeria. Tanah Abang market in Indonesia has a close business relationship with markets Lagos, Nigeria, long before economic diplomacy to Africa was officially announced by the Indonesian government(Online interview RD, July 2021).

By using several aspects of the global production networks (GPN) approach, the Tanah Abang trade network can be used as an alternative approach for Indonesia's economic diplomacy to Africa. First, this study shows important actors who are directly involved in trade between Indonesia and Africa but are not given much attention in the narrative of official economic diplomacy that is usually issued by the state. First, we have to look at the role of Igbo traders from Nigeria, who controlled the trade networks from Indonesia to West Africa. The Igbos from Eastern Nigeria have long been known to have a strong entrepreneurial spirit. They mostly control the business line, in contrast to the Hausa and Fulani who control the bureaucracy and the military in Nigeria. This difference is important to comprehend to be able to lobby properly, whether it will be directly to businessmen or formal diplomacy involving the bureaucracy and government officials. This differs based on ethnicity is also seen, for example in Kenya, which is in East Africa. In Kenya, the textile and garment trade network is mostly controlled by the Somali and Kikuyu tribes, while modern manufacturing and retail products are controlled by Kenyan Indian entrepreneurs. Diaspora or Africans who have lived in Indonesia for a long time and become agents for African importers have rarely been included as important actors in economic diplomacy to increase trade, especially from SMEs.

Part of the African diaspora in Jakarta comes from Mali. Most of them are garment businessmen. They buy from traders in Tanah Abang, or even directly to producers in Bandung, Cirebon, or other cities. Although there are many fellow Malians, they do not do business together. One person from Mali worked to deliver goods to different companies, both in Mali and in other countries in West Africa (Interview IC, 13 April 2022). Indonesia for the Malian became an ideal place to buy merchandise. The priceS are affordable, the network is already established, and the Muslim majority country also makes Malians feel comfortable coming from Africa to Indonesia (Interview IC, 13 April 2022). Although working separately, the Malians have associations in Jakarta. One of them is IC the elder. He is the owner of Sate DombaAfrika Restaurant in K. S. Tubun Street area. According to IC, it is not easy to make Malian people believe, especially about business. They will establish trade relations only with people who have been with them for a long time and are trusted. Not only garments, they will also find any ordered items requested by their company in Africa, like shoes, bags, daily items, or other household needs.

Model 2 shows how the Tanah Abang trade network connects actors in Indonesia and Africa, in this case Nigeria. The Tanah Abang trade network connects Indonesia with West Africa, but not with East or South Africa. One of the important actors is agent A. Agent A is an African who represents company A from his country. In the Tanah Abang area, there are several Africans who act as agents A. According to one of them, there are now only seven people due to the influence of the COVID-19 pandemic which has made the economy decreased (Interview EK, August 2021). One of the agents we met is a person who has lived in Jakarta for a long time, more than 15 years, so he already knows the ins and outs of Jakarta and its surrounding.

The role of agent A is to find goods demanded by traders from Africa and arrange the delivery to Africa. Many African traders came to Jakarta and Bandung to look for merchandise. They use the services of agent A to help arrange the delivery of the goods they buy to Africa. Likewise, traders in Africa can simply contact company A or agent A to find and send the goods they want. Because they have lived in Indonesia for a long time, they can easily find and get the goods ordered. They know where to buy or get the goods, whether directly from the factory, through wholesalers, or retailers in Indonesia.

Another very important factor in this trading network is company B. Company B is the company usually asked by agent A to take care of the delivery of goods, including various documents and import–export permits. They serve small and large-scale deliveries. Usually, company B would collect the goods from the buyer or book by company A. Company B sends the goods to company A. Then company A distributes the goods to traders in Africa. Before 2010, one of the companies B claimed to be able to ship more than 20 containers in a week (Interview HE, August 2021). But now, with more and more goods from China entering Africa, the company can only ship two containers per week.

Delivery of goods from company B to company A is usually done through the TanjungPriok port in Jakarta. From TanjungPriuk, these containers are then shipped to Singapore. From Singapore, the goods were transferred to a larger ship and then brought to Onne Port in Port Harcourt (Interview HE, August 2021). Many export goods from Indonesia have to pass through Singapore because large ships are not yet available in Indonesian ports. Usually, it takes about a month for the goods to arrive in Africa.

There are at least two B companies that regularly deliver goods to Nigeria. They have very close and longstanding relationships with Agent A and many African entrepreneurs. One example is the CTM company which has been serving trade between Indonesian and Nigerian entrepreneurs since 1997. Company B also facilitates Agent A and African traders so that they can get cheap accommodation while in Jakarta.

The Tanah Abang network is one of the important channels for Indonesia's economic diplomacy to Africa, especially for increasing trade for SMEs. The existence of company B and company A facilitates small-scale entrepreneurs or SMEs to trade between countries without worrying about the difficulty of processing export–import documents. The existence of companies A and B also makes international trade more efficient for SMEs because they collect from many buyers and shipping them together can reduce logistics costs.

Many of Indonesia's brands have a special place in the hearts of consumers in Africa (Interview HE, August 2021). According to HE, the demand for Indonesian goods, including from SMEs, is also quite large. However, they are constrained by the availability of dollars that can be obtained officially by African importers. With the lack of availability of dollars for imports, African entrepreneurs have limitations to import goods from Indonesia. The limited availability of dollars for Nigerian traders, for example, pushes them to buy US dollars from the black market, at a higher price, to be able to import. In August 2021, for example, the official value of 1 US dollar is 411 Naira, but they have to buy dollars at a price of around 520 Naira per US Dollar. This causes the price of Indonesian goods less competitive or more expensive for importers and consumers in Africa.

The issue of the availability of the dollar and the foreign exchange rate can be seen as a systemic problem concerning the policies and economic situation in African countries. Many African countries, such as Tanzania and Ethiopia, have serious problems regarding foreign debt and the availability of foreign exchange reserves. Meanwhile, Nigeria has a long history of dualism in the Naira exchange rate to the

US dollar between the official market and the black market. Countries with limited foreign exchange reserves and high foreign debt do not have the flexibility to provide enough US dollars for their importers.

By understanding the existing conditions, and how the issue of the availability of dollars has hampered Indonesia's trade with African countries, there is a desire to be able to trade with local currencies. As expected the actors involved in the trade network in Tanah Abang, Local Currency Settlement (LCS) expected to be used for trade between Indonesia and Nigeria. The Indonesian Embassy in Windhoek, Namibia has also expressed the same thing to facilitate small-scale traders to import goods from Indonesia. It seems that the aspirations of the actors in the field still need a process to be realized. Until now, Indonesia has only approved the use of the LCS with Malaysia, Thailand, Japan, and China.

## 5 Conclusion

Economic diplomacy is a priority for the Ministry of Foreign Affairs of Indonesia during President JokoWidodo's period. Indonesia's economic diplomacy to Africa has been conducted in several measures, such as the Indonesia-Africa Forum, Trade Expo, trade promotion and facilitation through ITPC, negotiations of FTA/PTA. No less important in economic diplomacy is the role of non-state actors, particularly from the private business sector.

Tanah Abang is an important global production site connecting Indonesia to African Market. The unconventional trade network in Tanah Abang shows the mobility of goods from Jakarta to West Africa. The trade is facilitated by export and import logistic companies in Jakarta and Port Harcourt. Garment and textile are the main commodities traded in this network. The characteristic of the traded commodity is not requiring high technology production process. Therefore, the process of upgrading process tends to operate within the chain. This is where the role social network among African takes its precedence through simplifying trading processes. This could be done by taking control of the logistic and competing for first-hand supplier.

The Iqbo tribe becomes the main player in this trade network. The Mali's especially from the Fulani Tribes also gain some benefits from the trade networks. Both of these ethnic groups have similar traditional backgrounds as an entrepreneur for their livelihood. As entrepreneur business opportunity is keyword for their relationship and network. Therefore, it is not too difficult for these cosmopolitan tribes to set broker business in Tanah Abang as well as have social and religious relationships with the surrounding neighborhood in Petamburan.

The African diaspora in Tanah Abang, Jakarta, which represents Nigerian importing companies to do business with Indonesian entrepreneurs, is important to increase the role of SMEs in trade to Africa. Indonesia's economic diplomacy strategy to Africa must pay attention to the network pattern that is formed, with various actors, business culture, and bargaining power.

## References


1. Acharya A (2008) Bandung's 1955 Asia-Africa Conference and Indonesia. Asia rising: who is leading? World Scientific, pp 51–54
2. Acharya A, Tan SS (eds) (2008) Bandung revisited: the legacy of the 1955 Asian-African conference for international order. NUS Press, Singapore
3. Acharya A (2016) Studying the Bandung conference from a Global IR perspective. Aust J Int Aff 70(4):342–357. https://doi.org/10.1080/10357718.2016.1168359
4. Amalina AAF, Novianti T, Asmara A (2018) AnalisisKinerjaPerdagangan Indonesia ke Negara PotensialBenuaAfrika. JurnalEkonomidanKebijakan Pembangunan 7(1):43–59
5. Buchan N et al (2019) Globalization and human cooperation. PNAS Proc Natl Acad Sci USA 106(11):4138–4142. https://doi.org/10.1073/pnas.0809522106
6. Coe NM, Hess M, Yeung HW, Dicken P, Henderson J (2004) "Globalizing" regional development: a global production networks perspective. Trans Inst Br Geogr 29(4):468–484
7. Coe NM, Dicken P, Hess M (2008) Global production networks: realizing the potential. J Econ Geogr 8(3):271–295. https://doi.org/10.1093/jeg/lbn002
8. Dicken P, Kelly PF, Olds K, Wai-Chung Yeung H (2001) Chains and networks, territories and scales: towards a relational framework for analysing the global economy. Global Netw 1(2):89–112
9. Dicken P, Henderson J (2003) Making the connections: global production networks in Britain, East Asia and Eastern Europe
10. Dlamini K (2019) Analysing the relevance of the New Asia-Africa Strategic Partnership (NAASP). Institute for Global Dialogue. http://www.jstor.org/stable/resrep23048
11. Erman E (2021) Gambaran umum republik bersatu tanzania, In Modal, Model, dan Memori: pembangunan Infrastructure Tanzania, Kanisius: Yogyakarta. pp 17–34
12. Ewing C (2019) The colombo powers: crafting diplomacy in the third world and launching Afro-Asia at Bandung. Cold War History 19:1, 1–19
13. Gereffi G, Korzeniewicz M (eds) (1994) Commodity chains and global capitalism. Praeger, Wesport
14. Grimalda G, Buchan N, Brewer M (2015) Globalization, social identity, and cooperation: an experimental analysis of their linkages and effects. Global Cooperation Research Papers
15. Hall PA, Soskice D (eds) (2001) Varieties of capitalism: the institutional foundations of comparative advantage. In: Academy of management review, vol 28. Oxford University Press, Oxford
16. Henderson J, Dicken P, Hess M, Coe N, Wai-Chung Yeung H (2002) Global production networks and the analysis of economic development. Rev Int Polit Econ 9
17. Indonesia Eximbank Institute danDirektoratJenderal Asia PasifikdanAfrika, KementerianLuarNegeri R.I.: Road to Africa: KajianPotensiEkonomidanRisiko Negara-Negara BenuaAfrika. Jakarta, Indonesia Eximbank Institute (2018)
18. Lee CJ (2009) At the rendezvous of decolonization the final Communiqué of the Asian-African conference, Bandung, Indonesia, 18–24 April 1955. J Interv Int J Postcolonial Stud 11(1)
19. Marthini NMA (2020) Manfaatkan Indonesia-Mozambique PTA: DorongPerdagangankeBenuaAfrika. Paparanpada Webinar Series 17 Juni 2020
20. Porter ME (1985) Competitive advantage: creating and sustaining superior performance. The Free Press, New York
21. Rahmawati VM (2019) UpayaPerluasanPasar Non-Tradisional Indonesia di KawasanAfrikaMelalui Indonesia Africa Froum (IAF). FISIP UniversitasPasundan, Thesis
22. Sabaruddin SS (2016) Grand Design DiplomasiEkonomi Indonesia: SebuahPendekatanIndeksDiplomasiEkonomi. JurnalIlmiahHubunganInternasional 12(1):69–90
23. Sabaruddin SS (2016) PenguatanDiplomasiEkonomi Indonesia Mendesain Clustering TujuanPasarEkspor Indonesia: PasarTradisionalvsPasar Non-Tradisional. JurnalIlmiahHubunganInternasional 12(2):205–219
24. Shimazu N (2014) Diplomacy as theatre: staging the Bandung conference of 1955. Mod Asian Stud 48(1):225–252

25. Sydow J, Schüßler E, Helfen, M (2022) Managing global production networks: towards social responsibility via inter-organizational reliability? In the relational view of economics: a new research agenda for the study of relational transactions, Springer. pp 133–158
26. Walker D (2005) Nervous outsiders: Australia and the 1955 Asia-Africa conference in Bandung. Hist Stud 36(125):40–59
27. Wicaksono P, Priyadi L, Erizaputri S (2019) Global production networks and social well-being: evidence from the Indonesian automobile industry. Int J Bus Soc 20(S1):107–126
28. Zeleza PT (2010) African diasporas: toward a global history. Afr Stud Rev 53(1):1–19

# Plague Mobility of Covid-19 in Upper Sembakung Mediated by Cross-Border as Materiality Actor-Network Theory (ANT)

**Puji Hastuti**

**Abstract** Not only a mere natural science-biological problem, but human mobility is also the root cause of the spread of the Covid-19 virus. The study of Anthropology of Infection Disease written by Merrill Singer confirms that disease transmission is no longer a question of natural causal biological aspects. Still, it is also tied to human socio-cultural systems, including human mobility activities in Hulu Sembakung North Borneo. Kathleen Coyne Kelly's critique of the study of mobility in "Mapping the mobility of the Plague" makes me, as a social researcher, warn to avoid getting caught up in capturing cultural phenomena that are mono-fragmented in mobile materiality. So Latour's Actor-Network Theory (ANT) analysis can solve the paradox-static problem of mobile materiality entities. The cyclical rite of Tempayan in Hulu Sembakung became an "intermediary" for the mobility of cross-border communities that revived Covid-19 into moving materiality. The Sembakung River, which flows through the Sabah region of Malaysia-North Kalimantan Indonesia, is the main route for community movements to carry out the rites uncontrolled from surveillance, which has resulted in the materiality of the virus moving freely without any "state control". Therefore, using the ethnographic method and the ANT analysis, this article will describe cross-border rites during the Covid-19 pandemic second wave and quality-measure the function of Covid-19 security control at nation-borders. The final analysis shows traditional rituals become "intermediary"—vehicles for cross-border mobility of the Hulu Sembakung community, which are "tolerated" by the state without any Covid-19 checks and control. This permeates people's mobility risks spreading the virus beyond state control due to the two countries' lack of data recording on cross-border mobility.

**Keywords** Rites · Covid-19 · Materiality · ANT · Mobility · Cross-border · North Borneo

P. Hastuti (✉)
Center for Population, National Research and Innovation Agency (BRIN), Jakarta, Indonesia
e-mail: pujisht@gmail.com

Department Anthropology, University of Indonesia, Jakarta, Indonesia



Nawawi et al. (eds.), *Managing Disruption and Developing Resilience for a Better Southeast Asia*, Springer Proceedings in Humanities and Social Sciences,
https://doi.org/10.1007/978-981-96-2116-3_44

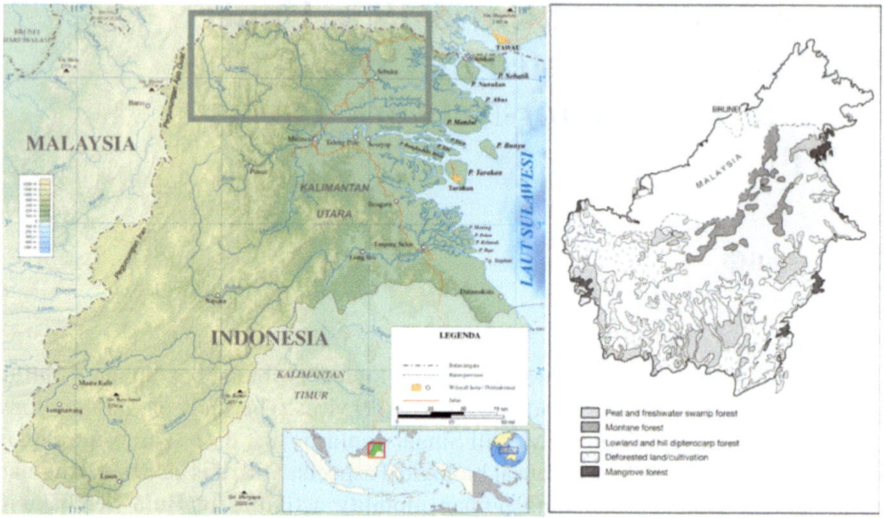


**Fig. 1** Map of North Kalimantan and the Upper Sembakung (source: commons.m.wikimedia.org[1] and [1] reprocessed by author)

## 1 Introduction

Upper Sembakung is a solitary area river path but also has contention between two border states. The area is a catchment area in a tropical forest on the border of North Kalimantan, Southeast Asia, with a mountainous topographic landscape and steep hills (montane forest). Being in a montane forest landscape forms the morphology of the catchment area of the Sembakung River, the more upstream, the more filled with rocks. Hulu Sembakung is an axis that connects the pillars of the boundary-crossing with the Pensiangan River, Sabah Malaysia, in a landscape of hilly forest wilderness extending to the northwest part of what is now known as the Nabawan area. Nabawan is now known as the administrative center of the Malaysian state of Sabah for residents who live along the Pensiangan River, formerly known as the Tiagang Sinsilog area, an old mountainous area. During the covid-19 outbreak in 2021, plague mobility was out of state control in this isolated-tense area (Fig. 1).

In the Gazetir document, an archive of data on the geographical location of the Sabah area carried out by JUPEM (Malaysian Measurement and Mapping Department), it is known that the Bukit Tiagang Sinsilog Trig has been mapped at coordinates 5° 6′ 50,644" South Latitude 116° 24′ 54,556" East Longitude [2] (Fig. 2).

---

[1] The North Kalimantan map material was obtained from Creative Commons Wikimaps at the following link https://commons.m.wikimedia.org/wiki/File:North_Kalimantan_(Indonesia)_topographic_map_-_id.svg which the author has reprocessed to obtain a focused landscape overview at the research locus in Hulu Sembakung.

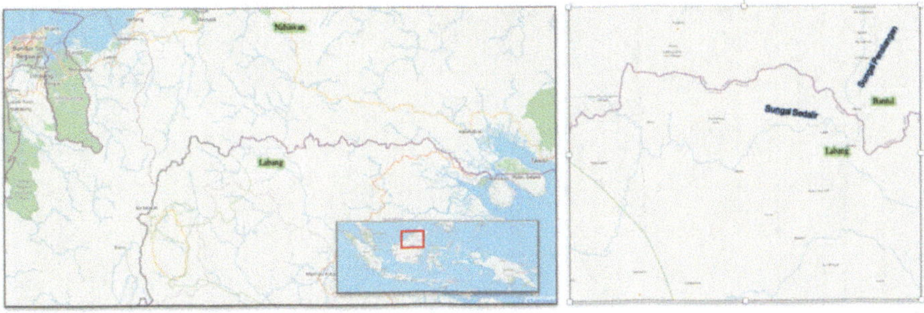

**Fig. 2** Upstream Sembakung connectivity map that penetrates National Boundary Demarcation (source: openstreetmap.org, reprocessed by author)

Hulu Sembakung River is the estuary of two major rivers, the Pensiangan River and the Sedalir River. The area at the intersection of these two rivers is known as the residential area of the Labang Village Group, which is part of the administrative area of Lumbis Pansiangan District, Nunukan Regency, North Kalimantan Province. Lumbis Pansiangan District is a new administrative area divided in 2019 after previously being part of the Lumbis Ogong District. According to the Nunukan Regency Regional Statistics 2021 document, the area of Lumbis Pansiangan District reaches 964.42 $km^2$[3]. Currently, the settlement formation in Lumbis Pansiangan District consists of 13 villages, namely Bokok Village, Bulu Laun Hilir Village, Kuyo Village, Labang Village, Lagas Village, Langgason Village, Nantukidan Village, Ngawol Village, Panas Village, Sumantipal Village, Sumentobol Village, Tambalang Hulu Village, and Tantalujuk Village [4]. Lumbis Pansiangan sub-district is an administrative area directly adjacent to the Bantul settlement—a village in the interior of the Pensiangan River, the Malaysian state of Sabah (see Fig. 3). Because the location of Lumbis Pansiangan District is a pillar of the intersection of state borders, there is a border security military post at the intersection of the Pensiangan River and Sedalir River (see Fig. 4). At this intersection, you can see the difference in the color of the water where the water flow from the Pensiangan River is more murky than the Sedalir River. Penetrating the Pensiangan River before reaching the settlement of Kg Bantul, several large pieces of rocks are considered a challenge for the people of Hulu Sembakung when crossing the river by boat, known by the community as Giram Luyu.

In August 2021, when Indonesia encountered the second wave of Covid-19, I had the opportunity to conduct pandemic research on Hulu Sembakung. Breaking the boundaries imposed by pandemic social restrictions, this study follows the local people who continue to practice the Tempayan exchange rite across the border, It explores how this cultural ritual sustains cross-border mobility despite government-imposed limitations, highlighting how the central state's authority cannot fully control the movement and resilience of borderland communities in the remote Hulu Sembakung region. Following people crossing the border and exploring how Tempayan rites move plague mobility amid the restrictions imposed and how the

**Fig. 3** Map of Kuala Hulu Sungai Sembakung (*source* openstreetmap.org, reprocessed by author)

state's central power cannot stem the mobility of the people in solitary Hulu Sembakung areas. For this reason, this paper will discuss how Materiality ANT mediates plague mobility in an isolated area. Latour framework in Actor-Network Theory (ANT) places materiality as a tool that records path nodes. The Tempayan rite as materiality is not placed in a figurative representation. The ANT analysis will reveal the contestation of actors and frame the plague mobility trajectory of the outbreak of Covid-19 in Hulu Sembakung.

## 2 Population

Residents in Hulu Sembakung were often associated with border communities living in remote areas. The distance of the Hulu Sembakung landscape from the center of the country creates the assumption that this place is an isolated residential area of the indigenous people of Kalimantan. In fact, the folklore of the sacred Tiagang Sinsilog stone found by the ancestors when traveling across the Keningau region to Pensiangan [5] is evidence that the people of Hulu Sembakung have traveled across borders through a landscape that was considered isolated for thousands of years.

The discovery of human skulls from the excavations of the Niah Cave site in Sarawak conducted by Tom Harrisson in the late 1950s became archaeological evidence that the island of Borneo is estimated to have been a human habitation since 4000 years ago [6]. Based on these findings, it is estimated that the Australoid Race reached the mainland of Borneo in the Pleistocene interglacial phase that connected

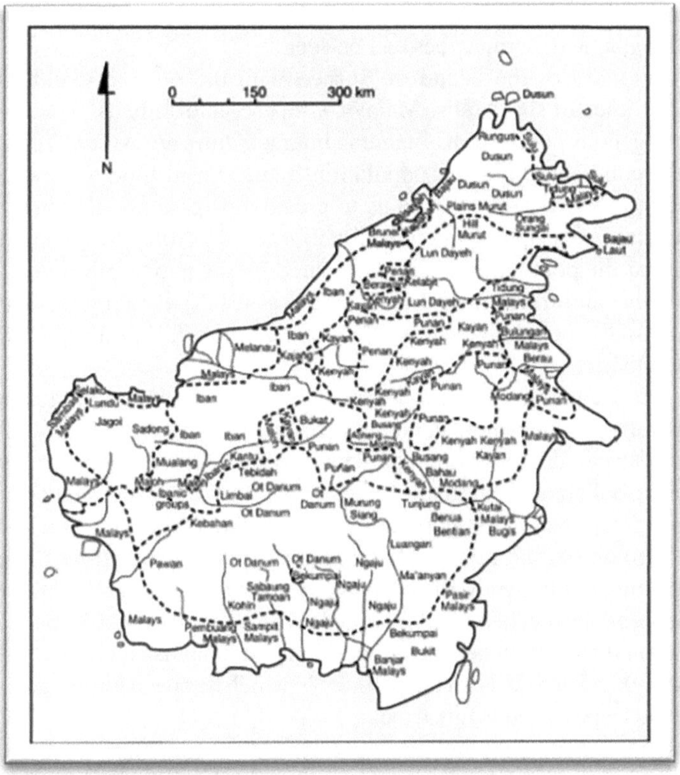


**Fig. 4** Map of the distribution of the Dayak tribe on the island of Borneo [1]

the Greater Sunda Islands with mainland Asia. Other archaeological traces found at Madai-Baturong, Sabah, reveal human life in the 28,000 who still live in the cave [7]. To meet their food needs, humans at that time wandered into tropical rainforests and approached rivers and lakes to meet their food needs. At that time, the humans who inhabited Kalimantan met their food needs by hunting and gathering. Hunting and gathering activities are very dependent on the availability of limited resources in the life niches they explore so that these conditions make them live nomadic lives.

The nomadic life was lived by humans at that time to seek and conquer territory by fighting or headhunting so that the group's food sources could be fulfilled. The search for food sources underlies the distribution or activity of human migration throughout Kalimantan. Over the centuries these humans migrated to the interior, mountains, hills, jungle forests, and river banks. Technological developments created the knowledge to make houses with materials obtained from the forest so that humans no longer depend on caves as a place to live. These humans came to be known as the Dayak, a term that refers to the original inhabitants of the island of Borneo. In Fig. 7, you can see a map of the distribution of the original inhabitants of Kalimantan by territory [1]. In the northern area of the island of Borneo, the distribution of the

Murut, Hamlet, Bajau, Bisayah, Kadahan, Tidung, Sungai Orang, Lundayeh, Malay, Punan, Bulungan, and Berau tribes can be seen.

The connectivity of the island of Borneo with the outside world was opened by the trade routes of the Arabs, Malays, Chinese, and Indians. Trading activities made the indigenous people of Kalimantan interact with various foreign nations, thus affecting the composition of the population living. From time to time, population migration continues dynamically so as to create a diverse population composition in the territorial landscape of the island of Borneo. In North Kalimantan, now, the composition of the population is not dominated by the native tribes of Kalimantan, but the Javanese and tribes from South Sulawesi [5]. These migrants from outside Kalimantan usually populate the urban landscape in North Kalimantan, as is the case in Nunukan District.

In Nunukan Regency, population density is concentrated on Nunukan Island as the administrative and business center. According to 2019 BPS data, 43.54% of the population lives centered on Nunukan Island, which actually only covers 5.21% of the total territorial area of Nunukan Regency [3]. In the population census in 2000, the Bugis made up the largest population in Nunukan Regency, namely 43.3% [8]. There has been no official update of ethnic survey data released by BPS; however, referring to Nunukan Regency BPS data, it was recorded that in 2019 the population of Nunukan Regency reached 209,922 people with a density of 14.73 people/km$^2$ [3]. The population distribution is concentrated in Nunukan District by 32.7%, followed by South Nunukan District as much as 10.84%, which has been known as a residential territorial landscape of the Bugis tribe.

In Nunukan Regency, the indigenous people of Kalimantan are actually widely spread outside Nunukan Island, namely in the mainland landscape of Kalimantan Island, namely the Krayan, South Krayan, Lumbis, Sembakung, and Sebuku areas [9]. Hulu Sembakung, until 2010, covered only the Lumbis sub-district. Administratively, Hulu Sembakung covers the territory of Lumbis Pansiangan District, Lumbis Hulu District, Lumbis Ogong District, and Lumbis District having a total population of 12,246 or about 5.83% of the total population of Nunukan [3]. Meanwhile, the Upper Sembakung landscape spans 25.6% of the total territory of Nunukan Regency as a whole. So it can be said that the population density in Upper Sembakung is still low when compared to some areas of Nunukan Regency on Nunukan Island and Sebatik.

Residents in Hulu Sembakung were often associated with border communities living in remote areas. However, over time, various government programs to reach developments at national borders have made the Hulu Sembakung area more connected. Upstream Sembakung Region, referring to the Presidential Regulation of the Republic of Indonesia No. 63 of 2020, is no longer part of remote areas of Indonesia [10]. The current development landscape makes the movement of the population easier and ultimately affects the composition of the population of Hulu Sembakung which is increasingly heterogeneous.

Accumulatively, the population of Hulu Sembakung is dominated by the Agabag tribe, although in each region the configuration is different. Lumbis District, which consists of 28 villages, is dominated by the Agabag tribe. At the administrative center of Lumbis District, namely Mansalong Village, the Agabag tribe dominates the population [11]; however, this area is also a residential landscape of the Tidung, Banjar, Bugis, Javanese, and Toraja tribes. Upstream entering the Sedalir River, there is a settlement of the Akolod tribe, known as the Panas Village Group which is now part of the administrative area of Lumbis Pansiangan District. Finally, entering the upper reaches of the Sedalir River, in the last village known as the Tau Lumbis Village, there is the Tahol tribe which is now Lumbis Hulu District.

Inland North Borneo by W. B. Pryer, in his On the Natives of British North Borneo, is considered a head hunting land [10]. The British colonial government records that until 1885, the indigenous people of North Borneo were still practicing head-hunting [12]. In this phase, the population of Hulu Sembakung carried out headhunting practices between village groups ('sampagun')—the Agabag, Akolod, and Tahol ethnic groups—with the 'one for one' rule. For example, if an Akolod person is killed by an Agabag person, the head of an Agabag person will be replaced with the head of an Agabag person in return. If you head more than one head, you are subject to the 'Ambasa' law. According to Pak Lumbis, an Agabag traditional leader at this time is known as 'Antabug' which is estimated to take place in the 1650-1900s. [13] In addition to the practice of headhunting between 'sampagun' in Hulu Sembakung, at that time, Dayak ethnic groups from other regions wandered into Hulu Sembakung so that the practice of headhunting also involved Dayak ethnic groups such as Baukan, Iban, Lundayeh—Agabag people called it Putuk and Kenyah—residents call it Ulun Nilui [14]. Unlike the war between the indigenous people of Hulu Sembakung, which has a 'one pay one' rule, the practice of headhunting with outside Dayak groups becomes an arena for consuming opposing troops.

The groups that have the origin of the 'one pay one' rule, except for the Akolod (Pemukiman Panas) and the Tahol (Pemukiman Tau Lumbis) ethnicity, are now in consensus to build the Agabag ethnic identity. This consensus is reinforced by the historical background of the ancestors of the people of Hulu Sembakung who in the past made a peace agreement at 'Batu Pengesahan', [14] an event that marked the end of the practice of headhunting between villages. Now Agabag has become an ethnic identity that is associated with the political efforts of the local elite in Hulu Sembakung to strengthen agency [13] as a marginal group in the iconicity of indigenous people. However, ethnicity in the census does not segregate group boundaries. What happened in the Batu Pengesahan Agreement became a group bond in the marriage scheme, which later incarnated in the rite of exchange of Tempayan.

## 3 Cycle Rite of Tempayan

Tempayan is archaic external object known as porselen obtained from trading tropical forest commodities with the Chinese [14]. People in Hulu Sembakung try to adopt the object function as a valuable sacred object. Its existence becomes a sacred object of the clan binding medium in every stage of the cyclical ritual of the Hulu Sembakung people. The cultural rite of "Tempayan exchange" upstream of Sembakung is in line

**Fig. 5** Hulu Sembakung map and village cluster sketch

with the theory-based "the gift" from Marcel Mauss which is "total presentation" [15]. The exchange of Tempayan became an arena of cultural rites that solidified the social cohesion of society. The implementation of the Tempayan exchange rite marks an essential stage in the cyclic life of the community into a period of population migration activities between villages in the upper reaches of the Sembakung River cross-border state (Fig. 5).

Hulu Sembakung people adhere to the patrilineal kinship system, namely the lineage following the father's side. This patrilineal relationship is usually accompanied by a patrilocal sedentary pattern. However, now, there are some families who ultimately choose a neolocal habitation pattern, namely living in a new place. Something that the locals could not leave behind until recently was the kinship bond to the extended family that was still very strong. This can be seen from the habits of residents who everywhere settle carrying one member of the wife's family or husband. Every family member in a broad family is obliged to take care of his relatives. This makes no residents of Hulu Sembakung hungry or displaced. Solidarity between relatives in the extended family is very maintained. This condition can be understood as the remains of relics of communal life in baloi aduat.

Although calculating the line based on the father's ancestry, it does not make the relationship with the male family become severed. The obligation to carry out a series of reciprocity activities still continues to occur between 'Tambuluy' and 'Ngampunon'. The division of the role of gift-giving as Tambuluy who is a guest is the party of a male family who acts as a giver of berian objects to be exchanged for women who are married. Meanwhile, 'Ngampunon' is the female family as the recipient of berian goods in return for giving female family members. In this activity, both parties have status and roles that have implications for a series of obligations that must be carried out cyclically, for life.

The activity of 'giving' involves three elements, namely the individual, the incarnation of the feelings of the soul, and society (body, soul, and social) (Mauss in [16]). All of them work in units of the tradition of reciprocity of the rite of life cycle. This tradition cannot be seen as cultural particles that are separated from each other to other aspects so that the activity of giving is termed as total service and total counter-services [17]. The rite of giving not only displays the activities of the exchange of objects, but also represents the "morals" of the units of society that exchange each other to maintain alliances between clans. In every reciprocal rite, it will certainly create a relationship between two parties, namely 'giver' and 'recipient' Hulu Sembakung people who know the reciprocal relationship between 'Tambuluy' and 'Ngapunon'. Tambuluy is a term for the family of the man who acts as a 'giver'. Ngampunon is a term for the family of women who act as 'recipients' and are obliged to repay berian who has been given with pleasant service.

The people who belong to the Tambuluy group are a broad family on the part of men, usually relatives who have a kinship of six descendants. They will be honest with each other, namely shoulder to shoulder to collect the 'pulut' requested by the female family, such as 'Tempayan', 'Agung', 'Bungkas', 'Tapih', and some other 'pulut' requested. This condition makes the nuclear family will have debts berian to broad relatives that must be reciprocated at a time when the relatives will also hold rituals. There is a kind of note to remember the 'pulut' items that have been donated by his relatives because they have a responsibility to return them. This is a consequence of reciprocal activities. As revealed by Marcel Mauss [17], a gift that is not reciprocated by the receipient may be seen as degrading, especially when the receipient has no intentation of returning it at all.

At the time the ritual is carried out, the 'Tambuluy' will come to the 'Ngampunon' place with 'Berian' objects. 'Ngampunon' has a reciprocity responsibility to serve the arrival of the 'Tambuluy' and provide entertainment so that they are happy. 'Tambuluy' comes in numbers that are not small, usually between 30 people to reach 300 people (usually at the time of the wedding ritual). It is impossible if the one who acts as a Ngampunon is only a member of the nuclear family. Servants or servants must also involve an extended family within the limit of six generations. In return for his help as a Ngampunon usually they will get a share of the goods. This division will usually be arranged by the chairman of 'Ngampunon' or parents of the female family.

Serving 'Pengasih' and 'Tuak' is a dish as a sign of respect for the 'Tambuluy'. Loving is made of fragmentation of cassava grater while the harvest can be made from rice base material. Yeast to make loving and pour or commonly referred to as burak is usually purchased from Mansalong or Keningau. But there are how many people who make it themselves. Related to the manufacture of Tuak, often residents in Hulu Sembakung also use 'Bulog' rice as the basic ingredient for making 'Tuak'.

In line with the reciprocity principle of Mauss, receiving 'Berian or Pulut' is sign of an obligation and in return, Tambuluy must receive respect from Ngampunon by drinking alcoholic drink 'Pengasih' or Tuak [15]. Alternately, Tambuluy will drink

Pengasih water in Tempayan using a straw made of bamboo. Usually, in the first and second straws Pengasih is not directly drunk, but thrown away. According to local residents, this is intended to avoid diseases that may be carried by people who have previously drunk. Tempayan that have run out of Pengasih will be poured again clear water, because the alcohol content is still contained in the dregs. Tambuluy has the task of making the loving in the Tempayan a bargain. Tempayan will be fresh in three days to a week. One week is specifically for the ritual of recitation ('Pangulunan'). The offering of all the compassionate water in the Tempayan marks the completion of the cyclical ritual.

Such is the reciprocal relationship between 'Tambuluy' and 'Ngampunon'. The activity displays not only a reciprocal relationship over the gift, but also an attempt by an individual to show his presence in a group or clan. Genetic affinity is not enough to make a person recognized as a member of a clan. Each member is required to show his role in a clan when the rite of giving is performed. The tradition of giving and receiving (gift-giving) represents the activity which Mauss [17] calls total social as wholes, that is, as where "body, soul, society" everything merges, a social totality that involves "body, soul, and society" in an integrated whole. The "total gift" from the 'Tambuluy' will be rewarded with a "total service" by the 'Ngampunon'. A total offering from one group to another. A total prestation (préstation totale) carried out in an integrated manner connected cross-border state villages in the upper Sembakung to become a cultural need for the community (Fig. 6).

Figure 7 is a kinship chart obtained from tracing an Indonesian female ego from the Desa Binter group who married a young man from Sikait, Pensiangan, Malaysia. After being traced, the grandfather of the youth came from Binter Village. In addition,

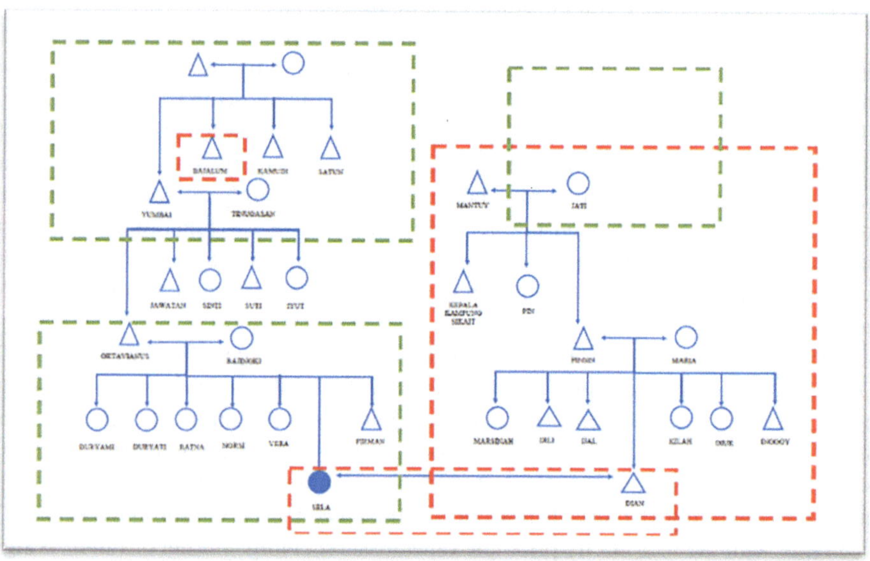


**Fig. 6** Cross-border kinship

**Fig. 7** Anti-coronavirus herb 'Limpasu'

the woman also has a relative who is the younger brother of her grandfather who lives in Fontas, a village in the state of Sabah, Malaysia. This kinship chart showed us that cyclical rites of Tempayan make social boundaries that break through state border.

## 4 Plague Mobility at Border

In August 2021, Indonesia was hit by the second wave of the Covid-19 pandemic [16]. This situation has made conditions outside the central region of Indonesia feel the real impact of the pandemic, including the hinterland of Kalimantan. In Hulu Sembakung, the situation of the second wave of the Covid-19 pandemic made the rules for social restrictions called PPKM (Pemberlakuan Pembatasan Kegiatan Masyarakat) increasingly stringent. Likewise, in Malaysia, at the time, social regulation restrictions increasingly stretch out to border areas. As Rothmüller notes, borders during states of emergency tend to materialize in various forms, including historical processes of separation through border-making practices. This condition affects cyclical ritual activities, which are often restricted or forbidden under the legal frameworks of the two nation-states, Indonesia and Malaysia [18]. This condition impacts cyclical ritual activities forbidden by two nation-states' legal regulations, Indonesia-Malaysia.

The Covid-19 case in Hulu Sembakung was initiated by the infection of dozens of PT Adikarya workers who were working on the border state-building project, PLBN

(Pos Lintas Batas Negara), in Labang Village. The workers of PT Adikarya who were mostly came from Java strengthened the fear of the people of Hulu Sembakung about the arrival of people from the center of the country as carriers of the virus. Meanwhile, the movement of local residents in Hulu Sembakung between villages is considered insusceptible to the plague. The conception of the outsider develops in following social boundaries that are not in line with national boundaries. However, this is in contrast to the residents of villages across national borders who are bound by the cyclical ritual relationship of the Tempayan.

When going into one of Hulu Sembakung villages, namely in Kalampising, in August 2021, I was to wash my own entire body with the 'Limpasu' concoction. This herb comes from local plants, usually used to acidify fish, which is believed to eliminate viruses in the body. This anti-Covid-19 concoction is hot water mixed with lemongrass leaves, oranges, lemons, and several other spices. Residents are used to eating processed fish from these ingredients, so consuming this food is considered prevention of people's habits against Covid-19. However, they feel the need to be wary of people who come from cities in Java, who are used to living in air-conditioned rooms, where they are the virus-carrying hosts. In addition to eating 'Limpasu' and believing that food served hot will eliminate the coronavirus, gardening is thought to make their bodies more immune to exposure to the Covid-19 virus. There is a local taboo to mention corona disease straightforwardly—people call it 'that disease (anu penyakitno).' Because it is believed that if you say the name of an epidemic disease, it will become more and more common. As stated by Singer in The Anthropology of Infection Disease, food habits, daily physical activities, and perceptions shaped by biosocial and biocultural contexts play a key role in preventing infectious diseases [19].

In contrast to the outsider's view as a virus carrier that must be watched out for when it is included in the social boundary of the community, the cyclic rite of Tempayan forms a movement that is still carried out even amid Covid-19 restrictions. Tempayan became 'Actant' in transmitting the cohesive population values and determinants of the social restrictions [20]. The movement of cyclic rites is separated between 'Spirit' and 'Matter' which is referred to in Tempayan as artifact material. The movement of Tempayan does not only produce a relationship that is casualty that is diadic, but the reality is also 'Indeterminacy' and 'Contingency', something termed by Peirce as thirdness [21]. For this reason, the Ferdinand de Saussurean semiological framework which only pays attention to the signifiers and signal (significance) becomes very limited to explore the phenomenon of material movement that occurs in the upstream of the Sembakung. Triadic semiotics becomes very appropriate for medium analysis that will accommodate various kinds of possible action of the relationship between 'Sign' and 'Interpretant' in the practice of Tempayan rites.

Methodologically, Actor-Network Theory or ANT Latour is flattened in restoring the disadvantages of social phenomena [22]. ANT materiality is in line with the idea of "Enframing" Heidegger [23] in carrying out "tracing" of the paths produced by the process of processing material artifact of Tempayan. Tempayan as a 'thirdness' moderates the way Peirce's thinking about the logic of signification, which displays the vulnerability of inherent from 'material artifact' to 'causality' and 'contingency', thus reducing Tempayan as a moving entity. For this reason, it is necessary to recognize how the materiality of signification is not only a factor for sign interpreters but raises and transforms the modalities of actions and subjectivity. Therefore, in triadic semiotics, the relationship between sign and object is not only 'iconicity' and 'indexicality'. The presence of thirdness allows the relationships formed by Tempayan materiality is symbolic-ontology, which can be explained by causal logic.

Thirdness in materiality of Tempayan moderates the relationship between 'sign' and 'object' into 'potentiality' and 'futurity'. If 'iconicity' has limitations in determining the actuality of the object cannot be determined by itself. While 'indexicality' is bound to the 'actual fact' that has occurred, then thirdness becomes a token that allows marking logic to display and provide vulnerability space for causal relations that occur in the cyclic rite of Tempayan. The presence of 'ontological thridness' makes semiotic ideology not only about 'sign', but also about what is called the subject of agent and its relationship with objects that manifest in the world to produce what is called a general law that governs possible instance caused from the practice of Tempayan exchange (Fig. 8).

Tempayan became a 'thirdness' who ignited the people to make a move to cross the state boundary in carrying out the customary rites. Residents who come from Sikait Village, retirement, are trying to penetrate the borders of the country to attend

**Fig. 8** Tempayan in Sikait Village, Malaysia, at marriage rites

a marriage rite in the village of Binter in the midst of the Covid-19 situation. His boat brought a Malaysian singer who filled the entertainment program to the marriage rite. Although he was arrested by the Malaysian border safety and entourage was told to return, they managed to penetrate the Malaysian border secretly to get to the village of Binter at night.

General Law through the idea of 'quali-sign' by Peirce has manifested in particular materiality co-represents/bundling with other qualities. Tempayan has become a particular material bundled with customary rites that penetrate state border even in the middle of Covid-19 social restrictions. Keane [21] refers to this condition as bundling, a term that resonates with Kopytoff's notion of the "conditions of possibility" and Appadurai's concept of the "biographx of things." These frameworks help explain how material movements become inherent to the Tempayan as an entity. Through the combination of quali-signs, the Tempayan gains 'sensuous quality'—Shifting in its relative value, utility, and contextual relevance over time. In September, the Sikait family returned to the border area to attend a death ritual called Amakan. Their journey took place during the day and involved carrying Malaysian commodit items-such as boilers, instant processed fish products, and sugar-concealed under a Tempayan. The Tempayan itself served as a quali-sign of their intention to cross the border, a symbolic gesture that had been informally acknowledged by the border milita officer (Fig. 9).

**Fig. 9** Massive crowd at death rite 'Amakan' in pandemic situation

Quali-Sign of Tempayan mediating the plague mobility also celebrated the Amakan rite in Tanjung Hulu village, which occurred during the PSBB level 3 period in Nunukan Regency. Mr. Yohanes Maluin, the vice chief of Agabag ethnic, died and created a cyclical rite to celebrate it. At that time, the Hulu Sembakung area, which was included in the administrative area of Nunukan Regency at level 3, which included the spread of the virus, was still quite virulent. A few weeks earlier, residents of Tanjung Hulu had alternately experienced symptoms of the coronavirus, such as loss of taste and smell, fatigue, fever, caught, and sore throat. However, they did not check for these symptoms at the medical center Puskesmas, so no antigen test was carried out because the disease infection was not detected. Tanjung Hulu village is still detected as a green area safe from Covid-19, and the implementation of traditional rites is still being carried out. Tanjung Hulu village was still detected as a green area safe from Covid-19, and the implementation of the rituals event is still being carried out. Even the crowded traditional rites attended by cross-district Agabag ethnic leaders, government bureaucrats, military officials, and members of the DPRD. One of the stages of the Amakan rite, namely the cockfighting event ('sabung ayam'), can still be carried out with a letter of recommendation from a traditional institution with an attention mark of the Tempayan ritual to become a representative sign for the event of cyclical rite to be legal to be carried out in Pandemic situation.

## 5 Conclusion

Tempayan has become an essential material culture for the continuity of the traditional rites of the Sembakung River community. Excluding being an object of exchange, as is the tradition of the archaic society described in The Gift, the Tempayan is a determinant of the nodes of ANT plague mobility in a pandemic situation. The existence of material culture, Tempayan, has been established in the life cycle of the people of Hulu Sembakung, North Kalimantan—Pensiangan, Sabah, Malaysia, in the plague situation. Tempayan, which is not a set of tools, does not come from indigenous material knowledge. The material things have been transformed into technology as Heidegger's phenomenological perspective shapes how we live and perceive fellow humans and other entities in the world and incarnated as moral status is potential and futurity day by day [24].

Back to the historicity, Tempayan is outsider materiality generated by the bartering activity of inland forest Borneo commodities mediated by the Tidung ethnic group since the fourteenth century in the Chinese trade chain. Even though the material object is the same, the essence of the Tempayan has been enframed by the Hulu Sembakung people in a different way from the Chinese merchants [23]. Still quoting Heidegger, the practice of revealing the people in Hulu Sembakung has been enframing the technology of Tempayan materials into traditional sacred objects [23]. The presence of Tempayan formed the way of life of the people of Hulu Sembakung, becoming a hybrid material culture that unites cross-river to cross-country communities. In contrast to the logic of regulating modern state administrative boundaries, the "way of life" for the Hulu Sembakung people, which has merged with the "moral status" of Tempayan, is "Bricolage" (Levi Strauss in Haraway [25] the population makes discoveries of technology according to their needs). In many communities, culture and sacred objects serve as key elements in fostering social cohesion. The community enframes the Tempayan as hybrid technology. The community enframes the Tempayan as a form of hybrid technology. This resonates with Donna Haraway's concept of hybrid creatures, particularly the cybrog, which she describes as a medium of liberation from fixed categories of identity and function [25]. Tempayan has brought the communities in the hinterland of Hulu Sembakung into the chain of cosmopolitan civilization into transboundary hybrid population entities.

In the Covid-19 plague situation in Hulu Sembakung, the lesson learned that could be carried out is that humans as individuals or collectives always can display the rhetoric of indeterminacy. Suppose de Abreu finds this in the condition of the temporal medium of threat from society here [26]. In that case, the author interprets the rhetoric of indeterminacy in the shape of society in contact with material technology as objects that legitimize crossing borders to attend crowd rite. Tempayan was previously a technological material originating from this Chinese trader, becoming inherent in the community's life cycle activities and creating a cohesive culture that is dynamic in Covid-19 plague situation and potentially transforms practical value in any future condition.

**Acknowledgements** I have to express gratitude to the people of Hulu Sembakung as informants who were generous to open the door and accept me as an outsider amid suspicion as a carrier of the Covid-19 virus during the pandemic. And also, I have thankfulness to BRIN and IPSH for the opportunity to fund this research with schema by research scholarship.

## References

1. MacKinnon K, Hatta G, Halim H, Mangalik A (1996) The ecology of Kalimantan: Indonesian Borneo. Ecol Indones Ser 3:287
2. JKNG, M. Dokumen Gazetir. 2–258 Preprint at (2012)
3. Nunukan BK (2021) Statistik Daerah Kabupaten Nunukan 2021. Preprint at
4. Nunukan BK (2021) Kecamatan Lumbis Hulu Dalam angka 2021
5. Arifin MB, Rijal S (2019) Bahasa Daerah di Kalimantan Utara (CV Istana Agency, 2019)
6. Barker G et al (2002) Prehistoric foragers and farmers in south-east Asia: renewed investigations at Niah Cave, Sarawak. Proc Prehist Soc 68:147–164
7. Bellwood P, Hughes P (1988) Archaeological research in south-eastern Sabah. The environmental setting (Chapter 1). Compiled and Edited by Petter Bellwood Australian National University
8. Lenggono PS (2012) "Jaringan Perdagangan Bugis" dan Pola Penguasaan Sumber Agraria di Kawasan Perbatasan Nunukan-Tawau
9. Nunukan BK (2011) Profil Kabupaten Nunukan 2011. Preprint at 2011
10. Pryer WB (1887) On the Native of British North Borneo 16:229–236

11. Suryana NK (2021) Analisis Kepuasan Kerja Dan Produktivitas Penyuluh Pertanian Di Kecamatan Lumbis Kabupaten Nunukan. Jurnal AgroSainTa: Widyaiswara Mandiri Membangun Bangsa 5:55–61
12. Fernandez C (1999) Contesting colonial discourse: rewriting Murut history of resistance in British North Borneo from 1881 to 1915. Akademika 54:81–103
13. Giddens A (1984) The constitution of society: outline of the theory of structuration. Polity Press. https://doi.org/10.2307/590448
14. Finlay R (1998) The pilgrim art : the culture of porcelain in world history the pilgrim art : the culture of porcelain in world history * In i619 Philip III of Spain made a ceremonial entrance into Lisbon 9:141–187
15. Mauss M (2002) The Gift. Routledge Classics
16. Annisa D (2021) Situasi Terkini Perkembangan coronavirus disease (COVID-19) 2 Agustus 2021. https://infeksiemerging.kemkes.go.id/situasi-infeksi-emerging/situasi-terkini-perkembangan-coronavirus-disease-covid-19-2-agustus-2021
17. Bell C (2009) Ritual theory, ritual practice. Oxford University Press
18. Rothmüller N (2021) Covid-19. Borders, world-making, and fear of others. Res Glob 3:1–9
19. Singer M (2015) The anthropology of infectious disease. Left Coast Press, Inc.
20. Latour B (1990) Technology is society made durable. In: The sociological review, vol 38, pp 103–131. Preprint at https://doi.org/10.1111/j.1467-954x.1990.tb03350.x
21. Keane W (2003) Semiotics and the social analysis of material things. Lang Commun 23:409–425
22. Latour B (2005) Reassembling the social an introduction to actor-network-theory. Oxford University Press
23. Heidegger M (1977) The question concerning technology and other essay (Translated by William Lovitt). Garland Publishing INC. https://doi.org/10.7312/vatt16696-004.
24. Risse M (2019) Human rights, artificial intelligence and Heideggerian Technoskepticism: the Long (Worrisome?) view. Preprint at 2019
25. Haraway D (1991) Simians, cyborgs, and women: the reinvention of nature. Routledge/New York
26. de Abreu MJA (2013) Technological indeterminacy: medium, threat, temporality. Anthropol Theory 13:267–284

# Guilt and Gratitude: A Comparison of Singaporean and Filipino Responses to Ilo Ilo (2013)

**Abel Agbayani Ubaldo**

**Abstract** Andrew Chen's *Ilo Ilo* (2013) is part of an increasing number of East and Southeast Asian films that examine the impact of migrant domestic work on the family structures of the host country and the migrant worker's home community. Partly autobiographical, Ilo Ilo looked into the experiences of a middle-class Singaporean family and their newly hired Filipino maid against the backdrop of the Asian Financial Crisis. Chen used the characters to explore the contradictions of a transactional transnational family, while the central conflict addressed the trauma coming from the disintegration of such a family and the hope for eventual reunification. Critically acclaimed and commercially successful, Singaporeans celebrated Ilo Ilo for its empathy, sentimentality, and rejection of the stereotyped images of domestic workers. While not a box office hit in the Philippines, the film did inspire a highly publicized campaign to reunite Chen with his Filipino "surrogate" mother. This paper will compare and contextualize these responses using the Philippines' history of exporting domestic labor to Singapore. Doing so will reveal the similarities and differences of how the home and host countries reconcile the traumas created by labor migration and how such reconciliation is dramatized and consumed in discursive forms.

**Keywords** Ilo Ilo · Trauma · Transnational family · Domestic labor

## 1 Introduction

Ilo Ilo opens with a shot of its protagonist, Jiale Lim, ordered by his teacher to clean the windows for an arriving school executive. A rebellious student, Jiale refuses to follow and bites his teacher to escape. The school informed his furious mother, Hwee Leng, who scolded and canned the boy upon returning home. Troubled by Jiale's misbehavior, Hwee Leng and her husband, Teck, decided to hire a maid who can look

A. A. Ubaldo (✉)
Ateneo de Manila University, Quezon City, Philippines
e-mail: aubaldo@ateneo.edu



Nawawi et al. (eds.), *Managing Disruption and Developing Resilience for a Better Southeast Asia*, Springer Proceedings in Humanities and Social Sciences,
https://doi.org/10.1007/978-981-96-2116-3_45

after their son while they are at work. They hired Teresa, a young Filipino domestic worker who left her child in the Philippines to earn better wages in Singapore. Jiale immediately rejected Teresa's presence, resenting the fact that he has to share his room, and by extension, his life, with a stranger.

In these first few scenes, director Anthony Chen establishes the dynamics of transnational families found in middle-class households in Singapore. Both parents work to maintain a middle-class lifestyle while child-rearing is left to contractual domestic workers from countries like Indonesia and the Philippines. Ironically, these workers also left their families behind in pursuit of higher wages and better lives. Treated as outsiders in a foreign land, domestic workers often find themselves vulnerable to systematic prejudice and abuse. Yet, some did find a 'home' abroad, forming bonds with the strangers they raised and becoming nominal members of the families they work for. They filled in the familial gaps produced by capitalism and provided motherly care and companionship for a generation of Singaporeans.

Chen himself is part of this generation. Ilo Ilo's story is inspired by the director's experiences of growing up in 1990s Singapore. Chen populated the film with images, products, and edifices that recreate and accentuate the period; from the pager and Toyota Corolla to Tamagotchi and Gardenia bread. The Asian Financial Crisis, one of the most defining events of the decade, looms in the background of Jiale's everyday life. His father lost his job, his mother became part of a pyramid scheme, and their neighbor committed suicide due to financial woes. Chen also consciously modeled the character of 'Teresa' after Teresita Sajonia, an Overseas Filipino Worker who took care of the director and his brothers during their childhood. The financial crisis forced his family to cut ties with Sajonia, who returned to the Philippines and lost all contact with her former employers. Chen described this separation as brutal, citing how the trauma of family separation influenced the film's portrayal of Singapore. Ilo Ilo weaves the social history of Singapore and the personal story of Chen to narrate and examine the experiences of a specific generation. The collapse and rebirth of Singapore during the financial crisis are framed through the lens of the formation and break up of Jiale's transnational family.

The experiences narrated in Ilo Ilo are put at the forefront of Asian film discourse when it won the Camera d'Or at the Cannes film festival. In Singapore, the press interpreted Jiale's story as a protest against Singapore's official nationalism and the film images that it produced [10]. Critics observed how Chen humanizes the characters, particularly Jiale and Teresa. The former's 'troublesome' behavior is framed not as a product of a spoiled upbringing, but as a consequence of a society trying to silence a misunderstood young soul. Likewise, Teresa's problems are never sensationalized to create emotional conflict, a deviation from the usual depiction of domestic workers as an oppressed or dangerous Other. For the Singaporean press, Ilo Ilo's departure from these cinematic conventions is a sign of the maturation of the film industry. Indeed, they cast Chen not only as a potential auteur but also as the face of Singaporean cinema's emerging 'new wave'.

In the Philippines, Ilo Ilo's success led to a very public campaign to find Sajonia, whom the press fondly referred to as 'Auntie Terry'. Major news and broadcast outlets follow Chen as he traces Sajonia's whereabouts in the province that inspired the film's title. The drama of the search for Auntie Terry also seeped into the film's reception. Local critics lauded Ilo Ilo's portrayal of Overseas Filipino Workers while also celebrating Sajonia as a national hero. Filipino audiences called the film accurate, realistic, and empowering in its premier. As Chen himself observed, despite the linguistic boundaries and foreign origins of Ilo Ilo, Filipinos seem to have embraced the film as their own [8].

## 2 Filipino Domestic Workers in Singapore

The different responses of Singaporeans and Filipinos to Ilo Ilo can be rooted in the Philippines' history of exporting domestic labor to Singapore. In the 1970s, the Philippine government began a labor exportation program to offset the country's high unemployment rate. At first, male workers comprised the majority of labor outflows. Over time, labor exportation undergoes a period of feminization. In 1975, only 12% of Overseas Filipino Workers are women. By 2002, the percentage has already increased to 73% [9]. A significant number of these female workers are engaged in domestic labor. Singapore is among the top destinations of Filipino domestic workers due to its proximity, both geographically and culturally, to the Philippines. At the same time, there is also a strong demand for Filipino domestic workers in Singapore, where the Filipinos' proficiency in speaking English is highly valued by the Singaporean middle-class. Indeed, a study conducted by [13] suggests that approximately 86% of migrant maids in Singapore are Filipinos.

Reports of abuse and maltreatment of Filipino domestic workers encouraged the Philippine government to implement a deployment ban in 1988, 1990, and 1991. Countries interested in employing Filipino domestic workers were required to negotiate the terms of employment with the Philippine government before the ban could be lifted. While it did force destination countries like Singapore to improve the employment conditions of Filipinos, it also encouraged foreign employers to hire domestic workers through illegitimate employment channels. This made it harder for the Philippine government to monitor the working conditions of Filipino domestic workers, making them more susceptible to exploitation.

The status and welfare of Filipino domestic workers became a major diplomatic issue in 1995 when Singaporean authorities sentenced Flor Contemplacion, a Filipino housemaid, to death for the murder of a three-year-old Singaporean boy and his Filipina nanny. Despite evidence of her innocence and negotiations between the Philippine and Singaporean governments, Contemplacion was executed by hanging on March 17, 1995. The case created a public backlash in the Philippines, as Filipinos blamed the government for failing to protect domestic workers like Contemplacion. Friendly relations and economic cooperation between the Philippines and Singapore also deteriorated. The Philippines implemented another deployment ban against Singapore and canceled all scheduled bilateral exchanges. At the same time, Singaporean investments in the Philippines dropped by 94.3% in the aftermath of Contemplacion's execution [4]. The situation was so bad that the Philippines and Singapore considered severing diplomatic ties. While relations eventually normalized, the case soured the bilateral cooperation between the two countries for several years.

It is worth noting that Ilo Ilo is set several years after Contemplacion's execution, and it provided glimpses of the living conditions of migrant domestic workers. Chen used the character of Teresa to present the structural and systematic injustices experienced by domestic workers in Singapore. She must surrender her passport to Hwee Leng, a common practice at the time that ensures maids will not run away from their employers. In the next scene, she is apprehended because of Jiale's mishaps in a bookstore. Chen also used Lucky Plaza, a popular shopping mall and meeting hub for Filipinos, as a setting for some of the film's key scenes. Here, the director observes how domestic workers navigate Singaporean society and culture. They spend their day-offs meeting with friends, sending remittances and souvenir boxes back home, hanging out in food stalls, and forming romantic relationships with their compatriots. Many accept part-time gigs to supplement their earnings. The last one is a minor plot point, as Teresa works as a part-time hairdresser in a Filipino-owned salon. The film made it clear that this is illegal because migrant workers cannot work part-time and Teresa risks repatriation. Nevertheless, she has no choice because her salary is not enough for the needs of her family in the Philippines.

Despite showing her problems, Chen did not use Teresa's presence in the film to sensationalize the plight of domestic workers. Teresa is never victimized or portrayed as a powerless character. She can stand up for her own when bullied by Jiale. Teresa even broke through the boy's delinquent exterior and provided motherly guidance and wisdom. Teck and Hwee Leng also treated her as a close confidant for their concerns and problems. Chen presented her as an integral part of the Lim family. But the director also ensures that the barriers that differentiate Teresa from her employers are visible. In one hilarious sequence, Teresa awkwardly follows the Lims as they perform a death rite for Jiale's grandfather. Several scenes later, she is forced to sit at a separate table when the clan had a family reunion. These scenes illustrate the existence of cultural and structural barriers that define domestic workers as an outsider. Teresa may be welcomed as a member of the transnational family, but she is still an outsider in Singapore.

Teresa's status as an outsider highlights her similarities to Jiale. Both suffer from sublime prejudices and suspicions that position them as an 'Other' in Singaporean society. The motherly bond that they formed is not just a consequence of Teck and Hwee Leng's absence but a product of their shared experience of being outcasts in a strict disciplinarian community.

## *2.1 Maids in Singaporean Cinema*

Chen's characterization of Teresa goes against the typical representation of domestic workers in Singaporean cinema. Maids are often depicted as passive and oppressed characters whose presence accentuates the characteristics of their employers. In Li Lin Wee's '*Gone Shopping*' (2007), an Indonesian domestic worker works for an annoying woman who tends to display her wealth to her peers. The maid's presence enhances her employer's status and communicates the privilege she enjoys. In Kelvin Tong's *The Maid* (2005), the director presented the harsh and violent nature of the Teo family when their Filipino domestic worker, Rosa, discovered that they murdered their former maid to cover up the sexual abuse that happened within the household. Woo Yen Yen and Colin Goh took a different approach in *Singapore Dreaming* (2006). The domestic worker in the film, Pinky, has a very cordial relationship with Mrs. Mei Teo, her employer. Their relationship changed when Mrs. Teo accused her of theft. Pinky fought back and proved her innocence. The guilt over the incident forced Mrs. Teo to a path of self-reflection and self-discovery. In the films mentioned, the domestic worker's relationship with her employer reflects the problems of contemporary Singapore, from conspicuous consumption (Gone Shopping) to class and ethnic tension (Singapore Dreaming and The Maid).

Singaporean cinema has always been defined by how it engages the issues stemming from its position as a transnational link to Western modernity and Easter tradition [12]. While this position brings economic progress to Singapore, it also disenfranchises vulnerable sectors of the population such as foreign workers. The role of Singaporean cinema then is to provide possible solutions to the contradictions of the nation. In this sense, Singapore's local film industry embodies the characteristics of a national cinema. According to [11], national cinemas create images of the nation that mobilize subjects into recognizing their membership in the national community. These images also resolve contradictions that may refute established nationalist myths. In the case of Singapore, these myths revolve around the idea that national discipline, ethnic harmony, and the rule of law lead to national progress. The execution of Flor Contemplacion exposes the gaps in Singapore's official nationalism. The case exposed the lack of transparency in the judicial process and the structural problems that foreign domestic workers faced. It dilutes the narrative of economic progress that Singaporean nationalism promotes. It is not surprising then that there is a subsequent attempt to visualize the plight of domestic workers in the 2000s. Their inclusion allows filmmakers to tackle issues about a disenfranchised community without challenging the narratives that serve as the foundation of Singaporean identity.

Nevertheless, how domestic workers have been portrayed in Singaporean films reinforced their secondary status in Singaporean society. The minor roles given to domestic workers in Gone Shopping and Singapore Dreaming mirror their real-life subordination. Likewise, the sensationalized violence in The Maid strengthens the image of a weak and powerless migrant worker. In this sense, the Otherness of migrant domestic workers in these films suggests that they are still outside the bounds of national belonging.

It is worth mentioning that Singapore has been conscious of its international image ever since Contemplacion's execution. As a result, the local media became wary in its portrayal of foreign workers. There is also a recognition that Singapore has and will continue to be dependent on immigrant workers, especially concerning domestic labor. In this case, cinema must include foreign domestic workers in Singapore's national narrative. But it must also avoid stereotyped images that limit national discourse about domestic workers. Ilo Ilo's benign representation of the Lim family captures this zeitgeist. It represents a national cinema that embodies the spirit of a more transparent, sympathetic, and inclusive Singapore. Indeed, the film ended with Teresa leaving the family and Hwee Leng giving birth to Jiale's sister. Framed within the national narrative, this signifies the birth of a new Singapore after a tumultuous decade. This Singapore is built not just by Singaporeans, but also by the toil and hard work of migrant workers.

On the surface, the response seems to embody the idea of liberal guilt. Ellison (1996) described liberal guilt as a "*symptomatic and embarrassed position that nobody wants to occupy.*" It is a collective performance of guilt for the colonial and racial violence committed in the past. Originating from the Civil Rights Movement in the United States, the concept became more mainstream in the 1980s and 1990s. Since then, the showcase of liberal guilt has extended to include the recognition of violence committed against a disenfranchised group. Foreign domestic workers are a disenfranchised group in Singapore. Because of this, gestures towards Ilo Ilo can be interpreted as a performance of remorse toward their victimization. Performative guilt and victimhood culture are part of post-modern multiculturalism. As a product of local and global capital, Chen's film can adopt such narratives.

Local interpretations of the film suggest otherwise. John Lui of the Strait Times argued that Ilo Ilo's strength lies in its ability to humanize both sides of the economic divide [5]. Anthony Kao of Cinema Escapist observed that the film criticizes Singaporean nationalism and the loss of passion and soul of its members in pursuit of national progress. For him, Teresa represents the more intimate side of the city-state concealed by the desire for academic excellence and obedience to the law (*Review: Ilo Ilo (Singapore 2013),* 2015). These interpretations do not emphasize remorse or correcting societal sins. Instead, they recognize how transnationalism shaped a generation of Singaporeans' understanding of the nation. The general theme of these interpretations is the nationalization of Singapore's transnationalism.

Chen did imply that there is a sense of guilt present in the film. In one of his interviews, Chen lamented how the transactional nature of hired domestic labor leads to the 'brutal erasure' of one's sense of family [8]. In the same interview, the director claimed that Ilo Ilo is inspired by his own experience of pain, of trying to reconnect with repressed memory. In this sense, the 'guilt' transpiring in the film is more personal and intimate rather than performative. It connects to a specific generation that shares Chen's memory of growing up with foreign maids functioning as their surrogate mothers. Such guilt does not criticize like its Western counterpart. Instead, it is a means for a generation to reconcile their transnational childhood with their national identity.

## 2.2 Domestic Workers as Cinematic Heroes

Just like in Singapore, domestic laborers are a fixture in Filipino films. Their depiction ranges from sassy gossipers to innocent provincial girls. Domestic workers, however, are usually depicted as tragic mothers. They face abuse and exploitation abroad to provide for an uncaring family. Joel Lamangan's *The Flor Contemplacion Story* (1995) established this stereotype. The film reenacts the plight of Contemplacion from her impoverished life in the Philippines to her execution in Singapore. Contemplacion became a saint-like figure who endures even if her husband is having an affair and her children become more emotionally distant. Rory Quintos' *Anak* (2000) investigates the experience of Josie, an Overseas Filipino Worker who returned to the Philippines after working as a nanny in Hong Kong. While initially happy, she eventually discovered that her children now consider her a stranger, but she persevered to mend their strained relationship. Tikoy Aguiluz's *Bagong Bayani* (1995) elevate Filipino domestic to the status of an unsung hero. The film suggests that the sacrifice of domestic workers abroad is the best representation of Filipino heroism. The image of sacrifice, endurance, fortitude, and martyrdom in the films mentioned serves as the primary template of how Filipinos see domestic workers working abroad.

Popular imaginings of a martyr mother can be traced back to religious theatrical plays called *senakulo* [2]. It is a dramatic adaption of the Pasyon, a Philippine epic narrative that chronicles the passion, death, and resurrection of Christ. Christ's mother, the Virgin Mary, is one of the protagonists of the senakulo. Throughout the play, Mary must endure the pain of seeing her son suffer and die. Her endurance is her primary virtue. In the Philippines, Mary manifests the image of an exemplary mother. Her relationship with Christ is the ideal image of a motherly bond. Mary is a good mother because of her martyrdom. Christ is a good son because he shows *utang na loob* (debt of gratitude) to her mother. In the Filipino context, one cannot repay this debt. Children honor their utang na loob by showing gestures of gratitude to their parents. Failure to do so will suggest that a person is *walang hiya* (shameless) and *walang utang na loob* (ungrateful). For Filipinos, gratitude is more than a showcase of respect. Gratitude is the recognition of parental worth. It is the fulfillment of parenthood.

Folk Catholicism's influence on Philippine culture allows the translation of religious images to the national cinema. The Virgin Mary functions as the model for cinematic images of good motherhood. A mother's martyrdom is her virtue. The more she suffers for her children, the more she proves her nobility. National cinema echoes this narrative through the plight of the domestic workers working abroad. They sacrifice their well-being for their family while the remittances they send back home help bolster the national economy. They also function as ambassadors of Philippine culture. They take care of children abroad and teach them Filipino songs, values, and traditions. By mothering the foreign, Filipino domestic workers connect the Philippines to the rest of the world. But despite all their contributions, the needs of domestic workers are often neglected by the state. National cinema transforms domestic workers into folk-like heroes by presenting them as martyr mothers. As both tragic and heroic figures, their stories become an avenue for the expression of national pride and disappointment.

At first glance, the narrative of martyr motherhood is not present in the Filipino response to Ilo Ilo. The local press focused on the film's universal themes and Teresa's positive characterization. In an article for the Philippine Daily Inquirer, columnist Rito Asilo observed that the film refused to treat Terry as a 'self-effacing domestic helper'. Asilo writes, "*Ilo Ilo has "a lot of memorable dramatic highlights that schmaltz for something thoughtful and provocative*" [1]. Ricky Lo of Philippine Star Global agrees while also praising Ilo Ilo's universality. Lo pointed out that Ilo Ilo's story and themes make "*any viewer, whether of Filipino or other nationality, tear up*" [3]. Both argued that Chen effectively narrated the plight of domestic workers without taking away their dignity.

The narrative that completely captured the Filipinos' imagination has ties to Chen's search for Teresa Sajonia. The local press followed the director as he searched through Ilo Ilo for his former nanny. The provincial government and private entities assisted Chen until they located Sajonia in the town of San Miguel. Their reunion became news in the Philippines, occupying the front pages of popular broadsheets like the Philippine Star and Philippine Daily Inquirer. Chen brought Sajonia to Ilo Ilo's premiere in Singapore. In the Philippines, popular broadcast outlets refer to her as a new hero, effectively making Sajonia the face of Overseas Filipino Workers.

Cinematic imaginings of domestic workers shaped this narrative. The press described Sajonia's life after working in Singapore to be filled with hardship and poverty. She never had children of her own, suffered from poor health, and did not have enough savings to live a comfortable life. Worse, the nephews whose education she helped finance offer no financial help. In this sense, Sajonia's experiences fit the image of the suffering mother. Chen is the returning son who fulfills Sajonia's motherhood. The director showed that he is grateful to his 'surrogate' mother. Sajonia's sacrifices are not in vain because Chen grew up to be a person with utang na loob. Their reunion becomes the completion of Sajonia's motherhood.

Chen and Sajonia's reunion also came at a time of strengthening diplomatic relations between the Philippines and Singapore. Bilateral cooperation between the two countries improved with multiple high-level exchange visits from 2000 to 2015. During this period, Singapore became the Philippines' fifth-largest export market. More importantly, Filipinos standing in Singapore also improved. Professionals and skilled workers began to replace Filipino domestic workers in Singapore's labor market. As of 2015, 60% of Filipinos working in Singapore are professional and skilled workers [7]. Likewise, the average wage of Filipino domestic workers in Singapore also improved. The Philippine embassy set the minimum wage of Filipino domestic workers in Singapore to be $550. The average salary of new recruits is $592 while those with experience earn $638. Experienced domestic workers transferring from another country to Singapore have an average monthly wage of $709 [6]. Overall, the monthly earnings of Filipino domestic workers are higher than their Indonesian and Sri Lankan counterparts.

Framed within the national narrative, Chen and Sajonia's motherly bond constitute the strong relations that Singapore and the Philippines forged decades after Contemplacion's execution. For Filipinos, Chen represents a grateful Singapore that recognizes the importance of the Philippines and Filipino domestic workers. Much like in the senakulo, the reunion of Chen and Sajonia represents a narrative of redemption.

The heroic sacrifices of domestic workers are vindicated while both the Philippines and Singapore are redeemed.

## 3 Nations and Domestic Workers

Ilo Ilo is a film that narrates the transnational experience. It weaves the narratives of different nationalities, tells its story through multiple languages, and engages the impact of a globalizing world on the family. Its transnationality is distinctly Singaporean, but Ilo Ilo's depiction of the everyday life of the Lim family is easily relatable. It is not surprising then that the film's appeal goes beyond its home country. Ilo Ilo's humanity knows no borders.

Despite this, narratives embedded in national cinema molded the public reaction to the film. In Singapore, the desire to integrate migrant workers, specifically foreign domestic workers, into the national narrative shaped the Singaporean response to Ilo Ilo. This response is a product of the problems concerning the treatment of foreign domestic workers that Singapore experienced in the 1990s. At the same time, the film appeals to a generation of middle-class Singaporeans whose transnational experience structured the definition of Singaporean identity. They wanted to depart from how Singaporean national cinema presents domestic workers. Ilo Ilo is the manifestation of this departure.

In the Philippines, the image of the martyr mother and the national experience of exporting labor coalesced to create the cinematic images of domestic workers. Filipino films often depict domestic workers as tragic figures whose redemption lies in the gratitude of their children and the nation. The Filipino reaction to Ilo Ilo is an extension of this tradition. Filipinos saw Chen's search for Teresita Sajonia as a gesture of gratitude. Chen himself becomes the personification of Singapore. For Filipinos, the success of his film on the international stage expresses the world's recognition of the sacrifices of Filipino domestic workers. Thus, the discourse surrounding Ilo Ilo became a narrative of redemption. For Filipinos, this is not just redemption for domestic workers. It is the redemption of the nation itself.

Reactions to Ilo Ilo suggest that the importance of domestic workers for the state goes beyond the labor and remittance that they provide. Both in the Philippines and Singapore, domestic workers have become the embodiment of the national images that the state wanted to project. Their experiences, both positive and negative, serve as a vehicle for the expression and reproduction of national ideologies. Through cinema, the story of the domestic workers becomes the story of the nation.

## References

1. Asilo RP (2013) Filipino migration tales vie for Oscar honors. INQUIRER.net. https://entertainment.inquirer.net/114343/filipino-migration-tales-vie-for-oscar-honors

2. Deocampo N (2007) Cine: Spanish influences on early cinema in the Philippines. Anvil Pub
3. Lo R (n.d.) *Anthony Chen: nothing will be the same as Ilo Ilo.* Philstar.com. Accessed 27 Apr 2022, https://www.philstar.com/entertainment/2016/06/14/1592603/anthony-chen-nothing-will-be-same-ilo-ilo
4. Lucero JJ (1998) Philippine labour migration: critical dimensions of public policy. Institute of Southeast Asian Studies
5. Migration (2013). Film review: Ilo Ilo is a heartland tale from the heart | The Straits Times. www.straitstimes.com, https://www.straitstimes.com/singapore/film-review-ilo-ilo-is-a-heartland-tale-from-the-heart
6. Network TSTN (2016) Bosses in Singapore must now pay Filipino maids at least $550 a month. INQUIRER.net. https://globalnation.inquirer.net/135340/bosses-in-singapore-must-now-pay-filipino-maids-at-least-550-a-month
7. Overview of Philippines-Singapore Relations - Embassy of the Philippines in Singapore (2018) https://www.philippine-embassy.org.sg/about-us-2/overview-of-philippines-singapore-relations/#:~:text=An%20estimated%20200%2C000%20Filipinos%20live
8. Rose S (2014) Ilo Ilo director Anthony Chen: "a lot of maids have forsaken their own children." The Guardian. https://www.theguardian.com/film/2014/may/01/ilo-ilo-director-anthony-chen-interview
9. Sayres N (n.d.) An analysis of the situation of Filipino domestic workers ILO special action programme to combat forced labour: mobilizing action for the protection of domestic workers from forced labour and trafficking in Southeast Asia. https://www.ilo.org/wcmsp5/groups/public/---asia/---ro-bangkok/---ilo-manila/documents/publication/wcms_124895.pdf
10. Shen KX (n.d.) Minoritizing sinophone cinema? Relocating Ilo Ilo through the trans/national lens of an independent film [Review of Minoritizing Sinophone Cinema? Relocating Ilo Ilo through the Trans/national Lens of an Independent Film].
11. Shohat E, Stam R (2014) Unthinking Eurocentrism: multiculturalism and the media. Routledge, Taylor & Francis
12. Uhde J, Yvonne NU (2010) Latent images: film in Singapore. Ridge Books
13. Yeoh BSA, Huang S, Gonzalez J (1999) Migrant female domestic workers: debating the economic, social and political impacts in Singapore. Int Migr Rev 33(1):114–136. https://doi.org/10.1177/019791839903300105

# Halal Tourism Development in Improving the Social Welfare of Indonesian Muslim Community in Taiwan

**Rita Pawestri Setyaningsih and Ety Rahayu**

**Abstract** This study focuses on how the Indonesian Muslim community in Taiwan responds to create welfare for themselves in the context of Taiwan Halal Tourism development. Though Taiwan has developed its Halal tourism industry, the Indonesian Muslim Community has faced some problems including in finding halal foods. However, there are also opportunities to empower themselves to achieve welfare, by creating apps or information in social media that are beneficial for the individual creator and Muslim community in Taiwan in general. It is argued that despite the difficulties they face, the Indonesian Muslim community in Taiwan has also played a role in developing Taiwan halal tourism. They share their good experiences of having halal foods and Muslim friendly environment on social media. They also create halal apps to help Muslims find halal restaurants, or check halal ingredients of products available in the market. This research aims to analyze the kind of problems they face and how to manage them; the kind of needs that must be met; and the kind of opportunities that are available to empower themselves. This is qualitative research based on secondary and primary data. Data is obtained by on-line interviews with some Indonesian Muslim communities in Taiwan.

**Keywords** Halal tourism · Taiwan · Welfare · Indonesia Muslim Community

## 1 Introduction

Currently, a lot of countries in the world, both the Muslim-majority and Muslim-minority countries have developed a halal tourism industry. Taiwan, among others, has also developed the Muslim-friendly tourism industry, also well known as

R. P. Setyaningsih (✉) · E. Rahayu
Research Center for Area Studies, National Research and Innovation Agency (BRIN), Jakarta, Indonesia
e-mail: rita003@brin.go.id

Department of Social Welfare Studies, Social and Political Sciences Studies, University of Indonesia, Depok, Indonesia



Nawawi et al. (eds.), *Managing Disruption and Developing Resilience for a Better Southeast Asia*, Springer Proceedings in Humanities and Social Sciences,
https://doi.org/10.1007/978-981-96-2116-3_46

the Halal tourism industry. Its development is so fast which can be seen from the increasing level of achievement. According to the Global Muslim Travel Index (GMTI) published by International Mastercard, among the Non-Organization of Islamic Cooperation (OIC) countries, Taiwan that in 2015 ranked 10th as the most Muslim-friendly tourism destination, jumped into ranked 2nd in 2021. Hence, within six years, the performance of Taiwan's halal tourism industry has increased significantly and must be appreciated.

Two aspects that become the focus in the development are halal certification and creating Muslim-friendly environment. To provide halal foods, the Taiwan authority has encouraged owners of restaurants both Muslim and non-Muslims to get halal certification. Along with the increasing number of halal certification bodies in Taiwan, the number of halal-certified restaurants increased significantly. In 2020 there were 276 certified restaurants and accommodations across the whole of Taiwan. Besides, availability of the halal manufactured foods products has also increased. More and more foods with halal-certified logos are available in some conveniene stores or supermarkets in Taiwan. However, Indonesian Muslim communities in Taiwan still find some difficulties in finding out the halal food [13]. Hence this research tries to identify what kind of problems have Indonesian Muslim community faced? What do they need? How do they cope with these problems to achieve their welfare? This paper argues that when facing difficulties, the community will try to find solutions to achieve their welfare.

In the global era, the role of mass media is vital. It does not only act as a source of information but is also used to direct the goals of community empowerment and development ([7]: 40). The mass media include newspapers, magazines, radio, books, television, and the internet. Besides, mass media is also important as a tool for social change and societal change. Due to the importance of the role of the mass media, every individual must be literate in the mass media. Through mass media, every individual can take advantage of both as a medium of entertainment, information, and learning media.

This research is a follow-up to my previous study on the "Taiwan Halal Tourism: Policy and Practice.[1]" This research focuses on the Indonesian Muslim community in Taiwan, which includes workers, students, and professionals. While aspects of the development of the Taiwan halal tourism industry will be focused on availability of the halal foods. Among the other Muslims in Taiwan, the Indonesian Muslims community shares the largest number. Related to the development of the Taiwan halal tourism industry, they can be categorized as domestic/local tourists whose needs should be catered or facilitated. Meanwhile, halal food constitutes a primary need for Muslim. The restaurant sector is one of the most significant sectors relevant to Muslim tourists [30]. The availability of halal food is one of the mandatory elements in the development of halal tourism [18, 23].

This article is organized into several subsections. After the introduction, it will discuss some concepts. Then it is followed by the development of Taiwan's halal tourism industry and the Indonesian community in Taiwan. After that, it will discuss

[1] Sponsored by The Posco TJ Park Foundation-Korea, 2018.

some difficulties that the Indonesian Muslim community has faced, how they manage them, what kind of needs should they meet, and finally kind of opportunities that are available to empower themselves.

## 2 Research Method

This is qualitative research in which the data was obtained via literature study and interviews. All of the interviews were conducted online, since that time was still under pandemic COVID-19, thus it did not allow us to do field research in Taiwan. In total within November 2021, we interviewed 10 Indonesian people, consisting of 1 person from an NGO, 4 students, and 5 professionals. They mostly were residing in Taiwan, but 2 of them have returned to Indonesia. All of the informants were people who understood the issue and the situation of the halal industry development in Taiwan. They were selected based on our previous knowledge of the halal tourism industry development in Taiwan. The length of the interviews was about 1.5 hour, using an interview guide. Besides, some of them were consumers and producers of halal food, some involved in starts-up related to Halal Apps, and the other was the PIC of the Halal Information Center of the Indonesian Muslim Student Association in Taiwan. We made three different classifications of the questions based on the type of the interviewee, including the problems faced by the Indonesian Muslims in Taiwan; what they need related to halal foods, and problems in managing the existing Apps related to halal.

In addition, in December 2021 one of us also attended three of four times of the online trainings on the Taiwan Halal Awareness (THA). The trainings were organized by the Department of Halal Information Center (HIC) of the Indonesian Muslim Student Association in Taiwan (FORMMIT). The first training was held on December 5, 2021, on "The Innovation of the "Halalin Apps" development to increase the awareness toward Halal products in Taiwan". The second one was held on December 11, 2021, on "how to select foods and *syiar* strategy of halal food in Taiwan". The third training was carried out on December 19, 2022, on the "Halal Guideline and introduction to halal products." The data was analyzed using descriptive analysis and the social welfare approach.

## 3 Concepts

### *3.1 Concept of Halal Tourism*

In Islam, halal means allowed by Islamic way (Syariah Law) [37]. It is not only related to food and beverages but also various aspects of life [16], including the way to behave, the way to get sustenance, the way to dress, etc. The opposite term of halal is haram, which means not allowed by Islamic Law. Hence, any kind of activities that are not allowed by Islamic law is not halal. The term halal in which in Islam refers to moral behavior that covers all areas of life is an important concept in the motivation and attitude of a Muslim [36].

In defining halal tourism, there are two approaches that are commonly used. First, namely the general approach which assumes that halal tourism is the same as religious tourism—Islamic tourism [31], or Sharia tourism ([11]: 29). For example, Duman [12] defines Islamic tourism as tourism activities by Muslims that originate from Islamic motivations and are realized according to Sharia principles. Carboni and Idrissi Janati [9] define halal tourism as tourism that is in accordance with Islam, involving Muslims who are interested in maintaining their personal religious habits when they are traveling. Meanwhile, Djakfar [11] defines it as tourism carried out according to the Sharia perspective because in the tourism environment is sought to avoid things that are forbidden. However, some researchers use the two terms halal tourism interchangeably with halal hospitality, Syaria tourism, Islamic tourism, and Muslim tourism [16, 28]. Even though the two have different meanings, using them interchangeably can lead to confusion [8]. Religious tourism or Islamic tourism is any type of tourism that is partially or exclusively motivated for religious/religious reasons [3, 19]. According to Thomson Reuters, as quoted by Djakfar [11], religious tourism is only 1/8 of the total halal tourism market which reached USD 169 billion in 2016.

The second approach assumes that halal tourism is similar to general tourism but there are wider services for Muslim visitor [9, 18, 22, 27]. Halal tourism is defined as travel intended for recreation, leisure or social reasons to understand culture and glorify God's creation [36]. While Battour and Ismail [8] simply defines it as a tourism object or action that is allowed according to Islamic teachings to be used by Muslims in the tourism industry. Thus, this is actually similar to nature tourism, historical tourism, etc., but is framed in a halal style. Halal tourism is a variety of tourism activities that are supported by various facilities and services from the community, entrepreneurs, and government (central and regional) in accordance with sharia principles. This article applies the second term of definition.

In halal tourism, every activity carried out while Muslim visitors (no matter where they come from, both domestic or foreign countries) are in tourist destinations needs to be facilitated to meet their needs, so that they can travel and worship at the same time. Mastercard-Crescentrating [23] categorizes three things that are mandatory, recommended, and good if they exist.

a. Must meet the following elements, i.e.: availability of halal food, worship facilities, toilets with available water and no Islamophobia. Some of the elements above are obligatory as a minimum element of halal tourism.
b. Recommendations that should be fulfilled i.e., the existence of social causes, services during the month of Ramadhan and experiences with local Muslims; and

c. Good if exists: a recreation room with privacy, and no non-halal services. That would be nice if these elements are available, but there is no obligation to provide this.

Hence, it is clear that the availability of halal food is a must in the development of the halal tourism industry. Although not all Muslims have similar needs, the availability of halal food constitutes as vital [6]. Halal food is the most important service sought by Muslim tourists when traveling, because this halal principle is perceived as being able to provide a guarantee of quality, safe, healthy, and clean halal products/services at a satisfactory level [20]. In the halal tourism industry, it becomes a factor that attracts tourist destinations and has an impact on tourist attitudes and behavior [36]. Nonetheless, acceptance rates of different levels of halal food assurance vary widely among Muslim travelers [18, 23]. Therefore, having food outlets that are halal guaranteed and easy to find, will ease Muslim tourists and this is the key to reducing suspicious attitudes ([23]: 15) or anxiety (Dugan in [18]: 2). Halal is one of the important attributes for tourist satisfaction with halal hospitality.

Related to food, Islam forbids everything that is prohibited by the Qur'an[2] and Hadith. The Qur'an forbids Muslims from consuming carrion, blood and swine, and what is offered to other than Allah, and that which is strangled, and that which dies from being beaten, and that which dies from falling from a height, and which people kill from the horns, and devour wild beasts, and what is enshrined in idols. Therefore, all types of food except those mentioned above are halal. Islam allows all types of food that are lawful and good (*Thayyib*). *Thayyib* itself comes from the Arabic "taba" which means delicious, clean or holy. It also means delicious, good, healthy, peaceful, and most importantly [33]. It is concerned with standards of appropriateness, hygiene and functional effects for humans [5]. Halal is also related to the quality of clean and hygienic food [24]. Therefore, halal and *thayyib* are two prerequisites for Muslims to consume food. Since having halal food has been regulated in the Qur'an, a good Muslim should follow it and avoid haram food. For this reason, Muslims need to be convinced that halal foods and drinks are available where they are traveling [36].

Some of the reasons for consuming halal food include maintaining a strong and healthy physique, and getting the best quality nutrition. The prohibition against consuming those types of non-halal food above is to protect their faith, physical and spiritual well-being [2]. Based on the characteristics above, halal food is not only intended for Muslims, because everyone can also enjoy it [15, 24], including non-Muslims [14]. Because consuming halal and *thayyib* food is obligatory for Muslims, the presence of halal restaurants is important in the halal tourism industry. The problem is how to guarantee that the food served to Muslim consumers is halal? There is no definite answer because there are various religious sects and also different interpretations of Islam [36].

The need to respond to Islamic values in developing halal tourism has raised awareness of the importance of ensuring product and service businesses can serve

---

[2] In relation to food, Islam regulates it in the Qur'an (Surah al-Baqarah [2]: 168; 172), QS. An-Nahl [16]: 114; 412); QS. al-Ma'idah [5]: 87; 88), Al-Anfal [8]: 69). Meanwhile, related to the prohibition of food is regulated in QS. al-Ma'idah [5]: 3, QS. Al-An'am [6]: 14.

consumers, the Islamic market share, Muslim tourists' satisfaction with halal requirements usually refers to halal hospitality. However, if the demand for halal hospitality services occurs when consumers are using their free time, this refers to the term halal tourism (halal tourism). This concept was introduced in countries with Muslim minorities, such as Canada, Australia, including Taiwan ([16]: 11). This is why the commercialization and commodification of halal as a product and brand has led to the emergence of various efforts to regulate and certify halal products in both Muslim and non-Muslim countries due to increased international trade for halal products, recognition of consumer rights and desire to give confidence in halal brands ([16]: 11). Hence, halal certification is defined as a product/service certification process regulated by Sharia Law ([4]: 14). Products that have been certified halal will get a logo in accordance with the halal standards from the Halal Certifying Organization that certifies them. According to Ab Talib et al., [1] companies are asked to serve the satisfaction of consumers' demand for halal food through halal certification.

From various studies related to halal certificates, there are at least two perspectives that can be used, namely from the perspective of entrepreneurs and consumers. From the perspective of an entrepreneur (commercial), service providers want to provide services according to the religion of their guests for financial reasons, halal certificates other than as an encouragement for entrepreneurs to meet halal standards (Ariff in [17]), and as a guarantee of *thoyyib*'s integrity. According to the consumer perspective, halal certification and logos are a guarantee that everything that is consumed is halal so that Muslims feel comfortable consuming it [4, 5].

Given the importance of this halal dimension for Muslim consumers, tourism service providers must consider the importance of "becoming halal" so that the tourism industry gains a competitive advantage [27]. With the existence of halal certification from the authorities, this will increase the positive perception and reputation of entrepreneurs. However, failing to do so could lead to a loss of clientele and competitiveness for tourist destinations. The issue of food safety on consumer behavior can have an impact on the loss of their trust and when the food they consume turns out to be not what they want [21]. But the most important thing of all is that it requires a full understanding of the service provider regarding this halal concept. Hall et al. [16] divide halal hospitality and tourism service providers into two categories, namely (1) certified (officially recognized by the competent authorities), and (2) claimants, namely those who claim that they provide halal services, for example through advertisements/according to consumer demand.

A product/service that has been certified will receive a halal logo from Halal Certification Organization (HCO). The HCO itself is a registered Islamic organization or agency. However, some entrepreneurs do not show the halal certificates they received because they believe that providing halal food is a Muslim's responsibility. That as a good Muslim, his words should be trusted [16]. Whereas, some other entrepreneurs claim to provide halal products but without official halal certification because of several reasons, namely: limited knowledge and lack of the halal concepts, costs, problems with the supply chain, consumers demand for non-halal products, bureaucracy, and because entrepreneur's assumption that it is not mandatory [29]. An entrepreneur who has limited knowledge about halal products has impacts on consumer's confidence in the services he/she provides. Even though, restoring consumers' trust takes time and money; hence establishing relationships is a valuable asset to survive in the halal market ([16]: 13).

### 3.2 *Concept of Social Welfare*

A wide concept of social welfare is defined as various actions to achieve a better standard of living physically, economically, socially, and spiritually. According to ([25]: 5), welfare is defined as a condition where the social problems can be managed, needs can be met and opportunity to advancement is provided or facilitated by the government. Social welfare will be achieved if the community experiences a high degree of social welfare. Though it is difficult to measure social well-being, if social problems within a community can be managed well, they can experience a degree of well-being. Besides, a community has social needs that must be met. They are not only basic needs, but also any kind of needs that exist at the level of community and society. Community that meets these needs will experience a collective sense of well-being. Finally, social welfare exists in a society whose social opportunities to advance and realize their potential. The absence of social welfare will cause the society illfare, the opposite of welfare. Those three dimensions combined together to achieve social welfare. It may be argued that when a society or community meets all those elements, they enjoy a satisfactory level of welfare.

The concept of welfare in this study is limited to the availability of halal foods. Hence, related to the welfare of the Indonesian Muslim community in Taiwan, it will be achieved if they can manage their social problems, especially in finding halal food easily, meet their need for halal food, their needs can be met and there is an opportunity that can be developed or can be facilitated by government. In short, it can be drawn up through the Fig. 1.

## 4 The Development of Taiwan Halal Tourism Industry

The development of Taiwan's halal tourism industry could be traced from the brochure published by Chinese Muslim Association (CMA), where in 2009 for the first time Taiwan tried to target Muslim tourists. Besides introducing some tourism destinations for Muslim tourists, it also provided information on halal restaurants. However, since then, there has been no explicit and detailed regulation on how the halal tourism industry must be implemented. In 2016, when Taiwan launched the New Southbound Policy (NSP) it was formally mentioned as part of the resource-sharing flagship. However, the gap from 2009 to 2016 becomes the reason why the development of this industry was very slow [32]. Nevertheless, Taiwan has put its best efforts into developing the halal tourism into account. As a result, Taiwan ranked

**Fig. 1** Research framework

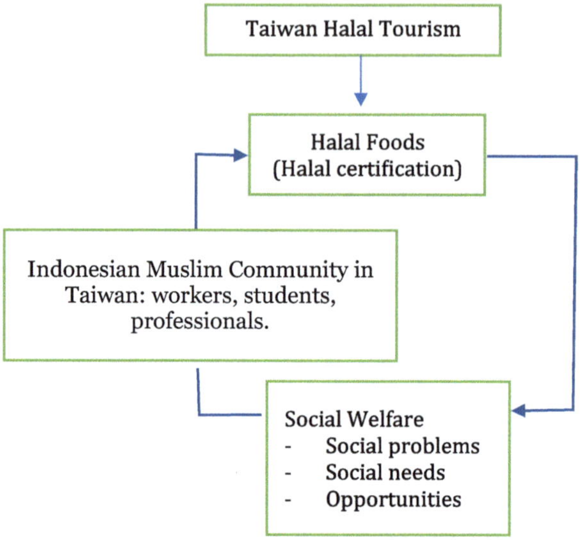


from no 10th in 2015 to no 2nd in 2021 as the best Muslim-friendly destination among the Non-OICs.

To develop it, two strategies are made, namely boosting halal certification and creating a Muslim-friendly environment. In boosting the halal certification, the Taiwan authority focuses on accommodation and restaurants. In the beginning, there are five categories of halal certifications. There were Muslim Restaurants (MR) labeled to that belong to Muslim; Muslim-Friendly Restaurants (MFR) that belongs to non-Muslim owners; and Halal Kitchen (HK) for those who own the Kitchen that provide services for transportation, hotel, etc. Whereas Muslim Hotel (MH) for the accommodation; and the rest is Muslim-Friendly Guide. Later on, more terms related to halal certification were made, following the establishment of new halal certification bodies in Taiwan. According to Taiwan Halal there are nine certification bodies in Taiwan, in which each of them has its own task. As a consequence, number of the halal certified restaurants increased. According to Tourism Bureau of the Republic of China (2019) until 2020 there were more than 276 halal certified restaurants and hotels. The number increased significantly from less than 100 in 2018 compared to that in 2012 where there were fewer than 20 halal-certified restaurants [34]. This indicates that within eight years, awareness of the owners of restaurants and accommodations toward the importance of halal foods and accommodation has increased.

Those restaurants are owned by Muslim ethnics in Taiwan, such as Indonesian, Malaysian, Indian, Turkey, Pakistan, as well as Taiwanese (Fig 2). Among the Southeast Asian countries, number of the halal restaurants from Indonesia is quite limited. There are six restaurants only spread in Taipei. There are some reasons for the restaurant not applying for the halal certification. According to the director of the Indonesian-Taiwan Business Association (APIT), some Indonesian restaurants in

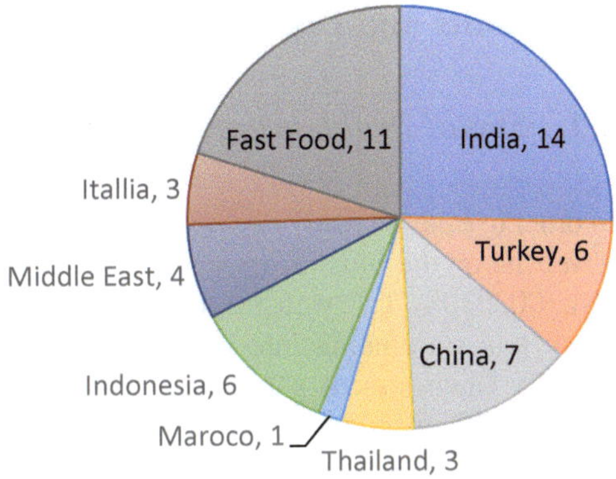


**Fig. 2** Halal restaurants in Taipei. *Source:* [35]

Taiwan are owned by Indonesian Chinese from Singkawang, Kalimantan.[3] They claim that halal certification they achieved does not necessarily increase the number of customers at their restaurant. Even though, they had spent time, energy and material to achieve that. Besides, some restoring got it difficultly, even though the location of the restaurant is very close to the Taipei Grand Mosque, where the CMA and the Taipei Grand Mosque certification bodies offices exist.[4] Halal certification is only valid for 2 years, which according to the businessman, this time duration is too short.

However, the number does not include the number of the manufacturing products sold in Taiwan. Halal Products available in Taiwan also constituted those made in Taiwan or exported products. They are available in conveniene stores and supermarkets.

## 5 Indonesian Muslim Communities in Taiwan

There are many elements of Indonesian Muslim communities in Taiwan. They come from different backgrounds and professions, i.e workers, students and professionals, mixed married couple and their descendants, etc. There is no fixed data explaining the number, however according to the national immigration of ROC, number of the Indonesians in Taiwan there are approximately 350 thousand people. The highest number is the worker, accounting for 230 thousand, followed by mixed married couples around 27 thousand and students which accounted for 4,000 and the rest are professionals. Since there is no exact data about the number of the Muslim community, it is assumed that 80% of the workers are Muslim. Hence, the number is around 184,000. They live distributed along Taiwan. They mostly live in urban areas, while some others live in remote areas.

[3] Based on the interview with the director of APIT via online on December 22, 2021.

[4] Based on interview with Mr. D, the owner of the Muslim restaurant in Taipei via online, on December 22, 2021.

# 6 Results and Discussion

## *6.1 Social Problems of Indonesian Muslim Communities*

In order to ease the Muslims living in Taiwan, the Taiwan Tourism Bureau has created a website on the Muslim-friendly Environment (https://eng.taiwan.net.tw/m1.aspx?sNo=0020308). This website provides any kinds of information about Taiwan tourism to all tourists coming into Taiwan. Especially for the Muslim, there is Muslim-friendly Environment part that provides information about what can be done by Muslim in Taiwan, particularly the dining and accommodation, places for praying, mosque, etc. It shows all of the halal certified restaurants available in every place in Taiwan, including the types of the restaurants, locations, statuses either Muslim restaurant or Muslim-friendly restaurants, and who issued the certificate.

However, Indonesian Muslim community there still find some problems. The problems come from internal, i.e. from the Muslim community itself and from external, from out of the community.

1. Limited availability of halal food

Compared to the other districts in Taiwan, most of the halal restaurants are available in Taipei city. This is because Taipei city has become the main tourist destination where many of Muslim visitors go there. Whereas, many Indonesian Muslim communities also live in other areas, even in remote area. Although no exact data on the number of Indonesian Muslim communities living in those areas, the data of the Indonesian workers living in Taiwan shows that a lot of Indonesian communities live in remote areas in Taiwan, as shown in the figure below. Due to the limited availability of the halal restaurants there, hence their access to halal food is limited. As a consequence, they sometimes have to buy food from no-halal -certified restaurants, to the vegetarian ones, or cook by themselves.

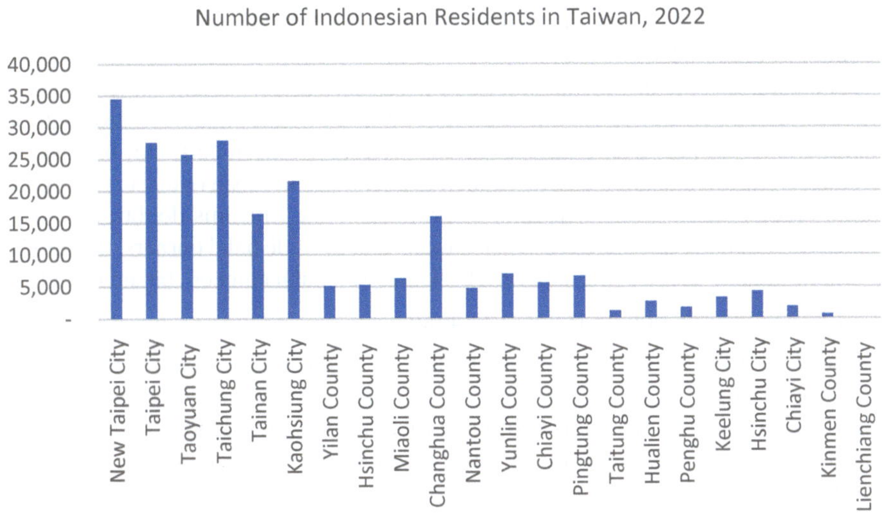


*Source* Ministry of Interior [26]

2. Lack of Mandarin language ability

The internal problem of some of the Indonesian Muslim community in Taiwan is the lack of language capability. A lot of Indonesian community in Taiwan are lack of Mandarin capability, since they are not equipped with sufficient Mandarin language skills before departing to Taiwan. As a consequence, when they visit the non-halal-certified restaurants, or food outlets or street vendors, they do not know how to communicate with the restaurant owners to ensure that the menus do not contain of non-halal ingredients. Moreover, not all of the restaurant owners provide menus in English. Even though it is not pork, Taiwanese sellers probably add it with pork oil or mix it with other things that contain pork in processing. As a consequence, it makes worrisome and anxious for the Indonesian Muslims to eat. However, the more difficult one is to ensure the ingredients of the food products are available in stores since they use specific terms that not all of the people can understand.

3. Limited number of Halal restaurants availability

Most of the problem is related to finding halal restaurant. Even though there are some websites showing where the location of the halal restaurants, a lot of Indonesian Muslim communities are not familiar with using it. As a result, some of them have to travel for quite a long journey to find halal food in halal-certified-restaurants. It creates difficulty for them. On one hand, they have to keep their faith, but on the other hand they have been busy with their activities as students.[5] Some of them forcefully eat chicken in the no-halal certificate Indonesian restaurants close to their school

[5] Some of the Indonesian students study the field of in science and they spend their time in laboratories to conduct experiments can be between 10 and 15 h a day [10].

by saying *Bismillah*, which means in the name of Allah. Hence, it rises the term of "*ayam bismillah*" [10].

In addition, some of the manufactured foods sold in conveniene stores or supermarkets do not clearly show the halal logo. Not all of the manufactured factories include it on the package, even though the product has been certified, because the product is exported to other countries such as to Korea and Japan or due to the repackaging process in Taiwan.[6] This kind of products make Muslims doubtful about its halalness. Even though there are supermarkets that provide halal corners, the number is still limited. Even, in some supermarkets, they sell halal chicken, but no halal logo.

4. Limited information on Halal restaurants

Especially for the Muslim workers that take care of the elderly, some of them do not have enough time to go out for many reasons. As a consequence, they are lack of information about the availability of halal food. Hence, they depend on information through social media. Some other Muslim workers live in remote areas in which the availability of halal restaurants is limited.

## *6.2 Meeting the Needs of the Indonesian Muslim Community*

Based on the problems, the Indonesian Muslim community needs to solve them. Indonesian people are creative; they have solutions based on their own problems.[7] There are some efforts that have been made by some actors, namely the Taiwan authority, entrepreneurs, certificate bodies, and Indonesian Muslim community members. They provided information related to halal foods. For example:

1. Creating halal card

As a lot of Indonesian Muslim communities are lack of Mandarin language, they need something that can help them to help them communicate with the restaurant owners or with the shop sellers when getting a halal food. FORMMIT, an organisational forum of Indonesian Muslim students, created a halal card whose aim is to ease other Muslims in finding halal food. This card contains some characters in Mandarin showing haram stuffs. For example, pork and its derivatives, pork oil or ham. A Muslim who would like to use it must print it and bring it whenever they are shopping. This card is shown to the seller. Though it is very useful, problems come when the have to buy something incidentally and they do not bring the card. Then the card is

[6] Some of the snacks imported from Malaysia originally have halal certificate on it. However, due to the repackaging process in Taiwan for the sake of adding local flavour, the logo was eliminated. Based on interview with Dr. I, one of the managerial staffs of the halal XYZ via online, on November 8, 2021.

[7] Based on interview with Dr. I, one of the managerial staffs of the halal XYZ via online, on November 8, 2021.

made into a digital form, that can be accessed via smartphone. In this way, it makes Muslims easier to access, since people are very often bringing their mobile phones everywhere.

2. Creating Halal Information Center (HIC)

This center is launched by the FORMMIT. It is aimed at assisting Muslims community in Taiwan to provide information related to halal products or Muslim-friendly places.[8] Taiwan authority as the provider of the database, "halalin" Taiwan other halal products provides any kind of information related to halal that can be found in Apps line and special addressed to Muslim group members.

3. Creating Taiwan Halal on Social Media

One of the Indonesian Muslim professionals in Taiwan creates it on Instagram Apps. Instagram constitutes as the easiest way to operate. Besides it does not need much funding, it can be operated individually. However, it needs creative content.

4. Creating halal Apps

Some of the Indonesian students in Taiwan created Halal Apps in the smartphone to assist the Muslim community in Taiwan, namely the "Halal XYZ" and "Halalin". Halal XYZ provides information about halal restaurants, prayer rooms, places Muslim community in Taiwan, etc. This effort in creating the Apps that was started from a competition at the university level further won the competition in the national level and was dedicated as a start-up company. However, this Apps only existed for several years, due to some problems,[9] including (1) human resources availability to manage it since most of the people involved the management have graduated from university and they have to return to Indonesia. (2) lack of finance. As a start-up, they have to pay the salary to the people involved in and any kind of expenses. To finance the expenses, they have relied on the funding gained from the prize of competition. However, they are lack of financial support to develop it.

The other Apps is "Halalin".[10] This apps aims to help Muslims find halal foods by scanning the code of the package, hence information will appear saying that this product is either halal or not. This apps really helps the Muslim community since it is easy to use. By scanning it, they can easily find out the status of the foods.

[8] Based on the information during the launching and webinar on Halal Information Center: *Syiar Halal di Negeri Minoritas*, held by FORMMIT on February 27, 2021 via online.

[9] Based on interview with Dr I, one of the managerial staffs of the halal XYZ via online, on November 8, 2021.

[10] Based on the "Training Taiwan halal awareness" by Robihamanto, organized by FORMMIT via online, on December 5, 2021.

### 6.3 Opportunities to Self-Development

Midgley [25] explains that one of the conditions to achieve social welfare is there are opportunities for self-development or government facilitated. Creating various ways to assist Indonesian Muslims in Taiwan is really appreciated, including creating Apps through smartphones. The problem is how to make those kinds of creativity can be long-lasting or sustained since they are useful. To make it sustained or developed, it needs support from the government. Even though the Indonesian Muslim community has contribution in developing Halal tourism in Taiwan, as Indonesian people live in Taiwan, they have some limitations. For example, they have a limited amount of stay duration in Taiwan, or terms and conditions to set up a business. Hence, doing the transfer of technology is another way with support from Indonesia but using particular standards.

The existing Apps gives advantages to Taiwan authorities since they can get information on the number of the halal-certified restaurants. The higher number of the certified restaurants, the more halal restaurants and foods available. The authority needs to input the database. It will ease Muslims in Taiwan to get halal foods. Moreover, their number has been increasing. Hence, the authorities may have no problem collaborating with them. Moreover, the university where they study has helped them in doing incubation process. In terms of financing the start-up, they have tried to search for foreign investors to get support, however, it is not easy to get it. One of the possibilities to make it sustainable is by getting support from the government. However, so far they have utilized the personal relation with the Representative officer of the Indonesian Economic and Trade Office.

## 7 Conclusion

From the explanation above, it can be concluded that even though Taiwan has developed a halal tourism industry and provides more and more halal food, the Indonesian Muslim community in Taiwan still faces some problems. The problems are related to the access to get the halal food. As a result, some of them still face worrisome, anxiety or doubt that may create unsatisfactory for them as foreign Muslim communitie in Taiwan. However, they have tried to manage all the problems by creating apps in the smartphone so the Indonesian Muslim community can solve their problems and can get what they need. Hence, they have a social degree of well-being. However, to make it sustainable, it needs support from the government so that it can have opportunities to self-developed.

## References


1. Ab Talib MS et al (2016) Emerging Halal food market: an institutional theory of Halal certificate implementation. Manag Res Rev 39(9):987–997. https://doi.org/10.1108/MRR-06-2015-0147
2. Ab Talib MS (2017) Motivations and benefits of halal food safety certification. J Islamic Mark 8(4):605–624. https://doi.org/10.1108/JIMA-08-2015-0063
3. Abrori F (2020) Pariwisata Halal dan Peningkatan Kesejahteraan, 1st edn. In: Rizki FA (ed) Literasi Nusantara. Literasi Nusantara, Malang. https://books.google.co.id/books?hl=en&lr=&id=iVIjEAAAQBAJ&oi=fnd&pg=PR1&ots=TK2KgRBpuX&sig=ewwnr8w1CAc2VzB6xg6kQ9GR47M&redir_esc=y#v=onepage&q&f=false
4. Akim A, Purnama C, Konety N (2020) Isu Halal Internasional dan Regional. In: Anugrah F (ed) Pertama. ITB Press, Bandung. https://www.researchgate.net/publication/343040551_Isu_Halal_Internasional_dan_Regional.
5. Alzeer J, Rieder U, Hadeed KA (2018) Rational and practical aspects of Halal and Tayyib in the context of food safety. Trends Food Sci Technol 71(October 2017):264–267. https://doi.org/10.1016/j.tifs.2017.10.020
6. Amadeus (2016) Halal Travellers 2016, (Amadeus Traveller Trend Observatory)
7. Anwas OM (2014) Pemberdayaan masyarakat di era global. Alfabeta, Bandung
8. Battour M, Ismail MN (2016) Halal tourism: concepts, practises, challenges and future. Tour Manag Perspect 19:150–154. https://doi.org/10.1016/j.tmp.2015.12.008
9. Carboni M, Idrissi Janati M (2016) Halal tourism de facto: a case from Fez. Tour Manag Perspect 19:155–159. https://doi.org/10.1016/j.tmp.2015.12.007
10. Dewi EY (2021) Ayam Bismillah. In: Fauzan FA (ed) Merajut Hikmah: Menemukan Makna Islam di Bumi Formosa. Penerbit Rana, Makassar, pp 164–171
11. Djakfar M (2017) Pariwisata Halal Persepektif Multidimensi, Uin-Maliki Press
12. Duman T (2017) Attributes of muslim-friendly hospitality service in a process. In: Hall CM, Prayag G (eds) The Routledge handbook of Halal hospitality and Islamic Tourism-Routledge. Taylor and Francis, London and New York, pp 53–69
13. Dywantari et al (2021). Merajut Hikmah: menemukan makna Islam di bumi Formosa (F. A. Fauzan (ed.)). Penerbit Rana.
14. El-Gohary H (2016) Halal tourism, is it really Halal? Tourism Manag Perspect 19(December 2015):124–130. https://doi.org/10.1016/j.tmp.2015.12.013
15. Gunita D (2017) Halal acceptance of non-muslim consumers in three Asian countries towards halal food halal acceptance of non-muslim consumers in three Asian countries towards Halal food. National Taiwan University of Science and Technology (NTUST)
16. Hall CM, Razak NHA, Prayag G (2020) Introduction to Halal hospitality and islamic tourism. In: Hall CM, Prayag G (eds) The Routledge handbook of halal hospitality and islamic tourism. Routledge, London and New York, pp. 1–18. https://doi.org/10.4324/9781315150604-26
17. Hanzaee KH, Ramezani MR (2011) Intention to Halal products in the world markets. Interdiscip J Res Bus 1(May):1–7. https://www.academia.edu/6019170/Intention_To_Halal_Products_In_The_World_Markets
18. Henderson JC (2016) Halal food, certification and halal tourism: insights from Malaysia and Singapore. Tour Manag Perspect 19(July 2016):160–164. https://doi.org/10.1016/j.tmp.2015.12.006
19. Jaelani A (2017) Halal tourism industry in Indonesia. Int Rev Manag Mark 7(3):25–34. https://doi.org/10.2991/aebmr.k.201116.027
20. Lestari YD et al. (2019) Halal-based business study: a case study in Taiwan. In: Aprianingsih A et al (eds) The 4th ICMEM 2019 and The 11th IICIES. Bali: Unit Research and Knowledge, SBM ITB, pp 641–651. https://journal.sbm.itb.ac.id/index.php/ProceedingSBMITB/article/download/3556/1434
21. Marzuki SZS, Hall CM, Ballantine PW (2012) Restaurant managers' perspectives on halal certification. J Islamic Mark 3(1):47–58. https://doi.org/10.1108/17590831211206581

22. Marzuki SZS, Hall CM, Ballantine PW (2014) Measurement of restaurant manager expectations toward halal certification using factor and cluster analysis. Procedia Soc Behav Sci 121:291–303. https://doi.org/10.1016/j.sbspro.2014.01.1130
23. Mastercard-Crescentrating (2019) Global muslim travel index 2019. Singapura
24. Mathew VN, Binti AMR, Abdullah A, Ismail SNBM (2014) 'Acceptance on Halal food among non-muslim consumers. Procedia—Soc Behav Sci 121:262–271. https://doi.org/10.1016/j.sbspro.2014.01.1127
25. Midgley J (1995) Social development: the developmental perspective in social welfare. SAGE Publications. London. https://doi.org/10.4135/9781446221839
26. Ministry of Interior, N. I. A. R. (Taiwan) (2019) Foreign residents by nationality 2021 (9-1-1101英文版-16現持有效居留證-在臺-外僑統計-按國籍及區域分). Taipei City. https://www.immigration.gov.tw/5475/5478/141478/141380/253654/
27. Mohsin A, Ramli N, Alkhulayfi BA (2016) Halal tourism: emerging opportunities. Tour Manag Perspect 19(2015):137–143. https://doi.org/10.1016/j.tmp.2015.12.010
28. Musa G, Ali SBM, Moghavvemi S (2016) Understanding Islamic (Halal) tourism through Leiper's tourism system. https://doi.org/10.2139/ssrn.2813023
29. Nur I, Rahman A, Saleh R, Rahman SA, Hashim DM (2011) Factors Contributing to Non-Compliance of the Halal Standard among Restaurant Operators in Malaysia. 2nd International Conference on Business, Econ Tour Manag, 24, 88–92. https://www.ipedr.com/vol24/18-CBETM2011-M10024.pdf
30. Said MF et al (2020) Exploring halal tourism in Muslim-minority countries: Muslim travellers' needs and concerns. J Islamic Mark. https://doi.org/10.1108/JIMA-07-2020-0202
31. Samori Z, Md Salleh NZ, Khalid MM (2016) Current trends on Halal tourism: cases on selected Asian countries. Tour Manag Perspect 19:131–136. https://doi.org/10.1016/j.tmp.2015.12.011
32. Setyaningsih RP (2020) Taiwan Halal tourism industry: policy and practice. In: Proceedings of the 3rd international conference on economics, business and economic education science, ICE-BEES 2020, 22–23 July 2020, Semarang, Indonesia. Semarang, Indonesia: European Alliance for Innovation (EAI). https://doi.org/10.4108/eai.22-7-2020.2307875
33. Shihab Q (2014) Halalan Thayyiba. http://quraishshihab.com/article/halalan-thayyiba/. Accessed 11 June 2021
34. Ting NNH (2019) Muslim-friendly tourism. Taipei, pp 1–44. https://isef.co.id/presentation/ISEF2019/15Nov2019/IndonesiaHalalTourismSummit/Sesi3-1-Muslim-FriendlyTourism.pdf
35. Tourism Bureau of Republic of China (Taiwan) (2019). Dining & Accommodation, 15.3, https://eng.taiwan.net.tw/m1.aspx?sNo=0020323&page=19.
36. Vargas-Sánchez A, María MM (2013) Halal tourism: the importance of halal food. J Chem Inf Model 53(9). https://www.academia.edu/38424117/Halal_Tourism_the_importance_of_halal_food
37. Wahab AR (2004) HALAL guidelines for manufacturers guidelines for the preparation of halal food and goods for the Muslim consumers halal guidelines for manufacturers. Malaysia: Halal and Safety Institute, pp 1–12. http://www.halalrc.org/images/ResearchMaterial/Literature/halalGuidelines.pdf

# Indonesian Professional Diaspora in Malaysia: Potentials, Roles, and Networks

**Lamijo**

**Abstract** Since the first Diaspora Congress in 2012, the government of Indonesia has paid more attention to the Indonesian diaspora because of its potential. Diaspora is an important asset for every country, including Indonesia. Indonesian diaspora spread over 193 countries in the world. Indonesian diaspora in Malaysia, especially Indonesian professional diaspora, have a pivotal role in the development of both home and host countries. They have the potential to help increase the competitiveness of the Indonesian nation. Based on the field research conducted in Malaysia in 2019, most Indonesian professionals diaspora were working in several strategic sectors such as oil and gas, information and technology (IT), transportation, aerospace, and transnational corporations. In addition, they also have a good network, either through alumni network, ethnicity, organization, or religious affiliation. This paper discusses how the potential of Indonesian professional diaspora in Malaysia can support the national development of Indonesia through their roles, networks, and transfer of knowledge.

**Keywords** Indonesian professional Diaspora · Malaysia · Diaspora potentials · Networks

## 1 Introduction

Discussing about Indonesian diaspora is very complex. For the first step to know about Indonesian diaspora is from the data of Indonesian diaspora. To date, there is no accurate and valid data on Indonesian diaspora. According to the ASEAN Trade Union Council (aseantuc.org),

Lamijo (✉)
Research Center for Area Studies—National Research and Innovation Agency, Jakarta, Indonesia
e-mail: lami002@brin.go.id



Nawawi et al. (eds.), *Managing Disruption and Developing Resilience for a Better Southeast Asia*, Springer Proceedings in Humanities and Social Sciences,
https://doi.org/10.1007/978-981-96-2116-3_47

> It is estimated that more than 10 million people have migrated from Indonesia to various overseas destinations to seek for opportunities. The people who emigrated from Indonesia in finding better opportunities abroad have formed a global community of 'Indonesian Diaspora'.

Besides, there is also a significant number of talented and highly skilled Indonesians who chose to move overseas to seek a better life and economy or to get high-quality education and access. While many Indonesians ventured aboard to study, a significant portion of them went overseas to work as nurses, caregivers, plantation workers, domestic helpers, professional workers, and many other career destinations. Thanks to globalization and demographic transition, skilled workers are more mobile.

However, according to Sari et al., [19], Indonesian diaspora living overseas is not less than 8 million. She added that more than 4 million Indonesian diaspora lived in over than 87 countries in 2019, in which Saudi Arabia being the first top country hosting about 37% of Indonesian diaspora. Meanwhile Malaysia being the second top country with 27% of Indonesian diaspora. However, if undocumented Indonesian are also included, the actual number of Indonesian diaspora residing in Malaysia would be four time higher. Moreover, according to survey data conducted by a research team from the Research Center for Area Studies, Indonesian Institute of Sciences, in 2021, Indonesian diaspora is spread in 193 different countries worldwide.

Regarding the definition of diaspora , the International Organization for Migration [8] mentioned that

> There is no single accepted definition of the term "diaspora", neither is there a legal recognition of the term which consequently has given rise to many different meanings and interpretations. The term "diasporas" conveys the idea of transnational populations, living in one place, while still maintaining relations with their homelands, being both "here" and "there".

However, Brubaker ([4]: 1) defined diaspora based on three general criteria, namely dispersal, homeland orientation, and boundary maintenance. Meanwhile, Ember et al. ([6]: xxvi) proposed a definition of diaspora by emphasizing the relationship among diaspora communities worldwide. It means that diaspora may not be fully assimilated into their host country due to their relationship and network with other diaspora communities.

Furthermore, IOM [8] also explained that, in terms of contributions, diaspora has been making significant distributions for a long time, without waiting for a particular policy to both mobilize and push them. However, at least from existing diaspora studies, the contributions of diaspora are seemingly often related to socio-economic background, institutional framework, political issues and society trust and perceptions, both in the sending and receiving countries. Based on the above background, this paper will broadly propose the "Indonesian professional diaspora" as Indonesian highly-skilled who have left the home country, but still maintains and links with Indonesia as their country of origin.

As mentioned earlier, among the Indonesian diaspora who are living in Malaysia, they work as nurses, caregivers, plantation workers, domestic helpers, university lecturers, entrepreneurs, as well as professional workers. The Indonesian professional diaspora in Malaysia seemed to be increasing in the early decade of the 2000s along with the growth of the information and technology (IT) and industrial sectors in Malaysia. Anis [2], cited from Immigration Statistic of Malaysia, revealed that there were 140,598 expatriates and their dependents in Malaysia as of October 2021. Of this figure, 82,280 are active expatriates with the highest number coming from India, followed by China, Japan, the Philippines, and Indonesia. It should be underlined that in the context of Malaysia, skilled workers or professional class of employees are often refferred to as expatriates.

However, Sari et al., [19] explained that the significant movement waves of highly-skilled and professional Indonesians to Malaysia since 2000s have also generated unfinished debates on brain drain. Related to brain drain debates, my fieldwork found an important answer that even though Indonesian professional diasporas continue living in Malaysia, but they still use their own knowledge and networks to help Indonesia. According to them, contributing to their home country does not mean staying in Indonesia. In addition, our research also found that alumni organizations become one of the most important key chains in shaping networks among them. In short, it can be said that research on Indonesian diaspora, especially on the Indonesian professional diaspora in Malaysia, is very rare. Therefore, this paper tries to fill the lack on Indonesian diaspora study as well to contribute new paradigm on Indonesian diaspora, especially professional diaspora.

This paper is divided into five sections. It will begin with an introduction, followed by a brief explanation of the methodology used in this study. The third section will discuss the history of Indonesian diaspora in Malaysia. The fourth section will be the analysis of Indonesian professional diaspora and the context of expatriates employees, it will assess the life history of Indonesian Professional diaspora in Malaysia. The last section of this paper is the conclusion.

## 2 Methodology

In the process of collecting data and information, this research uses triangulation methodolgy. The data for this research were obtained from literature review, both from photos, documents or textbooks, in-depth interviews, and point of view of Indonesian professional diaspora in Malaysia. The study of Indonesian professional diaspora in Malaysia was analyzed in accordance with the information collected from the literature reviews and then combined with the interview. The empirical research of this study was carried out in Malaysia, especially in Kuala Lumpur, Putra Jaya, Cyber Jaya, Petaling Jaya, as well as Selangor, for about two weeks in March–April 2019. In-depth interview was conducted with 13 Indonesian professional diaspora from various sectors such as entrepreneurs, oil and gas, trade, banking, services, and so on. In-depth interview was also carried out with officials from the Indonesian embassy in Kuala Lumpur. All interviewees in this article use pseudonyms.

## 3 The History of Indonesian Diaspora in Malaysia

There is a lot of literature discussing on the history of Indonesian migration to Malaysia, which was previously well-known as Malaya. Theoretically, the history of diaspora is the distribution of ethnic groups to various countries due to political reasons, in which later it also related to economic issues. Historically, many ethnic groups from Indonesian islands have migrated to various countries since long time ago. They have a long history of moving to many countries, especially Malaysia. Among the most popular ethnic groups in Indonesia in migrating to overseas is Bugis-Makassar. The current King Gowa from South Sulawesi, Mr. Andy, mentioned that Bugis-Makassar had massively migrated to Johor Bahru, Malaysia since the Bongaya Treaty between the Netherlands-VOC and Sultan Hasanuddin of Gowa in 1667 (Interview on May 27, 2021).

There were some scholars who discussed on the history of Indonesian ethnic groups in Malaysia. Among of them, Jani and Husain [10] discussed about the long history of Minangkabau diaspora; Lineton [12], Noorduyn [15], Maunati [13] and Kotarumalos [11] discussed on the Bugis diaspora in Peninsular Malaysia, especially in Johor. Another scholar, Ito [9] also discussed on the Bugis diaspora in Sabah. Ito mentioned that the differences in the identity of the Bugis diaspora in Malaysia, which is divided into Malay Bugis, Sabah Bugis, and Indonesian Bugis.

In addition, Sari et al., [19], cited from Lineton ([12]: 173), explains that Bugis have migrated to Peninsular Malaysia since the end of the seventeenth century. Meanwhile a study by Maunati [13] explains more about the Bugis identity which is still preserved in certain elements of their daily life. Besides the Bugis and Minangkabau diaspora in Malaysia, there are also scholars who had studied on the Javanese diaspora in Selangor [21], the Acehnese diaspora [14], the Mandailing diaspora [18], and various other ethnic groups.

## 4 Indonesian Professional Diaspora in Malaysia

Malaysia is an excellent country in which to study the main features and implications of regional labour mobility. It has developed faster and more steadily than its two more populous neighbours -Indonesia and the Philippines. Moreover, its impressive and rapid improvements in global industry, services, and education have created a relative shortages of skilled workers needed in high-skilled sectors such as oil and gas, finance, aerospace, information and technology, global base services and high-tech manufacturing [5]. However, Del Carpio added, that although the reliance on foreign workers began in the early 1970s and throughout the 1980s to support Malaysia's rapid growth, formal guidelines pertaining to foreign workers were only introduced in the early 1990s. According to Sari and Lamijo [20],

> The basis for the increasing demand for skilled labour in Malaysia is related to its industrialization programs, namely the New Economic Policy (NEP) between 1971 and 1990 and the National Development Policy (NDP) between 1991 and 2000. These two policies sought to diversify the nation's economy by engaging in export promotion and establishment of an educated workforce.

In addition, in the early 2000s, Indonesia sent many professional workers to Malaysia, particularly to work in the regional representative offices and multinational companies. In relation to this phenomenon, Hasanah ([7]: 383) explained that since the 2000s there were new groups of Indonesian immigrants to Malaysia. They were expatriates who were needed by both local and international companies' branches in Malaysia. Besides, Sari and Lamijo [20] mentioned that there were numerous Indonesian highly-skilled and professionals who moved to Malaysia to work at international companies and universities due to the economic cricis that still affected Indonesia.

The discussion on Indonesian professional diaspora in Malaysia cannot be separated from the diaspora definition of "migrant workers" in Malaysia. As mentioned by Aminuddin ([1]: 1), in the context of Malaysia, "migrant workers" is not a commonly used term for non-Malaysian nationals working in the country. Generally, foreign workers in Malaysia are divided into two distinct groups: (1) expatriates and (2) foreign workers (FWs). She added that the former are the highly skilled, highly paid managerial and professional class of employees and the latter are unskilled or semi-skilled labours. There is a stark difference in the number of each group currently working in the country. Accurate and up-to-date statistics are difficult to come by, especially for unskilled labour, which again is often divided into two categories, legal and illegal (or documented and undocumented).

Based on these two types of foreign workers in Malaysia, Indonesian professional in Malaysia can be recognized as expatriate category. This analysis is in accordance with our research findings in which all Indonesian professional diaspora interviewed recognized themselves as expatriates. According to the Work and Labor and Statistics, issued by the Ministry of Human Resources on a quarterly basis in 2019, out of the total workforce in Malaysia, stands at 15.6 million, only a small percentage of the workforce were expatriates, which was 122,169 in 2019. About 21 percent of these expatriates are from ASEAN member countries. Table 1 lists the origins and numbers of expatriate employees from ASEAN countries in 2019. The total number of expatriates from ASEAN countries is 26,213.

From Table 1, it can be seen that among ASEAN countries, Indonesian ranks second with 8,106 expatriates after the Philippines, which ranks first with 8,579 expatriates. It is also clear that Lao PDR has the lowest number of expatriates among Southeast Asian countries with only 16.

Furthermore, Aminuddin [1] also states that the number of expatriates employed in various sectors in 2019 were: 64,795 in services; 38,685 in information technology; 6,979 in construction; 6,898 in manufacturing; 2,382 in education; 1,451 in

**Table 1** Origins and numbers of expatriate employees from ASEAN countries

| Country of origins | Number of expatriates |
|---|---|
| Philippines | 8,579 |
| Indonesia | 8,106 |
| Thailand | 3,471 |
| Singapore | 2,714 |
| Vietnam | 2,323 |
| Myanmar | 832 |
| Brunei | 98 |
| Cambodia | 74 |
| Lao PDR | 16 |
| Total | 26,213 |

*Source* Statistik Pekerjaan dan Perburuhan Siri 22, Bil. 4/2019 (Work and Labour Statistics), issued by the Ministry of Human Resources on a quarterly basis

petroleum; 270 in tourism; 260 in commerce; 179 in agriculture; 73 in finance; 64 in medical services; 63 in sports; 53 in transportation, and 17 in minerals. Although Indonesian expatriates or professionals in Malaysia place at second rank among ASEAN countries in Malaysia, but unfortunately there is no data available on the number of them at each sectors they work at. However, during our field research in Malaysia, we interviewed Indonesian professional diaspora from various sectors, such as oil and gas, information and technology (IT), services, financial, telecommunications, and other agencies.

Interestingly, most of the Indonesian professional diaspora in Malaysia that we interviewed were affiliated with the Indonesian Brain Gain (IBG) Association. IBG was initiated by Mr. Rusdi Nandar Sigit in 2017. One of the most important reasons of the establishment of IBG was to counter the ‘brain drain’ phenomenon, where many Indonesian professionals diaspora are expected to work in their own country, but instead contribute their energy and thoughts in other countries. This phenomenon has not only happened in Indonesia, but also in other Asian and ASEAN countries. Many countries have issued policies to attract these professionals back home. For example, the government of Malaysia issued Talent Corp program since 2001, by providing various incentives in the form of tax cuts and other facilities. Likewise, South Korea exempts taxes for certain professionals who want to return home. . But it seems that these efforts are not very fruitful. The Indonesian government has also been trying to attract overseas professionals to return and work in the country.

Indonesian Brain Gain (IBG) is an Indonesian overseas professional community that aims to provide a forum for Indonesian professionals to contribute professional experiences (best practices), ideas, or inspiring things while living abroad to the Indonesians in Indonesia. Shortly, IBG reveals that Indonesian professionals living overseas can still contribute to their home country. It means that the debate on brain drain should be changed to brain gain concept. Better understanding on the concepts of brain brain gain are important elements to understand why it is important to know the potential of Indonesian professional diaspora. Related to brain gain or brain circulation, Patterson [17] discusses about the notion of "brain circulation" for the case of Chinese and South Korea diaspora, where diaspora from advanced countries play important role in transfer of technology in their home countries. Furthermore, Pande ([16]: 62) says that previously Indian diaspora had been referred to the notion of brain drain, but since the 1990s they have been considered to be resulted in a positive point as brain-regain. It means that brain circulation or brain gain is the positive result of diaspora in their home country. This could be seen in various forms, including transfer of technology, transfer of knowledge and so forth.

## 5 Life Story of Indonesian Professional Diaspora in Malaysia

Networking is one of the important key among Indonesian professional diaspora in Malaysia. Networking among them can be derived from campus alumni, ethnic group, religion, and hobbies. Among those networking dots, campus alumni is the most popular. However, there is common reason among those Indonesian professionals who continue to stay in Malaysia. As mentioned by Asmara et al. [3], geographical proximity and cultural similarity between the two countries are also mentioned as the other drivers for the Indonesian professional diaspora to choose Malaysia. Push factors also come from internal conditions in Indonesia, such as wariness and disappointment with the system, long and complicated bureaucracy, and feeling under-appreciation by the country, which become critical points in deciding to work overseas.

We found many different stories of Indonesian professional diaspora pursuing their careers in Malaysia from some sectors such as telecommunications, oil and gas, finance, information and technology, aerospace, and so on. We will illustrate here the life story of some Indonesian professional diaspora. Mr. Abdul is the secretary of Ikatan Alumni Geologi Indonesia (IAGI - Indonesian Geology Alumni Association) and has been working in Malaysia since 2008. He works at Petronas Oil and Gas Company as manager. As an expatriate and working for international company, he works based on work contract for certain period. Since 2008 to 2019, he has signed 4 work contract agreements. The first contract was for 5 years, the second one is for 3 years, and for the third and fourth ones were for 3 and 2 year respectively. (Interview on March 27, 2019). He added that if a professional foreign workers does not want to prolong his work contract, he has to go back home. He was initially working with work permit, but now he holds a talent pass which allows him to stay in Malaysia for more than 10 years. He also told us that there were many Indonesian professional diaspora who went back home and did not extend the work contract. However, they did not stay longer in Indonesia as well as could not adapt because of some reasons such as salary, bureaucratic system, uncertain policies, and so on. As a result, most of them went back to Malaysia or other countries such as the Middle East.

Another important story is that of Mr. Ben, one of the Indonesian professional diaspora or foreign workers in Malaysia who holds the highest rank at Petronas as a principal since 2015. He graduated from the Engineering Department, Gadjah Mada University. He tells us that previously, there were 200 Indonesian professionals working in Petronas. However, due to the crisis that hit Malaysia in 2014, most of them were sent back home. Mr. Ben, who was born in Belitung in 1972, started working for Petronas in 2006. At that time, the oil and gas industry was booming. In May 2006, he accepted a 5-years work contract as a senior process engineer with Petronas. According to him, the longer he works, the higher his salary will be. In 2007, Petronas established a new department for deepwater exploration. Since then, Mr. Ben has been assigned to this new department. In 2013, his career was promoted to a specialist and then to a principal in 2015. Principal position is the second rank in Petronas, only under the custodian, where it is only for Malaysian. As an expert on deepwater exploration, he has been several time to transfer his knowledge to the government of Indonesia since Indonesia has huge potential of deep water in eastern Indonesia territorials (interview on April 5, 2019).

Mrs. Corry also has a fascinating story. She obtained both her bachelor's and master's degrees in geology from Gadjah Mada University. She started working in Petronas in 2012 at the Development and Project Department. She is currently working at the Petronas Research Department. Before joining Petronas, she worked at Chevron Indonesia for 7 years. Thanks to the campus network, she then joined Petronas in 2012. She is working at Petronas under employment contract. This year is the fourth contract. The first contract was for three years, from 2012 to 2015. The second contract period and forward was only for two years. As a professional and expatriate, she received expatriate package, an expatriate facilities such as housing, healthcare, and tuition fees for her children. Since the oil crisis in 2014, Petronas has a shortages of foreign skilled workers. As a result, she added, from 700 Indonesian professionals working in Petronas, currently only 200 remain. She was actually eager to go back home Indonesia, but there were no better opportunities in Indonesia. She added, universities alumni networking was one of the popular way to work in Malaysia.

Mrs. Deasy has been staying in Malaysia since 1993, following her husband who is an entrepreneur. She is the owner of East Heritage Furniture and Handicraft, one of the most well-known furniture and handicraft showrooms in Malaysia. Currently she lives in Petaling Jaya. She obtained her bachelor's degree from the University of Indonesia and her master's degree from Oregon University, United State of America. Previously, she was a lecturer at a private School of Economics in Jakarta. A year after moving to Malaysia, she started teaching at University Kebangsaan Malaysia (UKM) until she resigned in 2000. She then pursued her doctoral degree at the University of Malaya (UM).

Since 2000, Mrs. Deasy and her husband started importing handicrafts and furniture from Jepara, Central Java, Indonesia. She said that in 2000s, especially during Gus Dur regim, everything from Indonesia, including teak furniture, was very cheap due to high inflation and economic crisis in Indonesia. Therefore she imported the best quality of furniture from Jepara and sold it in Malaysia. The market of teak furniture from Indonesia was very good from 2000 to 2014. After 2014, the market of furniture seemed to be decreasing due to the economic crisis that hit Malaysia. Even though the furniture market in Malaysia tends to decrease in the last decade, but East Heritage still exist because of Mrs. Deasy's expertise in managing the furniture market. She is also very open to her employees, so all her employees are very happy to work.

Another Indonesian professional diaspora story comes from Mr. Samin, coordinator of Ikatan Keluarga Miang (IKM - Minang Family Association). He was born and grew up in Bukit Tinggi, West Sumatra. He left for Malaysia in 1977, when he was still 17 years old. When he first arrived in Malaysia, he lived in Kampung Baru, Kuala Lumpur, with his older sister who has been living there. In order to develop his expertise as a tailor, he moved to Shah Alam—his current place of living—to open his boutique in 1990. He is the only Indonesian diaspora in Malaysia who was trusted to make uniforms for the Malaysian Army. He was also often commissioned by the royal families of Selangor to make their chlotes. His two children are Malaysian citizens, but he still keeps his Indonesian citizenship, because he still loves Indonesia. He tries to introduce Padang's batik pattern in his work. Through IKM, he and his IKM member, about 60 persons, still maintain Padang culture.

Mr. Donny is an expert on Information and Technology (IT). He has been living in Kuala Lumpur for nearly two years. He works at Telin Malaysia, an international branch of Telkom Indonesia. Before moving to Kuala Lumpur, he was posted in Taiwan as a Head of Development Program. His work focuses on the development of prepaid cards, especially for Indonesian workers in Malaysia. There are more than 1.3 million workers in Malaysia. They need cheap prepaid card to both call and video call to their families in Indonesia. This is great opportunity for Telin to expand and promote their new products, especially prepaid card. According to Mr. Donny, Indonesian workers in Malaysia frequently call their family in Indonesia. Matrix and Digi cards are the most used by those Indonesian workers to contact their family. The remaining prepaid cards are Celcom, U Mobile, Yes, and TM.

Mr. Waren also has an interesting story living in Kuala Lumpur. He works at Mandiri Bank, especially international branch in Kuala Lumpur since 2016. In Kuala Lumpur, Mandiri focuses on remittance sector. Mandiri Remittance in Kuala Lumpur was established in 2009 after receiving the remittance license. Mandiri Remittance has 78 staffs. It consists of 3% Indonesians, including Mr. Waren, and the remaining staffs are Malaysians. According to Mr. Waren, currently Bank Negara Malaysia allows Bank Mandiri to open public account for Indonesian, not only Mandiri Remittance. Having permit to open new public account for Indonesian, Bank Mandiri uses RAOS (Remote Account Opening System). This system to facilitate and cover Indonesian workers who live in remote areas in Malaysia, especially at palm oil plantations. With this system, they do not need to come to Kuala Lumpur to open an account at Bank Mandiri. This program helps Indonesian workers to send money to their family in Indonesia. In addition, having Mandiri account in Malaysia also assist them to avoid illegal money sending to Indonesia. With this program, every month Bank Mandiri allowed to visit plantations, so the workers can easily transfer money to Indonesia.

Mr. Derry's story is also fascinating. He is also an expert in IT program. He graduated from Gunadarma University. He is currently working for an international company from Germany in Cyberjaya, the most well-known area for international companies in Malaysia, about one and a half hours drive from Kuala Lumpur. Mr. Derry has been working for nearly 20 years. Even though he is an expert and works for international company, but his salary is equal to that of the locals. However, he is very happy working at Cyberjaya Complex because of its complete facilities. He does not want to go back to Indonesia unless there is guarantee from Indonesian government to provide all such facilities he gets in Malaysia.

Based on these life story of some Indonesian professional diaspora above, it can be said that they have potential and play important role in transfer of knowledge to home country using their potentials, roles, and networks.

## 6 Conclusion

The Indonesian professional diaspora in Malaysia is apart of Indonesian diaspora overseas. As highly-skilled workers, they have better access and opportunity to help their home country. Therefore, in order to contribute to their home country, they do not need physically or diasporically return to their country of origin. This model provides an alternative way to transfer the knowledge and skills of diasporas through social and professional networks and to link a diaspora to the country of origin through these networks. It means that skilled and professional emigration might not harm the country of origin, as their skills can be utilized abroad; they may even produce resources for development in the form of funds and ideas that can be transferred to their country of origin.

In terms of their potentials and roles, most of them had ever transfer their knowledge by giving training or giving general lecture through their networks, especially the university link. This study has certain limitations and, therefore, a further study of the Indonesian professional diaspora in many different aspects and in different countries could be very important topics for future study.

## References

1. Aminuddin M (Maimunah) (2020) Comparative study on laws and policies in the management of migrant workers in ASEAN. National Report: Malaysia. Putra Jaya: Ministry of Human Resource, Malaysia
2. Anis MN (2021) Study being run on who qualifies for expat status. https://www.thestar.com.my/news/nation/2021/12/01/study-being-run-on-who-qualifies-for-expat-status. Accessed 09 April 2022

3. Asmara IJ, Berliana NG, Achelia E, Ramdhan D, Akbar M, Zulhamdani M (2020) Saintist Diaspora Indonesia: Kembali ke Tanah Air atau Berkarya di Luar Negeri? Policy Brief, No. 2020–03.P2kmi. Jakarta: LIPI
4. Brubaker R (2005) The 'Diaspora' Diaspora. Ethn Racial Stud 28(1):1–19
5. Carpio SD et al (2017) Foreign workers in Malaysia: Labour market and firm level analysis. Labour Market in Malaysia: Selected Works. Ministry of Higher Education, Malaysia
6. Ember M, Ember C, Skoggard I (eds) (2005) Encyclopedia of diasporas, immigraant and refugee culture around the world. Springer, New York
7. Hasanah T (2015) Potential capital of Indonesian immigrants in Malaysia: a preliminary research. Procedia Soc Behav Sci 211(2015):383–389
8. IOM (International Organization for Migration) (2006) Engaging diaspras as development partners for home and destination countries: challenges for policymakers. IOM Migration Research Series No. 26
9. Ito M (2002) The nature of Bugis migration and their networks, In: Miyazaki (ed) Making of multicultural Sabah. Tokyo: Research Institute for Languages and Culture of Asia and Africa, pp 21–30
10. Jani MD, Mohd H (2014) Reclaiming the loss of the Minangkabau cultural landscape in Negeri Sembilan. Procedia Soc Behav Sci 153:317–329
11. Kotarumalos NA (2019) Ethnic belonging among Bugis Malays in Johor, Malaysia. J Malays Br Roy Asiat Soc 92, 2(317):79–98
12. Lineton J (1975) Pesompe 'Ugi': Bugis Migrants and Wanderers. Archipel 10:173–201. https://www.persee.fr/doc/arch_0044-8613_1975_num_10_1_1248. Accessed 1 March 2025
13. Maunati Y (2016) Translocal and transnational movements of bugis and the construction of multiple identities: the case of Bugis in North Kalimantan of Indonesia and Sabah and Johor of Malaysia. Suvarnabhumi: Multidiscip J Southeast Asian Stud 8(2):15–49
14. Misbach A (2012) Separatist conflict in Indonesia: the long-distance politics of the acehnese diaspora (1st ed). Routledge Contemporary Southeast Asia Series. Routledge, Taylor & Francis Group
15. Noorduyn J (1988) The Bugis Genealogy of the Raja Muda family of Riau-Johor. J Malays Br Roy Asiat Soc 61(2):63–92
16. Pande A (2013) Conceptualising Indian Diaspora diversities within a common identity. Econ Polit Rev xlviii(49):59–65
17. Patterson R (2006) Transnationalism: Diaspora homeland development. Soc Forces 84(4):1891–1907
18. Rozi F (2018) Mandailing diaspora and their cultural role in Malaysia, in strengthening the identity, enriching regional commonality. In: Proceeding of the 12th international conference on malaysia-Indonesia relations, Kuala Lumpur, 1–2 Agustus 2018
19. Sari BR, Maunati Y, Wuryandari G, Lamijo (2022) The widening global network of Indonesian Diaspora scholars in Malaysia. Diaspora Stud: 1–25
20. Sari BR, Lamijo (2020) Diaspora Dosen dan Profesional Indonesia di Malaysia. In: Lamijo et al (ed) Brain Drain atau Brain Gain? Jaringan Diaspora Akademisi dan Profesional Indonesia di Malaysia. Yogyakarta: Penerbit Ombak
21. Sunarti L (2018) Formation of Javanese Malay identities in Malay Peninsula betweem the 19th and 20th centuries. In: Budianta et al (eds) Cultural dynamic in globalized world. Routledge, Taylor & Francis Group, London
22. UNESCAP (2020) Asia-Pacific Migration Report 2020: assessing implementation of the global compact for migration. Social development division economic and social commission for Asia and the Pacific (ESCAP), Bangkok

# Identifying Vulnerabilities of Women Migrant Workers During the Pandemic

**Sylvia Yazid and Nada Gavrila Wasisto**

**Abstract** Feminization of labor migration, meaning the continuously dominant presence of women in the global migration has been observed and discussed for decades. Concerns have evolved around the topics on inequalities and vulnerabilities throughout the migration process. The COVID-19 pandemic has not only exacerbated the challenges faced by women migrant workers, but also increased their vulnerabilities. Despite the fact that policies have been made to respond to the pandemic, most countries are lacking an instrument which specifically ensures the safety of migrant workers, addresses the challenges they are facing, and most importantly, addresses the safety and vulnerability issues faced by women migrant workers. Departing from the belief that policies can become both the cause and the solution for vulnerabilities of women migrant workers, depending on how they are formulated and implemented, this paper aims at proposing how pandemic-related policies can actually address the vulnerabilities of women migrant workers. It uses the concept of intersectionality and structural vulnerability to argue that pandemic-related policies need to acknowledge the specific needs and conditions of women migrant workers and ensure that equality is highly considered, which unfortunately are still lacking.

**Keywords** Vulnerability · Women migrant workers · COVID-19 pandemic

S. Yazid
International Relations Department, Parahyangan Catholic University, Bandung, Jawa Barat, Indonesia
e-mail: s_yazid@unpar.ac.id

N. G. Wasisto (✉)
Political Science, University of Amsterdam, Amsterdam, Netherlands
e-mail: nada.wasisto@student.uva.nl



Nawawi et al. (eds.), *Managing Disruption and Developing Resilience for a Better Southeast Asia*, Springer Proceedings in Humanities and Social Sciences,
https://doi.org/10.1007/978-981-96-2116-3_48

## 1 Introduction

The inability to freely move from one point to another, caused by COVID-19 pandemic, has significantly impacted the global society, particularly those who have been moving regularly, migrant workers. The closing of borders between countries and local lockdowns have disrupted migrant workers' activity since their mobility is restricted [25]. At present, more than two years since the pandemic "officially" declared, cross-border movements have re-started but the speed has been low and the pattern has changed. Data from UN DESA (2020) shows how the international migrants flow has decreased by approximately 2 million migrants compared to mid-2019 and 2020.

While all migrant workers are affected, for women migrant workers, the ongoing inequalities they are experiencing in the societies are mirrored in their labor migration experience. They are usually less privileged and at the same time are frequently burdened by various roles and responsibilities.[1] Changes and limitations to migration have raised concerns regarding inequalities and vulnerabilities throughout the migration process, particularly for women migrant workers.

By 2020, approximately 42% of women are working in informal sectors where high-risk may occur, 10% higher than the number for men [23]. The presence of women in the informal sector has been subject to discussions and advocacy for it puts them in a more dangerous situation [10]. During the pandemic, the risk has become higher since informal sectors tend to be not covered by national labor law. This condition often denies them the rights to being protected from getting infected by the COVID-19 and the guarantee to receive the required treatment. Those with illegal status tend to be left out from getting COVID-19 vaccine, due to the requirements in the regulations [15]. There are also cases where women migrant workers were left stranded and homeless after they were tested positive on COVID-19. The COVID-19 pandemic has not only exacerbated the challenges faced by women migrant workers but has also created new problems causing double-burden which threaten their economic situation as well as their overall safety.

The vulnerability of women migrant workers has generally been discussed through the description of the challenges they face during their migration process, particularly during the employment period [2]. Efforts have been made to guarantee safe migration for women and to address the problems they face. However, these efforts need to be based on policies which specifically address the needs and the challenges faced by women migrant workers. To date, policies which specifically address the fulfillment of women migrant workers' rights and the prevention of discrimination acts against them are still limited. UN WOMEN has recognized that there is a double-burden faced by women migrant workers which gives the urgency to establish the Gender Responsive Guideline on Global Compact for Migration [38]. The necessity of gender equality is mentioned several times in the documents which urges policymakers to see migration from a gendered perspective. Furthermore, the document

[1] Yazid and Natania [45] explain how in the case of refugee crisis in Europe, women refugees have to bear multiple roles and responsibilities while facing specific challenges and conditions.

provided particular standards and parameters which can be utilized by countries as a basis in formulating their national policies. Nonetheless, countries are still facing challenges in ensuring that their national and local policies comply with the international conventions, mechanisms, and guidelines that can guarantee the safety and well-being of women migrant workers.

There are already a number of works on how women migrant workers are discriminated. Nardon et al. [30], found that skilled immigrants ended up being put in informal sectors or low-skilled positions. They found that gender, non-citizen status, and race are influencing their employment experience which then make them experience particular vulnerabilities. Furthermore, a research focusing on Chinese women migrant workers has shown how COVID-19 has created economic vulnerability to this group and has highlighted the impact of COVID-19 which reinforced traditional gender roles and also increased the inequalities in the labor market [46]. A journal article which discusses the impact of COVID-19 towards Indian women migrant workers has highlighted the insecure conditions of working in informal sectors and its possible long-term impacts towards women migrant workers, also how it heightens extreme poverty and food scarcity [31]. These body of literatures has highlighted how COVID-19 has indeed created more problems towards women migrant workers. They have extensively discussed the forms of vulnerability but not so much the policies, which are supposed to address the issue, particularly how the existing policies have not covered the vulnerability of women migrant workers during the pandemic. In fact, policies can actually be the reason for inequality to still exists, which are actually rooted in aspects of the society. As argued by Collins [6], when discussing race, gender, and class, policies may reinforce inequalities thus creating a discriminative outcome among societies.

This paper departs from an argument that policies on labour migration need to specifically address the vulnerabilities of women migrant workers. To do so, the policies need to recognize the specific needs of various groups in the society and supported by a social structure that promotes equality to ensure non-discriminative implementation. In this light, this paper aims to identify why the existing policies during the pandemic have not been able to address the vulnerabilities of women migrant workers. This question is answered using the concept of intersectionality and structural vulnerability. This paper looks into a number of policies by governments and international organizations and identifies the weaknesses of the policies that have led to the failure to address the vulnerability of women migrant workers.

A general definition of vulnerability would be the quality of being able to get hurt easily [4]. According to Kuran et al., the term ‘vulnerability’ can be defined as “the result of different and interdependent societal stratification processes that result in multiple dimensions of marginalisation” [28]. They describe vulnerable groups as populations within a country whose specific characteristics make them need more humanitarian assistance since they tend to be excluded from the community and have limited access to certain resources [28]. Vulnerability is the result of a nonfulfillment of an individual’s needs with the reasons of a homogenized characteristic of groups [28]. Therefore, vulnerability needs to be observed not just from one categorization, but instead from multilayered dimensions, such as race, gender, ethnicity, immigrant status, disability, and others [28]. In short, vulnerability is a result of generalization of the needs of the individuals in a society.

Vulnerability is further worsened by the existence of hierarchy within a society. As argued by Bourgois et al., in the context of personal health, individuals' ability to access health care is determined by their location within the power hierarchies, and their institutional and policy-level statuses, for instance immigration status [3]. Structural vulnerability is a condition of being at risk due to socioeconomic, cultural, and political hierarchy which tends to be enforced by institutions and policy [3]. It argues that hierarchical social order and broader sets of power relations can limit individuals' access to resources which create disparities and inequality to one another [3].

This paper uses these two perspectives of vulnerability to explain how women migrant workers are made vulnerable because their needs and problems are generalized (intersectional vulnerability) and they are not in the position to have easy access to resources (structural vulnerabilities) during the COVID-19 pandemic. The argument is explained by identifying the (non) existence of women within the policies made during the pandemic which should have provided a basis to address the specific needs and conditions of women migrant workers.

In discussing women migrant workers, it has been widely acknowledged that they have specific needs and conditions. Unfortunately, in most policies regarding labour migration, it is still difficult to find stipulations that provide specific categorization, let alone policies, for them. According to the perspective of intersectionality there are categorizations which can make people vulnerable (e.g. gender, age, wage, race, migratory status, geographic location, ethnicity, disability), therefore there needs to be a mapping of the existing groups in society based on their needs [28]. Similarly, structural vulnerability focuses on stereotypes, based on social hierarchy, which differentiate groups within the society and limit their access to resources [3]. Therefore, in analyzing the pandemic-related policies, this paper looks into two required aspects that need to exist in the policies on addressing pandemic to ensure that the policies can actually address the vulnerability of women migrant workers. First, to address the vulnerability of women migrant workers, the acknowledgement of specific needs and increased problems of this group is needed within the policies. As suggested by Kuran, this can be shown by public policies which categorizes groups in the context of their vulnerability to dangerous situations [28]. Thus, this paper assesses whether or not the pandemic related policies acknowledge the marginalized groups that are more prone to be vulnerable, which in this case, are women migrant workers. Second, policies also need to promote the necessity of relatively equal access towards resources. This can be achieved by gradually diminishing the hierarchical structure within the society which has led to discrimination in access to resources.

The analysis in this paper aims to identify to what extent the above two aspects exist in policies on pandemics, particularly in regard to women migrant workers. This analysis is crucial because the gendered impacts of COVID-19 has worsened the discrimination and gender inequalities, putting this group in a more vulnerable situation.

## 2 The Importance of Acknowledging Specific Needs and Conditions

Adequate protection from violence and exploitation such as sexual harrasment, low wages, and excessive working hours are still scarce for women migrant workers. A woman migrant worker who migrate to work abroad often experience a different reality in the destination country since she found her working environment distressing with long working hours [32]. The expectation tend to be a safer and more accommodative working conditions but the reality is very much different, not only in the case of undocumented migrations or informal sectors, but also in a documented and formal one. It has been argued that to eliminate the violence happening towards women migrant workers, migration policies both of origin and destination country need to be improved and formulated using gendered perspective and equipped with means to provide protection towards women migrant workers' rights [24, 38] to counter bad practices such as abusive employers and discriminative working conditions which are often the result of lack of employment contract and workplace regulation [43]. Standardized employment contract and form of protection are continuously demanded since many women migrant workers are excluded from destination countries' labour laws [13]. Protection needs to be based on inclusive policies which are supported by policy instruments that accommodate specific needs.

Generalization of migrant workers' needs tend to make women migrant workers invisible in the context of policies. Consequently, their specific needs are not identified and addressed accordingly. Also, there are needs which are basically universal, but for women, the need may become more urgent. As an illustration, adequate hygiene is required for both men and women, but for women unhygienic working condition may bring higher risks. As recommended by OHCHR [5], women migrant workers need to accommodate working situations with adequate hygiene. Women migrant workers working in informal sectors doing 3D (dirty, dangerous, demeaning) jobs, such as cleaners and helpers, tend to face inadequate working conditions which are lacking in hygiene and poor in quality [9]. For women migrant workers, hygiene does not only mean working in a place with clean conditions, but it further refers to menstrual hygiene and sufficient running water because it is important in ensuring their reproductive and sexual health [43]. The specific needs may include sanitary washroom, privacy, and running water [26] and realistic working hours, break time and working condition [26], While these needs and conditions are known to many, they are rarely written in policies. Responding to this, UN WOMEN has provided an international standard of the Terms of Employment for women migrant workers, especially for the domestic workers [39]. It can be said that arrangements at the global level have actually identified the specific needs of women migrant workers and suggested standards and measures that can be used by governments in formulating policies which may protect them.

As identified by a number of researches, the need for specifically addressing women migrant workers' particular needs has increased during the pandemic of COVID-19. Sanitation and protection against violence are becoming more crucial since many of them are trapped in their working conditions with insecurities [37]. Women migrant workers need to be equipped with personal protective equipment (PPE), such as masks and hand sanitizers, which are crucial to prevent infection. However, in many cases, their employees do not provide such protective equipments and women migrant workers do not have the resources to get them [33]. As identified in the policy brief prepared by ILO-UN WOMEN in the context of COVID-19 and ASEAN women migrant worker, there is an increased health risk of women migrant workers during the pandemic, especially because women in Asia–Pacific region spend 4.1 times more taking care of people that are sick than men [20]. The document has also given recommendations for the government in handling the issue.

Restriction of movements imposed during the pandemic, despite their scale, has made women migrant workers struggle to go back to their home country and instead put them in uncertain conditions with lack of adequate protection and security from experiencing violence. In Thailand, for example, restrictions on inter-provincial travel and border closure have created difficulties for international migrants to return to their home country [16]. Migrants from Myanmar were left stranded in Thailand with uncertain information on when they can return home [16]. It took approximately 2 months for those migrants to finally be able to return to Myanmar. For women migrant workers, this prolonged wait may lead to domestic abuse. As identified by UN WOMEN [37], domestic violence is increasing during COVID-19, due to the country's policy in restricting mobility, border closure, and implementing lockdown [37].

The issues of protecting women migrant workers and fulfilling their rights during COVID-19 have been addressed by various international institutions in their recommendations. For instance, in April 2020, the International Labour Organization (ILO) has put out a policy brief on how to protect migrant workers during the pandemic. This document which is intended to help the government and other stakeholders to create fair and effective national policy, explicitly mention "men" and "women" migrant workers, specifically identify risks for women migrant workers, and suggested for gender-sensitive and rights-based policies and measures which may ensure the fulfillment of the rights of women migrant workers [18]. The document mentions the importance of recognizing individual capacity and promoting legal assistance during COVID-19 including the provision of masks and hand sanitizers and protection of the rights to be free from discrimination and violence abusive incidents against workers and family members.

At the national level, countries have been trying to develop their national policies in enhancing the protection towards migrant workers, knowing that countries' lockdown implementation tend to not consider the needs of this group. For instance, the Indonesian Ministry of Women Empowerment and Child Protection Indonesia has formulated a Protocol for Handling Gender-Based Violence and Trafficking during COVID-19 on December 8, 2020 [8]. The protocol not only addresses the vulnerability faced by women migrant workers, but also provides specific step-by-step guidelines on how to handle gender-based violence victims. This document urges collaboration between local facilities in providing hotline and other services which women migrant workers can access during the pandemic.

On 26 November 2021, National Action Plan on Forced Labour (NAPFL) was established by the Malaysian government aimed to respond to the COVID-19 impacts on migrant workers and to commit with the ILO's Protocol of 2014 to the Forced Labour Convention [19]. It stated that "Forced labour is not always immediately visible and indeed forced labour often takes place in hiding from public view," thus it acknowledges the vulnerability of migrant workers. The document mentions specific problems faced by migrant workers such as violence, poor working condition, human trafficking, and other [11]. However, this document does not specifically address women thus the stipulation is still quite general.

The World Health Organization (WHO) produced "Global Evidence Review On Health and Migration" to address the overlapping impacts caused by COVID-19 towards migrant workers [42]. This policy does not specifically address women workers, however it can be used as guideline for policymakers in addressing vulnerability faced by women migrant workers and the special needs of the groups. A more women-oriented document was produced by the UN WOMEN, "Policies And Practice: A Guide To Gender Responsive Implementation Of The Global Compact For Migration", which is intended to be a guideline for policies and practices to be gender-responsive in the context of implementing the Global Compact for Migration during the COVID-19 pandemic [38]. In this document, issues specifically related to women migrant workers are identified, measures are suggested, and checklists are provided to be used in the governance of migration based on the Global Compact on Migration.

Hygiene, risk of sexual violence, and proneness to COVID-19 are only several of more possible vulnerabilities faced by women migrant workers during the pandemic. At the global level, it has been strongly suggested that pandemic related policies identify and address issues specifically faced by women migrant workers. However, at the national level, pandemic related policies tend to be general and policies intended for women are more on addressing issues arise from the pandemic such as abuses, not yet on the prevention or fulfillment of rights.

Women migrant workers are in need of specific attention from the government since they have been exposed to such problems even before the COVID-19 pandemic existed. Any general policy move should calculate the particular risks it may create on women migrant workers. The social distancing and border closure policy, for example, should also consider the existence of women migrant workers. Policymakers should take into consideration the impact of these policies towards women migrant workers in order to mitigate an increase in vulnerabilities faced by this group. The needs and conditions faced by women migrant workers have been highlighted by various global institutions. Policymakers have been urged to address this issue using a gendered perspective while acknowledging their vulnerability. However, the existing national policies tend to overlook specific needs of women such as hygiene, accommodative working arrangement, and safety from abuses, which require acknowledgement from the government in the policies they make.

## 3 The Importance of Acknowledging Equality

In the context of gender, UN defines equality as having equal rights, responsibilities and opportunities of women and men and girls and boys (UN WOMEN n.d.). It should not be understood as making women and men the same, instead it ensures that everyone's rights, responsibilities, and opportunities are not dependent on the sex when they were born (UN WOMEN n.d.). In 2021, ILO predicted that there is a possibility for the number of women in international migration—which had reached 41.5% or approximately 70 million women—to decrease, due to the never-ending unequal treatment against them [17]. Women migrant workers are more prone to face economic and non-economic obstacles, including gender discrimination and sexual violence [17]. The main reason is because most of them are working in the informal sectors (e.g. housecleaner, childcare, hotel maid) [35]. Race and gender are considered to play a big role in choosing concentration in job sectors. Meanwhile, the gender inequality among societies continues to occur, making them socially differentiated from the majority groups, thus creating barriers for them to work in formal sectors [35]. The existing education gap and stereotype against this group have been rooted in the gender inequalities among societies. This has not only created an outcome of women domination in informal sector but also unequal wage between male and female migrant workers [38].

The existing intersection of gender, age, and race is another cause of access limitation to formal and more decent working sectors [35]. The chance of getting jobs overseas is 0.07% lower for women with high education compared to women with low education [12]. This has created an overrepresentation of women in the informal sector. Women are encouraged to migrate to work in such conditions with no working permit, nor clear employment contract [37]. These occurrences tend to happen, which is why gender discrimination often takes place in these sectors. In ASEAN, women and girls contributed approximately 48.7% of the remittance flows in the labour market [40]. However, they still receive unequal treatments in the society such as less wage (30–35%) than migrant workers [40]. In European Union (EU) countries, female migrant workers experience worse employment outcomes and more inequalities than male migrants [9].

Worsened by the existing pandemic, unclear employment contracts can create another form of exploitation for women migrant workers since the employers tend to reduce wages which impact women migrant workers' personal income [41]. Because of COVID-19, around 8.5 million women migrant workers working in domestic sectors experience income loss and are at risk of exploitation due to their unclear contract [37]. Women migrant workers are also at high risk of being unpaid and deported [37]. Women domestic workers in the Middle East have been reported of experiencing unlimited working hours and increased work demand, especially in disinfecting homes [1]. Many women migrant workers have been trying to escape the upsetting working conditions, however the nonexistent exit permit due to unclear contract exacerbated with close-border policy making them hard to go home.

Furthermore, women migrant workers tend to be left out when it comes to health service provision. The existing barriers in accessing health services and vaccines due to their immigrant status are making them more prone to get infected by COVID-19 [44]. This is due to gender-related barriers to information on how to access the services and because countries tend to prioritize their citizens first [44]. The situation could be worse for those lacking in legal documents, such as work permits. Therefore, women migrant workers tend to be systematically not considered and included within the national COVID-19 responses. In Malaysia, the government used to arrest undocumented migrants that are seeking to get the COVID-19 vaccine because they do not have any legal documents [14]. It was also "impossible" to give vaccine doses to undocumented migrants since their status cannot be tracked [14]. Based on the structure of the society, women migrant workers, especially those working in the informal economy, are often not considered a priority, making them excluded from accessing vaccination.

Regional and global institutions have made the efforts to address the impacts of unequal social structure towards the discrimination of women migrant workers. For instance, ILO and UN WOMEN, through the policy brief on Women's Labour Migration, stated that the existing social structure has limited opportunities and benefits, which this group could actually receive [21]. They have also identified that there is a gender gap causing different wages between men and women migrant workers [21]. Therefore, the document acknowledges the importance of gender equality in order to alleviate the vulnerabilities faced by women migrant workers. Another international organization that argues for the importance of equality is the International Organization for Migration (IOM) through its report on Covid-19 Impacts On The Labour Migration And Mobility Of Young Women And Girls In South-East Asia And The Pacific. It mentions the existence of structural inequalities which gives more barriers for women migrant workers during COVID-19, such as barriers to accessing state assistance service, health support, technology and information [29]. The document stated that in the Asia Pacific region, 80% of migrant domestic workers are women. This group is at risk of being vulnerable and may face stigma and discrimination due to disproportionately effect of hostile migration policies.

In Indonesia, a Guideline for the Protection of Women Migrant Workers during COVID-19 was formulated by the Indonesian Deputy for The Protection of Women's Rights to provide the solution towards gender based violence and other problems faced by women migrant workers [34]. The guideline has acknowledged that women migrant workers are the group prone to be vulnerable amidst the pandemic by arguing that in a normal condition, women migrant workers had faced stigma, discrimination, and gender inequality which this condition is worsen due to COVID-19. The document specifically mentioned the importance of helping women migrant workers to receive health support and social assistant services in order to prevent COVID-19 infection. However, it has not elaborated on the problem from the root cause, which is actually necessary if the aim is to eradicate the vulnerability.

The above discussion has shown how vulnerability of women migrant workers during the COVID-19 pandemic has generally been acknowledged at the national and global levels. However, the suitable solution is yet to be found due to the tendency to overlook the rooted gender inequality that happens in the society that put women migrant workers in a vulnerable situation. With the mandate and resources it has, an international organization may be able to conduct specific analysis of the issues and conditions, based on its field of work. However, they are limited to giving recommendations which later need to be adopted by states. Hence, solutions given tend to be general, often do not reflect the specific conditions in each country. Thus, despite the fact that many international organizations and countries have mentioned the necessity of gender equality, it will never be enough to cover the whole problems since the assesment tends to be on generalized and serves as guidance for countries to establish their own national policy which should be more feasible to reach the core of the problems. With that being said, the most significant initiative can only come from national policies and their implementation in the society. The first much needed step would be to acknowledge more specific needs and conditions of women migrant workers in pandemic related policies.

Acknowledging equality does not merely mean putting the word "equality" in policies, but rather to include the principle of ensuring equality in all the stipulations and implement policies which ensure equality in every aspect of labour migration without having to consider its relations with gender. Thus, even though the importance of equality has been mentioned by international institutions or in national migration policies, it needs to be followed with the willingness to alleviate inequalities which eventually can diminish the vulnerability faced by women migrant workers. Moreover, women migrant workers will remain in the vulnerable situation if countries still have gender-based inequality within its social structure. Countries need to continue working on the elimination of inequality to address the vulnerability of women migrant workers. Thus, the second step should be for policymakers to acknowledge the necessity of equality in the policies they make and where possible explicitly state and elaborate the required policy actions.

## 4 Conclusion

Assessing existing pandemic related policies with the perspective of intersectionality and structure vulnerability, this paper has argued for the need to identify the root causes which lie within the existing social structure and the specific needs and conditions of women migrant workers. Policymakers should explicitly identify these in the policies they made to address the impacts of the pandemic. Policies which understand the vulnerabilities of women migrant workers and include measures to specifically address them are very much needed. Using the intersectionality perspective to comprehend the complex relations between the needs and conditions of various individuals within the society will assist policy makers in formulating such policies. As long as women migrant workers remain "implicitly" included in generalized policies, they remain vulnerable to risks during the pandemic.

The pandemic has also amplified inequality which has long existed between men and women, both in the formal and informal sectors. Inequality is strongly observed in the context of access. Limits to mobility triggered by the spread of the COVID-19 virus have created more barriers for women migrant workers in accessing services. Restrictions of mobility have also put women migrant workers in a more vulnerable situation, making them more prone to violations and various forms of gender-discrimination. At the bottom of this is the lack of gendered perspectives in the policy making and implementation process. Policymakers should acknowledge the importance of gender equality in the policies they make and promote gender equality through the policy implementation. Acknowledging the specific needs and conditions of women migrant workers and ensuring equal access between female and male migrant workers will allow better treatments toward women migrant workers and reduce their vulnerabilities. Reducing the structural vulnerability of women migrant workers, particularly in terms of equality of access to services, protections, and opportunities, will contribute to the wellbeing of women migrant workers.

## References


1. Aoun R (2020) COVID-19 impact on female migrant domestic workers in the middle. https://www.alnap.org/system/files/content/resource/files/main/covid-19-and-impact-on-vulnerable-female-migrant-domestic-workers_english.pdf
2. Arisman A, Jaya RK (2021) Labour migration in ASEAN: Indonesian migrant workers in Johor Bahru, Malaysia. Asian Educ Dev Stud (Emerald Publishing Limited) 10(1):27–39. https://doi.org/10.1108/AEDS-02-2019-0034
3. Bourgois P, Holmes SM, Sue K, Quesada J (2017) Structural vulnerability: operationalizing the concept to address health disparities in clinical care. Acad Med 92(3):299–307.https://doi.org/10.1097/ACM.0000000000001294
4. 2022. Cambridge Dictionary. Cambridge University Press. https://dictionary.cambridge.org/dictionary/english/vulnerability
5. CEDAW (2008) General recommendation No. 26 on women migrant workers. UN Committee on the Elimination of Discrimination Against Women (CEDAW). https://www.refworld.org/docid/4a54bc33d.html
6. Collins PH (2009) Emerging intersections: race, class, and gender in theory, policy, and practice. Rutgers University Press
7. Cyment CG, Paola (2020) How COVID-19 affects women in migration. Friedrich Ebert Foundation, July 9. https://www.fes.de/en/displacement-migration-integration/article-page-flight-migration-integration/how-covid-19-effects-women-in-migration-1-1
8. EEAS (2020) New guidelines launched to protect women migrant workers' rights from violence during COVID-19. The European External Action Service (EEAS), August 12. https://eeas.europa.eu/headquarters/headquarters-homepage/90091/new-guidelines-launched-protect-women-migrant-workers%E2%80%99-rights-violence-during-covid-19_kk
9. EIGE (2020) Gender and migration. Luxembourg: Publications Office of the European Union. https://doi.org/10.2839/051711
10. GAATW (2019) The lived experiences of women migrant workers. Global Alliance Against Traffic in Women (GAATW) Publications, Bangkok
11. Government of Malaysia, Ministry of Human Resources (2021) National action plan on forced labour (2021–2025). https://www.mohr.gov.my/ebook/National%20Action%20Plan%20On%20Forced%20Labour/NAPFL%202021-2025.pdf
12. Hanim A, Zainuri A, Sudaryanto S (2019) Rationality of gender equality of Indonesian. Int J Sci Technol Res 8(9):1238–1242

13. Hennebry J, Grass W, McLaughlin J (2016) Women migrant workers' journey through the margins: labour, migration and trafficking. UN WOMEN, New York
14. Human Rights Watch (2020) Malaysia: raids on migrants hinder vaccine access. Human Rights Watch. March 14. https://www.hrw.org/news/2021/06/30/malaysia-raids-migrants-hinder-vaccine-access
15. Hutchinson B (2021) Rite Aid apologizes after undocumented immigrants denied COVID-19 vaccine. ABC News, March 22. https://abcnews.go.com/US/rite-aid-apologizes-undocumented-immigrants-denied-covid-19/story?id=76590963
16. ILO (2020) COVID-19: impact on migrant workers and country response in Thailand. International Labour Organization
17. ILO (2021) ILO global estimates on international migrant workers: results and methodology. International Labour Organization
18. ILO (2020) Protecting migrant workers during the COVID-19 pandemic: recommendations for policy-makers and constituents. International Labour Organization, Geneva
19. ILO (2022) TRIANGLE in ASEAN quarterly briefing note: Malaysia. International Labor Organization. https://www.ilo.org/wcmsp5/groups/public/---asia/---ro-bangkok/documents/genericdocument/wcms_614381.pdf
20. ILO-UN WOMEN (2020) COVID-19 and women migrant workers in ASEAN. International Labour Organization
21. ILO-UN Women (2015) Valuing the contributions of women migrant workers in ASEAN. ILO-UN Women
22. IOM (2019) As education empowers women, migration allows them to go to where opportunities Beckon. International Organization for Migration, March 8. https://weblog.iom.int/education-empowers-women-migration-allows-them-go-where-opportunities-beckon#:~:text=higher%20education%20levels%20have%20been,a%20lower%2Dskilled%20job%20abroad. Accessed 22 March 2022
23. IOM (2020) COVID-19 Analytical snapshot #49: impacts on migrants in informal economies. International Organization for Migration. The International Organization for Migration. June 24. https://www.iom.int/sites/g/files/tmzbdl486/files/documents/covid-19_analytical_snapshot_49_-_migrants_in_informal_economies.pdf
24. IOM (2010) Labour migration from Indonesia: an overview of Indonesian migration to selected destinations in Asia and the Middle East. International Organization for Migration, Jakarta
25. Jones K, Mudaliar S, Piper N (2021) Locked down and in limbo: the global impact of COVID-19 on migrant worker rights and recruitment. International Labour Office, Geneva
26. Jose D (2020) Period, an added worry for migrant women on the move. The New Indian Express. May 27. https://www.newindianexpress.com/states/telangana/2020/may/27/period-an-added-worry-for-migrant-women-on-the-move-2148440.html
27. Kementerian Pemberdayaan Perempuan dan Perlindungan Anak Republik Indonesia (2016) "Employment, Migration and Access to Finance." Kementerian Pemberdayaan Perempuan dan Perlindungan Anak Republik Indonesia, March 6. https://www.kemenpppa.go.id/lib/uploads/list/f3455-81aaf-4.-employment-migration-and-access-to-finance.pdf
28. Kuran CHA, Morsut C, Kruke BI, Krüger M, Segnestam L, Orru K, Nævestad TO et al (2020) Vulnerability and vulnerable groups from an intersectionality perspective. Int J Disaster Risk Reduc 50:2212–4209. https://doi.org/10.1016/j.ijdrr.2020.101826
29. McAdam M (2020) COVID-19 impacts on the labour migration and mobility of young women and girls in South-East Asia and the Pacific. International Organization for Migration, Geneva
30. Nardon L, Hari A, Zhang H, Hoselton LPS, Kuzhabekova A (2021) Skilled immigrant women's career trajectories during the COVID-19 pandemic in Canada. Int J (Emerald Publishing) 41(1):112–128. https://doi.org/10.1108/EDI-09-2020-0255
31. Abdul Azeez PE, Negi DP, Rani A, Senthil Kumar AP (2020) The impact of COVID-19 on migrant women. Eurasian Geogr Econ (Taylor & Francis) 62(1):93–112. https://doi.org/10.1080/15387216.2020.1843513
32. Phromkade P (2021) I feel safe here—defending the rights of women migrant workers in Singapore. Spotlight Initiative, September 26. https://spotlightinitiative.org/news/i-feel-safe-here-defending-rights-women-migrant-workers-singapore

33. Phromkade (2020) Reaching Malaysia's women migrant workers amid COVID-19 crisis. European Commission. December 17. https://ec.europa.eu/international-partnerships/stories/reaching-malaysias-women-migrant-workers-amid-covid-19-crisis_en
34. RI, Deputi Bidang Perlindungan Hak Perempuan Kementerian Pemberdayaan Perempuan Dan Perlindungan Anak (2020) Panduan Pelindungan Bagi Perempuan Pekerja Migran Indonesia Dalam Situasi Pandemi Covid-19. https://pse.litbang.pertanian.go.id/ind/index.php/covid-19/regulasi-kebijakan/554-panduan-perlindungan-bagi-perempuan-pekerja-migran-indonesia-dalam-situasi-pandemi-covid-19
35. Thukral J (2010) Race, gender, and immigration in the informal economy. *Race/Ethnicity:* Multidiscip Global Contexts (Indiana University Press) 4(1):65–71. https://doi.org/10.2979/racethmulglocon.2010.4.1.65
36. UN WOMEN (n.d.) Concepts and definitions. UN WOMEN. https://www.un.org/womenwatch/osagi/conceptsandefinitions.htm#:~:text=Equality%20between%20women%20and%20men,men%20and%20girls%20and%20boys
37. UN WOMEN (2020) Guidance note: Addressing the impacts of the COVID-19 pandemic on women migrant workers. UN WOMEN
38. Women UN (2021) Policies and practice: a guide to gender responsive implementation of the global compact for migration. UN WOMEN, New York
39. UN WOMEN (2016) Template on Standard Terms of Employment (STOE) for women migrant domestic workers. UN WOMEN Asia Pacific
40. UN WOMEN (2017) Women migrant workers in the Asean economic community. UN WOMEN
41. UNICEF (2020) Impact of Covid-19 on gender-based violence refugee and migrant response. UNICEF
42. WHO (2021) Refugees and migrants in times of COVID-19: mapping trends of public health and migration policies and practices. World Health Organization, Geneva
43. WHO (2017) Women on the move: migration, care work and health. World Health Organization, Switzerland
44. World Health Organization (2022) Strengthening COVID-19 vaccine demand and uptake in refugees and migrants. World Health Organization
45. Yazid, S, Natania AL (2017) Women refugees: an imbalance of protecting and being protected. J Hum Secur 13(1). https://doi.org/10.12924/johs2017.13010034
46. Yueping S, Wu H, Dong X-Y, Wang Z (2021) To return or stay? The gendered impact of the COVID-19 pandemic on migrant workers in China. Feminist Econ 27(1-2):236–253. https://doi.org/10.1080/13545701.2020.1845391

# From Upstream to Downstream: Cascading Risks in the Jeneberang Watershed, South Sulawesi, Indonesia

**Dwiyanti Kusumaningrum, Tria Anggita Hafsari, Dicky Rachmawan, Deny Hidayati, Robert Siburian, Sudiyono, Rusli Cahyadi, and Ratna Indrawasih**

**Abstract** The Jeneberang watershed is one of degraded watersheds and is included in the 15 national priority watersheds in Indonesia. By using an ecosystem approach, this study aims to analyze the deforestation in Jeneberang that pose a cascading risks to the ecosystem sustainability throughout the watershed, starting from the upstream, middle-stream to downstream areas. The methods consist of a literature review, spatial analysis, focus group discussions (FGD), in-depth interviews, and field observations. This study reveals that human activities dominate deforestation along the Jeneberang watershed with activities varying by watershed areas. The forest cover in the upstream area is only 16.8% of 78,883.9 hectares. The deforestation is mainly caused by horticultural agriculture and tourism development. Meanwhile, in the middle and downstream areas, massive land-use changes and technological interventions occur through infrastructure development such as Bili-Bili Reservoir, dykes, and sand pockets. These activities coupled with physiography of Jeneberang River and extreme weather conditions which have a high impact on cascading risks, including landslides in the upstream which affect high sedimentation in the Jeneberang River and Bili-Bili Reservoir as well as flash floods during the rainy season and the risk of drought in the dry season. The cascading risks in Jeneberang Watershed also affects the decline in quantity and quality of water in the river and Reservoir leading to a lack of water sources for irrigating rice fields and a shortage of clean and drinking water for residents in the downstream and urban areas including Makassar City.

**Keywords** Deforestation · Disaster · Cascading risks · Jeneberang watershed

D. Kusumaningrum (✉) · T. A. Hafsari · D. Hidayati · R. Cahyadi
Research Center for Population Studies, National Research and Innovation Agency (BRIN), Jakarta, Indonesia
e-mail: dwiy005@brin.go.id

D. Rachmawan · R. Siburian · Sudiyono · R. Indrawasih
Research Center for Society and Culture, National Research and Innovation Agency (BRIN), Jakarta, Indonesia



Nawawi et al. (eds.), *Managing Disruption and Developing Resilience for a Better Southeast Asia*, Springer Proceedings in Humanities and Social Sciences,
https://doi.org/10.1007/978-981-96-2116-3_49

# 1 Introduction

Exploitation of natural resources, especially forests and sand mining in Jeneberang Watershed, is practically a necessity for the life and livelihood of the community and development in South Sulawesi and particularly in the surrounding area. Forest conversion was initially seen as the impact of population growth, especially farmers in forest areas, turned into a massive exploitation activity after many actors played a bigger role in the use of forests for economic development and commercial purposes. Forest exploitation is no longer carried out merely to meet the needs of the communities, but for the development of various sectors in many cities, such as the tourism, mining, industry, and infrastructure development as well as various city facilities. This exploitation is increasing with the increase in economic and development activities which generally rely on natural resources.

In many regions in the world, deforestation has become one of anthropogenic activities that destructively degrades biodiversity and environmental services which is actually very important for humans [8]. According to Meyer et al. [20], the simple definition of deforestation is the conversion of forest areas to become non-forest areas, usually for agriculture activity, settlements, or public infrastructures such as dams or roads. In short, deforestation will reduce the strategic function of forest areas and will be more complicated and more difficult to control when the human population is still increasing [13]. Moreover, the risk of deforestation could increase in recent times because of technological development that is more advanced to extract forest resources than the last time.

In the context of Jeneberang Watershed, the forest in the upstream is protected by law through the Government Regulation no. 37/2012 and the people especially those who live in the upstream area [21]. Unfortunately, the Jeneberang Watershed in fact has a worrisome condition that relates to forest covers, because majority of forest cover (83.18%) in Jeneberang Watershed were converted to horticultural crops (41.20%), paddy field (28.29%), and settlements (8.86%) [32]. Despite knowing that the forest is part of a conservation area, the authorities tend to ignore it so that deforestation becomes more massive and uncontrolled. Moreover, there are some agrarian issues that complicate the situation, such as land certificates issues which emerged within communities living near protected forest areas.

Exploitation of natural resources which is full of economic interests and financial benefits often leads to environmental destruction and thus affects people's vulnerabilities in many regions. Excessive consumption of natural resources results in environmental degradation due to reduced effectiveness of important ecosystem services, such as disruption of infiltration and water discharge which causes soil erosion, sedimentation, flooding in the rainy season and drought in the dry season. This in turn leads to a *cascading risks*, a condition where there is an increase in natural hazards that can further damage the environment and risk the communities [1, 9, 10].

Disaster risk reduction approaches are becoming a challenge in today's world as hazards become more frequent and more complex. This is fueled by population and economic growth, increasing interrelated exposures leading to more systemic vulnerabilities. The quantification and prediction of risk is therefore not easy, mainly because of the complexities underlying cascading risks.

Cascading risks is a risk that is endogenous, does not stand alone, but has the potential for latent or cumulative risks that can have a negative impact on the system, occurring when some characteristics of the system change. Cascading risks events may occur suddenly or may increase over time, especially if the response to signal changes is inappropriate. The degree of damage inflicted therefore depends on the underlying process and the severity of the triggering event, how extreme the event triggering the risk is [36].

Some cascading risks focus on national-scale risks required for public policy and provide guidance for disaster risk reduction. However, risks are interconnected across geographic areas, with larger and/or smaller scales. Cascading risks affects areas from upstream to downstream or across urban and/or rural areas, due to the unique characteristics of urban/rural areas as part of a complex system. For example, urban areas in coastal zones are at high risk of sea level rise and flood risk especially in areas without adequate structural measures or behavioral adjustments to avoid precipitating events or cascading hazard processes [36].

Within the Sendai Framework for disaster risk reduction, it was argued that understanding of cascading risks is needed to manage multidimensional and interdependent cascading risks with different systems or across different geographic or spatial scales. An understanding of cascading risks therefore must consider the risk from occasional or extraordinary events, such as flash floods, earthquakes, landslides, extreme weather events and sea level rises [36].

In attempt to understand cascading risks, this research uses ecosystem approach to analyze the process of cascading risks and its impact to the communities. Various literatures have explained that the ecosystem approach is part of integrated natural resource management which is defined as the process of combining various aspects of natural resource use into a sustainable management system to meet the objectives of environmental benefits (e.g., profitability, as well as risk reduction) and the goals of the broader community. In the context of this study, the ecosystem is a socio-ecological system that spans across Jeneberang watershed area, consisting of an upstream area, a middle-stream, and a downstream area, from Gowa Regency to Makassar City.

Watershed damage in Indonesia is increasing every year, so that it's causing very detrimental excesses. Every year there are always floods, landslides, droughts and other natural disasters. One of the causes of watershed damage is due to land use planning and management practices that are not in accordance with the right pattern [23]. The level of watershed damage can be determined from several physical indicators, namely the ratio of maximum/minimum river discharge, run-off coefficient, erosion, and sedimentation, ground water level, and spring discharge [27].

In this article, we aim to answer two research questions: 1. How anthropogenic activities especially deforestation in the upstream of Jeneberang watershed lead to a cascading risks within the whole Jeneberang watershed? 2. How is the process of cascading risks and what are the impacts to the communities in South Sulawesi particularly those who live within Jeneberang watershed? Hypothetically, we believe that deforestation or forest degradation in Jeneberang watershed has caused vulnerabilities that pose a cascading risks to ecosystem sustainability throughout the watershed, starting from the upstream, middle-stream to downstream areas. This critical condition of forest areas in Jeneberang Watershed envisages the emergence of risk disasters that could affect the middle stream and downstream area according to Soewarno in 1991 [12] and Noordwijk et al. [22]. This condition is supported by the position of South Sulawesi Province which is geographically prone to disasters [7]. Thus, the level of vulnerability to disasters may increase with the large number of people living in disaster-risk areas, from the upstream to the downstream areas of the watershed.

## 2 Methods

This article aims to elaborate on how deforestation or forest degradation in Jeneberang watershed has caused vulnerabilities that pose a cascading risks to ecosystem sustainability throughout South Sulawesi particularly in Jeneberang watershed area. We use ecosystem approach to analyze chronologically the process of cascading risks from upstream to the downstream in Jeneberang Watershed and its impact to the communities. The methods consist of a literature review, spatial analysis, FGD, in-depth interviews, and field observations.

For technical analysis and writing, we divide Jeneberang watershed into three segments, namely: upstream, middle stream, and downstream areas. The Jeneberang watershed has an area of ± 78 thousand hectares, with the Malino Nature Tourism Park (TWA) upstream in Gowa Regency, then crossing through Gowa Regency and ending in the downstream coast of Makassar City and Gowa Regency (Fig. 1).

## 3 Results and Discussions

In this section, we will explain the physiography of Jeneberang watershed and land degradation before explaining in detail how each watershed segment has created cascading risks in Jeneberang watershed. In attempt to make it chronological, this section consists of five sub-sections: (1) physiography and land degradation, (2) upstream: deforestation, horticulture, and tourism development (3) middle stream: sand mining and sedimentation on Bili-Bili Reservoir (4) downstream: damages and its impacts, (5) cascading risks and challenges.

### *3.1 Physiography of Jeneberang and Land Degradation*

Geologically, the Jeneberang watershed is dominated by volcanic and marine sedimentary rocks in the upstream to middle stream areas [31]. Thus, the upstream area

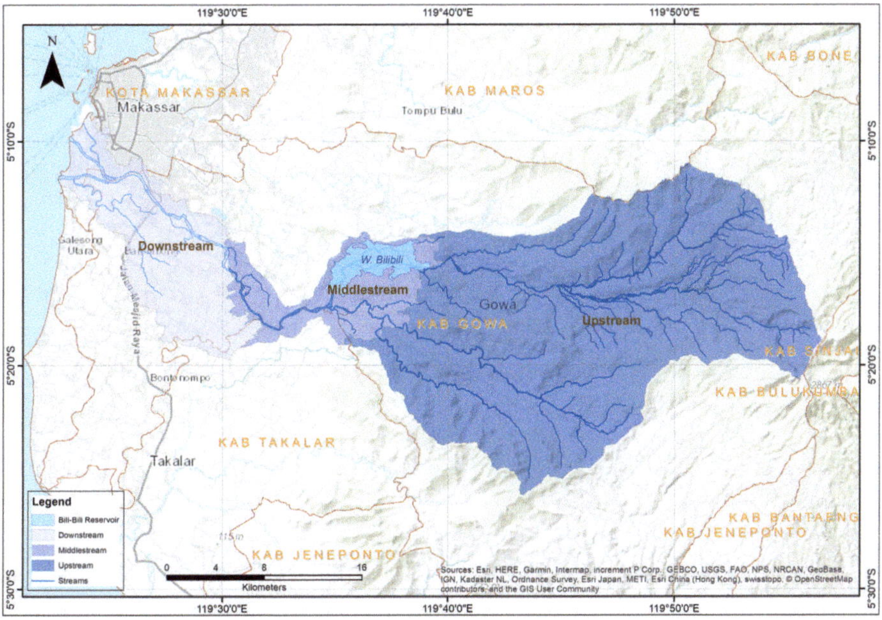


**Fig. 1** Study area in Jeneberang Watershed, South Sulawesi

and some part of the middle stream area have fertile soil which is very beneficial to the economy of communities. In terms of geomorphology, recent study has also explained that Jeneberang River is a braided river which is characterized by abundant supply of sediment and high stream gradient [19]. In the upstream, the slope has a tilt degree over 45° that covers 71.1% areas [11]. Jeneberang River also has the highest maximum river discharge among the 20 major rivers in the South Sulawesi region, which is 315.20 m$^3$/s [18]. Therefore, with the highest river discharge and physical attributes, Jeneberang River is naturally rich in mining materials, such as sand and gravel [19].

Despite having fertile soils and abundant supply of mining materials in the river areas, the land in Jeneberang watershed has been slowly degraded. The Ministry of Environment and Forestry has classified the land degradation level for every region in Indonesia. Based on the map below (Fig. 2), land degradation in Jeneberang watershed is varied but dominated by *potentially degraded, moderately degraded, degraded*, and *highly degraded.* Based on the overlay results, 19.40% (11,314.71 ha) of the upstream area is *highly degraded*. In addition, 47.52% (27,718.43 ha) of the upstream area is in a *potentially degraded* condition. Likewise, what happened in the middle stream, 81.52% (8035.64 ha) of land in the middle region was in a *potentially degraded* condition followed by *degraded* conditions (5.99%) and *highly degraded* (5.81%). Meanwhile, in the downstream area, 89.09% (3428.05 ha) of the area is classified as *non-degraded.* For more details, see the following graph below (Table 1).

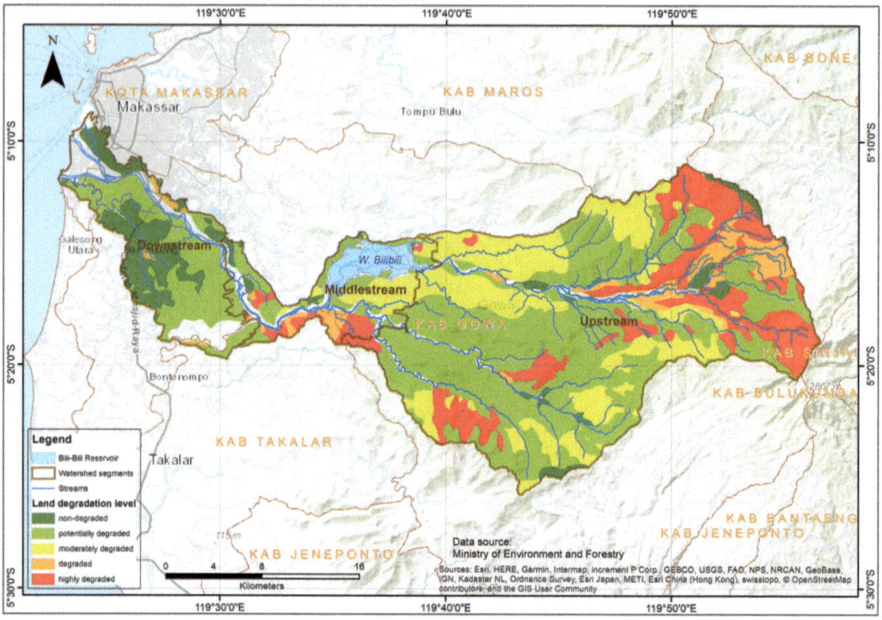


**Fig. 2** Distribution of land degradation in Jeneberang watershed

**Table 1** Proportion of land degradation in Jeneberang Watershed

| Watershed segments | Land degradation level (%) | | | | |
|---|---|---|---|---|---|
| | Non-degraded | Potentially degraded | Moderately degraded | Degraded | Highly degraded |
| Upstream | 3.94 | 47.52 | 24.26 | 4.88 | 19.40 |
| Middle stream | 5.51 | 81.52 | 1.16 | 5.99 | 5.81 |
| Downstream | 89.09 | 3.04 | – | 7.87 | – |

## *3.2 Upstream: Deforestation, Horticulture, and Tourism Development*

Based on land degradation data, more than 50% area of the upstream is degraded 35,236 ha (57.08%) indicating that there are quite massive land use changes in the upstream. Human activities such as forest exploitation, tourism development, and the horticultural industry in the upstream have greatly affected the ecological conditions of the Jeneberang watershed and have degraded the soils, making it prone to disasters such as landslides and floods. The land use changes particularly forest conversion caused by several factors which are mostly close to socio-political aspects.

Furthermore, forest conversion in Jeneberang Watershed into horticultural fields by communities has worsen due to the local government's support on vegetable production in the upstream area. The local government, especially provincial government, have their own interest to boost vegetables production for their regional economic growth. Besides, there is another crucial issue that cause the problem becomes more complex. That is the unclear delineation between conservation/ protected areas and communities' arable land. Informant in the upstream stated that the authorities did not really know where exactly the border of conservation areas are. The people said they have been cultivating the land for years, while the forest agency from the central government did not have the document that prove that certain border. This complex and difficult situation could happen because the local government has not signed the conservation borderline which had stated by the central government. Moreover, it had become more complicated because of the land certificate or at least the annual property tax (SPPT-PBB[1]) had been published by the land registry office (BPN). These land certificates or annual property tax (SPPT-PBB) as the retribution from people to local government become the justification for their right to their arable land. These conditions made the government authorities who has same interest to conserve forest areas difficult to battle the encroachment in Jeneberang Watershed.

Massive encroachment in Jeneberang Watershed leave 16.82% of forest areas remained, where approximately 41.2% of the areas are used for horticulture cultivation and 28.3% areas are used as the rice field [32]. In specific data, around 1.688,76 hectares (48.25%) from 3.500 hectares are converted in Malino Nature Park (TWA Malino). While the other source stated that the total area removed outside of Malino Nature Park in Bawakaraeng-Lompobattang's forest area has reached 5.000,34 ha.

In the context of land degradation, there is a dilemma between communities and the government. Historically, before massive encroachment in the upstream of Jeneberang, many people around the forest had depended on the logging that were sold to the Gowa Paper Factory [12]. In the 1980s, horticultural cultivation was brought by farmers from West Java with satisfied output especially in the profit aspect. It later then started to become mainstream until now. The horticultural sector has proved their role in Gowa Regency that they have contributed around 60.9% of agriculture production and 19.6% of Gross Regional Domestic Product [34]. Beside horticultural industries, there is also tourism development in the upstream. The rise of the tourism industry in Malino region could be seen by the sporadic "*villa boom*" or massive construction of villas in the middle of agricultural lands, especially in Batulapisi area. Extensive built-up area will disturb the hydrology system in Jeneberang watershed.

Therefore, deforestation in the upstream of Jeneberang Watershed affects many aspects including water availability in a dry season. The water tends to dry quickly affecting the process of horticultural cultivation production. Some of the farmers tried to stem the water with those who live in lower areas who also need the water for horticultural cultivation. The stem of the upper on the hill by higher upstream people reduces the flow of water for lower upstream people, the flow becomes slow or completely dry in lower upstream areas. They also come up with other strategies, such as trying to dig a well to water their crops. Some of them may have the capacity

[1] Surat Pemberitahuan Pajak Terutang—Pajak Bumi dan Bangunan.

in tackling the water issue when the dry season comes, but some other people may not. So, the water issue in the upstream especially in the dry season could be one of the issues that could cause conflict between the people.

The further effect of forest degradation areas in the upstream of Jeneberang Watershed is the high inequality of water discharge that reaches a ratio of 1: 60 compared with normal watershed water discharge at 1:25 [38]. The ratio is showing that water discharge can be very low when the dry season comes, while in rainy seasons, there will be plenty of water flowing in Jeneberang Watershed. The condition of low water discharge of Jeneberang in the dry season is utilized by sand miners to extract sand directly from riverbeds. On the other hand, the amount of wat.er discharge will be double compared to the water discharge on normal conditions. This higher water discharge in Jeneberang could raise the risk of floods.

### 3.3 *Middle Stream: Sand Mining and Sedimentation on Bili-Bili Reservoir*

The main issue in the middle stream area of Jeneberang Watershed is massive sand mining activities and sedimentation due to the poor management of Bili-Bili Reservoir. Based on land degradation data, 81.52% (8035.64 ha) of area in the middle stream is considered as a *potentially degraded* condition followed by *degraded* conditions (5.99%) and *highly degraded* conditions (5.81%). The existence of sand mining including dredging on the banks has caused the river widens and when it rains, the riverbank cannot hold water, water overflows into settlements (Fig. 3).

**Fig. 3** Middle stream of Jeneberang

Recent study stated that sand mining activities on the Jeneberang River were first carried out traditionally and later operated in a more modern way for more than 19 years in the Jeneberang River with 35 construction materials mining in Gowa Regency [3, 19]. Sand mining activities are practically very beneficial to support the economy of the communities. However, sand mining can lead to excessive exploitation if it is not carried out properly in accordance with conservation principles. Sand miners who do not pay attention to environmental aspects will risk the surrounding area with the danger of erosion and landslides [4].

Beside sand mining activities, sedimentation and the poor management of Bili-Bili Reservoir is also an issue. Bili-Bili Reservoir, located right in the middle of the watershed, was first built in 1992 with the assistance of the Japanese government. It is expected to prevent flooding in the downstream area due to the swift flow of the Jeneberang river from upstream. In 2004, there was massive landslide (167.2 million $m^3$) occurred in the caldera of Mount Bawakaraeng, causing large amount of sediment carried by the Jeneberang River [5, 16, 24, 25]. Bili-Bili was silted up due to the large amount of landslide sediment carried by the Jeneberang River (75.2 million $m^3$). In 2009 the total volume of deposits was estimated more than 244.9 million $m^3$ and unstable sediment deposits which is still exist in the caldera were estimated at 82.7 million $m^3$, so that the total volume of sediment flowing along the main Jeneberang river channel was 162.2 million $m^3$ [28]. In 2019 the sedimentation level in the Bili-Bili Reservoir reached a total of 75,055,327 $m^3$. This sedimentation rate increased very significantly in 2015 reaching an elevation above 60 m [17]. There is already a work plan to carry out dredging in the reservoir, BBWS already has the tools, but the dredging has never been carried out.

Based on our research, we found that sand mining activities are mostly carried out in Tinggimoncong and Parangloe District. According to the Head of Regional Company (*Perusahaan Daerah*), illegal sand mining activities carried out at those areas indirectly damage the artificial embankments (sand pockets). The sand pockets were built to avoid landslides and floods. Sand mining in the riverbanks can destroy both natural and artificial dikes in the Jeneberang River.

Despite its positive impact on regional economic development, a development approach in the context of sand mining will result in market failure due to failure to anticipate environmental impacts or negative externalities of an economic activity. One of the negative externalities of construction material mining comes from mining trucks which can cause conflicts. Our research found that there is contestation of power especially in Parangloe District. Mining activities that are expected to support the local economy of the surrounding communities, in fact, were not beneficials to all parties. The dominance of control over mining points (legal or illegal) carried out by entrepreneurs or individuals has an impact on the welfare of the grassroots community around the Parangloe District and Bili-Bili Reservoir.

WALHI revealed that there were three things that were mutually sustainable because of the exploitation of sand mining activities in the Jeneberang River. First, the silting of the Bili-Bili Reservoir, sand and non-sand material after erosion from mining activities will be carried away by currents and sediment in the Bili-Bili Reservoir. Second, floods and landslides are getting wider because of the silting of the Bili-Bili Reservoir. The amount of sedimentation in the Bili-Bili Reservoir has decreased its function as a water reservoir. As a result, when the rainfall is high, flooding and landslides are inevitable. And this brings us to the third thing, which is if floods and landslides continue to be unresolved, there will be more casualties and damage. This has been proven in 2019 when floods took many lives in Gowa (53 died), Makassar (1 died), Jeneponto (15 died), and Maros (4 died) [29].

## *3.4 Downstream: Damages and Its Impacts*

The downstream area of Jeneberang Watershed is a densely populated and a rapidly growing urbanized area.[2] But it is still dominated by paddy fields, covering an area of 12,999.46 ha, or 59.3% of the total area. In addition to paddy fields, the downstream area around the riverbank is dominated by built-up areas, especially settlements with an area of 6557.47 ha or 29.9% of the total area. With its diverse land use and outlet of the watershed, the direction of land use zoning in the downstream is permanent cultivation area or 80% utilization area and 20% buffer zone area [30]. In terms of land degradation, 89.09% (3428.05 ha) of the downstream area is classified as *non-degraded*. Meanwhile, the area in *degraded* condition is 302.79 ha or 7.87% of the total downstream area.

Even though most of the areas are classified as *non-degraded*, the downstream area of Jeneberang has become the most vulnerable areas compared to other segments. In 2019, hundreds of houses were flooded in Pangkabinanga Village, Pallangga District, Gowa Regency with an inundation height of about 2 m [2]. This flood was the result of the opening of the floodgates of the Bili-bili Reservoir. A total of 2,121 flood victims living in the riverbank took refuge in several shelters provided by the government [15]. WALHI also recorded that floods and landslides occurred in Gowa, Jeneponto, Maros and Makassar City [29, 32]. The downstream of the watershed also experiences inundation flooding caused by poor drainage. The affected areas include the Tamarunang area [35].

Beside floods, the downstream area becomes more vulnerable due to sedimentation carried by Jeneberang River. As explained in the previous section, sedimentation has not only occurred in the middle stream, but also in the downstream, spreading along the river mouth. The sedimentation[3] that occurred downstream of the Jeneberang River is an example of *cascading risks* caused by the natural processes

[2] Based on our observations, there are many ornamental plant traders who set up kiosk, scavenger activities, chicken farms, food traders as well as plantations activities and illegal gracing, all of which are along the downstream border of the Jeneberang River, which starts from the mouth of Jeneberang River until the rubber dam. All these activities have been contributed to the increase of sedimentation rate and increase watershed pollution. Likewise, fish farming activities in downstream of the Jeneberang River around the Somba Opu Bridge, Gowa Regency.

[3] Some of the sedimentation has created a delta that rises to the surface of the river when the sea water recedes. The delta in some places have been polluted by overgrown of nipah plants (*Nypa fruticans*), water hyacinth plant (*Eichhornia crassipes*), and other weeds.

in the upstream and middle stream areas including the most notable Bawakaraeng's caldera landslide[4] in 2004 [5]. The potential for sediment due to a large avalanche will flow downstream especially in the rainy season, making it prone to floods in the settlements located nearby the river.

Sedimentation in the downstream of Jeneberang is not only caused by natural processes, but also by waste carried by waterways from settlements that flow into the river. This is because certain spots have become waste accumulations in water bodies especially in riverbanks which are close to settlements. According to Yosafat [37], the waste that reaches the river mouth and sea flows from river/streams in the area. Besides, some channels are not optimally functioning. One of them is Jongaya channel in District Tamalate. The same condition has occurred in several drainage areas in each district. About 30% of the existing waterways in the coastal districts of Makassar City (especially Biringkanaya, Tamalanrea, Tallo, and Tamalate are not functioning properly [26]. Beside waste, sedimentation in the downstream is also influenced by fishery activities, cargo ships activities and other activities that have been increasing damage to the riverbanks.

Sedimentation also leads to contamination on the river. Previous report stated that the water quality of the Jeneberang River which has been one of the main raw sources of drinking water for Makassar and its surroundings is quite alarming. The Regional Environment Agency (BLHD) of South Sulawesi classified the water quality of the river crossing Gowa Regency and two districts in Makassar as *very bad*. Jeneberang River water pollution comes from erosion on the riverbanks caused by deforestation, as well as sand mining activities on the banks of the river, so that increasing sedimentation in the river flow. Another problem is anthropogenic activities such as agriculture, plantations, waste disposal, household waste, hotels garbage, and tourism activities.

In Malino and Palangga district for example, Gowa Regency and Tamalate district in Makassar City many housing and markets contribute domestic waste to river bodies. Besides, livestock manure that enters to the river caused getting worse of quality water river [14]. Jeneberang River water is heavily polluted. From observations in the field, not only in rivers, piles and garbage are also found at several points of the Jeneberang embankment in Gowa Regency, because used as garbage dumps by residents around the watershed areas.

The cascading risks downstream also caused by the decreasing function of the water catchment area. The decrease in water catchment areas is caused by rapid urban development, including violations of land use by the community with the constructing buildings on the riverbanks. Many factors cause change in the use of river border areas, including the high rate of urbanization in Makassar City. Population growth in Makassar and its suburban areas is associated with a decrease in agricultural land and an increase in building density [33]. The increasing number of lower-middle income residents has resulted in high demand for settlements, and this has triggered

[4] Nurdin et al. [25] stated that landslides occur due to natural processes, namely there is a disturbance in the stability of the soil making up the slopes which is influenced by geomorphological conditions, especially the slope factor.

the rise of illegal settlements or squatter areas in riverbanks which later affect the risks in Jeneberang Watershed.

### 3.5 Cascading Risks and Challenges

In the Jeneberang watershed, deforestation has a significant effect on environmental changes in this area. The use of forests that are dominated by human activities, either individually or as a community or as a corporation, and government policies & programs increase the frequency and intensity of hazards, as well as exposure and vulnerability to hazard threats. This condition causes an increase in the danger of landslides and floods due to the reduced/lost function of the forest to absorb rainfall and hold soil and release water periodically. When forest cover is lost, rainwater runoff that carries soil (mud) quickly flows to the lower reaches of the river, thus raising the river level (sediment) and overflowing water causing flooding of agricultural land, surrounding villages, and towns, especially during the rainy season. In contrast, during the dry season, areas downstream of deforestation are vulnerable to drought for months [9, 10].

Agriculture was the main driving factor for forest conversion in the Jeneberang watershed area, but its activities vary between upstream, middle-stream, and downstream areas. In the upper watershed, forest conversion was dominated by two main activities, namely horticultural crop farming and tourism activities. In the middle and downstream areas, deforestation and watershed damage were mainly related to infrastructure development policies and programs. Massive land use change and technological intervention through the construction of the Bili-Bili Reservoir, embankments, and sandbags. These activities were carried out in this watershed area with a steep slope geomorphology.

Vulnerability in the middle and downstream watersheds has increased significantly, resulting in higher systemic and disaster risks, including landslides that have caused high sedimentation in the Jeneberang River and Bili-Bili Reservoir. High sedimentation is a major challenge because it affects the quantity and quality of water in reservoirs which are the source of irrigation water and clean/drinking water. The vulnerability in this area was getting worse due to weather anomalies, especially extreme weather, which tended to increase in frequency. This condition caused an ecological disaster, marked by floods in the rainy season and drought in the dry season, especially the long dry season. Hundreds of families in the downstream area were affected by floods as high as 50 cm that often occurred, especially in the Somba Opu Fort area. On the other hand, during the dry season, the water discharge in the rivers and reservoirs dropped significantly, which often caused drought. Consequently, farmers face a high risk of crop failure due to drought, and residents, especially in downstream and urban areas, including Makassar City, are at high risk of lack of clean and drinking water sources.

Flash flood is an extraordinary event that is characterized by very large floods from higher areas that wash away a lot of material such as water, sand, soil, stones, mud and wood that move to lower places. This disaster generally begins with a landslide in the upstream river through the slopes along the river. Besides being caused by natural processes, flash floods can also be caused by high deforestation and the event of a dam or reservoir bursting due to heavy rain that flushes the ground for a long time which can result in additional water discharge in the reservoir or dam [6].

## 4 Conclusions

Communities in watershed areas face high risks stemming from natural hazards and non-natural factors. The Jeneberang watershed area, especially with its geomorphological attributes and high river gradient, is an area that is prone to various types of disasters, especially landslides, floods, and droughts. This condition is exacerbated by extreme weather that is increasingly occurring in this area. Meanwhile, non-natural risks are closely related to structural factors related to development policies and activities in this area. Forest conversion, which was initiated by community agricultural activities, was then encouraged by various tourism sectors, sand mining and policy activities and infrastructure development programs permeated through various economic and service sectors. Economic activities and infrastructure development seen by massive land use changes in every segment (upstream, middlestream, and downstream) have become a systemic trap that results in the destruction of these natural resources. The complexity of these activities has a cascading impact and varies by region in the watershed area. This indicates the high threat and risk of disaster faced by the community starting from the upstream, the middle to the downstream, including in Makassar City.

Cascading risks in the Jeneberang watershed area are marked by the occurrence of several disasters that trigger the emergence of further disasters in the future, considering that one disaster event has the potential to increase the risk of another disaster when community resilience decreases due to continuous disaster intensity. Landslides and floods in the watershed area are examples of the causes of increased vulnerability of the region to disasters.

Poor governance of Jeneberang Watershed, which tend to overlap, also needs to be addressed because it has greatly affected the physical condition of Jeneberang watershed which caused cascading risks in the region. Integration between the central government, local governments, CSOs, and the community is needed to achieve equally just and sustainable watershed management and regional governance. In addition, law enforcement in terms of spatial planning and zoning needs to be done, so that all anthropogenic activities can be carried out by considering land capabilities and in accordance with conservation principles.

## References


1. Adnyana IGNS (2003) Tantangan Pemerintah Daerah dalam Pengelolaan Sumber Daya Air yang Berkelanjutan [Regional government challenges in sustainable water resources management]. In: Peran Budaya Lokal dalam Menunjang Sumber Daya Air yang Berkelanjutan [The role of local culture in supporting sustainable water resources]. BAPPENAS and FAO, Kuta Beach, Bali
2. Amir H (2019) Ratusan Rumah Terendam Banjir di Palangga, Warga Dievakuasi [Hundreds of houses submerged in floods in Palangga, residents evacuated]. https://makassar.sindonews.com/berita/19992/4/ratusan-rumah-terendam-banjir-di-pallangga-warga-dievakuasi. Accessed 22 July 2021
3. Arjan A, Afifah AN, Patila YA, Anas AV (2020) Valuation of environmental impact due to material construction mining, Gowa, South Sulawesi. EPI Int J Eng 3(1):90–94. https://doi.org/10.25042/epi-ije.022020.13
4. As'ad (2005) Pengelolaan Lingkungan Pada Penambangan Rakyat [Studi Kasus Penambangan Intan Rakyat di Kecamatan Cempaka Kota Banjarbaru Propinsi Kalimantan Selatan [Environmental management in artisanal mining [Case study of artisanal diamond mining in Cempaka District, Banjarbaru City, South Kalimantan Province]]. Universitas Diponegoro
5. Asrib AR, Purwanto YJ, Sukandi S (2011) Dampak Longsoran Kaldera terhadap Tingkat Sedimentasi Di Waduk Bili-Bili Provinsi Sulawesi Selatan [The impact of caldera landslides on sedimentation levels in the Bili-Bili reservoir, South Sulawesi Province]. J Hidrolitan 2(3):135–146
6. BNPB (2016) Indeks Risiko Bencana Indonesia [Indonesia disaster risk index]. Jakarta
7. BNPB (2021) Indeks Risiko Bencana Indonesia 2020 [Indonesia disaster risk index 2020]. Jakarta
8. Bodo T, Gimah BG, Seomoni KJ (2021) Deforestation and habitat loss: human causes, consequences and possible solutions. J Geograph Res 4(2):22–30
9. Butler RA (2012) Consequences of deforestation. https://rainforests.mongabay.com/0901.htm. Accessed 05 April 2022
10. Chandra W (2019) Environmental degradation exacerbates Indonesia flooding, landslides. https://news.mongabay.com/2019/01/environmental-degradation-exacerbates-indonesia-flooding-landslides/. Accessed 05 April 2022
11. Danial M, Arsyad U, Demmallino EB (2020) Strategi Pengelolaan Hulu Daerah Aliran Sungai Jeneberang Provinsi Sulawesi Selatan [Upstream area management strategy for the Jeneberang watershed, South Sulawesi Province]. Ecosolum 9(2):11–31. https://doi.org/10.20956/ecosolum.v9i2.11890
12. Firnawati (2018) Perencanaan Lanskap Pertanian Kawasan Hulu DAS Jeneberang dengan Pendekatan Bioregion [Agricultural landscape planning of the upper Jeneberang watershed area with a bioregion approach]. Universitas Hasanuddin. https://ieeeauthorcenter.ieee.org/wp-content/uploads/IEEE-Reference-Guide.pdf%0A, http://wwwlib.murdoch.edu.au/find/citation/ieee.html%0A10.1016/j.cie.2019.07.022%0A, https://github.com/ethereum/wiki/wiki/White-Paper%0A, https://tore.tuhh.de/hand
13. Gregersen HM, Ffolliott PF, Brooks KN (2007) Integrated watershed management: connecting people to their land and water. In: Integrated watershed management: connecting people to their land and water. CABI Pub. https://doi.org/10.1659/mrd.mm042
14. Halide J (2014) Air Sungai Jeneberang tercemar berat [Jeneberang river is heavily polluted]. https://daerah.sindonews.com/berita/862915/25/air-sungai-jeneberang-tercemar-berat. Accessed 07 April 2022
15. Haq A (2019) Banjir Landa Gowa, 2121 Warga Mengungsi, Satu Anak Balita Tewas [Floods hit Gowa, 2121 residents evacuated, one toddler died]. https://regional.kompas.com/read/2019/01/23/10491831/banjir-landa-gowa-2121-warga-mengungsi-satu-anak-balita-tewas. Accessed 22 July 2021

16. Hardjosuwarno S (2008) Community based warning and evacuation system against debris flow in the Upper Jeneberang River, Gowa, South Sulawesi. Forum Geografi 22(1):13. https://doi.org/10.23917/forgeo.v22i1.4922
17. Istiqfarah AN (2021) Studi Laju Sedimentasi Waduk Bili-Bili Pasca Pengembangan Bangunan Penahan Sedimen [Study of sedimentation sate of Bili-Bili reservoir after development of sediment retaining structure]. Universitas Bosowa. https://repository.unibos.ac.id/xmlui/handle/123456789/105
18. Kementerian Pekerjaan Umum dan Perumahan Rakyat (2015) Pola Pengelolaan Sumber Daya Air Wilayah Sungai Jeneberang [Water resources management in the jeneberang river basin]. Indonesia
19. Kusumaningrum D, Hafsari TA, Syam L (2021) Sand and the city: the historical geography of sand mining in Jeneberang River and its relation to urban development in South Sulawesi. ETNOSIA: Jurnal Etnografi Indonesia 6(2):200–216. https://doi.org/10.31947/etnosia.v6i2.17918
20. Meyer AL, Van Kooten GC, Wang S (2003) Institutional, social and economic roots of deforestation: a cross-country comparison. Int Forest Rev 5(1):29–37. https://www.jstor.org/stable/43739299
21. Morrison-métois S, Lundgren H (2016, April) Forests and sustainable forest management. OECD Evaluation INSIGHTS
22. Noordwijk M, Agus S, Hairiah, Faarida (2004) Peranan Agroforestri dalam Mempertahankan Fungsi Hidrologi DAS [The role of agroforestry in maintaining watershed hydrological functions]. Agrivita 26(1):1–8
23. Nugroho SP (2003) Pergeseran Kebijakan dan Paradigma Baru dalam Pengelolaan Daerah Aliran Sungai di Indonesia [Policy shifts and new paradigms in watershed management in Indonesia]. Jurnal Teknologi Lingkungan 4(3). https://doi.org/10.29122/JTL.V4I3.283
24. Nurdin PF, Kubota T (2018) Gis-based landslide susceptibility assessment and factor effect analysis by certainty factor in upstream of Jeneberang River, Indonesia. Geoplanning: J Geomat Plann 5(1):75. https://doi.org/10.14710/geoplanning.5.1.75-90
25. Nurdin PF, Kubota T, Soma AS (2019) Investigation of flood and landslide in the Jeneberang catchment area, Indonesia in 2019. Int J Erosion Contr Eng 12(1):13–18. https://doi.org/10.13101/ijece.12.13
26. Nurmawati Gaol JL, Ling MM (2018) Tingkat Kerentanan Wilayah Pesisir Kota Makassar Terhadap Pencemaran Sampah [Vulnerability of coastal areas of Makassar City to waste pollution]. Jurnal Ilmiah Wawasan Pendidikan 4(3)
27. Prastowo (2011) Masalah Sumber Daya Air di Indonesia: Kerusakan Daerah Aliran Sungai dan Rendahnya Kinerja Pemanfaatan Air [Water resource problems in Indonesia: damage to river watersheds and low performance of water utilization].
28. Pratama AM (2015) Persepsi masyarakat sekitar Waduk Bili-Bili terhadap aktivitas penambangan di Sungai Jeneberang [The perception of the community around the Bili-Bili reservoir regarding mining activities in the Jeneberang river]. Universitas Negeri Makassar
29. Rosmila (2019) Potret Penanganan Korban Banjir dan Longsor di Sulawesi Selatan. Makassar [Portrait of rapid response of flood and landslide victims in South Sulawesi].
30. Rusdi (2013) Analisis Penggunaan lahan DAS Jeneberang (Permasalahan dan Solusi) [Analysis of land use of Jeneberang watershed [Problems and solutions]]. Universitas Gadjah Mada. https://www.researchgate.net/publication/337830605_Analisis_Penggunaan_lahan_DaS_Jeneberang
31. Sukamto R, Supriatna S (1982) Geologic Map of the Ujungpandang, Benteng, and Sinjai Quadrangles, Sulawesi Scale 1:250.000. Bandung: Geological Survey of Indonesia, Ministry of Mines
32. Sulfitra A, Mirajanna, Saputra R, Haidar A, Ihsan N, Arsenio M, ... Sulaiman MA (2019) Degradasi Lingkungan dan Bencana Ekologis di Sulawesi Selatan [Environmental degradation and ecological disaster in South Sulawesi]. Catatan Akhir Tahun WALHI Sulsel [WALHI South Sulawesi's end of year notes]. Makassar

33. Surya B, Salim A, Hernita H, Suriani S, Menne F, Rasyidi ES (2021) Land use change, urban agglomeration, and urban sprawl: a sustainable development perspective of makassar city, indonesia. Land 10(6). https://doi.org/10.3390/land10060556
34. Syafruddin RF, Sari DP, Kadir M (2018) Penentuan Komoditas Unggulan dan Sturuktur Tinggimoncong Kabupaten Gowa Berdasarkan Location Quotient (LQ) Dan Klassen Typology (KT) [Determination of superior commodities and tinggimoncong structure of Gowa regency based on Location Quotient (LQ) and Klassen Typology (KT)]. Jurnal Galung Tropika 7(1):22–32
35. Ummah NR (2021) Banjir Sudah Masuk Rumah, Warga di Gowa Pilih Bertahan dan Enggan Mengungsi [Flood has entered homes, residents in Gowa choose to stay and reluctant to evacuate]. https://makassarmetro.com/2021/03/10/banjir-sudah-masuk-rumah-warga-di-gowa-pilih-bertahan-dan-enggan-mengungsi. Accessed 22 July 2021
36. UNDRR (2019) Global assessment report on disaster risk reduction 2019 | UNDRR. Geneva, Switzerland. https://www.undrr.org/publication/global-assessment-report-disaster-risk-reduction-2019
37. Yosafat FE (2017) Pergerakan Sampah Lautan dengan Pendekatan Model Trajektori Partikel di Perairan Selat Bali [Movement of marine debris using a particle trajectory model approach in the waters of the Bali Strait]. Institut Teknologi Bandung
38. Yusran, Abdullah N (2010) Analisis performansi dan disain kelembagaan pengelolaan hutan di wilayah Pegunungan Bawakaraeng-Lompobattang Provinsi Sulawesi Selatan [Analysis of performance and institutional design of forest management in the Bawakaraeng-Lompobattang mountains area, South Sulawesi Province]. Jurnal Hutan Dan Masyarakat 2(2):200–208

# Democracy, Security and Human Rights in Southeast Asia: National and Sub-National Context

# Back to the Ground: Recognizing the South East Asian Local Wisdom and Indigenous People for Future Resilience

**Dessy Maeyangsari**

**Abstract** Southeast Asia is one of regions that has over millions of indigenous people along with their traditional knowledges and values. Even though the peoples are internationally subjected to collective rights recognized by the United Nations, however legal protection with a regional approach still does not exist within the ASEAN community. On the other hand, the member countries often have conflicts related to indigenous land due to the lack of formal recognition over their land and the other rights. This paper focuses on the capacity of indigenous people as a stakeholder and legal subjects in ASEAN, follows by a brief comparison to Inter-American Commission on Human Rights which have adopted the American Declaration on the Rights of Indigenous Peoples. The study will specifically point on the role of indigenous people in various fields related to national and regional resilience, be it in terms of the environment protection or food security.

**Keywords** Indigenous people · ASEAN · Resilience · Traditional knowledge

## 1 Introduction

Asia is home to the largest number of indigenous peoples with an estimated 260 million from the 370 million original inhabitants worldwide. Whilst, two states in South East Asia include as countries with the highest of indigenous people in the world. Even though all ASEAN members are parties to UNDRIP, however the identity has not been taken into account during preparations of national censuses. Therefore, it is very difficult to give accurate or a proper approximate figure of the populations of Indigenous People in the South East Asia Region.

Within these facts, all ASEAN Member States have basically recognized the existence of indigenous people by ratifying UNDRIP. However, on a regional scale, unlike other international organizations, ASEAN does not have an instrument that

D. Maeyangsari (✉)
UPN "Veteran": Jawa Timur, Surabaya 60294, Indonesia
e-mail: Dessy.maeyangsari.ih@upnjatim.co.id



Nawawi et al. (eds.), *Managing Disruption and Developing Resilience for a Better Southeast Asia*, Springer Proceedings in Humanities and Social Sciences,
https://doi.org/10.1007/978-981-96-2116-3_50

regulates all participating countries to protect and provides the collective rights of the indigenous peoples. Instead, conflicts between entities with indigenous peoples in Southeast Asia keeps going. In some cases, indigenous people forced to leave their lands because of violent conflicts, and to move to another country, like Thailand, Vietnam or Laos [1]. On other cases, the force resettlements due to land acquisition by the government policies or companies are commonly found. Indigenous peoples notwithstanding with the big corporation.

This paper focuses on the capacity of indigenous people and its traditional knowledge as helping part to national and regional resilience, emphasize in food and environmental resilience. It follows by a brief comparison to Inter-American Commission on Human Rights which have adopted the American Declaration on the Rights of Indigenous Peoples.

## 2 The Local Wisdom for National and Regional Resilience

### *2.1 Indigenous People and Traditional Knowledge*

In the context of international law, there is no treaty or international policy which formally establishes the legal definition of indigenous people. In fact, the international declaration focusing on the rights of indigenous people, United Nation Declaration on the Rights of Indigenous People (UNDRIP), does not stipulate any specification for a community to be classified as indigenous. Even though normally any prominent terms relating to the core subject of an international agreement get addressed in the definition clause, it does not apply to the current subject. The absence of formal definition on indigenous people is seen as a necessity to provide flexibility in order to respecting the desire and the right of each indigenous people to define themselves.

Nevertheless, International Labour Organization (ILO) provides a statement to coverage on the term of indigenous people in Convention No. 169. This statement, rather than a definition, is established to indicating that the Convention applies to:

(a) tribal peoples in independent countries whose social, cultural and economic conditions distinguish them from other sections of the national community and whose status is regulated wholly or partially by their own customs or traditions or by special laws or regulations;
(b) peoples in independent countries who are regarded as indigenous on account of their descent from the populations which inhabited the country, or a geographical region to which the country belongs, at the time of conquest or colonization or the establishment of present state boundaries and who irrespective of their legal status, retain some or all of their own social, economic, cultural and political institutions.

Meanwhile, within the United Nations system, various terms have not been formally defined, the most vivid examples being the notions of "peoples" and of "minorities". Yet, the United Nations has recognized the right of peoples to self-determination and has adopted the Declaration on the Rights of Persons Belonging to National or Ethnic, Religious and Linguistic Minorities.

However, the lack of formal definition of "peoples" or "minorities" has not been crucial to United Nations successes or failures in those domains nor to the promotion, protection or monitoring of the rights recognized for these entities. Similarly, in the case of the concept of "indigenous peoples", the prevailing view today is that no formal universal definition of the term is necessary.

## *2.2 The Role of Indigenous People and Traditional Knowledge for National and Regional Resilience*

The major special characteristic of traditional knowledge is their long relation with the land, ecosystem and its people. Due to this character, while traditional knowledge is strongly rooted into the community, it also is limited narrowly on the exact land territory and indigenous community. This condition results to the lack of attention from the authorities to study or to acknowledge the potential of traditional knowledge, mainly on the environmental protection and food resilience.

**Traditional Knowledge for the Environmental Protection**. International law instrument has recognized the vital role of indigenous people and their communities in the environmental management and development. Principle 22 of the early threshold for international environmental instrument, 1992 Rio Declaration, obliges the states to duly support the identity of indigenous people, culture and interests and enable their effective participation in the achievement of sustainable development. This recognition has been brought to the Rio Convention with the same notion in The Convention on Biological Diversity (CBD), that the close ties of indigenous peoples and local communities to their land and biological resources and traditional knowledge has vital roles in the environmental management and environmental development.

The CBD itself has established a working group to address the implementation and protection of traditional knowledge, particularly in Article 8(j) of the CBD, which emphasizes the importance of traditional indigenous knowledge, for conservation and for the purposes of the equitable sharing of the benefits derived from the utilization of such knowledge. The working group has developed important international policy guidance which reflects the need to protect biocultural heritage with the participation of Indigenous in the working group. Whilst other UN entities also have relevant policies and programs that recognize the role of traditional knowledge in securing the rights of indigenous peoples as elaborated in the UN Declaration. Nevertheless, the concept has not been fully implemented by many states.

Directing back to the global environmental concerns, factually many of areas with highest biological diversity on the planet are inhabited by indigenous community.

One example is the "Biological 17",[1] which refers to 17 nations home to more than two-thirds of the Earth's biological resources and are also the traditional territories of most of the world's indigenous peoples.[2] This link is particularly significant in rainforest areas[3] [OHCHR], which also actively becomes part of environmental development programs, such as REDD+.[4]

Out of seventeen nations of "Biological 17", seven countries are part of REDD+, while three of them are located in Southeast Asia and members of ASEAN, with the numbers of indigenous people are living and depending on the forest, the indigenous communities are certainly get affected by forest related project. However, it cannot be denied as well that REDD+ in theory is programmed to help boost the incomes of forest communities, including indigenous people, who depend on the forest for their livelihoods[5]; make it possible for positive and negative impact.

One study about the implication of REDD+ national plan in South and South East-Asia found the high intensity connection between the forests related plan and indigenous people. One of issue linked to indigenous people is regarding to Cambodia REDD+ project site in Seima which is settled by more than 11,000 indigenous ethnic minority people who largely depend on forest resources. Since the site's categorization changed from Production to Protection Forest in 2009 activities such as cutting and clearing forest, hunting, building infrastructure (e.g. housings, roads) as well as commercial extraction and agricultural activities are strictly prohibited within the core of the Seima Protection Forest (SPF) Area. The issue came up when the territory was being designated as a protection forest, the traditional land use practices had been restricted (e.g. shifting agriculture) because extended forestland clearance was not allowed in the protected forest area. However, referring to the 2002 Forestry Law, the Forestry Administration stated that traditional rights of local people are always respected, especially for the purpose of traditional customs, spiritual and basic living. This kind of conflicts related to the use natural resources and land tenure are easily found in national forest management, especially in developing countries [2].

On the contrary, another example of forest management with the contribution of indigenous people turns into positive outcome. In Panama, the country's indigenous

---

[1] The countries comprise the "Biological 17" are: Australia, Brazil, China, Colombia, the Democratic Republic of the Congo, Ecuador, India, Indonesia, Madagascar, Malaysia, Mexico, Peru, the Philippines, South Africa, Papua New Guinea, the United States of America, and Venezuela.

[2] Food A http://www.fao.org/3/a-i0838e.pdf.

[3] Office of the United Nations High Commissioner for Human Rights. https://www.ohchr.org/Documents/Publications/GuideIPleaflet10en.pdf.

[4] REDD+ is financial aid system adopted at COP 16 and COP 17. The COP 16 Decision urges Parties, in particular developed country Parties, to support, through multilateral and bilateral channels, the development of national strategies or action plans, policies and measures and capacity-building, followed by the implementation of national policies and measures and national strategies or action plans that could involve further capacity-building, technology development and transfer and results-based demonstration activities. The initial focus of the mechanism was on deforestation, but it has subsequently expanded to also cover reducing emissions from forest degradation, in addition to the role of conservation, sustainable management of forests and the enhancement of forest carbon stocks in developing countries.

[5] http://www.cifor.org/publications/pdf_files/media/MCCMP1001.pdf.

groups (Bribri, Bugle, Embera, Guna, Naso Tjër-Di, Ngäbe and Wounaan) teamed up with the UN-REDD Programme take part in the monitoring of the forests using drones and other technology. In the joint project, some indigenous participants have already developed maps and other documents to support land claims and a more integrated use of land. The experience and knowledge of the indigenous technicians have learned has led to South-South cooperation, in the form of workshops held in other countries like Guatemala, Paraguay and Peru.

From both of studies above, while it is undeniable that environmental management in "modern" term is more engaging for the investor, easier in some ways, and faster in giving the result, however the procedures easily can harm the indigenous peoples and in the worst case, exacerbating environmental conditions. To tackle this possibility, an active contribution from indigenous peoples is prominent. As a significant party of environmental policy management, the indigenous have the ability to assess the environment with proper traditional knowledge of the ecosystem, which can be beneficial in reduce the possibility of failures or errors that result in damage to biodiversity or the environment.

**Traditional knowledge for food resilience**. Consisting mostly of developing countries, some of ASEAN member states are still struggling in providing proper foods for their citizens. The 2016 Association of ASEAN Regional Report on Nutrition Security reported an alarming proportion of children, adolescents and adults in the region suffer from malnutrition and consume poor-quality diets, this phenomenon is not getting better in 2021 Report. This phenomenon is partly related to the global pandemic started from early 2020.

The COVID-19 epidemic is expected to worsen existing challenges to the availability, accessibility and affordability of nutritious food. It is estimated that nearly three-quarters of households in ASEAN Member States experienced a decline in income as a result of the pandemic due to disruptions of food supply chains. This condition is also changing food environments and access to essential, quality nutrition services. As a result, individuals and families are increasingly shifting away from traditional and indigenous diets based on whole foods, towards processed foods that are higher in salt, sugar and unhealthy fats and low in essential nutrients (ASEAN Report 2022).

In order to resolve the food scarcity due to the pandemic and for long term resolution, ASEAN Member States have been making agendas in agricultural sector to encourage the production of corps for food commodities. A sample of extensive agenda is carried out by the Indonesian government called food estate.

To maintain Indonesia's long-term food security, the government is planning a food estate program in Merauke Regency, Papua Province. Food Estate is a food development concept that is carried out in an integrated manner including agriculture, plantations, and livestock in a certain area [3]. The Ministry of Agriculture together with the Merauke Regional Government empowers potential uncultivated land to be used as land for food crop production. It was planned that 1.2 million ha of land will be cultivated by 2019. Apart from Papua, food estate development is also carried out in Western Borneo (120,000 ha), Central Borneo (180,000 ha), East Borneo

(10,000 ha), and Maluku (190,000 ha). As it is considered large scale program with large consequence, food estate program is highly criticized for its lack of concern to the environment and indigenous community. The use of high scale land on peat forest and protected forest is certainly something that needs to be watched out for, especially historically, this food estate has often failed from time to time.

Contrary to this mega project, some reports state that indigenous communities have been able to overcome food scarcity during pandemic. Indigenous mountain communities, from Peru to Kenya to Tajikistan, Bhutan and Papua New Guinea, were able to ensure the food security and health of their communities thanks to their localized, biodiverse, circular food systems founded on ancestral knowledge and cultural values [4]. The same report of a traditional farming culture, as practiced by the indigenous Dayak Bakatik people in Bengkayang Regency, West Kalimantan.

Through their practices, sociocultural traditions and profound knowledge, indigenous peoples have long maintained rich biocultural diversities. However, they have historically been marginalized and their rights have been threatened. Therefore, it is essential to promote and protect the integrity of the natural environment through maintaining or regaining Indigenous Peoples' full control over their lands, territories and its resources and enhancing their sustainable resource management systems, including their skills and traditional knowledge related to food security, livelihood and the protection of biodiversity.

## 3 Comparison on the Recognition and Protection System of Indigenous People in South East Asia and Organization of American States

The basic system of international human rights protection can be found in the United Nation Human Rights Regime, both in regards with the Social Political Rights or Economic Social and Cultural Rights. In term of regional organization, mostly human rights systems were already established to complement the protection of human rights, such as: The African, Inter-American, and European human rights systems. Each systems developed binding regional human rights treaties reflecting international standards contained in the Universal Declaration of Human Rights (UDHR) and other international human rights treaties. Unlike some of regional organizations, ASEAN does not have such judicial system (Table 1).

As a proper comparison stud.

On 4 March 2018, the Latin American and Caribbean region adopted the Regional Agreement on Access to Information, Public Participation and Justice in Environmental Matters in Latin America and the Caribbean, at Escazú, Costa Rica. As indicated by the title of the agreement, this legal instrument is established for environmental protection. The main aim is to ensure the right of all persons to have access to information in a timely and appropriate manner, to participate significantly

**Table 1** ASEAN comparison to organization of American States

| OAS | ASEAN |
|---|---|
| Seven states are parts of Biological 17 | Three states are parts of Biological 17 |
| Regional legal instruments on the recognition of indigenous people | It does not have legal instruments related to indigenous people |
| The Inter-American Court of Human Rights (IACHR or IACtHR) | The ASEAN Intergovernmental Commission on Human Rights (AICHR) |
| Members from South American countries as developing countries | Some of member states are developing countries |

in making the decisions that affect their lives and their environment, and to access justice when those rights have been infringed.

Moreover, this agreement is not only regulating environmental issue, but is also a human rights treaty. From a rights-based approach, the agreement recognizes core democratic principles and seeks to address the region's most important challenges, namely the scourge of inequality and a deep-rooted culture of privilege. Through transparency, openness and participation, the Regional Agreement contributes to the shift towards a new development model and tackles the region's inefficient and unsustainable culture of narrow, fragmented interests. Related provision can be seen under Article 9 about human rights defenders in environmental matters; where each state party shall guarantee a safe and enabling environment for persons, groups and organizations that promote and defend human rights in environmental matters, so that they are able to act free from threat, restriction and insecurity.

Regarding to recognition of indigenous people the parties set it up under Article 5 (4), which states that each Party shall meet the needs of persons or groups in vulnerable situations including indigenous peoples and ethnic groups, receive assistance in preparing their requests and obtain a response. After signatory, this agreement will give huge favor for the development of environmental law in the region for various stakeholders, also becomes one of legal instrument that gives indigenous people a basis to environmental democracy.

By forming a regional court, human rights commission and the upcoming regional agreement, Inter-American region has become one of the leading parties in providing environmental and human rights legal instrument for indigenous people. On the other hand, ASEAN has been lacking behind in terms of legal system to facilitate the people with active participation and litigation system inside the organization.

## 4 Conclusion

Compared to other regional legal frameworks, Indigenous peoples in Southeast Asia are fall behind the standard. The recognition of their legal status is need to be strengthened by the legal framework, and the participation of the communities to be heard during the national and regional hearing.

On the other hand, while it is undeniable the management of ecosystem in “modern” term is way easier and faster, the procedure (for example REDD+ and ICSS method), are in fact business centric. The difference with traditional knowledge are the people are recognized themselves as part of the ecosystem, instead of the manager of the environment. Therefore, it is necessary to enhancing the study on traditional knowledges to support regional resilience.

## References


1. Asia Indigenous Peoples’ Pact (AIPP), the International Work Group for Indigenous Affairs (IWGIA) and Asian Forum for Human Rights and Development (FORUM-ASIA), Chiang Mai (2010)
2. Dhiaulhaq A et al (2016) Conflict In Redd+: an analysis of sources of conflict based on case studies from South And Southeast Asia
3. Indonesia Baik. https://indonesiabaik.id/infografis/food-estate#:~:text=Food%20Estate%20merupakan%20konsep%20pengembangan,bahkan%20peternakan%20di%20suatu%20kawasan. Last Accessed 20 March 2022
4. Madden C, International Institute for Environment and Development. https://www.iied.org/indigenous-food-systems-prove-highly-resilient-during-covid-19. Last Accessed 05 March 2022
5. ASEAN, UNICEF and WFP (2022) ASEAN food and nutrition security report 2021, Vol 1. Jakarta, UNICEF
6. Hohmann J, Weller M (2018) The UN Declaration on the Rights of Indigenous Peoples: A Commentary. Oxford Commentaries on International Law
7. LNCS Homepage. http://www.springer.com/lncs. Last Accessed 21 Nov 2016
8. Syarifuddin (2021) Buku Ajar Kearifan Lokal Daerah Sumatera Selatan, 1st edn. Bening Media Publishing, Palembang
9. De Lucia V (2019) The ‘Ecosystem Approach’. In: International environmental law genealogy and biopolitics, 1st edn. Routledge, Oxon
10. Wales HGQ (1951) The making of Greater India: A study in south-East Asian culture change. Bernard Quaritch, London

# Road to Territorial Politics Through Special Law of Yogyakarta Number 13 of 2012

**Septi Satriani**

**Abstract** The five privileges of authority have been regulated under Specialty Law of Yogyakarta Number 13 of 2012 (UUK) in order to fulfill governor positions, land, culture, institutions, and spatial planning affairs. Particularly in regard to fulfilling the Governor position, this law guarantees that Sri Sultan Hamenku Buwono (HB) X reigning and serving as the king to automatically become the Governor of DIY. Therefore, he does not need to consider about how to reach his power over the next 5 years alike governors in other regions in Indonesia. Moreover, this law does not stipulate restrictions on the governor's position limited to only 2 periods. This paper argues that the UUK paved the way for Sri Sultan HB X to control his territory. He organizes, distributes his power, and implements the policy of arranging the sultanate's land in contrast with the basic agrarian law to return the 'lost' land belonging to the sultanate upon the implementation of the Basic Agrarian Law. Sri Sultan HB X stipulated a policy of withdrawing and amending the status of village land certificates which was not only perceived as a form of exclusion and restriction but also as part of regional control as well as economic accumulation. He further utilized the historical social support as a justification for amending village treasury land certificates from state land to sultanate lands. In implementing this policy, he implemented the privileged institutions with a different nomenclature from other regions in Indonesia. Thus, such various policies are considered as the forms of his strategy to defend territory. This paper was accomplished through field research conducted from January 2020 to December 2021 in DIY with qualitative methods. The data was obtained through in-depth interviews with competent sources related to the issue of Yogyakarta Special Law Number 13 of 2012 as primary data along with secondary data sources.

**Keywords** Territorial politics · Special law of Yogyakarta Number 13 of 2012 · Sri Sultan HB X

---

S. Satriani (✉)
Research Centre for Politics, National Research and Innovation Agency (BRIN), Jakarta, Indonesia
e-mail: sept001@brin.go.id



Nawawi et al. (eds.), *Managing Disruption and Developing Resilience for a Better Southeast Asia*, Springer Proceedings in Humanities and Social Sciences,
https://doi.org/10.1007/978-981-96-2116-3_51

## 1 Introduction

The fall of Suharto tenure in 1998 triggered extraordinary changes in Indonesia, demanding the participation opportunity in electing the leaders and in organizing and managing the regions through decentralization policies and direct regional head elections. This policy accentuates the idealism of executing close service delivery and improving the economic welfare of local communities. Decentralization policies and direct regional head elections are applied in almost Indonesia regions, including Daerah Istimewa Yogyakarta (DIY/Special Region of Yogyakarta). However, the election of regional heads in DIY only applies to regional heads at the district/city level because regional heads at the provincial level are closed only to kings reigning the Sultanate of Yogyakarta and the Kadipaten Pakualam. In particular, the position is legally regulated under the Privileges Law Number 13 of 2012 (UUK).

The five privileges are regulated by UUK, comprising the procedure for fulfilling the positions of the Governor and Deputy Governor; Regional Government Institutions; cultural; land, and spatial planning; thereby expanding the authority of Sri Sultan HB X and Sri Paduka Paku Alam X indicating a source of cultural legitimacy as Kings in the Sultanate and Duchy; thus providing formal legal legitimacy as Governor and Deputy Governor in Yogyakarta.

The five privileges affairs provide a complete package for Sri Sultan HB X to control his territory [4] to organize and distribute his power including commandeering the rights of residents of DIY to elect a governor. The automatic provision as Governor of DIY enables and accommodates Sri Sultan HB X to effortlessly maintain his power for the next 5 years unlike governors in other Indonesia regions. Moreover, the UUK never stipulates a limitation on the position of the governor as in other regions limited to only 2 times for a 5-year period.

In the institutional sector, Sri Sultan HB X issued the DIY Governor Regulation Number 25 of 2019 concerning Guidelines for Institutional Privileges in Regency/City and Urban Governments, containing an amendment in nomenclature of the government structure for districts/cities and sub-districts in exercising the assignment of privileges affairs by considering the original form and structure of government in DIY. Thus, such an amendment in nomenclature does not merely act as it names but describing the original government structures (different and special) of DIY from other regional government structures in Indonesia, indicating the mechanism of Sri Sultan HB X in utilizing the Indonesian state institutions to execute the five privileges in accordance with his interests, such as privileges regarding land often leading to problematic implementations.

This paper navigates that the problem lies in changing the position of Sultanate of Yogyakarta and Duchy of Pakualaman to become legal entities ([12]: 12–15). The change in position as legal entities allows both of them to have land rights as regulated in Article 4 of Law Number 5 of 1960 concerning Basic Agrarian Regulations (UUPA). Additionally, article 21 paragraph 2 of UUPA provides an exception that the government is deemed eligible to establish a legal entity in land ownership. However, the legal entities referred to here are banks established by the State, acknowledged as State banks, associations of agricultural cooperatives, religious bodies appointed by the Minister of Agriculture/Agrarian Affairs after hearing the Minister of Religion, and social agencies appointed by the Minister of Agriculture/ Agrarian after hearing the Minister of Social Welfare. Meanwhile, both Sultanate and Duchy are excluded from the four categories of legal entities, hindering the determination of legal entity type for both Sultanate and Duchy.

In addition, the position of Sultanate and Duchy as self-governing autonomous regions [40] based on Article 88 paragraph 3 of the Transitional Regulations of Law of the Republic of Indonesia Number 18 of 1965 concerning the Principles of Regional Government is revoked, dismissing the authority as an autonomous region. Moreover, with the issuance of Decree of the President of the Republic of Indonesia Number 33 of 1984 concerning the Full Enforcement of UUPA in the Province of DIY and the Regional Regulation of the Province of DIY Number 3 of 1984 concerning the full implementation of the UUPA, all the provisions of laws and regulations of DIY that regulate agrarian affairs are revoked as well. This notion asserts that upon the presence of this regional regulation, UUPA is fully applicable to DIY. Accordingly, the full implementation of UUPA revokes the position and authority of Sultanate of Yogyakarta and Duchy of Pakualaman as former self-government bodies in the land sector further transferred to the State. Consequently, UUPA serves as the basis for Sultanate of Yogyakarta and Duchy of Pakualaman in executing land affairs.

The enactment of the UUK in DIY, however leads to the opposite outcome, enabling Sri Sultan HB X to own a dual role and position as a cultural leader (King) and political leader (Governor). As a result, the interests of Sri Sultan HB X as the Head Governor of DIY who has to prosper the people of DIY with the interests of Sri Sultan HB X as the Sultan remains undefinable. This benefitting dual position and role allow Sri HB X to occupy state institutions, exercise power, issue various policies, and control State resources including returning the sultanate land into Stateland-based on the UUPA.

## 2 Territorial Politics and Special Law of Yogyakarta Number 13 of 2012

Territorial politics according to Tarrow, do not refer to territory, instead of how the politics fight for territory [4]. This paper focuses on the study of Sri Sultan HB X in defending his territory, based on Yogyakarta Privileges Law Number 13 of 2012 enabling Sri Sultan HB X authority as a king in Sultanate of Yogyakarta and as a political leader in DIY. Further, such Privilege Law limits the local political arena, especially in the contestation of power at the provincial level, limited to Sri Sultan HB X and Kanjeng Gusti Pangeran Adipati Arya Paku Alam X as the reigning king and his descendants, thereby controlling local politics at the DIY Province level leading to the monopoly of power in the local political arena.

In defending the territory, subnational regimes utilizes the economic strength [19], historical social support [16, 17], and institutional [4]. Sidel further interprets subnational authoritarianism as a local regime controlling state institutions based on families, clans, cliques, or organizations and relishing state power and resources outside of electoral challenges, democratic governance that demands effectiveness and accountability, and the rule of law. Here, Sidel argues that the level of economic autonomy of citizens greatly influences the presence or absence of power to oppose local authorities, thus allowing subnational authoritarianism to the extent that the economic autonomy of residents is limited and the concentration of local economic control is executed and dominated by authoritarian rulers. The consequences of control concentration over the local economy in the hands of individuals, families, and clans inevitably generates the population prone to clienteles, coercion, and financial inducements during elections [19].

When the degree of economic autonomy affects the emergence of opposing forces, subnational authoritarianism survives as long as it dominates and monopolizes economic power. Stronger economic dominance in the grip of a subnational authoritarian regime, leads to longer regime's lifespan, emerging subnational authoritarianism regimes through primitive accumulation processes such as the acquisition and concentration of land ownership, and natural resources, and the construction of monopolies on production and distribution sites in certain locations with the approval of supra-local authorities [19].

In contrast to Sidel, Nishizaki [17] argues that the social base and skills of an authoritarian ruler serve as the key factors in the survival of the authoritarian regime at the local level. Nishizaki specifically debates that the existed studies have emphasized a strong man named Banharn Silpa-Archa in the Suphanburi Province of Thailand as closely related to the characteristics of a *nakleng* or local strongman. *Nakleng* is characterized as a man acknowledged by his violence, brutality, toughness, fearlessness, ruthlessness, cruelty, hedonistic, breaking the law yet practicing generousity, compassion, big-hearted, loyalty, caring, and defensiveness [17].

Nishizaki [17] contends that Baharn's victory in every election was inseparable from the present social support due to his versatile and charisma. His meticulous nature was manifested in his way of supervising the implementation of all local development project completion. His expertise in supervising civil servants despite inherently corrupt, callous, inefficient, and irresponsible, otherwise contributed to local development efficiently.

Nishizaki establishes an argument that historical factors before Banharn became a politician contributed to getting support from the citizens. The patrimonial practice in Thailand at that time allowed Banharn to execute his leadership effectively from 1976. Although many scholars place patrimonialism as a negative thing, Nishizaki [16] however applauded it as a gift leading to positive contribution to Banharn's revival, resulting in various public development projects due to the strict supervision of local civil servants under Banharn tenure. Interestingly, despite receiving a lot of support from Suphanburi province, Banharn was incapable of obtaining the support at the national level.

Gibson [4] offers an analysis of subnational authoritarianism in the context of national politics, highlighting the emergence of authoritarian enclaves at the local level as a limitation consequence towards the central authority in expanding its influence in a region. Gibson adds that 'border control' by authoritarian regimes at the local level involves institutional strategies in various territorial arenas. Thus far, continuity and discontinuity of subnational authoritarianism are not only locally driven but also involving the interaction between existing local politics and national territorial system. As a result, the resilience of subnational authoritarianism is driven by an active strategy of institutional and political control by local authorities, as well as by strategic interactions and coalition-building between often democratic local and national leaders [4].

Authoritarian subnational governments are institutionally linked to democratic national politics represented in national politics through institutions grasping both the national and subnational areas, in which financial, political, and other resources flow between arenas through political-institutional channels such as representation in legislatures and political parties. The important factor that influences the existence of subnational authoritarianism lies in the capability of local authorities to control the territory and to localize the scope of the conflict. Thus, more open boundaries of the conflict leads to a more difficult control towards the ruler, indicating the monopoly of power such as manipulation in the local political arena.

For the local political context in DIY, the three concepts proposed by Sidel [19], Nishizaki [16, 17], and Gibson [4] are applicable simultaneously as Sri Sultan HB X uses institutions to maintain control over the DIY region under UUK for the accumulation of economic capital through the authority of land management additionally supported by socio-cultural support base. In terms of institutions, UUK provides an expansion of authority which allows Sri Sultan HB X to issue various policies in amending the status of land ownership and legitimizing new rights to apply exclusion, eviction, and management restrictions.

The most common form of exclusion is certification which is a formalized form of exclusion providing certainty for the owner. Typically, the certification process is accompanied by land measurement, record of ownership status, sale rights, and transfer of the land. As a result, the value of land is certain as a commodity that can be traded or offered for rent. In addition, this certification provides official recognition of access for certain people to control the land [6]: 45).

In the context of DIY, the policy of Sri Sultan HB X of revoking and amending the status of village land certificates was seen as a form of exclusion and restriction as well as part of regional control and economic accumulation. The village is utilized as a unit of practice for economic accumulation due to its lowest territorial area directly related to community members. When the land is controlled and the village head is subjugated through the politics of service (H, 19 November 2021), the territory at the local level is under the control. Therefore, the village as the lowest territorial unit becomes the defensive anchor for Sri Sultan HB X's wealth. It is however potential to control the arena at the village level, conducted from top-down through the village head, compared to bottom-up control over the area at the top level. In sum, the territorial politics practiced by Sri Sultan HB X at the same time limited the governor's power to his family.

## 3 Defending the Territory Through Economic, Institutional, and Historical Social Support

Sri Sultan HB X initiated to implement the policy of land structuring of Sultanate and Duchy in DIY after the issuance of UUK Number 13 of 2012. Through the Governor of Yogyakarta Province's letters Number, 593/4811 on November 12, 2012, and Number 593/0708 on February 15, 2013, Sri Sultan HB X tasked the Head of the Regional Office of the National Land Agency (*Kakanwil* BPN) DIY to regulate the control of requests for rights in the form of letter to state land controlled by the Government of DIY area, containing the inventory and arrangement of State land given to individuals, government agencies, private institutions, and foundations based on the Governor's Decree before and after the enactment of the UUK.

In the letter, the Governor of DIY ordered the Regional Head of BPN DIY to control every application for building rights (HGB), use rights, rights enhancements, and transfer of land rights controlled by the Government of DIY Region, mandating the suspension of the rights until the completion of arrangement or inventory of the land. Extensions are executed by amending the status of HGB on State land to HGB on land belonging to the Sultanate or Pakualaman as a Cultural Heritage Legal Entity [15. As a result of the enacted Governor's Letter, at least 100 certificates of property rights were published for residents in Gunung Kidul were canceled. In the certificate, the status of the property rights was amended into utilization rights [12].

Additionally, the policy of land structuring for Sultanate and Duchy resulted in an immense amendment of village treasury lands from utilization rights on State land to utilization rights on Sultanate and Duchy lands. Whereas initially, Sri Sultan HB X admitted that the village treasury land referred to land owned by the village through DIY Governor's Regulation Number 11 of 2008 concerning the Management of Village Treasury Land. Similarly, article 1 point 8 states that village treasury land is owned by the village whose utilization is declared in active under the approval of the *lurah* or the Regent/Mayor. Sri Sultan HB X securely strengthened the position of village land as one of the utilized village assets without changing the status of village treasury land as village assets through the Governor of DIY Regulation No. 65 of 2013. The position of village land is also regulated in the Law of the Republic of Indonesia Number 6 of 2014 concerning Villages, in which article 76 stated that village assets could be in the form of village treasury land, communal land, village markets, animal markets, boat moorings, village buildings, fish auctions, auctions of agricultural products, village-owned forests, village-owned springs, public baths, and other assets belonging to the village.

However, through the Regulation of the Governor of the Special Region of Yogyakarta Number 112 of 2014 concerning the Utilization of Village Land, Sri

Sultan HB X amended the position of the village land. In article 1 point 10 of this regulation, it is stated that village treasury land refers to the land whose origin is from Sultanate and/or Duchy with *anggaduh,*[1] and is utilized for village treasury, *bengkok/lungguh,*[2] and *pengarem-arem.*[3] As such, this Governor Regulation was later strengthened by the issuance of Special Region of Yogyakarta Regulation Number 1 of 2017 concerning the management and utilization of Sultanate lands and Duchy lands. If the utilization of village treasury land could initially be carried out by the Village Head/*Lurah* under the approval of the Regent/Mayor, then through this regional regulation, the utilization, and management of village land must be authorized by Sultanate and Duchy.[4] In spite of the Regulation of the Governor of the Special Region of Yogyakarta Number 34 of 2017, village land that has been certified with the status of utilization rights on State land must be returned to its status in accordance with the provisions of this regulation.[5]

The issuance of various regulations related to the status of land in DIY encouraged the Head of the Regional Office of the BPN DIY, Tri Wibisono to send a letter to the Minister of Agrarian Affairs and Spatial Planning/Head of BPN dated May 9, 2019, inquiring for instructions on the registration implementation of Sultanate and Duchy lands in DIY. The letter was then replied with the issuance of technical instructions Number 4/JUKNIS-HK.02.01/X/2019 concerning the Administration of Sultanate and Duchy Land of DIY dated on October 29, 2019, issued by the Minister of ATR/Head of Central BPN, Sofyan Djalil. The technical guidelines in their implementation were based on article 32 of UUK stipulating that in the exercise of land authority, Sultanate and Duchy are declared as legal entities which are subject to rights recognized by the State and have property rights to the untransferrable Sultanate or Duchy land. In the technical guidelines, it is also particularly stated that Sultanate and Duchy land which is used and utilized by the Village Government in DIY Region shall be administered under activities that include bookkeeping, inventory, and reporting of state/regional property by applicable regulations.

Since the issuance of this technical guideline, approximately 150 village land certificates in DIY have been adjusted. The Department of Land and Spatial Planning (Dispertaru) DIY noted that the 150 certificates were proliferated over 50 certificates which further increased each in regencies of Gunung Kidul, Sleman, and Bantul [24] by targeting the readjustment of 2,090 certificates in 2021 and 7,727 certificates in 2022 [24]. Additionally, this technical guideline Number 4/JUKNIS-HK.02.01/X/2019 concerning the Administration of Sultanate Land and Duchy Lands gives

---

[1] The anggaduh right is the right to use the land given by the Sultanate and/or the Duchy to the Village.

[2] Bengkok/lunguh land is part of Village Land used for additional income for the Village Head and Village Apparatus.

[3] Arem-arem land is part of the Village Land which is used for retired Village Heads and Village Apparatuses.

[4] See article 38 of the transitional provisions of the Yogyakarta Special Region Regulation Number 1 of 2017.

[5] Article 11 Regulation of the Governor of the Special Region of Yogyakarta Number 34 of 2017 concerning Village Land Utilization.

legality to the Sultanate and Duchy through BPN Sleman to withdraw 130 parcels of land or about 45 hectares of land in Sidoluhur Village previously certified as village land. Of the 130 plots of land, 50 plots or 15 hectares have amended their ownership status from State land to Sultanate and Duchy land [41].

Similarly, problem also occurred in Sinduadi Village during three years of applying for land certification to BPN, in which the village government experienced uncertainty. Instances include Sinduadi Village, Mlati District, Sleman which have 110 hectares of village land used for agricultural warehouses, Liquid Club entertainment venues, Jogja City Mall, and Sindu Kusuma Edupark. The certification which originally utilized the use rights on State land had amended into use rights on land owned by Sultanate and the Duchy. Consequently, this regulation legally amended the ownership status of village land certificates to Sultanate and Duchy land. According to Achiel, the legal representative of Sultanate, village land certification aims to provide legal status certainty that the land belongs to Sultanate, thereby hindering the selling or renting without the permission of Sultanate [37]. Further, Achiel as the representative of Sultanate emphasized that there are no new rights as this certification only recognizes or formalizes the mere existing rights.

Meanwhile, in Kulon Progo, a land certification case occurred in Karangwuni Village comprising an area of 540.434 square meters registered as land belonging to Duchy of Pakualaman. In 2016, the Regional Office of BPN DIY also handed over 500 parcels of land certificates for Sultanate and 150 plots of land for Duchy [25]. Undertaking the policy problem of land certification in several villages in DIY, several villages were concerned that the policy for land structuring of Sultanate and Duchy could feasibly erode the village's original income due to the ownership shifting of assets to Sultanate under Village Law Number 6 of 2014. Their main objection to this policy was the possibility of village land being privately owned by Sultanate, thereby risking the loss of village land and assets [41].

Adjustment of village land titling in DIY indicates the existence of new rights deliberately created by amending and eliminating the past rights. Elimination of rights from the implementation of this land management policy tends to benefit the authorities (Sri Sultan HB X and KGPAA Paku Alam IX). This certification policy focuses on managing the assets of Sultanate and Duchy and the defensive mechanism of Sri Sultan HB towards his territory and sovereignty [4] within the DIY region. Sri Sultan HB X attempted to control the territory by monopolizing power through automatic positioning as Governor and land ownership at the local level generating the birth of a more durable local political monopoly [2].

The monopoly of land ownership through adjustment of village land certificates has increased the percentage of Sultanate and Duchy land area which was originally 1.38% in 1993 to 9.43% in 2015 [22] and 10.67% in 2017 [45] of the total area of the DIY Province. If the area of DIY comprises 3,133.15 sq km, then 10.67% or 334.31 sq km belongs to Sultanate and Duchy. As such, this land accumulation continues to grow considering that Dispertaru DIY has a target of adjusting 7,727 land certificates in 2022. From a political perspective, land is considered as an economic resource fueling a political resource. Through land tenure, a person becomes advantaged encouraging the possession of power because the source of power other than position and trust is generated from wealth [1].

Surprisingly, the process of withdrawing village land certificates in various areas in DIY was relatively smooth without any significant turmoil due to the operation for withdrawing village land certificates executed through village officials, most of whom are servants of Sultanate of Yogyakarta [47]. As a result, the concentration and monopoly on land ownership and local resources practiced by Sri Sultan HB X was relatively 'smooth' because both local communities and authorities had contributed to assist and support the implementation of the policy for withdrawing village land certificates. This fact is inseparable from the symbolic power to define meaning for others. Otherwise, this symbolic power refers to the power to build and reproduce reality [13], thus any issued policies tend to be implemented by relevant agencies in DIY which are relatively acceptable to the community with or without violence. Accordingly, the scope of its actions has implications at the national level although this land management policy occurs in local level. Although the National Law on Villages regulates village land to belong to the village, this regulation is revoked in DIY and villages inevitably have to comply with land policies in DIY.

Another land management policy affected approximately 30–50 families of Suryatmajan residents, Danurejan District, Yogyakarta (Solopos Editor, 2014). The transfer of the main gate of Kepatihan complex from the west side to the south side had caused 4 residents who have title certificates, 12 descendants of Indonesian citizens who occupy HGB, 1 customary right, and 1 Quwwatul Islam mosque building on land with usage rights to experience eviction. All of these residents can no longer occupy their homes after the application for an extension of HGB experiencing disapproval for a building permit [35]. Upon the issuance of UUK and Governor's Letter of DIY regarding the control of HGB applications, usage rights, increasing rights, and transferring land rights until the inventory of the sultanate and duchy lands was completed, the impact of the uncertain land ownership was experienced by some residents in DIY hindering the access or land ownership for years.

This eviction and expulsion thus indicates a form of exclusion or removal, in which exclusion refers to an act imposed by Sultanate and Duchy through the Regional Government of DIY (Governor of DIY and Deputy Governor of DIY) on parties with legal access to land in certain areas. Exclusion also refers to actions on a large scale accompanied by violence causing people to be evicted from their lands on behalf of those in power ([6]: 5). The power of exclusion will operate through four aspects including regulation, market, coercion, and legitimacy ([6]: 25).

Arrangements typically relate to regulations or legal instruments and official rules containing conditions for land access and use. As the Governor of DIY, Sri Sultan HB X has the authority to issue various regulations and policies reflecting his interests as a ruler King in Sultanate of Yogyakarta. When in power, Sri Sultan HB X made plans, implemented programs, and appointed new implementers who were initiated to execute the program in accordance with the assigned tasks, thereby securing the longer duration of holding the power.

In the context of Indonesian politics post the New Order, Sri Sultan HB X faced the challenge of actualizing the democratization at the local level such as by demanding every citizen to vote and to be elected. If implemented in DIY, Sri Sultan HB X's position as the governor succeeding his father's position—Sri Sultan HB IX—could be under the threat. Hence, the presence of UUK guarantees that political power as governor in DIY remains in the hands of Sultan and Duke who reigns in Sultanate of Yogyakarta and Duchy of Pakualaman. This law further grants monopoly power at the DIY Province level and enables the expansion of authority for both of them; thus influencing and supporting each other in addressing their interest as the political leader and king in DIY.

The Privileges Law provides free tickets for both of them and their successors for continuously political positions as long as UUK is still in effect. This position also gives them the authority to issue various policies aimed at maintaining wealth and power, restoring the lost wealth, as well as increasing their wealth and power securing the political and economic monopoly. If referring to the oligarchy concept Winters [11, 21], wealth has served as a determining factor of oligarchic power, concentrating on wealth which demonstrates the challenge of maintaining such concentration of wealth. In this system, there may be a few rich people exercising their power to defend their interests benefitting financially while disregarding the public interest [8].

The presence of political authority for Sri Sultan HB X through this Privilege Act provided an opportunity for him to further increase his wealth. As reported in 2012, Sultan's wealth on land, buildings, and movable property amounted to IDR 6.8 billion, in 2014 Sri Sultan HB X's wealth on land, buildings, and movable property amounted to IDR 30.77 billion [30]. The wealth of Sri Sultan HB X continues to experience an extraordinary increase, especially after the issuance of the village land arrangement policy in 2017 where Sri Sultan HB X's wealth amounted to US $ 250 million or Rp 6 trillion and placed him in the ranks of the richest people (125 worldwide) based on the Indonesia version of Globe Asia [39].

## 4 Conclusion

Territorial politics according to Tarrow, does not solely regard to territory, but about how politics fight for territory [4]. The Yogyakarta Privileges Law 13/2012 enabled Sri Sultan HB X to expand the authority not only as a king in Sultanate of Yogyakarta but also as a political leader in DIY. This Privilege Law thus limits the local political arena contestation, especially for the power at the provincial level, to Sri Sultan HB X and Kanjeng Gusti Pangeran Adipati Arya Paku Alam X (after the passing of KGPAA Sri Paduka Paku Alam IX) as the reigning king and his descendants, securing local politics at the DIY Province level organized under their control to gain the monopoly of power in the local political arena [4]. The Special Law of Yogyakarta Number 13/2012 additionally feeds the power to Sri Sultan HB X in terms of land sector, including the amendment status of village treasury land from state land to land belonging to the Sultanate. This transfer of Sultanate treasury lands becomes a form of economic accumulation accelerating Sri Sultan HB X's wealth.

The form of economic accumulation, historical social support, and institutional forms of privilege endowed by Sri Sultan HB X are considered as the forms of territorial politics to defend his territory.

## References

### *Book*


1. Budiardjo M (2003) Dasar-dasar Ilmu Politik - HC,Ed. Revisi. Gramedia Pustaka Utama.
2. Buehler M (2018) The ephemeral nature of local political monopolies. In: Routledge handbook of contemporary Indonesia. Routledge, pp 106–117
3. Ford M, Pepinsky TB (2014) Beyond oligarchy: wealth, power, and contemporary Indonesian politics. Cornell University
4. Gibson EL (2013) Boundary control subnational authoritarianism in federal democracies. Cambridge University Press
5. Hadiz VR (2010) Localizing power in post authoritarian Indonesia A Southeast Asia perspective. Stanford University Press
6. Hall D, Hirsch P, Li TM (2020) Kuasa Eksklusi: Dilema Pertanahan di Asia Tenggara. Insist Press
7. Nordholt HS, Klinken GV (2007) Renegotiating boundaries: local politics in post-Soeharto Indonesia. KITLV Press, Leiden
8. Pye LW, Robison R, Hadiz V (2005) Reorganising power in Indonesia: the politics of oligarchy in an age of markets. Foreign Aff 84(1):196. https://doi.org/10.2307/20034258
9. Ratnawati T, Afadlal, Aziz LL (2009) Studi tentang Pemekaran Daerah: Pemetaan Problematika Politik, Ekonomi, dan Sosial Budaya di Daerah-Daerah Pemekaran era Reformasi: Upaya Menuju Penyusunan Konsep Alternatif. LIPI Press
10. Widyatama B (2017) Demokrasi Sebagai Siasat: Menafsirkan Tapak Politik Demokrasi Sultan HB IX. Penerbit Polgov
11. Winters JA (2011) Oligarchy. Cambridge University Press. https://doi.org/10.1017/cbo978051 1793806


### *Journal*


12. Antoro KS (2015) JournalAnalisis Kritis Substansi dan Implemenasi Undang-Undang Nomor 13 Tahun 2012 tentang Keistimewaan Daerah Istimewa Yogyakarta dalam Bidang Pertanahan, Jurnal Bhumi 1(1):12–32. https://doi.org/10.31292/jb.v1i1.38
13. Bourdieu P (1979. Symbolic power. Crit Anthropol 4(13–14):77–85. https://doi.org/10.1177/ 0308275x7900401307
14. Hamid A (2014) A family mater: political corruption in Banten Indonesia. Asian Polit Policy 6(4):577–593
15. Lestarini R (2018) Kebijakan Pertanahan Bagi WNI Keturunan Tionghoa DI Yogyakarta: Diskriminasi atau Diskriminasi Positif, Jurnal Hukum dan Pembangunan 48(1):44–63. https:// doi.org/10.21143/jhp.vol.48.no.1.1595
16. Nishizaki Y (2005) The moral origin of Thailand's provincial strongman the case of Banharn Silpa-Archa. South East Res 13(2):184–234
17. Nishizaki Y (2006) The domination of a fussy in provincial Thailand: the case of Banharn Silpa-Archa in Suphanburi. J Southeast Asian Stud 37(2):267–291. https://doi.org/10.1017/ S0022463406000555

18. Ratnawati T (2011) Antara Otonomi Sultan dan Kepatuhan pada Pusat di Era Reformasi: Studi Kasus Daerah Istimewa Yogyakarta (DIY). Governance 2(1):42–68
19. Sidel JT (2014) Economic foundations of subnational authoritarianism: insights and evidence from qualitative and quantitative research. Democratization 21(1):161–184. https://doi.org/10.1080/13510347.2012.725725
20. Thompson MR. Asia's Hybrid Dynasties, Asian Affair 43(2):203–220. https://doi.org/10.1080/03068374.2012.682366
21. Winters JA (Oktober 2013) Oligarchy and Democracy in Indonesia. JSTOR 96, Special Issue: Wealth, Power and Contemporary Indonesian Politics 11–23. https://doi.org/10.5728/indonesia.96.0099

## *Thesis*

22. Kurniadi BD (2019) Defending the Sultan's land: Yogyakarta, aristocratic power and control over land in post-autocratic Indonesia (pp 1–333) [Pdf]. https://openresearch-repository.anu.edu.au/items/ecb30ce2-1f22-41c7-a65b-daed14278e0b

## *Online News*

23. Aan (2006, Juli 06) Pro Kontra Keistimewaan Yogyakarta Mengemuka di DPR. news.detik.com. https://news.detik.com/berita/d-630292/pro-kontra-ruu-keistimewaan-yogyakarta-mengemuka-di-dpr
24. Adhi IS, Aprian D (2021, September 22) UU Keistimewaan, Pintu Masuk Klaim Tanah oleh Keraton Yogyakarta (1) Halaman all - Kompas.com. KOMPAS.com; Kompas.com. https://regional.kompas.com/read/2021/09/22/211626478/uu-keistimewaan-pintu-masuk-klaim-tanah-oleh-keraton-yogyakarta-1?page=all#page2
25. Admin LBH Yogyakarta. (2017, January 23) TAHTA UNTUK RAKJAT ATAU TAHTA UNTUK RAJA? - LBH Yogyakarta. LBH Yogyakarta. https://lbhyogyakarta.org/2017/01/23/tahta-untuk-rakjat-atau-tahta-untuk-raja/
26. Afandi M (2016, Mei 11) Deklarasi Perjuangan Warga Pesisir Selatan Kulon Progo. Selamatkanbumi.com. https://selamatkanbumi.com/id/2016/05/11/deklarasi-perjuangan-warga-pesisir-selatan-kulon-progo/
27. Apriando T (2015, Agustus 25) Ketika Para Petani Pesisir Kulon Progo Berjuang Menjaga Lahan. Mongabay.co.id. http://www.mongabay.co.id/2015/08/25/ketika-para-petani-pesisir-kulon-progo-berjuang-menjaga-lahan/
28. Arifin K, Rochman LF (2012, Mei 01) Menalar Kembali Makna Keistimewaan ala Yogyakarta. balairungpress.com. https://www.balairungpress.com/2012/05/menalar-kembali-makna-istimewa-ala-yogyakarta-2/
29. Bagus & Try (2012, Agustus 30) RUUK DIY Disahkan, Warga Yogya Gelar Syukuran. news.detik.com. https://news.detik.com/berita/d-2003516/ruuk-diy-disahkan-warga-yogya-gelar-syukuran.
30. Fatoni M (2017, Maret 27) Sri Sultan HB X Masuk Daftar Orang Terkaya di Indonesia, Ini Fakta Seputar Kekayaannya. jogja.tribunnews.com. https://jogja.tribunnews.com/2017/03/27/sri-sultan-hb-x-masuk-daftar-orang-terkaya-di-indonesia-ini-fakta-seputar-kekayaannya
31. Kementerian Perencanaan Pembangunan Nasional/Bappenas (2013) White Paper Kebijakan Pengelolaan Pertanahan Nasional. bappenas.go.id. https://www.bappenas.go.id/files/kajian-trp/White_Paper_Pengelolaan_Pertanahan_Nasional.pdf
32. Kresna M (2018, Agustus 27) Untung Pakualaman di Tengah Nasib Buntung Petani dari Proyek NYIA. tirto.id. https://tirto.id/untung-pakualaman-di-tengah-nasib-buntung-petani-dari-proyek-nyia-cU5q

33. Kurniawan AB (2012, Agustus 29) Aktivis Pro Keistimewaan Gelar Doa Bersama. megapolitan.kompas.com. https://megapolitan.kompas.com/read/2012/08/29/20170377/~Regional~Jawa
34. Laksono MY (2021, Oktober 06) Kurun 2018–2020, Ada 3.145 Kasus Sengketa Pertanahan yang Belum Diselesaikan. kompas.com. https://www.kompas.com/properti/read/2021/10/06/090000721/kurun-2018-2020-ada-3.145-kasus-sengketa-pertanahan-yang-belum?page=all.
35. Liputan 6 (2014, January 29) Warga Tolak Pembangunan Gerbang Kepatihan DIY. Www.liputan6.com. https://www.liputan6.com/news/read/813082/warga-tolak-pembangunan-gerbang-kepatihan-diy
36. Noroyono B, Pitakasari AR (2013, September 24) BPN: Kasus Sengkeeta Lahan Indonesia Tinggi. republika.co.id. https://www.republika.co.id/berita/nasional/umum/13/09/24/mtn2q0-bpn-kasus-sengketa-lahan-indonesia-tinggi
37. Nugraha F (2021, September 22) Siasat Mencaplok Tanah Desa Atas Nama Keistimewaan Yogyakarta. Project Multatuli. https://projectmultatuli.org/siasat-mencaplok-tanah-desa-atas-nama-keistimewaan-yogyakarta/
38. Redaksi Solopos (2014, Januari 24) Penataan Kepatihan: Warga Suryatmajan Tolak Digusur. Solopos.com. https://www.solopos.com/index.php/penataan-kepatihan-warga-suryatmajan-tolak-digusur-484511?utm_source=bacajuga_desktop&PageSpeed=noscript
39. Rony TK (2018, July 26) Masuk Daftar Orang Terkaya RI, Berapa Harta Sultan Hamengkubuwono X? Www.liputan6.com. https://www.liputan6.com/bisnis/read/3600120/masuk-daftar-orang-terkaya-ri-berapa-harta-sultan-hamengkubuwono-x?page=2
40. Setiawan E (2024) Arti kata swaprajadiaksespada - Kamus Besar Bahasa Indonesia (KBBI) Online. Kbbi.web.id. https://kbbi.web.id/swapraja
41. Somad A (2021, September 21) Main Coret atas Nama Kesultanan. Jaring. https://jaring.id/main-coret-atas-nama-kesultanan/
42. Somad A (2017, April 7) Pasir, Musik dan Penolakan Bandara. Selamatkanbumi.com. http://selamatkanbumi.com/id/pasir-musik-dan-penolakan-bandara/
43. Sutaryono. (2018). Prona Zaman Now. krjogja.com. https://www.krjogja.com/angkringan/analisis/prona-zaman-ae%CB%9Cnowae/
44. Wicaksono & Rudiana (2012, Juli 10). Petani Tuntut Miliki Tanah Sengketa Keraton Yogya. Tempo.co. https://nasional.tempo.co/read/news/2012/07/10/058415937/petani-tuntut-miliki-tanah-sengketa-keraton-yogya/


## *Presentation*


45. Antoro KS (2019, December 19) Keistimewaan dan Masa Depan DIY. Diskusi Publikasi Refleksi terhadap Keistimewaan DIY Hukum Pertanahan di Kasultanan Yogyakarta, Departemen Hukum Administrasi Fakultas Hukum UII dan Pusat Studi Hukum Agraria UIII


## *Interview*


46. JPB, 30 April 2020
47. HN, 11 November 2021
48. KSA, 6 Novemer 2021

## *Regulations*


49. Keputusan Presiden Republik Indonesia Nomor 33 Tahun 1984 tentang Pemberlakuan Sepenuhnya UUPA di Provinsi DIY
50. Peraturan Daerah Istimewa Yogyakarta Nomor 1 Tahun 2017 tentang Pengelolaan dan Pemanfaatan Tanah Kesultanan dan Tanah Kadipaten
51. Peraturan Daerah Provinsi DIY Nomor 3 Tahun 1984 tentang pelaksanaan berlaku sepenuhnya UUPA
52. Peraturan Gubernur Daerah Istimewa Yogyakarta Nomor 112 Tahun 2014 tentang Pemanfaatan Tanah Desa
53. Peraturan Gubernur Daerah Istimewa Yogyakarta Nomor 34 Tahun 2017 Tanah Desa
54. Peraturan Gubernur DIY 25/2019 tentang Pedoman Kelembagaan Urusan Keistimewaan pada Pemerintah Kabupaten/Kota dan Kelurahan
55. Peraturan Gubernur DIY Nomor 11 Tahun 2008 tentang Pengelolaan Tanah Kas Desa
56. Peraturan Gubernur DIY Nomor 65 Tahun 2013
57. Peraturan Pemerintah Nomor 38. Tahun 1963 tentang Penunjukan Badan-Badan Hukum Yang Dapat Mempunyai Hak Milik atas Tanah.
58. Permendagri Nomor 1 Tahun 2014 Tentang Pembentukan Produk Hukum Daerah
59. Petunjuk Teknis Nomor 4/JUKNIS-HK.02.01/X/2019 tentang Penatausahaan Tanah Kesultanan dan Tanah Kadipaten DIY tertanggal 29 Oktober 2019
60. Undang Undang Nomor 2 Tahun 2012 tentang Pengadaan Tanah bagi Pembangunan untuk Kepentingan Umum
61. Undang-Undang Nomor 12 Tahun 2011 tentang Pembentukan Peraturan Perundangan
62. Undang-Undang Republik Indonesia Nomor 18 Tahun 1965 tentang Pokok-Pokok Pemerintahan Daerah
63. Undang-Undang Republik Indonesia Nomor 6 Tahun 2014


**Septi Satriani** is a researcher at the Research Centre for Politics of the National Research and Innovation Agency, Ph.D. candidate in the Department of Political Science at the Faculty of Social and Political Science at the University of Indonesia and this paper is part of her dissertation proposal.

# 'Gender Equal Civil Society': Framework for Mapping Women's NGOs' Capacity in Supporting Women's Political Participation in Indonesia

**Kurniawati Hastuti Dewi, Ade Latifa, Nur Iman Subono, and Dian Ratna Sari**

**Abstract** Several studies revealed strategic role of women non-governmental organizations (women's NGOs) in Indonesia, from the New Order (*Orde Baru*) to the reform era (*era reformasi*). However, there are not studies have assessed capacity of women's NGOs in post-*reformasi* Indonesia, especially to supporting women's political participation. The existing framework such as gender mainstreaming (*Pengarusutamaan Gender*, PUG) that was introduced in 2000 does not sufficient to assess capacity of Indonesian women's NGOs. Therefore, this study fills the gap by utilizing a bottom-up approach and feminist research methodology to hearing voices and collecting thoughts of various women's NGOs activists in Jakarta, West Java, Yogyakarta, West Sumatra, North Sumatra, and East Nusa Tenggara. Data were collected by means of 21 Focus Group Discussions from 2020 to 2021. This paper develops a genuine and locally-based framework called MSSG (*Masyarakat Sipil Setara Gender*) or the Gender Equal Civil Society, as framework for mapping the capacity of women's NGOs, and their actions in promoting gender equality to supporting women's political participation. The MSSG consists of two dimensions: gender mainstreaming and women's empowerment, each of which consists of five elements namely (i) representation (descriptive & substantive), (ii) autonomy, (iii) consolidation, (iv) local context & intersectionality, and (v) social bases. Locating into the classical study of women's representation by Norris and Lovenduski (1995,

K. H. Dewi (✉) · D. R. Sari
Research Center for Politics, National Research and Innovation Agency (BRIN), Jl. Gatot Subroto 10, Jakarta 12710, Indonesia
e-mail: kurn008@brin.go.id

A. Latifa
Research Center for Center for Population, National Research and Innovation Agency (BRIN), Jl. Gatot Subroto 10, Jakarta 12710, Indonesia

N. I. Subono
Faculty of Social and Political Sciences, Universitas Indonesia (UI), Jl. Prof. Dr. Selo Soemardjan Depok, Jawa Barat 16424, Indonesia



Nawawi et al. (eds.), *Managing Disruption and Developing Resilience for a Better Southeast Asia*, Springer Proceedings in Humanities and Social Sciences,
https://doi.org/10.1007/978-981-96-2116-3_52

1997) which introduces the "supply and demand" model based on the western democracy experience. The MSSG contributes to the supply-side, based on the experiences and voices of women's NGOs of the Global South.

**Keywords** Women's NGOs · Gender equality · Framework · Women's political participation

## 1 Introduction

Civil society assists in strengthening democracy beyond the existence of a general election [1, 2]. Women's non-governmental organizations (women's NGOs) become one of the important elements of civil society because it immensely contributes to Indonesia's development from the colonial, the Old Order, the New Order, and the post-Reform era (*pascarefomasi*). During the post-reform era, Indonesian women's NGOs contribute in strengthening the "consolidation phase of democracy" to borrow from Alagappa's term [3]. This contribution tends not to be denied, but no specific study seriously analyzes the capacity of Indonesian women's NGOs, especially by using a gender perspective.

In 1996, Mansour Fakih published book entitled *Analisis Gender dan Transformasi Sosial* or Gender Analysis and Social Transformation. This book underscores the importance of gender analysis among Indonesian non-governmental organizations (NGOs) and grouped the Indonesian NGOs into three groups: (i) "conformism" (*konformisme*), (ii) "reformist" (*reformis*), and (iii) "transformative" (*transformatif*) [4]. Since Fakih's research and book on the importance of gender perspective in Indonesian NGOs, so far, there is no comprehensive study assessing capacity of Indonesian women's NGOs.

Attention on civil society in Indonesian democracy are mainly focused on good governance framework [5] without gender perspectives. Studies on women's NGOs by using a gender perspective are still limited. Thus, it is still unclear whether women's NGOs as part of civil society in Indonesia, will always encourage gender equality. Previous studies showed women's NGOs failed to always empower women, as some organizations perpetuate gender-biased norms and values [6]. Furthermore, Women Research Institute [7] showed that women's role through various women's NGOs is getting stronger, but it does not necessarily means achieving substantial gender equality. Given the importance of understanding the various issues and challenges faced by Indonesian women's NGOs, an analytical framework is needed to mapping the problems faced by women's NGOs in Indonesian post-reform era.

Indeed, there are already several gender analysis frameworks in Indonesia. There is gender mainstreaming framework (*Pengarusutamaan Gender*, PUG) issued by Presidential Instruction No. 9/2000 which regulates gender mainstreaming in various government institutions from national to local level. The PUG framework encouraged bureaucratic apparatus to have gender perspectives in delivering their services, to ensure justice and equality for women and men's access, participation, control and benefit in various development programs. Furthermore, the Knowledge Sector Initiative (KSI) proposed the Gender Equality, Disability, and Social Inclusion (GEDSI) that was adopted by Indonesian National Development Planning Agency (*Bappenas*) [8]. The GEDSI are seen not only as fundamental aspects of human rights and social justice, but also as a precondition to improve the development process [9].

Generally, the PUG and GEDSI are mainstreaming gender in government institutions or civil society organizations. However, PUG and GEDSI framework are not sufficient to assess capacity of women's NGOs in post-reform era Indonesia.

Having understood all the needs and circumstances, the Gender and Politics research team of National Research and Innovation Agency (BRIN) have conducted research from 2020 to 2021, in order to create an analytical framework by using gender perspectives to asses capacity of Indonesian women's NGOs. As presented in this paper, the framework developed by the Gender and Politics research team is called 'Gender Equal Civil Society' (in Indonesian language called *Masyarakat Sipil Setara Gender*, here in after in this paper called MSSG). The next section explains the method, followed by MSSG dimensions and elements, its contributions to encourage women's political participation, and end up with the conclusion.

## 2 Method

A qualitative research method with gender perspective was used to capture the voice and opinion of women's NGOs activists, in this study. Specifically, it uses feminist research methodology by using women's experiences in certain context as the source of knowledge [10]. The MSSG was developed by an inclusive approach including: (i) it was carried out by a bottom-up approach by inviting various women NGO activists in Jakarta, West Java, North Sumatra, West Sumatra, East Nusa Tenggara, and Yogyakarta. This is to consider the diversity of Indonesian women's NGOs. (ii) inclusiveness of MSSG is reflected in one of the elements of MSSG namely 'local contexts and intersectionality. The element of local context and intersectionality will enable researcher to reveal the multi-layered discrimination faced by women such as intersection gender with issues of race, ethnicity, or social class in different context across Indonesia.

The data were collected by means of 21 Focus Group Discussions (FGDs) with women's NGOs activists (especially chairwomen or secretary general) within two years, from 2020 to 2021. By involving participation of various Indonesian women's NGOs in developing the analytical framework of MSSG, thus the MSSG grows together with these women's NGOs.

## 3 Result and Discussions

### *3.1 Development of the Framework: 'Gender Equal Civil Society'*

The MSSG was developed based on the concepts of gender mainstreaming and women's empowerment as inspired by various scholars such as Lopes et al. [11], Aruna Rao et al. [12], Awan [13], Weldon [14], and Kabeer [15].

Aruna Rao et al. [16] in the book of *Gender at Work Theory and Practice for 21st Century Organizations* introduced the "Gender at Work Analytical Framework" with the initial aim of understanding gender inequality and power relations between women and men in the community, analyzing and making strategies to change gender relations. The "Gender at Work Analytical Framework" consists of four quadrants, namely: (i) quadrant I consists of individual consciousness and capabilities of leaders and members of the organization (are they aware of their rights, respects gender equality, or willing and able to take actions to create more gender equitable communities, (ii) quadrant II consists of resources within organizations to promote gender equality such as access to leadership, budgets and mechanisms for protection against sexual violence, (iii) quadrant III consists of rules and regulations such as whether the organization provides policy that promote gender equality, (iv) quadrant IV consists of social norms and deep structures including ideology, social norms, and practices which govern an ideal gender roles, which perhaps hinders women's opportunities to exercise their rights or limiting their ability to change; here, the organization should formulate strategies to address these problems [16].

Lopes et al.[11] also conducted a study on the role of civil society in Portugal in promoting gender equality through two analytical axes, namely mainstreaming and empowerment. Lopes et al. said that the concept of empowerment is more focused on looking at: (i) organizational capacity including mission, participation, management, accountability, (ii) strategic capacity and inter-organizational networks. Through Lopes et al., it can be understood more clearly how mainstreaming and empowerment strategies are applied to intervene in inequalities that exist in social groups or in organizational structures. Mainstreaming strategy is also considered as one way that can precisely ensure the effectiveness of a design. Initially, the mainstreaming strategy was widely used by women activists to influence public strategy and policy. In its development, it turns out that this strategy can be systematically integrated in all policies to adopt the needs of women and men equally and can explicitly be used to mobilize public policies to promote gender equality.

On empowerment, Rowland said empowerment does not simply refer to participation in decision making, but must include the process by which a person is able to achieve self-awareness to be able to make decisions; empowerment must include the 'power to' dimension namely to exercise decision-making authority to overcome problems, as well as the 'power within' dimension where a person has self-confidence, self-awareness and self-assertion [17]. Rowland further noted that empowerment includes three dimensions, namely: first, 'personal' where a person is able to build self-confidence, capacity, and escape from oppression from within; second, 'relational', namely the ability to negotiate or influence relationships or decisions in it; third, 'collective' where one can work together to achieve a more optimal impact such as joint efforts in the political structure emphasizing cooperation and not competition [17, p. 15]. Not much different, Kabeer noted [15] that women's empowerment is a process in which a person (especially woman) who initially did not have the opportunity to make strategic choices in her life, is then able to master this ability.

Here, mainstreaming is the efforts to improve life position, role, and quality to enable women and men entitle to justice. Thus, dimension of empowerment in MSSG is focused to explore how does women's NGOs are able to encourage women to: (i) gain access to resources, (ii) encourage critical awareness, (iii) empower them in decision-making in the household and public, and (iv) to enable them to have control over the decisions.

The two dimensions of MSSG namely gender mainstreaming and women's empowerment are further detailed into five elements including representation, autonomy, consolidation, local context & intersectionality, and social bases to strengthen women's participation in politics. In fact, initially MSSG was only consists of three elements namely representation, autonomy, consolidation. However, through suggestion of various women's NGOs in FGDs from 2020 to 2021, the three elements are expended into five elements with two additional elements: local context & intersectionality, and social basis.

Women's NGOs as the subject in this study are defined as organizations that are: (i) voluntarily formed by women or men regardless of their religion, culture, profession, and society, (ii) targeting women individually or in groups, (iii) independent and autonomous from the state, (iv) providing socio-economic and political benefits for women, (v) trying to influence the state and its policies, (vi) either have the Statutes and Bylaws (*Anggaran Dasar dan Anggaran Rumah Tangga,* AD/ART) or not, and (vii) either have registered in the Ministry of Home Affairs, or in the Ministry of Law and Human Rights or not.

Dewi Candraningrum from Jejer Wadon, Solo as one of the participants in the FGD [18] explained the importance of adopting Kimberly Crenshaw's theory of intersectionality which is more critical in looking at issues of gender discrimination, injustice, exploitation and violence against women that intersect with other issues such as race, ethnicity, class and masculinity in state policies, spatial disparity (rural–urban), and intergenerational dimension gap. In addition, Syarif Hidayat from BRIN [18] emphasized the importance to consider local context as an MSSG element because of the diversity context across Indonesia, as he said:

> ...there are three elements of MSSG including autonomy, representation, and consolidation. But social inclusion and local context should be added. This makes the various context of Indonesian society to be accommodated within the MSSG .... [19]

The local context and intersectionality was finally included in MSSG, in where gives room for various voices of women's NGOs and community members to be accommodated during the data collection and observations. The addition element of local context and intersectionality helps in understanding women's challenges in terms of gender, race, ethnicity, and social class across Indonesia.

The last element of MSSG which was added based on the suggestion from women's NGOs activists is social bases. According to Dwi Septiawati Djafar, Head of the Indonesian Political Women's Caucus (*Koalisi Perempuan Politik Indonesia*, KPPI) [20], social bases enables women to be able to win political competition, to counter the influence of material power or vote buying in politics. The power of social bases is potential in electoral politics as it contributes to increase popular electability to countering the influence of transactional politics. For example, Dwi Septiawati Djafar [20] indicated that social bases owned by women farmers, fisher women, and women's group of Family Welfare Empowerments (PKK) are potential to gather grassroot political support.

In conclusion, the MSSG consists of two dimensions namely gender mainstreaming and women's empowerment, which further includes element of representation, autonomy, consolidation, local context & intersectionality, and social bases. The MSSG is not only comprise of the theoretical aspect, but also practical elements as the analytical tools than can be used by other institutions or NGOs.

## 3.2 The 'Gender Equal Civil Society': Dimensions and Elements

This section explains the two dimensions and five elements of the Gender Equal Civil Society (MSSG). Each element of MSSG (representation, autonomy, consolidation, local context & intersectionality, and social bases) consists of two parts including: (i) the internal capacity of women's organization and, (ii) their strategies to interact with partners, as presented in Table 1.

Each element of MSSG is explained as follows:

First, representation which includes two things, namely descriptive representation and substantive representation. The element of representation is derived from the concept of political representation in legislative studies. In the MSSG, the representation is divided into two aspects: (i) 'descriptive representation' that focuses on symbolic or numerical issues, for example whether women's NGOs have a high enough representation of women in their management; (ii) 'substantive representation', namely whether female or male NGO administrators have a gender perspective, or the organization perpetuates gender inequality. This includes whether women's NGOs' programs also have a gender perspective. Ideally both aspects of 'descriptive representation' and 'substantive representation' can be fulfilled by women's NGOs.

Second, autonomy, in this case it is important to understand whether women's NGOs have their own source of funding, have a bargaining position to formulate the goals of the organization and to allocate funds (either from donor institutions or from central/regional governments) to support policies and programs that are directed towards achieving gender equality and strengthening democracy. Autonomy is not

**Table 1** Dimensions and elements of gender equal civil society (or MSSG)

| Gender mainstreaming | Women's empowerment |
|---|---|
| Descriptive representation<br>• *Institutional capacity*<br>• *Women's NGO strategy* | Descriptive representation<br>• *Institutional capacity*<br>• *Women's NGO strategy* |
| Substantive representation<br>• *Institutional capacity*<br>• *Women's NGO strategy* | Substantive representation<br>• *Institutional capacity*<br>• *Women's NGO strategy* |
| Autonomy<br>• *Institutional capacity*<br>• *Women's NGO strategy* | Autonomy<br>• *Institutional capacity*<br>• *Women's NGO strategy* |
| Consolidation<br>• *Institutional capacity*<br>• *Women's NGO strategy* | Consolidation<br>• *Institutional capacity*<br>• *Women's NGO strategy* |
| Local context and intersectionality<br>• *Institutional capacity*<br>• *Women's NGO strategy* | local context and intersectionality<br>• *institutional capacity*<br>• *women's ngo strategy* |
| Social bases<br>• *Institutional capacity*<br>• *Women's NGO strategy* | social bases<br>• *institutional capacity*<br>• *women's ngo strategy* |

*Source* Created by the team

only limited in terms of funding management but also includes the autonomy to use power to influence policy.

Third, consolidation refers to the understanding women's NGOs organizational capacity to make democratic decisions on any arising issues or internal conflicts, and to synergize and cooperate with other parties. Consolidation is ideally indicated while a joint decision is made to reject, accept, and implement a program. This element assists in achieving gender equality and strengthening democracy because women mutually agreed on particular issues while working with their partners. Putnam [21] as quoted by Alagappa [22] showed the enhancement of networks by involving society strongly affects people's lives. This cooperation tends to develop social trust which in turn facilitates and strengthens communication and reputation.

Fourth, local context and intersectionality. Nina Lykke [23] explained that intersectionality was introduced by Kimberle Crenshaw in the late 1980s. Crenshaw introduced concept of 'intersectionality' as an analytical tool to look at the occurrence of discrimination and exclusion of women of color, because the existing analysis, often cannot see the intersection between the existing socio-cultural categories and gender. Intersectionality is more critical in looking at issues of gender discrimination, injustice, exploitation and violence against women that intersect with other issues. Gadis Arivia [24] has the same opinion that 'intersectionality' is more critical in identifying discriminatory issues, injustice, exploitation, and violence against women. The element of local context and intersectionality will enable researcher to reveal the multi-layered discrimination faced by women such as intersection gender with issues of race, ethnicity, or social class in different context across Indonesia.

Fifth, social bases which in this study is defined as social capital or the capacity of women's NGOs to associate or interact regularly and continuously based on friendship, social ties, and common interests with particular group. In this study, the social bases can be seen from two interrelated perspectives: (i) from the perspective of women's NGOs, it refers to the bonds, relationships, and work done with women so that mutual trust and cooperation are formed; (ii) from the point of view of women who are partners with women's NGOs, the social bases is the involvement of women in various community activities at the local level that can contribute to increasing self-confidence, courage to make decisions, and courage to participate in the surrounding politics. The ability of these women NGO's partner to capitalize on the social bases in electoral political contestations in grass roots level is clearly important. The social bases social bases can provide potential supporters in electoral political contestations.

Having all of the elements of MSSG, Mike Verawati Secretary-General of the Indonesian Women's Coalition [25] said that women's NGOs will gain benefit from the MSSG analytical framework as it will help them to understand their capacity and strategy to address various problems. Member of the women's NGOs can further take parts in various activities and increase self-confidence to participate in politics such as in village meetings, village head competition, or legislative election. Thus, MSSG can encourage women's NGOs to increase women's political participation in Indonesia, as will be explained in the next section.

### 3.3 Contribution of MSSG to Supporting Women's Political Participation

Dahl's (1971) as cited by Paxton [26] showed that democracy consists of two dimensions including (1) competition and (2) participation. The contestation was marked by the existence of general elections because citizens, including women, use their right to vote to participate to changing leaders and policies. Paxton [26, p. 49] reiterated that democracy emphasizes the importance of universal suffrage and the political participation of all social groups including women. Therefore, this study used the dimensions of political participation as the target point of the MSSG to strengthen Indonesian democracy.

Barnes et al. [27] emphasized that political participation is voluntary activities that directly and indirectly influence elections at a different system. Nelson [28] defined it as citizens' action to affect the composition of national and local governments. Therefore, in this paper political participation is defined as the people's activities to directly or indirectly influence actions, or preferences at the local or national levels.

Furthermore, based on a gender perspective, political participation is not only related to the formal system at the local or national level but also involves daily activities. In the late 1960s, Carol Hanisch as quoted by Eisenstein [29] indicated the slogan of the women's movement as "the personal is political". This slogan emphasizes that personal experience is closely related to social and political structure in society. Therefore, this study believes that: (i) daily politics is part of political participation, and (ii) women do not always influence political policies at the local or national level, but they do play political participation through various civil society organizations, including women's non-governmental organizations.

Therefore, in this study defines political participation includes two aspects: (i) daily politics in the form of various actions in daily life, including their role in networking with women's NGOs or participate actively in community at the local level (neighborhood associations, or village level). Women who are consistently active in various meetings encouraged by women's NGOs will have a promising constituency base which attracted political parties to recruit them; (ii) electoral politics including women's political participation in the 2024 general election at the legislative or executive level. In this context, political parties become the key element in political recruitment which then can nominate potential women as legislative candidates. Political participation is closely related to "personal is political" because women's activities comprise either in the private or public sphere.

Thus, academically, the MSSG contributes to encourage political participation of women in a broader sense (in daily politics and electoral politics) which in turn help to increase women representation in parliament. Norris and Lovenduski introduced the "demand" and "supply" model for understanding representation of women in parliament [30, 31]. Here, the MSSG contributes in the supply-side by encouraging the role of women's NGOs in providing spaces and pools of talents of potential women to compete in electoral politics. It is expected that women's NGOs can encourage the emergence of more women activists from grass roots level to be politicians, to compete in electoral politics, especially in the forthcoming 2024 General Elections.

## 4 Conclusion

This paper has explained development of the MSSG or 'the Gender Equal Civil Society' as framework to mapping capacity and strategy of Indonesian women's NGOs in post-reform era. As explained, the two dimensions of MSSG namely gender mainstreaming and women's empowerment, and the five elements of MSSG (representation, autonomy, consolidation, local context & intersectionality, and social bases) were developed by a bottom-up approach by hearing the voices of various women's NGOs activists, from 2020 to 2021. The MSSG does not replicate any framework from other institutions. It is based on empirical conditions of Indonesian women's NGOs.

Currently, the MSSG is further developed into an operationalization tool consists of variables and indicators as basis for constructing the questionnaire for an online national survey for Indonesian women's NGOs that is distributed in May 2022. The result of the MSSG survey will be the first-ever data on Indonesian women NGO's capacity and strategy in the post-reform era. The results of the MSSG survey will help in improving Indonesian women's NGOs capacities in two aspects including:

(i) an internal institutional capacity and (ii) organizational strategies to collaborate with partner.

In sum, this study contributes in two ways: *first,* it provides academic novelty because the MSSG explores the supply-side element especially showing the role of Indonesian women's NGOs (in the Global South) in encouraging political participation of women in broader sense (daily politics and electoral politics). It contributes to the classical theory of women's representation in parliament, which is so far mainly based on the western democracy experience. *Second,* it practically will present a new understanding of Indonesian women's NGOs institutional capacity and strategy in the post-reform era.

Placing into the national effort to increase representation of women parliament, the MSSG contributes to the national grand design to achieve minimum of 30 percent of women in national parliament by the 2024 General Election as enacted by Ministry of Women's Empowerment and Child Protection (*Kementerian Pemberdayaan Perempuan dan Perlindungan Anak Republik Indonesia*). At the international level, the MSSG can be further used and developed by other organizations beyond Indonesia to contribute academically and practically.

**Acknowledgements** Kurniawati Hastuti Dewi, Ade Latifa, Nur Iman Subono are the main contributor of this paper. We thank National Research and Innovation Agency (BRIN) for funding this research from 2020 to 2022. LPDP of Indonesia also supported this research in 2020.

## References

1. Weiss ML (2015) Civil society and democratization in Southeast Asia: what is the connection? In: Case W (ed) Routledge handbook of Southeast Asian democratization. Routledge, London and New York, pp 135–146
2. Aspinall E (2013) A nation in fragments: Patronage and neoliberalism in contemporary Indonesia. Crit Asian Stud 45(1):27–54. https://doi.org/10.1080/14672715.2013.758820
3. Alagappa M (2004) Civil society and political change in Asia: expanding and contracting democratic space. Stanford University Press, California, pp 5–6
4. Fakih M (2010) Masyarakat sipil untuk transformasi sosial pergolakan ideologi LSM Indonesia (cetakan ke-5). Pustaka Pelajar & INSIST Press, Yogyakarta, pp 116–122
5. Hidayat S (2016) Menimbang ulang konsep good governance: Diskurus teoretis. Jurnal Masyara kat Indonesia 42(2):151–165
6. Barnes K, Albrecht P (2008) Civil society oversight of the security sector and gender. In: Bastick M, Valasek K (eds) Gender and security sector reform toolkit. DCAF, OSCE/ODIHR, UN-INSTRAW, Geneva
7. Women Research Institute (2013) Indonesian women's movements: Making democracy gender-responsive. WRI, Jakarta
8. Knowledge Sector Initiative, "Kesetaraan Gender, Disabilitas dan Inklusi Sosial dalam Praktik: Pengalaman Riset dan Advokasi Mitra Knowledge Sector Initiative. https://www.ksi-indonesia.org/id/pengetahuan/publikasi. Last aAccessed 16 April 2022
9. GEDSI in AIPJ2. https://aipj.or.id/pages/publication/kesetaraan-gender-disabilitas-dan-inklusi-sosial-gedsi-di-aipj2. Last Accessed 16 April 2022
10. Harding S (1987) The method question. Hypatia 2(3):19–35

11. Lopes M, Ferreira V, Ferreira S, Coelho L (2008) Civil society organizations and gender equality: Mainstreaming and empowerment in the public policies towards civil society. [Paper for the ISTR Eighth International Conference and 2nd EMES-ISTR European Conference, The Third Sector and Sustainable Social Change: New Frontiers for Research]. Barcelona, Organized by ISTR, EMES in partnership with CINEFOGO, Barcelona, July 9–12. https://www.researchgate.net/publication/237613718_Civil_society_organisations_and_gender_equality_mainstreaming_and_empowerment_in_the_public_policies_towards_civil_society. Last Accessed 10 April 2022
12. Rao A, Sandler J, Kelleher D, Miller C (2016) Gender at work: theory and practice for 21st-century organizations. Routledge, USA
13. Awan SZ (2012) Role of civil society in empowering Pakistani women. Res J South Asian Stud 27(2):439–458
14. Weldon SL (2004) The dimensions and policy impact of feminist civil society democratic policymaking on violence against women in the fifty US States. Int Fem J Polit 6(1):1–28. https://doi.org/10.1080/1461674032000165914
15. Kabeer N (1999) Resource, agency, achievements: Reflections on the measurement of women's empowerment. Dev Chang 30:437–438
16. Rao A, Sandler J, Kelleher D, Miller C (2016) Gender at work: theory and practice for 21st century organizations. Routledge, USA
17. Rowlands J (1997) Questioning empowerment: Working with women in Honduras. Oxfam, Ireland, p 14
18. Dewi Candraningrum's opinion in a research design seminar held on July 13, 2020
19. Syarif Hidayat's opinion, during the research design seminar on July 13, 2020
20. Dwi Septiawati Djafar's opinion in a focus group discussion on October 16, 2020
21. Putnam RD. Bowling alone: America's declining social capital. In: Diamond L, Platner MF (eds) The global resurgency of democracy. Baltimore, The Johns Hopkins University Press
22. Alagappa M (2004) Civil society and political change in Asia: expanding and contracting democratic space. Stanford University Press, California
23. Lykke N (2010) Feminist studies a guide to intersectional theory, methodology and writing. Routledge, New York & London
24. Arivia G (2020) Perspektif feminisme: Interseksionalitas dan covid-19. Jurnal Perempuan 25(4):7–25
25. Mike Verawati's opinion in the 20th FGD on October 12, 2021
26. Paxton P (2008) Gendering democracy. In: Goertz G, Mazur AG (eds) Politics, gender, and concepts: Theory and methodology. Cambridge University Press, UK, p 48
27. Barnes SH, Kaase M et al (1979) Political action: mass participation in five western democracies. Sage Publication, Beverly Hills, California, p 42
28. Nelson JM (1979) Access to power: politics and the urban poor in developing nations. Princeton, Princeton University Press, p 8
29. Eisenstein H (1984) Contemporary feminist thought. Unwin Paperbacks, London, Sidney, p 12
30. Norris P, Lovenduski J (1995) Political recruitment: gender, race, and class in the British parliament. Cambridge University Press, Great Britain, p 143
31. Norris P (1997) Introduction: theories of recruitment. In: Norris P (ed) Passage to power: legislative recruitment in advanced democracies. Cambridge University Press, Great Britain

# Prediction of Upcoming Sales for New Home-Scale Businesses Making Handmade Bags with Time Series Analysis Method

**Debira Paramita Siregar and Besar Agung Martono**

**Abstract** To add insight and income, many housewives currently carry out small-scale home-based businesses that are carried out from home, where the business goals are different, one of which is to increase income from developing their hobbies. Dhandmade is one of the home businesses developed by a housewife which is the business making handmade bags. Developed from what was originally a hobby, then ventured to accept orders and began to develop. To estimate or predict the continuity of her home-scale business, Dhandmade dares to start a forecast to estimate the number of orders that will be received in the coming year. This research method uses a quantitative method through forecasting which will use Time Series Analysis using POM QM software. This method was chosen because it is quite simple for a home-scale business forecasting measure. Time series data can be seen as a representation of the real variables which usually have the same time interval. The data collection is obtained from bag sales data for the last year which is processed using the Microsoft Excel program to see the trend of bags order in a year and is also supported by literature studies to examine it. The results of the research show that there is a trend of stability in ordering the handmade bags in the coming year for Dhandmade and the Linear Trend method of the Time Series Analysis is the suitable method because it has the smallest error rate value for the prediction. This research result aims to obtain the best demand forecast based on historical data on Dhandmade bags production demand for the last year that can be used as information and reference in planning future production activities and establishing steps in continuing the production of handmade bags home-scale business.

**Keywords** Forecasting · Time series · Home-scale business · Dhandmade bags

D. P. Siregar (✉) · B. A. Martono
Universitas IPWIJA, Jakarta, Indonesia
e-mail: debirasiregar@gmail.com

B. A. Martono
e-mail: agungmartono@gmail.com



Nawawi et al. (eds.), *Managing Disruption and Developing Resilience for a Better Southeast Asia*, Springer Proceedings in Humanities and Social Sciences,
https://doi.org/10.1007/978-981-96-2116-3_53

# 1 Introduction

In the pandemic era, besides the negative, there are some positive things that come up around us, like entrepreneurship among women world in Indonesia. Entrepreneurial work by housewives is currently mostly done through the development of hobbies. At first, it was only used for their own, but eventually, it became a producing commodity. That's usually the start of the home-scale industry. One that has developed a business starting from a hobby is Dhandmade by producing handmade bags which are starting to be marketed through social media and from friendship. With the increasing demand for handmade bags orders since the start of the business, Dhandmade feels the need to forecast future product demand based on monthly orders for the past year.

Forecasting is a method to count future values come by using past data. Forecasting on a business is widely used to describe the situation of the business in the future that can be used to help make decisions about what steps can be taken to meet consumer demand. And forecasting is a way to measure, estimate, and predict what needs are needed to prepare the demand for goods or services to consumers [1].

A sales forecast is one of the most important things in a production plan. Too much production will result in wastage which makes a loss in a home-based business. For that, it needs to take a sales forecasting to calculate sales in the next period to consider how many raw materials need to prepare, workers, and many more. With the background of the problem as described, several problems were formulated, namely "how many orders of Dhandmade bags for the next period based on the historical data?"

This study aimed to determine the best type of demand forecasting method that can be used, to match the demand conditions of Dhandmade bags based on its historical data. This study is important that the chosen forecasting method can be used widely among other home-scale businesses whether it's the same product or a different one. In this study, forecasting will be carried out using the POM QM application in which there is already a time series application with several of the methods mentioned above. The author will choose the most suitable method for forecasting sales or demand for Dhandmade bags for further use.

# 2 Research Method

Research is carried out by going through several stages as follows:

1. Conduct literature studies and field studies

The literature study conducted in this research is to read and find references to the theory of forecasting. The field studies in this research by looking directly at the home-scale business situation and collect sales data from previous.

2. Problem formulation

After conducting a literature study, study field researchers formulate problems contained in the business, namely "how many orders of Dhandmade bags for the next period based on the historical data?"

3. Setting goals

The purpose of this research is to determine the best type of demand forecasting method that can be used, to match the demand conditions of Dhandmade bags based on its historical data by doing forecasting.

4. Method selection

After getting historical data research company chooses method suitable forecasting to complete existing problems. POM QM method is a predictive method that estimates sales or demand in the future period using historical data. Several methods included in the Times Series method include moving average, linear regression, and additive decomposition (seasonal) but are equipped with other production modules [2].

5. Calculation of data with the selected method

The method chosen is the method linear regression forecast.

6. Conclusions and furthermore, the conclusions obtained are used to provide suggestions for improvement to Dhandmade business and research.

## 2.1 Time-Series Forecasting Method

The time series method is used to examine a series of data that is a function of time. The value for a variable has been set over time where supply for demand is associated with a fairly close relationship with the time series method. This method can be used to examine a set of one or more data based on a function of time, which is the definition of the time series method. Regression methods can be divided into several methods, including the linear, constant, cyclical, quadratic, seasonal method (Seasonal), trend method, and causal methods [3].

## 2.2 Linear Regression Method

Linear regression method is a statistical method that makes predictions through the development of relationships between variables. The dependent variable (Y) and the independent variable (X) are the variables. The dependent variable is the variable that is affected, while the independent variable is the cause or the variable that influences. Value prediction of the dependent variable is done if the independent variable is known. Generally, the demand or sales of a product is expressed as the dependent variable which value is influenced by the independent variable.

The formula for linear regression with a simple method is:

$$a = \frac{(\sum y)(\sum x^2) - (\sum x)(\sum xy)}{n(\sum x^2) - (\sum x)^2} \tag{1}$$

$$b = \frac{n(\sum xy) - (\sum x)(\sum y)}{n(\sum x^2) - (\sum x)^2} \tag{2}$$

$$y = a + bx \tag{3}$$

which $y$ is the sales quantity, $x$ is the month of sales, $a$ is a constant which refers to $y$ if $x = 0$, and $b$ is the amount change value of $y$.

## 2.3 POM QM Software

The POM QM application is a mathematical application for operational management and science management created by Pearson education Inc. Available in management science, fields of production and operations management, operations research, and quantitative methods. It is a user-friendly software package for management [4].

In its application, POM QM provides several different types of modules, including:

Forecasting (Forecasting), Assignment, Aggregate Planning, Balancing Assembly Line, Decision Analysis (Decision Making), Break Even/Cost-Volume Analysis, Inventory (Inventory), Job Shop Scheduling, Learning Curve, Linear Programming, Location, Lot Sizing, Material Requirements Planning, Operations Layout, Project Management (PERT/CPM), Quality Control, Reliability, Simulation, Transportation, Waiting Lines [5].

## 2.4 Accuracy Test

The forecast accuracy is determined by the magnitude of the error or deviation between the predicted data and the actual data. Forecasting accuracy here is used to select the best model from the existing methods by looking at the smallest mean square error or MSE [3].

The magnitude of the error can be caused by unexpected factors, where there is no forecasting method that can produce accurate forecasts or it can also be caused by the forecasting method used cannot accurately predict the trend component, seasonal component, or cyclical component contained in the data series [6].

Among the various ways to calculate the size of the error, some of them are mean absolute percentage error or MAPE and mean square error or MSE. MSE is the mean of the difference in squares between the predicted and observed values, and MAPE is an average of the absolute differences between the value of predicted and actual. Forecasting results are declared good if the MSE value is low, the lower the value, the better the forecasting is done [2].

the formula of the test is shown in the following equation:

$$MSE = \frac{1}{n}\sum (Yt - Y^{t}t)^{2} \quad (4)$$

$$MAPE = \frac{1}{n}\sum_{t=1}^{n} \frac{(Yt - Y^{t}t)}{Yt} \quad (5)$$

where the actual value of period *t* is *Yt*, $Y^{t}t$ is the forecast of period *t*, and the number of periods is *n*.

## 3 Results and Discussion

Researchers collected data based on data from bag sales during 2021, starting from January to December (Table 1).

**Table 1** Dhandmade bag sales data for January–December 2021

| No | Month (2021) | Sales quantity (Unit) |
|---|---|---|
| 1 | January | 22 |
| 2 | February | 26 |
| 3 | March | 23 |
| 4 | April | 20 |
| 5 | May | 35 |
| 6 | June | 28 |
| 7 | July | 18 |
| 8 | August | 24 |
| 9 | September | 29 |
| 10 | October | 21 |
| 11 | November | 30 |
| 12 | December | 42 |

*Source* Dhandmade sales data, 2021

**Fig. 1** 2021 bag sales results

### *3.1 Data Pattern Test*

In this study, the data pattern test was carried out using Microsoft Excel software to determine the movement pattern of demand for Dhandmade bag products. The results of the data pattern test can be seen in Fig. 1.

Based on the results of the data pattern test conducted, it can be said that the data is not stationary because data does not fluctuate.

### *3.2 Forecasting Demand Through Software Applications*

The software application used is forecasting with the POM QM software with the forecasting module to estimate the number of forecast orders with Time Series Analysis and takes four methods, including naïve method, moving average method, linear regression, and adaptive decomposition method. The results of demand forecasting are obtained by processing past demand data, precisely during 2021, and inputting them into the software [5].

In Fig. 2, the naïve method is what happened in the previous period of time and predicted the same thing will happen again. The table result shows MAPE 28% and MSE 68.91.

In Fig. 3, a moving average forecasting method is used for long-term trends of statistical. The technique takes an average of a set of numbers in a range while moving the range. The table result shows MAPE 28% and MSE 68.91.

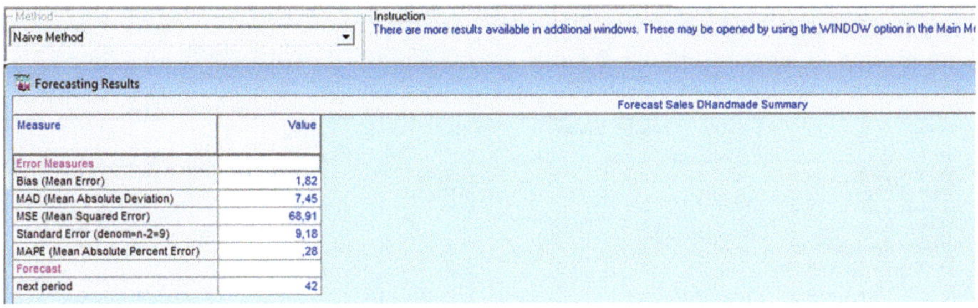


| Measure | Value |
|---|---|
| Error Measures | |
| Bias (Mean Error) | 1,82 |
| MAD (Mean Absolute Deviation) | 7,45 |
| MSE (Mean Squared Error) | 68,91 |
| Standard Error (denom=n-2=9) | 9,18 |
| MAPE (Mean Absolute Percent Error) | ,28 |
| Forecast | |
| next period | 42 |

**Fig. 2** Naïve method

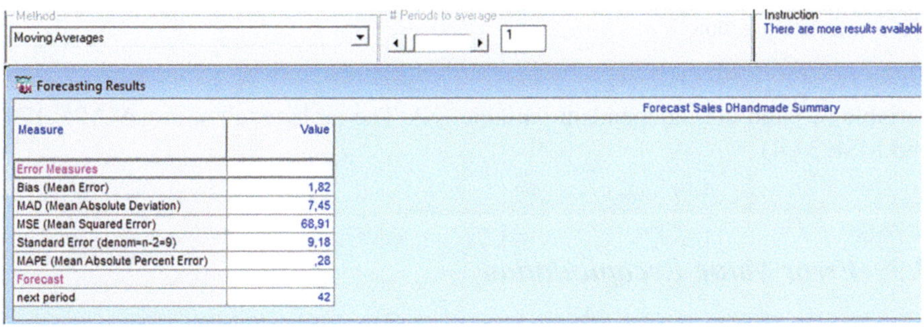


| Measure | Value |
|---|---|
| Error Measures | |
| Bias (Mean Error) | 1,82 |
| MAD (Mean Absolute Deviation) | 7,45 |
| MSE (Mean Squared Error) | 68,91 |
| Standard Error (denom=n-2=9) | 9,18 |
| MAPE (Mean Absolute Percent Error) | ,28 |
| Forecast | |
| next period | 42 |

**Fig. 3** Moving average method

In Fig. 4, an additive decomposition is to forecast the seasonal component of a decomposed time series. Usually assumed that the seasonal component is unchanging. The table result shows MAPE 17% and MSE 34.58.

In Fig. 5, a statistical method that makes predictions through the development of relationships between variables is linear regression, and variables are the dependent

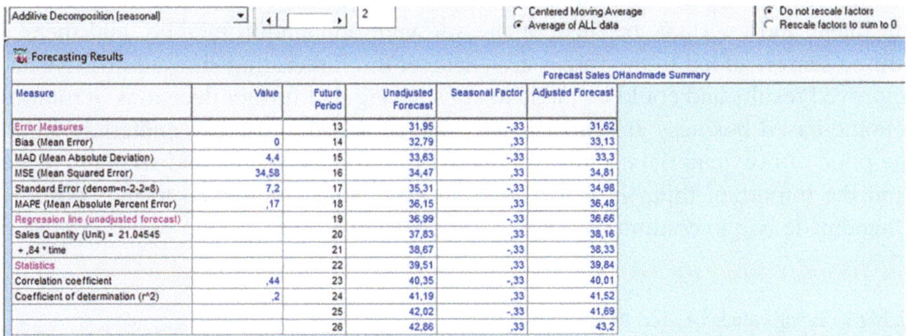


| Measure | Value | Future Period | Unadjusted Forecast | Seasonal Factor | Adjusted Forecast |
|---|---|---|---|---|---|
| Error Measures | | 13 | 31,95 | -,33 | 31,62 |
| Bias (Mean Error) | 0 | 14 | 32,79 | ,33 | 33,13 |
| MAD (Mean Absolute Deviation) | 4,4 | 15 | 33,63 | -,33 | 33,3 |
| MSE (Mean Squared Error) | 34,58 | 16 | 34,47 | ,33 | 34,81 |
| Standard Error (denom=n-2-2=8) | 7,2 | 17 | 35,31 | -,33 | 34,98 |
| MAPE (Mean Absolute Percent Error) | ,17 | 18 | 36,15 | ,33 | 36,48 |
| Regression line (unadjusted forecast) | | 19 | 36,99 | -,33 | 36,66 |
| Sales Quantity (Unit) = 21.04545 | | 20 | 37,83 | ,33 | 38,16 |
| + ,84 * time | | 21 | 38,67 | -,33 | 38,33 |
| Statistics | | 22 | 39,51 | ,33 | 39,84 |
| Correlation coefficient | ,44 | 23 | 40,35 | -,33 | 40,01 |
| Coefficient of determination (r^2) | ,2 | 24 | 41,19 | ,33 | 41,52 |
| | | 25 | 42,02 | -,33 | 41,69 |
| | | 26 | 42,86 | ,33 | 43,2 |

**Fig. 4** Additive decomposition (seasonal)

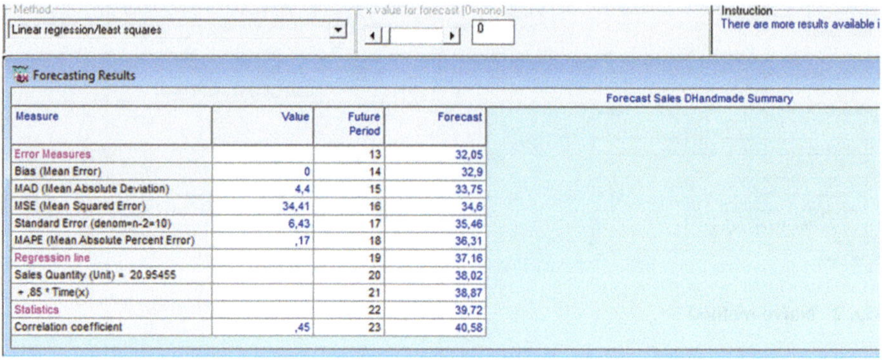


**Fig. 5** Linear regression

variable (Y) and the independent variable (X). The table result shows MAPE 17% and MSE 34.41.

## 3.3 *Error Value Recapitulation*

The recapitulation of the error or error value of each application method used is shown in Table 2.

In determining the best forecasting method, by looking at the magnitude of the error value in the method, the smaller the error value in a method, the better the forecasting results. From the results of this forecasting, the linear regression method has the smallest error with a MAPE value of 17% and an MSE of 34.41. This can be said that linear regression is a method that will be used to forecast sales demand for Dhandmade bags in the coming year (Table 3; Fig. 6).

The forecasting result shows that the upcoming sales of Dhandmade bags will continue to scale up from the numbers of last year's quantity. The forecasting numbers are linear and constant, because of the software application method, and there is still no season added to the forecast. Whatever the forecasting showed positive and improved results and could be made to considering that further decisions in running a home-based business are carried out, such as spending on raw materials where the price of raw materials is always changing, adding workers, and so many more. And the important thing is that result can give more confidence to the owner of Dhandmade bag to continue her home-scale business.

**Table 2** Error values of used time series methods

| | Moving average | Additive decomposition | Naive | Linear regression |
|---|---|---|---|---|
| MAPE | 28% | 17% | 28% | 17% |
| MSE | 68.91 | 35.58 | 68.91 | 34.41 |

**Table 3** Upcoming sales based on forecasting

| No | Month | Sales quantity 2021 | Up coming sales forecast |
|---|---|---|---|
| 1 | January | 22 | 32.05 |
| 2 | February | 26 | 32.9 |
| 3 | March | 23 | 33.75 |
| 4 | April | 20 | 34.6 |
| 5 | May | 35 | 35.46 |
| 6 | June | 28 | 36.31 |
| 7 | July | 18 | 37.16 |
| 8 | August | 24 | 38.02 |
| 9 | September | 29 | 38.87 |
| 10 | October | 21 | 39.72 |
| 11 | November | 30 | 40.58 |

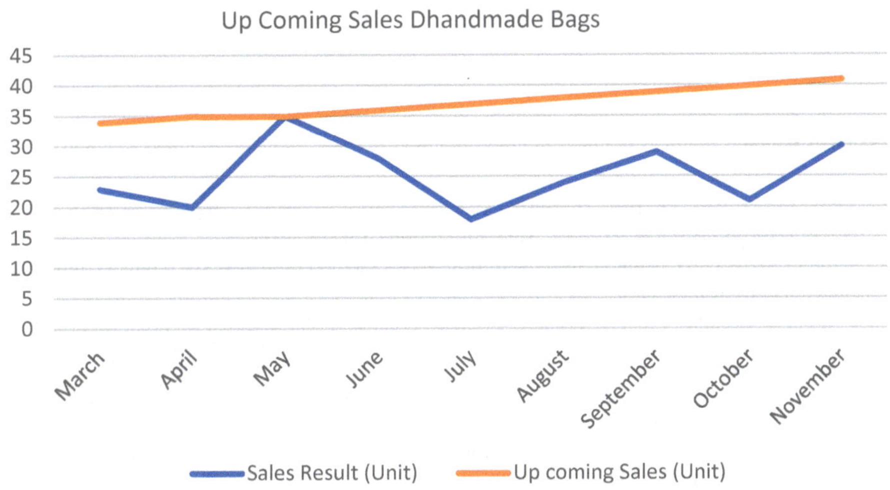


**Fig. 6** Upcoming sales of Dhandmade bags. *Source* Sales data forecast using linear regression

## 4 Conclusion

- Forecasting the sale of Dhandmade bags using the POM QM application with the linear regression method provides satisfactory results with MAPE 17% and MSE 34.41 and encourages business owners to continue and be consistent and improve her home-scale business in the years to come.
- Forecasting results obtained from the use of the POM QM application are only estimates for a certain period of time. However, this data information can be used by the Dhandmade bag business owner to make considerations on a business in

the future that can be used to help make decisions about what steps can be taken to meet consumer demand in the future.

## 5 Recommendation

- Using POM QM application is a good choice for small businesses to help its operation. And to make it socialized, the author will:
  - Publish the journal that I have written so that it can be reached by small business people who like to access information and materials from internet.
  - Sharing on sharing forums for small business and social media.
- In connection with this study taking very limited subjects and simple research, the researcher suggests to other parties to conduct further research on forecasting using the POM QM application with a longer time period and include seasonal elements so that generalizations can be drawn.

## References

1. Aji Prakoso I, Kusnadi, Billy N (2021) Sales Forecasting using Linear Regression Method And POM QM Application in PT XYZ. Scientific Journal Teknik 20(1)
2. Aulia I (2020) Forecasting analysis with time series method on hair dryer products. https://talentaconfseries.usu.ac.id/ee
3. Daryanto (2021) Production management. Yrama Widya, Bandung
4. www.pearson.com/us/higher-education/program/Weiss-POM-QM-for-Windows-v-3-3rd-Edition/.html (2006)
5. Danjunism (2020) POM QM Software Tutorial Ep. 04 | Forecasting/Forecasting Complete with Description. pom for windows forecasting time series, youtube
6. Ayuni GN (2019) Application of the linear regression method for property sales at PT XYZ. Journal.ithb.ac.id/telematika/article/view/321

# Preserving Democracy: Strengthening "Checks and Balances Mechanism" to Prevent Democratic Breakdown in Indonesia

**Devi Darmawan**

**Abstract** As a democratic country undertaking a democratic transition in 1998, Indonesia has gained worldwide attention and recognition for the practice toward good democratic governance. However, the existence of a democratic government practically goes hand in hand with the domination of elites, transactional politics, or cartel politics in government, allegedly due to the absence of resilient control as a manifestation of the mechanism of checks and balances among the branches of state power. This condition thus indicates the quality of democratic practice which tends to be artificial. In the end, this condition leads to the weakening quality of the democratic transition in Indonesia, thereby deteriorating democracy. This article implements a qualitative method and focuses on the practice of checks and balances in executives, legislative, and judicial level by looking at the practice of the opposition as well as the role of parliament and the judiciary in performing its control and balancing functions. This article concludes that weak practice of the checks and balances mechanism in Indonesia could subsequently threaten the sustainability of the democratic transition in the future. In this regard, attempts such as institutionalization of the opposition, strengthening DPD, harmonization, and synchronization of supervision within the judicial power are deemed pivotal to prevent the democratic setbacks in the future.

**Keywords** Checks and balances · Democracy · Democratic breakdown

## 1 Introduction

Indonesia experienced a democratic transition during the fall of the authoritarian regime led by Suharto in 1998. Indonesia has ever since attracted worldwide recognition as a country capable of administering democratic government, denoting successful periodic democratic elections both at national and local levels. However,

D. Darmawan (✉)
Research Center for Politics, National Research and Innovation Agency, Jakarta, Indonesia
e-mail: devi011@brin.go.id



Nawawi et al. (eds.), *Managing Disruption and Developing Resilience for a Better Southeast Asia*, Springer Proceedings in Humanities and Social Sciences,
https://doi.org/10.1007/978-981-96-2116-3_54

Indonesia democratic journey has been challenged, deteriorating the resilience of democracy in the future, indicated by the domination of elitists in government, and thus, political practices are based on consensus and transactions, as well as massive corruption by democratic institutions and law enforcement institutions. Hence, the entire phenomenon exacerbates the quality of democracy in Indonesia. Various factors are regarded to contribute to such condition.

The democratic scholars argued that the state of democracy should institutionalize the checks and balances principles to push back against the backsliding into the authoritarian regimes in order to preserve democratic consolidation. Otherwise, the democratization would remain stagnant signposted by the domination of elite shadowing democratic process within Indonesia political stage.

## *1.1 Problems and Significance*

This article evaluates the checks and balances practices among the legislative, executive, and judicial branches and the feasible influence toward the democratization in Indonesia. This study aims to contribute to political discourse in order to prevent democratic erosion by highlighting the checks and balances practices in Indonesia.

## *1.2 Literature Review*

Recent studies by several *Indonesianists* revealed that the practice of oligarchy [1, 2] or elitism [3] in Indonesia remains apparent despite the longstanding democracy practice of Indonesian political life. In general, observations toward contemporary Indonesian political indicate a paradox that Indonesia provides an excellent example of the phenomenon if the mechanism of democracy and the existence of oligarchy or elitism complement each other or coexist at the same time [4]. Meanwhile, regarding the relationship between the executive and the legislative, the established pattern has not indicated a solid form of democracy, denoted by the existence of political cartel relations, such as between the two institutions that tend to be mutually beneficial, both disguised and manifest, which in turn causes weak control of power [5–7]. Such phenomenon is in accordance with previous study [8] affirming the concept of "delegative democracy", referring that democracy lives in the midst of weak implementation of checks and balances. The aforementioned view apparently indicates that the existence and growth of democracy in Indonesia has been far from perfect, due to providing an ample space for the emergence of political practices reducing the nature of democracy itself.

Within Indonesia political practice, efforts to apply the principle of checks and balances are simultaneously conducted with efforts to actualize the post-reform democratic governance, as evidenced by the amendment of the constitution serving as the legal basis of the Indonesian state and the rules regarding the constitutional order through the formation of regulations in the field of politics such as Election Law, Political Party Law, and MD3 Law. Additionally, efforts include the establishment of regulation on Election Law limiting the term of office for the president, regulation on political parties to guarantee the right to serve as members and form political parties, and composition of representative institutions at the national level which contains changes in the roles and positions of high state institutions such as MPR and birth of new institutions in the composition of the Indonesian constitutional order, such as DPD, KY, and Constitutional Court.

Judging from the objectives, the amendments to the constitution and regulations were stipulated to abolish the rule of law that institutionalizes authoritarian power in Indonesia political. Therefore, changes in the state administration are conducted in a way that equal monitoring mechanism (checks and balances) could prevent potential abuse of power as emerged in the past. Unfortunately, this change leaves a problem undermining the state collective efforts toward a consolidated democracy, such as weak principle of checks and balances within Indonesia political system. In fact, democracy without a mechanism of checks and balances only leads to an artificial democracy. Democracy requires a mechanism of checks and balances to maintain the accountability of democratic government and keep the government from being dominated or co-opted by a group of elites. In fact, if the practice of checks and balances weakens, democratic governance is deemed endangered along with the fading of public confidence in the performance of democratic institutions as the pillars of the state.

### *1.3 Methodology*

This study employs qualitative research method, intended to explore the practice of checks and balances between branches of state power and between state high institutions in strengthening presidential democracy in Indonesia. In the process, this research implements data collection method through literature studies. Subsequently, literature and documents related to strengthening democracy such as the application of checks and balances in democratic institutions will be covered in this paper.

## 2 Discussion

### *2.1 Checks and Balances in Executive Branch*

The manifestation of checks and balances in the executive power refers to the opposition formed in the government system, as one of the barometers for a strong democracy is evident from the solidity of the opposition established in its political system. Opposition in the context of democratic life according to Dahl [9] refers to one of the inseparable foundations of democratic government, interpreted as a collective effort from an external group outside the government that legally holds the right to voice opinions and perform activities aimed at criticizing and controlling the attitudes, views, or policies of the government based on ideological perspectives, reality, empirical, or of particular interest [10].

In the political context, particularly in democratic life, the opposition has several functions. Firstly, it acts as a balance of power, indicating the existence of forces outside the government that provide alternative thoughts or attitudes to sustain the government track, not too far from the interests of the majority of the people. Secondly, it acts to keep the policy alternatives to be voiced, enabling the emergence of more policy options or alternative improvements to government policies which is in accordance with the fact that no government is free from mistakes. Even the best government requires indirect support from opposition groups to better capture the aspirations and interests of the people. The barrenness of the opposition, therefore, limits the options for upholding the aspirations of the people, deteriorating the government when running for a long time. Thirdly, the opposition acts as a stimulus for healthy competition between the political elites and the government. A government will stagnate, even decline, if it does not get a challenge from competent parties capable of publicly exhibiting that there are other sensible policies than those of government. The existence of opposition will awake the ruling government, realizing that there are other parties offering better policies. The opposition, therefore, needs the government as a stimulus to improve performance and maintain its good image in the eyes of the public. In this situation, a healthy competition emerges between the government and the opposition toward improvement. Therefore, it is necessary to strengthen the opposition, so that the government generates policies that are in accordance with the interests of the people and most importantly to avoid the occurrence of an oligarchy within the government.

In Indonesia political practice, the formation history of opposition in the government demonstrates its ups and downs. In the early era of independence, the practice of opposition was well institutionalized, initiated by two major nationalist and Islamic parties (PNI and Masyumi) [11, 12]. Some of the policies that became a source of opposition resistance included a number of benefitting agreements for the Dutch (the colonialist). However, the opposition did not reflect the collective views of the party because several ministers were from the two major parties defended government policies vigorously when serving in the cabinet.

Following the guided democracy period (1959–1966), the opposition no longer existed or at least moved in a very covert way. Soekarno attempted to ensure that the party leaders who were "left alive" at that time were those who were willing to work with him, thereby establishing his authoritarian regime under the name of "Guided Democracy". In an effort to build the regime, Soekarno put forward anti-democratic ideas by demolishing parties, further stating that democracy was incompatible with the character of the nation. Soekarno believed that the parliamentary democracy that had been practiced was improper for the Indonesian people and that the liberal democratic system was incapable of offering the political stability required by the nation. It was thus assumed that it was at such time that the roots of the opposition were forcibly relocated by the state.

Moreover, the situation in the New Order (1966–1998) did not prove any significant difference. At first, this new government seemed to provide great hope for the establishment of democracy. Numerous critical circles, students, intellectuals, as well as pro-democracy social activist figures were initially enthusiastic about supporting Suharto's leadership [13]. However, the reality later denoted that not long after the New Order regime was established, Suharto practiced a systematic suppression of the opposition or those who had the potential to become the opposition for both political and non-political parties.

Undertaking the reform era, democracy was re-established. However, even though Indonesia is recognized as a democratic country, the life of the opposition has not been present at an encouraging level. The legacy of the past political system, characterized by weak opposition, remained significant. During the administrations of Presidents Abdurrahman Wahid (Gus Dur) and Megawati Soekarnoputri (1999–2004), the opposition was less-regarded, considering that all the potential of national political power was absorbed in the government. During Gus Dur reign, all large and medium-sized parties (PDIP, Golkar Party, PAN, PKB, PPP, PBB, PKS, and PKP) obtained positions in the cabinet that was led together with PDIP General Chair Megawati Soekarnoputri, making PDIP as the only party with the majority holding positions in the government.

Several other issues were utilized as an excuse to fight, such as the misuse of aid funds from the Sultan of Brunei and Bulog (which were not legally proven) and the most crucial one was when Gus Dur unilaterally dissolved the parliament. However, the resistance leading to impeachment chronologically and substantively was inseparable from the question regarding change or reshuffle, which was not in line with the spirit of opposition. Resistance, in other words, would not have occurred if Gus Dur had not practiced his controversial maneuver. It was later proven that Megawati was able to safely complete her term of office as Gus Dur replacement, because she did not perform any detrimental movements to her supporting parties.

In the contemporary situation, the joining of several parties supporting the Red and White Coalition (KMP) into the ranks of the government becomes the proof that the opposition situation remains substantially weak. Parties that initially declared themselves in opposition to the government and even became competitors to the government coalition at the time of the presidential election, easily changed direction by declaring themselves as government loyalists, as did by PAN, PPP, and Golkar. Uniquely, during the SBY administration era (2004–2014), a pattern of "cartel politics" emerged when the opposition had little meaning and groups that had the potential to play an opposition role were actually absorbed in the government [5]. The reality revealed that the opposition was not working effectively.

Although there is a slight improvement in the quality of the opposition, especially at the beginning of Jokowi's administration, there are parties that firmly declare in opposition to the government, such as Gerindra and PKS. The current opposition phenomenon in its development tends to exhibit a continuation of the old pattern of relations between the government and the opposition. The function of the opposition, performed by KMP to the fullest, actually marks the phenomenon of an opposition that is limited and ineffective.

Until almost two decades into the reformation, the role of the opposition was performed by non-party and extra-parliamentary circles, which was sporadic and could not be used as a barometer of control over an effective government. As a result, instead of becoming a sphere for a healthy democratic life, Indonesia is currently trapped in an oligarchic practice by positioning the interests of the few above the masses. Government policies for the people are often manipulated by the interests of a group of people who are close to power [14]. Democracy which tends to be artificial, thus, is the result that is reaped by the situation of government without effective opposition.

The failure of institutionalizing the opposition in the government indicates the non-functioning of checks and balances against the president in conducting the governance within the executive power. Even existing, the opposition only exists before the election in the context of electoral contestation marked by the joining of all ranks of the leaders of the opposition parties to the elected president. Hence, the existing opposition is not based on program conflicts, differences in political views, or ideologies, indicating no practice of checks and balances to balance the executive power of the president.

## *2.2 Checks and Balances in Legislative Branch*

Checks and balances is apparent from the relationship between the parliament, both DPR and DPD and the President and the relationship between DPR and Constitutional Court in forming laws and regulations. The function of checks and balances in the legislative only emerged when Constitution was amended after the reform.

Before amendment, there are a number of problems in the system of political representation in Indonesia. Firstly, the problem of representation does not reflect the actual conditions. When referring to the existence of MPR in the 1945 Constitution which mentions regional delegates and group delegates as part of the MPR, it does not represent actual community groups, particularly regarding the appointment with uncertain accountability, easily controlled by those in power. Secondly, the adopted representative system does not reflect the checks and balances mechanism, indicating that there is only one room that performs the legislative function (Susanti 2008), not requiring control or supervision of DPR within the parliament.

Furthermore, there is an idea to change the representative system to be more representative, not only consisting of party representatives who occupy in DPR, but also regional representatives directly elected by the people and not appointed as group delegates. The representation of the selected regions is pivotal so that there are ties and linkages for Indonesian and various political processes, including the process of representation in policy-making. In addition, the mechanism of checks and balances is deemed pivotal to avoid any arbitrariness or abuse of power between institutions (Satya Arinanto: 2006). In this regard, the presence of a second chamber after DPR is a necessity. Despite DPD strong legitimacy as a directly elected regional representative, its authority remains weak, not having a constitutionally adequate position (UUD 1945) as its functions and authorities are not much different from that of Non-Governance Organizations (NGOs) or informal organizations.

The weak position of DPD in terms of authority compared to DPR places it in a subordinate or inferior position, thereby making DPR as a sole player in the formation of almost all national legislation products. Thus, the mechanism of checks and balances that occurs between the parliament and the president is merely played by DPR without meaningful involvement of DPD. Meanwhile, the checks and balances that exist between DPR and the President in the formation of *Trias Politica* tend to be compromising.

As acknowledged on the Indonesian constitutional system, the 1945 Constitution of the Republic of Indonesia allows DPR the constitutional rights and authority to form laws together with the President. This condition is considered as a form of checks and balances by the executive against the legislative in performing its function of establishing laws and regulations. Unfortunately, the President in the practice of checks and balances is overshadowed by the interests and intervention of DPR. Saldi Isra pointed out that the political weakness of the President's legislation was proven, when he surrendered to the majority of power of DPR who wanted the election organizers (KPU and Bawaslu) to be dominated by members of political parties. This condition also occurred in the discussion and approval of the amendment draft to KPK law, finally ratified with the content of "weakening and amputating the previous authority". The system of checks and balances in the formation of laws within the framework of the "presidential system through this back door" has resulted in numerous compromises of interest in determining the content of law.

## 2.3 Checks and Balances in Judicial Branch

The mechanism of checks and balances on judicial power is performed by the Judicial Commission (KY), newly established after the reform through the amendment of the 1945 Constitution, aimed at eradicating corruptions within the judiciary by ensuring that the exercise of judicial power runs in an authoritative, fair, and transparent manner. However, the Judicial Commission fails to perform the checks and balances role optimally, not reaching all actors of judicial including the Supreme Court which oversees the four following judicial circles and the Constitutional Court, due to juridical problems. Firstly, the legal construction regarding the existence of the Judicial Commission as a state institution only has the authority to propose, considered inappropriate because in such circumstances the Judicial Commission has no authority at all. Secondly, in terms of monitoring the performance of judges, it may overlap with the internal supervision by the Supreme Court or the Constitutional Court itself. In line with this opinion, Indiriyanto Seno Adji asserted that the Supreme Court and the Constitutional Court become the main organs of the judicial power. Meanwhile, another body such as Judicial Commission become the supporting organ ensuring harmony at the level of implementing fair and authoritative judicial power.

As the direction of power distribution, it cannot be justified that there is a will of checks and balances from the supporting organs to the main organs, as the constitutional relations between state institutions are only as a justification for attitudes and actions based on constitutional relations. Meanwhile, according to Busyro Muqaddas (Chairman of the Judicial Commission), the position of the Supreme Court, Constitutional Court and Judicial Commission in the state administration system is equal to one another. The Judicial Commission does not act as a state auxiliary body, but as an institution authorized to supervise a function of checks and balances on technical aspects of the judiciary, while the powers and duties of the Supreme Court and the Constitutional Court are judicial executor.

In the midst of the unclear position and authority of the Judicial Commission as a state institution, the implementation of its authority creates an open conflict between the Judicial Commission and the Supreme Court which occurs when KY issues a list of violations of the code of ethics committed by judges within the Supreme Court. This conflict has made efforts to carry out checks and balances against the Supreme Court to stagnate due to the absence of good communication between the two.

In addition, the condition of checks and balances in the judicial branch is perceived to be dysfunctional when associated with the Constitutional Court. In its decision Number 005PW-IV/2006, the Constitutional Court stated that constitutional judges could not be supervised by KY because constitutional judges are not the object of KY supervision, which is considered as professional judges in general. Although in its development, the Constitutional Court established an ethics board and an honorary court in the context of internal control within the Constitutional Court. Consequently, there is no control and balancing function from the Judicial Commission as an external party that could be performed on the Constitutional Court. In other words, despite designed in such mechanism, practically the checks and balances function performed by the Judicial Commission in relation to the Supreme Court and the Constitutional Court in relation to the parliament and the president does not run as expected.

The checks and balances function of KY is different from the checks and balances function attached to the Constitutional Court, as the Constitutional Court is an actor of judicial power that is different from the Supreme Court, functioned to test the constitutionality of legal products made by DPR together with the President. Judging from its functions and authorities, the Constitutional Court is the mere organizer of the checks and balances function both in relation to the President and in relation to DPR. In this regard, the Constitutional Court acts as a counterweight to the substance of the content of the regulations established by DPR together with the President through its function of conducting a judicial review for the constitutionality of laws against the Constitution. Meanwhile, in relation to the President, the Constitutional Court becomes the judiciary that follows up on allegations of abuse of power by the President and/or Vice President proposed by DPR. Through this function, the Constitutional Court acts as a counterweight to DPR in carrying out the process of impeachment against the alleged violations committed by the President and/or

Vice President. Thus, the function of the Constitutional Court in implementing the principle of checks and balances is evident in the realm of legislation by reviewing the constitutionality of the contents of the Act against the Constitution, indicated in relation to the executive by examining and adjudicating the proposed dismissal of the President and/or Vice President.

However, the Constitutional Court is a state institution with minimal supervision, in which there is no institution that could compensate or control the Constitutional Court from potential abuse of authority such as acts of corruption in the judicial level or branch, including KY. Thus far, this notion creates problems in the future, as internal supervision by the ethics council established by the Constitutional Court in the internal environment is considered incapable of actualizing constitutional judges according to the mandate of the constitution. Such an internal control model is considered not optimal in taking action against several cases of abuse of authority and judicial corruption that have ensnared several constitutional judges. Instances include the entanglement of Judge (Akil Mochtar) in the bribery case related to the dispute over the election of Palangkaraya, Central Kalimantan which was won by Riban Satia, and Judge (Patrialis Akbar) who was proven to have accepted a bribe of USD 10,000 (equivalent to 133 million). Likewise, the case of violation of the code of ethics by the chairman of the Constitutional Court, Arief Hidayat was based on a decision from the Ethics Council of the Constitutional Court, stating that Arief was proven to have held meetings (political lobbies) by giving promises related to the review of Article 79 paragraph (3) of Law No. 17 of 2014 concerning MPR, DPR, DPD, DPRD (MD3) regarding DPR inquiry rights in relation to the existence of KPK inquiry committee. These aforementioned cases have indicated that the purpose of establishing the Judicial Commission to become a catalyst for the functioning of checks and balances in the context of eradicating corruption within the judicial branch or level remains far from being ideal.

This condition is exacerbated by the dominance of the executive and legislative in governance, thereby positioning judicial power as a "stepchild". In some cases, judicial power is merely employed as a tool or means to support the decisions or policies of the President or DPR. This notion is increasingly possible as there is inadequate controlling function in the realm of judicial power that could offset the enormous dominance of the President and DPR, whereas judicial power becomes the only pillar of the rule of law as a prerequisite for a democratic state. In practice, the condition of the perpetrators of judicial power tends to be neglected within the management of the state.

## 3 Findings and Solutions

The aforementioned conditions have indicated that there are serious problems related to the implementation of checks and balances mechanisms in governance. Firstly, it is due to the absence of a checks and balances mechanism in the executive power which is marked by the absence of a solid opposition in the government. Secondly, the weak position of the DPD as the second chamber in the representative system discourages DPD to carry out the checks and balances role in intra-parliamentary relations with DPR. Thus, this condition also provides a great opportunity for DPR to become the sole player in the formation of laws and regulations proposed by the parliament as in the New Order era. This condition further provides ample space for compromises and transactions between DPR and the President in forming a national legal product that risks harming the interests of the regional constituents represented by DPD and the collective interests of the wider community. In other words, the weak checks and balances mechanism in the judicial level will have an impact on the quality of legislation that is compromising and transactional. Thirdly, the role of KY is not optimal in carrying out the role of checks and balances against the Supreme Court judicial power environment along with the absence of checks and balances role from external parties to the Constitutional Court. This condition further risks for opening up opportunities for the use of judicial power for the sake of electoral contestation or the President popular policies or DPR agenda. Through the conditions of practice in each branch of state power, this article concluded that the checks and balances mechanism does not optimally function. Consequently, the weak mechanism of checks and balances threatens the sustainability of democratic transition toward a consolidated democracy, because a government without a proper checks and balances mechanism would generate an authoritarian government resembling if it is a democracy with a shield for holding regular elections.

As previously stated, the checks and balances mechanism serves as the pillars of democracy, without which democracy could simply collapse. To avoid a decline in democracy, the practice of checks and balances in every branch of state power is required to be optimally enforced. There are at least three agendas to improve the current pace of democracy. Firstly, the agenda is initiated by encouraging the institutionalization of the opposition in the government as the existence of the opposition in Indonesia remains not solid. Secondly, the agenda is conducted by strengthening the functions and authorities of DPD, which is deemed pivotal to align with DPR, thereby strengthening the adopted bicameral system in performing the checks and balances mechanism in the implementation of legislative functions within the parliament. Lastly, the agenda is performed by strengthening the synergy of supervision by KY, both to the Supreme Court and to the Constitutional Court.

## 4 Conclusion

Various literature studies have revealed that the trend of democratic decline is influenced by several factors. One of them is due to the non-functioning of the checks and balances role, in which the state power among institutions is not monitored, leading to the absence of supervision among democratic institutions. If such conditions continue, they will place future democratic transitions at risk and gradually weaken the democratic regime. This decline can be observed in the intensification of political transactions, the formation of compromise-based coalitions that embed corruption, and the strengthening of political cartels across state institutions.

## References


1. Winters JA (2004) Oligarchy. Cambridge University Press, New York
2. Robison R, Hadiz VR (2004) Reorganising power in Indonesia: the politics of oligarchy in an age of markets. Routledge Curzon, London
3. Tornquist O (2006) Assessing democracy from below: a framework and Indonesian pilot project. Democratization 13(2):227–255
4. Ford M, Pepinsky TB (eds) (2014) Beyond oligarchy. wealth, power and contemporary Indonesian politics. Cornell Southeast Asia Program Publications, Cornell
5. Ambardi K (2009) Mengungkap politik kartel. Studi tentang sistem kepartaian di Indonesia era reformasi. Kepustakaan Populer Gramedia, Jakarta
6. Rodan G, Jayasurya K (2009) Capitalist development, regime transitions, and new forms of authoritarianism in Asia. Pac Rev 22(1):23–47
7. Mietzner M (2014) Oligarchs, politicians, and activists: contesting party politics in Post-Soeharto Indonesia. In: Ford DM, Pepinsky TB (eds) Beyond oligarchy. Wealth, power and contemporary Indonesian politics. Cornell: Cornell Southeast Asia Program Publications, Ithaca, 77–99
8. O'Donell G (1996) Delegative democracy. In: Diamond DL, Plattner MF (eds) The global resurgence of democracy. John Hopkins University Press, Baltimore and London, 94–108
9. Dahl R (1971) Poliarchy: participation and opposition. Yale University Press, New Haven, CT, and London
10. Noor F (2016) Oposisi dalam Kehidupan Demokrasi: Arti Penting Keberadaan Oposisi sebagai Bagian Penguatan Demokrasi di Indonesia. https://media.neliti.com/media/publications/152332-ID-oposisi-dalam-kehidupan-demokrasi-arti-p.pdf
11. Lucius RE (2003) A house divided: The decline and fall of Masyumi (1950–1956), Master thesis, Naval Postgraduate School, Monterey
12. Feith H (1968) The decline of constitutional democracy in Indonesia. Cornell University Press, Itacha, New York
13. Buehler M (2014) Elite competition and power brokerage: The politics of decentralisation in Indonesia. In: Ford M, Pepinsky TB (eds) Beyond Oligarchy: Wealth, Power, and Contemporary Indonesian Politics. Cornell Southeast Asia Program Publications, Ithaca, 101–122
14. Sabri M (2012) Presiden tersandera, melihat dampak kombinasi sistem presidensial-multipartai terhadap relasi presiden-DPR di masa pemerintahan SBY-Boediono. RMBooks, Jakarta

# Indonesia Political Condition Post-COVID-19 Pandemic: The Continuation of Democracy Stagnation Tendency and Its Potential Solutions

**Firman Noor, Dini Rahmiati, and Devi Darmawan**

**Abstract** Indonesia nowadays is in the situation of stagnant democracy. Several recent studies indicate that the quality of Indonesian democracy remains low. Numerous studies from survey institutions also indicate similar tendencies. Several fundamental grounds indicating low democracy include: weak public participation, impeded civil liberty, the existence of oligarchy, elitism, problematic law enforcement, political injustice and rampant corruption. This paper will employ qualitative method and documents study by using a multi-dimensional approach that involves the dimensions of leadership, structural, institutional, procedural and cultural in responding to the problem. Specifically, there are 6 conditions that become the focus of this paper to measure the stagnancy tendency, including: (1) national leadership condition, (2) political party condition, (3) trias political condition, (4) civil society condition, (5) political independence of the society condition and (6) the rule of law condition. This paper will lead to the conclusion that since the whole 6 conditions have not been fully fulfilled yet as previously expected, as the consequences, Indonesia's democratic condition will not differ from the situation either in the pandemic era or before. In this relation, a significant breakthrough is deemed pivotal to improve all six conditions to lead Indonesia to be free from democracy stagnation.

**Keywords** Democracy · Stagnation · Government · Leadership · Party · Civil society

F. Noor (✉) · D. Rahmiati · D. Darmawan
Research Center for Politics, National Research and Innovation Agency, Jakarta, Indonesia
e-mail: firman.noor@yahoo.co.id

D. Rahmiati
e-mail: dini005@brin.go.id

D. Darmawan
e-mail: devdarmawan@gmail.com



Nawawi et al. (eds.), *Managing Disruption and Developing Resilience for a Better Southeast Asia*, Springer Proceedings in Humanities and Social Sciences,
https://doi.org/10.1007/978-981-96-2116-3_55

## 1 Introduction

Democracy refers to a government system desired by the founding fathers of the nation, reflected in the existence of the fourth precept of *Pancasila* which mandates the formation of a state on the basis of consultation. The enforcement of democratic life is also the mandate of reform, the core of which lies in the implementation of a state of law under the spirit of popular sovereignty. Indonesian nation continues to strive to live a democratic life in terms of systems, procedures and substance. Indonesian people's support for democracy remains significant based on the survey results. Currently, there has been a regular change of leadership in which there is no longer a ruling party and the military is also not actively on the stage of power. There was a decentralization of power and local government formed from local elections. Parties were free to be founded, as was the mass media.

However, the recent Reformation Era has been marked by several phenomena of democratic decline. Some political observers perceive the positive side of our democratic life [1]. Observers of Indonesian politics, especially today, are aware that something goes wrong in democratic life, which has the potential to lead to stagnation or even a setback in Indonesia political life [2–10]. Several other studies lead to similar conclusion, as reported by Indonesian Democracy Index indicating a stagnation in the quality of Indonesia democracy [11]. Likewise, the results of studies from several institutions such as the Economist Intelligence Unit [12], Freedom House [13] and also IDEA [14] also reported stagnation and even democratic regression. The practice of oligarchy did not subside in the post-New Order era, only transformed according to the existing political situation [15, 16].

Referring at the various aforementioned trends, it is assumed that our political condition is at a crisis point for the development of democracy, both in terms of substance and procedure. If the government as well as the people in general are not careful and are not critical of the potential for the emergence of an elitist form of government, the potential for stagnation and even a decline in democracy remains open.

**Problem**

This article will evaluate the future democratic stagnation in Indonesia by considering the political position of the regime which will not change, at least until 2024, and the opportunity for certain potential groups to continuously support a presidential figure bearing similar perspective and support, where there is a chance for stagnation to continue. This article will analyze the aspects leading to the potential for democratic stagnation in Indonesia to occur. This study is expected to contribute to efforts for deeper understanding toward the development of democracy in the reform era and to anticipate the efforts to establish and maintain democracy in the future.

## 2 Literature Review

Several studies revealed that the decline in democracy was due to several factors, generated from various dimensions. In a situation when democracy is hijacked and does not produce conditions that are truly conducive to strengthening the quality of democracy itself, the problem is not solely cultural problem, but also relates to structure, leadership and institutional institutions. The classical theory of the political system indicates that to understand the political condition of a nation, a multi-dimensional understanding is required which includes problematic, cultural, structural, institutional and procedural events that have passed [17–19]. Meanwhile, democratic life itself is understood or approached procedurally, especially by regarding the electoral aspects, as well as more complex aspect, such as substantial aspect [20–29], discussing some fundamental aspects outside the election that affect the quality of democratic life, including the work of democracy. Contemporary studies on democratic life have also discussed various aspects and have given rise to several definitions and perspectives in perceiving the situation of democracy in Indonesia [3–5, 8, 15, 16, 30–40]. The results of these various analyzes concluded that several aspects should be considered in measuring the quality of democracy in Indonesia, denoting that a multi-dimensional approach is required in understanding the conditions of democracy.

## 3 Methodology

This research utilized a qualitative research method with data collection obtained through literature studies and media coverage. This paper will employ a multi-dimensional approach that involves the dimensions of leadership, structural, institutional, procedural and cultural in responding to the problem. Specifically, there are 6 conditions that become the focus of this paper to measure the stagnancy tendency, including: (1) national leadership condition, (2) political party condition, (3) trias political condition, (4) civil society condition, (5) political independence of the society condition and (6) the rule of law condition.

The main reason why those six conditions become the main issues of this article is because they represent main aspects to understand the political conditions, in particular democracy, in a country. Understanding the quality of democracy could not be done by merely using one or single variables. Several studies on the current political conditions, including on Indonesian politics, as has been discussed in the literature review part, indicate using one of those aspects—whether procedural, structural, cultural, substance, personal, political environment or institutional—as their fundamental argument and main discussion. We realize that there are other aspects that might be useful to give more insight to comprehend about current Indonesia political condition. However, we believe that those six conditions could be used as the main allusions in evaluating the current and future of Indonesia democracy condition.

Also, as the main foundation for the solutions to increase and maintain the quality of Indonesia democracy in the future.

## 4 Discussion

1. **National Leadership Condition**

Democracy requires democratic leadership based on the public interest and conducted by principles such as accountability and participation. However, a democratic system does not always produce democratic leadership. Democracy sometimes gives rise to leadership that is ultimately hijacked by the interests of a handful of people (oligarchs) [2], or by a leadership that neglects the efforts for strengthening and maintaining democratic values. As a result, a leadership emerges which is ultimately counterproductive to democratic values.

This leadership tendency has been experienced even before the COVID-19 pandemic. President Jokowi's speech in 2019 which marked the beginning of his second term of leadership indicated the government's strong orientation that prioritized economic development [41]. The speech delivered by the president notably leads to create a comprehensive support capacity for economic acceleration. Conversely, political development experienced lack of attention, where there is no discussion on corruption, democratic development and protection of human rights and strengthening of civil society.

Indonesia's political conditions after the 2019 presidential election or shortly before the COVID-19 pandemic have finally indicated a turning point for democratic life, reflected in the weak opportunity for the people to participate in policy-making, creating some policies to be substantially unaspirational. Among these policies is the revision of the KPK Law. In addition, the Omnibus Law Bill began to be discussed, which in the following year was set to become the Job Creation Law. Additionally, the national leadership tends to be anti-criticism. Practically, anti-democratic policies and policy proposals continue to emerge despite the claim of open-to-criticism. The criminalization of critical groups with the nuances of human rights violations and political injustice continued to occur. This condition was in line with the omission of the buzzer to the indecisiveness of the oligarchic practice in political life. The implementation of the ITE Law has drastically escalated from SBY Administration period, in which 233 Cases were in the Jokowi Era until 2020 versus 73 Cases during the SBY Era (2004–2014) [42].

Violence against residents in Wadas Village for the sake of building a dam, which reminded us of the repressive actions of the apparatus in the New Order Era [43], also received less attention and did not appear to have been completely and democratically resolved. Likewise, the omission of circles including several cabinet ministers proposed the idea of extending the presidential term, which was clearly unconstitutional. Ironically, one minister who supported the idea was entrusted an additional position.

In fact, there have been several protests from various groups regarding the practice of government which is no longer in line with the spirit of democracy. Various credible survey institutions have also reported various weaknesses in democratic life in Indonesia; however, the current national leadership does not seem to care. Instead of making improvements, the government has performed political maneuvers by allowing anti-democratic political maneuvers to occur, some of which even involved the palace circles [44, 45].

With the strength and support it has, the government is potential to accomplish efforts for the betterment of democracy without obstacles. However, since it is far from the accomplishment, the quality of our democracy from several circles remains poor. Under such kind of leadership, it seems certain that a democratic government will not be in the existence in the near future.

2. **Condition of Political Parties**

Political party serves as a bridge for the community to convey aspirations, a channel for political participation and a control over the rulers. With this function, the party has a significant role in maintaining democratic norms and practices. On such basis, some perceive the inconceivableness of democracy without political parties [46]. Empirically proven in countries with strong democracy, the quality of political parties and institutions play a decisive role. In non-democratic countries which are characterized by strong elitism and oligarchy, political parties do not play an important role in political life due to their high dependence on certain figures or on the government.

The current condition of Indonesia political parties has been far from ideal. Most parties are strongly dependent on figures or groups who have political modalities, due to historical or financial factors or both. In general, it becomes more personalized than before [47]. In addition, the dependence of political parties on oligarchs, as the main sponsors of funding party activities, continues to occur, which is in line with political parties that are not financially independent. Hence, some political parties nowadays are basically led or dominated by business people or oligarchs. It is also not surprising that 55% of the current total members of DPR are business people or community, of which 25% are company owners and 25% of DPR members are actively managing their companies [48].

In addition, the recent regeneration process in most parties has been far from the expected one. The absence of this cadre has contributed to the growth of a pragmatic-opportunist mindset and attitude. As a result, money or materials, and not ideas or ideals, become the glue and main motivation for people to be involved in political life and party activities [49]. Party cadres subsequently fight for their interests and or utilize all means to achieve their goals, becoming the beginning of the attitude of justifying all means in politics, including the practice of corruption and collusion in the political maneuvers of party cadres. With these various conditions, it is understood that parties in Indonesia are incapable of playing a maximum role in strengthening democracy.

Political parties could improve their condition and quality, only if actualizing serious efforts to institutionalize the party. Institutionalization relates to efforts in establishing the democratic internal procedure and encouraging the strengthening of idealism of all its members, seriously conducted by all cadres. In addition, institutionalization is ultimately related to the enactment of a set of rules that encourages the implementation of regeneration, financial independence and a merit system, thereby minimizing the potential for dynastic politics within the party [50, 51]. This improvement effort will have a greater chance when driven by an independent and critical community of existing parties.

However, these efforts have not been executed comprehensively. The party is mostly controlled by a group of elites and oligarchs who are reluctant to institutionalize the party. In addition, the existing party regulations have been incapable of improving the quality of political parties. Given these various situations, it is predicted that in the next few years the quality of political parties will be stagnant.

3. **Conditions of *Trias Politica* Implementation**

The concept of trias politica comprises a milestone in the institutionalization of a democratic country. This conception requires an apparent and firm separation of powers to avoid centralized absolute power in government, thereby establishing the three branches of power in government, which include the executive, legislative and judicial. Among the three, there is an equal relationship of each branch to monitor the implementation accountability of their respective functions or the potential for abuse of state power.

The implementation of a strict separation of powers is apparent from the existence of an executive function by the President, a legislative function by DPR and a judicial function by Supreme Court (MA) and Constitutional Court (MK). However, in the context of state administration, the principle of *Trias Politica* has been inseparable from one to another, as the relationship is formed among the three in executing certain functions. Example includes the legislative function which is performed by DPR together with the President, judicial function by Supreme Court and Constitutional Court with the consideration of the President and DPR. The complexity of the formed relations among the three branches of power determines the quality of democracy in the future [52].

In the dynamics of politics in Indonesia, the checks and balances model is more determined by the President and DPR (as the first chamber in parliament). According to Lili Romli [53] this notion ultimately leads other state institutions such as the DPD as a second chamber and judicial institutions such as the Supreme Court and the Constitutional Court to be incapable of performing their control roles both in legislative functions and in law enforcement. This practice undermines the role of the judiciary, which tends to be a tool to support executive power or support DPR policies in performing their functions. The absence of the coalition as the final hope to institutionalize the checks and balances function has also contributed to the degradation for the quality of democratic governance in Indonesia. This condition is exacerbated by the design of a representative institution that places a second chamber with limited functions, solely in matters of legislation. As a result, under this condition it is obvious that the implementation of checks and balances is almost non-existent [54].

There is an imbalance of function and authority between the first and second chambers in the parliament, leading to the absence of internal checks and balances in the parliament. Equally, the continued dominance of the DPR in coalition with the government tends to eventually produce transactional and compromising legal products. In addition, efforts to improve the quality of democracy in Indonesia, especially the checks and balances mechanism, have not been able to run properly. With the various aforementioned facts indicating that there are no concrete steps to improve the implementation of *Trias Politica*, it is understandable that the quality of our democracy will eventually stagnate.

4. **Civil Society Conditions**

Civil society serves as one of the supporters of the existence of democracy whose domain lies between the family and the state [55]. The ideal civil society refers to one that has a high spirit of community solidarity, obeys the law, respects freedom of expression, is self-sufficient and has high political awareness. With this character, civil society could function against various challenges to democracy, such as oligarchy, corruption and nepotism, considering that these three negative phenomena have rooted in a society that is not independent, unable to build self-sufficiency or self-sufficiency, underestimates the law, is not intelligent and careless and has low solidarity.

The condition of democracy and civil society in Indonesia has faced considerable challenges, especially in the last 2 years. Several cases demonstrated the pressure from the state, including attacks on the existence of civil society groups and attempts to criminalize democracy activists. Indeks Demokrasi Indonesia scored 58.82/100 on the issues of state apparatus violences that hamper people's freedom of expression [56]. Various cases thus prove that the state is considered to no longer respect the struggle of civil society, presenting a significant challenge for the people, especially the civil society movement [57].

On the other hand, the quality of the existence of civil society itself is not always satisfactory [58]. As asserted by Mutiah Alagappa, civil society has the potential to develop democracy, but at the same time it could also undermine the democracy [59]. In fact, there is civil society with bad character, in addition to many civil society groups who are actually in the stronghold of power. The issue of internal divisions has also become an unresolved issue and has practically caused the power of civil society to never be intact and has maximum strength.

In the end, this situation causes civil society to be the separable element that can be expected to participate in a critical watchdog on the actions of the government in order to stay within the corridors of democracy. On the one hand, a hope of optimism has emerged. Findings of Prakarsa October 2021 [60, 61], for example, indicate that civil society has initiated to improve itself and to play a more role in strengthening democracy in some areas [55]. However, the findings also indicate that significant changes among civil society have not been seen evenly. In addition, the opportunity for state repression, intervention and co-optation remains wide open, given the weakness of law enforcement and complete independence that our civil society has not fully owned. It was indicated by the decrease of public participation in policy-making process and the increase of state repression toward several NGO demonstrations [60, 61]. On the other hand, lack of financial and distorted internal management still becomes main problem of Indonesia NGO [62].

With these various situations, the strengthening of civil society in Indonesia remains problematic, requiring a longer time to grow into a solid entity. Meanwhile, the state does not seem to care in strengthening such circles. On the other hand, there are efforts by the state to suppress these groups, especially those who are considered too vocal. Under such situation, it is concluded that in the next few years, efforts to strengthen democracy through strengthening civil society have not really been able to actualize.

## 5. Conditions of People Political Independence

The existence of an independent or autonomous society becomes a prerequisite for strengthening democratic life, because democracy is a form of government that places the community or people as the holder of the highest sovereignty. As a consequence, it is only in conditions where the holder of the highest sovereignty is independent, sovereign and understands how democracy can work well. On the other hand, in a situation where the community is ignorance, always dependent on the authorities, and does not understand what they want, there will always be parties "on behalf of the people" who in the end put their self-interests above the interests of the people themselves.

Thus, independence is deemed important requiring an effort to complement the community's ability to be independent; one of them is by promoting good education particularly political education. John Dewey pointed out that a democratic system will work well, if both those who govern and those who are governed are educated [63]. Education refers to a means of forming a character that is in accordance with democracy, where its nature becomes an important supporting element for democracy [64–66]. As ignored people will become "soft-spot" for tyranny, oligarchy or a group of ordinary people who will destroy the essence of democracy [67].

In addition, independence is also formed if the community is financially prosperous by not depending on the oligarchs. The condition for a country to be free from oligarchs occurs when the economic inequality is minimized. According to Flavin, states with higher levels of economic inequality also tend to be the most politically unequal, in which states with a big divide in rich and poor in income also tend to have a bigger chance to be divided in political representation [68].

The current level of political literacy of Indonesian, especially in the context of political life, is not yet sufficient. This is exacerbated by the high level of economic disparity, since our economic life has been controlled by a few people [16, 69]. With this situation, society in general is in a position that is not ready, thereby becoming fragile, still politically and economically dependent, having an inequal position, particularly in determining the political life. The impact of the weak independence of the people is the emergence of government by, for and of the elites, characterized by the limited involvement of the community in the world of politics. In 2020, Economist Intelligent Unit, for instance, scored political participation only 6.11, which made Indonesia become a "flawed democracy country" in more than five consecutive years

[70]. Likewise, democratic institutions that are actually mouthpieces for the people's voice, such as political parties and the DPR, do not work effectively in voicing their aspirations due to the inability of the people to take advantage of them, or due to the domination of the oligarchs.

Unfortunately, various conditions have not been adequately responded to by various parties, especially by the government. There is no visible systematic effort that is measured and managed professionally and massively to increase the political independence of the community. In short, a form of political education that is systematic and disseminated by various institutions also does not run sporadically.

6. **Conditions of the Rules of the Game**

The support for the rules of the game plays an important role in regulating, encouraging and maintaining democratic development [71, 72]. In the Indonesian context, there are at least three significances of support for the rules of the game. Firstly, the existing regulations of the game can reduce corrupt practices. Secondly, the existing regulations must encourage party independence, especially in terms of seeking funds, in order to avoid dependence on the oligarchs. Lastly, the existing regulations encourage the development of idealism in political life, by fostering idealism in the cadres. Thus, these three significances of support will be a conducive pre-condition for strengthening democracy [51].

Currently, several regulations have been stipulated as an effort to strengthen democracy, including those related to the existence and role of political parties and elections, reflected in the 1945 Constitution in Article 6A (2) and Article 22E (3), stating that constitutional role of parties. Various rules of the game regarding political parties as well as elections have been established and changed from time to time, evident in the Law on Political Parties and the Law on Elections.

However, several required things do not exist or are not regulated within the existing rules of the game. Among of them is the necessity to perform the regeneration on a regular basis, tiered and sustainable. Good cadreization tends to strengthen the idealism of cadres, maintains loyalty to the party, prevents pragmatism and seriously performs obligations as cadres who prioritize party ideals over individual interests [73]. Although most parties admit that regeneration is deemed important, it has not been carried out with the party eventually lost its commitment to internal coaching and development. Despite the existence of subsidy, it still does not fully meet the party's needs. Several studies on the weakness of party performance have linked between the financial problems and the maintenance of oligarchy and corruption [5, 74–79].

The preparation of the list of candidates has also not obtained an adequate legal solution. Existing regulations have not facilitated political parties to obtain mandates from existing laws to be more transparent, objective and responsible in determining candidates. Thus, apart from the quality of the candidates being questioned, the potential involvement of oligarchs in determining the list of candidates remains open. The determination of legislative candidates currently becomes one of the links in the chain of maintaining the role of the oligarchs, both at the party and government levels.

Presidential Threshold (PT) also serves as a rule of the game that has the potential to trigger a decline in the quality of democracy, related primarily to the practice of high-cost politics that encourages money politics in all its forms [80]. Further, PT causes cattle trading politics or rent politics which increases political costs and leads to the strengthening of oligarchy or cartel politics. Under such atmosphere, the agendas for strengthening democracy, both in terms of cultural awareness, institutional maturation, as well as in the relationship among the branches of *Trias Politica*, are therefore neglected. Given this situation, it is predicted that in the next few years the condition of democracy in Indonesia will be stagnant.

# 5 Main Findings and Solutions

From the aforementioned study, it is perceived that there are several problems which are counterproductive to the growth of democratic life in Indonesia. The study above indicates that the national leadership has not accommodated the efforts to strengthen democracy in Indonesia. The leadership orientation is still aimed at improving economic development. As a result, democracy runs partially, is held hostage by elite interests and does not provide many benefits for the community at large, even being the cause of corruption, thereby fostering anti-democratic spirit. Democracy also generates a strong executive tendency by weakening the implementation of checks and balances, requiring solid commitment from national leaders and encouragement from various parties to the current national leadership to be more oriented and committed to political development, especially democracy. With the attitude and support of the national leadership, it is expected that efforts to improve democracy will be more effective and efficient by prioritizing the greater benefits for the people (citizen).

Furthermore, political parties have not yet been able to institutionalize themselves. Parties that should play a major role in strengthening and maintaining democracy are trapped within the oligarchic circles and networks. With such a strong constitutional support, political parties should be able to do much and become one of the determining elements of the movement to improve democracy. However, the internal problems and the environment in which they grow and develop are insufficient to encourage the improvement of political parties' quality, leading to stagnation, which in turn causes the quality of democracy to not improve. Thus, a commitment for serious institutionalization is deemed pivotal.

In addition, the separation of powers in *Trias Politica* conception does not work as it should, due to the dominance of the executive and legislative roles which tend to place the judiciary as a supporter of their functions and powers. The judiciary is frequently utilized as a mere tool to legitimize the power of the President or DPR for decision-making or policy formation. As a result, checks and balances among the three branches of state power are challenging to maintain. This condition causes a tendency to concentrate state power without effective control, resulting from a compromise between the executive and legislative. For this reason, encouragement is required to strengthen the function of DPD as a counterweight in intra-parliamentary and new political catalysts in the relationship between the executive and the legislative. There is also a need for a push for party elites in parliament to form an opposition coalition within the government. On the other hand, the dignity of the independence of the judiciary is required to be enforced on an equal basis, not under the executive or legislative branches, so as not to become an instrument of state power in the future political system.

The current conditions, especially the two years post the COVID-19 pandemic that hit Indonesia, have also caused the civil society movement as an element of democracy to face serious challenges. Civil society currently has to deal with lack of funding, difficulties in recruiting volunteers, as well as occurrence of community divisions and fragmentation among civil society. Behind the stagnation trend of the civil movement, based on a study by Kompas Research and Development [81], the public, however, has high hopes, especially for the student movement and NGOs. Civil society movement serves as one of the forces that can oversee policy, as well as become a "partner" for the government, which is deemed instrumental in order to build a balanced relationship between the state and the people as an effort to build a qualified democracy. For this reason, civil society volunteers must continue to improve themselves and collaborate with various parties in order to play their roles more effectively.

Meanwhile, community independence has not yet been established in a steady and comprehensive manner. This independence is an apparent indication of the low quality of people's skills related to politics as well as an indication that the state, oligarchy and its supporting groups are dominant and robust. With this condition, the rulers and elites have the freedom to formulate an agenda of activities and policies exclusively in accordance with their interests, thereby encouraging the creation of an elitist form of democracy. In the future, the community is expected to be supported for its independence to improve democratic quality.

Democracy is also far from its better performance due to numerous inconducive regulations for political improvement, especially democracy. Some of the existing regulations basically perpetuate corruption, leading to high-cost politics thereby relying on the support from the oligarchs, weakening the quality of political party cadres, especially those related to maintaining and fighting for the ideals they believe in. All of this ultimately contributes to the weakening or stagnation of the quality of democracy in Indonesia. Therefore, as a solution, there is no other options but the authorities to make an overhaul in some of the existing rules of the game.

## 6 Conclusion

The existence of democracy in Indonesia, especially during the Jokowi administration era, seems to be far from the expected one. Some of the aforementioned facts indicate and confirm the tendency of stagnation, highlighting that the decline is apparent. The findings also indicate that although this problem is deep, complex and rooted, there has been no sign of improvement that will essentially be performed or achieved by the Jokowi government. The declining condition or stagnation of democracy is thus possible under the Jokowi government, yet it does not appear to be a priority for the government to improve. With this trend onward, it is predicted that the decline of democracy in Indonesia will continue for the next years.

## References

1. Diamond L (2010) Indonesia's place in global democracy. In: Mietzner M, Aspinall E (eds) Problems of democratization in Indonesia, elections, institutions and society. ISEAS, Singapore
2. Ford M, Pepinsky TB (2014) Beyond oligarchy. wealth, power and contemporary Indonesian politics. Cornell Southeast Asia Program Publications, Cornell
3. Davidson JS (2015) Dilemmas of democratic consolidation in Indonesia, the Pacific Review 22(3):293–310
4. Power TP (2018) Jokowi's authoritarian turn and Indonesia's democratic decline. Bull Indones Econ Stud 54(3):307–338
5. Aspinall E, Berenschot W (2019) Democracy for sale, election, clientism and the state in Indonesia. Cornell University Press, Itacha
6. Aspinall E (2020) Elites, masses, and democratic decline in Indonesia. J Democratization 27(4):505–526
7. Power TP, Waburton E (2020) Democracy in Indonesia: from stagnation to regression. ISEAS, Singapore
8. Noor F. Demokrasi Indonesia dan Arah Perkembangannya di Era COVID-19. http://www.politik.lipi.go.id/kolom/kolom-2/politik-nasional/1394-demokrasi-indonesia-dan-arah-perkembangannya-di-masa-pandemi-covid-19. Last Accessed 01 March 2021
9. Fealy G. Jokowi's repressive pluralism. https://www.eastasiaforum.org/2020/09/27/jokowis-repressive-pluralism/. Last Accessed 05 March 2022
10. Wijayanto, Ruslan M, Bakarudin FN, Wiratraman HP, Nursahid F, Buadiatri AP, Fahmi I (2021) Nestapa Demokrasi di Masa Pandemi: Refleksi 2020, Outlook 2021. LP3ES, Jakarta
11. Indeks Demokrasi Indonesia (IDI) Menurut Indikator 2018–2020. https://www.bps.go.id/indicator/34/638/1/indeks-demokrasi-indonesia-idi-menurut-indikator.html. Last Accessed 01 March 2022
12. https://www.eiu.com/n/campaigns/democracy-index-2018/. https://www.eiu.com/n/campaigns/democracy-index-2019/. https://www.eiu.com/n/campaigns/democracy-index-2020/. https://www.eiu.com/n/campaigns/democracy-index-2021/.
13. https://freedomhouse.org/countries/freedom-world/scores
14. https://www.idea.int/gsod/asia-pacific
15. Robison R. dan Hadiz VR (2004) Reorganising power in Indonesia: the politics of oligarchy in an age of markets. RouledgeCurzon, London
16. Winters JA (2014) Oligarchy and democracy in Indonesia. In: Ford M, Pepinsky T (eds) Beyond oligarchy. wealth, power and contemporary Indonesian politics. Cornell Southeast Asia Program Publications, Cornell
17. Almond GA, Verba S (1963) The civic culture: the political attitudes and democracy in five nations. Princeton University Press, New Jersey
18. Masoed M, MacAndrews C (1997) Perbandingan Sistem Politik. Gajah Mada University Press, Yogyakarta
19. Apter D (1985) Pengantar Analisa Politik. Rajawali Press, Jakarta
20. Gutmann A, Thompson D (2004) Why deliberative democracy? Princeton University Press, New Jersey

21. Dahl R (1971) Poliarchy: participation and opposition. Yale University Press, New Haven CT, and London
22. Diamond L, Morlino L (2004) The quality of democracy: an overview. J Democr 15(2):20–31
23. Held D (1960) Models of democracy. Oxford University Press, Oxford
24. Mayo H (1991) An introduction to democratic theory. Polity Press, Cambridge
25. Pateman C (1970) Participation and democratic theory. Cambridge University Press, Cambridge
26. Przeworski A (1991) Democracy and the market: political and economic reforms in Eastern Europe and Latin America. Cambridge University Press, Cambridge
27. Roberts KM (1999) Deepening democracy: the modern left and social movements in Chile and Peru. Stanford University Press, Stanford
28. Schumpeter J (1975) Capitalism socialism and democracy. Harper and Row, New York
29. Young IM (2002) Ian Shapiro's democratic justice. Good Soc 11(2):76–77
30. Slater D (2004) Indonesia's accountability trap; Party cartels and presidential power after democratic transition. Indonesia, pp 61–92
31. Weber D (2006) A consolidated patrimonial democracy? Democratization in Post-Soeharto Era. J Democratization 13, hal:396–420
32. Klinken GV (2009) Patronage democracy in provincial Indonesia. In: Törnquist O, Webster N, Stokke K (eds) Rethinking popular representation Palgrave Macmillan, London, pp 141–159
33. Mietzner M (2009) Indonesia and the pitfalls of low-quality democracy: a case study of the gubernatorial elections in North Sulawesi. In: Bunte M, Ufen A (eds) Democratization in Post-Suharto Indonesia. Oxon, Routledge Contemporary Southeast Asia Studies, pp 124–149
34. Ambardi K (2009) Mengungkap Politik Kartel. Studi tentang Sistem Kepartaian di Indonesia Era Reformasi. Kepustaan Populer Gramedia, Jakarta
35. Rahmawati D (2018) Demokrasi dalam Genggaman Para Pemburu Rente. Departemen Politik dan Pemerintahan, UGM, Yogyakarta
36. Bunte M, Ufen A (2009) The new order and its legacy: reflections on democratization in Indonesia. In: Bunte M, Ufen A (eds) Democratization in Post-Suharto Indonesia. Routledge Contemporary Southeast Asia Studies, Oxon
37. Warburton E, Aspinall E (2019) Explaining Indonesia's democratic regression: structure, agency and popular opinion. Contemp Southeast Asia 41(2):255–285
38. Bland B (2019) Politics in Indonesia: resilient election and defective democracy. Lowy Institute for International Studies, Sydney
39. Hadiz V (2017) Indonesia's year of democratic setbacks: towards a new phase of deepening illiberalism? Bull Indones Econ Stud 53:261–278
40. Aspinall E, Mietzner M (2019) Indonesia's democratic paradox: competitive elections amidst rising illiberalism. Bull Indones Econ Stud 55(3):295–317
41. Naskah Lengkap Pidato Presiden Joko Widodo dalam Pelantika Periode 2019–2024. https://jeo.kompas.com/amp/naskah-lengkap-pidato-presiden-joko-widodo-dalam-pelantikan-periode-2019-2024. Last Accessed 01 March 2021
42. Hamid U. Indonesia's Information Law Has Threatened Free Speech for More a Decade. This Must Stop. https://theconversation.com/indonesias-information-law-has-threatened-free-speech-for-more-than-a-decade-this-must-stop-127446
43. Kemelut Wadas dan Memori Kelam Waduk Kedung Ombo. https://amp.kompas.com/nasional/read/2022/02/15/07170011/kemelut-wadas-dan-memori-kelam-waduk-kedung-ombo. https://www.republika.co.id/berita/r7320z328/tragedi-desa-wadas-ingatkan-publik-pada-pembangunan-waduk-kedung-ombo. Last Accessed 01 March 2021
44. Kudeta di Demokrat: Penunjukan Moeldoko hingga Rasa Bersalah SBY. https://amp.kompas.com/nasional/read/2021/03/06/08430311/kudeta-di-demokrat-penunjukan-moeldoko-hingga-rasa-bersalah-sby. Last Accessed 01 March 2021
45. Mendalami Cacat Hukum Moeldoko Kudeta AHY di Partai Demokrat. https://tirto.id/gaYd. Last Accessed 01 March 2021
46. Schattschneider EE (1942) Party government. Holt, Rinehart and Winston, New York, p 1
47. Budiarti AP, Haris S, Romli L, Nuryanti S, Nurhasim M, Darmawan D, Hanafi RI (2018) Personlaisasi Partai Politik di Indonesia. Yayasan Obor Indonesia, Jakarta

48. Margiansyah D, Aidulsyah F, Kurniawan FE, Kusumaningrum D, Aini YN, Sabilla K. Peta Pebisnis di Parlemen Potert Oligarki di Indonesia. https://www.researchgate.net/publication/344890558_PETA_PEBISNIS_DI_PARLEMEN_POTRET_OLIGARKI_DI_INDONESIA. Last Accessed 01 March 2021
49. Mietzner M (2013) Money, power, and ideology. Political parties in post-authoritarian Indonesia. ASAA Southeast Asia Publication Series, Singapore
50. Randall V, Svasand L (2002) Party instutitionalization in new democracies. Party Polit 8 Januari/1
51. Noor F (2018) Partai Politik Sebagai Problem Demokrasi. LIPI Press, Jakarta
52. Evans K (2020) The way to strengthen bicameral political representation system. In: Focus Group Discussion on Mapping on Political Representation System at the National Level. Unpublished, Jakarta
53. Romli L (2021) Bicameralisme: strengtening political representation at national level. Election Team Report-Center for Political Studies. Unpublished, Jakarta
54. Haris S (2020) The way to strengthen bicameral political representation system. In: Focus Group Discussion on Mapping on Political Representation System at the National Level. Unpublished, Jakarta
55. Cohen J, Arato A (1993) Civil society and political theory. Polit Theory 21(3):544–547
56. https://www.bps.go.id/indicator/34/638/1/indeks-demokrasi-indonesia-idi-menurut-indikator.html
57. Chandra W. Masyarakat Sipil Tak Boleh Lagi Disepelekan. https://www.walhi.or.id/masyarakat-sipil-tak-boleh-lagi-disepelekan. Last Accessed 21 Apr 2022
58. Hadiwinata BS (2006) Un–Civil Society dan Problematika Penegakan Hukum di Indonesia. Jurnal Hukum Pro Justitia 24(3):203–211
59. Alagappa M (2004) Civil society and political change. In: Alagappa M (ed) Civil society and political change in Asia expanding and contarcting space. Stanford University Press, Stanford
60. Prakarsa. https://theprakarsa.org/category/publikasi/policy-brief/PolicyBrief
61. Tata Kelola Civil Society Organization (CSOs) dan Demokrasi Subtansif di Indonesia. Last Accessed 22 Feb 2022
62. Praja. Ageng Nata (2009) Thesis. Distorsi Peran LSM dalam Perpektif Civil Society di Kab. Grobogan. https://core.ac.uk/download/pdf/11718707.pdf. Last Accessed 15 July 2022
63. Dewey J (1916) Democracy and education: an introduction to the philosophy of education. The Macmillan Company, New York
64. Barro RJ (1999) Determinants of democracy. J Polit Econ 107(S6):158–183
65. Chen J (2008) Democratization and government education provision in East Asia. J East Asian Stud 8(2):175–209
66. Turedi S, Terzi H (2017) The relationship between education and democracy in Turkey. In: Yilmaz R, Loschnigg G (eds) Studies on Balkan and Near Eastern social sciences. Frankfurt am Main, Peter Lang
67. Rosenberg S. Democracy devouring itself: the rise of the incompetent citizen and the appeal of right wing populism. https://escholarship.org/uc/item/8806z01m. Last Accessed 25 Jan 2022
68. Flavin P (2015) Direct democracy and political equality in the American States. Soc Sci Q 96(1):119–132
69. Winters JA (2004) Oligarchy. Cambridge University Press, New York
70. https://www.eiu.com/n/campaigns/democracy-index-2020
71. Shapiro SA, Tomain JP. Regulation and Democracy. https://www.theregreview.org/2014/03/24/24-tomain-shapiro-regulation-democracy/. Last Accessed 27 Jan 2022
72. Rule of Law and Democracy: Addressing the Gap Between Policies and Practices. https://www.un.org/en/chronicle/article/rule-law-and-democracy-addressing-gap-between-policies-and-practices. Last Accessed 27 Jan 2022
73. Noor F (2015) Perpecahan dan Soliditas Partai Islam: Studi Kasus PKB dan PKS di Dekade Awal Reformasi LIPI Press, Jakarta
74. Mietzner M (2007) Party financing in Post-Soeharto Indonesia: between state subsidies and political corruption. Contemp Southeast Asia 29(2):238–263

75. Minam A (2018) Partai Politik, Sistem Proporsional Terbuka Dan Pembiayaan Kampanye Pada Pileg 2014. In: Sukmajat M, Perdana A (eds) Pembiayaan Pemilu di Indonesia. Bawaslu, Jakarta
76. Baer BSD (2005) Money in politics: a study of party financing practices in 22 countries. National Democratic Institute for International Affairs
77. Yadav V (2011) Political parties, business groups, and corruption in developing countries. Oxford University Press, Oxford
78. Noor F, Siregar SN, Hanafi RI, Sepriwasa D (2021) The implementation of direct local election (Pilkada) and money politics tendencies: the current Indonesian case. Indones Polit Sci Rev 6(2)
79. Aspinall E, Sukmajati M (2015) Politik Uang di Indonesia, Patronase dan Klientisme pada Pemilu Legislatif 2014. Polgov, Yogyakarta
80. Noor F (2021) Partai dan Kemunduran Demokrasi: Identifikasi Penyebab dan Usulan Solusi. In: Wijayanto, Budiatri AP, Wiratraman HP (eds) Demokrasi Tanpa Demos. LP3ES, Jakarta
81. Lembaga Swadaya Masyarakat dan Kampus Jadi Harapan Publik Kritisi Pemerintah. https://www.kompas.id/baca/polhuk/2022/03/28/lembaga-swadaya-masyarakat-dan-kampus-jadi-harapan-publik-kritisi-pemerintah. Last Accessed 27 Jan 2022

# The Indonesian Democratic Party of Struggle (PDIP) in Thought and Action

**Luky Sandra Amalia**

**Abstract** This paper aims to critically examine the Indonesian Democratic Party of Struggle's (Partai Demokrasi Indonesia Perjuangan/PDIP) orientation in thought and action. Through media, this article elaborates on several aspects of the PDIP orientation at the level of thought and how it was implemented when PDIP became an opposition and a ruling party. Soekarno's idea, *Pancasila* (five foundations) of 1 June 1945, was clearly stated in the PDIP Struggle Charter (*Piagam Perjuangan*) and repeated in the PDIP Articles of Association (*AD/ART*). Since party documents are a guideline for a party to realize their work programs, the manifestation of the five foundations that Soekarno gave birth should be seen in the PDIP work under Megawati Soekarnoputri's leadership. This paper argues that PDIP is more pro-poor (*marhaen*) during its tenure as an opposition than a ruling party.

**Keywords** A ruling party · Indonesian Democratic Party of Struggle/Partai Demokrasi Indonesia Perjuangan/PDIP · *Marhaenism* · Megawati Soekarnoputri · Opposition

## 1 Introduction

As one of the top parties in Indonesian politics, the Indonesian Democratic Party of Struggle (PDIP) over the 23-year leadership of Megawati Soekarnoputri is interesting to be researched. PDIP has won three of the five legislative elections and two of the four presidential elections. PDIP's victory in the 1999 general election reached a fantastic figure of more than 33%, which has not been repeated. The PDIP vote gained in the 2004 and 2009 legislative elections only put PDIP in second and third positions. Likewise, in the 2004 and 2009 presidential elections, PDIP failed to

L. S. Amalia (✉)
The University of Sydney, Sydney, NSW 2000, Australia
e-mail: luky001@brin.go.id

Research Center for Politics, National Research and Innovation Agency, Jakarta 12710, Indonesia



Nawawi et al. (eds.), *Managing Disruption and Developing Resilience for a Better Southeast Asia*, Springer Proceedings in Humanities and Social Sciences,
https://doi.org/10.1007/978-981-96-2116-3_56

bring its general chairwoman, Megawati, to the presidency. For ten years as party opposition, PDIP has returned to the ruling party after winning the 2014 and 2019 legislative and presidential elections.

PDIP claims to be the successor to Soekarno and his ideas. Some people say that PDIP is the successor of the Indonesian National Party (Partai Nasional Indonesia/PNI), which was founded in 1927 by Soekarno, Megawati's father, whereas others state that PDIP is a transformation of the PNI, which was founded in 1946, which is in some ways different from Soekarno [19, 35]. Regarding party orientation, PDIP claims to carry Soekarno's ideas, including *Pancasila* (five foundations), born on 1 June 1945. PDIP mentions *Pancasila* in its Charter of Struggle (Piagam Perjuangan) and Articles of Association (AD/ART). Since party documents are a guideline for parties to realize their programs, the manifestation of the five foundations that Soekarno gave birth to should be seen in the PDIP works. Despite claiming to be a pro-poor (wong cilik or Soekarno called them *Marhaen*), the PDIP took several opposite policies when it became the ruling party. Through media analysis regarding the policies and actions taken by PDIP, this paper argues that the face of *Marhaenism* is more visible when PDIP becomes an opposition party than when it becomes the ruling party. Before answering this argument, this paper first describes the genealogy of PDIP and PDIP's orientation and *Pancasila*, which has shaped the party policy.

## 2 *Reformasi* Era

The collapse of Suharto's authoritarian regime in May 1998 led to dramatic changes in the Indonesian political system. This change is known as the reformation era, marked by the faucet's opening for freedom of expression and organization after more than 32 years of silence. This situation has contributed to hundreds of new political parties with various ideologies besides the three existing parties. The three established parties created by the New Order era are Golkar (the regime's political vehicle, which later transformed into the Golkar Party), the Indonesian Democratic Party/PDI (later transformed into the Indonesian Democratic Party for Struggle/PDIP before the 1999 general election), and the United Development Party (PPP). The electoral system was also reformed from closed-list Proportional Representation (PR) (for the 1999 and 2004 elections) to semi-open-list PR (for the 2009 election) to open-list PR (from the 2014 election to the present) to reduce the number of parties naturally.

The three established parties inevitably should adapt to changes in the political system, including competing in democratic elections with many parties. The electoral system affects the party system, particularly regarding the number of political parties in the party system and their ideological distance [9, 12]. The PR system produces a competitive multiparty compared to other electoral systems, making it difficult for a party to achieve a majority [9, 22, 37]. In addition, a party member in conflict also tends to break away and form a new party as there is an opportunity for new parties to gain seats in parliament [9, 22]. Although in the 1999 general election (the first democratic election of the reform era), the three established parties managed to occupy the top three positions in the vote, they failed to manage the victory in the next elections. The Democratic Party, one of the new parties, succeeded in winning the 2009 general election, overtaking Golkar as the winner of the 2004 election. Previously, the Democratic Party also won the 2004 (and 2009) presidential elections after defeating Megawati Soekarnoputri (PDIP chairwoman, incumbent candidate for the 2004 presidential election).

PDIP is a stalwart of the secular (nationalist) position. Since its inception, the PDIP has strongly opposed any special role for Islam at the state level, such as applying the Jakarta Charter and the passage of the Anti-Pornography Bill [1], ([10], 33). PDIP regularly wins landslide victories in electoral districts where most voters are non-Muslims and secular (abangan) ([24], 518). Following its successive defeats, PDIP, widely rumored as a communist party, changed its electoral strategy amid the rise of the Islamic stream in society. One of them is by embracing Islam. PDIP established an Islamic party wing, the Baitul Muslimin Indonesia (Bamusi), in 2007. PDIP also provides opportunities for Islamic groups to serve as party administrators and become legislative candidates to embrace Muslim voters.

## 3 Genealogy of PDIP

The name of PDIP just emerged before the 1999 general election, but three other important historical points also influenced the party. In its Charter of Struggle, PDIP declares itself as a transformation of the Indonesian Democratic Party (PDI), born on 10 January 1973. PDI is a combination of five secular (nationalist) and non-Islamic political parties, namely the Indonesian National Party (PNI), the Indonesian National Party Many People's Deliberations (Murba Party), Indonesian Independence Supporters Association (IPKI), Indonesian Christian Party (Parkindo), and Catholic Party.

Although in its Charter of Struggle, PDIP mentions that the joining of the five parties was driven by awareness of the responsibility to realize the noble ideals of the people's struggle, the merger of five parties with different ideologies was coercion by Soeharto's authoritarian regime [11, 19, 24]. In the early 1970s, Soeharto forced existing parties to merge into two groups, namely Islamic and non-Islamic parties. Non-Islamic parties with the ideology of nationalism, socialism, Christianity, and Catholicism were forced to join the PDI and change their ideology to *Pancasila*. On the other hand, Islamic parties were forced to join the United Development Party (PPP), although their streams differed. Meanwhile, the government formed the Golkar (Functional Group) as their political vehicle [11, 19, 24].

Despite agreeing to abandon their respective existences, conflicts between factions were unavoidable within the PDI. In addition, there was intervention from the New Order government to control the party by placing their people as PDI leaders. During its journey, the PDI split into two camps, the one supported by the government and the other rejected by the government. Soerjadi led the PDI supported by the government, while Megawati headed the one government rejected. Soeharto considered Megawati's appearance on the political stage to threaten his power. Since the regime did not recognize her PDI, Megawati announced that her PDI did not participate in the 1997 election [19]. As a result, PDI's vote fell sharply to only 3% in the 1997 election from 11% in the previous election [19].

## 4 PDIP's Orientation and *Pancasila*

Except for PPP and PKS, all political parties made *Pancasila* the basis of their parties, including PDIP. If other parties refer to the *Pancasila* version of the Jakarta Charter, PDIP follows the *Pancasila*, born by Soekarno on 1 June 1945. On 1 June 1945, Soekarno gave a speech before the Investigating Agency for Preparatory Efforts for Indonesian Independence (Badan Penyelidik Usaha-Usaha Persiapan Kemerdekaan Indonesia/BPUPKI), known as the birth of *Pancasila*. In his speech, Soekarno mentioned the five foundations of the state, namely nationality, internationalism (humanity), consensus (democracy), welfare (social justice), and divinity [19, 36]. These five principles are the forerunner of *Pancasila* as the basis of Indonesia stated in the Jakarta Charter. It was ratified by the Indonesian Independence Preparatory Committee (Panitia Persiapan Kemerdekaan Indonesia/PPKI) on 18 August 1945, where Soekarno was the chairman. Soekarno linked nationalism and internationalism (humanity) as socio-nationalism, while consensus (democracy) and welfare (social justice) became socio-democratic. All of them are based on divinity. Soekarno called these three precepts (socio-nationalism, socio-democracy, and divinity) the *Trisila*. He summarized the *Trisila* into one precept, cooperation (*gotong-royong* (AD/ART PDIP), [19, 36].

At the Indonesian Party (Partindo) Congress in 1933, Soekarno emphasized that the concept of socio-nationalism and socio-democracy was to free all Indonesian people from the shackles of poverty and misery (AD/ART PDIP; [23, 35]). Partindo is the PNI transformation, which Soekarno founded in 1927. The 1927 PNI was different from the PNI as part of the PDI. The PNI, which Soekarno founded on 4 July 1927, was dissolved by its administrators in 1931 after the Dutch arrested Soekarno and several party leaders as the Dutch accused them of treason [23, 35]. The PNI fought for Indonesian independence and the realization of Indonesian socialism [23, 35]. Instead, the PNI board established the Indonesian Party (Partindo) in 1932–1933. After being released from prison in 1933, Soekarno joined Partindo and became its chairman. The first Partindo conference in Yogyakarta released the principles and ideology of *Marhaenism* [23]. Unfortunately, the Dutch Colonial Government froze Partindo in 1934 and banished Soekarno to Ende, Flores [23].

In 1946, the PNI was re-established without Soekarno's involvement. Rocamora [35] explained that the PNI was re-established as a fusion of many elements of the movement. Different interests and factions contributed to the PNI's split after the 1955 elections. The split peaked when Ali Sastroamidjojo led the PNI in 1963. There was a dualism in the management of the PNI, the PNI led by Ali Sastroamidjojo and Surachman (left faction), and the PNI led by Osa Maliki and Usep Ranuwidjaja (right faction). After the G30S in 1965, the right faction controlled the PNI and became closer to the Soeharto regime [23]. Thus, the regime only accepted and ratified the Osa-Usep's PNI while disbanding and crushing the Ali-Surachman's PNI faction [23].

Regarding party ideology, Rocamora [35] explains that since returning in 1946, the PNI has looked at *Marhaenism* as the party's principle, although its interpretation has changed several times. In the third congress in 1948, they translated *Marhaenism* as socio-nationalism and socio-democracy, but the conception did not reflect Marxism which opposed individualism and emphasized class conflict [35]. Rocamora [35] links it to the background of the PNI leaders, which was dominated by conservative noblemen (*priyayi*). Until 1958, Soekarno criticized those who pretentiously understood *Marhaenism*, and he explained that *Marhaenism* is Marxism that is organized, adapted, and implemented in Indonesia [35].

## 5 PDIP and Elections in *Reformasi* Era

As the election rules prohibit two parties with the same name, Megawati changed the party's name she led to PDI for Struggle (PDIP) prior to the 1999 general election. In this first democratic election during the reformation era, PDIP garnered a fantastic vote of 33.7%. This achievement has not been repeated yet. Using the elitist-populist cleavage related to how the elites communicate to voters, Evans [10] explains how Megawati's silence led to the party's victory. The elitist spectrum regards personal loyalty and identification with the party's national leadership as less important than attachment to a political process/policy position. Elites seek to judge leaders and parties more by their actions and policies than their symbolic behavior [10].

Meanwhile, the populist spectrum considers their relationship with the national parties' leaders to be more emotional, even mystical [10]. Therefore, the educated middle-class considers Megawati's silence as a barrier to holding a dialogue, whereas the poor captured her silence as a feeling of being a victim of the New Order [10]. Megawati represents a symbolic bond through her silence in sharing experiences with the poor and the voiceless lower class [10]. They found an emotional connection with Megawati as victims of the New Order.

However, PDIP failed to maintain its dominance. In the 2004 election, PDIP was only in second place with 18.53% of the votes, below the Golkar Party's (21.58%). PDIP's ranking declined to third in the 2009 election with 14.03% of the vote, below the Democratic Party (20.85%) and Golkar (14.45%). PDIP also failed to lead Megawati to win the 2004 and 2009 presidential elections. After its defeat, PDIP decided to be an opposition party during the Susilo Bambang Yudhoyono (SBY) administration between 2004 and 2014.

Interestingly, Megawati's position as party chairperson is immovable even though she failed to maintain her party victory. Megawati has been reelected by acclamation at each party's Congress. Most candidates who lost in Congress left the party or were fired by Mega. For example, Eros Djarot, a senior PDIP politician, ran for general chairman at the PDIP first Congress in Semarang in 2000, but he failed. Then, he left PDIP and founded the National Bull of Independence Party (Partai Nasional Banteng Kemerdekaan/PNBK) [39]. Dimyati Hartono also experienced a similar situation. After losing in Congress, he left the PDIP and founded the Indonesian Our Homeland Party (PITA) [39].

After the Second PDIP Congress in Bali in 2004, Megawati fired some PDIP cadres, such as Laksamana Sukardi and Roy B.B. Janis's group, as they demanded that Congress should conduct a massive evaluation following the PDIP's successive defeats [39]. Other cadres wanted a democratic succession of party leaders such as Arifin Panigoro, Sukowaluyo Mintohardjo, Noviantika Nasution, Pius Lustrilanang, Postdam Hutasoit, Angelina Pattiasina, Didi Supriyanto, Peter Sutanto, Sophan Sophiaan, and Tjandra Widjaya, also ended in dismissal [39]. Later, some founded the Democratic Reform Party (PDP) and ran in the 2009 election [39]. While the PDIP splinter parties only survived in one or two elections, the PDIP has survived until today.

Political parties adapt their ideological positions in response to the changing social and political environments, such as a decrease in electoral support or electoral system change [9, 4, 8, 5, 13, 32]. The increasing Islamic stream also influences the strategy. The reformation era also opens the freedom of expression's faucet, including Islam. For instance, participation in Islamic studies increases, especially among middle-class Muslims; the use of Islamic headscarves by women has also increased compared to that of the 1970s, and TV and film broadcasts—which the West and East Asia once dominated—feature many Islamic-themed programs. Pew Research Center [33] mentions that 71% of Indonesian Muslims support the state's idea of reinforcing Islamic law. This figure is above average compared to other Muslim countries [33, 9].

Many previous studies have discussed the party system, political parties, and their ideologies/orientations at the global level and post-New Order Indonesia. At the global level, for example, party studies discuss more the characteristics and shifts of the party system from mass parties to catch-all parties [9, 13, 15, 17, 30, 32, 43]. In the era of catch-all parties, parties tend to decline their ideological commitment and weaken their ties to their traditional base to get wider votes [17].

However, in the Indonesian case, some of the core parties are rooted in a specific socio-cultural constituency where they articulate the interests of the people they represent (Aspinall in Hefner 2017). PDIP, for example, has a clear relationship with certain constituents and has moderately strong roots in society [11, 24] compared to later-born parties that were established as electoral vehicles for their chairmen ([3]; Aspinall in Hefner 2017).

Regarding party orientation, Soekarno's ideas stated in the PDIP Struggle Charter and Articles of Association should be seen in the PDIP work program under Megawati's leadership. Unfortunately, Megawati's administration (2001–2003) was known for its policies of privatizing state companies and divesting banks. PT Indosat and the gas field exploration rights at a low price are examples of privatized state-owned companies [18, 21]. BCA, Danamon, Lippo, BII, Permata, Niaga, Mandiri, and BRI Bank are examples of banks that experienced divestment [18, 21]. Although this unpopular policy was conducted to cover the state budget deficit and restore the country's economy following the ending of the IMF cooperation program in December 2003, it triggered a wave of street protest [18, 31].

After PDIP lost the 2004 and 2009 legislative elections and Megawati lost the 2004 dan 2009 presidential elections, PDIP decided to be an opposition party. This party strongly rejected various government policies which were considered not pro-poor. Unlike Megawati's tenure's controversial policies, PDIP showed its siding with the poor during Yudhoyono's reign. PDIP has been seen as keen to voice the rejection of some of the Yudhoyono government's policies throughout its ten years of opposition, especially when this government raised fuel prices. PDIP politicians in parliament are trying to block the 2013 state budget amendment (Draft State Revenue and Expenditure Budget—Amendment/Rancangan Anggaran Pendapatan dan Belanja Negara-Perubahan/RAPBNP), which contains a reduction in fuel subsidies [7], (Kompas 2013). They also walked out when most DPR members did not accommodate their proposal [27].

On the sidelines of the plenary meeting, the PDIP faction also distributed small books, 20 × 10 cm, to journalists and people outside the plenary meeting. The 24-page book contains the proposed 2013 APBN-P version of the PDIP through a pro-village program to match the government version [7, 27]. The book describes the PDIP position, the definition of the state budget dan why it is in deficit so that the administration needs to address it by increasing fuel prices in detail [27]. PDIP suspected the political imagery motive behind this unpopular policy. By increasing the fuel prices, Yudhoyono administration disbursed IDR 43 trillion for Community Temporary Direct Assistance (bantuan langsung sementara masyarakat/BLSM) and social assistance (bantuan sosial/bansos) [7, 27]. Outside parliament, PDIP cadres also staged street protests at the state palace to pressure the government to cancel the fuel price increase [7, 27]. The action of a member of the DPR from the PDIP faction who cried amid a demonstration had gone viral in the mass media [7, 26].

Nevertheless, the decision of PDIP to become an opposition party could not be separated from Megawati's problem with Yudhoyono. Yudhoyono is the chairman of the Democratic Party and the sixth Indonesian president, who defeated Megawati in the 2004 and 2009 presidential elections. Previously, Yudhoyono was a minister of the Megawati administration (2001–2004). Before the 2004 election, Mega repeatedly asked her ministers, including Yudhoyono, whether they would run for president. Yudhoyono repeatedly answered that he would not compete for president and supported the Megawati administration until the end [6, 26, 41]. Ahead of the 2004 election, Yudhoyono founded the Democratic Party (Partai Demokrat) and ran for president, even defeating Megawati in the 2004 and 2009 presidential elections [6, 26, 41]. This situation became one of the reasons why PDIP decided to be the opposition party during the Yudhoyono administration (2004–2014). In addition, Megawati rejected Yudhoyono's offer to seat her cadres as ministers in his cabinet [14].

After ten years of being an opposition party (2004–2009 and 2009–2014), PDIP has regained the voters' trust. It is reflected in winning the 2014 election with 18.95% of the vote and delivering Joko Widodo (Jokowi), his cadre, as the seventh president of Indonesia. PDIP also maintained its victory by getting 19.33% of the vote in the 2019 election and maintaining Jokowi as president until 2024. Jokowi delivered pro-poor policies, such as increasing village funds every year, launching a land certificate distribution program for low-income communities (MBR), and issuing the Indonesian Workers Social Security Program (BPJS labor) to protect the low-class workers [40]. Jokowi also distributed Smart Indonesia Cards (KIP) to 18.9 million students, Healthy Indonesia Cards (KIS), which reached 96.7 million people, and implemented the family hope program (PKH) to 10 million families [40]. During the Covid-19 pandemic, Jokowi provided cash assistance in Wage Subsidy Assistance (BSU) worth Rp. 2.4 million to 12.4 million active Jamsostek participants who met the criteria of the Minister of Manpower Regulation 14/2020 to alleviate the economic burden from the impact of the Covid-19 pandemic [20, 16].

However, the Jokowi administration has also known for its unpopular policies. The Jokowi administration has revoked energy subsidies three times, the 3kg liquefied petroleum gas (LPG), 900-W electricity, and fuel subsidies [25, 38]. Although the government diverted the subsidy for infrastructure development, education budget, and social assistance [29], street protests occurred since it triggered an increase in the price of basic needs and reduced people's purchasing power [28, 34, 42]. This unpopular policy had drawn satire from politicians from other parties, especially the Democrat Party cadres whose policies were protested by PDIP cadres.

## 6 Conclusion

As one of the top parties on the Indonesian political scene, PDIP, over the 23 years of Megawati Soekarnoputri's leadership, is interesting to be studied. Some people say that PDIP is the successor of the PNI founded in 1927 by Soekarno, Megawati's father, while others argue that PDIP is a transformation of the PNI founded in 1946, which is in some ways different from Soekarno. However, PDIP has embraced Soekarno's ideas, including *Pancasila* and *marhaenism*, and explicitly stated them in the Charter of Struggle and the party's Articles of Association. Since party documents are a guideline for parties in realizing their work programs, the manifestation of those ideas should be seen in the PDIP works under Megawati Soekarnoputri's leadership. Having lost two elections in a row, the PDIP decided to be the opposition party. During its ten years as an opposition party, PDIP strongly rejected the Yudhoyono policies, which were considered detrimental to the poor, especially the policy of increasing fuel prices. PDIP cadres in parliament refused the policy while other cadres shouted through street protests. Ironically, PDIP adopted similar unpopular policies, including rising fuel prices, when its party was in charge.

## References


1. Ambardi K (2009) Mengungkap Politik Kartel Studi tentang Sistem Kepartaian di Indonesia Era Reformasi. Kepustakaan Populer Gramedia, Jakarta
2. Aspinall E (2018) Democratization travails and achievements. In: Hefner RW (ed) Routledge handbook of contemporary Indonesia. Routledge, London and New York
3. Aspinall E, Sukmajati M (2016) Electoral dynamics in Indonesia: money politics, patronage and clientelism at the grassroots. NUS Press, Singapore
4. Buckler S, Dolowitz DP (2009) Ideology, party identity and renewal. J Political Ideol 14(1):11–30. https://doi.org/10.1080/13569310802649102
5. Demker M (1997) Changing party ideology gaullist parties facing voters, leaders and competitors. Party Politics 3(3):407–426
6. Detik (2009) Kronologi Konflik SBY-Mega, 16 March. https://news.detik.com/pemilu/d-1099903/kronologi-konflik-sby-mega
7. Detik (2013) PDIP dan PKS Tolak APBN-P 2013, Ajukan APBN-P Tandingan, 17 June. https://news.detik.com/berita/d-2275634/pdip-dan-pks-tolak-apbn-p-2013-ajukan-apbn-p-tandingan
8. Diamond L, Gunther R (eds) (2001) Political parties and democracy. Johns Hopkins University Press, London
9. Duverger M (1963) Political parties. John Wiley, New York
10. Evans K (2009) Politik "Aliran" yang Mana? Majalah Tempo, 31 Maret–6 April
11. Fionna U, Tomsa D (2017) Parties and factions in Indonesia: the effects of historical legacies and institutional engineering. In: Guan LH (ed) Working paper series. ISEAS, Singapore
12. Gallagher M, Mitchell P (2005) The politics of electoral systems. Oxford University Press, Oxford
13. Ghunter R, Diamond L (2003) Species of political parties: a new typology. Party Politics 9(2):167–199
14. Jawa Pos (2019) Megawati Pernah Ditawari 8 Menteri oleh SBY ketika PDIP Jadi Oposisi, 8 August. https://www.jawapos.com/nasional/politik/08/08/2019/megawati-pernah-ditawari-8-menteri-oleh-sby-ketika-pdip-jadi-oposisi/
15. Katz RS, Mair P (2012) Parties, interest groups and cartels: a comment. Party Politics 18(1):107–111
16. Kementerian Sekretariat Negara (2020) Presiden Jokowi Luncurkan Bantuan Subsidi Upah, 27 August. https://www.setneg.go.id/baca/index/presiden_jokowi_luncurkan_bantuan_subsidi_upah
17. Kirchheimer O (1966) The transformation of the western European party systems. In: LaPalombara J, Myron W (eds) Political parties and political development. Princeton University Press, Princeton
18. Kompas (2019) Perjalanan Politik Megawati, 3 Warisannya yang Dipuji dan Di-bully, 26 July. https://nasional.kompas.com/read/2019/07/26/15130301/perjalanan-politik-megawati-3-warisannya-yang-dipuji-dan-di-bully?page=all
19. Lay C (2019) Melawan Negara PDI 1973–1986. PolGov UGM, Yogyakarta
20. Liputan6 (2020) Jokowi Resmi Luncurkan Program Subsidi Gaji Rp 2,4 Juta, 27 August. https://www.liputan6.com/bisnis/read/4340807/jokowi-resmi-luncurkan-program-subsidi-gaji-rp-24-juta
21. Ma'arif S (2019) Privatisasi BUMN dan Reorientasi Peran Negara di Sektor Bisnis Pasca Orde Baru (Studi Komparasi Tiga Masa Pemerintahan). Jurnal Analisis Sosial Politik 5(1) 45–58
22. Mair P (1990) The west European party system. Oxford University Press, Oxford England, New York
23. Majalah Historia (2016) Partai Nasional Indonesia dan Ahli Warisnya
24. Mietzner M (2012) Ideology, Money and dynastic leadership: the Indonesian democratic party of struggle, 1998–2012. South East Asia Res 20(4):511–531
25. Merdeka (2020) Era Jokowi Aneka Subsidi Energi Dicabut, Ini Daftarnya, 17 January. https://www.merdeka.com/uang/era-jokowi-aneka-subsidi-energi-dicabut-ini-daftarnya.html

26. Merdeka (2018) Kisah 'perseteruan' Megawati dan SBY, berawal dari Pilpres 2004, 26 July. https://www.merdeka.com/politik/kisah-perseteruan-megawati-dan-sby-berawal-dari-pilpres-2014.html
27. Merdeka (2015) Mengenang galaknya PDIP tolak kenaikan BBM, 30 March. https://www.merdeka.com/politik/mengenang-galaknya-pdip-tolak-kenaikan-bbm.html
28. Merdeka (2017) Tolak kenaikan BBM, ratusan mahasiswa gelar demo di Bundaran Gladag, 9 January. https://www.merdeka.com/peristiwa/tolak-kenaikan-bbm-ratusan-mahasiswa-gelar-demo-di-bundaran-gladag.html
29. Ministry of Finance (2016) Selain Infrastruktur, Pengalihan Subsidi BBM Juga Untuk Perlindungan Sosial, 17 May. https://www.kemenkeu.go.id/publikasi/berita/selain-infrastruktur-pengalihan-subsidi-bbm-juga-untuk-perlindungan-sosial/
30. Neumann S (1956) Towards a comparative study of political parties. In: Neumann S (ed) Modern political parties. University of Chicago Press, Chicago
31. Okezone (2009) Privatisasi di Era Megawati karena Krisis Ekonomi, 30 May. https://news.okezone.com/read/2009/05/30/268/224502/privatisasi-di-era-megawati-karena-krisis-ekonomi
32. Panebianco A (1988) Political parties: organisation and power. Cambridge University Press, Cambridge
33. Pew Research Center (2013) The world's Muslims: religion, politics and society. 20 April. https://www.pewresearch.org/religion/wp-content/uploads/sites/7/2013/04/worlds-muslims-religion-politics-society-full-report.pdf
34. Republika (2014) Hujan, Demonstrasi Tolak Kenaikan BBM Tetap Berlangsung, 15 November. https://www.republika.co.id/berita/nf2vh9/hujan-demonstrasi-tolak-kenaikan-bbm-tetap-berlangsung
35. Rocamora JE (1991) Muncul dan Tenggelamnya Nasionalisme Mencari Idelogi Bangkit dan Runtuhnya PNI 1946–1965. Pustaka Utama Gravity, Jakarta
36. Rudiyanto R (2017) Sosialisme Bung Karno: Memahami Imajinasi Sosial Bung Karno. Jurnal Abdiel: Khazanah Pemikiran Teologi, Pendidikan Agama Kristen dan Musik Gereja 1(1):1–12
37. Shugart M, Wattenberg P (ed) (2003) Mixed-member electoral systems: the best of both worlds? Oxford University Press, Oxford, Incorporated
38. Tirto (2016) Dilema Subsidi Setrum 900VA, 21 June. https://tirto.id/dilema-subsidi-setrum-900va-bnRP
39. Tirto (2019) Sejarah Perlawanan Kader PDIP terhadap Feodalisme Ketua Umum Partai, 16 August. https://tirto.id/eggl
40. TNP2K (2018) Program Bantuan Pemerintah Untuk Individu, Keluarga, dan Kelompok Tidak Mampu Menuju Bantuan Sosial Terintegrasi. Jakarta: Sekretariat Wakil Presiden Republik Indonesia
41. Viva (2018) Politikus PDIP Ungkap Sebab Mega Sakit Hati pada SBY, 1 August. https://www.viva.co.id/berita/politik/1059886-politikus-pdip-ungkap-sebab-mega-sakit-hati-pada-sby?page=2&utm_medium=page-2
42. Wartakota (2018) Gelombang Demonstrasi Tolak Kenaikan Harga BBM Pecah di Solo dengan Aksi Jokowi Tebar Uang Receh, 3 April. https://wartakota.tribunnews.com/2018/04/03/gelombang-demonstrasi-tolak-kenaikan-harga-bbm-pecah-di-solo-dengan-aksi-jokowi-tebar-uang-receh
43. Wolinetz SB (2006) Party systems and party system types. In: Katz RS, Crotty W (eds) Handbook of party politics. Sage Publications, London

# Organising the Outbreak: Introducing Indonesia's Covid-19 Regulations and Media Statement Dataset, March 2020–March 2021

**Putri Ariza Kristimanta, Mario Surya Ramadhan, Rosita Dewi, and Sarah Nuraini Siregar**

**Abstract** There is a growing academic consensus that Indonesia's responses to the Covid-19 pandemic are more economic-oriented than public health. However, to strengthen the argument, recent studies are short on quantifying the regulations and statements issued by the related authorities during the first year of the outbreak. This article introduces a national dataset covering all the regulations and media statements of the central government, DKI Jakarta local government, and West Java local government. The dataset is a part of greater research about governing non-traditional security challenges involving PRP-BRIN researchers. The dataset recorded 1577 data, consisting of 610 national government regulations, 364 national government media statements, 93 DKI Jakarta government regulations, 198 DKI Jakarta government media statements, 128 West Java government regulations, and 184 West Java government media statements. Firstly, this article introduces the rationale for the dataset and explains the basic coding procedures and quality controls. Secondly, the paper discusses some of the data's potential limitations in representing the rapid and vast pandemic responses and some potential biases induced by the operationalisations. Thirdly, the paper provides an example of how the data can be used by illustrating and affirming the heavy economic orientation of Indonesia's national government outbreak responses. The dataset is valuable for policy analysis and discourse analysis of national and local government outbreak responses.

P. A. Kristimanta (✉) · M. S. Ramadhan · R. Dewi
Research Center for Politics, The National Research and Innovation Agency, Jakarta, Indonesia
e-mail: putr007@brin.go.id

M. S. Ramadhan
e-mail: mari017@brin.go.id

R. Dewi
e-mail: rosi008@brin.go.id

S. N. Siregar
Directorate of Politics, Law and Security Policies, The National Research and Innovation Agency, Jakarta, Indonesia
e-mail: sara002@brin.go.id



Nawawi et al. (eds.), *Managing Disruption and Developing Resilience for a Better Southeast Asia*, Springer Proceedings in Humanities and Social Sciences,
https://doi.org/10.1007/978-981-96-2116-3_57

**Keywords** Covid-19 · Dataset · Regulations · Media statements

## 1 Introduction

Since the declaration of a global pandemic in March 2020, Covid-19 has been pushing the boundaries of national and global efforts to handle this multidimensional threat. The national government's response varies from country to country depending on the political system, local-national dynamics, and national security interests. Also, Covid-19 has been testing international health cooperation at the international level, which is failed to be solidly established during the early chaos.

Scholars and policymakers in Indonesia have studied Indonesia's outbreak responses, particularly during the initial wave of Covid-19 cases in March 2020, including building new datasets related to Covid-19 and its handling. One fine example is the Covid-19 cases databases created by LaporCovid-19, community-based datasets built by local volunteers across all regions in Indonesia. Currently, LaporCovid-19 databases are one of the most reliable data to refer to while analysing Indonesia's Covid-19 in numbers. Other dependable Covid-19 databases were built by KawalCovid-19, Ministry of Health Republic of Indonesia, and, the notable databases related to Covid-19 responses and regulations are built by HukumOnline.com. The regulation data contained in HukumOnline provide comprehensive coverage of national government responses to regulations. However, this database lacks coverage of the local government regulations, resulting in incomplete data to capture the local-national dynamics during the outbreak.

Furthermore, the HukumOnline database also lacks media statement records, said by prominent leaders and policymakers in handling the pandemic. This dataset would like to fill the academic gap that previous scholars are failed to do so. Our Covid-19 datasets cover the regulations and media statements of the national government, DKI Jakarta province government, and West Java province government in handling the pandemic.

This dataset only covers the regulations and media statements issued from March 2020 to March 2021 to capture Indonesia's initial responses to the Covid-19 pandemic. This time frame was filled with local power struggles and fragmented responses to the pandemic, which may result in inward-looking responses that sacrificed a united national response. Also, the time limitations were established because of the research team's time and budget constraints.

This study selected DKI Jakarta and West Java as a sample of local government responses because of two reasons. The first reason is that the national and Jakarta's tug of war in the outbreak handling authority has been demonstrated in the initial months of responses. Another reason is that West Java is the most populated province in Indonesia with a vast region, which might be more challenging to establish a solid local response.

This article proceeds as follows, firstly, we expand on the rationale for the new dataset and its many possible contributions. Secondly, we detail our definitions, operationalisations, data collection procedures, coding, and mechanisms to ensure data quality and consistency. Thirdly, we briefly outline the limitations of the dataset and explain our reasoning behind some of the theoretical and operational choices. Fourthly, we present some descriptive statistics and an example of how this dataset can be used to illustrate the specific actors (in this case, the president) issued related to the national responses to the pandemic. With this illustration, we hope to stimulate interest in the many potential uses of the dataset for research questions at the local-national level of analysis.

This dataset is available upon request on the website of Repositori Ilmiah Nasional (RIN), developed and managed by Badan Riset dan Inovasi Nasional, with the link https://data.lipi.go.id/dataset.xhtml?persistentId=hdl:20.500.12690/RIN/OJXBQV. The potential user should click the "Request Access" button provided by RIN's Dataverse to contact and access the complete data. After the contributor receives the request, the user will receive the files.

## 2 Why a New Dataset?

During the Covid-19 pandemic outbreak, several datasets were released to capture the Indonesian situation in the middle of the pandemic. Most datasets released are datasets on the number of Covid-19 cases [1] and also the dataset on the economic impact of Covid-19 on the community [2]. These datasets are released by the government. The result shows that the economic condition of the community is impacted due to pandemics, even though the survey results show that only a few businesses had to close their business due to Covid-19. This situation severely impacts the community, who face the salary cut off or become unemployed because their company faces financial difficulties. This result influenced the government policy in facing the pandemic. The formation of Komite Penanganan Covid-19 dan Pemulihan Ekonomi Nasional (KPC-KPEN) under the Coordinating Minister for Economic Affairs, Airlangga Hartarto is one of the government efforts to minimise the economic impact toward community due to Covid-19. Another dataset is the dataset on the community's obedience to obey the health protocol during the pandemic [3]. Another important dataset on Covid-19 is a study on hoax information on Covid-19 in Indonesia analyses by arranging datasets from social media. The dataset shows interesting results that the fake news on covid-19 in Indonesia mainly spread through Facebook and WhatsApp. This study analyses that missing information on Covid-19 makes the problem of Covid-19 in Indonesia more complex [4].

The mentioned datasets contribute to analysing the community's situation during the pandemic. However, there is no dataset on regulations and government media statements. This dataset is essential to show how the central and local government's readiness to respond to the pandemic. This dataset will complement the previous datasets. This new dataset can be used to analyse the government approaches to respond to the Covid-19. This new dataset is important to contribute to the research agenda concerning on Covid-19 pandemic in Indonesia.

Moreover, this new dataset can be cultivated to analyse the range of authority (rentang kendali) of central and local governments in facing the Covid-19. It can show whether there is a gap or not between central and local government, whether the local government can translate the central government's will to handle the pandemic, or the dataset will show the contradiction between the local and central government approaches to handling the pandemic based on the regulations has been released by central and local government. This new dataset can show the government's priority in response to Covid-19. Furthermore, this new dataset can indicate the shifting of government policies during the pandemic, which will regulate and carry many impacts on Indonesian communities during the Covid-19 pandemic.

## 3 Criteria, Data Collection, and Limitations

Indonesia's Covid-19 Regulations and Media Statement Dataset recorded regulations and statements in the media by the central government, the Jakarta provincial government and the West Java provincial government from March 2020 to March 2021. Those three entities represent the central government as the leading policymaker, the provincial government of DKI Jakarta as the administrative authority of Indonesia's capital city, and the West Java provincial government as the province with the highest population in Indonesia. Regulations and statements reflect the policies of the Indonesian government to deal with the Covid-19 pandemic. Regulations and statements in the media by central and local governments can provide insights into the development and the effectiveness of Covid-19 policies in Indonesia.

Type and the hierarchy of Laws and Regulations in Indonesia refer to Law No. 12 of 2011 concerning the Establishment of Laws and Regulations. Article 7 of Law No. 12 of 2011 regulates the type and hierarchy of Laws and Regulations, consisting of the 1945 Constitution of the Republic of Indonesia, The Decree of the People's Consultative Assembly, Government Laws/Regulations in Lieu of Laws, Government Regulations, Presidential Regulations, Provincial Regulations, and Regency/City Regulations [5]. Laws and regulations in Indonesia also include decrees stipulated by the People's Consultative Assembly and the House of Representatives, the Regional Representative Council, the Supreme Court, the Constitutional Court, the Financial Audit Board, the Judicial Commission, Bank of Indonesia, ministers, bodies, institutions, or commissions of the same level formed by law or government at the order of the Law, the Regional House of Representatives, Governor, Regent/Mayor, and Village Head [6].

This dataset recorded various types of regulations of the central government, the provincial government of DKI Jakarta, and West Java province's government. At the central government level, the dataset recorded regulations ranging from government regulations in lieu of laws, presidential regulations, ministerial regulations, and letters in specific ministries or institutions. In the provincial scope, both in DKI Jakarta and West Java, the dataset recorded Governor regulations, Governor instruction, and Governor letters. The source of the regulations dataset comes from government websites, such as https://covid19.go.id/p/regulasi to track regulations issued by the central government https://corona.jakarta.go.id/id/kebijakan for regulations issued by DKI Jakarta province, and https://pikobar.jabarprov.go.id/info/documents for the regulations issued by the province of West Java.

In addition to government-issued regulations, this dataset also recorded the government's response to handling Covid-19 in the form of statements by government officials in the media. Media has a vital role in becoming a platform for communication, education, and socialisation of public health during the Covid-19 pandemic [7]. The government's response in the media is direct or indirect sentences of government officials reported by online media and websites in text or video news. The online media used in data collection are tempo.co as a national media with high credibility, and PikiranRakyat, an online media based on West Java. The government officials' statements in the form of videos are taken from the Kompastv YouTube channel as one of the independent and trusted online media.

The statements of government officials in the media reflect the government's response and approach to the Covid-19 outbreak. In the central government, government officials who are recorded giving statements in response to the handling of Covid-19, ranging from the President, Vice President, Chairman and Members of the House of Representatives, the Minister of Health, spokesperson for the Covid-19 Task Force, and other officials. Meanwhile, at the provincial level in DKI Jakarta and West Java, regional officials who gave statements included the Governor, the Head of Health Affairs Office, to other agency officials who served in the provincial scope, such as the Regional Police Chief.

Collecting regulations and government officials' statements in the media is conducted by observing online sources. Human coders observe on government websites and online media mentioned earlier. The observation process is also followed by a data sorting process which is then documented and stored for further data processing. The human coder explored the media archives of Tempo and Pikiran Rakyat during the data collection using Google News. The collected news is searched, for example, using the keyword "Media Online (Ex: PikiranRakyat) (space) Regional Focus (Ex: Jakarta) (space) "Covid-19" and sorted monthly based on the starting date from January 2020. The identified regulations are then recorded in a table by filling in the date of issue, name, type, content, and technical implementation of the regulation. Meanwhile, the data of media statements are recorded by identifying the date when statements appear in the media, the name of the official, the position of the official, the content of statements and media sources.

This dataset has some limitations. First, it only records the regulations and statements of officials for a limited time, starting from March 2020 to March 2021. This period only covers the first year of the Covid-19 pandemic in Indonesia. Meanwhile, the pandemic is still ongoing until 2022. Second, this dataset relies entirely on the ability of the human coder as it did not use automation in collecting data, especially statements of government officials in the media. The weakness of the human coder is the possibility of skipping some statements of government officials in the media. Third, the variants of online media sources targeted by data collection are limited.

# 4 Brief Descriptive Statistics

This section presents several descriptive statistical results that provide an overview of Indonesia's policies and response to the Covid-19 pandemic. The description refers to three dimensions: regulations, actors, and response, concerning three levels: the central government, DKI Jakarta, and West Java.

Based on the results of the general dataset, there are 610 regulations at the central level in dealing with the Covid-19 pandemic, followed by a central response of 364. Figure 1

shows that the number of responses from the central government is not linear with the number of regulations. Meanwhile, it is the opposite at the level of the two provinces in this dataset. In DKI Jakarta, the number of regulations issued was 93. However, the provincial government's response in dealing with Covid-19 was even stronger at 198. The same is the case with West Java, where there are 128 regional regulations, followed by the response of the West Java government, which exceeds the number of regulations, which is 184.

The following descriptive statistical explanation is for each section: the central government, the regional government of DKI Jakarta, and West Java. At the central government level, the dataset results show four dominant regulations (Fig. 2). The number of regulations in the form of Circulars is the largest (307), followed by Ministerial Regulations (83), Ministerial Decrees (42), then finally regulations at the government/presidential level (Perppu, UU, Keppres, Inpres, Perpres) (11). Others show a less significant number (Fig. 2).

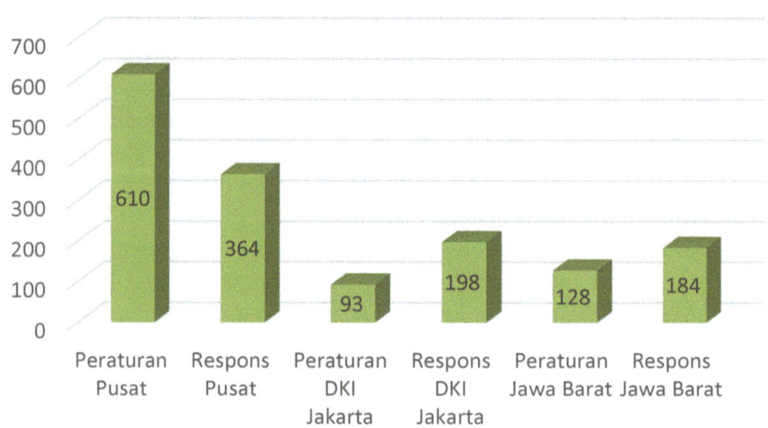


**Fig. 1** Number of data collected

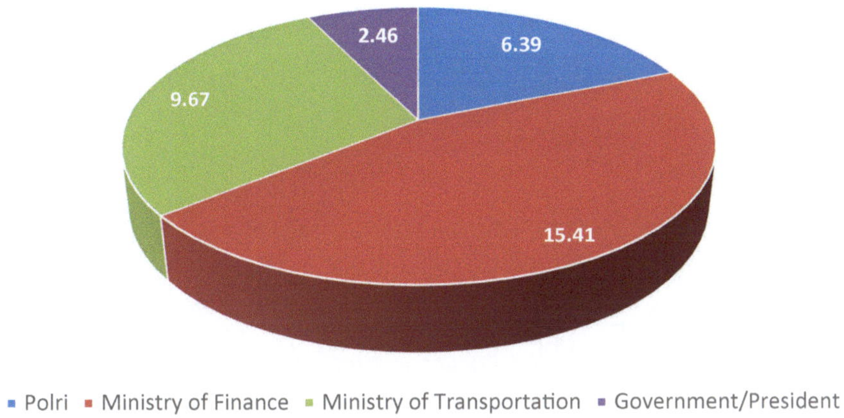


**Fig. 2** The proportion of regulation at the national level

Then, nine actors and institutions show a significant number of those who carry out the 610 regulations above. The Ministry of Finance is the institution that implements this regulation the most (94), followed by the Ministry of Health (65), Ministry of Transportation (59), Police (39), Ministry of Religion (24), OJK (24), Government/President (15), the Covid-19 Task Force (8), and finally the Covid-19 7 Task Force. These figures show that the Ministry of Finance plays the most significant role compared to the Ministry of Health. The impact and economic considerations are the government's main steps in dealing with the Covid-19 pandemic.

Figure 3 shows the percentage of each of these actors.

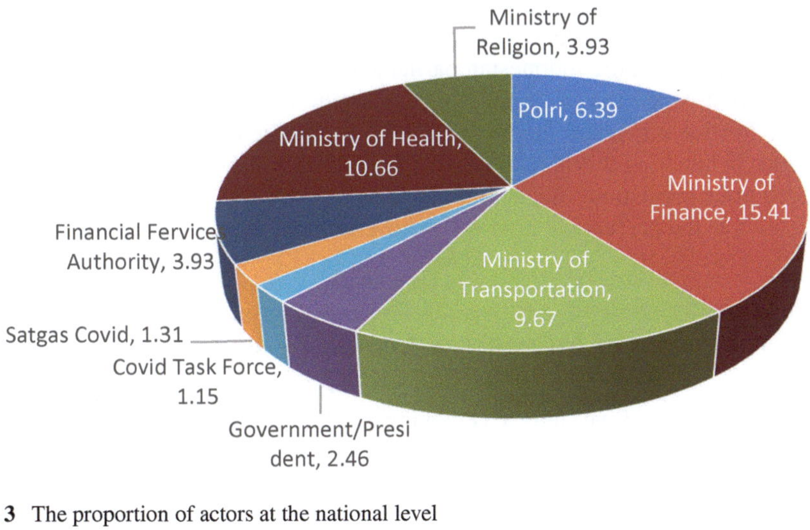


**Fig. 3** The proportion of actors at the national level

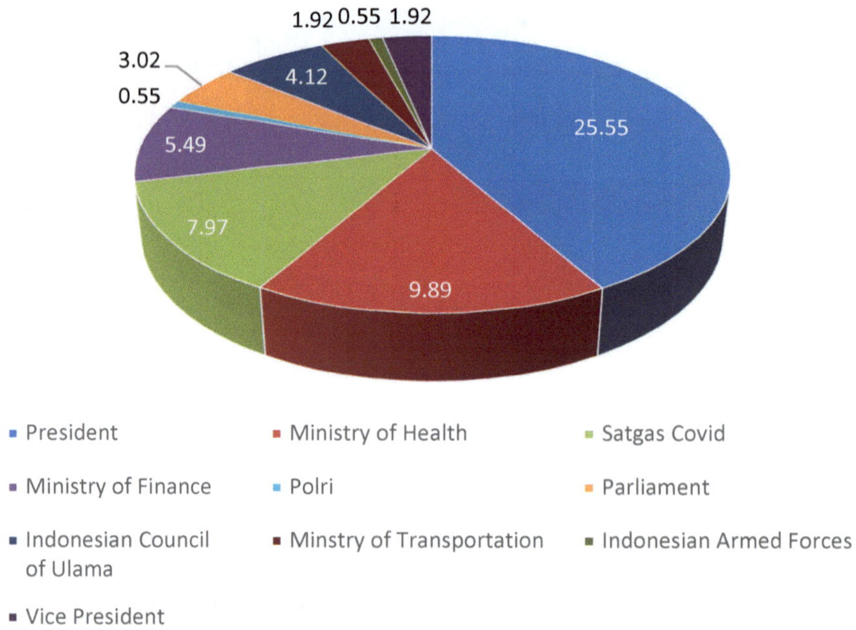


**Fig. 4** The proportion of national-level responses

## 4.1 *Proportions of Actors at the Central Level*

The following data at the central level is the government's response. From a total of 364, the government's response ranks first with 97, followed by the Ministry of Health (36), the Covid-19 Task Force (29), the Ministry of Finance (20), the Indonesian Ulema Council (15), the Indonesian parliament (11). Meanwhile, other institutions whose responses are below the number 10 are the Ministry of Transportation (7), the Vice President (7), and the National Police (2). The data set also shows 2 TNI responses in handling this pandemic. It is interesting considering that the TNI is not included in its regulations and actors.

Figure 4 is the percentage in terms of government response as described above.

## 4.2 *Proportions of Response at Central Level*

The following descriptive statistic is looking at DKI Jakarta and West Java. Of the 93 regulations in DKI Jakarta province, the dataset shows four regulations with more than 10. These regulations are 32 Governor Decrees, 24 Circulars, 16 Governor Regulations, and 10 Governor Appeals. Of the 93 regulations, the Governor of DKI Jakarta is the dominant actor in handling the pandemic in this province, namely 66.

**Table 1** Number of regulations and percentage of DKI Jakarta Covid-19 handling regulations

| Regulation | Total | Percentage |
|---|---|---|
| Governor's Decree | 32 | 34.40 |
| Circular Letter | 24 | 25.80 |
| Governor's Regulation | 16 | 17.20 |
| Governor's Instruction | 10 | 10.75 |

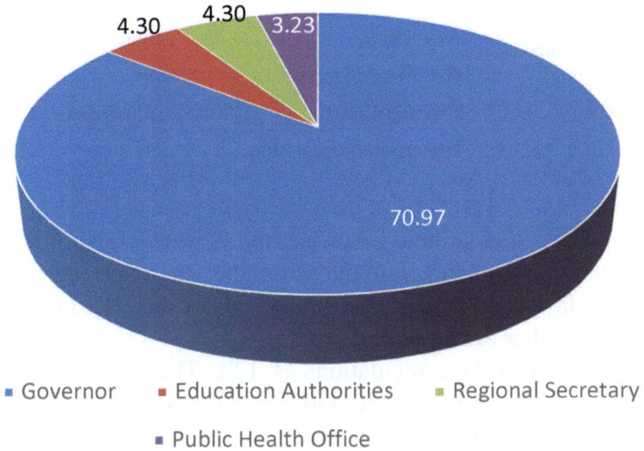


**Fig. 5** The proportion of actors in DKI Jakarta

The rest are related agencies whose numbers are below 10, namely the Education Office (4), Regional Secretary (4), and Health Office (3). Table 1 describes the number of regulations and percentages in DKI Jakarta based on the data set.

Figure 5 also illustrates the percentage of the dominant actor's role in handling Covid-19 in DKI Jakarta. The previous description shows the role of the Governor as a significant regional head in implementing these regulations.

## *4.3 Proportions of Actors in DKI Jakarta*

Out of 198 responses, the Governor of DKI Jakarta remained leading with 76 responses for the government's response. This data was followed by the Deputy Governor of DKI Jakarta with 31 responses, Polda Metro with 12 responses, and the Transportation Service with ten responses. All four are the results of a dataset whose responses are above the number 10. Table 2 describes the number of responses and their percentages.

Then the descriptive statistical picture in West Java also shows the same pattern as DKI Jakarta. The similarity is the number of local government responses that

**Table 2** Number of responses to handling Covid-19 DKI Jakarta

| Actors | Total | Percentage |
|---|---|---|
| Governor | 76 | 38.38 |
| Deputy Governor | 31 | 15.66 |
| Regional Police of Jakarta | 12 | 6.06 |
| Department of Transportation | 10 | 5.05 |

**Table 3** Number of regulations and percentage of regulations for handling Covid-19 West Java

| Regulation | Total | Percentage |
|---|---|---|
| Governor's Decree | 68 | 53.12 |
| Circular Letter | 25 | 19.53 |
| Governor's Regulation | 24 | 18.75 |

exceed the applicable regulations. Likewise, the Governor also plays a significant role compared to other agencies from the actor side. Then in terms of the number of regulations, West Java is more than DKI Jakarta. However, DKI Jakarta is still above West Java in the number of responses.

The number of West Java regulations is 128. The dataset results show that three regulations are above 10, namely Governor Decrees (68), Circulars (25), and Governor Regulations (24). The thing that is of concern in West Java is that there are 4 Ministerial Decree regulations and 1 Government Regulation which are central rules but are the basis for handling Covid-19 in West Java. Table 3 describes the number of these regulations.

Meanwhile, the Governor of West Java became the most dominant among other actors in terms of actors. The central government and the Ministry of Health are also two other actors who play a role in West Java. Figure 6 shows the percentage of these actors.

## *4.4 Proportions of Actors in West Java*

Then the response of the West Java government, out of 184 responses, the Governor of West Java also dominates in this data set, which is 151. The Covid-19 Task Force follows other actors, as many as 7, the Health Office and the Regional Secretary each, and the Education Office 1. Table 4 illustrates the number of responses and their percentage.

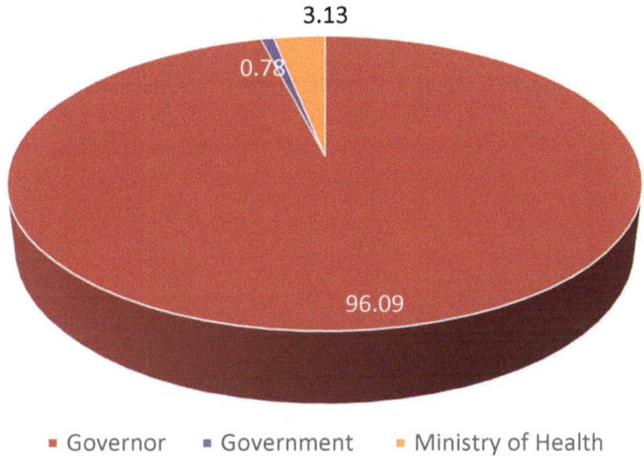


**Fig. 6** The proportion of actors in West Java

**Table 4** Number of responses for handling Covid-19 West Java

| Actors | Total | Percentage |
|---|---|---|
| Governor | 76 | 41.30 |
| Satgas Covid-19 | 31 | 16.84 |
| Regional Secretary | 12 | 6.52 |
| Public Health Office | 10 | 5.43 |
| Education Authorities | 1 | 0.54 |

## 5 Explaining Indonesia's Covid-19 Responses Through Presidential Regulations and Media Statements

This dataset is helpful to potential users who are deeply concerned with analysing the dynamics in national-local pandemic policies and plan to utilise the discourse analysis by capturing the delivered discourses by policymakers. This section demonstrates the use of the dataset by capturing the regulations and media statements issued by President Joko Widodo during the first year of the global pandemic.

President Joko Widodo was selected as the sample data because the executive branch is the most influential stakeholder in handling the national threat with its power exercise and budget allocation. Therefore, every national response is part of the presidential responses and statements, including ministerial directions, task forces, security mobilisation, or other circular letters. President Widodo, a prominent figure from the dominant party in the parliament, should ensure the checks and balances mechanism between the executive and legislative running properly, especially during the extraordinary situation.

First, there are 14 regulations issued in the presidential level in March 2020–March 2021, which are consists of one Act (Undang-Undang), one government regulations

**Table 5** Distribution of legislation issued by the president (March 2020–March 2021) in three sectors

| Legislation | Economic sector | Health sector | Other social sectors | Total |
|---|---|---|---|---|
| Undang-Undang | 1 | | | 1 |
| Perppu | 1 | | 1 | 2 |
| PP | 4 | | 1 | 5 |
| Perpres | 1 | 2 | | 3 |
| Keppres | | 3 | | 3 |
| **Total** | **7** | **5** | **2** | **14** |

in-lieu-of Acts (Peraturan Pemerintah Pengganti Undang-Undang or Perppu), five government regulations (Peraturan Pemerintah or PP), three presidential regulations (Peraturan Presiden or Perpres), and three presidential decrees (Keputusan Presiden or Keppres). This article coded the issued regulations into three sectors: economic, health, and other social sectors, because of the need to test the academic consensus that Widodo's default position is prioritising economic over health concerns. Other social sectors include local elections and holiday allowances for civil servants.

According to Table 5, the number of legislation forms issued at the presidential level in economics, health, and other social sectors has increased. In a broader context, Widodo's administration has responded most effectively through government regulations on economic incentives and arrangements. The point of the study is not to arrive at the conclusion that the greater the number, the higher the priority will be. However, a further examination of media statements will be conducted to confirm this preliminary pattern.

Based on the data collected, the president has imposed regulations on the economic sector in order to prevent a more severe economic disaster. The first legal basis for accomplishing this will be the first Perppu, released in March 2020 under the pretext of an "exceptional situation." According to the Minister of Finance, exceptional measures[1] were required to "save the people and their economy," as documented in the dataset. These included implementing fiscal expansion policies, loosening monetary policies, lowering Central Bank interest rates, pumping liquidity or quantitative easing measures, and loosening regulations in the financial sector. Following this, in May 2020, the extraordinary measures were incorporated into the Law of Number 2 of 2020 about State Financial Policy and Financial Stability for Handling the Covid-19 Pandemic [8], which was signed into law. In addition, as part of the Law of

[1] Government Regulations in Lieu of Law (Perppu) is a statutory regulation set by the president in matters of compelling urgency. The president can issue a Perppu on the basis of three things. First, there is an urgent need to resolve legal issues quickly based on the law. Second, the required law does not yet exist so that there is a legal vacuum, or third, there is a law but it is not sufficient. The legal vacuum cannot be overcome by making laws procedurally because it takes a long time. The government guarantees that the Perppu does not threaten freedom of expression because it is already guaranteed in Article 28 of the 1945 Constitution.

Number 2 of 2020s operational regulatory framework, four government regulations (PP) are relevant to Covid-19-induced financial settlements.

Besides other regulatory frameworks at the presidential level, there is other derivative legislation at the ministerial level, such as the ministerial directions, decrees, and circular letters, to translate the substantive points into more operational. As a part of the cabinet, the ministries took necessary measures according to their mandates. One prominent example is the Ministry of Health, which issued 65 regulations regarding the public health system and the handling of the Covid-19 pandemic. Then, the Ministry of Finance issued 94 regulations regarding financial arrangements. Last, the Ministry of Transportation issued 59 regulations regarding human mobility restrictions and other arrangements. The dataset also recorded the mentioned ministerial legislation.

The dataset also recorded media statements released by the president regarding the pandemic and how the government was trying to contain the outbreak and save the state's economic tensions. There are 91 media statements from the president in major national news media (KompasTV, Tempo, and Pikiran Rakyat). For the needs of this article, we coded 90 statements into the same three sectors: economic, health, and other social sectors. The coding is based on our interpretation, which might experience the researcher's bias about the delivered languages. However, we put objectivity to the standard. Also, the president's messages contained mixed interpretations from time to time due to economic and health matters being put on one occasion. To interpret this type of sentence, we count the words and decide which sectors are delivered in more words.

There are 22 statements regarding economics, 50 statements regarding health, and 19 statements regarding other social sectors (motivational public message, information about vaccine acquisition, human mobility, holiday, etc.). The dataset recorded Widodo's fluctuated statements between economic concerns, health concerns, and other social concerns in one-year period.

The fluctuation was demonstrated in the early outbreak in Wuhan, China, when the president had lost the sense of crisis and urgency. President Widodo was one of the populist leaders who actively downplayed the outbreak threat and prioritised the economy over health during the initial yet critical time frame in January–February 2020. Along with his ministers, including the Minister of Health himself, he established a public narrative to downplay and deny the outbreak in Wuhan to avoid social unrest in the community [9]. Also, the administration complacently omitted the World Health Organization (WHO)'s recommendations to increase testing and preventative measures when Indonesia has not reported any cases yet [10]. The concern escalated when Indonesia recorded its first two cases. Widodo said on 15 March 2020, when the first large-scale social restriction was imposed: "*we must work hard to contain the outbreak and minimise the economic impact by working, studying, and praying from home. This moment is the time when we should help each other to get this over with.*" However, in other occasions, the president also relied in the wishful messages that not evidence-based, when saying: "*I believe the pandemic will be over in the end of the year and next year there will be a booming in tourism*" (16 April 2020) and "*we have to live side by side with Covid to have a more productive and safe society. It is inevitable by doing the new normal*" (15 May 2020). Later he said, "*our positivity rate is still high; this is our homework*" (3 August 2020), and "*the society must obey the health protocols and the 2-weeks social restrictions*" (9 August 2020).

After analysing the regulations and media statements, it is clear that the delivered messages by the presidents have fluctuated, with health concerns dominating the discourse. The president constantly reminds the public that health protocols and social restrictions should be obeyed at any time. With constant and participative measures, the president also promised that the country could minimise the economic crisis caused by the pandemic. It is often perceived as Widodo's lip service. However, the legislations are more economic oriented, illustrated by the financial arrangements in the highest form of legislation, the law (undang-undang), and the numerous legislations issued by the financial sectors. Not to mention that the Covid-19 handling task forces were filled by prominent financial/economic leaders. Widodo's message and measures in handling the pandemic were inconsistent.

## 6 Conclusion

From the explanation above, this article portrays the uses of the government regulations and media statements on Covid-19 datasets from March 2020 until March 2021. This article shows that the dataset indicates that the central government tried to minimise the economic contraction caused by the pandemic by releasing several regulations which are primarily on economic and financial orientation. However, the use of this dataset is not only limited as provided in this article. This dataset can be used for further study and analysis of the policies or regulations response to the pandemic and the motive of central or local government in response to the Covid-19 pandemic or the reason why there are several contradictions between central and local government policies in response the pandemic.

**Acknowledgements** The authors would like to thank LPDP Rispro Mandatori as the primary funder of the development of the dataset. We also acknowledge assistance from Rizky Bintang Pratama (Indonesia Defence University) for collecting and organising the data.

## References


1. Satuan Tugas Penanganan COVID-19 (2022) Kasus Covid-19 Di Indonesia (Jakarta), https://covid19.go.id/. Satgas Covid
2. Badan Pusat Statistik (2020) Analisis Hasil Survei Dampak Covid-19 Terhadap Pelaku Usaha (Jakarta). https://www.bps.go.id/publication/2020/09/15/9efe2fbda7d674c09ffd0978/analisis-hasil-survei-dampak-covid-19-terhadap-pelaku-usaha.html
3. Badan Pusat Statistik (2021) Perilaku Masyarakat Pada Masa PPKM Darurat, Hasil Survei Perilaku Masyarakat Pada Masa Pandemi Covid-19, Periode 13–20 Juli 2021 (Jakarta). https://www.bps.go.id/publication/2021/08/02/29234b08faa4910dee5279af/perilaku-masyarakat-pada-masa-ppkm-darurat--hasil-survei-perilaku-masyarakat--pada-masa-pandemi-covid-19--periode-13-20-juli-2021.html
4. Muzykant V, Barabas V, Muqsith MA (2021) Fake news on Covid-19 in Indonesia. In: Berube DM (ed) Pandemic communication and resilience. Springer, Cham, pp 363–377. https://doi.org/10.1007/978-3-030-77344-1_22
5. Law of the Republic Of Indonesia Number 12 of 2011 on Legislation Making, Article 7
6. Law of the Republic Of Indonesia Number 12 of 2011 On Legislation Making, Article 8
7. Anwar A et al (2020) Role of mass media and public health communications in the COVID-19 pandemic. Cureus 12(9). https://doi.org/10.7759/cureus.10453
8. Ministry of Finance (2020) Law No. 2 of 2020 is evidence of the state to provide protection from Covid-19 impact. Ministry of Finance. https://www.kemenkeu.go.id/en/publications/news/law-no2-of-2020-is-evidence-of-the-state-to-provide-protection-from-covid-19-impact
9. Fealy G (2020) Jokowi in the Covid-19 era: repressive pluralism, dynasticism and the overbearing state. Bull Indones Econ Stud 56(3):301–323. https://doi.org/10.1080/00074918.2020.1846482.
10. Jaffrey S (2020) Coronavirus blunders in Indonesia turn crisis into catastrophe. Carnegie Endowment for International Peace. https://carnegieendowment.org/2020/04/29/coronavirus-blunders-in-indonesia-turn-crisis-into-catastrophe-pub-81684

# Impaired Institutionalisation of Special Autonomy and Perpetuation of Conflict in Papua, Indonesia

**Mardyanto Wahyu Tryatmoko**

**Abstract** Scholars have been debating the role of autonomy in resolving ethnic or separatist conflict. As the conflict persists despite the application of autonomy, scholars have been trying to identify factors that make autonomy perpetuates conflict. Due to ongoing humanitarian concerns in Papua, this article discusses how special autonomy (SA) has affected conflict in this region. Different from existing studies that tend to disregard comprehensive dimension of autonomy and focus merely on the role of institutions in conflict, this study examines institutionalisation of SA by scrutinising its three facets (relationship between SA institutions and their external environment, institutional changes and continuities, and internal dynamics of local institutions) in three dimensions of autonomy (political, fiscal, and administrative). This article shows that the institutionalisation of special autonomy in Papua has perpetuated separatist conflict and led to various internal conflict because it is impaired by three issues. First, external influences and pressures particularly from central state do not conform to local needs, values, and expectations. Second, institutional change and continuity are uncertain and ceremonial due to a combination between the domination of the central state and unresolved political contestation in the local dynamics. Third, internal dynamics of institutions are marked by competing logics and forms of dissociated agency due to the ambiguity of institutional rules and structures alongside ethnic contestation.

**Keywords** Special autonomy · Institutionalisation · Conflict · Papua · Indonesia

## 1 Introduction

The use of many forms of decentralisation or autonomy to resolve types of separatist conflict has been endorsed by some scholars and international agencies since the late of 1990s (see [1, 26, 34]). However, amidst this support, some scholars [7, 18, 27]

M. W. Tryatmoko (✉)
National Research and Innovation Agency, Jakarta, Indonesia
e-mail: mardyanto@gmail.com



Nawawi et al. (eds.), *Managing Disruption and Developing Resilience for a Better Southeast Asia*, Springer Proceedings in Humanities and Social Sciences,
https://doi.org/10.1007/978-981-96-2116-3_58

have shown the drawback of autonomy in addressing conflict. They not only show the failure of autonomy policy in a region or single case but also provide detailed insight of factors or dimensions of autonomy that contribute to conflict perpetuation. Despite rich studies of the failure of autonomy, existing studies tend to neglect institutionalisation processes and the comprehensive dimensions of autonomy in analysing why autonomy failed or even contribute to conflict perpetuation.

Different from studies focusing on the role of institutions under autonomy or decentralisation in contributing conflict, this article aims to show how the processes of institutionalisation of special autonomy in Papua contribute to conflict rather than ceasing separatist movement. By employing a single case study, this study presents detailed issues of the institutionalisation of special autonomy in Papua, Indonesia, covering three dimensions of autonomy and three facets of institutionalisation that have impacts on conflict perpetuation.

This study employs sociological institutionalism as the most appropriate approach in the new institutionalism to analyse the processes of institutionalisation where multiple pressures from the environments shape actors' behaviour in internal dynamics (see [17, 41]). There is various theorising of institutionalisation in institutional theory, but that in the sociological institutionalism is more relevant to analyse institutions within multiple institutional environments than others in the new institutionalisation. Institutionalisation in the perspective of sociological institutionalism mainly concerns to changes in institutional structures and rules [8, 11, 17, 25]. The changes of structures can occur at any time and this affects either stability or instability (deinstitutionalisation) of institutions [46]. Institutions can have their stability when changes strengthen commitment of members. In contrast, instability or deinstitutionalisation will be likely if changes erode the legitimacy of institutions that maintain the continuity of institutions. This approach is particularly useful to understand problematic institutionalisation of SA in Papua in three facets: the relationships of institutions with external environments, the continuities and changes of institutions, and the internal dynamics of institutions.

The institutionalisation of SA in Papua has run far from initial expectation of the central government and Papuan supporters to end conflict. Rather, it contributes to conflict because the institutionalisation is impaired by high pressures and influence from the central state, uncertain continuity and change, and internal fragmentation. In elaborating analysis, this article consists of four sections. The first section provides overview of the relationship between autonomy and conflict. The second section presents the application of special autonomy and the development of conflict in Papua. The third section analyses impaired institutionalisation of special autonomy in Papua and its contribution to conflict. The last section discusses conflict as the impact of impaired institutionalisation of SA in three dimensions of autonomy: political, fiscal, and administrative.

## 2 Autonomy and Conflict

The use of autonomy currently is beyond what scholars [9, 10, 49] define as a mean to transfer power or authority from central government to lower-local administrations. In dealing with conflict resolution, some scholars [14, 27, 28, 33, 58] perceive unique types of decentralisation or autonomy which can be able to address ethnic conflict particularly related to separatist movement. In this context, the delegation of more power and authority to specific regions is aimed to be part of policy to accommodate the interests of ethnic groups in order to address secessionist demand [48] or to "contain intrastate conflict" [3].

The impact of decentralisation or regional autonomy on either perpetuating or resolving conflict has become prolonged debate among scholars. The debate remains prevalent especially in the countries where separatist-related insurgencies emerge. There are some arguments that have been developed by both proponent and opponent of autonomy in managing conflict to defend each of stance.

Many scholars [5, 22, 26, 31, 51, 40, 43, p. 59, 59] and leading agencies such as United Nations Development Programme (e.g. [1]) not only believe but also support the application of autonomy as a democratic way to manage separatist insurgencies related to religious, economic, and ethnic issues. Success story in the application of autonomy in some countries including Canada, Belgium, India, the United Kingdom, and Spain [3, 9, p. 652, 10] supports advocates for autonomy. These cases, then, are used by the proponents of autonomy or federalism to justify that no secession movement has succeeded in democratic decentralising countries [5]. The advocates of federalism or autonomy argue that political accommodation and collective power sharing embedded in the measure are effectively used to regulate the diversity of ethnic groups, including to address ethnic conflict, while keeping the states unified and democratic.

Meanwhile, unexpected evidence in Czechoslovakia, Yugoslavia, Southern Sudan, and Eritrea shows that autonomy has little positive impact in reducing ethnic tensions or conflicts. For some scholars [7, 18], autonomy measure or federalism to resolve ethnic conflict can be counterproductive, leading to secession and further conflict instead of accommodating local rights. Institutions become main variable in determining the occurrence of conflict as they may escalate secessionism, ethnic mobilisation, and violent conflict [14, 23].

Recently, the discussion has apparently been shifted from the debate between the supporters and the critics of autonomy to the discussion on why autonomy failed to address conflict. Rather than showing the best practices of autonomy, currently more researchers have been interested in scrutinising the negative effect of autonomy on conflict. The failure of autonomy to address conflict in some regions has brought some scholars to question what makes autonomy failed. Some of them believe that autonomy has indirect impact upon conflict dynamics, but they tend to present big picture of autonomy issues. Some scholars go advance by explaining the conditions of autonomy that contribute to conflict. Siegel for instance argues that autonomy likely contribute to conflict in the situation where established federal structures experience higher level of sub-national tax revenue and residual governing authorities exercised by sub-national legislatures. The existing literatures suggest that there lacks study that explicitly examine particular aspects of autonomy arrangements which may contribute to conflict.

Studies connecting between autonomy and conflict have developed in two aspects. In the first aspect, scholars deal with institutional factors explaining how autonomy leads to conflict. Including in this aspect is the explanation of institutional failure leading to conflict due to the issues of institutional arrangement [2, 4, 19, 47) and power sharing [37]. Different institutional perspective is discussed by Bakke and Wibbels [4] emphasising on how the capacity of federal institution to discern the characteristic or situation of their societies determines the preservation of peace. In the view of Bakke and Wibbels [4], the operation of decentralisation is likely to produce conflict in the situation where interregional inequality is high, when minority regions are not to be included in national political institutions, and when there is a concentration of ethnic groups in a region.

Different institutional perspective is raised by Miodownik and Cartrite [42] focusing on the role of institutions in conflict. According to Miodownik and Cartrite [42], conflict is likely to emerge as the minority controls political institutions. In the operation of autonomy or decentralisation, conflict is also perpetuated because political parties at the local level mobilise ethnic groups in conflict.

The last type of institutional explanation of conflict emergence is the institutional history or condition that shapes the performance of autonomy leading to conflict. This perspective can be found in Bertrand's [6] analysis explaining the history of national political landscape that contributes to the failure of autonomy in Papua, Indonesia.

From the discussion of institutional factors explaining how autonomy contributes to conflict, it shows variety of perspectives that scholars can put in. However, none of them is aware of the process of institutionalisation as the institutions may need sometimes to adjust with their environments. Thus, this is important for this article to analyse how autonomy can contribute to conflict by explaining the process of institutionalisation.

The second aspect of how scholars identify the connection between autonomy and conflict is to explain closely the dimensions of autonomy. In this aspect, the most scholars are interested in examining the political dimension of autonomy that contributes to conflict. Political dimension of autonomy mainly deals with matters related to representative institutions, political parties, and electoral systems. The attention to behaviour or action of political parties in local autonomy has been brought by, for instance, Brancati. By examining the role of political parties in an autonomy scheme in Czechoslovakia in the early 1990s, she argues that regional parties contribute to conflict because they mobilise groups, create regional fragmentation, and advocate policies that discriminate against minorities. For some regions, including Indonesia in its most cases of autonomy arrangements, such attention to the practice of political parties is absence because they do not apply autonomy for political parties. However, other factors than political parties, such as party and electoral system under autonomy practice and the degree of autonomy that vary in different countries may determine the likelihood of conflict. As Cohen [12] points out, political parties within multi-party system in a proportional system tend to generate less conflict than those in majoritarian system. According to Cohen [12], the majoritarian system tends to reinforce ethnic division and this possibly contributes to aggravated ethnic tension. Moreover, federalism provides more political vents to sub-national government than does a unitary system. This is similar to what Linz and Montero [35] emphasise that new representative institutions, different processes of regional election, and devolved resources are challenges to inclusive political integration. In this case, it contributes to conflict.

Fiscal dimension of autonomy is the second attention of scholars in analysing the contribution of autonomy to conflict. Although the examination of fiscal autonomy in relation with conflict is underdeveloped compared to political dimension of autonomy, most scholars use cross-country analysis to examine fiscal arrangements of autonomy contributing to conflict. Fiscal transfer is desirable for the minority groups [55]. Thus, in order to reduce secessionist demands, as Sorens [53] argues, central states should make locals fiscally dependent upon them by restricting the capability of regional tax-collection and providing more grants to secessionist groups. The contribution of fiscal dimension of autonomy to conflict has been indicated by some scholars. According to them, fiscal decentralisation has contributed to regional disparities that are likely to increase the likelihood of conflict. However, the ability of locals to generate local revenues will contribute to lower number of violent incidents [39].

Different from the two dimensions (political and fiscal) of autonomy, administrative dimension of autonomy gets little attention from scholars who examine the relationship between autonomy and ethnic secessionist conflict. However, current studies on administrative dimension of autonomy provide useful insights for further examination of autonomy contributing to conflict. Zhou [60], for instance, emphasises on capacity of local institutions in running decentralised policies that in some cases also disregard its effect on preventing conflict. Meanwhile, Oberst [44] focuses on conflict in internal bureaucracy as a result of actions conducted by bureaucrats and political officers to benefit their own interests. Other attention paid by some scholars (see [21, 56]) is about the interaction or conflict between government administration and public at local level due to problems of resource allocation. The last insight is issues of relationships among tiers of government in managing public service deliveries (see [15, 20]). The examination of the administrative relationship is necessary in analysing its impact on conflict, but most literature [32, 36] tends to conflate delegation with deconcentration, with the result that it does not adequately comprehend the impacts of administrative processes on conflict. Basic assumption of delegation in special autonomy is that relationships among tiers of government should not be heavily determined by the central government. In this context, local political institutions have relative autonomy to influence local bureaucracy in implementing administrative tasks [38].

As it lacks from current literature, the examination of autonomy in three comprehensive dimensions is necessary to be brought to get full picture of how autonomy affects conflict in Papuan case. In public administration perspective, autonomy is commonly divided into three dimensions: political, fiscal, and administrative. This categorisation aligns with common package of autonomy policy in most countries as to provide greater political participation of locals, better public services, and encourage fiscal independency of locals. The examination of the three comprehensive dimensions of autonomy is applicable in assessing special autonomy for Papua because the dimensions cover most strategic provisions in SA.

## 3 The Arrangements of Special Autonomy and the Development of Conflict in Papua

There are various terms for asymmetrical autonomy such as territorial and cultural autonomy [14], asymmetrical federalism [13], or asymmetrical devolution [57]. In Indonesia, this type of autonomy is best known as special autonomy (SA, *otonomi khusus*). Special autonomy formalised under the Law 21 Year 2001 is one of measures to resolve conflict in Papua. This measure is likely more promising than other policies such as military approach, development, and regional proliferation because it covers relatively comprehensive aspects dealing with the roots of conflict.

In Papua, the existing arrangement of SA covers some areas including three conceptual dimensions of autonomy: political, fiscal, and administrative. In political dimension, SA regulates gubernatorial elections, the establishment of Papuan People Council (MRP, *Majelis Rakyat Papua*), and the establishment of special seats in the provincial parliament. From this dimension of autonomy, Papuans expected that the representation of their people in representative organisations at local level increases [52, pp. 99–101]. As Papuans felt that they did not have enough space to decide their own needs, through political autonomy they would have greater political power in decision-making processes [52, pp. 170–173].

The fiscal dimension of autonomy especially refers to redistribution of fiscal transfers from the national government to indigenous Papuans (local ethnic people), so the provision of a special fund under SA is in this category. One of the goals of the provision is to improve the welfare of Papuans. Papuans expected that the allocation of SA funds from the central government would increase their income and their participation in modern economic activities. The improvement of Papuans' welfare is required to eliminate their dissatisfaction or resentment at their economic marginalisation as under Indonesian rule [52, p. 174].

Meanwhile, the category of administration autonomy covers special management of public service sectors such as education, health, infrastructure, and socio-economic policy. From this dimension, indigenous Papuans expected that they would enjoy better living conditions, especially the improvement of their health and education [52, p. 180]. Papuans hoped that they would no longer suffer from low quality of life because of insufficient health and education services, particularly in remote areas [52, pp. 114–115]. The initiators of SA believed that such promising provisions under this administrative dimension of SA would eliminate Papuans' feelings of alienation and discrimination by the central state.

Such promising arrangements in fact, have not been smoothly met. In political aspect, Papuans enjoyed their native governors who have been elected from among themselves since 2005 election. But, in the operation of SA the electoral systems (nomination and voting procedures) have been frequently changing following central directions without having local consent. As locals are in nonconformity with central changes, they develop traditional voting practices. Instead of harmonising voting system, the local practices contribute to complex system in which fraud and manipulation take place.

The MRP was successfully established in 2005. But this institution was frequently in confrontation with the central government as some Papuan activists being members of MRP fought to defend Papuan rights. Since then, the central government restricted activists from being involved in the MRP nomination. This leads to serial protest from Papuan and rejection of the continuity of MRP.

Different from the two political arrangements, the establishment of special seats in local parliament was disrupted by prolonged debates between proponents and opponents of this arrangement. The debate lasted for about 16 years and hence the special seats have just been established in 2018.

In the fiscal arrangement, large amounts of money go to Papua from the central government every year from 2003. But Papuans especially those who are in village feel to have no improvement in their living while the number of corruptions tends to increase since the allocation of SA funds.

In the meantime, poor public service delivery indicates the problem of administrative sector of SA. The number of literation rate that remains low (below national standard) shows education services under SA is far from Papuans' expectation. The problem of public service delivery is also in health sector, where Papua remains experiencing malnutrition and disease outbreak in some areas.

Such issues of SA implementation show that the policy is still far from expectation of Papuans. They feel that there is no SA implemented as they got nothing from the implementation of SA. Many protests from Papuans that have been delivered to central government indicate dissatisfaction and resentment. In 2005 MRP and many Papuan activists rejected the continuity of SA. The rejection and protest then continue in years after.

Data from national violence monitoring system of Indonesia shows that conflict in Papua tends to increase during the implementation of SA. The conflict emerges in various categories including separatist, political, and government-related conflict. This indicates that SA cannot work as a mean to resolve conflict in Papua. Instead, the institutionalisation of SA is likely to contribute to conflict.

## 4 Impaired Institutionalisation of SA and Conflict in Papua

This section discusses how the institutionalisation of SA in political, fiscal, and administrative dimensions leads to conflict. The examination shows contrast situations from regular theorising of institutionalisation in sociological institutionalism describing stable and persistent institutionalisation. Institutionalisation of SA in Papua, however, shows impairment which is indicated by three issues. First, the relationships of institutions with external environments bring non-conformity of values, norms, and expectations with locals due to insensitive policy transfer and unintended political and administrative pressures from the central state. Second, continuities and changes of SA institutions are uncertain or loose durable trajectories because they are the product of political contentions and partially and exclusively follow interests of either central state or local elites. Third, internal dynamics of institutions are fragmented and conflictual and this hinders local actors to get a consensus to develop SA structures based on local preferences. These three characteristics of impaired institutionalisation of SA erode the legitimacy of SA, create more fragmentation within Papuans, and contribute to various conflict, including perpetuation of separatist conflict between Papuans and the central government. The following three sub-sections discuss the problems in more detail.

### *4.1 Institutional Unconformity with External Pressures*

To understand the process of institutionalisation of SA and its impact on conflict, the first facet of institutionalisation to examine is in how local institutional practices and actors deal with pressures and influences of their external environments. In relation to the operation of SA, the external pressures and influences can come from central state agencies, various groups of local society, modus operandi of Indonesian political parties, and global norms and values about the recognition of indigenous and minority protection and empowerment. From the examination of this facet of institutionalisation, my finding indicates that the local institutions (practices and actors) of SA have been struggling to conform to complex pressures and influences of values, interests, and structures that are inflected by contradictory approaches and ideologies to ethnicity and nationalism. These differences frequently manifest in conflicting views and approaches to questions of autonomy and independence and views about how these are to be managed and negotiated through SA.

Among external agencies, the central state is the most dominant agent that largely puts pressure on the operation of SA. The central pressures become problematic as these disrupt, instead of bringing in sustainability, the institutionalisation of SA. This is somewhat paradoxical as the central state should contribute to effective institutionalisation of SA as this is a way to reduce separatist demands. However, my analysis shows, across three dimensions of institutionalisation, that the central government routinely intervenes in and acts upon SA provisions and operationalisation in a way that compromises SA and the goal of conflict reduction because it tends to see elements of SA as a threat or an opportunity to install national order. My findings indicate the national state agencies disrupt the institutionalisation of SA through indirect and direct interventions.

Indirect pressures manifest not as specific imposition of the central state that usually comes with special rules and directives. Rather, the pressures indirectly force local institutions to meet national standards that are not in accordance with SA arrangements. Including this is how local institutions are required to comply general regulation in managing SA funds distribution and providing public service function. This compliance with general regulation is needed because provision of SA law is unclear and there is no support from central state for clarifying the provision.

The ways local actors comply with national standards hinder them to develop local rules and structures to operationalise prescribed structural SA arrangements. This situation brings the operation of SA being away from the goals of SA. Besides, my findings indicate that local bureaucracy is also unable to meet national standard for public services especially in education and health sector. Local bureaucracy experiences poor performance of public services in the administrative dimension of SA. This, then, leads to indirect conflict because local dissatisfaction with institutional practices fuels separatist sentiments.

In the meantime, direct pressures of the central state that are aimed at institutional practices of SA are conducted through formal imposition by using special regulations and directives. The central state directly imposes rules and policies mostly on political dimension of SA including direct voting system in the gubernatorial elections and restrictions on Papuan activists in any political recruitment at local level. In gubernatorial elections, although SA law (21/2001) regulates voting process through local parliament (DPRP), central government has never given chance to administer the process under SA. Central government changed the voting system from indirect to direct (by people) without having proper consultation with Papuans. Moreover, direct political intervention also occurs in every selection of Papuan People Council (MRP) member, whereas the central determines the last proper list who can sit in the council. It seems that there are at least two reasons why central government intensively and directly intervenes the operation of SA: to prevent the development of secessionist movement and to install national order.

My finding shows that central impositions are in fact not uniform. There are different views or responses to local structures and processes. In some cases, as in responding the use of the *Noken* system in the elections and the establishment of special seats of the DPRP, state agencies made conflicting directions. The Ministry of Home Affairs was in its position to reject Noken system while the Constitutional Court was allowing the application of this system. These differences in turn generate turmoil in the internal dynamics of Papuan institutions.

The direct interventions have impaired the institutionalisation of SA. This is because the pressures do not align with local values and expectations. Moreover, the pressures have clearly irritated Papuans. Thus, the non-conformity has led to conflict.

Central pressures can be identified in all dimensions of SA (political, fiscal, and administrative). In political dimension of SA, central government has intervened the process of institutionalisation of gubernatorial elections, Papuan People Council, and special seats in local parliament (DPRP).

In the perspective of sociological institutionalism, external institutional pressures can bring more stable institutions when internal expectation conform to external values, needs, and interests.

The mainstream of sociological institutionalism tends to perceive that pressures from state and society lead to conformity among institutions and to organisations that support the sustainability of legitimated institutional practices (see [17, 45, 50, 54]). The implementation of SA closely engages with external environments that also contribute to the direction of institutions. After 17 years of its implementation, it seems that SA has been challenged by non-conformity with values, norms, and expectations of such external environments. Challenging the mainstream of sociological institutionalism, the Papuan case illustrates that sustaining institutionalisation is difficult, as local practices and actors face the strain of adapting to diverse pressures and norms shaped by competing ideologies of ethnicity and nationalism. These tensions often surface in divergent perspectives on autonomy and independence, as well as in disagreements over how such issues should be addressed and negotiated within the framework of SA.

## 4.2 *The Uncertainty of Institutional Change and Continuity*

The second facet of institutionalisation that is examined in the operation of SA is the continuity and change of institutions. For this facet, my analysis shows that the bureaucratic practices and processes of SA institutions are unstable, lack of consistency and durable trajectories, and ineffective. Besides, governance environment of SA institutions is challenging and troubled. When continuity of institutional practices, structures, and rules seems to get stable trajectories, it tends to be disrupted by either political tensions or external institutional pressures that bring unnecessary institutional change. As the uncertain change and continuity are marked by contested nationalism and ethnic politics, this contributes to conflict perpetuation in Papua.

The disruptive change of rules in the institutionalisation of SA is clearly seen in the imposition of central government in changing voting mechanism of gubernatorial elections from indirect (through local parliament), as originally prescribed in SA law, to direct voting system. The quick change to adopt direct system was only based on agreement between central government officials and few local elites, without giving an opportunity to Papuans to internalise prescribed mechanism and having public consultation with Papuans (interview, Moha1 and DPRP2, 2018). As not expected by locals, the imposed change led to their non-conformity.

Instead of consolidating SA institutions, the change of electoral system contributed to complex political landscape of Papua. Local non-conformity with the change appeared as Papuans struggled to follow direct voting system. The resistance of local agencies to imposed voting system emerged. Local parliament insisted the application of indirect voting system as this is the most agreed system. The most moderate demand of local parliament is that they need to administer the elections.

Another non-conformity with central imposition is also shown by the demand of some elements of tribal groups to apply traditionally oriented voting system called *Noken* system in gubernatorial elections. For some tribal groups, direct voting system contradicts their custom that usually comes out with a solid decision or vote of one group. Thus, the Noken system is more accommodative to local needs than direct voting system. The Noken system allows one voice representing a tribal group to vote a pair of candidates in the election. It seems democratic voting mechanism when a group claims that a vote is resulted from local deliberation. However, many Papuans agree that *Noken* system is vulnerable to manipulation and fraud. A candidate might approach a head of tribal group to buy votes (with money or by funding a village cultural party) to get support in the election (interview, MRP3, DPRP1, Uncen1, and MOHA1, 2018). This kind of practice is very possible because head of tribal group can provide one vote on behalf the entire voters within the group.

The changes of institutional structures and rules are not only driven by external pressures. My finding indicates that the changes of structures and rules are likely due to the manoeuvre of political dominant actors. The change is brought by local actors who use the idea of change to get recognition of central state and to gain political support in elections or to preserve their power. I call the actors as politico-institutional entrepreneurs. How Suebu administration distributed SA funds is the case of politico-institutional entrepreneurship as they follow central ideology.

In some cases, external pressures make an important contribution to change and continuity in the institutionalisation of SA. Institutional changes in the operation of SA are mostly influenced by political agendas of external actors, including central state rather than evolving from internal commitment of institutions. This is problematic and brings issues of legitimacy as the institutionalisation accommodates more external values, needs, and expectations than local preferences and believes.

The changes of structures and rules in the institutionalisation of SA are problematic and do not promote stability of institutions. Instead, the changes have contributed to institutional disruption.

### *4.3 Internal Dissociation*

The last facet of institutionalisation that I examined in the operation of SA is in internal dynamics. My findings show that the institutionalisation of SA has not been supported by strong commitment of local actors. Instead, local actors have lacked consensus among them in operationalising SA arrangements. I have identified two issues indicating the lack of consensus among local actors. First, after 16 years of SA implementation, among them, local actors have remained to have different perspectives in the development of arrangements of SA. In the case of the establishment of special seats of Papuan People Representative Council, among local politicians and customary proponents have been debating whether this structure is needed or not, although SA law clearly regulates this. In additions, after 16 years they have not reached yet agreement on what element of society the representatives must be from, whether from purely customary or having engagement with political party. The appearance of such different perspectives from different logics or competing logics in SI terms would lead to issues of institutionalisation if there is no dominant logics adopted [16, 29, 30]. In Papuan case, competing logics among actors tend to persist because the complexity of actors' perspectives or logics is shaped not only by contesting nationalism (between central orders and Papuans' needs and expectations) but also political interests of local actors. Because local actors are not able to meet a consensus, this leads to uncertainty and disrupts institutionalisation of SA.

The second issue is a fact that institutional agencies are fragmented in administering SA. This is because a shared interpretive scheme of values, as it is understood by institutionalists [24] as a basic element toward a stable institution, is absent in the coordination of action. In the operation of SA in Papua, the fragmentation of bureaucratic agency clearly occurs with disharmonious relationships and power tension not only among provincial institutions (governor, MRP, and DPRP) but also between provincial and district government. The fragmented agency or I term "dissociated agency" is clearly seen in the institutionalisation of fiscal decentralisation under the SA.

In the distribution of SA funds, both provincial and district government seem to discern and therefore administer the practice of fiscal transfer in accordance with their own logics, thereby giving rise to dissonant bureaucracy. The dissonance is identified by the ambiguity of role, authority, and responsibility of both provincial and district government. The bureaucracy of SA fund distribution follows central orders, but Papuan provincial government adopts the role of dominant authority, following a key principle of SA law (Law 21/2001). Under this principle, the provincial government assumes that it is the leading authoritative agency in distributing SA funds at the local level, including for directing the management of SA fund allocation to district. Meanwhile, because of allowing greater autonomy, district governments use general regulations such as Law Number 32 Year 2004 on local governance, and Law Number 33 Year 2004 on Fiscal Balance between the Central Government and the Regions, as a basis for disbursing money. For districts, this stance provides more benefits, allowing more flexibility in managing the funds, than following provincial orders as directed by the SA law (interview, Gov6, 2018). Due to this flexibility, districts tend to manage SA funds as part of general revenue rather than treat it as special budget for special purposes. However, such tendency and dissonant practices of fund management especially between provincial and district government lead to a serious problem in attaining the outcome.

Internal dissociation of SA institutions marked by competing logics and dissociated agency leads to disengagement of institutional practices from SA arrangements stated in SA law. Such disengagement refers to institutional decoupling, a popular concept in sociological institutionalism. The decoupling in the case of

SA institutionalisation explains how the operation of SA is away from the formal arrangement.

Some empirical evidence showing institutional decoupling can be seen in some cases. In the case of MRP, the central state overly intervened the results of selection process by rejecting some activists selected from process. In the establishment of special seats, local elites tend to do manipulation. In the meantime, the implementation of gubernatorial elections also employed complex systems whereas local people are allowed to use traditional oriented voting system beside formal direct voting system ruled by the central government. Such complex system is not in accordance with the original scheme of SA nor Papuan needs and expectations.

### 4.4 *The Impact of Impaired Institutionalisation on Conflict by Dimensions of SA*

In addition to the analysis of above three facets of institutionalisation contributing to the conflict in Papua, this article presents different types and degrees of conflict in different three dimensions of autonomy (SA). My findings show that among three dimensions of SA, political dimension of SA has led to more conflict than fiscal and administrative dimension.

In the political dimension of SA, the process of institutionalisation of gubernatorial elections, the establishment of MRP, and special seats of DPRP as main cases in which I examined has resulted not only institutional conflict but also violent conflict. Among the three cases, my findings indicate that the institutionalisation of gubernatorial elections and the MRP contributes to similar types of conflict: institutional conflict, friction among and within societal groups, direct violence, and perpetuation of separatist conflict. The effects of both are also relatively expansive because they involve and impact upon a wide range of organisations and societal involvement, including the politics of ethnicity. Meanwhile, conflicts arising from the institutionalisation of special seats in the DPRP tend to be both less violent and less expansive because they are usually limited to political tensions among elites. In addition, the conflicts arising from the gubernatorial elections tend to involve more direct violence than those associated with either the MRP or the DPRP. This is because the complexity of successive changes to electoral systems is directly mobilised in electoral contestations by politicians. Nonetheless, taken together, the conflicts arising from the political dimension of the institutionalisation of SA tend to be more violent and directly linked with violence than in the other dimensions of SA.

In contrast to the political dimension, my findings indicate that issues in fiscal dimension of SA, especially in the institutionalisation of SA fund distribution lead to relatively less political and violent conflict at the local level, particularly taking account of the violence arising from gubernatorial elections. This is because the tensions generated by the impaired institutionalisation of the fiscal dimension of SA tend to play out within and among local institutions rather than through more extensive societal—and especially ethnic—competition and contestation. As with other dimensions, though, the impact of the institutionalisation of SA fund distribution is multifaceted and does contribute directly to some violent conflict at the grassroots in the form of village level conflicts about distribution of funds. However, it does not contribute directly to widespread conflict as the political dimension does.

Meanwhile, as shown in Table 1, the impaired institutionalisation of the administrative dimension of SA indicates no contribution to political and violent conflict. However, this dimension of SA has a relatively more severe impact on the perpetuation of separatist conflict because it undermines the efficacy of SA and hence Papuan perceptions about the promise of SA. This in turn provides fertile ground for activists to point to SA—and by extension the central government—as a failure. Overt local conflict does not arise because communal mobilisation does not occur as it does in the case of the institutionalisation of SA fund distribution. However, poor local administration leads to poor service delivery and health and education outcomes. Regular disease outbreaks are evidence to Papuans of poor health administration performance due to bureaucratic stagnation. Papuan activists mobilise these problems and this fuels tensions between Papua and the Indonesian central government.

From the points above, some reflections can be highlighted. First, the complexity of institutionalisation and the area of competition, both of which are high in the political dimension, tends to determine the degree of conflict with both positive correlated with greater violence. This is especially so when layers of complex changes are imposed through time, and where these structures or systems are applied widely. Second, and not yet noted immediately above, the extent of central pressure determines the degree of conflict. The more the central state imposes structures by coercion, the more likely conflict emerges and the more intense it is likely to be. Third and in contrast, important political and institution tensions—including various forms of fractured relationships—arising from impaired institutionalisation can affect perceptions of the promise of SA and feed into the wider separatist conflict, yet these have less direct effects on violence.

Overall, it seems clear that those dimensions of institutionalisation that are more directly related to political contestation and widely engaged with the populace (elections and fund distribution) generate more conflict and more violent conflict. Meanwhile, those aspects more related to tensions among political elites and institutional operations are relatively less likely to contribute directly to conflict. However, we should not discount the impact of the fiscal and administrative dimensions of SA on conflict because are likely to be central to the failures of SA and thus its undermining and the perpetuation of separatist conflict.

**Table 1** The institutionalisation of SA and its contribution to conflict in Papua

| | Three facets of institutionalisation | | | Effect on conflict |
|---|---|---|---|---|
| | Institutional relationships | Continuity and change | Internal dynamics | |
| *Political dimension* | | | | |
| – Gubernatorial elections | High direct coercion | Complex change | Fragmentation | – Institutional (political) tensions<br>– Friction of societal groups<br>– High-level violent conflict<br>– Perpetuation of separatist conflict |
| – The establishment of MRP | – Insensitive policy transfer<br>– High level of coercion | No substantive changes due to central pressures | 'Institutional decoupling' | – Institutional conflict<br>– Friction of societal groups<br>– Low-level violence<br>– Perpetuation of separatist conflict |
| – Special seats in DPRP | – Intervention of external agency<br>– Political pressures from local sources<br>– Central influence | Lack of change | 'Competing logics' | Political tension, possibly fuelling conflict |
| *Fiscal dimension* | | | | |
| Distribution of SA funds | – Central influence<br>– Narrow political pressures from local sources | Changes due to local politics | – 'Dissociated agency'<br>– 'Institutional decoupling' | – Bureaucratic tensions<br>– Low-level violence at the grass roots |
| *Administrative dimension* | | | | |
| Public service functions | Indirect central pressure | Lack of change | 'Dissociated agency' | – Bureaucratic tensions<br>– Perpetuation of separatist conflict |

# 5 Conclusion

My overall findings indicate that SA in the Papuan case does not achieve stable or effective regional governance. The three-middle columns show issues in three key facets of the institutionalisation of SA. In the relationship between SA institutions and external environments, pressures from the central state dominate the development of special autonomy. This domination hinders the ability of local actors to develop institutional practices that accommodate local Papuan needs, values, and expectation. In terms of institutional change and continuity, SA institutions are affected by forces that either restrain or disrupt (rather than accelerate or consolidate) the process of institutionalisation. Meanwhile, in the internal dynamics of institutions, institutional actors and their practices are fragmented through the play of "competing logics", "dissociated agency", and "institutional decoupling".

These issues are interrelated, and generally appear across the three dimensions of SA, making its institutions impaired rather than stable. This impaired institutionalisation manifests in three ways. First, SA is unable to cope with issues of adaptation to multiple pressures from external environments due to the lack of consensus among local actors and Papuans in general. Second, institutional changes and continuities do not have consistent or durable trajectories because they are the product of political contentions rather than the pursuit of efficiency, effectiveness, and legitimacy. Third, internal fragmentation among local actors has diminished or prevented consensus in developing SA structures based on local preferences, and this has caused prolonged political contestation among them.

The threefold nature of this impaired form of institutionalisation diminishes the legitimacy of SA, destabilises ethnic relationships among Papuans, contributes to conflict among them, and perpetuates separatist conflict between Papuans and the central government. As shown in Table 1, various types of conflict emerge from different issues in the processes of institutionalisation. The most common type of conflict is institutional conflict in the form of political and bureaucratic tensions among institutional actors. Both tensions involve the play of ideology (nationalism) and ethnicity (including as related to differences of view about questions of autonomy and independence) that make them entrenched and difficult to resolve. These kinds of conflict emerge because actors adopt different stances in developing and operationalising institutional structures of SA when it comes to issues "beyond" efficiency and effectiveness. Ideological influences from both external and internal groups shape the identity-based interests of actors and lead them to defend their institutional logics when dealing with SA. The second type of conflict is the perpetuation of separatist conflict. This pattern emerges due to state interventions that prevent activists from participating in local political recruitment and via the consequences of poor SA practices that, in the perspective of Papuan activists, lead to the continued suffering of Papuans. The third type of conflict is friction among and within Papuan societal (customary, religious, and women) groups and within activist organisations. These conflicts occur, inter alia, due to political competition for seats in representative organisations and effects of SA funds distribution. The final type of conflict identified through the analysis is direct violence, which occurs in dynamics surrounding the institutionalisation of gubernatorial election, the establishment of the MRP, and SA fund distribution. The accompanying causes of violent conflict stem from complexities related to the institutionalisation of multiple electoral systems, insensitive policy transfer in the development of the MRP, and fraud and manipulation as part of institutional decoupling in the institutional practices of fund distribution.

In sum, three problematic facets of SA institutionalisation—institutional relationships with external environments, institutional change and continuity, and internal dynamics within institutions—contribute to a form of impaired institutionalisation and thus various types of conflict. These diminish the legitimacy of SA, destabilise ethnic relationships among Papuans, contribute to conflict among them, and perpetuate separatist conflict between Papuans and the central government.

## References

1. Altmann J, Carino L, Flaman R, Kulessa M, Schulz I (2000) The UNDP role in decentralization and local governance: a joint UNDP-Government of Germany evaluation. Evaluation Office UNDP, New York. http://web.undp.org/evaluation/documents/decentralization_final_report.pdf
2. Anderson LM (2006) Exploring the paradox of autonomy: federalism and secession in North America. Reg Fed Stud 14(1):89–112. https://doi.org/10.1080/1359756042000245188
3. Bakke KM (2015) Decentralization and intrastate struggles: Chechnya, Punjab, and Québec. Cambridge University Press, New York
4. Bakke KM, Wibbels E (2006) Diversity, disparity, and civil conflict in federal states. World Polit 59(1):1–50. https://doi.org/10.1353/wp.2007.0013
5. Bermeo N (2002) A new look at federalism: the import of institutions. J Democr 13(2):96–110. https://doi.org/10.1353/jod.2002.0021
6. Bertrand J (2014) Autonomy and stability: the perils of implementation and "divide-and-rule" tactics in Papua, Indonesia. Natl Ethn Polit 20(2):174–199. https://doi.org/10.1080/13537113.2014.909157
7. Bieber F (2002) Bosnia-Herzegovina: developments towards a more integrated state? J Muslim Minor Aff 22(1):205–218. https://doi.org/10.1080/13602000220124917
8. Boasson EL, Wettestad J (2013) EU climate policy: industry, policy interaction and external environment. Ashgate, Surrey and Burlington
9. Brancati D (2006) Decentralization: fueling the fire or dampening the flames of ethnic conflict and secessionism? Int Organ 60(3):651–685. https://doi.org/10.1017/S002081830606019X
10. Brancati D (2009) Peace by design managing intrastate conflict through decentralization. Oxford University Press, Oxford and New York
11. Brint S, Karabel J (1991) Institutional origins and transformations: the case of American community colleges. In: Powell W, DiMaggio P (eds) New institutionalism in organizational analysis. The University of Chicago Press, Chicago, pp 337–360
12. Cohen FS (1997) Proportional versus majoritarian ethnic conflict management in democracies. Comp Pol Stud 30(5):607. https://doi.org/10.1177/0010414097030005004
13. Congleton RD (2006) Asymmetric federalism and the political economy of decentralization. In: Ahmad E, Brosio G (eds) Handbook of fiscal federalism. Edward Elgar, Cheltenham and Northampton, pp 131–153
14. Cornell SE (2002) Autonomy as a source of conflict: Caucasian conflicts in theoretical perspective. World Politics 54(2):245–276. https://doi.org/10.1353/wp.2002.0002

15. Crouch WW (1965) Conflict and co-operation among local governments in the metropolis. Ann Am Acad Pol Soc Sci 359:60–70. https://doi.org/10.1177/000271626535900108
16. DiMaggio P (1983) State expansion and organizational fields. In: Quinn RE, Hall RH (eds) Organizational theory and public policy. Sage, Beverly Hills, CA, pp 147–161.
17. DiMaggio P, Powell W (1983) The iron cage revisited: institutional isomorphism and collective rationality in organizational fields. Am Sociol Rev 48(2):147–160. https://doi.org/10.2307/2095101
18. Dorff RH (1994) Federalism in Eastern-Europe—part of the solution or part of the problem. Publius 24(2):99–114. https://doi.org/10.1093/oxfordjournals.pubjof.a038138
19. Erk J, Anderson L (2009) The paradox of federalism: does self-rule accommodate or exacerbate ethnic divisions? Reg Fed Stud 19(2):191–202. https://doi.org/10.1080/13597560902753388
20. Faust J, Harbers I (2012) On the local politics of administrative decentralization: applying for policy responsibilities in Ecuador. Publius 42(1):52–77. https://doi.org/10.1093/publius/pjq046
21. Gebremichael M (2011) Federalism and conflict management in Ethiopia: case study of Benishangul-Gumuz regional state. Ph.D., Department of Peace Studies, University of Bradford (United Kingdom)
22. Ghai Y (2000) Autonomy as a strategy for diffusing conflict. In: Druckman D, Stern PC (eds) International conflict resolution after the Cold War. National Academies Press, Washington, pp 483–530
23. Green ED (2008) Decentralisation and conflict in Uganda. Confl Secur Dev 8(4):427–450. https://doi.org/10.1080/14678800802539317
24. Greenwood R, Hinings CR (1988) Organizational design types, tracks and the dynamics of strategic change. Organ Stud 9(3):293–316. https://doi.org/10.1177/017084068800900301
25. Greenwood R, Hinings CR (1996) Understanding radical organizational change: bringing together the old and the new institutionalism. Acad Manag Rev 21(4):1022–1054. https://doi.org/10.5465/AMR.1996.9704071862
26. Gurr TR (1994) Peoples against states: ethnopolitical conflict and the changing world system: 1994 presidential address. Int Stud Quart 38(3):347–377. https://doi.org/10.2307/2600737
27. Hannum H (2004) Territorial autonomy: permanent solution or step towards secession? In: Wimmer A et al (eds) Facing ethnic conflicts: toward a new realism. Rowman & Littlefield, Lanham, MD, pp 274–282
28. Haryanto C, Lay B, Purwoko B (2018) Asymmetrical decentralization, representation, and legitimacy in Indonesia: a case study of the Majelis Rakyat Papua. Asian Surv 58(2):365–386. https://doi.org/10.1525/as.2018.58.2.365
29. Hensmans M (2003) Social movement organizations: a metaphor for strategic actors in institutional fields. Organ Stud 24(3):355–381. https://doi.org/10.1177/0170840603024003908
30. Hoffman A (1999) Institutional evolution and change: environmentalism and the U.S. chemical industry. Acad Manag J 42(4):351–371. https://doi.org/10.2307/257008
31. Horowitz DL (2007) The many uses of federalism. Drake Law Rev 55(4):953–969
32. Kingsbury D, Aveling H (eds) (2003) Autonomy and disintegration in Indonesia. Routledge-Curzon, London and New York
33. Kirn T, Khokrishvili E (2008) Will an asymmetrical system of fiscal decentralisation resolve the conflicts in the Republic of Georgia? University of Potsdam. https://publishup.uni-potsdam.de/opus4-ubp/frontdoor/deliver/index/docId/1707/file/paperG9_A1b.pdf
34. Lapidoth R (1994) Autonomy: potential and limitations. Int J Minor Group Rights 1(4):269–290. https://doi.org/10.1163/157181194X00229
35. Linz JJ, Montero JR (1999) The party systems of Spain: old cleavages and new challenges. Estudio/Working Paper 1999/138. Centro de Estudios Avanzados en Ciencias Sociales, Instituto Juan March de Estudios e Investigaciones
36. Loew D (2013) Decentralisation as a model for conflict transformation: the case of Kosovo. Philipps-Universitat Marburg, Marburg

37. Lustick I, Miodownik D, Eidelson R (2004) Secessionism in multicultural states: does sharing power prevent or encourage it? Am Polit Sci Rev 98(2):209–229. https://doi.org/10.1017/S0003055404001108
38. Manor J (2006) Renewing the debate on decentralisation. Commonw Comp Polit 44(3):283–288. https://doi.org/10.1080/14662040600996967
39. Mansoob Murshed S, Tadjoeddin MZ, Chowdhury A (2009) Is fiscal decentralization conflict abating? Routine violence and district level government in Java, Indonesia. Oxf Dev Stud 37(4):397–421. https://doi.org/10.1080/13600810903305224
40. McGarry J, O'Leary B (eds) (1993) The politics of ethnic conflict regulation: case studies of protracted ethnic conflicts, 1st ed. Routledge. https://doi.org/10.4324/9781315003641
41. Meyer JW, Scott WR (1983) Organizational environments: ritual and rationality. Sage, Beverly Hills, CA
42. Miodownik D, Cartrite B (2010) Does political decentralization exacerbate or ameliorate ethnopolitical mobilization? A test of contesting propositions. Polit Res Q 63(4):731–746. https://doi.org/10.1177/1065912909338462
43. Nordquist K-A (1998) Autonomy as a conflict-solving mechanism: an overview. In: Suksi M (ed) Autonomy: applications and implications. Kluwer Law International, The Hague, pp 59–77
44. Oberst R (1986) Administrative conflict and decentralization: the case of Sri Lanka. Public Adm Dev 6(2):163–174. https://doi.org/10.1002/pad.4230060205
45. Oliver C (1991) Strategic responses to institutional processes. Acad Manag Rev 16(1):145–179. https://doi.org/10.2307/258610
46. Oliver C (1992) The antecedents of deinstitutionalization. Organ Stud 13(4):563–588. https://doi.org/10.1177/017084069201300403
47. Roede PG (2009) Ethnofederalism and the mismanagement of conflicting nationalisms. Reg Fed Stud 19(2):203–219. https://doi.org/10.1080/13597560902753420
48. Safran W (1994) Non-separatist policies regarding ethnic minorities: positive approaches and ambiguous consequences. Int Polit Sci Rev 15(1):61–80. https://doi.org/10.1177/019251219401500105
49. Saideman SM, Lanoue DJ, Campenni M, Stanton S (2002) Democratization, political institutions, and ethnic conflict: a pooled time-series analysis, 1985–1998. Comp Pol Stud 35(1):103–129. https://doi.org/10.1177/0010414002035001008
50. Scott WR (1987) The adolescence of institutional theory. Adm Sci Q 32:493–511. https://doi.org/10.2307/2392880
51. Siegle J, O'Mahony P (2006) Assessing the merits of decentralization as a conflict mitigation strategy. Workshop on Decentralization and Democratic Local Governance, USAID, Washington, DC, September 18–19, 2006
52. Solossa, JP (2005) Otonomi Khusus: Mengangkat Martabat Rakyat Papua di dalam NKRI [Special autonomy: conferring the dignity of Papuans within the unitary state of Republic of Indonesia]. Pustaka Sinar Harapan, Jakarta
53. Sorens JP (2016) Secession risk and fiscal federalism. Publius: J Fed 46(1):25–50. https://doi.org/10.1093/publius/pjv037
54. Tolbert PS, Zucker LG (1983) Institutional sources of change in the formal structure of organizations: the diffusion of civil service reform, 1880–1935. Adm Sci Q 28(1):22–39. https://doi.org/10.2307/2392383
55. Tranchant J-P (2008) Fiscal decentralisation, institutional quality and ethnic conflict: a panel data analysis, 1985–2001. Confl Secur Dev 8(4):491–514. https://doi.org/10.1080/14678800802539358
56. van Klinken GA, Schulte Nordholt HGC (2007) Renegotiating boundaries: local politics in post-Suharto Indonesia. KITLV Press, Leiden
57. Wehner JHG (2000) Asymmetrical devolution. Dev South Afr 17(2):249–262. https://doi.org/10.1080/713661401
58. Weller M, Nobbs K (2011) Asymmetric autonomy and the settlement of ethnic conflicts. Purposes of paradise. University of Pennsylvania Press, Philadelphia

59. Weller M, Wolff S (eds) (2005) Autonomy, self-governance, and conflict resolution: innovative approaches to institutional design in divided societies. Routledge, London and New York
60. Zhou Y (ed) (2009) Decentralization, democracy and development recent experience from Sierra Leone. The World Bank, Washington. https://openknowledge.worldbank.org/bitstream/handle/10986/2672/503610PUB0Box31601OFFICIAL0USE0ONY1.pdf?sequence=1

# Reification of Political Parties in Indonesia: Between Organization and Personalization

**Mouliza K. Donna Sweinstani, Esty Ekawati, and Ridho Imawan Hanafi**

**Abstract** Reification is an essential aspect of the institutionalization of a political party. It assesses the extent to which the public knows the party. However, in Indonesia, political parties are likely better known to the public because of certain factors. Thus, elite individuals appear to hold a more significant position than their party organizations and other collective identities that bind the party as a whole. This article examines the issues of reification of political parties in Indonesia, focusing on four parties: the PDIP, the Gerindra Party, the Nasdem Party, and the Democrat Party. The authors employ a concurrent mixed research method, combining qualitative methods using literature studies with quantitative methods in using online public surveys administered to 264 respondents using random sampling techniques. The findings indicate that reification, which should be one of the supporting factors for the institutionalization of political parties, can be a factor that strengthens the phenomenon of political party personification. This finding differs from previous studies on the personalization of political parties, which focused solely on the party's internal dynamics. This study reveals that personalization in political parties occurs because of the presence of powerful figures and the public's perception of these figures. The public recognition of a figure in a political party can make opportunities for internal party parties to further connect the figure as a part of the party's identity. This condition makes it difficult for political parties to manage internal democracy and to provide political education to the public about party knowledge as an organization, which can be one of the party institutionalization variables.

**Keywords** Reification · Political parties · Personalization · Internal party democracy

M. K. D. Sweinstani (✉) · E. Ekawati · R. I. Hanafi
Research Center for Politics, Nasional Research and Inovation Agency (BRIN), Jakarta, Indonesia
e-mail: moul001@brin.go.id



Nawawi et al. (eds.), *Managing Disruption and Developing Resilience for a Better Southeast Asia*, Springer Proceedings in Humanities and Social Sciences,
https://doi.org/10.1007/978-981-96-2116-3_59

## 1 Introduction

The existence of political parties is critical in building democracy since they create democracy and modern political democracy is not possible without political parties [43]. A political party is a political group that participates in general elections; through these elections, political parties can place their candidates to fill public positions [39, p. 57]. Effectively functioning parties will help ensure that political demands are voiced against the government and can later shape policies based on the public's voice [11].

To fulfill their role in a democratic system, parties need institutionalization [13, 33]. Well-institutionalized parties will be able to perform their functional duties better than less-institutionalized parties [3]. Institutionalized parties tend to be strong in society, assisting in the resolving of collective problems and channeling effective preferences from citizens to political elites. Institutionalization of parties can encourage the stability of the pattern of party competition, institutionalize the party system, and encourage electoral accountability [5]. Thus, parties have the potential to contribute to the democratization process, particularly the consolidation of democracy [32].

Party institutionalization is not a single concept. Harmel et al. [15] note several institutionalization studies, some of which are classic studies from Huntington [16], Panebianco [26], and Rose and Mackie [35]. Several studies including Levitsky [20], Randall and Svasand [31], and Basedau and Stroh [3] followed this study. Randall and Svasand's study uses a multidimensional approach to analysis. In this context, institutionalization is understood as the process by which political parties are formed in terms of integrated patterns of behavior and attitudes or culture. Randall and Svasand's approach includes both internal and external dimensions. The internal aspect considers the party's internal development, while the external aspect perceives the party's relationship with the community in which it is located, including other institutions. They are dimensions of the system, value infusion, decisional autonomy, and reification in this internal and external aspect.

Political parties in Indonesia have been facing problems related to institutional development. In the institutionalization process, political parties in post-reform Indonesia keep in the problem of party-personalization where parties are still dominated by one particular figure or individual based on their charisma and patron-client culture [10]. One of the factors that cause party personalization is the "*charisma*" of a party leader, making him a very influential individual for both the party and its constituents [4]. Another factor that also causes personalization is the patronage culture [7]. This culture is built from a patron-client relationship where this relationship makes someone who has strong resources (especially in terms of material) become the holder of power while the others are just followers.

Personalization of political parties can be interpreted as a condition where elite individuals have a more significant position than their party organizations or other collective identities [18, 22, 30]. Political personalization occurs due to internal factors, as stated by Sartori because parties have limited ability to make choices and changes to their institutions [21]. The high level of constituent loyalty to party leaders, increasing roles and influence of the leader [28], the charisma of robust figure [34], and a growing patronage culture within the party [4] all contribute to the limitations of party management. Political personalization within the party can also occur due to several external factors, such as the political system and the electoral system, in particular, the presidential system combined with the direct election mechanism [2, 23, 37, 38] and the multi-party party system [39, 44]

Personalization issues in political parties are also intertwined with voter rationality in the heat of the general election. Nugroho [24] wrote that voters in Indonesia are used to voting based on sentiment factors, identity politics, or party figures, not on the programs offered by parties [24]. The issue of personalization that has emerged in several Indonesian political parties since the New Order has become a challenge in efforts to build the institutionalization of political parties. When the party is not institutionalized or weak, personal leadership tends to be more prominent than party programs. Party labels or identities have become meaningless, making it difficult for citizens or voters to distinguish a party; and party politicians no longer have orientations or special issues as work targets [36].

The concept of institutionalization, as proposed by Kenneth Janda [17] in Harmel et al. [15], relates to how the party exists in the public mind or, in the term of Randall and Svasand, reification. Reification refers to the extent to which the existence of the party is implanted in the public imagination and as a factor shaping the behavior of actors. The party's ability to build on this depends on part on the particular history as well as the party's symbolic values [31, 32]. So reification is one of the crucial variables in institutionalizing political parties in Indonesia.

Studies on reification are still rarely done. However, some of them noted the efforts of political parties in forming a positive party image in the eyes of the public [1], so this has an impact on vote acquisition in the general election [19]. The previous study on reification is also reviewed by Tomsa. Tomsa wrote that the Golkar Party made various efforts to shape its image, so the conclusion shows that the Golkar Party is still well-reified [40].

In post-New Order Indonesia, the issue of reification closely relates to the phenomenon of personalization of political parties. Some previous studies have seen that the causes of personalization in political parties are internal factors such as charisma, client patrons, and others, as well as external factors such as the electoral system and party system. However, the authors observe that, in addition to this external factor, other factors, namely reification, influence the occurrence of personalization. This article argues that the public is more familiar with the party based on its character than the programs owned by the party. This article aims to analyze that reification as a factor strengthening the personalization of several political parties in post-reform Indonesia.

It consists of four segments: an introduction that reviews the background and issues raised and early studies. The second part is research methods. In the third part, survey data related to reification and analysis are presented. The last part is the conclusion.

## 2 Data and Method

The method used in this study is a mixed research method. It combines quantitative and qualitative research methods in collecting and analyzing data in a series of studies to understand the problem [9], in this case, the reification of political parties in Indonesia. The type of mixed method used in this study is a mixed parallel/concurrent convergent method, Creswell [9]. The qualitative method in this study is by performing literature studies and the quantitative method by conducting surveys simultaneously. The analysis and interpretation of the data from these two methods were carried out simultaneously and with equal weight to conclude this study. The object of this study is the four political parties in the reform era, namely PDIP Party, Gerindra Party, Nasdem Party, and the Democratic Party. These four parties were chosen because all four had powerful figures who later became the inherent identity of these parties.

In a qualitative method, the writers conduct a study on references related to the topic of reification of political parties, institutionalization of political parties, and personalization of political parties, both from academic publications and from other popular publications. Meanwhile, in the quantitative method, the authors conducted an online survey to see how far the public is familiar with political parties. This survey is part of a massive survey conducted by the Political Party Team of the BRIN Political Research Center, in the context of compiling the Political Party Institutional Index. The three authors are part of this team. The survey was conducted over some time from 10 June 2021 to 5 July 2021 via the LimeSurvey platform. Although the sampling technique is carried out incidentally to anyone who gets access to the survey link obtained from the communication network, the filter on the sample taken is still carried out. The authors stipulate that the criteria for respondents are Indonesian citizen voters, namely those who are 17 years old and/or married. With this method, the authors managed to collect 264 respondents from various regions in Indonesia (Fig. 1).

Indicators used to measure public knowledge of parties are: the public's knowledge of symbols or anything that describes the party, which can be in the form of colors, images/mascots, logos, organizations close to parties and party leaders, as well as public knowledge about party leaders or leaders at the national level. The questions in this survey questionnaire are open-ended questions that allow respondents to answer more than one answer for each party. Therefore, the authors make coding to determine the frequency of the respondent's answers. If the answer is correct, then code 1 is given, which means the respondent knows the symbol or party figure. Meanwhile, a score of 0 is given for incorrect answers, out of context, or questions left unanswered, indicating that the respondent is unfamiliar with the symbol or party figure.

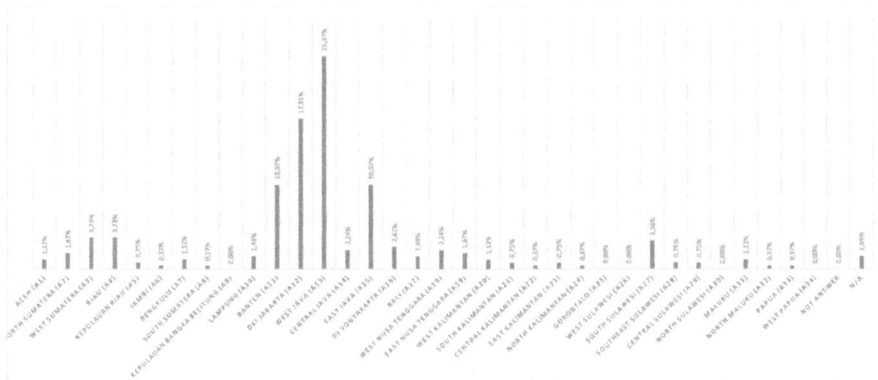


**Fig. 1** Distribution of survey respondents by province/domicile region. *Note* Data entry 275. Invalid data 11. *Source* Political Party Team Survey, BRIN Political Research Center, processed by the author

## 3 Public Knowledge of Political Parties

Based on the survey results, the public is aware of the political parties that became the object of this study. However, people tend to know more about the political figures of the four political parties studied than other party symbols such as logos, colors, ideology, and other attributes. It is shown by the percentage of respondents' knowledge of party leaders or national figures, which is higher than the percentage of respondents' knowledge of other party symbols. From the four parties, respondents generally knew the Gerindra Party quite well, both the party symbols and party figures. However, it is known that respondents know a little more about Gerindra Party figures than other party symbols. 92.8% of respondents said they knew national political figures or elites in the Gerindra Party. As for the symbol of this party, 86.7% of the respondents said they knew. Similar conditions also occur in the Democratic Party. Respondents quite well know the figures and symbols of this party. However, like the Gerindra Party, the percentage of respondents who know party figures are higher than respondents who know party symbols.

Different things happened to the Nasdem Party and PDIP. For the Nasdem Party, it can be concluded that respondents know much more about party figures than other symbols of this party. This can be seen from the range of significant differences between respondents' knowledge of symbols and parties when compared to the previous two parties. For party symbols, only 68.2% of respondents claimed to know other symbols of this party. Meanwhile, for party leaders, 88.6% of respondents said they knew. Meanwhile, for PDIP, the survey results show that respondents are quite familiar with the symbols and figures of this party. This can be seen from the similarity in the percentage between respondents who know party symbols and respondents who know party figures. Possibly, two factors cause a balance between public knowledge about the symbols and figures of PDIP. First, PDIP is the most senior party and has a longer history than the other three parties. In addition to having a strong figure who is well known to the public, namely Megawati Soekarno Putri, the logo and colors of this party have also taken root in the public's memory. As is well known, PDIP was born as a result of the factions that existed within the Indonesian Democratic Party (PDI) during the New Order era. Although there were changes and differences, both PDI and PDIP are made the red color of their greatness and the bull their main symbol. Therefore, when PDI was no longer part of the eligible participants in the last few elections in the reform era, people increasingly recognized the PDIP's red and bull identity, which has long been prominent since the New Order era. Complete data for the comparison of respondents' knowledge of the four parties can be seen in Table 1 and Fig. 2.

Focusing on respondents' knowledge of party symbols, the authors provided open questions for this indicator in the survey conducted. It encourages respondents to answer questions for this indicator by answering logos, colors, ideology, and other party symbols, including party leaders. In fact, on average, there was 9–16% of respondents answered party symbols with figures as the party's symbol, either explicitly answering with the full name of the person concerned or with their respective popular nicknames, such as SBY and AHY. For the symbol of the Gerindra Party, several respondents answered with Prabowo Subianto. Likewise,

**Table 1** Comparison of respondents who know and do not know party symbols and party figures in the Gerindra Party, PDIP, Nasdem Party, and the Democratic Party

**Gerindra: Symbols**

| | | Frequency | Percent | Valid Percent | Cumulative Percent |
|---|---|---|---|---|---|
| Valid | 0 | 35 | 13.2 | 13.3 | 13.3 |
| | 1 | 229 | 86.1 | 86.7 | 100.0 |
| | Total | 264 | 99.2 | 100.0 | |
| Missing | System | 2 | 0.8 | | |
| Total | | 266 | 100.0 | | |

**Gerindra: Figures**

| | | Frequency | Percent | Valid Percent | Cumulative Percent |
|---|---|---|---|---|---|
| Valid | 0 | 19 | 7.1 | 7.2 | 7.2 |
| | 1 | 245 | 92.1 | 92.8 | 100.0 |
| | Total | 264 | 99.2 | 100.0 | |
| Missing | System | 2 | 0.8 | | |
| Total | | 266 | 100.0 | | |

**PDIP: Symbols**

| | | Frequency | Percent | Valid Percent | Cumulative Percent |
|---|---|---|---|---|---|
| Valid | 0 | 21 | 7.9 | 8.0 | 8.0 |
| | 1 | 243 | 91.4 | 92.0 | 100.0 |
| | Total | 264 | 99.2 | 100.0 | |
| Missing | System | 2 | 0.8 | | |
| Total | | 266 | 100.0 | | |

**PDIP: Figures**

| | | Frequency | Percent | Valid Percent | Cumulative Percent |
|---|---|---|---|---|---|
| Valid | 0 | 21 | 7.9 | 8.0 | 8.0 |
| | 1 | 243 | 91.4 | 92.0 | 100.0 |
| | Total | 264 | 99.2 | 100.0 | |
| Missing | System | 2 | 0.8 | | |
| Total | | 266 | 100.0 | | |

**Nasdem: Symbols**

| | | Frequency | Percent | Valid Percent | Cumulative Percent |
|---|---|---|---|---|---|
| Valid | 0 | 84 | 31.6 | 31.8 | 31.8 |
| | 1 | 180 | 67.7 | 68.2 | 100.0 |
| | Total | 264 | 99.2 | 100.0 | |
| Missing | System | 2 | 0.8 | | |
| Total | | 266 | 100.0 | | |

**Nasdem: Figures**

| | | Frequency | Percent | Valid Percent | Cumulative Percent |
|---|---|---|---|---|---|
| Valid | 0 | 30 | 11.3 | 11.4 | 11.4 |
| | 1 | 234 | 88.0 | 88.6 | 100.0 |
| | Total | 264 | 99.2 | 100.0 | |
| Missing | System | 2 | 0.8 | | |
| Total | | 266 | 100.0 | | |

**Demokrat: Symbols**

| | | Frequency | Percent | Valid Percent | Cumulative Percent |
|---|---|---|---|---|---|
| Valid | 0 | 37 | 13.9 | 14.0 | 14.0 |
| | 1 | 227 | 85.3 | 86.0 | 100.0 |
| | Total | 264 | 99.2 | 100.0 | |
| Missing | System | 2 | 0.8 | | |
| Total | | 266 | 100.0 | | |

**Demokrat: Figures**

| | | Frequency | Percent | Valid Percent | Cumulative Percent |
|---|---|---|---|---|---|
| Valid | 0 | 21 | 7.9 | 8.0 | 8.0 |
| | 1 | 243 | 91.4 | 92.0 | 100.0 |
| | Total | 264 | 99.2 | 100.0 | |
| Missing | System | 2 | 0.8 | | |
| Total | | 266 | 100.0 | | |

*Source* Political Party Team Survey, BRIN Political Research Center, processed by the author

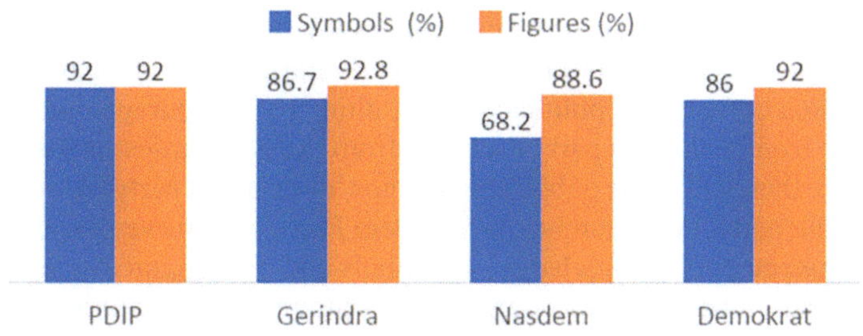


**Fig. 2** Comparison of respondents' knowledge of party symbols and figures. *Source* Political Party Team Survey, BRIN Political Research Center, processed by the author

with PDIP, some respondents answered questions for this indicator with answers from Megawati Soekarno Putri, Joko Widodo, to Ganjar Pranowo (although with a very small frequency). Likewise for the Nasdem Party and the Democratic Party, the names Surya Paloh for the Nasdem Party and Susilo Bambang Yudhoyono and Agus Harimurti Yudhoyono. Complete data from the breakdown of respondents' knowledge of party symbols can be seen in Fig. 3.

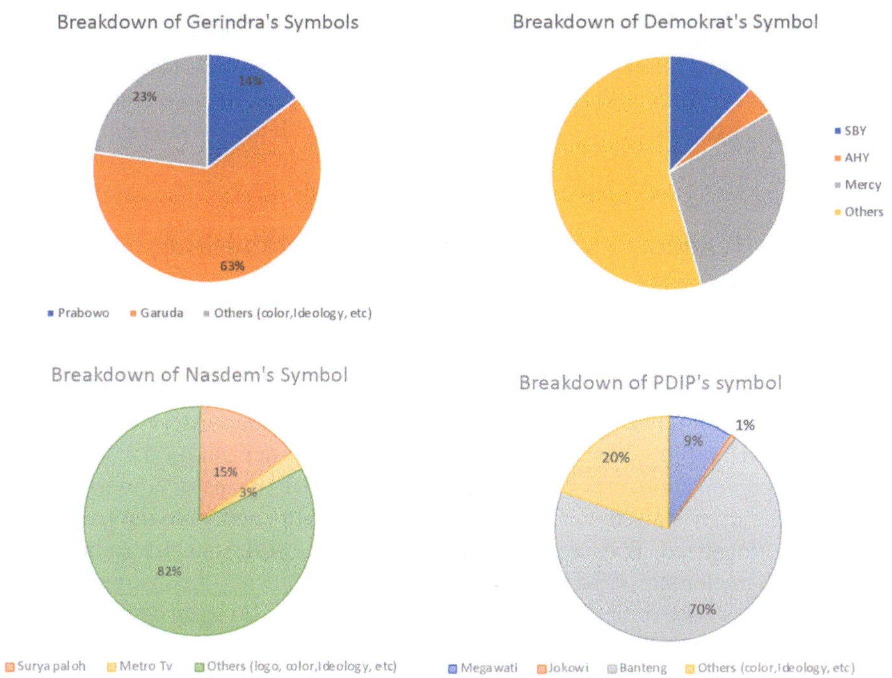


**Fig. 3** Breakdown of respondents' answers to respondents' knowledge of party symbols. *Source* Political Party Team Survey, BRIN Political Research Center, processed by the authors

The fact that the majority of respondents know more about the figures' party rather than other symbols can be caused by several factors. First, because of the strong charisma of figures in political parties, ultimately encourages wider exposure to them, both from within the party itself and from external parties such as the media. This exposure then makes the public tend to know more about party figures than other symbols of the party. For example, the Nasdem Party with survey results showed a large gap between public knowledge of symbols and party figures compared to the results for other parties. As the youngest party among the three parties in this study, bringing up a social figure as the identity of a party is a natural thing so that people can get to know the party. This condition often makes the public not pay too much attention to other things within the party, such as logos, colors, and even the platform and party programs. However, parties need to be careful so that this charisma figure does not necessarily lead to party personalization [4, 8, 10, 25] which can hinder the growth of internal party democracy and party institutionalization processes [10].

Apart from the charisma factor, a factor that causes more public to recognize party figures more than other party symbols is a misunderstanding of a party symbol. For example, misinterpretation of the colors of the party's greatness, symbols, or party logos to the party's ideology. This misunderstanding ultimately resulted in the respondent's answer getting a score of 0. It can occur because the public is not familiar with the party as an institution. Therefore, to avoid the negative impact of not knowing the public about the party as a whole, either in terms of figures, symbols, ideology, platform, or party programs, political parties need to carry out comprehensive political socialization. Thus, people can understand that the function of the party is as a bridge between public aspirations with the government.

## 4 Figure Tendency in Party Reification: Establishing Personalization

The extent to which political parties are institutionalized can be seen in how deeply their existence is embedded in the public imagination [31, 32]. The ability of a political party to establish itself will depend in part on the particular history and symbolic values it can claim to represent. In addition, it will also depend on the strength of the party's organization, especially its access to effective means of communication [31, 32]. The party's ability to build such reification will encourage the party to be more institutionalized. Widows, as referred to by Tomsa [40], state that reification is a defining characteristic of the party institutionalization process. An institutionalized party is a party whose reification is good in the public's mind, a party can be regarded as an existing organization if it does not depend on its temporary leader.

The parties in Indonesia seem to be easy to identify as organizations with strong personal figures, as illustrated among others in the PDIP, Gerindra Party, Nasdem Party, and the Democratic Party. The public is more likely to record their greater memories of these parties on powerful figures or their leaders. This phenomenon poses a challenge to the process of building party institutionalization. In the reification process, Mainwaring, as quoted by Tomsa [40], points out that the label or name of a party is important in an election, but usually, only a few of the public know in detail what the party's programs and policies are.

The prominence of such a figure in the reification process implies that the party institutionalization process will be hampered. Parties in Indonesia will rely on personal attractiveness or figures based on the charisma of character rather than relying on party organizational capabilities. Such symptoms make the party focus on the charisma of certain figures, not only distancing the organization from their work agenda but also hindering organizational development [12]. By focusing on individual charisma, making the party moves to certain characterizations. The role of strong party figures or individuals becomes more prominent compared to institutions or party issues which then leads to personalization [12, 42].

Figures in several parties such as Megawati Soekarnoputri in PDIP, Prabowo Subianto in Gerindra, Surya Paloh in the Nasdem Party, and SBY in the Democratic Party are figures who not only have charisma and are strongly attached to the party but are also influential in the party's policy process [6, 7, 12, 42]. These parties tend to experience symptoms of personalization with what is narrated by Karvonen [18], that individuals or political actors are more prominent than the collective identity of the party. It makes the centrality of individual actors increase within the internal party. Meanwhile, the emphasis on party organization is decreasing [29].

By having an introduction to the figures, the party may have its advantages as well as the party is easily known. Electoral advantages can be obtained when these figures become the main figures in marketing the party for votes. This short-term gain will be followed by the challenge of failing to build a solid party program and organization [12]. When a party relies on a figure as a voter, and as a factor for forming party cohesion, the agenda, platform, and values developed by the party can be weakened. Situations like this make the party depend on the leader or main figure of the party [27]. The party thus opens up the possibility that control over party authority is exercised by personal power rather than organizational prowess.

Such a personalization phenomenon becomes a stumbling block or obstacle to party institutionalization in general. This tendency puts decision-making authority in the hands of a figure who mostly has power that is difficult to match with others [14]. In the reification process, such personalization is also driven by how the party interacts with the public through communication channels or the media used to convey its messages [40]. Indonesian politics has recently used communication channels such as television and internet media to disseminate information and increase the popularity of candidates [41]. With the massive spread of messages, the party socialization process is also carried out by actors or candidates to attract or instill an image in the public.

Although this is also one of the media for message dissemination, as Ufen [41] explains that such efforts, if not balanced by organizational strength at the lower level, can create a distance between party organizations and voters. Voters are easier to identify the identity of the figure than the party institution [24]. Party socialization through such communication channels is related to the design of electoral institutions by implementing direct elections from national to local levels [41]. Within that framework, personal figures can build a personal image through media channels that allow them to be popular.

In the reification process, which tends to be caught by the public with such strong figures or figures, what is needed is to strengthen party organizations. Political parties can show, through their real performance, that they have an impact on people's welfare. Planting the party's image is balanced by building and implementing party programs consistently at the grassroots [24]. Institutionalized parties have strong relationships with organized groups in society. Besides, policy linkages are not based on personalism and patron-client [11]. The ability of parties to build reification through which the process of party institutionalization in Indonesia can run and support the process of consolidating democracy through the party's role in recruitment, training of the political elite, its role in building conflict resolution, institutionalizing democratic behavior and attitudes [31, 32].

## 5 Conclusion

An institutionalized political party, as well as having a stable relationship with the public and a strong organization, is one of the prerequisites for the consolidation process [13]. In the process of party institutionalization, the relevant aspect to be considered is reification. Reification is related to external recognition and legitimacy [31]. The potential that emerges in the reification process is that the public knows the charismatic figure or leader of the party. The introduction of the party to the figures makes the party more dependent on the figures than the party's ability to introduce other symbols and programs. This phenomenon leads to political personalization. Symptoms of personalization hinder the party's institutionalization process. Because the process of developing party organizations is more focused on personal abilities in attracting support in the community.

Symptoms of personalization make the reification process of political parties not accompanied by efforts to socialize party functions. Reification on the institutionalization of this party can be a double-edged coin. On the one hand, the reification of political parties as an indicator of the institutionalization of political parties can show the existence of political parties in society. But on the other hand, reification can be one of the factors that support the personalization of political parties. In political parties that are not yet fully institutionalized, public knowledge of political parties by knowing more about party figures as in the case of the four parties above can be a gap to legitimize the personalization of political parties.

## References


1. Agung S, Putra RS (2015) Studi Dimensi Systemness dan Reification dalam Pelembagaan Partai Persatuan Pembangunan (PPP) Kabupaten Tasikmalaya Pasca Reformasi. Jurnal Ilmu Politik Dan Pemerintahan 2(1):47–59
2. Alhamid A, Perdana A (2018) Presidentialized Party di Indonesia: Kasus Perilaku PDI-P dalam Pencalonan Joko Widodo pada Pilpres 2014. Jurnal Politik 3(2):237. https://doi.org/10.7454/jp.v3i2.125
3. Basedau M, Stroh A (2008) Measuring party institutionalization in developing countries: a new research instrument applied to 28 African political parties. GIGA Working Papers, 69
4. Blondel J, Thiebaut J-L (2010) Political leadership, parties and citizens: the personalisation of leadership. Routledge, London
5. Bolleyer N, Ruth SP (2017) Elite investments in party institutionalization in new democracies: a two-dimensional approach. J Polit 80(1):288–302
6. Budiatri AP (ed) (2018) Personalisasi Partai Politik di Indonesia Era Reformasi. Yayasan Pustaka Obor, Jakarta
7. Budiatri AP et al (2018) Faksi dan Konflik Internal Partai Politik di Indonesia. Yayasan Obor Indonesia, Jakarta
8. Calise M (2015) The personal party: an analytical framework. Rivista Italiana Di Scienza Politica 45(3):301–315. https://doi.org/10.1017/ipo.2015.18
9. Creswell J (2015) Research design: qualitative, quantitative and mixed methods approaches. Pearson Education Inc
10. Ekawati E, Sweinstani MKD (2020) Dampak Personalisasi Partai Terhadap Demokrasi Internal Partai di Indonesia Pasca Orde Baru. Jurnal Wacana Politik 5(2):111–123
11. Ezrow NM (2011) The importance of parties and party system institutionalization in new democracies. Briefing Paper (IDCR-BP-06/11). Institute for Democracy & Conflict Resolution
12. Fionna U (2016) The trap of pop-charisma for the institutionalization of Indonesia's post-Suharto parties. Asian J Polit Sci 24:124–141
13. Geyikci YS (2015) Party institutionalization and democratic consolidation: Turkey and Southern Europe in comparative perspective. Party Polit 21(4):527–538
14. Harmel R, Svasand LG (2019) Introduction. In: Harmel R, Svasand LG (eds) Institutionalisation of political parties comparative cases. Rowman & Littlefield, London
15. Harmel R, Svasand L, Mjelde H (2016, April) Party institutionalization and de-institutionalization: concepts and indicators. Prepared for presentation at the workshop "Institutionalization and De-Institutionalization of Political Organizations". ECPR Joint Sessions of Workshops, Pisa.
16. Huntington S (1968) Political order in changing societies. University Press
17. Janda K (1980) A note on measures of party system change. Comp Political Stud 12
18. Karvonen L (2010) The personalization of politics: a study of parliamentary democracies. ECPR Press, Colchester
19. Kaypama OD (2019) Dominasi Partai Golkar di Kabupaten Tanah Datar pada Pemilihan Legislatif Tahun 2014. Jurnal Demokrasi Dan Politik Lokal 1(2):149–159
20. Levitsky S (1998) Institutionalization and peronism: the concept, the case, and the case for unpacking the concept. Party Politics 4(1):77–92
21. Mair P (2002) Party system change, aprroaches and interpretations. Oxford University Press, Oxford
22. Mancini P, Swanson DL (1996) Politics, media, and modern democracy: introduction. In: Swanson DL, Mancini P (eds) Politics, media and modern society. Praeger, Westport, pp 1–26
23. Noor F (2009) Menimbang Masa Depan Sistem Presidensial di Indonesia Problematika Demokrasi dan Kebutuhan Perbaikan Sistemik. In: Nurhasim M, Bhakti IN (eds) Sistem Presidensial dan Sosok Presiden Ideal. Pustaka Pelajar, Yogyakarta
24. Nugroho K (2022) Kompas.id. Elektabilitas Partai Politik. Dalam https://www.kompas.id/baca/artikel-opini/2022/04/11/elektabilitas-partai-politik

25. Nurhasim M (2013) Kegagalan Modernisasi Partai Politik Di Era Reformasi. Jurnal Penelitian Politik 10(1):17–28
26. Panebianco A (1988) Political parties: organization and power. Cambridge University Press
27. Pedahzur A, Brichta A (2002) The institutionalization of extreme right-wing charismatic parties: a paradox? Party Polit 8(1):31–49
28. Pilet J-B, Cross W (2015) Uncovering the politics of party leadership. In: Cross W, Pilet J-B (eds) The politics of party leadership: a cross national perspective. Oxford University Press, Oxford, pp 1–15
29. Pruysers S, Cross WP, Katz RS (2018) Personalism, personalization, and party politics.In: Pruysers S, Cross WP, Katz RS (eds) The personalization of democratic politics and the challenge for political parties. ECPR Press, Colchester
30. Rahat G, Sheafer T (2007) The personalization(s) of politics: Israel, 1949–2003. Polit Commun 24(1):65–80. https://doi.org/10.1080/10584600601128739
31. Randall V, Svasand L (2002a) Party institutionalization in new democracies. Party Politic 8(1):5–29
32. Randall V, Svåsand L (2002b) Introduction: the contribution of parties to democracy and democratic consolidation. Democratization 9(3):1–10
33. Randall V (2006, July 9–13) Party institutionalization and its implications for democracy. Paper for Session MT 07.239 Political Parties and Democratization, at the IPSA Congress, at Fukuoka
34. Rhodes ERAW, Hart P (2014) The Oxford handbook of political leadership. Oxford University Press, Oxford. https://doi.org/10.1093/oxfordhb/9780199653881.001.0001
35. Rose R, Mackie TT (1988) Do parties persist or fail? the big trade-off facing organizations. In: Lawson K, Merkl PH (eds) When parties fail emerging alternative organizations. Princeton University Press
36. Sagarzazu I (2011) Weak party institutionalization and the dynamics of political dialogue. APSA 2011 Annual Meeting Paper
37. Samuels DJ (2002) Presidentialized parties: the separation of powers and party organization and behavior. Comp Pol Stud 35(4):461–483. https://doi.org/10.1177/0010414002035004004
38. Samuels D, Shugart MS (2010) Presidents, parties, and prime ministers: how the separation of powers affects party organization and behavior. Cambridge University Press, Cambridge
39. Sartori G (2005) Parties and party systems: a framework for analysis. ECPR Press, Colchester
40. Tomsa D (2008) Party politics and democratization in Indonesia Golkar in the post-Suharto era. Routledge, London
41. Ufen A (2010) Electoral campaigning in Indonesia: the professionalization and commercialization after 1998. J Curr Southeast Asian Aff 29(4):11–37
42. Ufen A (2006) Political parties in post-Suharto Indonesia: between politik aliran and 'Philippinisation'. GIGA Working Papers, No. 37, Desember 2006, GIGA German Institute of Global and Area Studies
43. Van Biezen I, Katz RS (2005) Democracy and political parties. ECPR Joint Sessions, Granada
44. Yudha H (2010) Presidensialisme Setengah Hati: dari dilema ke kompromi. Gramedia Pustaka Utama, Jakarta

# The Failure of Special Autonomy as a Final Solution to Separatist Conflict in Papua

**Riris Katharina and Poltak Partogi Nainggolan**

**Abstract** A special autonomy status has already been given to Papua since 2001 as Law 21/2001 agreed by the central government and the parliament. Its realization was supported by the allocation of an enormous development budget, the enlargement of the province and the extension of its financing for the next two decades. This essay analyses why separatist movements were more active throughout Papua provinces though special autonomy status and its privileges have been given since two decades ago. Field researches were conducted in provinces, municipalities and districts, as well as in cities and inlands of Papua and West Papua. Data was analysed with a qualitative methodology, for which in-depth interviews with stake-holders from different background have been made. Research findings disclose that the budget for the special autonomy has not been properly used. Some were illegally delivered to separatist movements to increase their armed struggles for independence. With a proper development planning, transparency and good supervisions, the writers recommend the extension of an extra budget for the special autonomy of the Papua provinces for the next two decades.

**Keywords** Papua · Special autonomy · Otsus · Separatist movements

## 1 Introduction

The failure of Otsus policy for twenty years in fulfilling its main goal to eliminate poverty among Papuan native people (*Orang Asli Papua* or OAP) has fuelled the fast rise of new separatist movements after the fall of Soeharto's New Order authoritarian regime in 1998. Severe situation, worsened by new gross human rights violations conducted by security forces in addressing separatist conflict [1, 2], provides opportunities for the separatist movements to boost their propaganda to gain wider political supports from overseas. Further, at the absence of proper responses of Jakarta, the

R. Katharina (✉) · P. P. Nainggolan
National Research and Innovation Agency (BRIN), Jakarta, Indonesia
e-mail: riri008@brin.go.id



Nawawi et al. (eds.), *Managing Disruption and Developing Resilience for a Better Southeast Asia*, Springer Proceedings in Humanities and Social Sciences,
https://doi.org/10.1007/978-981-96-2116-3_60

struggle for an independence conducting by pre- and post-2000 OAP generations has been intensifying in Papua that joint Indonesia in 1969 through a free referendum (*Penentuan Pendapat Rakyat* or Pepera) supervised by United Nations Temporary Executive Authority, allegedly has been unfair organized. The two different OAP generations [3] had same aspirations to struggle for self-determination, demanding a new referendum to build a new Papua separated from the Unitary State of the Republic of Indonesia [4].

Wrong responses have provided more opportunities for the rebels to obtain more supports from inside and outside Indonesia. The first twenty years of the realization of the Otsus in the Papua province, which followed up with the creation of the new province of the West Papua, have not been effective to stop separatist movements existing since 1960s. New symphatisants of the separatist movements are growing and spreading across South Pacific islands inside governments, parliaments, campuses and NGOs.

Separatist movements rapidly develop in since 2019, through which their propaganda has drawn international attentions [5] and supports across the regions [4]. They perform their stronger opposition to Otsus and increase their hostilities to pro-Jakarta local administrations and elites. They use negative issues such as the 1969 'unfair' Pepera, Jakarta's 'genocide policy' and 'discriminations' toward Melanesian race as political weapons to confront Jakarta's position.

This essay analyses the relevance between Otsus as a final conflict resolution with the development of separatist movements in Papua since the Otsus introduced in 2001. Its discussions will make clear how far the policy can achieve its goal to respond the growing of separatist movements there. Research findings will be aimed to help the government and parliament in improving the conflict resolution which has its new legal basis on Law No. 2/2021.

## 2 Development Malfunction and Escalations of Conflict

Poverty and conflict are widely understood to be closely interconnected, with poverty making countries more prone to civil war, and armed conflict weakening governance and economic performance, thus, increasing the risk of conflict relapse [6]. Poverty caused vulnerability at the individual and community level by lowering the opportunity cost of mobilizing for violence. Further, high rates of unemployment and inequality, combined with low levels of education and development, are thought to soften the ground for recruitment and provide motives to fight [7]. Ross underlined that resource governance plays a key role in shaping countries' economic and structural vulnerability to conflict [8].

Ted Robert Gurr, a conflict analyst, has highlighted the danger of unequal opportunities and persistent poverty in a region to security that undermined the power and authority of the national government [9]. The development malfunctions have produced rebellions in developing countries whose people since long time ignored and marginalized by their own governments [10, 11]. Further, Amartya Sen [12], who linked poverty and representativeness in politics found that the absence of policy corrections for decades in the one hand, and democracy, which provided people equal access to development, on the other, made the poverty and backwardness impossible to be diminished [11].

Terry Terriff et al. [13] have identified all sorts of these insurgencies as today's world challenging security threats produced by traditional motives [13]. In addition to this, Mark Duffield [14] and also Homer-Dixon [15] highlighted that the development malfunction is a clear indication of the crisis of developmentalism that will continue to occur and bring about the so-called complex emergencies due to unstopped deforestations and natural disasters and the rise of armed uprisings of the native people awakened at the same time [14, 15].

Barry Buzan [16], who focuses his researches on post-Cold War security problems, mentioned that economic insecurity is a major cause of today's non-traditional security threats, which has created internal conflicts that generate national instability in developing countries [16]. Siregar [17] in her recent research revealed that there is the relevance between excessive exploitation of natural resources which results in environmental degradations and conflicts between outsiders (businessmen and investors, as well as security forces who protect the activities) and native people who resists the investment projects and became the victims of natural disasters [17].

Since poverty eradications and a relevant national development policy are a crucial solution, a correction to development malfunction is required, meaning that good governance must be introduced. With these efforts, practices of mismanagements, nepotism, collusions, corruptions and other conflicts of interests, which have incited various human rights violations in the new era of devolution of power can be systematically eradicated [18]. Meanwhile, pouring money for military operations to crush insurgency or rebellion is a myopic way of addressing an old problem that has its roots in poverty [19]. The military solution may work for a while, but the problems would remain, and they will surely spawn a new batch of insurgents or rebels to substitute who would die in the conflict.

## 3 Research Methodology

Recent investigation reports from *Tempo* and formal reports of annual state budget spending for Papua's special autonomy since 2002 were examined to check whether the Otsus money has been properly used to improve OAP welfare at the grassroots level. Basic data from government institutions and NGOs were also employed. Field researches were conducted in both mountainous and coastal regions as well as in remote areas and cities of Jayapura, Manokwari, Wamena, Fakfak and Jayawijaya, supported by in-depth interviews with government apparatus and security officers: the military and national police.

## 4 Results and Discussions: Poverty and Rebellion

Since the beginning, this research wants to clearly explain why do separatist activities increase though the central government has offered a special autonomy policy since 2001? Why do they still challenge the Otsus and its derivative development projects when the UN does not simultaneously give support until recently? Development malfunction resulting from improper and inconsistent Otsus development projects materializes the emergence of new conflict against Jakarta, reflecting stronger opposition against integration mandated by the referendum results seven decades ago. Contrastly, until 2022, a large amount of Otsus money worth Rp. 144,476 trillion has been disbursed to both provinces in Papua, as an affirmative action to eradicate poverty and backwardness [20]. In fact, Otsus has not yet been successful in eliminating poverty and decreasing gaps between indigenous Papuans who mostly live from farming in hinterland and hunting in mountainous areas and the forests with migrants who live in cities and work in formal sectors and government offices [21].

Table 1 informs that since five years of the introduction of the Otsus, in 2005, the number of OAP lived in poverty in the Papua province was 1,028.20. It contributed 43.50 increase from 984.70 in 2002. Although in 2006, the policy could reduce poverty, its figures were not generally and significantly changed. Even, after it touched 709.30 in 2008, the lowest one, poverty number returned to increase again in 2009 before it fluctuated with a slight differences afterward. A consistent trend of poverty reduction since 2006 can be seen in the West Papua region, the new province formatted in 2008. Nevertheless, the diminution of the figure from year to year was not substantial before fluctuating for one year with a slight difference.

After one decade of the implementation of Otsus, in 2011, the gini coefficient ratio in West Papua surpassed the national figure, before it reached its peak in 2015, made it as the province with highest income gaps of its people in the whole regions of Indonesia! [22]. Our interviews disclosed that much of the Otsus money went to the wrong decision-makers, bureaucrats or elites due to the emergence of corruptions, collusion and nepotism practices of governance at the absence of systematic planning and supervisions. Otsus projects gave the non-OAP more opportunities to enjoy its results rather than the OAP at grassroots.

Paradigm change, from multi- to monoculture, in agricultural sector is also responsible for the development malfunction occurred during 2002–2022, which weakened OAP's food resilience who live since long time with different sources of daily consumptions, mainly sago and cassava [23]. Otsus provides more opportunity for outsiders, national and foreign investors, to exploit vast areas of Papua for cultivating lucrative agricultural products in global market. For two decades, paddy, corn and palm oil plantations dominated Papua, replacing traditional foods, reducing dense forest cover. A massive land clearing for infrastructure development and the new monoculture of OAP which influences their changing pattern of consumption brought about negative consequences to their health security.

In 2018, in highlands or coastal areas, and in municipalities or cities, OAP is threatened by infectious diseases. Both in Papua and West Papua, infectious diseases,

**Table 1** Development of poverty in Papua (2002–2019, in thousand)

| No | Year | Papua | West Papua |
|---|---|---|---|
| 1 | 2002 | 984.70 | NA |
| 2 | 2003 | 916.90 | NA |
| 3 | 2004 | 966.80 | NA |
| 4 | 2005 | 1028.20 | NA |
| 5 | 2006 | 816.7 | 284.1 |
| 6 | 2007 | 793.4 | 266.8 |
| 7 | 2008 | 709.3 | 237.3 |
| 8 | 2009 | 709.4 | 227.6 |
| 9 | 2010 | 981. 2 | 217.4 |
| 10 | 2011 | 946.6 | 227.1 |
| 11 | 2012 | 916.4 | 219.6 |
| 12 | 2013 | 960.6 | 226.2 |
| 13 | 2014 | 864.1 | 225.5 |
| 14 | 2015 | 859.15 | 225.36 |
| 15 | 2016 | 911.33 | 225.81 |
| 16 | 2017 | 897.69 | 228.38 |
| 17 | 2018 | 917.63 | 214.47 |
| 18 | 2019 | 926.36 | 211.50 |

*Source* BPS (Biro Pusat Statistik—Centre Statistical Bureau), 2020

particularly malaria, TB and HIV/AIDS, are dangerous and still a main human security threat when Otsus targeted to eliminate poverty. Though Jakarta has allocated special budget for the provinces, the local governments in Papua have lowest capability to prevent and control the outbreak of the infectious diseases comparing to all provinces in the country.

Regarding Human development Index (HDI) score, both Papua provinces still left behind other provinces in Indonesia until recently, meaning that the Otsus failed to developed education, economy and health sectors, especially in Asmat, Mamberamo Raya and Nduga. There is also a big gap of HDI score among municipalities/cities caused by their geographical problems. Most of HDI in remote areas, such as inlands and highlands only reached 50.0, for instances in Puncak Jaya, Asmat, Yahukimo, Pegunungan Bintang, Tolikara, Nduga, Lanny Jaya, Mamberamo Tengah, Yalimo Puncak, Intan Jaya and Deiyai. This condition, if not immediately improved, will permanently provide fertile grounds for separatist movements to grow, with their damaging activities in the future. Meanwhile, in coastal and lowlands areas, such as Merauke, Nabire and Yapen, HDI score can respectively reach above 66.0, annually, showing the regions are easier to cooperate with Jakarta [23].

There are several evidences of the development malfunction, namely: (1) Local markets have been built not in suitable locations; (2) The new markets have been built by moreover ignoring local values and wisdoms. The local government ignored the reality that OAP cannot live within the concept of modern markets, with dividing small shops. OAP used to do activities in open and large places without partitions; (3) The new houses built for OAP are not conducive with their local culture. The roofs of their new *honai* did not use *rumbia*, leaves of *nipah* or *sago* trees, but tin materials. The new houses are too hot at day time, and too cold at night; (4) The local governments built modern houses in compounds like mostly exist in Jayapura. They did not take into account that OAP since many years live together as big families in big houses without partitions; (5) Schools were built in remote areas, far from OAP's villages; (6) The presence of new hospitals, clinics and other healthcare facilities are not followed with the presence of sufficient barefoot doctors, nurses and other health workers; In general (7), the new infrastructures are more favourable for migrants rather than OAP's primary needs.

Many more findings can be presented as further evidences of development malfunction, in addition to the improper quality of Otsus projects due to corrupt behaviours of the local bureaucrats and heads of regions [24]. An example of their corrupt behaviour was the misuse of Otsus money in Nabire for the fake recruitment of 1000 new state employees as reported by Panaian regent.[1,2] The new infrastructures and public facilities are more enjoyed by migrants rather than OAP because since the beginning their creations lacked of OAP's participations. As previously, they were likely to more resume the top-down, instead of introducing a bottom-up, approach. The Otsus projects have alienated OAP from their modes and means of productions. Accesses to natural resources have been widely opened, managed and then controlled by big businesses owned by national and foreign investors, allegedly involving Jakarta's elites currently reported by NGOs [17, 25]. Therefore, Otsus projects during the first period (2001–2022) have drastically pushed migration in Papua to 5 percent, making it as the highest in the world! [17]

At the absence of the central government's supervisions [26], Otsus failed to implement good governance to lift up Papua provinces out of poverty line. The development projects have resulted in environmental degradations as the forests, especially conservation areas, have rapidly disappeared. This environmental degradation strengthens OAP's resistance to Jakarta's poverty alleviation solution. Together with the raise of the maternal and infant mortality rates, malnutrition, the wide spread of infectious diseases produced OAP's worst HDI score though Otsus had been introduced since 2001.

It can be generally inferred that the Otsus still could not meet its main objective as an alternative solution to self-determination conflicts [27]. The results of Otsus in the first period have dissatisfied Jakarta because the bad performance of health, education and economic sectors as the main pillars for improving OAP's social welfare [27]. The limited results of Otsus became more obviously since OAP still lacks of capability and knowledge to organize themselves and to plan and implement a

[1] Interview with John Tabu, former Tolikara Regent in Jayapura, on 29 May 2019.

[2] Interview with Let. Col (inf.) Leon Pangaribuan, social-communication affairs officer from Kodam Cenderawasih, in Jayapura, on 29 May 2019.

relevant development model suitable to solve their own problems, especially poverty [28]. Even, after 15 years the Otsus has been implemented, many OAP still does not know what was actually the Otsus policy? [29] Therefore, Jakarta's claim that Otsus is a bottom-up policy has been questioned since previously [30].

The absence of policy corrections for decades in the one hand, and democracy, which provided people equal access to development, on the other, made the poverty and backwardness impossible to be diminished [11]. Together with infectious diseases, low quality of life contributes to OAP depopulation [31]. Irrelevant development projects since Otsus was hastily made as the only and fast solution to referendum for independence produced development malfunction in many sectors. At the absence of Jakarta's supervisions, Otsus has generated corruptions and further tolerated many practices of mismanagement.

With lack of access of native Papuans to voice their aspirations and get involved in the decision-making process of Otsus projects, these problems produced accumulation of disappointments that eventually caused horizontal conflict between OAP versus migrants and vertical conflict between the local versus central governments. With long ignorance and injustice, Otsus contributed to the emergence of stronger resistance and more cases of unrests, ambushes, kidnappings and killing of civilians and security apparatus. The longer the cases last, the more disharmony occurs and threatens Indonesia's integrity [32].

A vicious circle between the need to push development and end conflict is then inevitably emerged [33]. Security forces who wants to secure Otsus projects and separatist movements who want to struggle for OAP's interests have been trapping in a prolonged conflict caused spread of insecurity and uncertainty due to the ongoing loss of trust. Police's operation, the Nemangkawi task force, has been deployed and later replaced with, using a softer name, Cartenz Peaceful Operation, but it cannot stop the conflict and violence until the moments.

Infrastructure development projects to eliminate poverty and backwardness are now a routine target of the separatist groups' attacks. Instead of finding a breakthrough to stop this vicious circle and building peace and preventing more innocent casualties, security personnel were more interested in rising take home pay by doing unclear routine tasks with no results [34]. TNI Chief Commander, Gen. Andhika, admitted the phenomenon, based on the investigation report of the 27 January 2022 of rebels' assault, which caused the death of three soldiers of Kodim YR 408 in Puncak municipality [34]. Such irresponsible behaviour of the security forces' routine tasks caused the rebels' backlash, resulted in circular conflicts between them [35]. The decline of welfare and quality of OAP's life in general, and the upsurge of human security threats from time to time explain why non-traditional security threats stemming from rebels' attacks in the name of OPM (*Organisasi Papua Merdeka*—Free Papua Movement) or KKB (*Kelompok Kriminal Bersenjata*—armed criminal group, a terminology used by the security forces) tends to increase today.

## 5 The Growing Separatist Movements During Otsus

Nduga, a remote municipality in highlands, which since 4 January 2008 has been enlarged with Law. No. 6/2008, can be picked-up as an example of Otsus failure. Of total Papua regions, after almost one decade it received Otsus funds, it has lowest HDI score in 2016, namely 26.56 [36]. Therefore, it is easy to explain why Nduga, the new municipality with 106,354 inhabitants, which has been enlarged and developed with Otsus funds, supported with the presence of 15–20 police from Polsek and 15–20 soldiers from Koramil levels, become an important base of OPM. It has not yet changed as a red zone for security forces, where OPM more frequently launched attacks to destroy the new infrastructure which has just been built. Meanwhile, TNI requests to place more soldiers, from only 40 percent capacity [36], to protect the new infrastructures and their workers in remote areas and highlands bring a new consequence to OAP regarding human rights violations. OPM has, however, anticipated that genocide will create a sufficient condition that can support their efforts to demand a new referendum for independence.

During two decades of Otsus implementation, new separatist generation with new leader plays important role in other regions of Papua. Kelly Kwalik, the old leader, has been replaced by Egianus Kogoya, the son of Daniel Yudas Kogoya, who involved in kidnapping and killing Lorentz Expedition team in January 1996. Egianus was the KKB masterminder who allegedly organized recent attacks against state apparatus and migrants in various locations and since long time have been consolidating different groups of rebels.[3] Kwalik was shot dead by the police in a routine surveillance in Timika on December 2009. Nevertheless, it did not stop separatist groups and their armed struggle in Papua. A clear evidence of this is the formation of the Second Division of OPM Armed Defence, subordinated to the OPM Fourth Paniai Military Command.

With the new commander, KKB more often launched guerilla attacks in various regions of the new enlarging province of West Papua, from August 2012 until June 2018. KKB continued its attacks to civilian targets, including the Twin Otter of Trigana Air, which was transporting logistics for regional elections, injuring two Brimob personnels. They further organized armed attacks to Kenyam district, causing three civilians killed. In a larger incident, on 3 October 2018, they took hostage teachers and health workers in Mapenduma for two weeks, during which one of them reportedly raped [36].

Subsequently, on 1 December 2018, KKB assaulted and took hostage 25 Istaka Karya workers who were building road in Yigi District, part of Trans-Papua project, causing 17 workers and 1 soldier died and 2 others seriously wounded [36]. Less than one month, on 27 February 2019, KKB and Egianus burnt an escavator operating to open access in the hinterlands. They intensified their activities, as on 7 March 2019, they attacked TNI Law Enforcement Task Force that wanted to secure road project in Mugi district to bring Papua out of isolation, resulted in 3 soldiers died [36]. Within

[3] Interview with AKBP (Lt.Col) Tony Ananda, Jayawijaya Police Resort Chief, in Wamena, on 31 May 2019.

two weeks, on 20 March 2019, with 40–50 personnels, KKB launched new attacks in Mugi district, caused 1 police died and 2 others wounded [36].

Since the end of 2011, separatist movements have been more active in conducting attacks on security forces and civilians. During 2021, there were 92 cases organized by separatist groups in Yahukimo, Pegunungan Bintang, Intan Jaya, Puncak and Nduga [37]. Comparing with 2020, the cases of shootings increased 87.75 percent. To respond these attacks, the police had launched 13 law enforcements operations in different names [37].

After a passive period in 2012–2017, since the beginning of 2018, the rebels have been reactivating their attacks, claimed more victims until the end 2021. Furthermore, as the new year 2022 began, separatist groups continued their armed struggle [38]. Not surprisingly, they looked more aggressive and braver than previously by intensifying their guerrilla warfare [39] to destroy infrastructures such as bridges, schools, health facilities, airports, police offices and other public facilities costly funded with Otsus money. Their actions also targeted state apparatus, especially military and police officers, in addition to their barracks and posts, which produced more incidences in the first quarter of 2022.In more recent attacks, they even attacked OAP inside TNI and the police, for instance, a man who was shot dead in early February 2022 and buried in his kampong (village) in Timika [39].

Apart from this, Jakarta's attempts to prosecute past cases of gross human rights violations mandated by Law No. 21/2002 on Otsus was not seriously implemented until today. The Attorney General Office (AGO) did not want to follow up the cases because they have no sufficient supporting documents. This is an important issue in UU No. 21/2002 that must be simultaneously realized in Papua in addition to the affirmative action to address poverty. Jakarta's recklessness to heal the old wound blocks new initiatives to address separatism comprehensively in the most eastern part of Indonesia [40].

## 6 Conclusion

The Otsus solution has been introduced as an immediately response offering an open check to stop the fast-growing aspirations demanding referendum for independence after the fall of Soeharto autoritarian regime. Its legal base, Law No. 21/2002, which excluded supervision and accountability, has been shortly passed by the parliament to utterly end separatism in Papua. Nevertheless, this alternative solution has failed to meet its main and strategic objective due to the limited trickledown effect obtained by both provinces there.

Poverty condition and OAP's HDI that have never significantly improved during two decades of Otsus were clear evidence of Jakarta's policy failure. The Otsus money has fallen into the wrong hands of bureaucrats and local leaders, with their irrelevant development projects. It has been further enjoyed by the separatist rebels and their symphatisants inside and outside local governments in all levels, as well as

Jakarta bureaucrats and elites, at the absence of good planning and supervision since the beginning.

With poor education, the OAP has been continuously marginalized and threatened by depopulation because of development projects their elites decided and implemented under the Otsus policy. Understandably, they could not compete with migrants in all sectors, to make money and seek new jobs. Many must leave their land because of landclearing projects for building infrastructure like Trans-Papua road, airports, modern markets, hotels, shopping centre, mal, football stadium as well as food estates, palm oil plantations, housing compounds for government employees and new military bases and compounds. Therefore, development projects with a proper planning must be introduced in the new Otsus policy, in accordance with Law No. 2/2021, its new legal base which has been passed by DPR. Pre- and Post-Legislative Scrutiny must be there and experts must play roles in the preparations and the realizations of the new development plan and projects in order to better overcome poverty and backwardness problems in all Papua regions.

In line with this, to stop genocide accusations, a security-focused plan must be replaced with a prosperity-focused approach, bearing in mind that the new infrastructures built are not intended to help security forces easier crush the rebels. This means that vicious circle of the violent separatist conflict must be cut and ended by replacing securitization with relevant development projects adopting good governance involving wide OAP's participations. Without all of these improvements, the new Otsus policy for the next two decades will predictably meet its same failure as previously.

**Acknowledgements** The writers extend their appreciation to Dr. Hendricus Andi Simarmata, senior lecturer on urban development studies from University of Indonesia and Dr. Thung Ju Lan, senior researcher on ethnicity and nation building from BRIN for their reviews and feedback which are important for improving this article.

**Contributorship** Both writers are equal contributors for this article.

## References

1. Araf A (2021) Papua securitization. Imparsial, Jakarta
2. International Crisis Group (2006) Papua: the dangers of shutting down dialogue
3. Meteray B (2012) The dual nationalism of the Papuans. Kompas, Jakarta
4. Elisabeth A, Budiatri AP, Wiratri A, Pamungkas C, Wilson (2017) Executive summary: updating Papua road map: peace process, youth politics, and Papuan diaspora. Yayasan Pustaka Obor Indonesia
5. Nainggolan PP (2014) International activities of Papua separatist movements. Kajian 19:181–199. https://doi.org/10.22212/kajian.v19i3.555
6. Goodhand J (2001) Conflict assessments—a synthesis report: Kyrgyzstan. Mold. Nepal Sri Lanka. King's College, London
7. Humphreys M, Weinstein JM (2008) Who fights? The determinants of participation in civil war. Am J Pol Sci 52:436–455. https://doi.org/10.1111/j.1540-5907.2008.00322.x
8. Ross ML (2004) What do we know about natural resources and civil war? J Peace Res 41:337–356. https://doi.org/10.1177/0022343304043773

9. Gurr TR (2015) Why men Rebel. Routledge
10. Litvack J, Ahmad J, Bird R (1998) Rethinking decentralization in developing countries. World Bank Publications
11. Thies CG (2010) Of rulers, rebels, and revenue: state capacity, civil war onset, and primary commodities. J Peace Res 47:321–332. https://doi.org/10.1177/0022343310361841
12. Sen, Amartya (1999) Development as Freedom. Oxford University
13. Terriff T, Croft S, James L, Morgan P (2000) Security studies today. Sage
14. Duffield M (1994) Complex emergencies and the crisis of developmentalism. IDS Bull 25:37–45. https://doi.org/10.1111/j.1759-5436.1994.mp25004006.x
15. Homer-Dixon TF (2010) Environment, scarcity, and violence. Princeton University Press
16. Buzan B (1991) People, states & fear: an agenda for international security studies. The University of Michigan, Harvester Wheatsheaf, MI
17. Siregar LA (2022) Papua enlargement for whom?
18. Nainggolan PP (2012) The Indonesian military response to reform in democratic transition: a comparative analysis of three civilian regimes, 1998–2004
19. Cruz Jr R (2017) Rebellion against poverty
20. Katharina R (2018) Measuring of special autonomy achievements in Papua. Yayasan Pustaka Obor Indonesia, Jakarta
21. Subarkah T (2022) Not only built infrastructure
22. Azis NLL, Zuhro RS (2018) Politics of special autonomy and special region budget. Yayasan Pustaka Obor Indonesia, Jakarta
23. Notohamijoyo A (2022) Papua development paradox
24. Enembe L (2016) Papua: between money and authority. RM Books, Jakarta
25. Haris Azhar Reported Luhut (2022)
26. Badan Akuntabilitas Keuangan Negara (2020) Reviews on special autonomy and special budget of Papua, West Papua, Aceh and D.I. Yogyakarta Provinces, Jakarta
27. Autonomy for Papua (2003) Opportunity or illusion. FES, West Papua Network and Watch Indonesia, Jakarta
28. Majelis Rakyat Papua (2020) Assessments on the effectiveness of the implementation of Law No. 21 Year 2001 on Papua Special Autonomy, Jayapura
29. Azis NLL, Zuhro RS (2018) Dynamics of supervisions of budget of special autonomy and special region. Yayasan Pustaka Obor Indonesia, Jakarta
30. Katharina R (2018) Deliberative formulation of Papua special autonomy policy. BISNIS BIROKRASI J Ilmu Adm dan Organ 24:69–77
31. Sitokdana MN (2022) Enlargement of Papua with new autonomy provinces amid OAP depopulation threat
32. Sudira IN (2020) Development, marginalization, and disintegration of Papua. Imparsial, Jakarta
33. Chairullah E (2022) The fruit's choice in Papua
34. Sudebang F (2022) General Andika disclosed anomaly in Gome Koramil assault
35. Violence in Papua difficult to stop (2022)
36. Heat in Nduga (2019)
37. KKB's violent attacks in Cen-drawasih land continued (2022)
38. Terror occurs again, more soldiers died (2022)
39. Three more soldiers died (2022)
40. Zen APM (2005) Inconsistency and separatism: why does Papua continue to resist? Jakarta

# Does the Government Sponsor Religious Violence? An Analysis of Mob Violence and Sectarian Violence Due to Restrictive Religious Policies

**Wasisto Raharjo Jati**

**Abstract** This paper examines the impact of restrictive religious policies on the ongoing mob and sectarian violence in some developing countries. Some prohibitive regulations such as banning religious clothing symbols and harassing the certain group of believers are two main examples of governments' misconduct. Interestingly, the freedom of religion is likely to have an adverse effect because of the constitution. Drawing on datasets from Pew Research Centre on Global Restriction on Religion in 2018, this paper runs a panel data regression analysis to investigate the link between restrictive religious policies and violence. It argues that while the relationship between state-sponsored harassment and mob violence is statistically significant, the link of some restrictive policies and sectarian violence has been salient in recent times. Particularly, it takes place in predominantly certain religious countries in some Asian countries.

**Keywords** Religion · Religious policy · Violence · Asian countries · Religious symbols

## 1 Introduction

The extent of religious freedom expression has been a long debatable issue in almost countries in the world. One central debate point is the incitement of religious hatred [22, p. 218]. It means that religious freedom expression subsequently takes a form of religious violence to different religious beliefs. This shows how religions have been an ideological living force for those believers. Religious violence also encourages believers to defend their faith from others to attract potential followers. These two logics seem to follow a principle, which says the more people stick with religions, the closer access to power. Furthermore, "religion is strongly associated with power, and with the state" [17, p. 14]. In another word, defending of religion means defending of

W. Raharjo Jati (✉)
Research Center for Politics, National Research and Innovation Agency, Jakarta, Indonesia
e-mail: wasisto.raharjo.jati@brin.go.id



Nawawi et al. (eds.), *Managing Disruption and Developing Resilience for a Better Southeast Asia*, Springer Proceedings in Humanities and Social Sciences,
https://doi.org/10.1007/978-981-96-2116-3_61

power. This results in the unequal power relationship among religions, particularly between the dominant believers and the minorities. Consequently, disputes have been profound for decades.

It has been widely acknowledged that religious violence has been already existing before nation-state formation. The consensus of literatures, commonly referred to the school of constructivist, has argued that religious violence is the product of long-established disputes among believers prior to modern civilisation [4, 6]. The emergence of the modern state serves the institutionalised shape of religious violence. The way state-run errands for himself in sparking religious violence is the main attention of the school of constructivist. An example of this argument is the ongoing Hindu-Islam conflict in India. These two religions have raised from the prejudices and hostilities between two religions [4, p. 10]. It has its conflict roots from some classical underlying causes like Hindus have labelled Muslims as obstacles to achieve an ideal Indian state since independence movements [4, p. 7. The obstacles itself include the distinctive religious orientation and the foundation of the state.

Likewise, the misinterpretation concept of "jihad" among Muslims often triggers violence against non-Muslims. The latter group includes Christians, Jews, and even Westerners like Americans. Jihad itself literally means "fighting" that addressed to non-believers whom perceived as an enemy [6, p. 85]. This narrow-minded definition might be not represented as the true meaning of jihad. However, the consensus of Jihad among Muslim scholars seems to conclude that it is compulsory duties for Muslim to defend their faith [6, pp. 82–84]. Following this line of thought, the concept of Jihad has grown up across the period from caliphate to modern nation-state period.

Another scholarly framework that focuses on religious violence is the school of secularists. According to this school of thought, religious violence is a part of government-led religious discrimination policies [5, 9, 23]. This means that the government-based restriction policies have restricted the religious minorities under the dominant believer rule. This also means that the government wants to enact secularisation policies by excluding religious matters [5, p. 44]. However, it is important to note that the relationship between restrictive religious policies and citizens depends on the policies level. While the restrictive policies only target to the aggregate level, the state still recognises the individual freedom of religious observance [23, p. 161].

This paper challenges the two above existing theories by revealing that the states get more intense over religious violence through a series of restrictive religious policies. The question I want to ask here: does the government ignite religious conflict? More specifically, to what extent, the state exercises its power when it comes to responding to violence? Drawing on the statistical results, the states are likely to spark conflict among citizens by issuing some limited religious expression rules. Furthermore, this kind of policies has widely increased gap between state and society. The latter findings I will elaborate in the Asian country case level.

This paper will proceed as follows. The first section discusses the broad concept of religious violence and its connection with state restrictive policies. It also includes the interplay between certain religious group, minorities, and policy-makers. Second, I will explain theories, causal mechanisms, and some hypotheses. These three will enable us to test the correlation between some restrictive religious policies as the independent variable and mob/sectarian violence as the dependent variables. Third, I will elaborate the statistical findings into Asian country case level like India, Indonesia, and also Saudi Arabia. These first two countries represent the country which has a secular view of religious expression. But it ends up with one dominant religion has a strong influence on policy preferences. The latter represents the one single religious country which has a long-established sectarian dispute with Shia Muslims.

## 2 Religious Violence and Restrictive Religious Policies

The violence that fuelled by religions may be more detrimental than ethnicity-driven factor. Religion has a strong psychological influence that encourages followers to defend their faith. It usually comes to underlying than the main factor when it comes to conflict escalation. Previous causes like economy have been the classical conflict root in human history. This, therefore, puts religion as the underlying factor that is able to trigger violence. The interplay between certain religious groups and state policy-making process should be important here. I would like to elaborate on these two factors in accordance with the previous theories above.

As mentioned earlier, the long-established religious dispute primarily serves religious violence according to the school of constructivist. The long-established religious dispute constructs the way state forcefully against its citizens thorough unbalanced policy-making process. The position of the state is a crucial case in point here because it will determine the outcome of religion policies. This may withdraw attention for many scholars to further investigate it. One plausible correlation with regard to the position of the state is if the government builds a cohesive connection with the certain religious group, it will result in restrictive and inegalitarian policies. Apart from the former, if the government stays away from a certain religious group, it will result in the neutral religious policies.

With regard to these two hypothetical situations above, most of the time, the long dispute between dominant and minorities eventually affects the behaviour of the state. This particularly points out the ruling elites to take long-term benefit. More specifically, they take benefits from the deep hostile views amidst contested two or more groups of believers. Usually, the politicians maintain close ties with leading or majoritarian believers. By exchanging their influence on the policy-making process to prominent religious leaders, the politicians expect to gain more votes on election day. However, this bargaining method certainly sacrifices the civil rights of those minorities. As a result, religious violence always happens all the time.

One leading theory on the school of a constructivist is clientelism theory. It says that religious violence is the way politicians use religion for their own political benefits like seeking for re-election chances [1, p. 374, 2, pp. 417–420, 3]. It is also meant to reconvince the dominant believers to cast a vote for those politicians who share the same religious affiliation, politicians. The constructivist scholars have focused on the long-established religious that causes the emergence of far-right politicians.

They construct religion is not only as of the way of life but then it expanded to political ideologies. This latter from constitutionally issues some restrictive policies such as limiting access to public service for those minorities and banning minorities' religious expressions. An example of this discrimination is a separation of neighbourhood communities [7, pp. 38–40]. The government would like to support one sect loyal to the government.

Some above-mentioned restrictive religious policies basically show how ruling elites take advantages on a long dispute between majoritarian and minorities. By scapegoating the religious minorities, the politicians spearhead a campaign to religious minorities to attract potential voters. Furthermore, politicians use religion to justify their action. It could also reach out to far-right voters. Constitutionally, when government is backing some certain religious groups, it has many unbalanced consequences for those minorities, specifically education and other public sectors [1, p. 372].

One main critic for the school of a constructivist is to what extent either elites or state build a special relationship with the majoritarian believers. This does not clearly enough to explain the root of restrictive religious policies. Putting aside the role of religion, the state seems to be a major factor in restricting freedom of religious expression on behalf of national stability.

In sum, the school of constructivist seems to suggest that the ingrained religious dispute has opened the windows of opportunity for those elites. They set up religious principle within some inegalitarian policies. This surely makes the current religious conflict become more embroiled in public spheres. As a result, the violence gets worse in society.

Compared with the school of constructivist, the secular approach has a different point of view on religious violence. It says that neutrality of the state in managing the relationship with the group of believers is the root of violence. This means some religious persecutions addressed by the state to ensure law and order. Some scholars have focused on the constitution that could be the source of violence. One leading scholar John Caiazza argues that religious violence committed by the state has two consequences: first, the elimination of the religious influence in order to ensure modern environment and second, advocating for the centralisation of state power to disable religious violent doctrine [5, pp. XV and 44]. These two purposes mean that while the increasing role of state prevails over the religions, this makes neither majoritarian nor minorities at the vulnerable position. Through its restrictive religious policies, the government want to centralise the power by monopolising violence.

This basic explanation above shows that the more centralised government equals to more coercive religious regulations are. This may open a debate whether or not the state constitution "officially" legitimises the religious violence. Many scholars have looked into the way the constitution can do so. It is important to note that the secular constitution strongly emphasises the state over religion. This may be debatable, but some country cases show religion should be in private, not in public matters. As a result, this may also make the constitution inadequate to support secular values.

Given that complex situation above, Finke and Martin argue that the secular constitution causes restrictive religious religions [8, p. 693]. This argument also means that while governments recognise the freedom of religion, they are less supportive in guaranteeing those expressions [8, p. 696]. As a result, the government wants to limit the religious expressions particularly certain religious organisations. This aims to show that religion does not override the state when it comes to exercising authorities.

The secular constitution may also affect greatly minorities. The consensus of literature argues that a lack of respect to religious freedom is the main problem [9, p. 887]. This problem happens because the government only acknowledges few official religion. This limited acknowledgement means the government wants to incorporate religions with the state system. Certainly, this policy has detrimental consequences for those believers, particularly minorities. This allows the state to supress the believers. Furthermore, this also potentially harms the relationship between religion and state as government administratively regulate the requirement of religion. It should have a God, prophet/holy figures, scripture, and the house of worship [16, pp. 86–87]. Moreover, social acceptance somehow is important to evaluate the requirement of religion. These two make the minorities as the second citizen.

Although the school of secular emphasises the role of the state in igniting the conflict, one missing point here is why state intervenes religious matters. This does not enough get attention from most secular scholars.

In sum, the school of secular seems to suggest that the state constitution may harm the freedom of religious expression. This results in inegalitarian attitudes towards minorities. As state attempts to incorporate religions within regulations, some believers would suffer unpleasant responses from either government or public itself. Ideally, the constitution should be neutral, but it practically suppresses believers, particularly minorities. An example of this might be intolerance attitudes such as religious discrimination and religious persecutions [19, 20]. Both often occurs in some religious countries.

## 3 Religious Violence, Causal Mechanisms, and Its Hypotheses

Following up the above-mentioned explanations, it seems that religious violence could be imminent according to two main reasons. The first factor is if the government builds a cohesive relationship with a certain group of believers, this may result in the inegalitarian religious policies. The government would like to adopt one single religion as the main preference to regulate religions. This can end up with strong objections, particularly for those minorities. The second factor is if the government puts himself over religions, this may result in the restrictive religious policies. The government would target either minorities or certain believers. This aims to maintain order and stability that minimise the role of religion in society.

Some scholars argue that religious violence has shaped the public understanding of those people who have a different background. These premises are notably argued by Sonia Ghumman and Ryan. They said that religious discrimination that occurred at work is usually driven by four main reasons such as (1) disparate treatment, (2) religious harassment, (3) failure to reasonably accommodate religious belief, and (4) retaliation against employee fellow who alleges religious discrimination [10, p. 441]. These four prohibitions have shown that the government tend to be the secular protector in daily life. Regarding segregation of religion from social life, the government particularly in Western countries attempted to issue policies for regulating religious symbol use in public space. It keeps a neutral condition among society members. However, as the right-wing political parties and its non-state actors being grown up in some countries, it directly harms the social relationship because they tend to oppose multicultural societal background. Furthermore, they had a strict and one-sided view in observing diversity because they preferred to advocate supremacist ideologies in the policy-making process.

In sum, there are two possible causal mechanisms we can draw from the theory of religious violence. First, the more the coercive government's attitude to the group of believers, the more restrictive religion-related policies would be. Second, the closer the government builds a relationship with certain group of believers, especially the majoritarian believers and far-right people, the more likely the religion policies would be inegalitarian for those minorities. We will look up to these two causal mechanisms within the statistical analysis.

Moving on to the position of religion within the state constitution, the position of state and religion has turned bias because the non-state actors suppressed the state to be more supportive with the majority religion. These include the implementation of law based on religion principle and banning other minority religions. It frequently found in several countries which constitutionally adopt official religion policies such as in the Middle East and North Africa (MENA) and some parts of Asia and few cases in European and America. The interesting findings of those regions are freedom of religious expressions has been threatened by the state's strict constitution and repression from non-state actors. To put it simply, there has been an inegalitarian constitution with regard to the position of religion. In these contexts, we assume that a weak state is the main factor why state-sponsored oppression by non-state actors intensively occurs. Persecutions repeatedly led to mob violence because most non-state actors would like to deny other religions emerge as rivals. Therefore, religion-based constitution often threatened minorities in public spheres. These cases visible in several Muslim majority countries which embraced religion is part of the constitution. The implementation of sharia law arguably led to discrimination because non-Muslims should obey and follow the rule [11, p. 7].

In sum, there are some possible causal mechanisms we can draw from the position of religion within the state constitution. First, the more the increasing influence of certain religious preference in the policy-making process, the more likely the religious policies will be unbalanced. Second, the more the inegalitarian religious policies, the more likely the involvement of non-state actors in policies reinforcement. These four causal mechanisms I will narrow it into several hypotheses. This will help us to test existing theories. Furthermore, the four hypotheses enable us to look up to previous findings. It could be the result of this research that would confirm or refute the findings.

Following up the four above-mentioned causal mechanisms, I already proposed some relevant hypotheses. This will enable us to test the arguments from the existing literature. The hypotheses I put down as follows:

*H1: Religious discrimination policies and public view are more likely to promote mob and sectarian violence. These two types of violence often led by a group of dominant believers.*
*H2: When the government stipulates strict religion constitution, it is more likely to cause minorities harassment. This potentially causes a series of violence.*
*H3: The intimidation, which based on one single religious preference likely to target the minorities. Furthermore, this official intimidation promulgated by the state has been continuously increasing.*
*H4: The mob and sectarian violence are likely to advocate their religious teaching into policymaking processes.*

These four hypotheses are worth testing as there is a few of literature that highlights the linkage between violent actions and the role of the state. In the next section, I will elaborate one of the data and methodologies in this paper.

## 4 Data and Methodology

This research has used datasets from Pew Research Centre about Global Restriction on Religion 2018. By and large, these datasets have combined two kinds of data such as time-series data and cross-sectional data. These two kinds of data also include nine reports on global violence trend, which started from 2008 until 2016. In addition, these datasets already observed 200 countries and self-governing entities based on two main indexes.

The first is the Government Restriction Index that explained the government policies on religions based on 20 variables. This index specifically monitored the trend of restrictive religious polices by each state in the world. The second is the Social Hostilities Index that explained the way people and communities intimidated other religion followers and also minorities members with several mob violence, sectarian conflict, and religiously biased crimes based on 13 variables [18, pp. 1–2]. From these two, I use these two datasets to further investigate the causal linkage between government policies and the hostile view of violence.

Both datasets mainly build on yes and no question. All variables are coded in binary models (0 = no and 1 = yes). This kind of answer enables us to obtain precise answers from the respondents. However, the phrase it is important to note that in some variables, there are third indicators that in-between between 0 and 1—for example: 0.45, 0.67, and 0.80. Those numbers indicate the variation of agreement that possibly has a dissenting opinion. It reflects the alternative answers instead of "yes" and "no". It also either relevant or irrelevant depends on the country cases.

Moving on to how to analyse the datasets, this research uses a quantitative analysis. More specifically, I use linear regression analysis and panel data model to examine correlation analysis between dependent variables and independent variables. These two variables I already put down. Both models seem to be suitable in this research since variables on datasets observed the behaviour and attitudes per each entity in the given time.

The use of regression analysis here gives us the basic insight tool for investigating the causal relationship between mob/sectarian violence and restrictive religious policies. With regard to panel data regression here, it enables us to understand the causal relationship particularly in the country case and even the year itself. Given that the datasets are longitudinal data with multiple units, it means that the institution that creates these datasets has repeated the questions towards the respondent across the given countries and periods in ensuring relation between all the variable has been under control [15, pp. 4–5]. In addition, some tested policies such as policies and violence have been reflecting the dynamic social phenomenon that may have specific tendencies.

I would like to explain the research strategy here. First, the regression analysis will investigate whether or not the restrictive religious regulations affect mob/sectarian violence. After that, we could have the first findings in general explanations. Second, the panel data will retest the findings of regression analysis with specific control variables. As mentioned above, I use the variable of year and country case. We are interested to see that tendency across the time and regions by controlling them into certain periods. The specific aim from these analyses shows us the trend change on variables such as policies and public response in a particular issue. We can measure the percentage of increased or decreased figure. In this respect, states are the entities that coded 1, 2, 3, 4, and so on and were observed during 10 years (2006–2016). However, in these datasets, there is no control variable (GDP and gender) that becomes the determinant factor why some variables had changed over the given periods. We already tested the fixed effect on panel data regression that showed us, all the data were controlled across the given years. However, we should acknowledge that this research is going to estimate the associate relation and not causal link because the variable of years gives different meaning in each given year. Moreover, we can still examine the associate relation between regions and time-effect.

With regard to variables, six variables are divided by two categories: 2 dependent variables and 4 independent variables.

1. Independent variable (GRI_Q_10) / binary data (yes/no): does the government regulate wearing religious attire and symbol?
2. Independent variable (GRI_Q_1) / binary data (yes/no): does the constitution protect freedom of religion?
3. Independent variable (GRI_Q-11) / binary data (yes/no): does the government harass/intimidate religious groups?

4. Dependent variable (SHI_Q_2) / binary data (yes/yes but death data were not reported): was there mob violence related to religion?
5. Dependent variable (SHI_Q_3) / binary data (yes/no): was there an act of sectarian or communal violence between religious groups?

All the independent variables represent the government's policies on religion while dependent variables represent religion harassment. We make two regression analysis (Pooled OLS and Panel Regression) based on two variables, namely "Nations" from Nation and "Year" from Question Year. We assume that both variables are "control variables" in this research.

## 5 Data Analyses

The first thing we do in data analysis is to make panel data by making xtset command on STATA based on two "control variables": Nation_fk and Question_Year. However, we dropped sub-Saharan Africa in my nations variable because the data taken from those regions were sufficient and missed some answers on the given survey questions. Therefore, we got a strongly balanced relation between variable years and nations. Then, we run the Pooled Regression model to show us the correlation between variables and after that we run the fixed effect test. We use fixed effect analysis because Hausman test shows that all the variables have a $p$-value less than 0.05 in OLS Regression. We control all the variables to ensure that the results are not different from the hypotheses and theoretical frameworks. Regarding control variables, we use country fixed effect and time fixed effect to examine all the variable relation. Most importantly, we can compare the comparative result between OLS Regression and the Panel Data Regression.

To test our hypotheses, we have two main estimation frameworks that summarised as the following equation:

$$SHI_{Q_{2_{irt}}} = \alpha_0 + \alpha_1 GRI_{Q_{10_{irt}}} + \alpha_2 GRI_{Q_{11_{irt}}} + \alpha_3 GRI_{Q_{1_{irt}}} + \gamma_i + \theta_t + \rho_{rt} + \upsilon_{irt}$$

where in my first equation $SHI_{Q_{2_{irt}}}$ is an indicator variable whether there was mob violence related to religion in the country $I$, at region $r$, at year $t$. $GRI_{Q_{10_{irt}}}$ is a dummy variable with value one if the government regulates wearing religious clothing or symbols, and zero otherwise. $GRI_{Q_{11_{irt}}}$ is a dummy variable with value one if the government harasses or intimidates religious groups, and zero otherwise. $GRI_{Q_{1_{irt}}}$ is a dummy variable with value one if the nation has the constitution that protects freedom of religion. R analysis would focus on discussing the magnitude and statistical significance of coefficients $\alpha_1$, $\alpha_2$, and $\alpha_3$

$$SHI_{Q_{3_{irt}}} = \beta_0 + \beta_1 GRI_{Q_{10_{irt}}} + \beta_2 GRI_{Q_{11_{irt}}} + \beta_3 GRI_{Q_{1_{irt}}} + \gamma_i + \theta_t + \rho_{rt} + \upsilon_{irt}$$

Our second equation is like my previous equation except for different dependent variable. In the second model, my main interest is $SHI_{Q_{3_{irt}}}$ which is an indicator variable with value one if there was sectarian violence between religious groups in country *i*, at region *r*, at year *t*. In my preferred specification, we use the country-specific fixed effect ($\gamma_i$) to control heterogeneity among countries. Also, we allow the time-specific variable to capture dynamic change over time. Lastly, we also control for the interaction of regional dummies and time dummies to capture any change overtime at the regional level. Our analysis would focus on discussing the magnitude and statistical significance of coefficients $\beta_1$, $\beta_2$, and $\beta_3$. All the analyses are remarkably robust in both regression tables because it is such easier for us to infer the meaning of the tables.

Following the comparative results as mentioned before, we categorise the panel data results as follows:

Model 1: OLS Regression without control variables
Model 2: Panel Data Regression with country fixed effect
Model 3: Panel Data Regression with country fixed effect and time fixed effect
Model 4: Panel Data Regression with country fixed effect, time fixed effect. And the interaction between region area and time fixed effect.

## 6 The First Statistical Analysis: Panel Data Regression Estimator Analysis Between Government's Religion Policies and Mob Violence During 2007–2016

I begin my analysis with the relationship between restrictive religious policies and mob violence. This relationship will reveal the findings of why mob violence could appear. I test several variables below that might be relevant. According to Table 1, there are no religious policies that might cause violent religious actions, particularly mob violence. Some variables I use such as regulating religious clothing and freedom of religious expression, which enacted by constitution seems to be unparallel with mob violence. The statistical results show statistically insignificant ($p > 0.005$). Instead, the harassment of certain believers by the state is likely the major cause. The statistical results show statistically significant ($p < 0.005$). The latter result shows that the perpetrators of mob violence are not certain believers, but the state itself.

This OLS regression analysis shows that in general, the state bears the responsibility for orchestrating the mob violence. Statistically, it also shows that the mob violence can be imminent through policy-making and non-policy-making processes. In another word, the state seems to monopolise the violence upon himself.

In sum, this OLS regression result rejects the first hypothesis that says religious discrimination policies and public view are more likely to promote mob and sectarian violence and the second hypothesis that says when the government stipulates strict religion constitution, it is more likely to cause minorities harassment. In reality, evidence explains the policies are the source of violence. This may open debate that

**Table 1** Summary statistics: relation between restrictive religion policies and mob violence

| Policies indicators | Statistics indicators | Model 1 | Model 2 | Model 3 | Model 4 |
|---|---|---|---|---|---|
| Does the government regulate wearing religious clothing or symbols? | Standard errors | 0.043 | −0.009 | −0.019 | −0.024 |
| | Coefficient | (0.018) | (0.024) | 0.024 | 0.024 |
| | p-values | 0.016 | 0.696 | 0.421 | 0.319 |
| Did the government harass or intimidate religious groups? | Standard errors | 0.167 | 0.026 | −0.003 | −0.012 |
| | Coefficient | (0.017) | (0.022) | (0.022) | (0.023) |
| | p-values | 0.000 *** | 0.241 | 0.883 | 0.611 |
| Does the constitution protect freedom of religion? | Standard errors | −0.061 | −0.233 | −0.223 | −0.215 |
| | Coefficient | (0.024) | (0.092) | (0.096) | (0.096) |
| | p-values | 0.011 | 0.013 | 0.021 | 0.027 |
| Relationship with the control variables | | | | | |
| Country-specific fixed effect | | No | Yes | Yes | Yes |
| Year fixed effect | | No | No | Yes | Yes |
| Region x year effect | | No | No | No | Yes |
| r-square | | 0.072 | 0.000 | 0.000 | 0.013 |
| N *(observation)* | | 1970 | 1970 | 1970 | 1970 |

*Note* * $p < 0.1$. ** $p < 0.05$. *** $p < 0.01$

the state uses other instruments to spark the conflict. Moreover, the type of regime can be determinant here as state singlehandedly conducts the violence. It can state regime be the main actor behind the mob violence.

Turning to the relationship between restrictive religious policies and sectarian violence, this analysis will further investigate the first findings. More specifically, it will involve several control variables in the analysis. In general, the second analysis seems to reverse the previously-mentioned findings. It said that the restrictive religious policy does not affect directly violence. My second finding in Table 2 already underscored the importance of policies in shaping violence. Particularly the sectarian violence, this may also show that the state seems to build a cohesive relationship with a certain group of believers. This can be visible in several religious policies like regulation on wearing religious symbols. While the harassment of believers has been continuously happening, surprisingly the constitution is likely to become an underlying violent factor.

According to Table 2, the prohibition of religious symbols has been the leading factor in shaping sectarian violence. The statistical analysis shows the statistically significant result in the question "does the government regulate wearing religious clothing or symbols?", which has the *p*-value ($p < 0.005$). When it comes to the year

**Table 2** Summary statistics: relation between restrictive religion policies and sectarian violence

| Policies indicators | Statistics indicators | Model 1 | Model 2 | Model 3 | Model 4 |
|---|---|---|---|---|---|
| Does the government regulate wearing religious clothing or symbols? | Standard error | 0.073 | 0.067 | 0.060 | 0.063 |
| | Coefficient | (0.021) | (0.025) | (0.024) | (0.024) |
| | p-values | 0.001** | 0.008* | 0.012 | 0.009** |
| Did the government harass or intimidate religious groups? | Standard error | 0.148 | 0.023 | 0.044 | 0.042 |
| | Coefficient | (0.017) | (0.016) | (0.021) | (0.021) |
| | p-values | 0.000*** | 0.154 | 0.043 | 0.048 |
| Does the constitution protect freedom of religion? | Standard error | 0.100 | 0.194 | 0.210 | 0.244 |
| | Coefficient | (0.033) | (0.089) | (0.086) | (0.092) |
| | p-values | 0.003** | 0.032 | 0.015 | 0.008 |
| Relationship with the control variables | | | | | |
| Country-specific fixed effect | | No | Yes | Yes | Yes |
| Year fixed effect | | No | No | Yes | Yes |
| Region x year effect | | No | No | No | Yes |
| r-square | | 0.087 | 0.059 | 0.082 | 0.106 |
| N *(observation)* | | 1970 | 1970 | 1970 | 1970 |

and country case in model 4, it seems that this policy entirely affects some countries case during 2017–2016.

Compared with the first variable, it seems the following variables such as state harassment to believers and constitution are likely unparallel with the country and specific period. Regardless of that, the results are statistically significant when it comes to sectarian violence. This result likely shows that the state uses secular preference in the policy-making process. As a result, there will neglect minorities to express their belief and faith publicly. This may signal the religious discrimination is still salient in society.

## 7 The Second Statistical Analysis: Panel Data Regression Estimator Analysis Between Government's Religion Policies and Sectarian Violence During 2007–2016

These panel data results above are also partially agreed with the rest of the two hypotheses such as H3: the intimidation, which is based on one single religious preference likely to target the minorities; and H4: the mob and sectarian violence are likely to advocate their religious teaching into policy-making processes.

Overall, the two above-mentioned statistical results contribute to two major findings. It is worth to further elaborate in the discussion section. The first, state-sponsored violence is particularly mob violence. This may reflect the secular stance of the state that wipes out any violent expression on behalf of religion. Second, the state intentionally uses specific religious preference and builds a relationship with a certain group of believers. This may result in egalitarian religious policies, particularly for those minorities.

With regard to two previously-mentioned findings, I will follow up these two into country and case experiences.

# 8 General Discussions

Let us return to the research question: does the government ignite religious conflict? More specifically, to what extent, religious preference can affect state policy-making process? According to the above-mentioned both regression and panel data analysis, I have two statistical analyses with which to provide answers.

1. The state naturally has the intention to spark conflict, specifically mob violence. The purpose of harassment to preserve the secular condition.
2. The state could issue some inegalitarian and restrictive religious policies when it comes to spark sectarian violence. This result strongly connected to the specific country and year period.

These two results ultimately show that the government ignites religious conflict. Basically, my result seems to suggest that while the harassment of believers still continuously occurs, this is more likely a side effect of the inegalitarian religious policies. This finding, however, is uncertain to make further link whether certain religious preference or close connection with specific dominant believers in shaping sectarian violence.

I would like to elaborate these two statistical analyses into several paragraphs below here. From these two findings, I also want to whether to confirm or challenge the current literature on religious conflict issues.

In general, my two main findings are likely to support the school of secularists instead of constructivist theory. The root of violent religious itself lies in the constitution. This subsequently causes religious conflict due to a lack of respect for religious freedom expression [9, p. 887]. The form of the constitution itself could be the secular constitution. This has aimed to limit the influence of religion over society. Furthermore, this less supportive religious expression potentially causes discrimination. I will further elaborate this in country case experiences.

I will take India and Indonesia in elaborating statistical findings. Both countries have a secular constitution but they also often have numerous religious conflicts at home. This verifies my findings become worth to elaborate in area case. One recent article that argued by Sumaktoyo confirmed with finding. He argues that the "level of religious policies and social discrimination have deteriorated significantly due to more assertive parliament" [21, p. 38]. Furthermore, he also argues stricter religious policy presumably due to explicit favour with certain religion [21, p. 38]. Given these two plausible arguments, I would pick up the former than latter arguments because it sounds reasonable with the current situation. The more assertive parliament in stipulate restrictive religious policies may represent the role of the state to restrict the number of religions [12, p. 733]. Moreover, through the national ideology of *Pancasila,* the government would like to implement "mild secularism" by regulating religion into state control [12, p. 731]. As a result, this kind of restricted religious policies dearly those religious minorities, particularly the heretics [16, pp. 87–88]. This Indonesian experience seems to suggest the religious violence could become vigilante attacks if the government were silent in responding conflict.

Similar to Indonesia, India has religiously-divided society. While Hindus still predominantly occupy at the top position, there are some other groups of believers like Muslims, Sikhs, Christians, and Buddhists. These interreligious relationships sometime could be deteriorated depending on the current regime. Indian case shows that there is a long debate whether the state can secularise the religious principle or state gives freedom of religious expressions [14, p. 621]. This condition subsequently causes the status quo condition for religion protection. However, the current Indian government suppresses religious minorities, particularly Muslims [13, pp. 209–210 and 216–217]. While Indian officially declared that the constitution is secular, in reality, there has been ongoing restrictions towards minorities. This condition surely confirms my findings that when the state intervenes the religious, it would deteriorate the religious violence.

## 9 Conclusion

The state has an important role in igniting religious conflict over society. The more assertive elites in implementing secular principles have caused huge consequences. Religious discrimination for those religious minorities is something the government should pay off. To be more specific, the state constitution ideally should have neutral in maintaining the harmonious relationship. But then ruling elites take advantages on it for their own political benefits.

As I mentioned earlier, India and Indonesia are the best examples of religious violence in Asian countries. Although both nations adopt secular principles within the constitution, religious policies seem to be inegalitarian and discriminative. My statistical analysis reveals that some freedom of religious expressions such as wearing religious symbols and attire is limited according to the law. This subsequently could drive the state to harass certain believers if the latter persist to express their faith publicly. Furthermore, these policies often target to those minorities. Consequently, the interreligious relationship could be harmful due to restrictive religious policies.

In the end, this research seems to suggest that the governments should revise or even revoke some inegalitarian policies regarding religious matters. The state should facilitate the mutual consensus when it comes to religious regulations.

## References

1. Anderson E, Longkumer A (2018) “Neo-Hindutva”: evolving forms, spaces, and expressions of Hindu nationalism. Contemp South Asia 26(4):371–377
2. Berenschot W (2009) Rioting as maintaining relations: Hindu-Muslim violence and political mediation in Gujarat, India. Civ Wars 11(4):414–433
3. Berenschot W (2012) Riot politics: Hindu-Muslim violence and the Indian state. Columbia University Press, New York
4. Brass PR (2003) The production of Hindu-Muslim violence in contemporary India. University of Washington Press. http://www.jstor.org/stable/j.ctvcwn5mp (January 6, 2021)
5. Caiazza J (2017) Religion, violence, and the secular state. Routledge, New York
6. Emanuilov R, Yashlavsky A (2011) Terror in the name of faith: religion and political violence. Academic Studies Press, Boston, MA
7. Fibiger T (2020) Mom, are we Shi’a? Neg(oti)ating sectarian identity in everyday life in post-2011 Bahrain. Rev Faith Int Aff 18(1):34–42
8. Finke R, Martin RR (2014) Ensuring liberties: understanding state restrictions on religious freedoms. J Sci Study Relig 53(4):687–705
9. Fox J, Finke R, Eisenstein MA (2019) Examining the causes of government-based discrimination against religious minorities in western democracies: societal-level discrimination and securitization. Comp Eur Polit 17(6):885–909
10. Ghumman S, Ryan AM (2013) Not welcome here: discrimination towards women who wear the Muslim headscarf. Hum Relat 66(5):671–698
11. Iffat I (2018) Threats to and approaches to promote freedom of religion or belief. Helpdesk report. Knowledge, Evidence, and Learning for Development, London
12. Iskandar P (2016) The Pancasila delusion. J Contemp Asia 46(4):723–735
13. Kronstadt KA (2018) India: religious freedom issues. Curr Polit Econ South Southeast Cent Asia 27(1/2):203–237
14. Lerner H (2013) Permissive constitutions, democracy, and religious freedom in India, Indonesia, Israel, and Turkey. World Polit 65(4):609–655
15. Longhi A, Nandi A (2015) A practical guide to using panel data. Sage, London
16. Marshall P (2018) The ambiguities of religious freedom in Indonesia. Rev Faith Int Aff 16(1):85–96
17. Mondal AA (2016) Articles of faith: freedom of expression and religious freedom in contemporary multiculture. Islam Christ-Muslim Relat 27(1):3–24
18. Pew Research Center (2018) Codebook for Pew Research Center’s global restrictions on religion data. Pew Research Center, Washington, DC
19. Raharjo Jati W (2022, November) Polarization of Indonesian society during 2014–2020: causes and its impacts toward democracy. Jurnal Ilmu Sosial dan Ilmu Politik 26(2). https://jurnal.ugm.ac.id/jsp/article/view/66057
20. Raharjo Jati W et al (2022) From intellectual to advocacy movement: Islamic moderation, the conservatives and the shift of interfaith dialogue campaign in Indonesia. Ulumuna 26(2). https://ulumuna.or.id/index.php/ujis/article/view/572 (January 31, 2023)
21. Sumaktoyo NG (2020) A price for democracy? Religious legislation and religious discrimination in post-Soeharto Indonesia. Bull Indones Econ Stud 56(1):23–42
22. Thompson S (2012) Freedom of expression and hatred of religion. Ethnicities 12(2):215–232
23. Wright JD (2016) More religion, less justification for violence: a cross-national analysis. Arch Psychol Relig 38(2):159–183

# An Epidemic of Human Rights Violations: The Authoritarian Response to COVID-19 in Duterte's Philippines

**Benjamin Velasco**

**Abstract** Philippines President Duterte imposed one of the longest lockdowns to control the spread of COVID-19 yet recorded at various times the highest number of infections in Southeast Asia. This paper asserts that it is precisely the authoritarian nature of the Duterte regime that has caused the tragedy. Further, the authoritarian response to COVID-19 exacerbated impunity and disregard for human rights in the country. The law and order paradigm of an authoritarian government is utterly unsuitable in managing a public health crisis. The regime exploited the pandemic to escalate its repression of political rivals and continue the bloody drug war. Policies implemented during the lockdown reveal a consistent bias for business interests and against workers' rights. The pandemic exposed the regime's ineptitude and this contrasts with its image of toughness in dealing with the manufactured crisis called the drug war. While it may be argued that an authoritarian response and the sacrifice of civil liberties are necessary in controlling COVID-19, it has not been the case for the Philippines.

**Keywords** Rodrigo Duterte · COVID-19 pandemic · Authoritarianism

## 1 Introduction

Philippines President Rodrigo Duterte imposed one of the strictest and longest lockdowns in the world, lasting 17 straight months, to control the spread of COVID-19 [6]. But despite severe restrictions on people's mobility and draconian limitations on civil liberties, the Philippines recorded 342,816 cases, the highest number of COVID-19 infections in Southeast Asia as of October 2020 [28]. Again, it had the most infections in the region during the surge in early 2021 that severely strained the healthcare system [13]. Then, the Philippines had the worst one-week average of new cases in Southeast Asia in January 2022 [29].

B. Velasco (✉)
University of the Philippines Diliman, Quezon City, Philippines
e-mail: bbvelasco@up.edu.ph



Nawawi et al. (eds.), *Managing Disruption and Developing Resilience for a Better Southeast Asia*, Springer Proceedings in Humanities and Social Sciences,
https://doi.org/10.1007/978-981-96-2116-3_62

The most serious challenge Duterte had faced in his administration has been controlling the spread of COVID-19 and mitigating its impact on the economy. In the war against COVID-19, Duterte has failed miserably. In contrast, similarly situated countries in Southeast Asia such as Vietnam and Thailand have resoundingly tamed the pandemic and escaped the worst of its economic impact.

This paper posits that a key reason for the ineffective response in the Philippines to the COVID-19 pandemic is authoritarian governance. Deconstructing the factors leading to the disastrous outcome of Duterte's response is relevant to understanding the relationship between authoritarian governance and crisis management. Likewise, it is important to observe the differentiated distribution of the costs and benefits of policies imposed on the population during the period of the lockdown in the Philippines. Finally, it is necessary to identify the contestations that are engendered by the authoritarianism of Duterte, and to observe the limits and possibilities of scenarios in the immediate term.

## 2 Duterte: Authoritarian and Neoliberal

Duterte has been called populist despite differences in how the term has been understood and the various nuances of the description [1, 8, 9, 8–9, 20, 8–9]. At one edge of the continuum, populism can be understood as an ideology or program [21] while on the other extreme, it can be described as a style or method [30]. This author posits that Duterte is a president whose populism is more appearance than content. And that Duterte's populism is style not ideology.

In contrast, Santos [27] and Viajar [34] describe Duterte as authoritarian. Authoritarianism is a relevant category to use in examining the question of Duterte's COVID-19 response. The adoption of a law and order framework that aims at strict social control and restriction of civil liberties is a defining characteristic of his response to the pandemic.

Useful in studying Duterte are the concepts of Tansel [31] and Brown [3] about the integral link between authoritarianism and neoliberalism. Tansel [31] understands neoliberalism as constituting specific means of reproducing capital accumulation. Thus, the primacy of the state as an instrument and the deployment of coercive means to safeguard capital accumulation in the face of opposition. Brown [3] calls this depiction of neoliberalism as neo-Marxist since it stresses the economic substructure. Tansel [31] and Brown [3] comprehend authoritarianism not as a pathology but as organic to neoliberalism.

The Great Recession of 2008 opened the floodgates to the rise of authoritarian leaders in places where frustration could be so channeled. In the time of COVID-19, neoliberalism faces a momentous challenge as an economic and social crisis once more threatens the world. Yet COVID-19 also presents a remarkable opportunity for neoliberalism to advance. If emergency measures are skewed toward protecting corporate profit rather than providing assistance to the working class, then inequality is even worsened [26]. Even during a pandemic, neoliberalism must function, capital needs to make a profit and capital should accumulate. Thus, the need for policies privileging capital even though it might be in the guise of emergency measures for public health or law and order.

It behooves then to examine the dynamics of the COVID-19 response in the Philippines under Duterte's authoritarian rule. Who are reaping the benefits and who are bearing the sacrifices?

## 3 Pre-pandemic Authoritarianism

The war on drugs is a defining characteristic of the Duterte administration. He won on the basis of that platform. His popularity even rests mainly on that issue [15]. Duterte's law and order governance hinges on the drug war. In the first 14 months of Duterte's term, more than 12,000 were shot to death, either in police operations or in so-called vigilante killings [16]. No reliable figure has been released since then except the Philippine Drug Enforcement Agency's tally of 5601 people who supposedly fought back and were killed in police operations [17]. This number excludes those killed by alleged vigilantes.

Duterte's authoritarian reign has also been characterized by the suppression of his political rivals. A woman senator, Leila de Lima, was jailed on controversial drug charges just eight months into Duterte's reign and after she initiated hearings on the extra-judicial killings in Davao City, where the Philippine president served as mayor for over 22 years. The Supreme Court chief, Maria Lourdes Sereno, another woman who was vocal against the drug war, was ousted on contentious grounds in 2018. Duterte personally made overtures to the Communist Party of the Philippines (CPP) upon assuming power and even appointed five of its nominees to key executive positions. But peace talks with the rebel movement formally collapsed in late 2017 and led to Duterte's listing of the CPP as a terrorist group. Killings of political activists and journalists have continued in the country as impunity was rampant. Political killings definitely pre-date Duterte's rise to power but it festered in the violent climate of the drug war.

Duterte's government proposed several laws seeking to circumscribe the exercise of human rights. Among these are the lowering of the age of criminal liability from 15 to 12, the re-imposition of the death penalty, a national ID system and a new anti-terror legislation. Of these, the last two were enacted into law.

While there were corruption scandals here and there, Duterte managed to ride them out. He simply dismissed tainted officials and then re-appointed many of them to other positions after a few months. Before the pandemic, the biggest trial Duterte confronted was putting down an Islamic fundamentalist rebellion in the southern city of Marawi. Duterte had previously belittled the threat of the Islamist group Maute but it took the military five months before the insurrection was suppressed.

Going into year 2020, Duterte's reign was on solid ground and faced no major controversy. In the mid-term election of 2019, the political opposition was massively defeated. No one among the opposition senate slate won and Duterte's anointed ones dominated the ballot.

## 4 Duterte's Authoritarian Response

### *4.1 Cognitive Bias*

Duterte downplayed the danger of COVID-19 and did not take immediate action to secure the population from local community transmission. Under Duterte, the country pivoted to China and it led to an influx of Chinese tourists and migrant workers who were employed in online gambling sites or in yuan-funded construction projects. At the onset of COVID-19, the government was notoriously tone-deaf to calls for banning flights from China. At one point, the head of the health department admitted that it was not prohibiting flights out of deference to China. On January 30, 2020, a Chinese woman was the first recorded COVID-19 case in the Philippines. The next day, a Chinese tourist in the Philippines was the first COVID-19 death outside of mainland China [4]. Thus, on February 2 an official ban took effect but flights from China, including Wuhan, continued nonetheless [24].

It took a month of complacency before the first case of local community transmission was confirmed on March 7. With the threat of runaway infection becoming a clear and present danger, the first month-long lockdown was imposed on March 15. At his State of the Nation address in July 2020, Duterte stated that he is pinning his hope on a vaccine coming after a few months. This was the closest to an admission that the government had given up hope of taming the infection through a pro-active plan [5]. Duterte suffered from the same cognitive bias and lack of anticipation to the danger of COVID-19 as that of Donald Trump of the US, Boris Johnson of the UK, and Joko Widodo of Indonesia [19].

### *4.2 Law and Order Framework*

The lockdown ushered in a clampdown not just on mobility but on freedoms. A high-level task force was set up to oversee the COVID-19 response and to enforce the lockdown. Instead of dealing with the pandemic using a public health lens, it was handled as a law and order issue in an authoritarian fashion.

To implement the stay-at-home order, police and soldiers were massively deployed, at times in full battle gear and with armored vehicles. Checkpoints manned by personnel in long firearms created havoc for the mobility of people who were allowed to work, including frontline health employees.

Amid the months-long lockdown, with overt resistance effectively shackled, the repression of Duterte's rivals escalated. Congress shut down the media network ABS-CBN by denying the renewal of its franchise. Despite official pronouncements that the executive did not influence the legislative's action, Duterte in his ad libs admitted that he wanted the media giant closed because of a personal slight.

Next in line was the chief executive officer of an online media outlet that was a vocal critic of the administration. Maria Ressa, of the online news portal Rappler, and a colleague were convicted of cyber libel and are out only on bail. The case is only one of eight filed against Ressa and Rappler during Duterte's term [25]. It was also in the midst of the lockdown when a new Anti-Terror Act was enacted. The law was criticized as draconian with the meager safeguards of a previous anti-terror legislation removed.

But even without the Anti-Terror Act, the law and order regime instituted during the lockdown effectively suppressed the right to assembly and redress of grievances. All attempts to hold protests at the height of the lockdown were dispersed and protesters arrested for allegedly violating the quarantine rules. During the State of the Nation address in 2020, liberal to radical opposition groups united in a plan to hold a physical rally but were denied a permit. They were forced to hold the gathering inside the campus of the national university. Critics of the administration have harped on the double standard during the lockdown, as thousands were arrested, mostly poor people trying to earn an income, while administration personalities violating quarantine rules were excused.

The war on drugs continued even during the war against COVID-19. Government data revealed there were 50% more people killed by police in drug operations between April and July 2020 compared to the previous period [7].

The crackdown on protests and activities did not just apply to the political opposition but also to organized labor. In the middle of the lockdown, a picket line of workers inside an export processing zone was dispersed by local police and security guards in the guise of enforcing quarantine rules [22]. In a region to the north of Metro Manila, police distributed aid to furloughed workers while lecturing them on the alleged evils of unionism as part of an open campaign to prevent union organizing within export zones.

The Philippines had one of the lowest rates of COVID-19 testing and the administration was dismissive of calls for mass testing. The law and order perspective of Duterte's COVID-19 response contrasts with the public health framework of other countries in Southeast Asia which had a better track record in controlling the pandemic.

## *4.3 Prejudice Not Science*

With the administration unable to put a lid on community transmission, it sought recourse to the narrative of blaming undisciplined Filipinos for the spread of the virus. This rhetoric was propagated by public officials and amplified in the social media through internet influencers.

Yet analysis of big data, culled from movement of Filipinos tracked using their cellphones, reveals that the population generally followed the quarantine rules and definitely disproves the "lack of discipline" narrative [10].

This narrative played into the law and order paradigm of the administration. An undisciplined mass putting public safety at risk deserves a policing if not militaristic response by the state. Moreover, this deflected questions about the effectiveness of the administration's COVID-19 response and its accountability for the failure to contain the pandemic.

Thus, disinformation was a weapon in the hands of the Duterte regime. Lassa and Booth [19] calls this leadership ambiguity and ignorance of science in their observation of the case of the US, Brazil, and Indonesia. Similar to Trump's outrageous promotion of a malaria drug as an antidote to COVID-19, Duterte advocated recycling masks by washing it with kerosene [18]. The presidential spokesperson stereotypically waved it away as a joke. Lassa and Booth explain that ignorance of science is part of the repertoire of populists.

### 4.4 Business-First Policy

Finally, the policies laid down by the Duterte regime during the lockdown reveal a consistent bias in favor of capital instead of labor. This correlates with the thesis of Tansel [31] and Brown [3] that authoritarianism springs from the demands of neoliberal reproduction. Likewise, it connects to the point of Salgado [26] that even during the pandemic the drive for investment returns and capital accumulation must be satisfied.

With the lockdown shuttering a large part of the economy and putting both formal and informal workers out of work, the Duterte government implemented an assistance program which came to be known as *ayuda.* There was a separate aid for formal workers and for informal workers. However, the *ayuda* got entangled in the complexities of a program that was targeted instead of universal. Moreover, the aid to informal workers was to be distributed by local politicians and so the dynamics of political patronage led to discriminatory practices. More than 400 local government officials were to be charged with anomalies in the aid distribution as of August 2020 [12]. Distribution of the *ayuda* was tied down in delays and entailed thousands of poor people lining up without much regard for social distancing rules.

The aid for formal workers was similarly lacking. In all some 2 million wage and salary workers were recipients of *ayuda* [23]. In comparison, some 16 million formal workers were furloughed due to the lockdown and the overwhelming majority were unpaid.

Organized labor vigorously called for aid for all affected. But as with appeals for mass testing and equal application of the quarantine rules, it fell on deaf ears. The labor movement also criticized the COVID-19-related issuances of the labor department for being pro-business and promulgated without social dialogue. During the lockdown, inspections of companies, filing of complaints, and union certification elections were all suspended. After determined lobbying by organized labor, a new order in August 2020 reinstated labor inspections and workers' complaints.

Meanwhile, a loophole in the issuances permitted employers to use workers' paid leaves during the lockdown. Another contested provision allowed employers to reduce wages, even those protected by collective bargaining agreements. These issuances have not been repealed or revised.

After a month and a half of the total lockdown, the stay-at-home rules were relaxed in parts of the country except for a few areas including the capital Metro Manila. This was motivated by the desire to restart the economy which had descended into a recession with a 16.5% negative growth in the second quarter of the year, the biggest on record [11].

Business lobbied strongly for the lifting of the total lockdown. In fact, even at the height of the total lockdown, factories in export zones and call centers in Metro Manila were operating. These factory workers and call center employees had to bear the daily grind of risking life and limb by traveling without public transportation and with lax enforcement of safety protocols by employers. With the lockdown relaxed, more workers went back to work.

Another glaring example of the use of the lockdown to ram through policies discriminatory to workers was the forcible phase out of the *jeepney,* an informal mini-bus system of public transport. The *jeepney* modernization program has been stalled for years due to resistance. But during the lockdown half a million informal drivers were furloughed as the *jeepney* was banned on the streets. It also forced millions of workers who still had jobs to walk or use bicycles to commute to and from work. Scores of *jeepney* drivers were forced to beg on the streets while a group who protested were jailed for several days. It was only in September 2020 that a few thousand *jeepneys*, whose owners had complied with the modernization program, were allowed to ply their routes.

In summary, it can be seen that the pandemic and the lockdown were exploited by the neoliberal state to ram through policies that debilitate labor rights such as standards enforcement, dispute resolution, social dialogue, and freedom of association. Organized labor boldly criticized the labor department as exercising "social distancing" by refusing to negotiate with workers concerning their grievances. This experience during the lockdown came on top of organized labor's earlier three-year lobbying and campaign for the concretization of Duterte's famous populist promise to abolish precarious work. After a series of twists and turns, a bill marginally promoting regular employment was passed in parliament only to be vetoed by Duterte. The veto came after an open letter by almost all employers' groups calling on the president to kill the bill. Duterte's satisfaction ratings dipped significantly among the lower classes after the veto.

## 5 Resistance to Authoritarianism

Protest and resistance against Duterte's ineffective response and crackdown on dissent during the lockdown had not been absent but it had been muted. In one notable instance, hungry urban poor living in a slum at the center of Metro Manila held an impromptu action in a major thoroughfare to demand assistance in the early days of the first lockdown. The leaders were quickly arrested to set a lesson even as *ayuda* was quickly delivered to the community to assuage their grievances.

Since mass gatherings were prohibited, activists and critics shifted to online protests. The liberal and radical opposition groups tried to reclaim the streets but could not physically confront the prohibition. This was due to the weakened state of the opposition and the lack of mass outrage. There was evident fear generated by the security presence during the lockdown even as the anti-terror law had a chilling effect.

The situation in the Philippines stood in stark contrast to other countries where mass resistance broke out even at the height of the pandemic—the Black Lives Matter movement in the US, and the protests in Hong Kong, Lebanon, and Belarus. In all these countries, the mass actions in the time of COVID-19 were clearly a continuation of movements generated in the year before. A historic number of mass protests surged in 2019 and the pandemic merely stopped its momentum for a time.

However, in the Philippines, mass protests had been on a secular decline even before COVID-19. This author posits that the absence of significant outrage is mainly due to the demoralization among the population stemming from the failures of three successive people power or EDSA uprisings (named after the main thoroughfare in the capital) within one generation. The first two EDSAs toppled a hated dictator in 1986 and then a corrupt president in 2001. The third uprising just a few months after the second was immediately quelled by force. The uprisings created expectations among the people for social change and social reform which were dashed by the cosmetic political changes that were actually delivered. As Bello [2] and Heydarian [14] explained, the failures of the EDSA regimes paved the way for the rise of the populist Duterte. In fact, it can be argued, there would not have been a populist president if instead there had been a popular movement that could have captured the imagination of the frustrated Filipino people. Unfortunately, the failures of the EDSA experience demoralized the people and quelled their enthusiasm for collective action. As atomized discontented individuals, they looked to a charismatic leader instead of finding strength in their unity.

Nonetheless a new generation of young students, who had no memory of the failed EDSA uprisings but were in turn frustrated by the authoritarianism of Duterte, are the most willing to reclaim the streets and take up the banner of collective action. They are however a small minority though vocal and influential in social media.

A resurgent student movement still has no reliable ally in a working-class movement that has been weakened by neoliberal economic restructuring and the political demoralization among masses of workers. Aside from civil society organizations, the other main EDSA actors like the Catholic Church, big business, and military [32] have refrained from political action and found accommodation within the status quo and even the authoritarian regime of Duterte.

## 6 Conclusion

The imposition of one of the longest and strictest lockdowns in the world was not able to control the spread of COVID-19 in the Philippines but directly led to the worst economic recession in Southeast Asia in 2020. This paper asserts that it is precisely the authoritarian nature of the Duterte regime that caused the tragic outcome for the country.

First, the law and order paradigm of an authoritarian government is utterly unsuitable in managing a public health crisis. The Duterte administration was riding high on the wings of a manufactured crisis—the war on drugs. But when it was confronted by a real crisis, it unraveled and could not muster a coherent response.

Second, instead of uniting the country to combat the spread of the infection, the Duterte regime exploited the pandemic to escalate its repression of political rivals and continue the bloody drug war.

Third, the Duterte government is populist only in rhetoric but not in substance. It is an authoritarian regime based on the neoliberal state. As such, it safeguards primarily capital accumulation even in a pandemic. Policies implemented during the lockdown reveal a consistent bias for business interests and the passing on of the costs of the crisis on the backs of workers.

The economic crisis created by the failed COVID-19 response contrasts with its image of toughness in dealing with the manufactured crisis called the drug war. Ironically, despite the incoherent and inept response of the Duterte regime, his popularity remained high up to very end. Identifying the reasons for this is beyond the scope of this paper. So is analyzing the factors that led to the victory in the 2022 national elections in the Philippines of the son of the former dictator Marcos and the daughter of Duterte as president and vice president, respectively. Nonetheless, it can be said that while the majority win of Marcos and Duterte in the 2022 election is extraordinary, also historic was the grassroots-led campaign of the opposition slate led by Vice President Leni Robredo. It is the vibrant activism of sections of an erstwhile passive population that provides hope for an empowered citizenry that values civic spaces and human rights in the Philippines.

## References

1. Abao CV (2017) Engaging Duterte: that space in between populism and pluralism. In: Curato N (ed) A Duterte reader: critical essays on Rodrigo Duterte's early presidency. Ateneo de Manila University Press, Quezon City, pp 301–318

2. Bello W (2017) The spider spins his web: Rodrigo Duterte's ascent to power. Philipp Sociol Rev 65:19–47
3. Brown W (2019) In the ruins of neoliberalism: the rise of antidemocratic politics in the west. Columbia University Press, New York
4. Cepeda M (2020, 11 March) Philippines records 1st local death due to coronavirus. Rappler. https://rappler.com/nation/philippines-first-local-death-coronavirus, last accessed 2021/06/15
5. Cepeda M (2020, 29 July) Robredo hits Duterte SONA: don't just wait for COVID-19 vaccine. Rappler. https://rappler.com/nation/robredo-hits-duterte-sona-2020-do-not-just-wait-covid-19-vaccine, last accessed 2021/06/15
6. Chiu PDM (2021, August 20) Why the Philippines' long lockdowns couldn't contain covid-19. The BMJ. https://doi.org/10.1136/bmj.n2063, last accessed 2022/07/25
7. Conde CH (2020, 8 September) Killings in Philippines up 50 percent during pandemic. Human Rights Watch. https://www.hrw.org/news/2020/09/08/killings-philippines-50-percent-during-pandemic, last accessed 2021/06/15
8. Curato N (2016) Politics of anxiety, politics of hope: penal populism and Duterte's rise to power. J Curr Southeast Asian Aff 35(3):91–109
9. Curato N (2017) We need to talk about Rody. In: Curato N (ed) A Duterte reader: critical essays on Rodrigo Duterte's early presidency. Ateneo de Manila University Press, Quezon City, pp 1–36
10. de Guzman W, Guido E (2020, 1 July) What Google mobility data say about Filipinos amid COVID-19 pandemic. ABS-CBN News. https://news.abs-cbn.com/business/07/01/20/what-google-mobility-data-say-about-filipinos-amid-covid-19-pandemic, last accessed 2021/06/15
11. de Vera BO (2020, 6 August) Officially a recession: PH GDP shrank 16.5% in Q2. Inquirer.net. https://business.inquirer.net/304543/officially-a-recession-ph-gdp-shrank-16-5-in-q2, last accessed 2021/06/15
12. Gonzales C (2020, 23 August) Over 400 officials, civilians linked to SAP anomalies facing raps—DILG. Inquirer.net. https://newsinfo.inquirer.net/1325868/over-400-local-execs-linked-to-sap-anomalies-facing-raps-dilg, last accessed 2021/06/15
13. Gonzales C (2021, May 8) PH had highest new COVID-19 cases in Southeast Asia during surge—ex DOH chief. Inquirer.net. https://newsinfo.inquirer.net/1429072/ph-had-highest-new-covid-19-cases-in-southeast-asia-during-surge-ex-doh-chief, last accessed 2021/06/15
14. Heydarian R (2018) The rise of Duterte: A populist revolt against elite democracy. Palgrave, Quezon City, Philippines
15. Holmes RD (2017) Who supports Rodrigo Duterte? In: Curato N (ed) A Duterte reader: Critical essays on Rodrigo Duterte's early presidency. Ateneo de Manila University Press, Quezon City, pp 57–75
16. Human Rights Watch (2018, 18 January) Philippines: Duterte's 'drug war' claims 12,000+ lives. HRW. https://www.hrw.org/news/2018/01/18/philippines-dutertes-drug-war-claims-12000-lives, last accessed 2021/06/15
17. Human Rights Watch (2020, 7 May) Philippines: lasting harm to children from 'drug war'. HRW. https://www.hrw.org/news/2020/05/27/philippines-lasting-harm-children-drug-war, last accessed 2021/06/15
18. Johnson I H (2020, 31 July) Rodrigo Duterte: I'm not joking—clean masks with petrol. BBC. https://www.bbc.com/news/world-asia-53605108, last accessed 2021/06/15
19. Lassa J, Booth M (2020, 8 April) Are populist leaders a liability during covid? The Conversation. https://theconversation.com/are-populist-leaders-a-liability-during-covid-19-135431, last accessed 2021/06/15
20. Mendoza RU, Jaminola III LM (2020) Is Duterte a populist? Rhetoric vs. reality. J Int RelatS Sustain Dev 15:266–279
21. Mudde C (2004) The populist Zeitgeist. Gov Oppos 39(4):541–563
22. Partido Manggagawa (2020, 11 April) Police disperse picketline using lockdown as alibi. PM. http://partidongmanggagawa2001.blogspot.com/2020/04/police-disperse-picketline-using.html, last accessed 2021/06/15

23. Patinio F (2021, 11 February) Over 2M workers, displaced OFWs get P12-B cash aid. Philippine News Agency. https://www.pna.gov.ph/articles/1130362, last accessed 2021/06/15.
24. Ramos CM (2020, 21 February) Senate probe sought on continuous China flights amid travel ban, virus woes. Inquirer.net. https://newsinfo.inquirer.net/1231704/marcos-wants-inquiry-into-alleged-continued-flights-from-china-amid-covid-19-travel-banlast accessed 2021/06/15
25. Regencia T (2020, 15 June) Maria Ressa found guilty in blow to Philippines' press freedom. Aljazeera. https://www.aljazeera.com/news/2020/06/philippine-court-rappler-maria-ressa-guilty-cyberlibel-200614210221502.html, last accessed 2021/06/15
26. Salgado P (2020, 14 September) COVID as the (second) death of neoliberalism. IRGAC. https://www.irgac.org/2020/09/14/covid-as-the-second-death-of-neoliberalism/, last accessed 2021/06/15
27. Santos VO (2016, 15 November) Duterte's descent into authoritarianism. The New York Times. https://www.nytimes.com/2016/11/16/opinion/dutertes-descent-into-authoritarianism.html, last accessed 2021/06/15
28. Tadem EC et al (2021) Marginalized societies and the state in the time of a pandemic: the Philippine case. Public Policy Monograph Series 2021-01, University of the Philippines Center for Integrative and Development Studies. https://cids.up.edu.ph/wp-content/uploads/2022/04/UP-CIDS-Public-Policy-Monograph-2021-01.pdf, last accessed 2022/07/25
29. Tadem EC et al (2022) Southeast Asian peoples in pandemic times: challenges and responses. Alternative Development Program of the University of the Philippines Center for Integrative and Development Studies. https://tinyurl.com/AltDevSEAcovid19v2, last accessed 2022/07/25
30. Taguieff P (1997) Populism and political science: from conceptual illusions to real problems. Vingtième Siècle. Revue d'histoire 56(4):4–33
31. Tansel CB (2017) Authoritarian neoliberalism: towards a new research agenda. In: Tansel CB (ed) States of discipline: authoritarian neoliberalism and the contested reproduction of capitalist order. Rowman & Littlefield, London
32. Teehankee J (2016) Weak state, strong presidents: situating the Duterte presidency in Philippine political time. J Dev Soc 32(3):293–321
33. Thompson R (2016) Introduction to the special issue. J Curr Southeast Asian Aff 35(3):3–14
34. Viajar V (2020, 22 July) Unravelling Duterte's iron hand in the time of Covid. IRGAC. https://www.irgac.org/2020/07/22/unravelling-dutertes-iron-hand-in-the-time-of-covid-19/, last accessed 2021/06/15

# Foreign Policy, Diplomacy and State Sovereignty in Contemporary Southeast Asia

# A Constructivist Analysis of ASEAN Centrality in Indo-Pacific Geopolitics

**Azza Bimantara and Rangga Tri Nugraha**

**Abstract** This paper explains why the Association of Southeast Asian Nations (ASEAN) needs its centrality in Indo-Pacific (IP) geopolitical discourse. The "centrality" here refers to ASEAN member states' concordance with the ASEAN Outlook on the Indo-Pacific (AOIP), aiming for ASEAN's leadership in promoting their vision on IP geopolitics and its following regional order. By using "constructivist geopolitics" and strategic narrative analytical frameworks, this paper argues that the normative structure of international relations in Southeast Asia (SEA)—consisting of the historical entanglement of SEA's geographical reality, ASEAN, and the "ASEAN Way"—has incarnated into an (institutional) strategic narrative called AOIP. This new institutional strategy redefines what the IP region means for ASEAN member states and reasserts their ideals on regional governance according to ASEAN centrality. As an implication, IP geopolitics will reproduce the initial SEA's normative structure. Such perpetuation establishes a new geopolitical (counter)-discourse on IP against dominant ones from external actors (e.g., Australia, China, India, Japan, and the US) and creates a sort of geopolitical system that respects ASEAN's "sphere of influence" as the "core" and external actors' "peripherality" within IP. This study contributes to the academic debate on ASEAN's institutional strategy by offering a new perspective on IP great power politics dominated by non-ASEAN policy discourses and neorealist perspectives in international relations academia.

**Keywords** ASEAN · Indo-Pacific · ASEAN Outlook on the Indo-Pacific · Constructivist Geopolitics · Strategic Narrative

A. Bimantara (✉)
Department of International Relations, Universitas Muhammadiyah Malang, Malang, Indonesia
e-mail: azzabima@umm.ac.id

R. T. Nugraha
Hankuk University of Foreign Studies, Seoul, South Korea
e-mail: rangga.nugraha@hufs.ac.kr



Nawawi et al. (eds.), *Managing Disruption and Developing Resilience for a Better Southeast Asia*, Springer Proceedings in Humanities and Social Sciences,
https://doi.org/10.1007/978-981-96-2116-3_63

# 1 Introduction

The Association of the Southeast Asian Nations (ASEAN) member states approved ASEAN Outlook on the Indo-Pacific (AOIP) in 2019 to reassert their shared perspective on the Indo-Pacific (IP) region, its objectives and principles to manage the region in cooperative and prosperous ways, its proposal for areas of cooperation, and a brief mechanism. AOIP aims for the ASEAN centrality in the Indo-Pacific governance in two senses. First, geopolitically, we can assume that ASEAN aims to (re)claim its geographical centrality and importance in the Indian and Pacific Oceans intersection. Hence, AOIP reflects ASEAN's new geostrategy to contain great powers' rivalry in inclusive, multilateral engagement. Second, such an ASEAN institutional discourse can be understood as ASEAN member states' desire for their own "one common voice" in IP politics [42]. Through AOIP, they hope to realise their regional stability and security plan: inclusive cooperation on sustainable economic development, connectivity, and maritime affairs [5, p. 2].

This paper proposes the ultimate research question concerning AOIP: Why do ASEAN member states need ASEAN centrality in IP politics? The following questions should also scrutinise our analyses throughout the paper: What is their perception of the relationship between the geographical conditions of Southeast Asia (SEA) as an existential buffer for ASEAN and the IP concept? How can they accept AOIP as a blueprint for ASEAN's new institutional strategy towards the IP? What factors influence their acceptance of AOIP? This paper derives those questions by reviewing a set of IP geopolitics literature that comes in three tenets. The first one concerns each conception and strategy on the IP from each pertinent country [15, 24]—e.g., Indonesia [4], Taiwan [46], China [21], Australia [13], US [16], Japan [34], and India [10]. The second tenet focuses on great power relations analyses—e.g., the US-China rivalry [45], the Sino-Indian rivalry [47], and the US-Russian feud [37]. The third tenet emphasises ASEAN institutional strategy [23, 33].

As this paper seeks to understand ASEAN centrality in IP geopolitics, the literature review focuses more on it than other general themes such as constructivism, ASEAN centrality, and the IP region. However, upon a thorough literature review on the topic, two existing literature gaps in preceding studies were identified, which include a need to generate a novel analysis/interpretation of IP based on a perspective that promotes ASEAN centrality—which still lacks—and the domination of the neorealist perspective in institutional strategy analyses.

By showing that the social constructivist school of thought can also contribute to institutional strategy studies, particularly international/regional organisations like ASEAN, this paper argues that the normative structure of international relations in Southeast Asia (SEA) and its geographical reality have incarnated into an (institutional) strategic narrative called AOIP. This new institutional strategy redefines what the IP region means for ASEAN member states and reasserts their ideals on regional governance according to ASEAN centrality. As an implication, IP geopolitics will reproduce the initial SEA's normative structure. Such perpetuation implies two things: (1) the establishment of a new geopolitical (counter)-discourse on IP against dominant ones from extra-regional actors and (2) the creation of a new geopolitical system that respects ASEAN's "sphere of influence" as the "core" and external actors' "peripherality" within IP.

This paper will be written based on the following structure. After initially introducing the analytical framework—constructivist geopolitics—and its operationalisation through this paper's methodology—interpretative case studies—this paper will explicate the normative structure of ASEAN through two steps. First, it will identify the linkage between Southeast Asia (SEA)'s geographical reality—based on its spatiality and temporality—and the evolution of SEA's geopolitics and international system throughout the region's history. By understanding the historicity of the linkage, we can relate to ASEAN's demand for "centrality" in contemporary SEA and IP geopolitics. Second, this paper continues to explain the establishment of ASEAN, its unique normative governance through the "ASEAN Way," the effect of such institutionalisation on ASEAN society's perception of geopolitical phenomena such as great power relations and IP governance, and the impact of the similar process towards member states' norm entrepreneurship in responding to the AOIP. The final substantial part of this paper will be the explication of AOIP through the strategic narrative framework. This part shall see how ASEAN "translates" its demand for centrality within the IP geopolitics—reflected in ASEAN's aforementioned normative structure—into a sort of institutional "speech act" called AOIP. As for the timeline, this paper will stick to after the AOIP was promoted, i.e., after the 34th ASEAN Summit in 2019—while also involving some historical background to provide a contextual understanding.

## 2 Constructivist Geopolitics: An Analytical Framework and a Methodology

This paper utilises constructivist geopolitics as its analytical framework in two senses simultaneously. On the one hand, the framework is derived from the critical geopolitics approach, which postulates geopolitics as a social phenomenon in which sociocultural dynamics—through social practices and discourses—define geography and, therefore, international politics [44, p. 193]. Such geodeterminism confirms this paper's tendency for geopolitics definition as a "mode of representation of the world" [18, p. 34] instead of mere mutual construction of politics, geography, and geographic entities [19, p. 3] or one's "strategy or analysis" that encase links and causal relationships between political power and geographical space within "ideological propensities" [43, p. 192]. The framework allows us to trace back the construction of geopolitical reality based on its spatiality—the influence of space on politics—and temporality—the historical development of the space-politics relationship [18, pp. 48–49].

On the other hand, the framework also represents this paper's attempt to apply the social constructivist theory of international relations to geopolitical phenomena.

Social constructivism—the international society-centric one—argues that social normative structure—a set of autonomous and constitutive norms that exist relatively independently from the state—determines a state's identities, interests, and behaviours in international politics [26, p. 148, 39]. The international realm as the "realm of obligation" consists of two sub-structures or tiers: the "deep structure" of the principal socialising norms and the "surface structure," which is international organisations [26, p. 150]. Any dynamics from the international level will shape the state's behaviour—as a norm entrepreneur [1, pp. 151–153]—to conform to internationally "appropriate" behaviours and reproduce the pertinent normative structure. In return, the state's norm entrepreneurship will reassert the pre-existing "deep" and "surface" structure.

For this paper, constructivist geopolitics' geographical spatiality-temporality elements will be supplemented to the constitution of normative structure alongside "deep-surface structures." Moreover, to capture institutional behaviours (e.g., action, policy, or strategy) that reproduce the international society following its normative structure, this paper also adds a strategic narrative analysis based on its ability to manifest three forms—i.e., order/system-oriented, issue/policy-oriented, and identity-oriented [40, pp. 2–3]. Finally, this paper believes that the "modified" analytical framework can capture AOIP's role in reasserting ASEAN centrality within IP geopolitics. Its operationalisation is shown in Fig. 1.

This paper follows a "pragmatic-constructivist" research paradigm [50]. It seeks the "middle ground" of tension between the objectivity of observable pertinent phenomenon as part of inter-state behaviours (e.g., the network of actors, institutions, material capabilities) and its inherent tendency to be driven by "non-material/intangible factors" (e.g., norms, identities, and ideas). It manifests in an interpretative

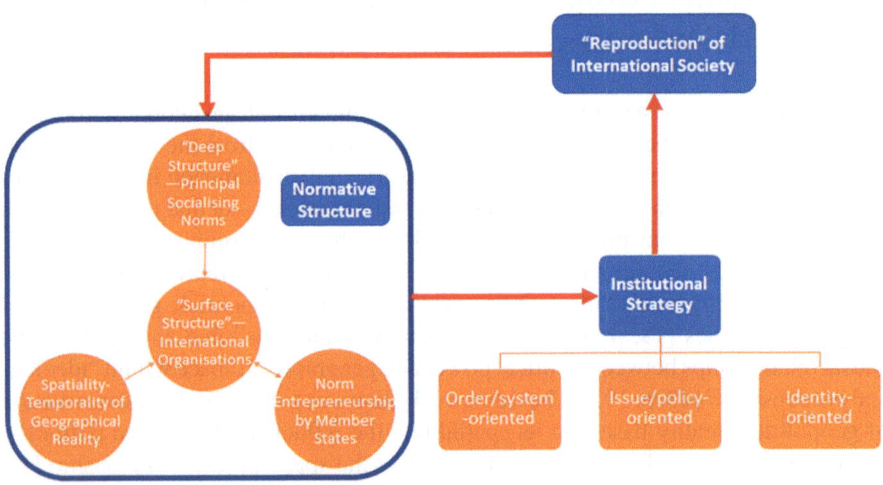


**Fig. 1** Analytical framework of constructivist geopolitics. *Source* Authors

case study design that explicates a specific case—AOIP as ASEAN's institutional strategy and its implication for IP politics—to throw light on the subject [36, p. 692].

The obtained data consist of three references: (1) ASEAN's institutional profile, (2) the AOIP document, and (3) ASEAN member states' official statements. They are primarily qualitative data—be it from primary or secondary sources—found through desk-study activity [35, pp. 79–91] in official documents or press releases, online archives, media reports on journalistic websites, and academic works that issue news and studies related to pertinent countries' activities related to the making of AOIP. The analytical method will be qualitative, with a tendency to go to both content and discourse analysis [29, p. 65]. The data will be positioned and analysed based on this paper's analytical framework and writing structure.

## 3 Geographical (Re)Interpretation of SEA and IP for ASEAN Centrality

The SEA's geopolitics can be examined based on the historical configuration of its geographical reality, which consists of its spatiality and temporality. On its spatiality, the SEA region as a "geographical hub" (between the Indian and Pacific Oceans and Mainland Asian and Australian continents) has allowed higher mobilities from land and sea. Its demography is highly diverse in ethnicities, languages, cultures, religions, and races. The region has also been attached to a warmer climate with rich tropical biodiversity and various geological conditions, making SEA contains enormous potential natural resources. Therefore, inter-civilisational encounters that shape this region's "melting pot" nature have been inevitable. Any geostrategic venture—political, trade, or religious missions from regional insiders and outsiders like Arabs, Indians, Chinese, and European traders and settlers—is possible.

On its temporality, the SEA region has evolved dynamically. Therefore, one must look at how it has evolved since the pre-colonial time to understand it. It is in line with the argument of Hobson and Lawson [27]—which was supported by Buzan and Little [12]—that understanding history is needed to fully grasp the world of international relations. In addition to that, knowing history can help one to be able to explain a particular phenomenon better using constructivism [32].

The pre-colonial SEA had its inter-polity relations system called *mandala*, statecraft based on a Brahmanic-Buddhist concept of concentric circle/sphere of influence from one polity (as the centre of the "galaxy") towards its peripherals—be it "challengers" or "allies," regional insiders or outsiders like Chinese and Indian empires [38, pp. 6–7]. Governing the "mandala polity" thus meant controlling people rather than territory, domestic/foreign demarcation was created based on (unstable, fluid) dynamics of loyalty [49, pp. 286–292]. European imperialism/colonialism between the fifteenth and twentieth centuries divided, conquered, and fixed the region's territoriality based on a Westphalian model of sovereignty and inter-state relations [49, pp. 316–318]. It has remained until now, even after the spread of nationalism in the region drove the decolonisation of SEA nations after the Second World War. However, modern geopolitical thinkers (or geostrategists) during the Cold War era, such as Nicholas J. Spykman, Henry Kissinger, and Zbigniew Brzezinski, were influenced by classical geopolitical thinkers like Alfred Thayer Mahan and Halford Mackinder to argue that Cold War Southeast Asia was part of the Western bloc's geostrategy in the "Asiatic rimland" to "ideologically contain" the"domino effect" of the "Eurasian heartland unification" by the Eastern bloc [22, p. 11]. Vietnam War, Indonesian-Malaysian *Konfrontasi*, the Cambodian Civil War, and the Cambodian-Vietnamese War reflected the region's political, economic, and ideological contestation at that time. Even after the end of the Cold War in the 1990s, SEA still becomes a "great powers arena" to establish its spheres of influence. While establishing the Quadrilateral Security Dialogue (QSD) and AUKUS security pact with allies such as Australia, India, Japan, and the UK, the US also promoted the notion of a "Free, Open Indo-Pacific" (FOIP) to balance China's economic and military prowess in the said region presented through the Belt and Road Initiative—BRI [30]. Therefore, the term "Indo-Pacific" here does not come initially from ASEAN citizens.

The aforementioned SEA's geographical reality shows us that, over its modern history, the region's geopolitics has been subjugated by narratives from extra-regional political actors. The establishment of ASEAN in 1967 exemplified efforts from intra-regional political actors to not only "label" the region—which had been reduced to larger geographical notions like Far East, Asia Pacific, or even Indo-Pacific by external powers—but also make it "functional" through their political institutions [19, p. 32]. Of course, they cannot go back to the pre-colonial era when its polities have distinctive "international relations," but at least it can demand its centrality in modern international politics. Historically speaking, it is justifiable to say that ASEAN centrality means that the importance of the ASEAN and SEA region as the "core geopolitical constituent" of IP must be prioritised.

## 4 ASEAN and the ASEAN Way: Perceptions of IP

ASEAN is a regional organisation established by signing the Bangkok Declaration on 8 August 1967 by the five founding countries: Indonesia, Malaysia, the Philippines, Thailand, and Singapore. Since then, its membership has extended to Brunei, Cambodia, Laos, Myanmar, and Vietnam. As a regional organisation, one should understand that ASEAN is not equal to the SEA region—though it has been trying to portray itself that way. For instance, Timor Leste and Papua New Guinea are not a part of it despite being located in the geographical proximity of ASEAN—with both countries bordering Indonesia [17]. Also, ASEAN has always seen the European Union as its role model and sometimes its counter-model. Although they are very different initially, they are becoming much more similar regarding objectives and aims—though the structure and legal means remain distinct [25, p. 857].

ASEAN, as an embodiment of "surface structure," can be called a "norm entrepreneur," i.e., it diffuses certain "appropriate" or "proper" norms and behaviour amongst its member states—the ASEAN Way [2, p. 10, 31]. Amongst the most prominent features of the concept are the informal way of solving issues and the non-interference in domestic affairs. The "informal way" refers to consultations to reach a consensus amongst its members. Some scholars argue that it originates from Indonesian culture—particularly the rural Javanese culture—where people would not meddle in others' affairs, avoid (direct) confrontation, and discuss their issues to reach an agreement though sometimes with latent dissatisfaction. However, some other scholars reject it because ASEAN society consists of various customs and religious backgrounds despite Indonesia being one of the most dominant members. They see the ASEAN Way as an adaptation of values from other international organisations that have existed before—for instance, the United Nations [31]. In short, ASEAN Ways is a "deep structure" for ASEAN as its "surface structure."

ASEAN and its "Way" influence how ASEAN leaders and citizens perceive IP politics. Being located in one of the most dynamic regions in the world, they are aware that ASEAN's prone to any conflict due to the current rise of material powers such as economic and military worldwide. Therefore, their interest is to ensure that the organisation will not fall into a regional zero-sum game. It is why 56.3% of ASEAN citizens' respondents are concerned that the threat of "decoupling" will divide Southeast Asia into two exclusive blocs led by China and the US [7, p. 29]. Regarding the "non-choice" policy against major powers, 46.1% of ASEAN citizens believe that ASEAN needs to enhance its resilience and unity to fend off pressure from the two major powers, in comparison, 26.6% insist that ASEAN not choose a side [8, p. 31]. Therefore, 54% of ASEAN citizens perceived IP as a solution for a new regional order [6, p. 32].

ASEAN leaders translate such notions as putting ASEAN's centrality, ASEAN Way, and ASEAN-led mechanisms as a foundation of IP governance. AOIP reflects these modalities. However, according to several data from ASEAN Studies Centre [6–8] from ISEAS-Yusof Ishak Institute, ASEAN citizens hold a mixed view on IP strategy in general. In 2021, about 11.8% of them need further elaboration on the IP strategy. Around 11% of ASEAN citizens hold an optimistic view of the IP strategy handling regional order in SEA. 16.7% also believe that all IP strategies should be defined and not discriminate against particular countries. Even their mixed view in 2022 extends to other forms of IP governance like the Australia-UK-US Trilateral Security Arrangement (AUKUS) and the Quadrilateral Security Dialog (QUAD) between Australia, India, Japan, and US. However, being asked about AOIP, about 40.3% of ASEAN citizens argued that ASEAN needs to articulate AOIP more clearly, indicating that AOIP would still seem like the potential to answer their concerns about regional stability and order in favour of ASEAN interests. It also shows that AOIP, as ASEAN's institutional strategy, wants to accommodate extra-regional stakeholders' interests in making ASEAN Community more inclusive.

The fact that ASEAN member states can individually and collectively agree on one specific outlook—established during the ASEAN Summit 2019— and generally give positive responses is also something which departs from the feature [20]. Indonesia fully agrees with the concept of AOIP—as it was the first to table it [4, 41]. Indonesia here even co-worked with ASEAN as the norm entrepreneur in the sense that, unlike many theories that argue for the centrality of non-state and intergovernmental actors as norm entrepreneurs, the state agency can also give input, if not exchange, with other actors. Thai Prime Minister Prayut Chan-o-cha, as the Chair of the Summit, highlighted the significance of AOIP in making ASEAN possess a common approach to the issue [42]. President of the Philippines, Rodrigo Duterte, positively responded to the existence of AOIP to strengthen ASEAN's centrality despite its weakness in holding external stakeholders accountable [3]. Singaporean Prime Minister Lee Hsien-loong was happy with ASEAN's endorsement of AOIP, hoping that it "can strengthen the existing inclusive, ASEAN-led regional architecture and maintain a stable region that all of us will benefit from" [9]. During a bilateral telephone talk, Malaysian Prime Minister Ismail Sabri Yaakob shared his support and commitment to AOIP with Japanese Prime Minister Kishida Fumio [11]. Even Cambodian Prime Minister Hun Sen thanked President Joko Widodo for initiating AOIP, an essential document of ASEAN in managing its relations with external partners [48].

## 5 Re-reading AOIP as ASEAN's Institutional Strategic Narrative

AOIP as a strategic narrative fulfils three forms: (1) a statement of the actor's understanding of international order/system, (2) narratives employed to develop an action/policy, and (3) an assertion of identity. First, AOIP translates the geographical reality of the IP region and its embedded, dynamic geopolitics and geoeconomy into an understanding of "opportunities and challenges" presented by the region for pertinent actors. In the text of AOIP, this understanding is inherent in a new geographical discourse in which the SEA region becomes the central constituent of the said map/region and its immanent dynamics [5, p. 1]. Second, AOIP narrates an urgency to act or develop policy in given circumstances on a new geographical reality. AOIP text states that the "[…] needs to consistently come up with its collective leadership in forging and shaping the vision for closer cooperation in the Indo-Pacific and to continue to maintain its central role in the evolving regional architecture in Southeast Asia and its surrounding regions" [5, p. 1]. Third, in the text as well, AOIP asserts ASEAN's identity/role in realising the action/policy previously mentioned. For example, AOIP text states that "it is in the interest of ASEAN to lead the shaping of their economic and security architecture and ensure that such dynamics will continue to bring about peace, security, stability and prosperity for the peoples in the Southeast Asia as well as in the wider […] Indo-Pacific" [5]. The last two narratives emphasise ASEAN's centrality and leadership in SEA and IP consistently reasserted in the following articles of the AOIP texts. Not to mention when AOIP text also promotes similar imperatives on cooperation within the IP region that prioritises ASEAN-led mechanisms, such as East Asia Summit (EAS), the ASEAN Regional Forum (ARF), the ASEAN Defence Ministers Meeting Plus (ADMM-Plus), the Expanded ASEAN

Maritime Forum (EAMF), and others such as the relevant ASEAN Plus One/Three/Six mechanisms [5, p. 5].

All these strategic narrative forms lead to an idealised international society—in this case, IP—that is envisioned as (1) "a closely integrated and interconnected region," (2) a polity of "dialogue and cooperation instead of rivalry," (3) "a region of development and prosperity for all," and (4) a regional evolutionary architecture modelled on "the importance of the maritime domain and perspective" [5, p. 2]. Such idealism accommodates areas of cooperation, ranging from maritime cooperation, connectivity, the fulfilment of Sustainable Development Goals (SDGs) 2030, to other forms of economic, trade, and development cooperation [5, pp. 3–5]. All of them must be governed according to the principles of strengthening ASEAN centrality, openness, transparency, inclusivity, a rules-based framework, good governance, respect for sovereignty, non-intervention, complementarity with existing cooperation frameworks, equality, mutual respect, mutual trust, mutual benefit and respect for international law [5, p. 2].

These visions are nothing but a portrayal of the long-standing ASEAN Way as a main feature of the organisation. They are ASEAN's discursive influence instrumentalised in altering the geographical reality of the intersection between SEA and IP. Such alteration puts the SEA region as the IP region's centre, positioning ASEAN as the core actor in IP politics and influencing other peripheral actors. It should be noted that AOIP is not exempted from any flaw, such as a lack of actionable policy and comprehensive/detailed mechanisms, a flawed assumption that existing ASEAN-led fora are stable, sufficient, and adequate platforms, weak institutional/legal binding, and highly dependent on ever-dynamic political consensus [14, 28]. Nevertheless, recalling analysis in the previous section, ASEAN's new sphere of influence resembles modern geostrategy inspired by the geopolitical *mandala* of pre-colonial SEA polities. In short, countries like Australia, China, India, Japan, and the US are incorporated into the IP sphere by conforming to ASEAN's centrality and leadership, so must other new countries who want to participate in IP politics and governance.

## 6 Conclusion

This paper has explicated the rationale behind AOIP demanding ASEAN centrality and leadership within IP discourse following international society-centric constructivism, constructivist geopolitics, and strategic narrative theory. It has demonstrated the setting of normative structure—"deep" and "surface"—that shapes ASEAN and the configuration of geographical spatiality and temporality of SEA that becomes the foundation of ASEAN's existence. Moreover, it has examined the AOIP in two senses: (1) how it reflects given ASEAN's normative structure and SEA's geographical reality and (2) how it fulfils the requirements to be an institutional strategic narrative.

In conclusion, the existence of ASEAN, the role of the ASEAN Way, and the SEA's geographical configuration are inseparable in shaping ASEAN's outlook in perceiving IP discourse and responding to external discursive forces. ASEAN's norm entrepreneurship is also complemented by Indonesia's. Their exchange allows the translation of given normative and geographical settings into an institutional strategic narrative called AOIP. There are two implications. First, the instrumentalisation of AOIP establishes a new geopolitical discourse in which ASEAN offers counter-discourse on IP against dominant ones based on ASEAN's centrality and leadership. Second, ASEAN's geostrategy resembles a modern geopolitical *mandala* that includes external actors like Australia, China, India, Japan, and the US into ASEAN's sphere of influence to respect ASEAN's "core" and its "peripherality."

This study contributes to the academic debate on ASEAN's institutional strategy. It offers a new perspective on great power politics—conflict or cooperation management—in SEA and even IP regions. It complements the previous study by giving an alternative (i.e., normative explanation) on what justifies ASEAN's choosing a particular institutional strategy aside from material power configuration in the region. Moreover, this study has tried to offer an ASEAN perspective to enrich IP discourse dominated by non-ASEAN countries' perspectives.

## Bibliography


1. Aggestam K, True J (2020) Gendering foreign policy: a comparative framework for analysis. Foreign Policy Anal 16(2):143–162
2. Allison-Reumann L (2017) The norm-diffusion capacity of ASEAN: evidence and challenges. Pac Focus: Inha J Int Stud 32(1):5–29
3. Aning J (2021, October 28) Duterte: ASEAN must assert central role, leadership amid new regional pacts. Retrieved April 24, 2022, from Inquirer.net: https://globalnation.inquirer.net/199891/duterte-asean-must-assert-central-role-leadership-amid-new-regional-pacts
4. Anwar DF (2020) Indonesia and the ASEAN Outlook on the Indo-Pacific. Int Aff 96(1):111–129
5. ASEAN (2019, June 22) ASEAN Outlook on the Indo-Pacific. Retrieved 3 2022, from ASEAN: https://asean.org/asean2020/wp-content/uploads/2021/01/ASEAN-Outlook-on-the-Indo-Pacific_FINAL_22062019.pdf
6. ASEAN Studies Centre (2020) The State of Southeast Asia: 2020 survey report. ISEAS-Yusof Ishak Institute, Singapore
7. ASEAN Studies Centre (2021) The State of Southeast Asia: 2021 survey report. ISEAS-Yusof Ishak Institute, Singapore
8. ASEAN Studies Centre (2022) The State of Southeast Asia: 2022 survey report. ISEAS-Yusof Ishak Institute, Singapore
9. Au-Yong R (2019, June 24) Asean nations on their own cannot control big powers, but together can make their voices heard: PM Lee. Retrieved April 24, 2022, from The Strait Times: https://www.straitstimes.com/asia/south-asia/asean-nations-on-their-own-cannot-control-big-powers-but-together-can-make-their
10. Barthwal-Datta M, Chacko P (2020) The politics of strategic narratives of regional order in the Indo-Pacific: free, open, prosperous, inclusive? Aust J Int Aff 74(3):244–263
11. Bernama (2022, April 22) Ismail Sabri, Japan PM Kishida discuss regional, international issues during telephone talk. Retrieved April 24, 2022, from TheStar: https://www.thestar.com.my/news/nation/2022/04/22/ismail-sabri-japan-pm-kishida-discuss-regional-international-issues-during-telephone-talk

12. Buzan B, Little R (2010) World history and the development of non-Western international relations theory. In: Non-Western international relations theory: perspectives on and beyond Asia. Routledge, New York, pp 197–220
13. Carr A, Baldino D (2015) An Indo-Pacific norm entrepreneur? Australia and defence diplomacy. J Indian Ocean Reg 11(1):30–47
14. Chong JI (2019, September 3) ASEAN needs more than an 'outlook' on the Indo-Pacific. Retrieved November 3, 2022, from East Asia Forum: https://www.eastasiaforum.org/2019/09/03/asean-needs-more-than-an-outlook-on-the-indo-pacific/
15. Choong W (2019) The return of the Indo-Pacific strategy: an assessment. Aust J Int Aff 73(5):415–430
16. Dubrovskiy IR, Thanh CD (2021) Ideological and conceptual content of the US approach to structuring the Indo-Pacific Macroregion. In: 2021 International Conference on Social Science: Public Administration, Law and International Relations (SSPALIR 2021). Atlantis Press, Dordrecht, pp 164–168
17. Emmerson D (2007, December) Challenging ASEAN: a "topological" view. Contemp Southeast Asia: J Int Strat 29(3):424–446
18. Fard R (2021) Towards a new concept of constructivist geopolitics: bridging classical and critical geopolitics. Cent Eur J Int Secur Stud 15(1):26–57
19. Flint C (2021) Introduction to geopolitics, 4th edn. Routledge, Oxfordshire
20. Frécon E (2020) L'ASEAN face à la redéfinition de sa centralité – diplomatique, opérationnelle et géographique. Hérodote 176:9–24
21. Gong X (2020) Non-traditional security cooperation between China and south-east Asia: implications for Indo-Pacific geopolitics. Int Aff 96(1):29–48
22. Guan AC (2018) Southeast Asia's Cold War: an interpretive history. University of Hawai'i Press, Honolulu
23. He K (2008) Institutional balancing and international relations theory: economic interdependence and balance of power strategies in Southeast Asia. Eur J Int Rel 14(3):489–518
24. He K (2018) Three faces of the Indo-Pacific: understanding the "Indo-Pacific" from an IR theory perspective. East Asia 35(2):149–161
25. Henry L (2007) The ASEAN Way and community integration: two different models of regionalism. Eur Law J 13(6):857–879
26. Hobson JM (2000) The state and international relations. Cambridge University Press, Cambridge
27. Hobson J, Lawson G (2008) What is history in international relations? Millennium 37(2):415–435
28. Jaknanihan A (2022, January 26) What critics miss on ASEAN's Indo-Pacific Outlook. Retrieved November 3, 2022, from East Asia Forum: https://www.eastasiaforum.org/2022/01/26/what-critics-miss-on-aseans-indo-pacific-outlook/
29. Johannesson P, Perjon E (2014) An introduction to design science. Springer, Cham
30. Kachiar Y, Poojary PV (2021, October 27). AUKUS? Quad? FOIP? A fragmented approach cannot counter China. The Lowy Institute. Retrieved July 11, 2022, from TheInterpreter: https://www.lowyinstitute.org/the-interpreter/aukus-quad-foip-fragmented-approach-cannot-counter-china
31. Katsumata H (2003) Reconstruction of diplomatic norms in Southeast Asia: the case for strict adherence to the "ASEAN Way." Contemp Southeast Asia 25(1):104–121
32. Kennedy-Pipe C (2000) International history and international relations theory: a dialogue beyond the Cold War. Int Aff 76(4):741–754
33. Koga K (2018) ASEAN's evolving institutional strategy: managing great power politics in South China Sea disputes. Chin J Int Polit 11(1):49–80
34. Koga K (2019) Japan's "Free and Open Indo-Pacific" strategy. Contemp Southeast Asia 42(1):286–313
35. Lamont CK (2015) Research methods in international relations. Sage, London
36. Lijphart A (1971) Comparative politics and the comparative method. Am Polit Sci Rev 5(3):682–693

37. Lukin A (2022) Russia and the United States in the Asia-Pacific: a perspective of the English school. In: Christoffersen G, Christoffersen G (eds) Russia in the Indo-Pacific: new approaches to Russian foreign policy. Routledge, New York, pp 35–51
38. Manggala PU (2013) The mandala culture of anarchy: the pre-colonial Southeast Asian international society. J ASEAN Stud 1(1):1–13
39. March J, Olsen J (1989) Rediscovering institution. Free Press, New York
40. Miskimmon A, O'Loughlin B, Roselle L (2017) Introduction. In: Miskimmon A, O'Loughlin B, Roselle L, Miskimmon A, O'Loughlin B, Roselle L (eds) Forging the world: strategic narratives and international relations. University of Michigan Press, Ann Arbor, pp 1–22
41. MOFA Indonesia (2019) Connecting the connectivity in the Indo-Pacific: Indian Ocean and Rim. Centre for the Study and Policy Development in Asia-Pacific and Africa, Jakarta
42. Nathalia T (2019, June 23) Asean leaders approve Outlook on Indo-Pacific cooperation concept. Retrieved February 21, 2022, from Jakarta Globe: https://jakartaglobe.id/context/asean-leaders-approve-outlook-on-indopacific-cooperation-concept
43. Østerud Ø (1988) The uses and abuses of geopolitics. J Peace Res 25(2):191–199
44. O'Tuathail G, Agnew J (1992) Geopolitics and discourse: practical geopolitical reasoning in American foreign policy. Polit Geogr 11(2):190–204
45. Scobell A (2021) Constructing a US-China rivalry in the Indo-Pacific and beyond. J Contemp China 30(127):69–84
46. Scott D (2019) Taiwan's pivot to the Indo-Pacific. Asia-Pac Rev 26(1):29–57
47. Singh AG (2016) India, China and the US: strategic convergence in the Indo-Pacific. Journal of the Indian Ocean Region 12(2):161–176
48. Sokhavuth T (2022, January 5) PM thanks Indonesia for initiating new ideas for Asean enhancement. Retrieved April 24, 2022, from Khmer Times: https://www.khmertimeskh.com/501000663/pm-thanks-indonesia-for-initiating-new-ideas-for-asean-enhancement/
49. Spruyt H (2020) The world imagined: collective beliefs and political order in the Sinocentric, Islamic and Southeast Asian international societies. Cambridge University Press, Cambridge
50. Tran TT (2017, November 7) Pragmatism: how to connect positivism and constructivism in doing research. Retrieved March 3, 2021, from WebQDA: https://www.webqda.net/pragmatism-how-to-connect-positivism-and-constructivism-in-ng-research/?lang=en

# Reciprocal Asymmetric Relations in Taiwan's Education Diplomacy to Indonesia Under the New Southbound Policy

**Tonny Dian Effendi**

**Abstract** This study maps and analyzes Indonesian students' research on Taiwan and Taiwanese students' research topics on Indonesia from 2016 to 2021. This study found that Indonesian students discuss Taiwan on limited topics: the cross-strait relations and Indonesian migrant workers, while Taiwanese students discuss Indonesia on diverse issues from domestic politics, migrant workers, education, and the Chinese Indonesian community. This situation shows a reciprocal asymmetric relation where, on the one hand, there is a gap between the number of Indonesian students in Taiwan and Taiwanese students in Indonesia, and on the other hand, fewer number and limited topic of Indonesian students' research on Taiwan compared to Taiwanese student's research on Indonesia. From the public diplomacy perspective, Taiwan's education diplomacy reached the third level, the engagement stage, but it seems to struggle to bring Taiwan into the discussion among Indonesian students. Therefore, Taiwan should consider the post-study program by involving Taiwan's alumni in Indonesia to participate in public diplomacy while including Taiwanese students who did research on Indonesia in the education diplomacy project.

**Keywords** Asymmetry · Research · Student · Taiwan · Indonesia

## 1 Introduction

Tsay Ching-lung argues that migration between Taiwan and Southeast Asia shows an asymmetric relationship when the number of migrations from Southeast Asia to Taiwan is much greater than from Taiwan to Southeast Asia [1]. In 2014, the number of Taiwanese students studying in Southeast Asian countries was 11 times smaller than that of Southeast Asian students in Taiwan, or only 1.3% of Taiwanese students

T. D. Effendi (✉)
Institute of Political Science, National Sun Yat-Sen University, Kaohsiung, Taiwan (ROC)
e-mail: tonny@umm.ac.id

Department of International Relations, University of Muhammadiyah Malang, Malang, Indonesia



Nawawi et al. (eds.), *Managing Disruption and Developing Resilience for a Better Southeast Asia*, Springer Proceedings in Humanities and Social Sciences,
https://doi.org/10.1007/978-981-96-2116-3_64

studying abroad. Among Southeast Asian countries, Singapore is the favorite destination for Taiwanese students, followed by Thailand and Malaysia. In the same year, no Taiwanese students were studying in Indonesia. Since the Taiwanese government implemented the New Southbound Policy (NSP) in 2016, the number of Southeast Asian students in Taiwan has increased significantly. In 2018, NSP countries reached 40.9%, where students from Malaysia had the largest population (32.2%), followed by Vietnam (25%) and Indonesia (22.7%) [2]. However, only 4.25% of Taiwanese students study abroad, studying in NSP countries, while most of them study in Australia (86.4%) and New Zealand (9.8%). Furthermore, Taiwanese universities are also increasing their attention to studying Southeast Asia.

Several universities in Taiwan established Southeast Asian research centers. In 1994, center of Southeast Asian studies was established in Academica Sinica, but then it expanded to Asia Pacific studies in 2001 [3]. Tamkang University in Taipei was the first campus that offered the master's program for Southeast Asian studies, but in 2009, this program was expanded under the Graduate Institute of Asian Studies. Recently, at least three state campuses have had Southeast Asian research centers: National Cheng Chi University in Taipei, National Sun Yat-Sen University in Kaohsiung, and National Chi-Nan University in Nantou. Several campuses also established Southeast Asia programs at the undergraduate level (Department of Southeast Asia at National Kaohsiung Normal University), master's (Wenzao Ursuline University of Languages), and doctoral (National Chi-Nan University).

However, when the interest in studying Southeast Asia increased in Taiwan, the contrast situation occurred in the region. There is only one Center for Taiwan Studies in Jakarta. In Malaysia, Taiwan established the Taiwan Resource Centre for Chinese Studies at Universiti Tunku Abdul Rahman (2013) and Universiti Malaya (2014), and then the center was also established at Chulalongkorn University (2018) in Thailand [4]. Starting in 2003, the Ministry of Education of the Republic of China (Taiwan) created Taiwan Studies Project to promote Taiwan studies while strengthening Taiwan's soft power and influence, but it focused more on European and North American countries. Among the 34 ongoing projects under this program, Indonesia received the project to establish the Taiwan Studies Project at BINUS University and the Taiwan Studies Consortium at the University of Indonesia [5]. The National Economics University in Vietnam also received a project for research on the local carbon economy, while Naresuan University became the first university in Thailand which receives the Taiwan Studies project in 2017 [6]. When Southeast Asian studies are growing in Taiwan, Taiwan studies in Southeast Asian countries are relatively slow progress. This situation raises the question, do Southeast Asian countries less interested in discussing Taiwan? If they discuss Taiwan, what topics do they discuss Taiwan?

This study focuses on the research on Taiwan by Indonesian students and Indonesia by Taiwanese students and discusses them in the public diplomacy analysis. This study begins with the theoretical framework (public and educational diplomacy) and Taiwan education diplomacy; then, it describes an analysis of the student's research topic in Indonesia and Taiwan. The last section explains the implication of reciprocal asymmetric relations to Taiwan's education diplomacy and soft power development in Indonesia.

## 2 Public Diplomacy and Educational Diplomacy

The NSP is a "people-centered" policy that focuses on the involvement of people [7, 8]. Since this policy has many programs related to people exchange [9], public diplomacy is critical in implementing the NSP. Public diplomacy targets the public in another country. Unlike traditional diplomacy, which targets governments or representatives of other countries, public diplomacy places the public in other countries as objects and, if possible, involves them as subjects [10, 11] and aims to strengthen soft power [12]. This new public diplomacy differs from propaganda [13] when it uses two-way communication and involves the public [14].

Leonard et al. [14] develop four hierarchical stages in public diplomacy. The first stage is the introduction and familiarity stage when a state introduces itself and attempts to make public in other states familiar with it. At this level, the state attempts to update the image while decreasing the negative image and making the targeted public think about it. This stage is the foundation of public diplomacy because this is where the initial perception of the state is formed. The second stage is appreciation. When the targeted public is familiar with the state, the state enhances its positive image by creating an opinion of the importance of the state at the international or global level. This stage aims to show some issues from the state's perspective. The third stage is engagement, an effort to attract the targeted public to be involved in the public diplomacy program. The state usually promotes tourism, education scholarship, and scientific cooperation. This stage's primary goal is to involve the targeted public while sub-scribing to the state's values. The fourth stage is influence, which attempts to influence other countries through the public. When the public in other countries are familiar with and participate in public diplomacy programs, they will understand and spread a positive image while influencing the government in their country and ultimately influencing their foreign policy. Since public diplomacy is mainly conducted in cultural diplomacy, education is one of the critical elements of public diplomacy.

Scholars discuss educational diplomacy globally rather than in an individual state. Jacqueline J. Batey argues that educational diplomacy is an attempt to improve the quality of education by sharing ideas, theories, and concepts across disciplines and transnationals [15]. Educational diplomacy is an instrument for creating global education policies to achieve three main goals: education coalition, cooperation between educational institutions, and building education management [16]. Therefore, education diplomacy is a means to overcome various global education problems [17]. In educational diplomacy, diplomacy skills and approaches are used to create a mutual understanding in addressing educational problems while promoting a transformative agenda to improve the quality of education [18].

This study focuses on the individual state's perspective on education diplomacy, where education is a critical element under Taiwan's NSP. From the individual state perspective, education diplomacy is related to education as a means to pursue public diplomacy goals, including enhancing soft power. China implements educational diplomacy by sending students abroad, inviting international students to study at Chinese universities, conducting research collaborations, and establishing Chinese branch campuses abroad [19]. China also builds its soft power through educational diplomacies, such as the Chinese Government Scholarship (EU Windows) to European Union countries [20]. India uses its education diplomacy to help Afghanistan create education equality and infrastructure [21]. Meanwhile, international education in Australia is part of public diplomacy, which aims to influence the public in other countries while increasing soft power [22].

## 3 Taiwan Education Diplomacy Under the NSP

Higher education in Taiwan is a critical element of the importance of Taiwan in a global context [23]. Taiwan is active in developing and advancing its educational diplomacy through the internationalization of its education by sending Taiwanese students abroad and accepting international students to study at universities in Taiwan. However, the situation of Taiwan as a semi-periphery country makes it difficult for Taiwan to sell higher education to core countries or fellow semi-periphery countries; therefore, Taiwan has marketed its higher education to peripheral countries in Southeast Asia [1]. According to Tsay, Taiwan markets higher education to Southeast Asia because of the low level of enrollment in higher education, geographical and cultural proximity, significant ethnic Chinese presence, and substantial economic ties.

Taiwan has an excellent source to support its education diplomacy. It has several universities that rank well at the world and Asian levels. Based on the World University Rankings report by Times Higher Education (THE), Taiwan has a relatively higher campus ranking than countries in Southeast Asia (except Singapore). At the Asia level, according to QS Asia University Rankings 2022, National Taiwan University is ranked 19th, under the National University of Singapore and the University of Malaya in first and eighth, respectively. Chulalongkorn University ranks 36, followed by Universiti Brunei Darussalam at 69th, the University of Indonesia at 56th, the University of the Philippines at 77th, and Ton Duc Thang University at 142nd (Table 1).

Education diplomacy for Taiwan is part of cultural diplomacy and soft power development. The focus on education diplomacy began at the end of President Ma Ying-jeou's administration and was further strengthened by President Tsai Ing-wen through the NSP [26]. This educational diplomacy is part of Taiwan's cultural diplomacy in conveying ideas and information about Taiwan since Taiwan considers the limitations of diplomatic relations. However, Chey noted that Taiwan's cultural diplomacy until 2014 encountered problems due to several factors such as cross-strait

**Table 1** Taiwan and Southeast Asian University Rank

| Country | THE World University Rankings 2022 | QS Asia University Rankings 2022 |
|---|---|---|
| Singapore | 21 (National University of Singapore) | 1 (National University of Singapore) |
| Taiwan | 113 (National Taiwan University) | 19 (National Taiwan University) |
| Malaysia | 301–350 (University of Malaya) | 8 (University of Malaya) |
| Brunei Darussalam | 351–400 (Universiti Brunei Darussalam) | 69 (Universiti Brunei Darussalam) |
| Vietnam | 401–500 (Duy Tan University) | 142 (Ton Duc Thang University) |
| Thailand | 601–800 (Mae Fah Luang University, Mahidol University) | 36 (Chulalongkorn University) |
| The Philippines | 601–800 (University of the Philippines) | 77 (University of The Philippines) |
| Indonesia | 801–1000 (University of Indonesia) | 56 (University of Indonesia) |

*Source* Times Higher Education [24] and QS Top Universities [25]

relations, weak consensus on national identity and coordination between agencies in government, and inconsistent strategies [27]. NSP seeks to overcome these problems and places education as an essential aspect of strengthening relationships through people-to-people relations [28], while it also strengthens Taiwan's soft power [29].

In Taiwan-Indonesia relations, Taiwan's educational diplomacy accompanies economic diplomacy in building Taiwan's soft power. Education follows economic diplomacy to strengthen Taiwan's soft power in Indonesia [30]. Initially, the promotion of Taiwan's higher education targeted the Indonesian Chinese ethnic group representing the middle-class group in Indonesia and then progressed to scholarships for international students from Indonesia. At the same time, universities in Taiwan also collaborate with several universities in Indonesia to conduct joint research. Education diplomacy has become a critical element in Taiwan's soft power development in Indonesia, where Taiwan is one of the destinations for Indonesian students to study abroad, and they are expected to play positive roles in the cooperation between Indonesia and Taiwan [31].

However, Taiwan's education diplomacy also faces some critics. Taiwan's higher education internationalization in Southeast Asia attempted to dominate and benefit from talented Southeast Asian human resources for Taiwan's development [32]. Besides the imbalance in student mobility, the uneven distribution is another problem when Brunei Darussalam and Laos do not have significant interactions with Taiwan [33]. Miscommunication, lack of socio-cultural knowledge, and legal issues become Indonesia-Taiwan education cooperation problems [34].

# 4 Research Method

This study surveyed Indonesian students' research topics about Taiwan and Taiwanese students about Indonesia. Data for Indonesia were obtained from oneres earch.id database provided by the Indonesian National Library, while data for Taiwan were obtained from the Taiwan National Central Library database. Data range from 2016 to 2021 or after the implementation of NSP, and the topics are limited to social and humanities. Indonesian students in this study are Indonesian students who study in Indonesia, while Taiwanese students are Taiwanese students who study in Taiwan. This study performs bibliographic analysis using the VOSviewer program.

# 5 Result and Discussion

## *5.1 Indonesian Student's Research on Taiwan*

There are 48 theses in the oneresearch.id database that discusses Taiwan from 2016 to 2021. An analysis by VOSviewer shows the research topics of Indonesian students in Taiwan, which are dominated by the topic of cross-strait relations and Indonesian migrant workers (Fig. 1). In 2017, the topic of research on migrant workers and physical violence became the main topic and then developed into a discussion on cross-strait relations and relations between the United States and Taiwan in 2018. After 2019, topics related to domestic Taiwan began to emerge, such as LGBT (Fig. 2). There are four clusters of research topics by Indonesian students about Taiwan (Table 2), but they can be grouped into two main groups: research on cross-strait relations and Indonesian migrant workers.

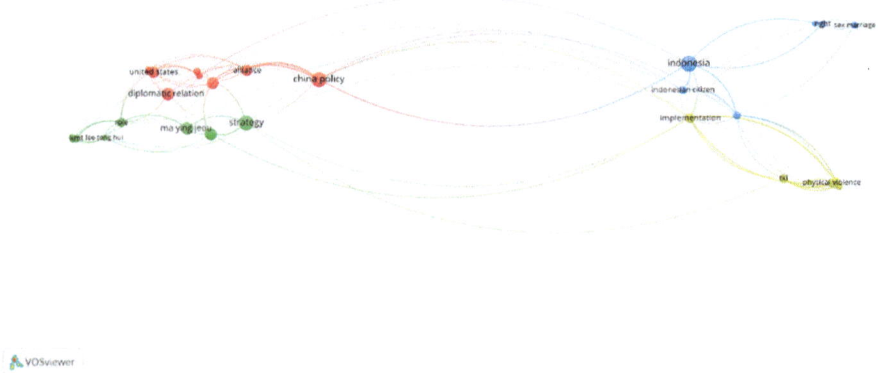


**Fig. 1** Indonesian student research topic on Taiwan (2016–2021)

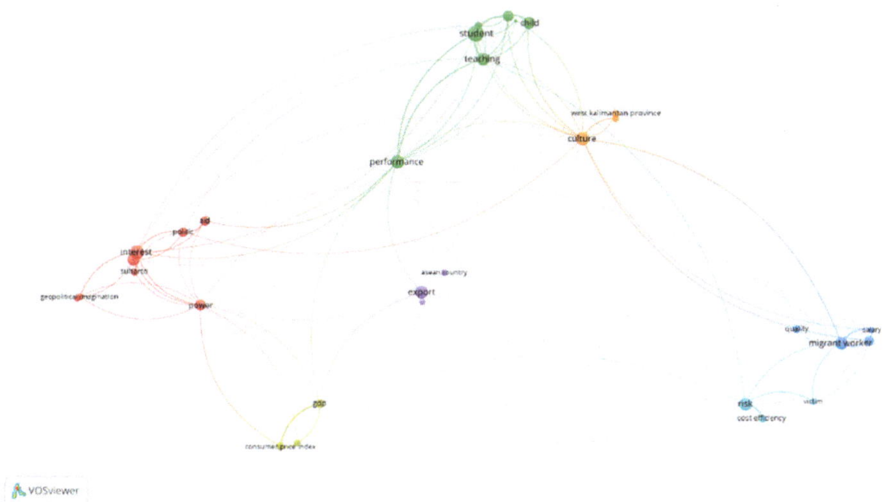


**Fig. 2** Taiwanese students' research topic on Indonesia (2016–2021)

**Table 2** Cluster topic of Indonesian student research on Taiwan (2016–2021)

| Cluster | Topics |
|---|---|
| 1 | Alliance, China policy, diplomatic relations, East Asia region, international relations, national interest, South China Sea, United States |
| 2 | Cross-strait policy, cross-strait relations, KMT, Lee Teng Hui, Ma Ying Jeou, New Southbound Policy, role, strategy, Tsai Ing Wen |
| 3 | Discrimination, Indonesia, Indonesian citizen, legalization, representative, right, sex marriage |
| 4 | Implementation, Indonesian migrant worker, insurance, claim, physical violence, placement, TKI |

## 5.2 *Taiwanese Students' Research on Indonesia*

There are 77 theses about Indonesia by Taiwanese students from 2016 to 2021. However, when looking at the total of student research in Taiwan (not limited to nationality), the number of research on Indonesia in the National Central Library database is 487. If these data are compared with research data conducted by Taiwanese students, it can be assumed that most research on Indonesia in Taiwan was conducted by Indonesian students studying in Taiwan. In other words, even though Indonesian students study in Taiwan's universities, they choose their research topic about Indonesia.

Taiwanese students discussed Indonesian culture and politics, such as Chinese culture in Indonesia, education and the Indonesian economy, Indonesian migrant workers, and domestic politics (Fig. 2). In 2017, Taiwanese student research

**Table 3** Cluster topic of Taiwanese students' research on Indonesia (2016–2021)

| Cluster | Topics |
|---|---|
| 1 | Aid, CCP, geopolitical imagination, interest and politics, power, reform, Suharto |
| 2 | Child, curriculum, performance, student, Taiwanese |
| 3 | Teacher, teaching |
| 4 | Employer, migrant, worker, quality, salary |
| 5 | ASEAN country, economic growth, export, product |
| 6 | Cost efficiency, risk, victim |
| 7 | Culture, Teochew Chinese, West Kalimantan province |

discussed domestic politics in Indonesia and then developed into research on the economy and Indonesian migrant workers in 2018–2019. Since 2020, their research has discussed a lot about the culture of the Chinese community in Indonesia. Taiwanese student studies in Indonesia are grouped into 7 clusters (Table 3).

### 5.3 *Reciprocal Asymmetrical Relations in Taiwan's Education Diplomacy with Indonesia*

This study's result shows another asymmetric relationship to Tsay's [1] study. When Tsay defines the asymmetrical relationship in terms of the gap in student mobility, this study shows the other asymmetric relationship in terms of the number and topics of research. In other words, the results of this study show an asymmetric relationship in ideational factors, whereas previous studies show an asymmetric relationship in material factors (population and migration). These two asymmetric relationships occur in two directions: the number of Indonesian students studying in Taiwan is more than Taiwanese students studying in Indonesia, and the number and topic of research about Indonesia by Taiwanese students are more than Indonesian students' research about Taiwan. Therefore, this study defines this relationship as reciprocal asymmetric relations.

Table 4 shows the disparity in the number of studies between the two groups of students. In terms of numbers, research by Indonesian students about Taiwan is less than Taiwanese students' research about Indonesia. Moreover, Taiwanese students discussed Indonesia as a broader topic than Indonesian students' research on Taiwan. This result indicates that Indonesian students' understanding of Taiwan is limited to cross-strait relations and the destination of Indonesian migrant workers. However, post-2019, some Indonesian students began studying Taiwan's domestic issues.

From the hierarchical stage of public diplomacy perspective, Taiwan's educational diplomacy through the NSP has succeeded in reaching the third stage but may still be heading to the fourth stage. The first and second stages of introduction, familiarity, and appreciation of Taiwan seem to have been achieved. The third stage

**Table 4** Number of Indonesian and Taiwanese students' research (2016–2021)

| Year | Research about Taiwan | Research about Indonesia | Research about Indonesia (ALL)* |
|---|---|---|---|
| 2016 | 5 | 10 | 86 |
| 2017 | 7 | 10 | 60 |
| 2018 | 12 | 13 | 67 |
| 2019 | 14 | 11 | 85 |
| 2020 | 10 | 19 | 90 |
| 2021 | | 14 | 99 |

*ALL here is the total research about Indonesia in Taiwan regardless of students' nationality (it includes Indonesian students in Taiwan)

is also achieved when many Indonesian publics are interested in studying Taiwan. The number of Indonesian students in Taiwan is increasing yearly with increasingly diverse student backgrounds—not only dominated by Chinese Indonesian students. This situation shows that Taiwan is relatively successful in engaging the Indonesian public, and the Indonesian public recognizes the positive image of Taiwan's higher education.

However, the increasing number of Indonesian students studying in Taiwan does not align with the other Indonesian students' interest in studying Taiwan at home. The limited number and topic of Indonesian students' research on Taiwan indicate that Taiwan is less discussed in Indonesian academics (at least at the university student level). Indeed, many factors influence these limited topics, like information access and involvement of these students in Taiwan's education diplomacy activity in Indonesia. However, this situation also represents that Taiwan's education diplomacy still needs more effort to bring Taiwan into Indonesian student discussion. When the lack of information becomes the leading cause, it means the information about Taiwan is either limited or does not encourage Indonesian students to study it. Taiwan education diplomacy that promotes higher education to encourage Indonesian students to study in Taiwan should be balanced to encourage Indonesian students to discuss Taiwan. This situation may impact Taiwan's soft power development in Indonesia.

### *5.4 The Implication of Reciprocal Asymmetric Relations to Taiwan's Soft Power in Indonesia*

The reciprocal asymmetric relationship presents challenges and advantages for Taiwan's soft power building in Indonesia. The asymmetric relation in student mobility shows the positive image of Taiwan's higher education in Indonesia when Taiwan becomes the destination of Indonesian students to study abroad. However, the lack of Taiwanese students in Indonesia may affect the low or limited understanding of Indonesia. The asymmetric relations regarding a limited number of Indonesian students' research about Taiwan bring two main challenges. First is the limitation of Taiwan's public diplomacy to bring Taiwan into Indonesian students' discussion. Taiwan may become a popular destination for Indonesian students to study abroad, but it may not be popular as a topic of research or discussion. Therefore, education diplomacy other than promoting higher education like research collaboration in social science and humanity and establishing more Taiwan studies in Indonesia may be the solution. Second is the dependence of the Taiwan discussion on other actors. The topic of research by Indonesian students, which is dominated by research on cross-strait relations and Indonesian migrant workers, shows that the Taiwan-China conflict and Indonesian perspectives dominate discussions about Taiwan in Indonesia. Therefore, Taiwan may need more strategies to disseminate information about Taiwan to the Indonesian public. Nondiplomatic relation is a critical issue, but at least in the academic discussion that provides freedom of thinking, discussing Taiwan's cultural, social, environmental, economic, and other non-political issues will attract Indonesian academia's attention.

Nevertheless, the reciprocal asymmetry relationship also provides opportunities to develop Taiwan's soft power in Indonesia. The increasing number of Taiwanese students' interest in research about Indonesia shows a positive development. They should positively impact Taiwan's soft power when more Taiwanese scholars on Indonesian studies increase. They can contribute as a bridge and actor when involved in various Taiwanese public diplomacy activities in Indonesia. Indonesian people, especially academics, including students, will see this situation as attention for Indonesia. Several countries such as Japan, the United States, and Australia have succeeded in producing experts on Indonesia in their countries, and in Indonesia, their presence is welcomed and bridges various educational collaborations between their countries and Indonesia. Therefore, this study suggests the Taiwan government should pay attention to students studying Indonesia to make them a part of public diplomacy in Indonesia, including encouraging more research on Indonesia or other NSP target countries.

## 6 Conclusion

Education diplomacy plays a critical role in NSP's implementation since it enhances Taiwan's higher education positive image and successfully invites students from NSP partner countries to study in Taiwan. However, the asymmetrical relations in student mobility or migration between Taiwan and NSP partner countries become a challenge. This study finds another asymmetrical relationship in Taiwan's education diplomacy with Indonesia. The number of research about Taiwan by Indonesian students is lower than Taiwanese students' research about Indonesia, while Taiwanese students discuss Indonesia in broader topics than Indonesian students on Taiwan. This study describes this situation as reciprocal asymmetric relations, where the asymmetric relations do not happen only from Indonesia to Taiwan but also from Taiwan to Indonesia.

Bringing Indonesian students to study in Taiwan is critical but bringing Taiwan into the discussion among Indonesian academics is essential to reach wider public attention. Therefore, promoting higher discussion should be balanced with promoting discussion about Taiwan by increasing research collaboration and Taiwan studies in Indonesia. Moreover, Taiwan should pay more attention to the Taiwan alumni by creating post-study programs in public diplomacy to enhance their role in disseminating information about Taiwan. Taiwan's educational soft power should be measured in the number of international students in Taiwan and the effect of the Taiwan alumni in the home country that brings Taiwan influence. The increasing number of Taiwan students' research on Indonesia with diverse topics also provides Taiwan opportunities to deal with asymmetrical relations regarding the number of Taiwanese students studying in Indonesia. They may become Indonesia's specialists in Taiwan in the future. The Taiwan government should consider involving them in public diplomacy to Indonesia.

## References


1. Tsay C-l (2016, February 10) Migration between Southeast Asia and Taiwan: trends, characteristics and implications. JAS (J ASEAN Stud) 3(2):68. https://doi.org/10.21512/jas.v3i2.842
2. CSIS (2018) Taiwan's New Southbound Policy: Data Repository. CSIS. https://southbound.csis.org/data
3. Chiung W-vT (2013) Features and prospects in comparative studies of Vietnam and Taiwan. In: 2013 International Conference on Vietnamese – Taiwanese Studies; 6th Taiwanese Romanization. National Cheng Kung University, Tainan
4. Center for Chinese Studies (2022) Taiwan Resource Center for Chinese Studies. National Central Library. https://ccs.ncl.edu.tw/en/academy2.aspx
5. Taiwan Studies Project (2022) Projects. Ministry of Education. https://taiwanstudies.moe.edu.tw/ProjectIntroEN?page=B3732B8F9CCC46B7&continents=&countryRegion=&school=&qstr=#Intro
6. MOE (2017) First MOE Taiwan Studies Project in Thailand launched at Naresuan University. Ministry of Education, Republic of China (Taiwan). https://english.moe.gov.tw/cp-117-22323-5C03B-1.html
7. Yang AH (2017) Strategic appraisal of Taiwan's New People-Centered Southbound Policy: the 4Rs approach. Prospect J (18):1–34
8. Yang AH, Chiang JHC (2019, April 15) Enabling human values in foreign policy: the transformation of Taiwan's New Southbound Policy. J Hum Values 25(2):75–86. https://doi.org/10.1177/0971685819826707
9. Chen PK (2020, September) Taiwan's 'People-Centered' New Southbound Policy and its impact on US–Taiwan relations. Pac Rev 33(5):813–841. https://doi.org/10.1080/09512748.2019.1594349
10. Szondi G (2008) Public diplomacy and nation branding: conceptual similarities and differences. Discussion Papers in Diplomacy. Den Haag
11. Effendi TD (2011) Diplomasi Publik Jepang: Perkembangan Dan Tantangan. Ghalia, Jakarta

12. Melissen J (2011) Concluding reflection on soft power and public diplomacy in East Asia. In: Lee SK, Melissen J (eds) Public diplomacy and soft power in East Asia. Palgrave Macmillan, New York, pp 247–62
13. Melissen J (2005) The new public diplomacy: soft power in international relations. Palgrave Macmillan, New York
14. Leonard M, Stead C, Smewing C (2002) Public diplomacy. Foreign Policy Centre, London
15. Batey JJ (2014, January 2) Education diplomacy: global diplomacy awareness developed through short-term international internships. Child Educ 90(1):77–80. https://doi.org/10.1080/00094056.2014.872524
16. Kyvliuk O et al (2018, July) Educational management as education diplomacy: strategies for Ukraine. Naukovyi Visnyk Natsionalnoho Hirnychoho Universytetu (3):139–144. https://doi.org/10.29202/nvngu/2018-3/23
17. Fuller S (2019, September 3) Education diplomacy at the intersection of gender equality and quality education. Child Educ 95(5):70–73. https://doi.org/10.1080/00094056.2019.1663103
18. Murphy Y (2018, May 4) Education diplomacy: the two sides of innovation. Child Educ 94(3):3–3. https://doi.org/10.1080/00094056.2018.1475742
19. Paradise J (2012, May 5). International education: diplomacy in China. Brown J World Aff 19(1):195–205. http://www.jstor.org/stable/24590938
20. Hong NY (2014) EU-China education diplomacy: an effective soft power strategy? Eur Foreign Aff Rev 19:155–171. http://www.kluwerlawonline.com/api/Product/CitationPDFURL?file=Journals%5CEERR%5CEERR2014026.pdf
21. Singh B et al (2021). The double whammy of pandemic and war: a systematic review of India's education diplomacy to address educational inequities in Afghanistan. Educ Sci 11(10). https://doi.org/10.3390/educsci11100651
22. Byrne C, Hall R (2013, August 1) Realising Australia's international education as public diplomacy. Aust J Int Aff 67(4):419–438. https://doi.org/10.1080/10357718.2013.806019
23. Rigger S (2011) Why Taiwan matters: small island, global powerhouse. Rowman & Littefield, Lanham, MD
24. THE World University Rankings 2022. https://www.timeshighereducation.com/world-university-rankings/2022#!/page/0/length/25/locations/BRN+IDN+MYS+PHL+SGP+TWN+THA+VNM/sort_by/rank/sort_order/asc/cols/stats, accessed July 15, 2022
25. QS Asia University Rankings 2022. https://www.topuniversities.com/university-rankings/asian-university-rankings/2022, accessed July 15, 2022
26. Verre F (2021) Hydro-diplomacy in Southeast Asia: the Taiwanese case. J Manag Policy Pract 22(1):34–46
27. Chey J (2014) Culture and diplomacy: the case of Taiwan. J Orient Soc Aust 46:41–73
28. Marston H, Bush RC (2018) Taiwan's engagement with Southeast Asia is making progress under the New Southbound Policy. Brookings. https://www.brookings.edu/opinions/taiwans-engagement-with-southeast-asia-is-making-progress-under-the-new-southbound-policy/
29. Haime J (2021) Taiwan's education soft power push. supchina.com. https://supchina.com/2021/11/15/taiwans-education-soft-power-push/
30. Paramitaningrum, Herlijanto J (2016) Economic diplomacy, soft power, and Taiwan's relations with Indonesia. Contemp Chin Polit Econ Strat Relat 2(3):1173–1194
31. Yustiningrum E et al (2022) Building people-to-people connection for a stronger Indonesia-Taiwan relationship. Jakarta
32. Surya P (2021) Kritik Terhadap Internasionalisasi Pendidikan Tinggi Ala Kebijakan Politik the New Southbound Taiwan. Jurnal Akuntabilitas Manajemen Pendidikan 9(2):203–212. https://doi.org/10.21831/jamp.v9i2.42586
33. Lin AF-Y (2020, January 1) Internationalization initiatives of Taiwan's higher education: a stepping stone to regional talent circulation or reproduction of unbalanced mobility scheme? High Educ Eval Dev 14(2):69–91. https://doi.org/10.1108/HEED-06-2020-0017
34. Mursitama TN, Ying Y, Shidarta (2020) Indonesia-Taiwan relations: searching for better understanding. Penerbit Andi

MIX
Papier aus verantwortungsvollen Quellen
Paper from responsible sources
FSC® C105338

If you have any concerns about our products,
you can contact us on
**ProductSafety@springernature.com**

In case Publisher is established outside the EU,
the EU authorized representative is:
**Springer Nature Customer Service Center GmbH**
**Europaplatz 3, 69115 Heidelberg, Germany**

Printed by Libri Plureos GmbH
in Hamburg, Germany